Credits

Acquisitions editor: Jeff Marshall
Senior marketing manager: Charity Robey
Production manager: Lari Bishop
Designer: Kris Pauls
Illustration editor: Benjamin Reece
Cover image: Copyright © Paul Stover/Stone

This book was set in Minion and printed and bound by Von Hoffmann Press.

ISBN 0471-22292-5

Printed in the United States of America

10   9   8   7   6   5   4   3   2   1

Strategic Management

Of Resources
And Relationships

Concepts and Cases

Jeffrey S. Harrison
Cornell University

John Wiley & Sons, Inc.

New York   Chichester   Weinheim   Brisbane   Singapore   Toronto

http://www.wiley.com/college

Dedication

*To Marie, for her unconditional
love, support, and friendship*

Contents

Part 1: Analysis of the Competitive Situation

Chapter 1
Strategic Management   2

Part 2: Strategy Formulation

Chapter 4
Strategic Direction   *116*

Chapter 5
Strategy Formulation at The Business-Unit Level   *146*

Part 3: Strategy Implementation and Control

Chapter 8
Strategy Implementation: Resources and Relationships   *260*

Chapter 9
Strategy Implementation: Design and Control   *298*

Chapter 10
Global Strategic Management and The Future   *342*

Cases

Case Summary Table

	Alliances/ Partnerships	Information Technology
ABB in China: 1998	X	
Agilent Technologies' Initial Public Offering		X
AOL Time Warner Merger		X
AT&T: Twenty Years of Change	X	X
Beijing Jeep Co. and the WTO	X	
Blinds To Go: Evaluating the Blindstogo.com Retail E-Commerce Venture	X	X
Cessna: Turbulence at 2000		
Citibank: The Confia Acquisition in Mexico (A)	X	
CNET Networks, Inc.	X	X
Cognex Corporation: "Work Hard, Play Hard"		X
The Comeback of Caterpillar, 1885–2001	X	
Competition in the Global Wine Industry: A U.S. Perspective	X	
The Department of Justice Versus Microsoft		
Drkoop.com		X
Excellence at Motorola		
Gannett Comany, Inc.		X
General Motors Corporation: Tooling Up and Scaling Back to Compete Globally		
Kerkhov Karpets, Inc.		
Kikkoman Corporation in the Mid-1990s: Market Maturity, Diversification and Globalization		
Kmart Corporation: Seeking Customer Acceptance and Preference	X	X
Lofty Ambitions at Cirrus Design and NASA	X	X
Moss Adams, LLP		
Peapod, Inc. and the Online Grocery Business	X	X
Perdue Farms Inc.: Responding to Twenty-First Century Challenges		
Philip Condit and the Boeing 777: From Design and Development to Production and Sales		
The Rise and Fall of Iridium	X	X
Seven-Eleven Japan: Managing a Networked Organization	X	X
Rocky Mountain Chocolate Factory, Inc.		
Wal-Mart Stores, Inc.: Strategies for Dominance in the New Millennium		
Weaving an Effective Strategy: The Quaker Fabric Corp. Case		
Workbrain Corporation	X	X

International Issues	Entrepreneurship	Competitive Dynamics	Corporate-Level Issues	Financials	Manufacturing	Service Sector
X			X			X
	X		X	X		
X		X	X	X		X
X		X	X		X	
	X					X
		X	X	X	X	
X			X			X
	X	X	X	X		X
				X	X	
X		X	X	X	X	
X		X			X	
		X	X	X	X	
	X	X				X
X			X	X	X	
				X	X	
X		X	X	X	X	
X	X			X	X	
X		X	X	X	X	
		X	X	X		X
X	X				X	
		X	X			X
	X	X		X		X
X					X	
X	X					X
X	X					X
X			X			X
X	X	X		X	X	X
X		X	X	X		
				X	X	
	X					X

Preface

What is it that strategic managers actually do? On one hand, they acquire, develop, and manage internal *resources* such as people, knowledge, financial capital, and physical assets. However, of equal importance, they acquire, develop, and manage *relationships* with external stakeholders such as customers, suppliers, and venture partners. The result of this external management process is a network of relationships and partnerships. Furthermore, these two activities overlap. For instance, firms use relationships with external stakeholders to enhance their resource positions.

Strategic Management of Resources and Relationships provides a realistic, balanced view of the field. It draws heavily from the resource-based perspective that firms can develop competitive advantages through the acquisition, development, and management of resources. It also uses stakeholder theory to help explain when firms should form partnerships, the form partnerships should take, and how to manage them. Finally, this book contains the most relevant theory and models from what might be called the traditional approach to strategic management. Consequently, combining the resource-based view and the stakeholder view with traditional theory and models provides a very complete, comprehensive, and managerially useful perspective of strategic management.

Special Features

In addition to the balanced approach found in this book, it also contains several other features that are a direct result of current trends in strategic management:

- *International flavor.* Many examples of global strategic management are included in the text material, as well as special highlighted examples in every chapter. Global strategic management theory is woven into many of the chapters and included in a separate international chapter.

- *Section on strategic thinking.* Strategic thinking is different from other aspects of strategic management. In fact, some strategists have argued that strategic planning processes can stifle strategic thinking. The perspective taken in this book is that strategic thinking is an essential, creative aspect of the strategy process.

- *Chapter on entrepreneurship and innovation.* Innovation and entrepreneurship are vital to strategic success. The entrepreneurship chapter contains elements of both starting a business (such as what a business plan contains) and entrepreneurship within existing organizations (organizational entrepreneurship or "intrapraneurship").

- *Section on competitive dynamics.* Firms do not create strategies in a static environment. They need to account for the dynamic elements of industry competition. This book reflects the reality of a dynamic environment in every chapter. Also included is a separate section on strategies that account for the actions of competitors.

- *Innovative and comprehensive treatment of implementation and control.* Consistent with the balanced theme of the book, implementation is treated from the perspective of managing internal processes as well as external relationships. A fully-integrated strategic control model, which is a major innovation in the text, pulls the whole implementation process together.

- *Up-to-date cases with breadth.* The cases are an excellent mix of large, small, and medium-sized companies from many types of industries, including high-tech, manufacturing, and services. All cases were selected by the author after extensive analysis and review to assure the best possible fit. Many of the cases are global in their focus or contain global elements.

- *Concise presentation.* In spite of all this coverage, the book contains only ten chapters. The essential material is included, without all the "fluff." Principles and theories are explained with brief examples that get right to the point. The smaller size of the book allows instructors to use more cases, simulations, exercises, or readings.

- *Strategic applications.* Special application assignments apply the theory found in each chapter to real companies. These applications reinforce important models, theories, and tools.

- *Strategic Internet applications.* The Internet has become an excellent learning resource. Each chapter contains an exercise that makes use of one or more Internet Web sites. The material in the chapters literally comes alive as students apply it to actual companies and industries in real time. Other Internet applications are found in the Web site materials that support the text.

Cases

The exciting cases selected for *Strategic Management of Resources and Relationships* include a variety of large and small, public and private firms from many industries. International issues cover a range, from simple exporting (Perdue Farms) to foreign operations of a U.S. company (Seven-Eleven Japan, Citibank) to non-U.S. companies operating globally (Kikkoman, ABB). Most of the cases are very current, with the exception of a few "classic" cases. A wide variety of information technologies are included, from dot-coms (drkoop.com) to companies providing technology-based operating support (Workbrain). In fact, most of the cases include information technology issues, a reflection of the current business environment. Also included are several excellent examples of entrepreneurship (Peapod) and intrapraneurship (Blindstogo.com). In addition, three cases involve IPOs (Agilent Technologies, GM, and CNET). A table summarizing the topics covered in each case can be found on pages xvi–xvii.

All of the cases may be used to teach resource-based and stakeholder concepts; consequently, there is no column for these categories in the case summary table. Competitive dynamics issues include both domestic (Wal-Mart) and global (Kikkoman) markets. Corporate-level issues represented within the cases include diversification (Kmart) and governance (Agilent). Many of the firms have been involved extensively in mergers and acquisitions. However, AOL Time Warner focuses specifically on merger issues.

The companies are classified as primary participants in the manufacturing or service sectors (far right columns of the case summary table on page xvi–xvii), although some of the companies have businesses in both areas. Most cases include excellent financial information; however, in some cases this information was not available to the case writer, either because the company is private or because it is the subsidiary of a larger corporation.

The Scaffold Plank Incident and Robin Hood (not listed in the case summary table) are brief but rich descriptions of ethical dilemmas. In fact, most cases can be used to discuss ethical issues.

Streamlined, Innovative Design

Strategic Management of Resources and Relationships also has several design elements that should be very appealing to students and instructors. Most of the examples are in-text rather than boxed, since boxes are often distracting to the flow of the material. Important terms are defined in the margins of the text. End-of-chapter materials include a key points summary, discussion questions, and exercises called Strategic Applications and Strategic Internet Applications. Because many people learn better when they receive more visual stimulation, the book has been produced in full color.

A Comprehensive Support Package

The Web Companion

A very comprehensive Web site has been created for students and instructors. The student's site contains chapter objectives, summary, additional readings, cases, and two-to-three strategic applications per chapter. The strategic applications provide hands-on exercises that illustrate concepts discussed in the chapter. Many of the strategic applications involve Internet use for research analysis and reporting. The Harrison site, www.wiley.com/college/harrison, will be updated regularly with links, relevant news, and case updates.

The instructor's site contains PDF versions of the instructor's manual, test bank, power point slides, case notes, and a link to xanedu.com where an extensive customized case packet can be created for classroom use. The author has created a substantial list of alternative cases in addition to the thirty-three cases contained in the textbook. Simply go to the Harrison Web site at www.wiley.com/college/harrison and click on the xanedu link. It will take you to xanedu.com, where you will be asked to register and follow the links to the strategic management course where you will find the Harrison case package option.

Test Bank

A comprehensive test bank consisting of more than 750 questions comprised of multiple choice, true/false, and essay questions is available.

Power Point Presentation Files

Prepared by the author, these slides go beyond merely outlining the chapter by providing key figures, tables, and concepts summaries.

The Instructor's Manual and Case Notes

Prepared by the author, this excellent teaching tool contains many of the features that are found on the Web site, only in paper format. These include lecture notes, solutions to end of chapter Strategic Applications, chapter objectives, and summaries. The manual also includes case notes. Each case note follows a similar format for consistent case analysis. In addition, key or unique aspects of each case are pinpointed so instructors will have a consistent framework directly linked to the text framework. At the same time, flexibility is provided by the high quality of the case notes applied to the strategic management process.

Strategic Management Simulation

You may package this book with Capstone's Strategic Management Simulation, by Management Simulations, Inc. This market-leading, Web-based simulation comes with a team member guide and instructions for setting up the simulation. Give your students the opportunity to make strategic management decisions in a competitive and dynamic environment. Please contact your Wiley representative for more information, or visit the text Web companion at www.wiley.com/college/harrison.

Acknowledgements

Book writing is a team activity and my team has been absolutely wonderful to work with. I would first like to thank my good friend and CEO of Leyh Publishing, Rick Leyh, for his many years of excellent work on several of my past writing projects, for encouraging me to write this book, and for helping me to produce a high-quality and innovative product. I am also grateful to Lari Bishop of Leyh Publishing for her guidance, patience, and excellent project management. Jana Pitts, another part of the Leyh team, and Christine Klepak, my graduate assistant, were absolutely essential in putting together an outstanding case list. I am also grateful to the people at Wiley for their enthusiasm and support of this project. In particular, Jeff Marshall and Susan Elbe were instrumental in shepherding this project along. Finally, my team included the best set of reviewers I have ever had the opportunity to work with. They were thorough, insightful, and sometimes very tough; however, their toughness resulted in a vastly better book. They are:

Michael Russo, University of Oregon

Sanjay Goel, University of Minnesota

Joseph Bensen, New Mexico State University

Michael Goldsby, Ball State University

Michael Coombs, California State University

W. Jack Duncan, University of Alabama at Birmingham

Vikas Anand, University of Arkansas

Rose Mary Cordova-Wentling, University of Illinois

Olav Sorenson, University of California at Los Angeles

William Schultze, Case Western Reserve University

Andrew Inkpen, Thunderbird

Grant Miles, University of North Texas

Garry Bruton, Texas Christian University

Richard Menger, St. Mary's University

I also need to acknowledge the excellent work of Caron St. John who, through past writing projects, helped me to develop some of the material found in this book. She is a great friend and cherished co-author. Finally, I am so grateful to my wife, Marie, and to the children who are still at home—Jared, Joseph, and Rebekah—for being patient with me when I was working late into the night and for supporting me in a multitude of ways so that I could work on this book.

Jeffrey S. Harrison
Cornell University

About the Author

Jeffrey S. Harrison is the Peelen Professorship Chair of Global Hospitality Strategy at the School of Hotel Administration, Cornell University. He received his Ph.D. at the University of Utah in 1985 and served on the faculties at Arizona State University, Clemson University, and University of Central Florida prior to his appointment at Cornell.

Dr. Harrison's research interests include corporate-level strategic management, the hospitality industry, and business ethics. Much of his work has been published in prestigious academic journals such as *Academy of Management Journal*, *Strategic Management Journal*, *Journal of Management*, and *Journal of Business Ethics*. His articles have been published in North America, Europe, and Japan. He has also published many articles in journals specifically targeted at managers such as *Academy of Management Executive, Long Range Planning* (European), and *Prevision* (Japanese). His other book projects include *Foundations in Strategic Management, Strategic Management of Organizations and Stakeholders, Blackwell Handbook of Strategic Management*, and *Mergers and Acquisitions: A Guide to Creating Value for Stakeholders*. Dr. Harrison's contributions to research have been recognized through many research awards.

Dr. Harrison is also an extraordinary teacher who has received awards for his teaching at both the undergraduate and graduate levels. In addition, Dr. Harrison provides highly visible service to the field of management through his positions on the editorial review boards of both *Academy of Management Journal* and *Academy of Management Executive*. He recently guest co-edited a special research forum of the *Academy of Management Journal* entitled "Stakeholders, Social Responsibility and Performance." Many high-level executives seek Dr. Harrison's advice on a wide range of issues. He has consulted or provided executive training to managers at Lockheed Martin, Siemens Westinghouse, Volvo, Southdown, and many other companies.

Part 1

Analysis of the Competitive Situation

Chapter *1*

Strategic Management

Learning Objectives

After reading and discussing this chapter, you should be able to:

1. Recognize and understand the components of strategic management.

2. List and describe three important theoretical foundations upon which modern strategic management is based.

3. Differentiate between the strategic planning process and strategic thinking.

4. Explain why globalization is such an important trend in strategic management.

Federal Express

FedEx Corporation is a premier worldwide provider of transportation services. One of its largest U.S. competitors is the U.S. Postal Service. These powerful rivals have come together in two service agreements. In the first agreement, the U.S. Postal Service will ship up to 3.5 million pounds of freight per day via FedEx jets. Most of the shipping will take place during the day, when many FedEx aircraft are idle. Consequently, the arrangement makes use of excess airlift capacity to generate an expected $6.3 billion in additional revenue for FedEx. The primary benefit to the U.S. Postal Service is that its fleet of aircraft will not have to expand to meet increasing demand for rapid delivery services. The second agreement allows FedEx to place a self-service drop box at every U.S. postal location. The 10,000 drop boxes FedEx will install are expected to result in $900 million in extra revenue. The public will benefit by having more convenient locations to drop off FedEx packages. According to Frederick W. Smith, chief executive officer of FedEx Corporation, "Whenever the public and private sectors work together, the real beneficiary is the American public. These two service agreements will create a winning business situation. The U.S. Postal Service will gain a single air transportation provider for most of its Express and Priority Mail which cannot travel solely by surface. FedEx will gain an expanded retail network to grow our business. Most importantly, our customers and the American public will win with greater choice, flexibility and convenience."[1]

Within the past few decades, the business environment has changed in fundamental ways. Through much of the past century, for example, much of the literature pertaining to what is now called Strategic Management has emphasized a warlike philosophy. The term "strategic" comes primarily from the literature on war. From this perspective, business is a battle, competitors are the enemy, and government makes and enforces the rules. The U.S. government reinforced this mentality with antitrust legislation that reflected a mistrust of cooperation among businesses, especially among competitors. However, the emergence of a fiercely competitive global economy meant that firms had to expand their networks of relationships and cooperate with each other to remain competitive.[2] For example, a firm that assembles cellular phones may have to buy parts from firms in five countries because that is where the best parts are made. This cooperation has even extended to relationships among direct competitors, as the FedEx example illustrates. This example is especially indicative of the times because the relationship is between a private business and a quasi-governmental organization!

Why are some companies successful, while so many other businesses fail? Some organizations may just be lucky. They may have the right mix of products and/or services at the right time. But even if luck leads to success, it probably won't last. Most companies that are highly successful over the long term effectively acquire, develop, and manage resources and capabilities that provide competitive advantages. For example, FedEx enjoys outstanding brand recognition and a world-class distribution system. Successful companies have also learned how to develop and manage relationships with a wide range of organizations, groups, and people that have a stake in their firms. These important constituencies are called stakeholders. **Stakeholders** are groups or individuals who can significantly affect or are significantly affected by an organization's activities.[3] They have (or believe they have) a legitimate claim on some aspect of the company or its activities because they are involved with or are influenced by the company.[4] Just as stakeholders have a stake in the organization, the organization depends on its stakeholders to survive and prosper.

This book focuses on how organizations satisfy their most important stakeholders through successful execution of the strategic management process. **Strategic management** is a process through which organizations analyze and learn from their internal and external environments, establish strategic direction, create strategies that are intended to move the organization in that direction, and implement those strategies, all in an effort to satisfy key stakeholders. Firms practicing strategic planning processes tend to outperform their counterparts that do not.[5] In fact, in a recent survey of executives, strategic management provided significantly higher levels of satisfaction than did most other management tools. Furthermore, 81 percent of companies worldwide reported doing strategic planning. In North America, the figure was even higher (89 percent).[6]

This book also recognizes that there is a difference between the strategic planning process and strategic thinking, and that both are a part of effective strategic management. The **strategic planning process** tends to be a rather rigid and unimaginative process in many organizations. It is sometimes accompanied by detailed instructions pertaining to every aspect of the process, which reduces flexibility and creativity. **Strategic thinking,** on the other hand, leads to creative solutions and new ideas. A firm that combines strategic thinking into the strategic planning process has the best of both worlds.

stakeholders
Groups or individuals who can significantly affect or are significantly affected by an organization's activities

strategic management
A process through which organizations analyze and learn from their internal and external environments, establish strategic direction, create strategies that are intended to move the organization in that direction, and implement those strategies, all in effort to satisfy key stakeholders

strategic planning process
The formal planning elements of strategic managment that result in a strategic plan; this process tends to be rather rigid and unimaginitive

strategic thinking
A somewhat creative and intuitive process that leads to creative solutions and new ideas

The Origin of Strategic Management

Prior to the twentieth century, most of the human race was engaged in producing the basic necessities of life. However, during the Industrial Revolution, many family farms and businesses were replaced by professionally managed firms. International trade increased with advances in transportation. Communications became a major global industry. Service industries such as entertainment and travel flourished. These trends accelerated during the post–World War II era. Prosperity during the Industrial Revolution also resulted in the creation of large and diversified business organizations. By the middle of the twentieth century, approximately 40 percent of the business-related assets in the United States were controlled by the largest 200 companies.[7]

In the immediate post–World War II era, U.S. companies dominated the global economy due to technological superiority and because the infrastructures of many countries were badly damaged during the war. However, these countries, most notably Japan and Germany, gradually but consistently improved their standing in the world economy. In particular, the United States lost its dominance in industries such as automobiles and electronics. Changes in the global and domestic business environments during the twentieth century gave rise to the need for new management techniques, especially from the perspective of the top manager. The dual tasks of efficiently running a large, often multinational firm and guiding its course became too difficult for any one leader to handle alone. New organizational forms emerged, with new divisions of managerial labor and new managerial techniques. Also, while the large organizations that formed during the early part of the century were internally focused on efficiency (a management science approach combined with basic financial planning), they soon learned that effective management in a rapidly changing business environment required more of an outward orientation.

Business schools responded to changing top management needs by offering a course called business policy. The business policy course applied general administrative principles to a variety of business situations through cases, which described real-world businesses and the challenges they faced. Competitiveness problems of U.S. firms also gave rise to substantial growth in consulting firms who specialized in top management issues and questions. Additionally, the topics of strategy and strategic management became major research thrusts in many business schools across the United States and elsewhere. By the early 1970s, teachers and researchers of business policy began meeting to discuss changes that were taking place in the field of business policy and how they should respond to them. Then, in May 1977, a major conference was held at the University of Pittsburgh. This conference confirmed the birth of a field now known as strategic management.[8]

Since that critical meeting in 1977, strategic management has continually grown in importance, as researchers in almost every country in the world attempt to discover the strategies and strategic management techniques that differentiate successful from unsuccessful organizations. Strategic management processes are widely recognized for their value to organizations. Most large corporations in the United States and abroad have staffs dedicated to strategic management activities. Smaller organizations have also found the tools and techniques of strategic management helpful.

In the past two decades, many perspectives on strategic management and the strategic management process have emerged. The approach found in this book is based predominantly on three of these perspectives: the traditional perspective, the resource-based view of the firm, and the stakeholder approach. These three perspectives, outlined in Table 1.1, will now be introduced.

The Traditional Perspective

As the field of strategic management began to emerge in the latter part of the twentieth century, scholars borrowed heavily from the field of economics. For some time, economists had been actively studying topics associated with the competitiveness of industries. These topics included industry concentration, diversification, product differentiation, and market power. However, much of the economics research focused exclusively on industries, and some of it even assumed that individual firm differences didn't matter. Other fields also had an influence on early strategic management thought, including marketing, finance, psychology, and management. Academic progress was slow in the beginning, and the large consulting firms began to develop their own models and theories to meet their clients' needs. Scholars readily adopted many of these models into their own articles and books.

Eventually, a consensus began to build regarding what is included in the strategic management process. The **traditional approach to strategic management** consists of analyzing the internal and external environments of the company to arrive at organizational strengths, weaknesses, opportunities, and threats (SWOT). The results from this "situation analysis," as this process is sometimes called, are the basis for developing missions, goals, and strategies.[9] In general, a company should select strategies that (1) take advantage of organizational strengths and environmental opportunities or (2) neutralize or overcome organizational weaknesses and environmental threats. After strategies are formulated, plans for implementing them are established and carried out. Figure 1.1 presents the natural flow of these activities.

traditional approach to strategic management Analysis of the internal and external environments of the organization to arrive at organizational strengths, weaknesses, opportunities, and threats (SWOT), which form the basis for developing effective missions, goals, and strategies

Table 1.1	**Three Perspectives on Strategic Management**		
	Traditional Perspective	**Resource-Based View**	**Stakeholder View**
Origin	Economics, other business disciplines, and consulting firms	Economics, distinctive competencies, and general management capability	Business ethics and social responsibility
View of Firm	An economic entity	A collection of resources, skills, and abilities	A network of relationships among the firm and its stakeholders
Approach to Strategy Formulation	Situation analysis of internal and external environments leading to formulation of mission and strategies	Analysis of organizational resources, skills, and abilities. Acquisition of superior resources, skills, and abilities	Analysis of the economic power, political influence, rights, and demands of various stakeholders
Source of Competitive Advantage	Best adapting the organization to its environment by taking advantage of strengths and opportunities and overcoming weaknesses and threats	Possession of resources, skills, and abilities that are valuable, rare, and difficult to imitate by competitors	Superior linkages with stakeholders leading to trust, goodwill, reduced uncertainty, improved business dealings, and ultimately higher firm performance

The model contained in Figure 1.1 is still valid and will provide a framework for understanding the various activities described in this book. However, the traditional approach to strategy development also brought with it some ideas that strategic management scholars have had to reevaluate. The first of these ideas was that the environment is the primary determinant of the best strategy. This is called **environmental determinism.** According to the deterministic view, good management is associated with determining which strategy will best fit environmental, technical, and human forces at a particular point in time, and then working to carry it out.[10] The most successful organization will be the one that best adapts to existing forces. There is some evidence that the ability to align the skills and other resources of the organization with the needs and demands of the environment can be a source of competitive advantage.[11] However, after a critical review of environmental determinism, a well-known researcher once argued:

> There is a more fundamental conclusion to be drawn from the foregoing analysis: the strategy of a firm cannot be predicted, nor is it predestined; the strategic decisions made by managers cannot be assumed to be the product of deterministic forces in their environments...On the contrary, the very nature of the concept of strategy assumes a human agent who is able to take actions that attempt to distinguish one's firm from the competitors.[12]

This is basically an argument that firms may choose their environments. For example, a larger firm may decide not to compete in a given environment. Or, as an alternative, the firm may attempt to influence the environment to make it less hostile and more conducive to organizational success. This process is called **enactment,** which means that a firm can influence its environment. The principle of enactment assumes that organizations do not have to submit to existing forces in the environment—they can, in part, create their environments through strategic alliances with stakeholders, investments in leading technologies, advertising, political lobbying, and a variety of other activities.[13] Of course, smaller organizations are somewhat limited in their ability to influence some components of their environments

environmental determinism
The perspective that the most successful organization will be the one that best adapts to existing forces—in other words, the environment "determines" the best strategy

enactment
The perspective that firms do not have to submit to existing environmental forces because they can influence their environments

FIGURE 1.1

The Traditional Strategic Management Process

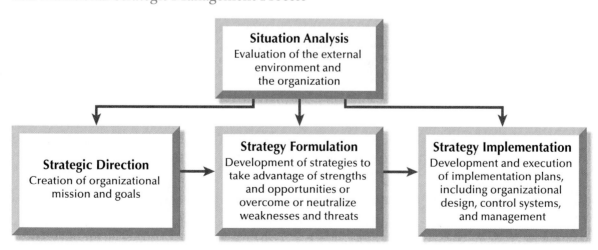

on their own. For example, a small firm may have a difficult time influencing national government agencies and administrators. However, smaller organizations often band together into trade groups to influence government. Also, they may form alliances with larger entities. In addition, even a small firm may be able to exert a powerful influence in its local operating environment. The key to enactment is understanding that a firm does not necessarily have to adapt completely to the forces that exist in its operating environment. It can at least partly influence certain aspects of the environment in which it competes.

The traditional school of thought concerning strategy formulation also supported the view that managers respond to the forces discussed thus far by making decisions that are consistent with a preconceived strategy. In other words, strategy is deliberate. **Deliberate strategy** implies that managers *plan* to pursue an *intended* strategic course. On the other hand, in some cases, strategy simply emerges from a stream of decisions. Managers learn as they go. An **emergent strategy** is one that was not planned or intended. According to this perspective, managers *learn* what will work through a process of trial and error.[14] Supporters of this view argue that organizations that limit themselves to acting on the basis of what is already known or understood will not be sufficiently innovative to create a sustainable competitive advantage.[15]

deliberate strategy
Implies that managers plan to pursue an intended strategic course

emergent strategy
Implies that the existing strategy is not necessarily planned or intended, but rather a result of learning through a process of trial and error

 The story of the small Honda motorcycle offers support for the concept of emergent strategy. When Honda executives decided to market a small motorcycle, they had no idea it would be so successful. In fact, the prevailing wisdom was that small motorcycles would not sell very well. But Honda executives broke the rules and made the decision to market a small motorcycle. As sales expanded, they increased marketing, and ultimately captured two-thirds of the American motorcycle market. In another example, General Motors had a minivan on the drawing boards long before Chrysler. On the basis of rational analysis, GM decided that the minivan probably would not sell.[16]

In spite of the strength of this example of emergent strategy, it is not a good idea to reject deliberate strategy either. One of the strongest advocates of learning and emergent strategy recently confessed, "We shall get nowhere without emergent learning alongside deliberate planning."[17] Both processes are necessary if an organization is to succeed.

In summary, scholars have determined that both adaptation and enactment are important to organizations. They should adapt to environmental forces when the costs of enacting (influencing) the environment exceed the benefits. However, they should be proactive in creating their own opportunities. In addition, organizations should engage in deliberate strategic planning processes, but they should also be willing to make mistakes and learn from them as they chart a strategic course. In other words, strategy should be both deliberate and emergent, and firms should both adapt to and enact their environments, with the situation determining which option to choose.

The Organization as a Bundle of Resources

resource-based approach to strategic management
Considers the firm as a bundle of resources; firms can gain competitive advantage through possessing superior resources

In recent years, another perspective on strategy development has gained wide acceptance. The **resource-based approach to strategic management** has its roots in the work of the earliest strategic management theorists.[18] It grew out of the question, "Why do some firms persistently outperform other firms?" An early answer to that question was that some firms are able to develop distinctive competencies in particular areas.[19] One of the first competencies identified was general management capability. This led to the proposition that firms with "high quality" general managers will outperform their rivals. Much research has examined this issue. Clearly, effective leadership is important to organizational performance. However, it is hard to specify what makes an effective leader. Also, although leaders are an important source of competence for an organization, they are not the only important resource that makes a difference.

Economic thought also influenced development of the resource-based view. Nearly two centuries ago, an economist named David Ricardo investigated the advantages of possessing superior resources, especially land.[20] One of Ricardo's central propositions was that the farmer with the most-fertile land has a sustained performance advantage over other farmers. More recently, another economist, Edith Penrose, expanded on Ricardo's view by noting that various skills and abilities possessed by firms can lead to superior performance. She viewed firms as an administrative framework that coordinates the activities of numerous groups and individuals, and also as a bundle of productive resources.[21] She studied the effects of various skills and abilities possessed by organizations, concluding that a wide range of skills and resources can influence competitive performance.

A common thread of reasoning in the distinctive competency literature and the arguments of Ricardo and Penrose is that organizational success can be explained in terms of the resources and capabilities possessed by an organization. Many modern scholars have contributed to this perspective of the firm.[22] According to this view, an organization is a bundle of resources, which fall into the general categories of (1) financial resources, including all of the monetary resources from which a firm can draw; (2) physical resources, such as plants, equipment, locations, and access to raw materials; (3) human resources, which pertains to the skills, background, and training of managers and employees, as well as the way they are organized; (4) organizational knowledge and learning; and (5) general organizational resources, including firm reputation, brand names, patents, contracts, and relationships with external stakeholders.[23] The organization as a bundle of resources is depicted in Figure 1.2.

Envisioning the firm as a bundle of resources has broad implications. For example, the most important role of a manager becomes that of acquiring, developing, managing, and discarding resources. Also, much of the research on the resource-based perspective has demonstrated that firms can gain competitive advantage through possessing superior resources.[24] Superior resources are those that have value in the market, are possessed by only a small number of firms, and are not easy to substitute. If a particular resource is also costly or impossible to imitate, then the competitive advantage may be sustainable. A sustainable competitive advantage may lead to higher-than-average organizational performance over a long time period.[25]

 The success of Marriott is largely attributable to advantages created by resources that have been difficult to duplicate by other companies in the hotel industry. The first is financial controls. Marriott can determine and anticipate construction and operating costs with nearly exact precision. Second, Marriott has developed a distinctive competence in customer service, or "becoming the provider of choice." Looking to the future, Marriott is actively engaged in creating a third organizational capability as the "employer of choice." Marriott executives reason that with fewer people entering the labor force in the 18- to 25-year old age group, good

FIGURE 1.2

The Organization as a Bundle of Resources

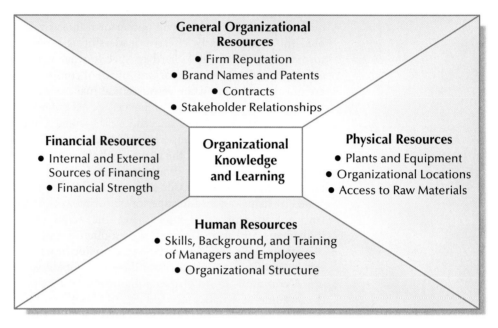

workers will become increasingly difficult to attract. Also, good workers are especially important in a service business like hotels because they interact directly with customers.[26]

Many strategy scholars believe that acquisition and development of superior organizational resources is the most important reason that some companies are more successful than others.[27] Most of the resources that a firm can acquire or develop are directly linked to a company's stakeholders. For example, financial resources are closely linked to establishing good working relationships with financial intermediaries. Also, the development of human resources is associated with effective management of organizational stakeholders. Finally, organizational resources reflect the organization's understanding of the expectations of society and the linkages it has established with stakeholders. Consequently, the stakeholder perspective of strategic management, which will be explained next, is complementary to the resource-based perspective.

The Organization as a Network of Relationships with Stakeholders

A *Fortune* magazine cover story described modern business in these terms: "Business already is moving to organize itself into virtual corporations: fungible modules built around information networks, flexible work forces, outsourcing, and webs of strategic partnerships."[28] Negotiating and contracting have always been important to business. However, the trend in business is toward more strategic alliances, joint ventures, and subcontracting arrangements with stakeholders. The fact is that some of a firm's most valuable resources may extend beyond the boundaries of a firm.[29] Consequently, business organizations are becoming a tangled web of alliances and contracts. For example, Toyota, the automobile giant, chooses to rely on outside suppliers rather than produce supplies in-house. Only two suppliers are owned outright by Toyota, with everything else provided by more than two hundred outside sources.[30]

In the mid-1980s, a **stakeholder approach to strategic management** began to emerge. It was developed as a direct response to the concerns of managers who were being buffeted by increasing levels of complexity and change in the external environment.[31] The existing strategy models were not particularly helpful to managers who were trying to create new opportunities during a period of such radical change. The word "stakeholder" was a deliberate play on the word "stockholder." Much of the strategy literature at the time was founded, either explicitly or implicitly, on the idea that stockholders were the only important constituencies of the modern for-profit corporation. Stakeholder theory contradicted this idea by expanding a company's responsibility to groups or individuals who significantly affect or are significantly affected by the company's activities, including stockholders.[32] Figure 1.3 contains a typical stakeholder map. A firm has internal stakeholders, such as employees, that are considered a part of the internal organization. In addition, the firm has frequent interactions with stakeholders in what is called the operating (or task) environment. The firm and stakeholders in its operating environment are both influenced by other factors such as society, technology, the economy, and the legal environment. These other factors form the broad environment, which will be discussed in Chapter 2.

The stakeholder model has several advantages. First, relative to a model that includes only a few stakeholders, it more accurately depicts the complicated nature of the management task by enlarging the group of relevant constituencies to which managerial attention is drawn. This accuracy is important so that managers understand the many forces that influence organizational behavior and success. Second, consideration of a broader group of stakeholders during the strategic management process can help prevent an organization from being surprised by a dissatisfied stakeholder. For example, looking at a new strategy from the perspective of a union can help a company prevent a strike. Also, considering the needs of a local community can prevent bad press, lawsuits, and adverse legislation. Third, the stakeholder model provides more choices when selecting strategic options. For example, an organization that has fostered excellent relationships with many stakeholders has more options to consider when difficulty is experienced. The following example demonstrates this point.

stakeholder approach to strategic management
Envisions the firm at the center of a network of constituencies called stakeholders; firms can gain competitive advantage through superior stakeholder management

 Stonyfield Farm, Inc. (Londonderry, New Hampshire) was in trouble when the company that manufactured its yogurt went bankrupt. Stonyfield responded with an innovative recovery plan that involved several key stakeholders, including employees, suppliers, a government agency, stockholders, managers, and customers. First, the company ran its product-development plant on a seven-day, three-shift schedule to maintain volume until a new plant could be built. This required the support of employees, which management fostered through weekly meetings. Due to financial strain during construction, workers were asked to take lower wages with the expectation of future bonuses. The company instituted flexible-time scheduling, improved benefits, increased training, and participative decision making in an effort to maintain good relationships with employees.

FIGURE 1.3

A Typical Stakeholder Map

Note: Two-headed arrows signify both two-way influence and a two-way dependent relationship between an organization and its stakeholders.

Stonyfield also tapped into the goodwill of external stakeholders through partnerships with suppliers and engineers, who agreed to provide their services up front without payment in exchange for exclusive supply agreements. A government agency, the Small Business Administration, provided a loan guarantee, and stockholders provided bridge loans so that the company could remain solvent until longer-term financing was arranged. After the new plant was opened, the company was still strapped for cash, resulting in a small marketing budget. They decided to involve their customers directly, and created a "Moo Patrol" program, complete with a newsletter and an "Adopt-a-Cow" program for children. These efforts resulted in a growth rate of more than 60 percent in some customer groups, and the introduction of several new product lines to be distributed nationally.[33]

Many companies in a financial condition as weak as Stonyfield's would not have even considered the option of building a new plant. However, through the creative use of a broad range of stakeholders, the company was able to achieve a high level of success. Now Stonyfield is the fourth-largest producer of yogurt in the United States.[34] With a huge recent investment by Group Danone SA of France, the company expects growth to continue at an accelerated pace.

Traditionally, at least in the United States, management theory has focused on internal (e.g., employees) rather than external stakeholders, with organizational boundaries drawn around the individuals and groups over which managers had direct supervisory control. An inherent assumption in the drawing of organizational boundaries was that external stakeholders could not be "managed," in the traditional sense of the word, because they were not a part of the organization. However,

subcontracting
Acquiring goods and services that used to be produced in house from external companies

traditional organizational boundaries are blurring.[35] Firms are **subcontracting** the creation of many goods and services that used to be produced in-house.[36] For example, Nike subcontracts its shoe-assembly operations, and Liz Claiborne has its apparel manufactured overseas. Subcontracting of vital activities requires a high level of communication and control. A company such as Nike has to ensure that the quality of its shoes is maintained, especially in a global marketplace that requires high quality. After the crash of one of its airliners in the Florida Everglades, ValuJet was sharply criticized, whether justifiably or not, for subcontracting its maintenance activities. The perception of the media and others, whether accurate or not, was that ValuJet was not able to exercise adequate oversight over an external contractor. Consequently, the public has now come to expect that firms will, to some extent, manage their external stakeholders.

Table 1.2 demonstrates that the differences in techniques between managing internal and external stakeholders are not that significant. American workers, in particular, have become more independent in their thinking, and the span of control of managers in most industries has increased. Effective managers use persuasion and rewards more than direct control to motivate their employees to fulfill obligations and move the organization toward its goals. Also, many companies have begun to break down traditional boundaries that excluded external stakeholders from internal processes. For example, firms in the automobile industry often include suppliers on their product-design teams, and many boards of directors now include representatives from financial institutions, the community, or labor unions. As the rest of this book will demonstrate, this attitude applies to a broad range of external stakeholders.

Table 1.2	Can External Stakeholders Be Managed?	
	Internal Stakeholder Management	**External Stakeholder Management**
Nature of Relationship	Contractual, contract longevity sometimes based on loyalty	Contractual, legal (regulatory), or informal (in the case of activists); contract longevity may also be based on loyalty
Physical Location	Predominantly inside organizational structure, sometimes geographically dispersed	Predominantly outside organizational structure, sometimes included in official structure
Motivation to Perform	Regular payments, retention, promotions, perks, bonuses, common purpose, persuasion	Regular payments, retention, incentives, and bonuses for performance, common purpose, persuasion
Direct Control	Schedules, plans, sometimes direct supervision	Schedules, plans, less often direct supervision
Communication	E-mail, much face-to-face contact, telephone, memos, directives, policies	E-mail, face-to-face contact, telephone, memos, directives, policies
Involvement in Organizational Decisions	Level of employee involvement in organizational decisions varies from one organization to the next, but recent trends are that this involvement is increasing (i.e., participative decision making, total quality management)	Level of external stakeholder involvement in organizational decisions varies also, but recent trends are that this involvement is increasing (i.e., product-design teams, board-of-director involvement, joint ventures)
Importance of Trust	High	High

The stakeholder view offers a realistic compromise between the two theoretical extremes of adaptation and enactment that were discussed earlier. External stakeholder analysis involves identifying and prioritizing key external stakeholders, assessing their needs, collecting ideas from them, and integrating this knowledge into strategic management processes such as the establishment of strategic direction and the formulation and implementation of strategies. These are processes associated largely with adapting to the external environment. On the other hand, stakeholder management includes communicating, negotiating, contracting, and managing relationships with stakeholders, and motivating them to behave in ways that are beneficial to the organization and its other stakeholders. These processes are most closely associated with efforts on the part of organizations to influence, or enact, their environments. In reality, the two processes of stakeholder analysis and stakeholder management overlap. That is, managers tend to analyze and manage relationships with stakeholders simultaneously.

Effective management of relationships with external stakeholders is even more important today than it was even a few years ago. Figure 1.4 illustrates this point. Increasing global competition means that organizations are dependent on companies in a wider range of countries to supply world-class goods and services that are necessary to compete effectively. Also, increasing technological complexity means that firms are dependent on more companies to provide needed supplies, parts, and

FIGURE 1.4

Need for and Outcomes from Trustworthy Partnering Behavior

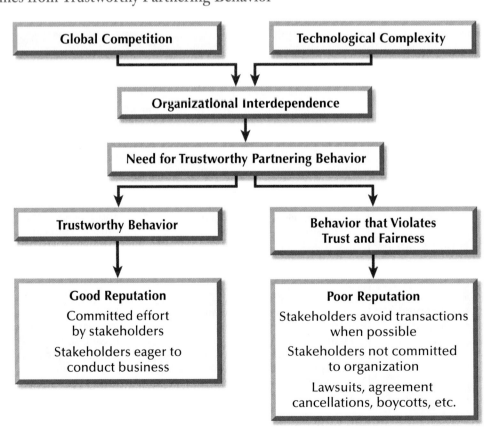

services. Both of these trends have led to increased organizational interdependence. That is, companies need each other now more than ever if they expect to prosper.

With increasing interdependence has come the need for trustworthy partnering behavior, which is associated with high levels of trust and effective partnering, since organizations are willing to work with companies only if they believe that outcomes will be favorable.[37] Effective partnerships are associated with high communication quality and participation, joint problem solving, commitment, coordination, and trust.[38] Stakeholders develop expectations concerning the way an organization should behave and the outcomes they expect to receive. When stakeholders become openly dissatisfied with organizational practices or performance, the company's ethical image and reputation are tarnished. Furthermore, this lack of consistency between the organization and its key stakeholders may result in financial losses due to lawsuits, lost contracts, and lost revenues.

 Bridgestone/Firestone recently severed a century-long relationship with Ford Motor Company. The action was a direct result of alleged problems with Bridgestone/Firestone tires on certain Ford models. After months of quarreling and casting blame between the two companies, John Lampe, CEO of Bridgestone/Firestone, concluded: "Business relationships, like personal ones, are built on trust and mutual respect. We have come to the conclusion that we can no longer supply tires to Ford since the basic foundation of our relationship has been seriously eroded." At one point, Ford even met directly with federal investigators to discuss possible problems with even more tires. Bridgestone/Firestone was not even invited. Commenting on the incident, Lampe stated: "We have always said that in order to insure the safety of the driving public, it is crucial that there be a true sharing of information concerning the vehicle as well as the tires. Ford simply is not willing to do that."[39]

This section has laid a foundation upon which the rest of this book will be built. The three perspectives that will be incorporated are the traditional, the resource-based, and the stakeholder views of strategic management. Now the strategic management process will be introduced in more detail.

The Strategic Management Process

Three perspectives on strategic management have been discussed: the traditional model, the resource-based view, and the stakeholder approach. In this book, these three approaches are combined (see Table 1.3). The basic strategic management process is most closely related to the traditional model. However, each one of the stages of this process is heavily influenced by each of the three approaches.

Chapter titles have been added to the simple model of the strategic management process introduced earlier (see Figure 1.5). The typical sequence of activities begins with (1) a situation analysis of the broad and operating environments of the organization, including internal resources, and both internal and external stakeholders; (2) establishment of strategic direction, reflected in mission statements and organizational visions; (3) formulation of specific strategies; (4) strategy implementation, which includes designing an organizational structure, controlling organizational processes, managing relationships with stakeholders, and managing resources so as to develop competitive advantage. While these activities may occur in the order

Table 1.3	A Combined Perspective of Strategic Management
Process	Firms conduct external and internal analysis (situation analysis), both of which include analysis of stakeholders. On the basis of information obtained, they create strategic direction, strategies, and tactics for implementing strategies and control systems.
Origin	Traditional, resource-based, and stakeholder perspectives.
Adaptation vs. Enactment	Influence the environment when it is economically feasible to do so. Take a proactive stance with regard to managing external stakeholders. Monitor, forecast, and adapt to environmental forces that are difficult or costly to influence.
Deliberate vs. Emergent	Firms should be involved in deliberate strategy-creating processes. However, they should learn from past decisions and be willing to try new things and change strategic course.
Source of Competitive Advantage	Firms can obtain competitive advantage from superior resources, including knowledge-based resources, superior strategies for managing those resources, and/or superior relationships with internal or external stakeholders (which are another type of resource).
Creation of Strategic Alternatives	Firms develop strategies to take advantage of strengths and opportunities or overcome weaknesses or threats. They arise as organizations conduct resource analysis, analysis of organizational processes, and through analyzing and partnering with external stakeholders.

specified, especially if a firm is engaging in a formal strategic planning program, they may also be carried out in some other order or simultaneously.

The feedback loops at the bottom of Figure 1.5 indicate that organizations often cycle back to earlier activities during the strategic management process, as new information is gathered and assumptions change. For instance, a company may attempt to develop strategies consistent with its strategic direction and, after a trial period, discover that the direction was not reasonable. Also, an organization may discover rather quickly (or over a longer period of time) that a proposed strategy cannot be implemented feasibly. As a result, the firm may have to cycle back to the formulation stage to fine-tune its strategic approach. In other words, organizations may learn from their own past actions and from environmental forces, and may modify their behavior in response.

Entrepreneurial start-up firms rarely engage in all of the processes depicted in Figure 1.5. Start-ups often begin with an entrepreneur who has an idea for a product or service that he or she believes will lead to market success. Venture capital is raised through a variety of public or private sources, and a new business is born. The entrepreneur may establish an informal sense of direction and a few goals, but the rest of the formal strategy process may be overlooked. If the organization is successful, it will typically expand in both sales and personnel until it reaches a critical point at which the original entrepreneur feels a loss of control. At this point, the entrepreneur may attempt to formalize various aspects of strategic planning, either by hiring outside consultants, by creating planning positions within the firm, or by involving other managers in planning activities. This same process is typical of nonprofit start-ups as well, except that the nature of the cause (i.e., humanitarian, educational) may place tighter constraints on the way the firm is financed and organized.

Consequently, the model in Figure 1.5 is not intended to be a rigid representation of the strategic management process in all organizations as they currently operate. Nevertheless, the progression of activities—from analysis to plan to action and control—provides a logical way to study strategic management. Furthermore, the activities relate equally well to for-profit, nonprofit, manufacturing, and service entities, although some of the differences in the way these organizations approach strategic management will be described throughout the text.

FIGURE 1.5

The Strategic Management Process

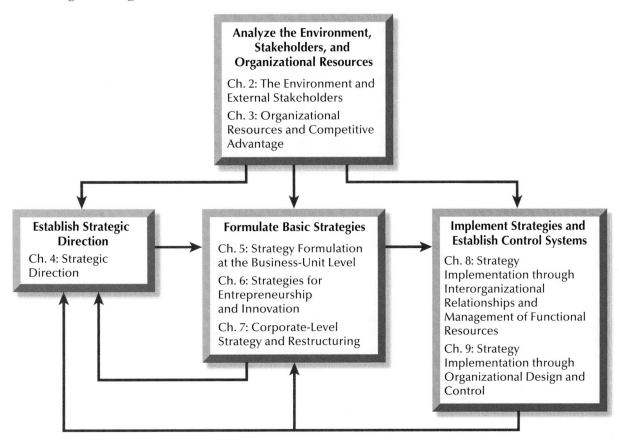

Now that the strategic management process has been introduced, each of its components will be described in more detail—situation analysis, strategic direction, strategy formulation, and strategy implementation.

Situation Analysis

situation analysis
Analysis of stakeholders inside and outside the organization, as well as other external forces; this analysis should be concluded at both the domestic and international levels, if applicable

Many of the stakeholders and forces that have the potential to be most important to companies were presented in Figure 1.3. When performing a **situation analysis,** all of the stakeholders inside and outside of the firm, as well as the major external forces, should be analyzed at both the domestic and international levels. Chapter 2 will deal with the external environment, which includes groups, individuals, and forces outside of the traditional boundaries of the organization that are significantly influenced by or have a major impact on the organization.[40] External stakeholders, part of a company's operating environment, include competitors, customers, suppliers, financial intermediaries, local communities, unions, activist groups, and government agencies and administrators. The broad environment forms the context in which the company and its operating environment exist, and includes sociocultural influences, economic influences, technological influences, and political/legal influences, domestically and abroad. One organization, acting independently, can have very little influence on the forces in the broad environment; however, the forces in this environment can have a tremendous impact on the organization. The internal organization, discussed in Chapter 3, includes all of the stakeholders, resources, knowledge, and processes that exist within the boundaries of the firm.

Analyzing the environment and the company can assist the company in all of the other tasks of strategic management. For example, a firm's managers should formulate strategic direction and specific strategies based on organizational strengths and weaknesses and in the context of the opportunities and threats found in its environment. Strengths are company resources and capabilities that can lead to a competitive advantage. Weaknesses are resources and capabilities that a company does not possess, to the extent that their absence places the firm at a competitive disadvantage. Opportunities are conditions in the broad and operating environments that allow a firm to take advantage of organizational strengths, overcome organizational weaknesses, and/or neutralize environmental threats. Threats are conditions in the broad and operating environments that may stand in the way of organizational competitiveness or the achievement of stakeholder satisfaction.

Strategic Direction

strategic direction
Pertains to the longer-term goals and objectives of the organization; this direction is often contained in mission and vision statements

Strategic direction pertains to the longer-term goals and objectives of the organization. At a more fundamental level, strategic direction defines the purposes for which a company exists and operates. This direction is often contained in mission and vision statements. Unlike shorter-term goals and strategies, the mission is an enduring part of planning processes within the company. Often missions also describe the areas or industries in which an organization operates. For example, the mission of the New York Stock Exchange is as follows:

> Support the capital-raising and asset-management processes by providing the highest-quality and most cost-effective, self-regulated marketplace for the trading of financial instruments; promote confidence in and understanding of that process; and serve as a forum for discussion of relevant national and international policy issues.[41]

vision
Expresses what the organization wants to be in the future

A **vision** statement expresses what the organization wants to be in the future, which may involve a fundamental change in its business. For example, a start-up firm may have a mission to provide software design and support for its clients, but its long-range vision may be to become a fully integrated Internet provider. While the mission directs the business for now, the mission will gradually change as the company moves over time toward fulfillment of its vision. A well-established strategic direction provides guidance to the stakeholders inside the organization who are largely responsible for carrying it out. A well-defined direction also provides external stakeholders with a greater understanding of the company and its activities. Strategic direction is the central topic of Chapter 4. The next logical step in the strategic management process is strategy formulation.

Strategy Formulation

A strategy can be thought of in either of two ways: (1) as a pattern that emerges in a sequence of decisions over time or (2) as an organizational plan of action that is intended to move a company toward the achievement of its shorter-term goals and, ultimately, toward the achievement of its fundamental purposes. In some organizations, particularly those in rapidly changing environments and in small businesses, strategies are not "planned" in the formal sense of the word. Instead, managers seize opportunities as they come up, but within guidelines or boundaries defined by the firm's strategic direction or mission. In those cases, the strategy reflects the insight and intuition of the strategist or business owner, and becomes clear over time as a pattern in a stream of decisions.

Strategies as "plans" are common in most organizations. **Strategy formulation,** the process of planning strategies, is often divided into three levels—corporate, business, and functional. One of the most important elements of **corporate-level strategy formulation** is to define a company's domain of activity through selection of business areas in which the company will compete. **Business-level strategy formulation,** on the other hand, pertains to domain direction and navigation, or how businesses should compete in the areas they have selected. Sometimes business-level strategies are also referred to as competitive strategies. **Functional-level strategy formulation** develops the details of how functional resource areas such as marketing, operations, and finance should be used to implement business-level strategies and achieve competitive advantage. Basically, functional-level strategies are strategies for acquiring, developing, and managing organizational resources. These characterizations are oversimplified, but it is sometimes useful to think of corporate-level strategies as "Where to compete?", business-level strategies as "How to compete in those areas?", and functional-level strategies as "The functional details of how resources will be managed so that business-level strategies will be accomplished."

Perhaps a more accurate way to distinguish among the three levels is to determine the level at which decisions are made. Corporate-level decisions are typically made at the highest levels of the organization by the CEO and/or board of directors, although these individuals may receive input from managers at other levels. If an organization is involved in only one area of business, then business-level decisions tend to be made by these same people. However, in organizations that have diversified into multiple areas, which are represented by different operating divisions or lines–of–business, business-level decisions are made by division heads or business-unit managers. Functional-level decisions are made by functional managers, who represent organizational areas such as operations, finance, personnel, accounting,

strategy formulation
The process of planning strategies, often divided into the corporate, business, and functional levels

corporate-level strategy formulation
The selection of business areas in which the organization will compete and the emphasis each area is given; also includes strategies for carrying out the corporate-level strategy

business-level strategy formulation
Pertains to domain direction and navigation, or how businesses should compete in the business areas they have selected

functional-level strategy formulation
The details of how functional resource areas, such as marketing, operations, and finance, should be used to implement business-level strategies and achieve competitive advantage

FIGURE 1.6

Strategy Formulation in a Multibusiness Organization

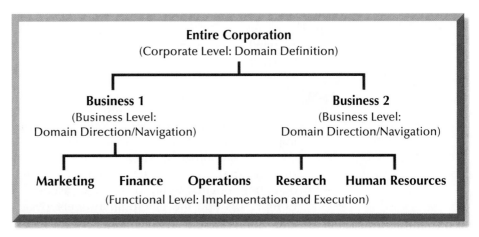

research and development, or information systems. Figure 1.6 shows the levels at which particular strategy decisions are made within a multibusiness firm.

Chapter 5 is concerned primarily with business-level strategies. Chapter 6 focuses on growth strategies, with a particular emphasis on entrepreneurship in both independent companies and in corporations. Chapter 7 contains a more detailed discussion of the corporate-level strategies of concentration, vertical integration, and diversification. Functional-level resource-management strategies are used to support all other types of strategies. You will find them discussed throughout the entire book, beginning in Chapter 3, when the various functions are presented as potential sources of competitive advantage. However, they are revisited again in Chapter 5 as tools to carry out business-level strategies; in Chapter 6 as they relate to entrepreneurial activities; and in Chapter 8, where they become tools of strategy implementation. The order in which the strategy formulation activities are discussed is not important. For example, many instructors prefer to discuss corporate-level strategies before business-level strategies.

Strategy Implementation

strategy implementation
Managing stakeholder relationships and organizational resources in a manner that moves the organization towards the successful execution of its strategies, consistent with its strategic direction

Strategy formulation results in a plan of action for the company and its various levels. On the other hand, strategy implementation represents a pattern of decisions and actions that are intended to carry out the plan. **Strategy implementation** involves managing stakeholder relationships and organizational resources in a manner that moves the business toward the successful execution of its strategies, consistent with its strategic direction. These topics are discussed in Chapter 8. Implementation activities also involve creating an organizational design and organizational control systems to keep the company on the right course. Organizational control refers to the processes that lead to adjustments in strategic direction, strategies, or the implementation plan, when necessary. Thus, managers may collect information that leads them to believe that the organizational mission is no longer appropriate or that its strategies are not leading to the desired outcomes. On the other hand, a strategic-control system may tell managers that the mission and strategies are appropriate, but that they have not been well executed. In such cases, adjustments should be made to the implementation process. Chapter 9 deals with organizational design and organizational control systems.

In summary, the four basic processes associated with strategic management are situation analysis, establishment of strategic direction, strategy formulation, and strategy implementation. Although larger companies tend to make use of the strategic management process, this process is also a vital part of decision making in smaller companies. In fact, it is important in companies of all sizes. Greater Construction Inc., one of the largest home builders in central Florida, recently completed the first cycle of a strategic management process.

Ex. The first step was a stakeholder and organizational resource analysis. This was conducted during a retreat involving operating managers and executives in the company. Robert (Bobby) Mandell, CEO, was impressed with what the company had discovered, so he decided to continue the process. Greater Construction then conducted a full strategic analysis, including an analysis of the broad environment, the operating environment, and each aspect of internal operations. Competitors and the environment were evaluated; employees, managers, and other key stakeholders were interviewed; and customers were surveyed. A full analysis of the financial situation of the company was conducted. Greater Construction was also compared to one of the leading companies of the industry with regard to strategies, organization, and financial results. In addition, Mandell rented a luxury bus and took executives, managers, and a few key external stakeholders on a two-day trip to building sites in other geographic locations in an effort to get new ideas. Results from this analysis of the situation were presented at a meeting of the board of directors.

Based on findings from the situation analysis, top managers were divided into committees representing each of the key operating areas of the company—home construction, land development and acquisition, ancillary businesses, and so forth. The goal was to develop specific strategies in each area as well as plans for implementation. The resulting strategies and implementation plans were then collapsed into a single comprehensive strategic plan. With regard to control, a timeline was created, and specific managers were assigned to report to the board by particular dates. To ensure that the strategic management process would continue, a rotating schedule was created so that particular areas would be reviewed and new strategies developed on an annual basis.[42]

Did this process make a difference? As a result, Mandell led Greater Construction into a bold new strategy involving new markets and new products.

Global Competitiveness

Most successful organizations eventually find that their domestic markets are becoming saturated or that foreign markets offer opportunities for growth and profitability that often are not available domestically. Many forces are leading firms into the international arena.[43] For example, global trends are leading to a more favorable environment for foreign business involvement. Trade barriers are falling in Europe (i.e., the European Community) and North America (i.e., the North American Free Trade Agreement). Also, newly industrialized countries such as Korea, Taiwan, and Spain are leading to increasing global competition and new marketing opportunities. There is a worldwide shift toward market economies, as in Germany and China, and financial capital is now readily exchanged in global markets. In addition, communication is easier due to satellites and the Internet, and English is becoming a universally spoken business language. Finally, technical standards have started to become uniform in industrialized countries around the world.

In addition to global trends, organizations have a variety of firm-specific reasons for international involvement. Sometimes firms are so successful that they have saturated their domestic markets, so they look overseas. For example, McDonald's expects more growth in international markets than in the well-saturated United States. Also, in some cases, international markets are more profitable than domestic markets. For example, Coke makes higher profits in its foreign operations than it does at home.[44] Hasbro, the toy maker, also enjoys much higher prices and higher margins in other countries than it does in the United States. Latin America has substantial business potential. Chile, in particular, has enjoyed rapid development in recent years.[45] Other once-battered nations such as Vietnam are emerging as profitable places for investment (see Global Insight). Both Eastern Europe and China, despite political turmoil, offer substantial investment opportunities, due to low labor rates and untapped consumer markets.

 Over the past decade, few developments in international economics have been more important than the sudden emergence of China as a dominant recipient of foreign direct investment (FDI) in the world. From an almost isolated economy in 1979, China has become the largest recipient of FDI in the developing world, and globally the second-largest recipient (after the United States), since 1993.[46]

In order to remain competitive, organizations need to acquire state-of-the-art resources at the lowest prices possible. Sometimes the best product or service is not available in the home country, but in a foreign country. The same is true of lowest-cost goods and services. For example, many companies acquire much of their labor from emerging nations such as Indonesia, India, Mexico, or Chile, where the wage rates are relatively low. Finally, foreign investments offer opportunities to acquire technical knowledge and managerial techniques that can then be applied across all the businesses of the firm.

The strategic management implications of increasing globalization are profound. Managers cannot afford to ignore opportunities in foreign markets. However, business methods and customs differ from country to country. These differences make stakeholder analysis and management even more important. Analysis of broad environmental forces such as society, technology, and political influences must also be expanded to each of the areas in which an organization conducts business. People also differ greatly from country to country. They cannot be managed in the same way.

The tools, techniques, and models found in this book apply well to strategic management in a global environment. The methods and theories are used by top strategic planners in business situations around the globe. However, there are differences between strategic management in a domestic setting versus in an international setting. Each of the four basic parts of the strategic management process (e.g., situation analysis, strategic direction, strategy formulation, and implementation) is a little different when applied to an international environment. First, analysis of the environment associated with a situation analysis is complicated by the fact that the organization is involved in multiple environments with varying characteristics. Second, strategic direction must consider stakeholders with a much broader range of needs. Third, the number of alternative strategies is greatly increased as a firm considers options arising from foreign environments. Finally, the specific details associated with implementing strategies will be very different from country to country due to differences in customs, resources, and accepted business practices.

International issues associated with strategic management will be handled in various ways in this text. First, the theory of strategic management will be illustrated with a variety of U.S. and non-U.S. organizational examples. Second, theories and models dealing with global strategy will be included in various chapters of the book and in Chapter 10. Finally, many country-specific illustrations will be used to demonstrate how strategic management is likely to differ in a variety of global contexts. Some of these illustrations will be included in special exhibits, such as the Global Insight on doing business in Vietnam.

The challenges of an increasingly competitive global marketplace can be addressed through a well-devised strategic management process. However, strategic planning does not always lead to the kinds of changes that are necessary to remain competitive over the long term. Ineffective strategic planning is often the result of a missing ingredient, strategic thinking, the topic of the next section.

Global Insight
Vietnam Possibly Emerging as an Investment Option

Once war-torn and destitute, Vietnam is emerging as a potential source of profitable business opportunities. Tran Xuan Gia, planning and investment minister, has a very optimistic view of his country's recent progress. In a recent interview, he expressed this optimism:

> The advantages of Vietnam include political and socioeconomic stability, which minimizes risk for foreign investors. The country has a record of continued development in recent years (especially 1991–1997, when our economy grew more than 8 percent per year.) Even though the growth rate slowed in 1998 (5.8 percent) and 1999 (4.7–5 percent), Vietnam stayed outside the regional crisis. Our country remains committed to our Doi Moi (Renovation) Policy. Internally, we are changing from a planned economy to a market economy in accordance with a socialist orientation; externally, we are changing from a closed economy to an open and integrated one.[1]

The regional economic crisis to which Mr. Gia refers began in Thailand in 1997 and quickly spread to other countries in Southeast Asia, including South Korea and Indonesia. As an excellent example of the kind of resilience demonstrated by Vietnamese firms, Vietnam Airlines increased its passenger loads during the period. Discussing that accomplishment, Dao Manh Nhuong, CEO of Vietnam Airlines, stated:

> It is true that Vietnam Airlines has overcome difficulties resulting from the recent economic-financial crisis.… Particularly in the context of this crisis, we rationalized our route network, strengthened the organization and its operations, maximized turnover (meaning asset turnover), and minimized expenditures.[2]

Nevertheless, Western business executives need to exercise due care when conducting business in Vietnam. For example, the Vietnamese often communicate through subtle messages in the stories they tell. Also, the concept of "right relationship," with roots in ancient ancestor cults and Confucianism, means that every person has his or her place in the organization, which defines rights, duties, and responsibilities. In addition, relationships should be developed over time in a step-by-step fashion. Relationships in Vietnam move through layers. First-time visitors are graciously welcomed acquaintances, second-time visitors return as friends, third-time visitors as old friends.[3]

Notes: 1. J. R. Schermerhorn Jr., "Planning and Investment Minister Tran Xuan Gia on Foreign Investment and the Vietnamese Business Environment," *Academy of Management Executive* (November 2000): 9–10. **2.** J. R. Schermerhorn Jr., "Vietnam Airlines' CEO Dao Manh Nhuong on Strategic Leadership," *Academy of Management Executive* (November 2000): 19. **3.** L. Borton, "Working in a Vietnamese Voice," *Academy of Management Executive* (November 2000): 23.

Strategic Thinking

Industry Revolutionaries
Firms that invent new business concepts

What does it take for a company to be on the cutting edge in its industry? Organizational leaders can learn a great deal from studying the strategies of competitors. Clearly, there are things an organization can learn from competitors that will lead to improvements in performance. However, by the time a firm develops the skills and acquires the resources that are necessary to imitate industry leaders, those leaders probably will have moved on to new ideas and strategies. Consequently, industry leaders break out of traditional mind-sets and defy widely accepted industry practices. Gary Hamel, a well-known strategic management author and consultant, calls these firms **"Industry Revolutionaries."** He says that revolutionaries don't simply seek incremental improvements to existing business systems to increase efficiency, nor do they focus exclusively on individual products or services. Instead, they invent new business concepts. According to Hamel, "Industry revolutionaries don't tinker at the margins; they blow up old business models and create new ones."[47] For instance, IKEA broke with tradition in the home-furnishings business by offering customers high-quality furniture that can be taken home the same day. They do very high volume by selling at low prices.

Bill Gates, CEO of Microsoft, has said that his company is "always two years away from failure."[48] At any time, a competing firm may develop a software product that is perceived as superior to whatever version of Windows Microsoft is selling, and, within a couple of years, become the market leader. Indeed, Microsoft almost missed a huge opportunity with the Internet and had to play catch-up to Netscape. Strategic thinking does not mean that a firm should randomly try new things until something works. Instead, it allows creative thought to emerge, which should then be accompanied by systematic analysis to determine what should actually be done.

Much will be said in this book about the importance of innovation and how to foster organizational entrepreneurship. An excellent way to start this discussion is with the topic of strategic thinking, since such thinking runs parallel to both innovation and entrepreneurship. It is important to understand from the outset that strategic thinking is not a replacement for the strategic planning process. There are certain aspects of the process, such as analysis of the external environment, that foster strategic thinking. Also, parts of the strategic planning process should be done very systematically, such as the evaluation of alternatives and the development of control systems. However, strategic thinking helps organizations move beyond what is tried and proven. *Effective strategic management includes both strategic thinking and the essential elements of the strategic planning process.*

Strategic Planning Can Drive Out Strategic Thinking

The term "strategic thinking" is used in so many different ways that it is difficult to determine what people mean when they use it. In fact, most people probably don't know exactly what they mean. They may use the word to mean "thinking about strategy," or use it interchangeably with "strategic management" or "strategic planning."[49] According to a well-known strategist, Henry Mintzberg, strategic planning is an analytical process aimed at carrying out strategies that have already been identified. Strategic planning results in the creation of a plan. On the other hand, strategic thinking involves intuition and creativity. It is a way to synthesize stimuli from the internal and external environments to create an "an integrated perspective of the enterprise."[50] According to Mintzberg, strategic planning is so rigid that it tends to drive out creative-thinking processes. The following true story illustrates this point. The actual name of the company is disguised to protect the firm from embarrassment. However, many companies, especially larger ones, have strategic planning processes that mirror the ones described in the following example.

 One of the largest companies in the world, with vast operations around the globe, has a very systematic strategic planning process. The organization is divided into many companies. Each year, all of the companies prepare a two-day presentation for corporate administrators to whom they report. They present highly detailed plans of the objectives the company will reach over the next few years, and the specific strategies that will be pursued in order to reach them. Hundreds of PowerPoint–style slides are used. A rigid format is followed, so that the presentations of each company contain the same elements, and corporate executives know what to expect. In preparing for the presentations, company managers are very cautious. They are hesitant to bring up highly innovative ideas that could lead to dramatic changes because they know that once they commit to performance targets they will be held accountable for achieving them. The managers are afraid to fail because the organization penalizes failure. In general, the organization doesn't reward unconventional thinking. Consequently, the company has been limping along for several years now, with many performance problems and low shareholder returns.[51]

This kind of approach to strategic planning can be referred to as "strategy as form filling," whereas strategic thinking is "crafting strategic architecture."[52] The next section provides more detail on the essential elements of strategic thinking.

Characteristics of Strategic Thinking

Strategic thinking is intent focused, comprehensive, opportunistic, long-term oriented, built on the past and the present, and hypothesis driven. A summary of these characteristics is found in Table 1.4.[53]

Intent Focused

strategic intent
A vision of where an organization is or should be going; similar to the strategic concept of "vision" defined previously

Strategic thinking is not a random process of trial and error. Instead, it involves **strategic intent,** which is a vision with regard to where an organization is or should be going. Strategic intent "implies a particular point of view about the long-term market or competitive position that a firm hopes to build over the coming decade or so. Hence, it conveys a *sense of direction.* A strategic intent is differentiated; it implies a competitively unique point of view about the future. It holds out to employees the promise of exploring new competitive territory. Hence, it conveys a *sense of discovery.* Strategic intent has an emotional edge to it; it is a goal that employees perceive as inherently worthwhile. Hence, it implies a *sense of destiny.* Direction, discovery, and destiny. These are the attributes of strategic intent."[54]

Comprehensive

Strategic thinking is based on a "systems perspective" that envisions the firm as a part of a complete end-to-end system of value creation. Furthermore, strategic

Table 1.4	Elements of Strategic Thinking
Intent Focused	Built on a managerial vision of where the firm is going and what it is trying to become. This is called strategic intent.
Comprehensive	A "systems" perspective. Envisions the firm as a part of a larger system of value creation. Understands the linkages between the firm and the other parts of the system.
Opportunistic	Seizes unanticipated opportunities presented to the firm.
Long-Term Oriented	Goes beyond the here and now. Looks several years into the future at what the firm will become, based on its strategic intent.
Built on Past and Present	Does not ignore the past or present. Instead, learns from the past and builds on a foundation of the realities of the present.
Hypothesis Driven	A sequential process in which creative ideas are then critically evaluated. Is willing to take a risk. Learns from mistakes.

Source: This table was strongly influenced by J. M. Liedtka, "Strategy Formulation: The Roles of Conversation and Design," in *The Blackwell Handbook of Strategic Management,* ed. M. A. Hitt, R. E. Freeman, and J. S. Harrison (Oxford: Blackwell Publishers, 2001), 70–93.

mental model
A view of how the world works; mental models should include an understanding of both the internal and external organization and the interaction between the two

thinking means that decision makers are very aware of the interdependencies in the system.[55] This type of thinking fits very well within the stakeholder view of the organization, which is one of the important perspectives upon which our model of strategic management is based. Organizational managers each possess a **"mental model,"** which is a view of "how the world works."[56] Mental models should include an understanding of both the internal and external organization. An industry-based model of the external environment has dominated for many years.[57] However, a more promising model views the company not as a member of a single industry, but as a part of a larger business system that crosses a variety of industries. Companies coevolve around innovations, and they work both in competition and cooperatively to satisfy the demands of a wide variety of stakeholders, including customers, suppliers, and broader society and its governments, as well as to create or absorb the next round of innovation.[58] Organizations are a part of one or more value chains, to which they can contribute in a number of ways.

Managers who want to think strategically must also understand and appreciate the internal pieces that make up the whole of their companies. The role of each person within the larger system must be identified, as well as the effect of that role on other people and groups within the organization and on the outcomes of the organization. It is impossible to optimize an organizational system in, for example, satisfying customer needs, without understanding how individuals fit into the system.[59] So the strategic thinker observes and understands the connections between and among the various levels of a business, as well as the linkages between the business and stakeholders in the external environment.

Opportunistic

intelligent opportunism
The ability of managers to take advantage of unanticipated opportunities to further intended strategy or redirect a strategy

Although strategic thinking is based on strategic intent, there has to be room for what might be called "intelligent opportunism."[60] **Intelligent opportunism** can be defined as the ability of managers at various levels of the organization to take advantage of unanticipated opportunities to further intended strategy or even redirect a strategy. For example, CEO Carlos Gutierrez redirected strategy at the struggling cereal manufacturer Kellogg's by buying the snack-foods giant Keebler.[61] Gino Tsai, president of JD Corp., originally developed the Razor Scooter to get around his bicycle factory in Taiwan. The scooter had a sleek aluminum frame and wheels similar to those found on in-line skates. However, Tsai saw the potential for the scooter and took it to a convention in Chicago. Sharper Image Corporation bought four thousand of them, and the new idea was launched.[62] Intelligent opportunism is consistent with the traditional strategic planning model. According to that model, strategies often come from taking advantage of opportunities that arise in the external environment.

Long-Term Oriented

Managers, especially in America, are often accused of making shortsighted decisions.[63] Perhaps a research project is canceled because the payoff looks too far away, or employees are laid off only to be rehired within a few months. In contrast, strategic thinking is long-term oriented. Actions that a firm must make now should be linked to a vision of what the firm should become, based on the strategic intent of its top managers. Kellogg's paid a large premium over market value to buy Keebler. The short-term ramifications of such a purchase are negative. However, Gutierrez envisions a Kellogg's with a broader product line that offers better growth opportunities. Mark Levin, CEO of Millennium Pharmaceuticals, Inc., was able to raise $1.8 billion from big drug companies and others because of his vision that information about the human genome can be used to revolutionize the pharmaceutical industry. With the same kind of long-term thinking, Sunil B. Mittal transformed his small bicycle-parts business into India's most profitable cellular-phone company, Bharti Telecom Ltd.[64]

Built on Past and Present

thinking in time
Recognition that the past, present, and future are all relevant to making good strategic decisions

Although strategic thinking is long-term oriented, it does not ignore the present or the past. In fact, it might be referred to as **"thinking in time"**:

> Thinking in time (has) three components. One is recognition that the future has no place to come from but the past, hence the past has predictive value. Another element is recognition that what matters for the future in the present is departures from the past, alterations, changes, which prospectively or actually divert familiar flows from accustomed channels.... A third component is continuous comparison, an almost constant oscillation from the present to future to past and back, heedful of prospective change, concerned to expedite, limit, guide, counter, or accept it as the fruits of such comparison suggest.[65]

Strategic thinkers need to consider the past. The past forms a historical context in which strategic intent is created. Learning from past mistakes helps the firm avoid making them again. Also, analysis of the past behaviors of important stakeholders such as customers, competitors, unions, or suppliers can help a firm anticipate how the stakeholders will react to new ideas and strategies.

The present is also important to strategic thinking, because it places constraints on what the organization is able to accomplish. While strategic thinking is a creative process, it is also a well-reasoned process. Although it may lead firms to *consider* unconventional ideas, the ideas that are actually pursued are selected based on rational analysis, including consideration of the organization's current resources, knowledge, skills, and abilities.

Hypothesis Driven

hypothesis development and testing
Organizations should test their decisions to see if they are appropriate or likely to be successful; hypothesis development is a creative process, whereas hypothesis testing is an analytical process

Organizations should test their decisions to see if they are appropriate or likely to be successful. This process is similar to the scientific method, in which hypotheses are developed and tested. **Hypothesis development** is a creative process, whereas **hypothesis testing** is an analytical process. For instance, in the example of Greater Construction Inc. that was discussed earlier, managers suggested ideas regarding new businesses the firm might want to consider. Those that were considered reasonable were then subjected to rigorous analysis of potential using a well-developed methodology. After analysis, managers considered several of the ideas worthy of implementation. However, the company decided not to make a full commitment to them at first. Instead, the CEO has allocated enough resources to the ventures so that Greater Construction will be able to tell whether they are going to work out. The businesses that are successful will be given additional resources. In this example, hypothesis testing occurred twice. The first test was the rigorous analysis conducted by managers in the organization. The second test is occurring now as the company tries the ideas in the marketplace.

If you combine all six of the elements of strategic thinking, what you have is a long-term thinker who builds a vision for the future on the foundation of the present and the past. It is someone who understands how the organization fits within its external environment, and who has a firm grasp of relationships with external stakeholders. Furthermore, it is someone who is willing to break out of traditional mindsets and to seize opportunities, but who uses a rational approach to test ideas to prevent the organization from moving indefinitely in an inappropriate direction.

Motivating Managers and Employees to Think Strategically

We live in a fast-paced world. To keep up, organizations should encourage strategic thinking. However, some companies are content to rest on their past successes instead of making needed changes. The decline of General Motors in the 1970s and 1980s is a legendary example. The world auto industry changed in fundamental ways due to a shortage of gasoline and accompanying high prices. Smaller cars were already very popular in Europe and Asia, but during this time period they also became popular in the United States. Toyota, Honda, and Datsun (Nissan) gained a great deal of market share. General Motors continued to produce large, inefficient automobiles, assured that the market would correct itself and that the company would once again be in a strong competitive position. However, consumers continued to favor the smaller cars even after gasoline prices became more stable. The effect of a lack of strategic thinking at GM during that period is still felt by the company today.

Organizations can encourage strategic thinking in a number of ways. First, managers and employees can receive training that describes strategic thinking and how to do it. Second, an organization can encourage and reward employees that generate new ideas (hypotheses). For example, Disney allows some of its employees an opportunity each year to present new ideas to top managers. With a similar philosophy, Virgin Airline created a new one-stop bridal-services company because one of its flight attendants was having a hard time lining up those services for a friend's wedding.[66] Virgin Bride, the name of the venture, is now Britain's largest bridal emporium. Lincoln Electric, the largest arc-welder manufacturer in the world, provides huge bonuses to its employees based, in part, on suggestions for improvements that were made during the year. Third, a company can actually implement a strategic planning process that incorporates the elements of strategic thinking. Such a process would include a thorough evaluation of the external environment, with a special emphasis on relationships with stakeholders. It would also include the generation of new ideas and facilitate their testing. Finally, to encourage strategic thinking, an organization has to be willing to take risks. It was risky for Sam Walton to build large discount department stores in rural areas; however, the strategy worked so well that Wal-Mart is now the largest department-store retailer in the United States.

Summary

This chapter emphasized the important role of the strategic management process in modern organizations. The strategic management process includes (1) analysis of the external environment and the organization, (2) the establishment of a strategic direction, (3) strategy formulation, and (4) strategy implementation and development of a system of controls. Each of these processes was described in detail. Organizations seldom begin with a thorough strategic management process. Instead, they usually begin with basic financial planning or forecasting. Over time, they develop methods that are more closely associated with what we refer to as strategic management.

A historical summary illustrated that the field of strategic management was born out of the need for better and more-refined models and methods for dealing with the challenges of doing business in the latter part of the twentieth century. The traditional approach to strategy development was that firms should adapt to their environments. According to this deterministic view, good management is associated with determining which strategy will best fit environmental, technical, and human forces at a particular point in time, and then working to carry out that strategy. However, strategists determined that organizations may, in part, create their own environments. The principle of enactment assumes that organizations do not have to submit to existing forces in the environment—they can, in part, create their environments through strategic alliances with stakeholders, investments in leading technologies, advertising, political lobbying, and a variety of other activities. The traditional strategy formulation model also supported the view that managers create strategies in a very deliberate fashion; however, a more reasonable approach also suggests that, through trial and error, managers can also learn as they go.

The resource-based view of the firm explains that an organization is a bundle of resources, which means that the most important role of a manager is that of acquiring, developing, managing, and discarding resources. According to this view, firms can gain competitive advantage through possessing superior resources. Most of the resources that a firm can acquire or develop are directly linked to an organization's stakeholders, which are groups and individuals who can significantly affect or are significantly affected by an organization's activities. A stakeholder approach depicts the complicated nature of the management task. This book combines the best of the traditional, resource-based, and stakeholder perspectives of strategic management.

Many trends and forces are leading firms into global markets at increasing rates, which has led to a high level of global economic interconnectedness. While the tools, techniques, and models of strategic management apply well to a global environment, there are differences between managing in a domestic or an international arena. Consequently, global examples and well-accepted international theories will be woven into each of the chapters. In addition, a separate chapter will be devoted to international topics.

Often industry leadership is associated with breaking out of traditional mind-sets and defying widely accepted industry practices. Strategic planning results in the creation of a plan. On the other hand, strategic thinking involves intuition and creativity. It is intent focused, comprehensive, opportunistic, long-term oriented, built on the past and the present, and hypothesis driven. Organizations can encourage strategic thinking through training, rewards systems, integrating elements of strategic thinking into the strategy-making process, and by encouraging risk taking.

Discussion Questions

1. Explain each of the activities in the definition of strategic management. Which of these activities do you think is most important to the success of an organization? Why?

2. Where did the field of strategic management come from? Explain its origin.

3. Explain the traditional, resource-based, and stakeholder perspectives of strategic management.

4. What are some of the considerations that are motivating U.S. companies to go global?

5. What is the difference between the strategic planning process and strategic thinking? Which of these is essential to effective strategic management?

6. What are the important characteristics associated with strategic thinking? How can an organization encourage this sort of thinking?

Strategic Application

Identifying the Strategic Management Process

Think of an organization with which you are familiar. Can you bring to mind any evidence that the organization engages in any of these strategic management activities?

Environmental Analysis

- Does the organization make any efforts to assess trends or influences in its industry?

- Does it track the needs or desires of its external stakeholders through surveys, interviews, or direct contact?

- Is the organization systematically engaged in collecting information about social trends, financial trends, or advances in technology?

- How does the organization use information about the industry and external stakeholders?

Strategic Direction

- Does the organization have a formal mission statement? How is it communicated to employees and other stakeholders?

- If no formal mission statement exists, have organizational managers provided a sense of corporate direction? Do employees know what the organization is trying to achieve? Do members of the external environment understand the organization and its purposes? How is this direction communicated?

Strategy Formulation

- Does the organization apply a consistent approach to the way products and services are produced and marketed? How would you describe this approach? For example, does the organization stress low cost and efficiency, customer satisfaction, high quality, innovation, or flexibility? Does the organization seem to focus on one particular type of customer or client?

Strategy Implementation and Control

- Is there a formal reporting structure or line-of-communication in the organization?

- How do each of the functional areas (i.e., finance, marketing, manufacturing, etc.) contribute to the overall organization? Are there any functional plans?

- Does the organization hold groups and individuals accountable for their performance?

- What are the reporting mechanisms used to measure performance?

Strategic Internet Application

Using a Web search engine such as www.Google.com, do two searches, each with the name of a major competitor in the aircraft manufacturing industry (or an industry selected by your instructor). The competitors should be based in different countries. For example, you could use Boeing (currently www.Boeing.com) and Airbus Industrie (currently www.airbus.com). Go to their websites. Most websites have a section called "Company Overview" or "About <company name>." Read this overview and as much other information as you need to capture the essence of what the company does. Also, by searching the Web site of a major company, you can usually find an annual report. Most often it is offered under a heading such as "Investor Information." Read some of the opening remarks in the annual report, as well as a description of the products, services, and performance in each of the segments of the company. If an annual report is not available, this type of information is almost always available somewhere else on the Web site. When you have done this research for both of your companies, answer the following questions:

1. How are these companies similar in their approaches to doing business?

2. How are they different?

3. Which company do you think is a better investment? Why?

4. What are some of the key issues each of the companies is addressing?

Notes

1. Business Editors, "FedEx, USPS Forge Two New Service Agreements; American Public Gains Greater Choice, Reliability, and Convenience," www.fedex.com, 31 August 2001.

2. J. S. Harrison and C. H. St. John, "Managing and Partnering with External Stakeholders," *Academy of Management Executive* (May 1996): 46–59.

3. This is essentially the definition used by Edward Freeman in his landmark book on stakeholder management: R. E. Freeman, *Strategic Management: A Stakeholder Approach* (Marshfield, Mass.: Pitman Publishing, 1984).

4. This view is explained in detail in M. B. E. Clarkson, "A Stakeholder Framework for Analyzing and Evaluating Corporate Social Performance," *Academy of Management Review* 20 (1995): 92–117.

5. C. C. Miller and L. B. Cardinal, "Strategic Planning and Firm Performance," *Academy of Management Journal* 37 (December 1994): 1649–1665.

6. D. Rigby, "Management Tools and Techniques: A Survey," *California Management Review* 43 (Winter 2001): 139–160.

7. L. W. Weiss, "The Extent and Effects of Aggregate Concentration," *Journal of Law and Economics* 26 (1983): 429–455.

8. D. E. Schendel and C. W. Hofer, eds., *Strategic Management: A New View of Business Policy and Planning* (Boston: Little, Brown, 1979).

9. C. W. Hofer and D. E. Schendel, *Strategy Formulation: Analytical Concepts* (St. Paul: West Publishing, 1978).

10. L. J. Bourgeois III, "Strategic Management and Determinism," *Academy of Management Review* 9 (1984): 586–596; L. G. Hrebiniak and W. F. Joyce, "Organizational Adaptation: Strategic Choice and Environmental Determinism," *Administrative Science Quarterly* 30 (1985): 336–349.

11. T. C. Powell, "Organizational Alignment as Competitive Advantage," *Strategic Management Journal* 13 (1992): 119–134; N. Venkatraman, "Environment-Strategy Coalignment: An Empirical Test of Its Performance Implications," *Strategic Management Journal* 11 (1990): 1–23.

12. Bourgeois, "Strategic Management," 589.

13. L. Smircich and C. Stubbart, "Strategic Management in an Enacted World," *Academy of Management Review* 10 (1985): 724–736.

14. H. Mintzberg and A. McHugh, "Strategy Formation in an Adhocracy," *Administrative Science Quarterly* 30 (1985): 160–197.

15. H. Mintzberg, "The Design School: Reconsidering the Basic Premises of Strategic Management," *Strategic Management Journal* 11 (1990): 171–196.

16. H. Mintzberg, "Learning 1, Planning 0: Reply to Igor Ansoff," *Strategic Management Journal* 12 (1991): 463–466.

17. Mintzberg, "Learning 1, Planning 0," 465.

18. J. B. Barney and Asli M. Arikan, "The Resource-based View: Origins and Implications," in *The Blackwell Handbook of Strategic Management*, ed. M. A. Hitt, R. E. Freeman, and J. S. Harrison (Oxford: Blackwell Publishers, 2001), 124–188.

19. L. G. Hrebiniak and C. C. Snow, "Top Management Agreement and Organizational Performance," *Human Relations* 35, no. 12 (1982): 1139–1157; M. A. Hitt and R. D. Ireland, "Corporate Distinctive Competence, Strategy, Industry, and Performance," *Strategic Management Journal* 6 (1985): 273–293.

20. D. Ricardo, *Principles of Political Economy and Taxation* (London: J. Murray, 1817).

21. E. T. Penrose, *Theory of the Growth of the Firm* (New York: Wiley, 1959).

22. Perhaps the first publication to clearly delineate what is now known as the resource-based view of the firm was B. Wernerfelt, "A Resource-based View of the Firm," *Strategic Management Journal* 5 (1984): 171–180. However, no other scholar has contributed more on this view than Jay Barney. See, for example, J. B. Barney, "Firm Resources and Sustained Competitive Advantage," *Journal of Management* 17 (1991): 99–120.

23. Barney and Arikan, "Resource-based View," 124–188; Barney, "Firm Resources," 99–120; J. B. Barney, *Gaining and Sustaining Competitive Advantage* (Reading, Mass: Addison-Wesley, 1997); J. S. Harrison et al., "Synergies and Post-Acquisition Performance: Differences versus Similarities in Resource Allocations," *Journal of Management* 17 (1991): 173–190; J. T. Mahoney and J. R. Pandian, "The Resource-based View within the Conversation of Strategic Management," *Strategic Management Journal* 13 (1992): 363–380; B. Wernerfelt, "A Resource-based View of the Firm," *Strategic Management Journal* 5 (1984): 171–180.

24. Barney and Arikan, "Resource-based View," 124–188.

25. Barney, "Firm Resources"; Mahoney and Pandian, "Resource-based View."

26. D. Ulrich and D. Lake, "Organizational Capability: Creating Competitive Advantage," *Academy of Management Executive* (February 1991): 79.

27. Barney and Arikan, "Resource-based View," 124–188.

28. J. Huey, "The New Post-Heroic Leadership," *Fortune,* 21 February 1994, 44.

29. J. H. Dyer and H. Singh, "The Relational View: Cooperative Strategy and Sources of Interorganizational Competitive Advantage," *Academy of Management Review* 23 (1998): 660–679.

30. G. G. Dess et al., "The New Corporate Architecture," *Academy of Management Executive* (August 1995): 7–20.

31. R. E. Freeman and J. McVea, "A Stakeholder Approach to Strategic Management," in *Blackwell Handbook,* 189–207.

32. This is essentially the definition used in Freeman, *Strategic Management.*

33. "Stonyfield Farm, Inc.," *Strengthening America's Competitiveness: The Blue Chip Enterprise Initiative* (Warner Books on behalf of Connecticut Mutual Life Insurance Company and the U.S. Chamber of Commerce, 1991), 56–57.

34. S. Branch, "Group Danone Scoops Up 40% Stake in Stonyfield Farm," *The Wall Street Journal,* 4October 2001), B9.

35. These arguments are also found in Harrison and St. John, "Managing and Partnering," 46–60.

36. M. Pastin and J. S. Harrison, "Social Responsibility in the Hollow Corporation," *Business and Society Review* (Fall 1987): 54–58.

37. E. C. Kasper-Fuehrer and N. M. Ashkanasy, "Communicating Trustworthiness and Building Trust in Interorganizational Virtual Organizations," *Journal of Management* 27 (2001): 235–254; B. Nooteboom, H. Berger, and N. G. Noorderhaven, "Effects of Trust and Governance on Relational Risk," *Academy of Management Journal* 40 (1997): 308–338.

38. J. Mohr and R. Spekman, "Characteristics of Partnership Success: Partnership Attributes, Communication Behavior, and Conflict Resolution Techniques," *Strategic Management Journal* 15 (1994): 135–152.

39. Associated Press, "Bridgestone, Firestone to End Dealings" www.dailynews.nets, 21 May 2000.

40. Freeman, Strategic Management; M. Pastin, *The Hard Problems of Management: Gaining the Ethics Edge* (San Francisco: Jossey-Bass, 1986).

41. Taken directly from New York Stock Exchange, *Annual Report* (1990).

42. Based on actual experiences and observations in the company.

43. H. Henzler and W. Rall, "Facing Up to the Globalization Challenge," *McKinsey Quarterly* (Winter 1986): 52–68; T. Peters, "Prometheus Barely Unbound," *Academy of Management Executive* (November 1990): 70–84; M. E. Porter, *Competition in Global Industries* (Boston: Harvard Business School Press, 1986), 2–3.

44. "As a Global Marketer, Coke Excels by Being Tough and Consistent," *The Wall Street Journal,* 19 December 1989, 1.

45. C. Larroulet, "Look to Chile for an Answer to the Latin Malaise," *The Wall Street Journal,* 24 August 2001, A9.

46. Taken directly from K. H. Zhang, "What Attracts Foreign Multinational Corporations to China?" *Contemporary Economic Policy* 19 (2001): 336.

47. G. Hamel, *Leading the Revolution* (Boston: Harvard Business School Press, 2000).

48. G. Hamel, "The Challenge Today: Changing the Rules of the Game," *Business Strategy Review* 9, no. 2(1998): 19–26.

49. J. M. Liedtka, "Strategy Formulation: The Roles of Conversation and Design," in *Blackwell Handbook,* 70–93.

50. H. Mintzberg, *The Rise and Fall of Strategic Planning* (New York: Prentice Hall, 1994).

51. This story comes from actual consulting experience.

52. G. Hamel and C. Prahalad, *Competing for the Future* (Boston: Harvard Business School Press, 1994).

53. Many of these points come from Liedtka, "Strategy Formulation."

54. Hamel and Prahalad, *Competing for the Future,* 129–130.

55. Liedtka, "Strategy Formulation."

56. P. Senge, "Mental Models" *Planning Review* (March/April 1992): 4–10.

57. M. E. Porter, *Competitive Strategy* (New York: The Free Press, 1980).

58. J. Moore, *The Death of Competition* (New York: Harper Business, 1996).

59. Liedtka, "Strategy Formulation."

60. Liedtka, "Strategy Formulation."

61. J. Muller, "Thinking Out of the Cereal Box," *Business Week,* 15 January 2001, 54–55.

62. D. G. Neeleman, "The Top Entrepreneurs," *Business Week,* 8 January 2001, 84–85.

63. J. S. Harrison and J. O. Fiet, "New CEOs Pursue Their Own Self Interests by Sacrificing Stakeholder Value," *Journal of Business Ethics* 19 (1999): 301–308.

64. Neeleman, "Top Entrepreneurs."

65. R. Neustadt and E. May, *Thinking in Time: The Uses of History for Decision Makers* (New York: The Free Press, 1986), 251.

66. Hamel, *Leading the Revolution.*

Chapter 2

The Environment And External Stakeholders

Learning Objectives

After reading and discussing this chapter, you should be able to:

1. Differentiate between the broad and operating environments.

2. Analyze the various components of the broad and operating environments.

3. Explain how managers can use information from environmental analysis to help devise strategies for their firms.

4. Describe each of the five major forces that drive competition in an industry.

5. Evaluate important stakeholders on the basis of their interest in and the extent of their power over a particular firm.

6. Understand the various forms of interorganizational relationships and how they are used to increase firm competitiveness.

Enron

On December 2, 2001, Enron, once the seventh-largest Fortune 500 company, filed for bankruptcy. Less than a year earlier, Enron's CEO, Jeff Skilling, said in an interview: "Our business is not a black box. It's very simple to model. People who raise questions are people who have not gone through it in detail. We have explicit answers, but people want to throw rocks." In retrospect, a black box was a very good description of Enron in 2001. Debt was hidden behind partnerships. Financial disclosures were kept to a minimum. Earnings were intentionally inflated. Executives made exaggerated statements about how well the company was doing. They have been accused of arrogance, greed, deceit, and financial chicanery.

The Enron collapse tarnished the reputation of what was previously one of America's most trusted organizations, Arthur Andersen LLP. Andersen, the huge accounting firm that audited Enron's financial statements, not only failed to provide realistic assessments of Enron's financial condition, but also sought to cover up its own mistakes through destroying documents. An October 12, 2001, memo directed workers to destroy all audit materials except for some basic working documents.

The fallout from the Enron implosion has had a sweeping impact on firms and industries in America and throughout the world. Many Enron employees had significant retirement investments tied up in company stock. Their losses have signaled to other companies and employees that they should seriously reconsider whether holding a large investment in their own companies is a financially sound strategy. The whole accounting profession is now under a high level of scrutiny, and a wave of new government regulation is expected. Investors and financial analysts have lost more of their already eroding confidence in the accuracy of financial statements. The financial community is now looking more closely at the statements of a wide range of companies, wondering whether they, too, have hidden debt or manipulated numbers. As Dennis Kozlowski, CEO of Tyco International Ltd., put it, "A lot of companies are going to suffer for Enron's sins."[1]

Many companies did suffer as a result of what Enron started. Due to a loss of investor confidence, Kozlowski's own firm lost so much value in the market after the Enron collapse that it was worth less in early 2002 than the combined value of its acquisitions from 1996–2000.[2] The Enron case is an excellent example of how the external environment can influence firms and industries.

The terrible events of September 11, 2001, sent even greater shock waves through the business community in the United States and abroad. Organizations and governments increased security, especially in the transportation and entertainment industries. Reduced travel had a large negative effect on tourism and the airlines. The decline in tourism also had a ripple effect on state tax revenues and an assortment of businesses in U.S. states and foreign countries that rely on tourism for a large part of their revenue. This provided another shock to an already slumping U.S. economy, which impacted most businesses either directly or indirectly. Meanwhile, military action in Afghanistan resulting from U.S. retaliation triggered an increase in the market values of civil-defense contractors, an indication that an environmental shock does not influence all companies or industries in the same way.

Successful organizations stay abreast of changes in their external environments to predict trends, anticipate concerns, and generate ideas. These activities lead to the identification of external opportunities and threats, which are then considered by managers as they develop strategic direction and formulate and implement organizational strategies. The **external environment** can be divided into the broad and operating environments. The operating environment is different for each firm, although similarities may exist among firms in the same industries. On the other hand, the broad environment is not firm specific or industry specific. In other words, the major trends and influences that occur in the broad environment impact many firms and industries, although the type and level of influence may be different from one industry to the next. For example, an event such as the Enron debacle has been felt most strongly in the energy and accounting sectors; however, virtually every industry has been influenced in some way.

The major components of the broad and operating environments are displayed in Figure 2.1. An organization can have a much more significant influence on events that transpire in its operating environment than it can in its broad environment. In fact, this is one way to distinguish between the two environments. For example, it would be difficult for a firm, working independently, to dramatically influence societal views on abortion, drug abuse, free trade with China, or migration to the Sun Belt states in the United States. However, an organization can have a profound impact on the attitude of its customers or suppliers, competitive rivalry, or even government regulations (assuming proactive political activities). Since organizations typically can have only a minimal influence on forces in the broad environment, the emphasis in the first section will be on analyzing and adapting to those forces.

external environment
Stakeholders and forces outside the traditional boundaries of the firm; they can be divided into the broad and operating environments

Assessment of the Broad Environment

This section describes some of the most important forces in the broad environment and how some organizations respond to them. The emphasis in this section will be on monitoring, forecasting, and adapting to broad environmental influences.

FIGURE 2.1

The Organization, Its Primary Stakeholders, and the Broad Environment

The **broad environment** forms the context in which the firm and its operating environment exist. The most important elements in the broad environment, as it relates to a business organization and its operating environment, are sociocultural influences, global economic influences, political influences, and technological influences. These four areas will now be described, as well as examples of successful and unsuccessful organizational responses.

broad environment
Forms the context in which the firm and its operating environment exist, including sociocultural influences, global economic influences, political/legal influences and technological influences

The Sociocultural Context

Society is composed of the individuals who make up particular geographic regions. Some sociocultural trends are applicable to the citizens of an entire country. For example, a few of the major social issues currently facing the United States are:

- Role of government in health care and child care
- Declining quality of education
- Legality of abortion and stem-cell research
- Terrorism and levels of crime in general
- Security of travel and public places
- Importance and role of the military
- Levels of foreign investment/ownership in the United States
- Social costs of restructuring, especially layoffs
- Pollution and disposal of toxic and nontoxic wastes

- General increase in environmental awareness
- Drug addiction and drug traffic
- Continued migration toward the sun belt states
- Graying of America
- AIDS and other health problems
- Major global issues
- Immigration restrictions and programs

sociocultural environment
Influences and trends that come from groups of individuals who make up a particular geographic region

On the other hand, attitudes and beliefs can relate to geographic areas that are larger or smaller than individual countries. For example, people refer to the South, which alludes to the southern states of the United States; to Western culture (globally speaking); to Latin American countries; or to the EC (European Community). These **sociocultural environments** have meaning to most well-educated people, because of the widely held beliefs and values that are a part of the culture in these areas.

Analysis of societal trends is important from at least four perspectives. First, broader societal influences can create opportunities for organizations. For example, societal interest in fitness has led to business opportunities in home fitness. Also, many baby-boomer couples had babies later in life than did past generations, causing a demographic trend toward older couples with children. The higher levels of income of these more established parents have led to the development of higher-quality baby accessories, clothing, and supplies, and to new business opportunities in child care and specialized education. Seemingly unrelated industries, such as the motion-picture and television industries, have taken advantage of these trends by producing many movies and television shows that center on birth, babies, and children. Although the baby-boomer parents and their children have provided growth and profit opportunities for child-related businesses, the countercycle of the baby-boomer trend, the baby-bust generation, will likely threaten the growth and profits of those child-related businesses.

Second, awareness of and compliance with the attitudes of society can help an organization avoid problems associated with being perceived as a "bad corporate citizen." For example, Exxon gained a terrible reputation in the United States because it spilled oil in Alaska and then resisted cleaning it up completely. On another level, a class-action suit was filed against Wal-Mart, alleging discrimination against women employees.[3] Both of these cases demonstrate a lack of sensitivity to the views of a large segment of the population. Although evidence concerning the relationship between social responsibility and financial performance is not very clear, it is obvious that firms may reduce the risk of gaining a bad "ethical" reputation by anticipating and/or adjusting for social beliefs and trends.[4] For example, Denny's was known for many years as one of America's most racist companies. However, Ron Petty, Denny's CEO, introduced initiatives that turned the company into a model of multicultural sensitivity.[5] Similarly, General Motors took the initiative to fix relationships with its minority dealers.

Ex. General Motors hired Weldon Latham, a high-profile civil-rights attorney, to lead an investigation into how the company could 'fix' its diversity plan. The company began a diversity effort many years ago that was largely unsuccessful. GM was accused of overcharging for dealerships, withholding training, and providing minority candidates with only the least-favorable locations. Things came to a head when a white GM executive punched a black colleague in the face during an argument over a black dealership candidate. After a year of study, Mr. Latham delivered a 150-page report with 215 specific actions that the company needed to take to improve its program. Although it was an overwhelming report, the company responded very favorably, embracing 213 of the 215 suggestions. As a result, things have really changed. For example, one in six minority dealerships are now earning over $1 million per year, compared to one in eight for white dealerships.[6]

Third, a positive organizational reputation among stakeholders such as customers and suppliers may increase demand for products or lead to increased business opportunities. Companies such as Coca-Cola, Procter & Gamble, Rubbermaid, and Johnson & Johnson go to great lengths to present themselves in a positive light. Each year, *Fortune* magazine rates corporations on the basis of their reputations. One of these issues began, "Each year we hear of more companies that have made an explicit corporate goal of improving their performance in *Fortune*'s annual survey of corporate reputations."[7] A corporate reputation can be a very important organizational resource, since it cannot be imitated completely. The value of this resource will be discussed further in Chapter 3.

Fourth, correct assessment of social trends can help businesses avoid restrictive legislation, which can be a threat to organizational success. Industries and organizations that police themselves are less likely to be the target of legislative activity. Legislative activity is often in response to a public outcry against the actions of firms or industries, as has been the case with some intrusive and unethical telemarketing activity. Business practices of U.S. firms in foreign countries continue to be an issue of social debate. This debate is complicated by a strict government regulation called the **Foreign Corrupt Practices Act.**

Foreign Corrupt Practices Act (FCPA)
A response to social concern about bribes paid by U.S. companies to foreign government officials; it defines the "rules-of-the-game" for U.S. companies when they operate in foreign countries

Ex.
The Foreign Corrupt Practices Act (FCPA) was passed by Congress and signed into law by President Carter in 1977. The act was a response to social concern about bribes paid by U.S. companies to foreign government officials. The public and Congress seemed to believe that foreign governments work similarly to the government of the United States. Unfortunately, the "rules-of-the game" are different in many foreign countries, where payments are demanded as a regular part of business. In the United States, while these types of payments may occur, they are illegal.

Some business writers believe that the FCPA reduced the competitiveness of U.S. firms in foreign markets for two reasons. First, U.S. firms can't compete fairly with firms from countries that do permit bribery. Second, the FCPA requires detailed record keeping and reporting, which adds another administrative expense to foreign operations and makes them less efficient. The lesson for businesses is fairly clear: "Once legislation that is supposedly ethically motivated is passed, it is almost impossible to rescind. The time to participate forcefully in discussion of ethically motivated legislation is before it is passed, no matter how difficult this appears to be at the time."[8] Another example of avoidable legislation is the **United States Sentencing Guidelines (USSG),** compulsory guidelines courts must use to determine fines and penalties when corporate illegalities are proven. These guidelines, which substantially increase corporate punishments, are a direct response to social distress over the increasing incidence of white-collar crime.[9]

United States Sentencing Guidelines (USSG)
Compulsory guidelines courts must use to determine fines and penalties when corporate illegalities are proven

Correct evaluation of societal forces can help direct organizational planning. For instance, understanding of demographic forces can help an organization forecast industry demand. Annual demand for washing machines, for example, is created for the most part by the number of new-household formations, which is influenced by the number of young adults in the population. Currently, the aging U.S. population is providing opportunities for companies in recreation, health care, and nursing homes. However, companies in many other industries are also taking advantage of this trend by offering special services and discounts to senior citizens.

The Economic Context

Economic forces can have a profound influence on organizational behavior and performance. Economic forces that create growth and profit opportunities allow organizations to take actions that satisfy many stakeholders simultaneously, particularly owners, employees, and suppliers. On the other hand, when economic trends are negative, managers face tremendous pressures as they balance potentially conflicting stakeholder interests, often between employees and owners.

economic environment
Influences and trends associated with domestic or global economics, such as economic growth rates, interest rates, the availability of credit, inflation rates, foreign exchange rates, and foreign trade balances

Economic growth, interest rates, the availability of credit, inflation rates, foreign-exchange rates, and foreign trade balances are among the most critical factors in the **economic environment.** Table 2.1 lists factors that are worthy of monitoring and, depending on the organization and its business, possibly forecasting as well. These forces should be considered for every country or region in which a firm is involved, as well as tracking global trends as a whole. Of course, many of these forces are interdependent. Organizations should constantly scan the economic environment to monitor critical but uncertain assumptions concerning the economic future, and then link those assumptions to the demand pattern and profit potential for their products and services. These assumptions often form the base upon which strategies and implementation plans are built.

Economic growth can have a large impact on consumer demand for products and services. Consequently, organizations should consider forecasts of economic growth in determining when to make critical resource-allocation decisions such as plant expansions. Inflation and the availability of credit, among other factors, influence interest rates that organizations have to pay. High interest payments can constrain the strategic flexibility of firms by making new ventures and capacity expansions prohibitively expensive. On the other hand, low interest rates can increase strategic flexibility for organizations and also influence demand by encouraging customers to purchase goods and services on credit. Volatile inflation and interest rates, such as those experienced in the United States in the 1970s and in

Table 2.1 A Few of Many Global Economic Forces to Monitor and Predict	
Force	**Potential Influences**
Economic Growth	Consumer demand, cost of factors of production, availability of factors of production (especially labor and scarce resources)
Interest Rates	Cost of capital for new projects, cost of refinancing existing debt, consumer demand (due to customer ability to finance purchases)
Inflation	Interest rates, cost of factors of production, optimism or pessimism of stakeholders
Exchange Rates	Ability to profitably remove profits from foreign ventures, government policies toward business
Trade Deficits	Government policies, incentives, trade barriers

South American and Eastern European countries, increase the uncertainty associated with making strategic decisions. Therefore, they are worthy of forecasting efforts in most organizations, but especially in those that are highly dependent on debt or have customers who finance their purchases.

foreign exchange rates
The rates at which currencies are exchanged across countries; this is a major source of uncertainty for firms operating in foreign countries

foreign trade balance
A measure of the relative value of imports to exports from one country to another

Foreign exchange rates are another major source of uncertainty for global organizations. Companies sometimes earn a profit in a foreign country, only to see the profit turn into a loss due to unfavorable currency translations. Furthermore, the organization may have billings in one currency and payables in another. Finally, **foreign trade balances** are highly relevant to both domestic and global organizations because they are an indication of the nature of trade legislation that might be expected in the future. For example, the United States tends to run a trade surplus with the European Union. As a result, American manufacturers who export to the EU are concerned about new protectionist legislation such as high tariffs that may be enacted to reduce the trade imbalance.[10]

The Political Context

political environment
Influences and trends associated with governments and other political or legal entities; political forces, both at home and abroad, are among the most significant determinants of organizational success

Political forces, both at home and abroad, are among the most significant determinants of organizational success, and make up the **political environment.** The stakes are often high. For instance, a pact among the governments of Kazakstan, Russia, and Oman allowed Chevron to recover a $715 million investment in the Tengiz oil field.[11] In another example, Israel once asked the White House to limit the ability of U.S. satellite companies to survey Israel from space. However, an Israeli company that is about to enter the same business would not face similar restrictions.[12] In the United States, a Supreme Court ruling allows liability lawsuits against manufacturers of medical devices even though the devices are regulated by law.[13] Also, court rulings have made banks liable when their customers pollute.[14]

Governments provide and enforce the rules by which organizations operate. These rules include laws, regulations and policies. Governments can encourage new-business formation through tax incentives and subsidies; can restructure companies, as in the case of the AT&T breakup; and can totally close firms that do not comply with laws, ordinances, or regulations. Furthermore, alliances among governments provide an additional level of complexity for businesses with significant foreign operations. Also, some countries have established independent entities to counsel them on government policy. For example, the Global Insight describes how the Australian government uses task forces to help devise policy.

Global Insight
How the Australian Government Uses Task Forces to Set Policy

The Australian government uses task forces as vehicles to periodically intervene in and adjust policy frameworks, and to create new policy and a new set of dynamics for business-government relations and behaviors. The task forces are independent of both business and government, attempting to find policy solutions that will be acceptable to the range of players in the game, including government. In recent cases, government has attempted to achieve step changes by using independent task forces that examined technological progress and the needs of the businesses in each industry to evolve and become more competitive. The challenge for government is to develop a set of rules and regulations that provide a stable basis for businesses to set strategy and operate in, yet at the same time keep policy up to date as forces such as technological change and globalization affect economies. For business executives, their opportunities are to lobby government and influence the frequency and nature of task-force processes in the pursuit of step changes.

Wool was a mainstay of the Australian economy for more than one hundred years. The past decade, however has seen failed policies and a lack of productivity improvement and innovation in the industry lead to a serious decline. With the industry in decline and disarray, and a vote of no confidence from the central-wool-authority farmers, the government sought to achieve a step change in policy. The Wool Industry Future Direction Task Force, headed by Ian McLachlan, was charged with setting the direction for the industry. As a result of substantial analysis and investigation, the task force prescribed a new set of rules for taxing the industry via a collective fund for supporting industry research and industrial marketing of wool, new performance standards and commercial incentives, new quality standards, and a need for much reform and restructuring of the farms themselves.

Financial services is another arena that has been subject to tight government regulations that have severely affected business strategies in Australia. Furthermore, drastic changes in the industry made a reinvestigation of the role and form of regulation inevitable. The Financial System Inquiry, under the leadership of Stanley Wallis, considered how to bring the industry up to date and set in place an institutional and regulatory framework that would be advantageous in the new economy of the information and knowledge age. The Wallis task force was conducted essentially independently of government, and involved wide and deep consultation with the major business players, as well as with consumer groups, government departments, and other stakeholders. Their recommendations were to create a simpler, sleeker regulatory system that would foster competition, lower costs, and move the industry toward efficiency.

Source: Adapted from V. Chaudhri and D. Samson, "Business-Government Relations in Australia: Cooperating Through Task Forces," *Academy of Management Executive* (August 2000): 19–29, used with permission.

Some organizations find themselves in a situation in which they are almost entirely dependent on government regulators for their health and survival. In many countries, tight regulatory controls are found in a wide variety of industries. In communist countries, such as China or Cuba, the government has significant control over the economy. In the United States, utilities are a good example of a highly regulated environment.

Although all organizations face some form of regulation, there is a trend toward deregulation and privatization (transfer of government productive assets to private citizens) of industries worldwide. In Portugal, for example, the previously regulated government-owned banking industry is moving toward privatization.

In Eastern Europe, many industries are struggling to survive and prosper in an emerging free-market economy. In the United Kingdom, water utilities have been privatized. In the United States, the past twenty years have brought the deregulation of the airline, banking, long-distance telephone, and trucking industries. The previously highly regulated electric industry is undergoing partial deregulation, which is opening up new opportunities, but creating competitive threats as well. With deregulation, existing industry competitors face turbulence and unpredictability. Also with deregulation, however, new opportunities arise for new firms to enter the market.

The amount of time and effort organizations should devote to learning about regulations, complying with them, and fostering good relationships with regulatory agencies and their representatives depends, in part, on the industry. Some laws and regulations pertain to only one industry, such as nuclear energy. On the other hand, many regulations are crosscutting, in that they apply to organizations in general. In the United States, two of the most widely known regulatory agencies are the Occupational Safety and Health Administration (OSHA) and the Environmental Protection Agency (EPA).

Monitoring and complying with laws and regulations is a good idea from a financial perspective. Involvement in illegal activities can result in a significant loss of firm value.[15] Fines and penalties imposed by government units can run in the millions of dollars. The following example demonstrates what can happen when an organization mishandles or ignores government regulation.

 Buying California's most famous, most beautiful, most historic golf course—the one where Crosby kidded Hope and knocked out ashes from his pipe against the cypress trees—must have seemed the coup of coups to Minoru Isutani, owner of Cosmo World, a Japanese golfing conglomerate. True, the price he paid in September 1990—said to be somewhere between $800 million and $1 billion—seemed high. But Isutani had a plan. He would transform Pebble Beach into a private club, with memberships (at $740,000 each) sold primarily to wealthy Japanese. Golfers of lesser means protested. Under existing rules, anybody willing to endure a waiting list and pay a $200-per-person greens fee could play the course. But if Pebble Beach went private, the best hours would be reserved for members. Enter the California Coastal Commission, all powerful in matters of coastal access: Did the new owners have a commission permit for this conversion? Er . . . no, they didn't. They didn't think they needed one. The commission ruled they did, and withheld it.[16]

A simplified model of some of the major groups in the United States that influence the political environment of business is found in Figure 2.2. Government influences come from (1) lawmakers, (2) regulatory agencies, (3) revenue-collection agencies, and (4) the courts. Notice that each of these influences can occur at the federal, state, or local levels, which results in twelve major forces instead of four. Involvement in more than one country further increases the number of relevant government forces. All industrialized countries have counterparts for each of the four government influences found in Figure 2.2. For example, the Health and Safety Commission in the United Kingdom functions similarly to many state and federal U.S. regulatory agencies.

The mission of the United Kingdom's Health and Safety Commission is to ensure that risks to people's health and safety from work activities are properly controlled. The commission aims to modernize, simplify, and support the regulatory framework; to secure compliance with the law; to improve knowledge and understanding of health and safety; and to promote risk assessment and technological knowledge as the basis for setting standards and guiding enforcement activities.[17]

Lawmakers often pursue legislation in response to requests and pressures from constituents. Regulatory agencies and revenue-collection agencies develop the specifics of the regulations needed to carry out new laws, and they serve an enforcement role as well. The courts handle disputes, interpret laws as needed, and levy fines and penalties. Courts may also make decisions that alter the makeup or strategies of organizations, as in the case of antitrust actions. A federal court was involved in the AT&T restructuring that resulted in spinning off local telephone services into smaller, independent companies, sometimes called the "Baby Bells." The court's position was that AT&T held a monopoly position in phone services in the United States that made it difficult for other long-distance companies to compete.

FIGURE 2.2

Government Influences on Organizations in the United States

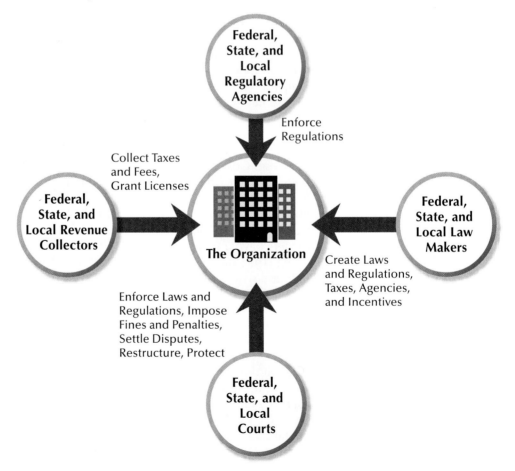

Source: Based on information contained in R. E. Freeman, *Strategic Management: A Stakeholder Approach* (Boston: Pitman, 1984).

Microsoft almost suffered a similar fate, as the courts originally determined that the company held monopoly power in the software industry and would need to be divided into two companies.

Although one organization may not be able to dramatically alter major political forces as a whole, it may have considerable impact within its own specific industries and operating domain. Consequently, major political forces are considered a part of the broad environment, while government agencies and administrators are considered a part of the operating environment. Political strategies for dealing with government within specific industries will be described later in this chapter.

The Technological Context

technological environment
Influences and trends related to the development of technologies both domestically and internationally

Technological change creates new products, processes, and services, and, in some cases, entire new industries. Changes in the **technological environment** can change the way society behaves and what society expects. Notebook computers, compact discs and players, direct satellite systems, and cellular telephones are technological innovations that have experienced extraordinary growth in recent years, leaving formerly well-established industries stunned, creating whole new industries, and influencing the way many people approach work and leisure. Computers and telecommunications technologies, for example, have played an essential role in creating the increasingly global marketplace. The Internet, in particular, added a new communications and marketing tool that has led to many new global business opportunities. Organizations that don't embrace technological change may live to regret it.

Ex. Technological change that disrupts whole industries might be called a "stealth attack." For example, steel minimill technology was scoffed at by the big steel manufacturers such as USX and Bethelehem Steel, but now accounts for 40 percent of steel production. Makers of sailing ships ignored the threat from steamships. Sears, Roebuck and Co. underestimated the potential of discount department stores such as Wal-Mart and Kmart. Now the Internet offers a similar challenge to many businesses. For instance, buying insurance over the Internet is radically different from buying from an agent in an office. The same holds true for stock brokerage, as Merrill Lynch is left wondering what to do to remain competitive.[18]

technology
Human knowledge about products and services and the way they are made and delivered

Technology refers to human knowledge about products and services and the way they are made and delivered. This is a fairly broad definition of technology. Typically, technology is defined in terms of such things as machinery, computers, and information systems. However, technologies don't have to be technically sophisticated. For example, there is a technology associated with teaching, cooking, and theater performance. Just because these technologies are simple does not mean that technological opportunities do not exist. There is still room for innovation and improvement.

Technological innovations can take the form of new products or processes, such as fax machines, air bags, cellular phones, and minimill steel technologies. When an innovation has an impact on more than one industry or market, it is referred to as a basic innovation. Examples include the microprocessor, the lightbulb, superconductors, and fiber optics. Basic innovations reverberate through society, transforming existing industries and creating new ones.

radical innovations
Major innovations that influence more than one business or industry

Technological change is difficult, but not impossible, to predict. An understanding of the three characteristics of innovation can help an organization develop a plan for monitoring technological change. They are: (1) new innovations often emerge from existing technologies, (2) a dominant design will eventually be widely adopted, and (3) **radical innovations** often come from outside of the industry group. These three characteristics will now be discussed.

Innovations from Existing Technologies

As James Utterback pointed out in his book *Mastering the Dynamics of Innovation*, most innovations draw from the existing technologies of the time, but, through a new configuration of some type, fulfill a new need or fulfill an existing need—better.[19] For example, the first personal computers were sold as do-it-yourself kits for electronics enthusiasts, and made use of existing electronics technology. It was only after Apple Computer provided a user-friendly interface and appearance, and software designers provided applications, that the personal computer began to gain legitimacy as a potential home and office machine. With the entry of IBM into the market, which further signaled the importance of the innovation, the market for personal computers exploded. Since then, innovations in semiconductor and microprocessor manufacturing have led to smaller, less-expensive components, which has improved affordability and design flexibility.

Adoption of a Dominant Design

Innovations in the personal-computer industry illustrate a second characteristic of technological innovation. Just like the invention process, commercial innovations tend to evolve through predictable stages—from chaotic efforts to develop new and different variations on the innovation, to emergence of a dominant design as customer needs become clear.[20] Emergence of a dominant design has strategic implications for firms in the industry, and for firms considering entering the industry. A dominant design suggests that the industry may evolve as a commodity—with customers comparing prices, and businesses finding fewer ways to create differences that customers will pay for. For example, when the personal computer was first emerging, many companies entered the market. They each had different target applications, different keyboard configurations, different operating systems, different microprocessor capabilities, and different overall appearances. Each manufacturer was struggling to create a computer that would appeal to a largely unknown target market. Over time, however, the personal computers began to converge toward a dominant design: operating systems with pulldown menus and user-friendly icons, a standard keyboard, standard word-processing/spreadsheet/graphics applications, and a standard microprocessor. Although computers made by different companies are not identical, they are so similar that few people have trouble moving from model to model.

Radical Innovations from Outside the Industry

A third characteristic of the innovation process is that radical innovations usually originate outside of the industry boundaries, which makes monitoring of trends outside the immediate competitive group so important. For example, it was not the existing office-machine companies that developed the personal computer, although office machines were ultimately displaced by personal computers. Many new innovations in electronics, telecommunications, and specialty materials have originated with space and military projects, and then have been adopted by other industries for use in various commercial applications. In general, when the rate of improvements with an existing technology begins to slow down, the likelihood of a new substitute innovation increases. Organizations should monitor the technological developments in industries other than their own, and conduct brainstorming sessions about the possible consequences for their own products and markets.

Dealing with Technological Change

To help identify trends and anticipate their timing, companies may participate in several kinds of technological-forecasting efforts. In general, organizations may monitor trends by studying research journals, government reports, and patent filings. Since the U.S. government is a major sponsor of basic research, government reports and federal technology assessments are often a rich source of information on emerging technologies. Another, more formal method of technological forecasting is to solicit the opinion of experts outside of the organization. These experts may be interviewed directly, or contacted as part of a formal survey, such as a Delphi study. A third method is to develop scenarios of alternative technological futures, which capture different rates of innovation and different emerging technologies. Scenarios allow an organization to conduct "what if" analyses and to develop alternative plans for responding to new innovations.

In addition to forecasting, some organizations establish strategic alliances with universities to engage in joint research projects, which allows them to keep abreast of new trends. Other organizations simply donate funds to universities for research in exchange for information about findings. The Partnership Data Net, a Washington, D.C.–based information center on partnerships, lists about three thousand partnerships between schools and businesses.[21] Akzo NV, the Dutch chemical giant, with more than eleven thousand employees at 161 locations in North America alone, created a massive partnership that paid healthy dividends.

 A few years ago, Akzo NV launched a "crash program" in research and development in the United States, in cooperation with twelve U.S. colleges. The goals for the university program were: (1) to create options for new business, either through the upgrading of present products or exploring new technologies; and (2) to identify talented people active in the academic scientific community and introduce them to Akzo for possible future recruitment. Within three years, the venture yielded forty patent applications, nine of which have been approved. The first estimate of the market size for six of these developments is greater than $2 billion.[22]

The Akzo example is a fitting conclusion for this section on analysis of the technological environment. Akzo not only stayed aware of technological changes in its broad environment, but it formed partnerships with members of that environment that resulted in the creation of new technology.

Organizations also form alliances with other firms as a way to monitor technological trends and prepare their organizations for the changes. Formation of strategic alliances between firms for purposes of technology sharing is a growing trend that will be discussed in detail later in this chapter. With a well-thought-out plan for monitoring technological trends, an organization can better prepare itself to receive early warnings about changes that will create opportunities and threats.

Change and Interdependence among the Broad Environmental Forces

Although each of the broad environmental forces has been discussed separately, in reality they are interdependent. For example, social forces are sometimes intertwined with economic forces. In the United States, birthrates (a social force) are low, and, because of improved health care and lifestyles (another social force), people are living longer. This demographic shift toward an older population is influencing economic forces in society. For instance, the older population means that there are shortages of young workers to fill the service jobs while demand for premium services by older consumers is increasing. Similarly, social attitudes can drive technological change. Hybrid electric- and gasoline-powered automobiles, such as the Honda Insight, were a direct response to broad societal trends favoring fuel-efficient automobiles.[23] Similarly, IBM is planning to produce a new energy-efficient microchip.[24] Baxter International has been very responsive to environmental concerns. As a result, the company saves millions of dollars through pollution-prevention efforts that eliminate or minimize pollution when it is created, instead of cleaning it up afterward.[25]

To assess the effect of broad environmental forces, including those that are interdependent, organizations often create models of their business environments using different scenarios. The scenarios are composed of optimistic, pessimistic, and best-case assumptions and interpretations of various economic, social, political, and technological data gleaned from an organization's business-intelligence system. Continuing the example of the aging population, a firm providing services for the elderly might develop different demand and wage-rate scenarios as a way of considering several different possible future business environments.

Information about broad environmental forces and trends is often available through public and private, published and unpublished sources, but organizations must take deliberate steps to find and make use of the information. For example, information about U.S. demographic patterns, investment patterns, economic trends, technological advances, and even societal views is widely available through published sources and government reports in libraries. For local economic and sociocultural trends, census data and chamber of commerce reports are just a few of the sources available.

Most well-managed firms collect broad environmental information regularly and understand its value in decision making. Perception, Inc., the world's largest producer of kayaks, has identified a sociocultural trend toward "extreme" sports that is helping its kayak business. Perception can track the interests of these sports enthusiasts through sports and recreation publications, and can associate the trend with a particular demographic profile. The number of individuals who fit that demographic profile provides an estimate of a target market for some of Perception's products, and can help the company in identifying new product directions and marketing programs.

Information about technological and economic trends is also widely available. Since a large portion of the technology investment in the United States is sponsored by the government, the findings of those research efforts are published through various government reports that are available to the public. Government reports also detail economic activity, investments, and trends within different regions and states, providing a rich source of information for business organizations.

As a review of this section thus far, Table 2.2 contains a chart that can help organizational managers track trends in their broad environments. It is also helpful to students in identifying opportunities and threats as a basis for developing alternatives during case analysis.

Collecting information on the broad environment in an international setting can be a significant challenge. Although most industrialized nations have similar sources of trend data, developing nations will not. Consequently, organizations often rely on a local firm to provide the kinds of broad environmental insights necessary for good strategic decision making. The next section briefly discusses some of the challenges firms face as they approach a global broad environment.

Table 2.2	**Assessment of the Broad Environment**			
	Implication for Organization			
Trends, Changes, or Forces	**Opportunity**	**Threat**	**Neutral**	**Organizational Response, If Any**
Sociocultural Influences • Attitude Changes • Demographic Shifts • Sensitive Issues • New Fads • Public Opinions • Emerging Public-Opinion Leaders				
Global Economic Forces • Economic Growth • Interest Rates • Inflation • Foreign-Exchange Rates • Trade Deficits • Other (depending on business)				
Technological Forces • New Production Processes • New Products/Product Ideas • Current Process-Research Efforts • Current Product-Research Efforts • Scientific Discoveries that May Have an Impact				
Political/Legal Forces • New Laws • New Regulations • Current Administrative Policies • Government Stability Wars • International Pacts and Treaties				

This chart is a useful tool for organizations that desire to track trends in their broad environments. It can also be used to generate strategic alternatives. On the left, a manager should describe the nature of each trend. The column in the middle can be used to identify each trend as an opportunity, a threat, or as neutral to the organization. The third column should list possible actions the firm could take to respond to the opportunities and threats, if appropriate.

Foreign Environments

So far in this chapter, international examples have included a partnership effort by Akzo NV, the Dutch chemical company; a new-product offering and a failed venture by Japanese companies; volatile interest rates in South America and Eastern Europe; a pact between the governments of Kazakstan, Russia, and Oman; the political actions of an Israeli satellite company; independent task forces that influence government policy in Australia; and industry deregulation in Portugal and the United Kingdom. It is evident from this discussion that broad environments extend beyond domestic boundaries.

As an organization becomes involved in or even interested in foreign business opportunities, the amount of data that must be collected and analyzed increases dramatically. The economic, social, and political environments of various countries can be very different. A few quotations from international business scholars will help to demonstrate this point further, beginning with an economic example.

 The Spanish capital market has recently undergone considerable change. Up to a few years ago it was a narrow market worked only by a very few people, as the public in general preferred to put their savings into lower risk, more traditional investments such as fixed term deposits, etc. However the way in which society and the economy in Spain have developed, together with a strong privatization policy, the increasingly global nature of the economy and the internationalization of markets have led to a considerable increase in shareholdings, so that many more Spaniards are now involved in the world of business and in the capital market.[26]

With regard to the political environment, differences also can be very significant.

 Hours after Prime Minister Lionel Jospin (of France) named Laurent Fabius his new minister of the economy, finance and industry, Socialist Senator Henri Weber hailed the new cabinet member as "the right man in the right place, who will set off fireworks." Fabius's appointment was the cornerstone of Jospin's cabinet reshuffle. . . . Jospin needed another powerful Socialist leader to become the second ranking person in the government. . . . Currently, as a part of a strategy being closely coordinated with Jospin—not unrelated to the emerging presidential race—he is working on further cuts in personal and corporate taxes, among the highest in Western, industrialized countries. The total tax burden in France represents 45.6 percent of gross national product and has been climbing.[27]

Of all the elements in the broad environment, perhaps societal differences are the most difficult to analyze, monitor, predict, and integrate into the strategic plan. For example, American firms often have difficulty in China due to differences in the sociocultural environment.

 China is known for rampant corruption that is tolerated by its citizens. Furthermore, Chinese/American relations are often strained due to China's poor attitude towards human rights and its unwillingness to conform to American policies on issues such as copyright protection and arms sales to politically unstable countries. Anti-U.S. sentiment can also be strong at times among some Chinese people. In a recent survey, 90% of Chinese youths feel that the U.S. behaves "hegemonistically." When some American movies are played in China, film authorities are swamped with phone calls complaining about the "unhealthy capitalist lifestyles" of some characters. Even the American icon, McDonald's, was attacked with complaints that they were undermining the health of children.[28]

Differences also exist within the technological environment; however, they tend to be a little less severe because of global information sharing and standardized technologies in many industries. The primary differences stem from the fact that some countries are more advanced in certain technologies than are others. Consequently, the global technological environment also deserves attention. In particular, organizations should try to identify where the most-advanced technologies exist so that they can be learned and applied to internal firm processes. As will be discussed later, one of the best ways to do this is through joint ventures with firms that possess the best technologies.

This section has been a discussion of the broad environment and the importance of collecting information on broad environmental trends. The emphasis in this section has been on monitoring, predicting, and adapting to trends in the sociocultural, economic, political, and technological environments. Attention will now turn to an analysis of the operating environment.

Analysis of External Stakeholders and the Operating Environment

operating environment
Consists of stakeholders with whom organizations interact on a fairly regular basis, including customers, suppliers, competitors, government agencies and administrators, local communities, activist groups, unions, the media and financial intermediaries

The **operating environment** consists of stakeholders with whom organizations interact on a fairly regular basis, including customers, suppliers, competitors, government agencies and administrators, local communities, activist groups, unions, the media, and financial intermediaries. Not all stakeholders are equally important to firm success, nor do any of them play the same roles. Furthermore, stakeholders have varying levels and types of power to influence an organization.

This section will briefly explore the characteristics that determine the nature of an industry, as well as relationships that exist between an organization and its external stakeholders. It will discuss the power particular stakeholder groups have to influence firm behavior and success. To begin, three of these stakeholder groups will be discussed with regard to economic power in an industry. They are customers, suppliers, and competitors. Other factors determining the dynamics of industry competition will also be presented. The section will then be expanded to include other important stakeholders such as government agencies and administrators, the media, activists, and local communities. Methods for managing external stakeholders and the operating environment will be presented. In particular, joint ventures and other cooperative relationships will be discussed, as well as political and economic strategies firms might pursue. Relationships with stakeholders and involvement in interorganizational relationships can be sustainable sources of competitive advantage.

Porter's Five Forces, Economic Power, and Industry Characteristics

Michael Porter developed a model that helps managers evaluate industry competition.[29] Industries are often difficult to define, but in general they refer to a group of organizations that compete directly with each other to win orders or sales in the marketplace. Porter described how the economic power of customers and suppliers influences the ability of a firm to achieve economic success. He reviewed factors that lead to high levels of competition among direct competitors. He also noted how entry barriers and the strength of substitute products increase or decrease the level of competition. These five areas of competitive analysis, referred to as the **five forces of industry competition,** are presented in Figure 2.3. According to Porter, the five forces largely determine the type and level of competition in an industry and, ultimately, the industry's profit potential.[30]

five forces of industry competition
Forces that largely determine the type and level of competition in an industry and, ultimately, the industry's profit potential; they include customers, suppliers, entry barriers, substitute products or services, and rivalry among existing competitors

An analysis of the five forces is useful from several perspectives. First, by understanding how the five forces influence competition and profitability in an industry, a firm can better understand how to position itself relative to the forces, determine any sources of competitive advantage now and in the future, and estimate the profits that can be expected. For small and start-up businesses, a five forces analysis can reveal opportunities for market entry that will not attract the attention of the larger competitors. An organization can also conduct a five forces analysis of an industry prior to entry to determine the sector's attractiveness. If the firm is already involved in the industry, a five forces analysis can serve as a basis for deciding to leave it. Finally, company managers may decide to alter the five forces through specific actions. Examples of such actions will be presented later in the chapter.

Economic Power of Customers

Customers provide demand for products and/or services, without which an organization would cease to exist. For instance, the Holland-based global retailer Koninklijke Ahold has determined that to remain successful, "A large body of customers must regard Ahold as committed, competitive, responsive to their ever-changing needs, and progressive on issues concerning the environment and health."[31] Because customers can withhold demand, they have **bargaining power,** a form of economic power. They can influence firm behavior. However, not all customers have the same amount of bargaining power. For instance, when retail giant Home Depot announced that it would no longer buy carpet from Shaw Industries (because Shaw, a carpet manufacturer, was moving into retail), Shaw's stock dropped by 11 percent in one day.[32] Similarly, Toys "R" Us has substantial influence over the products produced by toy manufacturers. If Toys "R" Us decides not to stock a toy, there is a high likelihood that the manufacturer will cease production of it. According to Porter, customers tend to exhibit greater bargaining power under the following conditions:[33]

bargaining power
Economic power that allows a firm or group of firms to influence the nature of business arrangements for factors such as pricing, availability of products or services, purchase terms or length of contract

- They are few in number. This creates a situation in which an industry competitor can't afford to lose a customer.

- They make high-volume purchases. High-volume purchasers can often dictate contract terms, force price concessions, or even tell their suppliers what to produce.

- The products they are buying are undifferentiated (also known as standard or generic) and plentiful. This means that customers can find alternative suppliers.

FIGURE 2.3

Porter's Five Forces Model of Industry Competition

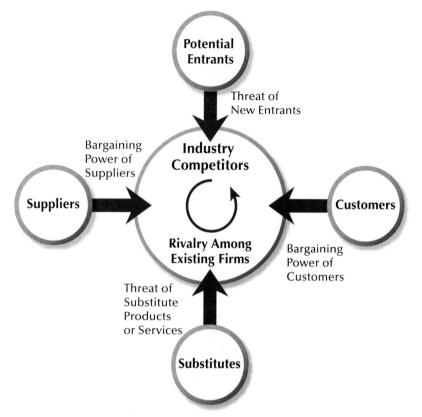

Source: Adapted with the permission of The Free Press, an imprint of Simon & Schuster Adult Publishing Group, from *Competitive Advantage: Creating and Sustaining Superior Performance* by Michael E. Porter, p. 5. Copyright 1985, 1998 by Michael E. Porter.

- They are highly motivated, as customers, to get good deals. This happens when customers earn low profits or when a lot of what they buy comes from the same industry. Terms of a deal may greatly influence whether the customer will be successful in the next year.

- They can easily integrate backward and thus become their own suppliers. **Vertical integration** means that a firm moves forward to become their own customer or, in this case, backward to become their own supplier. Both Sears and General Motors have been known to buy suppliers when they are unhappy with pricing.

- They are not concerned about the quality of what they are buying. This happens when the products or services don't influence the quality of their own products or services. Since quality is not affected, customers will be interested primarily in obtaining the lowest possible price. For example, office supplies don't influence the quality of microprocessor chips produced by Intel.

- They have an information advantage relative to the firms they are buying from. Information creates bargaining power. If a customer knows a

vertical integration
Exists when a firm is involved in more than one stage of the industry supply chain; a firm that vertically integrates moves forward to become its own customer or backward to become its own supplier

lot about the cost and profit structure of firms from whom they are buying, they can use this information to their advantage. For instance, *Consumer Reports* publishes information concerning how much dealers are paying for various makes and models of automobiles, and the costs associated with stocking, financing, and adding extras. Consequently, an astute customer can negotiate away almost all of the profit when purchasing an automobile.

- They are well organized. Sometimes weaker customers come together to increase their bargaining power. For example, smaller retailers may form buying clubs or associations to purchase items in bulk.

In combination, these forces determine the bargaining power of customers—that is, the degree to which customers exercise active influence over pricing and the direction of product-development efforts. Powerful customers must be given high priority in strategic management activities.

Economic Power of Suppliers

Powerful suppliers can raise their prices and therefore reduce profitability levels in the buying industry. They can also exert influence and increase environmental uncertainty by threatening to raise prices, reducing the quality of goods or services provided, or not delivering supplies when needed. Many of the factors that give suppliers power are similar to the factors that give customers power, only in the opposite direction. In general, supplier power is greater under the following conditions:[34]

- They are few in number, or, in the extreme case, there is only one supplier for a raw material, good, or service. This limits the ability of buying organizations to negotiate better prices, delivery arrangements, or quality. Makers of patented products frequently exercise great power.

- They sell products and services that cannot be substituted with other products and services. If there are no substitutes, the buying industry is compelled to pay a higher price and/or accept less-favorable terms.

- They do not sell a large percentage of their products or services to the buying industry. Since the buying industry is not an important customer, suppliers can reduce shipments during capacity shortages, ship partial orders or late orders, or refuse to accept orders at all, all of which can create turbulence for the buying industry, reduce profits, and increase competition.

- They have a dependent customer. In other words, the buying industry must have what the supplier provides in order to manufacture its own products or services. For example, companies that manufacture diet soft drinks must have artificial sweeteners, and microcomputer manufacturers need microprocessing chips.

- They have differentiated their products or in other ways made it costly to switch suppliers. For example, American Hospital Supply installs computer systems in hospitals to make ordering of supplies easy for its customers. However, if a hospital chooses to purchase from a different supplier, it must remove American Hospital's system, purchase a new system, and retrain employees to use it.

- They can easily integrate forward and thus compete directly with their former buyers. For example, a company that supplies electronic equipment to retail chains and is dissatisfied with prices or contract terms can open its own retail outlets to handle sales of its products.

- They have an information advantage relative to the firms they are supplying. If a supplier knows a lot about the cost and profit structure of firms to whom they are selling, the supplier can use this information to their advantage. For instance, if a supplier knows that a buyer is making high profits, a more attractive sales price can probably be negotiated.

- They are well organized. Sometimes suppliers form associations or trade unions to enhance their bargaining power.

These forces combine to determine the strength of suppliers and the degree to which they can exert influence over the profits earned by firms in the industry.[35] The laptop-computer industry is one that is particularly susceptible to the power of suppliers. Most manufacturers purchase microprocessors, batteries, operating-system software, and flat-panel displays from suppliers. Consequently, the manufacturing costs, performance characteristics, and innovativeness of the laptop computer are largely in the hands of suppliers.

Competition, Concentration, and Monopoly Power

In most industries, competitive moves by one firm affect other firms in the industry, which may incite retaliation or countermoves. In other words, competing firms have an economic stake in each other. Examples of competitive moves and countermoves include advertising programs, salesforce expansions, new-product introductions, capacity expansion, and long-term contracts with customers. In many industries, competition is so intense that profitability suffers, as has been the case in the airline, computer, and fast-food industries. Some of the major forces that lead to high levels of competition include the following:[36]

- There are many competitors in the industry, and none of them possess a dominant position. Economists sometimes call this pure competition. In a situation of pure competition, organizations must work hard to maintain their positions, since customers have so many options.

- The industry is growing slowly. Slow industry growth leads to high levels of competition since the only way to grow is through taking sales or market share from competitors.

- Products in the industry are not easily differentiated (i.e., they are standard or "generic"). Lack of product differentiation puts a lot of pressure on prices, and often leads to price-cutting strategies that appeal to customers but reduce the profitability of industry participants.

fixed costs
Costs associated with plants, machinery or other fixed assets

- High **fixed costs** exist, such as those associated with large plants or expensive machinery. High fixed costs mean that firms are under pressure to increase sales to cover their costs and eventually earn profits. It is not easy to cut back on production because the fixed costs will continue, so the manufacturers will cut prices or increase marketing expenses to increase demand.

exit barriers
Costs associated with leaving a business or industry

- High **exit barriers** exist. When exit barriers are high, firms may lose all or most of their investments in the industry when they withdraw from it. Therefore, they are more likely to remain in the sector even if profits are low or nonexistent.

The relative size of firms in an industry has a great deal to do with competitive dynamics. The first item in the list above describes pure competition as a situation in which sales are spread out over many companies without a dominant firm or firms in the industry. This type of situation fosters competitive rivalry, which in theory is good for consumers because it keeps prices at relatively low levels. At the other extreme are **monopoly** situations in which one company dominates all others in a sector. Monopolists may misuse their dominant positions through activities such as engaging in unfair practices that limit the ability of competitors to compete, erecting entry barriers to keep new competitors out of the industry, or charging too much for products or services. Consequently, some governments intervene to break up monopolies or penalize them for unfair practices. This is how AT&T was broken up. Another, more recent example is Microsoft.

monopoly
An industry in which one firm is the only significant provider of a good or service

 Microsoft holds a dominant position in software that runs on personal computers. Many competitors and customers have charged that Microsoft has used its might in unfair ways. For example, executives at Compaq Computer Corporation feared that Microsoft would retaliate if Compaq were to use software from other companies in their computers. In court, the plaintiffs listed twelve different retaliation tactics that Microsoft could pursue, including higher prices or reduced access to products, support, and training. Microsoft was also charged with requiring computer manufacturers to bundle the Microsoft Web browser, Explorer, into the Microsoft operating software, in an effort to put Netscape out of business. A U.S. federal judge described Microsoft as a "relentless, predatory monopolist." As a result of the findings, Microsoft was ordered to split into two operating companies; however, this order was later overturned to expedite a speedy conclusion to the legal case. The company still faced restrictions on its business practices. Across the Atlantic, the European Commission also charged Microsoft with anticompetitive behavior. The commission accused Microsoft of using its dominant position in PC software to push its way into the fast-growing market for Internet software.[37]

Relatively few firms are dominant enough to be considered a monopoly. Furthermore, even those businesses may not be able to keep their monopoly status for long. Besides government intervention, a rival company may develop a product or a technology that causes the dominant firm to lose its position, as in the case when AMD developed a microprocessor that was faster than the competing Intel product. However, industries are often characterized by the existence of a few very large firms. These industries are called oligopolies. For example, most automobile sales worldwide come from GM, Toyota, Ford, Nissan, and DaimlerChrysler.

Firms in oligopolies may informally cooperate with each other by not pursuing radical departures from existing pricing. They do this because they have learned that price wars hurt the profitability of the entire industry. Formal price-fixing, which is illegal in the United States, is called collusion. On the other hand, some oligopolies are known for severe price-cutting and high levels of competition. For example, the U.S. airline industry has struggled for many years as a result of price wars. If firms in an **oligopoly** sell products that are hard to differentiate, they are especially prone to a high level of competitive rivalry (see the previous list).

oligopoly
An industry characterized by the existence of a few very large firms

One of the global factors resulting in the creation of more-dominant companies and oligopolies is industry consolidation. Competitors in most industrialized countries are merging together to form larger companies with more market power. This trend is occurring in spite of resistance from many governments. For example, two midsize paper-and-packaging companies, Mead Corporation and Westvaco Corporation, merged in a stock swap to create a much larger company.[38] Internationally, Toshiba Corporation (Japan) plans to merge its memory-chip operations with those of Infineon Technologies AG (Germany).[39]

Richard D'Aveni has identified industries that experience what he calls **hypercompetition,** a condition of rapidly escalating competition based on price, quality, first-mover actions, defensive moves to protect markets, formation of strategic alliances, and reliance on wealthy parent companies.[40] Short product life cycles, international competitors, global market opportunities, and deep pockets are causing some industries to stay in turmoil. Firms take great risks as they jockey for position, but the results are not sustainable because their competitors match them move for move. Competitive practices are forcing profits to lower and lower levels. Personal computer manufacturers, with their expensive advertising and promotion programs, short product life cycles, and ruthless price-cutting, are one example of a hypercompetitive industry.

As a summary of what has been discussed so far, Figure 2.4 contains an abbreviated example of a five forces analysis for the brewing industry. In addition to the three forces just described, the figure also includes the similarity of substitute products, as well as barriers that keep new competitors from entering an industry. These forces will now be discussed.

Entry Barriers and Substitutes

Several forces determine how easy it is to enter an industry, and therefore how many new entrants can be expected. New entrants increase competition in a sector, which may drive down prices and profits. The new entrants may add capacity, introduce new products or processes, and bring a fresh perspective and new ideas—all of which can work to drive down prices, increase costs, or both. Forces that keep new competitors out, providing a level of protection for existing competitors, are called **entry barriers.** Examples of entry barriers that are found in many industries include:

- **Economies of scale.** Economies of scale occur when it is more efficient to produce a product in a larger facility at higher volume. For example, the big oil companies enjoy substantial cost savings through economies of scale in petroleum refinement. If a new entrant will be at a substantial cost disadvantage because of size, few firms will enter.

- **Capital requirements.** Also known as start-up costs, high capital requirements can prevent a small competitor from entering an industry. High capital requirements are sometimes associated with economies of scale, since new entrants need to invest in a large facility to be cost competitive. However, high capital requirements also result from research-and-development costs, start-up losses, or expenses associated with building inventories or extending credit to customers.

- **Product/service differentiation.** In some industries, established firms enjoy a loyal customer base, which comes from many years of past advertising, customer service, product differences, word of mouth, or simply being one of the first competitors in the industry. These factors make it very hard for a new entrant to compete. Consider, for example, how hard

hypercompetition
A condition of rapidly escalating competition

entry barriers
Forces that keep new competitors out, providing a level of protection for existing competitors

economies of scale
Cost savings that occur when it is more efficient to produce a product in a larger facility at higher volume

capital requirements
Costs associated with starting a business

product/service differentiation
Attributes associated with a product or service that cause customers to prefer it rather than competing products or services

FIGURE 2.4

Abbreviated Example of the Five Forces in the Brewing Industry

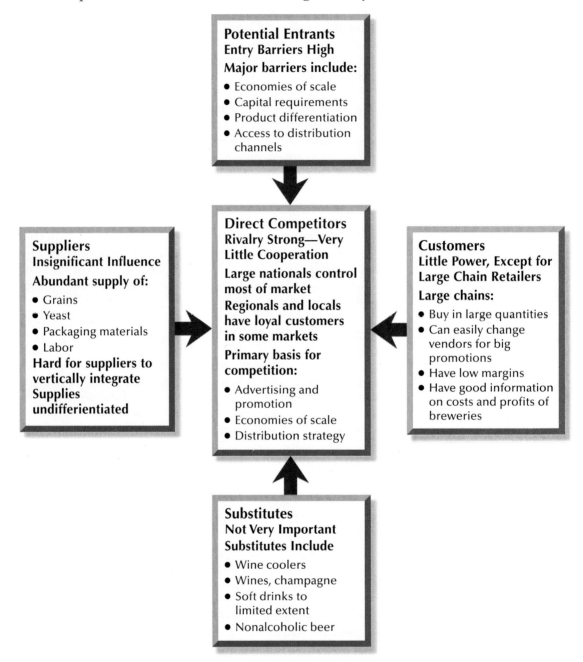

it would be to enter the automobile industry and compete with well-established advertising giants such as GM, Ford, and Toyota.

- High switching costs. Switching costs were mentioned earlier in our discussion of supplier and buyer power, but they can also serve as an entry barrier protecting competing firms.

- Access to distribution channels. In industries where supply networks are strong and competition is intense, access to distribution channels may effectively thwart new entry. Significant distribution-channel barriers exist in processed foods. Large companies such as Procter & Gamble can introduce new products into the markets with relative ease, due to their existing distribution networks. However, a new competitor would find it almost impossible to introduce a product on a large scale. Snapple, for example, was able to enter grocery retailing only after creating a strong name brand in delicatessens and convenience outlets, which created a form of pull-through demand

inimitable resources
Resources that are possessed by industry participants but are hard or impossible to completely duplicate

- **Inimitable resources.** Resources that are possessed by industry participants but are hard or impossible to completely duplicate may include patents, favorable locations, proprietary product technology, government subsidies, or access to scarce raw materials. Since these types of advantages are difficult or impossible for new entrants to duplicate in the short term, they often discourage entry. For example, the formula for the automotive additive Slick 50 was a carefully guarded secret. Only those who need to know had the combination to a fireproof vault with eight-inch-thick walls in which the sole printed copy of the formula was housed.[41] Unfortunately, the formula was recently revealed.

- Government policy. Sometimes governments limit entry into an industry, effectively preventing new competition. For example, airline companies for many years enjoyed a protected status, with their routes and prices protected from competitive pressures. However, when the airline industry became deregulated, many new competitors entered, and existing competitors greatly expanded their routes. These forces resulted in fare wars and lower profitability for all of the firms in the industry. Currently, airline companies are consolidating to build competitive strength.[42]

Taken together, these forces can result in high, medium, or low barriers. Examples of industries that traditionally are associated with high barriers to entry are aircraft manufacturing (technology, capital costs, reputation) and automobile manufacturing (capital costs, distribution, brand names). Medium barriers are associated with industries such as household appliances, cosmetics, and books. Low entry barriers are found in industries such as apparel manufacturing and most forms of retailing.[43]

substitute products/services
Products/services provided by another industry that can be readily substituted for an industry's own products/services

Substitute products/services are another force outside of the industry that can influence the level of industry competition. If organizations provide goods or services that are readily substitutable for the goods and services provided by an industry, these organizations become indirect competitors. Close substitutes serve the same function for customers, and can place a ceiling on the price that can be charged for a good or service.[44] For example, if the price of artificial sweeteners becomes too high, many consumers who typically prefer artificial sweeteners would probably switch back to sugar. In the service sector, credit unions are substitutes for banks, and bus travel is a substitute for airline travel. Close substitutes also set new performance standards. The availability of the smaller, direct satellites with pay-per-view options puts pressures on cable providers and video-rental stores to offer a broader selection of offerings at lower prices.

Whether a product or service qualifies as a substitute depends on how the boundaries of the industry are drawn. For example, health-care providers such as hospitals, private physicians, and health-maintenance organizations (HMOs) would be considered substitutes for one another if each type of provider were classified in a separate industry. However, if all of the providers were classified in the same industry—called, for example, the health industry—then hospitals, private physicians, and HMOs would be treated as direct competitors that exist in separate strategic groups. It is important to maintain consistency between whatever definition of industry is being used and the way substitutes are identified. Regardless of how they are defined, organizations should pay close attention to the actions of producers of close substitutes when formulating and implementing strategies.

External Stakeholders, Formal Power, and Political Influence

The emphasis throughout this section so far has been on economics and bargaining power. Economic analysis is important to strategic management. However, economic power is not the only type of power available to stakeholders, nor do economic factors completely determine the competitiveness of organizations. Figure 2.5 demonstrates that stakeholders can be classified based on their stakes in the organization and the type of influence they have. Such an analysis can help managers understand both the needs and the potential power of their key stakeholders.

FIGURE 2.5

Typical Roles of Various Stakeholders

Stake		Formal (Contractual or Regulatory)	Economic	Political
	Ownership	Managers who own stock in organization Directors who own stock in organization Stockholders in general Sole proprietors	Other companies that own stock in the organization	
	Economic Dependence	All paid managers and directors of for-profit and nonprofit firms Joint venture partners Creditors Internal revenue service	Employees Customers Suppliers Creditors Competitors	Competitors Foreign governments Local communities
	Social	Regulatory agencies (e.g., EPA, OSHA, and SEC) Unpaid trustees or managers of nonprofit organizations	Financial community at large (e.g., large brokerage houses, fund managers, and analysts)	Activist groups (e.g., Nader's Raiders) Government leaders The media

Influence on Behavior

Source: Adapted from R. E. Freeman, *Strategic Management: A Stakeholder Approach* (Boston: Pittman, 1984), p. 63. Reprinted with permission of the author.

Internal stakeholders are included in Figure 2.5 for completeness, although our attention in this section will be on external stakeholders.

In Figure 2.5, groups and individuals can have an ownership stake, an economic stake, or a social stake. An ownership stake means that a stakeholder's own wealth is dependent on the value of the company and its activities. Stakeholders also can be economically dependent without ownership. For example, employees receive a salary, debt holders receive interest payments, governments collect tax revenues, customers may be dependent on what they purchase to produce their own products, and suppliers receive payments for goods and services provided to the company. Finally, a **social stake** describes groups that are not directly linked to the organization, but are interested in assuring that the organization behaves in a manner that they believe is socially responsible. These are the "watchdogs" of our modern social order, such as Greenpeace.

On the influence side, groups and individuals may enjoy formal power, economic power, or political power. **Formal power** means stakeholders have a legal or contractual right to make decisions for some part of the company. Regulatory agencies and the Internal Revenue Service have formal power. **Economic power,** on the other hand, is derived from the ability to withhold services, products, capital, revenues, or business transactions that the firm values. Finally, **political power** comes from the ability to persuade lawmakers, society, or regulatory agencies to influence the behavior of organizations. Notice that some stakeholders have more than one source of power. For example, creditors sometimes have both economic and formal influence because they have formal contracts and may also have a seat on the board of directors.

In general, powerful stakeholders should be given more attention during strategy formulation and implementation. The most important external stakeholders are those with the greatest impact on the ability of the firm to survive and prosper. In for-profit organizations, the most important external stakeholders are typically customers.[45] For example, according to Tony Anderson, chief executive officer of H.B. Fuller Company, a *Fortune* 500 firm that makes glue and other products, "Customers are first, employees second, shareholders third, and the community fourth."[46] At Fuller, satisfaction of customers is the key to satisfying other stakeholders. However, the key to effective stakeholder management is that while some stakeholders are given more attention, none of the important stakeholders are ignored. In fact, consideration of a wide range of stakeholders can sometimes lead to creative strategies through partnerships and alliances.

Managing the Operating Environment

The operating environment may seem overwhelming to many managers. Powerful customers or suppliers can limit organizational success and profitability. Powerful competitors can make it difficult to remain competitive. Substitute products put pressure on prices and other product features. When entry barriers are low, new competitors enter the industry on a regular basis. Finally, external stakeholders can be powerful and difficult to deal with, based not only on economic power, but formal or political power as well. However, responding to challenges such as these defines the success of a manager. Fortunately, organizations can pursue a variety of actions to make their operating environments less hostile and thus increase the likelihood of organizational success. These actions tend to fall into three broad categories: economic actions, political actions, and partnering actions.

---

social stake
Occurs when a stakeholder group is not directly linked to the organization, but is interested in assuring that the organization behaves in a manner that they believe is socially responsible

formal power
Occurs when stakeholders have a legal or contractual right to make decisions for some part of an organization

economic power
Derived from the ability to withhold services, products, capital, revenues, or business transactions that the organization values

political power
Comes from the ability to persuade lawmakers, society, or regulatory agencies to influence firm behavior

Economic Actions

Firms may take a variety of economic actions to offset forces in the operating environment. For example, if entry barriers are low, companies may work to erect new entry barriers that prevent other firms from entering, thus preserving or stabilizing industry profitability. Although a difficult task, erection of entry barriers can be accomplished through actions such as increasing research and development or advertising to create product differentiation, or by constructing larger plants to achieve economies of scale. For example, service organizations such as banks may set up centralized loan-processing and credit-card departments that process large amounts of transactions somewhat more efficiently than do small-volume local banks. Similarly, large hospitals can support and utilize expensive laboratory and X-ray equipment more efficiently than a small hospital can. As another entry barrier, some firms make it hard for customers to switch. For example, for many years, IBM mainframe computer products were intentionally designed so that they would be compatible only with other IBM products. To make sales, a new entrant would have to convince an IBM user to drop the entire IBM system. IBM combined high switching costs with product differentiation based on outstanding service to gain the highest market share in mainframe computers.

competitive tactics
Techniques firms use, such as advertising, new product launches, cost reduction efforts, and quality improvements, to win market share, increase revenues, and increase profits at the expense of rivals

Industry rivals apply a variety of competitive tactics in order to win market share, increase revenues, and increase profits at the expense of rivals. **Competitive tactics** include advertising, new-product launches, cost-reduction efforts, new distribution methods, and quality improvements, to name a few. Typically, a particular industry can be characterized by the dominance of one or more of these tools. For example, the soft-drink industry is dominated by high levels of advertising as a competitive weapon. In addition, the presence of foreign competition in the automobile industry has placed an increasing emphasis on product differentiation through high levels of quality. Other common competitive tactics include providing high levels of customer service and achieving economies of scale through manufacturing a high volume of products in a large plant (which can lead to lower costs, thus allowing lower prices to customers). Notice that some of these competitive tactics can also lead to the erection of entry barriers, as previously discussed.

benchmarking
A tool for assessing the best practices of direct competitors and firms in similar industries, then using the resulting "stretch" objectives as design criteria for attempting to change organizational performance

Competitive benchmarking is a popular technique for keeping up with competitors. **Benchmarking** is a tool for assessing the best practices of direct competitors and firms in similar industries, then using the resulting "stretch" objectives as design criteria for attempting to change organizational performance.[47] For example, Federal Express is often cited as a model for customer satisfaction, Motorola in flexible manufacturing and quality, Procter & Gamble in marketing, 3M in new-product development, and Disney in worker training.[48] Xerox pioneered competitive benchmarking in the United States upon discovering that competitors were selling products at prices that were equal to Xerox's costs of producing them. The company responded by establishing benchmarks as a fundamental part of their business planning.[49]

While benchmarking may help a company improve elements of its operations, it will not help a firm gain competitive advantage. Benchmarking is a little like shooting at a moving target. While a firm is shooting, the target is moving. If an organization benchmarks against an industry leader, that leader will probably have moved on by the time the benchmark is achieved. Coincidentally, Xerox is no longer considered competitive in most of its markets (with the exception of the large copiers). Strategic thinking, described in Chapter 1, can help an organization move beyond what competitors are doing to set new standards and pursue new strategies.

Political Strategies

political strategies
All organizational activities
that have as one of their
objectives the creation of a
friendlier political climate for
the organization

Political strategies include all organizational activities that have as one of their objectives the creation of a friendlier political climate for the organization. For example, one of Enron's CEOs, Kenneth Lay, spent half an hour with U.S. Vice President Dick Cheney to outline what Lay saw as an effective energy policy. Many of his suggestions were incorporated into President Bush's energy plan. How did this happen? Enron had donated $888,000 to the Republican Party, $300,000 to the inaugural committee and $114,000 to the Bush campaign during the 2000 presidential campaign.[50] After the Enron collapse, this political influence was cast in a highly unfavorable light, but it is still an excellent example of how companies can influence their political environments.

Most organizations don't get half an hour with the vice president to talk about how they would like to be treated by government; however, many hire lobbyists to represent their views to political leaders. While lobbying can be part of a political strategy, it is only a small part of the bigger political picture. Companies may donate to political causes or parties, special-interest groups, or charities. They may pursue community-relations efforts or become involved in community service. Most large organizations have public-relations officers, and many do public-relations advertising.

Some scholars have suggested that individual firm lobbying efforts are often ineffective. Fragmented involvement, in which each company represents its own interests, have resulted in a free-for-all, and the collective interests of business have been the real loser.[51] One suggestion for fixing this problem is increased efforts to strengthen collective institutions such as the Business Roundtable and the Committee for Economic Development.

Collective actions can be very effective in influencing government. For example, the seven Baby Bells had to join political forces to win the ability to compete with AT&T in long-distance services and equipment.[52] General Motors, working through a trade group called the Diesel Technology Forum, is working with diesel-engine manufacturers and Exxon Mobil Corporation to influence the U.S. government to ease restrictions on diesel engines.[53] Some trade associations, such as the U.S. League of Savings Institutions, have had success influencing and sometimes even "rewriting" regulations before they are made law.[54]

 Automobile manufacturers in the United States, because of their size and limited number, might be expected to have almost overwhelming economic power in comparison to automobile dealers, who are numerous (more than twenty-five thousand) and widely dispersed. However, dealers have been effective in counteracting the power of manufacturers through unified political activity. An average of 57 auto dealers sit in every congressional district, and an average of 250 dealers reside in each senator's state. In contrast, auto manufacturing is concentrated primarily in six states. When conflict emerges between manufacturers and dealers, "grassroots" efforts are organized by the dealers' two powerful trade groups, the National Automobile Dealers Association and the American International Automobile Dealers Association. Dealers usually prevail in political conflicts with manufacturers. Consequently, the threat of legislation is a valuable bargaining tool for dealers when negotiating contract terms with manufacturers.[55]

Collective activity may include membership in trade associations, chambers of commerce, and industry and labor panels. Firms join associations to have access to information and to obtain legitimacy, acceptance, and influence.[56] Trade associations, although not as powerful in the United States as in Japan and Europe, often serve an information-management and monitoring purpose for member firms. They provide information and interpretation of legislative and regulatory trends, may collect market research, and sometimes provide an informal mechanism for exchanging information about competitors. Companies may also join industry and labor panels to manage negotiations with activist groups and unions. In addition, alliances of many types may form among competitors in an effort to influence stakeholders such as activist groups, unions, the media, or local communities.

Partnering with External Stakeholders

The foregoing discussion of collective political action is a good introduction to the concept of partnering. Organizations may partner for political reasons; however, many other types of partnerships exist. As mentioned previously, a firm's most valuable resources may extend beyond the boundaries of the company.[57] Table 2.3 contains a list and descriptions of common forms of **interorganizational relationships,** which is a term that includes many types of organizational cooperation.[58]

A **joint venture** is created when two or more firms pool their resources to create a separate, jointly owned organization.[59] Although traditionally joint ventures were formed to gain access to foreign markets or to pursue projects that were not mainstream to the organizations involved,[60] today they are being used to pursue a wide variety of strategic objectives, including development of new products or combining manufacturing or distribution processes to gain scale economies. For example, Kodak and Fuji have a joint venture to develop, manufacture, and distribute document-processing products in the Pacific Rim and Japan.[61]

interorganizational relationships
A term that includes many types of organizational cooperation or partnerships

joint venture
An entity that is created when two or more firms pool a portion of their resources to create a separate jointly owned entity

Table 2.3 Common Forms of Interorganizational Relationships	
Interorganizational Form	**Description**
Joint Venture	An entity that is created when two or more firms pool a portion of their resources to create a separate, jointly owned entity.
Network	A hub-and-wheel configuration with a local firm at the hub organizing the interdependencies of a complex array of firms.
Consortia	Specialized joint ventures encompassing many different arrangements. Consortia are often a group of firms oriented toward problem solving and technology development, such as R&D consortia.
Alliance	An arrangement between two-or-more-firms that establishes an exchange relationship but has no joint ownership involved.
Trade Association	Organizations (typically nonprofit) that are formed by firms in the same industry to collect and disseminate trade information, offer legal and technical advice, furnish industry-related training, and provide a platform for collective lobbying.
Interlocking Directorate	Occurs when a director or executive of one firm sits on the board of a second firm or when two firms have directors who also serve on the board of a third firm. Interlocking directorates serve as a mechanism for interfirm information sharing and cooperation.

Source: Adapted from *Journal of Management,* Vol. 26, B.B. Barringer and J.S. Harrison, "Walking a Tightrope: Creating Value Through Interorganizational Relationships," p. 383, Copyright 2000, with permission from Elsevier Science.

network
A hub and wheel configuration with a local firm at the hub organizing the interdependencies of a complex array of firms

Networks are constellations of businesses that organize through the establishment of social, rather than legally binding, contracts.[62] Typically, a focal organization sits at the hub of the network and facilitates the coordination of business activities for a wide array of other organizations. Each firm focuses on what it does best, allowing for the development of distinctive competencies. For example, Toyota is at the center of a tightly linked network of 180 firms that supply component parts and do joint research. Since network partners concentrate on the components part of the business, Toyota is able to focus specifically on design and manufacture of automobiles.[63] A special type of network form, called a *keiretsu,* is common in Japan. *Keiretsu* are organized around an industry, and work in much the same way as other networks; however, firms in a *keiretsu* often hold ownership interests in each other.

consortia
Specialized joint ventures encompassing many different arrangements; consortia are often a group of firms oriented towards problem solving and technology development, such as R&D consortia

Typically, **consortia** consist of a group of firms that have similar needs and thus band together to create a new entity to satisfy those needs. For example, CableLabs, a consortium of North American and South American cable-television operators, conducts research and development. Research findings are then reported to the approximately eighty members that make up the consortium. By banding together, these firms are able to accomplish much more research much more affordably than any one or a small group of firms could accomplish on their own.[64]

In another example, IBM, Microsoft, Intel, Oracle, and Hewlett-Packard launched a consortium to work out technology standards so that their equipment can communicate better across vendors.[65]

alliance
An arrangement between two or more firms that establishes an exchange relationship but has no joint ownership involved

Alliances are agreements among two or more firms that establish some sort of exchange arrangement but involve no joint ownership.[66] Alliances tend to be informal, and do not involve creation of a new entity. Two of the most common forms are marketing alliances and technology alliances.[67] For example, Walt Disney Company and Kellogg Company, the world's leading producer of cereals, formed an alliance in which Mickey Mouse and other Disney characters will show up on everything from cereal boxes to toothbrushes.[68] Technology alliances, on the other hand, involve cooperation in areas such as research and development, engineering, information systems, and manufacturing. For instance, in the aftermath of the September 11, 2001, attacks in New York City, the New York Stock Exchange and Nasdaq have begun discussions on how to trade each other's stocks.[69]

trade association
Organizations (typically nonprofit) that are formed by firms in the same industry to collect and disseminate trade information, offer legal and technical advice, furnish industry-related training, and provide a platform for collective lobbying

Trade associations typically are nonprofit organizations formed within industries to collect and disseminate information, offer legal or accounting services, furnish training, and provide joint lobbying efforts.[70] For example, the American Watchmakers-Clockmakers Institute offers a wide range of member services, including a database of hard-to-find parts, training, a library of industry-specific materials, and bulletins that contain up-to-date product information. Trade associations are especially important in industries that are heavily regulated or subject to frequent government interference. They are also important in industries in which technology is rapidly changing, since they offer to members the opportunity to stay abreast of recent advances. The primary advantages to belonging to a trade association are collective lobbying, learning, and cost savings through combining efforts in certain areas.

interlocking directorate
Occurs when a director or executive of one firm sits on the board of a second firm or when two firms have directors who also serve on the board of a third firm

Finally, **interlocking directorates** occur when an executive or director of one firm sits on the board of directors of another firm, or when executives or directors of two different companies sit on the board of a third company.[71] In the United States, the Clayton Antitrust Act of 1914 prohibits competitors from sitting on each other's boards. However, they are allowed to sit on the board of a third company. The primary advantage of interlocking directorates is the potential for what is referred to as "co-optation," defined as drawing resources from other firms to achieve stability and continued existence.[72] For example, if a firm develops a new technology, the interlocking director would have access to this information. Also, an organization may add to its board a director from a financial institution in an effort to facilitate financing.

The common characteristic behind all of these forms of interorganizational relationships is that they are an effort to combine resources, knowledge, or power to benefit each participant. They involve partnering and resource sharing. While the emphasis in much of this chapter has been on analysis of the environment in order to formulate strategy, the notion of partnering will be a common theme throughout the rest of this book. Successful interorganizational relationships can be an important source of sustainable competitive advantage.

This concludes our discussion of the broad and operating environments. Information collected during environmental analysis is used in every aspect of strategic planning, including creation of strategic direction, formulation of strategies, and creation of implementation plans and control systems. Organizations can pursue a variety of economic, political, and partnering actions to make their operating environments more hospitable. The next chapter will explore internal aspects of organizations and the ability of firm resources to provide other sources of sustainable competitive advantage.

Summary

The most important elements in the broad environment, as it relates to a business organization and its operating environment, are sociocultural influences, economic influences, technological influences, and political influences. The broad environment can have a tremendous impact on a firm and its operating environment; however, individual firms typically have only a marginal impact on this environment.

Analysis of society is important because broad societal changes and trends can provide opportunities for organizations. It is also important because awareness of and compliance with the attitudes of society can help a company avoid problems associated with being a "bad corporate citizen." A positive organizational reputation among stakeholders such as customers and suppliers may increase demand for products or lead to increased business opportunities. Finally, correct assessment of social trends can help businesses avoid restrictive legislation.

Economic forces such as economic growth, interest rates, availability of credit, inflation rates, foreign-exchange rates, and foreign-trade balances are among the most critical economic factors. Economic forces play a key role in determining demand patterns and cost characteristics within industries.

Technological forces in the broad environment have the power to create and destroy entire industries. In general, (1) innovations usually arise from existing technologies, (2) most products and processes evolve toward a dominant design, and (3) radical innovations tend to come from outside the established group of competitors. An understanding of these characteristics can help a manager develop a system for monitoring technology trends.

Organizations should also track political forces, particularly as they relate to increases and decreases in degree of regulation. Government influences come from (1) lawmakers, (2) regulatory agencies, (3) revenue-collection agencies, and (4) the courts. Each of these influences can occur at the federal, state, or local levels, which results in twelve major forces instead of four. Most industrialized nations have comparable government entities. Involvement in more than one country further increases the number of relevant government forces. Although one organization may not be able to dramatically alter major political forces, it may have considerable impact within its own specific industries and operating domain. Consequently, major political forces are considered a part of the broad environment, while government agencies and administrators are considered a part of the operating environment.

The operating environment includes stakeholders such as customers, suppliers, competitors, government agencies and administrators, local communities, activist groups, the media, unions, and financial intermediaries. One important distinction between the operating and broad environments is that the operating environment is subject to a high level of organizational influence, while the broad environment is not. A firm's industry is composed of companies that compete for the same sales dollars. The nature and level of competition in an industry is dependent on competitive forces that determine rivalry, such as the number of competitors and the growth rate of the industry, as well as the strength of customers and suppliers, the height of entry barriers, and the availability of substitute products or services. These competitive forces are known collectively as the five forces of competition.

Tactics for influencing stakeholders and the operating environment often involve interorganizational relationships, including joint ventures, networks, consortia, alliances, trade associations, and interlocking directorates. Other important tactics include contracting, various forms of stakeholder involvement in organizational processes and decisions, and exercising political influence to promote favorable regulations. Analysis of external stakeholders and the broad environment can result in the identification of opportunities and threats, which are then considered by managers as they establish a strategic direction and develop and implement strategies.

At this point, you should begin to appreciate that stakeholder analysis and management is a difficult and comprehensive management task. The themes, tools, and ideas contained in this chapter will be applied throughout the remaining chapters. The next chapter will focus on the internal organization and resource management.

Discussion Questions

1. Why is analysis of the broad environment important for effective strategic management?

2. What are the major components of the broad environment? Give an example of a trend in each area that could affect the welfare of a business organization.

3. Why should sociocultural influences be monitored? What are some of the current sociocultural forces in the United States?

4. What are some of the most important factors to track in the global economy? Why are these factors important to organizations?

5. Describe the roles of lawmakers, regulatory agencies, revenue-collection agencies, and the courts as they relate to doing business in the United States. Are these roles likely to be different in other countries?

6. Explain the three characteristics of technological innovation and how an understanding of those characteristics can be used to develop a technological forecasting process.

7. What are the major differences between the operating and broad environments? Can an organization effectively influence its broad environment? Its operating environment?

8. What are the five forces of competition? Describe their potential influence on competition in an industry with which you are familiar.

9. What are the primary factors that make some stakeholders more important than others? How should high-priority stakeholders be managed? How do management techniques for high-priority stakeholders differ from those of low-priority stakeholders? Give examples.

10. Describe the major forms of interorganizational relationships, and provide one possible advantage of each form.

11. What role can political strategy play in influencing favorable regulations? How can firms use political influence to balance power with strong competitors, suppliers, or customers?

Strategic Application

A Five Forces Analysis of Competition

Read the case assigned to you by your instructor or use an actual company of your choosing (check with your instructor for the specifics). Prepare a five forces analysis for the dominant industry in which the firm is involved. Remember that you are evaluating the firm's industry and not the firm itself. Additional library research is not required to complete this assignment, but you should fully utilize knowledge gained through your prior business training and life experiences. Make the reasonable assumptions you need to complete the assignment.

Fully evaluate each force. Consider each factor for each force, as described in the book. For example, there are eight factors that might give customers power. For each factor, you should decide whether it is relevant for your particular industry. In other words, does it apply to the industry, either to weaken or strengthen the force. In every case, determine whether it leads to greater power, less power, or does not apply to the industry. For example, if you analyze an industry in which there are many customers, you would say that this does not make the customers strong (weakens their power). On the other hand, if there are few customers, you would say that they have great power. If there are a moderate number of customers (in between), you would say that they have moderate power.

Clearly define your industry before you begin (in other words, how broadly are you defining your industry? If it is automobiles, does it include trucks too? If it is computers, does it include hardware and software? If it is entertainment, does it include movie production, music production, and/or theme parks?)

Customers—Who buys most of the products or services of this industry? It is possible that a company has more than one major customer group or industry. For this assignment, select the customer group or industry group that you think probably accounts for more of the sales than any other group or industry and conduct the analysis for this group or industry. It is possible, then, that two students may have analyses for different groups or industries.

- Number of customers
- Size of their purchases

- Differentiation of seller's products/services; also, is it costly or difficult to switch to a new seller if desired?
- Overall motivation of customers to get a good deal (perhaps based on financial weakness)
- Ease with which customers could vertically integrate backward and become their own supplier
- Concern about quality of what they are buying
- Ease with which customers can obtain accurate information on the seller
- How well organized are customers as a group?

Suppliers—Who are the major suppliers to this industry? Like customers, it is possible that more than one industry or group is a major supplier. Select the industry or group that you think is most relevant.

- Number of suppliers
- Availability of substitute products for what the supplier sells
- Percentage sold to a particular buying industry; is this buyer important?
- Determination of whether the buying industry must have the supplier's product/service to survive
- Differentiation of product/service supplier provides; is it costly or difficult to switch suppliers?
- Ease with which suppliers can vertically integrate forward and become their own customers
- Ease with which suppliers can obtain accurate information on the buyer
- How well organized are suppliers as a group?

Existing Industry Competitors—Who are the major competitors in this industry?

- Number of competitors and how well market share is divided
- Growth rate of industry
- Product/service differentiation
- Level of fixed costs (mostly fixed costs or variable costs or in between)
- Existence of exit barriers

Potential Competitors—Are there any significant entry barriers that keep new competitors out of the industry?

- Economies of scale
- Capital requirements
- Product/service differentiation
- Switching costs
- Access to distribution channels
- Inimitable resources held by current competitors
- Government policies and regulations that limit entry

Substitutes—What are the close substitutes for the products/services of the industry?

- To what extent could substitutes lure away customers from the products/services of the industry?

Now create a comprehensive summary of the major forces that are driving the dominant industry in which your firm is involved. For each of the five forces, *include only factors that are most influential.* Finally, summarize the results of your analysis (mention which forces are most important in the industry) and evaluate whether the combined forces create an industry in which it is easy or difficult to prosper (or something in between).

Strategic Internet Application

Select an industry or ask your instructor if an industry has been assigned. Go to www.Hoovers.com and click on the "Companies and Industries" section. On the left side of the window, click on "Industries." If Hoovers redesigns their Web site, this information may be organized differently, but it should still be available. Click on "Industry Snapshots." This will bring you to a page with many options. Spend some time reading everything that is available about your industry. If you page down on this screen, you will also find links to many other sources of information on your industry. Now go to www.Yahoo.com. You can either do a search for "industry news" or you can try to go directly to http://biz.yahoo.com/industry, which was the address for industry information at the time this book was printed. Click on your industry and read a few of the articles regarding what is currently happening. If you do not have enough information yet, you can do a Google.com search on "industry information." Google will provide you with many other links. After you have completed this research, answer the following questions:

1. Who are the major competitors in the industry? Who is the industry leader?

2. How well has the industry performed in recent years? Why?

3. What are the pressing issues in this industry right now?

4. If you were a major competitor in this industry right now, what would you do?

Notes

1. A. Bernstein and B. Grow, "Bracing for a Backlash," *Business Week,* 4 February 2002; J. R. Emshwiller and R. Smith, "Behind Enron's Fall, A Culture of Operating Outside Public's View," *The Wall Street Journal,* 5 December 2001, A1, A10; T. Hamburger and J. Weil, "Second Executive Tells of Andersen E-Mail," *The Wall Street Journal,* 21 January 2002, A3; B. McLean, "Why Enron Went Bust," *Business Week,* 24 December 2001, 59; M. Maremont, J. Hechinger, and K. Damato, "Amid Enron's Fallout, and a Sinking Stock, Tyco Plans a Breakup," *The Wall Street Journal,* 23 January 2002, A1, A4; R. Smith and J. R. Emshwiller, "Internal Probe of Enron Finds Wide-ranging Abuses," *The Wall Street Journal,* 4 February 2002, A3.

2. W. C. Symonds, "Is Tyco Looking at a Fire Sale?" *Business Week,* 18 February 2002, 35.

3. M. Conlin, "Is Wal-Mart Hostile to Women?" *Business Week,* 16 July 2001, 58–59.

4. J. B. McGuire, A. Sundgren, and T. Schneeweis, "Corporate Social Responsibility and Firm Financial Responsibility," *Academy of Management Journal* 31 (1988): 854–872.

5. F. Rice, "Denny's Changes Its Spots," *Fortune,* 13 May 1996, 133–134.

6. Taken directly from C. Daniels, "How to Love a Bad Report Card," *Fortune,* 10 July 2000, 189.

7. A. B. Fisher, "Corporate Reputations," *Fortune,* 6 March 1996, 90.

8. M. Pastin, *The Hard Problems of Management: Gaining the Ethics Edge* (San Francisco: Jossey-Bass, 1986), 123.

9. D. R. Dalton, M. B. Metzger, and J. W. Hill, "The 'New' U.S. Sentencing Commission Guidelines: A Wake-up Call for Corporate America," *Academy of Management Executive* (February 1994): 7–16.

10. R. A. Melcher, "Europe, Too, Is Edgy About Imports—From America," *Business Week,* 27 January 1992, 48–49.

11. A. Reifenberg, "Caspian Pact May Bolster Chevron Effort," *The Wall Street Journal,* 11 March 1996, A3, A6.

12. J. J. Fialka, "Israel Asks White House to Place Curbs on 3 U.S. Satellite-Surveillance Firms," *The Wall Street Journal,* 17 June 1996, A2.

13. Business and Finance, *The Wall Street Journal,* 27 June 1996, A1.

14. G. Hector, "A New Reason You Can't Get a Loan," *Fortune,* 21 September 1992, 107–112.

15. W. N. Davidson III and D. L. Worrell, "The Impact of Announcement of Corporate Illegalities on

Shareholder Returns," *Academy of Management Journal* 31 (1988): 195–200.

16. Taken directly from A. Farnham, "Biggest Business Goofs of 1991," *Fortune,* 13 January 1992: 83.

17. Taken directly from W. Altman, "Health and Safety Commission Chair Bill Callaghan on 'Good Health Is Good Business,'" *Academy of Management Executive* 14, no. 2(May 2000): 8.

18. G. Hamel, *Leading the Revolution* (Boston: The Harvard Business School Press, 2000); T. Mack and M. Summers, "Danger: Stealth Attack," *Forbes,* 25 January 1999, pp. 88–92.

19. J. M. Utterback, *Mastering the Dynamics of Innovation* (Boston: The Harvard Business School Press, 1994).

20. Utterback, *Mastering the Dynamics.*

21. S. A. Waddock, "Building Successful Social Partnerships," *Sloan Management Review* (Summer 1988): 18.

22. Taken directly from J. Vleggaar, "The Dutch Go Back to School for R&D," *The Journal of Business Strategy* (March/April 1991): 8.

23. D. Welch and L. Woellert, "The Eco-Car," *Business Week,* 4 August 2000, 62–68.

24. W. Bulkeley, "IBM Plans Energy-Efficient Chip to Counter High Electricity Costs," *The Wall Street Journal,* 1 October 2001, B6.

25. K. Dechant and B. Altman, "Environmental Leadership: From Compliance to Competitive Advantage," *Academy of Management Executive* (August 1994): 7–27.

26. Taken directly from M. Espinosa-Pike, "Business Ethics and Accounting Information: An Analysis of the Spanish Code of Best Practice," *Journal of Business Ethics* 22 (1999): 249.

27. Taken directly from A. Krause, "Laurent Fabius, France's Minister of the Economy, Finance, and Industry," *Europe* (July/August 2000): 16.

28. Adapted from J. Barnathan, "A Pirate under Every Rock," *Business Week,* 17 June 1996, 50–51; K. Chen, "Anti-U.S. Sentiment Surges in China, Putting a Further Strain on Relations," *The Wall Street Journal* , 15 March 1996, A11; L. Kraar, "The Risks Are Rising in China," *Fortune,* 6 March 1995, 179–180; K. Schoenberger, "Motorola Bets Big On China," *Fortune,* 27 May 1996, 116–124; K. Schoenberger, "Arco's Surprisingly Good Fortune in China," *Fortune,* 5 February 1996, 32.

29. This section is strongly influenced by M. E. Porter, *Competitive Strategy: Techniques for Analyzing Industries and Competitors* (New York: The Free Press, 1980).

30. This section on competitive forces draws heavily on the pioneering work of Michael Porter. See Porter, *Competitive Strategy,* 1–33.

31. Koninklijke Ahold NV, *Annual Report* (1990), 2.

32. Retail, *Orlando Sentinel,* 1 February 1996, C1.

33. Most of these factors came from Porter, *Competitive Strategy.*

34. Most of these factors came from Porter, *Competitive Strategy.*

35. R. W. Coff, "When Competitive Advantage Doesn't Lead to Performance: The Resource-based View and Stakeholder Bargaining Power," *Organization Science* 10 (1999): 119–133.

36. Most of these factors came from Porter, *Competitive Strategy.*

37. J. R. Wilke and D. Bank, "Microsoft Is Found to be Predatory Monopolist," *The Wall Street Journal,* 8 November 1999, A3; J. R. Wilke and T. Bridis, "Regulators Won't Seek Microsoft Breakup," *The Wall Street Journal,* 7 September 2001, A3, A6.

38. R. Sidel and Q. S. Kim, "Mead, Westvaco to Merge in Stock Swap," *The Wall Street Journal,* 29 August 2001, A3.

39. R. A. Guth, "Toshiba Talks with Infineon about Tie-up," *The Wall Street Journal,* 27 August 2001, A6.

40. R. D'Aveni, "Coping with Hypercompetition: Utilizing the 7S's Framework," *Academy of Management Executive* (AugusFt 1995): 45–57.

41. A. Reifenberg, "How Secret Formula for Coveted Slick 50 Fell into Bad Hands," *The Wall Street Journal,* 25 October 1995, A1, A9.

42. Barriers to entry form a major portion of the literature in industrial-organization economics. See J. S. Bain, *Barriers to New Competition* (Cambridge, Mass.: Harvard University Press, 1956); J. S. Bain, *Industrial Organization,* rev. ed. (New York: John Wiley, 1967); B. Gold, "Changing Perspectives on Size, Scale, and Returns: An Integrative Survey," *Journal of Economic Literature* 19 (1981): 5–33; Porter, *Competitive Strategy,* 7–17; W. G. Shepherd, *The Economics of Industrial Organization* (Englewood Cliffs, N.J.: Prentice Hall, 1979). For applications of barriers to entry to competitive strategy, see K. R. Harrigan, "Barriers to Entry and Competitive Strategies," *Strategic Management Journal* 2 (1981): 395–412.

43. Bain, Barriers to New Competition; H. M. Mann, "Seller Concentration, Barriers to Entry, and Rates of Return in Thirty Industries, 1950–1960," *Review of Economics and Statistics* 48 (1966): 296–307.

44. Porter, Competitive Strategy, 23

45. B. Z. Posner and W. H. Schmidt, "Values and the American Manager: An Update," *California Management Review* 3 (1984): 206.

46. P. Sellers, "Who Cares about Shareholders," *Fortune,* 15 June 1992, 122.

47. K. Jennings and F. Westfall, "Benchmarking for Strategic Action," *Journal of Business Strategy* (May/June 1992): 22.

48. O. Port, "Beg, Borrow, and Benchmark," *Business Week,* 30 November 1992, 74–75.

49. R. C. Camp, "Learning from the Best Leads to Superior Performance," *Journal of Business Strategy* (May/June 1992): 3.

50. B. Davis and R. Smith, "In Era of Deregulation, Enron Woos Regulators More Avidly Than Ever," *The Wall Street Journal,* 18 May 2001, A1, A6.

51. Empirical support of this phenomenon is found in K. B. Grier, M. C. Munger, and B. E. Roberts, "The Determinants of Industry Political Activity, 1978–1986," *American Political Science Review* 88 (1994): 911–925; a descriptive review of this problem is found in I. Maitland, "Self-defeating Lobbying: How More Is Buying Less in Washington," *Journal of Business Strategy* 7, no. 2 (1986): 67–78.

52. L. Cauley, J. J. Keller, and D. Kneale, "Battle Lines Harden As Baby Bells Fight to Kill Restrictions," *The Wall Street Journal,* 22 July 1994, A1–A2.

53. J. Ball, "GM Seeks to Ease Restrictions on Diesel Engines," *The Wall Street Journal,* 6 August 2001, A2.

54. M. Langley, "Thrift's Trade Group and Their Regulators Get Along Just Fine," *The Wall Street Journal,* 16 July 1986, A1, A14; I. Maitland, "Self-defeating Lobbying: How More Is Buying Less in Washington," *Journal of Business Strategy* (Fall 1986): 67–78.

55. B. Shaffer, "Regulation, Competition, and Strategy: Evidence from the Automobile Industry" (Ph.D. diss., University of California, 1992); F. M. Smith, "Franchise Regulation: An Economic Analysis of State Restrictions on Automobile Distribution," *Journal of Law and Economics* 25 (1982): 125–157.

56. W. R. Scott, *Organizations: Rational, Natural, and Open Systems,* 3d ed. (Englewood Cliffs, N.J.: Prentice Hall, 1992).

57. J. H. Dyer and H. Singh, "The Relational View: Cooperative Strategy and Sources of Interorganizational Competitive Advantage," *Academy of Management Review* 23 (1998): 660–679.

58. B. R. Barringer and J. S. Harrison, "Walking a Tightrope: Creating Value through Interorganizational Relationships," *Journal of Management* 26 (2000): 367–403.

59. A. Inkpen and M. M. Crossan, "Believing Is Seeing: Joint Ventures and Organizational Learning," *Journal of Management Studies* 32 (1995): 595–618.

60. Y. L. Doz and G. Hamel, *Alliance Advantage* (Boston: Harvard Business School Press, 1998).

61. Xerox, *Annual Report* (2000), 9.

62. C. Jones, W. S. Hesterly, and S. P. Borgatti, "A General Theory of Network Governance: Exchange Conditions and Social Mechanisms," *Academy of Management Review* 22 (1997): 911–945.

63. C. T. Edwards and R. Samimi, "Japanese Interfirm Networks: Exploring the Seminal Sources of Their Success," *Journal of Management Studies* 34 (1997): 489–510.

64. Barringer and Harrison, "Walking a Tightrope," 389.

65. D. Adamson, "Tech Giants Form Web Services Group," www.netscape5.marketwatch.com/news /story.asp 6 February 2002.

66. P. H. Dickson and K. M. Weaver, "Environmental Determinants and Individual-Level Moderators of Alliance Use," *Academy of Management Journal* 40 (1997): 404–425.

67. S. Das, P. K. Sen, and S. Sengupta, "Impact of Strategic Alliances on Firm Valuation," *Academy of Management Journal* 41 (1998): 27–41.

68. R. Verrier, "Disney, Kellogg Seal Honey of a Deal," *Orlando Sentinel,* 6 September 2001, A1.

69. K. Kelly, "Exchanges Reach Out to Avoid Future Disasters," *The Wall Street Journal,* 27 September 2001, C1, C17.

70. Barringer and Harrison, "Walking a Tightrope," 367–403.

71. Barringer and Harrison, "Walking a Tightrope," 367–403.

72. J. Pfeffer and G. R. Salancik, *The External Control of Organizations* (New York: Harper & Row, 1978).

Chapter 3

Organizational Resources and Competitive Advantage

Learning Objectives

After reading and discussing this chapter, you should be able to:

1. Determine which firm resources and capabilities are likely to lead to a sustainable competitive advantage.

2. Understand the value chain and its components and how a firm can use value chain activities to gain competitive advantage.

3. Recognize the important aspects of strategic leadership and the various leadership styles used by CEOs.

4. Understand the important functions of boards of directors, as well as the agency problems that sometimes exist when directors don't carry out their functions in a responsible manner.

5. Analyze a firm's culture and some of the pros and cons associated with it.

6. Appreciate the importance of organizational knowledge, interorganizational relationships, patents, brands and reputations in determining the competitiveness of a firm.

Eli Lilly and Company

Executives at Eli Lilly and Company, maker of the antidepressant drug Prozac, are more than a little concerned about the future performance of their company. Prozac was heralded by some as a "miracle drug" and a pharmaceutical innovation as important as aspirin. For many years, Lilly enjoyed huge profits. However, in late 2001, their patent ran out. Typically, generics will steal about 50 percent of the market from a brand-name drug within six months of patent expiration. Bruce Downey, CEO of Barr Labs, is excited about the potential. His company could sell as much as $250 million worth of fluoxetine, a generic for Prozac, within the first year. Lilly tried litigation to block generics, but the legal case was weak. They also introduced a weekly version of Prozac, complete with a free trial program for patients and a blitz of advertising. However, companies that manage health care fought back with a major campaign to switch consumers to the much cheaper generic drug. Merck-Medco, the pharmacy-benefit unit of Merck & Co., was able to persuade doctors to change the prescriptions of more than fifteen thousand patients. Blue Cross Blue Shield of Michigan launched a campaign called "Generic Drugs, the Unadvertised Brand" in an effort to get consumers to switch away from name brands.[1]

Lilly's dilemma is typical of a company that depends too heavily on a single innovation or patent to sustain organizational performance. Patents run out, innovations are copied, and high-performing managers are hired away by competitors every day. Heavy dependence on a single resource or capability is one of the reasons that today's great companies are often tomorrow's failures. Polaroid, originator of instant photography, recently filed for Chapter 11 bankruptcy protection. Xerox, synonymous with copy-machine technology, is struggling.

Resources and capabilities are the bread and butter of organizational success. Better resources and capabilities lead to higher levels of success. Poor resources and capabilities lead to failure. However, not all resources and capabilities are equal in their ability to help an organization achieve sustainable performance. This chapter is about how managers may identify and/or develop those resources and capabilities that are most likely to lead the firm to obtain a sustainable competitive advantage.

Internal Analysis and Competitive Advantage

Chapter 1 described internal resources and capabilities as falling into five general categories: financial, physical, human, knowledge-based, and general organizational. Figure 3.1 provides examples of the types of resources and capabilities that fall into each of these five areas.

sustainable competitive advantage
Exists when a firm enjoys a long-lasting business advantage compared to rival firms

The ability of a resource or capability to lead to a **sustainable competitive advantage** depends on the answers to six questions:

1. *Does the resource or capability have value in the market?* These types of resources allow a firm to exploit opportunities and/or neutralize threats. For example, Sony has developed the capability to design, manufacture, and sell miniaturized electronics. This capability has value to customers. Sony has applied this capability to numerous market opportunities such as stereos, tape players, disc players, televisions, and video cameras.

2. *Is the resource or capability unique?* If an organization is the only one with a particular resource or capability, then it may be a source of competitive advantage. If numerous organizations possess a particular resource or capability, then the situation is described as competitive parity—no company has the advantage. Note that uniqueness does not mean that only one organization possesses a capability or resource—only that few firms do. The uniqueness dimension also implies that a resource or capability is not easily transferable. That is, it is not readily available in the market for purchase.

3. *Is there a readily available substitute for the resource or capability?* Sometimes competing organizations may not have the exact resource or capability, but they have easy access to another resource or capability that will help them to accomplish the same results. For example, in Florida, a small number of cement manufacturers own their own rock quarries, and such resources are extremely limited in the state. However, competitors have been able to acquire this needed raw material at almost the same cost by importing through foreign vendors.

Positive answers to the first two questions and a negative answer to the third question mean that a resource or capability has the potential to lead to a competitive advantage for the firm. However, that potential is not realized unless two other questions are also answered in the affirmative:

FIGURE 3.1

Examples of Firm Resources and Capabilities

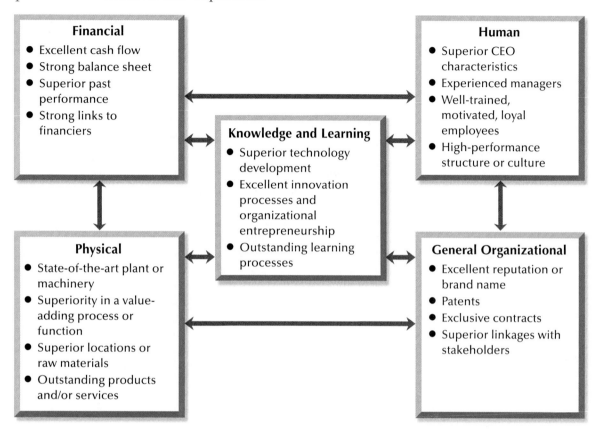

Financial
- Excellent cash flow
- Strong balance sheet
- Superior past performance
- Strong links to financiers

Knowledge and Learning
- Superior technology development
- Excellent innovation processes and organizational entrepreneurship
- Outstanding learning processes

Human
- Superior CEO characteristics
- Experienced managers
- Well-trained, motivated, loyal employees
- High-performance structure or culture

Physical
- State-of-the-art plant or machinery
- Superiority in a value-adding process or function
- Superior locations or raw materials
- Outstanding products and/or services

General Organizational
- Excellent reputation or brand name
- Patents
- Exclusive contracts
- Superior linkages with stakeholders

4. *Do organizational systems exist that allow realization of potential?* For potential to be realized, the firm must also be organized to take advantage of it. For example, Xerox formed a research laboratory called PARC, which, in the late 1960s and 1970s, developed an amazing assortment of technological innovations, including the personal computer, the "mouse," the laser printer, and Windows-type software. However, the company did not take advantage of many of PARC's innovations because it did not have an organization in place to do so. For instance, poor communications prevented most Xerox managers from knowing what PARC was doing, and a highly bureaucratic system mired a lot of the innovations in red tape. On the other hand, companies such as Wal-Mart and Disney are masters at exploiting their sources of competitive advantage.[2]

5. *Is the organization aware of and realizing the advantages?* One of the great differentiators between successful and unsuccessful companies is the ability of managers to recognize and tap into resource advantages. An organization may have employees that have great potential in an area, but the organization does not know it. The company may have the ability to produce a product that is highly unique and valuable to a particular market segment, but the firm does not realize it. In fact, an organization may even

have systems in place that would allow realization of potential. Nevertheless, managers have to be able to identify sources of competitive advantage and take positive actions for potential to be realized.

At this point, an organization is using its systems and knowledge to take advantage of a unique and valuable resource or capability. However, as the example about Prozac at the beginning of this chapter attests, resource advantages may not be sustainable. A final question determines the long-term value of a resource or capability:

6. *Is the resource or capability difficult or costly to imitate?* Competing firms face a cost disadvantage in imitating a resource or capability. The more difficult or costly a resource or capability is, the more valuable it is in producing a sustainable competitive advantage.[3]

Figure 3.2 demonstrates how resources and capabilities become sustainable competitive advantages. If a resource or capability is valuable, unique, nonsubstitutable, hard to imitate, and if it also can be applied to more than one business area, it is called a core competency or capability. For example, General Electric has been able to apply its skill in managing financial assets across a broad range of industries. In addition, Motorola has applied its skills in producing high quality across its diverse product portfolio. Procter & Gamble is known for its excellent marketing.[4] Finally, Circuit City is applying its "value priced," high-volume retailing capability to used cars through its CarMax outlets.[5] The most successful companies pay critical attention to developing and applying their core competencies.

tangible resources
Organizational assets that can be seen, touched, and/or quantified, such as plants, money, or products

intangible resources
Organizational assets that are hard to quantify, such as knowledge, skills, abilities, stakeholder relationships, and reputations

Tangible resources can be seen, touched, and/or quantified.[6] Examples include manufacturing processes and product variations. These resources tend to be easy to imitate. Although some products can be patented, a patent provides a measure of protection only until it runs out. On the other hand, some of the most important resources and capabilities are intangible; that is, they are hard to quantify **Intangible resources** and capabilities are the hardest to imitate. For example, knowledge about how to innovate is much harder to imitate than any particular product innovation. Organizational reputations cannot be fully imitated, even in the long term. Other intangibles include good relationships with external stakeholders, a high-performing culture, and a well-known corporate brand. One of the reasons that resources and capabilities are difficult for competitors to imitate is that it is difficult to determine exactly how the source of capability was created. Whereas a new product can be imitated, the processes used over time to hire, develop, retain, and build loyalty and shared values within the workforce are difficult to observe, and even more difficult to imitate. Consequently, intangible resources and capabilities are often the ones most likely to lead to competitive advantage.

The resources and capabilities that lead to competitive advantage are different in each industry, and can also change over time. For example, high-performing film studios during the period from 1936 to 1950 possessed superior property-based resources such as exclusive long-term contracts with stars and theaters. However, during the period from 1951 to 1965, knowledge-based resources in the form of production and coordinative talent and budgets were associated with high performance. These findings can be traced to the capabilities needed to deal with increasing uncertainty in the film industry.[7] Sometimes resource advantages within nations can lead to significant competitive advantages for the firms that compete there. For example, India is second only to the United States in the number of scientists and engineers its schools produce.[8] The following Global Insight demonstrates that this resource advantage has led to a competitive advantage for Indian companies in service industries.

FIGURE 3.2

Six Questions that Determine the Competitive Value of Resources and Capabilities

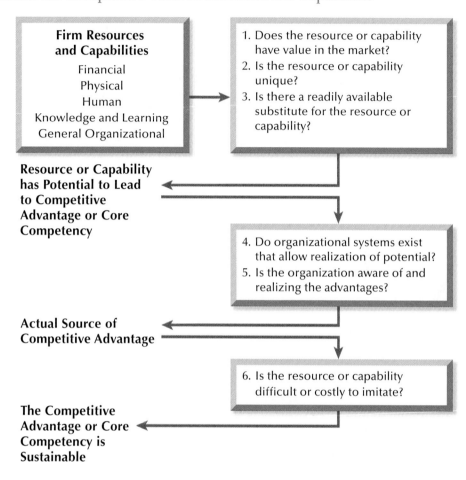

Global Insight

India's Emerging Competitive Advantage in Services

India has not yet caught the fancy of foreign investors—even though its population exceeds 1 billion, and its gross domestic product (GDP) of $500 billion ranks it as the eleventh-largest economy in the world. Political turmoil obviously explains why many global companies are hesitant to invest in India. Nevertheless, India has a potential source of competitive advantage that could fuel significant economic growth and foreign investment in the future.

India's competitive potential does not lie in the same fields as other low-income developing countries. Rather than enjoying competitiveness in natural-resource industries or low-skill, labor-intensive manufacturing, India is revealing surprising strength in skill-intensive tradable services, including software development, information-technology (IT)-enabled services, product/project engineering and design, biotechnology, pharmaceuticals, media, entertainment, and health care. New clusters are emerging in these activities in cities such as Bangalore and Hyderabad, where vibrant Indian firms are being joined by well-known multinationals. One interesting example is General Electric, which is investing $100 million in Bangalore to build its largest R&D lab in the world, employing twenty-six hundred scientists, including more than three hundred with Ph.D. degrees. It was while inaugurating this lab that GE's past CEO, Jack Welch, said: "The real treasure of India is its intellectual capital. The real opportunity of India is its incredibly skilled work force. Raw talent here is like nowhere else in the world."

India has received much attention recently on the prowess of its software industry, prompting Bill Gates to proclaim that "India is likely to be the next software superpower." For the better part of a decade, India's software industry has been growing at 50 percent annually. By 2000, the software sector's output had grown to $8 billion, and exports had risen to $6.2 billion. More than eight hundred firms provided a range of software services, targeted mostly at foreign customers. The United States accounted for nearly 60 percent of Indian software exports; followed by Europe, with 23.5 percent; and Japan, with just 3.5 percent.

Source: Adapted from D. Kapur and R. Ramamurti, "India's Emerging Competitive Advantage in Services," *Academy of Management Executive* (May 2001): 20–33, used with permission.

The rest of this chapter will discuss resources and capabilities in five sections. For the sake of simplicity, the term resources will sometimes be used to mean both resources and capabilities, unless a specific capability is being described. The five sections are financial resources, physical resources, human-based resources, knowledge-based resources, and general organizational resources. Although these resources will be discussed separately, it is important to note that in reality, they are all tied together. This point is demonstrated in Figure 3.3.

An organization can enter Figure 3.3 at any point, but we will start at financial resources. An organization with very strong financial resources can hire better-quality managers and employees and train them better. A strong financial position can also lead to increased investments in research and development and superior physical assets such as plants and machinery. If an organization is successful in hiring the most-talented people and training them well, the employees are more likely to learn and innovate better. This innovation and learning will result in better physical processes, which reinforces investments in superior physical assets. The result should be better products and services, which lead to a strong brand, an excellent organizational reputation, and excellent relationships with stakeholders. Strong brands and superior products and services are likely to lead to financial success. Thus, the cycle continues.

To be successful over the longer term, companies need to pay attention to *all five* resource areas. Lack of attention to any of the five areas can remove a firm from the loop. A solid investment strategy should focus on human-resource development and superior equipment and processes. If financial resources are misused, they will not result in better human resources or superior equipment and processes.

Eventually, the organization will no longer be competitive. Human resources need to be managed effectively so that learning and innovation are the result. If human-resource development is neglected or misguided, learning and innovation will cease, and the organization will eventually wear down, thus breaking out of the loop. Knowledge creation and innovative activities should be channeled so as to produce better processes and more-innovative products and services. If this does not happen, the value of a company's brand will be eroded, and its reputation may suffer. Finally, brand names, organizational reputation, and stakeholder relationships should be carefully guarded and developed in order to produce strong financial results. The point here is that all of the resource areas are interdependent, and an organization can't afford to neglect any of them.

Entrepreneurs enter the cycle at any of a number of stages; however, most often an entrepreneur will begin with an idea. He or she will then seek to build an organization around the idea. Financing will need to be arranged. Human resources will need to be acquired. Once a venture is formed, the innovation may lead to superior processes or products. If not, then it is unlikely to be successful. However, if superior processes or products result, financial success may be obtained. The entrepreneur then uses financial success as a platform for building the human resources of the organization. The cycle has begun.

FIGURE 3.3

Competitiveness and Resource Interconnectedness

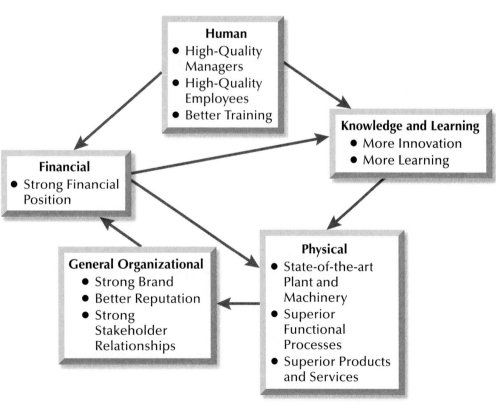

Financial Resources and Financial Analysis

Financial resources can be a source of advantage, although they rarely qualify as "unique" or "difficult to imitate." Nevertheless, strong cash flow, low levels of debt, a strong credit rating, access to low-interest capital, and a reputation for creditworthiness are powerful strengths that can serve as a source of strategic flexibility. Firms that are in a strong financial position can be more responsive to new opportunities and new threats, and are under less pressure from stakeholders than are their competitors who suffer financial constraints. Financial ratios, such as the ones found in Table 3.1, may be used to determine the financial strength of an organization and its ability to finance new growth strategies. Often companies will track trends of key ratios over several years. Also, organizations may compare their numbers against industry averages or ratios from a major competitor to assess comparative financial strength.

Profitability ratios are a common measure of overall financial success. They provide a barometer for management with regard to how well strategies are working, and may also provide warning of downward trends and thus the need for more-dramatic changes. External stakeholders pay critical attention to profitability ratios, as they are a primary determinant of share prices, the ability to repay loans, and future dividends. **Liquidity** ratios help an organization determine its ability to pay short-term obligations. Financiers are especially interested in these ratios because lack of liquidity can lead to immediate insolvency during downturns. Insufficient liquidity may be a sign that the company is performing poorly. However, it might also be an indication of the need for more long-term financing. For example, an organization may have relatively low levels of liquidity, but also low levels of long-term debt such as bonds. By selling bonds, the organization can increase its cash flow, thus relieving tight liquidity. This often happens when firms are growing. Consequently, liquidity needs to be measured against other ratios and trends to achieve an accurate picture of financial strength.

Leverage is a common measure of **financial risk,** which in simple terms may be thought of as the risk of bankruptcy. When a publicly held organization goes bankrupt, its shareholders, financiers, employees, managers, customers, local communities, and suppliers are all adversely affected. For example, the U.S. airlines had so much leverage and such low liquidity before the disaster on September 11, 2001, that the government had to give them billions of dollars within weeks just to help them continue to operate. Finally, Table 3.1 contains a few ratios that measure the efficiency of organizational activities. These ratios may be hard for outside observers to measure. For example, annual credit sales, a factor in two of these ratios, may not be reported. Consequently, students should not be frustrated if they can't get information to calculate all of these ratios. Instead, they should focus on information that is available. For example, information on sales and total assets, used to calculate asset turnover, is almost always available.

Financial resources are becoming particularly important in hypercompetitive environments, as described in Chapter 2. Deep financial resources are needed to wage battles in those markets where other forms of advantage are not sustainable for long. Also, the ability to invest in unique, valuable, difficult-to-imitate capabilities is often tied completely to the available financial resources. For example, the ability to build a brand name, to create a new, innovative process, or to compensate fairly and retain a highly creative workforce is dependent upon financial resources. While financial resources may not be unique or difficult to imitate, they provide the lever for developing those types of resources elsewhere in the organization.

liquidity
A measure of a firm's ability to pay short-term obligations

leverage
A measure of a firm's long-term or total debt relative to its assets or equity; a common measure of financial risk

financial risk
The risk that a firm will not be able to meet its financial obligations and may eventually declare bankruptcy

Table 3.1 Commonly Used Financial Ratios

Ratio	Calculation	What it Measures
Profitability Ratios		
Gross profit margin	$\dfrac{\text{Sales} - \text{COGS}}{\text{Sales}} \times 100$	Efficiency of operations and product pricing
Net profit margin	$\dfrac{\text{Net profit after tax}}{\text{Sales}} \times 100$	Efficiency after all expenses are considered
Return on assets (ROA)	$\dfrac{\text{Net profit after tax}}{\text{Total assets}} \times 100$	Productivity of assets
Return on equity (ROE)	$\dfrac{\text{Net profit after tax}}{\text{Stockholders' equity}} \times 100$	Earnings power of equity
Liquidity Ratios		
Current ratio	$\dfrac{\text{Current assets}}{\text{Current liabilities}}$	Short-run debt paying ability
Quick ratio	$\dfrac{\text{Current assets} - \text{inventories}}{\text{Current liabilities}}$	Short-term liquidity
Leverage Ratios		
Debt to equity	$\dfrac{\text{Total liabilities}}{\text{Stockholders' equity}}$	Extent to which stockholders' investments are leveraged (common measure of financial risk)
Total debt to total assets (debt ratio)	$\dfrac{\text{Total liabilities}}{\text{Total assets}}$	Percent of assets financed through borrowing (also financial risk measure)
Activity Ratios		
Asset turnover	$\dfrac{\text{Sales}}{\text{Total assets}}$	Efficiency of asset utilization
Inventory turnover	$\dfrac{\text{COGS}}{\text{Average inventory}}$	Management's ability to control investment in inventory
Average collection period	$\dfrac{\text{Receivables} \times 365 \text{ days}}{\text{Annual credit sales}}$	Effectiveness of collection and credit policies
Accounts receivable turnover	$\dfrac{\text{Annual credit sales}}{\text{Receivables}}$	Effectiveness of collection and credit policies

Physical Resources and the Value Chain

value chain
A representation of organizational processes, divided into primary and support activities that create value for customers

One way to think about organizational resources and capabilities is to visualize the activities and processes of an organization and determine how they add value to the products and services that the organization provides in the marketplace. Michael Porter developed a framework, called the value chain, that is a useful tool in identifying potential sources of competitive advantage.[9] The **value chain** divides organizational processes into distinct activities that create value for the customer. Value-adding activities are a source of strength or competitive advantage if they

inbound logistics
Primary activities of the value chain including those associated with acquiring inputs used in the product

operations
Primary activities of the value chain that refer to transforming inputs into the final product

outbound logistics
Primary activities of the value chain related to storing and physically distributing a final product to customers

marketing and sales
Primary activities of the value chain associated with customers purchasing the product and processes through which they are induced to do so

service
Primary activities of the value chain associated with providing service to enhance or maintain product value, such as repairing parts

resource procurement
Support activities of the value chain related to the purchase of inputs for the primary processes and support activities of the firm

technology development
Support activities of the value chain associated with learning processes that result in improvements in organizational function performance

human-resource management
Support activities of the value chain associated with human-based activities such as recruiting and training

administration
Support activities of the value chain consisting of general management activities, such as planning and accounting

meet the requirements identified earlier, such as value, uniqueness, nonsubsitutability, and inimitability.

The primary activities include inbound logistics, operations, outbound logistics, marketing and sales, and service (see Figure 3.4). **Inbound logistics** includes activities associated with acquiring inputs that are used in the product, such as warehousing, materials handling, and inventory control. The term **"operations"** refers to transforming inputs into the final product through activities such as machining, assembly, molding, testing, and printing. **Outbound logistics** are activities related to storing and physically distributing the final product to customers, such as finished goods warehousing, order processing, and transportation. **Marketing and sales** include processes through which customers can purchase the product and through which they are induced to do so, such as advertising, distribution of catalogs, direct sales, distribution channeling, promotion, and pricing. Finally, **service** refers to providing service to enhance or maintain product value, such as repair, parts supply, or installation.

Organizations also engage in activities that support these primary functions. These activities are placed above the primary activities in Figure 3.4. **Resource procurement** refers to the actual purchase of inputs, and not to the inputs themselves or to the way they are handled once they are delivered. All of the primary processes need purchased resources, many of which are not raw materials. Examples of these inputs include typewriters, accounting firm services, and computers. **Technology development** refers to learning processes, which result in improvements in the way organizational functions are performed.

Human-resource management includes human-based activities such as recruiting, hiring, training, and compensation. Finally, **administration** consists of general-management activities such as planning and accounting. The dotted lines connecting most of the support activities with the primary activities demonstrate that the support activities can be associated with each of the primary activities as well as support the complete chain. Administration is the only exception, since it applies to the complete chain instead of to any one unit. Profit is found at the right side of the chain, an indication that firms can achieve higher profit margins through the development of competencies and superior resources based on their value-chain activities.

An organization can develop a competitive advantage (1) in any of the primary or support activities, or (2) in the way they are combined, or (3) in the way internal activities are linked to the external environment. The cumulative effect of value-chain activities and the way they are linked inside the firm and with the external environment determine organizational performance relative to competitors. Each of the three means of creating a value-chain-based competitive advantage will now be discussed.

An organization can develop a competitive advantage in any of the primary or support activities. For each area, the relevant question is, "How much value is produced by this area vs. our cost of producing that value?" This analysis of value and costs is then compared with competing firms. For example, one firm may have superior customer service, accompanied by higher service costs, while another firm may have superior manufacturing quality accompanied by higher operations costs. These two firms may actually have products that are similarly valued in the market (as indicated by price and demand).

Competitive advantages can also occur through the manner in which activities are combined inside the firm. According to one expert, the success of Honda in moving from motorcycles into many other businesses is attributable at least partially to superior combinations of value-chain activities.

Another capability central to Honda's success has been its skill at "product realization." Traditional product development separates planning, proving, and executing into three sequential activities: assessing the market's needs and whether existing products are meeting those needs; testing the proposed product; then building a prototype. The end result of this process is a new factory or organization to introduce the new product. This traditional approach takes a long time—and with time goes money.

Honda has arranged these activities differently. First, planning and proving go on continuously and in parallel. Second, these activities are clearly separated from execution. At Honda, the highly disciplined execution cycle schedules major product revisions every four years and minor revisions every two years...when a new product is ready, it is released to existing factories and organizations, which dramatically shortens the amount of time needed to launch it.[10]

Finally, competitive advantages can be created through superior linkages with stakeholders in the external environment. For example, a firm may develop exclusive relationships with its suppliers or customers, which can lead to a cost advantage. For instance, Caterpillar's global electronic network with its suppliers and customers allows information to be passed from customers back to suppliers more quickly than its competitors can manage.[11] This source of competitive advantage is closely related to general organizational resources, which will be discussed further in the last section of this chapter.

FIGURE 3.4

The Value Chain

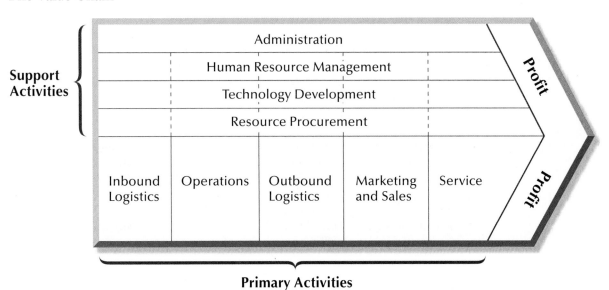

Human-Based Resources

The humans that make up an organization are its lifeblood—its unique and most valuable asset. Most of the other factors of production—such as properties, machinery, and even special knowledge—may be duplicated over the long term, but every human being is totally unique. General Electric puts it this way:

> Our true "core competency" today is not manufacturing or services, but the global recruiting and nurturing of the world's best people and the cultivation in them of an insatiable desire to learn, to stretch and to do things better every day.[12]

Internal stakeholders consist of managers, employees, and owners, including the boards of directors that usually represent them. This section will begin with a discussion of the importance of the chief executive officer in creating organizational success. This discussion will lead into a more general treatment of the characteristics of effective strategic leadership. Organizational-governance issues will then be presented, followed by a discussion of employees, structure, and culture.

Strategic Leadership

chief executive officer (CEO)
Common title for the highest-ranking manager in a firm

The highest-ranking officer in a large organization can be called by a number of titles, but the most common is **chief executive officer,** or **CEO.** Most of the research evidence indicates that CEOs have a significant impact on the strategies and performance of their organizations.[13] In fact, in some cases a CEO can be a source of sustainable competitive advantage. A CEO such as Michael Eisner at Disney, the retired Jack Welch at GE, or Bill Gates at Microsoft can leave little doubt that much of the success or failure of an organization is dependent on the person at the top. Bill Gates inspires fear and respect among employees, competitors, and customers.

> Ex. Employees speak knowingly of "Bill meetings," which sound only slightly better than the Spanish Inquisition. He challenges, he makes judgments, he finds flaws. Employees have been known to crib for weeks, even holding practice, for one sixty-minute session with Gates. "These meetings work," says software developer Neil Konzo. "He focuses in on the negative. He beats the living hell out of you. At the end he says: Hey, you're doing good."[14]

Just as excellent leadership can have an enormous positive influence, poor leadership can have a powerful negative influence. Coca-Cola enjoyed many years of double-digit growth under the leadership of Roberto Goizueta. However, since his death in 1997, the company has "fizzled." According to Daniel Fisher, a writer for *Forbes,* "Coke is run by has-beens and relatively recent hires."[15] In particular, he noted that Douglas Daft, CEO, brought back Brian Dyson, perhaps best known for the disastrous introduction of New Coke. Fisher continued his criticism by noting that Daft hurt morale with a big layoff, and "take-it-or-leave-it orders" that required longtime employees to relocate to far-off places. He also mishandled the acquisition of Quaker Oats by proceeding without the approval of the board of directors. Quaker Oats was later acquired by PepsiCo. Daft also botched a joint venture with Procter & Gamble to combine Coke's Minute Maid orange juice with P&G's Pringles potato chips in an effort to strengthen both brands. Synergies never materialized, and, according to a Coke observer, the deal is over. A beverage-industry analyst said it this way, "I've never seen so many faulty decisions in such a short time at Coke."[16]

In the traditional model of leadership, the CEO decides where to go, and then, through a combination of persuasion and edict, directs others in the process of implementation.[17] However, the traditional view of CEOs as brilliant, charismatic leaders with employees who are "good soldiers" is no longer valid in many organization settings. Turbulent global competitive environments and multibusiness organizations are far too complex for one person to stay on top of all the important issues. Shared leadership is needed because a leader cannot be everywhere at once. It would be naive to assume that a leader can, at any given time, control all the actions of members of an entire business. Also, companies are influenced by multiple stakeholders with competing demands. Consequently, while the CEO is the most important leader in a firm, other leaders are also vital to organizational success. While the smallest organizations may have a single owner/manager who makes all important strategic and operating decisions, in large organizations strategic leadership is distributed among a wide variety of individuals.[18]

The CEO has primary responsibility for setting the strategic direction of the firm; however, other executives and managers are expected to show leadership qualities and participate in strategic management activities. Many effective CEOs assemble a heterogeneous group of three to ten top executives that make up the **top management team (TMT)**.[19] Each member of the TMT brings a unique set of skills and a unique perspective of what the organization should do to respond to demands from a diverse set of stakeholders. CEOs work with TMT members to tap their skills, knowledge, and insights. Consequently, while this section will focus primarily on CEOs as the primary source of leadership in organizations, it is assumed that strategic leadership is distributed among the TMT and other influential managers and organizational members.

The literature on strategic leadership is vast, and there is no consensus on the characteristics that distinguish excellent leaders. However, most scholars would agree on five important responsibilities of **strategic leadership** that seem to be evident in most successful organizations. They are: (1) creating organizational vision, (2) establishing core values for the organization, (3) developing strategies and a management structure, (4) fostering an environment conducive to organizational learning and development, and (5) serving as a steward for the organization.

Creating Organizational Vision

The traditional view of leaders in organizations is that they set direction, make the important decisions, and rally the followers (usually employees). This traditional view is particularly common in the West, where leaders are often equated with heroes.[20] Our great leaders, our heroes, are the extraordinary men and women who take charge during times of crisis. There are many examples of visionary decision makers throughout political and business history. Lee Iacocca of Chrysler, Steven Jobs, the founding CEO of Apple Computer, and Ross Perot of Electronic Data Systems are just a few of the CEOs who are widely viewed as charismatic and visionary leaders. It is common for organizations to incorporate stories about their great leaders in the myths and rituals that form the organizational culture.[21]

Many CEOs have been described as visionaries. They have a vision of what the organization should become, and they communicate that vision to other managers

---

top management team (TMT)
Typically a heterogeneous group of three to ten top executives selected by the CEO; each member brings a unique set of skills and a unique perspective

strategic leadership
Generally refers to leadership behaviors associated with creating organizational vision, establishing core values, developing strategies and a management structure, fostering organizational learning, and serving as a steward for the firm

and employees. They make their vision a reality. Often described as charismatic and dynamic, their enthusiasm (or lack of it) can be contagious. Sam Walton, founder of Wal-Mart, was such an individual.

 Right up until his death, Sam Walton would fly his plane across the country visiting existing Wal-Mart stores, attending store openings and instilling in employees the value of customer service. There were only a handful of his hundreds of stores that he never had the time to visit. His visits included greeting customers, and asking them, "Ladies, are they treatin' you right? Do they look you in the eye and ask if they can help?" Actions like this communicate a sense of vision of what Wal-Mart is all about. And what a vision! Thirty years ago Sam Walton desired to make his retail chain the biggest and best in the country. Even when Sam discovered he was losing a battle with bone cancer, he did not slow down. He was not about to "kick back, congratulate himself, and let some sly devil like that Dayton Hudson discount chain, Target, sneak up behind him." Sam Walton's vision will live forever in the hearts of the associates who knew him.[22]

visionary leadership
Pertains to envisioning what the organization should be like in the future, communicating the vision, and empowering followers to enact it

Visionary leadership can be divided into three stages: (1) envisioning what the organization should be like in the future, (2) communicating this vision to followers, and (3) empowering these followers to enact the vision.[23] Sam Walton developed a vision of making Wal-Mart the biggest and best retailer in the country, then he tirelessly communicated this vision in word and deed to managers and associates. He also gave them the power to fulfill the vision by providing them with detailed computer analyses on a store-by-store and department-by-department basis and developing the most efficient distribution system in the industry. In short, Sam Walton was a model visionary leader.

Establishing Core Values

It would be naive to assume that a leader can, at any given time, control all the actions of members of an entire business. Effective leadership is much more subtle. Leaders basically establish a social system that establishes and reinforces desired behaviors. Consequently, when members of a company face an unexpected situation, they are guided by the social system.[24]

core values
The underlying philosophies that guide decisions and behavior in a firm; also called organizational values

One important way that leaders influence the social system in their organizations is through the **core values** they bring to the organization. These values can be conveyed in a number of ways. For instance, they can be communicated directly through public statements, memorandums, and e-mails. Linda Wachner, CEO of the apparel manufacturer Warnaco, runs her company with a near-fanatical devotion to three guiding principles: "Stay close to the customer, keep on top of the business, and watch the till."[25]

Highly visible decisions are also an effective way to communicate a value. For example, a CEO could overturn the decision of a subordinate in favor of a customer in an effort to communicate the importance of customer satisfaction: "The customer is always right." Also, "small talk" is vital to effectively establishing organizational values. Small talk refers to private discussions in offices or around watercoolers or in lunchrooms. Conversations of this kind are a forum for discussing issues, problems, situations, incidents, processes, and individuals.[26] Leaders can also influence value systems through the way they administer rewards. The organization's individuals that demonstrate the desired attitudes and behavior can be rewarded with salary increases, promotions, attention (i.e., awards), or special privileges.

In addition, core values can provide a basis for determining which alternative strategies to select, how they are to be selected, how strategic decisions will be communicated, and to whom. If leaders are responsive to the values of key stakeholders when making and communicating decisions, the decisions are more likely to be perceived as ethical by those stakeholders.

A strong value system can be a source of competitive advantage. However, putting too much emphasis on a particular factor can also be dangerous. For instance, a company that places too much emphasis on efficiency and the "bottom line" may give too little emphasis to particular stakeholder needs.

 Aircraft manufacturers are required to do evacuation tests whenever they make modification to their aircraft bodies. In one such test, McDonnell Douglas ran trials to see if 410 passengers could safely evacuate from its MD-11 jetliner in ninety seconds. In a morning test, twenty-eight people were injured, eighteen of whom were hospitalized. Many managers would have canceled the afternoon tests based on morning results. However, during the afternoon of the same day, the test was repeated with new volunteers, none of whom were informed of the earlier injuries. This evacuation resulted in twenty-two injured, with fourteen sent to the hospital. One sixty-year-old woman was paralyzed from the neck down as a result of her injury.[27]

Developing Strategies and Structure

Strategic leaders are directly responsible for overseeing the development of strategies the organization should follow. For example, Andrea Jung, CEO of Avon, has breathed new life into the company. She has put Avon in shopping malls by introducing Avon Centers in seventy-five J.C. Penney stores across the United States. Eiko Kono, president of Recruit in Japan, has turned around her company by putting its classified-advertising magazines on virtually every newsstand.[28] Effective strategy development implies a strong awareness of the resources and capabilities that an organization has or can develop or acquire that will lead to a sustainable competitive advantage.[29]

In small organizations, the entrepreneur typically serves as the sole strategist. As organizations grow, the top-management team (TMT) is assembled for the same purpose. Furthermore, as companies grow, they tend to have more managers and more levels of management. The variety and number of these other managers are as varied as the businesses themselves. Strategic leaders have the opportunity to "influence patterns of interaction and to assign responsibility to particular individuals."[30] They do this by creating a management-reporting structure. As organizations continue to grow, they often become involved in more than one business area. As this happens, typically the CEO will delegate responsibility for developing competitive strategies to the managers who are responsible for each business. The reporting structure is then altered accordingly. Specific strategies will be discussed in Chapters 5, 6, and 7, and organization structures will be treated at length in Chapter 8.

Fostering Organizational Learning

Many organizational scholars believe that the true role of a leader is to harness the creative energy of the individual, so that the organization as a whole learns over time.[31] Leaders should create an environment for organizational learning by serving as a coach, teacher, and facilitator.[32] Glen Hiner was the CEO who led a successful turnaround at Owens Corning. According to Hiner:

> A CEO can make acquisitions, which will account for about $1 billion of Owens Corning's sales growth. He can move capital to fund what's growing fastest and lend his presence and prestige to projects. He can hire, fire and reassign. But CEOs can't create internal growth; they can only help the people who concoct and execute plays, ploys and projects.[33]

A learning environment is created by helping organizational members question their assumptions about the business and its environment: what customers want, what competitors are likely to do, which technology choices work best, and how to solve a problem. For learning to take place, members must understand that the organization is an interdependent network of people and activities. Furthermore, learning requires that members keep their work focused on creating patterns of behavior that are consistent with strategy rather than reacting haphazardly to problems. Leaders play the essential role in creating an environment where employees question assumptions, understand interdependency, see the strategic significance of their actions, and are empowered to lead themselves.[34] Organizational learning will be treated further later in this chapter.

Serving As a Steward

steward
A leader who cares deeply about the firm, its stakeholders, and the socity in which it operates

Finally, effective leaders are **stewards** for their firms: they care about the company and the society in which it operates, both voluntary and involuntary stakeholders.[35] Leaders must feel and convey a passion for the organization, its contribution to society, and its purpose. They should feel that "they are part of changing the way businesses operate, not from a vague philanthropic urge, but from a conviction that their efforts will produce more productive organizations, capable of achieving higher levels of organization success and personal satisfaction than more traditional organizations."[36] This concept is best exemplified with a quote from Stanley Gault, former CEO of Rubbermaid, shortly after he left retirement to take over struggling Goodyear Tire & Rubber Company:

> People would say, "Why would you undertake this challenge?" Well, frankly, the decision was 98% emotional because Goodyear is the last major American-owned tire company… Therefore, I decided that I was willing to change my life for three years if there was any way I could lead the charge to rebuild Goodyear.[37]

So far, this section has emphasized some of the most important characteristics of effective strategic leadership, including (1) creating organizational vision, (2) establishing core values for the organization, (3) developing strategies and a management structure, (4) fostering an environment conducive to organizational learning and development, and (5) serving as a steward for the organization. Before leaving this section, a few common approaches to leadership will be presented. Also, the concept of fitting leadership characteristics to organizational circumstances will be discussed.

Leadership Approaches and Organizational Fit

There are many different ways to lead, depending on the circumstances and the personality of the individual. Bourgeois and Brodwin identified five distinct leadership approaches or styles.[38] The styles differ in the degree to which CEOs involve other managers and lower-level employees in the strategy formulation and implementation process. The first two styles correspond to the traditional model of leader as director and decision maker; the latter three styles represent more participative styles of leadership that are probably more relevant in today's global economy.

commander-style leadership
The CEO formulates strategy and then directs top managers to implement it

change-style leadership
The CEO formulates strategy and then plans the changes in structure, personnel, information systems, and administration required to implement it

collaborative-style leadership
The CEO works with other managers to create a strategy; participants are then responsible for implementing the strategy in their own areas

cultural-style leadership
The CEO formulates a vision and strategy for the company and then works with other managers to create a culture that will foster fulfillment of the vision

crescive-style leadership
The CEO encourages lower-level managers to formulate and implement their own strategic plans, while still filtering out inappropriate programs

- **Commander-style leadership.** The CEO formulates strategy and then directs top managers to implement it.

- **Change-style leadership.** The CEO formulates strategy, then plans the changes in structure, personnel, information systems, and administration required to implement it.

- **Collaborative-style leadership.** The CEO initiates a planning session with executive and division managers. After each participant presents ideas, the group discusses and agrees to a strategy. Participants are then responsible for implementing strategy in their areas.

- **Cultural-style leadership.** After formulating a vision and strategy for the company, the CEO and other top-level managers mold the organization's culture so that all organizational members make decisions that are consistent with the vision. In this approach, the culture inculcates organizational members into unity of purpose and action.

- **Crescive-style leadership.** Under this leadership model, lower-level managers are encouraged to formulate and implement their own strategic plans. The CEO's role is to encourage innovation while still filtering out inappropriate programs. Unlike the other models, the Crescive model of leadership makes use of the creative energies of all members of the organization, which is consistent with the philosophy of Total Quality Management (TQM) that is influencing American industry.

Not only do different executives have different leadership styles; they also have varying capabilities and experiences that prepare them for different strategic environments. While managers are capable of adapting to changing environments and strategies, it is not likely that they are equally effective in all situations. A manager who is part of the turbulent growth years of a start-up company may have serious difficulty adjusting to the inevitable slow-down in growth.

Ex. Steven Jobs, one of the highly successful founders of Apple Computer, had difficulty adjusting to the increasingly large and complex Apple Computer that success had created. He hired John Sculley, a former PepsiCo executive, to bring professional management techniques to Apple. Jobs's management style was incompatible with that of Sculley, and eventually Jobs was forced out of the organization he had created. Then, when Apple desperately needed Jobs's vision again, he was invited to return to the company. On the other hand, the founder of Microsoft, Bill Gates, has successfully managed Microsoft through its early start-up years to its current position as the largest computer-software company in the world.

The debate continues regarding whether it is appropriate to try to fit a manager to a particular organization's strategy.[39] Some research suggests that low-cost strategies are best implemented by managers with production/operations backgrounds because of the internal focus on efficiency and engineering. The research also suggests that differentiation strategies need to be managed by marketing- and R&D-trained executives because of the innovation and market awareness that are needed.[40] There is also some tentative evidence that strategic change or innovation in companies is more likely to occur with managers that are younger (both in age and in time in the company) but well educated.[41] Growth strategies may be best implemented by managers with greater sales and marketing experience, willingness to take risks, and tolerance for ambiguity. However, those same characteristics may be undesirable in an executive managing the activities of a retrenchment strategy.[42]

radical restructuring
Major changes to a firm's direction, strategies, structures, and plans

When **radical restructuring** is required, an outsider may be needed. The person who helped create problems in the organization is likely to be resistant to selling cherished assets, closing plants, or firing thousands of people. "In many cases, the emotional ties of the career CEO are just too strong," says Ferdinand Nadherny, vice-chairman of Russell Reynolds Associates, the nation's largest executive-recruiting firm. "The guy would be firing close friends."[43]

Organizational Governance

organizational governance
How the behavior of high-ranking managers is supervised and controlled; for example, the board of directors is responsible for ensuring that managerial behavior is consistent with shareholder interests

Effective leadership can be an important source of sustainable competitive advantage. As the previous section demonstrated, the definition of an effective leader varies somewhat depending on the nature of the environment in which a firm competes. **Organizational governance** is another aspect of leadership that can be associated with creation of a sustainable competitive advantage. Although organizational governance is a fairly broad topic, this chapter will focus on the board of directors, especially the role of the board in governing managers and ensuring that shareholder interests are protected and enhanced.

Establishment of Organizational Governance

Most larger companies, as well as smaller companies that need large amounts of capital to support growth, have issued stock. Therefore, their owners are the shareholders. Shareholders are interested primarily in receiving a steady and increasing stream of financial returns. Shares of stock have value because shareholders expect that, at some future point in time, they will receive dividends. However, many fast-growing or highly profitable organizations decide to reinvest most of their cash flow instead of paying out dividends. Consequently, the value of many stocks is dependent more on expectations of future dividends than on current payments. If a company does not pay high dividends but the stock increases in value, shareholders can receive the increase in value by selling their stock. Managers have a fiduciary duty to direct the organization in such a way that shareholders' financial returns are as high as they can be, given other constraints such as laws, regulations, formal and informal contracts, and ethics. Many companies have developed policies concerning the way they should manage shareholder interests. For example, the Bristol-Myers Squibb Pledge contains the statement: "We pledge a company wide dedication to continued profitable growth, sustained by strong finances, a high level of research and development, and facilities second to none."[44]

board of directors
In publicly-owned companies, a group of individuals who are elected by the voting shareholders to monitor the behavior of top managers, therefore protecting their rights as shareholders

The typical ownership structure found in most public corporations is illustrated in Figure 3.5. The interests of shareholders are protected by a **board of directors,** who are elected by the voting shareholders. In most corporations, each share of common stock has one vote in these elections. However, mutual funds and pension funds often make very large investments in companies. Therefore, they have significant voting power, which often equates to the ability to influence the board of directors and, through the board, even the decisions of top managers.

Boards of directors serve three primary functions.[45] First, the board monitors top managers to make sure they are acting responsibly with regard to shareholder and other stakeholder interests. Specific actions associated with this role include hiring, firing, supervising, advising, and compensating top managers within the firm. This function, sometimes called the "control" role, is a legal duty. The courts evaluate whether directors are fulfilling this fiduciary responsibility based on the business-judgment rule, which presumes that directors make informed decisions, in good faith, with the best interests of the corporation in mind, and independently of personal interests or relationships.

Second, directors provide services to top managers. Since they tend to come from diverse backgrounds and have varied skills, directors serve as excellent advisers on a wide range of issues from financing to operations to human-resource management. They can also provide information on what is happening in the external environment that could potentially influence the firm. Boards typically also reserve the right to reject major strategic decisions such as the development of a new line of

FIGURE 3.5

Typical Ownership Structure in a Public Corporation

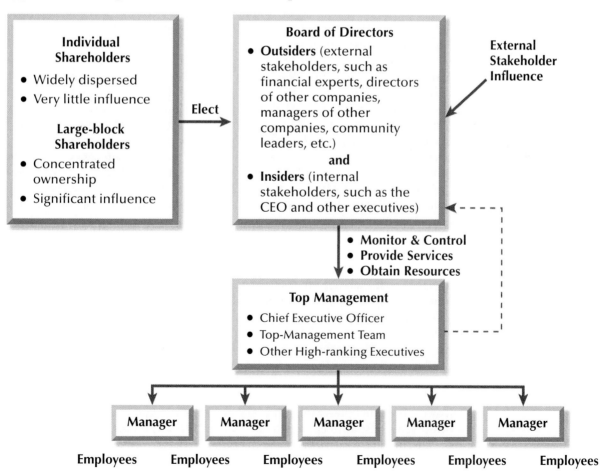

business, mergers, acquisitions, or entrance into foreign markets. Finally, directors can help establish important linkages with the external environment so that the organization can acquire needed resources. For example, a director may also sit on the board of a supplier company, thus allowing for easy contracting with that supplier. Also, many companies add bankers to their boards to facilitate financial arrangements. Each of the three functions is even more important when a company is in a crisis or experiencing stress.[46]

There are two major and interrelated issues of strategic importance concerning ownership in a publicly held corporation. The first deals with the conflicts of interest that sometimes emerge between owners and managers of the firm. The second major issue deals with the relationship between the composition and behavior of the board of directors and organizational performance. While this section will focus on governance structures in the United States, similar structures for publicly held organizations exist in most other industrialized countries.[47]

Conflicts of Interest and Agency Problems

In sole proprietorships, the owner and top manager is the same individual. Therefore, no owner/manager conflicts of interest exist. This is also the case in privately held or closely held companies in which all of the stock is owned by a few individuals, often within the same family. In these cases, the owners have direct control over their firms. However, as soon as ownership and management are separated, the potential for conflicts of interest exists. In this case, top managers become agents for the owners of the firm—they have a fiduciary duty to act in the owners' best interests.

Theoretically, in a publicly held corporation, both shareholders and managers have an interest in maximizing organizational profits. Shareholders want maximum organizational profits so that they can receive high returns from dividends and stock appreciation. Managers should also be interested in high profits to the extent that their own rewards, such as salary and bonuses, are dependent on profitability. However, top managers, as human beings, may attempt to maximize their own self-interests at the expense of shareholders. This is called an **agency problem. Entrenchment** occurs when "managers gain so much power that they are able to use the firm to further their own interests rather than the interests of shareholders."[48] Chief executives can become entrenched by recommending their friends and internal stakeholders such as other managers for board membership. Often the recommendations of the CEO are taken without much resistance.

agency problem
Exists when top managers, as human beings, attempt to maximize their own self interests at the expense of shareholders

entrenchment
Occurs when managers gain so much power that they are able to use the firm to further their own interests rather than the interests of shareholders

Agency problems are manifest in a number of ways. Some power-hungry or status-conscious top managers may expand the size of their empires at the expense of organizational shareholders. For example, a few years ago, Harding Lawrence led Braniff Airways to financial ruin through overzealous growth.[49] The highly unsuccessful unrelated acquisitions of the 1960s may have resulted, in part, from managers who were more interested in short-term growth than in long-term performance. This agency problem can be precipitated by compensation systems that link organizational size to pay.

Agency problems often arise because of the way executives are compensated. For example, an executive who is compensated according to year-end profitability may use his or her power to maximize year-end profits at the expense of long-range investments such as research and development.[50] Some business writers argue that the extremely high salaries of some CEOs, which often reach millions of dollars, are evidence that agency problems exist.[51] Sandy Weill's pay package of $151 million at

Citigroup or Steve Jobs's $872 million options grant at Apple seem to defy reason. Charles Elson, who runs the University of Delaware's Center for Corporate Governance, refers to such salaries as "outrageous in many cases and unrelated to services rendered."[52] Since shareholders are numerous and often not very well organized, their influence on decisions such as CEO compensation is nominal. Consequently, self-serving forces within the organization can sometimes prevail. For example, Roberto Goizueta of Coke once received an $81 million restricted stock award. The award was initiated by an old associate whose firm received $24 million in fees from Coke over the previous six years.[53] Unfortunately, conflicts of interest of this type are common.[54]

The real issue concerning salary is whether CEOs are worth what they receive. For example, in *Business Week's* annual report on executive pay, compensation is compared to the performance of the organizations for which the executives work. This analysis is revealing, and often demonstrates that some CEOs are a real bargain. CEOs that have more-demanding jobs, as indicated by the amount of information they have to process and the firm's strategy, tend to be more highly paid.[55] Because of all of the ramifications associated with executive pay, it is a decision that is as much ethical as it is financial.

To help overcome problems with excessive compensation of some CEOs, top management compensation should probably be linked to corporate perform-ance.[56] One risk in relating compensation to performance is that a lot of these schemes tie annual compensation to annual, as opposed to long-term, perform-ance. Whenever possible, compensation packages should be developed that encourage, instead of discourage, actions that will lead to high long-term per-formance. For example, if CEO bonuses are dependent on profit, board members in charge of compensation should add back R&D expenditures before calculating profits for the year. This helps ensure that CEOs will not be hesitant to allocate resources to potentially profitable long-term R&D projects. Another trend in CEO compensation is rewarding with stock instead of cash. When managers receive stock and stock options, they become owners, and their interests should converge with those of other shareholders.[57]

 Stock options are a very creative way to align CEO interests with the long-term interests of the organization. If a stock is currently selling at $50, a CEO might receive options to buy 100,000 shares of stock at $50, which is called the strike price. However, the options may not be exer-cisable for some specified time, such as three years. If, over the next three years, the stock price rises to $100, the options are now worth $5 million, since the CEO can buy 100,000 shares at $50 and sell them at $100. In this situation, if the stock price declines or remains the same, the options are worthless. Thus, it is in the best interests of the CEO to maximize the share price of the company, which is also in the best inter-ests of the shareholders.

Perhaps the greatest agency problems occur when top managers serve on the board of directors, which is often the case in U.S. corporations. In fact, it is not uncommon to find the CEO in the position of chairman of the board. This condition is known as **CEO duality.** As chairman of the board of directors, the CEO is in a strong position to ensure that personal interests are served even if the other stakeholders' interests are not. For example, a CEO/chairman may influence other board members to provide a generous compensation package. Also, a CEO/chairman

CEO duality
Occurs when the CEO also chairs the board of directors

is instrumental in nominating future board members, and therefore has the opportunity to nominate friends and colleagues who are likely to "rubber stamp" future actions and decisions.

In spite of these theoretical arguments against CEO duality, research findings are inconclusive.[58] However, when a relationship between CEO duality and performance is found, it typically supports the view that duality hurts performance. For example, one study examined the financial performance of 141 corporations over a six-year period, and discovered that firms opting for independent leadership consistently outperformed those relying upon CEO duality.[59] Of course, CEO duality is not a problem in privately held companies or in companies in which the CEO or the CEO's family owns a very large share of the stock.

Boards of Directors and Organizational Performance

The fiduciary responsibility for preventing agency problems lies with boards of directors. Some business experts believe that many boards of directors have not lived up to their fiduciary duties. These experts argue that for the most part, boards have not reprimanded or replaced top managers who were acting against the best interests of shareholders. However, the incidence of shareholder suits against boards of directors has increased.[60] In addition, large-block shareholders such as mutual-fund and pension-fund managers are putting lots of pressure on board members and directly on CEOs to initiate sweeping organizational changes that will lead to more accountability and higher performance.[61] Many boards have responded to these and other forces by taking a more active role in corporate governance, as the following example demonstrates.

 Lloyd E. Reuss was replaced by John F. "Jack" Smith as president of General Motors. The replacement was orchestrated by John G. Smale, past CEO of Procter & Gamble and a ten- year veteran of GM's board of directors. Smale, who was dissatisfied with GM's lackluster performance, convinced other board members to elect him to the position of chairman of the executive committee, which is a miniboard consisting of the chairmen of all board committees. This action effectively put Smale in control of GM. He then named Smith, who was the former chief of GM's successful international operations, as the new president.[62]

The GM board coup was followed by a wave of similar actions in many large companies, including IBM, Time Warner, American Express, and Westinghouse.[63] Even Greenpeace, the nonprofit environmental group based in Amsterdam, ousted its chairman, largely a result of the reduction in contributions and political clout.[64] More recently, Coca-Cola fired Doug Ivester after just two and a half years at the top. Rick Thoman at Xerox and Dale Morrison at Campbell Soup met similar fates with similar time frames. Durk Jager lasted only seventeen months at Procter & Gamble.[65]

Outside board members (external stakeholders who sit on the board) were an important factor in the board revolt at GM. The inclusion of several outsiders on the board should help ensure that shareholder interests are well served. In fact, the percentage of outsiders on the board of directors is increasing.[66] Boards with a large percentage of outside directors are referred to as independent. In theory, independent boards should lead to higher levels of organizational performance because they are more likely to look out for the interests of shareholders. However, inclusion of outsiders may not be a potent force in reducing agency problems if external board members are personal friends of the CEO or other top managers. These types of relationships limit the objectivity of outsiders. Consequently, a consistent relationship between board independence and firm performance has not been established, at least during normal circumstances.[67] In periods of crisis, board independence becomes more important.[68]

However, boards play other important strategic roles besides monitoring executive action. As mentioned previously, they provide services to top managers in the form of counseling and information. Boards can also provide guidance to top managers and participate in decisions. Higher performance is found in companies with boards that participate more actively in organizational decisions, compared to companies with "caretaker" boards.[69] Boards need sufficient power to both monitor and discipline CEOs. Vigilant boards are the best defense against executive entrenchment.[70]

In order to gain maximum benefits from the services directors provide to top managers, it is important to include both internal and external stakeholders on the board.[71] Internal stakeholders provide stability and enhanced understanding of internal operations. External stakeholders bring a breadth of knowledge and a fresh point of view to the challenges that face an organization. For example, inclusion of labor-union representatives on boards can help firms avoid decisions that are likely to be blocked by the union. By including environmentalists, firms can enhance their social image and decrease the likelihood that something that is proposed will be resisted due to potential damage to the environment. Some corporations appoint retired government officials, such as generals or presidential cabinet members, to their boards. The knowledge and contacts of these retirees can facilitate government contracting.

Inclusion of outside board members is also important with regard to establishing linkages to facilitate acquisition of needed resources. For example, interlocking directorates can lead to important strategic alliances. Interlocking directorates occur when executives from two companies sit on each other's boards or on a third company's board. As was mentioned in the previous chapter, this is a common practice in many countries, especially Japan (i.e., *keiretsu*). While it is illegal in America to have interlocking directors of direct competitors (i.e., Coke and Pepsi), firms often include representatives from suppliers or customers. Linkages such as these may reduce the monitoring ability of directors. For example, some stakeholders see the interlocking directorate between Millard "Mickey" Drexler of Gap Inc. and Steven Jobs of Apple Computer, Inc. as a conflict of interest.[72] The two CEOs may find it in their own best interests to support each other. However, interlocks can facilitate contract negotiations and the transfer of information and technology. In some cases, strategic alliances can even create barriers that make it hard for new firms to compete.

Nonprofit organizations are typically directed by a board of trustees and/or a board of directors, who perform many of the same functions that are performed by the board of directors in a for-profit corporation. The principal difference in responsibility between the director of a for-profit and that of a nonprofit organization is that the director of a nonprofit organization must ensure that the firm uses revenues from both internal operations and external donations in such a manner that the tax-exempt status granted by the Internal Revenue Service is maintained. This usually means that the organization is actively pursuing a philanthropic mission. Directors also provide service and resource-acquisitions roles in nonprofit organizations.

There are no owners, stocks, or shareholders of a nonprofit organization. However, agency problems do exist. For example, the CEO of the national organization of the United Way recently came under attack for his luxurious lifestyle, which was made possible by a high salary and perquisites, or "perks." Scandals like this happen in both the for-profit and nonprofit sector; however, in the nonprofit sector, they seem particularly offensive because donors give freely of their funds to support causes they think are worthy of support. A strong, active, and probing board of a nonprofit organization can have the same effect as the board of a for-profit organization in reducing agency problems.

In summary, boards of both for-profit and nonprofit organizations play a critical role in supervising managerial actions to ensure shareholder interests are served, providing services such as counseling and information to top executives, and establishing linkages that facilitate resource acquisition. The governance structure of an organization can be a source of competitive advantage that is hard for competitors to imitate. This completes a fairly thorough introduction to the leadership and ownership structure of modern corporations. This section will now turn to two other human-based sources of competitive advantage: employees and culture.

Employees

Lincoln Electric, the largest manufacturer of arc welders in the world, has been able to tap the capacity of its human resources in ways that its competitors have not been able to duplicate. This ability has led to a sustainable competitive advantage.

 Lincoln employees are twice as productive as employees in similar manufacturing operations. They are also paid twice as much, due to a year-end bonus that is approximately equal to base salary. How does Lincoln do it? Most experts agree that the key to Lincoln's success is the way employees are managed. According to George Willis, CEO: "Employees are our most valuable asset. They must feel secure, important, challenged, in control of their destiny, confident in their leadership, be responsive to common goals, believe they are being treated fairly, have easy access to authority and open lines of communication in all possible directions."

Lincoln is known for innovative personnel policies. Early in this century, James F. Lincoln, brother of the founder, asked employees to elect representatives to an "Advisory Board" to advise the CEO on company operations. An employees' association was formed in 1919 to provide health benefits and social activities. Other early innovations included a reduction in working hours from fifty-five to fifty, a stock-purchase plan, and paid vacations. A suggestion system was begun in 1929. Employee suggestions for process improvements have contributed to steadily increasing productivity levels at Lincoln ever since that time. Worker turnover is almost nonexistent. Employees are not, however, provided with lush working conditions. One of Lincoln's plants was described as a "cavernous, dimly lit factory" that looks a lot like a big-city YMCA. Most employees are not provided with base salaries either. To the extent possible, Lincoln has translated all of its work processes into piece rates. The piece-rate system, combined with year-end bonuses based on quality, dependability, output, and ideas and cooperation, provide substantial motivation to work hard and improve the manufacturing process.[73]

The strategic importance of employees became evident as the United States has lost its competitive edge in several global markets, including consumer electronics and steel. Shortages of qualified workers, especially in the technical areas, contribute to competitiveness problems.[74] Strategies that incorporate elements of quality, innovation, speed and flexibility, and reputation all have one organizational element in common: a well-trained workforce, capable of learning new methods and ways of doing business as the environment changes. Consequently, in the future, successful companies will have to devote even more attention to human-resource-development activities such as recruiting and training and development. For example, companies may have to form strategic alliances with educational institutions and local governments to help prepare qualified applicants for tomorrow's jobs.[75]

Employees and the way they are managed can be important sources of competitive advantage. Because of their importance to competitiveness, employees are being given increasing amounts of managerial attention in the organizational planning of a lot of large organizations. Research has shown that more-sophisticated human-resource planning, recruitment, and selection strategies are associated with higher labor productivity, especially in capital-intensive organizations.[76] Also, a large-sample study of nearly one thousand firms indicated that "High Performance Work Practices" are associated with lower turnover, higher productivity, and higher long- and short-term financial performance.[77] According to a well-known management scholar, Jeffrey Pfeffer: "Achieving competitive success through people involves fundamentally altering how we think about the work force and the employment relationship. It means achieving success by working with people, not by replacing them or limiting the scope of their activities. It entails seeing the work force as a source of strategic advantage, not just as a cost to be minimized or avoided. Firms that take this different perspective are often able to successfully outmaneuver and outperform their rivals."[78] Many companies have caught the vision.

 At Advanced Micro Devices' submicron-development facility, some 70 percent of the technicians come from older facilities at ADM. In keeping with ADM's emphasis on employment stability, as old facilities were closed, people were evaluated with respect to their basic skills. If accepted, they were put through a seven-month program at Mission College—and then went to work in the new facility. This training not only demonstrated the firm's commitment to its employees, which was then reciprocated, but also ensured that the facility would be staffed with highly qualified people who had been specifically trained for their new jobs.

At a Collins & Aikman carpet plant in Georgia, more than a third of the employees were high-school dropouts, and some could neither read nor write. When the firm introduced computers to increase productive efficiency, however, it chose not to replace its existing workforce but to upgrade employee skills. After spending about $1,200 per employee on training, including lost job time, the company found that the amount of carpet stitched increased 10 percent. Moreover, quality problems declined by half. The employees, with more skills and better morale, submitted some 1,230 suggestions, and absenteeism fell by almost half.

The Japanese are well known for their lifetime employment practices, although the practice is not as strong now as it once was. The Dutch oil giant Shell has a similar attitude. According to Ernest Van Mourik Broekman, coordinator of human resources and organization at

Shell: "In the first place, our company recruits and develops with the purpose of a full career. We recruit extensively in Europe at universities, and bring people to training programmes and job development programmes until they can be considered to be full professionals in their particular disciplines. The general characteristic is that a strong identification with the company is being pursued, so that people feel that there is a common interest building up between the objectives of the company and their personal aims. And on the whole, people feel that a full career in our company is worthwhile, rather than using it just as a stepping stone towards something else."[79]

Many organizations have established policies that govern the way they manage employees as stakeholders. For example, Johnson & Johnson's Credo includes the following passage:

We are responsible to our employees, the men and women who work with us throughout the world. Everyone must be considered as an individual. We must respect their dignity and recognize their merit. They must have a sense of security in their jobs. Compensation must be fair and adequate, and working conditions clean, orderly and safe. Employees must feel free to make suggestions and complaints. There must be equal opportunity for employment, development and advancement for those qualified. We must provide competent management, and their actions must be just and ethical.[80]

Effective stakeholder management of employees virtually always includes getting them involved in organizational improvements. For example, Dow Chemical Company discovered that employee suggestions and involvement were the key to high quality in one of their large aspirin facilities.[81] Employee empowerment, which is often associated with Total Quality Management (TQM), is also an important trend. The following excerpts come from an annual report of Union Pacific Corporation.

> The people in our empowerment programs are deliberately encouraged to take their work in their own hands—to become their own bosses—and they are taking to the process with terrific enthusiasm. Under empowerment, managers manage the people—but people manage the work. It's the only way that American industry and Union Pacific are going to stay ahead of the mounting competition of the Nineties. Empowerment, of course, is not an end in itself. It is a means to achieve the highest quality work and the greatest customer satisfaction.[82]

employee stock ownership plan (ESOP) Reward system in which employees are provided with an attractive method for acquiring stock in the companies where they work

performance-based compensation plan Reward system in which compensation varies depending on the success of the organization

Employee stock-ownership plans (ESOPs) are also becoming increasingly popular.[83] ESOPs merge the interests of employees with the interests of other shareholders. Since employees become owners, they are motivated to enhance shareholder welfare. **Performance-based compensation plans** can accomplish some of the same results.[84]

Structure and Culture

Leaders, managers, directors, and employees can all be sources of competitive advantage. However, the way they are organized can also lead to competitiveness.

organizational structure
Reporting relationships and the division of people into groups, teams, task forces, and departments within an organization

Organizational structure has a lot to do with how successful a firm will be. For example, in a world where innovations are widely understood by competitors within a year, a flexible structure is a key to success in many companies.[85] Big companies are trying to increase speed and flexibility by altering their organization structures and management systems. For example, some firms are attempting to become worldwide "modular corporations." A modular corporation nurtures a few core activities that it does best, and then lets outside specialists do the rest. "The new breed avoid becoming monoliths with plants and bureaucracy. Instead, they are exciting hubs surrounded by networks of the world's best suppliers. Those manufacturing or service units are modular: They can be added or taken away with the flexibility of switching parts in a child's Lego set."[86] Dell Computer and Chrysler are examples of companies that are pursuing flexibility in this way.

Another way large organizations are trying to improve flexibility is by decentralizing responsibility and rewarding employees for innovations and flexibility. 3M maintains a highly innovative, responsive organization by setting goals and establishing reward systems for encouraging flexible, creative behavior. Chapter 8 will explore in great detail various organizational structures that are used to support strategic objectives. It is sufficient to say at this point that structure is another potential source of sustainable competitive advantage.

organizational culture
The system of shared values of an organization's members

Closely related to structure is **organizational culture,** the system of shared values of its members. Organization culture often reflects the values and leadership styles of executives and managers, and is, to a great degree, a result of the past human-resource-management practices, such as recruitment, training, and rewards. Many companies are realizing the benefits of a shared set of values as a potential source of competitive advantage. There is an intangible quality that stakeholders look for when making decisions about the products and services that they purchase or in selecting alliance partners. They want to be able to *rely* on the company. They want promises and commitments to be fulfilled. There are many pragmatic benefits to a high-profile organizational culture that can help an organization in its recruiting, employee development, and relationships with customers.[87]

An organization's culture can be its greatest strength or its greatest weakness. Some firms have succeeded in creating cultures that are completely consistent with what the company is trying to accomplish. These are called high-performance cultures. At Nucor, the minimill steel company, the stated commitment to a low-cost strategy is supported by a culture that expects efficiency and tight fiscal policy. At Johnson & Johnson, the company's commitment to customers as its primary stakeholder is reflected in policy statements and is adopted by employees. Table 3.2 provides guidelines for identifying the culture of an organization based on factors such as attitude toward customer and competitors, risk tolerance, and moral integrity. For each of these factors, an organization should ask: (1) Which characteristics support the vision and strategies of the organization and should be sustained in the future? (2) Which characteristics do not support the vision and strategies and should be modified? (3) What efforts will be necessary to make the required changes happen?

A strong culture can be a two-edged sword. Sometimes very successful corporations so firmly attach themselves to their successful business practices that they exaggerate the features of the successful culture and strategy, and fail to adapt them to changing industry conditions. Four very common organization orientations associated with excellent performance can lead to four extreme orientations that can lead to poor performance:

craftsmen-type culture
Quality is the primary driver of the corporate culture

- **Craftsmen-type culture.** In craftsmen organizations, employees are passionate about quality. Quality is the primary driver of the corporate culture and a source of organizational pride. However, a culture that is focused on

Table 3.2	Defining an Organization's Culture		

Dimensions	Description
Attitude Toward Customers	Respect vs. indifference
Attitude Toward Competitors	Compliance, cooperation, or competitiveness
Achievement Orientation	Industry leader or follower
Risk Tolerance	Degree to which individuals are encouraged to take risks
Conflict Tolerance	Degree to which individuals are encouraged to express differences
Individual Autonomy	The amount of independence and responsibility given to individuals in decision making
Employee Relations	Cooperative vs. adversarial relationships among employees
Management Relations	Cooperative vs. adversarial relationships between managers and employees
Goal Ownership	Identification with goals and concerns of organization as a whole vs. identification with goals and concerns of a work group or department
Management Support	Cooperative vs. adversarial relationships between managers and employees
Perceived Compensation Equity	Perceived relationship between performance and rewards
Decision-making Style	Rational and structured vs. creative and intuitive
Work Standards	Diligent, high-performing vs. mediocre
Moral Integrity	Degree to which employees are expected to exhibit truthfulness
Ethical Integrity	Degree to which decisions are expected to be balanced with regard to stakeholder interests vs. focused exclusively on a key objective such as profitability

Source: Adapted from P. McDonald and J. Gandz, "Getting Value from Shared Values," *Organization Dynamics* (Winter 1992), 68; E.H. Schein, *Organization Culture and Leadership* (San Francisco: Jossey-Bass, 1985).

quality and detail can evolve to an extreme where craftsmen become *tinkers*. Obscure technical details and obsessive engineering perfection result in products that are overengineered and overpriced. Another version of the obsessive concern for quality is a passion for low costs, which paralyzes an organization's ability to make timely, necessary investments.

builder-type culture
Growth is the primary goal in the organization

- **Builder-type culture.** In builder organizations, growth is the primary goal. Managers are rewarded for taking risks that result in growth, new acquisitions, and new market niches. When efforts to grow and expand become careless, builders become *imperialists*, with high debt, too many unrelated businesses, and neglected core businesses.

pioneer-type culture
The emphasis is on new product and new technology development

- **Pioneer-type culture.** Pioneers build their businesses through leadership positions in new-product and new-technology development. The strengths of these organizations lie in their design teams and flexible structures, which promote idea sharing. Pioneers begin to decline when they evolve into *escapists*, who invent impractical products and pursue technologies with limited customer value.

salesman-type culture
These firms are excellent marketers who create successful brand names and distribution channels, and pursue aggressive advertising and innovative packaging

- **Salesman-type culture.** Salesmen are excellent marketers who create successful brand names and distribution channels, and pursue aggressive advertising and innovative packaging. They become so confident in their marketing abilities that they ignore product capability and quality, and begin to market imitative, low-quality products that customers do not value. They evolve into *drifters*.[88]

In all of the orientations described above, the organization becomes too focused on its own capabilities, and loses sight of its customers and evolving industry conditions. One stakeholder group becomes too dominant at the expense of others, and is resistant to change. Several contributing factors can drive a successful organization to an unsuccessful extreme. First, leadership may get overconfident from its past successes, and think that what has worked in the past will continue to work in the future. Second, one department may become overly dominant, attracting the best managerial talent, and exercising unbalanced influence over the decisions made within other departments. Third, the dominant managers and departments may keep the organization focused on strategies and policies that may no longer be relevant. An acknowledgment that change is needed would erode their base of power and influence. Finally, the successful strategies of the past may have become embedded in the routine policies and procedures of the organization. Those policies and procedures create an air of continuity that is very resistant to change.[89]

In summary, structure and culture can be added to an already impressive list of human-based sources of competitive advantage. Just as these factors can be sources of advantage, they can also be sources of weakness when they are neglected or poorly managed. Attention will now be drawn to knowledge-based and general organizational resources.

Knowledge-Based Resources

knowledge economy
Refers to the importance of intangible people skills and intellectual assets to developed economies

We live in what is sometimes called a **"Knowledge Economy."** More than 50 percent of the gross domestic product in developed economies is knowledge-based, which means that the GDP is based on intangible people skills and intellectual assets.[90] Consequently, wealth is increasingly being created through the management of knowledge workers instead of physical assets. According to David Teece:

> Fundamental changes have been wrought in the global economy which are changing the basis of firm level competitive advantage, and with it the functions of management. The decreased cost of information flow, increases in the number of markets…, the liberalization of product and labour markets in many parts of the world, and the deregulation of international financial flows is stripping away many traditional sources of competitive differentiation and exposing a new fundamental core as the basis for wealth creation. The fundamental core is the development and astute deployment and utilization of intangible assets, of which knowledge, competence, and intellectual property are the most significant.[91]

Knowledge is an intangible asset. Intangible assets differ from physical assets in fundamental ways. First, physical assets can be used only by one party at a time, whereas knowledge can be used by several parties simultaneously. Second, physical assets wear out over time and are depreciated accordingly. While knowledge does not wear out, its value depreciates rapidly as new knowledge is created. Third, it is relatively easy to set a price based on how much of a physical asset is sold or transferred, but it is difficult to measure the amount of knowledge transferred or its value. Finally, rights to tangible property are fairly clear and easy to enforce, whereas it is difficult to protect and enforce protection of intellectual property.[92]

core knowledge
Scientific or technological knowledge that is associated with actual creation of a product or service

integrative knowledge
Knowledge that helps integrate various activities, capabilities, and products

Knowledge can be divided into two general types: core knowledge and integrative knowledge.[93] **Core knowledge** is scientific or technological knowledge that is associated with actual creation of a product or service. For example, knowledge about integrated circuitry formed the foundation for creation of semiconductors. **Integrative knowledge** is knowledge that helps integrate various activities, capabilities, and products. For example, an organization that wants to be involved in selling personal computers has to understand how they are assembled and manufactured (core knowledge), but also has to understand how computer manufacturing fits into an entire system, which includes suppliers of component parts, marketing, financing, and even linkages between personal computers and other types of products (integrative knowledge).

Core knowledge is comparatively easier to acquire than integrative knowledge because integrative knowledge deals with a complex system. Consequently, integrative knowledge is probably more likely to lead to a sustainable competitive advantage. Wal-Mart, for instance, developed a complete and unique retailing system that involves complex coordination of codified information across suppliers, distribution centers, and stores; feedback from customers in the form of daily sales information; information about the products themselves; and forecasts of needs. Innovations have included cross-docking, which occurs when merchandise is unloaded from suppliers' trucks directly onto Wal-Mart's trucks for distribution to stores.[94]

codified knowledge
Knowledge that can be communicated completely via written means

tacit knowledge
Knowledge that is difficult to articulate in a way that is meaningful and complete

Another way to differentiate knowledge is based on whether it is codified or tacit. **Codified knowledge** can be communicated completely through written means. For example, blueprints, formulas, and computer code are codified. On the other hand, **"tacit knowledge** is that which is difficult to articulate in a way that is meaningful and complete."[95] Creation of an artwork such as a sculpture or a modern dance, for instance, would be very hard to describe in words that would have real meaning. You have to experience it. In general, the easier it is to codify knowledge, the less difficult it is to transfer. Tacit knowledge can be very valuable to organizations in creating a sustainable competitive advantage.

Internal Knowledge Creation and Organizational Learning

Some organizations are clearly more innovative than others. They consistently create greater numbers of successful new products or services. Other organizations may not develop a lot of new products or services, but they are adept at creating new, more-efficient ways of creating or delivering them. The distinction here is between product or service development and process development. Still other organizations seem better at both types of innovation. Knowledge creation is at the center of both product or service development and process development. One of the most important managerial tasks is facilitating knowledge (1) creation, (2) retention, (3) sharing, and (4) utilization. Outstanding execution of these tasks can lead to superior performance.[96]

Each of the four tasks requires different management skills and organizational arrangements. Knowledge creation requires systems that encourage innovative thinking throughout the firm. Most organizations tap only a fraction of the creative potential of employees and managers. An organization that wants to create knowledge will select employees and managers who contribute innovative ideas, and reward those employees and managers through salary increases, recognition, bonuses, and promotions. Some organizations even allow managers or employees the opportunities to lead in the execution of their ideas. Organizations also need to establish forums through which ideas can be conveyed to managers. A suggestion box is a rudimentary system to encourage ideas. Work meetings and interviews are other means of sharing knowledge. To create knowledge, organizations should also allocate human and financial capital to research and development.

 Sony, based in Japan, is one of the largest consumer-electronics firms in the world. Sometimes large companies have trouble staying innovative, but Sony is also one of the most inventive companies on the planet. Throughout its history, Sony has created many successful high-tech products. These products are well designed and attractive, and often alter the way people work or play. Among its success stories are the pocket-sized transistor radio, the battery-powered TV set, the VCR, the camcorder, and the Walkman. The company creates an average of four new products each business day. These new products are the work of thousands of engineers and scientists, who work very long days in workshops and laboratories around Tokyo. Sony spends between 6 and 7 percent of its total revenues on research and development.[97]

Knowledge gained through research and development can be important not only to product differentiation, but to technological advances leading to low-cost leadership as well.[98] Consequently, R&D is critical to competitiveness. Some top managers have been accused of maximizing short-term profits by cutting programs such as R&D or capital expenditures, taking large bonuses, and leaving before their companies experience performance problems. Johnson & Johnson, the large and highly diversified consumer-drug company, has adopted a corporate-wide policy to counteract these tendencies:

> Our final responsibility is to our stockholders. Business must make a sound profit. We must experiment with new ideas. Research must be carried on, innovative programs developed and mistakes paid for. New equipment must be purchased, new facilities provided and new products launched. Reserves must be created to provide for adverse times. When we operate according to these principles, the stockholders should realize a fair return.[99]

Knowledge retention is a second critical activity. A lot of knowledge exists in an organization. Only part of that knowledge is shared, but very little of that sharing gets recorded unless it is associated with an actual research or development project. Actually, the documenting procedures used in R&D would be helpful for recording other types of knowledge. Low-cost information systems have made it possible to record and store vast amounts of information very affordably. An important part of documentation is recording not only the new knowledge, but how a manager or the organization responded to it. Also, an organization should record information on whether such actions were a success or a failure.

Sharing of knowledge is as important as creating it. For example, Disney recently applied its knowledge in staging dramatic presentations (developed in its theme parks and moviemaking) to Broadway musicals. The results of R&D activities should be shared across an organization. For example, Lockheed Martin has a newsletter for its employees and managers that reports on research and development projects and other company programs and activities. Aside from research and development activities, new knowledge of all types should be shared with managers in the organization who have the authority to do something about the knowledge. There is a risk in doing this, of course, because information shared so openly with employees is likely to be picked up by competitors. However, information of this type does not have to be detailed. For example, suppose a division of Lockheed Martin develops a new way of managing some aspect of their billing process for government accounts. This information could be shared in the newsletter in summary form. Interested parties such as accountants from other parts of the company could then contact the innovative unit for the details. Creating an information system for the sharing of ideas is, by itself, a possible source of competitive advantage.

Finally, an organization has to clear the way for knowledge to be translated into new processes and programs. This sometimes means eliminating barriers to innovation. For example, some companies require many signatures and approvals on even the smallest projects before they will be funded. An organization should also encourage taking risks by not harshly penalizing managers whose projects or ideas fail and richly rewarding managers whose projects or ideas succeed. General Electric reflects these attitudes with regard to its employees, "By finding, challenging and rewarding these people, by freeing them from bureaucracy, by giving them all the resources they need—and by simply getting out of their way—we have seen them make us better and better every year."[100] Table 3.3 reviews the four tasks associated with knowledge creation and utilization. Attention will now be drawn to generating knowledge through partnerships with external stakeholders.

Knowledge Creation and Interorganizational Relationships

If firms perform the tasks associated with internal knowledge creation, they will still be limited in how much knowledge they acquire unless they also have a productive program for acquiring knowledge from outside their organizations. As discussed in Chapter 2, a part of obtaining knowledge from the outside is studying the innovations of others in the industry, other industries, and the technological environment in general. In fact, most of the knowledge that will revolutionize an industry actually comes from outside the industry. For example, semiconductors were developed in the computer industry, but had far-reaching implications for most other industries. Knowledge about innovations in other industries comes into an organization through hiring people with varied backgrounds, through hiring consultants and trainers, through providing educational programs and opportunities to employees, and through assigning researchers to specifically follow various scientific streams through journals, newsletters, books, and seminars.

Another important source of external knowledge comes from interorganizational relationships.[101] Organizations can learn from each other. In fact, knowledge is not always created within a single firm, but rather in a network of firms working together. An example of this phenomenon is found in the biotechnology industry, where there is a large-scale reliance on collaborations to produce innovation.[102]

Several factors can lead an organization to enhance organizational learning from interorganizational relationships. First, relational ability, defined as the ability to interact with other companies, can increase a firm's ability to obtain and transfer knowledge.[103] Firms can enhance their relational ability through practice (e.g., increasing the use of interorganizational relationships) or through hiring managers that have already developed relational skills.[104] Often CEOs develop excellent relational skills. Second, the more embedded into a network of interorganizational

Table 3.3   **Tasks Associated with Internal Knowledge Creation and Utilization**

Task	Description
Knowledge Creation	Develop reward systems that encourage innovative thinking. Create a forum whereby creative ideas are shared. Invest in research-and-development programs.
Knowledge Retention	Document findings from research and development programs. Create information systems that record and organize innovative ideas. Document both the ideas and managerial responses or organizational responses to them. Document successes and failures.
Knowledge Sharing	Create an information system that shares results from research and development projects with other parts of the organization. Routinely pass new ideas on to managers who can act on them. Create a database-management system to organize ideas generated from employees and managers so that they can be retrieved systematically at a later date.
Knowledge Utilization	Reduce bureaucratic barriers that prevent knowledge from resulting in new programs and projects. Encourage risk taking. Reward success.

relationships an organization becomes, the more it is able to acquire competitive capabilities.[105] Consequently, increasing the use of joint ventures, alliances, and other interorganizational relationships can position a firm in a more central location to what is happening in its industry and across relevant industries. Third, close proximity can lead to enhanced learning.[106] For example, high-tech firms have clustered in locations such as what is referred to as the Silicon Valley in northern California.[107] Finally, an organization needs to be very deliberate about taking steps to increase its absorptive capacity, which refers to the ability of a firm to absorb knowledge. Just like internally generated knowledge, if knowledge gained through interorganizational relationships is not retained, shared, and utilized, it is of no worth to the organization.

Andrew Inkpen, an expert on interorganizational relationships, studied forty American-Japanese joint ventures with the intention of finding out what organizational conditions facilitate effective transfer of knowledge. His conclusions, contained in Table 3.4, are a fitting summary to this section on the important role of knowledge in creating a sustainable competitive advantage.

General Organizational Resources

The final category of organizational resources is a varied collection of organizational possessions that can have a tremendous impact on financial success and survival. In this section, only a few of many such resources will be discussed. However, the ones that are discussed have been found to be very powerful sources of competitive advantage in some instances. They are patents and brand names, organizational reputation, and superior relationships with external stakeholders.

Patents and Brands

patent
Legal protection that prevents other companies from making use of a firm's innovation

Patents are the tangible result of knowledge creation. Organizations file for patent protection to prevent other companies from making use of their innovations. Patents can sometimes be a source of competitive advantage for a period of time. However, as mentioned in the previous chapter, they eventually run out. In addition, when a firm files for a patent, they have to describe, in detail, what they are patenting. This information is then available to the general public. Competitors may violate the patent, which is illegal, but the legal fees and other resources associated with pursuing legal remedies can be prohibitive. Also, in many foreign countries, patents do not provide protection.

trademark
Legal protection that prevents other companies from making use of a firm's symbol or brand name

Brands and their associated **trademarks** offer a higher level of protection. Consequently, if managed well, brands can be a powerful source of sustainable competitive advantage. John Reed, past CEO of Citicorp, worked to turn "Citibank" into a worldwide consumer brand, sort of like the Coca-Cola of financial services. What goes with the brand equity that those companies have, and he covets, is the ability to set themselves above the competition, either in the prices they can obtain or quantities sold or both.[108] Disney also takes full advantage of its brand, which is one of its core competencies. According to Michael Eisner, CEO:

Table 3.4 Facilitating Knowledge Transfer in Joint Ventures	
Facilitation Mechanism	**Description**
Flexible Learning Objectives	Organizations should enter into a venture with objectives regarding what the organization would like to learn from the venture. However, conditions often change, and managers should be willing to adjust those objectives if needed.
Leadership Commitment	At least one strong, higher-level manager must champion the learning objective. This person acts as a catalyst for knowledge transfer. For example, in one case, an American president had a long-standing relationship with the chairman of the Japanese partner. They worked together to facilitate transfer of both technical and management ideas.
A Climate of Trust	Trust is critical to the free exchange of knowledge. One of the greatest disadvantages of a joint venture is the risk of opportunistic behavior. This is the risk that one of the partners will use information gained in the venture to the disadvantage of the other partner. Consequently, trust must be carefully guarded or information transfer will be stifled.
Tolerance for Redundancy	This means that there is deliberate overlapping of company information, processes, and management activities. Redundancy leads to more interaction among participants, and interaction leads to more sharing of information.
Creative Chaos	Disruptive or high-stress events can enhance transfer of knowledge by focusing partners on solving problems and resolving difficulties.
Focus on Learning in Spite of Performance	Some ventures perform poorly, at least on financial measures, but organizations can still learn from them. The American firms tended to let poor performance reduce or eliminate learning, whereas the Japanese firms took a longer-term view and were less distracted by short-term performance.

Source: Based on A.C. Inkpen, "Creating Knowledge through Collaboration," *California Management Review* 39, no. 1 (Fall 1996): 123–140.

We are fundamentally an operating company, operating the Disney Brand all over the world, maintaining it, improving it, promoting and advertising it with taste. Our time must be spent insuring that the Brand never slides, that we innovate the Brand, nurture the Brand, experiment and play with it, but never diminish it. Others will try to change it, from outside and from within. We must resist. We are not a fad! The Disney name and products survive fads![109]

Business Week periodically reports the results of an analysis of the value of various brands. In a recent ranking, Coca-Cola was ranked first, Microsoft second, IBM third, GE fourth, and Nokia fifth with regard to value.[110]

Organizational Reputation

reputation

An economic asset that signals observers about the attractiveness of a company's offerings, based on past performance

A **reputation** can be thought of as an economic asset that signals observers about the attractiveness of a company's offerings. A reputation is also an assessment of past performance by various evaluators. It is a part of a social system and is based more on interpretation than fact.[111] Like a brand, an organization's reputation is difficult to imitate. A good reputation may be associated with excellent quality or highly innovative products or services, excellent human-resource management, or other factors. Merck was once rated first for quality products, first in human-resource management, and second in innovativeness in a *Fortune* poll of eight thousand corporate executives.[112] Reputation is something that can transcend international borders. and is thus a potential source of global competitive advantage.[113]

Much has been said in this book about how to develop a good reputation through socially responsible actions and stakeholder satisfaction. Some of the potential benefits of a good reputation include the ability to attract talented workers, charge premium prices, keep loyal customers, raise capital with less difficulty by attracting investors, avoid constant scrutiny by regulators and activists, or enter international markets with less difficulty.[114] Some business writers have argued that a corporate reputation may be the only source of truly sustainable competitive advantage.[115] They argue that it is the only component of competitive advantage that can't ever be duplicated in its entirety. Therefore, organizations should devote considerable time and effort to safeguarding a good reputation. Organizations with the best reputations in the *Fortune* survey had strong financial performance, but it was combined with strong performance in nonfinancial areas as well.[116]

Of course, an organization's reputation is often linked to a well-known brand name. Earlier-cited examples provided evidence that companies such as Disney, Citicorp, and Coke understand and foster the strength of their brands.

Superior Relationships with Stakeholders

Stakeholder relationships were described in detail in the previous chapter. Furthermore, the chapter demonstrated how strong relationships with stakeholders can lead to sustainable competitive advantage. This section will not be redundant with Chapter 2, but is included to demonstrate an important point. Stakeholder theory and the resource-based view are closely linked.

Relationships with external stakeholders can also be described as an organizational resource. The fact is that all five areas of resources and capabilities described in this chapter are closely linked to external stakeholders. For example, financial resources are based, in part, on relationships with financial intermediaries. The strength of human resources may depend on linkages with unions, trainers, human-resources associations, communities, or educational institutions from which an organization recruits. Valuable knowledge comes from interorganizational relationships with competitors, customers, suppliers, or other stakeholders. Raw materials and other inputs necessary to develop physical resources are provided by suppliers. Finally, contracts with many types of stakeholders are a general organizational resource.

Internal resource analysis may be combined with stakeholder analysis to identify strengths and weaknesses, and for uncovering opportunities for cost savings or ways to add value for customers. For instance, the intersection between activist groups and technology development could result in low-cost solutions to problems with pollution and other externalities. Also, customers may be able to help a firm increase the effectiveness of its marketing, sales, or service activities. The combination of stakeholder analysis with resource analysis holds great potential for developing strategies that are both efficient and effective.

The conceptual link between stakeholder theory and the resource-based view has important implications. Basically, an organization that is incapable of successful stakeholder management will have a very difficult time developing resources and capabilities that will lead to a sustainable competitive advantage. Also, an organization with weak resources and few capabilities will find it very difficult to develop strong stakeholder relationships because stakeholders will find them unattractive for partnerships and contracts.

Summary

This chapter evaluated organizational resources and capabilities and their ability to lead to competitive advantage. The value of a resource or capability in leading to a competitive advantage depends on the answers to six questions: (1) Does the resource or capability have value in the market? (2) Is the resource or capability unique? (3) Is there a readily available substitute for the resource or capability? (4) Do organizational systems exist that allow realization of potential? (5) Is the organization aware of and realizing the advantages? (6) Is the resource or capability difficult or costly to imitate? If a capability or resource is valuable, unique, and not easily substitutable, it has potential to lead to a competitive advantage. If the firm has systems to support the resource or capability and is using them, a competitive advantage is created. If the resource or capability is hard to imitate, then the competitive advantage will be sustainable.

Five resource areas were then discussed in detail. The areas are: financial, physical, human-based-, knowledge-based, and organizational resources. Although these resources were discussed separately, in reality they are all tied together. An organization must pay close attention to each of the five areas to remain competitive over the longer term.

Financial resources can be a source of advantage, although they rarely qualify as "unique" or "difficult to imitate." Nevertheless, strong cash flow, low levels of debt, a strong credit rating, access to low-interest capital, and a reputation for creditworthiness are powerful strengths that can serve as a source of strategic flexibility. Firms that are in a strong financial position can be more responsive to new opportunities and new threats, and are under less pressure from stakeholders than are their competitors who suffer financial constraints.

Physical resources were discussed through Porter's value chain. The primary activities include inbound logistics, operations, outbound logistics, marketing and sales, and service. Organizations also engage in activities that support these primary functions. Resource procurement refers to the actual purchase of inputs, and not to the inputs themselves or to the way they are handled once they are delivered. Technology development refers to learning processes, which result in improvements in the way organizational functions are performed. Human-resource management includes human-based activities such as recruiting, hiring, training, and compensation. Finally, administration consists of general-management activities such as planning and accounting. An organization can develop a competitive advantage (1) in any of the primary or support activities, *or* (2) in the way they are combined, *or* (3) in the way internal activities are linked to the external environment. The cumulative effect of value-chain activities and the way they are linked inside the firm and with the external environment determine organizational performance relative to competitors.

Human-based resources and capabilities were discussed next. The humans that make up an organization are its unique and most valuable asset. Several types of internal stakeholders were discussed, including managers, employees, and owners, as well as the boards of directors that usually represent them. The section began with a discussion of the importance of the chief executive officer in creating organizational success. This discussion then led into a more general treatment of the characteristics of effective strategic leadership. Organizational governance issues were then presented, followed by a discussion of employees, structure, and culture.

Owners in a for-profit, publicly held corporation, the shareholders, are typically represented by a board of directors, who act as their agents. Directors have the responsibility to oversee the activities of organizational managers and ensure that shareholder interests are protected. They are obligated to hold CEOs and other organizational officials accountable for their actions. They also provide services to top managers and create linkages with the external environment that can lead to acquisition of essential resources. Agency problems can exist when boards of directors are weak in carrying out these responsibilities, when CEOs also serve as chairmen of their own boards (e.g., CEO duality), or anytime CEOs or other managers act in their own personal interests at the expense of shareholders. Recently, boards of directors in the United States have been playing a more significant role in supervising top managers, participating in managerial decisions, and even replacing marginally successful CEOs.

Organizations need highly qualified employees if they are going to succeed in the global economy. These trends make training and other human-resource-management activities crucial to long-term competitiveness. Innovative human-resource-management techniques are increasing employee effectiveness for some successful companies.

An organization's structure and culture are also potential sources of competitive advantage. Organization culture is defined as the shared values of its members. Culture often reflects the values of management, the human-resource-management practices that create the working conditions, and the past experiences of employees. Culture can be a tremendous source of advantage for a firm, or a millstone.

Since we live in a knowledge-based economy, knowledge management is very important to organizational success. The section on internal knowledge management focused on knowledge (1) creation, (2) retention, (3) sharing, and (4) utilization. Also important is acquiring knowledge through interorganizational relationships. Several guidelines for facilitating knowledge transfer through interorganizational relationships were presented.

General organizational resources include superior brands, patents, and reputations. Also included in this category are relationships with external stakeholders, which create a conceptual overlap with Chapter 2 and stakeholder theory. The overlap is useful, since an organization that is incapable of successful stakeholder management will have a very difficult time developing outstanding resources and capabilities, and an organization with weak resources and few capabilities will find it very difficult to develop strong stakeholder relationships.

Discussion Questions

1. What are the six questions that must be asked to determine whether a resource or capability will lead to a sustainable competitive advantage?

2. What are the five resource areas that an organization should analyze to determine internal sources of competitive advantage? Why must a firm pay attention to all five areas?

3. Draw and explain the value chain, including primary and support activities. How can an organization use the value chain to help determine ways to create competitive advantage?

4. Describe the five distinct leadership approaches or styles CEOs use. Which of these styles is more authoritarian? Which is more participative? Is any one style the best? Why?

5. Describe the relationships that exist among shareholders, boards of directors, and CEOs. What is an agency problem? How can agency problems be avoided?

6. Why is human-resource management becoming an even more important part of strategic management in many organizations?

7. Name four very common cultural orientations that are often associated with excellent performance. How can these orientations lead to extremes that ultimately lead to poor performance?

8. What is the difference between core knowledge and integrative knowledge? Which type of knowledge is more likely to be associated with a sustainable competitive advantage? Why? What is the difference between tacit knowledge and codified knowledge? Which type of knowledge is more likely to be associated with a sustainable competitive advantage? Why?

9. Name several factors and organizational conditions that can lead an organization to enhance organizational learning from interorganizational relationships.

10. Which source of competitive advantage is usually more sustainable: a patent or a brand? Why?

11. What is an organizational reputation? What are the benefits of having an excellent organizational reputation? Are those benefits typically sustainable?

Strategic Application

Competitive Resources Associated with Human Aspects of the Organization

Answers to the following questions can help an organization assess strengths and weaknesses resulting from its human resources. These questions can be applied to a case assigned by your instructor (to the extent the case contains sufficient information) or to another company.

The CEO

- Is the background and training of the CEO strong for this type of firm and industry? Does the CEO have global experience?
- Is the CEO a visionary? Is he/she able to lead and inspire?
- Is the CEO well connected with other important stakeholders or potential stakeholders?
- Is his/her style commander, change, collaborative, cultural, or crescive? How well does this style fit the competitive situation?
- Is he/she willing to take risks?
- What is the reputation of the CEO among internal and external stakeholders?
- Does the CEO have a good track record for making strategic decisions? If there have been mistakes, can you tell why?
- Do the CEO's personal values prevent him/her from making decisions that would be beneficial to other stakeholders? Does the CEO ignore any important stakeholders?
- What is the CEO's ownership stake in the organization? Is there any evidence of agency problems related to the decisions of the CEO? Is salary tied to performance through stock payments and options? Is salary excessively high?

Employees

- Are human resource management practices different from those of rival firms? Are the differences, if any, a source of strength or weakness?
- Are employees happy with their situations and roles in the organization? How high is turnover?
- Are employees well trained? Do they have special skills? Are they cross-trained in various jobs?
- Are they socially, racially, and globally diverse? Is diversity important in this company and industry?
- Do women and minority employees have an opportunity to advance professionally?
- Are employees productive? Are they creative? Do they make suggestions for improvements?

Strategic Internet Application

Select a large company or ask your instructor if a company has been assigned. Go to www.Hoovers.com and then click on the "Companies and Industries" section. On the left side of the window, click on "Companies." Click on the company index and find your company. Once you are at your company's page, click on "Financials" and then click on "Annual Financials." If Hoovers redesigns their Web site, this information may be organized differently, but it should still be available. If you are successful, you will now have several years of annual financial figures on your screen. Use these figures to calculate as many ratios as you can based on the formulas found in Table 3.1. Now do the same thing for a major competitor of your firm in the same industry. If you do not know the name of a competing firm, the "Companies and Industries" section in Hoovers.com can help you with this information also (see the Strategic Internet Exercise in the Chapter 2). After you have completed your calculations, answer the following questions:

1. What are the major trends you see in the ratios for your company? Which ones seem to be favorable and which ones are unfavorable?

2. How do the trends of your company compare with the trends of the rival company?

3. Do you believe that your company is in a strong financial position? What are the implications of the financial position of your company with regard to its ability to take advantage of future opportunities? Overcome downturns? Overcome competitive threats?

4. Based on this analysis, would you like to invest in the company?

Notes

1. A. Barrett, "Bruce Downey, Generic Drug Lord," *Business Week*, 1 October 2001, 76–77; R. Winslow and B. Martinez, "Efforts to Switch Patients to Generic Prozac Advance," *The Wall Street Journal*, 20 August 2001, A3.

2. J. B. Barney, "Looking Inside for Competitive Advantage," *Academy of Management Executive* (November 1995): 49–61.

3. Most of these questions are based on Barney, "Looking Inside"; R. L. Priem and J. E. Butler, "Is the Resource-Based 'View' a Useful Perspective for Strategic Management Research?" *Academy of Management Review* 26 (2001): 22–40.

4. Some of these companies were cited in O. Port, "Beg, Borrow—and Benchmark," *Business Week*, 30 November 1992, 74–75.

5. L. Backman, "Circuit City to Add CarMax in Tampa Area," *The Tampa Tribune*, 10 June 1995, 1B.

6. M. A. Hitt, R. D. Ireland, and R. E. Hoskisson, *Strategic Management: Competitiveness and Globalization* (Minneapolis: West Publishing, 1995), 73.

7. D. Miller and J. Shamsie, "The Resource-based View of the Firm in Two Environments: The Hollywood Film Studios from 1936 to 1965," *Academy of Management Journal* 39 (1996): 519–543.

8. D. Kapur and R. Ramamurti, "India's Emerging Competitive Advantage in Services," *Academy of Management Executive* (May 2001): 20–33.

9. M. E. Porter, *Competitive Advantage: Creating and Sustaining Superior Performance* (New York: The Free Press, 1985), chap. 2.

10. Taken directly from G. Stalk, P. Evans, and L. E. Shulman, "Competing on Capabilities: The New Rules of Corporate Strategy," *Harvard Business Review* (March/April 1992): 57.

11. B. Bremner, "Can Caterpillar Inch Its Way Back to Heftier Profits?" *Business Week*, 27 September 1989, 75–78.

12. General Electric, *Annual Report* (2000), 2.

13. S. Finkelstein and D. C. Hambrick, *Strategic Leadership: Top Executives and Their Effects on Organizations* (Minneapolis: West Publishing , 1996), chap. 2.

14. Taken directly from K. Rebello and E. I. Schwartz, "Microsoft," *Business Week*, 24 February 1992, 60–64

15. D. Fisher, "Gone Flat," *Forbes Global*, www.forbes.com/global, 15 October, 2001.

16. Fisher, "Gone Flat."

17. P. Nutt, "Selecting Tactics to Implement Strategic Plans," *Strategic Management Journal* 10 (1989): 145–161.

18. C. Handy, *The Age of Unreason* (Boston: Harvard Business School Press, 1989).

19. R. D. Ireland and M. A. Hitt, "Achieving and Maintaining Strategic Competitiveness in the 21st Century: The Role of Strategic Leadership," *Academy of Management Executive* 13, no. 1 (February 1999): 43–57.

20. P. M. Senge, "The Leader's New Work: Building Learning Organizations," *Sloan Management Review* 32, no. 1 (Fall 1990): 7–24.

21. E. H. Schein, *Organization Culture and Leadership* (San Francisco: Jossey-Bass, 1985).

22. Taken directly from J. Huey, "America's Most Successful Merchant," *Fortune*, 23 September 1991, 46–59.

23. F. Westley and H. Mintzberg, "Visionary Leadership and Strategic Management," *Strategic Management Journal* 10 (1989): 17–18.

24. S. Sjostrand, J. Sandberg, and M. Thyrstrup, *Invisible Management: The Social Construction of Leadership* (London: Thomson Learning, 2001).

25. S. Caminiti, "America's Most Successful Businesswoman," *Fortune*, 15 June 1992, 102

26. Sjostrand, Sandberg, and Thyrstrup, *Invisible Management.*

27. A. Farnham, "Biggest Business Goofs of 1991," *Fortune*, 13 January 1992, 80–82.

28. A. Harrington, "The Power 50," *Fortune*, 15 October 2001, 194–201.

29. Ireland and Hitt, "Achieving and Maintaining."

30. Sjostrand, Sandberg, and Thyrstrup, *Invisible Management*, 8.

31. Senge, "Leader's New Work"; C. C. Manz and H. P. Sims, "SuperLeadership," *Organization Dynamics* 17, no. 4 (1991): 8–36.

32. Senge, "Leader's New Work."

33. T. A. Stewart, "Owens Corning: Back from the Dead," *Fortune*, 26 May 1997, 182.

34. Senge, "Leader's New Work"; Manz and Sims, "SuperLeadership."

35. Clarkson Centre for Business Ethics, *Principles of Stakeholder Management* (Toronto: Rotman School of Management, 1999), 3

36. Senge, "Leader's New Work," 13.

37. J. M. Graves, "Leaders of Corporate Change," *Fortune*, 14 December 1992, 106.

38. L. J. Bourgeois and D. R. Brodwin, "Strategic Implementation: Five Approaches to an Elusive Phenomenon," *Strategic Management Journal* 5 (1984): 241–264.

39. J. G. Michel and D. C. Hambrick, "Diversification Posture and Top Management Team Characteristics," *Academy of Management Journal* 35 (1992): 9–37; S. F. Slater, "The Influence of Style on Business Unit Performance," *Journal of Management* 15 (1989): 441–455; A. S. Thomas, R. J. Litschert, and K. Ramaswamy, "The Performance Impact of Strategy-Manager Coalignment: An Empirical Examination," *Strategic Management Journal* 12 (1991): 509–522.

40. V. Govindarajan, "Implementing Competitive Strategies at the Business Unit Level: Implications of Matching Managers to Strategies," *Strategic Management Journal* 10 (1989): 251–269.

41. K. A. Bantel and S. E. Jackson, "Top Management and Innovations in Banking: Does the Composition of the Top Team Make a

Difference?" *Strategic Management Journal* 10 (1989): 107–124; C. M. Grimm and K. G. Smith, "Management and Organizational Change: A Note on the Railroad Industry," *Strategic Management Journal* 12 (1991): 557–562; M. F. Wiersema and K. A. Bantel, "Top Management Team Demography and Corporate Strategic Change," *Academy of Management Journal* 35 (1992): 91–121.

42. A. K. Gupta and V. Govindarajan, "Business Unit Strategy, Managerial Characteristics, and Business Unit Effectiveness at Strategy Implementation," *Academy of Management Journal* 27 (1984): 25–41.

43. B. Brenner, "Tough Times, Tough Bosses: Corporate America Calls in a New, Cold-eyed Breed of CEO," *Business Week,* 25 November, 1991, 174–180.

44. "The Bristol-Myers Squibb Pledge," *Annual Report* (1989).

45. S. Chatterjee and J. S. Harrison, "Corporate Governance," in M. A. Hitt, R. E. Freeman, and J. S. Harrison, *The Blackwell Handbook of Strategic Management* (Oxford: Blackwell Publishers, 2001), 543–563; J. L. Johnson, C. M. Daily, and A. E. Ellstrand, "Boards of Directors: A Review and Critique," *Journal of Management* 22 (1996): 409–438.

46. Chatterjee and Harrison, "Corporate Governance."

47. Sjostrand, Sandberg, and Thyrstrup, *Invisible Management.*

48. S. Weisbach, "Outside Directors and CEO Turnover," *Journal of Financial Economics* 20 (1988): 431–460.

49. J. A. Pearce II and S. J. Teel, "Braniff International Corporation (A) and (B)," in *Strategic Management: Strategy Formulation and Implementation,* 2d ed. (Homewood, Ill.: Richard D. Irwin, 1985), 820–838.

50. J.S. Harrison and J.O. Fiet, "New CEOs Pursue Their Own Interests by Sacrificing Stakeholder Value," *Journal of Business Ethics* 19 (1999): 301–308.

51. J. A. Byrne, "How High Can CEO Pay Go?" *Fortune,* 22 April 1996, 100–122.

52. G. Colvin, "The Great CEO Pay Heist," *Fortune,* 25 June 2001, 64.

53. J. A. Byrne, "What, Me Overpaid? CEOs Fight Back," *Business Week,* 4 May 1992, 142–148.

54. Byrne, "Overpaid?,"147.

55. A. D. Henderson and J. W. Fredrickson, "Information Processing Demands As a Determinant of CEO Compensation," *Academy of Management Journal* 39 (1996): 575–606.

56. E. J. Zajac, "CEO Selection, Succession, Compensation, and Firm Performance: A Theoretical Integration and Empirical Analysis," *Strategic Management Journal* 11 (1990): 217–230.

57. C. W. L. Hill, "Effects of Ownership Structure and Control on Corporate Productivity," *Academy of Management Journal* 32 (1989): 25–46.

58. P. L. Rechner and D. R. Dalton, "The Impact of CEO As Board Chairperson on Corporate Performance: Evidence vs. Rhetoric," *Academy of Management Executive* (May 1989): 141–143; and "CEO Duality and Organizational Performance: A Longitudinal Analysis," *Strategic Management Journal* 12 (1991): 155–160.

59. Rechner and Dalton, "CEO Duality."

60. I. F. Kesner and R. B. Johnson, "Crisis in the Boardroom: Fact and Fiction," *Academy of Management Executive* (February 1990): 23–35.

61. M. Magnet, "Directors, Wake Up!" *Fortune,* 15 June 1992, 86–92.

62. A. Taylor III, "The Road Ahead at General Motors," *Fortune,* 4 May 1992, 94–95; J. B. Treece, "The Board Revolt," *Business Week,* 20 April 1992, 31–36.

63. J. A. Byrne, "Requiem for Yesterday's CEO," *Business Week,* 15 February 1993, 32–33; C. J. Loomis and D. Kirkpatrick, "The Hunt for Mr. X: Who Can Run IBM?" *Fortune,* 22 February 1993, 68–72; A. A. Morrison, "After the Coup at Time Warner," *Fortune,* 23 March 1992, 82–90.

64. T. M. Burton, "Greenpeace Is Battling Slide in Contributions and in Political Clout," *The Wall Street Journal,* 3 March 1993, A1.

65. G. Colvin, "Boards to CEO: One Strike and You're Out," *Fortune,* 26 June 2000.

66. I. F. Kesner, B. Victor, and B. T. Lamont, "Board Composition and the Commission of Illegal Acts: An Investigation of Fortune 500 Companies," *Academy of Management Journal* 29 (1986): 789–799; I. B. Kesner and R. B. Johnson, "An Investigation of the Relationship between Board Composition and Shareholder Suits," *Strategic Management Journal* 11 (1990): 327–336.

67. D. R. Dalton, C. M. Johnson, and A. E. Ellstrand, "Meta-analytic Reviews of Board Composition, Leadership Structure, *and Financial Performance,*" Strategic Management Journal 19 (1998): 269–290.

68. Chatterjee and Harrison, "Corporate Governance."

69. W. Q. Judge Jr. and C. P. Zeithaml, "Institutional and Strategic Choice Perspectives on Board Involvement in the Strategic Decision Process," *Academy of Management Journal* 35 (1992): 766–794; J.A. Pearce II and Shaker A. Zahra, "The Relative Power of CEOs and Boards of Directors: Associations with Corporate Performance," *Strategic Management Journal* 12 (1991): 135–153.

70. E. F. Fama and M. C. Jensen, "Separation of Ownership and Control," *Journal of Law and Economics* 26 (1983): 301–325.

71. M. J. Stahl and D. W. Grigsby, *Strategic Management for Decision Making* (Boston: PWS-Kent, 1992), 12–13.

72. D. Robson, "Apple and Gap: How Cozy Is Too Cozy," *Business Week,* 21 May 2001, 45.

73. E. I. Porteus and S. Whang, "On Manufacturing/Marketing Incentives," *Management Science* 37 (1991): 1166–1182; A. D. Sharplin, "Lincoln Electric Company, 1989," in *Strategic Management for Decision Making,* ed. M. J. Stahl and D. W. Grigsby (Boston: PWS-Kent, 1992), 788–812; P. T. Taplin, "Profit-Sharing Plans As an Employee Motivator," *Employee Benefit Plan Review* (January 1989): 10–11.

74. T. P. Summers and J. S. Harrison, "Alliances for Success," *Training and Development* (March 1992): 69–76; "Analysis of U.S. Competitiveness Problems," in *America's Competitive Crisis: Confronting a New Reality,* a report by the Council on Competitiveness (April 1987), 121–126.

75. Summers and Harrison, "Alliances for Success."

76. M. J. Koch and R. G. McGrath, "Improving Labor Productivity: Human Resource Management Policies Do Matter," *Strategic Management Journal* 17 (1996): 335–354.

77. M. A. Huselid, "The Impact of Human Resource Management Practices on Turnover, Productivity, and Corporate Financial Performance," *Academy of Management Journal* 38 (1995): 635–672.

78. J. Pfeffer, "Producing Sustainable Competitive Advantage through the Effective Management of People," *Academy of Management Executive* (February 1995): 55–72.

79. R. Calori and B. Dufour, "Management European Style," *Academy of Management Executive* (August 1995): 68; Pfeffer, "Sustainable Competitive Advantage," 62; information on Japan from E. Fingleton, "Jobs For Life: Why Japan Won't Give Them Up," *Fortune,* 30 March 1995, 120–125.

80. "Our Credo," Johnson & Johnson company documents, used by permission of Johnson & Johnson.

81. K. Bemowski, "People: The Only Thing That Will Make Quality Work," *Quality Progress* (September 1988).

82. Taken directly from Union Pacific Corporation, *Annual Report* (1991), 1.

83. J. W. Henry, "ESOPs with Productivity Payoffs," *Journal of Business Strategy* (July/August 1989): 32–36; C. Rosen, "The Growing Appeal of the Leveraged ESOP," *Journal of Business Strategy* (January/February 1989): 16–20.

84. A. Sharplin, "The Lincoln Electric Company, 1989" in *Strategic Management: A Choice Approach,* ed. J. R. Montanari, C. P. Morgan, and J. S. Bracker (Chicago: Dryden, 1990), 807–826.

85. W. M. Bulkeley, "The Latest Thing at Many Companies Is Speed, Speed, Speed," *The Wall Street Journal,* 23 December 1994; J. T. Vesey, "The New Competitors: They Think in Terms of 'Speed-to-Market,'" *Academy of Management Executive* (May 1991): 23–33.

86. S. Tully, "The Modular Corporation," *Fortune,* 8 February 1993, 106.

87. J. B. Quinn, *Intelligent Enterprise: A Knowledge and Service Based Paradigm for Industry* (New York: The Free Press, 1992).

88. Based on information from D. Miller, *The Icarus Paradox* (New York: Harper Business, 1990).

89. Based on information from Miller, *Icarus Paradox.*

90. G. G. Dess and G. T. Lumkin, "Emerging Issues in Strategy Process Research," in *Blackwell Handbook,* ed. Hitt, Freeman, and Harrison, 3–34.

91. D. J. Teece, *Managing Intellectual Capital* (New York: Oxford University Press, 2000), 3; see also R. M. Grant, "Toward a Knowledge-based View of the Firm," *Strategic Management Journal* 17 (Special Issue) (1996): 109–122.

92. Teece, *Intellectual Capital.*

93. C. E. Helfat and R. S. Raubitschek, "Product Sequencing: Co-Evolution of Knowledge, Capabilities, and Products," *Strategic Management Journal* 21 (2000): 961–979.

94. Helfat and Raubitschek, "Product Sequencing."

95. Teece, *Intellectual Capital,* 13.

96. D. M. DeCarolis and D. L. Deeds, "The Impact of Stocks and Flows of Organizational Knowledge on Firm Performance," *Strategic Management Journal* 20 (1999): 953–968.

97. S. Arimura, "How Matsushita Electric and Sony Manage Global R&D," *Research Technology Management* (March/April 1999): 41–62; P. W. Beamish, "Sony's Yoshihide Nakamura on Structure and Decision Making," *Academy of Management Executive* 13, no. 4 (November 1999): 12–16; B. R. Schlender, "How Sony Keeps the Magic Going," *Fortune,* 4 February 1992, 77.

98. V. Scarpello, W. R. Boulton, and C. W. Hofer, "Reintegrating R&D into Business Strategy," *Journal of Business Strategy* (Spring 1986): 49–56.

99. "Our Credo," Johnson & Johnson company documents.

100. General Electric, *Annual Report* (2000), 2.

101. J. B. Goes and S. H. Park, "Interorganizational Links and Innovation: The Case of Hospital Services," *Academy of Management Journal* 40 (1997): 673–696.

102. W. W. Powell, K. W. Koput, and L. Smith-Doerr, "Interorganizational Collaboration and the Locus of Innovation: Networks of Learning in Biotechnology," *Administrative Science Quarterly* 41 (1996): 116–145.

103. G. Lorenzoni and A. Liparini, "The Leveraging of Interfirm Relationships As a Distinctive Organizational Capability: A Longitudinal Study,"
Strategic Management Journal 20 (1999): 317–338.

104. B. L. Simonin, "The Importance of Collaborative Know-How: An Empirical Test of the Learning Organization," *Academy of Management Journal* 40 (1997): 1150–1174.

105. B. McEvily and A. Zaheer, "Bridging Ties: A Source of Firm Heterogeneity in Competitive Capabilities," *Strategic Management Journal* 20 (1999): 1133–1156.

106. P. Maskell and A. Malmberg, "Localised Learning and Industrial Competitiveness," *Cambridge Journal of Economics* 23 (1999): 167–185.

107. K. R. Harrigan, "Strategic Flexibility in the Old and New Economies," in *Blackwell Handbook,* ed. Hitt, Freeman, and Harrison, 97–123.

108. C. L. Loomis, "Citicorp: John Reed's Second Act," *Fortune,* 29 April 1996, 90.

109. Walt Disney Company, *Annual Report* (1995), 6–7.

110. G. Khermouch, "The Best Global Brands," *Business Week,* 6 August 2001, 50–57.

111. C. J. Fombrun, "Corporate Reputations As Economic Assets," in *Blackwell Handbook,* ed. Hitt, Freeman, and Harrison, 289–312.

112. J. Reese, "America's Most Admired Corporations," *Fortune,* 8 February 1993, 46.

113. J. A. Petrick et al., "Global Leadership Skills and Reputational Capital: Intangible Resources for Sustainable Competitive Advantage," *Academy of Management Executive* (February 1999): 58–69.

114. R. P. Beatty and J. R. Ritter, "Investment Banking, Reputation, and Underpricing of Initial Public Offerings," *Journal of Financial Economics* 15 (1986): 213–232; C. Fombrun and M. Shanley, "What's in a Name? Reputation Building and Corporate Strategy," *Academy of Management Journal* 33 (1990): 233–258; B. Klein and K. Leffler, "The Role of Market Forces in Assuring Contractual Performance," *Journal of Political Economy* 89 (1981): 615–641; P. Milgrom and J. Roberts, "Price and Advertising Signals of Product Quality," *Journal of Political Economy* 94 (1986): 796–821; P. Milgrom and J. Roberts, "Relying of the Information of Interested Parties," *Rand Journal of Economics* 17 (1986): 18–32; G. J. Stigler, "Information in the Labor Market," *Journal of Political Economy* 70 (1962): 49–73

115. S. Caminiti, "The Payoff from a Good Reputation," *Fortune,* 10 February 1992, 74–77.

116. Reese, "Most Admired."

Part 2

Strategy Formulation

Chapter *4*

Strategic Direction

Learning Objectives

After reading and discussing this chapter, you should be able to:

1. Appreciate the various uses of organizational missions.

2. Identify the strategic direction of a firm.

3. Create a mission statement, including the elements of vision, business definition and organizational values.

4. Understand the five ethical frames of reference and how they influence organizational values.

Stewart-Marchman

The mission of Stewart-Marchman Center is to improve the quality of life of individuals and families affected by substance abuse and delinquency through prevention, intervention and treatment. Stewart-Marchman Center is a private not-for-profit corporation formed in 1970 to provide treatment to people experiencing alcohol and other drug addiction. The Center is named after its founder—Leon F. Stewart, a circuit court judge, and Hal S. Marchman, a local pastor.

We envision that, as a premier provider of substance abuse prevention, chemical dependency treatment, and juvenile delinquency rehabilitation services, Stewart-Marchman Center is a model for the state and for the nation. We offer state-of-the-art services.

We ensure the highest service quality at the lowest cost. We treat each client with respect and dignity. Our innovative continuum of services is family oriented, outcome driven, easily accessible, and affordable to all. Our founders are the inspiration for our corporate values. Our future lies in continually seeking out and incorporating in our programs the ever-growing body of scientific knowledge

SMC provides a complete continuum of addiction prevention and treatment services for adults and adolescents, including outpatient, residential and crisis services. SMC also provides a variety of day treatment, residential and aftercare programs for delinquent youth. . . . Each year, the Center serves over 4,500 clients, mostly residing in Volusia and Flagler Counties.[1]

This mission statement of the Stewart-Marchman Center, located in Daytona Beach, Florida, is an excellent example of the major components of strategic direction. In this statement, we see that SMC has a vision of being a premier provider of substance abuse prevention, chemical-dependency treatment, and juvenile delinquency rehabilitation services using state-of-the-art technology. SMC's business definition is clearly explained. They provide a complete continuum of addiction-prevention and -treatment services for adults and adolescents, including outpatient, residential, and crisis services, and a variety of day-treatment, residential, and aftercare programs for delinquent youth. The mission also lays out corporate values, which include treating clients with respect and dignity, focusing on the family, being affordable and accessible, and continuously learning. While sometimes organizations keep statements of strategic direction simple, others go to great lengths to clearly elaborate every aspect of vision, business definition, and values. The following Global Insight contains excerpts from Nokia's extensive statement of strategic direction.

Global Insight
Nokia's Strategic Direction

Nokia, based in Finland, is the world leader in cellular phones. The company has gone to great lengths to clearly define every aspect of its strategic direction. The following are excerpts from Nokia's statement of strategic direction. They are only a small part of the dozens of pages in their Strategic Direction section. For example, the Environment section has nine separate subsections that provide more depth and detail.

Vision and Business Definition

We're living in the digital age. The shrinking, knowledge-based, global village—a world of opportunity and daily discoveries. The way we interact has been radically transformed, and central to that transformation is mobile communications. The mobile phone is fast becoming the centrepiece of personal communication, allowing us access to an ever-widening range of services. Today, we are moving from voice services to services driven by data and multimedia. As new industry structures emerge, we aim for the next wave of growth and innovation.

Welcome to the Mobile World!

Values—the Environment

Looking after the environment is a responsibility shared by everyone in the company and, in turn, by everyone associated with our production, products and services whether they are customers, suppliers, investors or other stakeholders. Our respect for the needs of future generations goes all the way from the production of raw materials to the recycling of obsolete equipment.

Mobile technology enables people to live and work in the way they choose, wherever they happen to be. It gives us all an opportunity to nurture natural resources rather than exhaust them. A technology that can put work and pleasure in the palm of your hand has the power to change lifestyles and do the environment a power of good. This, coupled with constant moves to improve product design, tighten production processes and make better use of recycling, means that the Mobile Age has a responsible role to play in reducing the use of scarce resources.

Taking care of the environment is part of Nokia's corporate culture. It means eliminating risks, but it also enables us to gain stakeholder acceptance as well as to achieve financial benefits and broader business opportunities.

Values—Employees and Society

Our aim is straightforward—to keep Nokia a safe and inspiring place in which to work, and to contribute to the welfare of the communities in which we operate. Every Nokia employee has influence over Nokia's performance and reputation in issues of health, safety, security, employee relations, corporate citizenship and human rights. Therefore, every employee is vital to the success of our business by carrying responsibility for the company's social performance.

Source: www.nokia.com/aboutnokia/our_objectives/business_strategy.html, 13 March 2002. If you discover that the Web site has changed and this page no longer exists at this location, you can find it by going through the Investor Relations section of www.nokia.com.

The central components of strategic direction—vision, business definition, and values—are the primary topics of this chapter. The chapter begins with a general discussion of the importance of strategic direction and the factors that influence it.

Influences on Strategic Direction

Top managers are charged with the responsibility of providing long-term direction for their organizations, while at the same time balancing the competing interests of key stakeholders. One of the critical errors that some organizations make is that they do not know who they are, how they got to where they are, or where they are going. They suffer an "identity crisis." For example, Josten's, the Minnesota-based manufacturer of class rings, yearbooks, and other products to schools, had a thirty-four-year record of sales and earnings increases. Then they diversified into computer systems and started losing money. A New York stock analyst who followed the company for years concluded that "Nobody was taking a hard look at what was going on—nobody seemed to be asking the right questions."[2]

Strategic direction is established and communicated through tools such as visions, missions, business definitions, and values, all of which will be discussed in this chapter. There are no widely-accepted guidelines managers use to provide strategic direction. In some companies, very little is written down. Other companies have adopted formal statements for each of these areas. However, regardless of the medium of communication, high-performing companies tend to create an organizational identity that is understood by both internal and external stakeholders. On the inside, a well-established organizational identity can provide guidance to managers at all levels as they make strategic decisions.[3] In addition, communicating strategic direction to external stakeholders can increase their understanding of the motives of the organization, and may also facilitate the creation of interorganizational relationships, since potential partners have a greater ability to judge the existence of common goals. One corporate president stated that "his company's mission statement has helped create a 'partnering attitude' instead of an adversarial relationship" between his company and its customers.[4]

As Figure 4.1 illustrates, both internal and external stakeholders influence strategic direction. The amount of influence stakeholders have is proportional to their economic, political, and formal (legal or contractual) power. The broad environment is also very influential. For example, an organization usually tries to establish a value system that is consistent with what society expects, or at least appears to be consistent. Also, economic, technical, and political/legal realities influence the selection of business areas in which to compete. Strategic direction forms the foundation from which plans of action are developed. Actions include the firm's competitive strategies, implementation strategies, control systems, and the way internal and external stakeholders and stakeholder relationships are managed.

Organizational actions lead to particular outcomes such as market successes or failures, and to financial performance, which includes sales growth. Also, stakeholders will respond to the actions of organizations in a variety of ways. For instance, customers could be very pleased with the products and services of an organization, or they could be angry and file a lawsuit against the company. Employees could be happy, or they could strike. Government regulators could be cooperative, or they could interfere with operations or levy fines and penalties. These outcomes translate into feedback that the organization can use to adjust strategic direction, actions, or both direction and actions.

Feedback becomes a part of the organization's history. History can potentially assist strategic planning processes, since organizations can learn from past successes and failures. Unfortunately, history can also be a weakness that stands in the way of forward progress. Past successes sometimes create strong **structural inertia,** the term for forces at work to maintain the status quo.[5] These forces can include systems, structures, processes, culture, sunk costs, internal politics, and barriers to entry and exit. Anything that favors the "status quo" has the potential to cause inertia. Inertia is stronger when an organization has been successful in the past because managers believe that past success will translate into future success, regardless of early-warning signals to the contrary. Inertia, then, is another potential threat to the survival and prosperity of an organization.

Structural inertia is related to human nature. Most humans desire a certain amount of predictability in their work. In other words, they have learned to cope with their organizational environment—they are comfortable. They may also fear that changes will reduce their own power or position in the organization or that they will no longer be considered competent. If the forces favoring inertia are

structural inertia
Forces at work to maintain the status quo, which may include systems, structures, processes, culture, sunk costs, internal politics, and barriers to entry and exit

strong and if the organization has been successful in the past, people will be highly resistant to any major shift in missions or strategies. Inertia based on past successes was one of the main reasons for the decline of the railroads as a form of passenger transportation. They continued to pursue the same strategies until it was simply too late.[6] According to Leslie Wexner, CEO of The Limited, Inc.:

> Success doesn't beget success. Success begets failure because the more that you know a thing works, the less likely you are to think that it won't work. When you've had a long string of victories, it's harder to foresee your own vulnerabilities.[7]

One of the most common means to communicate strategic direction is in a written mission statement. The next section is a general discussion of organizational mission statements and how they develop over time.

FIGURE 4.1

Influences on Strategic Direction

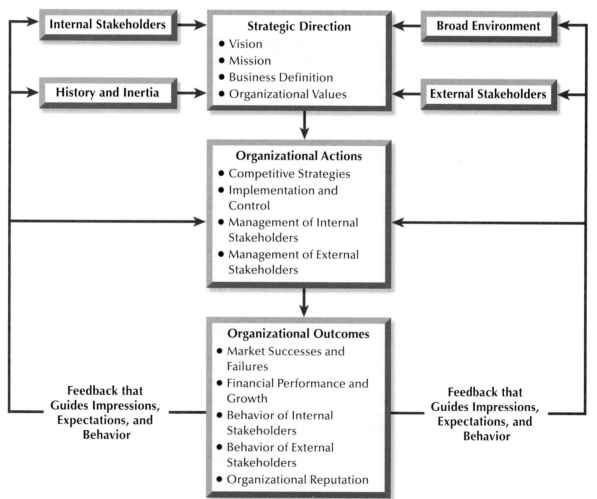

Mission Statements

mission statement
Defines what the organization is and its reason for existing; often contains all of the elements of strategic direction, including vision, business definition and organizational values

An organization's **mission statement** provides an important vehicle for communicating ideals and a sense of direction and purpose to internal and external stakeholders. It can inspire employees and managers. It can also help guide organizational managers in resource-allocation decisions. Clearly, not all "opportunities" that organizations face will be compatible with their missions. If used properly, an organization's mission should provide a screen for evaluating opportunities and proposals. Table 4.1 outlines the various uses of mission statements and considerations for writing them.

Sometimes students of strategic management confuse the terms mission and vision. In general, a mission is what the organization is and its reason for existing, whereas a vision is a forward-looking view of what the organization wants to become. However, when mission statements are written, they often include a vision statement. Many times, mission statements also include a business definition and statements about the values of an organization. The example of Stewart-Marchman Center at the beginning of this chapter is an excellent example of what might be called a "complete" mission statement.

Table 4.1   Multiple Uses of Mission Statements

Use	Primary Stakeholders Targeted	Considerations
Direct Decision Making and Resource Allocations	Managers and Employees	Mission statements should use terms that are understandable to internal stakeholders. For example, a clear business definition provides guidance with regard to where an organization should pursue business opportunities. Also, a statement like, "We use state-of-the-art technology" has clear implications for how resources should be allocated. To be effective, missions should be communicated to internal stakeholders on a regular basis.
Inspire Higher Levels of Performance and Pride in Association	Managers and Employees	Mission statements should be worded in such a way that they inspire the human spirit. A person should read the statement and feel good about working for the company. On the other hand, this can be a two-edged sword if the organization does not act accordingly. This can cause a sense of betrayal and hypocrisy.
Communicate Organizational Purpose and Values	Managers, Employees, Shareholders and Potential Investors	Organizational purpose and values help managers and employees resolve dilemmas when faced with tradeoffs. They also help external stakeholders know what to expect from the organization in particular situations.
Enhance Organizational Reputation	Society and Most External Stakeholder Groups, Especially Customers and Potential Venture Partners	Mission statements should be carefully articulated so that they enhance reputation. Catchy slogans (but not cliché) are helpful so that stakeholders will remember them. They should be short enough so that external stakeholders will attempt to read them and remember them. They should be widely dispersed to media sources and apparent in public settings such as the foyers of office buildings and factories.

As organizations are first established, their mission may be as simple as: "Provide software services to the local business community while generating a profit for the owner." The mission is often informal and is seldom written down. But notice that even in its simplest form, this mission encompasses a purpose, a brief definition of the business, and two important stakeholders, the owner and the customer. Most businesses begin with a mission that is just as simple as the example given. The mission is an extension of the entrepreneur or entrepreneurs who form the organization.

As companies succeed in their business environments, opportunities arise that allow the firm to grow in revenues and number of employees, and encourage it to expand into new product and market areas. The original mission may seem too restrictive. At this point, the organization will probably begin to pay more attention to previously overlooked or neglected stakeholders. For example, the company may increase employee benefits (employees), hire additional tax specialists (government), designate a public-relations officer (society), attempt to negotiate better discounts with suppliers (suppliers), or increase borrowing to help sustain growth (financial intermediaries). In addition, the firm will certainly pay more attention to the actions and reactions of competitors. These stakeholders and forces in the broad environment then become forces that are considered as the organization adjusts or enlarges its mission.

At some point in the growth of an organization, planning processes are formalized. At this point, the mission statement may be put into words. Articulating a mission forces top managers to come to terms with some key issues regarding the current direction of the firm and its future. A well-written mission statement can be an excellent tool for conveying the meaning and intent of an organization to its internal and external stakeholders. For example, the following mission statement of Rhône-Poulenc Rorer, a global pharmaceutical company, defines the goal as being the "best," but then goes on to define what that means.

 Our Mission is to become the BEST pharmaceutical company in the world by dedicating our resources, our talents and our energies to help improve human health and the quality of life of people throughout the world. Being the best means:

Being the BEST at satisfying the needs of everyone we serve: Patients, healthcare professionals, employees, communities, governments and shareholders;

Being BETTER AND FASTER than our competitors at discovering and bringing to market important new medications in selected therapeutic areas;

Operating with the HIGHEST professional and ethical standards in all our activities, building on the Rhône-Poulenc and Rorer heritage of integrity;

Being seen as the BEST place to work, attracting and retaining talented people at all levels by creating an environment that encourages them to develop their potential to the fullest;

Generating consistently BETTER results than our competitors, through innovation and a total commitment to quality in everything we do.[8]

A mission statement can also be an effective way to communicate to important stakeholders such as shareholders, customers, and employees that the company is aware there is a problem and is trying to fix it. This is important during a turnaround. Sears has experienced major setbacks in recent years, including market-share erosion in retailing and loss of the market-leadership position to Wal-Mart. Their mission statement reflects awareness of difficulties and the outline of a plan for fixing them.

 Sears is a company on the move. Our destination is clear. We're pursuing ways to generate profitable growth. We're striving to become more relevant to our customers. We're learning to celebrate our diversity, work together and perform with urgency. And we're establishing new benchmarks for productivity and continuous improvement. By turning individual success stories into models we can replicate across the organization, we can become the destination of choice for customers, employees and investors.[9]

Unfortunately, in many organizations, the process of developing a written mission statement has deteriorated into an exercise in slogan writing. Managers often worry more about writing a catchy, short phrase that can be printed on a business card than about managing with purpose. For an organization's mission to be a management tool, it must be grounded in the realities of the business. One of the first steps in creating a clear sense of mission is to fully understand the nature of the business in which the organization participates. This first step, business definition, will be discussed in the next section.

Business Definition

business definition
A description of the business activities of a firm, based on its products and services, markets, functions served, and resource conversion processes

One of the most vital questions management can ask is, "Who are we?"[10] A clear **business definition** is the starting point of all strategic planning and management.[11] It provides a framework for evaluating the effects of planned change, and for planning the steps needed to move the organization forward.

When defining the business, the question, "What is our business?" should be answered from three perspectives: (1) Who is being satisfied? (2) What is being satisfied? (3) How are customer needs satisfied?[12] The first question refers to the markets that the organization serves, the second question deals with the specific functions provided to the customers identified in question 1, and the third question refers to the capabilities and technologies the firm uses to provide the functions identified in question 2. In actuality, most business definitions also identify specific products or services provided by the organization. In this regard, a fourth question, which is an extension of the third question, can be stated as, "What are our products and services?" This approach is, admittedly, marketing oriented. Its greatest strength is that it focuses on the customer, a very important external stakeholder for most firms.

Table 4.2 contains three examples of firms and their business definitions, organized around the four areas of a business definition—products and services, markets, functions served, and resource-conversion processes. Notice that the concepts that have been discussed thus far apply equally well to both product and service firms. For illustration purposes, the firms described in Table 4.2 represent both product and service orientations, with Church & Dwight providing a tangible product, Toys "R" Us combining service with tangible products, and Delta Airlines focusing exclusively on services.

Sometimes there is a difference between the actual business definition and the one that is reported in a mission statement. An organization should clearly define each component of its business definition for internal uses such as directing the resource allocations of managers. On the other hand, what is reported as a part of the mission statement is typically more of a summary. The purpose is to provide to external stakeholders some notion as to what the company does. In their mission statement, Sara Lee Corporation defines their businesses in simple terms:

> Sara Lee Corporation will build leadership brands in three highly focused global businesses: Food and Beverage, Intimates and Underwear, and Household Products.[13]

On the other hand, Sypris Solutions, Inc. is very specific about what they do:

> Our company is a diversified provider of technology-based outsource services and specialized industrialized products. The Company performs a wide range of manufacturing and technical services, typically under long-term contracts with major manufacturers. We also manufacture and sell complex data storage systems, magnetic instruments, current sensors, high-pressure closures and a variety of other industrial products.[14]

Increasing the Scope of Operations

While defining a business is helpful in communicating to internal and external stakeholders what the organization is all about, the business definition should not constrain strategic choice. In other words, it is an excellent tool for identifying where a company is, but should not be used to determine where the company should go in the future.[15] Peter Drucker suggested that the business-definition question should be stated not only as "What is our business?" but also as "What will it be?" and "What

---

Table 4.2   Business Definitions of Three Well-Known Companies

	Church and Dwight	Toys 'R' Us	Delta Airlines
Markets	Grocery stores and bakeries	Children, parents, and grandparents	Business travelers, vacationers and occasional travelers
Functions Served	Baking ingredient, cleaner, odor absorbent	Availability of merchandise	Fast, long-distance and moderate distance transportation
Capabilities and Technologies Utilized	Chemical processing/packaging, promotion, and advertising	Buying, inventory management, service, promotion, and advertising	Flying, logistics, fleet management and service, baggage handling, reservations, promotion, and advertising
Product Groups and Services	Baking soda and related consumer products	Toys, clothing, and furniture for children	Air transportation

Note: Church and Dwight is the manufacturer of Arm & Hammer baking soda and other consumer products.

should it be?"[16] The second question refers to the direction that the firm is heading at the current time. In other words, where will the business end up if it continues in its current course? The third question, "What should it be?" allows for modifications to the existing strategy to move the company in an appropriate direction. Organizations that struggle to come to grips with those two questions are forced to look forward in time, and to think about a vision for the future. If the railroads had asked these questions soon enough, they might have realized that they should enlarge their business definitions to include transportation instead of just "railroads." Narrowness of definition may have been one of the leading causes of their decline in American industry.[17]

Sometimes it takes a major shock to cause a firm to rethink its business definition, as in the case of Total Logistic Control Group (TLC), a warehousing company based in Zeeland, Michigan.

 A rainstorm dumped 13.5 inches of rain in three hours and caused extensive damage to their 215,000-square-foot dry-goods warehouse. Shortly thereafter, TLC's president died from a heart attack. Three days after his death, a fire swept through TLC's corporate offices and refrigerated warehouse, destroying nearly 1 million cubic feet of refrigerated warehouse space. "TLC responded to these events by redefining their business." According to Keith Klingenberg, new president of TLC, "Usually it takes some significant event to knock you out of your comfort zone, to take you out of that complacent, ho-hum mode. And we have had our share of adversities and it has proven to be our blessing." Craig Hall, CEO, explained, "We found out that we were not in the warehousing business at all, but in fact, in the field of logistics, providing the warehousing function." This new approach to business resulted in 400 percent growth in sales in three years. TLC now distributes all Slim-Fast Products in the United States, and decided to move into the international marketplace by applying to become a foreign-trade zone.[18]

Gary Hamel suggests that rather than determine the future direction of an organization based on what it does, the organization should think in terms of what they know and the resources they own.[19] In other words, a company should determine future direction based on its resources and capabilities. This suggestion is consistent with the discussion of resource analysis contained in Chapter 3. As organizations become involved in businesses outside of their current operations, they are increasing what is referred to as their scope. In other words, the scope of an organization is the breadth of its activities both within a market and across markets.

Many organizations begin with a very narrow scope and then expand in various directions. For instance, Church & Dwight, traditionally a narrowly defined company, began a market-development program several years ago to find new applications for its basic product, baking soda.

 Initially, baking soda was advertised as an odor absorbent for the refrigerator and shoes. This move increased sales by increasing the number of functions served, but had no effect on the product (baking soda), the market (grocery-store consumers), or the capabilities and technologies used. Later the company began marketing products containing baking soda, such as rug and room deodorizers, as well as oven cleaner.

Notice that these later moves were still aimed at grocery stores (building on brand-name recognition), but greatly increased the number of products and functions. The capabilities and technologies used were altered only slightly to include new packaging (i.e., aerosol cans). However, Church & Dwight is still involved predominantly in chemical processing and packaging.

On the other hand, when Toys "R" Us entered the children's-apparel market through its Kids "R" Us retail outlets, the products and functions increased somewhat, but the markets and technologies remained the same.[20] Like Toys "R" Us, the Kids "R" Us chain requires buying, inventory management, distributing, limited service, promotion, and advertising. Toys "R" Us had mastered these skills before the Kids "R" Us chain was even envisioned. In addition, Toys "R" Us could draw on its rich experience in marketing to children, grandparents, and parents. Using these same skills and capabilities, the company entered the children's-furniture segment through an acquisition.

Delta Airlines has adhered to a very narrow business definition. Instead of venturing into new areas, in 1986 Delta acquired Western Airlines. This move allowed Delta to greatly increase its western U.S. route coverage and establish an international presence, thus expanding the geographic size of its markets.[21] However, the type of customer served, function, service, and technologies remained the same. Delta and other airlines are almost entirely dependent on one business. When the industry experiences downturns and shocks, they have no other businesses to offset losses. This became evident in 2001 when the terrorist bombings in the United States and the associated downturn in demand for air travel led to losses that the airlines could not sustain. When it looked as if many airlines would go out of business, the U.S. government provided a multibillion-dollar bailout.

Studying changes in business definitions can help determine the nature of the distinctive competencies a firm is trying to develop or has developed. For instance, Church & Dwight continues to focus on the same basic resource-conversion process. Although Toys "R" Us is in a completely different business from Church & Dwight, the basic approach to business, expanding into areas that draw on the same technologies, is the same. Both of these companies have expanded into sectors in which they could excel, due to their own areas of expertise. Delta, on the other hand, has concentrated on only one line of business, while expanding geographic territory and thus market size.

An organization may expand its business definition to include markets, functions, technologies, and/or products across a broad segment of the global economy, or it may decide to move forward or backward in the industry supply chains in which it is currently participating. An **industry supply chain** represents the flow of goods in a manufacturing industry from their crudest forms to their final forms, where they are ultimately consumed.

industry supply chain
The sequence of activities in an industry from raw materials extraction through final consumption

Moving Forward or Backward on the Industry Supply Chain

A typical industry supply chain, which is illustrated in Figure 4.2, begins with extraction of raw materials such as timber, ore, or crude oil. These raw materials are then manufactured into commodities such as wood pulp or iron. Primary manufacturing sometimes also involves the creation of components that are used to assemble final products. Therefore, the primary manufacturing stage can be short or long, depending on the nature of the final products.

Final-product manufacturing involves the creation of a product that is in its final form prior to consumption. At this point, branding becomes very important, since consumers associate brand names of final products with particular levels of quality, service, and reliability. Finally, wholesaling entails channeling final products to retail outlets, and retailing consists of selling these products to the ultimate consumer. Some products bypass the wholesaling and/or retailing stages due to direct sale by the manufacturer to customers.[22]

While the model in Figure 4.2 is intuitively appealing, the industry supply chain is actually more complex than it looks. For instance, some products, such as salt, are both final products and products that are used as raw materials in other products. An example of a complete industry supply chain for a simple product is found in Figure 4.3. Note that many of the outputs in this model are used in many more products than just the ones in this simplified supply chain. For example, both crude oil and cotton end up as part of literally thousands of products.

vertical integration
Exists when a firm is involved in more than one stage of the industry supply chain

An organization can be involved in all or a subset of the activities that make up the industry supply chain, depending on its business definition. **Vertical integration** is the term used to describe the extent to which a firm is involved in several stages of the industry supply chain. Oil companies such as Exxon are totally vertically integrated, since they explore for oil; extract it from the earth; refine it into gas and other products; and store, distribute, advertise, and sell the refined products to consumers. On the other hand, some oil companies are not at all vertically integrated. For example, several companies exist that do nothing more than provide engineering services to oil rigs. They are in the same industry, but they have chosen to limit their organizations to one specific activity in the industry supply chain.

As mentioned in Chapter 1, strategy formulation is often divided into levels, with corporate-level strategy at the highest level in the organization. Corporate-level strategy formulation refers primarily to the selection of business areas in which the organization will compete and the emphasis each area is given. Consequently, corporate-level strategy is directly linked to business definition, or the execution of a corporate-level strategy results in a particular business definition. For example, if a corporate-level strategy includes increased involvement in various stages of the vertical supply chain or an increase in the scope of operations, the business definition will be changed to reflect these changes. Corporate-level strategy will be discussed in depth in Chapter 7.

FIGURE 4.2

Industry Supply Chain for Manufacturing Firms

FIGURE 4.3

Simplified Industry Supply Chain for a Bed Sheet Purchased at a Department Store

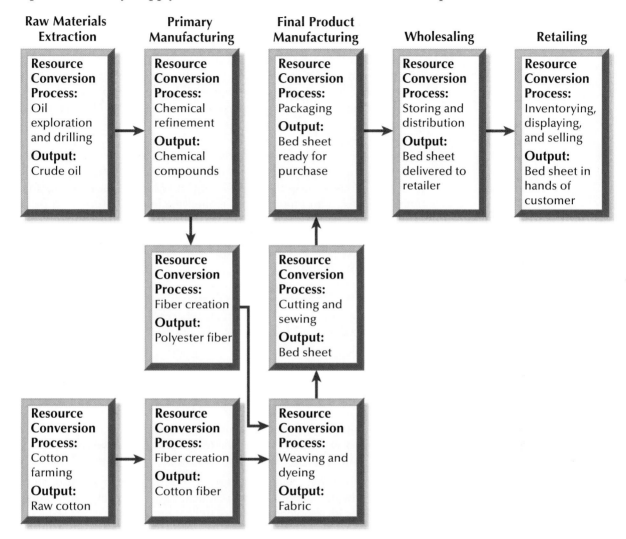

Organizational Vision

An organization with a vision has a definite sense of what it wants to be in the future. For example, Bill Gates has a clear vision of how he expects his industry to evolve and the role he wants to play in it. He wants Microsoft to dominate the software systems that link all digital transactions and communications, in business, entertainment, and leisure. His vision provides the framework for creating new businesses and forming new partnerships.

The CEO has primary responsibility for creating the organizational vision. For many years, Wal-Mart's vision was to become the largest discount retailer in the United States, a vision that was achieved shortly before founder Sam Walton's death. In the case of Wal-Mart, the organizational vision did not require a departure from the existing business definition, although it did require continued growth in markets served as new regions were entered. More importantly, Sam Walton and Wal-Mart illustrate how a well-articulated vision can be a strong motivational tool. Once it is stated, it may be used to focus the efforts of the entire organization.[23] For example, plans, policies, or programs that are inconsistent with the corporate vision may need to be altered or replaced. A well-understood vision can help managers and employees believe that their actions have meaning. Pharmacia Corporation also has an inspiring vision of what the company can be.

 We are passionate in our commitment to improving health and wellness around the world. Working in teams as part of a global organization, each one of us contributes to building the best-managed company in our industry . . . a company that is the best in responding as a partner to meet the diverse needs of the people we serve, through a flow of innovative medicines, products and services. By doing so, we deliver best-managed performance for our shareowners: superior long-term growth and profitability.[24]

The second half of Pharmacia's vision statement establishes priorities on serving customers and earning superior returns for shareholders. These statements are evidence of organizational values, which will be discussed next.

Organizational Values

organizational values
The underlying philosophies that guide decisions and behavior in a firm; also called core values or organizational ethics

A final, but certainly not less important, aspect of strategic direction is the establishment of **organizational values.** Values guide organizational decisions and behavior. Eli Lilly and Company has established the following three values:

1. Respect for people that includes our concern for the interests of all people worldwide who touch—or are touched by—our company: customers, employees, shareholders, partners and communities;

2. Integrity that embraces the very highest standards of honesty, ethical behavior and exemplary moral character;

3. Excellence that is reflected in our continuous search for new ways to improve the performance of our business to become the best at what we do.[25]

High-level managers, especially the CEO, have a great deal of influence on the values of the company. When a new top manager takes charge, his or her personal values help shape the entire company. Managers who work with the CEO quickly identify his or her value system and communicate it to lower-level managers and employees. The CEO may also discuss organizational values in speeches, news releases, and memos. To the extent that the CEO controls the rewards systems subjectively, managers who make decisions that are consistent with the values of the CEO are likely to be rewarded, thus reinforcing what is expected. Many of the people who strongly disagree with the new values will voluntarily leave the firm. Or, if their own behavior pattern is inconsistent with the new rules of the game, they will be "forced out" through poor performance evaluations, missed promotions, and/or low salary increases. Thus, over a period of time, the example and actions of the CEO are reflected in most of the major decisions that are made by the organization.[26]

In spite of the power of the CEO, he or she is not the only determinant of organizational values. The values of an organization are also a reflection of the social groups from which managers and other employees are drawn (which makes global management even more challenging). These individuals bring a personal value system with them when they are hired. Also, if value changes in society are not voluntarily incorporated into the firm, an employee or manager may "blow a whistle," which is an attempt to force the organization to cease a behavior that society currently finds unacceptable, or to incorporate a practice that is in keeping with the new social value. For example, antidiscrimination lawsuits have prompted many organizations to adopt more-stringent equal employment opportunity policies and even affirmative action programs. The values of various social groups are constantly changing. Therefore, strategic managers need to keep abreast of these changes in order to successfully position their firms. This task is especially difficult in global organizations.

Stakeholder theory is closely aligned with discussions of values and social responsibility, since one of the principles underlying the theory is that organizations should behave appropriately with regard to a wide range of stakeholder concerns and interests.[27] The increasing incidence of lawsuits against top managers and their companies in recent years provides evidence that many organizations are not satisfying all of their stakeholders' expectations very well.[28]

Social Responsibility

organizational ethics
A value system that has been widely adopted by members of an organization; often used interchangeably with the term "organizational values"

Virtually all strategic decisions contain ethical dimensions because they are directly linked to the way the organization interacts with its stakeholders.[29] As they relate to individuals, ethics are a personal value system that helps determine what is right or good. These values are typically associated with a system of beliefs that supports a particular moral code or view.[30] **Organizational ethics** are a value system that has been widely adopted by members of an organization. For example, Wal-Mart's values emphasize the worth of customers and employees, while Motorola has values that focus on participation and patriotism. To determine what the values of a firm are, a student can simply study the pattern of decisions in the company to discover what or who is given priority.[31]

Sometimes the stated values of an organization differ from the actual values that guide organizational decisions. For example, a company may publish an affirmative-action statement that condemns prejudice in hiring and promotion decisions on the basis of sex or race. However, that same company may not have a single minority member or female in its top-management team. Thus, studying the pattern of promotion decisions over a few years can determine whether the stated position differs from the actual behavior of the firm. This approach to ethics is consistent with the stakeholder model developed in this book, since stakeholders will naturally make these types of judgments when determining how well the organization is satisfying their needs and desires.

social responsibility
The duty of an organization, defined in terms of its economic, legal, and moral obligations, as well as discretionary actions that might be considered attractive from a societal perspective

Embedded within the application of ethics found here is the notion of social responsibility. **Social responsibility** contains four major components: (1) economic responsibilities such as the obligation to be productive and profitable and meet the consumer needs of society; (2) a legal responsibility to achieve economic goals within the confines of written law; (3) moral obligations to abide by unwritten codes, norms, and values implicitly derived from society; and (4) discretionary responsibilities that are volitional or philanthropic in nature.[32] Discretionary actions would include things such as Stonyfield Farm's donation of 10 percent of its profits to environmental causes. Also, Stonyfield promotes environmental issues on its yogurt cups.[33]

F. Hoffmann-La Roche Ltd., a leading European health-care company, clearly acknowledges its obligations to society:

> We want to maintain high ethical standards in our business dealings and in our efforts to protect the environment. We will also maintain these standards in adhering to local, national and international laws, in cooperating with authorities and in communicating with the public.[34]

In another illustration, the following are excerpts from a special environmental report published by General Motors.

 Global businesses must act responsibly in regard to their business and to the natural environments in which they operate. As we pursue our strategies worldwide, we accept a social and environmental responsibility as well. These responsibilities include the promotion of a sustainable global economy and recognition of the accountability we have to the economies, environments, and communities where we do business around the world. It is important to work for environmental protection in balance with economic objectives and to establish national policies to foster development that can be sustained over the long term. Indeed, sustainable development is supported by the fact that economic growth and environmental protection can be collectively achieved through cooperative efforts—and that's a key philosophy at General Motors.

We at GM have many challenges ahead in defining sustainable development within the context of the global automotive industry. One thing is certain: The managerial skills and technology that a global enterprise such as GM can mobilize provide considerable potential for sustainable development initiatives.[35]

GM means it. Its representatives have served on the President's Council on Sustainable Development. GM also collaborated with government and environmental organizations to develop action plans to foster U.S. economic vitality and support a set of directives adopted by participants at the United Nations Conference on the Environment. Why would the world's largest automaker devote resources to publishing an environmental report and becoming involved in environmental initiatives? Top executives are thinking long term. They realize that the environmental movement that began with a few special-interest groups half a century ago has become a part of mainstream social opinion, especially in the United States. GM is also establishing alliances with government and other organizations that keep them in this mainstream, and using public relations to promote their actions, as shown by the document quoted above.

Research evidence does not unequivocally support the idea that firms that rank high on social responsibility, based on the four components described above, are necessarily any more or less profitable than firms that rank low.[36] However, social responsibility is only one part of the stakeholder view. While a stakeholder approach can help an organization maintain an untarnished reputation, it should also provide opportunities to enhance economic performance. Organizations that apply stakeholder analysis and management well, including many that are featured in this book, can achieve higher-than-normal economic profits by learning from stakeholders; forecasting their needs; forming alliances; and avoiding negative outcomes such as strikes, lawsuits, boycotts, and stiffer government regulation.

Furthermore, firms that have an overall high rank in the four areas listed above (one of which is productivity and profitability) have achieved an end in itself. The old belief, espoused primarily by economists such as Milton Friedman, is that the only valid objective of a corporation is to maximize profits, within the rules of the game (legal restrictions). While it is true that profits are desirable, they are only one outcome of successful corporations. For-profit corporations are also in business to create products and/or provide services.

A corporation that becomes too focused on profits is likely to lose the support and cooperation of key stakeholders such as suppliers, activist groups, competitors, society, and the government. In the long run, this sort of strategy may result in problems such as lawsuits, loss of goodwill, and, ultimately, a loss of profits. One business-ethics expert argued that "there is a long-term cost to unethical behavior that tends to be neglected. That cost is to the trust of the people involved. Companies today—due to increasing global competition and advancing technological complexity—are much more dependent than ever upon the trust of workers, specialists, managers, suppliers, distributors, customers, creditors, owners, local institutions, national governments, venture partners, and international agencies. People in any of those groups who believe that they have been misgoverned by bribes, sickened by emissions, or cheated by products tend, over time, to lose trust in the firm responsible for those actions."[37] The case of Manville is illustrative of these points.

 Nearly fifty years ago, employees and managers of Manville (then Johns-Manville) started to receive information that asbestos inhalation was associated with various forms of lung disease. Manville chose to ignore this information and to suppress research findings. The company even went so far as to conceal chest X-rays from employees in their asbestos operations. When confronted about this tactic, a Manville lawyer was quoted as saying that they would let their employees work until they dropped dead, all in the interest of saving money. Eventually, this neglect of research findings and their own employees led to financial ruin for Manville.[38]

Concerning ethical decision making, the approach of many business organizations seems to be to wait until someone complains before actions are taken. This is the type of attitude that resulted in the savings-and-loan crisis, the Bhopal explosion tragedy in India, and the explosion of the space shuttle *Challenger*. In each of these situations, the organizations involved could have avoided problems by being more responsive to warning signals from key stakeholders. History has taught us that many human-induced disasters and crises could be avoided if organizations were sensitive to what one or another of their stakeholders is saying.

Enterprise Strategy

One fundamental question an organization should ask in determining its purpose is, "What do we stand for?" This question is the critical link between ethics and strategy. **Enterprise strategy** is the term used to denote the joining of ethical and strategic thinking about the organization.[39] It is the organization's best possible reason (assuming there is a reason) for the actions it takes.

enterprise strategy
Joins ethical and strategic thinking about the organization; it is the organization's best possible reason for the actions it takes

An enterprise strategy is almost always focused on serving particular stakeholder needs. For example, an enterprise strategy can contain statements concerning a desire to maximize stockholder value, satisfy the interests of all or a subset of other stakeholders, or increase social harmony or the common good of society.[40] In the mission statement of Rhône-Poulenc Rorer, the enterprise strategy is to "help improve human health and the quality of life of people throughout the world."

The development of an enterprise strategy is a legal requirement in not-for-profit organizations in the United States. In order to gain a tax-exempt status, not-for-profits have to be organized around a societal mission, whether it is educational, religious, charitable, or otherwise. The mission statement of the American Red Cross contains a clear expression of enterprise strategy: "The mission of the American Red Cross is to improve the quality of human life; to enhance self-reliance and concern for others; and to help people avoid, prepare for, and cope with emergencies."[41]

Some for-profit organizations also get very specific about how they will deal with stakeholder interests. For example, Harris Corporation, a maker of electronics, created broad goals concerning how the organization will endeavor to satisfy its customers, shareholders, suppliers, employees, and communities. Table 4.3 contains these stakeholder goals.

Organizational mission statements containing the elements of an enterprise strategy are more likely to be found in high-performing than in low-performing corporations.[42] Enterprise strategy is a natural extension of the ethics of the organization, which are an extension of the values of key managers within the organization (as was discussed in Chapter 3). The ethics of a firm are not just a matter of public statements. Ethical decision making is a way of doing business. A company that specifically works to build ethics into its business practice, to develop and implement an enterprise strategy, will have a frame of reference for handling potential ethical problems.

Ethical Frames of Reference

The pattern of decisions made by organizational managers establishes strategy and creates expectations among other organizational members and external stakeholders. For example, a firm that has specialized in the highest-quality products and services creates an expectation among customers that all products will be high quality. If the firm chooses to change its strategy to include lower-quality products, it runs the risk that customers will perceive the change as a breach of faith. Similarly, if a company has an established relationship with a customer as its sole source of supply of a particular product, then the customer comes to depend on that company. If the supplier then chooses to drop that product from its product line, what might seem to be a clear-cut business decision takes on an ethical dimension: Can the customer's business survive if the product is dropped? Should other alternatives be considered? What obligation does the supplier have to that customer?

These types of decisions carry an ethical dimension because they go against what some important stakeholders think is right. An ethical dilemma exists when the values of different stakeholders of the organization are in conflict. Although there is no real legal dimension, there is an issue of trust or good faith that is very apparent. The values that organizational members bring to their work—the shared values that make up the organizational culture—determine whether the issues of trust, good faith, and obligation are raised when decisions are being deliberated, as well as the degree to which these issues influence the final outcome.

In addition to decisions that violate stakeholder expectations, there are also ethical dilemmas related to the gray area surrounding legal behavior: the definitions of what society views as right and wrong. In some cases, they are part of an obvious organizational crisis such as a plant closing, product recall, or environmental or safety accident. However, employees face decisions all day that have ethical implications: whether to tell a customer the truth that their order will be shipped late, whether to exaggerate a travel-expense claim for a particularly inconvenient business trip, whether to ship a marginal product as first quality in order to meet the

Table 4.3   Harris Corporation's Broad Stakeholder Goals
Customers—For customers, our goal is to achieve ever-increasing levels of satisfaction by providing quality products and services with distinctive benefits on a timely and continuing basis worldwide. Our relationships with customers will be forthright and ethical and will be conducted in a manner to build trust and confidence.
Shareholders—For shareholders, the owners of our company, our goal is to achieve sustained growth in earnings-per-share. The resulting stock-price appreciation combined with dividends should provide our shareholders with a total return on investment that is competitive with similar investment opportunities.
Employees—The people of Harris are our company's most valuable asset, and our goal is for every employee to be personally involved in and share the success of the business. The company is committed to providing an environment that encourages all employees to make full use of their creativity and unique talents, and to providing equitable compensation, good working conditions, and the opportunity for personal development and growth that is limited only by individual ability and desire.
Suppliers—Suppliers are a vital part of our resources. Our goal is to develop and maintain mutually beneficial partnerships with suppliers who share our commitment to achieving increasing levels of customer satisfaction through continuing improvements in quality, service, timeliness, and cost. Our relationships with suppliers will be sincere, ethical, and will embrace the highest principles of purchasing practice.
Communities—Our goal is to be a responsible corporate citizen. This includes support of appropriate civic, educational and business activities, respect for the environment, and the encouragement of Harris employees to practice good citizenship and support community programs. Our greatest contribution to our communities is to be successful so that we can maintain stable employment and create new jobs.
Source: Annual Report.

daily-output quota. Although some of these decisions concern personal honesty more than business practice, the organization's culture—its system of shared values—determines in large part how employees deal with them.

In making decisions that deal with ethical issues, it is important to have a frame of reference. Very few ethical dilemmas have simple right-or-wrong answers. Instead, they are complex and require balancing the economic and social interests of the organization.[43] The following are five theoretical models that often influence organizational decisions.[44]

economic theory
Defines the purpose of a business organization as profit maximization

- **Economic Theory.** Under economic theory, the purpose of a business organization is to maximize profits. Profit maximization will lead to the greatest benefit for the most people. Other than profit maximization, there are no ethical issues in business. *Limitations of Economic Theory:* Assumptions of profits being evenly distributed is naive. Not all business decisions relate to profit making, and some ways of increasing profits hurt society.

legal theory
Ethical behavior is defined as legal behavior

- **Legal Theory.** Laws are a reflection of what society has determined is right and wrong. Compliance with the law ensures ethical behavior. *Limitations of Legal Theory:* The social and political processes used to formulate laws are complex and time-consuming. Since the processes are subject to manipulation, the laws may not truly reflect the interests of society.

religious theory
Religious teachings define appropriate behavior

utilitarian theory
The most appropriate actions generate the greatest benefits for the largest number of people

- **Religious Theory.** Everyone should act in accordance with religious teachings. *Limitations of Religious Theroy:* As a model for business decision making, religious values are difficult to apply. There are many different religious beliefs, and no consensus on the behaviors that are consistent with the beliefs.

- **Utilitarian Theory.** Utilitarian theory says to focus on the outcome of a decision. Everyone should act in a way that generates the greatest benefits for the largest number of people. *Limitations of Utilitarian Theory:* Under this model, immoral acts that hurt society or a minority group can be justified if they benefit the majority.

universalist theory
Appropriate behavior is defined by the question: "Would I be willing for everyone else in the world to make the same decision?"

- **Universalist Theory.** Universalist theory says to focus on the intent of the decision. Every person is subject to the same standards. Weigh each decision against the screen: Would I be willing for everyone else in the world to make the same decision? *Limitations of Universalist Theory:* This model provides no absolutes. What one person believes is acceptable for all in society may be offensive to others.

It is obvious that the five models do not provide absolute guidance on how to handle an ethical dilemma. Instead, they provide a departure point for discussing the implications of decisions.

Ex. Suppose an organization produces a small amount of toxic pollutant as a part of its manufacturing process. Although the law requires that the material be disposed of in a special, costly manner, the company is sure that the small amount of pollutant it produces is not enough to damage local water supplies. Furthermore, the disposal method costs more than the original cost of some raw materials. If the company releases the small quantities of toxin into the sewer system, it is unlikely that the firm will be caught or fined.

According to economic theory, since there is not a cost attached to disposal and it is unlikely that the firm will have to pay a fine, the profit-maximizing option would be to release the toxin into the sewer system. From a legal perspective, release of the toxin is illegal. In most religions, deceit of any kind is considered to be wrong. In utilitarian theory, the costs of complying with the law are material and paid by the company and its shareholders. The costs of not complying are borne by society in the form of cleaning up; however, in this case of a very small amount of toxin, there are no costs to society. Finally, from a universalist perspective, if everyone decided to release a small amount of toxin into the sewer, the problem would be overwhelming.

Codes of Ethics

code of ethics
Communicates the values of the corporation to employees and other stakeholders

Many organizations create a code of ethics to communicate the values of the corporation to employees and other stakeholders. **Codes of ethics** are also a part of strategic direction, an extension of the organization's enterprise strategy.

The code of ethics of United Technologies states:

> Our code of ethics, comprised of corporate principles and standards of conduct, governs our business decisions and actions. The integrity, reputation, and profitability of United Technologies ultimately depend upon the individual actions of our employees, representatives, agents and consultants all over the world. Each employee is personally responsible and accountable for compliance with our code.[45]

The detail within United Technologies' code of ethics addresses specific standards of conduct the organization will exhibit in its dealings with customers, suppliers, employees, shareholders, competitors, and worldwide communities. Employees are encouraged to report violations to their supervisors or to the vice president for business practices. One of the statements in the code of ethics specifies that corporate policy prohibits retribution against employees for making reports of violations. Some codes of ethics set a minimum standard of behavior by stating that employees are expected to obey all laws. Other organizations make specific statements about values, duties, and obligations to customers, employees, and societies. Clearly, in those cases, the organization expects members to maintain standards of ethical behavior that transcend minimum legal standards. Wendy's International Inc., one of the world's largest restaurant-operating and -franchising companies, has a very specific statement of values that should drive organizational decisions and operations.

Ex. *Integrity*—We keep our promises. All actions are guided by absolute honesty, fairness and respect for every individual.

Leadership—We lead by example and encourage leadership qualities at all levels. Everyone has a role to play.

People Focus—We believe our people are key to our success. We value all members of our diverse family for their individual contributions and their team achievements.

Customer Satisfaction—Satisfying internal and external customers is the focus of everything we do.

Continuous Improvement—Continuous improvement is how we think; innovative change provides competitive opportunities.

Community Involvement—Giving back is our heritage. We actively participate and invest in the communities where we do business.

Commitment to Stakeholders—We serve all stakeholders and, through balancing our responsibilities to all, we maximize value to each of them.[46]

To ensure that employees abide by the corporate code of ethics, some companies establish an ethics system, including an audit process to monitor compliance. However, sometimes formal systems are not enough to ensure ethical behavior, as the following case attests.

 Dow Corning established a highly regarded ethics system in the 1970s. Some of its features included ethics-training sessions, a section on the company's semiannual employee opinion survey regarding ethics, and routine ethics audits of each business operation. Six managers served on a Business Conduct Committee and conducted the audits, which included a three-hour review session with employees. Results were reported to a special committee of the board of directors. Apparently, even these efforts were not enough. During the same year the ethics system was implemented, an engineer resigned after the company paid no attention to warnings of the health hazards of silicone breast implants. Further investigation suggested that the company was aware of possible health problems and tried to conceal these problems from the public. When health issues were revealed in the 1990s, the ethics system was closely scrutinized. The system apparently was not enough to change the fundamental culture of the organization.[47]

In an award-winning article titled "The Parable of the Sadhu," Bowen McCoy, an investment banker with Morgan Stanley, discussed what he thought was the core, underlying problem when an organization handles ethical dilemmas poorly.[48] In his view, people who are part of an organization often do not personalize ethical issues. It is as if the "organization" is responsible, and the individuals are not. Even individuals who see themselves as very ethical will tend to pass through an ethical dilemma without recognizing it as one, or will view the dilemma as ultimately someone else's problem. For many ethical dilemmas, one person is not physically capable of correcting the problem alone.

When faced with a major crisis, such as finding that a key product is dangerous to the customers who buy it, many organizations do not know what to do. There is no guiding precept, no system of shared values, to unite the company behind a clear understanding of correct behavior. Although some company members may feel discomfort with the course of action being pursued by the firm, a change in action requires a structured, systematic effort by the entire organization. According to McCoy: "Some organizations have a value system that transcends the personal values of the managers. Such values, which go beyond profitability, are usually revealed when the organization is under stress.... Members need to share a preconceived notion of what is correct behavior, a 'business ethic', and think of it as a positive force, not a constraint."[49]

The individual has a critical role in the development of the shared values. McCoy writes: "What is the nature of our responsibility if we consider ourselves to be ethical persons? Perhaps it is to change the values of the group so that it can, with all its resources, take the other road."[50]

Ethics in Global Environments

Dealing with the ethics of employees, customers, and other stakeholders and the society from which they are drawn is a difficult task even in organizations that compete within a single domestic economy. However, the difficulty level increases for global organizations because value systems are highly divergent across international boundaries. For example, a survey of 3,783 female seniors attending 561 universities and colleges in Tokyo revealed that they not only expected sexism in the workplace, but didn't seem to mind it. "More than 91% said they would not mind being treated as 'office flowers.' Nearly 25% considered that to be a woman's role. Over 66% said acting like an office flower would make the atmosphere more pleasant."[51] This attitude concerning the role of women, which is widely held in Japan, is inconsistent with the values of Americans.

In fact, Japanese companies are responding to pressure to conform to the values of the countries in which they compete. For instance, Akio Morita, prior chairman of Sony, once argued that Japanese corporations must adapt the way they do business, in response to resentment from U.S. and European rivals. His formula was to "seek profits ahead of market share, increase dividends to shareholders, treat employees more humanely, (and) contribute more to the community and environmental protection."[52] This represents a major departure from the way some Japanese managers think. U.S and other foreign competitors in Japan also have a difficult time dealing with Japanese values. As Akio Morita suggests, American managers need to find ways to adapt to the countries in which they operate.

The clash of Japanese and American values is illustrative of the types of problems that exist across many international relationships. U.S. companies often experience cultural clashes when doing business with companies in China, Latin America, Russia, and many other countries. And, of course, firms from other countries often have difficulty understanding the values of Americans, Europeans, Australians, and so forth. The list goes on and on. The problem is a common one. The key to overcoming cultural clashes is working to understand the host-country culture, and developing strategies that are consistent with that culture instead of fighting it. The discussion of ethical frames of reference found earlier in this chapter is very helpful in doing this, since people in many countries tend to favor one or another of the ethical frames.

Although there are dissimilarities among international cultures, it would be an overstatement to say that everything is different. In fact, as organizations grow, develop, and internationalize, they tend to adopt values that are friendlier to a wider group of international constituents. This chapter will close with a statement from Luiz Alberto Garcia, chairman of the board of directors of Algar, a large and successful Brazilian company with investments in agribusiness, publishing, transportation services, and entertainment. The statement was found at the beginning of Algar's recent annual report. Many of the elements of values, social responsibility, and enterprise strategy are included in the chairman's message. In fact, it could just as well have been the opening statement in the annual report of a U.S., European, or Asian company.

 Algar is known today as being one of the most active companies in Brazil in terms of corporate citizenship as well as one of the best companies in which to work. We take great pride in such recognition. But above all, these are things that are part of our core values and beliefs. We have conducted training programs for our associates for many years now and our companies believe in—and invest in—actions of social responsibility. We know that these projects go hand in hand with the respect we give our human talents, our partners and, of course, our customers. All of these relationships merge into an overall chain of action involving ethics, quality, commitment, and attitude. And believing in a better Brazil is also a business investment.[53]

Summary

Strategic managers are charged with the responsibility of providing long-term direction for their organizations, while at the same time balancing the competing interests of key stakeholders. Strategic direction should be established based, in part, on an analysis of the internal and external environments and the history of success or failure of the business. However, managers need to be careful that past success does not lead to failure due to resistance to change. Inertia is the term used to describe the forces that cause a company to resist change.

One of the most common means to communicate strategic direction is in a written mission statement. An organization's mission statement provides an important vehicle for communicating ideals and a sense of direction and purpose to internal and external stakeholders. It can inspire employees and managers. It can also help guide organizational managers in resource-allocation decisions. Sometimes the terms mission and vision are confused. In general, a mission is what the company is and its reason for existing, whereas a vision is a forward-looking view of what the company wants to become. However, when mission statements are written, they often include a vision statement. Many times, mission statements also include a business definition and statements about the values of an organization.

A clear business definition is the starting point of all strategic planning and management. It provides a framework for evaluating the effects of planned change, and for planning the steps needed to move the organization forward. Businesses are defined with answers to three questions: (1) Who is being satisfied? (2) What is being satisfied? (3) How are customer needs satisfied? In actuality, most business definitions also identify specific products or services provided by the organization. In this regard, a fourth question, which is an extension of the third question, can be stated as, "What are our products and services?"

While defining a business is helpful in communicating to internal and external stakeholders what the organization is all about, the business definition should not be used to limit where the company should go in the future. The business-definition question should be stated not only as "What is our business?" but also as

"What will it be?" and "What should it be?" In answering these questions, the organization should think in terms of what it knows and the assets it owns, its resources and capabilities.

An organization may expand its business definition to include markets, functions, technologies, and/or products across a broad segment of the global economy, or it may decide to move forward or backward in the industry supply chains in which it is currently participating. An industry supply chain represents the flow of goods in a manufacturing industry from their crudest forms to their final forms, where they are ultimately consumed.

The final aspect of strategic direction discussed in this chapter was the establishment of organizational values. Values guide organizational decisions and behavior. Values help determine the firms's attitude toward social responsibility and treatment of various stakeholder groups. Enterprise strategies define how a company will serve particular stakeholder needs. Many organizations create a code of ethics to communicate the values of the corporation to employees and other stakeholders.

Dealing with the ethics of employees, customers, and other stakeholders and the society from which they are drawn is considerably more difficult as organizations become global. Value conflicts are common across international boundaries. The key to overcoming cultural clashes is working to understand the host-country culture and developing strategies that are consistent with that culture instead of fighting it. Viewing problems from multiple frames of reference is an important tool for understanding the values of other cultures, since very few ethical dilemmas have simple right-or-wrong answers. Common frames of reference include economic, legal, religious, utilitarian, and universalist.

Discussion Questions

1. What, really, is an organizational mission? What is the difference between a mission and a vision? What can a mission include? Does a mission have to be formally written down to be effective?

2. What are some of the key forces influencing strategic direction in an organization? What is inertia, and how can inertia lead a successful firm to failure?

3. Describe the four elements that are critical in defining the business or businesses of an organization. Define the business of a large, diversified organization with which you are familiar. Do not use a company that was described in this chapter.

4. What is vertical integration? Please answer this question by also describing the concept of an industry supply chain.

5. What is corporate-level strategy, and how does it relate to a firm's business definition?

6. What are five common ethical frames of reference? What are their limitations?

7. Due to a decrease in demand for its products, an organization is about to lose money. Managers are considering laying off 10 percent of their workforce. This would be the first layoff in company history. Employees are not organized into a union. The decrease in demand for products is expected to last into

the foreseeable future; however, there may be other options for cutting costs. Determine the major issues to consider with regard to this problem from the perspective of each of the five ethical frames of reference.

8.   What is an enterprise strategy? Why is an enterprise strategy important to an organization?

9.   Create a mission statement for the university or college you are attending. Make any logical assumptions that are necessary to complete the task. Include all the elements of strategic direction, including vision, business definition, enterprise strategy (what the organization does for its stakeholders), and a statement of what the organization values.

Strategic Application

Identification of Strategic Direction

You may use this application to identify the strategic direction of the company in a case assigned to you or some other firm. Every firm has a strategic direction, whether it is written down or not, and whether it is a good direction or not. If a company has a formal mission statement, it may contain clues with regard to strategic direction. However, mission statements are often written primarily for public consumption and not for direction. You should identify what you perceive is the actual:

- Mission—What the organization is now (brief description of the business definition).

- Vision—Where the firm seems to be headed over the long-term (5 years or more into the future). What do managers seem to be trying to do?

- Organizational values—What does the firm stand for and which stakeholders does it seem to give highest priority?

Now evaluate this strategic direction. Is this an appropriate direction? Does it fit what is going on in the external environment? Is it likely to continue to be successful? Does it fit with the strengths and weaknesses of the organization? Is the business definition appropriate, or should the company focus on fewer areas, or expand to other areas? If you think that change is needed, you should very specifically mention what needs to be changed.

Strategic Internet Application

Go to a search engine, such as www.Google.com. Do a search for the name of a company in which you have interest (or get an assigned company from your instructor). Go to the official Web site of the company. Spend time on the Web site finding out about the businesses and strategies of your company. Most Web sites have a section called "Company Overview" or "About <company name>." Read this overview and as many other links as you need to capture the essence of what the company does. Also, by searching the Web site of a major company, you can usually find an annual report. Most often it is listed under a heading such as "Investor Information." Read portions of the annual report that deal with strategic direction, as explained in this chapter. If an annual report is not available, this type of information is almost always available somewhere else on the Web site. After you have completed your research, answer the following questions, based on whether you found a mission statement on the website or not.

If you found a written mission statement:

1. Does the mission statement contain a clear definition of the businesses of the firm? If so, what are the major businesses of the firm? Does it capture the essence of what the company is all about?

2. Does the mission statement contain a vision of what the company is trying to do or can become? If so, what is this vision? If not, what do you think this company is trying to do or become?

3. Does the mission statement contain information about the company's values? For example, does it specify which stakeholders are important and what the company intends to do for them? Does it mention anything about the way the company will conduct itself in its business dealings?

If you did not find a written mission statement:

Every firm has a strategic direction, whether it is written down or not and whether it is a good direction or not. Based on your online research, write a mission statement that contains the following:

1. *Definition of the business.* What does your company do?

2. *Vision.* Where is your company headed over the longer term (5 years+)? What do managers seem to be trying to do?

3. *Organizational Values.* What does the firm stand for? Which stakeholders seem to be given highest priority? What does the company do for these stakeholders?

Notes

1. "Stewart-Marchman Center's Mission," www.stewartmarchman.org/corporate_profile.html, 18 October 2001.
2. K. Labich, "Why Companies Fail," *Fortune,* 14 November 1994, 53.
3. L. J. Bourgeois, "Performance and Consensus," *Strategic Management Journal* 1 (1980): 227–248; G. G. Dess, "Consensus on Strategy Formulation and Organizational Performance: Competitors in a Fragmented Industry," *Strategic Management Journal* 8 (1987): 259–277; L. G. Hrebiniak and C. C. Snow, "Top Management Agreement and Organizational Performance," *Human Relations* 35 (1982): 1139–1158; Labich, "Why Companies Fail."
4. S. Nelton, "Put Your Purpose in Writing," *Nation's Business* (February 1994): 63.
5. J. Betton and G. G. Dess, "The Application of Population Ecology Models to the Study of Organizations," *Academy of Management Review* 10 (1985): 750–757.
6. T. Levitt, "Marketing Myopia," *Harvard Business Review* (July/August 1960): 45–60.
7. G. G. Dess and J. C. Picken, "Creating Competitive (Dis)advantage: Learning from Food Lion's Freefall," *Academy of Management Executive* 13, no. 3 (1999): 97–111.
8. Taken directly from Rhône-Poulenc Rorer, company documents.
9. Taken directly from Sears, *Annual Report* (2000), 7.
10. G. Hamel, *Leading the Revolution* (Boston: Harvard Business School Press, 2000), 246.
11. D. F. Abell, *Defining the Business: The Starting Point of Strategic Planning* (Englewood Cliffs, N.J.: Prentice Hall (1980), 169.
12. Abell, *Defining the Business,* 169.
13. Sara Lee Corporation, "Mission," *Annual Report* (2000), 8.
14. Sypris Solutions, Inc., www.sypris.com/home.asp, 17 October 2001.
15. Hamel, *Leading the Revolution.*
16. P. F. Drucker, *Management—Tasks, Responsibilities, Practices* (New York: Harper & Row, 1974), 74–94.
17. T. Levitt, "Marketing Myopia," *Harvard Business Review* (July/August 1960): 45–60.
18. Adapted from "The TLC Group," *Strengthening America's Competitiveness: The Blue Chip Enterprise Initiative* (Warner Books on behalf of Connecticut Mutual Life Insurance Company and the U.S. Chamber of Commerce, 1991, 156–157.
19. Hamel, *Leading the Revolution.*
20. C. H. St. John, "Toys 'R' Us," in *Strategic Management for Decision Making,* ed. M. J. Stahl and D. W. Grigsby (Boston: PWS-Kent, 1992), 648–660.
21. J. S. Bracker, "Delta Airlines," in *Strategic Management: A Choice Approach,* ed. J. R. Montanari, C. P. Morgan, and J. S. Bracker (Chicago: The Dryden Press, 1990), 657–670.
22. J. R. Galbraith and R. K. Kazanjian, *Strategy Implementation: Structure, Systems, and Process,* 2d ed. (St. Paul: West Publishing, 1986), chap. 4.
23. D. J. Isenberg, "The Tactics of Strategic Opportunism," *Harvard Business Review* (March/April, 1987): 92–97.
24. Taken directly from Pharmacia Corporation, "The Pharmacia Vision," *Annual Report* (2000), 2.

25. Eli Lilly and Company, "Overview—Our Values," www.lilly.com/about/overview/values.htm.

26. E. H. Schein, *Organizational Culture and Leadership* (San Francisco: Jossey-Bass, 1985); E. H. Schein, "The Role of the Founder in Creating Organizational Culture," *Organizational Dynamics* (Summer 1983), 14; P. Selznik, *Leadership in Administration* (Evanston, Ill.: Row, Peterson, 1957).

27. Clarkson Centre for Business Ethics, *Principles of Stakeholder Management* (Toronto: Rotman School of Management, 1999).

28. I. F. Kesner, "Crisis in the Boardroom: Fact and Fiction," *Academy of Management Executive* (February 1990): 23–35.

29. R. E. Freeman and D. R. Gilbert Jr., *Corporate Strategy and the Search for Ethics* (Englewood Cliffs, N.J.: Prentice Hall, 1988), 20.

30. L. T. Hosmer, *The Ethics of Management*, 2d ed. (Homewood, Ill.: Irwin, 1991), 103.

31. This entire discussion of ethics as ground rules was strongly influenced by M. Pastin, *The Hard Problems of Management: Gaining the Ethics Edge* (San Francisco: Jossey-Bass, 1986).

32. A. B. Carroll, "A three dimensional model of corporate social performance," *Academy of Management Review* 4 (1979): 497–505.

33. N. Deogun, "Groupe Danone Scoops up 40% Stake in Stonyfield Farm," *The Wall Street Journal*, 4 October 2001, B9.

34. F. Hoffmann-La Roche Ltd., www.roche.com /home/company/com_aim_intro/com_aim_prin c.htm, 18 October 2001).

35. General Motors, *Environmental Report*, 1995.

36. K. E. Aupperle, A. B. Carroll, and J. D. Hatfield, "An Empirical Examination of the Relationship between Corporate Social Responsibility and Profitability," *Academy of Management Journal* 28 (1985): 446–463.

37. L. T. Hosmer, "Response to 'Do Good Ethics Always Make for Good Business,'" *Strategic Management Journal* 17 (1996): 501. See also L. T. Hosmer, "Strategic Planning As If Ethics Mattered," *Strategic Management Journal* 15 (Summer Special Issue) (1994): 17–34.

38. S. W. Gellerman, "Why 'Good' Managers Make Bad Ethical Choices," *Harvard Business Review* (July/August 1986): 85–90.

39. Hosmer, "Strategic Planning"; D. Schendel and C. Hofer, *Strategic Management: A New View of Business Policy and Planning* (Boston: Little, Brown, 1979).

40. Freeman and Gilbert, *Corporate Strategy.*

41. American Red Cross, *Annual Report* (1989).

42. J.A. Pearce II and F. David, "Corporate Mission Statements: The Bottom Line," *Academy of Management Executive* (May 1987): 109–115.

43. Hosmer, *Ethics of Management.*

44. Based on information in Hosmer, *Ethics of Management.*

45. United Technologies, *Code of Ethics* (1991).

46. Taken directly from Wendy's International Inc., *2000 Summary Annual Report to Shareholders* (2000), 1.

47. J.A. Byrne, "The Best-laid Ethics Programs," *Business Week*, 9 March 1992, 67–69; D. Driscoll, "The Dow Corning Case," *Business and Society Review* 100, no. 1 (September 1998): 57–64; M. B. W. Tabor, "Ex-Dow Corning Executive Faults Company's Ethics on Implants," *The New York Times*, 23 September 1995, 10.

48. B. McCoy, "The Parable of the Sadhu," *Harvard Business Review* (September/October 1983).

49. McCoy, "Parable of the Sadhu."

50. McCoy, "Parable of the Sadhu."

51. E. Thronton, "Japan: Sexism OK with Most Coeds," *Business Week*, 24 August 1992, 13.

52. "Why Japan Must Change," *Fortune*, 9 March 1992, 66.

53. Taken directly from Algar, *Annual Report* (2000), 5.

Chapter 5

Strategy Formulation at The Business-Unit Level

Learning Objectives

After reading and discussing this chapter, you should be able to:

1. Understand the responsibilities of a business-unit manager.

2. Evaluate the effectiveness of a generic business-level strategy, based on its strengths and weaknesses and how well it fits the resources and capabilities of a firm.

3. Analyze an industry to determine its stage in the life cycle. Understand how that stage determines the appropriateness of various business strategies.

4. Appreciate the competitive dynamics found in a particular industry and the implications of those dynamics for individual firms in the industry.

5. Select an appropriate competitive strategy for a firm based on its competitive environment.

Toys "R" Us

For many years, Toys "R" Us would enter a market with one of its stores and, primarily through low prices and large product variety, overwhelm competitors and put them out of business. However, consumers grew tired of poor service, and eventually began returning to remaining rivals with better customer service. Furthermore, Wal-Mart's low-cost toys grabbed the attention of bargain shoppers, so Toys "R" Us lost much of that business also. In an effort to regain prominence, Toys "R" Us recently hired John H. Eyler Jr. away from the high-end toy merchant FAO Schwarz. Eyler is attempting to inject fun and customer service into the struggling company. To restore prestige to the dwindling brand name, the company has opened a three-story, 110,000-square-foot flagship store at 44th Street and Broadway in New York City. The store is supposed to represent what Toys "R" Us is all about at its other thirteen hundred locations scattered around the world. The store has better service, more fresh offerings, a Ferris wheel, a 20-foot T. Rex, and more firsts and exclusives. In spite of these premium features, the company claims that toy prices will remain consistent with the low prices of its regular stores. [1]

business-level strategy
Defines an organization's approach to competing in its chosen markets

Business-level strategy defines an organization's approach to competing in its chosen markets. Sometimes this type of strategy is referred to as "competitive" strategy. However, all strategies should be competitive strategies, so, to avoid confusion, this book uses the term "business level" to describe strategies within particular businesses. The new strategy of Toys "R" Us can be described as a combination of low-cost leadership and differentiation, a combination called "best value," which is increasing in popularity. Toys "R" Us achieves low cost through high volume and a massive distribution network. However, the company is also attempting to differentiate its stores in the eyes of consumers.

Some of the major strategic management responsibilities of business-level managers are listed in Table 5.1. They include establishing the overall direction of the business unit, ongoing analysis of the changing business situation, selecting a generic strategy and the specific strategies needed to carry it out (strategic posture), and managing resources to produce a sustainable competitive advantage. These responsibilities and the methods for carrying them out are similar in for-profit and nonprofit organizations.[2] They are also similar in both manufacturing and service settings. This chapter will begin with a discussion of the basis for competing in particular markets through specific business-level strategies. Attention will then turn to **competitive dynamics**—the moves and countermoves of firms and their competitors.

competitive dynamics
The moves and countermoves of firms and their competitors

Table 5.1   Major Business-Level Strategic Management Responsibilities

Major Responsibilities	Key Issues
Direction Setting	Establishment and communication of mission, vision, ethics, and long-term goals of a single business unit
	Creation and communication of shorter-term goals and objectives
Analysis of Business Situation	Compilation and assessment of information from stakeholders, broad environmental analysis, and other sources
	Internal resource analysis
	Identification of strengths, weaknesses, opportunities, threats, sources of sustainable competitive advantage
Selection of Strategy	Selection of a generic approach to competition—cost leadership, differentiation, focus, or best value
	Selection of a strategic posture—specific strategies needed to carry out the generic strategy
Management of Resources	Acquisition of resources and/or development of competencies leading to a sustainable competitive advantage
	Ensuring development of functional strategies and an appropriate organizational design (management structure) to support business strategy
	Development of control systems to ensure that strategies remain relevant and that the business unit continues to progress toward its goals

Generic Business Strategies

generic business strategies
A classification system for business-level strategies based on common strategic characteristics

Business strategies are as different as the organizations that create them. That is, no two business strategies are exactly alike. However, classifying types into **generic business strategies** helps firms identify common strategic characteristics. For example, a firm that is trying to achieve a competitive advantage by producing at lowest cost should emphasize production efficiency, low levels of administrative overhead, and high volume. Also, since generic strategies are widely understood, they provide for meaningful communication. Instead of having to explain the strategy each time, managers can simply use the generic label.

The generic strategy types proposed by Michael Porter are perhaps the most widely used and understood. Porter advanced the idea that a sustainable competitive advantage is related to the amount of value a firm creates for its most important stakeholder, the customer.[3] According to Porter, firms create superior value for customers by either offering them a basic product or service that is produced at the lowest possible cost or by offering them a preferred product or service at a somewhat higher price, where the additional value received exceeds the additional cost of obtaining it. The first option, called **low-cost leadership strategy,** is based on efficient cost production. In this book, as in practice, the terms low-cost leadership and cost leadership are used interchangeably. The second option, referred to as **differentiation,** requires the company to distinguish its products or services on the basis of an attribute such as higher quality, more-innovative features, greater selection, better service after sale, or more advertising. Both of these strategies assume that an organization is marketing its products or services to a very broad segment of the market. For example, Nucor produces low-cost steel for a wide variety of users, and Disney attempts to differentiate its entertainment products and services so as to appeal to most of society.

low-cost leadership strategy
A firm pursues competitive advantage through efficient cost production. Also called cost leadership

differentiation
Requires the firm to distinguish its products or services on the basis of an attribute such as higher quality, more innovative features, greater selection, better service after sale, or more advertising

Porter identified a third strategic option, called focus, in which companies target a narrow segment of the market. According to Porter, a firm can focus on a particular segment of the market through either low-cost leadership or differentiation. Consequently, Porter's original generic strategies were low-cost leadership, differentiation, and focus through either low cost or differentiation (for a total of four strategic approaches).

Porter referred to companies that were not pursuing a distinct generic strategy as "stuck-in-the-middle."[4] According to Porter, these uncommitted firms should have lower performance than committed firms because they lack a consistent basis for creating superior value. He argued that companies that exclusively pursue one of the generic strategies center all of their resources on becoming good at that strategy. However, since that time, many firms have been successful at pursuing elements associated with cost leadership and differentiation simultaneously. In this book, we refer to this hybrid as "best value." Increasing global competition has made a best-value strategy increasingly popular. Combining low-cost, differentiation, and best value approaches with a broad-versus-narrow market focus results in six generic-strategy types, outlined in Table 5.2. Notice that for each strategy, the term "firms attempt" is used. These are descriptions of intended strategies, and do not depend on whether the strategies are successful. For example, five firms can pursue a cost-leadership strategy, while only one of them will be the cost leader. Each of the strategy types will now be discussed in detail.

Table 5.2   Generic Business-Level Strategies

Business-Level Strategy	Broad or Narrow Market	Desired Source of Advantage	Description
Low-Cost Leadership	Broad	Lowest-Cost Production	Firms attempt to manufacture a product or provide a service at the lowest cost to the customer. The product or service is targeted at a very broad segment of the market.
Differentiation	Broad	Preferred Product or Service	Firms attempt to manufacture a product or provide a service that is preferred above the products or services of competing firms. The product or service is targeted at a very broad segment of the market.
Best Value	Broad	Low Cost & Highly Desirable Product or Service	Firms attempt to manufacture a product or provide a service that is very attractive to customers, but also produced at a reasonably low cost, thus providing the best value for the cost. The product or service is targeted at a very broad segment of the market.
Focus through Low-Cost Leadership	Narrow	Lowest-Cost Production	Firms attempt to manufacture a product or provide a service at the lowest cost to the customer within a specific segment (niche) of the market.
Focus through Differentiation	Narrow	Preferred Product or Service	Firms attempt to manufacture a product or provide a service that is preferred above the products or services of competing firms within a specific segment (niche) of the market.
Focus through Best Value	Narrow	Low Cost & Highly Desirable	Firms attempt to manufacture a product or provide a service that is very attractive to customers, but also produced at a reasonably low cost, thus providing the best value for the cost in a particular segment (niche) of the market.

Cost Leadership

Firms pursuing cost leadership set out to become the lowest-cost providers of a good or service. The broad scope of cost leaders means that they attempt to serve a large percentage of the total market. For instance, Panasonic seeks to be the cost leader in consumer electronics. Chaparral Steel is another excellent example.

 Chaparral is remarkable because, like a sculling crew that pulls in flawless synchronism, it has all the basic elements of good management—customer service, empowerment, quality training, and more—working in concert. As a result, it produces steel with a record-low 1.6 hours of labor per ton, vs. 2.4 hours for other mini-mills and 4.9 hours for integrated producers. Making such products as skyscraper beams and concrete-reinforcing rods, Chaparral is in a down-and-dirty commodity business. But by sticking to its low-cost philosophy, it has shown that any company can make money in a mature industry, even when times are tough.

Behind Chaparral's success is a mild-mannered CEO Gordon Forward, a native of British Columbia with a Ph.D. in metallurgy. Texas Industries, a cement company that owns 81 percent of Chaparral, asked Forward in 1975 to leave his job at a Canadian steel company to help

Chapter 5   Strategy Formulation at the Business-Unit Level   **151**

found a mini-mill. To become the world's low cost producer, he focused on three ideas: the classless corporation, universal education, and freedom to act. In return for extraordinary freedom and trust (i.e., employees don't punch a clock), workers are expected to take the initiative, use their heads, and get the job done. To help them use their noggins, Chaparral makes sure that at least 85 percent of its 950 employees are enrolled in courses, cross-training in such varied disciplines as electronics, metallurgy, and credit history.[5]

To fully appreciate the significance of the cost-leadership strategy, it is important to understand the factors that underlie cost structures in firms. Companies pursuing a low-cost strategy will typically employ one or more of the following factors to create their low-cost positions: (1) accurate demand forecasting combined with high capacity utilization, (2) economies of scale, (3) technological advances, (4) outsourcing, or (5) learning/experience effects.[6] These factors will now be explained.

High Capacity Utilization

When demand is high and production capacity is fully utilized, a firm's fixed costs are spread over more units, which lowers unit costs. However, when demand falls off, the fixed costs are spread over fewer units, so unit costs increase. This basic concept suggests that a firm that is able to maintain higher levels of capacity utilization, either through better demand forecasting, conservative capacity-expansion policies, or aggressive pricing, will be able to maintain a lower cost structure than a competitor of equal size and capability.

 Williams Companies is one of the world's biggest pipeline companies. It builds steel pipelines that transport natural gas, and fiber-optic pipelines that can carry Internet traffic. To Williams, both businesses are essentially the same. "There are a lot of analogies between steel pipes and fiber pipes," says Chief Executive Keith Bailey. "Whether it's a piece of glass or a piece of steel," costs drop steeply as transport volume grows, he says. Riding that declining cost curve to profit is Williams's strategy. And that means sticking with its formula of big pipeline projects and big customers. In other words, Williams has found its core business.[7]

High capacity utilization is particularly important in industries in which fixed costs represent a large percentage of total costs (highly **capital-intensive** industries). In these situations, entry barriers exist that make industry participants extremely sensitive to even small fluctuations in customer demand. For example, in the pulp-and-paper industry and in the chemical-processing industry, fixed costs are high, and small variations in demand can cause wide fluctuations in profitability. In these types of businesses, where capacity utilization is so important, companies that are faced with falling demand typically attempt to stimulate sales by employing massive price-cutting.

Economies of Scale

The second major factor with the potential to lead to cost advantages is economies of scale. Economies of scale are often confused with increases in the "throughput" of a manufacturing plant or other facility. As described above, increases in capacity utilization that spread fixed expenses can lead to lower unit costs. However, true

capital intensity
The extent to which the assets of an organization are primarily associated with plants, equipment, and other fixed assets

economies of scale are associated with size rather than capacity utilization. The central principle of economies of scale is that in some industries, production costs per unit are less in a large facility than in a small facility. For example, the cost of constructing a 200,000-unit facility will not necessarily be twice the cost of building a 100,000-unit facility, so the initial fixed cost per unit of capacity will be lower.

Other scale economies are also evident in many industries. Continuing with the previous example, the manager of the larger facility will not generally receive double the salary of the manager of the smaller facility. Also, activities such as quality control, purchasing, and warehousing typically do not require twice as much time or twice as many laborers. In addition, the purchasing manager of the larger facility may be able to negotiate better volume discounts on orders. In summary, the larger firm may be able to achieve per-unit savings in fixed costs, indirect labor costs, and materials costs. If per-unit costs are not lower in the larger plant, then the company has not achieved economies of scale. In fact, diseconomies of scale occur when a firm builds facilities that are so large that the sheer administrative costs and confusion associated with the added bureaucracy overwhelm any potential cost savings.

Technological Advances

Companies that make investments in cost-saving technologies are often trading an increase in fixed costs for a reduction in variable costs. If technological improvements result in lower total-unit costs, then firms have achieved a cost advantage from their investments referred to as economies of technology.[8] While investments of this type are typically associated with the factory floor, it is just as common for investments to be made in office and service automation. For example, the automated distribution system at Wal-Mart, the automated ordering and warehouse system at Lands' End, and the reservation systems maintained by the major airlines all represent investments in technology that serve to lower overall costs and provide a degree of information and product control that was previously impossible. The order-filling technology of Amazon.com is designed to keep costs at a minimum.

 Several hundred—many young, unmarried, and well educated—work at the Seattle premises in gigantic landscaped offices split into tiny, shared cubicles. With their headsets plugged in and their eyes glued to the screen, they handle millions of e-mail orders a year. Some managers at Amazon refer to them as 'electronic peasants,' for when they are on-line with a customer they are not supposed to show off their literary skills. The focus in these modern times is on output: twelve e-mails an hour, and the sack for anyone who drops below seven and a half. On the phone, any conversation exceeding four minutes, in a voice that, according to a former employee, 'is supposed to be loud enough for the customer to hear and quiet enough to keep from distracting cubical mates,' earns the guilty party a warning. [9]

Outsourcing

Traditional thinking in management was that organizations should perform as many value-adding functions as possible in-house in order to retain control of the production process and gain technological efficiencies through creating synergies among processes. However, competitive reality has set in, and corporations realize that sometimes another company can perform a process better or more efficiently

outsourcing
Contracting with another firm to provide goods or services that were previously supplied from within the company. Similar to subcontracting

than they can. This has led to **outsourcing,** which means contracting with another firm to provide goods or services that were previously supplied from within the company. Ericsson, a leading supplier of telecommunications equipment with operations in more than 140 countries, actively pursues outsourcing to retain strategic flexibility.

> **Ex.** Ericsson signed a contract to outsource IT service and support to Compaq. The agreement covered twenty thousand end users in Ericsson's Swedish-based companies. Compaq will assume responsibility for "technology refresh, server management, help-desk and desk-side support, maintenance, and implementation services." The initial phase of the project included transfer of 170 employees from Ericsson to Compaq. According to Ericsson's chief information officer: "The agreement with Compaq is an important link in Ericsson's IT standardization agenda. Customers demand easy access to Ericsson and to our services. Flexibility in a truly global organization requires standardization of the IT platform." In addition to outsourcing itself, Ericsson also performs functions that are outsourced by others. For example, Telecom New Zealand signed an outsourcing agreement with Ericsson to operate and manage its entire mobile network, including "monitoring and surveillance of the end-to-end services, network performance improvements, hardware support and also managing the field and maintenance staff."[10]

Although firms can sometimes gain efficiency through outsourcing, it is important that they continue to control production of the unique features that provide competitive advantage to the company. In other words, they should "nurture a few core competencies in the race to stay ahead of rivals."[11] According to one Ericsson manager, "Outsourcing allows us to concentrate resources on our core business. . ."[12]

Learning Effects

learning curve
Demonstrates that the time required to complete a task will decrease as a predictable function of the number of times the task is repeated

A final factor that influences cost structures is learning effects.[13] You probably spent a long time the first time you registered for classes as a freshman. Now, as a veteran of several registrations, you know how to get through the process much faster. When an employee learns to do a job more efficiently with repetition, then learning is taking place. The **learning curve** effect says that the time required to complete a task will decrease as a predictable function of the number of times the task is repeated. In theory, the time required to complete the task will fall by the same percentage each time cumulative production doubles. For example, a firm might see a 10 percent reduction in the time required to manufacture its products between the first and second unit of product, another 10 percent reduction between the second and fourth units, and another 10 percent reduction between the fourth and eighth unit.

Clearly, dramatic time savings are achieved early in the life of a company. However, as the company matures, tangible cost savings from labor learning are harder to achieve because it takes longer to see a true doubling of cumulative volume, and because most of the opportunities for learning have already been exploited. Also, learning effects do not just happen. They require a relatively labor-intensive process since people learn but machines do not. Learning effects occur only when management creates an environment that is favorable to both learning and change, and then rewards employees for their productivity improvements.

There are many factors that can interfere with the achievement of learning effects. Products and processes that frequently change create an environment where employees do not gain sufficient experience with a particular activity and cannot improve upon it. Also, the technological innovations of competitors can wipe out a company's cost advantages from learning.

Learning effects can be described by a curve such as the one found in Figure 5.1.[14] Following from the logic of this curve, the market-share leader should enjoy a cost advantage relative to competitors because of the extra learning and experience that has occurred by producing the additional output. This concept has led many firms to fight aggressively on price in order to obtain the highest market share and thus move to the right on the curve as far as possible. As the curve flattens, it becomes increasingly difficult to gain cost advantages from learning and experience effects. The same sort of phenomenon exists with respect to economies of scale.

Companies that are able to achieve the lowest cost do not have to charge the lowest price. In other words, a *cost* leader does not have to be a *price* leader. If an organization is able to achieve the lowest cost, but charge a price that is the same as competitors, then it will still enjoy higher profits. However, if the low-cost producer's price is the same as or higher than the price others charge, then customers may switch to competing products, which can undermine the low-cost producer's efforts to benefit from capacity utilization, learning effects, or other sources of low cost. Consequently, many low-cost producers try to underprice competitors slightly in order to give customers an incentive to buy from them, and to keep their volumes high enough to support their low-cost strategies.

Risks Associated with a Cost-Leadership Strategy

There are some risks associated with a cost-leadership strategy. Firms pursuing cost leadership may not detect required product or marketing changes because of a preoccupation with cost. They run the risk of making large investments in plants or equipment only to see them become obsolete because of technological breakthroughs. Their large investments make them reluctant to keep up with changes that are not compatible with their technologies. Another risk is that competitors will quickly imitate the technologies that are resulting in lower costs. As Michael Porter observed, "A company can outperform rivals only if it can establish a difference it can preserve."[15]

Another risk associated with a cost-leadership strategy is that the company will go too far and perhaps even endanger customers or employees in the process. ValuJet's "penny-pinching" allowed it to achieve a very low cost position in the airline industry. ValuJet passed the savings on to consumers and experienced

FIGURE 5.1

A Typical Learning Curve

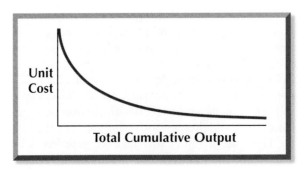

unprecedented growth. However, their stinginess came under close scrutiny after the crash of ValuJet flight 592 into the Florida Everglades. Federal investigators found some of ValuJet's procedures, especially maintenance procedures, unsafe, and ultimately shut down the airline until safety concerns could be worked out.[16]

Differentiation

In differentiation strategies, the emphasis is on creating value through uniqueness, as opposed to lowest cost. Uniqueness can be achieved through product innovations, superior quality, superior service, creative advertising, better supplier relationships, or in an almost unlimited number of other ways. The key to success is that customers must be willing to pay more for the uniqueness of a product or service than the firm paid to create it. As in the cost-leadership strategy, an organization pursuing a differentiation strategy is targeting a broad market; consequently, the differentiated product or service should be designed so that it has wide appeal to many market sectors. Examples of organizations that are pursuing differentiation strategies include Maytag, through its highly reliable appliances; L.L. Bean, through its reliable, high-quality mail-order services; and Coca-Cola, through promoting its well-known brand name.

 Google, the well-known search engine company, pursues a strategy that is unique in its industry. When a user submits a query, most search engine companies provide a list of links based on how much advertisers are paying them. For example, if a user puts in 'rental car,' the company will return a list of rental car companies in an order based on how much each rental company pays them. However, Google will try to pinpoint exactly what a user wants. Furthermore, Google does not accept banner adds. The result is that users get what they want in a relatively clutter-free environment. The browser technology is so good that other companies, such as Yahoo, pay Google to use it.[17]

Companies pursuing differentiation strategies cannot ignore their cost positions. When costs are too high relative to competitors, a firm may not be able to recover enough of the additional costs through higher prices. Therefore, differentiators have to keep costs low in the areas that are not directly related to the sources of differentiation. The only way a differentiation strategy will work is if the attributes that make a product unique are sufficiently valued by buyers so that the buyers are willing to pay a higher price for the product or choose to buy from that firm preferentially.

Resource-Based Differentiation

Chapter 3 contained a detailed discussion of resource-based sources of competitive advantage. No attempt will be made to repeat that discussion here. However, it is worth mentioning that some resources are more likely to lead to a source of sustainable differentiation. For example, reputations and brands are very difficult to imitate, whereas particular product or service features may be easy to imitate (unless protected by patents). An organizational culture that fosters a high level of customer service is hard to imitate, whereas a particular customer-service policy is easy to imitate. In general, intangible resources are more likely to lead to a sustainable advantage than are tangible resources. Intangible resources are associated with what internal stakeholders know or how they are organized, as well as with how external stakeholders feel about a particular organization or its products or how they are linked to the organization.

Risks Associated with a Differentiation Strategy

It is important to recognize that the difference in value may be a result of buyer perceptions rather than actual product or service attributes. For example, effective advertising may result in a strong brand preference even though the products in an industry are essentially the same (e.g., beer). Consequently, the major risks associated with a differentiation strategy center on the difference between added costs and incremental price. One risk is that customers will sacrifice some of the features, services, or image possessed by a unique product or service because it costs too much. For instance, NeXT computers were designed to be absolutely state–of–the–art. If you haven't heard of NeXT, that is because the venture, led by Steven Jobs, was largely unsuccessful. Another risk is that customers will no longer perceive an attribute as differentiating. They may come to a point at which they are so familiar with a product that brand image is no longer important.

If a source of differentiation is easy to imitate, then imitation by competitors can also eliminate perceived differentiation among products or services. This is what happened when a VCR manufacturer introduced the "HQ" (high-quality) feature into VCRs. Within a few months, all VCRs had "HQ," thus eliminating any basis for higher prices based on the "HQ" feature. Rivalry in an industry can make it very difficult to sustain a competitive advantage from innovation for very long. For example, competitors are able to obtain detailed information on 70 percent of all new products within one year after development.[18] Consequently, staying ahead of the competition in product development requires *constant* innovation. As one business writer put it: "For outstanding performance, a company has to beat the competition. The trouble is the competition has heard the same message."[19]

Best Value

Some strategy scholars argue that a combination of strategic elements from both differentiation and low cost may be necessary to create a sustainable competitive advantage: "The immediate effect of differentiation will be to increase unit costs. However, if costs fall with increasing volume, the long-run effect may be to reduce unit costs."[20] Volume is expected to increase because differentiation makes the product more attractive to the market. Then, as volume increases, costs will decrease. For example, Anheuser-Busch has been very successful in creating brewing products that have a good image and high quality, yet A-B is a cost leader due to efficiencies created by high-volume production and sales. Kellogg, best known for breakfast cereals, enjoys a similar situation of low-cost production due to economies of scale combined with higher prices made possible due to differentiation through advertising and new-product development.

Consumers are coming to expect a combination of high quality and low price.[21] John F. "Jack" Welch, a very famous CEO of General Electric, described the situation this way:

> We're playing in a game where we'll show up and we'll be selling an engine against another engine competitor. Now, to get the deal, you've got to have performance and all the other things, but you'd better have low cost. And as you go around the world, and you want to sell turbines to developing countries, you'd better have a low cost base. Because in the end, you could have performance, you can have quality, but you'd better have cost.[22]

best-value strategy
A firm pursues elements associated with cost leadership and differentiation simultaneously

The key to a **best-value strategy** is simple supply-and-demand economics. For example, assume that three organizations manufacture hunting knives. The first firm pursues a low-cost strategy. It is able to produce a knife for $10, and to sell one hundred thousand a year at $16—for a total profit of $600,000. On the other hand, the second firm uses a differentiation strategy. It produces a premium product with features that the market finds attractive. The premium product costs $40 to make. The firm can sell fifty thousand at $60. The total profit is $1 million. Both companies seem to be successful; however, they are each achieving success using a different generic strategy.

However, assume that a third company can create a very good product, through a variety of product and process technological advances, for $20. This product is almost as appealing as the product of the second firm. The third firm can sell 75,000 at $50. The total profit is more than $2 million, and consumers believe they are getting a great deal (saving $10). This is the essence of a best-value strategy—finding a level of differentiation that will bring a premium price while doing so at a reasonable cost. Unlike a differentiation strategy, in which the emphasis is on creating extra value, or a low-cost strategy, which stresses cutting costs, the best-value strategy gives approximately equal weight to both factors, while perhaps not maximizing either one. Wal-Mart has been successful with it. General Electric is pursuing it across a wide range of markets. It just may be the premier strategy of the future.

Technology is often a big part of a successful best-value strategy. Wal-Mart is successful at providing a large variety of high-quality products to customers at low cost. A key part of Wal-Mart's strategy is a technologically advanced distribution system that allows fast and efficient delivery of products.[23] Porter, who originally argued that it would be unlikely that a firm could successfully pursue cost leadership and differentiation simultaneously, conceded that such advances may allow a company to successfully pursue both strategies at the same time.[24] Many organizations have been pursuing best-value strategies through an emphasis on quality or speed.

Quality

Much has been said and written on the topic of quality. According to the American Assembly, which consisted of sixty-five leaders of business, labor, government, and academia: "This does not mean quality merely to specifications but that improves constantly, quality that is characterized by constant innovations that create a loyal customer. It means achieving this attitude from top to bottom, from the board room to the factory floor."[25] W. Edwards Deming, an expert on quality, argued that producing higher-quality products though superior designs also reduces manufacturing costs.[26] Also, high-quality production eliminates waste through reducing the amount of rework and minimizing the amount of discarded final products. It is less expensive to produce ten products right the first time than to build eleven products and have to throw one away because of quality defects.

Many organizations have implemented in the past, and some are still pursuing, Total Quality Management (TQM) programs in an effort to improve quality. The principles of TQM are presented in Table 5.3. TQM is so comprehensive in its scope that virtually all parts of an organization are affected.

Six Sigma
A philosophy based on minimizing the number of defects found in a manufacturing operation or service function

Six Sigma has also had a pervasive effect on organizations in the United States and elsewhere. It is a philosophy based on minimizing the number of defects found in a manufacturing operation or service function. The term comes from Sigma, the Greek letter that statisticians use to define one standard deviation from the center of the normal bell-shaped curve. At one Sigma, about one-third of whatever is being

Table 5.3   Principles of Total Quality Management

General

1. Get to know the next and final customer.
2. Get to know the direct competition, and the world-class leaders (whether competitors or not).
3. Dedicate to continual, rapid improvement in quality, response time, flexibility, and cost.
4. Achieve unified purpose via extensive sharing of information and involvement in planning and implementation of change.

Design and Organization

5. Cut the number of components or operations and number of suppliers to a few good ones.
6. Organize resources into chains of customers, each chain mostly self-contained and focused on a product or customer "family."

Operations

7. Cut flow time, distance, inventory, and space along the chain of customers.
8. Cut setup, changeover, get-ready, and start-up time.
9. Operate at the customer's rate of use (or a smoothed representation of it).

Human Resource Development

10. Continually invest in human resources through cross-training (for mastery), education, job switching, and multi-year cross-career reassignments; and improved health, safety, and security.
11. Develop operator-owners of products, processes, and outcomes via broadened owner-like reward and recognition.

Quality and Process Improvement

12. Make it easier to produce or provide the product without mishap or process variation.
13. Record and own quality, process, and mishap data at the workplace.
14. Ensure that front-line associates get first chance at process improvement—before staff experts.

Accounting and Control

15. Cut transactions and reporting; control causes and measure performance at the source, not via periodic cost reports.

Capacity

16. Maintain/improve present resources and human work before thinking about new equipment and automation.
17. Automate incrementally when process variability cannot otherwise be reduced.
18. Seek to have multiple work stations, machines, flow lines, cells for each product or customer family.

Marketing and Sales

19. Market and sell your firm's increasing customer-oriented capabilities and competencies.

Source: R.J. Schonberger, "Is Strategy Strategic? Impact of Total Quality Management on Strategy," *Academy of Management Executive* (August 1992): 83, used with permission.

observed falls outside the range. Two Sigmas means that about 5 percent falls outside the range. Six Sigmas is so far out that virtually nothing is out there. This is the goal with regard to the number of defects that are considered acceptable.

 In consultant-speak, it denotes the path to a corporate nirvana where everything—from product design to manufacturing to billing—proceeds without a hitch. In engineer-speak, it means no more than 3.4 defects per million widgets or procedures. In practice, Six Sigma is a statistical quality-control method that combines the art of the efficiency expert with the science of the computer geek. And a growing group of big, no-nonsense companies such as Allied Signal, Motorola, and General Electric swear by it. "Six Sigma has galvanized our company with an intensity the likes of which I have never seen in my forty years at GE," says John F. Welch, the chairman of General Electric.[27]

Although quality is extremely important, it does not guarantee success. The ability of quality to lead to sustainable differentiation depends on how long it takes for rivals to imitate the quality difference. For example, in the personal computer industry, in which product components are easily interchangeable, quality is easy to imitate. It is also difficult for firms competing in this segment to differentiate their products because many of the components of personal computers are manufactured by a core group of suppliers who sell to all competitors. As described in Chapter 3, if a resource or capability is easy to imitate, then it cannot provide a basis for a sustainable competitive advantage. Consequently, some PC manufacturers have turned to speed as a source of best value.

Speed

Speed is a powerful competitive weapon in some industries. If an organization can reduce the time it takes to provide a good or service, costs are likely to be reduced while customers may also be happier because their desires are satisfied more quickly. Dell Computer is a master at speed. Dell can make and deliver a computer within a day of receiving the order.

 Dell makes its OptiPlex desktop computers at a 250,000-square-foot facility called Metric 12 in Austin, Texas. Bar-code readers flicker incessantly as they follow each PC on its journey down the line. A steady stream of trucks drops off raw materials from suppliers and picks up finished computers. A Dell employee walks along the production line to show where the company's engineers have sped up production, bit by tiny bit (collectively, Dell engineers have more than two hundred process-related patents). Workers used to touch a computer 130 times in the process of assembling it; that number is down to sixty. At one station near the beginning of the line, workers attach mother-boards and power-supply units to a computer's chassis. This effort, which once required six screws, now takes one. Farther down, a forklift-like tool called the stacker moves piled PCs in groups of five; workers used to move them one at a time.[28]

Speed is sometimes accompanied by a flexible-manufacturing system (FMS), a battery of sophisticated machine tools that allow the manufacture of immense varieties of products in the same plant. A good illustration is Benetton, which has orders electronically relayed to manufacturing sites where computer-automated-design systems, which contain all of the specifications for various clothing items, control the machinery that make the clothes. Not only is the system fast, but Benetton employs only eight people in its warehouse, which ships 230,000 items of clothing daily.[29] In another example, Michelin, the French tire manufacturer, unveiled its "C3M" manufacturing process, which is a simultaneous manufacturing system designed to increase flexibility in manufacturing while cutting factory size and the required number of workers.[30]

Risks Associated with a Best-Value Strategy

To review, cost leadership is associated with risks (1) that a firm will become preoccupied with cost and lose sight of the market, (2) that technological breakthroughs will make process-cost savings obsolete, (3) that competitors will quickly imitate any sources of cost advantage, and (4) that the company will take the cost-reduction emphasis too far, thus endangering stakeholders. The risks associated with differentiation are (1) that the company will spend more to differentiate its product or service than it can recover in the selling price, (2) that competitors will quickly imitate the source of differentiation, and (3) that the source of differentiation will no longer be considered valid by customers.

A best-value strategy represents somewhat of a trade-off between the risks of a cost-leadership strategy and the risks of a differentiation strategy. The risk that technological breakthroughs will make the strategy obsolete is as much a problem with best value as it is with cost leadership. Also, the risk of imitation, found in both of the other two strategies, is evident in a best-value strategy as well. On the other hand, a firm pursuing best value is unlikely to become preoccupied with either cost or differentiation, but rather, should try to balance these two factors. Also, the company probably would not be prone to take the cost-saving strategy too far, thus endangering employees or customers. Finally, because of the balance between cost and differentiation, a firm pursing a best-value strategy is less likely than a pure differentiator to put so much into differentiating a product that the company will be unable to recover the additional costs through the selling price.

Focus

focus strategy
A firm targets a narrow segment of the market through low-cost leadership, differentiation, or a combination of low cost and differentiation

Focus strategies can be based on differentiation, lowest cost, or best value. The key to a **focus strategy** is providing a product or service that caters to a particular segment in the market. Firms pursuing focus strategies have to be able to identify their target market segment and both assess and meet the needs and desires of buyers in that segment better than any other competitor.

Cooper Tire & Rubber is an example of a company that pursues a focus strategy through cost leadership. Cooper is the only major tire company that does not sell tires to automobile manufacturers in the original-equipment market (OEM). Instead, the company focuses on replacement tires. Cooper is very efficiency oriented: "Its low-rise corporate headquarters could pass for a 1950s suburban elementary school, right down to the linoleum floors and the flagpole out front. The annual report is printed in living black and white."[31] Cooper saves on R&D costs by copying the designs of OEM manufacturers instead of designing its own products. The cost-focus strategy is so successful that Cooper provides the highest returns to its investors of any firm in the tire industry.

On the other hand, Porsche pursues a differentiation-focus strategy. The focus is on elite consumers. One time a group of students was taking a plant tour at Porsche headquarters in Germany. One of the students, looking at a particularly stylish sports car, asked the tour guide, who was a high official in the company, how Porsche had managed to create a bumper that was so elegant and yet conformed to U.S. safety regulations. This top company official told the student that Porsche had simply poured enough money into the bumper to make it work. This example demonstrates that Porsche spares no expense in meeting the precise needs and desires of its target customer.

Finally, focus through best value is probably more difficult than a broader best-value strategy because the narrow market focus means lower volume. At lower volume, it is hard to achieve low cost while still providing meaningful differentiation. Nevertheless, this is still an effective strategy for some firms. SawTech Corporation focuses on the precision-dicing-and-scribing industry through a best-value strategy.

The company seeks to "exceed customer expectations" by focusing on excellence and customer satisfaction, yet SawTech also seeks to keep costs at a minimum. Like companies that pursue best-cost strategies for broader markets, SawTech emphasizes speed and a rapid turnaround of customer orders. Also, the firm has implemented a rigorous quality-assurance program.[32]

The risks of pursuing a focus strategy depend on whether the strategy is pursued through differentiation, cost leadership, or best value. The risks of each of these strategies are similar to the risks faced by adopters of the pure strategies themselves. However, the focus strategy has two risks that are not associated with any of the three pure strategies. First, the desires of the narrow target market may become similar to the desires of the market as a whole, thus eliminating the advantage associated with focusing. Second, a competitor may be able to focus on an even more narrowly defined target and essentially "outfocus the focuser."

This completes our discussion of generic strategies. We have also devoted considerable attention to how to successfully implement those strategies. Low-cost leadership may be achieved through high capacity utilization, scale economies, technological advances, outsourcing, and learning effects. Differentiation is pursued on the basis of providing a preferred product or service. Meaningful differentiation can be achieved through a variety of firm resources and capabilities; however, the intangible resources tend to provide a more sustainable advantage. Best-value strategies combine elements from both differentiation and cost leadership. Many firms are pursuing a best-value strategy through an emphasis on quality or speed. Focus strategies apply one of the generic orientations to a specific market niche.

Business-level strategies should be formulated based on the existing or potential resources and abilities of the organization. However, they should also be selected based on how well the resulting products and services are expected to be received in the market. Otherwise, an organization might develop a wonderful product or service that is largely unsuccessful. "It would be a little like having a concert pianist in a street gang who has a skill that is unique in that environment, but that hardly helps to attain the gang's goals."[33]

Strategy and the Life Cycle

Strategies need regular adjustment. Organizations often find that a strategy that performed well in the past is no longer viable. The expectations of customers and the actions and abilities of competitors change constantly, which creates a dynamic environment in which strategies are formulated. In particular, a strategy that is appropriate at one point in the life of an industry may be inappropriate at another point.

Although there are certainly exceptions, industries tend to evolve along similar paths, creating somewhat predictable conditions, or stages, for strategy development. Although the stages of an industry life cycle do not dictate which business strategies should be chosen, they can help a strategist understand the context within which the chosen strategy will be implemented and the likely strategies of competitors. As an industry moves through the stages of the life cycle, different strategies and organizational resources are needed to compete effectively.

industry life cycle
Portrays how sales volume for a product category changes over time, from the introduction stage through the commodity or decline stage

The **industry life cycle** portrays how sales volume for a product category changes over its lifetime. As Figure 5.2 illustrates, demand gradually builds during the introduction stage, as customers come to understand the product and its uses. During the growth stage, demand greatly increases as product variations proliferate, new customer groups are developed, and new product applications are identified. Growth opportunities tend to attract new competitors, which intensifies efforts to achieve differentiation. Sales growth eventually begins to level off during the maturity stage of the life cycle, because markets are fully penetrated and opportunities for additional market growth or new applications are limited. This slowing of growth can lead to a competitive "shakeout" of weaker producers, resulting in fewer competitors.

During the commodity, or decline, stage, demand patterns can take on many shapes. The traditional curve is labeled *C* in Figure 5.2. This curve is fairly accurate with regard to a very specific individual product. For example, the original Nintendo video-game system was introduced and became very popular during the growth stage. However, after a few years, several factors, such as market saturation and an increase in popularity of competing products, led to a decrease in demand for the original system. Nevertheless, it is important to point out that demand for video-game systems as a group did not decline. Furthermore, the broader industry (e.g., electronic games) did not decline. Decline was associated only with the original system.

Whole product groups or whole industries rarely follow the path labeled *C*, and if they do decline in sales, it tends to happen after a long time has elapsed since the introduction of the original product. If the products of an industry become a commodity, which means they are used in many other products or become a basic part of life for some consumers, demand may just level off, as in *B*, or may gradually increase over an extended time period, represented by *A*.[34]

Understanding the industry life cycle helps an organization understand demand, but can also help the organization formulate strategies.[35] During the introduction stage, as demand for a product gradually builds, companies are concerned primarily with survival—producing the product at a low enough cost and selling it at a high enough price so that they will be able to sustain operations and enter the next stage of the life cycle. The competitive environment at this stage is often turbulent and fragmented. Often customer needs for the new product are not that well understood, and new firms enter with different product versions and new methods.

FIGURE 5.2

The Industry Life Cycle

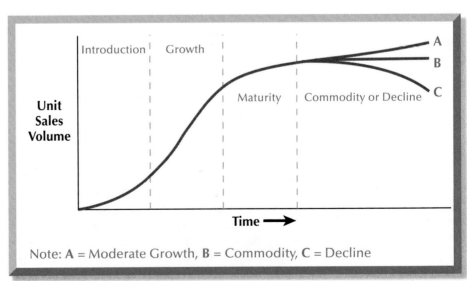

Note: **A** = Moderate Growth, **B** = Commodity, **C** = Decline

Those firms that identify, through their product and market development, those characteristics that matter most to customers are likely to be the most successful. Since businesses often lose money during this stage, this is a difficult challenge.

In the introduction stage, firms also attempt to produce a product that is of sufficiently high quality that they will be able to establish a good reputation in the market. The emphasis is often on research and development, and on market-penetration strategies. Early producers sometimes enjoy a "first-mover advantage" because of the experience they are gaining, the image they have the opportunity to build, and the opportunity they may have to create barriers to entry such as patents or exclusive distribution channels.[36] There is some evidence to support these ideas.[37] In fact, products sometimes come to be associated with early innovators, as in the case of Scott towels, Scotch tape, Linoleum floor coverings, and Xerox machines.

During the growth stage, sales volume increases as the number of competitors increases and as those competitors all pursue various market-penetration, market-development, applications-development, and product-development strategies. Industry competitors also attempt to differentiate themselves to customers through advertising or through new features and services. It is during the growth stage that some competitors will begin to gain the benefits of size. They will build plants that are large enough to enjoy economies of scale, locking in contracts for supplies or distribution of products, or differentiating products through advertising and new features or service. During the latter part of the growth stage, customer expectations will become more standardized, and competitors will begin to offer similar products of similar quality. Since products of the industry are increasingly similar, price will become more of a factor in the purchase decision. As growth begins to level off toward the end of the growth stage, price competition heats up, and some firms fail to develop product characteristics that customers value, or else try to grow faster than their resources allow. A competitive shakeout usually occurs. Since the market is no longer growing at an increasing rate, the weaker competitors discover that they can no longer generate enough sales or profits to sustain themselves. They sell off their assets, declare bankruptcy, or are acquired by stronger competitors.

During the maturity stage, as demand continues to level off, efficient, high-volume production tends to dominate manufacturing strategy. Since price is now one of the most important factors in the purchase decision, competitors must pursue cost reductions as a way to stay profitable. A dominant design for the product has probably emerged at this point, and therefore consumers typically focus on price and service. When an organization discovers a successful innovation, it is quickly incorporated into other firm's products. Consequently, product differentiation becomes increasingly difficult. Often firms will shift their focus from market penetration and product development to process development that will reduce costs and to international market development to support large-volume operations. Marketing, distribution efficiency, and low-cost operations gain increasing importance during this stage.

Finally, during the commodity, or decline, stage, tight cost controls leading to efficiency are essential to success. Since the product has become highly standardized at this point, price is still a very important basis for competition. Competition is intense, and firms may begin to drop out again, especially if demand completely levels off and exit barriers are low. Examples of exit barriers that might cause organizations to resist leaving the industry include owning a lot of assets that cannot be used for anything else, high costs of terminating contracts or tearing down buildings, or social costs such as laying off workers.[38]

Most of the world's industries have already matured, and are represented by one of the demand curves on the right side of Figure 5.2. However, even mature industries can experience growth in some product segments due to product innovations or other forms of differentiation that make older products undesirable or obsolete. To avoid the full effects of decline, companies may focus on a particular niche in the market that is still growing. Or, as demonstrated in Figure 5.3, innovative firms may be able to introduce a product that totally replaces the old product and makes it obsolete. For example, microcomputers replaced typewriters, and cassette tapes, followed by compact discs, replaced records. Finally, some organizations may just "hang on" until other firms have dropped out, at which time reduced competition can result in improved profitability and market share.[39] This is happening right now in the tobacco industry.

One of the lessons that we learn from the product life cycle is that organizations must adapt as their products move through the stages of evolution. Markets and industries are constantly changing. Consequently, a good product or service is not enough to ensure success over the longer term. Organizational managers need to evaluate and respond to the competitive dynamics within their industries.

Competitive Dynamics

Even well-designed strategies may not be as successful as anticipated due to the reactions of competitors. For instance, suppose an organization decides to pursue a low-cost-leadership strategy through cutting product price to increase sales volume. To meet anticipated demand, the company builds a larger, more technologically advanced plant that makes production more efficient. However, when the firm cuts prices, competitors do likewise. So the organization launches a major advertising campaign. Competitors also increase advertising. These actions may increase demand in the industry as a whole, but the increased demand probably is not enough to cover the increased expenses and loss of profit margins. The result is that the organization still has approximately the same market share as before, with an expensive new plant that is not being fully utilized.

creative destruction
The inevitable decline of leading firms because competitors will pursue creative opportunities to eliminate the competitive advantages they hold

Competitive dynamics are particularly important because of what a well-known economist, Joseph Schumpeter, called **"creative destruction."**[40] Creative destruction describes the inevitable decline of leading firms due to competitive moves and countermoves. Competitors pursue creative opportunities in an attempt to eliminate the competitive advantages of market leaders. As long as the playing field is level, which means that the government enforces rules of fair competition, eventually competitors will succeed. The principle of creative destruction can also be understood in terms of the process illustrated in Figure 5.3. Basically, as a firm's product begins to decline, another product is introduced to replace it. For a company to remain the market leader, it must constantly outpace its competitors in creating its own replacement products. Bill Gates, CEO of Microsoft, once said that his company is always only a few years away from potential failure because at any time a competitor could produce a product that is better than Windows. Intel, once dominant in producing state-of-the-art microprocessing chips, now has another major rival with which to contend.

 Advanced Micro Devices (AMD) was founded at about the same time as Intel by Jerry Sanders, a former employee of Fairchild Semiconductor. Mr. Sanders once described Intel as "a fascist organization that uses

FIGURE 5.3

Breaking Out of the Product Life Cycle

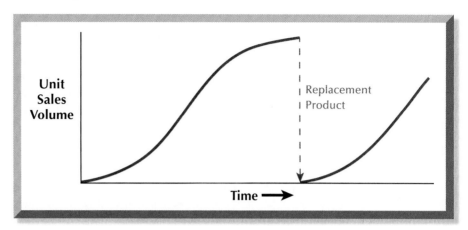

intimidation to make our lives difficult." Although AMD is the leader in "flash" chips (used in small electronic devices), anytime they have made headway in the highly profitable microprocessing segment, "Intel's zealous marketers found some way to thwart AMD, often by putting the squeeze on customers or by offering them advertising subsidies that they couldn't refuse in return for exclusive supply agreements." AMD filed an antitrust suit against Intel, but the suit was largely unsuccessful. In fact, the final settlement prevented AMD from building microprocessing chips that would simply plug into Intel's circuitry. AMD would have to design its own PC circuitry. In the end, this would help AMD score a major competitive victory.

The speed of a PC is dependent both on the speed of the microprocessing chip at the heart of the system and on the efficiency with which some lower-tech chips called "chipsets" handle the flow of information to the microprocessor and other parts of the computer. As Intel's powerful new microprocessors got faster and faster, they were often sitting idle due to low chipset speed. To solve this problem, Intel launched a new design created by a company called Rambus. However, the new design required costly modifications. AMD saw this as an opportunity. Working with VIA Technologies in Taiwan, they developed DDRAM, a chipset technology that doubled the transfer speed of data. For a period of time, this cheaper platform enabled AMD's processors to outperform Intel's Pentium chips. For the first time in decades, Intel did not have the premier product![41]

In the past few decades, increasing globalization of markets has made competitive dynamics even more important. Advances in communications and transportation have resulted in greater interdependence among manufacturers and suppliers. These factors have dramatically increased the number of potential actors that need to be considered. For example, early in the past century the U.S. automobile industry was somewhat isolated from foreign competition. Most of the automobiles purchased in the United States were made domestically, and most suppliers were based in the United States. However, foreign competitors increased their presence in the U.S. market—first the Europeans (i.e., Volkswagen, BMW, Mercedes-Benz), and then the

Japanese (i.e., Toyota, Nissan). The Arab oil embargo and resulting increases in gasoline prices during the 1970s increased the popularity of the more efficient Japanese models. To import fees, Japanese and European firms established manufacturing facilities in the United States, some in cooperation with an American partner.

On the supply side, U.S. companies began making more use of automobile parts produced outside the United States. Enhanced knowledge sharing from joint ventures and improved communications systems resulted in technological advances around the globe. Most recently, the Internet has made business-to-business transactions even easier. The result of these advances is that the competitive actions of an auto manufacturer anywhere in the world now have a ripple effect on all other industry participants. For example, if Nissan develops a new safety device, other competitors may need to match the innovation with one of their own. Such actions also affect suppliers of automobile parts. If General Motors announces zero percent financing, then other manufacturers feel pressure to do likewise to avoid losing sales. The automobile industry is representative of the competitive dynamics found in most industries today.

Markets are always in a state of flux, in the United States as well as other countries (see the following Global Insight). The actions of one competitor result in countermoves from other industry participants.[42] Countermoves set off another series of actions, and then reactions to those actions. Across all industries, the number of competitive moves and countermoves has been increasing.[43] In addition, the number of new products introduced and the number of patents issued have both increased. Along with these trends, brand loyalty has been dropping, and foreign imports as a share of U.S. gross domestic product have been steadily increasing. Consequently, increasingly disloyal consumers now have more to choose from, and it comes from a lot more places. It is not surprising, then, that the number of new-business failures is also increasing.[44]

Global Insight
Competitive Dynamics in the Thai Fast-Food Industry

Tricon Restaurants International, with its Kentucky Fried Chicken (KFC) and Pizza Hut brands, has been very successful in penetrating Asian markets. In fact, KFC is the best-known international brand in China, according to a recent ACNielsen survey. In Thailand, KFC ranks number one in sales volume in the fast-food segment, with three hundred stores at the end of 2001 (compared to 240 at the end of 1999). McDonald's is number two in sales volume in Thailand, with a mere 95 stores at the end of 2001. Tricon's other major brand, Pizza Hut, also made the top ten in sales volume in Thailand, coming in at number five.

Lucrative business segments tend to ignite competitive behavior, and the attractive chicken segment in Thailand is illustrative of this point. The Minor Food Group does business in Thailand under the brand names of Burger King, Sizzler, Dairy Queen, and Chicken Treat. Although a relatively small competitor in the chicken segment, Minor is trying to lure customers to its Chicken Treat restaurants through price-cutting. For example, an advertising campaign offered six pieces of chicken at 99 baht, down from the usual price of 160 baht. A similar dinner sells at KFC for about 150 baht, according to Kullavat Vichailak, the general manager of Chicken Treat. Chicken Treat also launched a new hot-and-spicy fried-chicken line, along with a 6-million-baht promotional campaign.

Bill Heinecke, CEO of the Minor Food Group, noted that KFC was forced to close a few locations in Bangkok, where Minor was expecting to increase its Chicken Treat stores by 50 percent within twelve months. Although Hester Chew, executive vice president at Tricon, acknowledged that some locations were below expected sales for the year, he was also quick to point out that KFC's overall presence in Thailand was increasing.

Sources: "KFC Sales Growth Proves Disappointing," www.siamfuture.com/thainews /thnewstxt.asp, 13 March 2002; "Chicken Treat Pitches Price Cuts Against Leader KFC," www.siamfuture.com/thainews/thnewstxt.asp, 3 October 2001; "Rank in Thailand," www.siamfuture.com/retailbuscenter/retailerscenter/foodchains.asp, 13 March 2002; "Kentucky Fried Chicken Tops International Brands in China," www.english.peopledaily .com.cn/200006/26/eng200006_43930.html, 28 February 2002.

Strategies That Reflect Competitive Dynamics

Given these trends, it is clear that competitive dynamics play an important role in strategy formulation. An organization can respond in a number of ways to the dynamics in its industry. Offensive strategies such as aggressive competition or seeking first-mover advantages are intended to increase market share and diminish the ability of competitors to compete. Defensive strategies such as threatening retaliation, seeking government intervention, or erecting barriers to imitation are intended to deter or slow down rivals from taking actions that would reduce the effectiveness of a firm's own strategies. Collaboration with stakeholders can be used offensively or defensively. Finally, a firm may avoid direct competition (avoidance) or be so flexible that it can easily leave an industry segment if the battle becomes too intense.

Aggressive Competition

aggressive strategy
These firms use every available resource in an effort to overwhelm rivals, thus reducing the chance that any countermove will be effective

Aggressive strategy competitors use every available resource in an effort to overwhelm rivals, thus reducing the chance that any countermove will be effective. For example, Pep Boys seeks to put their competitors out of business through offering lower prices, convenient hours, high levels of customer service, the widest selection of automobile parts, and a unique management system.

 Mitchell Leibovitz, CEO of Pep Boys—Manny, Moe, and Jack— wants to annihilate other auto-parts retailers. When intense competition from Pep Boys forces chains like Auto Zone, Western Auto, or Genuine Auto Parts to abandon a location, he adds a snapshot of the closed-down store to his collection. He burns and buries baseball caps bearing their corporate logos and videotapes the ritual to show his 14,500 employees. "I don't believe in friendly competition," he says. "I want to put them out of business." An accountant who got his MBA at Temple University at night, Leibovitz, 47, treats retailing like war. He says consolidation is under way in the $125 billion-a-year aftermarket for parts and servicing, so Pep Boys must be "a killer." That means offering superior selection, price, and service. For instance, Pep Boys stocks fan belts not just for current car models but for 98 percent of all cars on the road.[45]

Walt Disney Company is another example. Disney uses the most-advanced technologies and the most-talented workers in producing its animated feature films. Then the company floods the market with advertising and promotion. A similar offensive strategy is pursued in its theme parks. High-tech, innovative rides and world-class entertainment based on Disney characters and feature films create a "magical" place that is especially appealing to young people and families.

To be successful, aggressive competition requires significant resources that have high value and are at least somewhat rare. In addition, if those resources are difficult or costly to imitate, the attack may be effective over a longer time frame. Disney has been effective for many years at overwhelming competitors in theme parks and animated feature films due largely to its incredible brand name and its ability to attract the most-talented people for feature films and to attract and train low-cost laborers for its theme parks. Other resources that tend to provide a strong base for aggressive competition include a superior market position; a strong financial position; possession of patents or trade secrets; exclusive contracts; and involvement in a well-organized network of external stakeholders that includes major suppliers, financial institutions, government leaders, and other competitors.

One of the greatest risks of aggressive competition is that a rival will try to match the attack or even top it. In this regard, Oracle, the market leader in corporate software, is feeling new pressure from IBM.

 For every Oracle product, IBM has a counterpunch: databases, applications, and e-business foundation software. At the same time, the companies' philosophies are strikingly different. Oracle's strategy is to offer customers a complete and tightly integrated package of software—everything a company needs to manage its financials, manufacturing, sales force, logistics, e-commerce, and suppliers. In contrast, IBM Chairman and CEO Louis V. Gerstner Jr. is backing a "best-of-breed" approach in which it stitches together a quilt of business software from various companies, including itself.[46]

Another risk is that the basis for competition may lose power over time. Disney, for instance, enjoyed many decades of almost unchallenged domination in the theme-park industry. The company built their dominant position through a strategy that focuses on children and the families that bring them to the parks, with little that appealed directly to teenagers and young adults with no children. Now Americans are having fewer children and having them later in life. Furthermore, several major competitors have entered the scene with products that have specific appeal to teenagers and young adults. For example, in Orlando, Universal Studios was expanded to become Universal Escape, a complete vacation destination featuring themed resorts and Islands of Adventure, a state-of-the-art, high-tech adventure park that appeals to almost everyone under 40. Vivendi Universal, the French conglomerate that owns Universal, also owns Universal Studios Japan through a joint venture with Osaka Municipal Group. The venture is in direct competition with Disneyland Tokyo. Disney is still "top dog" in the theme-park market, but their position is weakening, and their original strategy in this segment is losing some of its power. In response, Disney has opened its own "adventure park" in California.

In spite of these hazards, aggressive firms tend to have higher performance than do laggards. For example, software firms that engage rivals with a greater number of competitive moves have the highest performance.[47] Also, these sorts of companies tend to elicit slower responses to their moves by competitors, an indication that intimidation is working.[48]

First-Mover Advantage

first-movers
Firms that stay at the forefront of technological advances in their industries

First-movers also tend to enjoy a competitive advantage. These are firms that stay at the forefront of technological advances in their industries. Microsoft is an excellent example. Although some observers argue that the original Windows operating systems was simply an imitation of Apple's Macintosh operating software, ever since that time Microsoft has led the pack with innovative software for personal computers. The company pursues this strategy through hiring extremely intelligent people from a variety of scientific areas as well buying technologies from early innovators or, in some cases, buying entire companies. Domino's Pizza is another example of a company that has benefited by being a first-mover.

 Domino's Pizza built an initial advantage over rivals by being the first to offer home delivery in an half hour or less with a free product guarantee. Rivals at first scorned that tactic, but eventually imitated it. Once most pizza retailers offered home delivery, Domino's initial advantage was gone. Domino's second action was to offer a giant pizza, the 'Big Foot,' its third was to distribute direct mail coupons, and fourth was to give its customers handy magnets for easy access to Domino's phone number. Only through a string of actions could Domino's maintain its advantage and keep rivals off guard.[49]

Consistent with the principle of creative destruction, industry leaders are often "dethroned" by aggressive moves by number-two competitors.[50] Consequently, to remain the first-mover in an industry, significant investments in research and development typically are required. Organizational learning ability is also important to this strategy.

Not only first-movers, but early imitators as well, may enjoy higher performance.[51] Some firms have a deliberate strategy of rapidly imitating the innovations of competitors. They enjoy many of the same benefits without all of the research-and-development costs.

Collaboration

collaboration strategy
Firms combine resources in an effort to gain a stronger resource position. Various forms of interorganizational relationships can lead to collaboration

Organizations often combine resources in an effort to gain a stronger resource position. This is called **collaboration strategy.** In some cases, a leading firm will collaborate with a "handpicked" group of firms and deliberately exclude others in an effort to weaken them or put them out of business. Or weaker rivals may join forces to gain position relative to a market leader. DaimlerChrysler (German) and Aerospace Matra (French) agreed to combine their aerospace businesses to create the third-largest aircraft and defense company in the world, trailing behind Boeing and Lockheed Martin.[52]

Collaborative relationships can be hard to duplicate, thus increasing their value as a competitive tool. For many years, Novell has used joint ventures and alliances to enhance its competitive position. This has resulted in the creation of a network of relationships that would be virtually impossible to imitate.

 Novell is one of the top system-software companies and a developer of services that support network-based computing solutions. Novell's NetWare computing products integrate desktop PCs with each other and with mid-range and mainframe computer systems. Novell has a commanding lead in network software, with about half of the world market.

About half of Novell's sales are outside of the United States. The company has developed an infrastructure of related businesses around Novell's core network-software business in an attempt to solidify its position in the computer industry. The infrastructure is continuously being created through joint ventures and a variety of other initiatives to "accelerate the momentum of networking." Some of Novell's joint ventures include a project with Apple Computer and Go Corp. to develop software that ties wireless devices to corporate networks, a venture with AT&T aimed at linking PC networks to corporate phone systems, and a technology project with Kodak to develop a way to send photos and other types of images across networks. Novell has ongoing ventures it calls "systems solution partnerships" with Compaq, Memorex Telex, Olivetti, Digital Equipment, IBM, Hewlett-Packard, and Unisys. Finally, Novell has provided about $25 million in seed money to nine start-ups that are developing new software to use on NetWare, including workgroup-applications software and an object-based services interface.[53]

It is interesting to note that Novell was unable to establish effective collaborative activity with Microsoft. Instead, Microsoft launched its own network-software product and stole significant market share from Novell. Microsoft soon became Novell's biggest rival, a situation that has intensified even more in recent years.

Threat of Retaliation

retaliation strategy
A firm threatens severe retaliation in an effort to discourage competitors from taking actions

multimarket competition
Firms compete in multiple markets simultaneously

Sometimes organizations will threaten severe retaliation in an effort to discourage competitors from taking actions. This is called **retaliation strategy.** For a threat to be believable, an organization should be perceived as having enough resources to carry on an effective battle if one ensues. High liquidity, excess manufacturing capacity, and new-product designs that are being held back for a "rainy day" can be significant in convincing competitors that they would lose more than gain from the conflict.[54]

Multimarket competition means that firms compete in multiple markets simultaneously. When this is the case, a company may fear that its actions in one market could lead to retaliation in another market. Lockheed Martin and Boeing compete in many of the same segments of the national-defense industry. If Lockheed were to launch a competitive strike in one segment, Boeing could retaliate in another. Industries consisting of competitors with a lot of multimarket competition are expected to demonstrate a lot of mutual forbearance, which limits rivalry.[55] Since rivalry is limited, profit margins are expected to be higher in these situations.[56] On the other hand, lack of multimarket contact can lead to more-intense rivalry and lower profit margins.[57]

Government Intervention

Chapter 2 discussed political strategies as a tool to create a more favorable operating environment in which to compete. There will be no attempt here to repeat that discussion. However, it is worth noting that political strategies can be used to attempt to change the rules of the game.

Ex. In a ruling that could reshape the nation's $1.3 trillion credit-card industry, a U.S. district court judge ruled that Visa and MasterCard will no longer be able to bar member banks from issuing cards from rivals. The decision . . . is a major victory for rival card brands American Express and Discover, which effectively have been banned from pursuing relationships with banks that issue Visa or MasterCard.[58]

Barriers to Imitation

One of the most common competitive countermoves is imitation. A "follower" organization can simply imitate the leader's strategy point by point. Consequently, some leading companies attempt to thwart imitation through erecting a variety of barriers. Some barriers to imitation are similar to barriers to entry discussed in Chapter 2. The primary difference is that **barriers to imitation** are intended to prevent existing competitors from imitating sources of cost savings or differentiation, whereas barriers to entry are created to discourage potential new companies from entering the industry. Also, many barriers to entry are possessed by most existing firms; therefore, they have an effect on new entrants rather than on incumbent firms. Most automobiles, for example, are built in large factories that enjoy economies of scale. Nevertheless, as a practical matter, many of the entry barriers are the same as imitation barriers.

barriers to imitation
Barriers intended to prevent existing competitors from imitating sources of cost savings or differentiation

Organizations may discourage imitation in a number of ways. A company may build a significantly larger and more expensive plant, thus achieving economies of scale that are hard to duplicate. A firm may patent its products or protect a brand name or trademark. In addition, special relationships with external stakeholders can be difficult to copy. For example, an organization may have special arrangements with a financial institution, an excellent relationship with its union, or an exclusive-supply agreement with one of its suppliers. In addition, an organization may deter entry through product proliferation, significant investments in advertising, cutting prices, or withholding information about the profitability of a product so that potential competitors will not be anxious to enter the segment.[59]

As discussed in Chapter 3, intangible assets are among the most difficult to imitate. For example, a product is fairly easy to imitate, but the research-and-development processes that went into creating the product are more difficult to reproduce. Consequently, an organization with an excellent ability to innovate may be able to create a barrier to imitation. By the time competitors have imitated a product, the company has produced its replacement. This is the strategy Intel has been using for many years with regard to its microprocessing chips. Organizational-learning ability is similarly very difficult to imitate. Organizational learning can lead to private information (secrets) that results in higher performance. Consequently, an organization can build a barrier to imitation by fostering learning processes (Chapter 6 will cover this topic in detail). Finally, a high-performance organizational culture is difficult to copy.

Strategic Flexibility

strategic flexibility
A firm can move its resources out of declining markets and into more prosperous ones in a minimum amount of time

Strategic flexibility allows a firm to earn high returns while managing the amount of risk it faces.[60] Flexibility means that a company can move its resources out of declining markets and into more-prosperous ones in a minimum amount of time. Exit barriers influence a firm to remain in a market or industry after it is no longer attractive for investment. For example, an organization may have a significant investment in a large plant. Selling the plant would result in a major loss, and closing it would mean losing everything. Strategic exit barriers can also reduce flexibility. These barriers are a result of reluctance to sacrifice the benefits of intangible assets that have accumulated through previous investments. Some of these may include loss of synergies created through linkages with other businesses, loss of customers or a market position, or loss of distribution channels. Organizations that have pursued vertical integration over time face particularly high exit barriers because they are involved in many interconnected stages of value creation.

Organizations can retain strategic flexibility by reducing investments in assets that are likely to create large exit barriers. The extreme case of strategic flexibility is what might be called the "virtual firm":

 The new economy is a world where journalists adulate the virtual firm—a company that sits in the middle of a network of electronically linked alliances, but own few physical assets. It is an extremely opportunistic model, in which alliance partners change frequently and rapidly. In this ideal world of virtuality, a concept company can sit in the middle of a spider's web of alliances, working its magic and its power over many smaller, partner companies that are easily replaced.[61]

Virtual firms must be masters at putting together deals, selecting partners, managing information, and integrating systems. Much of what is produced in the world today can be created through managing a network of subcontractors. However, this is an extreme example. Most organizations will want to establish themselves on the strategic-flexibility scale somewhere in the middle between the "old economy" vertically integrated manufacturing firm and the "new economy" virtual firms. The important thing to remember at this point is that the level of strategic flexibility is a decision.

Avoidance

avoidance strategy
Competitive strategy in which a firm avoids confrontation completely by focusing on a particular niche in the market in which other firms have little interest

Each of the strategies above can require a great deal of managerial attention and, in some cases, significant other resources. However, some firms simply use **avoidance strategy,** avoiding confrontation completely by focusing on a particular niche in the market in which other firms have little interest (Porter's focus strategy). A niche can be a particular type of specialized product, a small segment of the market, or a small geographic area. A dairy farmer, for instance, might specialize in a particular type of milk from cows that are fed only oats. Or the farmer might sell raw milk to people with special dietary needs. Or the farmer could focus exclusively on a smaller area of a state that would be inefficient for a larger operation to service anyway.

The French retailer Carrefour, the second-largest retailer in the world, has prospered in international markets where Wal-Mart does not have a foothold.

 Carrefour's most significant edge on Wal-Mart, though, is the French group's commanding presence in markets where the Americans—late arrivals on the international retail scene—are either at the startup stage or have yet to plant their flag. "Carrefour is the world's most successful international retailer," says Jaime Vasquez, an industry analyst at Salomon Smith Barney in London, adding, "Wal-Mart has no track record outside North America."[62]

Actually, Wal-Mart is ahead of Carrefour in Mexico and has made recent acquisitions in Germany and Britain. However, in all other international markets, Carrefour is way ahead. It can't last forever. As the two titans continue to grow, they will eventually clash.

Resources, Industry Structure, and Firm Actions

Many of the strategies contained in this section require a strong resource position or excellent stakeholder relationships.[63] For example, for aggressive competition to succeed, a firm must have better or more resources than competitors do. First-movers need significant resources associated with innovation and learning. Collaboration requires a network of excellent relationships with external stakeholders. Successful government intervention comes from excellent relationships with government leaders or parties. Firms with strong or unused (slack) resources are in a strong position to pursue most of the strategic options. On the other hand, firms with poor resources are limited in their abilities to pursue aggressive strategies. They may need to avoid direct competition or to develop strategic flexibility until their resource positions are stronger.

The characteristics of an industry determine, in part, the tactics an organization will pursue. Rapid industry growth typically is associated with lower levels of rivalry because firms do not have to steal market share to increase sales.[64] Also, a high level of concentration (a few firms hold most of the market share) should reduce the motivation of rivals to compete aggressively. If entry or imitation barriers are high, there is less competitive pressure from potential entrants.[65] Figure 5.4 illustrates the effect firm resources and industry structure have on firm actions and competitor reactions over time. After an organization acts, competitors will respond in turn, thus changing the resource positions of each company, as well as

FIGURE 5.4

The Relationship Among Resources, Industry Structure, and Actions Over Time

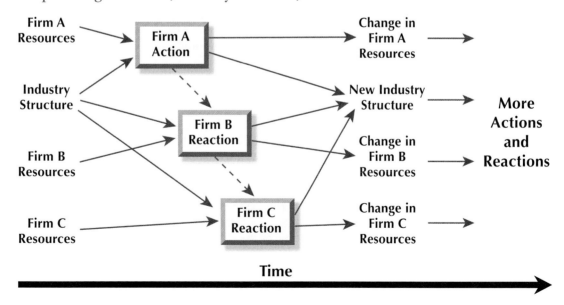

Source: This model was inspired by K. G. Smith, W. J. Ferrier, and H. Ndofor, "Competitive Dynamics Research: Critique and Future Directions," in *The Blackwell Handbook of Strategic Management,* ed. M. A. Hitt, R. E. Freeman, and J. S. Harrison, (Oxford: Blackwell Publishers, 2001), 315–368.

industry structure. The cycle then continues with moves, countermoves, and resulting changes.

Thus far, this discussion has centered on specific strategies firms might pursue to deal with competitive dynamics. Another important aspect of competitive dynamics is anticipating the countermoves of rivals. The question is, "How are competitors likely to respond to a strategic move?" Anticipation of competitor reactions is vital to understanding how effective a strategy may be. The two factors already identified in this section, resource position and industry characteristics, are very important to predicting countermoves. For example, a rival with a strong resource position is much more likely to respond with a countermove. Also, a slow-growing industry is more likely to elicit a response from competitors than is an industry that is growing rapidly. However, several other factors can play a role in determining whether a firm will countermove and what form the response will take.

Predicting the potential response of a competitor also has a lot to do with the goals of its managers.[66] If a planned strategy is likely to interfere with the goals found in a competitor organization, that organization is likely to respond with a countermove. For example, a company may launch a strategy to grow in a particular market. If another company's goals are dependent on that market, a strong reaction can be expected.

 Boeing has historically dominated the Japanese market for commercial aircraft. In fact, Boeing's planes account for 84 percent of the nation's commercial fleets. Recently, the European rival Airbus Industrie began an attack on Boeing's dominance through expanding its Japanese office and making allies of Japanese businesses. Airbus recently targeted Japan with its new A380 superjumbo jet, which holds up to eight hundred people. Large jets are important in Japan because its airports are so congested. Airbus should have expected a strong reaction. It came in the form of a newly designed Boeing 747X, a stretch model that will accommodate up to 520 passengers and will cost $20 million less than the Airbus A380.[67]

On the other hand, sometimes companies pursue different segments of the market (avoidance strategy), thus allowing a less aggressive atmosphere to develop. An organization should also try to understand the assumptions of competing firm managers about their organization and the industry. For example, managers may assume that a countermove will be detrimental because such moves have been harmful in the past. Or firm managers may see their organization as a follower.

Of course, a competitor is not likely to respond if it is unaware that a firm has pursued a strategic action. Consequently, the strength of a firm's environmental-scanning and -analysis abilities and the awareness of its top managers to significant events in the industry also play a role in whether a countermove will be pursued.[68] Newer or smaller organizations are less likely to be aware of precisely what larger, older competitors are doing.

In summary, some of the characteristics that help an organization anticipate the response of a competitor to a particular strategic move include strength of its resource position, characteristics of the industry, goals and assumptions of competing-firm managers, and awareness of competitive actions. When a strategy is formulated, managers should try to anticipate the reactions of competitors in order to more accurately assess the potential outcomes.

Tracking Competitor Movement

strategic-group map
Categorizes existing industry competitors into groups that follow similar strategies

One way to keep track of the strategies of competing firms is with a strategic-group map such as the one in Figure 5.5. A **strategic-group map** categorizes existing industry competitors into groups that follow similar strategies. To construct a strategic-group map, first identify strategic dimensions that are important in the industry, such as breadth of product line, quality level, or national-versus-regional distribution. The axes of a strategic-group map should describe strategy and not performance. Therefore, variables such as pricing strategy, customer-service approach, level of advertising, and product mix are appropriate, whereas return on assets and earnings per share are not. Furthermore, to reveal more about the industry, the dimensions should not be highly correlated with one another. Once the variables are selected, a grid may be constructed by plotting industry rivals on the relevant dimensions.

FIGURE 5.5

Strategic-Group Map of Department Store and Specialty Retailing

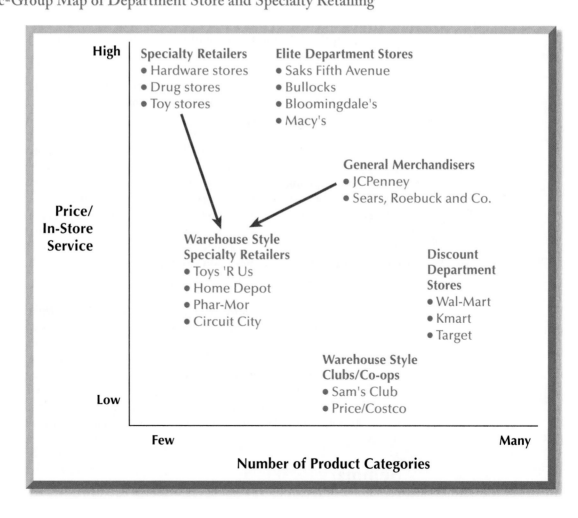

Organizations that end up in the same general location on a map are called strategic groups. Consequently, they have similar strategies based on the dimensions found in the map. Companies in one strategic group experience the external forces differently from companies in other strategic groups. For instance, in the retail industry, the recession of the early 1990s hurt traditional department stores but actually helped discounters.

Strategic-group maps can help an organization understand the strategies of competitors. For example, competitors within the same strategic group, such as Marriott and Hilton, are in direct competition for customers, whereas competitors in different strategic groups, such as Days Inn and the Ritz Carlton, do not compete directly. Strategic-group maps may also highlight an area in the industry in which no firms are currently competing (a strategic opportunity). For instance, short-haul, no-frills airlines occupy a competitive arena that was almost empty before airline deregulation.

 One time a group of business students at a major university created a strategic-group map for the global automobile industry. They selected pricing and safety of the automobile as their strategic variables. Through this analysis, they discovered that a low-priced, very safe automobile does not exist. This sort of car would be like a Volvo without all the frills. Parents probably would be delighted to buy such a car for their teenagers. It might also appeal to older drivers. Perhaps the automobile industry is missing an opportunity.

Strategic-group maps may also be used to track the evolution of an industry over time. In the past twenty years, general merchandisers such as Sears and J.C. Penney have come under siege from discounters. Some of the discounters have chosen to follow the lead of the old "dime store" chains by offering a full line of discount-priced products. Others—such as Toys "R" Us, Home Depot, and Phar-Mor—have taken one product category and offered extreme inventory depth and discount pricing in a warehouse-like environment. Consequently, traditional department stores are seeing entire segments of their industry closed out by these "category killers" that are pursuing their own unique strategies. For example, J.C. Penney and other regional department stores, who once carried large selections of toys, no longer do. Sears, once a general merchandiser, has responded by moving in the direction of the discounters. However, recent strategic shifts indicate that Sears may have dropped its discounting strategy. It is currently difficult to predict where the company will end up.

On the other hand, one of the weaknesses associated with strategic-group maps is that organizations can belong to several different strategic groups, depending on the dimensions that are used to form the groups. For example, Hilton and Marriott compete in both the high-end and the affordable (through Hampton Inn and Courtyard) hotel categories. Since the choice of dimensions is somewhat subjective and dependent entirely on the industry under study, strategic-group maps do not provide answers, but they help raise relevant questions about the current state and direction of competitive rivalry. As noted, they may also help firms discover untapped market opportunities.

Summary

The responsibilities of business-level managers include establishing the overall direction of a business unit, ongoing analysis of the changing business situation, selecting a generic strategy and a strategic posture through which to implement it, and acquiring and managing resources. The generic business-level strategies described in this chapter are cost leadership, differentiation, best value, and focus. Firms may focus through cost leadership, differentiation, or best value. The distinguishing feature of a focus strategy is that energy is focused on a narrow, as opposed to a broad, segment of the market.

Companies that pursue cost leadership actively seek resources that will allow them to produce products and services at the lowest possible cost. Organizations that pursue differentiation attempt to distinguish their products or services in such a way that they have greater value to their consumers. Best-value strategies combine elements of both differentiation and low cost. Many organizations have implemented programs that enhance speed or quality in an effort to produce a product or service that is the best value.

An understanding of the industry life cycle is useful in determining the distinct characteristics of a business-level strategy. Business strategies must be adapted to fit the circumstances of the industry as it evolves through the introduction, growth, maturity, and commodity (or decline) stages.

Organizational dynamics is defined as the moves and countermoves of industry competitors. Markets are in a constant state of flux, with a competitive move setting off a series of reactions and countermoves. Organizations can pursue a variety of strategies in response to competitive dynamics. They include aggressive competition, seeking a first-mover advantage, collaborative agreements with stakeholders, threats of retaliation, seeking government intervention, erecting barriers to imitation, remaining flexible enough to move in and out of markets with relative ease, and avoiding direct competition completely. Sometimes organizations combine these approaches.

Discussion Questions

1. What are the strategic management responsibilities of a business-unit manager? Please explain what each of these responsibilities entails.

2. Please describe the generic business-level strategies found in this chapter. Provide an example of companies that you think are pursuing each of these strategies.

3. How can an organization pursue the business-level strategy of low-cost leadership?

4. How can an organization pursue a differentiation strategy?

5. What are some of the risks associated with a cost leadership, differentiation, best value, and focus strategy?

6. What are two major programs that many firms are implementing in an effort to pursue a best-value strategy? How do these programs lead to best value?

7. What is the industry life cycle? What are some of the important factors to consider at each stage of the life cycle? How do those factors affect choice of business strategies?

8. What are competitive dynamics? Why has competition become more dynamic in the past few decades?

9. Describe the eight strategies that reflect competitive dynamics.

10. Of the strategies that reflect competitive dynamics, which one seems to be the highest risk? Why? Which one seems to be the lowest risk? Why?

11. If you were a market leader in an industry, which of the strategies that reflect competitive dynamics would probably be the most attractive to you? If you were a weak competitor with few resources, which strategy would you likely find attractive?

Strategic Application

Analysis of Business-Level Strategies

This application will provide you with an opportunity to compare and contrast business-level strategies of companies in a familiar industry. First, select an industry with which you feel comfortable. A few industries that will facilitate this analysis include airlines, hotels, and discount department stores. Now identify the five or six major competitors in the industry. For each competitor, answer the following questions:

- What is the generic strategy—cost leadership, differentiation, best value, or focus? Be specific about whether it is focus through cost leadership, differentiation, or best value.

- What is the strategic posture, or specific tactics used to execute the generic strategy?

- How successful has the strategy been in the past?

- Is the strategy likely to be successful in the future or will it need to change? If it needs to change, how will it need to change?

After answering each of these questions, determine if there are any strategic approaches that are not being used in the industry, but that might be applied with success.

Strategic Internet Application

Select an industry for study (or your instructor may assign one). With regard to competitive dynamics, some of the most interesting industries are airlines, restaurants, and soft drinks (or beverages). Go to www.yahoo.com. On the Yahoo! site, do a search for "Industry News," or go directly to http://biz.yahoo.com/industry—the address for industry information at the time this book was printed. Click on your industry and read several of the articles regarding what competitors are doing. If you do not have enough information, use Google.com to search for "Industry Information" and the name of your industry. Google will provide you with many other links. After you have completed this research, answer the following questions:

1. Who are the major competitors in the industry?

2. Is there a clear industry leader in terms of competitive strength (which is not necessarily the same as size)? What are the key strengths that make this company a leader?

3. Describe a few of the primary sources of competitive rivalry in this industry. For example, do companies tend to compete primarily on the basis of pricing, product features, advertising, promotions, customer service, speed to market, or other factors?

4. For each of these sources of competitive rivalry, what have one or more firms done recently, as reflected in the articles you read?

Notes

1. N. Byrnes, "Old Stores, New Rivals, and Changing Trends Have Hammered Toys 'R' Us," *Business Week,* 4 December 2000, 128–140; T. Howard, "Toys 'R' Us Rallies 'Round Flagship Store, Vows Superlative Staff, Stock," *USA Today,* 13 November 2001, 7B.

2. H. J. Bryce, *Financial and Strategic Management for Nonprofit Organizations* (Englewood Cliffs, N.J.: Prentice Hall, 1987).

3. This discussion of generic strategies draws heavily from concepts found in M. E. Porter, *Competitive Strategy: Techniques for Analyzing Industries and Competitors* (New York: The Free Press, 1980), chap. 2.

4. Porter, *Competitive Strategy.*

5. Adapted from B. Dumaine, "Unleash Workers and Cut Costs," *Fortune,* 18 May 1992, 88.

6. This discussion of factors leading to cost savings is based, in part, on Porter, Competitive Strategy; M. E. Porter, *Competitive Advantage: Creating and Sustaining Superior Performance* (New York: The Free Press, 1985); and R. W. Schmenner, "Before You Build a Big Factory," *Harvard Business Review* 54 (July/August 1976): 100–104.

7. Taken directly from B. Wysocki Jr., "Corporate America Confronts the Meaning of a 'Core' Business," *The Wall Street Journal,* 9 November 1999, A1.

8. As defined by Schmenner, "Before You Build."

9. Taken directly from "Electronic Peasants," *Le Monde Diplomatique,* www.monde-diplomatique.fr/en/2000.

10. Ericsson News Center, www.ericsson.com/infocenter/news/outsourcing_Sweden_and_France.html, 14 November 2001.

11. M. E. Porter, "What Is Strategy?" *Harvard Business Review* (November/December 1996): 61.

12. Ericsson News Center.

13. The same principles apply to "experience effects." In this book, the two terms will be used synonymously.

14. W. J. Abernathy and K. Wayne, "Limits of the Learning Curve," *Harvard Business Review* (September/October 1974): 109–119; Boston Consulting Group, *Perspectives on Experience* (Boston: Boston Consulting Group, 1972); W. B. FHirschman, "Profit from the Learning Curve," *Harvard Business Review* (January/February 1964): 125–139.

15. Porter, "What Is Strategy?" 62.

16. A. Paszton, M. Branningan, and S. McCartney, "ValuJet's Penny-pinching Comes Under Scrutiny," *The Wall Street Journal,* 14 May 1996, A2, A4.

17. Taken directly from M. Mangalindan, "Google to Name CEO As Strategy to Raise Profile," *The Wall Street Journal,* 6 August 2001, B1.

18. E. Mansfield, "How Rapidly Does New Industrial Technology Leak Out?" *Journal of Industrial Economics* (December 1985): 217.

19. P. Ghemawat, "Sustainable Advantage," *Harvard Business Review* (September/October 1986): 53.

20. C. W. L. Hill, "Differentiation versus Low Cost or Differentiation and Low Cost: A Contingency Framework," *Academy of Management Review* 13 (1988): 403. See also A. I. Murray, "A Contingency View of Porter's 'Generic Strategies,'" *Academy of Management Review* 13 (1988): 390–400.

21. H. Kahalas and K. Suchon, "Interview with Harold A. Poling, Chairman, CEO, Ford Motor Company," *Academy of Management Executive* (May 1992): 74.

22. "A Conversation with Roberto Goizueta and Jack Welch," *Fortune,* 11 December 1995, 98–99.

23. T. C. Hayes, "Behind Wal-Mart's Surge, a Web of Suppliers," *The New York Times,* 1 July 1991, D1–D2.

24. Porter, *Competitive Advantage,* 20.

25. M. K. Starr, ed., *Global Competitiveness: Getting the U.S. Back on Track* (New York: W. W. Norton, 1988), 307.

26. W. E. Demming, *Out of the Crisis* (Cambridge, Mass.: MIT Press, 1982); L. W. Phillips, D. Chang, and R. D. Buzzell, "Product Quality, Cost Position, and Business Performance," *Journal of Marketing* 47 (1983): 26–43; M. Walton, *Deming Management at Work* (New York: Putnam, 1990).

27. Taken directly from C. H. Deutsch, "Six Sigma Enlightenment," *The New York Times,* 7 December 1998; reprinted in E. H. Bernstein, *Strategic Management* (Guilford, Conn: McGrawhill/Dushkin, 2001), 151.

28. Taken directly from E. Brown, "Americas Most Admired Companies," *Fortune,* 1 March 1999, 68–73; reprinted in Bernstein, Strategic Management, 35.

29. J. B. Barney and R. W. Griffin, *The Management of Organizations: Strategy, Structure, Behavior* (Boston: Houghton Mifflin, 1992), 505; B. Dumaine, "How Managers Can Succeed through Speed," *Fortune,* 13 February 1989, 54–59.

30. B. Davis, "Automation Is Key to Efficiency," *European Rubber Journal* (Special Issue, 1992/1993): 32.

31. A. Talor III, "Now Hear This, Jack Welch!" *Fortune,* 6 April 1992, 94.

32. "About SawTech," www.sawtech.com/about.htm, 17 October 2001, 1.

33. G. G. Dess and J. C. Picken, "Creating Competitive (Dis)advantage: Learning from Food Lion's Freefall," *Academy of Management Executive* 13, no. 3(1999): 100.

34. R. H. Hayes and S. C. Wheelwright, *Restoring Our Competitive Edge: Competing through Manufacturing* (New York: John Wiley, 1984), 203.

35. This discussion of strategy during the stages of product-market evolution is based on C. R. Anderson and C. P. Zeithaml, "Stage of the Product Life Cycle, Business Strategy, and Business Performance," *Academy of Management*

Journal 27 (1984): 5–24; Barney and Griffin, *Management of Organizations,* 229–230; Hayes and Wheelright, *Competitive Edge,* chap. 7; C. W. Hofer and D. Schendel, *Strategy Formulation: Analytical Concepts* (St. Paul: West Publishing, 1978), chap. 5.

36. M. B. Lieberman and D. B. Montgomery, "First-Mover Advantages," *Strategic Management Journal* 9 (1988): 41–58.

37. M. Lambkin, "Order of Entry and Performance in New Markets," *Strategic Management Journal* 9 (1988): 127–140.

38. K. R. Harrigan and M. E. Porter, "End-Game Strategies for Declining Industries," *Harvard Business Review* (July/August 1983): 111–120.

39. Harrigan and Porter, "End-Game Strategies."

40. J. Schumpeter, *The Theory of Economic Development* (Cambridge, Mass.: Harvard University Press, 1934).

41. B. Schlender, "Intel Unleashes Its Inner Attila," *Fortune,* 15 October 2001, 174; J. Robertson and B. Gain, "AMD to Roll Out Its Fastest Two-Way Server Mpus, Zipping Past Intel—But Clock Speed No Magic Bullet in this Market," *Manhasset,* 15 October 2001, PG3.

42. K. G. Smith, W. J. Ferrier, and H. Ndofor, "Competitive Dynamics Research: Critique and Future Directions," in *The Blackwell Handbook of Strategic Management,* ed. M. A. Hitt, R. E. Freeman, and J. S. Harrison (Oxford: Blackwell Publishers, 2001), 315–361.

43. Predicasts, *Predicasts' Funk and Scott Index,* United States Annual Edition (Cleveland, Ohio: Predicasts, 1993).

44. All of these trends are well documented in C. M. Grimm and K. G. Smith, *Strategy As Action: Industry Rivalry and Coordination* (Cincinnati, OH: South-Western College Publishing, 1997).

45. Taken directly from A. Taylor III, "How to Murder the Competition," *Fortune,* 22 (February 1993, 87.

46. Taken directly from J. Kerstetter and S. E. Ante, "IBM vs. Oracle: It Could Get Bloody," *Business Week,* 28 May 2001), 65.

47. G. Young, K. G. Smith, and C. Grimm, "Austrian and Industrial Organization Perspectives on Firm-Level Competitive Activity and Performance," *Organization Science* 73 (1996): 243–254.

48. K. G. Smith, C. Grimm, and M. Gannon, *Dynamics of Competitive Strategy* (London: Sage Publications, 1992).

49. Taken directly from Grimm and Smith, *Strategy as Action,* 99.

50. W. Ferrier, K. Smith, and C. Grimm, "The Role of Competition in Market Share Erosion and Dethronement: A Study of Industry Leaders and Challengers," *Academy of Management Journal* 43 (1999): 372–388.

51. H. Lee et al., "Timing, Order, and Durability of New Product Advantages with Imitation," *Strategic Management Journal* 21 (2000): 23–30.

52. D. Michaels and C. Goldsmith, "Daimler and Aerospatiale Matra Agree to Combine Their Aerospace Businesses," *The Wall Street Journal*, 15 October 1999, A3, A4.

53. Novell, Inc., Annual Report (1992); D. Clark, "Novell in Talks to Sell Software Lines It Acquired in WordPerfect Purchase," *The Wall Street Journal*, 31 October 1995, A3–A4; E. I. Schwartz, "The Industry Needs an Alternative—But Will It Be Novell?" *Business Week*, 1 February 1993, 69–70; S. Stahl and C. Gillooly, "Perfect Office Unplugged," *Investor's Weekly*, 13 November 1995, 14–16.

54. P. Ghemawat, *Strategy and the Business Landscape* (Upper Saddle River, N.J.: Prentice Hall, 2001).

55. G. Young, K.G. Smith, C. Grimm, and D. Simon, "Multimarket Contact, Resource Heterogeneity,

and Rivalrous Firm Behavior," *Journal of Management* (2002): in press.

56. J. Gimeno and C. Woo, "Multimarket Contact, Economies of Scope, and Firm Performance," *Academy of Management Journal* 42 (1999): 323–341.

57. Smith, Ferrier, and Ndofor, "Competitive Dynamics."

58. Taken directly from J. Sapsford and P. Beckett, "Visa and MasterCard Must Allow Banks to Issue Rivals' Credit Cards, Judge Rules," *The Wall Street Journal*, 10 October 2001, A3.

59. Grimm and Smith, *Strategy As Action.*

60. K. R. Harrigan, "Strategic Flexibility in the Old and New Economies," in *Blackwell Handbook*, ed. Hitt, Freeman, and Harrison, 98–123.

61. Taken directly from Harrigan, "Strategic Flexibility," 107.

62. Taken directly from R. Tomlinson, "Who's Afraid of Wal-Mart," *Fortune*, 26 June 2000, 186–196.

63. Smith, Ferrier, and Ndofor, "Competitive Dynamics."

64. K. G. Smith et al,, "Predictors of Response Time to Competitive Strategic Actions: Preliminary Theory and Evidence," *Journal of Business Research* 183 (1989): 245–259.

65. Smith, Ferrier, and Ndofor, "Competitive Dynamics."

66. Porter, *Competitive Strategy.*

67. S. Holmes, C. Dawson, and C. Matlack, "Rumble over Tokyo," *Business Week*, 2 April 2001, 80–81.

68. Smith, Ferrier, and Ndofor, "Competitive Dynamics."

Chapter 6

Strategies for Entrepreneurship and Innovation

Learning Objectives

After reading and discussing this chapter, you should be able to:

1. Understand the importance of entrepreneurship and organizational entrepreneurship.

2. Create a simple business plan.

3. Understand the steps in the creation of an entrepreneurial venture.

4. Avoid the pitfalls associated with new venture failures.

5. Consider the various options for new venture funding.

6. Select an appropriate structure for an internal venture.

7. Create a plan for fostering innovation in an existing firm.

Turbine Technology Services

Turbine Technology Services, based in Orlando, Florida, provides aftermarket services for power-generation equipment around the world. David Hamilla, vice president of operations, saw a need for troubleshooting turbine-generator problems without sending an engineer to the location of the turbine. Existing information technology could be used to satisfy this purpose. For example, advanced satellite-communications systems could provide a continuous information flow. Furthermore, programming applications had already been developed that could process all the information and diagnose impending problems. General Electric already used a similar approach in the medical-systems area. However, the technology had not yet been applied to power-generation equipment.

David's plan was to establish a centralized worldwide monitoring and diagnostic system that would help companies anticipate problems before they became critical. He saw a potential $200 million market for the services his venture would provide. The board of directors was impressed with his analysis, which included a one-year payback on the initial investment. The venture was approved, and a monitoring and diagnostic command center was established in Orlando. The center is staffed with engineers who monitor gas and steam turbines 24 hours a day. These turbines are found in locations across the United States and Europe. It is sometimes difficult for turbine owners to relinquish operating control to engineers in a remote location. However, the payoff for doing so can be very significant. For example, during a six-month period, one of their customers saved an estimated $750,000 from not having to shut down turbines that otherwise would have shut down. The cost of TTS's service over that six-month period was a small fraction of the savings.[1]

entrepreneurship
The creation of new business

In the broadest sense of the term, **entrepreneurship** is the creation of new business. It involves opportunity recognition or creation, assembling resources to pursue the opportunity, and managing activities that bring a new venture into existence. Some ventures are complete start-ups, while other ventures are pursued within an existing organization. According to Arnold Cooper, widely acknowledged as a pioneer in the study of entrepreneurship: "Entrepreneurial ventures, whether independent or within established corporations, might be viewed as experiments. They test to determine the size of particular markets or whether particular technologies or ways of competing are promising. They have good internal communication and enormous commitment from their key people."[2]

This chapter discusses entrepreneurship, innovation, and growth. The first section discusses independent new-venture creation, followed by a section on entrepreneurship within established firms. The final section provides a link between the ideas in this chapter regarding internal growth and the external-growth options that will be treated in detail in Chapter 7.

Entrepreneurial Start-ups

The U.S. economy relies heavily on entrepreneurship as a source of growth and strength. Hundreds of thousands of small firms are created each year. Annually, more than 1 million new jobs are created by these firms, while *Fortune* 500 companies are cutting their workforces. More than half of the private workforce is employed in firms with fewer than five hundred employees. These businesses account for about half of the private-sector gross domestic product. Two-thirds of new inventions come out of smaller firms.[3] Nevertheless, entrepreneurship is a high-risk activity. Entrepreneurs in nations with highly developed economies often complain about how difficult it is to keep a new business going, and they are right. However, Global Insight demonstrates how much more difficult entrepreneurial efforts are in less-developed economies such as Russia.

Global Insight
Entrepreneurship in Russia

An unstable government, an undeveloped legal system, overregulation, a virtually unfathomable taxation system, a pervasive mafia, and an inadequate business structure characterize the maze that Russian entrepreneurs must navigate in their attempts to create successful ventures. This hostile environment stems from historical precedent as well as the government's mishandling of the economic transition during the 1990s.

Consider how the hostile environment presented huge obstacles to the following entrepreneurs in establishing and growing their firms:

- The founders of Premier Bank were forced to keep excessively high reserves on deposit with the central bank, limiting funds available for making business loans.

- The entrepreneurs who started Aquarius, an assembler and distributor of computers and cash registers, had to close their plant when the government unexpectedly passed laws making domestic assembly unprofitable and encouraging foreign competitors to export finished products to Russia.

- BusinessLink's founders—who built executive-search, consulting, advertising, and real-estate-development businesses—lost most of their client base in 1998. BusinessLink's international customers substantially cut their Russian activities after the ruble was devalued, making imports too expensive for Russian consumers.

- The founder of EpicRus, a software and systems company, was forced to incur heavy security expenses and take other extreme measures, such as not advertising in Russian-language media, to avoid the dangers of exposing the company's activities to the Russian mafia.

- The brothers who started Vybor, a trading and retail firm, found the complicated and ever-changing tax laws so perplexing that they resorted to tips from the how-to book *Twenty-five Ways to Avoid Taxes*.

Source: S. M. Puffer and D. J. McCarthy, "Navigating the Hostile Maze: A Framework for Russian Entrepreneurship," *Academy of Management Executive* (November 2001): 24, used with permission.

Much of what is found in this book is valuable to entrepreneurs. However, this section looks specifically at aspects of entrepreneurship that are different from other types of strategic planning. The topics include characteristics of entrepreneurs, the entrepreneurial tasks of opportunity recognition or creation, creation of a business plan, securing financing and managing a venture through its first year, and common causes of new-venture failures.

The Entrepreneur

Entrepreneurs have been studied for many years, and lists of their characteristics are numerous. However, some common traits exist among the lists. In general, entrepreneurs today are opportunists, in that they recognize and take advantage of opportunities. They are also resourceful, creative, visionary, hardworking, and optimistic. They are independent thinkers who are willing to take risks and innovate. They also tend to be excellent leaders.[4] Above all, they are dreamers.

 Would-be entrepreneurs live in a sea of dreams. Their destinations are private islands—places to build, create, and transform their particular dreams into reality. Being an entrepreneur entails envisioning your island, and, even more important, it means getting in the boat and rowing to your island. Some leave the shore and drift aimlessly in the shallow waters close to shore, while others paddle furiously and get nowhere, because they don't know how to paddle or steer. Worst of all are those who remain on the shore of the mainland, afraid to get in the boat. Yet, all those dreamers may one day be entrepreneurs, if they can marshal the resources—external and internal—needed to transform their dreams into reality.[5]

Not everyone has the internal stamina and drive to be an entrepreneur. Entrepreneurship causes a lot of stress. Disappointments are common. Uncertainty is a constant. However, successful entrepreneurs can also acquire great wealth and personal satisfaction.

Entrepreneurial Tasks

The primary tasks associated with a new venture are recognition or creation of an opportunity, creation of a business plan, securing start-up capital and actual management of the start-up through its early stages. These **entrepreneurial tasks** will now be described.

Opportunity Recognition or Creation

Entrepreneurship is often envisioned as a discovery process. **Entrepreneurial discovery** entails channeling resources toward the fulfillment of a market need.[6] For a start-up to be successful, this often means meeting a need better than other companies. Google, a popular Web browser, is an excellent example.

 In late 1995, Google cofounders Sergy Brin and Larry Page began working on its technology when they were Ph.D. candidates in computer science at Stanford University. The two dropped out and founded Google in August 1998. Not only does Google's technology look for keywords inside of Web pages, but it also gauges the importance of a search result based on the number and popularity of other sites that link to the page. This summer, a survey by market researchers NPD Group ranked Google the most effective search engine, with 97 percent of users saying they located what they were looking for "every time" or "most of the time."[7]

While this explanation of entrepreneurship is inherently satisfying, it is not a complete explanation. Entrepreneurial discovery may also be viewed as the intersection of a need and a solution. There are a lot of unmet needs in the world. For example, we need a cure for AIDS, and we need a more efficient way to enforce laws, and we need to be able to communicate more easily in a wide variety of languages. There are also a lot of solutions for which there may be no need at the present time. Scientists and even common people discover things every day. Human creativity is unbounded. Entrepreneurial activity occurs anytime an entrepreneur is able to link a need to a solution in such a manner that a new business emerges. Opportunities to do this are context specific.

Ex. What might be an opportunity today in Ukraine may not be an opportunity at all in the United States today or even in Ukraine tomorrow. This means that entrepreneurial opportunities do not necessarily lie around waiting to be discovered by the serendipitous entrepreneur who stumbles upon them, or even be "divined" by entrepreneurial geniuses, if any such geniuses exist. Instead, entrepreneurial opportunities are often residuals of

entrepreneurial tasks
Recognition or creation of an opportunity, creation of a business plan, securing startup capital and actual management of the startup through its early stages

entrepreneurial discovery
Entails channeling resources towards the fulfillment of a market need; the intersection of a need and a solution

human activities in non-economic spheres and emerge contingent upon conscious actions by entrepreneurs who continually strive to transform the outputs of those non-economic activities into new products and firms and in the process fulfill and transform human aspirations into new markets. In other words, before there are products and firms, there is human imagination; and before there are markets, there are human aspirations.[8]

The implication of this perspective is that entrepreneurial activity can emerge from anywhere. It is interesting to note that Microsoft employs top scientists from a lot of fields that seem to have nothing to do with computer software. This Microsoft strategy is an attempt to find needs in the software area that can be satisfied through solutions in other areas.

Sometimes organizations pass over ideas and then regret it. Scores of companies have been started by people who found no support for their ideas, and left their companies to form new ventures. In 1993, Tom Siebel formed Siebel Systems because one of his ideas was rejected while he was working at Oracle.

 Having made it into the top echelon of Oracle, Siebel got the itch to run his own show. He had an idea for a company based on a piece of technology he'd conceived of and used internally at Oracle to help sales reps communicate with one another about customer accounts. Siebel approached Oracle CEO Larry Ellison about commercializing the software, but Ellison, Siebel says, wasn't interested. . . . Before writing a single line of code, he and his co-founder, Pat House, also an Oracle veteran, went out and talked to customers about what kind of products they wanted. That was revolutionary. Most software companies are created by engineers designing a product that people with marketing and sales savvy then go out and hawk. Siebel thought that was stupid. Why not please the customer from the get-go, he reasoned, since happy customers buy more software? Siebel came to this logic at Oracle where, he reasoned, he learned a great deal about how not to run a business.[9]

Creation of a Business Plan

business plan
A plan that contains the details of how a new venture will be carried out

Everything associated with a new venture revolves around a **business plan.** Creation of the plan forces the entrepreneur to think through the details of the venture and determine whether it really seems reasonable. Table 6.1 contains a description of the various sections. The executive summary has the primary objective of catching the interest of the reader. This is followed by a description of the proposed business venture; an analysis of the environment; a resource analysis; and functional plans such as a marketing plan, operations plan, and a management plan. Financial projections are among the most important elements of a business plan, especially for potential investors. Projections determine when financing will be needed and in what quantity, as well as when investors can expect to begin receiving returns. Projections often

pro-forma financial statements
Forward-looking income statements, balance sheets, and cash flow statements that are based on predictions of what will happen in the future

take the form of **pro-forma financial statements,** including financial statements, balance sheets, and cash-flow statements. Pro-forma statements are hard to develop because entrepreneurs seldom have good data upon which to base them. But the process of developing pro-forma statements requires research on how much resources will cost and potential margins that might be expected. Pro-forma statements are an excellent way for an entrepreneur to communicate expected financial needs and performance.

Table 6.1   What's in a Business Plan?

Section	Description
Executive Summary	The executive summary contains a brief description of the venture and why it is likely to be successful. It must immediately catch the attention of potential investors and encourage them to read the entire business plan.
Business Description	The introduction provides a thorough description of the venture. It should include elements such as where it will be launched, who will be involved, the customers it will serve, and when everything is likely to happen.
Environmental Analysis	This section covers the most-relevant characteristics of the external environment in which the new venture will compete. These characteristics often include: ● Market analysis (including customer analysis and evaluation of past and expected growth in demand), ● Existing-competitor analysis ● Supplier analysis ● Evaluation of potential substitutes ● Discussion of entry and exit barriers and their influence on entering and exiting competitors ● Relevant government regulations and regulators ● Financial condition of the industry ● Availability of funding ● Overall economic factors for the host country ● Availability of technology ● Availability of personnel with appropriate qualifications
Resource Analysis	Resource analysis focuses on the special resources the venture already possesses and the resources that will be needed in order to make the venture a success. Such things as personnel, financial capital, equipment, patents and intellectual capital, and physical property are described. The most important resource and the one that should receive the most attention is the entrepreneur(s).
Functional Plans	The nature of the venture will determine which functional plans should be included. A marketing plan (how the market will be reached, advertising ideas, distribution strategy, etc.), a management plan (who will be responsible for which activities) and an operating plan are essential. Beyond these, other plans may include research and development, information management strategy, or personnel (training).
Financial Projections	Good data for projections typically is not available, but potential investors want to have some sense of the potential market size and growth and the projected margins that will be available. Financial projections (pro-forma statements) also help investors understand timing issues, such as when money will be needed, how much will be needed, and when their investment will begin to provide tangible returns.
Implementation Schedule	This is a plan outlining the steps that will be taken as the venture unfolds. It provides a time frame for the accomplishment of various activities.
End-game Strategy	Potential investors will be interested in knowing at what point they can exit the venture. Other important elements of an end-game strategy from the perspective of the entrepreneur include an executive succession plan and an exit strategy if the venture is not successful or when the venture has concluded.
Risk Analysis	All ventures entail risk. Potential investors appreciate a good analysis of risk. This section is also very helpful to the entrepreneur in determining whether to pursue the venture.

A fully developed implementation schedule may or may not be included in the initial business plan. However, even when a full schedule is not included, a business plan typically outlines a timeline for major events. Investors are also interested in what might be called an "endgame" strategy. This is a plan for concluding the venture, transferring control to others, or allowing potential investors to exit the venture with a high return on their investments. It may also include contingency plans in the event the venture does not succeed (i.e., alternative uses or sales potential for acquired resources), and an executive-succession plan in case the primary entrepreneur decides to leave the venture. Finally, potential investors will be very interested in the amount of risk found in a venture. Rather than sidestepping this issue, it is probably better to include a section that honestly evaluates financial and operating risks.

In most ways, a business plan closely resembles a strategic plan for an existing business. It contains the basic elements of situation analysis (external and internal), strategy formulation, and strategy implementation. However, in a business plan, there is more emphasis on financing. Also, the perspective from which the two types of plans are written is very different. For instance, strategic plans assume an ongoing business, whereas a new business venture may not be pursued if it is determined to be infeasible. Also, the target audiences of a business plan and a strategic plan are very different. Since a business plan will go to potential investors, it must be written in a concise format (no more than thirty to forty pages), and it must answer the types of questions that potential investors would like to have answered. A strategic plan usually includes a lot more detail in the implementation sections, since it serves as a guide for an existing organization. Potential investors are not interested in as much operating detail as are managers in an existing organization.

Securing Start-up Capital

start-up capital
The financing required to begin a new venture

Obtaining **start-up capital** is probably the most difficult problem facing a potential entrepreneur, and, as will be demonstrated later in this chapter, not obtaining sufficient capital is one of the biggest causes of failure. Some of the most common sources of start-up capital include commercial banks, personal contacts, venture capitalists, corporate partnerships, and business angels (see Table 6.2). Bank loans result in debt. Personal contacts, venture capitalists, corporate partners, and business angels may provide loans or receive equity (or both) in exchange for the capital they provide. After start-up, if the venture has enough of a track record so that potential investors believe that it will be highly profitable in time, an initial public offering may be pursued.

Some entrepreneurs are able to start with their own financial resources. For example, the first of Colonel Sanders's fried-chicken restaurants was financed with his Social Security check.[10] Others may turn to family and friends. For larger ventures or once these resources are exhausted, they often turn to a bank. Because of the risks involved, commercial banks don't tend to get very excited about financing entrepreneurial ventures unless substantial secured assets are involved. For example, entrepreneurs often mortgage their homes or offer their automobiles, jewelry, or financial investments as loan security. Banks also consider loans more attractive if a wealthy third party is willing to co-sign, thus taking on the financial obligation if the entrepreneur is unable to pay. Occasionally, a bank will make an unsecured loan based on the reputation or credentials of the entrepreneur or on a personal relationship. Another common form of financing for smaller ventures is credit cards. One or more entrepreneurs run their credit cards up to their limits to pay for needed

Table 6.2 Sources of Capital for Entrepreneurs

Source	Description
Commercial Banks	Includes asset-backed borrowing, small loans, third-party loan guarantees, leasing, credit cards, and credit lines. Once in a while, a bank will select a venture for funding with very little security, usually based on the track record and credentials of the entrepreneur.
Personal Contacts	Family and friends, asset sales
Venture Capitalists	Organizations or individuals who evaluate business plans and invest "seed money" in some of them for an ownership interest and other compensation. They expect very high returns on their investments because of the risk they are taking.
Corporate Partnerships	Many corporations seek opportunities to invest in new ventures with a high potential payoff. The corporation usually trades money or other resources for an ownership interest.
Business Angels	High net worth individuals who invest in entrepreneurial ventures as an opportunity to grow their wealth at a rate higher than a secure investment would provide. Many angels are also interested in providing opportunities to entrepreneurs.
Initial Public Offerings	These are usually used during a more advanced stage of the venture, rather than at start-up. The venture has existed long enough to provide adequate information that would lead potential investors to believe that it will be highly successful. The IPO basically provides the capital to pursue the venture at a larger scale.

Sources: J. A. Fraser, "How to Finance Anything," *Inc* (March 1999): 32–48; P. DeCeglie, "The Truth about Venture Capital," *Business Startups* (February 2000): 40–47; K. Schilit, "How to Obtain Venture Capital," *Business Horizons* (May/June 1987): 76–81; J. Freear, J. E. Sohl, and W. E. Wetzel Jr., "Angels and Non-Angels: Are There Differences?" *Journal of Business Venturing* (March 1994): 109–123.

venture capitalists
Individuals or groups of investors that seek out and provide capital to entrepreneurs

resources to finance the venture. This tends to be a very-high-risk option for the entrepreneur, since new ventures often fail.

Venture capitalists are another potential source of start-up capital. They are individuals or groups of investors that seek out and provide capital to entrepreneurs with ideas that seem to have the potential for very high returns. They may seek an annual return as high as 60 percent or more on "seed money" for a new venture.[11] In evaluating business plans, venture capitalists consider the entrepreneur's personality and experience, the product or service characteristics, market characteristics, financial potential, and the strength of the venture team.[12] Financing from a venture capitalist is often combined with capital from other sources such as banks or private investors. Entrepreneurs that seek financing from venture capitalists should prepare a thorough business plan and should answer questions as completely and accurately as possible. They should not expect an immediate decision, embellish facts, dodge questions, hide significant problems, or fixate on pricing.[13]

Entrepreneurs may also turn to corporations to obtain financing. From the entrepreneur's perspective, the chief disadvantage of this form of financing is a partial loss of control and ownership. Large corporations often seek investments in new ventures as a way to obtain new technology, products, or markets. For example, Novell frequently finances software developers that are working on projects that can enhance Novell's position in network software. Another example is Applied Materials, a half-billion-dollar leader in the production of computer chips.

Bob Buckwald, founder of CI Systems, developed infrared applications that proved valuable in Operation Desert Storm. Buckwald determined that his applications could be useful in measuring the temperature of silicon chips during manufacture, but his tiny company lacked the capital to do research and development, and also lacked a production line on which to test products. He found a strategic partner, Applied Materials, that could supply both. Applied Materials lacked expertise in infrared technology, but, as the ultimate consumer of the device, could see the benefit of the product.[14]

business angels
Wealthy individuals who provide startup capital to entrepreneurs

Another potential source of capital are **business angels,** wealthy individuals who provide start-up capital to entrepreneurs with promise. Many of them were once entrepreneurs themselves. They sometimes seek high returns, but many of them enjoy investing simply for the sake of helping an entrepreneur or advancing the state of technology in an area such as medicine, the arts, or computer technology. Unlike venture capitalists, business angels do not pursue investing full-time.

initial public offering (IPO)
Entails sale of stock to the public and investors

After a venture has established a record of performance, entrepreneurs or venture capitalists may pursue an **initial public offering (IPO).** An IPO entails selling stock to the public and investors (see Figure 6.1). Assuming a board of directors has been created, the first step is to receive approval from the board to proceed with the IPO. Then an underwriter (investment banker) is selected, and a "letter of intent" is drafted. The letter of intent outlines the financial relationship between the company and the underwriter (i.e., fees), and other conditions of the offering. Attorneys then begin work on a prospectus, being careful to follow guidelines set by the Securities and Exchange Commission. The investment banker will then oversee

FIGURE 6.1

The Initial Public Offering (IPO) Process

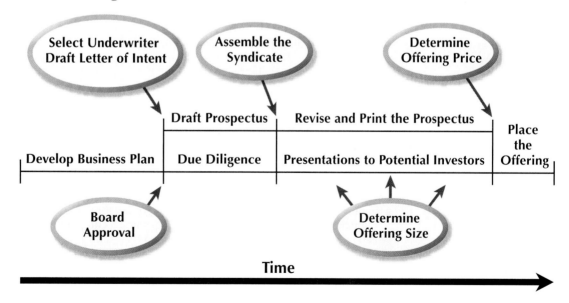

Source: This model is based on information found in Nasdaq, "Going Public" (New York: The Nasdaq Stock Market, Inc., 2000).

an elaborate "due diligence" process, which is a thorough examination of the company, its financial situation, markets, customers, creditors, and any other important stakeholders. After a printer is selected for the prospectus and a preliminary prospectus is filed, the underwriter assembles a syndicate of companies that will help sell the IPO to targeted investors. Venture managers and the investment banker then do a series of formal presentations to potential investors. If everything looks positive after these presentations, the final prospectus is printed, the offering is priced, the size of the offering is determined, and the IPO takes place.[15]

Managing the Venture

The early stages of an entrepreneurial start-up are the most difficult.[16] Some of the major tasks of entrepreneurs for the first year of a venture are outlined in Table 6.3. In the early stages, financing and financial management are difficult problems. Even after the difficult process of securing initial financing, the entrepreneur must still set up a system to manage financial flows and keep records necessary to satisfy venture capitalists, creditors, and the Internal Revenue Service. Fortunately, there are a lot of inexpensive software packages available in the market today that can help an entrepreneur track revenues and expenses and prepare to file tax reports. However, sometimes entrepreneurs are not familiar enough with personal computers to fully

Table 6.3	First Year Agenda For Entrepreneurial Startups
Activity	**Description**
Financial Management	Once external funding is obtained, the emphasis becomes establishing systems to track revenues and expenses and control costs. A record-keeping system must be established that will satisfy the demands of investors, creditors, and the Internal Revenue Service.
Marketing	Early marketing efforts may include providing a product or service to a few customers at a nominal price to establish a track record and gain references. Targeted advertising is also appropriate.
Product/Service Development	This includes establishment of a system for collecting feedback from early customers so that the product or service can be improved. Continuous improvement is essential.
Resource Acquisition	This process begins with site selection and construction of a building, if necessary. The site must also be equipped with necessary machinery, furnishings, information systems, utilities, and supplies. Contracts need to be established with suppliers of raw materials, components, and services.
Process Development	The focus is on production and operations management to ensure efficiency and quality. Once again, continuous improvement is essential.
Management and Staffing	One of the most essential activities is recruitment of motivated, well-trained employees and selection of managers, as needed. This area also includes assignment of responsibilities, establishment of personnel policies, overcoming administrative problems, training, and establishing a compensation system, which may include benefits. The entrepreneur is establishing an organizational culture in this first year. It should support the objectives of the venture.
Legal Requirements	The venture will need a legal form (sole proprietorship, partnership, corporation). If employees are hired, the venture will need an Employer Identification Number and will need to collect and pay payroll taxes. Patents and trademarks are sometimes necessary to protect the proprietary technology or brand image of the venture. Other legal requirements vary depending on the nature of the venture, and the country and industry in which it is formed.

understand how to implement even a simple system. In this case, it is helpful if one of the first employees hired has the skills to handle a basic financial program. Also, many entrepreneurs secure the services of a tax adviser during the first few years of the venture.

Entrepreneurs often experience cash-flow problems because typically inflows from sales take a while to materialize. Low sales can plague a new venture, especially in the first few months after introduction. If a product or service is new to the market, it may take a while before potential customers consider it worth trying. Many consumers and businesses wait to see if the new product or service is reliable and valuable. They look for a "track record." One strategy for overcoming resistance is to provide the first few products or services to customers at a nominal price on a trial basis. Those first customers then become references. Targeted advertising is also helpful. For example, if a company is selling products that appeal to modern women, a women's magazine may be an appropriate advertising outlet.

product/service development
Introduction of new products or services related to an existing competence of the firm or development of truly new-to-the-world products not related to the core business of the firm

Another important first-year activity is **product/service development.** Entrepreneurs seldom get a product or service exactly right the first time. Early users of the product or service will very quickly discover flaws. Entrepreneurs should set up a system that collects feedback from early customers so that the product or service can be improved. Continuous improvement is essential because if the product or service is a success, other firms will quickly imitate it. They may be larger firms with more resources. Therefore, it is important to stay one step ahead of the competition in order to enjoy first-mover advantages.

Many resources need to be acquired at start-up. One of the most important decisions in this regard is site selection. The entrepreneur has to select a site that is small enough to be cost-efficient, yet large enough to allow some growth as the venture grows. The site-selection decision is usually made during the development of the business plan, since potential investors will be interested in making sure that a suitable site is available. The site also has to be attractive to personnel that have the skills required for the venture to be a success. It should also be as close as possible to suppliers and customers. If the site does not yet include a building, then construction must be coordinated. Other physical resources that need to be acquired include machinery, furnishings, utilities, information systems, and supplies. Contracts need to be established with suppliers of raw materials and services.

In addition to product/service development, process development cannot be neglected. Once a site has been selected, it has to be prepared for production. The first units of a product or service are the most expensive to produce. Entrepreneurs should pay close attention to process issues, should establish a quality-control system, and should focus on obtaining raw materials and supplies at a minimum of cost. Costs of production should drop rapidly in the early stages of the product life cycle, consistent with the experience curve presented earlier. Other production- and operations-management issues will present themselves, and will require immediate attention.

Many entrepreneurial ventures begin with a single person or a small group of people; however, successful ventures need more personnel within a short period of time. The entrepreneur simply has too much to do. As the venture grows, recruitment and training of personnel and managers become important activities. The entrepreneur has to delegate responsibilities and establish a compensation system, which might even include benefits such as insurance. As the organization grows, it is important to have a culture in place that supports the objectives of the venture. The culture is established very early through the examples of the entrepreneur and other early employees. For example, if the entrepreneur works hard, a cultural norm that values hard work will be established. If customers are given highest priority, then a customer-oriented culture will emerge.

partnership
A business form in which the partners each contribute resources and share in the rewards of the venture

limited partnership
A business form in which the management responsibility and legal liability of partners are limited

S corporation
Formerly called the Subchapter S corporation, this corporate form allows tax advantages in the United States that are similar to those associated with a partnership

Legal requirements are also a major issue during the first year. First, the entrepreneur should decide which legal form the venture will take. In a sole proprietorship, the entrepreneur is the owner and is financially and legally liable for the venture in its entirety. In a **partnership,** the partners each contribute resources such as money, physical goods, services, knowledge, and external relationships to the venture. They also share in the rewards. Typically, articles of partnership are drawn up by the partners to define such things as the duration of the venture, contributions by partners, division of profits and losses, rights of partners, procedures for settlement of disputes, and employee management.[17] A **limited partnership** can be established in which the management responsibility and legal liability of partners are limited, except that at least one partner must be a general partner with unlimited liability. Several forms of limited partnerships exist.[18] A key advantage of a partnership over a corporation is that profits are passed through to partners instead of being taxed at higher corporate rates. Also, the problem of double taxation, where profits are taxed at the corporate level and then dividends are taxed at the personal level, is avoided.

Corporations and the agency issues surrounding them were discussed in Chapter 3. At this point, the only thing that needs to be added is that one of the advantages of forming a corporation is that the financial risk of a shareholder is limited to the amount invested in the corporation. However, shareholder control over the actions of the company is extremely limited. Also, the tax advantages found in partnerships are lost when a corporation is formed. The only exception is the **S corporation,** formerly called the Subchapter S corporation (from Subchapter S of the Internal Revenue Code), which allows tax advantages similar to what are found in a partnership. However, to qualify as an S corporation, organizations must have relatively few shareholders, and must adhere to other strict guidelines.[19]

If employees are hired, the entrepreneur will also need to file for an Employer Identification Number (EIN) and begin to pay (and collect) payroll taxes. Patents may need to be filed or trademarks protected. Other legal requirements depend on the nature of the venture and the regulations surrounding it.

This discussion is not intended to be complete, but it does provide an idea with regard to what an entrepreneur faces in the first year or so. For any would-be entrepreneurs, it adds a dimension of realism with regard to what it will take to make it through the first year. Entrepreneurs experience a lot of problems. Figure 6.2 demonstrates that from an external perspective, customer contact is an issue facing more than a quarter of entrepreneurs. Other major concerns are a lack of market knowledge, and problems with market planning. It is interesting to note that most entrepreneurs do not feel that competitors are much of a problem. This point attests to the advantages of being small and introducing a new product or service to the market. From an internal perspective, the most common issues are obtaining adequate capital and managing cash flow. Management problems are also experienced with inventory control, facilities and equipment, human resources, leadership, organization structure, and accounting systems. Some of these causes of failure will be discussed further in the next section.

Causes of Failure

According to both entrepreneurs and venture capitalists, the most common reasons new ventures fail are internal.[20] Specifically, the number-one reason cited by both groups is lack of management skill. Entrepreneurs often have enthusiasm, optimism, and drive, but do not possess the business skills they need to make a venture successful. A poor management strategy or inappropriate vision are also common

FIGURE 6.2

Internal and External Problems Faced by Entrepreneurs

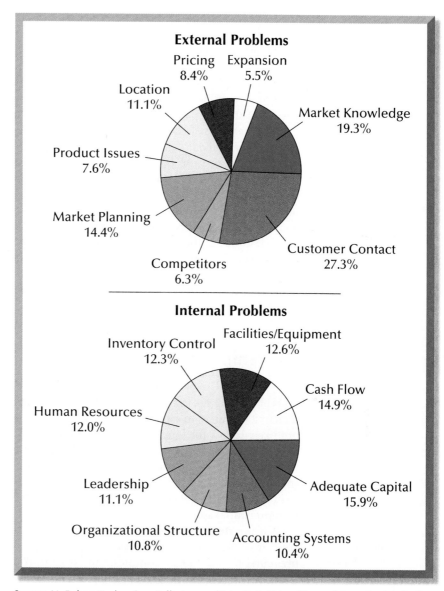

Source: H. Robert Dodge, Sam Fullerton, and John E. Robbins, "Stage of Organizational Life Cycle and Competition as Mediators of Problem Perception for Small Business," *Strategic Management Journal* 15 (1994): 129. Reprinted by permission of John Wiley & Sons, Ltd.

problems in failed ventures. In addition, many times entrepreneurs lack the ability to manage finances effectively.

Many new ventures fail because of a lack of capitalization. Often businesses need a lot of capital at the beginning if they are going to succeed. Without sufficient capital, the venture may fail even if the idea was good and the management skills were present. For example, a business may need to be a particular size to generate enough efficiency to make a profit. Or a venture may fail because not enough people know about a product or service due to insufficient advertising. A firm that does not initially have enough financial backing may also assume too much debt too early. Interest payments can divert funds away from more-important uses, and the risk of insolvency from not being able to make timely payments is a constant threat. When entrepreneurs feel high levels of financial risk, their behavior may change. They may be less willing to take other risks that are necessary for the venture to continue to progress.

Other factors that can lead to failure are associated with the product or service itself. Poor product design is a common problem, or it may be that the product or service is simply too early or too late into the market. A product can be too early if the market does not have enough skill to use it yet or if the market is not yet interested in using it. A late entry loses all of the early-mover advantages and may find that the market is already saturated or that consumers have already developed loyalty to other brands.

Even if a venture has excellent management, sufficient capitalization, and a good product or service, it can still fail if market conditions are not favorable. This is another timing issue. An entrepreneur may begin the launch of a new product or service right before a downturn in the domestic economy or in a foreign economy upon which the new venture is dependent. There are many other reasons a venture can fail; however, these are some of the most common. Table 6.4 contains a summary of common problems leading to failure of entrepreneurial ventures.

So far, this discussion has focused primarily on entrepreneurial start-ups. However, existing organizations also need entrepreneurship. The next section deals with entrepreneurship and innovation in established firms.

Corporate Entrepreneurship and Innovation

Entrepreneurial success comes from more effectively accumulating, combining, and directing resources to satisfy a need than other firms can. However, the advantage is not likely to last for long due to competitor imitation.[21] Consequently, continued growth requires continual innovation and entrepreneurship. Small companies tend to be better than large companies at innovation. One reason for the difference is that smaller companies are more flexible. They are not as subject to the constraints of a rigid bureaucracy that can stifle creative activity. They also tend to foster more of an entrepreneurial spirit.[22]

corporate entrepreneurship
Involves the creation of new business ventures within existing corporations

intrapraneurship
Corporate entrepreneurship, or the creation of new business ventures within existing corporations

Corporate entrepreneurship, sometimes called **intrapraneurship,** involves the creation of new business ventures within existing corporations.[23] This sort of entrepreneurship is more common in organizations that foster innovation. Consequently, this section will begin with a discussion of factors that encourage corporate innovation, followed by a description of the various structures firms use when they form internal ventures. Because so much entrepreneurial activity has been directed recently toward communications technology, this section will close with a discussion of the Internet and e-commerce.

Fostering Innovation in Established Firms

Among large companies, 3M is one of the most innovative. In fact, the company boasts a catalog of sixty thousand products, including Post-it Notes, antistatic videotape, translucent dental braces, and Scotch Tape.[24] The company follows some simple rules.

Table 6.4	Most Common Sources of Entrepreneurial Failure
Problem	**Description**
Management Skills	This is perhaps the most common problem. It can be manifest in poor planning, a poor management strategy or ineffective organization, or inadequate financial management. Or an entrepreneur may lack "people skills." Inflated owner egos, poor human-resource management, or control issues can stifle a venture.
Lack of Adequate Capitalization	Many entrepreneurial ventures begin "on a shoestring." They lack the financial backing necessary to be large enough to be efficient or effective in reaching the desired customer. Some organizations may also acquire too much debt too early, which can stifle a new venture.
Product/Service Problems	Poor product/service design or an inappropriate distribution strategy can hinder success. Or the venture may depend too much on a single customer. Timing is also an issue. A product/service may be too early or too late into the market to be successful.
External Market Conditions	An otherwise outstanding venture may still fail if economic conditions turn sour in a domestic or international economy upon which the new venture depends.

Sources: D. E. Terpstra and P. D. Olson, "Entrepreneurial Startup and Growth: A Classification of Problems," *Entrepreneurship Theory and Practice* (Spring 1993): 19; A. V. Bruno, J. K. Leidecker, and J. W. Harder, "Why Firms Fail," *Business Horizons* (March/April 1987): 50–58.

- *Don't Kill a Project.* If an idea is not applicable to the division in which an employee works, he or she can spend up to 15 percent of his or her time to try to find a home for it within the company. The company also provides "seed money" to corporate entrepreneurs so that they can pursue their projects. This money is provided in the form of Genesis grants of $50,000. Ninety of these grants are awarded each year.

- *Tolerate Failure.* Because the company encourages experimentation and risk taking, there is a greater likelihood that something will work out. The goal is that divisions of the company must derive at least 25 percent of their sales from products that were created during the past five years.

- *Keep Divisions Small.* Managers must know the names of each member of their staff. When a division gets too big, it is split up.

- *Motivate the Champions.* An employee with a good idea can recruit a team to pursue it. Salary and promotion prospects are then tied to the success of the product. Sometimes successful entrepreneurs are given the opportunity to run their own 3M product group or division.

- *Stay Close to the Customer.* Managers, researchers and marketing people visit frequently with customers to determine their reactions to 3M products and their future needs.

- *Share the Wealth.* Regardless of where ideas are developed within the company, they are shared by all.[25]

Researchers have studied innovative companies such as 3M for many years now, and have been able to identify several factors that seem to encourage innovation. In addition, they have discovered many impediments to innovative activity. Some of the major factors that encourage or prevent innovation in established firms are listed in Table 6.5

Large corporations that are successful innovators tend to have a clear-cut, well-supported vision that includes an emphasis on innovation.[26] Their cultures support

Table 6.5   Factors Encouraging or Discouraging Innovation in Established Firms

Factors Encouraging Innovation	Factors Discouraging Innovation
• Vision and culture that support innovation, personal growth and risk taking	• Rigid bureaucracy and conservatism in decision making
• Top management support and organizational champions	• Absence of management support or champions
• Teamwork and collaboration; a flat management hierarchy	• Authoritarian leadership and traditional hierarchy
• Decentralized approval process	• Difficult approval process
• Valuing the ideas of every employee	• Attention given to the ideas of only certain people (researchers or managers)
• Excellent communications	• Closed-door offices
• Innovation grants and time off to pursue projects	• Inadequate resources devoted to entrepreneurial activities
• Large rewards for successful entrepreneurs	• Harsh penalties for failure
• Focus on learning	• Exclusive emphasis on measurable outcomes

this vision by encouraging people to discuss new ideas and take risks. The organization should not only tolerate failures, but encourage employees and managers to learn from them.[27] Innovative cultures also promote personal growth in an effort to attract and retain the best people. The best people also seek ownership, and innovative companies often provide it to them through stock incentives and stock options.[28] This is one way to align the interests of the organization with the interests of talented individuals. Finally, a culture that supports innovation encourages employees and managers to challenge old ideas by instilling a commitment to continuous learning and strategic change. As Yoshio Maruta of Japan's second-largest diversified cosmetics and computer firm describes it:

> Past wisdom must not be a constraint but something to be challenged. Yesterday's success formula is often today's obsolete dogma. My challenge is to have the organization continually questioning the past so we can renew ourselves every day.[29]

On the other hand, rigid bureaucracies can stifle innovation. They are characterized by rules, policies, and procedures that make it difficult for an individual to vary from normal activities. People who feel as though they cannot or should not vary from established rules are unlikely to be sources of creativity and innovative thought.

Top-management support of innovation is essential, including efforts to develop and train employees with regard to innovation and corporate entrepreneurship.[30] Managers should be persistent in getting projects to market.[31]

 A decade ago, James McDonald was considered a dreamer when he predicted cable companies would soon offer digital movies on demand and push-button shopping from living rooms. Yet McDonald, chief executive of cable set-top box maker Scientific-Atlanta, never gave up—even after his first interactive TV cable box flopped in a 1993 test in Orlando. . . . Today Scientific-Atlanta supplies 52 of the 100 largest cable-TV systems with digital boxes. In the most recent quarter, the company's sales surged 51% to $663.7 million, and earnings doubled, to $76.2 million.[32]

Because they shape the vision and purpose of the organization, top managers must also serve a disruptive role, making sure that managers and employees don't get too comfortable with the way things are.[33] In addition to top managers, organizational champions are important.[34] A champion is someone who is very committed to a project and is willing to expend energy to make sure it succeeds. Two champions are needed. The first is a managerial champion, a person with enough authority in the company to gather the resources and push the project through the administrative bureaucracy. The second is a technical champion. This is an expert with the knowledge needed to guide the technical aspects of the project from beginning to end.

As top managers support innovation, they also have to be careful not to be too dictatorial in their decision making. Authoritarian management can stifle innovation. This type of management is being replaced by networking, teams and a "people friendly" style of management.[35] To maintain an adaptive, learning atmosphere at all organizational levels, many firms have created self-managed work teams and cross-functional product-development teams, so that multiple perspectives will be brought to problem solving. Teams cut across traditional functional boundaries, so that a single team might include representatives from engineering, research and development, finance, marketing, information systems, and human resources. These teams are kept small so that they are highly flexible, adaptable, and easy to manage.[36] The management hierarchy in these types of organizations tends to be flat, meaning that there are not a lot of levels in the management hierarchy between the customer and the top manager.[37]

The level at which projects are approved is also a key factor in determining support for innovative activities. Some large corporations require that an idea receive approval from five or more managers before any resources are committed to pursuing it. Innovative organizations allow project teams to form that do not report through the traditional lines of authority. Consequently, their work does not have to pass through multiple levels for approval.[38]

Lockheed used the term "Skunkworks" to describe these special teams. They are free from virtually all organizational requirements and boundaries. They have full authority and autonomy to create ideas and solutions. These sorts of teams were common in the early years of the microcomputer industry. Increasingly, these types of autonomous, entrepreneurial teams are needed to prevent the lethargy and inertia that can plague large organizations. In addition, managers in innovative companies encourage several projects to be pursued at the same time. This is important because some of the projects will not work out.[39]

Innovation is also more likely to emerge from a company with a culture that values the ideas of every person. Gary Hamel, an expert on innovation, talks about his work with companies in which secretaries come up with ideas for multimillion-dollar businesses. He says: "Many companies have succeeded in making everyone responsible for quality. We're going to have to do the same for innovation."[40] Unfortunately, many large companies don't give equal attention to everyone's ideas. They expect researchers or managers to come up with all of the innovations. Along with an egalitarian culture, excellent communications are found in innovative organizations. They encourage communication by having informal meetings whenever possible, forming teams across functions, and planning the physical layout of the facility so as to encourage frequent interaction (they don't let people hide in their offices).[41]

For corporate entrepreneurship to take place, organizations also have to commit resources such as people, money, information, equipment, and a physical location.[42] Some companies, such as 3M, even provide seed money in the form of innovation grants. Giving people time to pursue their ideas is also critical. At 3M, a corporate policy that supports internal venturing allows scientists to spend up to 15 percent of their time on personal research projects. "Post-it" notepads were invented through this program.[43]

Effective rewards systems are also important. Corporate entrepreneurship allows creative people to realize the rewards from their innovative talents without having to leave the company.[44] Innovation should be rewarded through raises, promotions, awards, perquisites, and public and private recognition. While the upside rewards for innovation should be high, the downside penalties for failed innovation efforts should be minimal.[45]

Corporate entrepreneurship can be viewed as an organizational-learning process directed at developing the skills and knowledge necessary to compete in new domains.[46] Organizational learning is at the center of innovative activities. Chapter 3 discussed activities associated with knowledge (1) creation, (2) retention, (3) sharing, and (4) utilization. As was demonstrated in that chapter, outstanding execution of these activities can be a source of competitive advantage leading superior performance.[47]

Many of the characteristics of innovative companies are found in General Electric, one of the largest and most successful conglomerates. Jack Welch, Jeff Immelt, and other board members of General Electric recently discussed the organization's transition to becoming a "learning company."

Our true "core competency" today is not manufacturing or services, but the global recruiting and nurturing of the world's best people and the cultivation in them of an insatiable desire to learn, to stretch and to do things better every day. By finding, challenging and rewarding these people, by freeing them from bureaucracy, by giving them all of the resources they need—and by simply getting out of their way—we have seen them make us better and better every year. We have a Company more agile than others a fraction of our size, a high-spirited company where people are free to dream and encouraged to act and to take risks. In a culture where people act this way, every day, "big" will never mean slow. This is all about people—"soft stuff." But values and behaviors are what produce those performance numbers, and they are the bedrock upon which we will build our future.[48]

This is a fitting summary of this section because it mentions so many of the elements of innovative companies. The next section will discuss methods for structuring internal ventures.

Structuring Internal Ventures

There are many design alternatives available to organizations for pursuing corporate entrepreneurship. The selection of an organizational design depends on the strategic importance of the venture and how closely related the venture is to current activities.[49] Strategic importance can be assessed based on factors such as the likelihood that the venture will lead to a competitive advantage relative to competitors, and what may be learned during the venture that can move the whole organization forward. Top management will want to maintain a high level of control over ventures that are strategically important, in that they are closely related to the organization's current or anticipated business activities. For example, managers of strategically important new ventures should probably report directly to top management, who will stay apprised of the project at every step.

Operational relatedness of the new venture to current organizational activities can be determined by asking whether the organization currently has the capabilities and resources that will be required to make the venture a success. Many new ventures are actually a result of combining organizational resources in new ways, as when Toys "R" Us ventured into children's-clothing retailing and when Microsoft created the Microsoft Network, a Web site on the World Wide Web. Consequently, new capabilities may not be required, but only new combinations of existing capabilities. Managers should also assess what effect the new venture will have on current processes. For example, will the new venture slow down production of other products or services because of the resources it uses? High levels of operational relatedness should result in a strong operational coupling between the new and existing businesses. Joint information systems should be established, and professionals from new and existing businesses should meet regularly. Depending on the nature of the project, work flows may even need to be coordinated.

Joining operational relatedness with strategic importance results in the model in Figure 6.3. The model contains suggested design configurations for each type of internal venture. They are described below.

- Strategically Important/Strongly Related. Top managers will want to maintain a high level of control over these ventures, and also create a strong coupling with existing operations. Direct integration can accomplish both of these ends, by integrating the new venture right into the mainstream processes of the organization.

- Strategically Important/Unrelated. Since these ventures are strategically important but do not draw on existing resources of the organization,

FIGURE 6.3

Designs for Corporate Entrepreneurship

Operational Relatedness		Important	Not Important
Unrelated		High Control/ No Operational Coupling **Special Business Units**	No Control/ No Operational Coupling **Complete Spinoff**
Related		High Control/ Strong Operational Coupling **Direct Integration**	No Control/ Strong Operational Coupling **Nurturing and Contracting**

Strategic Importance

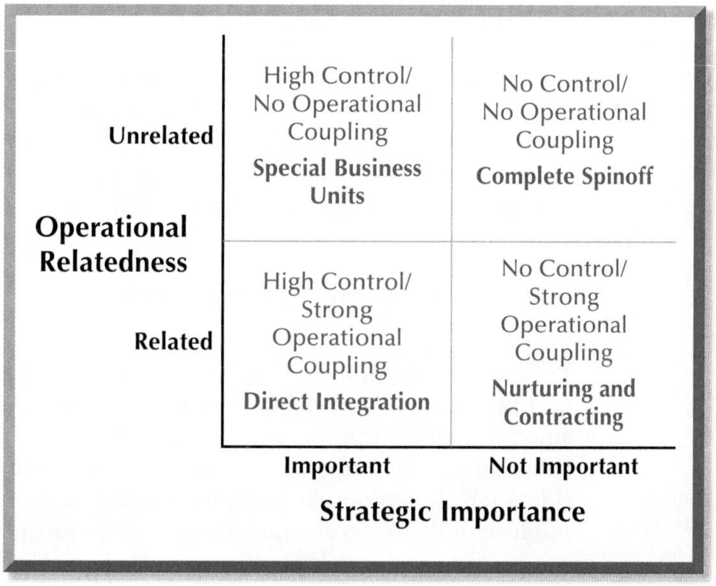

Source: Adapted from R. A. Burgelman, "Designs for Corporate Entrepreneurship in Established Firms," Copyright © 1984 by the Regents of the University of California. Reprinted from the *California Management Review,* Vol. 26, No. 3. By permission of the Regents.

special business units should be established. These units are still wholly owned by the organization, and their managers still report directly to top management.

- Not Strategically Important/Strongly Related. Since the business is not strategically important to the organization, there is no motivation to develop the venture in-house. However, operational relatedness may create the opportunity to sell services or excess manufacturing capacity to the new business. Also, the organization may be able to learn from the new business. Consequently, organizations should not create these ventures themselves, but should nurture entrepreneurs as they create their own independent companies.

- Not Strategically Important/Unrelated. A complete spin-off of a totally independent company is appropriate in these instances. The organization should not pursue any type of business relationship with the new company.[50]

For example, Norton Manufacturing Company of Fostoria, Ohio, established a separate business unit to pursue a venture that was considered critical to the company, but was unrelated to what they were currently doing.

 Norton Manufacturing Company was founded in 1950 as a tool-and-die shop. After many years of growth, Norton began to lose business to smaller machine shops with lower overhead. Refusing to become a victim of economic circumstances, the company searched for an opportunity that would be consistent with its resources and the talents of its employees. Managers found an opportunity to supply high-performance crankshafts to the auto-racing industry. Norton decided to pursue the opportunity as a separate venture, and used supplier communications to send a signal to potential customers that it would be pursuing the highest standards of excellence. Special training was provided to employees. The new focus led to 208 percent growth in sales over a three-year period.[51]

As an alternative to corporate venturing, some organizations choose to grow through acquiring other companies or engaging in joint ventures. A summary of various growth options is contained in the final section of this chapter. The next section focuses attention on a topic that has attracted a lot of entrepreneurial activities, both from independent entrepreneurs and within established firms.

The Internet and E-Commerce

We live in an age of expanding worldwide communication. The Internet is a major part of the Information Revolution. According to Peter Drucker, "The explosive emergence of the Internet as a major, perhaps eventually the major, worldwide distribution channel for goods, services, and, surprisingly, for managerial and professional jobs is profoundly changing economies, markets, and industry structures; products and services and their flow; consumer segmentation, consumer values, and consumer behavior; jobs and labor markets."[52] Firms are using the Internet for e-tailing, exchanging data with other businesses, business-to-business buying and selling, and e-mail communications with a variety of stakeholders. This is activity is generally referred to as **e-commerce.**

e-commerce
Describes business dealings that are electronically based, such as e-tailing (retailing through the Internet), exchanging data, business-to-business buying and selling, and e-mail communications

Webifying a business is not even half of it. Too often today's CEOs view the Web as yet another productivity tool—one that offers the promise of wholesale efficiencies. Yet, despite the fevered claims of Internet boosters and IT vendors, the Web's most profound impact on business will come not in the form of hyperefficient business processes, but in a riotous explosion of new products, new services, new content, new companies, and new organizational forms.[53]

In the 1990s, thousands of entrepreneurs started businesses that came to be known as **dot-coms.** These were companies that would register a domain name on the World Wide Web, typically with a dot-com extension, and begin providing some sort of service over the Internet. Companies spent millions of advertising dollars through many forms of media trying to attract users to their Web sites.

dot-coms
Internet-based businesses; the name comes from the fact that many of these businesses have an internet-based address that ends in .com, as in Amazon.com

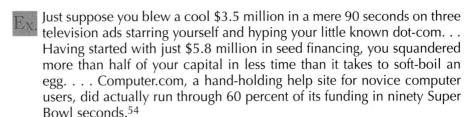 Just suppose you blew a cool $3.5 million in a mere 90 seconds on three television ads starring yourself and hyping your little known dot-com. . . Having started with just $5.8 million in seed financing, you squandered more than half of your capital in less time than it takes to soft-boil an egg. . . . Computer.com, a hand-holding help site for novice computer users, did actually run through 60 percent of its funding in ninety Super Bowl seconds.[54]

Early in the Internet craze, the race was not to achieve profits or even revenues, but to attract "eyeballs." The notion was that if a Web site could become a favorite for users throughout the world, eventually the business owners would figure out a way to make money from it. The founders of these types of Web sites had an inadequate business model for turning eyeballs into profits and cash flow.[55] Eventually, their initial investment capital ran out, and they were left with inadequate cash flow to continue operations. Some of these dot-coms were bought out. Others went out of business. A few of the most successful have continued to hold on. For example, priceline.com Inc., the travel retailer, announced its first-ever profit late in 2001. Other profitable ventures include the on-line broker Ameritrade Holding and Homestore.com, the real-estate-listings site.[56] Yahoo! boasts 145 million registered users, more than any other in the world, and is profitable.[57]

A variety of approaches to the Internet have been used. Some dot-coms provide retailing. Many of these dot-com retailers carry no inventory themselves. Rather, they connect buyers and sellers. Other dot-coms provide a service to consumers and sell advertising on their Web sites . For instance, Lycos.com has extensive road-map information, and Google.com is a Web browser. Monster.com is a job-placement service. Some companies use a combined approach. Amazon.com is a retailer that provides extensive services to its users and sells advertising.

Another interesting application of the Internet is test-marketing, such as Procter & Gamble's Web site, PG.com.

 Each month the $40 billion consumer-goods-marketing powerhouse invites on-line consumers to sample and give feedback on new prototype products. If an item gets rave reviews, P&G might decide to bring it to retail stores. If not, it's history. Since first dabbling in on-line research in 1998, the Cincinnati-based company had become the industry's most avid proponent of using the Internet as a fast, cost-effective means for gauging consumer demand for potential new products. It already conducts

40 percent of its six thousand product tests and other studies on-line. Procter & Gamble spends about $140 million annually on research, and the company believes it can cut that figure in half by shifting efforts to the Internet.[58]

Existing "brick and mortar" companies have used the Internet as an effective way to increase their market reach. They are marketing existing products and services through their Web sites. For example, Toys "R" Us has an extensive Web site that sells many of the same products found in its existing stores. Trane Company, the air-conditioner manufacturer, has a private exchange that allows its five thousand dealers to browse, buy, and schedule deliveries.[59] The Internet is a very cost-effective way to reach existing and potential customers. Some established companies spun off dot-coms as separate business entities, only to reclaim them later. According to Russell Miller, a consultant with SCA Consulting in New York, "Now, companies realize that their Internet divisions are not separate businesses at all, but just another distribution channel."[60] For example, Disney bought back the Walt Disney Internet Group.

Many business-to-business ventures have also been formed. These are companies that use the Internet to link established businesses to each other. They may provide information, products, services, or transactions assistance. For example, the cement giant CEMEX, working with the E-business expert Ariba Inc., formed an alliance with Alfa, Bradesepar, and Votorantim to create the leading E-procurement marketplace in Latin America. Latinexus, the name of the venture, is a "neutral business-to-business integrated supplier exchange."[61] Another example is a deal formed by General Motors Corporation, Ford Motor Company, and DaimlerChrysler AG to create a single dot-com source of auto parts. "This will be the world's largest Internet company and trade exchange," according to a representative from Ford. "We'll IPO it. It won't be a long time, but we want to have operating results."[62] The benefits of these business-to-business ventures to users can be very significant, as the following example attests.

 On his pig farm in Arena, Wis., Rick Lawinger is planning to sell some swine—namely, 230 castrated male feeders being fattened for market. But instead of making his way to the nearest livestock auction, Lawinger heads to his computer. For this herd, the journey to the slaughterhouse begins on-line. Lawinger has gone hog-wild for the pig auctions held every Tuesday at Farms.com, an Internet farming and livestock exchange. When Lawinger first tried the Web site in late February, the 47-year old farmer sold three hundred pigs at $63 a head, even though he had estimated their value at only $56 a head. Now, Lawinger hopes to cybersell ten thousand pigs this year—his entire herd. "When local dealers come around looking to buy, I refer them to the Web site," he says.[63]

So how do you make money on the Internet? According to Gary Hamel: "Electricity created dramatic productivity gains—and shrank margins. The Net is doing the same. The way for companies to avoid the crunch: Be unique. The collective delusion of the dotcom mob was that clicks could readily translate into customers and revenues. The collective delusion of the Fortune 500 is that productivity gains translate into plumper profits. Any company that plans to make money from 'e' must have a Web strategy that creates unique value for customers, confers unique advantages in delivering that value, and is tough to copy."[64]

It is hard to predict the future of the Internet. However, several trends seem apparent. First, the Internet is an increasingly important tool for the exchange of information, goods, and services. Retail sales via the Internet are increasing at an astronomical rate. Businesses are using the Internet as a tool for a wide variety of applications. Second, managers and investors are being much more careful as they design business models around the Internet, making sure that there is some way to use invested resources to generate positive returns. Finally, information technologies are changing at such an amazing rate that the Internet is likely to be a source of entrepreneurial ventures for many years to come.

Orientation Toward Growth

organizational scope
The breadth of an organization's activities across businesses and industries

prospector strategy
An offensive strategy in which firms aggressively seek new market opportunities and are willing to take risks

defender strategy
A conservative strategy intended to preserve market share

analyzer strategy
Occupies a position in between a prospector strategy and a defender strategy; firms attempt to maintain positions in existing markets, while locating growth opportunities on the fringes

reactor strategy
Describes firms that don't have a distinct strategy; they simply react to environmental situations

Entrepreneurship, whether independent or corporate, results in business growth. Thus far, most of this book has dealt with growth in one way or another. This section deals directly with the concept of growth, and serves as a brief summary of what has been said on the topic, as well as an introduction to the next chapter. Entrepreneurs have to determine how fast they are able or willing to grow their ventures. If they try to grow too fast, they may fail due to inadequate resources or insufficient management capacity.[65] In existing firms, top managers need to discuss and agree on a general orientation toward growth. This kind of understanding is vital to the effective allocation of resources. For example, growth orientation determines the amount of resources devoted to activities such as research and development and marketing. Microsoft, a very aggressive growth company, allocates nearly $5 billion per year to research and development.[66]

The **scope** of an organization's businesses also depends on the attitude of its managers toward growth. The findings of Raymond Miles and Charles Snow are illustrative of this point. Based on field studies in four industries, firms were classified into one of four categories based on the rate at which they changed their products and markets. The authors were able to identify four general categories. **Prospectors** pursue what could be termed an offensive strategy. They aggressively seek new-market opportunities and are willing to take risks. **Defenders,** on the other hand, are turf protectors that engage in little or no new-product/market development. Their strategic actions are intended to preserve market share through reducing the impact of offensive moves by competitors. **Analyzers** occupy a position in between prospectors and defenders. They attempt to maintain positions in existing markets, while locating growth opportunities on the fringes. **Reactors** don't have a distinct strategy. They simply react to environmental situations.[67] The Miles and Snow classifications illustrate two fundamentally different positions with respect to growth. Prospectors aggressively pursue growth, while defenders tend to pursue stability. Firms in the other two classifications are somewhere in between these two extremes.

Growth Tactics

In addition to determining how aggressively a company should grow, top executives (or entrepreneurs) need to decide which directions growth will take. The two general approaches are internal and external. Internal-growth strategies make use of internal resources to build sales in existing businesses or pursue new markets. External growth involves cooperation with or acquisition of other organizations.

Internal Growth

market penetration
Competing with a single product or service in a single market

Organizations typically begin with a single product or service in a single market. If they remain in one market, their strategy is called **market penetration.** Firms that are pursuing market penetration build market share through investments in advertising, capacity expansion, and/or the sales force. Eventually, organizations may decide to pursue diversification outside their traditional markets. The two basic types of internal diversification are market development and product or service development.

market development
Involves repositioning a product or service to appeal to a new market

Market development involves repositioning a product or service to appeal to a new market. To support market development, firms may need to invest in market research, advertising and promotion, a new sales force, or applications development and testing. For example, a nylon-fabric manufacturer who sells fabric to wind-suit manufacturers would likely have to invest in market and applications development in order to sell nylon fabric to tent or sleeping-bag manufacturers.

Product or service development may include introduction of new products or services related to an existing competence of the firm or development of truly new-to-the-world products not related to the core business of the firm.[68] Resource allocations focus on product development, applications development, basic research and development, and perhaps process development or market development, depending on the nature of new or modified products. For example, pharmaceutical companies continuously make investments in new and improved products. Johnson & Johnson manufactures an effective drug for the treatment of colon cancer. The drug actually started out as a sheep wormer sold through veterinarians! Through product and applications development, the drug now serves a very different function and serves a completely different customer group. In another example, Culligan Water Conditioning used product development to save the company.

 Culligan Water Conditioning has not only survived, but has grown in an economically depressed region by increasing the scope of its operations. The company, a water-conditioning-equipment dealer and bottled-water business, is based in Havre, Montana, a small community in the heart of an agricultural region. Its main challenge was to maintain cash flow and grow the business in an economically depressed region. After hitting the saturation point in water-conditioning equipment, Culligan used its own water conditioners to enter the water-bottling market. As demand grew, the company had to open two bottling facilities to create an effective distribution system.[69]

vertical integration
Exists when a firm is involved in more than one stage of the industry supply chain

Vertical integration is often classified as an external-growth option because many times it is accomplished through purchase of a supplier or a customer. However, vertical integration can also be accomplished "in-house" by enlarging the firm's scope to include more resource-conversion processes. The concept of vertical integration was introduced in Chapter 4. Vertically integrated businesses may appear, on the surface, to be highly related to existing businesses. However, vertical integration often involves a dramatic change in the scope of a firm's business—its products/services, markets (unless all goods and services of the new company are kept in-house), functions served, and certainly its technologies. Consequently, vertical integration provides substantial movement into "new" businesses (diversification), and a firm that can master one stage of the industry supply chain will not necessarily excel at other stages. For instance, Southland's (7-Eleven Stores) venture into petroleum refining (CITGO) proved to be unsuccessful.

External Growth

horizontal integration
Involves acquisition of an organization in the same line of business

related acquisitions
Occur when the acquiring company shares common or complementary resources with its acquisition target

unrelated acquisitions
Occur between companies that don't share any common or complementary resources

joint venture
An entity that is created when two or more firms pool a portion of their resources to create a separate jointly owned entity

External-growth tactics involve seeking resources from external organizations through acquisitions or joint ventures. **Horizontal integration** involves acquisition of an organization in the same line of business. Typically, horizontal integration is accomplished for the purpose of gaining market share in a particular market, expanding a market geographically, or augmenting product or service lines. This was the motivation behind the Delta Air Lines acquisition of Western Airlines. Organizations also use acquisitions to pursue related or unrelated diversification. **Related acquisitions** occur when the acquiring company shares common or complementary resources with its acquisition target. Resources to consider include products, markets, services, or technologies. For example, prior to their combination, the businesses of AOL and Time Warner were related in the sense that both companies were heavily oriented toward communications technology, and also complementary, because each of the companies had strengths in different markets. **Unrelated acquisitions** occur between companies that don't share any common or complementary resources.

Joint ventures, defined in Chapter 2, are partnerships formed with other organizations that result in a separate, jointly owned firm. They are used to accomplish a variety of purposes, such as penetrating new domestic or foreign markets, developing new products and services, or improving existing processes for producing products and services. For example, a joint venture between General Motors and Toyota led to the Geo. Also, CorningWare cookware was developed through a joint venture between Corning Glass Works and Dow Chemical called Dow Corning. The external-growth tactics of acquisitions and joint ventures will be explored in more detail in Chapter 7.

Internal or External Diversification

Assuming that top managers have decided that growth through diversification is worthy of pursuit, they must still decide whether to pursue that growth internally or externally. The most important strength an internal diversifier brings to a new business venture is its ability to make use of the combined resources and capabilities of its various operations, especially in the technological areas.[70] For example, IBM used its abundant resources in the computer industry to develop and market its very successful line of personal computers in the early 1980s. W. L. Gore & Associates has used its capabilities in Gore-Tex materials to venture into new businesses in health care, industrial applications, and outdoor apparel. Compared to some of the external-growth options, internal venturing provides an organization with complete control over the innovation and marketing processes, as well as the ability to fully exploit new innovations if the venture is a success.[71]

Nevertheless, research suggests that internal venturing is typically associated with slower growth than are external-diversification options. In fact, one researcher discovered that new ventures take, on average, eight years before they become profitable and generate a positive cash flow. Furthermore, it takes ten to twelve years before the return-on-investment of new ventures equals that of existing product lines.[72] Also, another researcher found that only 12 to 20 percent of new R&D-based ventures ever become profitable.[73] However, if organizations can quickly learn which new ventures are going to be successful, and respond to this knowledge before large amounts of resources have been expended, internal venturing can be a very successful approach to diversification. Also, both acquisitions and joint ventures have low success rates, so an organization is going to have to take risks regardless of tactic.

The point of this discussion is that there are trade-offs associated with all of the growth options, which means that organizations should constantly reevaluate whether their current tactics are working. Cisco Systems is an excellent example of the need to rethink a strategy.

 Over the past eight years, Cisco Systems, Inc. made a fortune for itself and its shareholders by perfecting the art of innovation-through-acquisition. The giant maker of Internet networking gear has used its turbocharged stock to gobble up more than seventy companies since 1993, integrating technology startups into a massive Silicon Valley powerhouse. Today, about half of its $22 billion in 2001 sales can be traced to an acquired company or technology. That strategy is about to change radically. With its shares off 79 percent, to just $17, since its March, 2000, high, Cisco's acquisition engine has slowed from twenty-three purchases in 2000 to just five this year. As a result, it has had to find a new way to stoke revenues and fix its tarnished image on Wall Street. So now CEO John T. Chambers wants to concentrate on developing products and technologies in-house through Cisco's own engineers.[74]

So far, this section has dealt specifically with the choices top executives make regarding both the amount of growth their firms will pursue and the tactics for pursuing it. It has served as a summary of much of the material on entrepreneurship dealing with internal growth. In addition, the external-growth tactics of vertical integration, diversification, and joint venture were introduced as external options for growth. These tactics will be explored in depth in the next chapter. All of these strategies assume that managers want their firms to grow. However, not all organizational missions stress growth. The next subsection deals with organizations that desire a stable investment strategy to maintain what they have.

Stability Strategies

While most for-profit organizations actively seek growth, some organizations do not. They may be family-owned businesses, nonprofit organizations that are satisfied with the current level of operations, or they may simply be business organizations that are content with their share of a mature market. In these situations, no overt actions are taken to achieve growth. The prevalent theme of operations is "business as usual." These types of organizations maintain fairly level investments in marketing, operations, and services, and engage in only enough R&D to maintain their share of the market. As mentioned previously, these firms are best described as defenders.

Some executives are bothered by the concept of limited or no growth. However, the stakeholder framework developed in this text provides a vehicle for understanding why and when a no-growth philosophy may be appropriate. The appropriateness of any strategic position depends on the attitudes of the stakeholders that the organization intends to serve. Some organizations are composed of people who enjoy stability and security. These firms may stress lifetime employment, a family atmosphere, and slow but certain promotion as managers age and retire. They may also take pride in excellent craftsmanship or superior service to long-standing clients. Lincoln Electric Company fits this description fairly well.

Nevertheless, a limited or no-growth position is hard to defend for organizations that are publicly held—because managers, as agents for the owners, are responsible for actions that will enhance shareholder wealth, and typically wealth is associated with growth. Lincoln Electric, the market leader in the production of arc welders, gets around this agency problem because its stock is owned almost entirely by managers and employees. However, there are also situations in which investing for the objective of growth is ineffective.

For instance, a firm may be in a mature, declining, or rigidly segmented market in which efforts to increase sales would cost more than they are worth. This situation is typical of industries with low profits, no growth, and high exit barriers. Exit barriers exist when the capital equipment and skills an organization possesses are not applicable to other businesses.[75] For example, equipment used in brewing has almost no potential for other uses. Consequently, many smaller breweries are barely able to survive against large organizations such as Anheuser-Busch, but they do not close down because their entire investment would be lost.

Organizations may also pursue a temporary no-growth strategy during periods of restructuring. Restructuring often involves streamlining and reorienting the organization. Product lines are trimmed, unnecessary workers are laid off, and investment priorities are altered to bring the organization more in line with the external environment. The intent is usually to place the organization on a sound footing, followed by more-effective growth in the future. Restructuring will be discussed in depth in Chapter 9.

Summary

The U.S. economy relies heavily on entrepreneurship as a source of growth and job creation. Entrepreneurship involves the creation of new business. Some ventures are complete start-ups, while other ventures are pursued within an existing organization. Entrepreneurs are opportunists and dreamers. They are resourceful, creative, visionary, hardworking, and optimistic. They are independent thinkers who are willing to take risks and innovate. They also tend to be excellent leaders.

Entrepreneurial tasks include opportunity recognition or creation, assembling resources to pursue the opportunity, and managing activities that bring a new venture into existence. Entrepreneurial discovery may be viewed as the intersection of a need and a solution. Entrepreneurial activity occurs anytime an entrepreneur is able to link a need to a solution in such a manner that a new business emerges. Opportunities to do this tend to be context specific, and they can emerge from anywhere.

Everything associated with a new venture revolves around a business plan. Creation of the plan forces the entrepreneur to think through the details of the venture and determine whether it is feasible. A business plan includes an executive summary; a description of the proposed business venture; an analysis of the environment; a resource analysis; and functional plans such as a marketing plan, operations plan, and a management plan. It also includes financial projections, which are especially important to potential investors. Some sort of implementation schedule or timeline for major events is also included. Investors are also interested in what might be called an "endgame" strategy, a plan for concluding the venture, transferring control to others, allowing potential investors to exit the venture with a high return on their investments, contingency plans in the event the venture does not succeed, and an executive-succession plan in case the primary entrepreneur decides to leave the venture. Finally, a business plan should include an honest assessment of potential risks.

Obtaining start-up capital is probably the most difficult problem facing a potential entrepreneur. Some of the most common sources of start-up capital include commercial banks, personal contacts, venture capitalists, corporate partnerships, and business angels. After a venture has established a record of performance, entrepreneurs or venture capitalists may pursue an initial public offering (IPO). An IPO entails selling stock to the public and investors.

Some of the major tasks of entrepreneurs for the first year of a venture include financing and financial management, marketing, product/service development, resource acquisition, process development, management and staffing, and satisfying legal requirements. Entrepreneurs also need to decide whether to form their new ventures as sole proprietorships, partnerships or corporations.

The most common reason for the failure of entrepreneurial ventures is lack of management skill. This is sometimes demonstrated by a poor management strategy, inappropriate vision, or an inability to manage finances effectively. Many new ventures fail because of a lack of capitalization. Other factors that can lead to failure are associated with the product or service itself, such as poor product design or poor timing. Even if a venture has excellent management, sufficient capitalization, and a good product or service, it can still fail if market conditions are not favorable.

Corporate entrepreneurship, or intrapraneurship, involves the creation of new business ventures within existing corporations. This sort of entrepreneurship is more common in organizations that foster innovation. Some of the factors associated with these types of firms include a well-supported vision that includes an emphasis on innovation and a culture that supports this vision, top-management support, organizational champions, teamwork and collaboration, a flat management hierarchy, a decentralized approval process, respect for the ideas of everyone, excellent communications, adequate resources devoted to entrepreneurial activities, a reward system that encourages innovation, and a focus on learning.

The selection of an organizational design for an internal venture depends on the strategic importance of the venture and how closely related the venture is to current activities. Top management will want to maintain a high level of control over ventures that are strategically important, in that they are closely related to the organization's current or anticipated business activities. High levels of operational relatedness should result in a strong operational coupling between the new and existing businesses. Joint information systems should be established, and professionals from new and existing businesses should meet regularly. Depending on the nature of the project, work flows may even need to be coordinated. Based on these determinations, an internal venture could be directly integrated into existing operations, managed as a special business unit, nurtured as an independent unit owned by others, or not pursued at all.

Finally, this chapter ended with a discussion of an organization's orientation toward growth and some of the common tactics firms use to pursue various growth strategies. Prospectors aggressively pursue growth, while defenders tend to pursue stability. The two general approaches to growth are internal and external. Internal-growth strategies make use of internal resources to build sales in existing businesses or pursue new markets. External growth involves cooperation with or acquisition of other organizations. Internal-growth tactics allow a firm more management control, but they tend to be slower than external-growth options. Both internal- and external-growth tactics have high rates of failure. Thus, firms may need to pursue a variety of options to ensure that at least some of them are successful. It is also important to be flexible and learn from mistakes. Some firms aren't pursuing growth. This is an acceptable option if all the key stakeholders agree, or during a period of restructuring. It may also be the only reasonable option in a mature, declining, or rigidly segmented market.

Discussion Questions

1.   What is entrepreneurship, and why is it important?

2.   What are some of the characteristics of entrepreneurs? Are you that sort of person? Do you know anyone who would be a good entrepreneur?

3.   Describe the entrepreneurial tasks.

4.   What does a business plan contain? Is a business plan the same as a strategic plan for an existing business? If not, how are they different?

5.   What are the primary reasons new business ventures fail?

6.   What are some of the typical activities of an entrepreneur during the first year of a venture?

7.   Describe the sources to which an entrepreneur can turn for venture capital.

8.   How can established firms foster innovation?

9.   What are two important variables that determine how internal ventures are structured? Name four ways to structure an internal venture, and when each structure is appropriate.

10.   What are the primary internal and external tactics available to firms in pursuit of growth? Describe each of them. Is vertical integration an internal or external tactic? Why?

11.   When might a no-growth strategy be appropriate?

Strategic Application

Analysis of Business Failure

Consider a situation in which a business failed or is struggling. You can choose a firm with which you are familiar or a case assigned by your instructor. Most communities have numerous examples of business failures all around them. Or you may be able to read about a failing or failed business in a current business periodical. You can evaluate a separate entrepreneurial venture or a venture within a larger company. Evaluate the venture on the basis of the following factors to provide a preliminary indication of why it is struggling or failed:

Quality of management skills

- Was the venture managed well?
- Did managers have the right kind of experience?
- Did they take enough risks?

Level of capitalization

- Was sufficient capital available to make the venture successful?

Product or service

- Was the product or service a good fit with the market?
- Did it have attractive features?
- Was it priced well for the market?
- Was the company too dependent on a single customer?
- Was entrance to the market well timed?

External market conditions

- How strong was the economy?
- Were there any conditions in the economy or the industry that were highly unfavorable?
- Did competitive responses make the situation more difficult?

In summary, why do you think the venture failed or is failing?

Internet Application

Table 6.1 contains an overview of what is contained in a business plan, but it is a summary without much detail. The purpose of this exercise is to provide you with more exposure to what is found in a business plan. The Edward Lowe Foundation is dedicated to encouraging entrepreneurship and helping entrepreneurs. Go to their website at http://edge.lowe.org. If they have changed their website address, do a Google search on Edward Lowe (or you can go to the Kauffman Foundation website at http://www.entreworld.org/ for similar material). If you get into the Edward Lowe website, you will discover a search engine for articles pertinent to entrepreneurship. Use the search engine and enter "Business Plan." This will take you to several articles on the subject. Click on the article that seems most pertinent. At the time this book was printed, an excellent article was found on the website entitled "Writing a Business Plan." After reading this or another article or articles on how to do a business plan, answer the following questions:

1. What are the major sections of a business plan, based on your research?

2. Does the website or article on the website emphasize anything as particularly important when writing a plan? If so, what is it and why is it important?

3. Which sections of a business plan seem like they would take the longest to write? Why?

4. What kind of research would you need to do in order to complete a plan? Specifically, which areas in the plan would require research and what kind of research would these sections require?

5. Are there any sections of the plan in which you would have to exercise a lot of judgment or "guesswork"?

Notes

1. Based on personal knowledge of the author and an interview with David Hamilla, 3 November 2001.

2. A. M. McCarthy and C. L. Nicholls-Nixon, "Fresh Starts: Arnold Cooper on Entrepreneurship and Wealth Creation," *Academy of Management Executive* 15, no. 1 (February 2001): 29.

3. P. D. Reynolds, M. Hay, and S. Michael Camp, *Global Entrepreneurship Monitor* (Kauffman Center for Entrepreneurial Leadership, 1999).

4. S. J. Min, "Made Not Born," *Entrepreneur of the Year Magazine* (Fall 1999): 80.

5. Taken directly from L. E. Shefsky, *Entrepreneurs Are Made Not Born* (New York: McGraw-Hill, 1994), 10.

6. R. Jacobson, "The 'Austrian' School of Strategy," *Academy of Management Review* 17 (1992): 782–807; J. Schumpeter, *The Theory of Economic Development* (Cambridge, Mass.: Harvard University Press, 1934).

7. Taken directly from B. Elgin, J. Kerstetter, and L. Himelstein, "Why They're AGOG Over Google," *Business Week,* 24 September 2001, 83.

8. Taken directly from S. Venkataraman and S. D. Sarasvathy, "Strategy and Entrepreneurship: Outlines of an Untold Story," in *The Blackwell Handbook of Strategic Management,* ed. M.A. Hitt, R. E. Freeman, and J. S. Harrison (Oxford: Blackwell Publishers, 2001), 652.

9. Taken directly from M. Warner, "Confessions of a Control Freak," *Fortune,* 4 September 2000, 136.

10. Shefsky, *Entrepreneurs Are Made,* 20.

11. W. K. Schilit, "How to Obtain Venture Capital," *Business Horizons* (May/June 1987): 78.

12. I. MacMillan, R. Siegel, and P. N. Subba Narasimha, "Criteria Used by Venture Capitalists to Evaluate New Venture Proposals," *Journal of Business Venturing* (Winter 1985): 119–128.

13. P. DeCeglie, "The Truth about Venture Capital," *Business Startups* (February 2000): 40–47

14. Shefsky, *Entrepreneurs,* 15–16.

15. Nasdaq, "Going Public" (New York: The Nasdaq Stock Market, Inc., 2000).

16. D. E. Terpstra and P. D. Olson, "Entrepreneurial Start-up and Growth: A Classification of Problems," *Entrepreneurship Theory and Practice* (Spring 1993): 19.

17. D. F. Kuratko and R. M. Hodgetts, *Entrepreneurship: A Contemporary Approach,* 5th ed. (Fort Worth, Tex.: Harcourt College Publishers, 2001).

18. Interested readers will find a wealth of information on this subject in K. W. Clarkson et al., *West's Business Law,* 7th ed. (St. Paul, Minn.: West Publishing).

19. R. L. Miller and G. A. Jentz, *Business Law Today,* 4th ed. (St. Paul, Minn.: West Publishing).

20. L. Zacharakis, G. D. Meyer, and J. DeCastro, "Differing Perceptions of New Venture Failure: A Matched Exploratory Study of Venture Capitalists and Entrepreneurs," *Journal of Small Business Management* (July 1999): 1–14.

21. K. G. Smith, W. J. Ferrier, and H. Ndofor, "Competitive Dynamics Research: Critique and Future Directions," in *Blackwell Handbook,* ed. Hitt, Freeman, and Harrison, 315–361.

22. J. Naisbitt and P. Aburdene, *Re-inventing the Corporation* (New York: Warner Books, 1985).

23. R. A. Burgelman, "Designs for Corporate Entrepreneurship in Established Firms," *California Management Review* (Spring 1984): 154–166.

24. 3M, *Annual Report* (1995).

25. Taken directly from E. Von Hipple, S. Thomke, and M. Sonnack, "Creating Breakthroughs at 3M," *Harvard Business Review* (September/October 1999): 47–57.

26. J. B. Quinn, "Managing Innovation: Controlled Chaos," *Harvard Business Review* (May/June 1985): 73–84.

27. Kuratko and Hodgetts, *Entrepreneurship.*

28. Naisbitt and Aburdene, *Re-inventing the Corporation.*

29. Taken directly from S. Ghoshal and C. A. Bartlett, "Changing the Role of Top Management: Beyond Structure to Process," *Harvard Business Review* 73 (January/February 1995): 94.

30. J. A. Pearce II, T. R. Kramer, and D. K. Robbins, "Effects of Managers' Entrepreneurial Behavior on Subordinates," *Journal of Business Venturing* 12 (1997): 147–160.

31. Kuratko and Hodgetts, *Entrepreneurship.*

32. Taken directly from A. Weintraub et al., "Little Niches That Grew," *Business Week,* 18 June 2001, 100.

33. Ghoshal and Bartlett, "Changing the Role," 86–96.

34. P. G. Green, C. G. Brush, and M. M. Hart, "The Corporate Venture Champion: A Resource-Based Approach to Role and Process," *Entrepreneurship Theory and Practice* (March 1999): 103–122.

35. Naisbitt and Aburdene, *Re-inventing the Corporation.*

36. Quinn, "Managing Innovation."

37. Ibid.

38. Ibid.

39. Ibid.

40. G. Hamel, "Avoiding the Guillotine," *Fortune,* 2 April 2001, 140.

41. Kuratko and Hodgetts, *Entrepreneurship.*

42. Burgelman, "Designs."

43. "Lessons from a Successful Entrepreneur," *Journal of Business Strategy* (March/April 1988): 20–24.

44. Naisbitt and Aburdene, *Re-inventing the Corporation.*

45. Kuratko and Hodgetts, *Entrepreneurship.*

46. R. Normann, "Organizational Innovativeness: Product Variation and Reorientation," *Administrative Science Quarterly* 16 (1971): 203–215.

47. D. M. DeCarolis and D. L. Deeds, "The Impact of Stocks and Flows of Organizational Knowledge on Firm Performance," *Strategic Management Journal* 20 (1999): 953–968.

48. Taken directly from J. F. Welch, J. Immelt, and other board members, *GE Annual Report* (2000), 2.

49. This discussion of corporate entrepreneurship draws heavily from Burgelman, "Designs."

50. Based on Burgelman, "Designs," 162–164.

51. Adapted from "Norton Manufacturing Company, Inc.," *Strengthening America's Competitiveness: The Blue Chip Enterprise Initiative* (Warner Books on behalf of Connecticut Mutual Life Insurance Company and the U.S. Chamber of Commerce, 1991), 94–95.

52. P. F. Drucker, "Beyond the Information Revolution," *Atlantic Monthly,* October 1999, 47–57.

53. Taken directly from G. Hamel, "Take It Higher," *Fortune,* 5 February 2001, 169.

54. Taken directly from Salon, "Business As Usual," www.salon.com, 8 May 2000).

55. G. Hamel, "Is This All You Can Build with the Net? Think Bigger," *Fortune,* 30 April 2001, 134–138.

56. J. Angwin, "Latest Dot-Com Fad Is a Bit Old-Fashioned: It's Called Profitability," *The Wall Street Journal,* 14 August 2001, A1, A6.

57. S. Rosenbush, "Empire Builders," *Business Week E. Biz,* 15 May 2000, EB27.

58. Taken directly from J. Gaffney, "How Do You Feel about a $44 Tooth-Bleaching Kit?" *Business 2.0* (October 2001): 125.

59. D. Little, "Let's Keep This Exchange to Ourselves," *Business Week,* 4 December 2000, 48.

60. D. Sparks, "The Prodigal Dot-Coms' Return," *Business Week,* 4 June 2001, 92.

61. CEMEX, "Building for the Future," *International Cement & Line Journal,* www.cemex.com/mc/m/mc_rn_bf2001.asp, 1 November 2001.

62. R. L. Simison, F. Warner, and G. L. White, "Big Three Car Makers Plan Net Exchange," *The Wall Street Journal,* 28 February 2000, A3.

63. Taken directly from D. Little, "Old MacDonald Has a Web Site," *Business Week E.Biz,* 15 May 2000, EB83.

64. G. Hamel, "Edison's Curse," *Fortune,* 5 March 2001, 175.

65. E. T. Penrose, *The Theory of the Growth of the Firm* (New York: John Wiley, 1959).

66. "Microsoft Research," www.microsoft.com /msft/ar01/low/inventing.htm, 17 October 2001.

67. R. E. Miles and C. C. Snow, *Organization Strategy, Structure, and Process* (New York: McGraw-Hill, 1978); R.E. Miles et al., "Organizational Strategy, Structure, and Process," *Academy of Management Review* 3 (1978): 546–562.

68. R. K. Kazanjian and R. Drazin, "Implementing Internal Diversification: Contingency Factors for Organization Design Choices," *Academy of Management Review* 12 (1987): 342–354.

69. Adapted from "Culligan Water Conditioning of Havre," *Strengthening America's Competitiveness,* 40–41.

70. R. A. Pitts, "Strategies and Structures for Diversification," *Academy of Management Journal* 20 (1977): 197–208

71. C. A. Lengnick-Hall, "Innovation and Competitive Advantage: What We Know and What We Need to Learn," *Journal of Management* 18 (1992): 399–429.

72. E. R. Biggadike, "The Risky Business of Diversification," *Harvard Business Review* (May/June 1979): 103–111

73. E. Mansfield, "How Economists See R&D," *Harvard Business Review* (November/December 1981): 98–106. See also B. T. Lamont and Carl R. Anderson, "Mode of Corporate Diversification and Economic Performance," *Academy of Management Journal* 28 (1985): 926–934.

74. Taken directly from B. Elgin, "A Do-It-Yourself Plan at Cisco," *Business Week,* 10 September 2001, 52.

75. K. R. Harrigan, "Deterrents to Divestiture," *Academy of Management Journal* 24 (1981): 306–323.

Chapter 7

Corporate-Level Strategy and Restructuring

Learning Objectives

After reading and discussing this chapter, you should be able to:

1. Understand the basic corporate-level strategies and their strengths and weaknesses.

2. Identify the factors that are necessary for a diversification strategy to produce synergy.

3. Analyze existing and suggest potential corporate-level distinctive competencies for a firm.

4. Suggest methods to avoid pitfalls and enhance the probability of success in mergers and acquisitions.

5. Understand the basic types of restructuring and how restructuring can be successfully executed.

6. Create a portfolio matrix for a corporation and understand what it means.

The ALFA Group

Dionisio Garza Medellin is CEO of a massive Mexican conglomerate called ALFA, S.A. de C.V. (the ALFA Group). With 2000 sales that translated to nearly $5 billion, the ALFA Group's operations cover a wide geographic region. Revenues were distributed 43 percent in North America, 27 percent in Central and South America, 17 percent in the Far East and Oceania, and 13 percent in Europe and the Middle East. ALFA is is engaged through subsidiaries in five major business activities:

- **Petrochemicals and Synthetic Fibers**—Through Alpek, S.A. de C.V., ALFA is engaged in the manufacture of petrochemicals and synthetic fibers for use primarily as raw materials in the textile, food, beverage-packaging, construction, and automotive industries in Mexico and abroad. Alpek also manufactures raw materials used in the production of polyester fibers and polymer products such as textile and industrial nylon, polyester, and Lycra, and produces specialty chemical products such as polyols for urethanes, polystyrene, glycol, and monoethylene glycol. This area accounts for 37 percent of revenues.

- **Steel and Transformation**—Through Hylsamex, S.A. de C.V., a publicly traded subsidiary, ALFA manufactures primary and value-added finished-steel products for use in the construction, auto-parts, and home-appliances industries. Hylsamex's products include thick-wall pipe, galvanized sheets, steel coil, tubing, painted sheets and coil, wire products, and foam-insulated products. Steel and transformation activities provide 35 percentof revenues.

- **Refrigerated Foods**—Through Sigma Alimentos, S.A. de C.V., a publicly traded subsidiary, ALFA produces and distributes processed meats, dairy products, and other refrigerated and frozen foods. Refrigerated foods provide 16 percent of revenues.

- **Auto-Parts Retailing**—Through Versax, S.A. de C.V., ALFA operates in four industries: auto parts, carpets, mattresses, and building-supplies retailing. Versax also produces aluminum cylinder heads.

- **Telecommunications**—through a joint venture with AT&T called Alestra.[1]

The Alfa Group pursues unrelated diversification on a global scale. Garza Medellin faces a huge corporate-level management task in coordinating financial flows and determining which businesses are in need of attention and which ones might need to be sold.

Concentration, vertical integration, and diversification are the three basic corporate-level strategies. This chapter begins with a comparison of these three strategies, followed by a detailed analysis of acquisition strategies, an important tactic firms use to diversify. Vertical integration, diversification, and mergers are corporate-level strategies and tactics, but they can also be applied within the business units of larger companies. For example, a division president could decide to diversify the business through an acquisition of a firm in a related industry. The acquisition might have to be approved at the corporate level, but it could still be executed at the business level. Nevertheless, the focus of this chapter will be on the corporate level, while recognizing that much of this discussion can sometimes apply to individual business units as well.

Corporate-level strategy is formulated by the CEO and other top managers. An organization may have several business units or divisions that are run by individual managers. Those managers establish strategy for their own units, but not for the corporation as a whole. At the corporate level, primary strategy-formulation responsibilities include setting the direction of the entire organization, formulation of a corporate strategy, selection of businesses in which to compete, selection of tactics for diversification and growth, and management of corporate resources and capabilities. These responsibilities and the key issues associated with each responsibility are listed in Table 7.1.

Organizations begin as entrepreneurial ventures with a single product or service or a small group of products or services in a single market. This type of corporate-level strategy, called **concentration,** is associated with a narrow business definition. As long as an organization has virtually all of its resource investments in one business area, it is still concentrating. With this strategy, a firm may pursue growth in the area through internal business ventures, mergers and acquisitions, or joint ventures. Some organizations never stop concentrating, in spite of their size. For instance, Delta Air Lines is still pursuing a concentration strategy.

Most successful organizations abandon their concentration strategies at some point due to market saturation, excess resources that they need to find a use for, or some other reason. Through internal ventures, mergers and acquisitions, or joint ventures, they pursue businesses outside their core business areas. Corporate strategy typically evolves from concentration to some form of vertical integration or diversification of products, functions served, markets, or technologies (see Figure 7.1).[2] **Diversification** that stems from common markets, functions served, technologies, or products and services is referred to as **related diversification. Unrelated diversification** is not based on commonality among the activities of the corporation. Organizations may continue to pursue vertical integration and/or diversification successfully for many years, each time expanding their business definitions.

Virgin spans industries as diverse as air travel, packaged holidays, music retailing, banking, and radio broadcasting. Says Virgin's Gordon McCallum, head of business development: "There is no assumption about what business Virgin should be in or shouldn't be in." Yet Virgin will enter an industry only if it believes it can (a) challenge existing rules, (b) give customers a better break, (c) be more entertaining, and (d) put a

---

concentration
A corporate-level strategy in which the firm has virtually all of its resource investments in one business area

diversification
Occurs when a firm expands its business operations into new products, functions served, markets, or technologies

related diversification
Diversification that stems from common markets, functions served, technologies or products and services

unrelated diversification
Diversification that is not based on commonality among the activities of a corporation

Table 7.1   Major Corporate-Level Strategic Management Responsibilities

Major Responsibilities	Key Issues
Direction Setting	Establishment and communication of organizational mission, vision, enterprise strategy, and long-term goals
Development of Corporate-Level Strategy	Selection of a broad approach to corporate-level strategy—concentration, vertical integration, diversification, international expansion
	Selection of resources and capabilities in which to build corporate-wide distinctive competencies
Selection of Businesses and Portfolio Management	Management of the corporate portfolio of businesses—buying businesses, selling businesses
	Allocation of resources to business units for capital equipment, R&D, etc.
Selection of Tactics for Diversification and Growth	Choosing among methods of diversification—internal venturing, acquisitions, joint ventures
Management of Resources	Acquisition of resources and/or development of competencies leading to a sustainable competitive advantage for the entire corporation
	Hiring, firing and rewarding business-unit managers
	Ensure that the business units (divisions) within the corporation are well managed, including strategic management; provide training where appropriate
	Develop a high-performance corporate management structure
	Developing control systems to ensure that strategies remain relevant and that the corporation continues to progress toward its goals

thumb in the eye of complacent incumbents. Says McCallum: "The culture is one of why not, rather than why."[3]

Many organizations eventually come to a point at which slow growth, declining profits, or some other crisis forces corporate-level managers to "rethink" their entire organizations. Disgruntled stakeholders—including stockholders, employees, and managers—often drive this process. The result of this process is usually some form of restructuring. **Restructuring** often involves reducing the business definition combined with refocusing efforts on the things the organization does well. Most successful restructuring efforts result in a leaner (i.e., fewer employees, less capital equipment), less-diversified organization. The organization may then cycle back and begin a cautious, better-educated, and more-focused program of diversification or vertical integration. Restructuring will be discussed at the end of this chapter.

restructuring
Involves major changes to an organization's strategies, structure and/or processes

Concentration Strategies

Concentration is the least complicated of the corporate-level strategies, but it is still pursued by many large and successful companies such as Federal Express, Domino's Pizza, and McDonald's. Many other companies, such as Eastman Kodak, built their reputations pursuing concentration strategies, but have since diversified into other businesses. In the case of Kodak, diversification was a necessity because too much

FIGURE 7.1

Corporate-Level Strategies

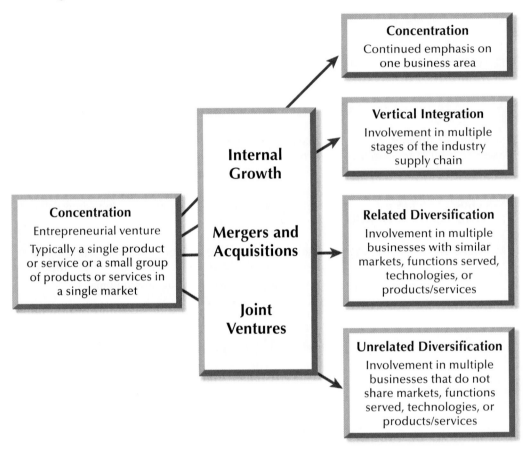

Concentration
Entrepreneurial venture

Typically a single product or service or a small group of products or services in a single market

Internal Growth

Mergers and Acquisitions

Joint Ventures

Concentration
Continued emphasis on one business area

Vertical Integration
Involvement in multiple stages of the industry supply chain

Related Diversification
Involvement in multiple businesses with similar markets, functions served, technologies, or products/services

Unrelated Diversification
Involvement in multiple businesses that do not share markets, functions served, technologies, or products/services

dependence on one business area became a substantial business risk. In the same industry, Polaroid never successfully diversified and is now in financial trouble. Consequently, a concentration strategy is associated with both strengths and weaknesses (see Table 7.2).

The strengths of a concentration strategy are readily apparent. First, concentration allows an organization to master one business. This specialization allows top executives to obtain in-depth knowledge of the business, which should reduce strategic mistakes. Also, since all resources are directed at doing one thing well, the organization may be in a better position to develop the resources and capabilities necessary to establish a sustainable competitive advantage. Furthermore, organizational resources are under less strain. Lack of ambiguity concerning strategic direction may also allow consensus to form among top managers. High levels of consensus are sometimes associated with superior organizational performance. In fact, a concentration strategy has sometimes been found to be more profitable than other types of corporate-level strategy.[4] Of course, the profitability of a concentration strategy is dependent largely on the industry in which a firm is involved.

On the other hand, concentration strategies entail several risks, especially when environments are unstable. Since the organization is dependent on one product or business area to sustain itself, change can dramatically reduce organizational performance. The airline industry is a good example of the effects of uncertainty on

Table 7.2   Advantages and Disadvantages of a Concentration Strategy

Advantages	Disadvantages
• Allows an organization to master one business • Less strain on resources, allowing more of an opportunity to develop a sustainable competitive advantage • Lack of ambiguity concerning strategic direction • Often found to be a profitable strategy, depending on the industry	• Dependence on one area is problematic if the industry is unstable • Primary product may become obsolete • Difficult to grow when the industry matures • Significant changes in the industry can be very hard to deal with • Cash flow can be a serious problem

organizational performance. Prior to deregulation in the airline industry, most of the major carriers were profitable. They had protected routes and fixed prices. However, deregulation and the ensuing increase in competition hurt the profitability of all domestic carriers. Since most of the major carriers were pursuing concentration strategies, they did not have other business areas to offset their losses. Consequently, several airlines were acquired or went bankrupt. However, the industry did not seem to learn its lesson. In the aftermath of the September 11, 2001, disasters, most airlines would have gone bankrupt without help from the U.S. government. Once again, inadequate diversification reduced their ability to deal with the shock.

Product obsolescence and industry maturity create additional risks for organizations pursuing a concentration strategy. If the principal product of an organization becomes obsolete or matures, organizational performance can suffer until the company develops another product that is appealing to the market. Some firms are never able to duplicate earlier successes. Furthermore, since they have experience in only one line-of-business, they have limited ability to switch to other areas when times get tough; consequently, many are eventually acquired by another company or go bankrupt.

Concentration strategies are also susceptible to problems when the chosen industry is undergoing significant evolution and is converging with other industries. For example, as the telecommunications industry evolves, entire segments are converging. Some local telephone operating companies are now offering cable-television services through a modified version of the telephone long-distance lines, which represents a substantial diversification away from local telephone services. Companies that fail to diversify in ways that are consistent with industry evolution and convergence can often find themselves short of the next generation of products and services.

Concentration strategies can also lead to cash-flow problems. While the business is growing, the organization may find itself in a "cash poor" situation, since growth often entails additional investments in capital equipment and marketing. On the other hand, once growth levels off, the organization is likely to find itself in a "cash rich" situation, with limited opportunities for profitable investment in the business itself. In fact, this may be one of the most popular reasons that organizations in mature markets begin to diversify.[5] Having exhausted all reasonable opportunities to reinvest cash in innovation, renewal, or revitalization, organizational managers may look to other areas for growth. Of course, the company might also consider increasing dividends, but at some point managers feel a responsibility to profitably invest cash rather than simply returning it to shareholders. Finally, a concentration strategy may not provide enough challenge or stimulation to managers. In other words, they may begin to get tired of doing the same things year after year. This is less true in organizations that are growing rapidly, since growth typically provides excitement and promotion opportunities.

Vertical Integration Strategies

Some industries, such as steel and wood products, contain firms that are predominantly vertically integrated. In other industries, such as apparel, vertical integration is limited, and most organizations are involved in only one or a few stages. Research has not generally found vertical integration to be a highly profitable strategy relative to the other corporate-level strategies.[6] However, many of the firms that have been studied are old and large. They may have used vertical integration with success as their industries were forming. As one vertical integration expert explained, vertical integration can "lock firms in" to unprofitable adjacent businesses.[7] However, this does not mean that all vertical integration is unprofitable.

Furthermore, one study suggested that vertical integration may be associated with reduced administrative, selling, and R&D costs, but higher production costs. The researchers believe that the higher production costs may be a result of a lack of incentive on the part of internal suppliers to keep their costs down. Since the internal suppliers have a guaranteed customer, they do not have to be as competitive.[8] *An important point to remember with regard to all of the strategies is that some companies are pursuing them successfully.*

From a strategic perspective, vertical integration contains an element of risk that is similar to concentration. If a firm is vertically integrated and the principal product becomes obsolete, the whole organization can suffer unless its value-chain activities are sufficiently flexible to be used for other products and services. Researchers have found that both high levels of technical change and high levels of competition reduce the expected profits from vertical integration.[9] Among the most significant advantages are internal benefits such as the potential for efficiency through **synergy** from coordinating and integrating vertical activities. Vertical integration can also help an organization improve its access to essential components or materials, differentiate its products, or gain greater control over its market. On the other hand, activities associated with vertical integration can increase overhead, link firms to unprofitable adjacent firms, or cause firms to lose access to important information from suppliers or customers. Other advantages and disadvantages of vertical integration are listed in Table 7.3.

synergy
Occurs when the whole is greater than the sum of its parts

Vertical Integration and Transaction Costs

Transaction-cost economics, which is the study of economic transactions and their costs, helps explain when vertical integration is appropriate.[10] From this perspective, firms can either negotiate with organizations or individuals on the open market for the products and services they need, or they can produce these products and services themselves. According to Oliver Williamson, an influential transaction-cost economist, "Whether a set of transactions ought to be executed across markets or within a firm depends on the relative efficiency of each mode."[11] If required resources can be obtained from a competitive open market without allocating an

transaction-cost economics
The study of economic transactions and their costs

transaction costs
The resources used to create and enforce a contract

undue amount of time or other resources to the contracting process or contract enforcement, it is probably in the best interests of an organization to buy from the market instead of vertically integrating. However, when **transactions costs** are high enough to encourage an organization to produce a good or service in-house instead of buying it from the open market, a market failure is said to exist.

For example, suppose a motorcycle manufacturer needs a new "high-tech" part for its top-of-the-line motorcycle. Unfortunately, the manufacturer does not currently have the capacity or the required skills to build the part in-house. For the sake of simplicity, we will assume that the manufacturer can either (1) purchase the required machinery and acquire the knowledge necessary to produce the part in-house or (2) contract with another company to produce the part. The easier solution would be to contract out the part. However, suppose that there is only one company in the world that, due to its "high-tech" nature, currently has the skills and machinery required to produce the part. Obviously, the potential part manufacturer would be in a very strong bargaining position and may try to take advantage of the motorcycle manufacturer. Suppose also that secrecy concerning the new part is critical to competitive advantage. The motorcycle manufacturer may determine that enforcing a contract that includes a covenant of secrecy would be prohibitively

---

Table 7.3   Advantages and Disadvantages of Vertical Integration

Advantages	Disadvantages
Internal Benefits	**Internal Costs**
• Integration economies reduce costs by eliminating steps, reducing duplicate overhead, and cutting costs	• Need for overhead to coordinate vertical integration
• Improved coordination of activities reduces inventorying and other costs	• Burden of excess capacity if the organization cannot efficiently use all of the output from one of its vertically linked businesses
• Avoids time-consuming tasks, such as price shopping, communication design details, and negotiating contracts	• Poorly organized vertically integrated firms do not enjoy synergies that compensate for the higher costs
Competitive Benefits	**Competitive Dangers**
• Avoids getting shut out of the market for hard-to-get inputs (i.e., raw materials, services) by competitors	• Obsolete processes may be perpetuated
• Improved marketing or technological intelligence since vertical businesses are "in house"	• Reduces strategic flexibility due to being "locked in" to one business
• Opportunity to create product differentiation through coordinated effort	• May link firms to unprofitable adjacent businesses
• Superior control of firm's market environment due to direct involvement	• Lose access to information from suppliers or distributors
• Increased ability to create credibility for new products	• There may not be much potential for synergy because vertically integrated businesses are so different
• Synergies could be created by coordinating vertical activities carefully	• Managers may use the wrong method for vertical integration (i.e., full integration instead of contracting)

Source: Adapted from K.R. Harrigan, "Formulating Vertical Integration Strategies," *Academy of Management Review* 9 (1984): 639; used with permission.

expensive. Either one of these conditions can lead to market failure, a situation in which it would be more efficient for the motorcycle manufacturer to develop the manufacturing capability in-house than to acquire it from the open market.

The market is likely to fail, which means that transactions costs are prohibitively high, under a variety of conditions.[12] First, if the future is highly uncertain, it may be too costly or impossible to identify all of the possible situations that may occur, and to incorporate these possibilities into the contract. In other words, humans cannot process enough information to identify all possible contingencies, especially where the future is uncertain. Second, if there are only one or a small number of suppliers of a good or service and these suppliers are opportunistic, which means that they are likely to pursue their own self-interests through a lack of candor or honesty, a market failure may occur. This second condition was illustrated in the example of the motorcycle manufacturer.

A third situation in which transactions costs may be too high is when one party to a transaction has more knowledge about the transaction or a series of transactions than does another party, once again resulting in opportunism. Finally, if an organization invests in an asset that can be used only for the purpose of producing a specific good or service for the other party to a transaction (called asset specificity), the other party can take advantage of the producer after the asset is in place.

Where transaction costs are low, an organization would usually be better off contracting for the required goods and services instead of vertically integrating. Remember that transactions costs are assumed to be low only if there are a large number of potential suppliers. Under these circumstances, there is probably no profit incentive to vertically integrate, since competition would eliminate abnormally high profits. Furthermore, vertical integration often requires substantially different skills than those currently possessed by the firm. In this regard, vertical integration is similar to unrelated diversification.[13] As mentioned previously, a firm that can master one stage of the industry supply chain will not necessarily excel at other stages.

Substitutes for Full Vertical Integration

Much of this discussion assumes that when a firm vertically integrates, it will do so at full scale. In other words, the firm will become fully involved in becoming its own supplier or customer. However, firms may pursue partial vertical integration to overcome some of the disadvantages of full integration.[14] Taper integration means that an organization produces part of its requirements in-house and buys the rest of what it needs on the open market. Quasi-integration involves purchasing most of what is needed of a particular product or service from a firm in which the purchasing organization holds an ownership stake. Also, some firms use long-term contracts to achieve many of the benefits of vertical integration. For example, General Motors signed a long-term contract with Simpson Industries that allowed GM to inspect Simpson's engine-parts facilities and books and to interview Simpson's employees. In return, Simpson became the sole supplier of a part to GM.[15]

Each of the alternatives to complete integration contains trade-offs. That is, while they each reduce the level of exposure to the ill effects of vertical integration, they also reduce the potential for benefits arising from vertical integration. For example, taper integration, quasi-integration, and long-term contracting all yield less control over resources than does full integration.

Because of the potential disadvantages of vertical integration and the limited potential for profitability that may exist at other stages in the industry supply chain, some organizations bypass vertical integration and pursue diversification directly. Other organizations may vertically integrate for a while, but eventually pursue diversification. Diversification is the topic of the next section.

Diversification Strategies

Diversification, which is one of the most studied topics in all of strategic management, can be divided into two broad categories.[16] Related diversification implies organizational involvement in activities that are somehow related to the dominant or "core" business of the organization, often through common or complementary markets or technologies. Unrelated diversification does not depend on any pattern of relatedness. Some of the most common reasons for diversification are listed in Table 7.4.[17] They are divided into strategic reasons, which are frequently cited by executives in the popular business press, and personal motives that CEOs may have for pursuing diversification. In addition to these strategic and personal reasons, some diversification may be simply a result of less familiarity with the diversified business areas than with the core business areas of the organization. In other words, diversification opportunities may look good because organizational managers do not possess enough information about problems and weaknesses associated with the diversified areas—they "leap before they look."[18]

Related Diversification and Synergy

Most of the research on diversification strategies indicates that some form or other of relatedness among diversified businesses leads to higher financial performance.[19] Related diversification can also reduce risk.[20]

Table 7.4 Commonly-Stated Reasons for Diversification	
Strategic Reasons	**Motives of the CEO**
• Risk reduction through investments in dissimilar businesses or less dynamic environments	• Desire to increase the value of the firm
• Stabilization or improvement in earnings	• Desire to increase personal power and status
• Improvement in growth	• Desire to increase personal rewards such as salary and bonuses
• Use of excess cash from slower-growing traditional areas (a form of organizational slack)	• Craving for a more interesting and challenging management environment
• Application of resources, capabilities, or core competencies to related areas	
• Generation of synergy through economies of scope	
• Use of excess debt capacity (also a form of organizational slack)	
• Ability to learn new technologies	
• Increase in market power	

Related diversification is based on similarities that exist among the products, services, markets, or resource-conversion processes of different parts of the organization. These similarities are supposed to lead to synergy, which means that the whole is supposed to be greater than the sum of its parts. In other words, one organization should be able to produce two related products or services more efficiently than can two organizations each producing one of the products or services on its own. The same reasoning applies to similar markets and similar resource-conversion processes. For example, Johnson & Johnson is involved in a wide variety of diversified businesses; however, virtually all of them are related to converting chemical substances into drugs and toiletries. Also, Del Monte has diversified into a wide variety of activities, but they center on food production, processing, and distribution.

Ex. Del Monte Foods Company, with net sales of approximately $1.3 billion in fiscal 2001, is the largest producer and distributor of premium-quality, branded processed fruit, vegetable, and tomato products in the United States. The Del Monte brand was introduced in 1892 and is one of the best-known brands in the United States. Del Monte products are sold through national grocery chains, independent grocery stores, warehouse-club stores, mass merchandisers, drugstores, and convenience stores under the Del Monte, Contadina, S&W, and Sunfresh brands. The Company also sells its products to the U.S. military, certain export markets, the food-service industry, and food processors. The company employs twenty-seven hundred full-time employees and approximately eleven thousand additional seasonal workers in twelve production facilities in California, the Midwest, Washington, Texas, and in seven strategically located distribution centers. The company has operations in Venezuela, and owns Del Monte brand marketing rights in South America.

Since 1997, growth in the company's core business has been enhanced effectively by strategic acquisitions and product innovations. The Contadina brand of canned-tomato products greatly expanded the company's offerings of cut and paste-based tomato products, with a particular emphasis on the "freshest ideas in Italian cooking." In 1999, Del Monte introduced nationally the Orchard Select brand of premium-quality fruit in glass jars—products that provide convenience and picked-at-peak-ripeness taste. In 2000, the Orchard Select specialty products were complemented with the acquisition of the Sunfresh brand of citrus- and tropical-fruit lines. The company continues to develop and market products to meet the active lifestyle demands of today's consumer—these products are easy to use and convenient for meals at home and on the go. For example, to meet consumers' healthy-snacking needs, the company has successfully introduced and expanded its Fruit To-Go and Fruit & Gel To-Go single-serve fruits in plastic cups. In January 2001, the company acquired the S&W line of fruits, tomatoes, dry-bean items, specialty sauces, and vegetable products, broadening Del Monte's offerings of top-quality branded products.[21]

tangible relatedness
Means that the organization has the opportunity to use the same physical resources for multiple purposes

Relatedness comes in two forms, tangible and intangible.[22] **Tangible relatedness** means that the organization has the opportunity to use the same physical resources for multiple purposes. Tangible relatedness can lead to synergy through resource sharing. For example, if two similar products are manufactured in the same plant, operating synergy is said to exist. This phenomenon is referred to as *economies of scope*. Economies of scope occur anytime slack resources that would not have been otherwise used are being put to good use.[23] Sharing production facilities can also lead to economies of scale through producing products or services in an optimally sized (typically larger) plant.[24]

Other examples of synergy resulting from tangible relatedness include: (1) using the same marketing or distribution channels for multiple related products, (2) buying similar raw materials for related products through a centralized purchasing office to gain purchasing economies, (3) providing corporate training programs to employees from different divisions that are all engaged in the same type of work, and (4) advertising multiple products simultaneously.

intangible relatedness
Occurs any time capabilities developed in one area can be applied to another area

Intangible relatedness occurs anytime capabilities developed in one area can be applied to another area. It results in managerial synergy.[25] For example, Toys "R" Us developed skill in retailing that was directly applicable to Kids "R" Us. Also, Campbell Soup has applied skills in manufacturing and packaging soup to a variety of other products. Both of these companies make effective use of another intangible resource, image or goodwill. Goodwill means that a company that has an established trade name can draw on this name to market new products. For instance, Singer, which has an established reputation in sewing machines, also began marketing small consumer appliances and furniture under the same label. Also, Heinz enjoys a high-quality reputation that is shared by all of its food varieties. Synergy based on intangible resources such as brand name or management skills and knowledge may be more conducive to the creation of a sustainable competitive advantage, since intangible resources are hard to imitate and are never used up.[26]

The potential for synergy based on relatedness in diversified firms is limited only by the imagination. However, some types of relatedness are more imaginary than real. For example, the relatedness between oil and other forms of energy such as solar and coal proved illusive to several of the large oil companies, who experienced performance problems in these "related business ventures." They found much greater synergy with plastics and other petrochemicals, which represented a form of forward vertical integration. In addition, even if relatedness is evident, synergy has to be created.[27] The requirements for synergy creation are outlined in Figure 7.2. Some examples of potential sources of synergy from related diversification are shown in Table 7.5.

Some managers seem to believe that if business units are somehow related to each other, synergy will occur automatically. Unfortunately, this is not the case. One factor that can block the ability of organizational managers to create synergistic gains from relatedness is a lack of strategic fit. **Strategic fit** refers to the effective matching of strategic organizational capabilities. For example, if two organizations in two related businesses combine their resources, but they are both strong in the same areas and weak in the same areas, then the potential for synergy is diminished. Once combined, they will continue to exhibit the same capabilities. However, if one of the organizations is strong in R&D, but lacks marketing power, while the other organization is weak in R&D, but strong in marketing, then there is real potential for both organizations to be better off—if managed properly. When AT&T purchased NCR as a vehicle for integrating telecommunications and computer technologies, AT&T was dismayed to find that NCR did not possess strong core technical skills. Consequently, the movement into computing did not yield the synergies that were expected, and NCR was divested some years later.

strategic fit
Refers to the effective matching of strategic organizational capabilities

Another factor that can block managers from achieving synergistic gains is a

FIGURE 7.2

Requirements for the Creation of Synergy

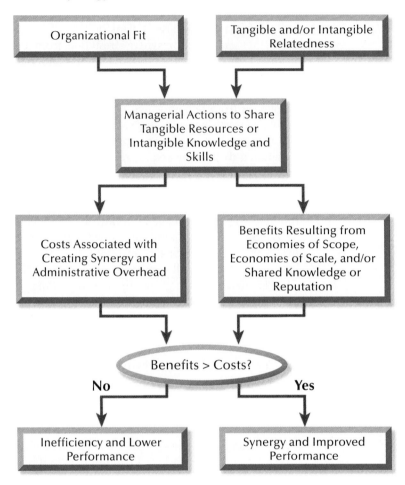

lack of organizational fit. **Organizational fit** occurs when two organizations or business units have similar management processes, cultures, systems, and structures.[28] This makes them compatible, which facilitates resource sharing, communication, and transference of knowledge and skills. Unfortunately, relatedness on a dimension such as common markets or similar resource-conversion processes does not guarantee that business units within a firm will enjoy an organizational fit. Lack of fit is especially evident in mergers and acquisitions. For instance, two related companies may merge in an effort to create synergy, but find that they are organizationally incompatible. When Federal Express and Flying Tigers joined forces, the intent was to create a total package-delivery company. Federal Express specialized in small packages, while Flying Tigers specialized in larger shipments. Unfortunately, the cultures of the two firms were so different that conflicts arose, communications broke down, and synergies never materialized.

The concept of dominant logic provides further insight concerning why

organizational fit
Occurs when two organizations or business units have similar management processes, cultures, systems, and structures

Table 7.5	Potential Sources of Synergy from Related Diversification

Potential Operations Synergies

- Common parts designs: Larger purchased quantities allow lower cost per unit
- Common processes and equipment: Combined equipment purchases and engineering support allow lower costs
- Common new facilities: Larger facilities may allow economies of scale.
- Shared facilities and capacity: Improved capacity utilization allows lower per-unit overhead costs.
- Combined purchasing activities: Increased influence leading to lower costs, and to lower-cost shipping arrangements
- Shared computer systems: Lower per unit overhead costs and can spreading out the risk of investing in higher-priced systems
- Combined training programs: Lower training costs per employee

Potential R&D/Technology Synergies

- Shared R&D programs: Spread overhead cost and risk of R&D to more than one business
- Technology transfer: Faster, lower-cost adoption of technology at the second business
- Development of new core businesses: Access to capabilities and innovation not available in the market
- Multiple use of creative researchers: Opportunities for innovation across business via individual experience and business analogy

Potential Marketing-based Synergies

- Shared brand names: Build market influence faster and at lower cost through a common name
- Shared advertising and promotion: Lower unit costs and tie-in purchases
- Shared distribution channels: Bargaining power to improve access and lower costs
- Cross-selling and bundling: Lower costs and more integrated view of the marketplace

Potential Management Synergies

- Similar industry experience: Faster response to industry trends
- Transferable core skills: Experience with previously tested, innovative strategies and skills in strategy and program development

dominant logic
Consists of the way managers deal with managerial tasks, the things they value, and their general approach to running their businesses; similar to a mental model

organizations may not fit. The **dominant logic** of an organization consists of the way managers deal with managerial tasks, the things they value, and their general approach to running their businesses: "The characteristics of the core business… tend to cause managers to define problems in certain ways and develop familiarity with and facility in the use of those administrative tools that are particularly useful in accomplishing the critical tasks of the core business."[29] Unfortunately, the administrative tools acquired while working in the core or dominant business unit of the organization may not work well in other business environments.[30] This explains, in part, why it is so hard for executives to manage diverse business units. Following this logic, some researchers suggest that organizations should invest only in businesses that would gain from the management style that permeates existing businesses.[31]

One of the best-known examples of diversification that was incompatible with dominant logic was when IBM entered the personal-computer industry. In the mainframe business, IBM's original computer business, customers expected high levels of technical service support and purchased computers through direct-sales groups. The personal-computer industry, on the other hand, did not make use of direct sales, and involved very little technical customer service. For IBM, the change in the basic way of doing business was very difficult. Because the dominant logics were so different, IBM was forced to separate the mainframe and personal-computer businesses completely, which reduced the opportunities for synergies.

Synergy creation requires a great deal of work on the part of managers at the corporate and business levels. The activities that create synergy include combining similar processes, coordinating business units that share common resources, centralizing support activities that apply to multiple units, and resolving conflicts among business units. Many organizations do not engage in these activities to any degree. Synergy, which is supposed to result in 2 + 2 = 5, often ends up 2 + 2 = 3. Not only are the coordinating and integrating activities expensive themselves, but corporate-level management creates an administrative-overhead burden that must be shared by all of the operating units.[32]

Consequently, organizational performance is increased only if the benefits associated with synergy are greater than the costs related to corporate-level administration, combining activities, or sharing knowledge and resources. When the economic benefits associated with synergy are highest, the administrative costs are highest also, because a lot more information and coordination are required to create the synergy.[33] For example, if two business units are unrelated to each other, they do not ever have to communicate or coordinate with one another. On the other hand, if they are related to each other and want to share knowledge or skills, they will have to engage in meetings, joint-training programs, and other coordination efforts. If two related businesses are using the same plant for production, they will have to work out production schedules. Coordination is also required when using the same sales force for related products, combining promotional efforts, and transferring products between divisions. Coordination processes can be costly in time and other resources. Consequently, the benefits of synergy may be offset, in part, by higher administrative costs. The various costs and forces that can undermine creation of synergies are listed in Table 7.6.

In summary, organizations may pursue related diversification by acquiring or developing businesses in areas that are related to each other on some basic variable, such as a similar production technology, a common customer, or any number of other dimensions. However, synergy is not instantaneously created if businesses are related. The creation of synergy requires related businesses to fit together common processes. This can be a difficult managerial challenge. The level of difficulty depends on the amount of strategic and organizational fit that exists among related businesses. In addition to the synergy that can be created through related diversification, corporate-level managers sometimes try to add value to their organizations through the development of corporate-level distinctive competencies that may or may not be associated with a relatedness strategy.

Unrelated Diversification

conglomerate
A large, highly diversified firm

Large, unrelated diversified firms are often called **conglomerates,** since they are involved in a conglomeration of unrelated businesses.[34] Kabushiki Kaisha Hitachi Seisakusho, or Hitachi, Ltd., is a conglomerate based in Tokyo. Hitachi's major products and services are divided into the following groups:

- *Information and Telecommunications Systems*—systems integration, software, RAID storage systems, servers, PCs, switches, and fiber-optic components

- *Electronic Devices*—semiconductors, LCDs, display tubes, semiconductor-manufacturing equipment, test and measurement equipment, and medical-electronics equipment

- *Power and Industrial Systems*—nuclear, hydroelectric, and thermal power plants; control equipment; compressors; rolling-mill equipment; plant engineering and construction; elevators; escalators; air-conditioning equipment; rolling stock; automotive equipment; construction machinery; environmental-control systems

- *Digital Media and Consumer Products*—room air conditioners, refrigerators, washing machines, microwave ovens, vacuum cleaners, heating appliances, kitchen appliances, lighting fixtures, TVs, VCRs, DVD drives, mobile phones, audiotapes, videotapes, batteries, optical-storage media, and floppy disks

- *High-Functional Materials and Components*—semiconductor-related materials, display-related materials, printed circuit boards, synthetic-resin materials and products, housing equipment, specialty steels, rolls for rolling mills, malleable cast-iron products, magnetic materials, pipe fittings, wires, cables, copper products, rubber products

Table 7.6	Forces that Undermine Synergies

Management Ineffectiveness

- Too little effort to coordinate between businesses means synergies will not be created
- Too much effort to coordinate between businesses can stifle creativity

Administrative Costs of Coordination

- Additional layers of management and staff add costs
- Executives in larger organizations are often paid higher salaries
- Delays from and expense of meetings and planning sessions necessary for coordination
- Extra travel and communications costs to achieve coordination

Poor Strategic Fit

- Relatedness without strategic fit decreases the opportunity for synergy
- Overstated (or imaginary) opportunities for synergies
- Industry evolution that undermines strategic fit
- Overvaluing potential synergies often results in paying too much for a target firm or in promising too much improvement to stakeholders

Poor Organizational Fit

- Incompatible cultures and management styles
- Incompatible strategies, priorities, and reward systems
- Incompatible production processes and technologies
- Incompatible computer and budgeting systems

- *Logistics, Services, and Other*—general trading, transportation, and property management
- *Financial Services*—leasing, auto financial services, retail, credit cards, securitized-asset sales, and payment and collection[35]

Richard Rumelt documented the rise in popularity of unrelated diversification during the 1950s, 1960s, and early 1970s.[36] The increase in conglomerates was precipitated by several forces, including government regulation and the popularity of financial theory and portfolio management. Rigid antitrust enforcement by the federal government made unrelated diversification attractive.[37] **Antitrust laws** were established to keep organizations from getting large and powerful enough in one industry to engage in monopoly pricing and other forms of noncompetitive or illegal behavior. Many organizational managers pursued unrelated diversification in an effort to use excess cash in ways that would not lead to conflicts with antitrust-enforcement agencies.

Another powerful force leading to unrelated diversification was an increase in the popularity of the Capital Asset Pricing Model (CAPM), financial-portfolio management, and related financial theories. These theories were developed in the field of finance as tools for managing portfolios of financial securities. The general proposition is that investors can reduce the risk of a portfolio of securities by investing in securities that have dissimilar return streams. For example, investors should try to invest in companies that prosper under different business conditions so that one or another of the companies will be prospering at any given time. This proposition was also applied, perhaps erroneously, to the business portfolios of individual organizations.[38] In particular, managers believed that by investing in business areas with uneven revenue streams, they would not only be able to reduce risk, but also maximize the profitability of a portfolio of businesses. CEOs, responding to their knowledge about the CAPM, pursued unrelated diversification. Nevertheless, Rumelt concluded that unrelated firms experience lower profitability than firms pursuing other corporate-level strategies. His findings have been generally, although not unequivocally, supported by other researchers.[39] Perhaps of greater concern, there is some evidence that unrelated diversification is associated with higher levels of risk than other strategies.[40] This is particularly distressing since one of the most frequently cited arguments for unrelated diversification is that it leads to reduced risk.

Unrelated diversification places significant demands on corporate-level executives due to increased complexity and technological changes across industries. In fact, it is very difficult for a manager to understand each of the core technologies and appreciate the special requirements of each of the individual units in an unrelated diversified firm. Consequently, the effectiveness of management may be reduced. By the late 1960s, conglomerates began suffering performance problems. In early 1969, the stock prices of many conglomerates fell by as much as 50 percent from their highs of the previous year, while the Dow Jones Industrial Average fell less than 10 percent during the same period.[41]

Now managers and researchers alike believe that unrelated diversification typically is not a high-performing strategy. However, some firms have had great success with it. Ford Motor is making billions of dollars each year in profits from its highly successful financial subsidiaries.[42] Also, General Electric, one of the biggest conglomerates in the world, has enjoyed many years of strong financial performance. Jack Welch, recently retired CEO of GE, explained his philosophy this way:

> All our industries don't grow at the same rate. Our plastics business might be more like [a fast-growing company] in terms of top line

antitrust laws
Established by governments to keep organizations from getting large and powerful enough in one industry to engage in monopoly pricing and other forms of noncompetitive or illegal behavior

growth. But in our other businesses, it allows us enormous staying power. For example, next year we'll go from A to B. I think I know exactly how I'm going to go from A to B, and I know the company in total will go from A to B. I'm not sure the 30 or so businesses are going to get from A to B exactly as they planned it, but I've got enough muscle that I can get from A to B.

If one of the businesses is going to be weak, and it's a great business but it's in a difficult moment, I can support it. If I'm a single-product guy in a weak business like that, in a business that cycles dramatically, I get whacked. So the staying power that our businesses have allows us to stay for the long haul.[43]

The 1980s were marked with a dramatic decrease in unrelated diversification, accompanied by an increase in related diversification.[44] The Reagan administration's "hands-off" approach to antitrust policy supported the trend toward mergers among related firms, even horizontal mergers among firms in the same industries. Related diversification, accompanied by sell-offs of unrelated businesses, is a continuing trend among U.S. firms.[45]

Mergers and Acquisitions

Some companies, such as Johnson & Johnson, rely on internal venturing for most of their growth and diversification. However, managers sometimes feel that their own firm's resources are inadequate to achieve a high level of growth and diversification. Consequently, they seek to acquire skills and resources through purchase of or merger with another firm. Compared to internal venturing, mergers and acquisitions are a relatively rapid way to pursue growth or diversification, which may partially account for the dramatic increase in their popularity over the past few decades.[46]

merger
Occurs any time two organizations combine into one; acquisitions are the most common type of merger

acquisition
An organization buys a controlling interest in the stock of another organization or buys it outright from its owners

Mergers occur anytime two organizations combine into one. **Acquisitions,** in which one organization buys a controlling interest in the stock of another organization or buys it outright from its owners, are the most common type of merger. Acquisitions are a relatively quick way to (1) enter new markets, (2) acquire new products or services, (3) learn new resource-conversion processes, (4) acquire needed knowledge and skills, (5) vertically integrate, (6) broaden markets geographically, or (7) fill needs in the corporate portfolio.[47] As a portfolio-management tool, managers often seek acquisition targets that are faster growing, more profitable, less cyclical, or less dependent on a particular set of environmental variables. For example, Mobil Oil once acquired Marcor, which consisted of Montgomery Ward and Container Corporation of America, because Marcor was not as dependent on factors connected to oil.[48]

industry consolidation
Occurs as competitors merge together

Industry consolidation, which occurs as competitors merge together, is a major trend. For example, significant consolidation has occurred in banking, hotel, health care, aerospace, and many other industries. As mentioned in the previous section, horizontal mergers that create consolidation are now blocked less often through antitrust enforcement. However, antitrust enforcement is not dead. For example, the U.S. government blocked the acquisition of Northrop Grumman by Lockheed Martin on antitrust grounds. Nearly one hundred countries have enacted antitrust laws to protect consumers from firms that become too powerful.[49] This Global Insight contains excerpts from the general director of Israel's Antitrust Authority.

corporate raiders
Organizations and individuals who engage in acquisitions, typically against the wishes of managers of target companies

hostile acquisition
An acquisition that is not desirable from the perspective of the managers of a target company, typically considered hostile

Corporate raiding is another interesting phenomenon associated with mergers and acquisitions. **Corporate raiders** are organizations and individuals who engage in acquisitions, often against the wishes of the managers of the target companies. This type of acquisition is called **hostile,** and tends to be more expensive than a friendly acquisition because the premium paid to acquire the firm is higher.[50] From a social perspective, some corporate raiders have argued that they are doing society a favor, because the threat of takeover motivates managers to act in the best interests of the organization's stockholders.[51] They believe that they are keeping managers from becoming "entrenched." However, this argument remains to be proved.

 On a summery afternoon in early May, Tyco International chief executive L. Dennis Kozlowski strode into the New Jersey boardroom of his latest prey, CIT Group Inc., the nation's largest independent commercial-finance company. Technically, CIT was not yet in Kozlowski's grip: Tyco's $9.2 billion offer wouldn't come up for a shareholder vote for another three weeks, and the deal wasn't expected to close until June 1. Kozlowski stunned investors and executives with his bid for CIT—an outfit that, ironically, once rejected him for a low-level auditing job. Skeptics question what an industrial conglomerate specializing in such mundane products as valves and garbage bags can possibly bring to the competitive world of commercial finance. It's a field that has proved to be a veritable graveyard for expansion-minded CEOs. "Kozlowski is putting his toe [into an area] that ostensibly he doesn't know anything about," says former AlliedSignal CEO Larry Bossidy.[52]

Global Insight
Comments from the General Director of Israel's Antitrust Authority

David Tadmor is general director of Israel's Antitrust Authority. The following are excerpts from a recent interview in which Mr. Tadmor was asked about Israel's position with regard to corporate mergers.

Corporate mergers, and in the large sense the market for corporate control, are an essential building block of our markets. Mergers and other forms of business combination generate tremendous efficiencies. Mergers, however, might also lead to inefficient concentration in markets that results in monopoly power, the exercise of which might harm consumers. Our legislation in the area of antitrust follows this string of thought. In line with current regulatory and economic thinking in the United States, the European Union, and the legal systems of other economically advanced nations, antitrust legislation in Israel assumes that mergers are a natural, positive economic phenomenon—but also one that should be evaluated and reviewed in circumstances that create a substantial likelihood that competition in the market might be compromised.

Our practice is very similar in its philosophy and implementation to that of advanced economies, applying solid economic analysis to assure that competition in the market is maintained. Indeed, we have not invented a single antitrust principle in Israel, but have applied internationally accepted standards. Of course, we apply those standards in the context of our markets and the preferences of our consumers. Like the legislatures of those 85 countries that have enacted antitrust laws and the additional 10 or 15 that are in the process of doing so, the legislature in Israel wishes to protect consumers through laws that preserve competition in the market.

Competition is the best way, often the only effective way, to protect consumers. Competition leads to efficient allocation of resources more than any other principle—efficient in the sense that limited resources are directed to produce those goods and services in which consumers are interested, to be sold at prices those consumers are willing to pay. Mergers between major competitors, for example, might result in substantial harm to consumers and are therefore scrutinized by the Antitrust Authority.

Source: Adapted from M. Lerner, "Israeli Antitrust Authority's General Director David Tadmor on Corporate Mergers," *Academy of Management Executive* (February 2001): 8–11, used with permission.

Merger Performance

The shareholders of an acquired firm typically enjoy a huge payoff because they receive an enormous premium over market value for the shares of stock they hold prior to the acquisition announcement.[53] However, most of the research evidence seems to indicate that mergers and acquisitions are not, on average, financially beneficial to the shareholders of the acquiring firm.[54] In one study of 191 acquisitions in twenty-nine industries, researchers found that acquisitions were associated with declining profitability, reduced research-and-development expenditures, fewer patents produced, and increases in financial leverage.[55] John Chambers, CEO of Cisco Systems, made seventy-one acquisitions between 1993 and 2000. Reflecting on that activity, he said, "I don't know how to make large mergers work."[56]

Table 7.7 provides several explanations for why acquisitions, on average, tend to depress profitability (at least in the short term). High premiums, increased interest costs, high advisory fees and other transaction costs, and poison pills (actions that make a target company less attractive) can cause acquisitions to be prohibitively expensive, and thus reduce any potential gains from synergy. In addition, strategic problems such as high turnover among target-firm managers, managerial distraction, lower innovation, lack of organizational fit, and increased leverage and risk can reduce any strategic benefits the organization was hoping to achieve. Many of these factors may be adversely affecting the merger between Daimler-Benz and Chrysler.

Ex. Chrysler's loss of edge is stunning considering its reputation for staying a step ahead of the market. Some believe the merger and the early morale problems that prompted many Chrysler execs to leave meant that U.S.

Table 7.7   A Few of Many Potential Problems with Mergers and Acquisitions

High Costs

- High Premiums Typically Paid by Acquiring Firms—If a company was worth $50/share in a relatively efficient financial market prior to an acquisition, why should an acquiring firm pay $75 (a typical premium) or more to buy it?

- Increased Interest Costs—Many acquisitions are financed by borrowing money at high interest rates. Leverage typically increases during an acquisition.

- High Advisory Fees and Other Transaction Costs—The fees charged by the brokers, lawyers, financiers, consultants, and advisers who orchestrate the deal often range in the millions of dollars. In addition, filing fees, document preparation, and legal fees in the event of contestation can be very high.

- Poison Pills—These antitakeover devices make companies very unattractive to a potential buyer. Top managers of target companies have been very creative in designing a variety of poison pills. One example of a poison pill is the "golden parachute," in which target-firm executives receive large amounts of severance pay (often millions of dollars) if they lose their jobs due to a hostile takeover.

Strategic Problems

- High Turnover among the Managers of the Acquired Firm—The most valuable asset in most organizations is its people, their knowledge, and their skills. If most managers leave, what has the acquiring firm purchased?

- Short-Term Managerial Distraction—"Doing a deal" typically takes managers away from the critical tasks of the core businesses for long durations. During this time period, who is steering the ship?

- Long-Term Managerial Distraction—Because they are too distracted running diversified businesses, organizations sometimes lose sight of the factors that led to success in their core businesses.

- Less Innovation—Acquisitions have been shown to lead to reduced innovative activity, which can hurt long-term performance.

- No Organizational Fit—If the cultures, dominant logics, systems, structures, and processes of the acquiring and target firms do not "fit," synergy is unlikely.

- Increased Risk—Increased leverage often associated with mergers and acquisitions leads to greater financial risk. Acquiring firms also take the risk that they will unable to successfully manage the newly acquired organization.

Source: M.A. Hitt, J.S. Harrison and R.D. Ireland, *Mergers and Acquisitions: A Guide to Creating Value for Stakeholders* (New York: Oxford University Press, 2001); S. Chatterjee, et al., "Cultural Differences and Shareholder Value in Related Mergers: Linking Equity and Human Capital," *Strategic Management Journal* 13 (1992); 319–334; J.S. Harrison, "Alternatives to Merger—Joint Ventures and Other Strategies," *Long Range Planning* (December 1987); 78–83; J.P. Walsh and J.W. Ellwood, "Mergers, Acquisitions, and the Pruning of Managerial Deadwood," *Strategic Management Journal* 12 (1991); 201–207.

managers spent more time around the watercooler worrying about internal dynamics between Stuttgart and Detroit than they did on how solid the business was. While Holden (CEO of Chrysler) and Schrempp (CEO of Daimler) have done a lot to smooth over relations, problems that were allowed to fester months ago may be eating into the carmaker's bottom line. "Have they taken their eye off the ball?" asks Casesa (from Merrill Lynch). "I can't help but sense that the merger has been a distraction."[57]

Perhaps the most condemning evidence to date concerning mergers and acquisitions was presented by Michael Porter. He studied the diversification records of 33 large, prestigious U.S. companies over a period of 37 years. He discovered that most of these companies divested many more of their acquisitions than they kept. For example, CBS, in an effort to create an "entertainment company," bought organizations involved in toys, crafts, sports teams, and musical instruments. All of these businesses were sold due to lack of fit with the traditional broadcasting business of CBS. CBS also bought the Ziff-Davis publishers, which they unloaded a few years later for much less than they paid after having run all its magazines into the ground. Porter's general conclusion was that the corporate-level strategies of most of the companies he studied had reduced, rather than enhanced, shareholder value.[58]

Successful and Unsuccessful Mergers and Acquisitions

Does the discouraging evidence about merger performance mean that all mergers are doomed to failure? Recently researchers have been able to identify factors associated with successful and unsuccessful mergers. Unsuccessful mergers are associated with a large amount of debt, overconfident or incompetent managers, poor ethics, changes in top management or organization structure, or diversification away from the core area of the acquiring firm.[59]

Some factors seem to lead to success in mergers. For example, some researchers have found that successful mergers are made by acquiring firms with relatively small amounts of debt. Merger negotiations are friendly (no resistance), which helps keep **acquisition premiums** to a minimum and helps make postmerger integration of the companies a lot easier.[60] Successful mergers also tend to involve companies that share a high level of complementarity among their resources, thus creating the potential for synergy. Complementarity occurs when two companies have strengths in different areas that complement each other.[61]

acquisition premium
The percentage paid for shares of stock above their market value prior to the acquisition announcement

 Finalized in February 1999, the $4 billion merger between Oryx Energy Company and Kerr-McGee Corporation is an example of a transaction that company executives believe will allow the sharing of complementary resources. As the world's fourth-largest independent oil and gas exploration and production company, the merged firm (with Kerr-McGee Corporation as its new name) is thought to have the potential needed to increase shareholder value. According to Luke R. Corbett, CEO: "This strategic merger creates value for both Kerr McGee and Oryx shareholders. The companies have complementary skill sets and assets, particularly in the Gulf of Mexico and the North Sea. Kerr-McGee brings a strong balance sheet, exploration and exploitation opportunities and development expertise [while] Oryx brings a significant inventory of exploration prospects and technical expertise, particularly in the deepwater area of the Gulf of Mexico."[62]

Furthermore, researchers have discovered that the largest shareholder gains from merger occur when the cultures and the top-management styles of the two companies are similar (organizational fit).[63] In addition, sharing resources and activities has been found to be important to postmerger success.[64] However, it is fair to say that "there are no rules that will invariably lead to a successful acquisition."[65]

One of the most important factors leading to a successful merger is the due-diligence process. Warren Hellman, former CEO of Lehman Brothers, suggests that because so many acquisitions fail, organizations should assume that all of them will fail. The burden is then on the shoulders of the managers who want the merger to take place to prove why their particular deal will be an exception to the general rule.[66] The due-diligence process is an excellent way to obtain the necessary

due diligence
Involves a complete examination of a merger or acquisition, including management, equity, debt, sale of assets, transfer of shares, environmental issues, financial performance, tax issues, human resources, customers, and markets

evidence. **Due diligence** involves a complete examination of the merger, including such areas as management, equity, debt, sale of assets, transfer of shares, environmental issues, financial performance, tax issues, human resources, customers, and markets. Typically, the process is conducted by accountants, investment bankers, lawyers, consultants, and internal specialists.[67] The due-diligence team should be empowered by top managers of both companies with responsibility and authority to obtain all of the necessary data.

Many of the major problems with mergers and acquisitions can be avoided through effective due diligence, even if it means avoiding the deal altogether. For example, the president of a billion-dollar division of one of the largest corporations in the United States recently walked away from an acquisition because of accounting irregularities discovered during due diligence.[68] On the other hand, for those acquisitions that finally occur, information gained during due diligence is invaluable for integration planning.

Chapter 3 discussed organizational learning through interorganizational relationships. Organizations can also learn through acquisitions. In fact, some experts have argued that "acquisitions may broaden a firm's knowledge base and decrease inertia, enhancing the viability of its later ventures."[69] However, mergers and acquisitions represent a paradox with regard to innovative activities. While organizations can learn from the companies they acquire, acquisitions can lead to reduction in research-and-development activities. This negative effect may come from a loss of focus on the core business or absorption of new debt that directs cash flow toward interest payments and away from research and development. Regardless of the reasons, acquisitions seem to be a way to "buy" innovation from external sources while damaging internal innovation. Consequently, some experts call acquisitions "a substitute for innovation."[70]

In summary, mergers and acquisitions have a high incidence of failure but, if carefully executed, may enhance firm performance. Once a firm has created a portfolio of businesses—either through acquisitions, joint ventures, or internal growth—the emphasis becomes managing those businesses in such a manner that high organizational performance is achieved. One of the keys to doing so is creating competencies that span multiple businesses. The next section will discuss this important topic.

Corporate-Level Distinctive Competencies

corporate-level distinctive competencies
Derived from the ability to achieve shared competitive advantage across the business units of a multi-business firm

Corporate-level distinctive competencies come from the ability to achieve shared competitive advantage across the business units of a multibusiness firm. They are dependent on a firm's ability to effectively and efficiently deploy combined resources. Many corporations attempt to build core capabilities that can be applied across many businesses in the domestic market or globally. Organizations can develop core capabilities based on skills and resources that "(1) incorporate an integrated set of managerial and technological skills, (2) are hard to acquire other than through experience, (3) contribute significantly to perceived customer benefits, and (4) can be widely applied within the company's business domain."[71] A firm can derive synergistic benefits if it can deploy its pool of experience, knowledge, and systems (core capabilities) from one business to another business so that the costs and time required to create and expand assets and resources are less than that of competitors.[72] For example,

AT&T has developed a corporate-level core competence in benchmarking methods, Disney in human resources, and 3M in supplier management.[73]

Strategy researchers identified fifty-five activities that corporations engage in to develop core capabilities and competencies.[74] These activities were based on general administration, production/operations, engineering and R&D, marketing, finance, personnel, and public and governmental relations. A few of their examples follow:

- Attracting and retaining well-trained and competent top managers (General Administration)
- Developing a more effective company-wide strategic-planning system (General Administration)
- Increased automation of production processes (Production/Operations)
- Improvement in research and new-product-development capabilities (Engineering and R&D)
- Improved marketing research and information systems (Marketing)
- Effective tax management (Finance)
- Effective relations with trade unions (Personnel)
- Better relations with special-interest groups such as environmentalists, consumerists, and others (Public and Governmental Relations)[75]

Notice that these activities cover a wide range of activities in the value chain. Any of these activities have the potential to lead to a competitive advantage. Whether the competitive advantage is sustainable depends on the ability of competitors to imitate the resulting competence or capability. However, many of these activities are long term by nature. For example, effective relations with trade unions and special-interest groups take many years to develop. Consequently, some competencies are harder to duplicate in the short term and are more likely to lead to a sustainable competitive advantage.

If a corporate-level strategy is successful, an organization may enjoy many years of growth and prosperity. However, at some point, organizations typically experience some sort of setback. The nature of the setback may be a result of declining performance or some other organizational shock. Regardless of the reason, such a setback is usually enough to prompt corporate-level managers to consider restructuring approaches. Some of the basic approaches to restructuring will be discussed in the next section.

Strategic Restructuring

Disgruntled stakeholders are often the force that causes corporate-level managers to consider restructuring. For example, stockholders may be dissatisfied with their financial returns, or debt-rating agencies such as Standard & Poor's may devalue firm securities due to high risk. If an organization has spent many years diversifying in various directions, top managers may feel as though the organization is "out of control." This feeling of loss of control is also related to organizational size. In the largest organizations, top managers may even be unfamiliar with some of the businesses in their portfolios. Also, many organizations have acquired high levels of debt, often associated with acquisitions. For these companies, even small economic downturns can be a rude awakening to the risks associated with high leverage.[76] For all of these reasons, restructuring has become commonplace in recent years.[77]

Researchers have observed that as organizations evolve over time, they tend to move through what is called a period of convergence, followed by a period of **strategic reorientation** or radical adjustment, and then another period of convergence.[78] During the convergence stage, the organization makes minor changes to strategies in an effort to adapt, but for the most part follows a consistent approach. During this time, the structure and systems are more or less stable, and performance is acceptable.

For many organizations, success during the convergence stage reinforces a certain way of doing business. During this stage, managers develop **mental models,** or mind-sets, about how the industry and the organization work. Mental models represent the knowledge managers have about the industry and the organization, and how specific actions relate to desired outcomes.[79] It is what they understand to be true about the organization and its industry. Mental models are derived from experiences, with past successes and failures contributing to the overall picture. As long as the premises that underlie these mental models do not change, they represent useful experience that should be brought to bear on decisions. When premises do change, however, mental models may prevent executives, managers, and employees from recognizing the need for change. Two well-known examples will illustrate this point.

strategic reorientation
A significant realignment of organization strategies, structure, and processes with the new environmental realities

mental model
A view of how the world works; mental models should include an understanding of both the internal and external organization and the interaction between the two

 In the automotive industry several years ago, and in the minicomputer industry more recently, established management mental models contributed to a sluggish response to industry change. In both industries, established competitors had achieved extraordinary, sustained success. They had effective strategies, useful structures, and strong cultures. When the assumptions underlying their industries changed, the existing competitors were slow to recognize what was happening. In the automotive industry, competitors failed to recognize the demographic, economic, and social trends driving demand for fuel-efficient economy cars, or the potential competitive threat from German and Japanese automakers. In the minicomputer industry, competitors failed to recognize that networked microcomputers would take the place of minicomputers. Not only were they slow to recognize the need for change, they were also slow to make changes once the need was recognized. In other words, the out-of-sync mental models combined with established organizational structures, resources, and processes to create high levels of inertia, or reluctance to change course.[80]

Managers in these firms did not recognize and respond to change until firm performance began to suffer. One of the limitations of human decision making is that often we succumb to perceptual distortion. The information that doesn't fit our preconceived mental model is just not seen at all. As one researcher recently described it, "The writing on the wall cannot be read."[81]

A period of convergence can continue indefinitely, as long as the industry conditions and organization characteristics are not significantly out of alignment.[82] However, when gradual drift results in a substantial misalignment or an environmental discontinuity does occur, the organization will be forced to reorient itself. A reorientation is a significant realignment of organization strategies, structure, and processes with the new environmental realities.[83] Transformation, renewal, reorientation, and restructuring are all words that describe the same general phenomenon: a radical change in how business is conducted. Some of the most common restructuring approaches will now be described. They include retrenchment or downsizing, refocusing corporate assets on distinctive competencies, Chapter 11 reorganization, leveraged buyouts, and changes to organizational design. Organizations may use any one or a combination of these strategies in restructuring efforts.

Retrenchment (Downsizing)

retrenchment
A turnaround strategy that involves tactics such as work force reductions, closing unprofitable plants, outsourcing unprofitable activities, implementation of tighter cost or quality controls, or new policies that emphasize quality or efficiency

Retrenchment is a turnaround strategy. It can involve such tactics as workforce reductions, closing unprofitable plants, outsourcing unprofitable activities, implementation of tighter cost or quality controls, or new policies that emphasize quality or efficiency. Chrysler Corporation, under the leadership of Lee Iacocca, combined many of these tactics in its amazing recovery more than a decade ago. Chrysler cut the workforce and emphasized quality, which included a five-year, fifty-thousand-mile warranty on its automobiles. Lee Iacocca used a variety of tools—including media releases, television commercials, and speeches—to convince the American public of the "New Chrysler Corporation."

The fiber and optics manufacturer Corning, in a major retrenchment program, announced plans to cut four thousand jobs and take a $1 billion charge.[84] ConAgra, the food-processing giant, eliminated sixty-five hundred jobs and closed or reconfigured twenty-nine production plants.[85] Boeing announced it would cut twelve thousand jobs in response to slowdowns after the attacks of September 11, 2001.[86] Of course, corporate retrenchment is also a global phenomenon. The next Global Insight describes the major retrenchment plan of Hitachi, the Japanese giant.

Workforce reductions, sometimes called downsizing, have become commonplace in organizations in the United States as a response to the burgeoning bureaucracies in the post–World War II era. Even the military has a new focus on a "lighter fighter" division that can respond faster to combat situations. The great mystery is that some companies continue to lay off employees in spite of record profits. For example, in 1995, Mobil posted "soaring" first-quarter earnings—and then announced plans to cut 4,700 jobs.[87]

The evidence is mounting that "downsizing does not reduce expenses as much as desired, and that sometimes expenses may actually increase."[88] Certainly, severance packages are one reason for the increase. Nabisco took a $300 million charge to cover its restructuring, while ConAgra spent $505 million. Also, a study of "white-collar" layoffs in the U.S. automobile industry found that most companies experienced problems such as a reduction in quality, a loss in productivity, decreased effectiveness, lost trust, increased conflict, and low morale.[89] According to H. Laurance Fuller, CEO of Amoco during its significant restructuring that included cutting 16 percent of the workforce, "The human impact of our decisions is very real and very painful."[90] Table 7.8 contains comments from middle managers that provide evidence of many of the problems associated not only with layoffs, but with retrenchment activities in general.

Many organizations cut muscle, as well as fat, through layoffs. One reason the muscle is cut is that some of the best employees leave, either because of attractive severance packages or fear of future job loss. Because the best employees can usually get new jobs fairly easily, they may decide to leave while all of their options are open to them. Also, studies have shown that the "surviving" employees experience feelings

Table 7.8   Voices of Survivors: Words that Downsizing CEOs Should Hear

Middle managers play a crucial role in corporate downsizing and restructuring as they evaluate and implement a strategy that is emotionally demanding and non-traditional. The following statements are from middle managers who survived layoffs in their companies. They demonstrate a full range of emotions, most of which are potentially damaging to the organization.

Anger

Stop blaming us! We've been loyal to the company. We've worked hard, and we did everything we were told. We've moved for the company; we've traveled for the company; and we've taken on extra work for the company. And now you say we did wrong. You told us to do it. Management told us to do it! And the company did pretty well while we did it. Stop blaming us!

Anxiety/Confusion

Who are we? The company used to stand for something. We all wore our company pins proudly. But now, I don't know who we are anymore. I've got a notion that we're meaner and leaner—but isn't everybody else? And is that who we want to be...?

Cynicism

I understand that these are hard times. But how come we are the worst? Everyone in the industry is going through a downturn, but not everyone is feeling the heat the way we are. We've downsized more, but our stock and credit rating are still bad. What happened to make us the worst?

Resentment

There's a double standard here. We lined up everything that needed to be cut. We set priorities. We participated. Did the executive dining room go? No! Did the corporate helicopter go? No! Who's kidding whom?

Retribution

Why don't you leave? Get out, and let us get on with the business. Leave the company, and let us build a new one.

Hope

We want to be the best. Lead us there!
Give us a mission, a vision.

Source: Adapted from H.M. O'Neill and D.J. Lenn, "Voices of Survivors: Words That Downsizing CEOs Should Hear," *Academy of Management Executive* (November 1995): 23–33, used with permission.

of guilt and fear that may hurt productivity or organizational loyalty.[91] It is not surprising, then, that the stock market often reacts unfavorably to announcements of major layoffs.[92]

A survey by the American Management Association of 1,142 companies that had been involved in workforce reductions indicates that about half of these companies were poorly prepared for these activities.[93] One of the keys to successful downsizing, then, may be sufficient preparation with regard to outplacement, new reporting relationships, and training.

Of course, another important element in all successful restructuring activities, especially workforce reductions, is effective communication with and examination of the needs of key stakeholders.[94] Managers anticipating layoffs should combine caring with cost consciousness and should "humanize" their approaches to workforce reductions.[95] Many organizations are avoiding layoffs through hiring freezes, restricting overtime, retraining and redeploying workers, switching workers to part-time, starting job-sharing programs, giving unpaid vacations, shortening the workweek, or reducing pay.[96]

Global Insight
Hitachi's Retrenchment Program

In response to poor business performance, the Japanese conglomerate Hitachi announced in August 2001 that it was embarking on an aggressive program to improve business results. Strategic measures included:

1. Comprehensive Cutting of Fixed Costs—on an unconsolidated basis, targets for cutting fixed costs will be set for each business group to reduce overall level of fixed costs by 60 billion yen by the end of fiscal 2001, the year ending March 31, 2002. In subsidiaries belonging to segments where results are particularly sluggish, such as Electronic Devices and High Functional Materials and Components, manufacturing facilities will be closed, merged or downsized.

2. Personnel Reductions—on a consolidated basis, the number of employees will be reduced by around 14,700 (10,200 in Japan and 4,500 overseas), by the end of fiscal 2001, mainly through natural attrition and restructuring of the Semiconductor Group and Display Group.

3. Top-to-Bottom Review of Planned Investment in Plant and Equipment—in response to a rapid deterioration in the operating environment, plant and equipment investment plans will be reviewed to reduce investment items to the minimum required.

4. Boosting Management Efficiency—the Company will continue to move forward with the Corporate Innovative Initiative (CII), encompassing the following elements.

    a. Procurement Renewal Project (PRP)—the procurement specifications and methods of the Hitachi Group are being reviewed to reduce consolidated procurement costs by a planned 20% (approximately 600 billion yen) over two years, by using such measures as net-based centralized purchasing and by making major reductions in distribution costs.

    b. Project C—the aim of project C is to ensure funds for strategic investments and reduce interest-bearing debt through a 25% decrease in the number of days it takes to turn over inventory and accounts receivable.

    c. Project A—each business group and division is developing businesses and services which aim at world leadership in 2 to 3 years. Compared to fiscal 2000 sales, the aim is to increase sales of products and services targeted by the project by 1.5 times in fiscal 2001, and to double sales by fiscal 2002.

Source: Taken directly from "Hitachi to Implement Emergency Management Measures and New Consolidated Management System," www.global.hitachi.com/News/cnews/E/2001, 31 August 2001.

Refocusing Corporate Assets (Downscoping)

Most restructuring companies are moving in the direction of reducing their diversification as opposed to increasing it.[97] Refocusing activities are generally viewed favorably by external stakeholders such as the financial community.[98] Refocusing entails trimming businesses that are not consistent with the strategic direction of the organization. For example, Xerox sold its "low-tech" circuit-board- and small-copier-manufacturing operations to Singapore's Flextronics International Ltd.[99] This type of refocusing is often called downscoping. **Downscoping** involves reducing diversification through selling off nonessential businesses that are not related to the organization's core competencies and capabilities.[100] Furthermore, R&D activities tend to increase in companies involved in this type of restructuring. You may recall from Chapter 7 that this is opposite of the impact of acquisitions.[101]

On the other hand, sell-offs that do not improve the strategic focus of the organization may signal failure or market retreat, which can cause concern among stakeholders such as owners, debt holders, and the financial community. For instance, the stock market tends to react positively to divestitures linked to corporate-level or business-level strategies, and negatively to divestitures that are portrayed as simply getting rid of unwanted assets.[102]

A **divestiture** is a reverse acquisition. One type of divestiture is a sell-off, in which a business unit is sold to another firm or, in the case of a leveraged buyout, to the business unit's managers. For example, Chrysler agreed to sell most of its aerospace and defense holdings to Raytheon, and Rockwell sold its aerospace and defense assets to Boeing.[103] The Xerox deal described above was also a sell-off.

Another form of divestiture is the **spin-off,** which means that current shareholders are issued a proportional number of shares in the spun-off business. For example, if a shareholder owns one hundred shares of XYZ company and the company spins off business unit J, the shareholder would then own one hundred shares of XYZ company and one hundred shares of an independently operated company called J. The key advantage of a spin-off relative to other divestiture options is that shareholders still have the option of retaining ownership in the spun-off business. General Motors spun off EDS, but kept a ten-year contract in which EDS would continue to provide computer services to GM. Also, Corning, unable to sell its $1.6 billion laboratory-testing business, spun it off to shareholders.[104] More recently, AT&T spun off Liberty Media, its television-programming unit.[105]

The businesses that should be divested during a restructuring include those that have little to do with the distinctive competencies of the organization. An obvious example is when Johnson & Johnson, the consumer-oriented drug and toiletry giant, sold their sausage-casings company.[106] Also, W.R. Grace, one of the largest chemical companies, refocused its efforts away from basic chemistry and toward chemical-conversion processes.[107] Other examples include the departure of General Mills from retailing, the withdrawal of Sears from mail-order catalogs, and the retreat of Xerox from financial services.[108]

Refocusing may also involve new acquisitions or new ventures to round out a corporate portfolio or add more strength in an area that is essential to corporate distinctive competencies.[109] For instance, Grand Metropolitan bought Pillsbury and simultaneously sold Bennigan's and Steak & Ale restaurants in an effort to redefine its domain in the food-processing industry.[110]

downscoping
Involves reducing diversification (refocusing) through selling off nonessential businesses that are not related to the organization's core competencies and capabilities

divestiture
A reverse acquisition; business assets are sold off or spun off as a whole business

spin-off
A type of divestiture in which current shareholders are issued a proportional number of shares in the spun-off business

Chapter 11 Reorganization

Chapter XI
A legal filing under the Federal Bankruptcy Code of the United States; allows an organization to work out a plan or arrangement for solving its financial problems under the supervision of a federal court

An organization that is in serious financial trouble can voluntarily file for Chapter 11 protection under the Federal Bankruptcy Code: "**Chapter XI** provides a proceeding for an organization to work out a plan or arrangement for solving its financial problems under the supervision of a federal court. It is intended primarily for debtors who feel they can solve their financial problems on their own if given sufficient time, and if relieved of some pressure."[111] For example, Kmart became the largest retailer in history to file for Chapter 11, "hoping to buy itself time to repay creditors while it restructures its businesses."[112] However, a company does not have to be huge to file Chapter 11.

 The FM Corporation of Rogers, Arkansas, is involved in the manufacture of custom molded structural plastics. A $3 million loss due to inventory problems almost put the company out of business, but instead, FM Corporation filed for Chapter 11 protection. The company then reviewed its costing system to confirm all costs. All employees pulled together, and FM Corporation instituted a new training program and improved management techniques, as well as a profit-sharing plan. The company also instituted a revamped marketing program and computerized its production schedule and inventory transactions to increase reliability and speed. Because of all these measures, FM Corporation was able to find new investors willing to provide the cash so that managers would have more time to put the company on sound financial ground. The court finally approved a plan allowing the corporation's successful emergence from Chapter 11, a feat achieved by only 20 percent of the companies that file for it. The FM Corporation is now a reliable supplier with an excellent reputation.[113]

Chapter 11 can be expensive. After Pacific Gas and Electric Company filed Chapter 11 in 2001, the company was billed more than $7 million in fees from lawyers, investment bankers, and accountants.[114] Another disadvantage is that, after filing, all major managerial decisions are subject to court approval. Thus, managerial discretion and flexibility are reduced. One organizational response to this problem is the prepackaged reorganization strategy. Firms using this strategy negotiate a reorganization plan with creditors before filing Chapter 11. Consequently, the courts stay out of the picture until after a tentative agreement is reached. Two attorneys who specialize in prepackaged reorganizations list four ingredients for success:

- A realistic assessment of financial problems by management.

- Willingness and ability of management to incur the professional fees that are necessary to carry out the prepackaged reorganization. Lawyers, accountants, investment bankers, and others are necessary to work out the details. Organizations will either have to pay the costs now or later—-they are not avoidable.

- Formulation of a reorganization plan that is acceptable to most of the organization's creditors. Also, if there are too many creditors, negotiations may not be feasible.

- A creditor group that is willing to negotiate. Some creditors insist on litigation instead of negotiation.[115]

While Chapter 11, if executed properly, can provide firms with time and protection as they attempt to reorganize, it is not a panacea for firms with financial problems. Also, researchers do not agree on the potential for successful reorganization. Some researchers have argued that it is in the best interests of organizations that are facing high amounts of adversity to quickly select Chapter 11 (instead of having it imposed on them), unless they have high levels of organizational slack.[116] On the other hand, in a study of firms that had voluntarily filed for Chapter 11 protection, only a little more than half of the companies were "nominally successful in reorganizing," and "two-thirds of those retained less than 50 percent of their assets on completion of the reorganization process."[117] While larger firms had a better chance of successfully reorganizing, Chapter 11 should probably still be used as a strategy of last resort.

Leveraged Buyouts

leveraged buyouts (LBOs)
Private purchase of a business unit by managers, employees, unions or private investors

Leveraged buyouts (LBOs) involve private purchase of a business unit by managers, employees, unions, or private investors. They are called leveraged because much of the money that is used to purchase the business unit is borrowed from financial intermediaries (often at higher-than-normal interest rates). Because of high leverage, LBOs are often accompanied by selling off assets to repay debt. Consequently, organizations typically become smaller and more focused after an LBO.

 Kelly Truck Line, Inc., located in Pittsburg, Kansas, has operations in Kansas, Missouri, Texas, Ohio, and Arkansas. The company was experiencing all sorts of problems when Michael Kelly entered into a leveraged buyout. For one thing, their insurance carrier went into receivership with more than $100,000 of their money. The company had negative net worth and an aging fleet. Kelly decided to specialize in one business, selling off all trailer types except flatbeds. Money from sale of the other trailers was used to retire debt. Kelly then developed a new sales and incentive program that involved salespeople, dispatchers, and drivers. The aging fleet was replaced with new trucks, and the size of the fleet was eventually tripled. The company bought a new computer system that allowed communications with customers through electronic-data interchange. Within five years, Kelly retired all of the debt from the leveraged buyout and completely replaced its aging fleet. Sales more than doubled, and the company has attracted major corporations as clients throughout the country.[118]

During the late 1970s and early 1980s, LBOs gained a reputation as a means of turning around failing divisions. For instance, Hart Ski, once a subsidiary of Beatrice, was revived through an LBO led by the son of one of its founders. Also, managers and the union joined forces to turn around American Safety Razor, a failing division of Philip Morris. These LBOs benefited many of these organizations' stakeholders, including employees and local communities.[119]

However, some researchers have discovered that LBOs stifle innovation and R&D, similar to what can happen with mergers and acquisitions.[120] Others have found that LBO firms have comparatively slower growth in sales and employees, and that they tend to divest a larger proportion of both noncore and core businesses, compared to firms that remained public.[121] Also, some executives who initiate LBOs seem to receive an excessive return, regardless of the consequences to others. For example, John Kluge made a $3 billion profit in two years through dismantling Metromedia following an LBO.[122] Plant closings, relocations, and workforce reductions are all common outcomes. Consequently, some businesspeople are starting to wonder if LBOs are really in the best interests of all stakeholders. LBOs can certainly do seemingly irreparable damage to organizational resources.

 In 1996, Robert Hass led a LBO of Levi Strauss & Co., putting its future in the hands of four people: himself, an uncle, and two cousins. Other family shareholders had a choice of staying in or cashing out. While most of them stayed, they probably should have cashed out. Under Robert's leadership during the 90s, "Levi's market share among males ages 14 to 19 has since dropped in half, it hasn't had a successful new product in years, its advertising campaigns have been failures, its in-store presentations are embarrassing, and it manufacturing costs are bloated." He launched an $850 reengineering that was a huge failure. From 1997 to 1999, the company announced plans to shutter twenty-nine factories in the United States and Europe and eliminate 16,310 jobs. *Fortune* estimated that during the first four or five years of the LBO, Levi Strauss's market value shrank from $14 billion to about $8 billion. In the same time period, Gap, a rival company, grew from $7 billion to over $40 billion.[123]

It is the responsibility of the board of directors to ensure that stakeholder interests are considered prior to approving an LBO.

 When considering a leveraged buyout, board members must treat fairly not only shareholders but other stakeholders as well. Corporate groups— employees, creditors, customers, suppliers, and local communities— claim the right to object to leveraged buyouts on the grounds that they have made a larger investment in— and have a more enduring relationship with— the corporation than do persons who trade share certificates daily on the stock exchanges. . . . Similarly, if short-run profit is at the expense of and violates the expectations of employees, customers, communities, or suppliers, companies will find themselves unable to do business. The better employees will leave. Customers will stop buying. Communities will refuse to extend services. Suppliers will minimize their exposure.[124]

Not surprisingly, reports of failed LBOs are becoming more common. Successful LBOs require buying a company at the right price with the right financing, combined with outstanding management and fair treatment of stakeholders.[125]

Changes to Organizational Design

Organizational design, which will be discussed in detail in Chapter 9, can be a potent force in restructuring efforts. As organizations diversify, top managers have a more difficult time processing the vast amounts of diverse information that are needed to appropriately control each business. Their span of control is too large. Consequently, an organization that is functionally structured may move to a more decentralized product/market or divisional structure. The end result is more managers with smaller spans of control and a greater capacity to understand each of their respective business areas.

 In the early 1990s, IBM broke off its personal computer business as a separate operating unit, which could eventually become a wholly owned subsidiary. In the old organization structure, one part of the corporation was responsible for marketing while another was responsible for producing the personal computers. The separate operating unit had responsibility for developing, manufacturing, distributing, and marketing all personal computers world-wide. About twelve hundred employees of the U.S. marketing and sales group were reassigned to the new operating unit. The purpose of the change in structure was to eliminate bureaucracy in decision making, cut overhead, and improve responsiveness, part of a long-term plan to decentralize authority and decision making in all of IBM's businesses. Other autonomous operating units were to be created around software, semiconductor, hardware and service businesses. The goal was to make IBM look much like a holding company—with the head of each operating unit functioning as the executive officer, and corporate headquarters serving an advisory function.[126]

In an effort to increase control, some organizations are actually splitting their operations into multiple public corporations. An extreme case of the spin-off tactic described earlier, this restructuring strategy might be called the "breakup." For example, Hanson PLC, the British conglomerate, split into four companies—chemicals, tobacco, energy and building materials, and equipment. All of these units have revenues of more than $3 billion.[127]

On the other hand, some organizations restructure by becoming more centralized. For instance, British Petroleum collapsed its structure to save costs. According to Robert Horton, former chairman and CEO of British Petroleum:

> Excessive differentiation and decentralization in the past has been a terrible mistake. We now run our European division from Brussels. We have one office and we run the whole of Europe from there. Now it has been a hell of a fight and you know Paris did not like it, and Hamburg did not like it, and Vienna did not like it, and I have to tell you London did not like it either. I mean, I run the corporation worldwide from London, but the operations for continental Europe are now run from Brussels. But of course, the savings are enormous. Instead of having twelve head offices, you just have one. Instead of having twelve research centers, you have one.[128]

In a similar move, Philip Morris merged Kraft and General Foods into one company. Prior to the restructuring, an executive familiar with the situation estimated that the consolidation would eliminate one hundred corporate jobs immediately.[129] Also, when Jack Welch took over General Electric, he dramatically altered the organization's structure by squeezing 350 product lines into thirteen large businesses.[130] On a smaller scale, Sara Lee combined ten meat companies into just three.[131]

Reengineering is a very popular restructuring approach that dramatically alters organizational design. "Business Process Reengineering involves the radical redesign of core business processes to achieve dramatic improvements in productivity cycle times and quality. Companies start with a blank sheet of paper and rethink existing processes, typically placing increased emphasis on customer needs. They reduce organizational layers and unproductive activities in two ways: they redesign functional

reengineering
A restructuring approach that involves the radical redesign of core business processes to achieve dramatic improvements in productivity cycle times and quality

organizations into cross-functional teams, and they use technology to improve data dissemination and decision making."[132] Based on a survey of the executives of large American firms, by 1995, more than three-quarters of firms in the United States were reengineering. However, satisfaction rates are lower for most other management tools in the survey, and use has dropped almost in half since then. Some business experts think that reengineering may have been just a fad.

Closely linked to changes in organizational structure are adjustments to the culture of the firm, the unseen glue that holds the structure together. The successful turnaround of Chrysler, described earlier, was accompanied by a dramatic change in culture that led to a leaner, meaner, and more focused organization. If restructuring activities are precipitated by unusually poor economic or competitive conditions, a strong strategy-supportive culture can be undermined by the actions taken during the restructuring.[133] In other retrenchment situations, the existing culture may be part of the problem: too little focus on quality, too little learning and sharing, a poor attitude toward customers, or lack of innovation. If the culture is part of the problem, then the restructuring effort has to address the necessary changes in culture. It is very difficult for an organization to throw off its old way of doing business. Following a hostile takeover, Linda Wachner, CEO of Warnaco, says she had to instill a new, hardworking "do it now" culture to improve the organization's performance:

> Don't get me wrong, getting these successes hasn't been easy. And some people felt that the pressure to succeed was too great. Some people left. So we said, "Okay, if you can't meet the goal or if you can't get under the limbo rack, good-bye, and we don't hold it against you." But of the 100 people we put in equity [ownership positions in the company] almost seven years ago, 86 are still here and have a major financial stake in the company.[134]

In 1999, Sony, the Japanese conglomerate with worldwide sales of more than $56 billion and 170,000 employees, combined a new structure with cultural change in order to create more of an entrepreneurial spirit. When Nobuyuki Idei became president of the company in 1995, he gave managers two slogans: "Regeneration" and "Digital Dream Kids." According to Yoshihide Nakamura:

> That's the spirit of being small and going back to when we started Sony in 1946. So we want to make Sony smaller. Instead of having this huge corporation, he wants to organize Sony into four divisional companies so that a small venture capital spirit can be brought into management. . . . The first of the three principal areas is the Home Networking Company, and the second is the Personal and Information Technology Network Company, and the third is the Core Technology and Network Company. The third one is the one I belong to and serve as deputy president. There is one additional company, Sony Computer Entertainment, which has only one product, PlayStation.[135]

Combined Restructuring Approaches

Companies sometimes combine restructuring tactics in an effort to turn their organizations around. For example, Lockheed Martin recently concluded a highly successful turnaround, topped off by winning a contract to produce the Joint Strike Fighter, a U.S. government contract that could be worth as much as $200 billion. "The victory marks a new era for Lockheed, which as recently as two years ago was mired in debt, saddled with a cumbersome organizational structure and plagued by high-profile financial and management blunders. Since then, the company has bounced back by implementing a broad program to control costs, divest noncore businesses and rebuild its badly damaged relationship with the Defense Department."[136] In another example, Navistar (International Harvester)—a former leader in the manufacture of trucks, engines, and agricultural and construction products—embarked on a restructuring that took place over most of a decade. The restructuring utilized several of the techniques that were discussed in this chapter.

 International Harvester nearly went bankrupt during the early 1980s, a result of two decades of complacency and mismanagement. By 1984, the company had lost more than $3 billion. The company renegotiated its debt with its two hundred lenders, but much more was needed. Subsequently, International Harvester developed a complete restructuring plan that involved closing plants, laying off employees, and selling many business units, including construction equipment and solar turbines. The company even sold one of its traditional strongholds, agricultural equipment, to Tenneco, and agreed to change its name to Navistar so Tenneco could keep the International Harvester trade name. Facilities were reduced worldwide from forty-two to seven. Employment went from nintey-five thousand to thirteen thousand. Navistar also made changes to organizational design by decentralizing decision-making authority, creating a new values-based culture, and establishing Continuous Improvement Teams.[137]

The successful Navistar turnaround demonstrates an important point—it is not enough to simply sell off unwanted business units or restructure debt. Permanent organizational changes are required if a company is going to emerge from a restructuring with increased competitiveness. These changes often include a renewed emphasis on research and development; better use of human capital through training and development; and the creation of an effective corporate culture that encourages entrepreneurial activity, high quality, and a global, long-term perspective.[138]

Unfortunately, efforts to fundamentally restructure companies do not have an attractive success rate. Some are very successful, some are dismal failures, but most create only minor improvements in the overall, sustained health of the organization.[139] Quite often the morale problems that follow a radical restructuring are so severe that it takes years for the firm to gain momentum in the new direction. Consequently, internal stakeholders should be given significant attention when contemplating a program of restructuring. Poorly executed restructurings can damage trust and thus long-term relationships. Even in the best-planned restructurings, some internal stakeholders are likely to be upset; however, if organizational managers make decisions in light of the needs of stakeholders, the negative effects can be reduced. Failed restructurings often lead to turnover at the top of the organization.

 When Jacques Nasser took over as Ford Motor Co.'s chief executive officer in January 1999, he made his agenda clear. He wanted to transform the auto giant in much the same way legendary CEO Jack Welch had done at General Electric Co. "Five years from now, we will be a different company, and five years from then, we'll be another different company," Mr. Nasser, 53, said, explaining his commitment to change.

Yesterday [October 30, 2001] Ford announced Mr. Nasser's abrupt departure, and the ascendancy of Henry Ford's 44-year-old great grandson, William Clay Ford Jr., as Ford's CEO, flanked by a team of veteran executives. The shake-up marks a dramatic warning to would-be agents of change that revolutions often backfire in big organizations.[140]

Some authors suggest that restructuring should be a continuous process.[141] Changes in global markets and technology have created a permanent need for firms to focus on what they do best and divest any parts of their organizations that are no longer contributing to their missions or long-term goals. This is basically the approach that GE has been using since Jack Welch took control of it a couple of decades ago. However, most organizations have a hard time achieving significant changes, and managers' mental models cause them to resist change. Consequently, continuous restructuring is a good idea, and perhaps even essential to remain competitive, but it is certainly difficult to accomplish.

Summary

Corporate-level strategy focuses on the selection of businesses in which the firm will compete, and on the tactics used to enter and manage those businesses and other corporate-level resources. At the corporate level, primary strategy-formulation responsibilities include setting the direction of the entire organization, formulation of a corporate strategy, selection of businesses in which to compete, selection of tactics for diversification and growth, and management of corporate resources and capabilities. The three broad approaches to corporate-level strategy are concentration, vertical integration, and diversification, which is divided into two broad categories, related and unrelated. These strategies, and their strengths and weaknesses, were discussed in depth.

Concentration is associated with a narrow business definition. As long as a company has virtually all of its resource investments in one business area, it is concentrating. However, most successful organizations abandon their concentration strategies at some point due to market saturation, excess resources for which they need to find a use, or some other reason. Through internal ventures, mergers and acquisitions, or joint ventures, they pursue businesses outside their core business areas. Corporate strategy typically evolves from concentration to some form of vertical integration or diversification of products, functions served, markets, or technologies. Diversification that stems from common markets, functions served, technologies, or products and services is referred to as related diversification. Unrelated diversification is not based on commonality among the activities of the corporation. Many firms eventually come to a point at which slow growth, declining profits, or some other crisis forces corporate-level managers to "rethink" their entire organizations. The result of this process is usually some form of restructuring. Restructuring often involves reducing the business definition combined with refocusing efforts on the things the organization does well.

Concentration strategies allow a company to focus on doing one business very well; however, a key disadvantage is that the company is dependent on that one business for survival. Vertical integration allows a firm to become its own supplier or customer. However, according to the theory of transaction-cost economics, if required resources can be obtained from a competitive open market without allocating an undue amount of time or other resources to the contracting process or contract enforcement, it is probably in the best interests of an organization to buy from the market instead of vertically integrating.

Unrelated diversification was very popular during the 1950s, 1960s, and the early 1970s. However, research results seem to indicate that it did not lead to the high performance that many executives had expected. Many organizations are now restructuring to reduce unrelated diversification. Related diversification, on the other hand, is still a very popular strategy. Businesses are related if they share a common market, technology, raw material, or any one of many other factors. However, for a related-diversification strategy to have its full positive impact, synergy must be created. In addition to some form of relatedness, organizational fit is required, as are actions on the part of managers to actually make synergy a reality. Corporate-level managers can help create value in their companies not only by combining and managing related operations, but by helping their organizations create a corporate-level distinctive competence.

Mergers and acquisitions are the quickest way to diversify; however, they are fraught with difficulties, and most of them fail to meet the expectations of the firms involved. Nevertheless, friendly acquisitions between companies that have complementary skills or resources, executed after a thorough due-diligence process, are more likely to succeed.

Restructuring has become a very popular corporate activity. Some of the most common restructuring approaches include retrenchment or downsizing, refocusing corporate assets on distinctive competencies, Chapter 11 reorganization, leveraged buyouts, and changes to organizational design. Retrenchment is a turnaround strategy. It can involve such tactics as workforce reductions, closing unprofitable plants, outsourcing unprofitable activities, implementation of tighter cost or quality controls, or new policies that emphasize quality or efficiency. Workforce reductions, sometimes called downsizing, have become commonplace in organizations in the United States. However, most of the recent evidence suggests that downsizing is a perilous activity that can hurt organizational culture while not really reducing expenses as much as expected. On the other hand, downscoping involves reducing diversification through selling off nonessential businesses that are not related to the organization's core competencies and capabilities. This sort of restructuring seems to be a very effective way to reorient the firm around a basic core of activities.

For companies in financial trouble, Chapter 11 provides an opportunity for an organization to work out a plan or arrangement for solving its financial problems under the supervision of a federal court. While Chapter 11, if executed properly, can provide firms with time and protection as they attempt to reorganize, it can also reduce managerial discretion and flexibility. Unfortunately, success rates for firms pursuing Chapter 11 are not high. Leveraged buyouts (LBOs) are another tactic for major restructuring. Because of high leverage, LBOs are often accompanied by selling off assets to repay debt. LBOs have helped some managers amass large sums of wealth. However, they may stifle innovation and R&D and result in slow growth. Finally, changes in organizational design may either centralize or decentralize decision making.

Efforts to fundamentally restructure companies do not have an attractive success rate. Most create only minor improvements in the overall, sustained health of the firm. Permanent organizational changes are required if a firm is going to emerge from a restructuring with increased competitiveness. These changes often include a renewed emphasis on research and development; better use of human capital through training and development; and the creation of an effective corporate culture that encourages entrepreneurial activity, high quality, and a global, long-term perspective.

Discussion Questions

1. Describe the three basic corporate-level strategies.

2. What are the strengths and weaknesses of a concentration strategy? What are the strengths and weaknesses of a vertical integration strategy?

3. How is a vertical integration strategy like a concentration strategy? How is it like an unrelated diversification strategy?

4. Why isn't an unrelated diversification strategy generally a good idea? Why, then, was this strategy so popular during the 1950s, 1960s, and early 1970s?

5. What is required for a related diversification strategy to produce synergy? Please explain.

6. Describe five ways organizations can develop a corporate-level distinctive competence. Give examples.

7. What are ten common reasons for mergers and acquisitions? What are some of the major reasons that mergers and acquisitions often produce unsatisfactory results?

8. Which of the major restructuring techniques is most likely to provide rapid results? Defend your answer.

9. Is downsizing or downscoping typically a more appropriate restructuring technique? Why? Also, what are some of the ill effects from layoffs? How can an organization avoid layoffs and still reduce labor costs?

10. Why doesn't Chapter 11 work out for most firms? Is there anything they can do to increase their chances of success?

11. What are some of the key factors that lead to success in restructuring, regardless of the technique used to restructure?

Strategic Application

Identification of Corporate-Level Strategy

Select a firm that has diversified into at least three different businesses (or use a case assigned by your instructor). You may need to access the Web site of the firm, its annual report, or an online database such as Hoovers.com to learn enough about the corporate strategy of the firm to complete this assignment.

- Begin by describing the business portfolio of the firm. What are the businesses of the company?

- Identify any forms of relatedness found among the businesses. For example, do they share a common customer, a common marketing channel, or a certain type of manufacturing? There are many ways businesses can be related. These are just examples.

- Identify any vertical linkages between the businesses of the company.

- Based on your responses to the last two items, identify the corporate-level strategy of your company as primarily related, vertically integrated, unrelated, or a combination of strategies.

● What are the tactics used for growth—acquisitions, joint ventures, internal growth, or a combination?

Now that you have identified the corporate-level strategy, evaluate its effectiveness. Do you think it is appropriate? Are the growth tactics working? One way to assess effectiveness is to compare the success of your company in a few of its businesses to the success of competitors in those same businesses. For example, if one of your firm's businesses is hotels, how successful has your company been in the hotel business relative to competitors in that industry? Finally, what recommendations would you make? Why?

Strategic Internet Application

Go to a search engine such as www.Google.com. Do two searches, each one with the name of a major competitor in the aircraft manufacturing industry (or an industry selected by your instructor). The competitors should be based in different countries. For example, you could use Boeing (currently www.Boeing.com) and Airbus Industrie (currently www.Airbus.com). Go to their Web sites. Most Web sites have a section called "Company Overview" or "About." Read this overview and as many other links as you need to capture the essence of what the company does. Also, in exploring the Web site of a major company, you can usually find an annual report. Most often it is listed under a heading such as "Investor Information." Read some of the opening remarks in the annual report, as well as a description of the products, services, and performance in each of the segments of the company. If an annual report is not available, this type of information is almost always available somewhere else on the Web site. When you have done this research for both of your companies, answer the following questions:

1. How are these companies similar in their approaches to doing business?

2. How are they different?

3. Which company do you think is a better investment? Why?

4. What are some of the key issues addressed by the companies?

Notes

1. Adapted from ALFA, S.A. de C.V., www.mex-i-co.com/mexcoys/Alfa1.htm, 23 November 2001.

2. A. D. Chandler Jr., *Strategy and Structure: Chapters in the History of the Industrial Enterprise* (Cambridge, Mass.: MIT Press, 1962).

3. Taken directly from G. Hamel, *Leading the Revolution* (Boston: Harvard Business School Press, 2000), 247.

4. R. P. Rumelt, *Strategy, Structure, and Economic Performance* (Boston: Harvard Business School, 1974); R. P. Rumelt, "Diversification Strategy and Profitability," *Strategic Management Journal* 3 (1982): 359–369.

5. H. I. Ansoff, *Corporate Strategy: An Analytical Approach to Business Policy for Growth and Expansion* (New York: McGraw-Hill, 1965), 129–130.

6. Rumelt, *Strategy, Structure*; Rumelt, "Diversification Strategy."

7. K. R. Harrigan, "Formulating Vertical Integration Strategies," *Academy of Management Review* 9 (1984): 639.

8. R. A. D'Aveni and D. J. Ravenscraft, "Economies of Integration versus Bureaucracy Costs: Does Vertical Integration Improve Performance?" *Academy of Management Journal* 37 (1994): 1167–1206.

9. S. Balakrishnan and B. Wernerfelt, "Technical Change, Competition, and Vertical Integration," *Strategic Management Journal* 7 (1986): 347–359.

10. O. E. Williamson, *Markets and Hierarchies: Analysis and Antitrust Implications* (New York: The Free Press, 1975); O. E. Williamson, *The Economic Institutions of Capitalism* (New York: The Free Press, 1985).

11. Williamson, *Markets and Hierarchies*, 8.

12. B. Klein, R. Crawford, and A. A. Alchian, "Vertical Integration, Appropriable Rents, and the Competitive Contracting Process," *Journal of Law and Economics* 21 (1978): 297–326; Williamson, *Markets and Hierarchies*, 9–10.

13. R. E. Hoskisson, J. S. Harrison, and D. A. Dubofsky, "Capital Market Implementation of M-Form Implementation and Diversification Strategy," *Strategic Management Journal* 12 (1991): 271–279.

14. K. R. Harrigan, "Exit Barriers and Vertical Integration," *Academy of Management Journal* (September 1985): 686–697.

15. J. B. Treece, "U.S. Parts Makers Just Won't Say 'Uncle,'" *Business Week*, 10 August 1987, 76–77.

16. D. D. Bergh, "Diversification Strategy Research at a Crossroads: Established, Emerging, and

Anticipated Paths," in *The Blackwell Handbook of Strategic Management,* ed. M. A. Hitt, R. E. Freeman, and J. S. Harrison (Oxford: Blackwell Publishers, 2001), 362–383.

17. Information on the strategic arguments can be found in Ansoff, *Corporate Strategy,* 130–132; C. W. L. Hill and G. S. Hansen, "A Longitudinal Study of the Cause and Consequence of Changes in Diversification in the U.S. Pharmaceutical Industry," *Strategic Management Journal* 12 (1991): 187–199; W. G. Lewellen, "A Pure Financial Rationale for the Conglomerate Merger," *Journal of Finance* 26 (1971): 521–537; F. M. McDougall and D. K. Round, "A Comparison of Diversifying and Nondiversifying Australian Industrial Firms," *Academy of Management Journal* 27 (1984): 384–398; and R. Reed and G. A. Luffman, "Diversification: The Growing Confusion," *Strategic Management Journal* 7 (1986): 29–35. The personal arguments are outlined in W. Baumol, *Business Behavior, Value, and Growth* (New York: Harcourt, 1967); D. C. Mueller, "A Theory of Conglomerate Mergers," *Quarterly Review of Economics* 83 (1969): 644–660; N. Rajagopalan and J. E. Prescott, "Determinants of Top Management Compensation: Explaining the Impact of Economic, Behavioral, and Strategic Constructs and the Moderating Effects of Industry," *Journal of Management* 16 (1990): 515–538.

18. Ansoff, *Corporate Strategy,* 130–131.

19. A detailed review of this literature is found in R. E. Hoskisson and M. A. Hitt, "Antecedents and Performance Outcomes of Diversification: A Review and Critique of Theoretical Perspectives," *Journal of Management* 16 (1990): 468. More-recent evidence is found in P. S. Davis et al., "Business Unit Relatedness and Performance: A Look at the Pulp and Paper Industry," *Strategic Management Journal* 13 (1992): 349–361; J. S. Harrison, E. H. Hall Jr., and R. Nagundkar, "Resource Allocation As an Outcropping of Strategic Consistency: Performance Implications," *Academy of Management Journal* 36 (1993): 1026–1051; J. Robins and M. Wiersema, "A Resource-Based Approach to the Multi-Business Firm: Empirical Analysis of Portfolio Interrelationships and Corporate Financial Performance," *Strategic Management Journal* 16 (1995): 277–299.

20. M. Lubatkin and S. Chatterjee, "Extending Modern Portfolio Theory into the Domain of Corporate Diversification: Does It Apply?" *Academy of Management Journal* 37 (1994): 109–136.

21. Adapted from www.delmonte.com/company /Profile.asp, 5 March 2002.

22. M. E. Porter, *Competitive Advantage: Creating and Sustaining Superior Performance* (New York: The Free Press, 1985), 317–363.

23. D. J. Teece, "Economies of Scope and the Scope of the Enterprise," *Journal of Economic Behavior and Organization* 1 (1980): 223–247.

24. B. Gold, "Changing Perspectives on Size, Scale, and Returns: An Integrative Survey," *Journal of Economic Literature* 19 (1981): 5–33

25. Ansoff, *Corporate Strategy.*

26. H. Itami, *Mobilizing Invisible Assets* (Cambridge, Mass.: Harvard University Press, 1987).

27. P. R. Nayyar, "On the Measurement of Corporate Diversification Strategy: Evidence from Large U.S. Service Firms," *Strategic Management Journal* 13 (1992): 219–235; Reed and Luffman, "Diversification," 29–36.

28. D. B. Jemison and S. B. Sitkin, "Corporate Acquisitions: A Process Perspective," *Academy of Management Review* 11 (1986): 145–163.

29. C. K. Prahalad and R. A. Bettis, "The Dominant Logic: A New Linkage between Diversity and Performance," *Strategic Management Journal* 7 (1986): 491.

30. R. M. Grant, "On 'Dominant Logic,' Relatedness, and the Link between Diversity and Performance," *Strategic Management Journal* 9 (1988): 639–642.

31. M. Goold and A. Campbell, *Strategies and Styles* (Oxford: Basil Blackwell, 1987).

32. M. C. Lauenstein, "Diversification—The Hidden Explanation of Success," *Sloan Management Review* (Fall 1985): 49–55.

33. G. R. Jones and C. W. Hill, "Transaction Cost Analysis of Strategy-Structure Choice," *Strategic Management Journal* 9 (1988): 159–172.

34. This section and portions of other sections in this chapter were strongly influenced by M.Goold and K. Luchs, "Why Diversify?: Four Decades of Management Thinking," *Academy of Management Executive* (August 1993): 7–25.

35. "Hitachi Global: Products and Services," www.global.hitachi.com/Prod/index.html, 23 November 2001.

36. Rumelt, "Diversification Strategy and Profitability," 361. See also Bergh, "Diversification Strategy Research."

37. A. Shleifer and R. W. Vishny, "Takeovers in the '60s and the '80s: Evidence and Implications," *Strategic Management Journal* 12 (Special Issue 1991): 51–59.

38. T. H. Naylor and F. Tapon, "The Capital Asset Pricing Model: An Evaluation of Its Potential As a Strategic Planning Tool," *Management Science* 10 (1982): 1166–1173.

39. A few examples of the many studies that demonstrate low performance associated with unrelated diversification are R. Amit and J. Livnat, "Diversification Strategies, Business Cycles, and Economic Performance," *Strategic Management Journal* 9 (1988): 99–110; R. A. Bettis and V. Mahajan, "Risk/Return Performance of Diversified Firms," *Management Science* 31 (1985): 785–799; D. Ravenscraft and F. M. Scherer, *Mergers, Selloffs, and Economic Efficiency* (Washington, D.C.: Brookings Institution, 1987); P. G. Simmonds, "The Combined Diversification Breadth and Mode Dimensions and the Performance of Large Diversified Firms," *Strategic Management Journal* 11 (1990): 399–410; P. Varadarajan and V. Ramanujam, "Diversification and Performance: A Reexamination Using a New Two-Dimensional Conceptualization of Diversity in Firms," *Academy of Management Journal* 30 (1982): 380–393. On the other hand, the following studies are among those that support the superiority of unrelated diversification: R. M. Grant and A. P. Jammine, "Performance

Differences between the Wrigley/Rumelt Strategic Categories," *Strategic Management Journal* 9 (1988): 333–346; A. Michel and I. Shaked, "Does Business Diversification Affect Performance?" *Financial Management* (Winter 1984): 18–25.

40. Lauenstein, "Diversification"; M. Lubatkin and R. C. Rogers, "Diversification, Systematic Risk, and Shareholder Return: A Capital Market Extension of Rumelt's 1974 Study," *Academy of Management Journal* 32 (1989): 454–465; M. Lubatkin and H. G. O'Neill, "Merger Strategies and Capital Market Risk," *Academy of Management Journal* 30 (1987): 665–684; M. Lubatkin, "Value-Creating Mergers: Fact or Folklore," *Academy of Management Executive* (November 1988): 295–302; C. A. Montgomery and H. Singh, "Diversification Strategy and Systematic Risk," *Strategic Management Journal* 5 (1984): 181–191.

41. R. S. Attiyeh, "Where Next for Conglomerates?" *Business Horizons* (December 1969): 39–44.

42. A. B. Fisher, "Ford Rolls Out a Money Machine," *Fortune,* 15 April 1996, 48.

43. Taken directly from "A Conversation with Roberto Goizueta and Jack Welch," *Fortune,* 11 December 1995, 98–99.

44. Hoskisson and Hitt, "Antecedents and Performance Outcomes," 461–509; Shleifer and Vishny, "Takeovers in the '60s."

45. Hoskisson and Hitt, "Antecedents and Performance Outcomes," 461.

46. M. A. Hitt, J. S. Harrison, and R. D. Ireland, *Mergers and Acquisitions: A Guide to Creating Value for Stakeholders* (New York: Oxford University Press, 2001).

47. Lubatkin, "Value-Creating Mergers"; J. Pfeffer, "Merger As a Response to Organizational Interdependence," *Administrative Science Quarterly* 17 (1972): 382–394.; J. H. Song, "Diversifying Acquisitions and Financial Relationships: Testing 1974–1976 Behaviour," *Strategic Management Journal* 4 (1983): 97–108; F. Trautwein, "Merger Motives and Merger Prescriptions," *Strategic Management Journal* 11 (1990): 283–295.

48. A. A. Thompson Jr., "Mobil Corporation (Revised)," in *Strategic Management: Concepts and Cases,* 4th ed., ed. A. A. Thompson Jr. and A. J. Strickland III (Plano, Tex.: Business Publications, 1987), 671–697.

49. M. Lerner, "Israeli Antitrust Authority's General Director David Tadmor on Corporate Mergers," *Academy of Management Executive* (February 2001): 8–11.

50. L. L. Fowler and D. R. Schmidt, "Determinants of Tender Offer Post-Acquisition Financial Performance," *Journal of Management* 10 (1989): 339–350.

51. T. B. Pickens, "Professions of a Short-Termer," *Harvard Business Review* (May/June 1986): 75–79.

52. Adapted from W. C. Symonds, "The Most Aggressive CEO," *Business Week,* 28 May 2001, 68.

53. Lubatkin, "Value-Creating Mergers."

54. One of the most active proponents of the view that mergers and acquisitions create value for acquiring-firm shareholders is Michael Lubatkin (see Lubatkin, "Value-Creating Mergers"). However, he recently reported strong evidence that contradicts his earlier conclusions in S.

Chatterjee et al., "Cultural Differences and Shareholder Value in Related Mergers: Linking Equity and Human Capital," *Strategic Management Journal* 13 (1992): 319–334. Other strong summary evidence that mergers and acquisitions do not create value is found in W. B. Carper, "Corporate Acquisitions and Shareholder Wealth," *Journal of Management* 16 (1990): 807–823; D. K. Datta, G. E. Pinches, and V. K. Narayanan, "Factors Influencing Wealth Creation from Mergers and Acquisitions: A Meta-Analysis," *Strategic Management Journal* 13 (1992): 67–84; K. M. Davidson, "Do Megamergers Make Sense?" *Journal of Business Strategies* (Winter 1987): 40–48; T. F. Hogarty, "Profits from Merger: The Evidence of Fifty Years," *St. John's Law Review* 44 (Special Edition 1970): 378–391; S. R. Reid, *Mergers, Managers, and the Economy* (New York: McGraw-Hill, 1968).

55. M. A. Hitt et al., "Are Acquisitions a Poison Pill for Innovation?" *Academy of Management Executive* (November 1991): 20–35.

56. S. Thurm, "Cisco Says It Expects to Meet Profit Estimate," *The Wall Street Journal*, 4 October 2001, A12.

57. J. Muller, D. Welch, and K. Kerwin, "The Merger That Can't Get in Gear," *Business Week*, 31 July 2000, 46–47.

58. M. E. Porter, "From Competitive Advantage to Corporate Strategy," *Harvard Business Review* (May/June 1987): 59.

59. M. Hitt et al., "Attributes of Successful and Unsuccessful Acquisitions of U.S. Firms," *British Journal of Management* 9 (1998): 91–114.

60. Hitt, Harrison, and Ireland, *Mergers and Acquisitions*. See also J. B. Kusewitt Jr., "An Exploratory Study of Strategic Acquisition Factors Relating to Success," *Strategic Management Journal* 6 (1985): 151–169; L. M. Shelton, "Strategic Business Fits and Corporate Acquisition: Empirical Evidence," *Strategic Management Journal* 9 (1988): 279–287.

61. J. S. Harrison, M. A. Hitt, R. E. Hoskisson and R. D. Ireland, "Resource Complementarity in Business Combinations: Extending the Logic to Organizational Alliances," *Journal of Management* 27 (2001): 679-690; J. S. Harrison et al., "Synergies and Post-Acquisition Performance: Differences versus Similarities in Resource Allocations," *Journal of Management* 17 (1991): 173–190; M. A. Hitt, R. D. Ireland, and J. S. Harrison, "Mergers and Acquisitions: A Value Creating or Value Destroying Strategy?" in *Blackwell Handbook*, ed. Hitt, Freeman, and Harrison, 384–408.

62. Adapted from Hitt, Harrison, and Ireland, *Mergers and Acquisitions*, 47–48. Quotation from Oryx home page, "Joint News Release," www.oryx.com. 15 October 1998.

63. S. Chatterjee et al., "Cultural Differences and Shareholder Value in Related Mergers: Linking Equity and Human Capital," *Strategic Management Journal* 13 (1992): 319–334; D. K. Datta, "Organizational Fit and Acquisition Performance: Effects of Post-Acquisition Integration," *Strategic Management Journal* 12 (1991): 281–297; Jemison and Sitkin, "Corporate Acquisitions."

64. T. H. Brush, "Predicted Change in Operational Synergy and Post-Acquisition Performance of Acquired Businesses," *Strategic Management Journal* 17 (1996): 1–24.

65. F. T. Paine and D. J. Power, "Merger Strategy: An Examination of Drucker's Five Rules for Successful Acquisition," *Strategic Management Journal* 5 (1984): 99–110.

66. M. L. Sirower and S. F. O'Byrne, "The Measurement of Post-Acquisition Performance: Toward a Value-Based Benchmarking Methodology," *Applied Corporate Finance* 11 (1998): 107–121.

67. Hitt, Harrison, and Ireland, *Mergers and Acquisitions*.

68. This is one of my private consulting clients. I am not at liberty to disclose the name.

69. F. Vermeulen and H. Barkema, "Learning through Acquisitions," *Academy of Management Journal* 44 (2001): 457.

70. Hitt, Harrison, and Ireland, *Mergers and Acquisitions*, chap. 7.

71. P. Haspeslagh and D. B. Jemison, *Managing Acquisitions* (New York: The Free Press, 1991), 23.

72. C. C. Markides and P. J. Williamson. "Corporate Diversification and Organizational Structure: A Resource-based View," *Academy of Management Journal* 39, no. 2 (1996): 340–367.

73. O. Port, "Beg, Borrow, and Benchmark," *Business Week,* 30 November 1993, 74–75.

74. M. A. Hitt and R. D. Ireland, "Corporate Distinctive Competence, Strategy, Industry, and Performance," *Strategic Management Journal* 6 (1985): 273–293; M. A. Hitt and R. D. Ireland, "Relationships among Corporate Level Distinctive Competencies, Diversification Strategy, Corporate Structure, and Performance," *Journal of Management Studies* 23 (1986): 401–416.

75. Hitt and Ireland, "Corporate Distinctive Competence," 289–291.

76. These arguments are outlined in M. A. Hitt, R. E. Hoskisson, and J. S. Harrison, "Strategic Competitiveness in the 1990s: Challenges and Opportunities for U.S. Executives," *Academy of Management Executive* (May 1991): 7–22.

77. R. E. Hoskisson and R. A. Johnson, "Corporate Restructuring and Strategic Change: The Effect on Diversification Strategy and R&D Intensity," *Strategic Management Journal* 13 (1992): 625–634.

78. C. J. Gersick, "Revolutionary Change Theories: A Multi-level Exploration of the Punctuated Equilibrium Paradigm," *Academy of Management Review* 16 (1991): 10–37; M. I. Tushman and E. Romanelli, "Organizational Evolution: A Metamorphosis Model of Convergence and Reorientation," in *Research in Organization Behavior*, ed. E. E. Cummings and B. M. Staw (Greenwich, Conn: JAI Press, 1985), 171–222.

79. N. A. Wishart, J. J. Elam, and D. Robey, "Redrawing the Portrait of a Learning Organization: Inside Knight-Ridder, Inc," *Academy of Management Executive* 10 (February 1996): 7–20; J. P. Walsh, "Managerial and Organizational Cognition," *Organization Science* 6 (1995): 280–321.

80. Taken directly from A. Saxenian, *Culture and Competition in Silicon Valley and Route 128* (Cambridge, Mass: Harvard University Press, 1994).

81. Gersick, "Revolutionary Change Theories," 22.

82. Gersick, "Revolutionary Change Theories"; Tushman and Romanelli, "Organizational Evolution."

83. Gersick, "Revolutionary Change Theories"; Tushman and Romanelli, "Organizational Evolution."

84. D. K. Berman, "Corning Sets a $1 Billion Charge to Cut 4,000 More Employees," *The Wall Street Journal*, 4 October 2001, B2.

85. J. Baily and R. Gibson, "ConAgra to Cut 6,500 Jobs, Close Plants," *The Wall Street Journal*, 15 May 1996, A3, A8; Y. Ono, "Nabisco to Cut 4,200 Jobs in Restructuring," *The Wall Street Journal*, 25 June 1996, A3, A6.

86. "Boeing to Cut 12,000 Jobs by Dec. 14," *Associated Press*, dailynews.netscape, 12 October 2001.

87. M. Murray, "Amid Record Profits, Companies Continue to Lay Off Employees," *The Wall Street Journal*, 4 May 1995, A1, A6.

88. W. McKinley, C. M. Sanchez, and A. G. Schick, "Organizational Downsizing: Constraining, Cloning, Learning," *Academy of Management Executive* (August 1995): 32.

89. K. S. Cameron, S. J. Freeman, and Aneil K. Mishra, "Best Practices in White-Collar Downsizing: Managing Contradictions," *Academy of Management Executive* (August 1991): 57–73.

90. Adapted from C. Solomon, "Amoco to Cut 8,500 Workers, or 16% of Force," *The Wall Street Journal*, 9 July 1992, A3.

91. J. Brockner et al., "Survivors' Reactions to Layoffs: We Get By with a Little Help from Our Friends," *Administrative Science Quarterly* 32 (1987): 526–541.

92. D. L. Worrell, W. N. Davidson III, and V. M. Sharma, "Layoff Announcements and Stockholder Wealth," *Academy of Management Journal* 34 (1991): 662–678.

93. D. A. Heenan, "The Downside of Downsizing," *Journal of Business Strategy* (November/December 1989): 18.

94. If you would like to read some of this literature, you can start with Brockner, et al, "Survivors' Reactions," and C. Hardy, "Investing in Retrenchment: Avoiding the Hidden Costs," *California Management Review* 29 (1987): 111–125.

95. M. Settles, "Human Downsizing: Can It Be Done?" *Journal of Business Ethics* 7 (1988): 961–963; Worrell, Davidson, and Sharma, "Layoff Announcements."

96. E. Faltermeyer, "Is This Layoff Necessary?" *Fortune*, 1 June 1992, 71–86.

97. R. E. Hoskisson et al., "Restructuring Strategies of Diversified Business Groups: Differences Associated with Country Institutional Environments," in *Blackwell Handbook*, ed. Hitt, Freeman, and Harrison, 433–463.

98. C. Markides, "Consequences of Corporate Refocusing: Ex Ante Evidence," *Academy of Management Journal* 35 (1992): 398–412.

99. W. F. Bulkeley, "Xerox to Sell Some Plants to Flextronics," *The Wall Street Journal*, 3 October 2001, B6.

100. Hitt, Hoskisson, and Harrison, "Strategic Competitiveness"; R. E. Hoskisson and M. A. Hitt, *Downscoping: How to Tame the Diversified Firm* (New York: Oxford University Press, 1994), 3.

101. Hoskisson and Johnson, "Corporate Restructuring"; Hoskisson and Hitt, *Downscoping*.

102. C. A. Montgomery, A. R. Thomas, and R. Kammath, "Divestiture, Market Valuation, and Strategy," *Academy of Management Journal* 27 (1984): 830–840.

103. J. Cole, "Chrysler Agrees to Sell to Raytheon Co. Bulk of Its Aerospace, Defense Holdings," *The Wall Street Journal*, 8 April 1996, A3; Business and Finance, *The Wall Street Journal*, 10 June 1996, A1.

104. W. Bounds, "Corning Will Spin Off Its Lab-Testing Division," *The Wall Street Journal*, 15 May 1996, B4; Business and Finance, *The Wall Street Journal*, 2 April 1996, A1.

105. S. Rosenbush and R. Grover, "A Spin-Off with a Hangover," *Business Week*, 27 August 2001, 50.

106. J. Weber, "A Big Company That Works," *Business Week* 4 May 1992, 125.

107. D. Hunter, "Grace Sharpens Its Focus," *Chemical Week*, 1 April 1992, 15.

108. T. Smart, "So Much for Diversification," *Business Week*, 1 February 1993, 31; P. Yoshihashi, "Unocal Corp. Will Revamp into Two Units," *The Wall Street Journal*, 9 July 1992, A4.

109. Hitt, Hoskisson, and Harrison, "Strategic Competitiveness," 7–21.

110. R. L. Daft, *Organization Theory and Design*, 4th ed. (St. Paul, Minn.: West Publishing, 1992), 94.

111. D. M. Flynn and M. Farid, "The Intentional Use of Chapter XI: Lingering versus Immediate Filing," *Strategic Management Journal* 12 (1991): 63–64.

112. A. Merrick, "Kmart Lays Out Plans to Trim Its Size, Increase Efficiency in Bankruptcy Filing," *The Wall Street Journal*, 23 January 2002, A3.

113. Adapted from "FM Corporation," in *Strengthening America's Competitiveness: The Blue Chip Enterprise Initiative* (Warner Books on behalf of Connecticut Mutual Life Insurance Company and the U.S. Chamber of Commerce, 1991), 89–90.

114. E. Thornton and C. Palmeri, "Who Can Afford to Go Broke?" *Business Week*, 10 September 2001, 116.

115. Taken directly from Based on T. J. Salerno and C. D. Hansen, "A Prepackaged Bankruptcy Strategy," *Journal of Business Strategy* (January/February 1991): 36–41.

116. Flynn and Farid, "Intentional Use."

117. W. N. Moulton, "Bankruptcy As a Deliberate Strategy: Theoretical Considerations and Empirical Evidence," *Strategic Management Journal* 14 (1993): 130.

118. Adapted from "Kelly Truck Line, Inc.," in *Strengthening America's Competitiveness*, 152

119. K. M. Davidson, "Another Look at LBOs," *Journal of Business Strategies* (January/February 1988): 44–47.

120. A good review of these studies, of which there are seven, is found in S. A. Zahra and M. Fescina, "Will Leveraged Buyouts Kill U.S. Corporate Research and Development?" *Academy of Management Executive* (November 1991): 7–21.

121. M. F. Wiersema and J. P. Liebeskind, "The Effects of Leveraged Buyouts on Corporate Growth and Diversification in Large Firms," *Strategic Management Journal* 16 (1995): 447–460.

122. Davidson, "Another Look at LBOs."

123. Taken directly from N. Munk, "How Levi's Trashed a Great American Brand," in *Strategic Management*, ed. E. H. Bernstein (Guildford, Conn.: McGraw-Hill/Dushkin, 2001), 163–168, first published in *Fortune*, 12 April, 1999.

124. Taken directly from Davidson, "Another Look at LBOs," 44–45.

125. M. Schwarz and E. A. Weinstein, "So You Want to Do a Leveraged Buyout," *Journal of Business Strategies* (January/February 1989): 10–15.

126. Taken directly from J. W. Verity et al., "The New IBM," *Business Week*, 16 December 1991, 112–118.; L. Hooper, "IBM to Unveil New Structure of PC Business," *The Wall Street Journal*, 3 September 1992, A3.

127. R. Bonte-Friedheim and J. Guyon, "Hanson to Divide into Four Businesses," *The Wall Street Journal*, 31 January 1996, A3, A16.

128. Taken directly from R. Calori and B. Dufour, "Management European Style," *Academy of Management Executive* (August 1995): 67.

129. S. L. Hwang, "Philip Morris to Reorganize Food Operation," *The Wall Street Journal*, 4 January 1995, A3, A4.

130. Hoskisson and Hitt, *Downscoping*.

131. J. Forster, "Sara Lee: Changing the Recipe—Again," *Business Week*, 10 September 2001, 125–126.

132. D. Rigby, "Management Tools and Techniques: A Survey," *California Management Review* 43, no. 2 (Winter 2001): 156.

133. B. O'Brian, "Delta Air Makes Painful Cuts in Effort to Stem Red Ink," *The Wall Street Journal*, 10 September 1992, B4.

134. Taken directly from J. M. Graves, "Leaders of Corporate Change," *Fortune* (December 14, 1992): 113.

135. Taken directly from P. W. Beamish, "Sony's Yoshihide Nakamura on Structure and Decision Making," *Academy of Management Executive* 13, no. 4 (November 1999): 13.

136. A. M. Squeo, "Fighter-Jet Contract Adds Crucial Thrust to Lockheed Rebound," *The Wall Street Journal*, 29 October 2001, A1.

137. C. Borucki and C. K. Barnett, "Restructuring for Survival—The Navistar Case," *Academy of Management Executive* (February 1990): 36–49.

138. Hitt, Hoskisson, and Harrison, "Strategic Competitiveness."

139. J. P. Kotter, "Leading Change: Why Transformation Efforts Fail," *Harvard Business Review* (March/April 1995): 59–67.

140. Taken directly from J. B. White and N. Shirouzu, "A Stalled Revolution by Nasser Puts a Ford in the Driver's Seat," *The Wall Street Journal*, 31 October 2001, A1.

141. J. F. Bandnowski, "Restructuring Is a Continuous Process," *Long Range Planning* (January 1991): 10–14.

Appendix

Portfolio Management

Portfolio management refers to managing the mix of businesses in the corporate portfolio. General Electric is a master at this type of management. The company invests in the businesses with the most promise, buys companies to round out their business portfolio, and eliminates businesses that have lost their ability to perform. CEOs of large diversified organizations such as GE continually face decisions concerning how to divide organizational resources among diversified units and where to invest new capital. Portfolio models are designed to help managers make these types of decisions.

Portfolio planning gained wide acceptance during the 1970s, and, by 1979, approximately 45 percent of Fortune 500 companies were using some type of portfolio planning.[1] Monsanto applied portfolio-management concepts in restructuring its business portfolio by divesting slow-growing commodity-chemical businesses and acquiring faster-growing businesses in areas such as biotechnology. More recently, executives from several large corporations—including GE, US West, and DuPont—indicated that they are still using portfolio-management techniques.[2] In spite of their adoption in many organizations, portfolio-management techniques are the subject of a considerable amount of criticism from strategic management scholars.[3] However, since these techniques are still in wide use, this book would be incomplete without them. Keep in mind that they are not a panacea and should not replace other types of sound strategic analysis.

This section begins with a description of the simplest and first widely used portfolio model, the Boston Consulting Group Matrix. The model has many shortcomings, stemming mostly from its simplicity. However, most of the other portfolio techniques are adaptations of it, and its simplicity makes it a good starting point.

The Boston Consulting Group Matrix

The Boston Consulting Group (BCG) Matrix, displayed in Figure 7A.1, is based on two factors, business growth rate and relative market share. Business growth rate is the growth rate of the industry in which a particular business unit is involved. Relative market share is calculated as the ratio of the business unit's size to the size of its largest competitor. The two factors are used to plot all of the businesses in which the organization is involved, represented as Stars, Question Marks (also called Problem Children), Cash Cows, and Dogs. The size of the circles in Figure 7A.2 represent the size of the various businesses of an organization. Remember that only one organization, consisting of many different business units, is plotted on each matrix.

The BCG Matrix can be useful in planning cash flows. Cash Cows tend to generate more cash than they can effectively reinvest, while Question Marks require additional cash to sustain rapid growth, and Stars generate about as much cash as they use, on average. According to BCG, Stars and Cash Cows, with their superior market-share positions, tend to be the most profitable businesses.

Consequently, the optimal BCG portfolio contains a balance of Stars, Cash Cows, and Question Marks. Stars have the greatest potential for growth and tend to be highly profitable. However, as the industries in which Stars are involved mature and their growth slows, they naturally become Cash Cows. Therefore, Question Marks are important because of their potential role as future Stars in the organization. Dogs are the least attractive types of business. The original prescription was to divest them. However, even Dogs can be maintained in the portfolio as long as they do not become a drain on corporate resources. Also, some organizations are successful at positioning their Dogs in an attractive niche in their industries.

One of the central ideas of the BCG Matrix is that high market share leads to high profitability due to learning effects, experience effects, entry barriers, market power, and other influences. In fact, there is evidence, both in the strategic management literature and in the economics literature, that higher market share is associated with higher profitability in some instances. However, some low-share businesses enjoy high profitability.[4] The real relationship between market share and profitability depends on many factors, including the nature of the industry and the strategy of the firm. For example, one researcher found that the market share–profitability relationship is stronger in some industries (capital goods) than in others (raw materials). He also discovered that beyond a certain market share, profitability tended to trail off.[5]

One of the shortcomings of the BCG Matrix is that it does not allow for changes in strategy due to differing

FIGURE 7A.1

The Boston Consulting Group (BCG) Portfolio Matrix

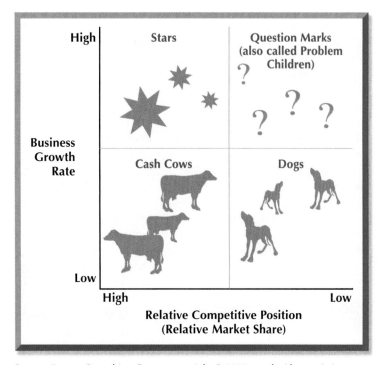

Source: Boston Consulting Group, copyright © 1970, used with permission.

FIGURE 7A.2

The General Electric Business Screen

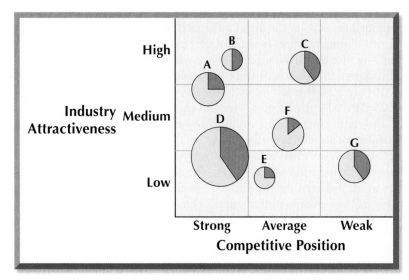

Source: From *Strategy Formulation: Analytical Concepts, 1st Edition,* by C.W. Hofer and D. Schendel, © 1978. Reprinted with permission of South-Western College Publishing, a division of Thomson Learning. Fax 800-730-2215.

environments. The standard BCG prescription is to achieve market-share leadership and become a Star or a Cash Cow. However, this prescription may not fit all settings. Other problems with the BCG Matrix are related to its simplicity. Only two factors are considered, and only two divisions, high and low, are used for each factor. Also, growth rate is an oversimplification of industry attractiveness, and market share is an inadequate barometer of competitive position. A common criticism that applies to many portfolio models, and especially the BCG Matrix, is that they are based on the past instead of the future. Given the rate of change in the current economic and political environments, this criticism is probably valid. Finally, another problem that is inherent in all matrix approaches is that industries are hard to define. Numerous organizational managers and business writers have developed portfolio matrices that overcome some of the limitations of the BCG Matrix. One of these approaches was developed by General Electric.

The General Electric Business Screen

Virtually any variables or combination of variables of strategic importance can be plotted along the axes of a portfolio matrix. The selection of variables depends on what the organization considers important. Many matrices contain factors that are composites of several variables. One of the most famous of these, developed at General Electric, is illustrated in Figure 7A.2. The GE model is referred to as the GE Portfolio Matrix, the Nine-Cell Grid, or the GE Business Screen.

In the GE Business Screen, the area in the circles represents the size of the industries in which each business competes. The slice out of the circle is the market share of the business unit in each of these industries. The variables that are used to assess industry attractiveness are typically derived from the objectives and characteristics of the organization (i.e., attitude toward growth, profitability, or social responsibility) and of the industries themselves. Assessment of competitive position is based on a firm's position with respect to the key success factors in an industry. An organization would like to have all of its businesses in the top-left cell. These

businesses are called Winners. However, some of these Winners should be established businesses that are not growing rapidly, so that a portion of their cash flow can be used to support developing winners.

By applying resource analysis and environmental analysis to a portfolio model such as the GE Business Screen, it may be possible to tap the potential of a business unit as well as its current competitive standing. For example, based on a thorough resource analysis, a firm's competitive position could be determined based on the strength of its human, physical, financial, knowledge-based, and general organizational resources, especially as they relate to competitive advantage. Industry attractiveness may be assessed by evaluating the power of suppliers and customers, the level of competitive rivalry, the threat of substitutes, the height of entry barriers, the amount and type of regulation, the power of unions, rate of growth, current profitability, and resiliency during downturns. From a portfolio-management perspective, businesses that are in a strong competitive position in attractive industries should be given the highest priority with regard to resource allocations.

In conclusion, while all portfolio-management models have weaknesses and limitations, they provide an additional tool to assist managers in anticipating cash flows and making resource-allocation decisions. The GE Business Screen, in particular, is flexible enough to accommodate a wide variety of indicators of industry attractiveness and competitive strength.

Notes: 1. P. Hapeslagh, "Portfolio Planning: Uses and Limitations," *Harvard Business Review* (January/February 1982): 58–73; **2.** G. S. Swartz, "Organizing to Become Market-Driven," *Marketing Science Institute Conference Summary,* report no. 90 (1990): 123; **3.** R. A. Kerin, V. Mahajan, and P. R. Varadarajan, *Strategic Market Planning* (Needham Heights, Mass.: Allyn & Bacon, 1990), 94; J. A. Seeger, "Reversing the Images of BCG's Growth Share Matrix," *Strategic Management Journal* 5 (1984): 93–97; **4.** R. G. Hammermesh, M. J. Anderson, and J. E. Harris, "Strategies for Low Market Share Businesses," *Harvard Business Review* (May/June 1978): 95–102; C. Y. Woo and A. C. Cooper, "Market Share Leadership—Not Always So Good," *Harvard Business Review* (January/February 1984): 50–54; **5.** Schwalbach, "Profitability and Market Share: A Reflection on the Functional Relationship," *Strategic Management Journal* 12 (1991): 299–306.

Part 3

Strategy Implementation and Control

Chapter 8

Strategy Implementation: Resources and Relationships

Learning Objectives

After reading and discussing this chapter, you should be able to:

1. Appreciate the advantages and potential disadvantages of various types of interorganizational relationships.

2. Analyze stakeholders to determine their strategic importance.

3. Select strategies for dealing with stakeholders based on their strategic importance.

4. Understand how to make partnerships effective.

5. Create plans for using functional-level resources to implement business strategies.

6. Determine how to effectively manage relationships with external stakeholders.

Harris Corporation

Harris Corporation has formed partnerships with a variety of external stakeholders to create opportunities and exploit Harris technology. Three of its ventures are with General Electric (GE). For example, the company owns 20 percent of GE-Harris Railway Electronics, a leading supplier of electronics for railroads. The venture acquired Harmon Industries, a railroad-equipment manufacturer with two thousand employees and worldwide sales of more than $300 million. Harris also owns 49 percent of GE Harris Aviation Information Solutions, which provides information-network products and decision-support systems to airlines. In addition, Harris owns 49 percent of GE Harris Energy Control Systems, a venture that provides technology and support to companies involved in power generation, transmission, and distribution. Harris also owns 40 percent of LiveTV, a venture with Sextant In-Flight Systems to provide live television to the seats of airline passengers. Some of their early customers included JetBlue, Legend, and Alaska Airlines. Harris also has a partnership with a venture-capital firm, Venture First, to exploit Harris technologies. Harris takes an equity position in each new venture. For example, a venture called AirNet led to an initial public offering and a stake worth nearly $100 million. Other ventures include Terion, a company involved in transportation tracking; ImageLinks, which provides aerial- and satellite-image processing; and AuthenTec, which is involved in creating integrated circuits for fingerprint imaging.[1]

As the Harris example demonstrates, formation of partnerships is one way to take advantage of opportunities that arise in the external environment. Productive interorganizational relationships can be sources of competitive advantage. On the other hand, companies may also develop competitive advantages through superior acquisition, development, and management of internal resources and capabilities. This chapter provides a detailed treatment of how organizations can use these two tools, partnerships and resource management, to develop competitive advantage as they implement their strategies. Of course, internal and external approaches to strategy implementation are not mutually exclusive. That is, a firm may use both approaches simultaneously.

The focus of this chapter is on **strategy implementation.** It presupposes that the firm has established an appropriate strategic direction and strategies at the corporate and business levels, as well as an effective growth strategy. The organization needs to develop specific tactics for executing those strategies. Managers often have to decide whether the company should attempt to implement a strategy with internal resources or seek a partner, as the following example illustrates.

strategy implementation
Managing stakeholder relationships and organizational resources in a manner that moves the organization towards the successful execution of its strategies, consistent with its strategic direction

 An organization that makes lighting equipment has determined that its business-level strategy should emphasize product differentiation through technological leadership. In other words, the firm wants to use research and development to become the industry leader in developing new technologies that will enhance the value of its lighting products. One approach would be to devote significant internal resources—including existing researchers, managers, and financing—to improving R&D in-house. However, the firm could also decide to form a research partnership with a more technologically sophisticated company, perhaps from another industry such as computers or electronics.

The first section in this chapter emphasizes the role of interorganizational relationships in the successful execution of strategies, as well as how to effectively manage relationships with external stakeholders. The second section deals with how companies can manage resources in each of the functional areas so as to develop competitive advantage. Taken together, these sections provide a wealth of ideas that can help firms achieve competitive success as they implement their strategies.

Interorganizational Relationships and Stakeholder Management

Chapter 2 introduced common forms of interorganizational relationships, including joint ventures, networks, consortia, alliances, trade groups, and interlocking directorates (see Table 2.4 for a review of these terms). All of these arrangements represent various types of partnerships; therefore, the term partnership will be used interchangeably with interorganizational relationship in the remainder of this text. This section will focus specifically on how such partnerships can be used to implement strategies. Some organizations make extensive use of partnerships as a part of their corporate-level strategies. For example, AT&T has joint ventures with Philips, a leading European electronics and communications firm; Olivetti, a giant in European information processing; Lucky Goldstar, a manufacturer of communications equipment in Korea; Compañía Telefónica Nacional de España, the Spanish telephone company; and three Taiwanese firms engaged in manufacturing switching equipment. Commenting on AT&T's attitude toward partnerships, James Olson, chairman of the board, stated:

 We can't do everything everywhere—we will need to cooperate and partner with other companies. And we will have to concentrate our resources on activities that contribute to the success of our business and our long-term strategy.

With partners that are established in the information industry overseas, AT&T will concentrate on bringing its evolving data networking capability to countries in the Triad (North America, Western Europe, and the Far East).[2]

Partnerships can help organizations achieve many of the same objectives that are sought through mergers and acquisitions. They can lead to improved sales growth, to increased earnings, or they can provide balance to a portfolio of businesses, which are some of the most commonly cited reasons for acquisitions.[3] For example, Monsanto and General Electric formed a joint venture called Fisher Control International to make regulators and control valves. Within one year, their joint venture ranked second in sales in the growing process-control-equipment industry. Also, one of the largest and most profitable robot manufacturers in the world is a joint venture between GM and Fanuc Ltd. called GMFanuc (GMF) Robotics Corporation.[4]

Advantages and Disadvantages of Interorganizational Relationships

Many of the potential advantages of interorganizational relationships are summarized in Table 8.1. These advantages are most easily illustrated through joint ventures, a form of interorganizational relationship that results in a separate, jointly owned entity. Consequently, many of the examples are joint ventures. However, most of the advantages are also available to some degree through the other types of partnerships.

One of the primary advantages of interorganizational relationships is that they can allow firms to gain access to particular resources. Examples of resource sharing are easy to find. Disney teamed up with the American Automobile Association (AAA) to provide a "Disney-style" multipurpose rest area for travelers.[5] CBS formed joint ventures with Twentieth Century Fox to develop videotapes, and with Home Box Office (owned by Time Inc.) and Columbia Pictures (owned by Coca-Cola) to develop motion pictures.[6] All of these joint ventures by CBS were similar in that they resulted in related diversification and drew on the combined strengths of all joint-venture partners. In the international sector, Airbus Industrie is a multicountry, multicompany European joint venture that is now the second-largest manufacturer of large jet aircraft.[7]

resource complementarity
Occurs when two businesses have strengths in different areas

Resource complementarity is helpful in partnerships just as it is in mergers and acquisitions.[8] Complementary skills, in particular, can help increase speed to market. For example, if two companies each have strengths in different areas, by combining those strengths, they can save a lot of time in bringing a product to market. In the successful alliance between Ford and Mazda, the companies have worked jointly on numerous automobile models, with Ford leading in design, and Mazda making contributions in engineering.[9] In addition, a partnership can enhance speed

Table 8.1	Potential Advantages of Participation in Interorganizational Relationships
Gain Access to a Particular Resource	Firms form relationships to gain access to a particular resource, such as capital, employees with specialized skills, intimate knowledge of a market, or a modern production facility.
Speed to Market	Firms with complementary skills, such as one firm that is technologically strong and another that has strong market access, partner to increase speed to market in hopes of capturing first-mover advantages.
Enter a Foreign Market	Partnering with a local company is often the only practical way to gain access to a foreign market.
Economies of Scale	In many industries, high fixed costs require firms to find partners to expand production volume.
Risk and Cost Sharing	Many types of partnerships allow two or more firms to share the risk and cost of a particular business endeavor.
Product and/or Service Development	Partnering can provide firms the opportunity to pool their skills to develop new products and/or services
Learning	Interorganizational relationships often provide participants with the opportunity to "learn" from their partners (e.g., lean manufacturing, product development, human resource management in an unfamiliar country).
Strategic Flexibility	Creation of partnerships can provide a valuable alternative to acquisitions because they do not have to be as permanent. They also require less of an internal resource commitment, which frees up resources for other uses.
Collective Political Clout	Interorganizational relationships can increase collective clout and influence governments to adopt policies favorable to their industries or circumstances.
Neutralizing or Blocking Competitors	Through a partnership, firms can gain the competencies and market power that are needed to neutralize or block the moves of a competitor.

Source: Adapted from *Journal of Management,* Vol. 26, B.B. Barringer and J.S. Harrison, "Walking a Tightrope: Creating Value Through Interorganizational Relationships," p. 385, Copyright 2000, with permission from Elsevier Science.

of entry into a new field or market. For instance, Hewlett-Packard once formed a joint venture with Yokogawa Electric to penetrate the Japanese market.[10] These types of partnerships also allow firms to draw on the specific strengths of countries, such as low-cost labor or advanced technology.[11]

In addition to the advantages associated with resource sharing, partnerships can lead to economies of scale through sharing physical facilities, where one firm may not be able to achieve those economies on its own. Risk and costs are shared among the partners, which minimizes the impact on any one organization if the venture should prove to be unsuccessful. Consequently, compared to mergers or internal venturing, joint ventures are sometimes considered a less risky diversification option. Partnerships also allow firms to pool their resources for product and/or service development, which can lead to more-competitive products and services. In addition, they provide participants with ample opportunity to learn from each other. Learning is considered to be one of the most important reasons to pursue interorganizational relationships.[12]

Since partnerships often have an ending date or can be canceled with a minimum of difficulty, firms may be able to retain their strategic flexibility by deciding whether to continue a particular venture or allocate venture-related resources elsewhere. Partnerships also have political advantages, since companies can combine their clout with respect to influencing government leaders and agencies. Trade groups are an excellent example of combined political clout. Finally, partnerships may be formed as firms try to improve their competitive positions against rivals by locking in exclusive-distribution arrangements or depriving competitors of raw materials. These actions can also deter the entry of new competitors.[13]

In spite of their strategic strengths, partnerships may be limiting, in that one organization has only partial control over the activity and enjoys only a percentage of the growth and profitability that are sometimes created. In addition, partnerships sometimes create high administrative costs associated with developing the multi-party equity arrangement and managing the venture once it is undertaken.[14] Company culture clashes can erode cooperation between firms, and prevent true partnering from taking place. Furthermore, joint decision making can be slow, and result in too many compromises. Also, there is some evidence that some types of partnerships may not be desirable in particular environments. For instance, one researcher discovered that joint ventures in the petroleum industry to produce productive oil and gas leases were more expensive and were no more successful than non-joint ventures.[15]

As was discussed in previous chapters, partnerships also entail a risk of opportunism by venture partners. Unfortunately, a stronger venture partner may take advantage of the smaller, or less experienced partner, and structure the deal so that the benefits accrue unfairly to the stronger partner. Good written contracts can help to alleviate, but cannot eliminate, this risk.

 In the late 1980s, Matsushita Electic Industrial Co., Ltd., Japan's largest electronics company, purchased a 52 percent share of workstation manufacturer Solbourne Computer, Inc, a Colorado company with $60 million in annual sales. At the time, the alliance seemed to make sense: Solbourne needed money and manufacturing capability, and Matsushita needed a presence in the workstation market and technology that Solbourne had licensed. The needs of each firm fit with the capabilities of the other. In 1992, Solbourne announced it was getting out of the workstation business, and dismissed one-third of its employees. The alliance had met none of Solbourne's objectives, although it had met all of Matsushita's objectives. Matsushita engineers were involved in all development projects and had gained access to the technology they needed, but Matsushita did not distribute Solbourne products in Japan or provide the quality manufacturing services that had been agreed upon. Coordination problems created delays, communication problems added to the frustration, and poor management decisions at Solbourne made things worse.[16]

As in mergers and acquisitions, organizational fit is important to interorganizational relationships. Lack of organizational fit can reduce cooperation and lead to venture failure. Potential differences among partners range from dissimilar ethics to different languages to disparate managerial techniques to incompatible manufacturing methods.[17] For example, a joint venture between Acme-Cleveland and Multi-Arc Vacuum Systems to market a coating technology fell apart because of vastly different management styles between the parent companies.[18]

Trust among partners is also critical. If trust breaks down, the venture can fall apart. Also, companies are more likely to form partnerships with firms they trust. Consequently, it is essential that partners manage their interorganizational relationships carefully so as not to violate trust.[19]

In summary, while interorganizational relationships have both benefits and drawbacks relative to other strategic options, many firms have found that they are essential to competitive success.[20] Consequently, partnerships of all types are very popular, and many types of partnerships, such as joint ventures, are increasing in use. The following Global Insight offers an interesting perspective on the importance of partnership activities to the growth of two very different national economies: Canada and China. One of the key decisions with regard to interorganizational relationships is selecting appropriate partners. The next section will address this important issue.

Global Insight

International Partnerships as a Source of Growth in China and Canada

Partnerships are an important vehicle for growth in both well-developed and in rapidly developing economies. With an average economic growth rate of more than 8 percent per year and with about 25 percent of the world's population, China is attracting large numbers of international partners. In fact, China is the most active joint-venture market in the world. Nevertheless, outside partners face enormous challenges in China due to the complexity of the legal and economic systems and differences in the way various types of joint ventures are treated. Consequently, while Chinese businesses most need critical resources such as technical knowledge and capital, Western and other foreign partners need knowledge and understanding of the complicated Chinese business environment.

Only a little more than two decades ago, China had an orthodox communist system with strong central control of nearly all economic decisions. Although government influence is still dominant, China has made progress in moving toward a market economy. Large government businesses still exist, but village and township enterprises have also emerged. The emergence of different types of businesses in China is also associated with a legal system that is not consistently applied throughout the entire country. Instead, general guidelines have been established, and significant legal authority has been delegated to individual judges to determine right and wrong. Also, joint ventures are treated differently depending on whether they are domestic or involve international partners, and whether they are formed with government or nongovernment businesses. Consequently, as Western firms enter into joint ventures with Chinese firms, the knowledge they need most relates to government issues such as understanding government behavior and learning national rules, policies, and laws. They also seek knowledge about the Chinese culture and market. While these knowledge goals may be met to some degree, Western firms are often dissatisfied with the profit performance of their joint ventures in China.

Canada, with its stable legal system, offers a very different type of partnership environment. The high-technology sector is experiencing significant growth in Canada. For example, in the province of British Columbia, high technology is growing at a rate that is four times faster than that of the economy as a whole. International partnerships have been an important tool in creating this growth, especially in the computer-software and biotechnology industries. The typical venture involves a foreign firm that is significantly larger than the Canadian firm. For example, ALI Technologies, with forty employees, entered into a partnership with IBM to develop a new automated-medical-archive server. ALI's CEO hopes that the venture will create the potential to enter developing Third World countries. Canadian firms tend to become involved in alliances related to their core competencies. This increases the risks associated with losing control of proprietary information. However, many Canadian firms report that communication and trust with their partners is good. In general, they report a fairly high level of satisfaction with the performance of their partnerships.

Sources: S. X. Si and G. D. Bruton, "Knowledge Transfer in International Joint Ventures in Transitional Economies: The China Experience," *Academy of Management Executive* (February 1999): 83–99; D. Cyr, "High Tech, High Impact: Creating Canada's Competitive Advantage through Technology Alliances," *Academy of Management Executive* (May 1999): 17–26.

Selection of Stakeholders for Partnerships

Managers have limited resources, and one of the most important of these is time. Clearly, managers do not have time to pursue interorganizational relationships with all stakeholders. Consequently, deciding when and with whom to partner are significant managerial decisions. In general, organizations should consider partnering with stakeholders that are strategically important. This means that they have a significant impact on the firm and its future success. Several factors, outlined in Figure 8.1, can increase the strategic significance of a stakeholder, thus making partnering more attractive. One of the most common reasons to partner is to acquire needed resources, and many of the interorganizational forms that have been described in this section can facilitate resource transfer. One of the most important resources a company may need is, of course, knowledge. Partnerships can facilitate organizational learning. However, stakeholders also become important when they hold formal power, which means that they a legal or contractual right to make decisions that affect some part of the organization (i.e., regulatory agencies).

Another factor that can dramatically affect the strategic importance of a particular stakeholder is its influence on the organizational uncertainty facing the firm.[21] For example, organizations are uncertain of the level of future demand; the price elasticity of demand; the strategic moves of competitors, suppliers, activists, unions, and other key stakeholders; the nature of future government regulations; and the ability to secure adequate resources, whether physical, financial, or human. Stakeholders that have high economic or political power have more influence on the environmental uncertainty facing a firm. Consequently, arrows are drawn from the economic-power and political-power boxes to the environmental-uncertainty box in Figure 8.1. For example, a customer can quit buying from an organization, or a bank can sever a financial agreement. These are examples of exerting economic power. On the other hand, stakeholders with political power have the ability to influence events and outcomes that have an impact on the organization. In one example, some of Wal-Mart's angry competitors have succeeded in convincing local communities and governments in several locations in the Northeastern United States that Wal-Mart, by causing small businesses to suffer, harms the community

FIGURE 8.1

Strategic Importance of Stakeholders and the Decision to Partner

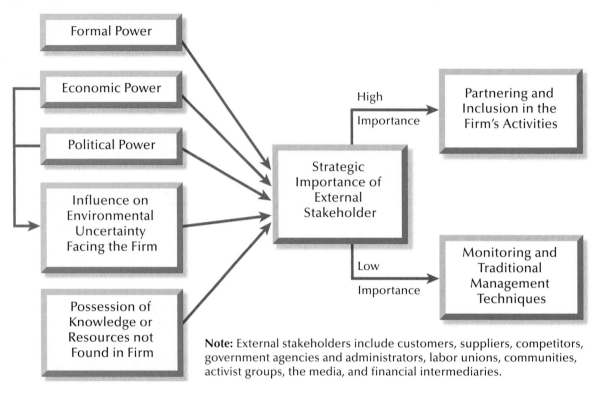

Note: External stakeholders include customers, suppliers, competitors, government agencies and administrators, labor unions, communities, activist groups, the media, and financial intermediaries.

more than it helps it. The result has been adverse legislation, causing Wal-Mart to lose several new locations for its stores.[22] Economic and political power were discussed previously in Chapter 2.

One way to understand the role of **environmental uncertainty** is to imagine a situation in which managers knew everything that would happen with regard to customers, suppliers, unions, competitors, regulators, financial intermediaries, and every other relevant external force for the next year. In such a hypothetical situation, management of the company would be a straightforward task of generating maximum revenues at minimum costs so that profits are maximized. Management is difficult because our hypothetical world does not exist. Managers have to make decisions without knowing how customers, suppliers, and competitors will react. Customers are particularly important because their actions have so much impact on how the firm will perform. In other words, they have a large influence on the uncertainty that the firm is facing.

While environmental uncertainty often originates in the broad environment (e.g., economic cycles, social trends), organizations feel most of its influence through external stakeholders. For example, the Arab oil embargo was a major shock in the broad environment of U.S. automobile companies. However, they felt the shock indirectly through changes in customer expectations about the size, fuel efficiency, and styling of new cars.

Establishment of the strategic priority of stakeholders provides direction as to the amount of attention they should be given during the development of strategy. However, prioritizing stakeholders also provides clues concerning the types of

environmental uncertainty
A result of not being able to predict precisely what will happen with regard to the actions of external stakeholders and other external influences; results in organizational uncertainty

strategies that may be appropriate in managing them. Strategically important stakeholders should be seriously considered for partnerships. According to Pfeffer and Salancik, two well-known organizational researchers, "The typical solution to problems of interdependence and uncertainty involves increasing the mutual control over each other's activities."[23] Companies may also want to consider including them in organizational processes, such as including a supplier on a research-and-development team to create a new product. Less-important stakeholders should not be ignored. They should be monitored and managed in more-traditional ways.

Effective Stakeholder Management

Chapter 2 provided a detailed description of the operating environment and the major stakeholders found therein, including customers, suppliers, competitors, government agencies, labor unions, local communities, activists, the media, and special-interest groups. The emphasis in that chapter was on analyzing stakeholders (as well as industry factors) as a foundation upon which to build effective strategies, although a few tactics for managing stakeholders were provided at the end. Thus far, this chapter has provided a thorough examination of interorganizational relationships, which are one of the most important tools for managing stakeholder relationships. It also provided guidelines for deciding which stakeholders are most attractive for the formation of partnerships. We are now in a position to discuss stakeholder management more broadly.

There are two basic postures organizations use when managing relationships with external stakeholders.[24] One posture involves **buffering** the organization from environmental uncertainty through techniques designed to stabilize and predict environmental influences and, in essence, raise the boundaries higher. They soften the jolts that might otherwise be felt as the organization interacts with members of its external environment. These are traditional stakeholder management techniques such as marketing research, creation of special departments to handle specific areas of the external environment (e.g., legal, recruiting, purchasing), efforts to ensure regulatory compliance, advertising, and public-relations efforts. Buffering techniques focus on planning for and adapting to the environment so that the needs and demands of critical stakeholders are met.

On the other hand, the previous section argued that stakeholders with attractive resources the firm needs; with high levels of formal, economic, or political power; and/or with a large influence on environmental uncertainty facing the firm are likely candidates for partnerships of one form or other. Partnering activities allow companies to build bridges with their stakeholders in the pursuit of common goals, whereas traditional stakeholder management techniques (buffering) simply reduce shocks and facilitate the satisfaction of stakeholder needs and/or demands. One analyst concluded that it is nearly impossible to be competitive in the aerospace industry without effective use of interorganizational relationships. Consistent with this view, United Technologies has more than one hundred worldwide collaborations.[25]

buffering
Techniques designed to stabilize and predict environmental influences and therefore soften the jolts that might otherwise be felt as the organization interacts with members of its external environment

Ex. Apple Computer is an example of a company that encountered problems because of its resistance to partnering with external stakeholders. Once the king of the personal computer industry, Apple resisted the notion that it should partner with other companies through license agreements for its hardware and software. Managers within Apple believed that technical superiority would be sufficient to sustain Apple's leadership, or at least a strong position in the industry. After several periods of decline in market share, Apple managers realized their mistake, and scrambled to create partnerships with a variety of companies. However, it was too late for Apple to regain its previous position as an industry leader.

Table 8.2 provides a list of examples of traditional stakeholder management techniques as well as partnering techniques, grouped by type of external stakeholder. The rest of this section will elaborate on effective management of the external stakeholders listed in Table 8.2, with an emphasis on creation of partnerships.

Customers

Since customers are so vital to organizational success, many firms place highest priority on satisfying customer needs. Occasionally, successful companies begin to lose sight of the importance of customers, perhaps due to their own success. Disaster inevitably follows such neglect.

 Once mighty Motorola lost three-quarters of its value in one year. One of the biggest reasons for the decline was that it lost sight of the fact that its customers are not only the people carrying their phones, but the wireless carriers that provide the phones to those customers. The carriers determine which phones will be offered in their stores and which phones will be promoted. "At the height of its cockiness in the mid-1990s, when its StarTAC model was hot, Motorola dictated how carriers had to display some of its phones in their own stores. More recently, it has often missed critical deadlines to deliver products and sometimes never sent the products at all." Verizon Wireless chief marketing officer John Stratton calls this Motorola's "arrogance."[26]

Because customers are so important, organizations pursue a number of what might be called traditional management tactics to satisfy them. Among the most important are customer-service departments, marketing research, on-site visits, and product/service development. Listening to customers is one of the most important strategies a firm can pursue. Sears for many years ignored the changing needs of their predominantly middle-class customers. Many middle-class consumers were forced to tighten up their finances due to a significant decline in their spending power. They switched their loyalties to lower-priced stores such as Kmart and Wal-Mart.[27] Of course, Kmart and Wal-Mart, as competitors, are also stakeholders of Sears. Therefore, Sears could have adjusted its strategy on the basis of information received from either of two stakeholders, customers or competitors. Instead, Sears, after more than a decade of restructuring, is just now beginning to recover its footing as a major retail chain. Now K-mart is struggling.

Firms are increasingly trying to include customers more in internal processes or form partnerships with them. Popular partnering approaches include joint planning sessions to identify driving forces for industry change, joint product- and market-development efforts, enhanced communication linkages, sharing of facilities, and joint training and service programs (other examples are found in Table 2.5). Efforts to strengthen linkages with customers often provide significant benefits. For example, sales representatives from U.S. Surgical coach surgeons during surgery in the use of their company's instruments. Experiences with surgeons led to the

Table 8.2   Examples of Tactics for Managing and Partnering with External Stakeholders

Stakeholder	Traditional Management	Partnering and Inclusion Strategies
Customers	Customer service departments Marketing and marketing research On-site visits 800 numbers Long-term contracts	Involvement on design teams or product testing Joint planning sessions Joint training/service programs Financial investments Appointments to board (interlocking directorate)
Suppliers	Purchasing departments Encouraging competition among suppliers Sponsoring new suppliers Threat of vertical integration Long-term contracts	Involvement on design teams for new products Integration of ordering system with manufacturing Shared information systems Coordinated quality control Appointments to board (interlocking directorate)
Competitors	Direct competition based on differentiation Intelligence systems Corporate spying and espionage (ethical problems)	Joint ventures or consortia for research and development, manufacturing, marketing, etc. Alliances to pursue a variety of objectives Trade associations for information sharing and collective lobbying Informal price leadership or collusion (may be illegal)
Government Agencies and Administrators	Legal, tax, or government relations offices Lobbying and political action committees Campaign contributions Personal gifts to politicians (ethical problems)	Jointly- or government-sponsored research Joint foreign development projects Problem-solving task forces on sensitive issues Appointment of retired government officials to board
Local Communities	Community relations offices Public relations advertising Involvement in community service Donations to local causes	Task forces to work on special community needs Cooperative training and educational programs Development committees/boards Joint employment programs
Activist Groups	Organizational decisions to satisfy demands Public/political relations efforts Financial donations	Consultation with representatives on sensitive issues Joint research and development programs Appointments to the board
The Media	Public/political relations efforts Media experts/press releases	Exclusive interviews or early release of information Inclusion in social events and other special treatment
Unions	Union avoidance through excellent treatment of employees Hiring professional negotiators Mutually satisfactory labor contracts Chapter 11 protection to re-negotiate contract	Contract clauses that link pay to performance Joint committees on safety and other issues Joint industry/labor panels Inclusion on management committees Appointments to the board
Financial Intermediaries	Financial reports Close correspondence Finance and accounting departments High-level financial officer Audits	Inclusion in management decisions requiring financing Contracts and linkages with other clients of financier Shared ownership of projects Appointments to the board

Source: Adapted from J.S. Harrison and C.H. St. John, "Managing and Partnering with External Stakeholders," *Academy of Management Executive* (May 1996), 53. Used with permission.

development of laproscopic instruments, which are used to perform procedures through tiny incisions. U.S. Surgical now holds a dominant position in the multibillion-dollar laproscopic-instruments market.[28]

Suppliers

Many firms are involving strategically important suppliers in product and process design, in quality-training sessions, and in on-line production scheduling. Most firms that rely on just-in-time delivery have involved suppliers in their internal processes. For example, Digital Equipment Corporation (DEC) and Hewlett-Packard include suppliers on their product-planning teams. DEC also asks managers to evaluate their suppliers as if they were part of the internal organization.[29] Bailey Controls, a $300-million-a-year manufacturer of control systems, does likewise, but they go a step further by providing Arrow Electronics, a major supplier, with a warehouse in a Bailey factory.[30] G&F Industries, a plastic-components manufacturer, has dedicated an employee to Bose, one of their major customers. The employee works full-time inside the Bose facility.[31]

A front-page story in *The Wall Street Journal* in the mid-1990s stated that the "next manufacturing revolution is under way, and U.S. companies are bringing airplanes, cars, even kitchen stoves to market faster and cheaper by leaning on their suppliers to help engineer and bankroll new projects."[32] These types of relationships are providing tremendous cost savings and other benefits. For instance, Whirlpool contracted with a supplier, Eaton Corporation, to develop the burner system for its new gas range. Also, McDonnell Douglas once saved $300 million by having suppliers pay up-front tooling and development costs and by subcontracting assembly of its new one-hundred-seat jetliner.

Competitors

Competitors pose a difficult stakeholder management problem because it is often in the best interests of one competitor to cause another competitor to falter. However, to combat collapsing product and process life cycles and to get a jump on new emerging technologies, competitors are joining forces in increasing numbers. Rival organizations are coming together to form alliances for technological advancement, for new-product development, to enter new or foreign markets, and to pursue a wide variety of other opportunities.[33]

 Very few international rivalries are as intense as the one between film manufacturers Kodak and Fuji. Consequently, some analysts were surprised when Kodak and Fuji began a joint research-and-development project with three Japanese camera makers to establish a new standard for photographic film. Eugene Glazer, an analyst at Dean Witter Reynolds, explained: "Fuji has to be granted the same technology. If they don't include Fuji, Fuji would fight very hard against the introduction of a new system." The venture has already produced a new Advanced Photo System (APS), including a new type of "smart" film that allows correction of photographer errors. In the computer-chip industry, IBM formed a joint venture with rivals Toshiba Corporation of Japan and Siemens AG of Germany to develop an advanced line of memory chips. Also, Advanced Micro Devices, Inc. formed an alliance with Fujitsu Limited of Japan to develop a new kind of memory chip. The alliance includes the purchase of each other's common stock.

In the automobile industry, rivals GM, Ford, and DaimlerChrysler joined forces to form a single automotive-parts exchange to be run through the Internet. In airlines, rivals have been teaming up to provide coordinated service on international routes. United has allied with Lufthansa, Delta with Swissair, Austrian Airlines with Sabena, Northwest with KLM, and American with British Airways. American Airlines CEO Robert Crandall, in justifying his own company's venture, said: "The government changed the rules. I don't have to like it, but we understand the rules and we will play by them."[34]

The underlying motive of some partnerships seems to be to put the remaining firms that are not included in an alliance at a competitive disadvantage. According to one industry analyst, "Regulatory barriers created by firm conduct may be used by groups in the industry as a competitive weapon against other groups."[35]

In oligopolies, where a few major rivals dominate an industry, the major firms may cooperate with each other in setting prices. Formal price-setting cooperation is called **collusion.** In the United States and many other countries, collusion is illegal. However, companies may still cooperate informally by being careful not to drop prices enough to start a price war. Price wars can damage the profits of all firms in the sector, as demonstrated several times in the airline industry since it was deregulated. Alternatively, some sectors have an established price leader, usually one of the largest companies in the industry, who establishes a pricing pattern that other firms follow.

In some countries and regions, collusion is not illegal, or it is widely practiced in spite of its illegality. For example, for many years, the OPEC cartel established the price charged for crude oil produced by Middle Eastern countries. Ultimately, the cartel lost some of its power when countries participating in OPEC discovered that great financial rewards were available for individual firms that were willing to violate OPEC agreements.

collusion

Formal price-setting cooperation among firms

Government Agencies and Administrators

Business organizations and governments share a number of common goals, among them creating a favorable environment for international trade, stable market conditions, a healthy economy, and production of desirable goods and services. Consequently, many organizations form alliances with government agencies and officials to pursue a wide variety of objectives, including basic research, finding answers to social problems, and establishing trade policies.

Government/business partnerships are even more widely used outside of the United States, where governments often play a more active role in economic development. One such effort resulted in the formation of the major aerospace company Airbus Industrie, jointly owned by aerospace firms from Britain, France, Germany, and Spain. The Japanese Ministry of International Trade and Industry (MITI) targets particular segments of Japanese industry and provides support for those that are determined to be most closely linked to the growth of the Japanese economy.

In one of the most interesting government/industry alliances to date, the U.S. Department of Justice actually helped aluminum manufacturers form a cartel to regulate the production and, ultimately, the price of aluminum. The accord resulted from fear of Russian influence in the world aluminum market. The former Soviet Union, rich in natural resources such as aluminum, and starved for foreign cash, began flooding the world market with aluminum. In response, major U.S. and European producers decided to offer $2 billion to close one huge smelter for two years to modernize it. President Bush (the elder Bush) squashed the deal. The dumping situation continued, and became so extreme that eventually U.S. aluminum makers begged the government for intervention. The administration changed, and Bowman Cutter, President Clinton's deputy of the National Economic Council, eventually took the aluminum manufacturers' situation to heart. The council brought together a broad group of government agencies, who could not agree on how to attack the problem. Finally, a group consisting of industry and government representatives from seventeen nations, including three antitrust lawyers from the U.S. Justice Department, met in Brussels to decide who would produce how much aluminum.[36]

In another interesting alliance, Loral Chairman Bernard Schwartz, due to his ties with the late Ron Brown, the secretary of the Department of Commerce, got a boost to his business that most managers just dream about. Schwartz was invited to accompany Brown to China, with the objective of helping the fast-growing nation develop their telecommunications capability. The trip was expected to bring Loral as much as $1 billion in Chinese contracts over a period of ten years. To keep this unusual alliance strong, Mr. Schwartz donated nearly $200,000 to Democratic interests favored by Mr. Brown. Although the relationship was advantageous in some respects to both the United States and Loral, the ethics of the situation were brought into question.[37]

Local Communities

Organizations take a proactive role in their local communities for a variety of reasons. Good relationships with local communities and governments can result in favorable local regulation or in tax breaks. For example, the Walt Disney Company received tax breaks and special treatment from the city of New York when the company invested millions of dollars in the development of one of the most crime-filled areas in the city—42nd Street between Times Square and Eighth Avenue in Manhattan. The company constructed a live-production theater, a Disney Store, cinemas, hotels, game parlors, and restaurants.[38]

Other organizations find opportunities to achieve financial or operating objectives while satisfying a need in the local community. For instance, Creative Apparel of Waldo County, Maine, helped a depressed local economy by establishing a partnership with a local tribe of Indians. A training program was put in place, and a grant was obtained from the Department of Commerce to assist with the construction of a new manufacturing building. The Department of Defense awarded Creative Apparel a $2.95 million contract for flame-retardant flier jackets.[39] Social partnerships are a good way to achieve common goals.

 A task force was formed among business leaders, educational institutions, and local-government representatives to address skilled-labor shortages in the upstate South Carolina region. The task force consisted of twenty-one members, including local employers, a county school-board executive, faculty members from a local university, and representatives from a literary society and a job service. Efforts of the task force resulted in specific recommendations to find more job applicants, improve the qualifications of applicants, and upgrade the skills of current employees. In addition, the task force developed a Human Resources Workforce Information and Preparedness Program (the WIPP) to address human-resource needs on a longer-term basis. Not only did companies participating in the upstate task force have an opportunity to promote goodwill with several stakeholder groups, but they could also work on filling unmet human-resource needs and potentially begin the development of a distinctive competence through the creation of a labor pool composed of better-skilled workers.[40]

Quasi-public alliances between local governments and business leaders are flourishing across many sections of the United States. For example, the Economic Development Commission of Mid-Florida Inc. represents four central Florida counties. The commission works with government and business leaders to create economic plans and initiatives. Recent activities include the development of an economic-action plan for Osceola County, promotion of an industrial park, matching companies that sell goods with foreign companies that buy them, and finding ways to make use of the Orlando Naval Training Center, one of several military facilities the navy has decided to abandon. The commission has a lot of cash, including $425,000 in state and local government grants.[41]

Martin Marietta, which is now merged with Lockheed (another corporation with a strong presence in central Florida), is among the companies that have formed a partnership with the commission to preserve employment, reduce operating costs, and bring new business to the central Florida economy. Rick Tesch, who heads the commission, describes their successes this way: "We've proven that partnerships like this work. By streamlining permitting, helping reduce operating costs and assisting them in obtaining state training and incentive dollars, we were able to solidify Martin's presence in metro Orlando and bring an additional 1,500 jobs into our community."[42]

Activist Groups

activist groups
Organizations formed with the purpose of advancing a specific cause or causes; public interest groups represent the position of a broad cross-section of society, while special interest groups focus on the needs of smaller subgroups

Activist groups such as the Sierra Club, Greenpeace International, the National Association for the Advancement of Colored People (NAACP), the National Organization for Women (NOW), and Mothers Against Drunk Driving (MADD) represent a variety of social and environmental perspectives. Public-interest groups (e.g., MADD) represent the position of a broad cross-section of society, while special-interest groups (e.g., the NAACP) focus on the needs of smaller subgroups. While these groups are most often seen in an adversarial role relative to the desires of other organizational stakeholders, this does not have to be the case. However, it is difficult for executives to break out of the old mind-set and adopt an attitude of common goal achievement. To adopt a win-win attitude with activist groups, executives should consider potential benefits from partnering activities, especially in situations in which an activist is strategically important.

One of the best ways to reduce unfavorable regulation in an industry is to operate in a manner that is consistent with the values of society. Organizations that respond to the widely held positions of public-interest groups on issues such as pollution, fair-hiring practices, safety, and waste management do not need to be regulated. They find themselves in the enviable position of solving their own problems, instead of having a regulatory body of individuals with less experience in the industry dictating how problems will be solved. Public-interest groups are particularly important in helping organizations avoid conflicts with social values, which can result in unfavorable media and a damaged reputation. Such groups are experts in the causes they represent. As a result, many companies invite public-interest-group members that may have an interest in what they are doing to participate in strategic-planning processes, either as advisers or as board members.

Organizations should also consider the needs of special-interest groups, which represent the views of smaller social groups. However, buffering techniques may be more applicable because these groups, by virtue of their smaller social scope, are likely to be less strategically important than are public-interest groups.

Both types of activists can also provide an alternative perspective on issues that affect the environment, consumers, minorities, or other interests. This alternative perspective can lead to new ways to solve organizational problems. For example, the Conservation Law Foundation, a New England–based environmental organization, formed a partnership with the New England Electric System, a medium-sized utility, on conservation, load management, and regulatory and rate adjustments. As a result of this collaboration, it is estimated that, out to the year 2010, one-third of the planned power plants in the region will not have to be built, thus releasing this capital for other uses. New England Electric saved capital, and the Conservation Law Foundation helped reduce, among other things, air pollution and respiratory problems in the affected areas. It was a win-win situation.[43]

Another benefit to allowing participation by important public-interest or special-interest groups during planning processes is that there may be fewer obstacles during strategy implementation. The groups involved would be less likely to protest or seek government intervention. This may also result in good public relations and publicity. For example, Sun Company (oil) worked directly with the Coalition for Environmentally Responsible Economies (CERES) in developing a new policy for health, safety, and the environment. Sun was cited by Friends of the Earth as a model company that other firms should follow.[44]

Alliances with activist groups can also help companies develop new products. The increasing social emphasis on environmental protection has left companies rushing to introduce products that are environmentally acceptable.[45] Examples include the conversion of McDonald's back to paper packaging, and Rubbermaid's environmentally friendly "Sidekick" lunch box. Also, organizations in the mature PC industry may find new growth opportunities in developing products for the physically and mentally challenged by partnering with the Institute on Applied Technology, a Boston-based nonprofit organization that does research and training on computer applications for these individuals.[46]

The Media

Not only must an organization assess the potential effects of social forces on its business, it must also manage its relationship and reputation with society at large. The media acts as a "watchdog" for society. It is a commanding force in managing the attitudes of the general public toward organizations. Executives have nightmares about their companies being the victims of the next *20/20* program or some other news show. On the other hand, a well-managed media can have a significant positive impact on the image of a firm. Burger King combined local social responsibility with astute media management by announcing that after fourteen years of sponsoring a float in the Orange Bowl Parade, moneys ordinarily used for the float would be used to support education (primarily scholarships) in Burger King's headquarters city of Miami.[47]

It is rather difficult to pursue an inclusion or partnering strategy in the case of the media. In general, companies will rely on traditional management techniques to deal with this stakeholder. To manage relations with the media, large firms typically employ public-relations (PR) experts. The public-relations staff is usually active in releasing information that will place their company in a favorable light, while being careful not to create the impression that their organization is withholding information from the public. Press conferences are sometimes held for important announcements. President Clinton's presidential-election-campaign "war room" is an interesting example of media management. The room operated twenty-four hours a day in Clinton's campaign headquarters, responding instantly with fast-faxed press releases to any political attack.[48]

While it is difficult to include the media directly in the organization, and formal partnerships are pretty much out of the question, managers can make individual reporters feel as though they have a special relationship with the company, thus prompting the reporters to portray the company in a more favorable light. Granting individual interviews to specific reporters, early release of information to a limited set of reporters, or treating a few media people to social activities such as luncheons or golf are some of the many efforts that firms make to cultivate the goodwill of the press.

Labor Unions

Unions are formed to protect and advance the welfare of their members. The strength of unions varies from state to state and country to country. In the United States, union strength has declined recently; however, unions are far from dead. For example, the Service Employees International Union (SEIU) employs shock tactics and harassment to influence janitorial contractors to pressure their employees to unionize.[49] As a result, the SEIU is growing steadily. Also, a very visible strike at a GM brake plant shut down the entire organization.[50]

The values of unions were reflected well in a statement by Owen Bieber, president of the United Auto Workers:

> I'm struck by the widespread confusion between means and ends that is hampering public understanding of the competitiveness issue. Competitiveness should be viewed as a means, useful only if it moves us toward such ends as full employment at decent wages, rising living standards, and fairness in the distribution of income and wealth. If competitiveness simply implies reducing costs, it can work against the goal of improving our quality of life. For example, the same company could improve its competitiveness by investing in training for its workers, forcing them to take wage cuts, or moving its production overseas. While all three strategies may improve competitiveness, they have very different consequences for employment, living standards, and quality of life.[51]

Unions are making great strides in pursuing common goals with managers. The AFL-CIO once urged the eighty-six unions it represents to "become partners with management in boosting efficiency."[52] This was an unprecedented move for the AFL-CIO.

Unions are being treated as partners instead of adversaries in some of the companies that have had the greatest success with programs such as self-managed work teams. For example, Xerox implemented three teamwork programs with its sixty-two hundred copier assemblers, represented by the Amalgamated Clothing and Textile Workers Union (ACTWU). The efforts worked so well that Xerox was able to bring three hundred jobs home from abroad to a plant it opened in Utica, where savings of $2 million a year were expected. Xerox shares internal financial documents with union leaders and provides executive development for them with their own managers. CEO Paul Allaire commented on the success of these programs: "I don't want to say we need unions if that means the old, adversarial kind. But if we have a cooperative model, the union movement will be sustained and the industries it's in will be more competitive."[53]

Organizations that are successful in labor/management relationships are starting to include representatives from labor unions in strategic-planning decisions. For example, Scott Paper Company formed a committee combining ten of its top executives with ten top officials from the union. They pledged to "work together to meet the needs of employees, customers, shareholders, the union and the community."[54] The results were so successful in terms of cutting costs and boosting quality that now other paper companies are doing the same thing.

Financial Intermediaries

financial intermediaries
A wide variety of institutions, including banks, stock exchanges, brokerage houses, investment advisors, mutual fund companies, pension fund companies, and other organizations or individuals that may have an interest in investing in the firm

Financial intermediaries consist of a wide variety of institutions, including banks, stock exchanges, brokerage houses, investment advisers, mutual-fund companies, pension-fund companies, and other organizations or individuals that may have an interest in investing in the firm. This list is not exhaustive, and many financial-service firms play more than one role.

Trust is especially important in dealing with creditors. Disclosure of financial records helps establish trust, as do timely payments. Many organizations, in an effort to manage their relationships with creditors and develop trust, have invited creditor representatives onto the board of directors. In some cases, this is a loan requirement. This type of involvement allows creditors to know firsthand the financial condition of the company and to have a say in major financial decisions such as acquisitions, restructuring, and new offerings of stock and debt. Another type of linkage occurs when an organization does business with a company that is represented by the same financial institution. This type of cooperation, which can facilitate contracting and financial transactions, is common among the *keiretsu* in Japan. Banks and other lenders may also participate as part owners of business ventures of client firms.

Financial intermediaries are the last of the external stakeholders that will be discussed in this chapter; however, it should be noted that other external stakeholders, of varying importance, exist on a firm-by-firm basis. For example, donors are a key stakeholder in nonprofit organizations. Donors should probably be treated more like customers than anything else. In fact, individuals who donate to charities or religious organizations are forgoing other purchases. Nonprofit organizations should communicate with donors, involve them in the processes of the organization, and create a high-quality service that donors will want to support. In the case of charities, the recipients of goods and services should also be treated as customers.

Managing Partnerships

Much of this chapter so far has dealt with creating successful partnerships with external stakeholders. This section will close with a few comments on how to manage partnerships so that they are likely to be successful. Managers should communicate the expected benefits of the venture to important external and internal stakeholders so they will understand the role the alliance will play in the organization.[55] They should also develop a strategic plan for the partnership that consolidates the views of the partners about market potential, competitive trends, and potential threats. There are several additional steps that may be used to improve the likelihood of success:

1. Through careful systematic study, identify an alliance partner that can provide the capabilities that are needed. Avoid the tendency to align with another firm just because allianceforming is a trend in the industry.

2. Clearly define the roles of each partner and ensure that every joint project is of value to both.

3. Develop a strategic plan for the venture that outlines specific objectives for each partner.

4. Keep top managers involved so that middle managers will stay committed.

5. Meet often, informally, at all managerial levels.

6. Appoint someone to monitor all aspects of the partnership, and use an outside mediator when disputes arise.

7. Maintain enough independence to develop your own area of expertise. Avoid becoming a complete "captive" of the alliance partner.

8. Anticipate and plan for cultural differences.[56]

This concludes our discussion of strategy implementation through the creation of partnerships and managing relationships with external stakeholders. The next section focuses on another element of strategy implementation—developing functional-support strategies

Functional-Level Resource Management

functional-level strategy
The collective pattern of day-to-day decisions made and actions taken by managers and employees who are responsible for value-creating activities within a particular functional area

Functional-level strategies are about paying attention to detail. Some of the most successful companies of our time are operating in low-growth, moderately profitable industries and are pursuing strategies that are not unique. The reason for their extraordinary success is their attention to the details associated with strategy implementation. Wal-Mart is in the discount-retail business, just like Kmart. They offer similar merchandise, with similar prices, in a similar discount-store facility. Why has Wal-Mart consistently outperformed Kmart, even to the point that Kmart is having severe financial difficulties? One reason is the attention to detail. For many years, Wal-Mart had a company policy that when a customer asked a Wal-Mart associate where something was, the associate should stop what he or she was doing and escort the customer to the proper aisle. Wal-Mart employees did not escort customers through the stores because they were nice people. They did it because management believed the gesture was an important element of service, they had established an operating policy that specified this tactic as the preferred way to handle a customer request, and they taught employees to do it and believe in it.

Nucor, a steel company, has been successful in the declining, virtually profitless steel industry while much larger foreign and domestic competitors have suffered. Year after year, Nucor uses its lean organization structure, incentive-pay systems, and technological investments to keep its costs lower than those of most competitors. In the case of Wal-Mart and Nucor, one company has outperformed its competitors primarily on the strength of its strategy implementation.

Organizations are made up of people who interact with each other and with external stakeholders as they perform functions that serve to meet the goals of the organization. Several years ago, researchers found that companies who were most successful in implementing their strategies created a "pervasive strategic vision" throughout the company, with the full involvement of all employees.[57] In those firms where strategies were implemented effectively, employees worked as a "coordinated system," with all of their separate but interdependent efforts directed toward the goals of the firm. Consequently, each functional area is one piece of a larger system, and coordination among the pieces is essential to successful strategy execution.

From a coordinated-systems perspective, well-developed functional-level resource-management strategies should have the following characteristics:

- *Decisions made within each function will be consistent with each other.* For example, if marketing chooses to spend a great deal of money creating a premium brand name for a new product, it should take advantage of distribution channels that allow the product to reach customers who will pay a price premium. If the wrong distribution channels are chosen, then the efforts spent on advertising, promotion, and product placement will be lost. Several years ago, one of the synthetic-fiber producers allowed one of its best branded products to become associated with discount, low-quality garments, and the company's investment in the trademark was lost.

- *Decisions made within one function will be consistent with those made in other functions.* Interdependencies and linkages exist among the many activities of a firm. It is common for the decisions made by one department to be inconsistent with those of another department. For example, financial policies may be in conflict with the goals of engineering. Although they are responsible for most of the primary value-adding activities, marketing and operations frequently advocate very different approaches to the many interdependent decisions that exist between them. Left to their own devices, with no guidance from the organization, it is likely that marketing, over time, will make decisions that implement a differentiation strategy, while manufacturing, over time, implements a low-cost strategy. Table 8.3 shows the many areas of potential conflict that exist between marketing and manufacturing groups.

- *Decisions made within functions will be consistent with the strategies of the business.* For example, if a company is pursuing a low-cost competitive strategy, then the bulk of the activities and resources should be focused on cost reduction to improve profitability. It is often difficult to adapt to changes in the competitive environment. Suppose a company is pursuing an aggressive-growth strategy in a healthy business environment. Under those conditions, marketing may pursue market-share increases and revenue growth as its top priority. If the business environment changes—demand slows down and profits are squeezed—then the focus of marketing may have to change to stability and profit improvement over sales-volume increases. Unless prodded by the organization, marketing may be very reluctant to change from its traditional way of doing business.[58]

The rapid success and subsequent decline of People Express Airlines is a good demonstration of what can happen when there is inconsistency in tactical decisions across departments or between a generic strategy and functional strategies.

Ex. Following the deregulation of the airlines, Donald Burr started the company People Express as a low-cost commuter airline. In the beginning, every management decision supported low costs: aircraft were bought secondhand, pilots kept planes in the air more hours per day than any other airline, terminal leases were inexpensive, and human-resource policies required cross-training, encouraged high productivity, and rewarded employees with profit-sharing plans. In line with its no-frills commuter approach, the company did not book reservations or provide in-flight meals. The airline was extraordinarily successful with its strategy, and achieved the lowest cost position in the industry. However, with success, People Express began to alter its pattern of decisions and, over time, drift from its low-cost strategy. It pursued longer routes, which pulled it into direct competition with the full-service airlines, even though People Express did not have the elaborate reservation systems and customer services. It contracted more-expensive terminal arrangements and purchased new aircraft at market prices. The close-knit, high-performance culture that encouraged an extraordinary work pace in exchange for profit sharing was undermined by rapid growth and too many new faces. Just a few years after its start-up, People Express was in serious financial trouble and was forced to sell out to another airline.

Table 8.3   Areas of Interdependency and Potential Conflict Between Marketing and Operations

1. Facility Size/Process Choice vs. Market Forecasts

For a firm to exploit economies of scale and achieve low costs, offer a broad product line, serve a large market region, produce standardized products, or produce customized products, it must have properly sized facilities and appropriate processes. To make correct decisions about size and technology, operations requires information from marketing about expected long-run volume, future product mix, low cost versus responsiveness competitive priorities, and the role of product and service quality. Often, marketing will complain that operations has failed to build enough capacity and properly plan facilities. Operations will, in turn, blame marketing for failing to provide accurate demand forecasts.

2. Facility Location vs. Market Planning

Depending upon the demands of the marketplace, facilities may be located near suppliers, low-cost labor, or customers. To make correct decisions about facility location, operations depends on marketing for information about the relative importance of low costs, responsiveness, and delivery speed, as well as the location of current and future customers and the demand patterns expected for each product and market region.

3. Production Schedules vs. Forecasts, Orders, and Promotions

Production schedules determine inventory levels, sourcing arrangements, labor utilization, capacity utilization, delivery performance, and cost structures. In making production scheduling decisions, operations depends on marketing for short-run demand forecasts and promotion plans by product and by market, firm customer commitments whenever possible, and guidance about the relative importance of low costs and delivery performance. When operations is unable to meet demands in the short-run, marketing complains about flexibility and commitment to the needs of the customers. Operations, in turn, blames marketing for failing to provide good forecasts and arrange for longer lead times on orders.

4. Operating Policies

On a daily basis, operations management makes decisions about the focus of continuous improvement activities and whether to schedule overtime, disrupt production schedules to meet the special requests of customers, stop shipment of marginal quality goods, or build inventory in anticipation of demand. Many of these decisions embody trade-offs. For example, it is difficult to maintain low costs if high stock levels are required to service unexpected demand. In all cases, those decisions are influenced by information from marketing about demand patterns and competitive priorities.

functional-strategy audit
Thorough evaluation of functional-level strategies on the basis of internal consistency, consistency across functional areas, and the extent to which each functional strategy is supportive of the overall strategies of the firm

A **functional-strategy audit** can be very helpful in determining whether functional strategies are internally consistent, consistent across functions, and supportive of the strategies of the firm. Table 8.4 contains an outline of some of the functional areas to be included in a functional audit. The first step is to determine what an organization is currently doing in each area. Internal consistency is evaluated, as is consistency across functional areas and consistency with the strategies of the organization. The next step is to develop plans to correct any inconsistencies. A functional-strategy audit is especially helpful as an implementation tool for new strategies. You may personally find it useful as you do case analyses in your Strategic Management course. If your instructor requires you to write an implementation section for a strategy you recommend, you can develop your plan, in part, based on the items for each functional area found in Table 8.4.

The collective pattern of day-to-day decisions made and actions taken by managers and employees who are responsible for value-creating activities result in the functional strategies that are used to implement the growth and competitive strategies of the business. In the following sections, we will discuss the responsibilities and patterns of decisions made by marketing, operations, information-systems, R&D/technology, human-resources, and finance functions in organizations. Management's challenge is to ensure that the pattern is consistent with what was intended.

Marketing Strategy

One of the most critical responsibilities of marketing employees is to span the boundary of the organization and interact with external stakeholders such as customers and competitors. Marketing is responsible for bringing essential stakeholder information about new customer needs, projected future demand, competitor actions, and new business opportunities into the organization as an input to plans for continuous improvements, capacity and workforce expansions, new technologies, and new products and services. Motorola sees their sales force in a vital boundary-spanning role between the customer and the organization.

 Members of our sales force are surrogates for customers. They should be able to reach back into Motorola and pull out technologists and other people they need to solve problems and anticipate customer needs. We want to put the salesperson at the top of the organization. The rest of us then serve the salesperson.[59]

marketing strategy
Plan for collecting information about customers or potential customers and using this information to project future demand, predict competitor actions, identify new business opportunities, create new products and services, and sell products and services

Marketing strategy evolves from the cumulative pattern of decisions made by the employees who interact with customers and perform marketing activities. To support growth strategies, marketing identifies new customer opportunities, suggests product opportunities, creates advertising and promotional programs, arranges distribution channels, and creates pricing and customer-service policies that help position the company's products for the proper customer groups. If a company pursues a stability or turnaround strategy within one of its businesses, the demands placed on marketing will change. Instead of pursuing growth, marketing may manage a reduction in the number of customer groups, distribution channels, and products in the product line—all in an attempt to focus on the more profitable and promising aspects of the business. Such was the case with Sturm, Ruger & Company, a maker of guns for hunters, target shooters, and collectors. Facing a decline in the gun industry, the company decided it could no longer support wholesalers who also sold Smith & Wesson weapons. Fifty percent of its distributors agreed to supply Ruger guns only, which reduced the company's marketing costs and helped create a prestigious, hard-to-find image for its products.[60]

The competitive strategy of the firm also influences marketing decisions.[61] Low-cost competitive strategies require low-cost channels of distribution and low-risk product- and market-development activities. If demand can be influenced by advertising or price discounts, then marketing may pursue aggressive advertising and promotion programs or deep price discounts to get demand to a level that will support full capacity utilization and economies of scale within operations, as when the soft-drink companies advertise and discount their products. Differentiation strategies require that marketing identify the attributes of products and services that customers will value, price and distribute the product or service in ways that capitalize on the differentiation, and advertise and promote the image of difference. Logitech, a leading producer of the personal-computer device called the "mouse," used an aggressive marketing strategy to implement a growth strategy.

 There are three ways to sell a mouse: (1) directly to original computer-equipment makers,(2) through distributors to retail outlets, and (3) through mail order. In its early start-up stage, Logitech bypassed the traditional mode of entry through distributors. Instead, the company sold direct to customers by advertising its mouse through personal-computer magazines at half the price of the leading model. The interest created by the mail-order approach fueled pull-through sales with distributors. Logitech also qualified as a supplier to AT&T. Logitech leveraged its AT&T contact into a European market entry when it won a contract with Olivetti, an AT&T alliance partner.[62]

The many stakeholder interests and the inherent trade-offs that are embedded in decision making make development of marketing strategies difficult and subject to inconsistencies. For example, one large market segment may be very price-competitive, while a much smaller segment will pay a premium price. Which is more consistent with the firm's strategy? When introducing a new product, is it better to offer the product at a competitive price and grow with the market, or offer the product at a deeply discounted price to gain market share in the early introduction period? Just how high can the price go on a "differentiated" product before the customer is no longer willing to pay? Is it desirable to participate in sole-supplier arrangements with customers? How marketing handles these types of questions reflects its understanding of stakeholder needs and influences the strategy that is created over time.

Operations Strategy

operations strategy

Emerges from the pattern of decisions made within the firm about production or service operations

Operations strategy emerges from the pattern of decisions made within the firm about production or service operations. The task of operations managers is to design and manage an operations organization that can create the products and services the firm must have to compete in the marketplace. An effective operations unit "is not necessarily one that promises the maximum efficiency or engineering perfection, but rather one that fits the needs of the business—that strives for consistency between its capabilities and policies and the competitive advantage being sought."[63]

Table 8.4 Conducting a Functional-Strategy Audit

Marketing Strategy

- Target Customers—few vs. many, what groups, what regions
- Product Positioning—premium commodity, multi-use, specialty use
- Product Line Mix—a mix of complementary products
- Product Line Breadth—a full-line offering of products
- Pricing Strategies—discount, moderate, premium prices
- Promotion Practices—direct sales, advertising, direct mail, Internet
- Distribution Channels—few or many, sole contract responsibilities
- Customer Service Policies—flexibility, responsiveness, quality
- Product/Service Image—premium quality, good price, reliable
- Market Research—accuracy, frequency, and methods for obtaining marketing information

Operations Strategy

- Capacity Planning—lead demand to ensure availability or lag demand to achieve capacity utilization
- Facility Location—near suppliers, customers, labor, natural resources, or transportation
- Facility Layout—continuous or intermittent flow
- Technology and Equipment Choices—degree of automation, use of computers and information technology
- Sourcing Arrangements—cooperative arrangements with a few vs. competitive bids
- Planning and Scheduling—make to stock, make to order, flexibility to customer requests
- Quality Assurance—acceptance sampling, process control, standards
- Workforce Policies—training levels, cross-training, rewards, use of teams

Information-Systems Strategy

- Hardware—local area network (LAN), mainframe, minicomputer, internal systems, links to Internet
- Software—data processing, decision support, Web management, computer automated design (CAD), computer integrated manufacturing (CIM), just-in-time inventory
- Personnel—in-house experts, subcontracting, or alliances
- Information Security—hardware, software, physical location and layout
- Disaster Recovery—off-site processing, backup procedures, virus protection and treatment
- Business Intelligence—management support, marketing, accounting, operations, R&D, human resources, finance
- Internet—uses of Internet in communications, marketing, resource acquisition, research, or management

R&D/Technology Strategy

- Research Focus—product, process, applications
- Research Orientation—leader, early follower, late follower
- Project Priorities—budget, quality, creativity, time
- Knowledge Creation—training, alliances and ventures, acquisitions, cross-functional teams
- Corporate Entrepreneurship—"seed money" grants, time off to develop a venture, management support, rewards for entrepreneurs, ideas come from everyone

(continued)

Table 8.4   Conducting a Functional-Strategy Audit (continued)

Human Resources Strategy

- Recruitment—entry level vs. experienced employees, colleges, technical schools, job services
- Selection—selection criteria and methods
- Nature of Work—part-time, full-time, or a combination; on-site or off-site; domestic or foreign
- Performance Appraisal—appraisal methods and frequency, link to rewards
- Salary and Wages—hourly, piece rate, commission, fixed, relationship to performance, competitiveness
- Other Compensation—stock-ownership programs, bonuses
- Management Compensation—stock awards, stock options, bonuses linked to performance, perquisites, low-interest loans
- Benefits—medical, dental, and life insurance; paid leave; vacations; child care; health club
- Personnel Actions—disciplinary plans, outplacement, early retirements
- Training—types of training, availability of training to employees, tuition reimbursement

Operations Strategy

- Sources of Capital—debt, equity, or internal financing
- Financial Reporting—frequency, type, government, shareholders, other stakeholders
- Capital Budgeting—system for distributing capital, minimum ROI for investments, payback
- Overhead Costs—allocation of overhead costs based on direct labor, machine use, sales volume, activity
- Financial Control—system to ensure accuracy of internal and external financial information, audits
- Returns to Shareholders—dividends policy, re-purchase of stock, treasury stock, stock splits
- Financial Targets—establishment of financial targets for functional areas and business units, method of reporting on progress

Operations managers, like marketing managers, must manage multiple stakeholder interests in their daily decision making. The Total Quality Management (TQM) movement was a direct result of operations managers' neglect of their most critical stakeholder—customers. In the 1970s, many operations managers took the position, "We made it—now it is up to marketing to sell it." The cavalier attitude toward the concerns of customers led to systemic quality problems that undermined entire industries. Faced with fundamental change in their industries, many operations organizations implemented extensive Total Quality Management and continuous-improvement programs to help focus operations decisions on the needs of customers.

 KL Spring and Stamping Corporation of Chicago, a supplier of parts to General Motors, was under pressure to change from its traditional focus on cost reduction. To implement a new strategy focused on quality, fast delivery, and service, KL Spring formed quality circles, initiated worker cross-training, increased employee involvement, provided quality and productivity incentives, and invested in new capital equipment. The improvement efforts paid off with acknowledgments from customers: a Mark of Excellence Award from GM and a Certified Quality Vendor Award from AT&T.[64] In some organizations, operations managers have enlisted the support of another stakeholder group, suppliers, in their efforts to better serve the needs of customers. Motorola, Xerox, and Ford have very active quality and technology programs in which they train tens of thousands of their suppliers' employees, including CEOs and executive managers.[65]

Although quality programs are still common, a lot of attention has focused recently on speed. According to Michael Porter, "It's gone from a game of resources to a game of rate-of-progress. Competition today is a race to improve."[66] Speed is often the result of rethinking processes and procedures. While small entrepreneurial organizations may be at a disadvantage relative to larger organizations in developing some of the other competitive weapons, they actually have an advantage when it comes to speed and flexibility.[67] Smaller firms are typically less constrained by large investments in capital equipment. Consequently, they may be more willing to fluctuate their output or produce in small batches to satisfy customer demands. In addition, less bureaucracy often means that changes that are required due to new technology can be made in a shorter period of time. This also means that managers are typically closer to their customers and have fewer customers, thus allowing them to really get to know customers and understand their needs. Consequently, many operations managers in larger companies are struggling to be competitive with regard to speed.

The interdependencies among stakeholders can also create difficulties for operations managers. Employees want good wages and benefits, reasonable work schedules, and a safe and pleasant work environment. Communities want nonpolluting industries that will provide stable employment for citizens of the community and add to the tax base. Suppliers want predictable demand for their products and services, and a fair price. Customers want excellent quality, prompt delivery, and reasonable prices. However, a change in customer demand can upset schedules with workers and suppliers. A problem with a supplier can create havoc with the schedules and quality levels that are intended to serve the needs of customers. A new labor contract can cause cost structures and then prices to go up. A new product for a customer may require new raw materials that may, in turn, require new pollution-control procedures. In managing these interdependencies, operations managers must be guided by an understanding of business-level strategies.

Every strategy affects operations in ways that have implications for stakeholder interests. For example, growth strategies put pressure on the systems and procedures used to schedule customer orders, plan employee work arrangements, order raw materials, and manage inventories. Turnaround strategies often target the activities of operations first: line employees are laid off, equipment is idled, plants (offices and stores) are closed. In implementing a quality-management program, an organization may choose to move to sole-source arrangements, which will increase dependency on one supplier and sever relationships with others. Differentiation strategies based on flexibility and high-quality service may require a flexible or temporary workforce, special arrangements with suppliers, and very high levels of training for employees. Major capital investments in new equipment depress earnings in the short run, which lowers earnings per share reported to stockholders. How operations managers handle these types of trade-off decisions can have a substantial influence on the performance of the firm.

Information-Systems Strategy

Since the early 1980s, the role of information systems in organizations has changed fundamentally. Before microcomputers, computer information systems were used primarily for accounting transactions and information record keeping. In the 1980s, computer technology revolutionized the way companies do business. In some firms, an information-systems department plans computer use organization-wide so that computer resources are compatible and integrated. However, as systems become more user-friendly and decentralized, many information-system activities are being managed within other departments. Then, in the 1990s, the increased use of the Internet caused another fundamental shift in the way companies use information technology. The Internet has had a profound impact on interorganzational communications, marketing, data collection, business transactions, and internationalization.

Organizations regularly make decisions about how to make use of information systems, such as which hardware and software to use, what kind of information and transactions will be available on computer, how information-systems resources will be linked, and how the Internet will be used to enhance organizational processes such as marketing and communications with external stakeholders. The pattern of information systems decisions creates an **information-systems strategy.**

information-systems strategy
Plan for using information systems to enhance organizational processes and strategy

Some firms have built their entire competitive strategies on use of the Internet. Chapter 6 contained a detailed discussion of use of the Internet in developing competitive strategy. This section will focus instead on other information-systems applications. Information systems can play a key role in developing competitive strategies. Information technology can provide both information efficiencies and information synergies.

 Information efficiencies (INE) are the cost and time savings that result when IT (information technology) allows individual employees to perform their current tasks at a higher level, assume additional tasks, and expand their roles in the organization due to advances in the ability to gather and analyze data. For example, as a result of the application of IT in the organization it is very likely that a reshuffling of tasks will occur as technologies increase peoples' or subunits' ability to process information. . . . On the other hand, information synergies (INS) are the performance gains that result when IT allows two or more individuals or subunits to pool their resources and cooperate and collaborate across role or subunit boundaries, a between-person or between-group effect. For example, information synergies occur when IT allows the different individuals or subunits to adjust their actions or behaviors to the needs of the other individuals or subunits on an ongoing basis.[68]

In many organizations, computer information systems affect every aspect of business operations and serve a major role in linking stakeholders. Local area networks (LANs) and internal webs sometimes called "Intranets" link employees and improve communications and decision making.[69] With spreadsheet packages, expert systems, and other decision-support software, employees at the lowest levels of the organization have the information and the tools to make decisions that once were reserved to middle managers. Computer-aided design (CAD) systems help marketing, manufacturing, and R&D employees develop designs faster and with fewer errors. In computer-integrated manufacturing (CIM) environments, product designs and production schedules are linked directly to manufacturing equipment, which increases accuracy, flexibility, and speed in meeting customer orders. Direct linkages with suppliers help in managing just-in-time (JIT) delivery arrangements. Real-time inventory systems linked to order-taking systems provide valuable information that improves customer service. Direct computer linkages with customers provide real-time sales data that the organization may use to plan for the future.

Other organizations create strategies that rely on effective use of information systems and creation of effective decision-support systems (DSS) that record data and present it in a format that assists managers in their decision making. For example, at Toys "R" Us and Wal-Mart, scanners are used to record sales data by product and by store. Store managers use the data to update inventory records and reorder products so that their in-stock position will be assured. The sales data from the hundreds of stores are transmitted daily to the corporate office, where they are studied by product and by store to determine patterns and trends in customer buying behavior. These companies have made such effective use of customer buying information that toy manufacturers regularly consult them before scaling up to manufacture a new product.

 Benetton, the largest producer of clothing in Europe, has also made information systems a central part of its strategy. Benetton maintains an integrated production, distribution, and sales-communication system that has removed much of the risk in the fashion-apparel business. The company subcontracts 80 percent of its clothing production through a large number of subcontractors, and sells through a network of four thousand franchised shops worldwide. Clothing is designed on computers that create patterns immediately. Patterns can be transferred to subcontractors within a matter of hours. All items are bar-coded, which allows shop owners to monitor sales by product and by sales assistant. Orders and customer buying information are transmitted to the headquarters in Italy so that new production lots can be planned.[70]

R&D/technology strategy
Plan for developing new products and new technologies

R&D/Technology Strategy

Technology can play a central role in the development of a firm's strategies, as it has for Kellogg, the cereal maker.

 Kellogg invested in proprietary technology that allowed the company to develop unique cereals and sell them at a premium in the grocery stores. With its unique technology, large share of market, fast product-development time, and efficient distribution channels, Kellogg was also one of the lowest-cost producers in the industry. Rather than make a trade-off between low costs and differentiation, Kellogg made investment decisions that served both causes interdependently.

Research and development (R&D) is a primary internal activity for developing new products and new technologies. Some firms seek to achieve differentiation through innovations, which usually requires aggressive investment in research and development. Product innovation, process innovations, and quality advantages often go hand in hand. The amount of R&D investment required to be competitive tends to vary by industry. Some sectors, such as the pharmaceutical and electronics industries, require large investments in R&D to keep up with changing customer expectations, and to stay ahead of competitor product and process innovations. In other industries, such as textile and building products, investments in R&D are minimal. Inadequate R&D expenditures for improvements in innovation and quality relative to foreign rivals led, in part, to the decline of American firms in several global industries in the 1980s.[71]

R&D involves four different activities: basic research, applications development, product development, and process development. Depending on the strategy of the firm as well as identification of core competencies and related technologies, some of these research activities may be more important than others. The strategy that emerges from the decisions and actions within R&D, engineering, and technical-support activities is the research-and-development strategy.

basic research
Activity associated with pushing back the boundaries of science as we know it

Basic research is commonly referred to as the activity associated with pushing back the boundaries of science as we know it. For the most part, government laboratories, universities, and some high-technology companies have the most-aggressive programs in basic research. Recombinant-DNA technologies, superconductors, and specialty materials are examples of the types of radical findings and inventions that have resulted from pure scientific exploration.

In most companies, R&D efforts are in support of the known strategies of the firm. For example, a firm that is pursuing a market-development growth strategy will invest in applications development so that its products can be tested and qualified for more uses. Fabric manufacturers put their industrial fabrics through extensive wear testing to qualify them for everything from conveyor belts to tents to bandages.

If the firm is pursuing a product-development strategy, the engineers and scientists within R&D will modify the product to improve its performance or extend its application to different markets. In some cases, they will develop a line of product variations to serve particular market segments. The widespread use of DuPont's Teflon fibers, coating, films, and membranes in everything from pots and pans to industrial equipment is the result of aggressive product-development activities within the company.

Once products and entire product lines begin to mature, the focus of much of the R&D effort often shifts to process development.[72] While some product changes may still be required, the firm is concerned primarily with reducing its costs of production. Engineers and scientists work to improve processing methods and conditions, and to design special-purpose equipment that can efficiently produce the company's products. For example, some of the R&D efforts within many computer and electronics firms have been redirected toward process development as product lines have matured and foreign competitors have achieved lower processing costs.

R&D decisions are also characterized by trade-offs that must be matched with the strategies of the business and the interests of internal and external stakeholders. Should the firm be a leader or a follower in its research-and-development activities? What stakeholder interests should take priority in product-design decisions? Should the emphasis be on what the customer and marketing want, or on what operations can produce? What should be the balance among product, process, and applications development? Should new-product modifications be worked on sequentially, or worked on by two teams operating in parallel so that new-product variations may be introduced more quickly? Under what conditions should the plug be pulled on a new-product-development project that is not proceeding as planned? When is it no longer profitable or worthwhile to continue to create product variations? As in marketing and operations, the pattern created in deciding among the trade-offs can either work for or against the planned strategy of the firm.

Of course, R&D is only part of a complete technology-development strategy. Organizations can also acquire technology through acquisitions, strategic alliances, and joint ventures.[73] In addition, organizations should encourage corporate entrepreneurship by providing resources to employees and managers for innovative activities, allowing employees and managers time to develop their ideas, providing management support through the vision of the firm and the establishment of an innovation-supportive culture, and by rewarding successful entrepreneurs.

Human-Resources Strategy

In the not-too-distant past, human-resources (HR) activities were considered to be more administrative than strategic. However, a shift has taken place.

 So what is different now? Why are people more important today? What is it about HR issues that bring them into a discussion of strategic management? Part of the answer to these questions has to do with shifting priorities and perspectives about competition and firm advantage. As theories of strategic management turn toward resource-based and knowledge-based views of the firm, where competitive advantage increasingly resides in a firm's ability to learn, innovate, and change, the human element becomes increasingly important in generating economic value.[74]

James Brian Quinn reinforced this idea by stating that, "with rare exceptions, the economic and producing power of the firm lies more in its intellectual and service capabilities that in its hard assets—land, plant and equipment."[75]

While some human-resources departments are still concerned primarily with avoiding people problems (strikes, turnover, lawsuits, unions), others have evolved to the point where HR managers are actively involved in the formulation of strategies.[76] Human-resources managers serve a coordinating role between the organization's management and employees, and between the organization and external stakeholder groups, including labor unions and government regulators of labor and safety practices such as the Equal Employment Opportunity Commission and the Occupational Safety and Health Administration. Human-resources management can play an important role in the implementation of a firm's strategies.[77] HR management can also be a source of competitive advantage.[78] Disney and Federal Express are two examples of companies that use training to create a competitive advantage.

The pattern of decisions about selection, training, rewards, and benefits creates a **human-resources strategy.** Different industry environments and organizational strategies tend to reinforce different HR practices. In high-technology and growth companies, employees are usually hired from outside the firm to fill positions at all levels, entry positions through top-level management. Compensation systems emphasize long-range performance goals, with frequent use of bonus and profit-sharing plans.[79] Therefore, in companies pursuing growth strategies, such as Microsoft in software and Merck in pharmaceuticals, the HR strategy focuses on hiring, training, and placing employees at all levels in the organization, and on developing performance-based compensation strategies.

Mature or cost-oriented businesses usually hire employees at the entry level and promote from within to fill higher-level positions. They are more likely to focus rewards on short-range performance goals and to include seniority issues in compensation systems.[80] Firms following turnaround strategies, such as Motorola and Delta Air Lines, have to focus their HR priorities on programs for early retirements, structured layoffs, skills retraining, and outplacement services.

The human-resources strategies that are in place create a workforce with certain skills and expectations, which then influences the strategy alternatives available for the future.[81] If, throughout the life of a growth organization, salespeople are rewarded for finding new customers, R&D is rewarded for frequent new-product variations, and operations is rewarded for maximizing throughput, then a retrenchment strategy that limits customer groups, product lines, and production levels can be very difficult to implement. A change in reward systems must precede or accompany the change in strategy. Because of the potential for conflict between existing

human-resources strategy
The pattern of decisions about selection, training, rewards, and benefits

HR policies and new organization strategies, HR managers play their most strategic role at the point when a major change in organization strategy is necessary. They must anticipate the change in skills and behavior that will be needed to support the strategy, modify the HR practices, and plan for an orderly, timely transition. Although General Motors has experienced severe labor problems in the past, effective HR practices have contributed to the success of its Saturn automobile project. The Saturn has been rated in the past by J.D. Power and Associates as the highest-quality American-made automobile.

 Saturn achieves its extraordinary quality by tying quality objectives to rewards. All employees are on salary, including the workers on the assembly line. Quality, productivity, and profitability are linked to 20 percent of each employee's pay. Recently, with customer demand at a very high level, Saturn management tried to increase factory output. Because of fears that machine stress and rushing would create quality problems, line workers insisted that output be returned to the original levels that were more compatible with highest quality. The change in rewards created changes in behavior that were completely consistent with the organization's strategy of high quality.[82]

Another trend that is affecting human-resource strategy in many firms is the tactic of outsourcing labor resources, and of outsourcing HR-department activities. For example, some companies keep a relatively low percentage of their direct labor on the full-time payroll. Instead, they keep a pool of temporary, part-time workers who can be called in as needed, or they contract with a temporary-services firm that will provide temporary workers as needed. The purpose of this tactic is to reduce the overall cost of human resources, by avoiding the payment of benefits and by avoiding the cost of idle labor. The downside of this strategy is that human resources may not develop the skills needed on the job, or may not develop a sense of loyalty to the organization. In addition, some organizations are outsourcing their HR-department activities, such as benefits planning and administration. The purpose is to reduce costs, and possibly improve quality, by turning those administrative activities over to external partners who can specialize and operate at large scale.

As companies become more global, the challenges for the HR staff are mounting. However, global firms can draw from multiple human-resource labor pools, which can be a source of competitive advantage relative to single-nation firms that draw from only one pool.[83] HR managers determine what skills are needed to manage people of different cultures, recruit top candidates worldwide, create training programs and experiences that help employees appreciate other cultures, and conduct relocations worldwide.[84] Furthermore, they need to create compensation strategies for employees who, because of their national culture, value different reward and benefit packages. For example, in cultures that value personal accomplishment, control of one's destiny, and independence, such as the United States and Britain, compensation strategies may focus on individual performance. In cultures that value team accomplishment, sacrifice for others, and external control or fate, the rewards may focus on group measures and seniority.[85]

Financial Strategy

The finance and accounting functions play a strategic role within organizations because they control one of the most important resources needed to implement

financial strategy
Primary purpose is to provide the organization with the capital structure and funds that are appropriate for implementing growth and competitive strategies

strategies—money. In implementing strategy, two sources of funds are needed: (1) large amounts of capital for growth- and maintenance-related objectives and strategies, and (2) expense budgets to support the ongoing daily activities of the business. The primary purpose of a **financial strategy** is to provide the organization with the capital structure and funds that are appropriate for implementing growth and competitive strategies.

In managing the funds of the business, finance is responsible for virtually all contact between the organization and some very influential stakeholders: stockholders, bankers, other investors, the Securities and Exchange Commission, and the Internal Revenue Service. The finance group decides the appropriate levels of debt, equity, and internal financing needed to support strategies by weighing the costs of each alternative, the plans for the funds, and the financial interests of various internal and external stakeholder groups. Finance also determines dividend policies and, through preparation of financial reports, influences how financial performance will be interpreted and presented to stockholders. In fact, financial reports may be the only contact many members of the investment community and most stockholders have with the organization.

Capital and expense budgets are an extremely important means for allocating funds to those departments, projects, and activities that need them to support strategies. In theory, all expenditures in capital and expense budgets should be linked back to the strategies of the firm. "The structure that a mature enterprise takes on at any point in time essentially represents the accumulation of a long series of prior resource allocation decisions. If a company wants to develop in a specific direction, it must make these resource allocation decisions in an organized fashion."[86]

Unfortunately, the financial policies that many companies have in place work against the "strategic" use of funds. In most firms, proposals for new equipment, new products, and new facilities must be described in terms of projected cash flows, which are then used in a payback or discounted cash-flow analysis. There are several problems with these types of capital-budgeting analyses, including the potential for inaccurate numbers, inappropriate assumptions, and trade-offs that undermine the future competitiveness of the company. The problems that underlie capital-budgeting techniques are described in more detail in Table 8.5.

The trade-offs that are embedded in financial decisions carry significant implications for strategy implementation. Should the firm pay earnings out in dividends to satisfy stockholders who want a fast return on their investment, or invest them back into the company to benefit employees, communities, and stockholders who want a longer-term increase in share price? In assessing expenses, investments, and earnings, should long-run or short-run performance be given more emphasis, and how should that information be presented to stockholders and the investment community? Which internal-stakeholder groups—marketing, operations, R&D, employees—should be most influential in capital-allocation decisions? As described in Table 8.5, how minimum acceptable rates of return, base comparisons, indirect cost-allocation processes, and qualitative issues are handled in investment and budgeting decisions also represents trade-offs. Since American industry is so burdened with obsolete factories and out-of-date equipment, it is worthwhile to consider that our financial policies and capital-investment processes may have worked to discourage timely investment in plant and equipment.[87]

Table 8.5   Problems with Capital Budgeting Systems

Inaccurate Cost Data
Traditional management accounting systems compute product costs by adding direct labor and materials to indirect and overhead costs. Typically, overhead and indirect costs are allocated on the basis of direct labor hours. While this procedure made sense years ago, direct labor hours represent a small proportion (<15%) of production costs in businesses now that the allocation procedure distorts true product costs.

Base Comparisons
When deciding whether to make an investment, many companies assume if no investment is made, business will continue as usual. Unfortunately, the decision to neglect or delay an investment may place the firm at a substantial disadvantage against competitors who did make the investment. The correct base case to have used was a substantial deterioration in position rather than business as usual.

Hurdle Rate
It is very common for firms to set hurdle rates (minimum acceptable return on investment) for capital projects at levels that are well beyond the cost of capital or the firm's current return on investment. Such high hurdle rates are unrealistic and discourage new investment.

Qualitative Factors
Many companies generate cash flows based on what they are sure about: existing customers, competitors, states of technology, and market conditions. Often a new investment—say, in new flexible automation—will open the door to new knowledge and opportunities. It is the difficult-to-quantify opportunities that may provide the greatest future return but are most often omitted in the analysis.

Source: R. Hayes, S. Wheelwright, and K. Clark, *Dynamic Manufacturing* (New York: The Free Press, 1988); R. Johnson and R. Kaplan, *Relevance Lost* (Boston: Harvard Business Press, 1990).

Summary

This chapter focused on implementing strategy from two perspectives. First, organizations can look outward to external stakeholders, especially through the formation of interorganizational relationships. However, another approach is to look inward to the way organizational resources are managed through the execution of functional-level resource-management strategies. These approaches are not mutually exclusive, but rather, include a range of options that executives may consider when devising implementation plans.

Interorganizational relationships are an increasingly popular technique for pursuing strategic objectives. One of the most important reasons for forming partnerships is to acquire needed resources, especially knowledge. Stakeholders with a large amount of formal, political, or economic power; stakeholders that have a large impact on the uncertainty facing an organization; and/or stakeholders that possess needed resources should be given high priority for partnerships. Other stakeholders should not be ignored, but can be managed with more-traditional stakeholder management techniques, with the objective of buffering the organization from their influence.

Strategies are implemented through the day-to-day decisions and actions of employees throughout the organization. Management's challenge is to create a pattern of integrated, coordinated decisions that meets the needs of stakeholders and fulfills the planned strategy of the organization. To this end, strategies are established for functional-level resource areas such as marketing, operations, information systems, R&D/technology, human resources, and finance. In each area, employees interact with different stakeholder groups and manage conflicting expectations. In managing functional strategies, managers must ensure that decisions within each area are consistent over time, with other functions, and with the stated strategies of the firm.

Discussion Questions

1.   Return to Chapter 2 (Table 2.4) and review the definitions of the following interorganizational relationships: joint ventures, networks, consortia, alliances, trade groups, and interlocking directorates.

2.   What are the major advantages of interorganizational relationships?

3.   Do interorganizational relationships have any disadvantages? If so, what are they?

4.   What are the primary factors that make some stakeholders more important than others? How should high-priority stakeholders be managed?

5.   How do management techniques for high-priority stakeholders differ from those of low-priority stakeholders? Give examples.

6.   What can organizations do to ensure that their partnerships are effective?

7.   What is a functional-level resource-management strategy? Give an example of how a functional-level resource-management strategy can be used to carry out one of the generic business-level strategies, such as low-cost leadership.

8.   From a coordinated-systems perspective, what characteristics should well-developed functional-level resource-management strategies have?

9.   What are some of the methods organizational leaders can use to effectively manage relationships with customers, suppliers, and competitors?

10. What are some of the methods organizational leaders can use to effectively manage relationships with local communities, activists, the media, unions, and financial intermediaries?

Strategic Application

Effective Management of Stakeholder Relationships

For a company with which you are familiar or based on a case assigned by your instructor, select four different external stakeholders that seem to be at least moderately important. Some possibilities include a major supplier organization, a major customer, a union, a special interest group, a competitor, or a particular regulating agency. For each of these stakeholders, do the following:

● Describe the nature of the relationship between the stakeholder and the firm.

● Determine the strategic importance of the stakeholder by evaluating its formal power, economic power, political power, influence on uncertainty facing the firm, and possession of knowledge or resources not possessed by the firm.

- Based on the level of strategic importance, suggest how this stakeholder could be effectively managed. If you recommend a partnership, please describe what the partnership would involve (the chapter contains numerous examples).

Strategic Internet Application

Although unions are not as powerful in some countries as they used to be, they are still a potent force in many countries and industries. Use a search engine such as www.Google.com to locate information on what is happening in the world unionization movement. One database that was available at the time this book was printed is found at http://www.global-unions.org. This database contains links to many recent articles about what unions are doing throughout the world and the positions they support. Read several of these articles and then answer the following questions:

1. What are some of the recent issues unions are facing throughout the world?

2. To what extent are the issues that surfaced in your answer to question 1 relevant in your own country? What industries in your country would be most affected?

3. Did you find any clues in the articles you read that might help a unionized firm in your country deal with its labor union? What were they and how should a firm respond?

4. Did you find anything in the articles you read that would help a nonunionized firm in your country avoid having its employees organize into a union?

Notes

1. Harris Corporation, *Annual Report* (2000), www.harris.com/harris/ar/00/jv.html, 15 October 2001.

2. J. E. Olson and T. A. Cooper, "CEOs on Strategy: Two Companies, Two Strategies," *Journal of Business Strategy* (Summer 1987): 53.

3. J. S. Harrison, "Alternatives to Merger—Joint Ventures and Other Strategies," *Long Range Planning* (December 1987): 78–83.

4. C. E. Schillaci, "Designing Successful Joint Ventures," *Journal of Business Strategies* (Fall 1987): 59–63.

5. L. Doolittle, "Disney Teams with AAA to Provide Multipurpose Rest Area for Travelers," *Orlando Sentinel*, 25 January 1996, B1.

6. R. M. Kanter, "Becoming PALS: Pooling, Allying, and Linking across Companies," *Academy of Management Executive* (August 1989): 183–193.

7. J. Cole, "United Air Orders Airbus Industrie Jets for about $3 Billion, Bypassing Boeing," *The Wall Street Journal*, 9 July 1992, A3.

8. J. S. Harrison et al., "Resource Complementarity in Business Combinations: Extending the Logic to Organizational Alliances," *Journal of Management* 27 (2001): 679-690.

9. J. B. Treece, K. Miller, R. A. Melcher, "The Partners," *Business Week*, 10 February 1992, 102–107.

10. P. Lorange and J. Roos, "Why Some Strategic Alliances Succeed and Others Fail," *Journal of Business Strategy* (January/February 1991): 25.

11. M. E. Porter, *The Competitive Advantage of Nations* (New York: The Free Press, 1990); W. Shan and W. Hamilton, "Country-Specific Advantage and International Cooperation," *Strategic Management Journal* 12 (1991): 419–432.

12. A. C. Inkpen, "Strategic Alliances," in *The Blackwell Handbook of Strategic Management*, ed. M. A. Hitt, R. E. Freeman, and J. S. Harrison (Oxford: Blackwell Publishers, 2001), 409–432.

13. B. Kogut, "Joint Ventures: Theoretical and Empirical Perspectives," *Strategic Management Journal* 9 (1988): 319–332.

14. K. R. Harrigan, "Joint Ventures and Competitive Strategy," *Strategic Management Journal* 9 (1988): 141–158; R. N. Osborn and C. C. Baughn, "Forms of Interorganizational Governance for Multinational Alliances," *Academy of Management Journal* 33 (1990): 503–519.

15. D. H. Kent, "Joint Ventures vs. Non-Joint Ventures: An Empirical Investigation," *Strategic Management Journal* 12 (1991): 387–393.

16. Adapted from P. Burrows, "How a Good Partnership Goes Bad," *Electronic Business*, 30 March 1992, 86–90.

17. Lorange and Roos, "Strategic Alliances," 25–30.

18. Schillaci, "Successful Joint Ventures," 62.

19. Inkpen, "Strategic Alliances"; E. C. Karper-Fuehrer and N. M. Ashkanasy, "Communicating Trustworthiness and Building Trust in Interorganizational Virtual Organizations," *Journal of Management* 27 (2001): 235–254; R. Gulati, "Does Familiarity Breed Trust? The Implications of Repeated Ties for Contractual Choice in Alliances," *Academy of Management Journal* 38 (1995): 85–112; B. Nooteboom, H. Berger, and N. G. Noorderhaven, "Effects of Trust and Governance on Relational Risk," *Academy of Management Journal* 40 (1997): 308–338.

20. Inkpen, "Strategic Alliances."

21. J. S. Harrison and C. H. St. John, "Managing and Partnering with External Stakeholders," *Academy of Management Executive* (May 1996): 46–50; J. D. Thompson, *Organizations in Action* (New York: McGraw-Hill, 1967); J. R. Lang & D. E. Lockhart,

"Increased Environmental Uncertainty and Changes in Board Linkage Patterns," *Academy of Management Journal* 33, no. 1 (1990): 106–128; A. D. Meyer and G. R. Brooks, "Environmental Jolts and Industry Revolutions: Organizational Responses to Discontinuous Change," *Strategic Management Journal* 11 (Special Issue 1990): 93–110.

22. J. Perreira and B. Ortega, "Once Easily Turned Away by Local Foes, Wal-Mart Gets Tough in New England," *The Wall Street Journal,* 7 September 1994, B1, B4.

23. J. Pfeffer and G. R. Salancik, *The External Control of Organizations: A Resource Dependence Perspective* (New York: Harper & Row): 43.

24. This is the view of many organization theorists. For example, see R. L. Daft, *Organization Theory and Design,* 4th ed. (St. Paul, Minn: West Publishing, 1992), chap. 3.

25. M. Schifrin, "Partner or Perish," *Forbes,* 21 May 2001, 26–28.

26. Taken directly from A. Petersen, "Once-Mighty Motorola Stumbled When It Began Acting That Way," *The Wall Street Journal,* 18 May 2001, A1

27. W. Weitzel and E. Jonsson, "Reversing the Downward Spiral: Lessons from W.T. Grant and Sears Roebuck," *Academy of Management Executive* (August 1991): 7–22.

28. J. Reese, "Getting Hot Ideas from Customers," *Fortune,* 18 May 1992, 86.

29. R. M. Kantar, "The New Managerial Work," *Harvard Business Review* (November/December 1989): 85–92.

30. E. Schonfeld, "The New Golden Rule of Business," *Fortune,* 21 February 1994, 60–64.

31. F. R. Bleakley, "Some Companies Let Suppliers Work on Site and Even Place Orders," *The Wall Street Journal,* 13 January 1995, A1, A6.

32. N. Templin and J. Cole, "Manufacturers Use Suppliers to Help Them Develop New Products," *The Wall Street Journal,* 19 December 1994, A1.

33. J. Hagedoorn, "Understanding the Rationale of Strategic Technology Partnering: Interorganizational Modes of Cooperation and Sectoral Differences," *Strategic Management Journal* 14 (1993): 371–385; E. R. Auster, "International Corporate Linkages: Dynamic Forms in Changing Environments," *Columbia Journal of World Business* 22 (1987): 3–13; Harrigan, "Joint Ventures and Competitive Strategy."

34. R. L. Simison, F. Warner, and G. L. White, "Big Three Car Makers Plan Net Exchange," *The Wall Street Journal,* 28 February 2000, A3, A16.; M. Maremont, "Will A New Film Click?" *Business Week,* 5 February 1996, 46; D. Rosato, "American Alliance Signals Something New in the Air," *USA Today,* 13 June 1996, 2B; J. Schneidawind, "Kodak Joins Fuji, Others for Project," *USA Today,* 26 March 1992, B1; L. Hooper, "Pragmatism Wins As Rivals Start to Cooperate on Memory Chips," *The Wall Street Journal,* 14 July 1992, B1.

35. S. Oster, "The Strategic Use of Regulatory Investment by Industry Sub-groups," *Economic Inquiry* 20 (1982): 604.

36. E. Norton and M. DuBois, "Don't Call It a Cartel, But World Aluminum Has Forged New Order," *The Wall Street Journal,* 9 June 1994, A1, A5; S.

Tavernise, "An Aluminum Behemoth Is Born in Russia," *The New York Times,* 6 April 2001, W1.

37. H. Cooper and R. Wartzman, "How Ron Brown Picks Who Joins His Trips Abroad Raises Doubts," *The Wall Street Journal,* 9 September 1994, A1, A4.

38. F. Rose, "Can Disney Tame 42nd Street?" *Fortune,* 24 June 1996, 95–104.

39. "Creative Apparel, Inc.," in *Strengthening America's Competitiveness: The Blue Chip Enterprise Initiative* (Warner Books on behalf of Connecticut Mutual Life Insurance Company and the U.S. Chamber of Commerce, 1991), 9–10.

40. T. P. Summers and J. S. Harrison, "Alliance for Success," *Training and Development* (March 1992): 69–75.

41. B. Kuhn, "Business Growth on the Rise: Central Florida Faces Good News, Bad News Scenario," *The Orlando Sentinel,* 10 January 1994, 24; J. DeSimone, "A Boost for Business," *The Orlando Sentinel,* 31 October 1994, 8; A. Millican, "Want New Industry? House It," *The Orlando Sentinel,* 7 October 1994, 1.

42. "How Can Central Florida Position Itself to Benefit from the Merger of Martin Marietta and Lockheed?" *The Orlando Sentinel,* 5 September 1994, 4.

43. T. A. Hemphill, "Strange Bedfellows Cozy Up for a Clean Environment," *Business and Society Review* (Summer 1990): 38–45.

44. A. VanBuren, "Shareholders Seek to Color the Corporate World Green," *Business and Society Review* (Summer 1994): 45–47.

45. J. J. Davis, "A Blueprint for Green Marketing," *The Journal of Business Strategy* (July/August 1991): 14–17; J. S. Scerbinski, "Consumers and the Environment: A Focus on Five Products," *The Journal of Business Strategy* (September/October 1991): 44–47; Z. Schiller, "At Rubbermaid, Little Things Mean a Lot," *Business Week,* 11 November 1991, 126

46. T. L. O'Brien, "Aided by Computers, Many of the Disabled Form Own Businesses," *The Wall Street Journal,* 8 October 1993, A1, A9.

47. M. R. Moskowitz, "Company Performance Roundup," *Business and Society Review* (Spring 1995), 74

48. G. F. Seib and M. K. Frisby, "As Opponents Gear Up, Clinton Prepares Pitch for His Economic Plan," *The Wall Street Journal,* 5 February 1993, A1, A4.

49. M. J. Ybarra, "Janitors' Union Uses Pressure and Theatrics to Expand Its Ranks," *The Wall Street Journal,* 21 March 1994, A1, A8.

50. Business and Finance, *The Wall Street Journal,* 9 March 1996, A1.

51. "Competitiveness: 23 Leaders Speak Out," *Harvard Business Review* (July/August 1987): 116–117.

52. A. Bernstein, "Why America Needs Unions But Not the Kind It Has Now," *Business Week,* 23 May 1994, 70–82.

53. Ibid., 71.

54. Ibid., 82.

55. Lorange and Roos, "Strategic Alliances," 25–30.

56. Adapted from various sources, including: Burrows, "Good Partnership"; G. Develin and M. Bleackley, "Strategic Alliances—Guidelines for Success," *Long Range Planning* 21, no. 5 (1988):

18–23.; Lorange and Roos, "Strategic Alliances"; Treece, Miller, and Melcher, "Partners."

57. F. W. Gluck, S. D. Kaufman, and A. S. Walleck, "Strategic Management for Competitive Advantage," *Harvard Business Review* (July/August 1980): 154–161.

58. R. Hayes and S. Wheelwright, *Restoring Our Competitive Edge: Competing through Manufacturing* (New York: John Wiley, 1984), 30.

59. Taken directly from B. Avishai and W. Taylor, "Customers Drive a Technology-Driven Company: An Interview with George Fisher," *Harvard Business Review* 67, no. 6 (November/December 1989): 107–108.

60. J. Millman, "Steady Finger on the Trigger," *Forbes,* 9 November 1992, 188–189.

61. P. R. Varadarajan and S. Jayachandran, "Marketing Strategy: An Assessment of the State of the Field and Outlook," *Journal of the Academy of Marketing Science* 27 (1999): 120–143.

62. V. K. Jolly and K. A. Bechler, "Logitech: The Mouse That Roared," *Planning Review* (November/December 1992): 20–32.

63. Hayes and Wheelwright, *Restoring our Competitive Edge,* 30.

64. "KL Spring & Stamping Corporation," in *Strengthening America's Competitiveness,* 91.

65. J. Welch, L. Cook, and J. Blackburn, "The Bridge to Competitiveness—Building Supplier-Customer Linkages," *Target* (November/December 1992): 17–29.

66. W. M. Bulkeley, "The Latest Thing at Many Companies Is Speed, Speed, Speed," *The Wall Street Journal,* 23 December 1994, A1.

67. A. Fiegenbaum and A. Karnani, "Output Flexibility—A Competitive Advantage for Small Firms," *Strategic Management Journal* 12 (1991): 101–114.

68. Taken directly from T. Dewett and G. R. Jones, "The Role of Information Technology in the Organization: A Review, Model and Assessment," *Journal of Management* 27 (2001): 316.

69. A. Cortese, "Here Comes the Intranet," *Business Week,* 26 February 1996, 76–80; A. L. Sprout, "The Internet Inside Your Company," *Fortune,* 27 November 1995, 161–168.

70. Cortese, "Here Comes the Intranet"; Sprout, "Internet Inside."

71. L. G. Franko, "Global Corporate Competition: Who's Winning, Who's Losing, and the R&D Factor As One Reason Why," *Strategic Management Journal* 10 (1989): 449–474.

72. W. J. Abernathy and P. L. Townsend, "Technology, Productivity, and Process Change," *Technological Forecasting and Social Change* 7, no. 4 (1975): 379–396.

73. B. Quélin and C. Mothe, "Cooperative R&D and Competence Building," in *Strategic Flexibility in a Turbulent Environment,* ed. G. Hamel et al. (New York: John Wiley, 1998), 29–50.

74. Taken directly from S.A. Snell, M. A. Shadur, and P. M. Wright, "Human Resources Strategy: The Era of Our Ways," in *Blackwell Handbook,* ed. Hitt, Freeman, and Harrison, 627.

75. J. B. Quinn, "The Intelligent Enterprise: A New Paradigm," *Academy of Management Executive* 6, (November 1992): 241.

76. W. E. Fulmer, "Human Resources Management: The Right Hand of Strategy Implementation," *Human Resource Planning* 12, no. 4 (1990): 1–10.

77. Ibid.

78. B. E. Becker et al., "HR As a Source of Shareholder Value: Research and Recommendation," *Human Resource Management* 36, no. 1 (Spring 1997): 39–47.

79. C. Fisher, "Current and Recurrent Challenges in HRM," *Journal of Management* 15, no. 2 (1989): 157–180.

80. Ibid.

81. C. A. Lengnick-Hall and M. L. Lengnick-Hall, "Strategic Human Resource Management: A Review of the Literature and a Proposed Typology," *Academy of Management Review* 13, no. 3 (1988): 466–467.

82. Adapted from D. Woodruff et al., "Saturn," *Business Week,* 17 August 1992, 86–91.

83. A. McWilliams, D. D. Van Fleet, and P. M. Wright, "Strategic Management of Human Resources for Global Competitive Advantage," *Journal of Business Strategies* 18, no. 1 (Spring 2001): 1–24.

84. N. M. Tichy, "Setting the Global Human Resource Management Agenda for the 1990s," *Human Resource Management* 27, no. 1 (Spring 1988): 1–18.

85. L. R. Gomez-Mejia and T. Welbourne, "Compensation Strategies in a Global Context," *Human Resource Planning* 14, no. 1 (Spring 1992): 29–41.

86. R. H. Hayes, S. C. Wheelwright, and K. B. Clark, *Dynamic Manufacturing* (New York: The Free Press, 1988), 61.

87. Ibid.

Chapter *9*

Strategy Implementation: Design and Control

Learning Objectives

After reading and discussing this chapter, you should be able to:

1. Understand the dimensions of organizational structure and how they are important.

2. Select an appropriate business-level structure for an individual business unit based on the characteristics of the unit and its strategies.

3. Select an appropriate corporate-level structure that combines the individual business units of a whole corporation.

4. Develop a comprehensive strategic control system.

5. Understand the characteristics of an accident-prone organization and a few things organizations can do to control organizational crises.

Algar

Algar is a Brazilian conglomerate that owns nine telecommunications, one entertainment, six service, and three agribusiness companies. The telecommunications businesses are involved in fixed-line and cellular telephones, engineering and maintenance of communications networks, long-distance transmission, cable-TV services, call-center services, and telecommunications consulting. The entertainment arm of the company runs one of the most successful hotel and leisure properties in Brazil. The services companies are engaged in providing communications, aviation, transportation, printing, security, and networking services to a broad range of customers and municipalities. In agribusiness, Algar is involved in the production of corn and soybeans and in developing new agricultural ventures.

Algar is organized as what management calls a company network, which includes up to three levels in the management hierarchy. Departments are organized as internal minicompanies, called profit centers. Each has its own budget, goals, autonomy, and participatory management. Subtle changes in the nomenclature are consistent with the values of the company. Instead of human resources, Algar has human talents, who are not known as "employees," but rather, "associates." In this philosophy, other factors are added, such as flexible hours ("flextime"), driven by the responsibility of each associate. A "Y" career path allows maximum opportunity to pursue advancement in either the technical side of the business or in management, depending on the skills of the associate.[1]

Organizations employ a wide variety of tactics to implement their strategies. In this example, Algar is using a very decentralized management structure to enhance implementation of its unrelated-diversification strategy. Organization structure can have a powerful influence on the execution of strategy.

One of the most important activities associated with strategy implementation is designing a strategy-supportive organization. While there were a few hints at how to do this in earlier chapters, this chapter will add a great deal of understanding. It will begin with a discussion of the various formalized structures and how they can be used to support a particular strategic focus. The section will close with a few comments on some of the newly emerging organizational structures.

The final section of these two chapters on implementation will review control systems. Beyond the traditional measuring and monitoring functions, top managers use control systems to overcome resistance to change, communicate new strategic agendas, ensure continuing attention to new strategic initiatives, formalize beliefs, set boundaries on acceptable strategic behavior, and motivate discussion and debate about strategic uncertainties.[2] Therefore, control systems may also be considered "tools of strategy implementation."[3]

Organizational Design

formal structure
Specifies the number and types of departments or groups and provides the formal reporting relationships and lines of communication among internal stakeholders

Since so many activities take place within organizations, the activities and people are usually subdivided into departments and groups so that employees may specialize in a limited number of activities, and focus on a limited set of responsibilities. The **formal structure** specifies the number and types of departments or groups, and provides the formal reporting relationships and lines of communication among internal stakeholders.

Alfred Chandler was the first researcher to recognize the importance of the structure-strategy relationship.[4] According to Chandler, an organization's structure should be designed to support the intended strategy of the firm.[5] The underlying assumption is that a strategy-structure fit will lead to superior organization performance, which seems logical but has not been proved conclusively.

Several principles or dimensions may be used to characterize an organization's structure. The dimensions, described in Table 9.1, capture the formal arrangements of people, activities, and decision-making authority. Each of these dimensions represents an organizational-design decision, and these decisions have ramifications with regard to organizational behavior. For instance, decentralized decision making is likely to encourage innovation and entrepreneurship, while a high level of formalization (rules and procedures) will have the opposite influence. Also, high levels of professionalism (well-educated employees) may be needed to support a strategy of technical leadership. These are just examples. The key point here is that managers need to be very deliberate about organizational-design choices because they have ramifications on a firm's ability to execute its chosen strategies.

When making decisions about how to structure an organization, it is important to remember the following:

- Structure is not an end; it is a means to an end. The "end" is successful organizational performance.

- There is no one best structure. A change in organization strategy may require a corresponding change in structure to avoid administrative

Table 9.1   Dimensions of Organizational Structure

Dimension	Description
Hierarchy of Authority	Formal reporting relationships among levels and across functions and departments. A tall, narrow structure means that there are multiple levels between the CEO and the customer. A flat, wide structure means fewer levels and a wider span of control for managers (more people report to them). A flat structure may be associated with more use of cross-functional, self-managed teams.
Degree of Centralization	Refers to where in the structure the decision-making authority lies. A highly centralized structure means that high-level managers make most of the critical decisions. A decentralized structure puts more decision-making authority in the hands of lower-level managers and teams.
Complexity	Describes the number of levels in the hierarchy, the number of units such as departments or teams, and the number of markets served.
Specialization	The degree to which the tasks of the organization are divided into separate jobs. Some organizations have a highly specialized structure, with people focusing on one particular task or function. The advantage is that people can get very good at what they do. Other organizations expect people to be skilled in a number of tasks, which improves scheduling flexibility and teamwork.
Formalization	This might also be called bureaucracy. It describes the extent to which formalized rules, policies, and procedures exist within the organization, and the extent to which people actually follow them. A high level of formalization can lead to efficiency, but may reduce the flexibility that is sometimes required to satisfy customers.
Professionalism	Refers to the amount of formal education and training possessed by employees and managers. High-technology firms tend to have more professionalism, while firms engaged in agriculture or basic assembly tend to have less-well-educated employees.

Source: R.L. Daft, *Organization Theory and Design* (Cincinnati, Ohio: South-Western College Publishing, 2001).

inefficiencies, but the organization's size, strategies, external environment, stakeholder relationships, and management style all influence the appropriateness of a given structure. All structures embody trade-offs.[6]

- Once in place, the new structure becomes a characteristic of the organization that will serve as a constraint on future strategic choices.

- Administrative inefficiencies, poor service to customers, communication problems, or employee frustrations may indicate a strategy-structure mismatch.

TransAmerica Telemarketing had structural problems that were hurting productivity and customer service. To implement their strategy as intended, they reorganized departments and responsibilities.

 TransAmerica Telemarketing, a telemarketing and direct-mail-services firm, had its operations located in Harrisonburg, Virginia, and its administrative, account-services, and marketing support located in Washington, D.C. However, over time, the Harrisonburg operations center began to handle many of the support staff's duties because it had quick answers to clients' questions. Lack of effective communication caused a mass of confusion between offices and among clients. Also, several people at each location performed the same duties, thus causing duplication of effort. To fix the situation, the company redefined duties and created a new structure. Account services was moved to Harrisonburg, where staff could keep in constant communications with operations managers. The marketing and account-services people began to have weekly meetings. Simple changes like these allowed the marketing people to allocate all of their time to sales. In addition, customer support has improved, and efficiency has increased.[7]

owner/manager, structure
In this form, the owner is the top manager and the business is run as a sole proprietorship

The simplest management structure is the entrepreneurial, or sometimes called **owner/manager, structure.** In this form, the owner is the top manager, and the business is run as a sole proprietorship. This means that the owner/manager makes all of the important decisions and directs the efforts of all employees. A successful entrepreneur will soon need to add personnel, making the managerial task more difficult. Eventually, the owner/manager will seek to create a more formalized structure. The various structural forms can be divided into two broad groups, business-level and corporate-level. These groups are consistent in their definitions with the way we have been using the terms business-level and corporate-level in describing strategies.

Business-level structures are methods of organizing individual business units, which are often called divisions if they are part of a larger corporation. Another way to think of these units is as separate operating companies. If an organization consists of only one operating company, then its business-level structure is its corporate structure. However, as organizations diversify and form multiple operating companies, they encounter the need to create a corporate-level structure to tie these separate companies together. It is interesting to note that a single corporation could have two or more business units using different business-level structures. For example, one unit could be organized according to functions, and another unit could be using a project-matrix structure. However, the corporate-level structure would tie these and other business units together. This will become clearer as we discuss the various structures.

Business-Level Structures

The business-level structures include functional, product/market, business matrix, and network. Some of the essential characteristics, strengths, and weaknesses of these structures are presented in Table 9.2.

Functional Structures

functional structure
A business-level structure organized around the inputs or activities that are required to produce products and services, such as marketing, operations, finance, and R&D

Functional structures are organized around the inputs or activities that are required to produce products and services, such as marketing, operations, finance, and R&D.[8] Organizations that are functionally structured usually have marketing, human-resources, operations, finance and/or accounting, and R&D departments, at a minimum. The structure is centralized, highly specialized, and most appropriate when a limited product line is offered to a particular market segment and when the needs of external stakeholders are relatively stable. The functional structure is oriented toward internal efficiency and encourages functional expertise. It is particularly appropriate in organizations that want to exploit economies of scale and learning effects from focused activities. Small businesses often employ functional structures very effectively (see Figure 9.1). A functional structure can also be effective

Table 9.2   Important Attributes of Business-Level Structures

	Functional	Product/Market	Project Matrix	Network
Organizing Framework	Functional inputs such as marketing, engineering, and manufacturing	Outputs such as types of products or various markets in which they are sold	Inputs and Outputs	Outputs
Degree of Centralization	Centralized	Decentralized	Decentralized with shared authority	Very Decentralized
Competitive Environment	Tends to work better if the environment is stable and demands internal efficiency or specialization within functions	Works well in a dynamic environment with pressure to satisfy needs of particular customers or markets	Responds to both internal pressure for efficiency or specialization and external market pressure to satisfy particular needs	Competitive conditions vary substantially from region to region
Growth Strategy	Supports market penetration well	Useful for market and/or product development	Frequent changes to products and markets	Suitable for market penetration and market development
Major Strengths	—Economies of scale within departments may lead to efficiency. —Allows development of functional expertise and specialization. —Best in organizations with few products or services	—Suited to fast change in an unstable environment —High levels of client satisfaction —High coordination across functions —Best in large organizations with several products or markets	—Achieves coordination —Flexible sharing of human resources —Best in medium-sized firms with multiple products	—Allows units to focus on the specific needs of markets —Provides high levels of client satisfaction —Best in larger organizations with highly differentiated markets
Major Weaknesses	—Slow response time to environmental changes —Hierarchy overload from decisions collecting at the top —Poor coordination across departments —Restricts view of organizational goals	—Lose economies of scale —Some functions are redundant within the organization —Lose in-depth specialization within functions —May lead to poor coordination and integration across product lines	—Dual authority can cause frustration and confusion —Excellent interpersonal skills needed —Additional training required can be expensive —Time-consuming due to frequent meetings —Great effort needed to maintain power balance	—Lose economies of scale —Duplication of resources —May be hard to coordinate units when coordination is required —May be confusing to customers with locations in multiple regions where the firm operates

Source: R.L. Daft, *Organization Theory and Design* (Cincinnati, Ohio: South-Western College Publishing, 2001); R. Duncan, "What is the Right Organization Structure? Decision Tree Analysis Provides the Answer," *Organization Dynamics* (Winter, 1979): 429–431.

for a firm pursuing a market-penetration strategy because organizational scope (i.e., number of products and markets) and customer requirements will be relatively stable over time.

The functional structure is not appropriate in an environment where customer needs are diverse or changing, as when a firm is trying to provide many products or services to many different customer groups. Hierarchy overload can lead to decisions piling up at the top of the organization. Also, the functional structure may

FIGURE 9.1

The Functional Structure

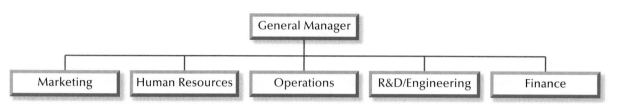

result in poor coordination across departments and thus impede the ability of the firm to adapt to changing needs. Over time, the different departments may become insular and focus on departmental goals at the expense of overall organizational goals.[9] In the late 1970s, the functionally organized maintenance activities of the U.S. Air Force's Tactical Air Command experienced just such a problem.

 In 1978, the U.S. Air Force's Tactical Air Command was responsible for a $25 billion fleet of planes, only half of which were capable of flying at any given time. Because of the aircraft shortage, TAC pilots were not getting enough flying time to keep their skill levels up. The accident rate was increasing, and frustrated pilots (trained at a cost of almost $1 million each) were leaving the service in frustration. When General W. L. Creech took command of TAC in 1978, he attributed many of the maintenance problems to the functionally structured, centralized maintenance unit. When a fighter plane needed repairs, the crew chief inspected the plane, then called a centralized maintenance unit to report the problem. If an electrical problem was suspected, then the central maintenance unit dispatched an electrician to the flight line. If the electrician discovered that a panel needed to be removed to repair the electrical problem, the electrician called the central maintenance unit to request someone from the mechanical group. If additional skills were needed, the procedure was repeated. It often took hours for all of the necessary people to arrive on the site, with expensive planes and frustrated pilots sitting idle the entire time.[10]

Product- and Market-based Structures

product/market structure
A business-level structure that organizes activities around the outputs of the organization system, such as products, customers, or geographical regions

A **product-** or **market-group structure** organizes activities around the outputs of the organization system, such as products, customers, or geographic regions.[11] When a business pursues a product- or market-development strategy, it adds products to its product line and interacts with more stakeholder groups, which may lead to administrative inefficiencies and confusion unless the organization structure is modified. It may be necessary to form smaller, more-decentralized market groups or divisions to handle the broader scope of activities and to be more responsive to the diverse needs of customers. A firm that expands its business from a regional market base to a national market base may form new units around geographic market segments. For example, a restaurant chain or retail toy chain may be divided into units responsible for eastern and western regions (see Figure 9.2a).

FIGURE 9.2

Types of Product/Market Structures

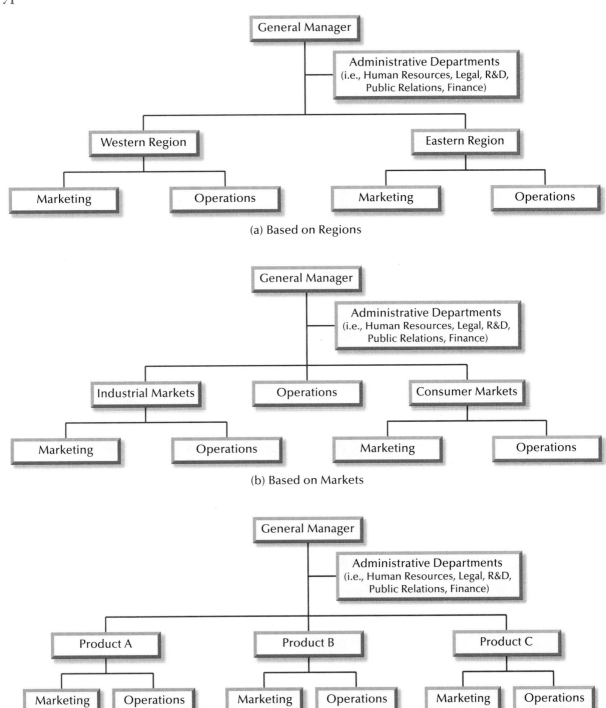

(a) Based on Regions

(b) Based on Markets

(c) Based on Products

Some firms that pursue growth through market development seek out new customer groups and new product applications. If sales to a particular new type of customer reach sufficient volume, the organization may reorganize around customer groups. For example, a soft-drink company may divide its business into "fountain" and "retail" segments, with the fountain unit targeting its marketing and sales efforts to restaurants and theaters, and the retail unit focusing on grocery and convenience stores. Similarly, a microcomputer company might organize its business around home-user, business, academic, and mail-order customer groups. Or an architectural firm might organize around commercial, military, and residential projects. When a business organizes around geographil regions or type of customer, it may continue to centralize its production or service operations in one area if economies of scale are significant (see Figure 9.2b). If not, then each geographic region or market unit may have its own operations facilities (as in Figure 9.2a).

To correct the maintenance inefficiencies described earlier, the Tactical Air Command's maintenance group was reorganized around a decentralized market structure. Technicians were assigned exclusively to one squadron. Eventually, they started taking personal responsibility for the condition of the aircraft and the safety of the pilots in their squadron. Six years later, nearly all planes were mission ready, and crashes from faulty maintenance had almost completely disappeared.[12] As illustrated in the TAC example, decentralized market activities can lead to improved service, responsiveness, and customer awareness. However, structuring around markets can lead to some complications. There is potential for duplication of staff resources, which can be expensive. Also, if the market regions or groups cultivate different strategies to serve their customers, then there may be a lack of overall organizational identity, with different segments trying to pull the organization in different directions.

A product group or division is often appropriate when a business pursues growth through product or service development. As a firm pursues product development, its product line increases, and often, as a result, its number and type of customer groups increase. A pharmaceutical company that pursues product development may eventually form one unit for cardiovascular drugs and another for cancer drugs. A bank may form separate units for personal accounts, mortgage loans, and bank cards (see Figure 9.2c). In all cases, the new organization units are intended to improve the organization's ability to respond to internal and external customer demands in a more timely and efficient manner.

Product- or market-based structures share some common strengths and weaknesses. They are suited to a fast-changing environment and lead to high coordination across functions and high levels of customer satisfaction. They are especially appropriate in larger businesses with multiple products, and are helpful if market or product development are the strategic focus. However, economies of scale are lost if operations are separated, and some functions will be redundant across locations. Also, the company loses some of its in-depth functional specialization, and coordination across product lines can be a problem.[13]

Matrix Structures

project-matrix structure
A hybrid business-level structure that combines some elements of both functional and product/market structures

A hybrid structure that combines some elements of both functional and product/market forms is called a **project-matrix structure.** The project-matrix structure is viewed by some as a transition stage between a functional form and a product/market-group structure, and by others as a complex form necessary for complex environments.[14] Either way, the many stakeholder influences that simultaneously pull an organization toward functional forms and the more diverse market/product forms reach an equilibrium in the matrix structure. Project-matrix structures are most common in turbulent or uncertain competitive environments where internal stakeholders are highly interdependent, and where external stakeholder demands are diverse and changing.[15] Matrix structures can improve communications between groups, increase the amount of information the organization can handle, and allow more-flexible use of people and equipment.[16]

In a matrix structure, the organization is simultaneously functional and either product, market, or project oriented (see Figure 9.3). Fluor Daniel, one of the world's largest engineering-design and construction companies, employs a matrix structure.

 At Fluor Daniel, it is very common for design engineers to report to two or more managers: the project manager on a particular contract, and the functional manager of their particular design area, such as electrical or mechanical systems. The dual-reporting relationships of the matrix structure emphasize the equal importance of functional-design performance and service on the particular project. The functional dimension encourages employees to share technical information from one project to the next (learning), and helps avoid unnecessary duplication of skills. The project dimension allows the organization to focus on serving the needs of the customer while simultaneously encouraging cooperation and coordination among the different interdependent functions.

Unfortunately, matrix structures can be disconcerting for employees because of the "too many bosses" problem. Power struggles may occur because it is difficult to

FIGURE 9.3

The Project-Matrix Structure

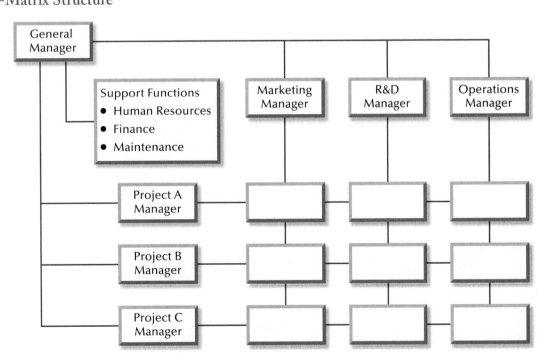

balance the different lines of authority. Matrix structures require a lot of interpersonal skill because of frequent communications. Meetings can take a lot of time, and it is sometimes difficult to coordinate the many people and schedules. The overall complexity of the structure can create ambiguity and conflict between functional and product managers and between individuals. The sheer number of people that must be involved in decision making can slow decision processes and add administrative costs.[17]

Network Structures

network structure
A business-level structure in which operating units or branches are organized around customer groups or geographical regions

Some organizations, particularly large integrated service organizations, use the network, or "spider's web," structure.[18] The **network structure** is very decentralized, and is organized around customer groups or geographic regions. As shown in Figure 9.4, a network structure represents a web of independent units, with little or no formal hierarchy to organize and control their relationship. The independent units are loosely organized to capture and share useful information. Other than information sharing, however, there is little formal contact among operating units. When formal contact is needed, committees and task forces are created on an "ad hoc" basis. The network structure is particularly appropriate in knowledge-intensive industries where decentralization and duplication of resources are required to service the market, yet manufacturing or technology economies of scale are not sufficient to drive centralization. Many large accounting firms use a network structure so that they can provide customized service to their clients based on regional needs.[19]

FIGURE 9.4

The Network Structure

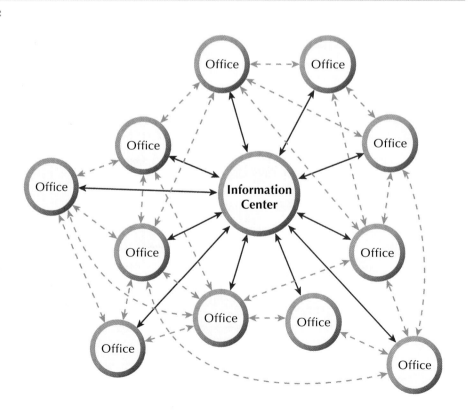

The California office of a big accounting firm aggressively recruited a particular accounting graduate not because he was a good student (in fact, he was a C student), but because he was fluent in Japanese. They needed him because they specialized in business relationships with Japan. His language ability was much more valuable in the California region than it would have been anywhere else in the United States.

A network structure allows the independent units to focus on the specific needs of the markets in which they compete, which can lead to high levels of client satisfaction. However, a network may not be appropriate when high levels of coordination and resource sharing are required. The network structure is an extreme form of decentralization, with executive-level management serving primarily an advisory function, and lower-level managers controlling most decisions. The weaknesses of the network structure include the potential for lost control of the autonomous units, a loss of economies of scale, and high costs from the extensive duplication of resources. Also, customers that make contact with more than one unit in a network structure may be confused or frustrated by the differences in approach. Network structures may be appropriate for large companies with diverse constituency needs such as universities, large medical and legal practices, investment banking, global distribution firms, consulting services, and charitable organizations such as United Way and Girl Scouts of America.

Corporate-Level Structures

Four general types of structures are used by multibusiness organizations: multidivisional, strategic business unit, corporate matrix, and transnational. Table 9.3 lists the major characteristics of these corporate-level structures.

Multidivisional Structures

multidivisional corporate-level structure
A corporate-level structure in which each business exists as a separate unit reporting to top management

If an organization has relatively few businesses in its portfolio, management may choose a **multidivisional (line-of-business) structure,** with each business existing as a separate unit. For example, a multidivisional organization may have an agricultural-chemicals division, industrial-chemicals division, and pharmaceuticals division. In this type of structure, a general manager—sometimes referred to as a divisional president or vice president—heads up each of the three divisions. Each division has its own support activities, including sales, accounting/finance, personnel, and research and development. Services that are common to all three businesses are housed at the corporate level, such as legal services, public relations, and corporate research.

International strategies are often implemented through multidivisional structures. If an organization chooses to produce and sell its products in Europe, management may form an international division to house those activities. If a firm pursues a multidomestic strategy that involves it in several independent national or regional businesses, management may form a separate division for each business. The multidivisional structure is appropriate when management of the different businesses does not require sharing of employees, marketing resources, or operations facilities.

The multidivisional structure, shown in Figure 9.5, has several advantages. By existing as a separate unit, each business is better able to focus its efforts on the

Table 9.3	Distinguishing Characteristics of Corporate-Level Strategies			
	Multidivisional	**Strategic Business Unit**	**Corporate Matrix**	**Transnational**
Number of Businesses	Few relative to the other corporate-level structures (but at least two independent businesses).	Many businesses grouped into SBUs based on commonalities such as products or markets.	Few or many businesses.	Many businesses, involvement in multiple nations.
Degree of Relatedness	No operational or marketing relatedness required; however, sometimes a low level of relatedness exists.	Related businesses are grouped into SBUs, but there may be little or no relatedness across SBUs.	Typically very high relatedness is required so that people can be transferred throughout the corporation without significant retraining or frustration.	Very high, similar to the corporate matrix and for the same reasons.
Need for Coordination Across Businesses	Typically low coordination across units; coordination required only to the extent that relatedness exists.	Coordination required within SBUs; little or no coordination required across SBUs.	Significant coordination required to make the structure work.	Significant coordination required; even more coordination than in a corporate matrix.
Expected Synergy	Financial synergy can be achieved; limited operational synergies, only to the extent that units are related and coordinated.	Financial synergy available across SBUs; operating synergy may be available within SBUs to the extent that strategies and activities are coordinated.	High operational synergies are available; may result in high levels of innovation, cost savings, or a greater ability to serve multiple markets.	High operational synergies are available; may result in high levels of innovation, cost savings, or a greater ability to serve multiple markets.

needs of its particular stakeholders, without being distracted by the problems of other businesses. Corporate-level management is freed from day-to-day issues and is able to take a long-term, integrative view of the collection of businesses. Corporate executives may monitor the performance of each division separately and allocate corporate resources for specific activities that show promise. This can lead to what is referred to as financial synergy. Financial synergy can be defined as the additional value added due to the ability to allocate financial resources to the areas that have the highest potential. The result may be increased returns, reduced risk (variability in earnings), or both.

With the multidivisional structure, it is often difficult to decide which activities will be performed at the corporate level and which ones will be held within each division. Competition for corporate resources (R&D, legal, investment funds) may create coordination difficulties among divisions. Also, organizational efforts may be duplicated, particularly when the different businesses within the corporate portfolio are highly related. It may be that shared distribution channels or common-process development could save costs for the two businesses, yet separation in the organization structure discourages cooperation.

A multidivisional structure is well suited to an unrelated-diversification strategy where there is no attempt to achieve operating synergies through coordinating

FIGURE 9.5

The Multidivisional Structure

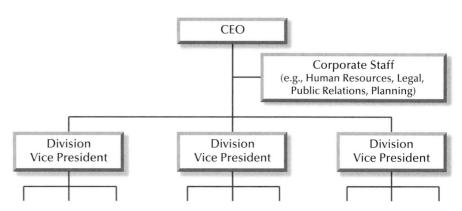

and combining activities. However, managers sometimes use a multidivisional structure while pursuing a related-diversification strategy. Unfortunately, to exploit operational synergies, managers must structure relationships among businesses and partners in ways that encourage interdependence, and manage them over time with shared goals, shared information, resource sharing, and cooperative program development.[20] The multidivisional structure makes resource sharing and cooperation difficult. Unfortunately, resource sharing and cooperation are necessary for operating synergy to occur.

Strategic-Business-Unit Structures

strategic business unit (SBU) structure
A multidivisional structure in which divisions are combined into SBUs based on common elements they each possess

When an organization is broadly diversified with several businesses in its portfolio, it becomes difficult for top management to keep track of and understand the many different industry environments and business conditions. Management may choose to form **strategic business units (SBUs),** with each SBU incorporating a few closely related businesses and operating as a profit center. Each SBU is composed of related divisions, with divisional vice presidents reporting to an SBU or group vice president. If an organization becomes very large, it may combine strategic business units into groups or sectors, thus adding another level of management. Johnson & Johnson uses an SBU structure in the management of its health-care businesses. The corporation has nearly two hundred separate operating companies that are grouped into nineteen SBUs. These SBUs are formed into sectors for pharmaceuticals, consumer products, and professional products.[21] The SBU structure is illustrated in Figure 9.6.

The SBU structure makes it possible for top management to keep track of many businesses at one time. It allows decentralization around dimensions that are meaningful to the business, such as markets or technologies. SBU vice presidents can encourage the members of the SBU to coordinate activities and share information. The intent of the structure is to provide top management with a manageable number of units to keep track of and to force responsibility for decision making lower into the organization, near the important internal and external stakeholders. Financial synergy is possible through allocating resources to the SBUs that have the greatest potential. Operating synergy is also available within SBUs, since they are

FIGURE 9.6

The Strategic Business Unit (SBU) Structure

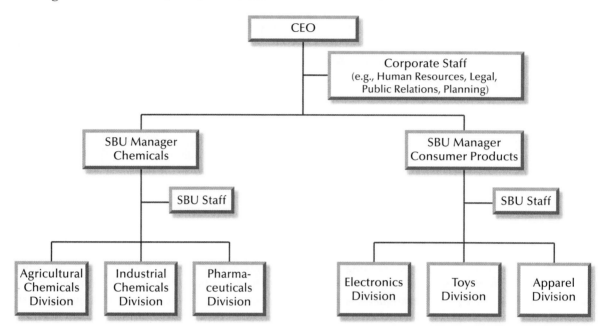

formed based on relatedness among businesses. Consequently, financial synergy is available across SBUs, while operating synergy is possible only within SBUs.

The difficulty of the SBU structure is that operating units, and therefore the customer, are even further removed from top management than in the multidivisional form. As with the multidivisional form, there is competition for corporate financial and staff resources, which may create conflicts and coordination problems. It is important to assign specific job responsibilities and expectations to business vice presidents, SBU vice presidents, and the corporate president, or conflicts may occur.

Corporate-Level-Matrix Structures

corporate matrix structure
The corporate-level counterpart to the project matrix structure described earlier; organizes businesses along two dimensions, such as product and function

The **corporate matrix** is the corporate-level counterpart to the project-matrix structure described earlier (see Figure 9.7). It is a way to achieve a high degree of coordination among several related businesses. Corporate-matrix structures are used when the individual businesses within a corporation's portfolio need to take advantage of resource, information, or technology sharing in order to succeed in their industries. The corporate-matrix structure tries to reach a balance between pressures to decentralize units closer to market and technological trends, and pressures to maintain centralized control to bring about economies of scope and shared learning.

As mentioned previously, 3M is a global company with more than twenty business units producing sixty thousand products in at least fifty-five countries. To interact with the many stakeholder groups in the different nations, 3M must have a flexible, responsive organizational structure. A 3M manager described the structure this way:

FIGURE 9.7

Types of Corporate Matrix Structures

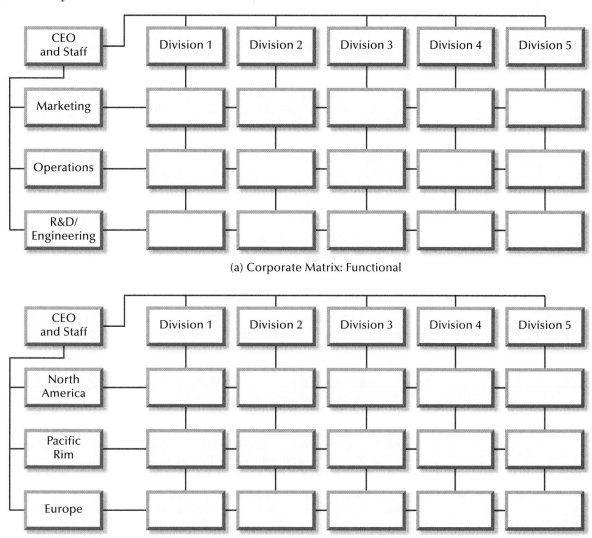

(a) Corporate Matrix: Functional

(b) Corporate Matrix: Regional

When people ask how we structure a corporation with such a disparate lot of variables, I begin by discussing 3M's matrix management structure. One side of the matrix represents the company's product divisions. Along the other axis are the international subsidiaries. For any business in an international subsidiary, responsibility is shared by the managing director of the subsidiary (who reports through area or regional vice-presidents to me as head of International Operations) and the product manager (who reports to the vice-president of his or her division).[22]

The corporate-matrix structure is particularly appropriate for related-diversification strategies and global strategies. For example, a consumer-products firm that has businesses in beverages, snack foods, and packaged foods may use a matrix structure to capitalize on economies of scale and capture operating synergies in marketing and distribution, as shown in Figure 9.7. Ideally, the corporate-matrix structure improves coordination among different internal stakeholders by forcing managers within related businesses to maintain close contact with each other. It can help the organization become more flexible and responsive to changes in the business environment, and can encourage teamwork and participation.[23]

The corporate-matrix form may also be effective in structuring a company that produces several products that are all sold in several nations. A multinational firm may create a matrix structure that groups all products under each national manager and simultaneously groups all nations under each product manager. This type of matrix structure allows the firm to achieve a national focus in its marketing and distribution practices, and encourages synergies through economies of scale and shared information within each product category. The corporate-matrix structure applied to a multinational organization is also shown in the bottom half of Figure 9.7.

Transnational Structures

transnational structure
A corporate-level structure that organizes businesses along three dimensions: nation or region, product, and function

A more complex version of the corporate-matrix structure is the transnational form.[24] Whereas the global-matrix structure organizes businesses along two dimensions, the **transnational structure** organizes businesses along three dimensions: nation or region, product, and function. The transnational form is an attempt to achieve integration within product categories, within nations, and within functions while simultaneously achieving coordination across all of those activities. As shown in Figure 9.8, the transnational form requires three types of managers who serve integrating roles: (1) country or region managers who oversee all products and functions performed in their area to maintain a focal point for customers, (2) functional managers who oversee the activities of a particular function (technology, marketing, or manufacturing) for all products in all nations, and (3) product or business managers who oversee all functions and markets supported by a particular product or product group.[25] Organizations that employ transnational structures can build three capabilities: responsiveness and flexibility at the national level; global-scale economies; and learning that transcends national, functional, and product boundaries.[26] Many large multiproduct global organizations, in industries ranging from computers to consumer products, are making the transition to a transnational structure. Xerox uses a transnational structure.

 We have created an organization that by its very design forces managers to confront—and manage—the necessary tensions between autonomy and integration. . . . In a sense, we have turned the traditional vertically organized company on its side. At one end is technology, and we have retained an integrated corporate research and technology organization. At the other end is the customer. We have organized our sales and service people into three geographic customer-operations divisions, so that we can keep a common face to the customer. Between these two poles are the new business divisions. Their purpose is to create some suction on technology and pull it into the marketplace.[27]

The corporate-matrix and transnational structures are plagued by one serious difficulty: sheer complexity may interfere with what they are designed to accomplish. It is difficult to balance the needs of the different functional, national, and product stakeholders. The unusual command structure can create an atmosphere of

FIGURE 9.8

The Transnational Structure

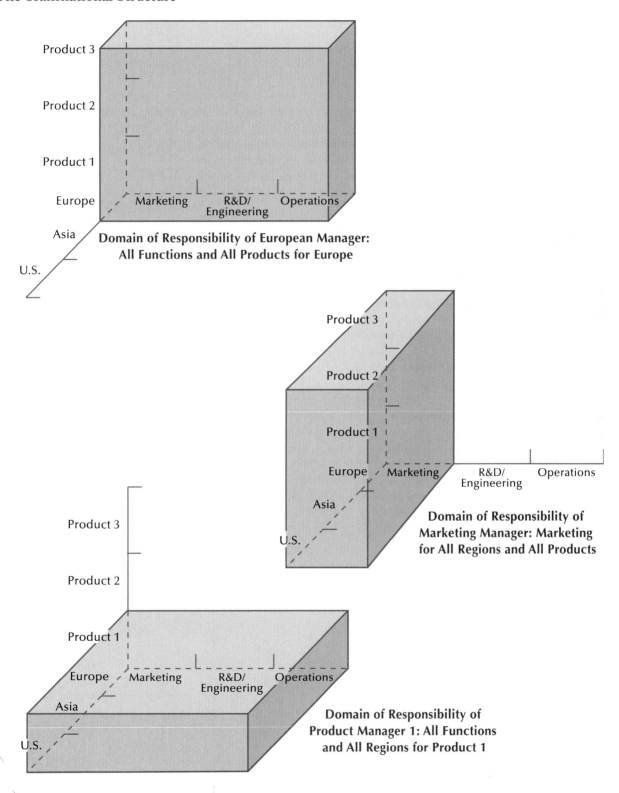

Domain of Responsibility of European Manager:
All Functions and All Products for Europe

Domain of Responsibility of
Marketing Manager: Marketing
for All Regions and All Products

Domain of Responsibility of
Product Manager 1: All Functions
and All Regions for Product 1

ambiguity, conflict, and mixed loyalties. The overall complexity and bureaucracy of the structure may stifle creativity and slow decision making because of the sheer number of people that must be involved. Furthermore, the administrative costs associated with decision delays and extra management may overwhelm the benefits of coordination.[28]

This concludes our discussion of the business- and corporate-level structures. Each of the forms contained in this section is a model that provides a general idea with regard to how to structure an organization. With the exception of the simpler forms, it would be unusual to find a firm structured exactly like one of the models in this chapter. Also, it would be unusual to find any two companies structured in exactly the same way. Organizations create their own designs based on their own needs. Also, many companies create hybrid structures that combine elements of two or more of the models discussed in this section.

Earlier chapters discussed the worldwide trends that are leading firms to increased interorganizational relationships. These trends are causing newer organizational forms to emerge. Modular-type structures outsource all the noncore functions of the organization. The organization is actually a hub surrounded by networks of suppliers. This type of structure allows the firm to minimize capital investments and focus internal resources on core activities. A second new form is referred to as the virtual type, a group of units from different firms that have joined an alliance to exploit complementary skills and resources in the pursuit of a common strategic objective. The term virtual comes from the computer industry, where computers can be programmed to seem as though they have more memory than they actually have. Paramount Communications, through strategic alliances, is currently positioning itself to exploit as many stages of the entertainment industry as possible. Modular and virtual-organizational forms present new management challenges for managers.[29]

This discussion has provided a lot of information with regard to the structural forms that might be useful in various competitive situations or in the pursuit of particular strategies. Organization structure can influence the successful execution of a strategy, but it is only one of many strategy-implementation tools. It is also important to note that the structures discussed in this section are strongly influenced by Western thought. As companies expand globally, they encounter differing perspectives on how firms should function. The following Global Insight demonstrates this with the example of *ubuntu* in South Africa. The next section describes how organizations create control systems to ensure that their strategies are both relevant and effective.

Global Insight
South African *Ubuntu*

Much of management theory is based on the writings of early-twentieth-century Western scholars whose disciplinary orientations were heavily grounded in economics and classical sociology. These writings depict *Homo sapiens* as an individualistic, utility-maximizing, transaction-oriented species. However, humans are social and communal beings. Along with rationality, we are guided by emotions such as anxiety, hope, disappointment, fear, anger, excitement, pity, and remorse. South Africa offers a unique opportunity for understanding the African concept of *ubuntu*. *Ubuntu* is rich with consideration for compassion and communality.

Ubuntu can be defined as humaneness—a pervasive spirit of caring and community, harmony and hospitality, respect and responsiveness—that individuals and groups display for one another. *Ubuntu* is the foundation for the basic values that manifest themselves in the ways African people think and behave toward each other and toward everyone else they encounter.

One of the most important attributes of *ubuntu* is the high degree of harmony and continuity throughout the system. An organizing concept of *ubuntu* is human interdependence. The driving norms are reciprocity, suppression of self-interest, and the virtue of symbiosis. Hence, it is often repeated that *umntu ngumntu ngabanye* ("a person is a person through others"). This statement conveys the notion that a person becomes a person only through his/her relationship with and recognition by others. One of the key advantages of this aspect of *ubuntu* is that people are intrinsically motivated to contribute more when they are valued members. Another aspect of *ubuntu* is that decisions are made by consensus. Although this may slow down decision making, the decision makers are more committed to the final decision. Actually, time is not as relevant in South Africa as it is to Westerners. There is a saying, "God gave the African time, and Westerners a watch."

Firms operating in South Africa need to be sensitive to *ubuntu* in their business operations. A major and costly strike at a South African mining company probably could have been avoided if top management had simply addressed the employees. According to an employee representative: "The only thing the employees wanted was for the top management to come and address us. Just to speak to us." It may also be possible for foreign firms working in South Africa to capitalize on the attributes of cohesion and respect that are so much a part of *ubuntu*. In fact, some aspects of *ubuntu* may be useful as organizations compete in other countries as well.

Source: Adapted from M. P. Mangaliso, "Building Competitive Advantage from Ubuntu: Management Lessons from South Africa," *Academy of Management Executive* (August 2001): 23–34, used with permission.

Organizational Control

control systems
Systems used to measure and monitor firm activities and processes, as well as motivate or encourage behaviors that are conducive to desired organizational outcomes; the tools of strategy implementation

As mentioned in the introduction to this chapter, top managers use **control systems** for a variety of important functions, such as overcoming resistance to change, communicating new strategic agendas, ensuring continuing attention to strategic initiatives, formalizing beliefs, setting boundaries on acceptable strategic behavior, or motivating discussion and debate about strategic uncertainties.[30] From the perspective of top executives, a strategic-control system is "a system to support managers in assessing the relevance of the organization's strategy to its progress in the accomplishment of its goals, and when discrepancies exist, to support areas needing attention."[31]

feedback control
Provides managers with information concerning outcomes from organizational activities

feedforward control
Helps managers anticipate changes in the external and internal environments, based on analysis of inputs from stakeholders and the environment

internal controls
A set of controls that firms use to guide internal processes and behaviors; specifically, behavioral, process and accounting controls

Several types of strategic control will be discussed. **Feedback control** provides managers with information concerning outcomes from organizational activities. With feedback control, managers establish objectives and then measure performance against those targets at some later time. **Feedforward control** helps managers anticipate changes in the external and internal environments, based on analysis of inputs from stakeholders and the environment. The learning processes associated with feedforward and feedback control form the basis for changes to strategic direction, strategies, implementation plans, or even the targets themselves, if they are deemed to be unreasonable given current conditions. In addition to feedforward and feedback controls, organizations make use of a special group of **internal controls**—specifically, behavioral, process, and accounting controls. These might be called functional controls, since each of them pertains to a particular functional area in the organization. Finally, this section will conclude with a discussion of crisis prevention and management.

Strategic vs. Financial Controls

A brief review of the evolution of organizational-control systems will help you to understand how they work and why so many of them fail to live up to expectations. Early in this century, the increase in diversified and vertically integrated organizations created the demand for systems that could help top managers allocate time, capital, and human resources where they were most needed. E.I. du Pont de Nemours Powder Company, formed from a combination of previously independent companies, was one of the early innovators in this area.[32] DuPont created one of the most enduring systems for controlling diversified businesses. The system was based on return on investment (ROI), which was defined as the operating ratio (return on sales) times the stock turn (sales to assets).[33] Sales cancels out, leaving return divided by assets. Using this summary measure of performance for each division, top managers could identify problem areas and allocate capital to the most successful operations and divisions.

Since financial-reporting requirements included figures for income, assets, and sales, managers could easily calculate ROI or related measures from existing data. As the multidivisional form of organization proliferated after 1950, the use of financial measures such as ROI gained wide acceptance and application.[34] In many organizations, they became the only important measure of success. In the words of Roger Smith, past CEO of General Motors: "I look at the bottom line. It tells me what to do."[35]

financial controls
Based purely on financial measures such as ROI

Unfortunately, organizational-control systems that rely primarily on **financial controls** are likely to have serious problems. The main problem with financial-control systems as a primary basis for control is that high-level managers typically do not have an adequate understanding of what must be done to improve value-adding activities within the organization. According to some control experts, financial-control measures based on accounting data are "too late, too aggregated, and too distorted to be relevant for managers' planning and control decisions."[36] Lateness refers to the long lag times between the organizational transactions themselves and the dates financial reports come out. For example, Pinkerton's didn't know they were in trouble until so much time had passed that the problem became very large.

In an effort to increase revenues, Pinkerton's engaged in a major acquisition program in 1991. They bought a host of small security-guard-contracting firms, with the intention of making the combined businesses more efficient through economies of scale. Executives were telling investors that business was booming. Instead, costs increased dramatically, and the recession hurt profit margins, but no one at Pinkerton's had any idea what was happening. The stock price fell from $36 at the beginning of 1992 to around $15 in September. A group of shareholders filed a lawsuit charging that executives misled them so that they could sell some of their own shares at an inflated price.[37]

The aggregation problem simply means that financial measures based on accounting data do not contain the detail that is necessary to make meaningful improvements to organizational processes. Finally, distortions associated with financial information are well documented (e.g., the Enron scandal). Differences in the way financial-control variables are created make meaningful comparisons difficult across departments, divisions, or companies. Also, changes in the way a department, division, or company calculates a variable from one period to the next can cause distortion. Distortion is especially evident in the way inventories, plant, and equipment are valued, and in the way overhead costs are allocated to various departments and divisions.

Ex. Going through IBM's 1999 financials, you quickly discover that the reported earnings per share of $4.12—a 25 percent increase over the previous year's—exaggerate the strength of the core business. You'll also find out that it's almost impossible to figure out what the core businesses' real earnings were. In that respect, the 1999 earnings are not unusual. You'd have the same problem figuring out 1998's true earnings, or those of just about any year you pick. And you wouldn't be alone. IBM's nearly impenetrable financial reporting has kept a cottage industry of accounting sleuths foraging through footnotes in financial statements for some years now.[38]

In addition, accounting-based financial measures sometimes prompt managers to behave in ways that are counterproductive over the long run. For example, financial measures such as ROI discourage investments in long-term research-and-development projects because expenses must be paid out immediately, while benefits may not accrue until many financial periods later.[39] Also, managers may shut down lines or cancel services that appear to be too costly, placing an emphasis on products and services that are most efficiently produced. If financial-control information is used as a part of an incentive system to reward managers, then organizations should consider adding back long-term investments such as R&D before calculating ROIs. Another alternative is to create separate accounts for longer-term-investment programs that are independent of the rest of the financial-reporting system.

Rather than establish a control system based purely on financial controls, top managers should establish a more complete strategic-control system. In the literature on strategic management, some scholars use the term **"strategic control"** to mean that corporate-level managers become integrally acquainted with the processes and operations of each of their divisions through sharing of "rich" information and face-to-face contact.[40] This kind of knowledge is necessary so that they can evaluate the performance of each division on the basis of factors that are relevant within their own companies and markets. A corporate manager that relies on this type of control puts less weight on financial controls as a source of information

strategic control
Refers to a combination of control systems that allows managers excellent control over their firms

for evaluating division performance. My use of the term "strategic control" is also based on the idea that financial controls should not be relied on exclusively to evaluate performance. They are one of many types of feedback-control systems that should be in place in an organization. The combination of control systems is what I refer to as strategic control.

Feedback-Control Systems

Anytime goals or objectives are established and then measured against actual results, a feedback-control system exists. Feedback-control systems perform several important functions in organizations.[41] First, creating specific targets ensures that managers at various levels and areas in the company understand the plans and strategies that guide organizational decisions. Second, feedback-control systems motivate managers to pursue organizational interests as opposed to purely personal interests, because they know they will be held accountable for the results of their actions. This alignment of interests reduces some of the agency problems discussed in Chapter 3. Finally, feedback-control systems help managers decide when and how to intervene in organizational processes by identifying areas requiring further attention. Without good feedback-control systems, managers can fall into the trap of spending too much time dealing with issues and problems that are not particularly important to the future of the firm.

Examples of feedback-control systems are easy to find. Budgets are feedback-control systems because they provide revenue and expense targets against which actual results are measured. Financial-ratio analysis is another example. Ratios such as ROI or a current ratio are measured against targets that are established on the basis of past performance or in comparison with competing firms. Audits are also a type of feedback-control system because firm conduct and outputs are measured against established guidelines, typically by independent auditors. Financial audits control accuracy within accounting systems, based on generally accepted accounting principles (GAAP). Social audits control ethical behavior, based on criteria that are established either totally in-house or in conjunction with activist groups, regulatory agencies, or editors of magazines that compile this sort of information (e.g., *Business and Society Review*).

Figure 9.9 contains a flowchart of activities for a feedback-control system as it applies to strategic control. The starting point is the strategic management process, beginning with establishment of strategic direction, followed by identification of basic strategies and implementation plans. Objectives are established as a part of the implementation process. Time passes, and eventually these objectives are measured against actual performance. Performance information is then used as feedback to guide the strategic management process, and the cycle continues. The steps in developing a feedback-control system for strategic control, shown in Table 9.4, will now be explained. They include determining broad goals, establishing links between those goals and resource areas or activities, setting measurable targets for each resource area or activity, and a variety of specific tasks that increase the probability that targets will be achieved.

Determination of Broad Goals

The first step in developing a strategic-control system is determining what needs to be controlled. One way to determine control factors is to ask, "If we achieve

FIGURE 9.9

Feedback Controls

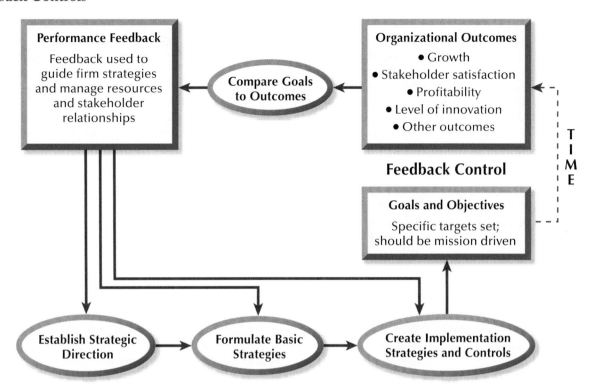

our vision, what will be different?" Robert Kaplan and David Norton have developed an approach to designing a strategic-control system that considers organizational performance from four perspectives: (1) financial, (2) customer, (3) internal business, and (4) innovation and learning.[42] Each of these performance perspectives has its own set of feedback controls, and is linked to particular stakeholder groups. For example, stakeholders who evaluate an organization's performance using financial targets will typically look to return on investment, cash flow, stock price, and stability of earnings. Customers, on the other hand, evaluate other types of information: pricing, innovation, quality, value, and customer service. From an internal-stakeholder and -processes perspective, another set of performance indicators becomes important, such as cost controls, skill levels and capabilities, product-line breadth, safety, on-time delivery, quality, and many others. From an innovation and learning perspective, an organization may consider the foundation it is building for the future, such as workforce morale, innovation, investments in R&D, and progress in continuous improvement.

While Kaplan and Norton's four areas are important and worthy of control, they do not capture everything that is important to the long-term success of a firm. The stakeholder perspective of organizations provides a fairly comprehensive view of who is important to a firm. Stakeholders that might be worthy of attention include shareholders, customers, employees and managers, suppliers, local communities, government regulators and taxing agencies, creditors, bondholders, unions, or even particular special-interest groups, among others. A company should not

Table 9.4	**Steps in Developing a Feedback-Control System**

Step	Description
1. Determine Broad Goals	If the organization achieves its vision, what will be different? Answer this question from the perspective of the organization and each of its key stakeholders. In other words, what is the organization going to do for each key stakeholder?
2. Establish Links between Broad Goals and Resource Areas or Activities of the Organization	Determine which areas are instrumental in achieving each of the broad goals. For instance, if one of the goals is to have the highest level of customer satisfaction, determine which activities, skills, and resources are needed to make this happen. Examples might be customer service, product quality, and pricing. The objective is to identify factors that can be measured.
3. Create Measurable Operating Goals for Each Resource Area or Activity.	The things that are measured and rewarded are the things that get done. Operating goals are established for each factor that was identified in the last step, including a date by which each goal should be accomplished. Monitoring systems should also be established as a part of this step.
4. Assign Responsibility	Each of the goals should be assigned to a specific manager, who is then responsible to make sure it is accomplished.
5. Develop Plans for Accomplishment	Each manager should develop an action plan for accomplishing each goal, including needed resources (technology, personnel, capital, supplies). Some resources may be available inside the organization, while others will have to be sought through outside contracts, joint ventures, or other forms of interorganizational relationships.
6. Allocate Resources	Resources should be allocated to the accomplishment of each goal, as needed.
7. Follow Up	At an agreed-upon time, each manager should report on the status of a goal. Following up also means rewarding managers and employees who are responsible for accomplishment of a goal.

establish control systems for every possible stakeholder, but only for those that are considered most important.

Examples of the kinds of broad goals an organization could set on the basis of achieving its vision include "We want to have the highest level of customer satisfaction," or "We want to give back to the community through community-service programs" or "We want to maximize shareholder return." The first goal pertains to customers, the second goal relates to the communities in which the organization operates, and the third goal pertains to shareholders.

Identification of Resource Areas or Activities

As shown in Table 9.4, the next step in establishing a feedback- control system is to identify resource areas or organizational activities that are key to accomplishing the broad goals identified in the first step. This identification of resource areas or activities should lead to factors the firm can measure, although the measures do not have to be financial in nature. For example, assume that one of the broad goals is to achieve a very high level of customer satisfaction. Specific factors that lead to customer satisfaction may include a high-quality product, excellent customer service, good value (price relative to features and quality), and excellent hands-on training or instructions. These things can be measured through direct customer surveys or interviews, quality-measurement systems, hiring a research firm, observing repeat business, or conducting competitor-comparison surveys. Notice that the factors identified as important to customers include both resources (a high-quality product) and activities (customer service, training, pricing).

Financial measures are appropriate to achieve broad financial goals. Consequently, if a broad goal is a high rate of return for shareholders, as it is in many public corporations, then things such as profitability, debt relative to assets, inventory control, and short-term cash management should be measured. Since the things that get measured are often the things that receive attention in organizations, managers need to be sensitive to the needs of stakeholders and make sure that the critical result areas identified reflect the priorities that have been established concerning satisfaction of various stakeholder needs and interests.

Sometimes a factor will need to be evaluated further so that an appropriate resource area or activity can be identified. For example, profitability is a good thing to measure, but what really causes profitability? Managers should analyze what they think are the key drivers of profitability in their industry and establish measures in those areas as well. They may determine that cost control is the primary driver, or they may decide that market reach is vital. Whichever factors they decide are most important should then become other factors to control. The same sort of thinking applies to a high-quality product. What causes high quality? These factors should be controlled also.

One of the great challenges associated with comprehensive feedback control is to determine how to measure results. Table 9.5 contains a list of stakeholder that are important to many firms, and some possible near-term and long-term measures of factors that they might find important.

Creation of Measurable Operating Goals

Once identified and linked specifically to financial, customer, internal-process, learning and other stakeholder-driven outcomes, the critical result areas become the objectives that pace strategy implementation. Vision and mission statements include broad organizational goals and lofty ideals that embrace the values of the organization. These ideals can provide motivation to employees and managers; however, they typically provide general, not specific, direction. Specific operating goals or objectives are established in an effort to bring the concepts found in the vision statement to life—to a level that managers and employees can influence and control. As time passes and operating objectives are met, then the broader goals will be met as well, and ultimately the vision will begin to be realized. By specifically linking objectives to the vision, the firm can structure a control system that is strategically relevant.

The terms "objectives" and "goals" capture the same basic concept: they each represent a performance target for an individual, a department, a division, a business, or a corporation. In fact, the term "target" is often used in practice. The important point to remember when using these words is to make sure that people understand how you are using them. In this section, a distinction is made between broad goals and operating goals. Unlike the broad goals contained in vision statements, **operating goals** in key result areas provide specific guidance concerning desired outcomes. Consequently, they are an important part of strategy implementation. Effective operating goals should be high enough to be motivation yet realistic. They should be specific, measurable, and cover a specific time period. They should be established through a participative process and should be understood by all affected employees.[43]

Goals are established at all levels in the organization. At the corporate level, they encompass the entire organization. At the business level, goals focus on the

operating goals
Established in an effort to bring the concepts found in the vision statement to a level that managers and employees can influence and control

Table 9.5   Key Result Areas and Possible Measures

Stakeholder Category	Possible Near-Term Measures	Possible Long-Term Measures
Customers	Sales ($ and volume) New customers Number of new customer needs met ("Tries")	Growth in sales Turnover of customer base Ability to control price

Suppliers	Cost of raw material
	Delivery time
	Inventory
	Availability of raw material
		Growth rate of:
		   raw material costs
		   delivery time
		   inventory
		New ideas from suppliers

Financial Community	EPS Stock price Number of "buy" lists ROE etc.	Ability to convince Wall Street of strategy Growth in ROE etc.
Employees	Number of suggestions Productivity Number of grievances	Number of internal promotions Turnover
Congress	Number of new pieces of legislation that affect the firm Access to key members and staff	Number of new regulations that affect industry Ratio of "cooperative" vs. "competitive" encounters
Consumer Advocate	Number of meetings Number of "hostile" encounters Number of times coalitions formed Number of legal actions	Number of changes in policy due to CA Number of CA-initiated "calls for help"
Environmentalists	Number of meetings Number of hostile encounters Number of times coalitions formed Number of EPA complaints Number of legal actions	Number of changes in policy due to environmentalists Number of environmentalist "calls for help"

Source: R.E. Freeman, *Strategic Management: A Stakeholder Approach* (Boston: Pitman, 1984), p. 179. Reprinted with permission of the author.

performance of a particular business unit. Goals are also developed at the functional level, where they provide functional specialists with specific targets. One of the keys to effectively setting goals is that they must be well integrated from level to level.

Once the goals and critical results areas are determined, systems for monitoring progress must be put into place. These systems typically involve the accounting, marketing-research, and information-systems departments, but other departments may be needed. Many larger organizations have an individual or department specifically devoted to strategic planning. If this is the case, then that individual or department typically coordinates the collection of data for monitoring progress.

Facilitation of Operating Goals

Goals do not get accomplished on their own. Behind each goal should be a manager with responsibility for making it happen. After managers are assigned responsibility for goal achievement, they should develop plans for accomplishment. Often these plans are evaluated and approved by higher-level managers. Plans should include a list of needed resources such as technology, personnel, capital, equipment, and supplies. Some of these resources may be available inside a department or business unit, while other resources might need to be acquired from other units of the organization. The plan might also include resource acquisition from outside the organization through purchases, contracts, joint ventures, or other types of interorganizational relationships.

The higher-level managers who assign managers responsibility for achieving a goal should also make sure that required resources are allocated. Then, at the agreed-upon time, the assigned manager should report on progress. When Jack Welch was CEO of General Electric, he used to have meetings in which goals were set. Afterward, Welch would "dispatch a highly specific written summary of commitments the manager made." Then, in following up, he would "refer to the previous summary." He used to do this consistently with dozens of managers.[44]

Reward systems should be linked to successful accomplishment of goals. While rewards are usually financial, they do not have to be purely monetary. Besides salary, bonuses, and profit sharing, recognition could include professional advancement, assignment of more responsibility or more personnel, tangible awards, and public recognition.

The purpose of all control systems is to provide information that is critical to decision making. If a control system reveals that something has changed or deviated from expectations, the managers should assess cause and effect in an effort to learn why. This will usually happen at the time goals and outcomes are compared. For example, assume that a passenger airline has established an operating goal that its planes should be 80 percent full for the first quarter of the fiscal year. At the end of the quarter, performance is at 70 percent, which causes enough concern that managers investigate the matter further. They look at other goals that were set in support of the 80 percent goal. They look specifically at marketing and other internal functions. They investigate competitor behavior and look at economic variables. Upon investigation, they discover that early indicators suggest a slowdown in the economy. The airline uses this information to revise its performance goals. In this case, an adjustment to the goal was warranted because of factors outside the influence of the organization. In other cases, adjustments to operations or marketing might have to be made.

Numerous control systems at multiple levels are necessary to keep an organization and its component parts headed in the right directions. However, they should be integrated in such a way that information can be shared. In other words, information from all parts of the organization should be accessible when and where it is needed to improve organizational processes. To enhance the quantity and quality of organizational learning, comprehensive organizational-control systems should have the following characteristics:

- Information generated by control systems should be an important and recurring item to be addressed by the highest levels of management.

- The control process should also be given frequent and regular attention from operating managers at all levels of the organization.

- Data from the system should be interpreted and discussed in face-to-face meetings among superiors and subordinates.

- The success of the control process relies on the continual challenge and debate of underlying data, assumptions, and strategies.[45]

Feedforward Control

Feedforward control helps managers anticipate what will happen in the external environment so that they can make timely adjustments to organizational strategies and goals. If good feedforward controls are not in place, managers may overlook something important, as the following example demonstrates.

> Ex. A major U.S. manufacturer of medical supplies was shocked to learn that an important Japanese competitor, Kokoku Rubber Industry, was going to dramatically increase its output through a new plant in Kentucky. As a result, the U.S. company decided to pursue a dramatic price cut in an effort to retain its share of the market. The shocking thing is that information about Kokoku's move had been available for years through a number of public sources such as newspapers. Also, some of their employees most certainly knew about Kokoku's plans, but the company had no system in place to tap this sort of knowledge. As the strategist Frederick the Great once said, "It is pardonable to be defeated, but never to be surprised."[46]

environmental discontinuities
Major, unexpected changes in the social, economic, technological, political or internal environments that necessitate change within organizations

Good feedforward-control systems are also important because of **environmental discontinuities,** which are major, unexpected changes in the social, economic, technological, and political environments that necessitate change within organizations.[47] Environmental discontinuities can also arise from inside the organization, such as the unplanned development of a new product, or a problem with labor turnover. Consequently, feedforward control also has an internal dimension.

Environmental discontinuities may lead to changes in the assumptions that underlie the organizational vision, goals, strategies, and, in some cases, organization structure and technology. For example, a merger between two competitors would cause a firm to reevaluate its goals and strategies. A serious problem with labor turnover might cause a firm to improve its wage-and-benefits plans, which would affect its cost structure. New industry regulations could influence new-product-development plans. A shortage of skilled labor could force a firm to consider investments in automation or relocate its factories. Even in stable environments, where environmental discontinuities play a minor role (e.g., production of commodities), feedforward control is essential to learning processes that allow organizations to move toward the accomplishment of their goals.

Business Intelligence and Strategic Surveillance

strategic surveillance
The process of collecting information from the broad, operating, and internal environments

business intelligence
The collection and analysis of information on markets, new technologies, customers, competitors, and broad social trends, as well as information gained from internal sources

In feedforward-control systems (see Figure 9.10), information is collected from the internal and external environments, compiled in a usable form, then compared to the premises or assumptions made by the organization. The process of collecting information from the broad, operating, and internal environments is called **"strategic surveillance."** Information gained through strategic surveillance becomes part of the business intelligence of the firm. **Business intelligence** is sometimes defined as "the collection and analysis of information on markets, new technologies, customers, competitors, and broad social trends."[48] However, a more comprehensive view of business intelligence includes information gained from internal sources and from the feedback-control system. All organizations have a business-intelligence system, although some systems are elaborate and formal, while others may be simple and informal. In many small businesses, the business-intelligence system consists of the information absorbed by the owner/manager.

FIGURE 9.10

Feedforward Control

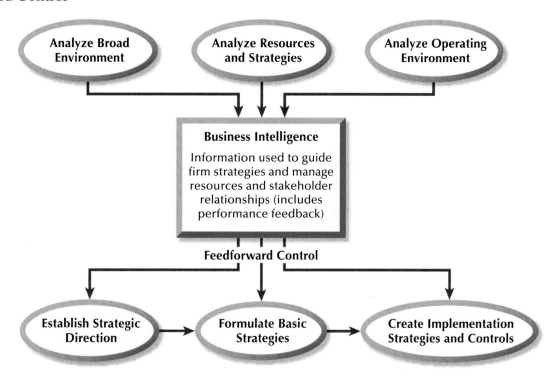

Preliminary efforts to develop business-intelligence systems include the creation of management-information systems (MIS), decision support-systems (DSS), and group-decision-support systems (GDSS). An MIS requires collection and use of information about products, services, costs, and quality, typically gathered from internal sources. Accounting-information systems are a type of MIS. DSS goes one step further in allowing individual or multiple managers to tap into databases and ask novel questions that are not answered through standard reports.[49] For example, Frito-Lay has an enormous DSS that collects sales information from ten thousand salespeople on a daily basis. The system is used by managers to fine-tune product and marketing decisions.[50]

Full-scale business-intelligence systems are similar to decision-support systems, except that their scope is comprehensive. They perform the functions of supporting the strategic-decision-making and feedback-control processes of the organization, providing early-warning signals of threats and opportunities, and tracking the actions and reactions of competitors.[51]

A well-developed business-intelligence system is a vital part of the strategic management process. Information in the system helps managers to identify strengths, weaknesses, opportunities, and threats. Also, the business-intelligence system is central to the development and application of organizational resources, which can help a company develop competencies leading to a competitive advantage. The system is also central to the strategic management activities of establishing strategic direction, developing strategies, and implementing those strategies.

Ex. Wachovia Bank uses customer-transaction data to support a modeling process that evaluates each branch's current and long-term profitability.

In Atlanta, the bank's largest market, Wachovia showed significant performance improvements when it used the outputs of the modeling process as a basis to decide which of its ninety-six branches to close and in which locations to open new ones.[52]

premise control
Use of information collected by the organization to examine assumptions that underlie organization vision, goals, and strategies

One of the most important functions of a business-intelligence system is to compare information collected to the premises, or assumptions, that underlie organization vision, goals, and strategy. This is called **"premise control."** Strategic direction and strategies are established based on premises about the organization and its external environment. These premises are assumptions about what will happen in the future, based on current conditions. For example, a firm may plan to expand its manufacturing facilities over a period of five years based on the assumption that interest rates will remain approximately the same. If interest rates change, it could make the planned expansion unprofitable. These types of situations demonstrate the need for premise control. Premise control helps organizations avoid situations in which their established strategies and goals are no longer appropriate.

 Premise control has been designed to check systematically and continuously whether or not the premises set during the planning and implementation process are still valid. Accordingly, premise control is to be organized along these premises. The premises should be listed and then assigned to people or departments who are qualified sources of information. The sales force, for instance, may be a valuable source for monitoring the expected price policy of the major competitors.[53]

The development of a business-intelligence system is a complex and difficult task, even for companies that have limited their activities to highly industrialized countries such as Japan, Germany, or the United States. However, this task is even more difficult in developing countries, where accurate information is often not readily available. Organizations have to learn to derive their information according to circumstances, relying on line managers in-house for much of what is collected. The sales force can still gather information about competitors' products, and can establish informally the level of competitors' sales. Accountants may be able to get some information through the strength of their contacts with banks. In general, successful strategic planning in developing countries relies more on fast feedback than on precision of information.[54]

The collection and dissemination of intelligence is loaded with ethical implications. People associate intelligence-gathering activities with spying. In fact, "spying" agencies such as the Central Intelligence Agency and the old Soviet KGB developed some of the most comprehensive and sophisticated information-management systems in the world. Clearly, organizations should always abide by the laws preventing surreptitious activities. But even when laws are not broken, scouting out information on competitors and customers can be laden with ethical implications. Effective information management often means organizing and making good use of available information rather than going to extreme lengths to find confidential information.

Responsibility for Intelligence Management

Responsibility for collecting and disseminating intelligence information should be assigned in a very deliberate fashion to the appropriate levels, areas, and individuals within the firm. For example, marketing departments are typically responsible for collecting information on consumer tastes and preferences; sales departments manage most of the interactions with customers; middle managers can collect information about union activities; and public-relations departments typically deal with the media, special-interest groups, and the general public. These are just a few examples of possible assignments.

chief information officer (CIO)
A high-level manager who oversees the collection, analysis and dissemination of information

Many firms have created a very high level officer sometimes called the **chief information officer (CIO)** to oversee the collection, analysis, and dissemination of information. Also, many "leading-edge" corporations are also experimenting with the creation of special units within their firms, called environmental scanning, or analysis, units. These units play a variety of different roles in the organization:

- *Public-Policy Role.* These units are assigned the tasks of scanning the environment for early detection of emerging issues that are suspected to be harbingers of widespread shifts in societal attitudes, laws, or social norms. Examples of these shifts are urban decay and women's rights.

- *Strategic Planning Integrated Role.* These units play an integral role in the corporate-wide strategic-planning process. The focus is on both the operating and broad environments. Typically, these units are required to prepare an environmental forecast and analysis for the entire corporation, to be distributed to line and/or staff executives during various stages in the planning cycle.

- *Function-Oriented Role.* The function-oriented role is just the opposite of the public-policy role. While the public-policy role means that scanning units search for broad issues, the function-oriented role focuses on only those aspects of the environment that impinge directly on the activities of one function, such as product development or public relations. These units are typically housed within the functional departments of an organization.[55]

In conclusion, feedforward-control systems take information collected through the business-intelligence system and compare it to the premises, or assumptions, that the organization is using in its strategic management activities. Business intelligence guides the development of strategic direction, strategies, and implementation plans. Top managers are already involved in a continuous process of collecting information, assessing key stakeholders, devising strategies that will satisfy their needs and desires, and delegating duties for stakeholder analysis and management. A good business-intelligence system can assist top management in these processes and in identifying external trends that will affect the organization.

Behavioral, Process, and Accounting Controls

Creation of control systems is a vital part of the implementation process. There are so many types of organizational controls that they are even hard to classify, and there is no consensus with regard to definition of terms or titles. Some controls help guide an organization's progress in the accomplishment of its goals. A special set of controls also ensures that reporting is accurate and that organizational processes are accomplished according to predetermined standards. This section describes a group of controls that are closely linked to the functional-level strategies discussed in the previous chapter. In a sense, they might be called "functional-level" controls. They include behavioral, process, and accounting controls. Figure 9.11 demonstrates that these types of control systems are created as a part of implementation planning.

Behavioral Controls

A special set of controls is used to motivate employees to do things that the organization would like them to do, even in the absence of direct supervision. They will be referred to here as **behavioral controls,** although other names could be used.[56] Behavioral controls work to encourage employees to comply with organizational norms and procedures. They are "realtime" in that they influence the employee as the job is being performed. Among the most important of these systems are bureaucratic controls, clan control, and human-resources systems.

Bureaucratic Controls

Bureaucratic control systems consist of rules, procedures, and policies that guide the behavior of organizational members. They are especially appropriate where consistency between employees is important. For example, in an effort to guarantee quality, McDonald's has established standard ways of doing everything from frying french fries to assembling orders.

Rules and procedures outline specific steps for an employee to follow in a particular situation. When a particular problem is routine or arises often, a rule or procedure may be developed so that every employee handles it in the way that is consistent with the organization strategy. Since rules and procedures outline detailed actions, they are usually relevant for very specific situations. Unusual situations and quickly changing business conditions can make an existing procedure obsolete or ineffective.

A policy is a more general guide to action. Some policies are stated in very broad terms and communicate the organization's commitment to a guiding principle. They serve to guide behavior in a general sense only (e.g., equal-opportunity employer), with specific procedures needed to translate that commitment into action. Other policies are more specific. For example, human-resource policies may

behavioral controls
A special set of controls used to motivate employees to do things that the organization would like them to do, even in the absence of direct supervision; they include bureaucratic controls, clan control and human resources systems

bureaucratic control
Rules, procedures, and policies that guide the behavior of organizational members

FIGURE 9.11

Behavioral, Process, and Accounting Controls

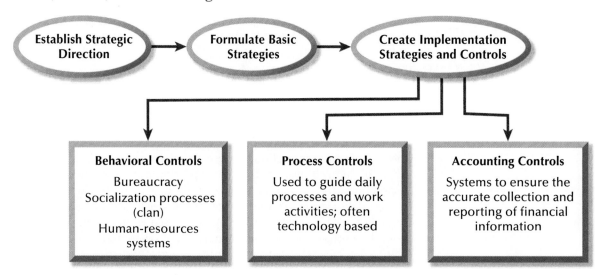

specify which employees are eligible for training programs or what employee behaviors deserve disciplinary actions. A marketing policy may specify which customers are to get priority, and an operations policy may describe under what conditions an order of raw materials will be rejected. The procedures and policies that most companies employ to govern daily activities such as check approval, returns, bid negotiations, overtime, maintenance, and customer service are all a form of concurrent control, and are intended to ensure consistency of action.

Unfortunately, many companies do not see everyday rules, procedures, and policies as "strategic." However, since they guide the decisions and actions of employees, they are a major determinant of how well strategies are implemented. For example, one of the most successful retailers in the United States, The Gap, makes extensive use of detailed procedures. The Gap replaces most of its merchandise in stores every two months. At that time, all store managers receive a book of detailed instructions specifying exactly where every item of clothing will be displayed. Company procedures also require that white walls be touched up once a week, and wood floors polished every three to four days.[57] Gap management believes this level of procedural detail is necessary to achieve consistency and high levels of performance.

It is also possible for policies and procedures to encourage behavior that works against the strategies of the firm. For example, rules and procedures may stifle employees from improving processes because they feel "rule-bound." Merchandise-return policies that alienate customers can undermine any attempt at a customer-service advantage. Purchasing policies that require bids to be awarded on the basis of price can erode quality. Frequently, reward policies create tensions among interdependent stakeholder groups.

 Several years ago, a large chemical company was pursuing an important project: a multimillion-dollar process-improvement and equipment modification. The project required around-the-clock activity by R&D and plant engineering for many months. When the product was finally commercialized, the improved product quality allowed the sales department to identify new markets and charge higher prices. After a record sales year, the marketing department, as part of a bonus-reward policy, was treated to a weekend planning session at an ocean resort with plenty of golf and tennis. The engineers and production employees who had worked around the clock were not included. The undermining of trust and respect among departments was tremendous. The success of the new process was clearly a team effort and required a team reward.

Clan Control

An expert on Japanese management provided the following description of control within Japanese firms:

> Japanese firms rely to a great extent upon hiring inexperienced workers, socializing them to accept the company's goals as their own, and compensating them according to length of service, number of dependents, and other nonperformance criteria. It is not necessary for these organizations to measure performance to control or direct their employees,

since the employees' natural (socialized) inclination is to do what is best for the firm.[58]

clan control

Socialization processes through which an individual comes to appreciate the values, abilities, and expected behaviors of an organization; closely linked to the concepts of culture and organizational ethics

According to this description, **clan control** is based on socialization processes through which an individual comes to appreciate the values, abilities, and expected behaviors of an organization.[59] Socialization also helps organizational members feel inclined to see things the same way, by espousing common beliefs and assumptions that in turn shape their perceptions. Socialization processes for existing employees take the form of intensive training; mentoring relationships and role models; and formal organizational communications including the vision, mission, and values statements. Clan control is closely linked to the concepts of culture and ethics that were discussed in earlier chapters.

Organizations that want to create, preserve, or alter their organization's culture and ethics often make use of formal and informal orientation programs, mentoring programs, rigorous selection procedures, skills and communications training, and other methods of socialization to instill commitment to organization values. The first step is to define those behaviors that the company finds important, and then stress them in selection, orientation, and training procedures. Some firms select employees on the basis of their existing personal work-related values. Other firms prefer to hire young people and then socialize them toward a required set of values that will support the culture of the organization. Either way, human-resource-management systems play an important role in controlling organizational behavior.

Process Controls

process controls

Use immediate feedback to control organizational processes

Process controls use immediate feedback to control organizational processes. For example, the warning systems that are built into navigational equipment on an aircraft tell the pilot immediately if the aircraft has fallen below an acceptable altitude. The systems don't just feed back an aggregate report at the end of the flight telling the pilot how many times the aircraft fell below acceptable standards. That aggregate feedback information might be important for some uses, such as designing new navigational systems, but it would not be useful for the pilot. Within a business environment, real-time feedback is also useful in some instances, but would be a disadvantage in others. Real-time financial feedback, for example, would make managing a business much like operating on the floor of the stock market—a frenzy. On the other hand, real-time controls in service-delivery environments and in production environments can be very useful.

Some of the most common types of process controls are those associated with production and service processes and with quality standards. Statistical process control involves setting performance standards for specific work activities. The employees performing the activities monitor their own performance and the "outputs" of their efforts. If their work is out of specification, they fix it before handing it off to someone else. In those cases, real-time controls work to encourage autonomy and improve quality and efficiency.

Other types of process controls are those associated with inventory levels and order taking. For example, the more successful mail-order firms have real-time inventory systems that allow them to know when stock is low for a particular item, so that a new order can be sent to their manufacturers as soon as needed. They also use the real-time inventory controls to give customers specific information about what items will be shipped, on what day, and when the customer will receive them.

Accounting Controls

accounting controls
Ensure that the financial information provided to internal and external stakeholders is accurate and follows generally accepted accounting practices (GAAP)

Well-devised **accounting controls** are an essential part of an organization's complete control system. They are supposed to ensure that the financial information provided to internal and external stakeholders is accurate and follows generally accepted accounting practices (GAAP). In the United States and many other countries, accounting systems and reports are audited by public accounting firms. If these firms give a company a clean bill of health, then, in theory, investors and the financial community can have confidence in what is reported. When apparent inconsistencies are found, tension and other problems can be created.

 Xerox Corp. dismissed its longtime auditor KPMG LLP amid continuing tension with the accounting firm over whether Xerox had taken adequate steps to shore up accounting in the wake of a financial scandal. The firing of its auditor, an unusual action among large corporations, signals Xerox still is struggling to put behind it the accounting woes that have afflicted it for more than a year. The company remains the subject of a wide-ranging probe by the Securities and Exchange Commission. . . . In a Friday SEC filing that announced the auditor shift, Xerox revealed that KPMG in recent months had leveled a range of criticisms of the copier company's accounting practices, having found "material weaknesses in the company's internal control systems," along with a failure by Xerox management to set "the appropriate tone with respect to financial reporting."[60]

With the collapse of Enron, the business community learned a sad lesson about what can happen when accounting controls are inadequate or are not used correctly. Arthur Andersen did not behave appropriately as an auditor, and employees and shareholders (many of whom were the same people) were the biggest losers. However, the Enron scandal set off a fury of interest in financial accounting, and reforms are under way to help prevent such situations in the future.[61] It is interesting to note that firms pay their own auditors. Consequently, as the KPMG example illustrates, there is pressure on an auditor to be reasonable in order to maintain the account.

A broader discussion of effective auditing procedures and policies is beyond the scope of this book; however, strategic managers need to ensure that adequate financial controls are in place and are being implemented correctly. The Enron environment was described as "ripe for abuse."[62] Also, we learn from Enron that managers should thoroughly understand where financial figures are coming from and what they mean. It is fairly apparent from the scandal that although they may have known more about finances than they admitted to at first, many high-ranking officials at Enron really didn't completely understand the financial information they were receiving.

Figure 9.12 shows how all the types of control systems fit together into a system of complete organizational control. At the top of the figure are the feedforward controls that were discussed in this section. Information is collected from the broad and operating environments, based on an analysis of internal resources and strategies. This information, in addition to information from the feedback-control system, becomes business intelligence. Intelligence information is used to guide strategic direction and formulate strategies and implementation plans. Moving to the bottom of the figure, as a part of strategy implementation, behavioral, process, and accounting controls are established. Specific operating goals and objectives are also set.

These goals form the basis for feedback control. The feedback-control process is to the right side of the figure. After a period of time, firm performance is measured and compared to the goals that were set. Variations are examined through an assessment of cause and effect. This feedback-performance information then becomes a part of business intelligence.

FIGURE 9.12

How Control Elements Fit Together

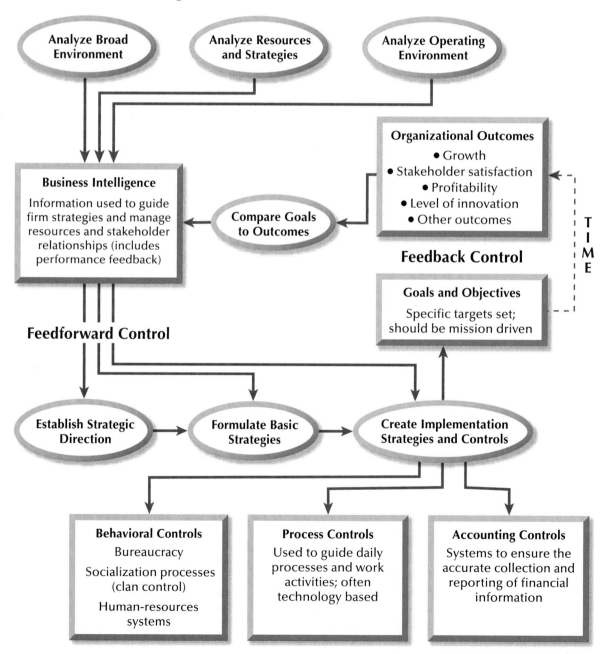

A well-designed strategic-control system should provide feedback for ongoing, iterative adjustments in direction, resource allocations, and management priorities. When performance suffers, a strategic-control system may provide early warnings of performance problems, but it cannot prevent them entirely. Most of this section has described techniques that organizations use to deal with change. Strategic-control systems help companies anticipate changes (feedforward control) and control change processes through establishing and monitoring goals (feedback control). Organizational crises are another type of change that require an immediate response from managers. The final section deals with how to prevent and manage crises.

Crisis Prevention and Management

organizational crises
Critical situations that threaten high priority organizational goals, impose a severe restriction on the amount of time in which key members of the organization can respond and contain elements of surprise

Organizational crises are critical situations that threaten high-priority organizational goals, impose a severe restriction on the amount of time in which key members of the organization can respond, and contain elements of surprise.[63] While crises such as natural disasters can sometimes be avoided, they are hard to control. On the other hand, managers have at least some control over the incidence and resolution of human-induced organizational crises. Examples of these types of crises include the explosion of the space shuttle *Challenger,* the injection of cyanide into Tylenol pain capsules, and the explosion of the Chernoble nuclear reactor in the Soviet Union.

crisis management
Processes associated with preventing, detecting or recovering from crises

Figure 9.13 contains a model of the five phases of **crisis management.** Firms that ignore crises until they are involved in one will spend most of their time in the containment and recovery stages, essentially mopping up the damage. On the other hand, crisis-prepared companies establish early-detection systems and prepare for crises, or even prevent them from occurring (left side of the model). The learning processes depicted at the bottom of the model are similar to the cause-and-effect processes in the model of feedback control introduced at the beginning of this chapter. An organization that learns from crises can improve its ability to prevent, detect, and recover from them.

FIGURE 9.13

The Five Phases of Crisis Management

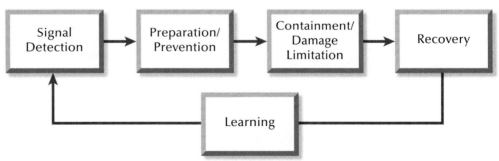

Source: Reprinted from "Crisis Management: Cutting Through the Confusion," by I. I. Mitroff, *MIT Sloan Management Review* (Winter 1988), p. 19, by permission of publisher. Copyright © 1988 by the Sloan Management Review Association. All rights reserved.

Some organizations are crisis-prone. Studies conducted at the University of Southern California Center for Crisis Management have identified crisis-prone organizations as those having the following characteristics:

- If these organizations prepare at all, they prepare for only a few of the possible types of crises. Furthermore, their preparations are fragmented and compartmentalized.

- They focus on only one aspect of a crisis, and only after it has already occurred.

- They consider only technical factors (as opposed to human or social) in the cause or prevention of crises.

- They consider few, if any, stakeholders in an explicit fashion.[64]

With regard to stakeholders, the key questions organizations should ask are: "Who are the individuals, organizations, groups, and institutions that can affect as well as be affected by CM (crisis management)? Can the stakeholders who will be involved in any crisis be analyzed systematically?"[65] As in other types of stakeholder management, open communication with important stakeholders is essential to success.

Organizations can take steps to control organizational crises. These activities fall into the categories of strategic actions, technical and structural actions, evaluation and diagnostic actions, communication actions, and psychological and cultural actions. Examples of these types of actions are found in Table 9.6. Above all, organizations have to plan ahead for things that might happen. Because of advance planning, Merrill Lynch was up and running when the U.S. stock market reopened on September 17, 2001, after the September 11 disaster that devastated New York City.

In the 1950s and 1960s, the surest way to get a job at Merrill Lynch was to be an ex-marine; the place was full of them. Though that is no longer the case, Merrill employees still pride themselves on being good marines. Like those graduates of Parris Island, they had planned for worst-case scenarios long ago. In 1999, Merrill installed a global-trading platform that meant all its business was on the same system—and that the system would operate even if part of it went down. And Merrill's chief technology officer, John McKinley, was well versed in disaster planning. The firm had prepared for all kinds of problems: loss of power, loss of water, loss of voice and data communications, loss of an entire builiding.[66]

In summary, organizational crises have the potential to thwart organizational efforts toward the accomplishment of goals. However, the Japanese symbol for crisis is made up of two characters. One elaborate character symbolizes threats, and one simple character symbolizes opportunities. Crisis-prevention and -management programs represent yet another opportunity for organizations to develop distinctive competencies. Distinctive competencies in these areas may be hard to detect, because it is hard to measure, in financial terms, savings from a disaster that does not occur or whose negative effects are reduced. However, as more and more organizations suffer blows from large-scale crises, it is evident that effective crisis prevention and management are critical to steady long-term performance.

Summary

This chapter described the organizational structures and control systems that are used in implementing strategies. In configuring the relationships among departments

Table 9.6 Crisis Management Strategic Checklist	
Strategic Actions 1. Integrate crisis management (CM) into strategic planning processes 2. Integrate CM into statements of corporate excellence 3. Include outsiders on the board and on CM teams 4. Provide training and workshops in CM 5. Expose organizational members to crisis simulations 6. Create a diversity or portfolio of CM strategies **Technical and Structural Actions** 1. Create a CM team 2. Dedicate budget expenditures for CM 3. Establish accountabilities for updating emergency policies/manuals 4. Computerize inventories of CM resources (e.g., employee skills) 5. Designate an emergency command control room 6. Assure technological redundancy in vital areas (e.g., computer systems) 7. Establish working relationships with outside experts in CM **Evaluation and Diagnostic Actions** 1. Conduct legal and financial audit of threats and liabilities 2. Modify insurance coverage to match CM contingencies 3. Conduct environmental impact studies	4. Prioritize activities necessary for daily operations 5. Establish tracking system for early warning signals 6. Establish tracking system to follow up past crises or near crises **Communication Actions** 1. Provide training for dealing with the media regarding CM 2. Improve communication lines with local communities 3. Improve communication with intervening stakeholders (e.g., police) **Psychological and Cultural Actions** 1. Increase visibility of strong top management commitment to CM 2. Improve relationships with activist groups 3. Improve upward communication (including "whistleblowers") 4. Improve downward communication regarding CM programs/accountabilities 5. Provide training regarding human and emotional impacts of crises 6. Provide psychological support services (e.g., stress/anxiety management) 7. Reinforce symbolic recall/corporate memory of past crises/dangers **Source:** I. I. Mitroff and C. Pearson, "From Crisis Prone to Crisis Prepared: A Systematic and Integrative Framework for Crisis Management," *Academy of Management Executive* (February 1993), p. 58. Used with permission.

in a single business, organizations usually employ a variation of one of the following structures: functional, product/market group, project matrix, or network. Each of the structures exhibits strengths, weaknesses, and fits with particular strategic choices. The functional form encourages functional specialization and focus, but discourages coordination between functions or departments. The product/market-group structures divide products and markets into smaller, more-manageable subunits that may improve service to customers but result in resource duplication. The project-matrix structure employs a dual-reporting relationship that is intended to balance functional focus and expertise with responsiveness to customer needs. However, it is expensive and may create ambiguity and slow decision making if managed improperly. The network structure is a very decentralized form that is particularly well suited to geographically dispersed offices, stores, or units that, except for some sharing of information and operating policies, operate independently. The network structure may result in extreme resource duplication and missed opportunities for sharing and learning.

In structuring relationships among multiple business units, managers attempt to create independence so that organizations are free and unencumbered, or to create interdependence to exploit operating synergies. Multidivisional and strategic-business-unit (SBU) structures divide businesses into divisions. The multidivisional structure creates the potential for financial synergy as managers allocate financial resources to the most promising divisions; however, the business units are typically so independent and share so few resource similarities that coordination and resource sharing among businesses is difficult. Consequently, operating synergy across divisions is hard to achieve. The SBU structure combines divisions into groups based on commonalities, thus allowing for the creation of operating synergy within an SBU. Corporate-matrix and transnational structures are intended to exploit economies, learning, and resource sharing across businesses; however, they require extra measures of coordination to avoid divided loyalties, slow decision making, and management conflicts.

Strategic controls consist of systems to support managers in tracking progress toward organizational vision and goals, and ensuring that organizational processes and the behavior of organizational members are consistent with those goals. Feedforward control helps managers anticipate changes in the external and internal environments, based on analysis of inputs from stakeholders and the remote environment. Feedback control provides managers with information concerning outcomes from organizational activities, which is then used as a basis for comparison with the targets that have been established. The learning processes associated with strategic control form the basis for changes to strategic direction, strategies, implementation plans, or even the goals themselves, if they are deemed to be unreasonable given current conditions. Control systems are developed at the corporate, business, functional, and operating levels in a company. These systems should be integrated in such a way that information can be shared. In other words, information from all parts of the firm should be accessible when and where it is needed to improve organizational processes. Goals should also be integrated from one level to the next and across the firm.

Development of a feedback-control system entails determining broad goals based on strategic direction, establishing links between broad goals and resource areas or organizational activities, setting measurable goals for each resource area or activity, assigning responsibility for completion of each goal to individual managers, allowing those managers to develop plans for accomplishment and allocating resources to them, and following up to ensure completion and provide rewards. The factors that are to be controlled should reflect the interests of various stakeholder groups inside and outside of the organization.

Closely related to the functional strategies are a special type of process controls that might be called "functional controls." These are internal systems that encourage accuracy in processes and reporting, as well as motivating employees to make decisions and behave in a way that will move the organization in the intended directions. They include behavioral controls such as bureaucratic controls and clan control, as well as process and accounting controls.

Crisis-prevention and -management systems are a special type of controls, specifically designed to prevent major disasters. Organizational crises are critical situations that threaten high-priority organizational goals, impose a severe restriction on the amount of time in which key members of the firm can respond, and contain elements of surprise. Companies can take steps to control organizational crises. Crisis-prevention and -management activities fall into the general categories of strategic actions, technical and structural actions, evaluation and diagnostic actions, communication actions, and psychological and cultural actions. While the potential for crisis is a threat to an organization, effective crisis prevention and management may also represent an opportunity to develop a distinctive competence.

Discussion Questions

1. Describe each of the dimensions of organizational structure. How are they important?

2. Use the resources of your college library and selected interviews in your community to describe each of the dimensions of organizational structure for a bank and a department store. How and why do the structures differ?

3. For each of the business-level structures presented in this chapter, discuss strengths and weaknesses, and when each structure might be most appropriate.

4. What are the primary differences between the functional structure and the product/market structure? How is a project-matrix structure a combination of the two?

5. Discuss the distinguishing characteristics of each of the corporate-level structures presented in this chapter.

6. How are the multidivisional and SBU structures the same? How are they different? When would one structure be more appropriate than the other?

7. How are the corporate-matrix and transnational structures the same? How are they different? When would one structure be more appropriate than the other?

8. What is a strategic-control system? Give examples.

9. Describe the problems associated with traditional accounting-based financial controls. Are they ever appropriate? In what circumstances?

10. What is feedback control? Describe the steps associated with developing a feedback-control system.

11. What are some of the most important factors that require feedback control in organizations? Name at least five, including the stakeholder perspectives they represent.

12. What is a business-intelligence system? For instance, where does business intelligence come from, and how is it used?

13. What are the characteristics of accident-prone organizations? Name ten things companies can do to control organizational crises.

Strategic Application

Development of a Business-Level Structure

Randy Bon owns a factory in the western United States that builds office furniture and distributes it across the country. He has five managers who report directly to him. Nancy Woo is responsible for finances and accounting and has five people working for her. Jon Straight takes care of marketing. He has fifteen sales agents spread around the country and an advertising specialist. Palmina Argyle-Hernandez runs the factory on a day-to-day basis. She has five supervisors and four hundred employees in the factory. She also has a purchasing department of three people who report to her directly. Shipping of products is subcontracted to a trucking company. R.J. Nargundkar is an attorney and handles all contractual and legal issues. Finally, Jostyn Amos heads up a staff of four in personnel. Create a functionally oriented organization chart that reflects this information.

The factory is no longer large enough to meet demand. Furthermore, Mr. Straight has found through some market research that furniture styles are very different in the western United States than they are in the eastern United States. Create a new organization structure that resolves these problems.

Strategic Internet Application

Use an Internet search engine, such as www.Google.com, to locate information on a recent and well-known organizational crisis. Remember that crises are defined as critical situations that threaten high-priority organizational goals, impose a severe restriction on the amount of time in which the organization can respond, and contain elements of surprise. If the crisis is well known, you should be able to find numerous articles written about it through Web site links to local and national newspapers, among other sources. After reading several articles about the crisis and the way the organization responded to it, identify each of the five phases of crisis management, as follows:

1. At what point and how did the organization detect the crisis?

2. What actions did the firm take to try to prevent damage from the crisis?

3. What actions did the firm take to try to contain damage from the crisis?

4. Has the firm recovered from the crisis? If so, how much time elapsed before the firm recovered, and what did the firm do during recovery? If not, what can the firm do to speed recovery?

5. What should the firm have learned from the crisis?

Notes

1. Adapted from Algar, *Social Report* (2000). This document is published by Algar of Brazil and provided to the public free of charge.

2. R. Simons, "How New Top Managers Use Control Systems As Levers of Strategic Renewal," *Strategic Management Journal* 15 (1994): 169–189.

3. R. Simons, "Strategic Orientation and Management Attention to Control Systems," *Strategic Management Journal* 12 (1991): 49–62.

4. B. Keats and H. M. O'Neill, "Organizational Structure: Looking through a Strategy Lens," in *The Blackwell Handbook of Strategic Management*, ed. M.A. Hitt, R. E. Freeman, and J. S. Harrison (Oxford: Blackwell Publishers, 2001), 520–542.

5. A. D. Chandler, *Strategy and Structure: Chapters in the History of the American Industrial Enterprise* (Cambridge, Mass.: The MIT Press, 1962).

6. P. R. Lawrence and J. W. Lorsch, *Organization and Environment* (Homewood, Ill.: Irwin, 1969), 23–39.

7. Adapted from "TransAmerica Telemarketing, Inc.," in *Strengthening America's Competitiveness*

(Warner Books on behalf of Connecticut Mutual Life Insurance and the U.S. Chamber of Commerce, 1991), 28.

8. A. C. Hax and N. S. Majluf, *The Strategy Concept and Process: A Pragmatic Approach* (Englewood Cliffs, N.J.: Prentice Hall, 1991).

9. R. Duncan, "What Is the Right Organization Structure? Decision Tree Analysis Provides the Answer," *Organization Dynamics* (Winter 1979): 429–431.

10. Adapted from J. Finegan, "Four Star Management," *Inc,* January 1987, 42–51.

11. Hax and Majluf, *Strategy Concept and Process.*

12. Finegan, "Four Star Management."

13. "Right Organization Structure?"

14. J. R. Galbraith and R. K. Kazanjian, *Strategy Implementation: Structure, Systems, and Processes,* 2nd ed. (St. Paul, Minn: West Publishing Company, 1986).

15. R. L. Daft, *Organization Theory and Design,* 3d ed. (St.Paul, Minn.: West Publishing, 1989), 240.

16. R. C. Ford and W. A. Randolph, "Cross-functional Structures: A Review and Integration of Matrix

Organization and Project Management," *Journal of Management* 18, no. 2 (1992): 267–294.

19. Ibid.

20. C. W. L. Hill, M. A. Hitt, and R. E. Hoskisson, "Cooperative versus Competitive Structures in Related and Unrelated Diversified Firms," *Organization Science* 3, no. 4 (November 1992): 501–521.

21. J. Weber, "A Big Company that Works," *Business Week,* 4 May 1992, 124–132; Johnson & Johnson, *Annual Reports* (1990–1991).

22. H. Hammerly, "Matching Global Strategies with National Responses," *The Journal of Business Strategy* (March/April 1992): 10.

23. Ford and Randolph, "Cross-functional Structures."

24. C. A. Bartlett and S. Ghoshal, *Managing Across Borders: The Transnational Solution,* (Boston: Harvard Business School Press, 1989).

25. C. A. Bartlett and S. Ghoshal, "The New Global Manager," *Harvard Business Review* (September/October 1992): 124–132.

26. Ibid.

27. Taken directly from R. Howard, "The CEO As Organizational Architect: An Interview with Xerox's Paul Allaire," *Harvard Business Review* (September/October 1992): 112.

28. Ford and Randolph, "Cross-functional Structures."

29. G. G. Dess et al., "The New Corporate Architecture," *Academy of Management Executive* 9, no. 3 (1995): 7–20.

30. Simons, "New Top Managers."

31. P. Lorange, M. F. Scott Morton, and S. Ghoshal, *Strategic Control* (St. Paul, Minn.: West Publishing, 1986), 10.

32. H. T. Johnson and R. S. Kaplan, *Relevance Lost: The Rise and Fall of Management Accounting* (Boston: Harvard Business School Press, 1987), 10–18.

33. J. F. Weston and E. F. Brigham, *Essentials of Managerial Finance,* 7th ed. (Hinsdale, Ill.: The Dryden Press, 1985), 154.

34. O. E. Williamson, *Markets and Hierarchies: Analysis and Antitrust Applications* (New York: The Free Press, 1975).

35. A. Lee, *Call Me Roger* (Chicago: Contemporary Books, 1988), 110.

36. Johnson and Kaplan, *Relevance Lost,* 1.

37. A. Barrett, "Feeling a Bit Insecure: Overexpansion and Too Rosy Forecast Plague Pinkerton," *Business Week,* 28 September 1992, 69–72; "Bogie's Men: Pinkerton," *The Economist,* 5 October 1991, 73; "Pinkerton's Reports Earnings Pressures, Revises 1992 Earnings Expectations," *Newswire,* 19 June 1992, 0618A1456; "Two Investors Charge Pinkerton's Misled Them to Inflate Stock," *The Wall Street Journal,* 26 June 1992, A7

38. Taken directly from B. McLean, "Hocus Pocus: How IBM Grew 27% a Year," *Fortune,* 26 June 2000, 165–166.

39. R. E. Hoskisson and M. A. Hitt, "Strategic Control and Relative R&D Investment in Large Mulitproduct Firm," *Strategic Management Journal* 6 (1988): 605–622.

40. M. A. Hitt et al., "The Market for Corporate Control and Firm Innovation," *Academy of Management Journal* 39 (1996): 1084–1119.

41. M. Goold and J. J. Quinn, "The Paradox of Strategic Controls," *Strategic Management Journal* 11 (1990): 43–57.

42. R. S. Kaplan and D. P. Norton, "Putting the Balanced Scorecard to Work," *Harvard Business Review* (September/October 1993): 134–147.

43. G. P. Latham and E. A. Locke, "Goal Setting—A Motivational Technique That Works," *Organizational Dynamics* (Autumn 1979): 68–80; M. D. Richards, *Setting Strategic Goals and Objectives,* 2d ed. (St. Paul, Minn.: West Publishing 1986); M. E. Tubbs, "Goal Setting: A Meta-Analytic Examination of Empirical Evidence," *Journal of Applied Psychology* 3 (1986): 474–475.

44. G. Colvin, "The Ultimate Manager," *Fortune,* 22 November 1999, 187.

45. Simons, "Strategic Orientation," 50.

46. R. S. Teitelbaum, "The New Race for Intelligence," *Fortune,* 2 November 1992, 104; "North American Supplies Directory Index," www.devicelink.com /company98/h/h00092.html, 20 January 2002.

47. Lorange, Scott Morton, and Ghoshal, *Strategic Control,* 2–8.

48. S. Ghoshal and S. K. Kim, "Building Effective Intelligence Systems for Competitive Advantage," *Sloan Management Review* (Fall 1986): 49.

49. J. P. Stamen, ""Decision Support Systems Help Planners Hit Their Targets," *The Journal of Business Strategy* (March/April 1990): 30–33.

50. J. Rothfeder, J. Bartimo, and L. Therrien, "How Software Is Making Food Sales a Piece of Cake," *Business Week,* 2 July 1990, 54–55.

51. J. P. Herring, "Building a Business Intelligence System," *Journal of Business Strategy* (May/June 1988): 4–9.

52. Taken directly from T. H. Davenport et al., "Data to Knowledge to Results," *California Management Review* 43, no. 2(Winter 2001): 118.

53. Taken directly from G. Schreyogg and H. Steinmann, "Strategic Control: A New Perspective," *Academy of Management Review* 12 (1987): 96.

54. W. R. Haines, "Making Corporate Planning Work in Developing Countries," *Long Range Planning* (April 1988): 91–96.

55. R. T. Lenz and J. L. Engledow, "Environmental Analysis Units and Strategic Decision-making: A Field Study of Selected 'Leading-Edge' Corporations," *Strategic Management Journal* 7 (1986): 69–89.

56. V. Govindarajan and J. Fisher, "Strategy, Control Systems, and Resource Sharing: Effects on Business Unit Performance," *Academy of Management Journal* 33 (1990): 259–285.

57. R. Mitchell, "Inside the Gap," *Business Week,* 9 March 1992, 58–64.

58. W. G. Ouchi, "Markets, Bureaucracies, and Clans," *Administrative Science Quarterly* 25 (1992): 129–141.

59. P. McDonald and J. Gandz, "Getting Value from Shared Values," *Organization Dynamics* (Winter 1992): 60–71.

60. Taken directly from W. M. Bulkeley and M. Maremont, "Xerox Fires Auditor KPMG As Tension Continues," *The Wall Street Journal,* 8 October 2001, A3.

61. A. Bernstein and B. Grow, "Bracing for a Backlash," *Business Week,* 4 February 2002; J. R. Emshwiller and R. Smith, "Behind Enron's Fall, A Culture of Operating Outside Public's View," *The Wall Street Journal,* 5 December 2001, A1, A10; T. Hamburger and J. Weil, "Second Executive Tells of Andersen E-Mail," *The Wall Street Journal,* 21 January 2002, A3; B. McLean, "Why Enron Went Bust," *Business Week,* 24 December 2001, 59; M. Maremont, J. Hechinger, and K. Damato, "Amid Enron's Fallout, and a Sinking Stock, Tyco Plans a Breakup," *The Wall Street Journal,* 23 January 2002, A1, A4; R. Smith and J.R. Emshwiller, "Internal Probe of Enron Finds Wide-ranging Abuses," *The Wall Street Journal,* 4 February 2002, A3.

62. J. A. Byrne and M. France, "The Environment Was Ripe for Abuse," *Business Week,* 25 February 2002, 118.

63. C. F. Hermann, ed., *International Crises: Insights from Behavioral Research* (New York: The Free Press, 1972).

64. I. I. Mitroff and C. Pearson, "From Crisis Prone to Crisis Prepared: A Systematic and Integrative Framework for Crisis Management," *Academy of Management Executive* 7 00 (February 1993): 48–59.

65. Ibid.

66. D. Rynecki, "The Bull Fights Back," *Fortune,* 15 October 2001, 132.

Chapter *10*

Global Strategic Management and The Future

Learning Objectives

After reading and discussing this chapter, you should be able to:

1. Appreciate the major trends in global strategic management and why internationalization is important.

2. Recognize the stage of global development of a particular firm.

3. Understand how to create a global mindset in firms.

4. Understand the roles of foreign subsidiaries.

5. Select an international expansion tactic that is appropriate to a competitive situation.

6. Analyze a foreign country to determine its attractiveness for investment.

Wal-Mart

Wal-Mart has experienced serious difficulties trying to enter global markets. In the past, rivals in many countries have scoffed at the American giant due to its "cookie-cutter" outlets that did little to adapt to local needs and customs. According to Hong Sun Sang, assistant manager for E-mart, a large South Korean chain, "We don't see Wal-Mart as a threat anymore." Wal-Mart learned some hard lessons about differences in consumers, regulators, and suppliers in international markets. However, Wal-Mart has learned from mistakes and kept trying. In 2001, Wal-Mart expected to open 120 stores outside the United States, about 26 percent of its total capital expenditures of $9 billion. With $32 billion in international sales, the company is now the largest retailer in Canada and Mexico. Things began to improve in a big way when John B. Menzer, chief financial officer, was put in charge of the international division. Menzer tightened financial discipline and decentralized operating authority. He is building a firstrate management team and spreading "best practices" developed in the United States and elsewhere throughout the world.

Wal-Mart's aggressive-growth strategies are reshaping some foreign markets. "Shopkeeper Carlos Huerta recently walked into a Sam's Club warehouse store here [Mexico City] and bought $6,000 worth of Act II brand microwave popcorn. Then he trundled across the street to resell it at his stall in Latin America's biggest wholesale market. Mr. Huerta used to buy the U.S.-made popcorn direct from the manufacturer's distributor here. But with the U.S.-Mexican border growing increasingly porous, Wal-Mart Stores Inc. now can deliver Act II to its Mexican Sam's Club outlets for only a few cents more than to its U.S. stores, undercutting the product's Mexican distributor."[1]

Wal-Mart and many other companies are making huge investments in foreign markets. One of the outcomes of increasing internationalization is that countries are economically interconnected at an unprecedented level. For example, in the wake of the September 11, 2001, terrorist attacks in the United States, many American businesses announced layoffs and cutbacks. However, across the Atlantic, British Airways cut seven thousand jobs, and Volkswagen announced weeklong shutdowns at two of its main plants in Germany. Both of these announcements occurred within one week of the tragedy, and analysts predicted that Europe would follow the United States into economic recession, with Germany the hardest hit.[2] In Japan, a much-heralded launch of a new GameCube console by Nintendo was overshadowed by the events in the United States. Early sales were disappointing. Speculation at the time was that the disasters would result in a decline in Asian exports, which would lead to economic woes across the region.[3] The United Nations predicted that the region's gross domestic product could decrease by 2.4 percentage points as a result of the attacks. In fact, "China's relative isolation from the U.S. may serve it well right now." [4]

Among the most popular reasons companies make foreign investments are to search for new markets or better resources, increase efficiency, reduce risk, or counter the competition (see Table 10.1).[5] Although many countries are significant in the world economy, they tend to fall into three dominant regions, which are sometimes called the "Triad" regions: North America, Europe, and the Pacific Rim. Some researchers have suggested that in order to remain competitive, larger organizations should be involved in all three of these regions.[6] For example, organizations may find that the best suppliers of a particular good or service are not in their own countries. If they are going to be "world class," they have very little choice but to develop business relationships where the best suppliers operate.

Some scholars have argued that global strategic management is "simply the application of strategic management in a larger arena." Others "point to the historical legacy of international economics and trade theory, to the powerful effects of cultural differences, to the role of exchange rate risk, and to the very different

Table 10.1 Primary Reasons Firms Make Foreign Investments	
Reason	**Description**
New Markets	As domestic markets become saturated, companies seek to expand their market reach into other countries.
Better Resources	Some countries have more-abundant resources than do others. Firms may seek resources such as raw materials, excellent suppliers, trained workers, advanced technologies, well-developed infrastructures, and good financial markets.
Efficiency	Organizations can create economies of scale through increasing production. Also, they can increase efficiency through cutting costs in countries with inexpensive labor. In addition, fixed investments in certain resources can be applied to multiple markets (economies of scope).
Risk Reduction	Although global markets are interconnected, their business cycles do not match up perfectly. Consequently, a recession in Europe may not coincide exactly with a recession in Japan or in the United States. By investing in multiple global regions, a company can theoretically reduce volatility in overall corporate earnings.
Competitive Countermove	If a major competitor invests in a particular global region, other competitors may feel obliged to do so to protect their own interests. For example, they may fear that one company will develop better resources or achieve more efficiency.

institutional conditions in different countries and see the strategic concerns of multi-national firms to be intrinsically different from their domestic cousins."[7] Both views are correct. Many of the tools you have learned—such as environmental, stake-holder, and resource analysis; creation of strategic direction; and development of control systems—can be directly applied to global firms. In this book, you have seen numerous applications of the theory and tools of strategic management to firms based or operating outside the United States. Nevertheless, significant differences exist between U.S. and other markets. These differences are worthy of discussion.

This chapter begins with a discussion of the general orientation a firm takes toward international involvement. Consistent with the underlying themes of this book, the next section will describe global stakeholder management and global resource development as they relate to competitive advantage. Various global strategies will then be described, and guidelines will be provided for selecting among countries for investment. The final section will briefly discuss some of the global trends that are likely to be a part of the competitive environment in the future.

Global Orientation

international expansion
The process of building an expanding operational presence; this can lead to global resource advantages

global integration
The process through which a multi-national organization integrates its worldwide activities into a single world strategy through its network of affiliates and alliances

domestic stage of international development
Organizations focus their efforts on domestic operations, but begin to export their products and services

international stage of international development
Exports become an important part of organizational strategy; operations and marketing are tailored to the needs of each country

multinational stage of international development
The organization has marketing and production facilities throughout the world

global stage of international development
The organization has become so global that it is no longer associated primarily with any one country

Multinational strategies tend to fall into two broad categories: international expansion and global integration.[8] **International expansion** is the process of building an expanding operational presence. As organizations expand their reach, they can enjoy benefits such as increased market size, economies of scale, increased opportunities for learning, a larger pool of resources from which to draw, more opportunities to create partnerships, and more advancement opportunities for their managers. **Global integration** is the process through which a multinational organization integrates its world-wide activities into a single world strategy through its network of affiliates and alliances. It is a process of coordinating decentralized activities so as to exploit the firm's capabilities across markets. Global integration can result in cost efficiency, global flexibility, and an ability to apply firm resources and skills across multiple markets.

Some organizations are more globally oriented than others. A company's attitude toward international expansion is another element of its strategic direction. Firms seem to evolve through four stages of international development.[9] In the first stage, the **domestic stage,** companies focus their efforts on domestic operations, but begin to export their products and services, sometimes through an export department or a foreign joint venture. Toys "R" Us, a fairly recent entrant into foreign markets, is currently in this stage. In the **international stage,** exports become an important part of organizational strategy. The firm typically forms international divisions to handle sales, service, and warehousing in the foreign markets. Marketing programs are custom-tailored to suit the needs of each country. Hasbro, the toy maker, is in this stage.[10]

In the third stage, **multinational,** the organization has marketing and production facilities throughout the world. More than a third of firm sales originate overseas, and the company has worldwide access to capital markets. Nike, the shoe company, is at the multinational stage, having passed the point at which one-third of revenues come from non-U.S. sales.[11] Finally, in the **global stage,** the organization is no longer associated primarily with any one country. Global firms—such as Philips Electronics N.V., Unilever, and Matsushita Electric—operate in as many as forty countries or more.

Unfortunately, not long ago, many U.S. companies were not ready for global expansion. According to Sheth and Eshghi, experts on international strategy:

Many companies become multinational reluctantly. They start off as export houses, and as international business grows and becomes a significant part of corporate revenues, they become more involved in foreign operations. However, the corporate culture still remains domestic, and the international division is treated as a stepchild. The situation becomes one of them vs. us. . . . What is lacking is a true worldwide orientation in product design, manufacturing, and marketing functions.[12]

structural inertia
Forces at work to maintain the status quo, which may include systems, structures, processes, culture, sunk costs, internal politics, and barriers to entry and exit

Structural inertia within U.S. companies has been a major impediment to their transformation into true global competitors. You may recall from Chapter 4 that inertia describes forces at work to maintain the status quo, including systems, structures, processes, culture, sunk costs, internal politics, and barriers to entry and exit.[13] Inertia is stronger in successful organizations because managers believe that past success will translate into future success. Historically, North American companies were able to prosper by selling goods to the largest and richest market in the world. In the past, some managers considered overseas operations nuisances or simply organizational appendages that generated a few extra dollars in sales revenue.[14] However, the United States had a "wake-up call," and now American companies are rushing to foreign markets in an effort to catch up.

International activities should be accompanied by a new mind-set for all members of an organization, from top managers to the lowest-level employees. Where will this new global mind-set come from? It has to start at the top of the organization. CEOs who want to create global companies can start by expanding their organizational visions to include overseas operations. However, they should also assign specific individuals to monitor global stakeholder groups, economic trends, and markets, and integrate this information into ongoing strategic management processes through the business-intelligence system.

CEOs can create a sense of urgency in the organization by constantly discussing global customers, operations, strategies, and successes and failures with subordinates, the board of directors, employees, and the media. They will also want to make visits to global operations as a part of their regular routines. Finally, CEOs can communicate the value of employees from countries that are outside of the home country by making sure that they are both hired and promoted as often as Americans.

To be fair, American companies are not the only companies that have been guilty of a narrow global vision. As this next example demonstrates, one of the largest and most successful Japanese companies was also in need of a "wake-up call."

 Some seasoned analysts see Mitsubishi Corporation of Tokyo as a "lumbering, prehistoric beast that has outlived its epoch" and "should roll over and die." Although harsh, these doomsday analysts have a point. The core business that built the trading company—hauling raw materials into Japan and speeding finished goods out into the world— has been declining for more than a decade. . . . Minoru Makihara, chief executive since 1992, is keenly aware of Mitsubishi's difficult plight. His challenge: to persuade subordinates, who may have become too comfortable, that the need for transformation is urgent. "We have to change the contents of our business," says Makihara. "But in order to change the business, I have to create a sense of crisis. If you are running IBM, you can create a sense of crisis by firing people.

Tradition won't allow me to do that here." Makihara believes he must impress on his troops how vital it is to become truly global, to invest in faraway businesses that have no ties to Japan.[15]

Makihara is still struggling to transform the slumbering giant.[16]

Global Stakeholders and Resources

Global strategic management provides challenges and opportunities that are not found in domestic markets. Stakeholder management is more complicated because of the diversity of people, organizations, and governments involved. However, a more diverse environment offers more opportunities to develop stakeholder-based competencies through effective management and interorganizational relationships. Also, global diversity provides a much larger pool of resources from which to draw.

Stakeholder Management in Foreign Environments

Global expansion requires an adjustment in the business definition of the organization. The answer to, "Who is being satisfied?" typically is enlarged to include worldwide customers. Also, "How are customer needs satisfied?" may involve relationships with a much broader range of suppliers and partners. Depending on the nature of the venture, any of the stakeholder groups may be enlarged. At a minimum, all global ventures rely on cooperation from a foreign government; however, most foreign ventures involve many other stakeholder groups as well. These new stakeholders add a new dimension to stakeholder analysis and management. They also increase the need for a state-of-the-art business-intelligence system.

Stakeholder analysis, a complicated process in domestic environments, becomes even more demanding when companies are significantly involved in countries other than their home countries. Organizations may respond to this complexity by evaluating stakeholders in all countries simultaneously. This process, which requires a high level of information-system sophistication, results in a very comprehensive view that provides the firm with a global picture and helps high-level managers craft missions, goals, strategies, and implementation plans that are applicable in a broad global setting. On the other hand, many companies use a decentralized approach to stakeholder analysis, allowing local managers to manage their own information and custom-tailor or modify strategic direction, goals, strategies, and implementation plans.

Of course, global stakeholder management is even more taxing than analysis. Going global offers many new management challenges. The fact is that Europeans and the Japanese have different views of business and manage differently than American managers, although management techniques are slowly converging.[17] Table 10.2 contains quotations from European managers that demonstrate some of the differences among the **Triad regions.** Within those statements are evidence of differences in culture, government intervention, and management philosophy.

triad regions
Three dominant economic regions in the world; namely, North America, Europe, and the Pacific Rim

Although there are similarities among countries in specific regions of the world, there are also significant differences that need to be addressed. It is a mistake to lump all European countries together, all Asian countries in another block,

---

Table 10.2   Management Differences Across the U.S., Europe, and Japan

The following quotations are based on a recent study of differences in management perspectives and styles across the three regions of the U.S., Europe and Japan, from a European manager perspective. They are illustrative of the types of challenges American managers face when doing business abroad.

Sir Anthony Pilkington, Chairman of Pilkington: "In Germany, in Sweden, in Denmark, and even in France, there are a lot of checks and balances against management freedom of actions, there are supervisors' reports, there are workers' representatives on the board and there is much more government intervention."

Jacopo Vittorelli, former Deputy Chairman of Pirelli: "If you have to close a plant in Italy, in France, in Spain or in Germany, you have to discuss the possibility with the State, the local communities with the trade unions, everybody feels entitled to intervene...Even the Church."

Andre Leysen, Chairman of the Supervisory Board of Agfa Gevaert: "...we work for profit, but also for people. On the other hand, in the U.S., profit dominates everything, and people are considered as a resource that you can take or leave. This is a major difference. Now you could say that the European philosophy is close to the Japanese. I do not think so. There is a fundamental difference between the two. Europe is an individualistic society whereas the Japanese society is based on the collective."

Willem H.J. Guitink, Corporate Director of Management Training and Education at Philips: "European business leaders are better equipped to deal with cultural diversity, geographical diversity, than most American managers. I don't think that that would necessarily hold for the Japanese."

Justus Mische, Member of the Board in charge of Personnel of Hoechst: "Europe, at least the big international firms in Europe, have a philosophy between the Japanese, long term, and the United States, short term."

Source: R. Calori and B. Dufour, "Management European Style," *Academy of Management Executive* (August, 1995), pp. 61–73, used with permission.

---

and all African or Middle Eastern countries in their respective groups. In fact, the difference between Indonesia and Korea is greater than that between Japan and the United States.

 The Danish culture is closer to the Indonesian culture than to the Swedish culture in terms of the mindscape characteristics. Let us take one aspect of the Danish culture as an example. In the Danish culture, the main purpose of interpersonal communication is to maintain a familiar atmosphere and convey affection. A small group of friends often sit together in the same café, eating the same pastry week after week, telling the same or similar gossips. Subtle variations are considered interesting. For example, everyone knows that Mr. X ties his left shoe first, then his right shoe. One day he reverses the sequential order. This becomes big news. Less subtle information is avoided because it may disturb the familiar atmosphere. It is impolite to explain things, because such an act assumes that someone is ignorant. It is also impolite to ask questions on anything beyond immediate personal concern, because the respondent may not know the answer. It is often considered aggressive to introduce new ideas. A foreign businessperson eager to discuss what is outside the immediate business needs is likely to be met with a strong, silent resistance.

In contrast, in Sweden, the purpose of daily interpersonal communication is transmission of new information or frank feelings. One prefers to be silent unless he or she can convey an important message, while in Denmark one must keep talking. While Danes are affect-oriented; Swedes are performance-oriented.

As this example demonstrates, your friendly behavior of asking questions or explaining things may have a negative effect in some cultures, and you may not know why it does not work. Unfortunately, Americans seldom have training programs on foreign cultures and languages, though there are exceptions such as Teradyne of Boston.[18]

Management of internal stakeholders such as employees becomes difficult and complex when an organization operates in more than one country. Figure 10.1 is an illustration of the wide differences that exist from country to country regarding assumptions about manager/subordinate relationships. In countries such as the

FIGURE 10.1

Cross-Cultural Human Resource Differences

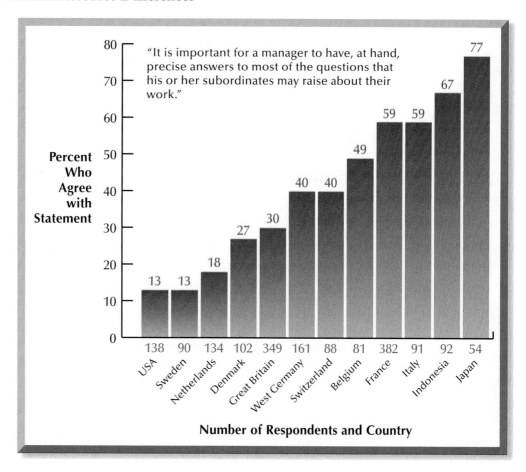

Source: A. Laurent, "The Cross-Cultural Puzzle of International Human Resource Management," *Human Resource Management* 25 (1986), p. 94, Copyright © 1986 by John Wiley & Sons, Inc. Reprinted by permission of John Wiley & Sons, Inc.

United States, Sweden, the Netherlands, and Denmark, managers are typically not expected to have precise answers to subordinates' questions. In France, Italy, Indonesia, and Japan, most employees expect managers to be able to deal with most of their questions in a precise manner.

Training programs can do a lot to help firms cope with global stakeholder management. Companies are sending some of their managers to special training programs to help increase their global awareness and vision. The University of Michigan recently provided an intensive, in-depth five-week program for twenty-one executives from Japan, the United States, Brazil, Great Britain, and India to help them become global thinkers. The program first made the participants more aware of the differences that existed between them. Then the trainers helped the participants to work out these differences. The training program was so successful that organizers are planning to make it an annual event.[19] Some Korean firms have very thorough training programs. An example is the use of "culture houses." An employee who will be sent to Germany, for example, is put in a "German house," where the employee is confined until he or she is able to eat, live, and sleep like a German.[20]

Government stakeholders are among the most difficult for a global firm to manage. The level of involvement of government administrators and regulators varies widely from nation to nation. A communist government such as China has firm control over economic factors, whereas the U.S. government favors more of an open-market system. The section on international market selection at the end of this chapter highlights some of these issues. How can organizations cope with such diversity? A very common approach is to enter a new country with a foreign partner that understands the government system. At a minimum, a firm should hire employees and managers who are natives of the host country and have significant business experience specifically to handle government issues such as regulations and taxes.

global resource advantage
A source of competitive advantage resulting from the ability of a global organization to draw from a much broader and more diversified pool of resources

Global Resource Advantages

One of the major advantages of global involvement is that organizations can draw from a much broader and more diversified pool of resources—including human resources; physical resources such as raw materials, supplies, and locations; and technological know-how.[21] Advanced worldwide technology is a resource that some companies are using as a primary basis for developing their competitive strategies.

 News Corporation is one of the few media giants that can truly call themselves global. The Australian-based owner of the Fox TV network and Fox movie studio controls a ring of satellite channels around the world that are upgrading to digital platforms. These platforms— BSkyB in the United Kingdom, STAR TV in Asia, and Sky Latin American—can essentially act like a broadband pipeline to distribute both video channels and Internet services to subscribers. . . . News Corporation's challenge is marketing its sprawling satellite system into actual subscriptions on the ground. The company is betting that satellites will be the preferred broadband-distribution pipeline outside the United States, but it isn't clear there is a market to support News Corporation's billion-dollar-plus investment to date.[22]

FIGURE 10.2

Factors That Lead to Competitive Advantages of Nations

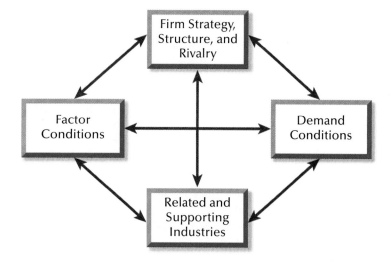

Source: Adapted with the permission of The Free Press, an imprint of Simon & Schuster Adult Publishing Group, from *The Competitive Advantage of Nations* by Michael E. Porter. Copyright 1980, 1998 by Michael E. Porter.

Michael Porter, whose name should now be familiar to you, expanded his analyses of competitive environments to include the global economy. In his book *The Competitive Advantage of Nations*, he developed arguments concerning why some nations produce so many stellar companies in particular industries. For example, Germany is the home base for several top luxury-car manufacturers, and Switzerland has many leading companies in pharmaceuticals and chocolate. The United States is the undisputed world leader in the entertainment industry. Porter explains that four characteristics of countries actually create an environment that is conducive to creating globally competitive firms in certain business areas (see Figure 10.2). The four characteristics are:

- *Factor Conditions.* Some nations enjoy special endowments such as uncommon raw materials or laborers with specific skills or training. Often countries with excellent schools or universities that excel in particular areas produce laborers with superior skills. For example, Japan is well known for producing graduates with outstanding quantitative and technical skills.

- *Demand Conditions.* If a nation's buyers of a particular product or service are the most discriminating and demanding in the world, then firms must achieve product and service excellence just to survive. Since they are so good, these companies can easily outperform foreign companies that compete in the same industry, even in the home countries of those foreign competitors. For example, American consumers are very discriminating in their consumption of movies and theme parks. Consequently, American entertainment companies are very competitive, even in foreign markets and against home-country rivals.

- *Related and Supporting Industries.* If suppliers in a particular country are the very best in the world, then the companies that buy from them are at a relative advantage. Firms in related industries that are also global leaders can also help create a nationally based competitive advantage.

- *Firm Strategy, Structure, and Rivalry.* If the management techniques that are customary in the nation's businesses are conducive to success in a particular industry, then the firms in that nation are at a competitive advantage relative to firms from other countries. Another advantage can come from having an industry that attracts the most talented managers in the nation. Finally, if industry rivalry is strong in a particular industry, then firms are forced to excel. This is similar to the argument with regard to discriminating buyers.

Basically, the reason companies can develop a highly competitive nucleus is that tough market environments can create world-class competitors only if the competitors are also endowed with the resources they need to compete. If home markets are uncompetitive, firms will not be sufficiently motivated to produce a superior product. On the other hand, if home markets are highly competitive but the factors of production, support industries, and human talent are not available, firms will likewise be incapable of producing globally competitive products. When these two conditions are met, however, an environment is created that both motivates and rewards excellence.

 Nokia is an excellent example of a company that was able to achieve great success due to operating in a country with specific resource advantages. Nokia, a global market leader in the cellular-phone industry, grew out of an unexpected location. "How could tiny Finland give birth to such a company? Simple. Though its population is only five million, Finland is by all accounts the world's most wired country, with a highly educated and technologically savvy population." According to a Nokia executive, the company is now heavily involved in creating "mobile phones and everything you have in between."[23]

Some firms buy foreign companies specifically to get a "foothold" in a world-class industry. For example, Vivendi, the French conglomerate, bought Universal Studios, with operations primarily in the United States. Vivendi Universal can now enjoy the learning benefits from competing head-to-head with other U.S. rivals in an environment with the most discriminating buyers. What Vivendi learns in the United States will help its theme-park joint venture in Japan and any other international theme-park ventures it decides to pursue.

The logical conclusion from Porter's analysis would seem to be to locate subsidiaries in the nations with the strongest home bases in particular industries. However, he argues that this is sometimes hard to do. First, it is difficult in some cases for an "outsider," a foreign firm, to become an "insider." In other words, it may be difficult for a foreign firm to tap into the sources of supply or obtain the highly valued resources that make home-base competitors so successful. Japan, in particular, is a tough nation to penetrate. Second, Porter suggests that it is difficult for the foreign subsidiary in the nation with the natural advantages to influence the parent company "long distance." For example, if Hershey locates a subsidiary in Switzerland to take advantage of the natural advantages that are found there, it is unlikely that the Swiss subsidiary would have much of an impact on Hershey's operations in the United States. In spite of the difficulty, it is worth pursuing when possible.

Porter suggests that firms should take advantage of their own nation's natural-resource advantages. He also recommends that some of the principles that apply to the competitive advantages of nations can be applied in any company that wants to become more competitive in the world economy. Specifically, organizations can seek out the toughest, most discriminating buyers, choose from the best suppliers in the world, seek to excel against the most outstanding global competitors, form alliances with outstanding foreign competitors, and stay abreast of all research findings and innovations that are relevant to their core businesses.

Management of Foreign Subsidiaries

The role of foreign subsidiaries in a multinational company is changing from being treated as simply "branch locations" to a full role in the development of new competencies, capabilities, resources, and products.[24] Some early models of multinational companies assumed that foreign subsidiaries would look more or less alike, except perhaps for size.[25] For example, if they were involved in marketing and sales, their structures and functions would be very similar. If they were involved in production, their production facilities would be alike. However, multinational firms evolved toward a system that allowed each foreign subsidiary to play a different yet integrated role in the overall organization. Three levels of subsidiary responsibility emerged.

- *Local Implementation*—These subsidiaries have very well defined roles to play and little independence. These local implementers have a single-country scope of operations and, at most, might make minor adjustments to strategy to satisfy local markets.

- *Specialized Contribution*—These subsidiaries belong to an interdependent network of subsidiaries, often in a production role. Each subsidiary makes a unique contribution to the network.

- *Global Mandate*—They have responsibility for an entire global business, and not just one part of the value chain. Activities are integrated by the subsidiary itself, instead of by the corporate office.[26]

The role each subsidiary will play depends on its capabilities and resources. If capabilities and resources are limited either by virtue of the country in which a subsidiary operates or by insufficient internal resources, then it might be assigned an implementation role. Subsidiaries that exist in countries with special advantages or that have specific internal-resource advantages are expected to make a specialized contribution. Subsidiaries with a global mandate must have substantial skills and resources from which to draw, both from the country environment and internally.

Matrix and transnational structures, described in Chapter 8, are helpful in integrating activities across subsidiaries, especially where those subsidiaries have highly related activities. As responsibilities for determining strategies become more decentralized, integration across subsidiaries becomes more important.

Ex. These decentralized activities, located in highly differentiated subsidiaries, are tied together through intensive and extensive use of electronic communications. Of great importance, though, is the condition that these communications are no longer primarily vertical, from headquarters to subsidiary and back, but horizontal, directly from subsidiary to subsidiary. The global center participates only in headquarters-relevant issues, such as financial reporting, key account management, executive level management, and the like.[27]

The head office is responsible primarily for determining the role each subsidiary will play; however, managers of subsidiaries themselves will have a lot of influence on those decisions. Corporate-level managers should envision each subsidiary as a semiautonomous unit that has different skills and resources to contribute to a global network of subsidiaries. In such a situation, strong centralized control is not advisable.

So far, this discussion has assumed that organizations would like to integrate activities and build one integrated global strategy. However, some firms do not pursue such integration. These are companies whose subsidiaries are unrelated to each other. They are pursuing a global unrelated-diversification strategy. If this is the case, then financial controls such as those described in Chapter 9 are suitable for corporate-level control. For example, corporate-level management could make resource-allocation decisions and reward subsidiary managers based on financial-performance indicators such as ROI. Also, corporate management could make decisions about buying and selling subsidiaries based on performance indicators or needs in the corporate portfolio. The integration activities described in this section are applicable only in situations in which organizations have enough commonality among their subsidiaries to pursue such things as economies of scale or economies of scope.

International Alliances and Joint Ventures

International strategic alliances are an outstanding way to acquire both resources and skills. Resource combinations can lead to superior products and services. For example, Toshiba built a new $1 billion chip-making facility that uses state-of-the art ultraviolet technology. The plant was completed, in part, though a joint venture between Toshiba, Siemens of Germany, and IBM. Also, Mitsubishi, a leader in one of the biggest Japanese keiretsu, is involved in a long-term joint venture with Caterpillar. The venture already has produced an excavator line manufactured in Japan, the United States, Indonesia, and China.[28]

 Sprint Corp. and Richard Branson's Virgin Group Ltd. (announced) they have formed a joint venture to offer prepaid wireless telecom services and handsets to the youth market in the United States. Sprint, the No. 3 U.S. long-distance telephone company, beat rivals including AT&T Corp. to supply the U.S. network for a Virgin-branded service modeled after Virgin's wireless ventures in Britain and Australia. The two companies have been in talks since July. The new venture targets fifteen- to thirty-year-old consumers. Virgin will sell digital phones with services such as voice mail, messaging, and games. The company will begin retail sales in Virgin Megastores in New York and Los Angeles (in 2002), said John Tantum, a senior Virgin executive.[29]

Global competition is also causing firms to reevaluate how they acquire knowledge. "New knowledge provides the foundation for new skills, which in turn can lead to competitive success," according to Andrew Inkpen, an expert on international alliances, "In bringing together firms with different skills, knowledge bases, and organizational cultures, alliances create unique learning opportunities for partner firms."[30]

In some cases, international joint ventures are born of competitive necessity.

Ex. Motorola, Inc. and Germany's Siemens AG are in talks to create a joint venture for either their wireless-infrastructure operations or their handset businesses, or potentially both, in a deal that could create ventures with a total value between $20 billion and $25 billion, people familiar with the situation say. The talks come as many of the world's biggest mobile-phone makers have been hit hard by the global economic slowdown. Philips Electronics N.V. responded recently by restructuring its unprofitable handset division, while other companies such as Sony Corporation and Sweden's Telefonaktiebolaget LM Ericsson have joined forces and created a joint venture to produce mobile phones.[31]

In summary, global organizations face a much more complicated management task due to diversity of stakeholders and resources. However, this diversity provides opportunities with regard to both stakeholder relationships and acquisition or development of resources that domestic companies do not enjoy. The way global firms manage their foreign subsidiaries has much to do with how they manage their resources. Also, firms can learn new technologies and acquire skills and other resources through international alliances. The next section deals with various strategies that companies apply as they approach global markets.

Global Strategies

As firms approach international markets, they have several strategic decisions to make. They must select a general approach to their markets, decide on expansion tactics, and formulate global business-level and corporate-level strategies. These strategic decisions are the subject of this section.

Product/Market Approach

multidomestic product/market strategy
Entails handling product design, assembly, and marketing on a country-by-country basis by custom tailoring products and services around individual market needs

global product/market strategy
Companies use one product design and market it in the same fashion throughout the world

One of the key issues facing top managers as their organizations pursue international development is selection of a product/market approach. A **multidomestic strategy** entails handling product design, assembly, and marketing on a country-by-country basis by custom-tailoring products and services around individual market needs. On the other hand, organizations pursuing a **global strategy** produce one product design, and market it in the same fashion throughout the world.[32]

Bausch & Lomb used a multidomestic strategy to significantly increase its global market share in several markets.

Ex. The key to success for Bausch & Lomb was to "Think globally, act locally," letting local managers make their own decisions. Until the big change, production and marketing policies all came from headquarters in Rochester, New York, treating foreign subsidiaries "as sales adjuncts to the U.S. divisions." For example, the company was unsuccessful in Japan with rigid, gas-permeable contact lenses because ophthalmologists there insist on a surface that goes well beyond clinical requirements to near perfection. So the company built a new plant in South Korea to manufacture lenses that met the requirements. B&L now has 11 percent of the Japanese market for those lenses. This strategy also extended to Bausch & Lomb's Ray-Ban division. More than half of Ray-Ban's new sunglasses are developed specifically for international sale. In Europe, Ray-Bans tend to be flashier, more avant-garde, and costlier than in the United States. In Asia, the company redesigned the sunglasses to better suit the Asian face—with its flatter bridge and higher cheekbones—and sales took off.[33]

Multidomestic strategies are intuitively appealing from a stakeholder point of view, since they emphasize the satisfaction of segmented customer needs. One of the reasons that Japanese firms are so successful in the U.S. market may be that they tailor their products to meet the needs of U.S. consumers. This is quite different from the attitude sometimes found in U.S. firms—that foreign consumers should naturally want to buy U.S. products just as they are. However, customization may add more costs to the products or services than can be successfully recaptured through higher prices. A well-known marketing scholar, Theodore Levitt, asserts that:

> Well managed companies have moved from emphasis on customizing items to offering globally standardized products that are advanced, functional, reliable—and low priced. Multinational companies that concentrated on idiosyncratic consumer preferences have become befuddled and unable to take in the forest because of the trees. Only global companies will achieve long-term success by concentrating on what everyone wants rather than worrying about the details of what everyone thinks they might like.[34]

As a counter-argument, some researchers explain that a global product/market strategy is appropriate only if: (1) there is a global market segment for a product or service, (2) there are economic efficiencies associated with a global strategy, (3) there are no external constraints such as government regulations that will prevent a global strategy from being implemented, and (4) there are no absolute internal constraints.[35]

transnational product/market strategy a hybrid product/market strategy that combines elements of the multidomestic and global strategies

Some organizations are now pursuing a hybrid **transnational product/market strategy.** An international counterpart to the best-cost strategy discussed previously, a transnational strategy entails seeking both global efficiency and local responsiveness. This difficult task is accomplished through establishing an integrated network that fosters shared vision and resources while allowing individual decisions to be made to adapt to local needs.[36]

International Expansion Tactics

Firms can apply a variety of expansion tactics as they pursue global opportunities. Among the most common are:

exporting
Transferring goods to other countries for sale through wholesalers or a foreign company

licensing
Selling the right to produce and/or sell a brand name product in a foreign market

franchising
The services counterpart to a licensing strategy; a foreign firm buys the legal right to use the name and operating methods of a foreign firm in its home country

wholly-owned foreign subsidiary
A business venture that is started from scratch; sometimes called a greenfield investment

- **Exporting.** Transferring goods to other countries for sale through wholesalers or a foreign company.
- *Contractual Arrangements,* such as:
  - **Licensing.** Selling the right to produce and/or sell a brand name product in a foreign market.
  - **Franchising.** This is the services counterpart to a licensing strategy. A foreign firm buys the legal right to use the name and operating methods of a foreign firm in its home country.
- *Foreign Direct Investment,* such as:
  - *Joint Venture.* Cooperative agreement among two or more companies to pursue common business objectives.
  - **Wholly Owned Subsidiary.** Venture is started from scratch, thus creating a wholly owned foreign subsidiary. These ventures are sometimes called a greenfield investment.
  - *Acquisition.* Purchase of a foreign firm or the foreign subsidiary of a foreign or domestic firm.[37]

Among the most important criteria when deciding on an option for international growth are cost, financial risk, profit potential, and control. In general, moving down the list of alternatives from first to last entails greater cost and greater financial risk, but also greater profit potential and greater control. Consequently, these alternatives represent a trade-off between cost and financial risk on one hand, and profit and control on the other. Of course, this is a gross generalization. Some of the options, such as joint ventures and acquisitions, are hard to judge on the basis of these four criteria because the exact nature of the agreement can vary so widely from deal to deal. For any international growth decision, these options should be weighed based on real data on cost, risk, profit potential, and control, rather than relying on generalizations.

Another factor that seems to influence the decision among international growth options is multinational diversity. Firms that operate in diverse multinational environments have a greater capacity to learn and develop resources and skills. These types of firms are more prone to starting a business in a foreign environment, with or without partners, rather than acquiring one.[38]

Research demonstrates some of the major differences between Western and Japanese firms in the way they enter foreign markets. U.S. firms tend to favor big overseas investments, often through acquisitions. On the other hand, Japanese firms favor sequential investment. They make frequent, smaller investments in foreign operations over a long period of time, "Typically, Japanese companies make a small initial investment in their core businesses and expand their operations if this investment performs well. The companies might later make big investments. . . ."[39] For example, Fuji began small, but continually increased its business investments in the United States over the past several decades. Recently, Fuji built a $100 million film-packaging plant in the United States.[40] Sequential entry can help an organization reduce the risks associated with foreign investments, regardless of which method of entry is used.

Global Business-Level Strategy

World markets also provide outstanding opportunities with regard to business-level strategy. Organizations that are involved in multiple global markets have advantages available to them in pursuing their business-level strategies. Examples of the many options available for improving competitive position vis-à-vis cost leadership through a global strategy include the following:

- Cost reductions through foreign assembly or manufacturing. Many firms are currently shipping components to foreign countries for assembly by low-cost laborers. The maquiladora industry in Mexico consists of hundreds of these assembly operations just south of the United States–Mexico border. The opening up of East Germany provides similar opportunities for European firms. Some companies are also manufacturing in foreign countries.

- Branding of finished products that are subcontracted to low-cost foreign manufacturers. Nike designs shoes, but manufactures them in developing nations according to Nike specifications. Likewise, Liz Claiborne products are produced overseas.

- Global sourcing. This involves purchase of low-cost foreign components or raw materials. Many U.S. firms buy Japanese semiconductors or Japanese steel for use in their products.

- Expanding markets leading to economies of scale. Some companies could not grow large enough to enjoy the lowest possible production costs on the basis of domestic demand alone. However, expansion into foreign markets can lead to significant increases in demand.

- Transfer of technological know-how through joint venture (learning from competitors). Some foreign firms are more efficient than U.S. firms in producing similar products. Joint ventures with these firms may provide opportunities to learn new technologies that can lead to significant cost reductions.[41]

Global strategies can also lead to competitive advantages through differentiation. Some strategies for doing this include:

- Distribution of foreign products in the United States. American firms can purchase elite products from foreign manufacturers for sale in the United States. This strategy is easy to imitate unless the companies sign a contract that provides the American firm exclusive rights to market the product in the United States.

- Sale of U.S. products in foreign countries. In some countries, American products command a premium price because of the image they convey. For example, Coca-Cola Company enjoys higher operating profits in Japan than in the United States.

- Superior quality through joint venture. Just as U.S. companies can learn cost-saving technologies through joint ventures, they can also learn how to better differentiate their products, through higher quality or some other unique feature.

- Licensing of product technology from abroad. Joint venture is not the only way to learn new technologies. U.S. firms sometimes have the option of licensing product technologies to differentiate their present products.

- Forcing an open, learning mind-set. U.S. companies that attempt to differentiate themselves on speed and flexibility in the international marketplace must develop an innovative mind-set or culture, and must be willing to learn from and adapt to a variety of conflicting circumstances. They can then bring what they learn back to the United States and apply it to local businesses.[42]

While world markets provide many opportunities, pursuing these opportunities creates additional costs and risks. Managing businesses in foreign countries can result in additional costs associated with such things as travel, communications (including translation costs), export and import duties and tariffs, transportation of products, advertising, taxes, and fees. In addition, managers may find themselves unable to understand or effectively manage businesses in countries that are unfamiliar to them. This is another reason that hiring a local manager may be desirable.

Many risks are also associated with global expansion. Organizations face the risk that citizens in some countries may not be receptive to some foreign products because of prejudices they hold against the countries in which the products were produced. The same sort of risk applies to service firms. Also, the risks associated with managing international joint ventures and currency translations were discussed previously. These are only a few of many potential risks. Wise selection of countries in which to pursue opportunities can reduce costs and risks associated with global expansion.

In conclusion, organizations can use global strategies to strengthen their cost positions or increase differentiation. However, they must be careful to choose foreign environments that are conducive to the type of enterprise they are considering. Several regions in the world economy offer significant opportunities for growth and development, for organizations that are willing and able to take the risks. Globalization of both operations and management thinking will be required for U.S. firms to remain strategically competitive.

Global Corporate-Level Strategy

The merger-and-acquisition wave that has been so prevalent in the United States has become a global trend, both within countries and across borders. In an effort to boost dairy-production capacity, China's Sanyuan Foods offered $9.3 million for the Beijing operations of Kraft Foods International, a U.S.-based company. According to reports in China, an "unprecedented wave of mergers and acquisitions is sweeping the nation. The number of M&As is expected to grow by as much as 40% in 2001, to $40 billion worth of deals. In some cases, state-owned companies are taking over other state-owned companies. In others, they are buying the local operations of a foreign multinational."[43] The M&A wave has hit Russia also: "Russia's industrial combines are on a buying binge. Moscow-based Alfa Group is snapping up stakes in telcos to diversify a portfolio dominated by oil holdings. Local rival Interros is adding a naval shipyard to its nickel-mining interests. And in Cheropovets, in the pine forests of northwestern Russia, the young managers of steelmaker Severstal are busy buying automotive, motor engine, and locomotive factories."[44]

The merger-and-acquisition wave has created some enormous, highly diversified global companies. For example, ABB, "a global electrical equipment giant that is bigger than Westinghouse and can go head to head with GE," was created by combining two Swiss engineering groups, ASEA and Brown Boveri, and then adding seventy more companies in Europe and the United States. All of this took place in a period of four years, resulting in a company that is a world leader in robotics, high-speed trains, and environmental controls. "ABB isn't Japanese, nor is it Swiss or Swedish. It is a multinational without a national identity, though its mailing address is in Zurich. The company's 13 top managers hold frequent meetings in different countries. Since they share no common first language, they speak only English, a foreign tongue to all but one."[45]

Another huge factor in all of the merger activity is industry consolidation. Many industries are consolidating, both within countries and globally.

 In one of Europe's biggest mergers, the Zeneca Group PLC of Britain announced a stock deal valued around $35 billion today to buy Astra AB of Sweden, creating a pharmaceutical giant. The deal, which had been expected, was the latest in a series of cross-border mergers and acquisitions in the European pharmaceutical industry. These deals reflect a quest for size to pursue costly research into new drugs and to compete in a market dominated by U.S. corporations. The new company, to be called AstraZeneca, will be the world's fourth-largest pharmaceutical concern, with a market value of $67 billion. It will also represent the tenth-largest of all mergers and acquisitions.[46]

Some large organizations are building global portfolios of related businesses in an effort to achieve economies of scope based on shared resources and reputation. Economies of scope, introduced in Chapter 7, occur anytime slack resources that otherwise would not have been used are being put to good use.[47] For example, when an organization invests in developing a new marketing technology, if the technology can be applied to more markets, then the cost of that investment per market is reduced. Economies of scope are especially applicable to organizational learning that leads to new technologies, patents, or management techniques, but they can apply to physical assets as well, so long as the physical asset can be shared.

 The British company Pearson PLC owns publishers Simon & Schuster, Scott Foresman, Prentice Hall, Addison-Wesley Longman, National Computer Systems, and Learning Network Pearson's Financial Times Group includes, in addition to its namesake,the French business paper Les Echos, the Spanish paper group Recoletos, and an on-line financial-data business. The Penguin Group includes the Penguin, Putnam, Dorling Kindersley, and Viking imprints. Marjorie Scardino, the charismatic Texan who runs Pearson, "contends that she's building a 21st century learning company, capable of delivering its products and services to any audience, on paper or online." She claims, "People are going to school longer, and people are reeducating themselves professionally."[48]

The chapter on corporate-level strategy provided evidence that large, unrelated diversified firms, or conglomerates, usually have relatively low-performing strategies. With a few notable exceptions, such as General Electric, conglomerates have a hard time generating high returns, and the risk-reduction benefits associated with allocating capital to the highest-performing businesses seem hard to achieve.

Consequently, many global firms have "learned their lesson," and are downscoping to fewer activities around a common core.[49]

While downscoping makes sense for many conglomerates in nations with advanced economies, it may be detrimental in developing nations in Asia or South America.[50] To understand why conglomerates might make perfect sense in developing nations, it is important to realize that one of the original theories about why conglomerates should be effective states that they are better than capital markets at allocating financial capital.[51] In a market-based economy, firms seek financial capital through borrowing and equity. However, bondholders, stockholders, and creditors have a limited view upon which to make decisions. In some cases, they don't have sufficient time to thoroughly evaluate each venture or company before deciding to provide capital. On the other hand, management has much-more-complete information upon which to base capital-allocation decisions.

 Suppose Onyx Company wants to raise capital for a new venture through a stock issue. They will provide a prospectus and other information to potential investors, who will determine whether they think the venture will be successful. Information available to investors is very limited, and they probably don't have a complete understanding of Onyx Company or the venture in which they want to invest. Now assume that Onyx Company is not a stand-alone company, but a part of the conglomerate Superior Inc. To raise the needed capital for the venture, Onyx management will have to go to Superior management. Managers at Superior know a lot about Onyx and its past performance. They know Onyx managers personally and are very familiar with their business. The point is that Superior is in a much better position than external market participants to make a good capital-allocation decision.

This argument about the efficiency of internal capital markets is hard to dispute. Poor performance found in many conglomerates is probably not because internal capital markets are inefficient, but because of other problems associated with managing unrelated businesses. Also, external capital markets in advanced economies are fairly efficient, which may mean that the advantages of internal capital markets do not offset the disadvantages of unrelated diversification. However, this is not the case in many developing nations that lack effective financial intermediaries and sound regulations. A country such as Brazil has an underdeveloped external market for capital. In fact, it is nearly impossible in Brazil to get capital to start up a business.[52] Consequently, for firms in developing nations, the conglomerate form of organization is probably a much more efficient means of allocating capital.[53] In those countries, the benefits of the form should offset the management disadvantages.

 Once diversified business structures are in place, business groups could then multiply the use of internal capital. This occurred in Korea. When a new subsidiary was established in a Korean business group of chaebol, equity and working capital could be provided by subsidiaries. Given the backwardness of external capital markets in the Korean economy, such internal financing capabilities were often essential to funding the rapid growth of business groups.[54]

International Market Selection

Significant changes in the global environment have created great opportunities for organizations that are willing to take a risk and wait patiently for returns. However, these changes have also created significant challenges. Some of the greatest management challenges are experienced by firms entering developing countries—an unstable government, inadequately trained workers, low levels of supporting technology, shortages of supplies, weak transportation systems, and an unstable currency. Furthermore, problems in the financial markets of one emerging nation can have ripple effects on financial markets in other emerging nations.

 Argentina's stock market jumped 8.2 percent, and emerging-market bonds rallied following an $8 billion rescue package from the International Monetary Fund, the IMF's latest effort to head off a potential default in emerging markets. Still, jitters remain. Both investors fear that the aid package won't stave off substantial restructuring of Argentina's $130 billion in public debt. If Argentina is forced to restructure, the process could be far more complicated than previous restructuring efforts by countries like Ecuador and Russia. "A really nasty restructuring would highlight the problems with lending to emerging markets," says Abigail McKenna, an emerging-markets portfolio manager for Morgan Stanley Asset Management. "If the restructuring in Argentina turns out to be a disaster, it could really mar prospects not just for Argentine bonds, but for other emerging-market bonds, too."[55]

Firms also have to struggle with managing stakeholders that are typically very different—in values, beliefs, ethics, and in many other ways—from stakeholders found in the industrialized countries. However, firms that are "first movers" into developing countries may be able to develop stakeholder-based advantages such as long-term productive contractual and informal relationships with host-country governments and organizations that followers won't have the opportunity to develop. For example, Spanish firms took huge risks by making major investments in Latin America during the first wave of privatizations; however, they are now firmly entrenched in one of the world's fastest-growing regions. According to one large Spanish bank executive with significant investments in Latin America: "It's not a new frontier for Spanish companies because we discovered America in 1492. But it's a growth frontier. It's a financial rediscovery of the Americas."[56] Actually, growth in gross domestic product in Latin America averaged 3.2 percent during the 1990s, while poverty decreased dramatically.[57]

In North America, the North American Free Trade Agreement has done much to open up borders and stimulate trade between the United States and its neighbors, Canada and Mexico. In fact, whether rightly or wrongly, NAFTA is sometimes credited with creating jobs in both Mexico and the United States.[58] Mexican President Vicente Fox, educated in the United States, has a very pro-business attitude. He and U.S. President George W. Bush have an excellent and productive relationship.[59] Some U.S. companies are now thriving in Mexico, which is reshaping the Mexican economy. Surprisingly, Canada offers economic advantages compared to other industrialized nations, especially with regard to starting new businesses.

A 1999 KPMG study of business costs in the United Kingdom, the United States, Japan, Italy, Austria, Canada, France, and Germany found that Canada was the least expensive country in which to build a business. The results are fairly consistent across nine industries studied.[60] Organizations that want to establish centralized call centers are finding that they can operate in Canada for 15 percent to 35 percent less than in the United States. In addition, Canada offers "an available quality labor force that delivers excellent and loyal customer-attracting-and-retaining service, sales and tech support."[61]

Another region with a lot of potential is Asia. The **"Pacific Century"** refers to a forecast that the world's growth center for the twenty-first century will shift across the Pacific Ocean to Asia. Asia is already the world's biggest consumer of steel, and the second-fastest-growing market for automobiles. It is General Electric's fastest-growing market.[62] The **newly industrialized economies (NIEs)** of South Korea, Taiwan, Hong Kong, and Singapore have experienced growth in real gross domestic product at a much higher level than Europe, Japan, or the United States.[63]

China, with more than 1 billion potential consumers, will provide much of the growth in demand for consumer products over the next several decades.[64] An "open door" policy on the part of the Chinese government has made China the largest recipient of foreign direct investment among developing nations, and second among all nations (after the United States).[65] Nevertheless, there are huge risks and difficulties for foreign firms operating in China. Management fraud is a widespread problem.[66] The government dominates the economy through its control over the infrastructure, utilities, pricing, and distribution networks (see Global Insight). A subsidiary's board must be chaired by a Chinese citizen, who is nominated by the Communist Party.[67] To encourage growth, China established Special Economic Zones that allowed considerable autonomy with regard to business practices. Much of the foreign direct investment that has flowed into China in recent years has taken place in these zones. Successful foreign companies in China form excellent relationships with the government, use joint ventures, make large investments, and "stick it out" over the long term.[68]

Pacific Century
Refers to a forecast that the world's growth center for the 21st Century will shift across the Pacific Ocean to Asia
newly industrialized economies (NIEs)
Countries that have recently experienced high levels of growth in real gross domestic product

Global Insight
Government-Led Reforms in China

China can be a frustrating place to do business. One of the biggest sources of frustration is the government. China's leaders insist on a high level of control over most aspects of business in their country. Furthermore, the whims of government leaders sometimes take precedence over official rules and laws. For example, Chinese leaders wanted their government's English-language television channel to be broadcast in America in exchange for allowing AOL Time Warner to connect its services to a few million Chinese homes. Also, Beijing often makes companies officially recognize China's claim on Taiwan before they are allowed to conduct business in the country.

When the Chinese government talks about reforms, they probably are not exactly what most Westerners would expect. According to President Shangquan Gao of the Chinese Economic Reform Foundation, one of the goals of the reforms is that "The state sector is to have more dominance in the national economy in accordance with the fundamental transformation of the economic structure and economic growth mode, and with the needs of opening up further to the outside world." It may seem like a contradiction to proclaim movement toward more state dominance combined with opening up to the outside world; however, this is the mind-set of a lot of Chinese leaders. Basically, China wants to retain its monopoly of state ownership in areas such as state security, all industries that supply major products or services to Chinese citizens, and in high or emerging technologies. Leaders also want to control many large and extra-large businesses or groups of businesses in major industrial sectors and highly profitable industries. A final goal is "Withdrawing state ownership from generally competitive industries in a step-by-step and planned manner." One might draw the conclusion from this reform plan that the Chinese government is interested in releasing absolute control only of areas that it sees as unprofitable or unimportant.

As Chinese government officials retire and are replaced by new leaders, China's economic policies may be revised. However, it is unlikely that China will relinquish its firm grip on the economy. Nevertheless, business opportunities in China will undoubtedly continue to draw foreign investors.

Sources: D. Roberts and M. L. Clifford, "Power Shift: China Gets Set for New Leaders," *Academy of Management Executive* (February 2002): 54–56; "China Trade(-Offs)," *Christian Science Monitor,* 7 September 2001, 10; quotations of President Gao are from Z. Wang, "Economic Reform Foundation's President Shangquan Gao on Organizational Reform and Sustainable Business Development," *Academy of Management Executive* (February 2000): 9.

Japan enjoyed a long period of economic growth and expansion during the 1980s and early 1990s. However, the so-called "economic bubble" burst in 1992. Over the next several years, the yen declined dramatically against U.S. currency, property prices plummeted, and the Nikkei stock-market index dropped precipitously. The unemployment rate increased to an unprecedented level, and business investment dropped off. Now an already competitive market has become even more competitive, especially for foreign companies.[69] "Personal care companies, such as Bristol-Myers, L'Oréal, Nippon Lever, and Procter & Gamble, typify the foreign companies that experienced a collapse of the prices their products commanded at retail levels. They encountered year-on-year manufacturing level price reductions of approximately five percent."[70] In what might be called "post-bubble" Japan, much is changing. Table 10.3 provides a description of some of these changes and their implications. Successful foreign companies in Japan are those that understand the Japanese market and play by Japanese rules.[71] High levels of technological capability are also important.[72]

Changes in Europe have made it increasingly important for U.S. companies to be involved there. Privatization programs in the United Kingdom and elsewhere and a fundamental restructuring of the financial capital markets in countries such as Germany have put a lot more assets into the hands of private citizens.[73] A common currency (the euro) and reduction of trade barriers among many European countries have created a more open market of 340 million consumers.[74] Reduction in

Table 10.3   Changes in Japan After the Economic Bubble Burst

Factor	Pre-Bubble Japan	Post-Bubble Change	Implications for Foreign-owned Affiliates
Japanese Business Environment	Major obstacles to success in Japan were high operating costs and extreme competitiveness.	Remains a tough, highly competitive environment; price destruction, distribution becoming more concentrated; increasing expectations of fast retailer response.	Power brands; vertical integration to encompass retail sector
Consumers	Japanese consumers very willing to adopt new products; they work hard and long to support radical spending habits.	Increased balance between work and family; some convergence with "international values."	More and different products consumed in the home.
Heritage	Cramped living conditions in Japanese cities and high concern for aesthetics made Japanese consumers a ready target for luxury products.	Luxury designer products hold strong, but consumers are more price/value conscious; luxury products sold through discount outlets.	Quality and image remain important but are supplemented by functional and value claims.
Consumer Interest	Japanese consumers delighted in foreign travel and out-of-home experiences; led to preference for foreign designer brands with premium pricing.	More focus on home; more value-for-money-driven behavior; increased emphasis on functional performance, less brand devotion.	Justify positioning of brands and price levels, value-driven positioning; stress on dependability and function.
Product Churning	Japanese companies were known for churning out new products regardless of justification.	Reduction in product-emulation activity.	Products must have genuine consumer justification.
Insider Strategy	Success for foreign-owned companies believed to be associated with becoming a part of Japanese "insider," an integral part of the business community.	May still be true, but foreign-owned companies attempting "insider" strategies are struggling.	Adopt those aspects of "insiderism" that are financially justified.
Marketing Skills	The pace of change in Japan required a sharpening of marketing skills.	Marketers in Japan still maintain dedicated dialogue with consumers.	Need to gear up to track consumer.

Source: Adapted with permission from *Journal of International Marketing,* published by the American Marketing Association, D.M. Reid, "Changes in Japan's Post-Bubble Business Environment: Implications for Foreign-Affiliated Companies," 7 (1999): 38-63.

trade barriers
Factors that discourage international trade, such as tariffs and import quotas

trade barriers means that companies involved in Europe can more easily take advantage of regional variations in wage rates and the cost of raw materials, which can lead to lower costs of production. Also, differentiation is easier to achieve because organizations can draw freely from the technological strengths of each nation. Companies that have businesses in Europe already enjoy the advantages of a typically well-educated workforce, a well-developed infrastructure, a sophisticated level of technology, and high consumer demand—all factors that are associated with "First World" countries. The recent changes in Europe make it even more attractive for investment.

Foreign investment in Russia and the old Soviet bloc is also increasing. The countries that make up the former Soviet Union may have up to a quarter of the world's undiscovered oil, about equal to the oil remaining in the Middle East. The former Soviet states also possess more natural gas than any other country. Dozens of companies are rushing to help bring this oil to market; however, instability in the region makes investment recovery difficult and risky.[75] Oil is not the only risky business in Russia. Although Russia's many regions are working to attract funds from foreign investors, investments often bring unexpected problems. For example, a British steelmaker that bought Kazakstan's largest steel plant had to negotiate for two months to get more than a dozen old KGB agents to leave their electronically sophisticated corner office in the factory.[76] Furthermore, communist ideals are still popular, and some Russian officials are working to reverse business privatization.[77] Nevertheless, in the aftermath of the September 11, 2001, attacks, Russian relations with the United States improved dramatically.

 When retired General Fyodor I. Ladygin, a former head of Russian military intelligence, first heard reports that U.S. military cargo planes had landed in the former Soviet republic of Uzbekistan in Central Asia, he figured the Americans had cut a sly deal with the Uzbeks without consulting the Russians. No way, Ladygin told Business Week on September 24, (2001), would Russian President Vladimir V. Putin give a green light to stationing the U.S. military in Russia's own backyard. Wrong prediction, General: In a speech that very evening on national television, Putin voiced support for such deployments to assist the U.S.-led campaign against international terrorism. Of all the surprising developments the world has witnessed since the attack on the World Trade Center, the sudden rapprochement between Russia and the United States is one of the most startling.[78]

Many characteristics must be evaluated when considering a foreign country for investment. Many of them fall within the general areas of the broad environment, including the social environment, the economy, the political/legal environment, and the state of technology. Other characteristics are related to specific industries and markets. Questions concerning each of these factors are listed in Table 10.4. These questions are a useful tool for evaluating a potential country for investment.

The wrong answers to any of the questions in Table 10.4 can make a country less attractive. The following are some examples that demonstrate this point: (1) an unstable government can greatly increase the risk of a total loss of investment; (2) an inefficient transportation system can increase total product costs to prohibitively high levels; (3) inadequate school systems can result in poorly skilled workers, who then may not have the ability to manufacture technical products; (4) a slowly growing GNP could mean that consumer demand will be sluggish; (5) high foreign tax rates can virtually eliminate profits; and (6) if the local currency cannot be translated into U.S. dollars, the organization will have a tough time removing profits from the country.

Answers to the questions should also be judged based on the type of activity the organization is considering. For example, a high per-capita income is favorable if the company is only going to sell U.S. products in the foreign market (export). On the other hand, low per-capita income could mean that wages are very low, which is positive if the firm is considering only foreign manufacturing or assembly.

One of the most important factors to consider when deciding whether to enter a country is the state of its capital markets. Some economies support very well developed capital markets with very efficient financial transactions, while other economies are less-well developed (see Figure 10.3). **Market-centered economies** have well-developed infrastructures, business environments, and external capital markets. Laws and regulations regarding capital markets are well developed and enforced. The capital market is not dominated by either equity or debt as a source of funding. Examples are the United States and the United Kingdom. **Bank-centered economies** also have well-developed infrastructures and business environments. However, capital markets are not as strong as in the United States or the United Kingdom. Banks and other financial institutions play the most significant role in the external capital markets. One of the advantages of this system is that banks are willing to let companies take on higher debt levels, and then are willing to help the borrowers through tough times. Examples of bank-centered economies are Japan and Germany.

market-centered economies
Economies with well-developed infrastructures, business environments and external capital markets

bank-centered economies
Banks and other financial institutions play the most significant role in the external capital markets

Table 10.4   Examples of Questions to Ask About a Potential Foreign Market

Social Forces
What currently are the hot topics of debate? How well organized are special-interest groups with regard to the environment, labor, and management issues? Are current policies or behaviors of the organization likely to be offensive in the new host country? What is the attitude of potential consumers toward foreign products/services? Will there be significant cultural barriers to overcome? How difficult is the language? How old is the population? What other differences could cause difficulty for the organization?

The Economy
What is the inflation rate? How large is the gross national product (GNP)? How fast is it growing? What is income per capita? How much impact does the global economy have on the domestic economy? How high is the unemployment rate? What actions does the government take to fuel economic growth? What is the trade balance with the United States? Can the currency be exchanged for the home currency? How high are interest rates? Is the financial sector well organized? How expensive are the factors of production?

Political/Legal Environment
What is the form of government? How much influence does the government have over business? Is the government stable? What is the attitude of the government toward private enterprise and U.S. firms? What is the attitude of the home government toward the foreign government? How high are tax rates compared with the home country? How are taxes assessed and collected? How high are import and export taxes? What is the nature of the court system? Is legal protection available through incorporation or a similar form?

Technology
Is the country technologically advanced? Do schools and universities supply qualified workers? Are the required skills available in sufficient quantity? Are suitable information systems available? Is the infrastructure sound (i.e., roads, transportation systems)? Is an appropriate site available?

Industry Specific
How large is the industry? How fast is it growing? Can it be segmented? How many competitors are there? How strong are they? What is the relative position of industry participants in relation to suppliers and customers? Are substitute products available? What is the primary basis for competition? Is there a possibility of reaching the market through a joint venture?

family-centered economies

Families hold a lot of the stock in large corporations, allowing them a lot of control

group-centered economies

Groups of companies manage the use of internal capital as a replacement for external capital markets

emerging economies

Economies that have historically been dominated by government influence, with poorly developed financial capital markets; some are now pursuing privatization programs to put economic assets in the hands of private citizens

In **family-centered economies,** families hold a lot of the stock in large corporations, allowing them control. A pyramidal structure is often used to maintain control.[79] At the lower levels, the parent company holds stock in its subsidiaries. At the next level, different parent companies are linked to a large financial institution. At the highest level, these financial institutions are interconnected through "capital networks and interlocking directorates." A good example of a family-centered economy is France, where about a third of the largest companies are still managed by their founders or heirs. Other examples are Sweden and Italy.

Group-centered economies such as Korea do not have strong financial systems. Groups of companies manage the use of internal capital as a replacement for external capital markets. This system is sometimes created because only the government is able to borrow abroad. The government then channels borrowed money into particular sectors. Firms in those sectors secure funds from the government, diversify their portfolios, and then recycle capital into other ventures. Finally, **emerging economies** historically are dominated by government ownership of the economic enterprise, with very little development of financial capital markets. Some of these economies are now pursuing privatization programs that put economic assets in the hands of private citizens. These programs are experiencing varying levels of success. Examples of emerging economies include Russia, China, and Argentina.[80]

Strategic Management in the Future

Without question, the greatest managerial challenges lie ahead. It is hard to predict with precision the kind of business environment the next generation of managers will face; however, judging from the recent past, it will probably be associated with increasing global complexity and interconnectedness. Major events like those that

FIGURE 10.3

Institutional Differences Across Countries

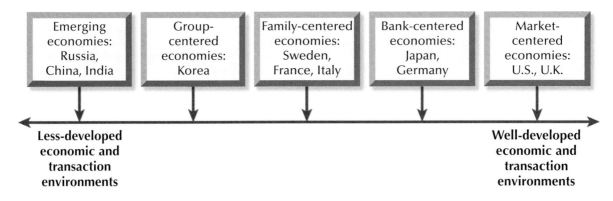

Source: R. E. Hoskisson et al., "Restructuring Strategies of Diversified Business Groups: Difference Associated with Country Institutional Environments," in *The Blackwell Handbook of Strategic Management,* ed. M. A. Hitt, R. E. Freeman and J. S. Harrison (Oxford: Blackwell Publishers, 2001), 444. Used with permission.

transpired on and after September 11, 2001, are hard to predict, yet they result in sweeping global changes in the business environment. Table 10.5 contains a few of the characteristics that, based on recent trends, might be expected to exist in the business environment of the early twenty-first century.

What kind of leaders will be needed to navigate through the business environment of the future? They will be strategic thinkers—people who are willing to break with conventional norms, but at the same time learn from and respect the past. They will be revolutionaries who don't simply seek incremental improvements to existing business systems to increase efficiency, but invent new business concepts. [81] As Bill Gates said of Microsoft, any company can be " two years away from failure."[82] At any time, a competitor may develop a product that makes another company's product obsolete. They will be global thinkers, eager to establish relationships with outstanding companies, to obtain the best resources, and to sell in the most advantageous markets, regardless of where they are found. They will be sensitive to the organizational and external environment, realizing that long-term success requires a broad attitude regarding what and who is important. Finally, they will be able to instill in organizational members an urgent sense of vision.

The tools, theories, and techniques found in this book can help you become an effective leader for the next century. I encourage you to apply what you have learned to current and future business situations in which you and your organizations are found.

Summary

One of the outcomes of increasing internationalization is that countries are economically interconnected at an unprecedented level. Among the most popular reasons companies make foreign investments are to search for new markets or better resources, increase efficiency, reduce risk, or counter the competition. For example, organizations may find that the best suppliers of a particular good or service are not in their own countries. If they are going to be "world class," they have very little choice but to develop business relationships where the best suppliers operate. Structural inertia within U.S. companies has been a major impediment to their

Table 10.5	Strategic Management for the Twenty-First Century

- Increasing levels of global trade and global awareness
- Global and domestic social turbulence
- Increased terrorism and a worldwide effort to eliminate it
- Increased sensitivity to ethical issues and environmental concerns
- Rapidly advancing technology, especially in communications
- Continued erosion of buying power in the U.S. and other economies
- Continued development of third world economies
- Increases in U.S. and global strategic alliances
- Revolution in the U.S. health-care industry
- Greater emphasis on security and crisis management

transformation into true global competitors. However, the United States had a "wake-up call," and now American companies are rushing to foreign markets in an effort to catch up. International activities should be accompanied by a new mind-set for all members of an organization, from top managers to the lowest-level employees. CEOs are instrumental in creating this mind-set.

Global strategic management provides challenges and opportunities that are not found in domestic markets. Stakeholder management is more complicated because of the diversity of people, organizations, and governments involved. However, a more diverse environment offers more opportunities to develop stakeholder-based competencies through effective management and interorganizational relationships. Also, global diversity provides a much larger pool of resources from which to draw—including human resources; physical resources such as raw materials, supplies, and locations; and technological know-how. Companies that operate in countries with uncommon factor conditions, demand conditions, related and supporting industries, or exceptional firm strategies, structures, or rivalry may be at a comparative advantage relative to other global competitors.

Multinational strategies tend to fall into two broad categories. International expansion is the process of building an expanding operational presence. Global integration is the process through which a multinational organization integrates its worldwide activities into a single world strategy through its network of affiliates and alliances. Some firms are more globally oriented than others. A company's attitude toward international expansion is another element of its strategic direction. Organizations seem to evolve through four stages of international development—the domestic stage, the international stage, the multinational stage, and the global stage.

The role of foreign subsidiaries in a multinational company is changing from being treated as simply "branch locations" to a full role in the development of new competencies, capabilities, resources, and products, depending on the company's capabilities and resources. If capabilities and resources are limited either by virtue of the country in which a subsidiary operates or by insufficient internal resources, then the subsidiary might be assigned an implementation role. Subsidiaries that exist in countries with special advantages or that have specific internal-resource advantages are expected to make a specialized contribution. Subsidiaries with a global mandate must have substantial skills and resources from which to draw, both from the country environment and internally. Matrix and transnational structures are helpful in integrating activities across subsidiaries, especially where those subsidiaries have highly related activities. International strategic alliances are an outstanding way to acquire both resources and skills.

One of the key issues facing top managers as their organizations pursue international development is selection of a product/market approach. A multidomestic strategy entails handling product design, assembly, and marketing on a country-by-country basis by custom-tailoring products and services around individual market needs. On the other hand, organizations pursuing a global strategy produce one product design, and market it in the same fashion throughout the world. Firms must also determine which expansion tactics they will pursue. Common options include exporting, licensing, franchising, joint ventures, wholly owned subsidiaries, and acquisitions. Among the most important criteria when deciding on an option for international growth are cost, financial risk, profit potential, and control. Another factor that seems to influence the decision among international growth options is multinational diversity.

World markets also provide outstanding opportunities with regard to business-level strategy. Organizations that are involved in multiple global markets have advantages available to them in pursuing their business-level strategies. They can use global strategies to strengthen their cost positions or to increase differentiation. The merger-and-acquisition wave that has been so prevalent in the United States has become a global trend. It has created some enormous, highly diversified global companies. Another major trend is industry consolidation. Some global firms are pursuing economies of scope through highly integrated, related businesses, while others are pursuing unrelated diversification. Unrelated diversification may be more appropriate in some developing countries because internal capital management in conglomerates may substitute, in part, for well-developed external capital markets.

Many characteristics should be evaluated before entering a foreign market. They fall into the areas of the broad environment, including the social environment, the economy, the political/legal environment, and the state of technology. Other characteristics are related to specific industries and markets. One of the most important factors to consider when deciding whether to enter a country is the state of its capital markets.

Discussion Questions

1. What are some of the outcomes from increasing global interdependence among companies? Why might a firm want to pursue internationalization?

2. Describe the four stages of global development. Give an example of a company that is in each of these stages.

3. How can an organization create more of a global mind-set?

4. Explain the conditions that can lead a nation to produce a disproportionate amount of global leaders in particular industries.

5. Describe the various roles played by foreign-owned subsidiaries. What determines which role they will play?

6. What is the difference between a global and a domestic product/market strategy, and what are the advantages and disadvantages of each? Is there a strategy in between these extremes?

7. What are the major expansion tactics, and what are the factors that determine which one is the preferred approach?

8. How can a firm use business-level strategy to strengthen its cost position or increase differentiation?

9. What are some of the major trends in global corporate-level strategy?

10. What should a company consider before entering a foreign market?

Strategic Application

Selecting a Foreign Market for Entry

Assume that you are the CEO of a retailer of exotic foods. You import foods from foreign countries for sale in your own country through about 40 store locations, but you haven't yet opened any stores in the countries from which you import. You would like to expand into a foreign market by opening one or two stores there, with the potential for future expansion if those stores work out. Select a foreign country and do some research (on-line or in the library) to determine whether it would be a reasonable choice for this type of expansion. Use Table 10.4 for ideas on what you should include in your evaluation.

Strategic Internet Application

Michigan State University provides a wealth of information to the public on global business climates. You can access their Web site at http://globaledge.msu.edu/ (or if it has changed recently, do a search for "Global Edge"). In that Web site, find the link to "Country Insights." You will be directed to a choice of world regions. For each of the regions of Asia, Latin America, Europe, Africa, and North America, select one country for further analysis. At a minimum, read the information on the economy, history, statistics, and the government for each country. Then answer the following questions:

1. Which of the countries would seem to be the greatest risk for business investment? Why?

2. Which of the countries seems to hold the greatest potential for business investment leading to growth? Profit? Why do you think so?

3. If you were exporting a basic food commodity, such as wheat or sugar, which country would seem to offer the greatest potential? Why?

4. If you were exporting a high-tech consumer product, such as a hand-held electronic device, which country would seem to offer the greatest potential? Why?

5. How do the countries you selected compare to your own country with regard to government stability, economic growth, and infrastructure (such as roads, transportation systems, information systems, and so forth)?

Notes

1. Quotations in first paragraph are from W. Zellner et al., "How Well Does Wal-Mart Travel?" *Business Week*, 3 September 2001, 82; the second paragraph came from D. Luhnow, "How Nafta Helped Wal-Mart Reshape the Mexican Market," *The Wall Street Journal*, 31 August 2001, A1.

2. J. Ewing, "The Fallout in Europe," *Business Week*, 8 October 2001, 52–53.

3. M.L. Clifford, "Trapped in the Tornado," *Business Week* 8 October 2001, 54.

4. J. Booth, "Terror Attacks to Harm Asian Economies," *The Wall Street Journal*, 16 October 2001, A23,

5. H. Henzler and W. Rall, "Facing Up to the Globalization Challenge," *McKinsey Quarterly* (Winter 1986): 52–68; T. Peters, "Prometheus Barely Unbound," *Academy of Management Executive* (November 1990): 70–84; M. E. Porter, *Competition in Global Industries* (Boston:

Harvard Business School Press, 1986), 2–3; S. Tallman, "Global Strategic Management," in *The Blackwell Handbook of Strategic Management*, ed. M. A. Hitt, R. E. Freeman, and J. S. Harrison (Oxford: Blackwell Publishers, 2001), 464–490.

6. K. Ohmae, "Becoming a Triad Power: The New Global Corporation," in *Global Strategic Management: The Essentials*, 2d ed., ed. H. Vernon-Wortzel and L. H. Wortzel (New York: John Wiley, 1991), 62–74.

7. Tallman, "Global Strategic Management," 464.

8. M. E. Porter, "Changing Patterns of International Competition," *California Management Review* 28, no. 2 (1986): 9–40; Tallman, "Global Strategic Management."

9. N. J. Adler, *International Dimensions of Organizational Behavior*, 2d ed. (Boston: PWS-Kent Publishing, 1991); R. L. Daft, *Organization Theory and Design*, 4th ed. (St. Paul, Minn.: West

Publishing, 1992), 228–229; T. T. Herbert, "Strategy and Multinational Organizational Structure: An Interorganizational Relationships Perspective," *Academy of Management Review* 9 (1984): 259–271.

10. D. W. Grigsby, "Hasbro, Inc," in *Strategic Management for Decision Making*, ed. M. J. Stahl and D. W. Grigsby (Boston: PWS-Kent Publishing, 1992), 725–738.

11. "Nike Net Surged 21% in Quarter to Record; Stock Rises by $6.375," *The Wall Street Journal*, 9 July 1992, B4

12. J. Sheth and G. Eshghi, *Global Strategic Management Perspectives* (Cincinnati, Ohio: South-Western Publishing, 1989), 13.

13. J. Betton and G. G. Dess, "The Application of Population Ecology Models to the Study of Organizations," *Academy of Management Review* 10 (1985): 750–757.

14. C. A. Bartlett and S. Ghoshal, "Global Strategic Management: Impact on the New Frontiers of Strategy Research," *Strategic Management Journal* 12 (1991): 5–16.

15. Adapted from L. Smith, "Does the World's Biggest Company Have a Future?" *Fortune,* 7 August 1995, 124

16. B. Bremner, "The President Has a Will, But No Way," *Business Week,* 15 March 1999, 92–95.

17. M. Muller, "Employee Representation and Pay in Austria, Germany, and Sweden," *International Studies of Management and Organization* 29, no. 4 (2000): 67–83; R. Calori and B. Dufour, "Management European Style," *Academy of Management Executive* (August 1995): 61–73.

18. Excerpted and adapted from M. Maruyama, "Changing Dimensions in International Business," *Academy of Management Executive* (August 1992): 88–96, used with permission.

19. S. Tully, "The Hunt for the Global Manager," *Fortune,* 21 May 1990, 140–144; J. Main, "How 21 Men Got Global in 35 Days," *Fortune,* 6 November 1989, 71.

20. Maruyama, "Changing Dimensions."

21. A. McWilliams, D. D. Van Fleet, and P. M. Wright, "Strategic Management of Human Resources for Global Competitive Advantage," *Journal of Business Strategies* 18, no. 1 (Spring 2001): 1–24.

22. E. H. Bernstein, ed., *Strategic Management* (Guilford, Conn.: McGraw-Hill/Dushkin, 2001), 81, first published in D. Bank, "You've Got Time Warner!" *The Wall Street Journal,* 11 January 2000.

23. Bernstein, *Strategic Management,* 23, first published in Y. M. Ibrahim, "Nokia: Made in Finland and Sold Just About Everywhere," *The New York Times,* 13 August 1997.

24. N. Nohria and S. Ghoshal, *The Differentiated Network* (San Francisco: Jossey-Bass, 1997).

25. G. S. Yip, *Total Global Strategy: Managing for Worldwide Competitive Advantage* (Englewood Cliffs, N.J.: Prentice Hall, 1992).

26. J. M. Birkinshaw and A. J. Morrison, "Configurations of Strategy and Structure in Subsidiaries of Multinational Corporations," *Journal of International Business Studies* 26 (1995): 729–754.

27. Tallman, "Global Strategic Management," 485.

28. B. Bremner et al., "Keiretsu Connections," *Business Week,* 22 July 1996, 52–54.

29. Reuters, "Virgin, Sprint in Wireless Venture," *Orlando Sentinel,* 6 October 2001, B9.

30. A. C. Inkpen, "Learning and Knowledge Acquisition through International Strategic Alliances," *Academy of Management Executive* 12, no. 4 (1998): 69.

31. A. Raghavan, A. Petersen, and N. Deogun, "Motorola Talks with Siemens about Venture," *The Wall Street Journal,* 1 October 2001, A3.

32. K. Ohmae, "Managing in a Borderless World," *Harvard Business Review* (May/June 1989): 152–161.

33. Adapted from R. Jacob, "Trust the Locals, Win Worldwide," *Fortune,* 4 May 1992, 76.

34. T. Levitt, "The Globalization of Markets," *Harvard Business Review* (May/June 1983): 92.

35. S. P. Douglas and Y. Wind, "The Myth of Globalization," *Columbia Journal of World Business* (Winter 1987): 19–29.

36. M. A. Hitt, R. D. Ireland, and R. E. Hoskisson, *Strategic Management: Competitiveness and Globalization* (Minneapolis: West Publishing, 1995).

37. H. G. Barkema and F. Vermeulen, "International Expansion through Start-up or Acquisition: A Learning Perspective," *Academy of Management Journal* 41 (1998): 7–26; C. W. L. Hill, P. Hwang, and W. C. Kim, "An Eclectic Theory of the Choice of International Entry Mode," *Strategic Management Journal* 11 (1990): 117–128; C. W. L. Hill and G. R. Jones, *Strategic Management: An Integrated Approach* (Boston: Houghton Mifflin, 1992), 254–259

38. Barkema and Vermeulen, "International Expansion through Start-up."

39. S. J. Chang, "International Expansion Strategy of Japanese Firms: Capability Building Through Sequential Entry," *Academy of Management Journal* 38 (1995): 383.

40. Business and Finance, *The Wall Street Journal,* 21 February 1996, A1.

41. Some of the options contained in this list were based on information found in M. L. Fagan, "A Guide to Global Sourcing," *Journal of Business Strategy* (March/April 1991): 21–25; Sheth and Eshghi, *Global Strategic Management Perspectives;* and Stahl and Grigsby, *Strategic Management for Decision Making,* 205–206.

42. Some of the options contained in this list were based on information found in Sheth and Eshghi, *Global Strategic Management Perspectives,* and Stahl and Grigsby, *Strategic Management for Decision Making,* 205–206.

43. D. Roberts and A. Webb, "Buying Binge: An M&A Wave Breaks over China," *Business Week,* 29 January 2001, 48–49.

44. P. Starobin and C. Belton, "The Big Are Getting Bigger Fast," *Business Week,* 16 July 2001, 50.

45. C. Rapoport, "A Tough Swede Invades the U.S.," *Fortune,* 29 June 1992, 76–77

46. Bernstein, Strategic Management, 25, first published in A. Cowell, "Zeneca Buying Astra As Europe Consolidates," *The New York Times,* 10 December 1998.

47. D. J. Teece, "Economies of Scope and the Scope of the Enterprise," *Journal of Economic Behavior and Organization* 1 (1980): 223–247.

48. S. Reed, A. M. Pascual, and W. C. Symonds, "Chapter 2 at Pearson," *Business Week,* 22 January 2001, 80.

49. R. A. Johnson, "Antecedents and Outcomes of Corporate Refocusing," *Journal of Management* 22 (1996): 437–481.

50. R. E. Hoskisson et al., "Restructuring Strategies of Diversified Business Groups: Difference Associated with Country Institutional Environments," in *Blackwell Handbook,* ed. Hitt, Freeman, and Harrison, 433–463.

51. O. E. Williamson, *Markets and Hierarchies, Analysis and Antitrust Implications: A Study in the Economics of Internal Organization* (New York: The Free Press, 1975).

52. Based on personal experiences as a trainer and consultant to South American companies.

53. Hoskisson et al., "Restructuring Strategies," 433–463.

54. C. Karmin and P. Murphy, "IMF Aid Lists Argentina Stocks, but Jitters Remain," *The Wall Street Journal,* 23 August 2001, C1.

55. T. Kamm and J. Friedland, "Spanish Firms Discover Latin America Business As New World of Profit," *The Wall Street Journal,* 23 May 1996, A1, A9.

56. C. Larroulet, "Look to Chile for an Answer to the Latin Malaise," *The Wall Street Journal,* 24 August 2001, A9.

57. C. J. Whalen, P. Magnusson, and G. Smith, "Nafta's Scorecard: So Far, So Good," *Business Week,* 9 July 2001, 54–56.

58. J. Cummings and N. King Jr., "Mexico's Fox Gets Commitment from Bush to Reshape Ties, Even If Congress Balks," *The Wall Street Journal,* 7 September 2001, A16.

59. O. Edur, "Setting Up Shop Abroad," *CMA Management* (September 2000): 54.

60. B. B. Read, "Scoring Points Up North," *Call Center Magazine,* September 2001, 36.

61. J. Rohwer, "GE Digs into Asia," *Fortune,* 2 October 2000, 165–178.

62. J. Labate, "The World Economy in Charts," *Fortune,* 27 July 1992, 62.

63. L. Kraar, "Asia 2000," *Fortune,* 5 October 1992, 111.

64. K. H. Zhang, "What Attracts Foreign Multinational Corporations to China?" *Contemporary Economic Policy* 19 (2001): 336–346.

65. P. M. Norton and L. Huang, "Management Fraud in China," *The China Business Review* (March/April 2001): 26–35.

66. R. N. Sanyal and T. Guvenli, "American Firms in China: Issues in Managing Operations," *Multinational Business Review* (Fall 2001): 40–46.

67. Ibid.

68. D. M. Reid, "Changes in Japan's Post-Bubble Business Environment: Implications for Foreign-affiliated Companies," *Journal of International Marketing* 7 (1999): 38–63.

69. Ibid., 46.

70. M. G. Allen, "Succeeding in Japan," *Vital Speeches of the Day* 60 (1994): 429–432.

71. H. Yoshihara, "Foreign Companies in Japan—Key Factors for Success and Failure," *Management Japan* 24, no. 1 (1991): 17–24.

72. A. Spicer, G. A. McDermott, and B. Kogut, "Entrepreneurship and Privatization in Central Europe: The Tenuous Balance between Destruction and Creation," *Academy of Management Review* 25 (2000): 630–649; S. Ogden and R. Watson, "Corporate Performance and Stakeholder Management: Balancing Shareholder and Customer Interests in the U.K. Privatized Water Industry," *Academy of Management Journal* 42 (1999): 526–538; M. Johnson, "Germany Gets a Makeover," *Global Finance* 14, no. 11 (November 2000): 31–39.

73. D. Fairlamb and G. Edmonson, "Out from under the Table," *Business Week,* 24 September 2001: 116–120; S. Tully, "Europe 1992: More Unity Than You Think," *Fortune,* 24 August 1992, 136–142.

74. P. Nulty, "The Black Gold Rush in Russia," *Fortune,* 15 June 1992, 126.

75. K. Pope, "A Steelmaker Built Up by Buying Cheap Mills Finally Meets Its Match," *The Wall Street Journal,* 2 May 1996, A1, A10.

76. N. Banerjee, "Russia's Many Regions Work to Attract Funds from Foreign Investors," *The Wall Street Journal,* 30 April 1996, A1, A13; S. Liesman,

"Some Russian Officials Are Moving to Reverse Business Privatization," *The Wall Street Journal,* 20 March 1996, A1, A6; C. Rosett, "Communists Mount Comeback in Russia, and Mean Business," *The Wall Street Journal,* 27 March 1996, A1, A4.

77. P. Starobin, C. Belton, and S. Crock, "Vladimir Putin, Washington's Pal?" *Business Week,* 8 October 2001, 56.

78. P. Windolf, "The Governance Structure of Large French Corporations: A Comparative Perspective," paper presented at the Sloan Project on Corporate Governance at Columbia Law School, May 1998.

79. Hoskisson et al., "Restructuring Strategies."

80. G. Hamel, *Leading the Revolution* (Boston: Harvard Business School Press, 2000).

81. G. Hamel, "The Challenge Today: Changing the Rules of the Game," *Business Strategy Review* 9, no. 2 (1998): 19–26.

Strategic Management
Of Resources and Relationships

Cases

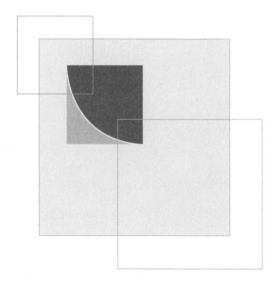

Learning Through Case Analysis

Strategic management is an iterative, ongoing process designed to position a firm for competitive advantage in its ever-changing environment. To manage an organization strategically, a manager must understand and appreciate the desires of key organizational stakeholders, the industry environment, and the firm's position relative to its stakeholders and industry. This knowledge allows a manager to set goals and direct the organization's resources in a way that corrects weaknesses, overcomes threats, takes advantage of strengths and opportunities, and, ultimately, satisfies stakeholders. The first ten chapters of this book contain a foundation for understanding these strategic management processes.

With case analysis, you can practice some of the techniques of strategic management. Case analysis, to some extent, mirrors the processes managers use to make real strategic decisions. Managers have somewhat of an advantage over students who analyze cases because they have more information available to them and more experience. For example, managers have ongoing relationships with internal and external stakeholders, from whom information can be gathered. They may also have a business intelligence-system and staff to help them make decisions. In addition, managers usually have substantial experience in the industry and company. Nevertheless, managers must still make decisions without full information. Like students, they never have all of the facts or the time and resources to gather them. In case analysis, you must decide what information is accurate and relevant.

Case authors attempt to capture as much relevant information as possible. They typically conduct extensive interviews with managers and employees, and gather information from public sources such as annual reports and business magazines. Many cases include a detailed description of the industry and competitors as well as an extensive profile of one organization. You can supplement this information through your own library research if your instructor thinks this is appropriate.

Case analysis typically begins with a brief introduction of the company. The introduction, which sets the stage for the rest of the case, should include a brief description of the defining characteristics of the firm, including some of its outstanding qualities, past successes, failures, and products or services. The industries in which the firm is involved are also identified.

The next section of a case analysis can be either an environmental analysis or an internal-resource analysis. Both types of analysis are required before all of the organization's opportunities can be identified. I typically treat environmental analysis first because it establishes the context in which firm strategies and resources can be understood. However, reversing the order of analysis would not be incorrect, and is even preferred by many strategic management scholars.

Environmental analysis is an examination of the external environment, including external stakeholders, the competition, and the broad environment. Systematic external analysis will help you draw conclusions about the potential for growth and profit in the industry and determine keys to survival and success in the industry.

An organizational-resource analysis, which follows the external analysis, is designed to evaluate the organization's strategic direction, business- and corporate-level strategies, resources, capabilities, and relationships with internal and external stakeholders, and then determine the strengths, weaknesses, vulnerabilities, and sources of competitive advantage exhibited by the firm. These determinations must be made against a background of knowledge about the external environment so that the full range of opportunities and threats can also be identified.

Structuring an Environmental Analysis

An analysis of the external environment includes an industry analysis and an examination of key external stakeholders and the broad environment. Findings are then summarized, with an emphasis on identifying industry growth and profit potential and the keys to survival and success in the industry. Some organizations are involved in more than one industry. Consequently, a separate industry analysis is done for each of the industries in which a firm is involved.

The Broad Environment

A complete environmental analysis includes an assessment of the broad environment, including social influences, economic influences, political influences, and technological influences. Each of these areas is evaluated only as it relates to the industry in question. The areas should be evaluated at the domestic and global levels, if appropriate. Forces in the broad environment may pose threats or provide opportunities.

Industry Analysis

The first step in industry analysis is to provide a basic description of the industry and the competitive forces that dominate it. Porter's Five Forces are evaluated, along with other relevant issues.

- What is the product or service? What function does it serve? What are the channels of distribution?
- What is the industry size in units and dollars? How fast is it growing? Are products differentiated? Are there high exit barriers? Are there high fixed costs? These are some of the forces that determine the strength of competition among existing competitors.
- Who are the major competitors? What are their market shares? In other words, is the industry consolidated or fragmented?
- Who are the major customers of the industry? Are they powerful? What gives them power?
- Who are the major suppliers to the industry? Are they powerful? What gives them power?
- Do significant entry barriers exist? What are they? Are they effective in protecting existing competitors, thus enhancing profits?
- Are there any close substitutes for industry products and services? Do they provide pressure on prices charged in this industry?
- What are the basic strategies of competitors? How successful are they? Are competitors likely to retaliate to competitive moves or countermoves? How rapidly do they respond?
- Is the industry regulated? What influence do regulations have on industry competitiveness?
- Are any other external stakeholders important in this industry? Examples might include labor unions, special-interest groups, financial institutions, or local communities.
- To what extent is the industry global? Are there any apparent advantages to being involved in more than one nation?

After describing the industry as it is now, you should try to capture the underlying dynamics that will create industry change and require new strategic approaches. One useful way to accomplish this is to group factors that influence the industry into two categories: those that create and influence industry demand, and those that create and influence industry cost structures and profit potential. The findings of this part of the analysis will help you decide whether the industry is "attractive" (growing and profitable) and worthy of further investment (i.e., time, money, resources). It will also help you identify areas in which the firm may be able to excel in an effort to create a competitive advantage.

Factors That Influence Demand   Many industry factors and stakeholder actions create and influence demand for products and services. Some of the factors are part of the broad environment of the firm, such as the state of the economy. Other factors are part of the operating environment, most of which are related to the actions of two key stakeholder groups: customers and competitors. If the underlying factors that create demand are changing, then it is likely that demand patterns will change. For example, demand for washing machines is a function of household formations and replacements. To predict future demand, you would study the numbers of people in the household-forming age bracket, durability of washers, and economic conditions.

Some of the factors that create and influence demand and growth prospects in an industry include:

- The function(s) served by the product
- The stage of the product life cycle (i.e., degree of market penetration already experienced)
- Economic trends, including income levels and economic cycles (i.e., recession, boom)
- Demographic trends (part of social-trend analysis) such as population and age
- Other societal/cultural trends, including fads and commonly held values and beliefs
- Political trends, which may include protectionist legislation such as trade barriers
- Technological trends, including new applications, new markets, and cost savings that make prices more competitive
- Programs developed by firms in the industry, such as new-product introductions, new marketing programs, new distribution channels, and new functions served
- Strong brand recognition, domestically or worldwide
- Pricing actions that stimulate demand

After analyzing the factors that create and influence demand, you should be able to draw some conclusions about growth prospects for both the industry and the firm. Since you can never be certain about the timetable and ultimate outcome of a trend that, by definition, is changing over time, one technique that may be useful is to develop alternative demand scenarios. For example, if the health of the economy is a major driver of a product's demand, you could consider the upside and downside of an economic recovery using the following type of format: "If the economy recovers within six months, then industry demand for the product could be the highest in five years. If the recovery does not materialize, then demand might linger at last year's levels."

Factors That Influence Cost Structures   After determining growth prospects for the industry, you will want to determine the cost structure and profit potential of the industry. As with demand, there are various factors and stakeholder actions that create and influence cost/profit structures in an industry. Among these factors are:

- Stage of the product life cycle. In the early stages of the life cycle, firms have large investments in product development, distribution-channel development, new plant and equipment, and workforce training. In the latter stages, investments are more incremental.

- Capital intensity. Large investments in fixed costs such as plants and equipment make firms very sensitive to fluctuations in demand—high levels of capacity utilization are needed to cover or "spread" fixed costs. Industries that have a lower relative fixed-cost investment but higher variable costs are able to control their costs more readily in turbulent demand periods.

- Economies of scale

- Learning/experience effects

- The power of customers, suppliers, competitive rivalry, substitutes, and entry barriers. Powerful customers, suppliers, competitive rivalry, substitutes, or low entry barriers can erode profit potential.

- The influence of other stakeholders, such as powerful foreign governments, joint-venture partners, powerful unions, strong creditors, and others.

- Technological changes that provide opportunities to reduce costs through investing in new equipment, new products, and new processes or that alter the balance of investments between fixed and variable costs

After systematically profiling the factors and stakeholder actions that influence cost structures and profits, you should be able to draw conclusions about industry profit potential. After the basic environmental analysis is complete, the next step is to perform a more detailed examination of the major strategic issues facing the industry.

Strategic Issues Facing the Industry

A thorough environmental analysis provides the information needed to identify factors and forces that are important to the industry in which your organization is involved—and, therefore, important to your organization. These factors and forces may be categorized as follows:

- Driving forces in the industry, which are trends that are so significant that they are creating fundamental industry change, such as the opening up of Eastern Europe or networked-computer communications. Of course, each industry will have its own unique set of driving forces.

- Threats, defined as noteworthy trends or changes that threaten growth prospects, profit potential, and traditional ways of doing business

- Opportunities, which are important trends, changes, or ideas that provide new opportunities for growth or profits

- Requirements for survival, identified as resources and capabilities that all firms must possess to survive in the industry. An example in the pharmaceutical industry is "product purity." These factors do not command a premium price. They are necessary, but not sufficient to be successful.

- Key success factors, which are factors that firms typically should possess if they desire to be successful in the industry. An example in the pharmaceutical industry is the ability to create products with new therapeutic qualities. This ability may lead to high performance.

Having completed an analysis of the external environment, you are ready to conduct a more specific analysis of the internal organization.

Structuring an Organizational-Resource Analysis

Understanding industry trends, growth prospects, profit potential, and key strategic issues can help you critique an organization's strategies and evaluate its strengths and weaknesses. For example, what might qualify as a strength in one industry may be an ordinary characteristic in another industry. A good organizational analysis should begin with a general evaluation of the internal organization.

Evaluation of Strategic Direction and the Internal Environment

The following questions are useful in beginning to assess the internal organization:

- What is the company's strategic direction, including its vision, business definition, and values? If these factors are contained in a formal mission statement, share it. If not, you may want to write one. Remember that organizations have a strategic direction even if it is not written down.

- How has the strategic direction changed over time? In what way? Has the evolution been consistent with the organization's capabilities and planned strategies?

- Who are the principal internal stakeholders? In particular, who are the key managers, and what is their background? What are their strengths and weaknesses? Are they authoritarian or participative in their management style? Is this appropriate for the situation? What seems to drive their actions?

- Who owns the organization? Is it a publicly traded company with a board of directors? If there is a board and you know who is on it, is the composition of the board appropriate? Is there an individual or group with a controlling interest? Is there evidence of agency problems? How active are the owners, and what do they value?

- What are the operating characteristics of the company—including its size in sales, assets, and employees; its age; and its geographic locations (including international operations)? Does the company have any unique physical resources?

- Are employees highly trained? If a union is present, how are relations with the union?

- How would you describe the organization's culture? Is it a high-performing culture? Is it supportive of the firm's strategies?

Most instructors also require a financial analysis, both to identify financial strengths and weaknesses and to evaluate performance. A financial analysis should include a comparison of ratios and financial figures with major competitors or the industry in which the organization competes (cross-sectional), as well as an analysis of trends in these ratios over several years (longitudinal). Financial-ratio analysis can provide an indication as to whether the firm is pursuing appropriate strategies. Poor financial trends are sometimes symptoms of greater problems. For example, a firm may discover that administrative costs are increasing at a faster rate than sales.

This could be an indication of diseconomies of scale or the need for tighter controls on overhead costs. Financial analysis is also used to indicate the ability of the firm to finance growth. For example, managers of a firm that has very high leverage (long-term debt) may have to be less ambitious in their strategies for taking advantage of opportunities. On the other hand, an organization with a strong balance sheet is well poised to pursue a wide range of opportunities. Strong financial resources are often hard to imitate in the short term.

When superficially analyzed, ratios can be more misleading than informative. For example, in comparing return-on-assets for two firms in the same industry, the one with the higher ratio could have superior earnings or devalued assets from too little investment. Two firms can differ in return-on-equity because of different debt-equity financing policies rather than from true performance reasons. When accurately interpreted and considered in the larger organization context, the analysis may also uncover strengths, weaknesses, or symptoms of larger organizational problems.

Analysis of Resources and Capabilities

The foregoing analysis of the internal environment provides an excellent starting point for identifying key resources and capabilities. For example, outstanding resources and capabilities may result from (1) superior management, (2) well-trained employees, (3) an excellent board of directors, (4) a high-performance culture, (5) superior financial resources, (6) effective knowledge-generating processes, or (7) the appropriate level and type of international involvement. However, these potential sources of competitive advantage barely scratch the organizational surface.

You also should evaluate the organization's primary value-chain activities to identify resources and capabilities. These activities include the company's (8) inbound logistics, (9) operations, (10) outbound logistics, (11) marketing and sales, and (12) service, as well as the support activities of (13) procurement, (14) technology development, (15) human-resource management, and (16) administration. In addition, an organization may have (17) an excellent reputation, (18) a strong brand name, (19) patents and secrets, (20) excellent locations, (21) outstanding learning capabilities, or (22) strong or valuable ties (i.e., alliances, joint ventures, contracts, cooperation) with one or more external stakeholders. All of these potential resources and capabilities (and many others) have been discussed in this book. They form a starting point that you can use to help identify the potential sources of competitive advantage. Each company will have its own unique list.

It is useful to screen resources and capabilities based on their long-term strategic value. This process entails asking several questions:

- Does the resource or capability have value in the market?

- Is the resource or capability unique?

- Is there a readily available substitute?

Positive answers to the first two questions and a negative answer to the third mean that the resource or capability has the ability to provide a source of competitive advantage. Two additional questions are then asked:

- Do organizational systems exist that allow realization of potential?

- Is the organization aware of and realizing the advantages?

Opportunities can exist if an organization is not taking advantage of sources of competitive advantage, either because it is unaware of them or because systems are not in place yet to take advantage of them. A final question is then asked:

- Is the resource or capability difficult or costly to imitate?

If it is difficult or costly to imitate a resource or capability, it can be a source of sustainable competitive advantage. A final part of this analysis is to determine whether the resource or capability can be applied to multiple business areas. If this is the case, it can be classified as a core competency or capability.

Performance Evaluation

The next step in internal analysis is to describe and critique the organization's past strategies. In critiquing strategies, you will need to describe them in detail, discuss whether they have been successful, and then *evaluate whether they fit with the industry environment and the resources and capabilities of the organization.*

- What is the company's pattern of past strategies (corporate-level, business-level, international)?

- How successful has the company been in the past with its chosen strategies? How successful is the company now?

- For each strategy, what explains success or failure? (Use your environmental- and organizational-resource analyses to support your answer.)

Many instructors require their students to evaluate the success of an organization on the basis of both qualitative and quantitative (financial) measures. The financial measures were developed during your financial analysis,

so you need only to make reference to them here. Some common qualitative measures include product or service quality, productivity, responsiveness to industry change, innovation, reputation, and other measures that indicate key stakeholder satisfaction (i.e., employees, customers, managers, regulatory bodies, society).

Summary of Situation Analysis

On the basis of your environmental and organizational analyses, you should be in a position to draw some conclusions about the situation your organization is facing, called a situation analysis. Many students will do this by creating lists of strengths and weaknesses, opportunities and threats. Strengths are defined as firm resources and capabilities that can lead to a competitive advantage. Weaknesses, on the other hand, are resources and capabilities that the firm does not possess, resulting in a competitive disadvantage. Consequently, each of the resources and capabilities identified during the organizational analysis should be measured against the factors identified in the environmental analysis.

Opportunities are conditions in the external environment that allow a firm to take advantage of organizational strengths, overcome organizational weaknesses, or neutralize environmental threats. Consequently, now that the organizational analysis is complete, you should reevaluate your list of opportunities to determine whether they apply to your organization. You should also evaluate threats to make sure they are applicable to your firm. Threats are conditions in the broad and operating environments that may stand in the way of organizational competitiveness or the achievement of stakeholder satisfaction.

At this point, you may also want to add to your list of opportunities some of the potential linkages and alliances that the firm could develop with external stakeholders. For example, if your company is strong in production but weak in foreign marketing, you may see an opportunity to enter a new foreign market through a joint venture with a strong marketing company. Another example may involve neutralizing a threat of new government regulation by forming an alliance with competitors to influence the regulating body.

Developing a Strategic Plan

Your environmental and organizational analyses helped you to evaluate the past strategies and strategic direction of the firm, as well as to develop a list of strengths, weaknesses, opportunities, and threats. The next step is to make recommendations concerning the strategies the company may want to pursue in the future. If the firm is not a stellar performer, this should be an easy task. However, even companies that have been highly successful in the past should consider taking advantage of opportunities and should respond to threats. History has taught us that organizations that are unwilling to move forward eventually decline.

Strategic Direction and Major Strategies

You should probably begin your strategic recommendations by focusing on the strategic direction and major strategies of the firm. Based on your earlier analyses, you may want to consider adjustments to the mission of the firm, including its vision or business definition. Determine whether the business definition is still appropriate, given your environmental analysis. Is your dominant industry stagnant? Is it overregulated? Is competition hurting profitability? Should you consider investing in other industries? If so, what are their defining characteristics? What core competencies and capabilities could be applied elsewhere? What opportunities could be explored that relate to the corporate-level strategies?

The business-level strategy should also be considered. If you determined earlier that the business-level strategy is not as successful as it should be, what adjustments should be made? Could the company have more success by focusing on one segment of the market? Or, if the company is pursuing a focus strategy, would broadening the target market be appropriate? If the company is following cost leadership, would a differentiation strategy work better? If differentiation doesn't seem to be working very well, would a cost-leadership strategy be better? Finally, would a best-value strategy be the most appropriate?

It is possible that you may want to leave the strategic direction and major strategies alone, especially if the organization has enjoyed recent success. Regardless of whether you altered the direction and strategies, at this point you have now established what you think they should be. The direction and corporate- and business-level strategies provide guidance for fine-tuning an organization's strategies. Each of the recommendations you make from this point on should be consistent with the strategic direction and major strategies of the organization. At this point, it is time to explore strategic opportunities further.

Evaluation of Opportunities And Recommendations

Using the strategic direction and corporate- and business-level strategies as guides, strategic opportunities should be evaluated further. These alternatives were generated during earlier analyses. They include:

- Opportunities that allow a firm to take advantage of organizational strengths. These opportunities may involve alternatives such as better promotion of current products and services, new products or services, new applications for existing products and services within existing markets, exploring new domestic or foreign markets, diversifying into areas in which strengths can be applied, or creation of joint ventures with companies with complementary strengths. These are only a few examples.

- Opportunities for the firm to overcome organizational weaknesses. Do any of the organizational weaknesses relate to an area that you described in your industry analysis as essential for survival? Do any of the weaknesses relate to key success factors? Firms can overcome their weaknesses through strategies such as learning from joint-venture partners, creating new alliances with other organizations that are strong where the company is weak, or fixing problems internally through R&D, better controls, efficiency programs, information technology, and so on. Again, these are only a few examples.

- Opportunities for the firm to neutralize environmental threats. These often involve creation of strategic alliances to offset the influence of a powerful stakeholder such as a government regulator, a strong union, a powerful competitor, or an influential special-interest group. The firm may form an alliance *with* the powerful stakeholder or with other stakeholders in an effort to balance the power. Companies may also form alliances to help cope with threats emerging from the broad environment.

Evaluation of opportunities means much more than simply accepting them on the basis of earlier environmental and organizational analyses. They should also be evaluated based on factors such as the following:

- Value added to the organization. Some alternatives may have high potential for growth in revenues, while others may be oriented toward improving efficiency, eliminating problems, taking advantage of organizational strengths, or any of a wide range of other factors. Any of these factors may add value to the organization. As you perform this part of the analysis, make sure that you look at long-term value as well as short-term value.

- Influence of the alternative on organizational costs. The actual dollar costs to an organization are often difficult for a student to estimate. (If you can make reasonable estimates, go ahead and do so—in some cases, you cannot). However, you should always provide a description of all of the costs. For example, assume you are evaluating an alternative such as "Imperial Toy Company should expand through exporting toys to Japan." Costs would include import/export duties, transportation, foreign taxes, time devoted by managers (existing and new), salaries, warehousing, marketing research, advertising, and so on. Describe the costs—don't just list them. Tell specifically the types of items each would include. The reason you are doing this is because you can still compare the costliness of one alternative to another alternative even though you may not be able to do so with specific dollar amounts.

- The extent to which the alternative fits within the organization. Base this part of your analysis on such things as whether the alternative takes advantage of current distinctive competencies; the ability of the firm to successfully execute the alternative; and whether the existing culture, management, and resources of the organization will support implementation of the alternative. Make sure to specify whether this alternative is consistent with the current strategic direction of the company or whether it requires new direction.

- Risks associated with the alternative. Consider such things as financial risk; risk to the reputation of the firm or its existing strengths; and risk to particular stakeholder groups such as employees, managers, special-interest groups (representing the environment, etc.), or suppliers. Part of this analysis should anticipate the reactions of competitors to the strategy and what could happen if they respond in an adverse manner.

- Stakeholder analysis. How will this strategy affect key stakeholders? Which ones are likely to support it? Are they high priority? Which ones are likely to oppose it? Are they high priority? What are the strategic ramifications of their support or opposition?

- Future position. Will the strategy continue to be viable as the industry and the broad environment undergo their expected changes? Will it provide a foundation for survival or competitive success?

The result of this analysis should be a recommendation or recommendations that the organization should pursue. Many evaluation tools can facilitate the evaluation process, such as a payoff matrix (illustrated in Table 1). However, the tools should never act as substitutes for in-depth analysis of the alternatives themselves. In other words, even if a numeric score-keeping system is used, the numbers should be explained based on detailed strategic analysis.

You may not be required by your instructor to conduct a formal analysis of alternatives based on a standard set of criteria; however, you should still make recommendations concerning changes the organization should make to remain or become competitive and satisfy its stakeholders. Through this entire process, remember that many companies identify areas of strength that are no longer capable of giving the company a competitive edge. What was a key to success yesterday may be a requirement for survival today.

Implementation and Control

Recommendations should always be accompanied by an implementation plan and basic controls. The following are major questions that should be addressed during this section of a case analysis. The last two items relate specifically to control.

- How do the recommendations specifically address concerns that were identified during the analysis?

- What will be the roles and responsibilities of key internal *and* external stakeholders in carrying out the recommendations, and how are they expected to respond? What actions should be taken to smooth out the transition period or avoid stakeholder discontent?

- Does the organization have the resources (funds, people, skills) to carry out the recommendations? If not, how should the organization proceed in developing or acquiring those resources?

- Does the firm have the appropriate systems, structures, and processes to carry out the recommendations? If not, how should the firm proceed in creating the appropriate systems, structures, and processes?

- What is the appropriate time horizon for implementing recommendations? What should the company and its managers do immediately, in one month, in six months, in a year, and so on?

- What are the roadblocks the organization could encounter while implementing the recommendations (e.g., financing, skilled-labor shortages)? How can the organization overcome these roadblocks?

- What are the desired outcomes or changes the company should expect once the recommendations have been implemented? How will the company know if the recommendations have been successful? In other words, what are the objectives associated with your recommendations?

- What were some of the major assumptions you made with regard to the external environment? Which of these factors, if different from expected, would require an adjustment to your recommendations?

Table 1   Payoff Matrices

You may decide to include a payoff matrix in one of your case analyses. If you do, a common way to set up a payoff matrix is as follows:

	Value Added	Cost	Fit	Risk	Total
Alternative 1	1	2	5	1	9
Alternative 2	5	3	2	3	13
Alternative 3	4	3	4	3	14

(Scale: 1 is the worst, and 5 is the best)

Of course, you would call your alternatives by their real names instead of calling them Alternative 1, Alternative 2, and Alternative 3. You could also weight the importance of the criteria on a scale from 1 to 5, and then multiply the values by the weight and sum them. This would more heavily weight the factors you think are important.

This kind of a payoff matrix is a useful way to numerically summarize your evaluation of alternatives. Nevertheless, it has limitations. For example, is there really a meaningful difference between Alternatives 2 and 3 in this matrix? If you select Alternative 3, do you realize that your recommendation did not receive the best score for Value Added? Is this a problem? Maybe it is or maybe it isn't. Notice that fit is much better for Alternative 3 compared to Alternative 2. An equally effective, non-numerical alternative comparison table is found below:

	Value Added	Cost	Fit	Risk	Total
Alternative 1	Not Much Value	High Cost	Excellent Fit	Many Risks	Not Strong
Alternative 2	Highest Value	Average Cost	Weak Fit	Moderate Risk	Fit Could be Big Problem
Alternative 3	Average Value	Average Cost	Good Fit	Moderate Risk	Best Overall

In addition, some instructors require separate functional plans for areas such as finance, human resources, or marketing. Chapter 8 contains detailed information that should help you develop these plans.

Following the implementation section, you may want to update your audience (your instructor or other students) concerning actions the firm has taken since the case was written. If a case update is required, it should center on actions that pertain to the focus of your case analysis. If you do an update, remember that what the organization did, even if it appears to have been successful, may not have been the optimal solution.

A Note to Students

If you are reading this appendix early in the course, you will have the rest of the semester or quarter to practice the case-analysis process and study the chapter readings. If you are reading this appendix later in the course, we encourage you to go back to earlier chapters and refresh your memory concerning the concepts that were covered. Just as this course integrates material you learned during your years of business study, the case-analysis process integrates material from all sections of the strategic management course.

Since there is not a standard method for analyzing cases, your instructor may teach a method of case analysis that differs from the approach contained herein. Also, cases can be treated in many different formats, including class discussions (complete with discussion questions to be answered before coming to class), written papers, formal presentations, and class debates. Finally, some cases do not lend themselves to comprehensive analysis. After reading this appendix, check with your instructor for specific instructions and requirements.

Case 1

ABB in China: 1998

Michael Lubatkin, *University of Connecticut,* **Suzanne Uhlen,** *Lund University*

"I want to make ABB a company that encourages and demands innovation from all of its employees, and a company that creates the environment in which teamwork and innovation flourish," declares ABB's CEO Göran Lindahl. In seeking new growth, CEO Göran Lindahl is moving out of the long shadow of his predecessor Percy Barnevik. The former CEO of ABB, Percy Barnevik, was argued to probably be one of the most successful international managers in Europe.

ABB, the world leader in electrical engineering, is a US$35 billion electrical engineering group, with companies all over the globe. It operates primarily in the fields of reliable and economical generation, transmission, and distribution of electrical energy.[1] Much has been written about the worldwide company. In 1996 ABB was ranked in the top forty of the first 500 companies listed by *Fortune* magazine. Recently, the company has announced their newest reorganization that will make the company more up-to-date with the global world as the current CEO, Göran Lindahl, expressed.[2] Göran Lindahl took over from Percy Barnevik as CEO in 1997 of the technology giant ABB, and the pressure from the shareholders and the market is highly demanding.

ABB has different priorities in different markets. Western Europe and North America are the company's biggest markets. However, the high-potential markets are the Middle East, Africa, Latin America, and Asia. These markets are growing fast and ABB expects to have half of its customers in these regions not long into the next century. The priority is on building local manufacturing, engineering, and other forms of added value. ABB wants to integrate these operations into the global networks to get full synergy effects and scale economies.

During 1998 it has been shown that the industrial production in OECD countries, in which ABB performs about 75 percent of its total business, continues to grow, although at a slower pace than the strong growth rates a year ago. Overall, industrial production in Europe is lower than a year ago, but still high compared to historical levels. Current economic activity in North America is slowing compared to the strong economy of recent years. In Latin America, high interest rates are delaying the financial closing of projects in an environment of reduced economic activity. The Indian economy is slowing, also due to reduced exports as a result of its strong currency compared to others in the region. Southeast Asia is gradually stabilizing at a low level with reduced consumption and investments.

As a result of the ongoing economic uncertainty, overall global demand is forecast to remain soft in the near future. ABB expects to benefit with its well-established local presence around the world from higher demand in various industries and world markets. Appropriate cost cutting, continued selective tendering, and successful working capital reduction programs are expected to continue contributing positively to the ABB Group results. The company recognizes the world to be rapidly changing and increasingly unpredictable. Efforts have paid off and the Group has taken its opportunities in Asia and positioned itself for future growth in what is seen to be "*the world's most dynamic market over a long term—China.*"[3]

The interest in China is growing steadily and companies in Japan, the Western European countries, the United States, and elsewhere today view the Chinese market as having enormous potential. With a population of a billion and a growing economy, it has appeared to be worthwhile to make a major effort to gain a foothold in the market.[4] On the one hand, China represents a huge and largely untapped market. The Chinese market alone is potentially bigger than that of the United States, the European Community, and Japan combined! On the other hand, China's new firms are proving to be very competitive, and China's culture is quite different from that of the West. However, on the Chinese market the growth remains at a relatively good level for a long row of enterprises such as Procter & Gamble, Motorola, Nestlé, and ABB. This market is regarded to act as a lifeboat to a lot of worldwide companies suffering from the financial crisis in the rest of Southeast Asia. Nevertheless, discussions exist about China devaluating their currency or not, which might also drag

China down into the crisis. Yet the country has, however, not shown any visible scratches from the surrounding crisis. China seems to be unshakable and analysts are still valuing China as the country of the future.[5] Thus, the changes in China are creating both opportunities and threats for established worldwide companies. This is a country, which, according to *Management Today*, will be one of the top 10 economies in the world by the year 2010.[6]

Chinese Influence

> China will enter the next century as the rising power in Asia after two decades of astonishing economic growth that has transformed the country and that has given rise to new challenges.[7]

Many cities in China have more than five million inhabitants. It is a country that has had a growing economy, which cannot be compared to any other country during almost three decades.[8] It is argued that China is not like any other developing country, due to the rapid changes that are taking place in certain areas. In some areas, such as with home electronics,[9] the development has surpassed the development in western countries, while in other areas China lags far behind.

The Chinese culture and society stretch back more than five thousand years. There is a unique cultural heritage of philosophy, science and technology, societal structures, and traditional administrative bureaucracy.[10] With this in mind it is no wonder, according to researchers, that conflicts often occur between Chinese and foreign cultures. This is due to the fact that foreign managers are accustomed to other values and norms, some of which may hardly be acceptable in China.[11]

In the current half-year reports from worldwide companies, a distinct trend is noticed according to *Dagens Industri*.[12] The more focus that the companies have put on basic industry, the more the Asian crisis tends to affect these companies. However, China is the country that can save these companies and others, but especially those companies operating in the business of infrastructure.[13] Now that the Cold War with China has ended, economic growth is stabilizing and the country is demanding a speedy reconstruction. The country has begun to enjoy unprecedented strategic latitude for the first time in 200 years and it no longer faces the threat of aggression from superior powers.[14] This has enabled the country to focus on economic developments as the driving force of both its domestic and foreign policies. According to Professor Yahuda, China's leaders also have come to base their legitimacy on providing the conditions of stability in which people can look forward to continued high levels of prosperity. The need for economic development is fuelled by many other factors, such as providing employment for a vast population that increases by some 15 million people a year. Additionally, there are significant regional inequalities that can only be addressed by further economic development.[15]

China is expected to evolve into a hybrid system of authoritarianism, democracy, socialism, and capitalism. Also recognized are the internal problems the country faces such as environmental disasters, political struggles, and tensions between the emerging entrepreneurial economy and the vast parts of China still under state control.[16] Today China receives the most direct investment and foreign aid of any developing country. Many companies are eager to establish their presence in China, which, it is argued, attracts more than its proportionate share of investments.[17] However, concluding remarks are; " … *westerners cannot expect to know how China will develop and need to expect that the Chinese will always be different from them. Instead of trying to change China, they should look for positive steps that take their differences into account*"[18]

According to China's Premier Zhu Rongji, China is indeed the largest market in the world. However, due to the problem of duplicate construction, there is a problem of oversupply in some areas. Nevertheless, the Premier states that the market is far from being saturated.[19] Since China opened up its doors to the outside world in the late 1970s, a large number of foreign investors have gained rich returns from their investments, yet some have ended in failure. Some guiding keys to ensuring success in business in China according to *China Daily* include:[20]

- Making long-term strategies for the Chinese market. Competition is intensifying and market exploitation needs time and patience. Foreign companies eager to get a quick return are usually disappointed at the results.

- Localizing staff. They are familiar with the local business environment.

- Being aware of changes in policies and regulation. China is in a process of transforming from a planned economy to a market economy. Various policies and regulations are being revised and replaced, while new ones are being issued. Foreign investors must keep informed of the ongoing changes.

- Undertake practical market research. Due to social, economic, and cultural differences, practical and down-to-earth market research is a must before and during investment in China.

Chinese Cultural Influence

There is a consensus among several authors concerning the belief that there is in China a traditional respect for age, hierarchy, and authority.[21] This originates from the Confucian concept of *li* (rite, proprietary), which plays an important role in maintaining a person's social position. *Li* can be seen today in the existing traditional bureaucracy and in vertical relationships concerning centralization of decision-making, and in corruption to some extent, which is acceptable in such a cultural context.[22]

Secondly, the family is viewed as an essential social unit and there is a strong tendency to promote the collective or the group. Members within the family or group must maintain harmonious relationships and these social relations are seen as more important than the individual.[23] Thus, the family or clan norms are adopted as the formal code or conduct, and members are bound to these standards. Other research found that in modern China, business and industrial enterprises were perceived as an extension of the family system.[24]

Thirdly, the concept of "face" (*mianzi*) is seen as an important characteristic. As Ju noted, the general idea of *mianzi*, is related to "*a reputation achieved through getting on in life through success and ostentation.*"[25] *Mianzi* also serves to enhance harmony within the family or group, so that the positive is expressed publicly and any conflicts remain private.[26] Hong has found that the concept of *mianzi* still plays an important role in social relationships and organizational behavior.[27] However, Yuan points out that there are two sides to this concept.[28] The first includes the individual's moral character and the strong fear of losing this limits the person's behavior. The second aspect of *mianzi* involves assertions about a person, which is not seen quite as serious as the former loss of face.[29]

The importance of personal relations (*guanxi*) is the fourth characteristic. According to Hong, persons with *guanxi* usually share a common birthplace, lineage, surname, or experience, such as attending the same school, working together, or belonging to the same organization.[30] A comparative study of decision-making in China and Britain has revealed that Chinese managers use their personal *guanxi* more widely to exchange information, negotiate with planning authorities, and accelerate decision-making processes than managers from British firms.[31] As it is, the network transmits information, and, because contacts and co-operation are built on trust, it is seen as very serious if that trust is broken. If a trust is broken, the whole network will soon know about the incident and it is maintained that the person involved will have a hard time doing business again.[32]

A company that has been doing business on the Chinese market since 1919 is ABB. At that time, this was the first product delivery to China, and it was not until 1979 that ABB established its first permanent office. Almost 11 years later, the heart of almost every chairman of an energy company started to pound with excitement if it heard the words 'Asia' and 'electricity.' There were billions to be had from the booming demand for electricity in Asia.[33] But in recent years, the emerging Asian market has slowed down due to the financial crisis in the area. At the moment it seems like China is the only country not affected by this financial crisis, and consequently there are many companies who are now trying to be successful in China.

ABB is argued to be a company with a good position on the Chinese market due to good performance, delivery, autonomy, and also its good name. Today the company has nine representative offices and 15 joint ventures and the number of employees has grown in four years from approximately 1,000 to 6,000 employees in China.

Local Roots

The strategy of ABB is to use its global strength to support the needs of its local customers around the world. However, in China, ABB has a fairly high import duty on its products, which limits how much the company can sell. The idea of setting up local production in China was to increase the market share, due to the fact that most Chinese customers do not have foreign currency[34] and are consequently forced to buy locally produced goods with the local currency. The reason for ABB to localize in China was furthermore not to achieve lower production costs, as some locally supplied components are actually more expensive in China than elsewhere. It was rather to be closer to the local market, and therefore facilitate a few local modifications to the products and provide shorter delivery times to the customer.

The phase "think global, act local," is said to reflect ABB's fundamental idea of strong local companies working together across borders to gain economies of scale in many areas.[35] In spite of ABB claims to be able to respond swiftly and surely to market conditions,[36] some of the products in China are not truly adapted to the local market. Most of the products are designed for the IEC—an international standard association based in Europe. The company manufactures products, which have to be tested according to different norms and standards. For example, North America ABB follows the ANSI-standard and in Canada the CSA-standard.

However, some of ABB's products would not pass a type test based on the Chinese standards. That is not because the quality is too low, on the contrary the quality of ABB products is sometimes too high. The quality of some of the products has evolved far beyond the requirements of Chinese standards—therefore these ABB products cannot meet the standards. The Chinese standards are based on what the local manufacturer can produce, because the country does not have much other information. As one manager at ABB in China stated:

> We are not going to redesign our products in order to meet the standards for the obvious reasons, why should we take our quality out, why shall we take the advances out. It does become an issue from time to time. Chinese are very risk averse, if we have not done the type test in China. It is more to cover themselves in case something goes wrong.

Some other managers expressed that they felt more that even though ABB tries to adapt the products to the Chinese local standard there was a negative response because the customer regards Western standards as superior and are actually asking for the superior product. The Chinese customers are seen as tough and sometimes demand more tests than ABB's products have gone through. Another reason put forward is insufficient feasibility studies when setting up new joint ventures in China. This delays the work when new information has to be collected about the market conditions. This aspect originates from the speed of changes in China and the difficulty for the company to catch up with what is going on.

However, when the so-called "type tests" of the product has been done, the company cannot change the design due to the high costs involved in this test. Some criticism has been heard that ABB should adapt more to the Chinese situation, which the company cannot respond to concerning the technical design, because then the tests have to be done all over again. Of course, it is different from product to product for some of the products, as one manager said,

> we have to adapt to the configurations the customers have a demand for, because they have an option—go to the competitor.

Still in most cases, the local ABB companies in China are not allowed to change the products other than according to agreements with the licensee. The reason for that is that the technology partners[37] have the overall view of the quality and performance. The ABB corporation definitely does not want to have different product performance from different countries. The products must have the same descriptions, in order that they are seen as the same product all over the world. Consequently the local ABB company can only do a few modifications to the standard product for the specific customer and cannot change the technology involved. The technology partners have a few alternatives that meet the demands of the Chinese customers and these products are also tested, but do not necessarily meet the Chinese standards.

The local ABB company tries to follow the ABB Group's policy, to be close to the customer and responsive to his or her needs.[38] In China, however, contracts are not commonly used, and this frequently obstructs satisfying the many customer demands.

> They keep on saying this is China and you should adapt to the Chinese way: Ok, if you want to buy a Chinese product that's fine, but this is our product—here are the terms and conditions. You can't just give in to that; otherwise you will kill your company, because they expect you to accept unlimited liability and lifetime warranty and the risks to which you would expose your company would eventually lead to its shutting down, so you just cannot do that.

To be close to the customer is stated within ABB to be the best guarantee that local requirements are met.[39] However, the headquarters in Zurich has also set up some rules about the kind of contracts that the local subsidiaries shall sign worldwide. In China contracts are as argued above, something rather new, and many Chinese customers do not want it that way. The consequence is that some ABB companies in China do not use the standard ABB contract and are actually responsive to the customers' needs. When another ABB company comes to the same customer to set up a standard contract, the customer will refer them to the previous ABB company who did not seem to find the contract necessary. The question asked by the confused customer is said to be: "Why do you then have to use a standard contract when the other ABB didn't?"

Profit Centers

ABB's strategy is to take full advantage of its economies of scale while at the same time being represented by national companies in many home markets where some 5,000 entrepreneurial profit centers are attentive to every local customer. These companies are quite independent and have to stand on their own economically. In addition, the individual company's profit can easily be compared to revenue. In other words, the individual ABB company is measured on its own performance and needs, of course, a profit when selling products or parts, even though it is within the ABB Group. It is recognized that the profit centers are efficient for decentralization and that the organization can act relatively fast. This also enables the company to be sensitive and responsive to potential problems. Each company has a fair amount of autonomy, which in turn makes the individual company flexible in the decision-making process. Even though, ABB brochures state that the strategy of having profit centers enables the easy transfer of know-how across borders,[40] it is argued that the direction is pretty much one way—from the technology partners, Business Areas and Country level to the subsidiary, rather than a two-way exchange.

Nevertheless, some conflicts of interest have occurred, due to the fact, for example, that the local ABB company and all other licensees are more or less dependent on their licensors in Europe.[41] In the local ABB company's case, a factory in X-city that is one of their technology partners is measured, like everyone else, on its performance and on its profit. If it gives the local ABB company support, it will cost the former money, and likewise, if it sells the local ABB company components, it wants to make a profit. The consequence is that it is charging the local ABB company 25–100 percent over and above the cost of its parts.

> So in the end you end up calling them as little as possible and we end up buying parts from local suppliers that probably we should not buy from local suppliers. And we reduce our quality. They have great profit figures, we have some profit figures but there are some real serious problems along the way.

The technology partner argues on the contrary, that the prices are high because it first has to buy from its supplier and then sell to the local ABB company. This, of course, makes the products more expensive, and also because the technology partners pay for the "type tests" and all the product development.[42]

These kinds of disagreements or conflicts have been occurring for a long time within ABB, but nobody has yet found a solution. It is said to be difficult for a company like ABB, which is working with so many different products, markets, and in different cultures to have anything else than sole profit centers. If the profit centers did not aim for a profit when selling within the ABB Group, it is argued that the companies would no longer be independent companies. Being independent is seen as a strength, and therefore it would be against the laws of nature if the companies were not always aiming for a profit. Nonetheless, between these independent companies with profit centers there are some extreme examples:

> Our partner in Y-country was selling the finished product in China before. Now he sells the parts to the joint venture in China and wants to charge more for the parts than he did for the finished product, and that is because it is in his interest and he will be evaluated on his performance. If he does not do that, his profits will be too low and he will be blamed for it. So he has got to do what he has got to do. That is what he is motivated to do and that is what he is going to do.

To some extent the technology partners are even selling indirectly to the Chinese market using non-official agents to avoid a high import tax and slip under the high market price that exists on the Chinese market. ABB China has tried to put a stop to these agents and they are trying to force ABB companies to use only two official channels for ABB goods into the Chinese market—the locally produced by the local ABB company and the directly imported from a technology partner.

Structure

ABB is a huge enterprise with dispersed business areas, which encompass the three segments: Power Generation, Transmission & Distribution, and Industrial Building systems. However, this has recently been changed and divided into six segments. Before the reorganization, every country had its national ABB head office with a country management who dealt with all the company business in that particular country. The other dimension of the matrix structure reflects the clustering of the activities of the enterprise into 36 Business Areas (or BAs). Each Business Area represents a distinct worldwide product market. Simplified, each BA is responsible for worldwide market allocation and the development of a worldwide technical strategy for that specific product line. Additional responsibilities for the BA are to coordinate who shall supply or deliver where, and also to work as a referee in potential disagreements between companies within the ABB Group.

However, in China, as in most developing countries, there is no BA in place and the decision-power of the Country management is consequently closer at hand. As a result, it is argued that the power of the decision-making tends to rest more heavily on the country level than on the BA level. Disagreements between licensees in western countries and subsidiaries in China have been, and are occurring, due to different business orientations. The local subsidiary in China has two or more licensors in western countries from which they buy components. Some of the licensees sold these components themselves before the local subsidiary was set up in China. In some cases the licensee feels that the market in China was taken from them and that they therefore can only compensate for potentially lost sales by charging the Chinese subsidiary a higher cost. Consequently, if the disagreeing partner seeks the BA as a referee in this kind of case, the following happens and is explained by one manager:

> The BA are looking at the global business—we can increase our global business if we set up a joint venture in China. But the technology partner can't increase their business if we set up a joint venture in China. If we set up a joint venture in China the technology partner wants to increase its business also, they are going to do some work, and of course want something for it. The BA is really powerless to push those along.

To date, the licensors have also been paying for all the technology development, which is, from their point of view, the reason for charging a higher price for the components they are selling. Since the enterprise is divided into 5,000 profit centers and because each of these profit centers wants a profit when selling a component or product, there have been some shortcomings in the coordination and cooperation between the licensors and the local Chinese subsidiary.

The licensor in X-country makes the same breakers that the local ABB company does, and when they run into quality problems they don't always inform each other. For example, in Germany they are ineffective in informing their licensee in China who will probably also run into the same quality problem in the near future. The problem is also discussed at the local ABB company, but if they suggest changes to the licensor, the licensor will evaluate on the basis of benefits to itself. Since they are going to invest their own resources they are, of course, going to invest in areas beneficial to themselves first or charge the local ABB company extra. The consequences are thus:

> We have had some things that would really help us here in China. But I don't even bother, because I know the reaction.

Over 80 percent of what the Centers of Excellence produce is going to be exported,[43] which makes it especially important that the partners of the licensor can manage the contemporary challenges and opportunities that can emerge. However, the BA divides the world markets into different areas in which the specific ABB companies are to be a so-called first source.[44] Between some

of the licensors and the local ABB company this has resulted in certain disputes. For example:

> We are responsible for the Peoples Republic of China's market and are supposed to be the sole source (or rather first source) because we have the expertise for this market. Our technology partner in X-country quotes into this market on a regular basis, does not inform us, and competes against us, and takes orders at lower prices. This can destroy our position in the market place.

According to the licensor, they do not quote in the local ABB company's market due to the fact that if a final customer has foreign currency they will prefer imported products. The licensor argues that they do not go into the Chinese market and offer their products, but do get inquiries from ABB in Hong Kong and deliver to them. Hong Kong sells, in their turn, the products directly to the Chinese customer after having increased the original price up to the market price that is often several times higher in China than in Europe, for example. It is a decision of the ABB China management that the Hong Kong coordinated sales force shall sell the local ABB company's products on the Chinese market among imported products and locally joint venture produced products. It is argued that it helps to have sales coordination, that is the decision as to whether the products should be imported or not.

The technology is owned today by the Centers of Excellence in Europe or so-called licensors, which are also the ones paying for all the product development. ABB has chosen these licensees to be responsible for becoming the company's world source of this specific technology. These units are responsible for developing new products, and look after the quality by arranging technical seminars about the technology, and by keeping special technology parts—so called "noble parts"—at only their factory. The strategic decision to keep special parts and the drawings of these parts at only one chosen factory enables the company to secure itself against competitors copying their products. Consequently, these parts will not be localized or purchased in China. However, for one product group (THS) there has been an organizational change including the establishing of a unit called CHTET, which shall now own all new technology that is developed and also pay for the product development. This change now involves all product groups.

Multicultural

The current fashion, exemplified by ABB, is for the firms to be "multicultural multinationals," which means for the company to be very sensitive to national differences.[45]

Barnevik did debate that a culturally diverse set of managers can be a source of strength. According to Barnevik, managers should not try to eradicate these differences and establish a uniform managerial culture. Rather, they should seek to understand these cultural differences, to empathize with the views of people from different cultures, and to make compromises for such differences. Barnevik believes that the advantage of building a culturally diverse cadre of global managers is to improve the quality of managerial decision making.[46]

ABB in China is typified by a culturally diverse set of managers with a mixture of managerial ideas, derived from the different managers' national backgrounds, different values, and different methods of working. It then depends on which stage in personal development the manager has reached if he or she is going to be influenced and absorb the new climate. Or as one manager said:

> If you are close to being retired you might not change so much, there isn't much point. But you can't work in the same way as you do at home—it just wouldn't work.

According to another manager, ABB is a very international company with a great deal of influence from Scandinavian culture. However, it is a mixture of many cultures and it really depends on where the ABB company is located. Here in China the ABB culture is influenced by Chinese culture, by the environmental circumstances, and by the laws. It is stricter in China than it is, for example, in Europe, because there are more rules. In spite of that, the managers do not feel that the result is a subculture of the ABB culture, rather a mixture of managers from different cultures—*"we are a multidomestic company."*

However, the top level of the ABB management is seen to be far away from the daily life at the subsidiary level in China, such as at the Local ABB company. Or as one manager expressed *"between that level and here, it's like the Pacific Ocean."* All the managers argue, though, that what the top level, including Barnevik and Lindahl,[47] says sounds very good and that is how it should be. Some managers continued the discussion and expressed this difference:

> Sounds like I'm working for a different ABB than these guys are. What they talk about is really good and that is how it should be. But then when I sit back and go into to the daily work and say that's not at all how it is. Somewhere along the line something gets lost between the theory and ideas at that level which is quite good. But when you get down to the working level and have to make it work something really gets lost along the way.

Expatriates

It is the BA with its world-wide networks that recommends, after suggestions from local offices, who is going to be sent as an expatriate to China or any other country. Thereafter, it is a cooperation between the BA and the Country level, but it is the latter that finally decides which potential foreign expatriate is appropriate. However, it is particularly noted that it is very important that an expatriate must be able to fit into the system when coming to China, due to the high costs involved in being there. It is estimated that an expatriate costs the company about $¼ million a year, due to the high taxes the company is paying to have a foreign employee.

As a corporation, ABB's identity is supported not only by its possession of a coordinating executive committee but also by an elite cadre of 500 global managers, which the top management shifts through a series of foreign assignments. Their job is intended to knit the organization together, to transfer expertise around the world, and to expose the company's leadership to differing perspectives.[48]

However, ABB in China is not yet a closely tied country unit, and there are argued to be several reasons for that. Firstly, the expatriates come from the outside and most of their contacts are back in the home country. Most expatriates argue, though, that they feel that the home office does not understand how difficult it can be to work abroad and that they need support—*"sometimes it just feels like I'm standing in the desert screaming,"* one expatriate expressed. The home office, on the contrary, often feels that the expatriates can be a burden because he or she needs so much support. It is the home office that is also a part of selecting candidates, along with the BA, to a foreign placement, even though it is argued they have brief knowledge, or no knowledge, of how it really is to work in the actual country. However, it would be an almost impossible task for all the local offices to have insights in how the working conditions are in the other operating countries.

Concerning growing a strong country unit, the expatriates themselves say that they are stationed in China on assignments for a relatively short time period, and are thus less able to build up informal networks, for example. It is argued that few efforts are put into establishing an informal network, because the few contact persons the managers have today will eventually return home after a while and there is no formal way of contacting the replacing person. Of course, there is the formal LOTUS notes, which is a computer based network with all managers world-wide included, but it is said to be deficient in building the preferred strong country unit within China. Finally, the managers do not feel that they can offer the time, or the effort, to establish informal networks if these have to be rebuilt due to the replacement of expatriates every two to three years. A worldwide policy within the company limits the expatriates to operating as such for not more than five years at a time. This, executives have questioned saying that:

> It is during the first year you learn what is going on and get into your new clothes. During the second year you get to know the people and the system, the third year you apply what you learned and the fourth year you start to make some changes—and this is very specific for developing countries.

Three years ago the expatriates did not get any information or education about the country specific situation before being sent out to ABB's subsidiaries in China. Today when there are about 100 expatriates with 25 different nationalities in China, it has changed to some degree, but still it is mostly up to the individual who is going to be an expatriate to collect material and prepare so that the acclimatization works out. Within the worldwide corporation there is no policy of formal training before being sent out as an expatriate; rather, it is up to the home office of the expatriates to prepare the managers for the foreign assignments. Some argue that *"you could never prepare for the situation in China anyway, so any education wouldn't help."* Others say that this has resulted in a lot of problems with the expatriates, which results in even higher costs for the company if the expatriate fails.

When the contract time as an expatriate is over and the time has come for the expatriate to return to the home office, it is maintained that he or she may feel unsure whether there is still a placement for the expatriate back home. It is argued thus, that it is very important for the expatriate to have as close a contact with the home office as possible and also to make use of the free trips home offered by the company. It is in most cases also expressed that the expatriates do not know what will happen when the contract expires and they are to return back home.

The Chinese Challenge

According to ABB they want to send out managers with preferably 10–15 years of experience. However, the task is argued to be difficult, especially when the location may be in a rural area overseas and most managers with 10–15 years experience have families who are less likely to want to move to these areas. It is even said that sometimes a manager gets sent to China when the company does not want to fire him.

So instead they send the manager to where the pitfalls are greater and challenges bigger and potential risks are greater.

After being located in China, the task of adapting to the new environment, whether located in a rural area or in a big city, is discussed. It is found throughout the research that most expatriates have strong feelings about living in and adapting to the new environment in China. Newly arrived expatriates seem to enjoy the respect they get from the Chinese, and several managers delightedly expressed:

> I love it here, and how could you not, you get a lot of respect just because you're a foreigner and life is just pleasant.

Some of the expatriates that have stayed a bit longer disliked the situation to a great extent and a number of expatriates have asked to leave because their expectations about the situation in China have not been fulfilled.[49]

Some country specific situations are argued to be how to teach the Chinese employees to work in teams. The worldwide company ABB is especially focusing on creating an environment that fosters teamwork and promotes active participation among its employees.[50] This is, however, a big challenge for Western managers (the expatriates) because it is argued that the Chinese employees have a hard time working in a group due to cultural and historical reasons. It is held that some of the local ABB companies have radically failed in their attempt with team working, *ad hoc* groups, and the like because they have been in too much of a hurry. Or as quoted:

> Here in China the management needs to encourage the teamwork a little bit, because it is a little against the culture and the nature of the people. This it not a question of lack of time for the managers, but I do not think we have the overall commitment to do it. Some of us feel strongly that we should, others that we can't.

Another consequence is that the expatriate management does not have the understanding or the commitment to teach local employees the company values, which has resulted in the quality at some companies not being acceptable.

It is stated that ABB has a great advantage in comparison to other worldwide companies due to its top priority of building deep local roots by hiring and training local managers who know their local markets.[51] Replacing expatriates with local Chinese employees, where the local employees are set to be successors to the expatriates after a certain amount of years, shows the commitment to the philosophy of having a local profile.

However, as the Chinese employees are coming from an extremely different system from the western expatriates, it is argued that it takes quite a long time for the former to get exposed to western management practices. To ease this problem and to teach western management style, ABB China, among other companies, has recently set up an agreement with a business school in Beijing to arrange training for Chinese employees with good management potential. This is in a way specific for ABB China because in developed countries the employees are responsible for their own development.[52] Just recently ABB had their own school in Beijing for Chinese employees to learn, for example, ABB culture and management. Unfortunately, this school had to close due to the profit center philosophy, where even the school had to charge the individual ABB companies for teaching their employees. This resulted in few companies that wanted to pay for the education and consequently the school had to close.

ABB is also regularly sending about 100 local Chinese employees to an ABB company in a western country every year. After having faced problems with several employees having quit after the invested training, ABB has now set up several precautions to secure this risk with a so-called service commitment. This includes in practice that the employee (or new employer) has to pay back the training investment if he or she quits or that the employee signs an agreement that he or she will continue working for ABB for a certain number of years. The problem with local employees quitting after ABB's investment in training for him or her has been experienced in more developing countries in Asia such as in India and Thailand. It is even shown in the personnel turnover rate, approximately 22 percent within ABB China, that many local employees are aiming for the experience of working for an international company such as ABB and then move on to another job, which might be better paid.

However, by having local employees, the local ABB company is responsive to local conditions and sensitive to important cultural objectives such as the Chinese "guanxi."[53] It has been decided that the local employees should take care of the customer contact since the expatriates are usually only stationed for a few years at one location and are consequently not able to build up strong connections with customers.

Reorganization

It is stated that the organization is a decentralized organization, based on delegated responsibility and the right to make decisions in order to respond quickly to customers' requirements. In the core of this complex organization are two principles: decentralization of responsibility and individual accountability. These principles have been very relevant in China, which is a relatively young country for ABB to be operating in.[54] Decentralization is highly developed and the expatriate[55] managers have a wide responsibility that would normally demand more than one specialist in a western company. However, in some instances the organization is criticized for being too centralized, such as that the country manager needs to accept if an employer is flying overseas.

The changes in China happen very fast and according to ABB brochures, the greatest efficiency gains lie in improving the way people work together.[56] Within the ABB China region communication has, however, its shortcomings when companies with overlapping products or similar products do not exchange their information to any large degree or coordinate their marketing strategies. On the technical side communication is used frequently, which can be seen when a manager during one day usually receives up to 100 e-mails from other ABB employees. However, tactics for building up effective informal communication are lacking between most ABB companies operating in China. The distances are large and, accordingly, a meeting demands greater efforts than in almost any other country in the world.

According to the former CEO, Percy Barnevik, the purpose with the matrix organization is to make the company more bottom heavy than top heavy: *clean out the headquarter in Zurich and send everybody out, have independent companies operating in an entrepreneurial manner,* as one respondent mentioned. It is further maintained in the company brochures that these entrepreneurial business units have the freedom and motivation to run their own business with a sense of personal responsibility.[57]

However, the result from the matrix organization in China is that the ABB subsidiaries have ABB China's objectives (the Country level) and the Business Areas (BA) objectives to follow. ABB China is measuring how the different companies are performing within China. The BA, on the contrary, is measuring how the specific products are performing on a worldwide basis and what the profitability is for the products. Each BA has a financial controller, and each Country level has one also.

> Rarely are the two coordinated, or do they meet. So you end up with one set of objectives from each ... Duplication! Which one shall you follow?

According to the ABB Mission Book, the roles in the two dimensions of the ABB matrix must be complementary.[58] It demands that both the individual company and at headquarter level are flexible and strive for extensive communication. This is the way to avoid the matrix interchange becoming cumbersome and slow. It is seen to be the only way to: "*reap the benefits of being global (economies of scale, technological strength, etc.) and of being multidomestic (a high degree of decentralization and local roots in the countries in which we operate)."*

For many years ABB was widely regarded as an exemplary European company, yet it is undergoing a second major restructuring within four years. CEO Göran Lindahl says restructuring is aimed at making the organization faster and more cost efficient.[59] Due to the demands of a more global market, there are reasons for getting rid of the regional structure and to concentrate more on the specific countries. The reorganization has basically dismantled one half of the matrix: the country management. Henceforth, the BA's will manage their businesses on a worldwide basis and it is said that there will no longer be the confusion between BA and country management setting different objectives. At the same time, segments are split up (many BA's form a segment) to make them more manageable (e.g. the Transmission and Distribution segment has been split into two segments: Transmission and Distribution). To conclude, the general managers of the individual joint ventures and other units will only have one manager above them in the organization who has a global view of the business. In China, it also means the dismantling of the Hong Kong organization as well as the Asia Pacific organization.

According to Göran Lindahl, the reorganization is preparation for a much faster rate of change on the markets and for the company to be able to respond more effectively to the demands of globalization. It is seen as an aggressive strategy to create a platform for future growth.

Future Vision

CEO Göran Lindahl was appointed in 1997 to be the new president and chief executive of ABB. His view of the future is that it can no longer be extrapolated but forecasted by creativity, imagination, ingenuity, innovation—action based not on what was, but on what could be. The corporate culture needs to be replaced by globalizing leadership and corporate values. ABB is focusing on this by creating a unified organization across national, cultural, and business borders.

On the path towards the next century, ABB is going to focus on several essential elements: a strong local presence; a fast and flexible organization; the best technology and products available; and excellent local managers who know the business culture are able to cross national and business borders easily, and who can execute your strategy faster than the competition.[60]

We are living in a rapidly changing environment, and our competitors will not stand still. In the face of this great challenge and opportunity, enterprises that adapt quickly and meet customer needs will be the winner, and this is the ultimate goal of ABB.[61]

Notes

1. 100 years of experience ensures peak technology today, ABB STAL AB, Finspong

2. *Dagens Industri*, 13 August 1998, p. 25

3. ibid.

4. Usunier, Jean-Claude, *Marketing across Cultures*

5. *Dagens Industri*, 2 July 1988

6. *Management Today*, April 1996, by David Smith, p. 49

7. Ahlquist, Magnus as editor; *The recruiters guide to China*, by preface of Professor Michael Yahuda.

8. *Bizniz*, 30 September 1997

9. Examples include VCR-player, CD-ROM player, mobile telephones, beepers, and video cameras.

10. Garten, Jeffrey E. "Opening the Doors for Business in China," *Harvard Business Review* (May-June, 1998): 160–172.

11. *Månadens Affärer*, 11 November 1996, searched through: AFFÄRSDATA via http://www.ad.se/bibsam/

12. *Dagens Industri* 19 August 1998, searched through: AFFÄRSDATA via http://www.ad.se/bibsam/

13. ibid.

14. Ahlquist, Magnus as editor; *The recruiters guide to China*, by preface of Professor Michael Yahuda

15. ibid.

16. Garten, Jeffrey E. "Opening the Doors for Business in China," *Harvard Business Review* (May-June 1998): 167–171.

17. See a recent report from *The Economist*, (www.economist.com, in October 1998).

18. Hong Yung Lee. "The Implications of Reform for Ideology, State and Society in China," *Journal of International Affairs* 39, no. 2: 77–90.

19. An interview with Premier Zhu Rongji in *China Daily*, 20 March 1998, p. 2.

20. *China Daily, Business Weekly*, Vol. 18, No. 5479, March 29-April 4, 1998, p. 2.

21. Hoon-Halbauer, Sing Keow; *Management of Sino-Foreign Joint Ventures;* Yuan Lu; *Management Decision-Making in Chinese Enterprises.*

22. ibid.

23. Ma, Jun, *Intergovernmental Relations and Economic Management in China.*

24. Laaksonen, Oiva; *Management in China during and after Mao in Enterprises, Government, and Party*

25. Ju, Yanan; *Understanding China*, p. 45.

26. Hwang, Quanyu; *Business Decision Making in China.*

27. Hong Yung Lee. "The Implications of Reform for Ideology, State and Society in China," *Journal of International Affairs* 39, no. 2: 77–90.

28. Yuan Lu; *Management Decision-Making in Chinese Enterprises.*

29. Yuan Lu; *Management Decision-Making in Chinese Enterprises.*

30. Hong Yung Lee. The Implications of Reform for Ideology, State and Society in China, *Journal of International Affairs* 39, no. 2: 77–90.

31. Yuan Lu; *Management Decision-Making in Chinese Enterprises.*

32. *Månadens Affärer*, 11 November 1996.

33. *The Economist*, 28 October 1995, searched from http://www.economist.com.

34. Due to China still being a quite closed country, Chinese people are not able to obtain foreign currency, other than in very limited amounts.

35. ABB, "The Art of Being Local," ABB Corporate Communications Ltd., printed in Switzerland.

36. ABB Brochure, "You can rely on the power of ABB," ABB Asea Brown Boveri Ltd., Department CC-C, Zurich.

37. Technology partner (in this case) = Center of Excellence (CE), = Licensors.

38. ABB's Mission, Values, and Policies.

39. HV Switchgear, ABB, ABB Business Area H.V. Switchgear, Printed in Switzerland.

40. ABB Asea Brown Boveri Ltd., You can rely on the power of ABB, Department CC-C, Zurich.

41. Licensing is defined here as a form of external production where the owner of technology or proprietary right (licensor) agrees to transfer this to a joint venture in China which is responsible for local production (licensee).

42. During the study this has changed to some degree due to a unit called CHTET being introduced.

43. http://www.abb.se/swg/switchgear/index.htm in November 1997

44. First source = you are the first source, but if you cannot meet the customers requirements the second source steps in.

 Appendix

Motorola

Motorola was involved with their business in Russia and faced some problems with Glasnost and decline of the country. At that time the founder of the company, Galvin, realized that there was no future in Russia and declared that China was the country where the growth was to be. Consequently, Motorola established their first representative office in China in 1987, and have grown very fast ever since. Today, China generates more than 10 percent of Motorola's sales and the company has its major businesses in China.

Motorola has found that modernization in China happens very fast and all their competitors are present in the country, but they are still predicting China to be the potential leader in Asia for their kind of business. The customers also have high expectations on the products Motorola are offering; because the products are regarded to be very expensive. However, the problem the company is facing in China is argued to be that the company is growing too fast, or as expressed below:

> The problem we have is that Motorola is growing very fast and it is like chasing a speeding train and trying to catch up with it.

Presently, Motorola has 12,000 employees and 200 expatriates in China, whereas the goal is that Chinese successors will take over the job of the expatriates. The expatriates are sent out on assignments for two to three years, with the possibility of renewal with a one-two rotation, but limited to a maximum of six years as an expatriate. High demands are set on the expatriates, especially concerning the difficulties experienced teaching teamwork to local employees. This is very important within the company since all the strategy planning is done in teams. When the contract time for the expatriate has expired the following is expressed:

> You have done your job when the time comes and you have left the company and everything is working smoothly, but if everything is falling apart, you are a failure as an expatriate and have not taught a successor.

However, progress has been made in developing the company's local employees. Motorola has set up training abroad. The training, nevertheless, is preferably held within China, with rotation assignments and training at Motorola University. This company university was set up in 1994 when the company found that the Chinese universities did not turn out sufficiently well trained students. Within the company there is, however, a requirement that every employee worldwide shall have at least 40 hours of training, which is argued to possibly be exceeded in China. It is held that there must be a combination of good training and mentor development to get successful people. Motorola does not deny, but instead admits that they do make a mistake by not providing enough training for foreign expatriates before they come to China. It is also said that they have noticed that overseas Chinese often do not do well fitting into the system, even though they speak Chinese, or as quoted;

> You get more understanding if you look like a foreigner and make some mistakes than if you don't. Overseas Chinese are measured through other standards than other foreigners.

Other problems the company is facing concerning expatriation, is that some expatriates just cannot handle the situation in China. If an expatriate fails, this has to be handled with care, otherwise the person loses face when coming back to the home office. The company also has pointed out that they need expatriates with 10–15 years of experience in order to teach the local employees the company values and to transfer company knowledge. However, the people that are willing to change addresses and move to China are the younger employees with less than five years of experience.

The expatriates are often responsible for transferring technology knowledge and helping to get projects started, especially in the case of the newly set up Center of Excellence in Tianjin, where $750 million was invested. This was Motorola's first manufacturing research laboratory outside the United States, and altogether the company has invested $1.1 billion in China and has plans to invest another $1 to 1.5 million. Motorola has also set up two branches of worldwide training universities to educate customers, suppliers, and government officials, as well as its own employees. The invested money in China is said to be from the earnings within the whole enterprise, with the motivation that the Chinese market is going to be huge. Sincere commitment has been made and the present CEO, Gary Tucker, is said to have expressed the following:

> When Motorola has come to your country they never leave … We manufacture in China, because this is where our market is. We get wealth by going to a lot of countries around the world and then doing well in that country.

The expansion strategy in China is through joint ventures. However, it is said that it is important that the Chinese partners bring something of value, which means that the partners have to be approved by the CEO. Other than that, it is argued that the company has become; "*so decentralized that it has become bad*," and that the company desires to reorganize more along customer than product lines. A practical reorganization has taken place to move everybody operating in Beijing to the same newly built headquarters. However, entrepreneurial activities are also argued to be of importance, but difficult in practice due to financial motivation and autonomy.

In China the products are localized by having Chinese characters on the cellular phones and pagers. In 1987 Motorola started selling pagers and thought there would not be a big market because the telephone-net was not well established, but then the company invented codebooks, which enabled two-way communication. Fortunately this also worked in Hong Kong, Singapore, and Taiwan. After five years of operation in China, the company has not yet been able to grow deep roots in the market. Nevertheless, the investments in the country and efforts to make the company a Chinese one are argued to be the reason for the deepness of the localization and make the company unshakable. To show the seriousness of attaining deep roots in China Motorola has invested huge sums in sponsoring environmental protection, providing scholarships to students, building labs at universities, and donating money to primary schools in rural areas.[1]

The worldwide organization is illustrated to be a "pyramid" with the corporate on top and Business Units underneath "*then put the apex at the bottom.*" The Corporate office works as the glue that holds the organization together. In 1997 Motorola conducted a reorganization to better reflect the global nature of the business.[2] The coordination is also said to be safeguarded by this new formal structure. However, the informal information flow is argued to be better, but pointed out as probably overused. The information flow is mostly through e-mails. A manager gets approximately 70–100 a day, of which less than 30 percent are regarded as really useful. Regarding the network communication, the following was expressed:

> Some days it feels like we have all these opportunities and we do not really communicate.

All the controllers or general managers in the joint ventures get together quarterly to counsel, solve problems, and give support to each other. Information is encouraged, but no system is developed to track what is going on in all the six districts in China where the company is operating. Competition between the different units is a common problem Motorola is experiencing, which is said to result in the customers getting confused. This is a problem that is said to have no solution due to the matrix organization, or as expressed below:

> We do not have the answers, because if we are too centralized then we miss new opportunities. How do you encourage creativity and yet keep people from competing with each other?

What makes Motorola a world-wide company is argued to be that it has a set of key common beliefs or guiding principles from the role model and father figure of the company, Galvin: *"uncompromising integrity and constant respect for people—that is what makes us Motorola."* This is the principal code of conduct that Motorola practices, and which the management has to reread and sign every two years.

Motorola has expressed that they *"obviously"* have to change the way the company does things because they are operating on the Chinese market: such as show face, building relations, and going to ceremonial meetings. In the issue regarding relations it is essential to make sure the partner is reliable, that the business makes sense, and then make sure that it is legal, which is pointed out to be opposite from the west. However, it is then stated that the Motorola company always looks the same all over the world, but it is the expatriates and their families that have made an effort to adopt to the surrounding changes.

The challenge for Motorola in China is said to be doing business in the country. China is argued to be very difficult for a huge company like Motorola to be operating in, or as quoted:

> … because they would like to control the system and everything takes a long time because they will make sure that you are not cheating. You must be able to work with all the people that come from different departments and to let them trust you. Ordinary things like getting water, electricity etc, is a huge problem. Doing business in the Chinese system is a challenge and therefore creates pressure because you get frustrated.

Procter & Gamble

In August 1998 China's largest international employer had been in China for ten successful years. Procter and Gamble—or P&G—has approximately 5,000 employees and 100 expatriates spread in 11 joint ventures and wholly-owned enterprises in the country. This success has also been paying off by being ranked this year on *Fortune* magazine's "World's Most Admired Companies" list. Currently, the biggest market for the company is China where new companies are being established. However, before establishing companies in China, a feasibility study was, of course, done. As with most other feasibility studies done in China, the information was outdated even though it was only one year old and people were criticized for not having sufficient knowledge about the country's specific situation.

The expatriates sent to China for the P&G account are claimed to be no more prepared for the situation, than that the company has a deep culture that will support them. Furthermore, a continuous effort exists within the company to put different cultural backgrounds together. Cultural values are also written down and are consistent all over the world. However, due to that, the different expatriates have a wide variety of cultural backgrounds and their culture is colored by their management style. It is pointed out that this mixture of management styles might confuse the local Chinese employees.

The main benefit gained for an expatriate is the one offered in the daily work. One exception is made, the expatriate sales people, who get a whole year orientation training and language training. In line with the localization demands, the number of expatriates is decreasing. Due to the high costs involved of having expatriates, who are mostly three to four levels up in the organization, one of key strategies is also to develop local employees. Everybody who is an expatriate for P&G has a sponsor back home, a contact. It is mentioned that it is essential to keep contact with the sponsor so that it is not just a name on a paper and people are also encouraged to go back home once a year at the company's cost. There is no official limit in expatriate policy within the company, however most expatriates are on a three-year contract. The expatriate network is not yet an issue, however the expatriates are said to be a very close group—*"we are all in this together and we have a common vision."*

The optimal goal for P&G is to develop the organization so that it can be a Chinese run company. Today, everything is made in the Chinese P&G factories for internal use and, just a couple of months ago, the company opened up a research center in Beijing, in cooperation with a prominent university.[3] A reason for opening a research center in Beijing is a bet on the future that the world's largest group of consumers will have a large say on how P&G will market and develop in the rest of the world. If the company has developed a good idea in China, the company will analyze how to re-apply those ideas in the rest of the world. This is also said to be done if the ideas have been developed at the headquarters in Cincinnati or in the previous Center of Excellence in Brussels.

Counterfeits are the greatest competition for the company, which is an extensive problem as the customer is offered counterfeit products that appear to the customer to be the real but are not. However, all the products from P&G are not sold in China and the quality of the products sold is not as high as it is in western countries. The Chinese customers are said to be unable to pay for better value, nevertheless, the company is trying to offer a consistency of quality the Chinese consumers are willing to pay for.

In the Chinese P&G organization, fewer layers are developed and the decision-making takes a shorter time within the organization. Because the company evolved very quickly and the market is argued to be so dynamic and changing that they have not had the time to implement the layers—*only tried to understand the market.*" Consequently, the Chinese organization and structure are not the same as in other countries, but it is argued that the Chinese organization is by all accounts, more efficient and that P&G will implement some of the things they have in China in other countries. At the current time a reorganization is taking place within the world-wide P&G where the organization is being changed along with the culture and reward system-all to make the company more flexible.[4]

As for the Chinese situation *guanxi* is mentioned, which is said to be difficult for the expatriates to establish and consequently the company rely on the local staff. On the contrary, the local employees get an immense amount of education at P&G's own school, for example. Also, expatriates exist that are present at the company with an explicit responsibility to deal with company principle, values, and all the technical specifics for P&G. It is, however, at the same time pointed out that the company falls short with the expatriates, because *"they are so into running the business that sometimes the coaching of the locals is not possible."*

One of the challenges Procter & Gamble faces in China is the difficulty in dealing with the government. The company has dealt with this by searching for a sophisticated government-relations manager who shall report not only to the head of operations in China but also to the chief executive of the company.[5]

Nestlé

In the beginning of the 1980s China asked the world's largest food company—Nestlé—to come and build "milk streets" in the country. China was unfamiliar with how to produce milk and turned to Nestlé, whose core business is actually milk powder. From that time the company has grown strongly in China and now has almost 4000 employees, where 200 of them are foreign expatriates.

Today Nestlé is regarded as having come from Swiss roots and turned into a transnational corporation.[6] Nestlé is argued to have their foundation in their history for being locally adaptive. During the First World War, Nestlé gave their local managers increasing independence from the beginning, to avoid disruptions in distribution.[7] This resulted in a great deal of Nestlé's operations being established at other locations than at their headquarters in Switzerland. Another cause was the company's belief that the consumers' taste was very local and that there were no synergy effects to be gained by standardizing the products. However, in 1993 the company

started to rethink their belief in localization due to the increasing competition in the industry. Nestlé has acquired several local brands, influenced by their own country culture, which has caused Nestlé to standardize where it is possible.[8]

However, although the company is growing in China, it must be pointed out that they are not always selling products with as much margin as desired. The company is argued to have as high a quality on their products as they have in other countries, but the downside is that they must have lower margins in order to be competitive, which might not always be profitable. On the question "Why Nestlé has to be in China?" the following was expressed:

> It is because China is a large country and if you have a company that is present in more than 100 countries, you see it as a must for all international companies to be present there. We supply all over the world and it is our obligation to bring food to the people—which is the Company's priority.

Nestlé entered China with a long-term strategy to be in the country for a long period of time and from then the strategy was always set to focus on the long run perspective. Nestlé's overall approach is stated to be *"Think global and act local!"* The Company's strategy is guided by several fundamental principles, such as the following:

> Nestlé's existing products will grow through innovation and renovation while maintaining a balance in geographic activities and product lines.[9]

With regard to the local Chinese employees—they get a few days of Nestlé education to learn about the Nestlé culture, but the expatriates have less training experience, regarding going to another country. It is up to the home country to decide if it is necessary to train expatriates before sending them on an often three year foreign assignment. However, the leadership talent is highly valued within the company and consequently Nestlé has developed courses for this. The managers can independently develop their leadership talent without any connection with the specific company style or culture. Community centers have been developed to help expatriates with their contacts, supporting these expatriates psychologically, and even offering language training.

In 1997 Nestlé's "The Basic Nestlé Management and Leadership Principles" was published, which is aimed to make "the Nestlé spirit" of the company generally known throughout the organization by discussions, seminars, and courses.[10] According to the CEO of Nestlé China, Theo Klauser, this publication is the key factor in Nestlé's corporate culture and started the company's international expansion 130 years ago.[11]

Within the organization of Nestlé China, the company has developed a specific structure due to the joint venture configuration. The information flow is seen as easy and smooth between these regions, thanks to the company concentrating its activities to only three regions in China. However, communication is said to be on a very high level, yet, it is argued that it is not even necessary to get all levels involved. As an example, only one unit in China takes care of all the marketing. At the same time each Nestlé company in China is responsible for its own turnover rate, which is said to create the flexible and decentralized company Nestlé is today. Quite unique for a worldwide company, Nestlé does not have any external e-mail network, and this is believed to concentrate the flow of information within the company.

A major challenge indicated for Nestlé in China is the effort in building long relationships to establish Nestlé as the leading food company. Difficulties are to bring the products to a more acceptable level in terms of profitability. Legal difficulties are also more important than in any other country. Other challenges are the issues concerning change, where the following was expressed:

Change happens every couple of months here, that is how the environment is, a lot of employees come from other more stable countries and sometimes find it difficult with all the changes. Change is how things are in China—it is normal. It is when something doesn't change, that is when you get worried! It is expected to change! Different from other countries where changes can be difficult to get.

Notes

1. Garten, Jeffrey E. "Opening the Doors for Business in China," *Harvard Business Review* (May–June 1998): 174–175.

2. Motorola Annual Report 1997.

3. Qinghua University.

4. Procter & Gamble Annual Report 1998.

5. Garten, Jeffrey E. "Opening the Doors for Business in China," *Harvard Business Review* (May–June 1998): 173–175.

6. http://www.Nestlé.com/html/home.html, September 1998.

7. Quelch, J. A. & Hoff, E. J. "Customizing Global Marketing," *Harvard Business Review* 3 (May–June 1986): 59–60.

8. Brorsson, Skarsten, Torstensson; *Marknadsföring på den inre markanden—Standardisering eller Anpassning*, Thesis at Lund University, 1993.

Case 2

Agilent Technologies' Initial Public Offering

Patricia A. Ryan, *Colorado State University*

> Exponential growth is based on the principle that the state of change is proportional to the level of effort expended. The level of effort will be far greater in the twenty-first century than it has been in the twentieth century.
> —*Bill Hewlett, Co-founder Hewlett-Packard*[1]

Edward (Ned) Barnholt had his work cut out for him over the next several months. A successful executive with Hewlett-Packard (HP) for ten years, Barnholt faced a unique challenge. On March 2, 1999, Hewlett-Packard announced a plan to create a separate company, which was to be comprised of Hewlett-Packard's Test and Measurement division as well as the Semiconductor Products, Healthcare Solutions and Chemical Analysis businesses. Barnholt, the General Manager of Hewlett-Packard's Measurement Organization, was named President and Chief Executive Officer of these spun-off divisions, soon to be known to the world as Agilent Technologies. Faced with many strengths and opportunities, Barnholt also knew the threats and risks that faced his business. At the helm of the ship, he was ultimately responsible for the company's success or failure. Now, November 2, 1999, Agilent Technologies was to go public with an initial public offering of stock on November 18, 1999. How could this IPO go as smoothly as possible? What are the long-term growth prospects and limitations for Agilent Technologies? What should the offering price for the stock be? How could the split from Hewlett-Packard, a long time ally and partner, work optimally for both companies? How might employee morale be affected by the spin-off? Perhaps most importantly, how might Barnholt continue to work to maximize shareholder wealth for this global diversified technology company in the midst of a run-away economy? These questions and many others ran through Barnholt's mind as he left his Palo Alto, California office to have lunch with his executive team.

After failing to meet analyst expectations for six of the past nine quarters, on March 2, 1999, Hewlett-Packard announced plans to spin off its Test and Measurement business, an $8 billion per year subsidiary. At that time, the company indicated the spun off division would go public within 18 months. Upon the announcement, Hewlett-Packard's stock rose four percent to $68.63. After the spin off, Hewlett-Packard would focus on computing and imaging and maintain revenues of approximately $40 billion annually. The new company would bundle the other businesses Hewlett-Packard operated including the chemical division which generated $1 billion is sales annually. It was now late on November 2, 1999 and Barnholt awaited the latest projections from his finance staff and underwriters regarding pricing the IPO. In an interview Barnholt commented,

> Where possible, customers in the chemical industry will be able to bundle together measurement instrumentation and computer software. … the split is something we have been working on for a long time.[2]

History of Hewlett-Packard

Two Stanford electrical engineering graduates, Dave Packard and Bill Hewlett set out on a small business venture upon the advice of their professor, Fred Terman. Professor Terman told the two friends to "make a run for it." After a two week camping trip to the Colorado mountains Packard and Hewlett decided to join collective forces to form the seedling of what was to become known to the world as Hewlett-Packard. Interestingly, the ordering of their names was determined by a coin toss in a small Palo Alto, California garage. In 1940, total revenues were $34,000 and Dave and Bill had three employees. In 1962, Hewlett-Packard joined the Standard and Poors 500 where the company remains today. In 1999, revenue topped $47.1 billion and HP employed over 124,000 throughout the world.

Walt Disney was one of HP's first customers with the purchase of eight audio oscillators to test the sound equipment in the movie "Fantasia." In the 1950s, Hewlett-Packard developed its corporate objectives and began globalization of HP. The philosophy that was to become known as the "HP Way" depictive of the innovative and generous relationships with employees was formally developed in this decade of change and growth. The company went public on November 6, 1957 with 373 products, $30 million in net revenue, and 1,778 employees. In the late Fifties, marketing emphasis was placed on European markets in Switzerland and West Germany. In the Sixties, the computing division bloomed and the Test and Measurement division became known for its progressive position in the market. Hewlett-Packard was well respected as a well-managed company that worked hard to assist its employees develop a balance between work and home life. The Sixties brought joint ventures in Japan and Germany. By the Eighties, the increasing global presence of Hewlett-Packard was partially due to the onslaught of personal computers and peripherals. Hewlett-Packard strove to provide high performance at reasonable cost. The Nineties brought accelerated web-based information and increased focus on the computing side of the company. In 1992, Hewlett-Packard introduced a new atomic clock that became the world's most precise timekeeper. In 1992, seasoned executive Lew Platt was named President and CEO of the computing and measurement giant. In the very fast growth period of that decade, Hewlett-Packard struggled to keep up with all the new technological breakthroughs while operating in multiple industries. It became clear that some action would now have to be taken to streamline the company.

Separation for Hewlett-Packard and Formation of Agilent Technologies

Hewlett-Packard wanted to revitalize its stifled business. On March 2, 1999, the company announced a strategic realignment that would essentially spin-off the Test and Measurement divisions of the business while maintaining the computing divisions. (See Table 1 for a sequential timeline.) Test and Measurement consisted of several business lines including Chemical Analysis, Healthcare Solutions, and Semiconductors. The new company went unnamed for four months as Hewlett-Packard attempted to realign with a new "HP Way;" one that would and could keep up with the lightning fast speed of change. At the same time, Lew Platt announced that he would retire after the spin-off, allowing a new chief executive to start with the revitalized Hewlett-Packard. Hewlett-Packard was to focus on computing, imaging, and peripherals and the new company would take the other business units and operate independently of Hewlett-Packard. On July 28, 1999, Hewlett-Packard announced the name of the new company, Agilent Technologies that was to be categorized in SIC Code 3825 "Instruments to Measure Electricity." The name was derived from the base word "agile," which was to be a focus for management and a concept to permeate the company. In July and August of 1999, many of Hewlett-Packard's Test and Measurement management team were named to senior positions in Agilent Technologies (See Table 2 for Agilent's management and Board of Directors). As former lead of the Measurement division, Ned Barnholt was named President and CEO of Agilent Technologies.

Table 1	Agilent's Road to Independence
Date	Event
March 2, 1999	Hewlett-Packard announces strategic realignment into two companies.
July 28, 1999	President and CEO Edward (Ned) Barnholt unveils Agilent's new name and logo.
August 16, 1999	Agilent files registration statement with the SEC for the IPO.
October 4, 1999	Agilent announces it will list on the NYSE with the ticker symbol "A".
October 13, 1999	Agilent purchased the rights to the Internet domain "Agilent.com".
October 25, 1999	Estimate IPO price $19–22 per share for a total of $1.1 billion per amended registration with the SEC; estimated date of IPO: November 18, 1999.
November 1, 1999	Agilent becomes a Hewlett-Packard subsidiary and operates independently.
November 17, 1999	Underwriters price Agilent IPO at $30 per share.
November 18, 1999	Agilent stock begins trading on the New York Stock Exchange under ticker symbol "A". Sold 72,000,000 shares at $30.
December 16, 1999	Agilent ends IPO quiet period and announced fiscal year 1999 financial results.
Mid-2000	Agilent's independence is achieved when Hewlett-Packard distributes its remaining Agilent stock holdings to Hewlett-Packard shareholders.

Sources: Agilent Press Releases and Agilent Technologies, *Innovating the HP Way In Brief* Booklet

I want Agilent to be one of the best decisions we ever made at Hewlett-Packard. All 42,000 Agilent people have the opportunity, and the responsibility, to take the superb hand we've been dealt as part of HP and turn it into something better. We're striving to live up to both our heritage and our potential.

—*Ned Barnholt, President and CEO, Agilent Technologies*[3]

Table 2	Senior Management and Board of Directors

Senior Management

Name	Title, Background	First year with Hewlett-Packard
Edward W. Barnholt, 56	President and Chief Executive Officer	1990
Byron Anderson, 56	Senior VP, Electronic Products and Solutions	1991
William R. Hahn, 48	Senior VP, Strategic Programs	1993
Jean M. Halloran, 47	Senior VP, Human Resources	1980
Richard D. Kniss, 59	Senior VP, Chemical Analysis	1984
D. Craig Nordlund, 50	Senior VP, General Counsel and Secretary	1987
Stephen H. Rusckowski, 42	Senior VP, Healthcare Solutions	1984
Thomas A. Saponas, 50	Senior VP and Chief Technology Officer	1986
John E. Scruggs, 58	Senior VP, Automated Test	1992
William P. Sullivan, 50	Senior VP, Semiconductor Products	1991
Robert R. Walker, 49	Senior VP and Chief Financial Officer	1975
Thomas White, 42	Senior VP, Communications Solutions	1994
Dorothy D. Hayes, 49	Vice President and Controller	1989

Board of Directors

Name	Position	Affiliation
Edward W. Barnholt, 56	Inside Director	President and CEO
Gerald Grinstein, 67	Chairman of the Board of Directors	Former Chairman for Delta Air Lines and Burlington Northern Santa Fe Corporation
Thomas E. Everhart, 67	Outside Director	President Emeritus California Institute of Technology
Walter B. Hewlett, 55	Outside Director	Independent Researcher and Director for the Center for Computer Assisted Research in the Humanities
David M. Lawrence, M.D.	Outside Director	Chairman of the Board and Chief Executive Office for Kaiser Foundation Health Plan, Inc. and Kaiser Foundation Hospitals
Randall L. Tobias, 57	Outside Director	Chairman Emeritus for Eli Lilly and Company
Robert R. Walker, 49	Inside Director	Senior Vice President and Chief Financial Officer
Dorothy D. Hayes, 48	Inside Director	Vice President and Controller
Thomas A. Saponas, 50	Inside Director	Senior Vice President and Chief Technology Officer

Sources: Agilent 1999 10-K, pp. 42–43, Agilent Annual Report, p. 36, and Filing S-1, p. 87.

Executive Compensation

Many managers are compensated with a combination of salary plus bonus and stock options with the intent being to better align shareholders' and managers' interests. Table 3 reflects the compensation structure for key Agilent executives for 1999. Barnholt's 1999 compensation (salary and bonus) was slightly over $1.1 million, but when considering stock options, his compensation package totaled approximately $18 million. Clearly, the vast majority of this was a pay for performance; that is, performance of the stock. Exercised stock options are options the manager chose to exercise that year.

Exercisable stock options are options that he could exercise to purchase stock at a discounted price but had not done so as of October 31, 1999 (end of fiscal year). Finally, in an attempt to better align long-term management interests with those of shareholders, each executive held options that could not yet have been exercised, but would be exercisable at some date in the future. As had become the case in recent years, the majority of senior executives' pay came in the form of stock options that would grant them revenue only if the stock price continued to rise. It was common practice to hold a significant portion of the options for several years in an attempt to induce shareholder wealth maximizing behavior.

Table 3	Agilent Technologies Executive Compensation and Stock Options for the Fiscal Year Ending October 31, 1999				
Executive	Salary	Bonus	Total Annual Compensation	All Other	Fiscal Year Total
Edward W. Barnholt— President, Chief Executive Officer and Director	$ 920,635	$ 210,892	$ 1,131,527	$ 415,626	$ 1,547,153
Robert R. Walker—Senior Vice President and Chief Financial Officer	$ 435,666	$ 26,015	$ 461,681	$ 26,057	$ 487,738
Byron Anderson—Senior Vice President, Electronic Products and Solutions	$ 425,000	$ 63,724	$ 488,724	$ 29,417	$ 518,141
Richard D. Kniss—Senior Vice President, Chemical Analysis	$ 388,025	$ 78,469	$ 466,494	$ 25,882	$ 492,376
John R. Scruggs—Senior Vice President, Automated Test	$ 415,167	$ 75,568	$ 490,735	$ 27,651	$ 518,386

Executive	Exercised Stock Options		Exercisable Stock Options		Non-Exercisable Stock Options	
	Number	$ Value	Number	$ Value	Number	$ Value
Edward W. Barnholt— President, Chief Executive Officer and Director	82,288	$ 6,757,816	178,500	$ 7,993,245	137,500	$ 2,111,675
Robert R. Walker—Senior Vice President and Chief Financial Officer	30,000	$ 1,904,800	24,600	$ 941,682	35,500	$ 567,035
Byron Anderson—Senior Vice President, Electronic Products and Solutions	36,400	$ 2,963,674	14,000	$ 304,165	38,000	$ 587,755
Richard D. Kniss—Senior Vice President, Chemical Analysis	9,200	$ 631,304	12,900	$ 309,259	32,300	$ 518,593
John R. Scruggs—Senior Vice President, Automated Test	16,000	$ 1,352,848	16,625	$ 380,054	40,875	$ 642,431

Source: SEC Filing S-1, pp. 92, 95

The Business of Agilent Technologies

Agilent Technologies' 60-year history under the umbrella of Hewlett-Packard allowed for the development of close relationships with many of its large customers. The company is a globally diversified company with four divisions:

- **Test and Measurement:** This was the primary division that Hewlett-Packard was known for prior to the spin-off. Test and Measurement provides test instruments as well as standard and customized test, measurement and monitoring instruments, and systems for design, manufacture, and support of electronics and communication devices. Additionally, Agilent Technologies provides software for the design of high frequency electronics and communication devices. Test and Measurement's solutions are used by a wide range of customers including communications and network equipment manufacturers, including providers of fiber optic, wireless and wireless components, products and systems. Additionally, designers and manufacturers of semiconductor products including microprocessors, memory boards, electronic equipment such as cellular handsets and avionics equipment, and communications and network equipment services such as telecommunications and Internet providers use Agilent's Test and Measurement expertise. Test and Measurement must carefully develop a strategy that allows the division to remain ahead of the rapid technological changes in the industries it serves and work to use new technology to access multiple customer applications. At the same time, it must maintain strong client relationships and continue to expand services and consulting globally. Major customers include AT&T, Boeing, General Motors, IBM, Intel, Lucent, Nokia, Sprint, and the United Stated Air Force.[4]

- **Semiconductor Products:** This business group provides fiber optic communication devices and assemblies, integrated circuits for wireless applications, application-specific integrated circuits, optoelectronics and image sensors. Major customers include Cisco, Motorola, 3Com, Tyco, Hewlett-Packard, Hitachi, Qualcomm, and Data General.[5] This business is largely directed by rapid technological advancement. In the semiconductor business, there is a concept known as Moore's Law, which states that the functionality and performance of a digital integrated circuit doubles roughly every 18–24 months. While the speed of change may present its own problems, there are significant business opportunities for Agilent because of the new challenges presented by new integrated circuits. The increased pervasiveness of semiconductor devices creates growth opportunities for many semiconductor products including electrical and optical components, high frequency and digital design equipment, and automated test equipment.

- **Healthcare Solutions:** This business unit provides patient monitoring, ultrasound imaging and cardiology products and services. Major customers include the Boston Medical Center, Columbia HCA Healthcare Corporation, Kaiser Foundation Hospitals, Mayo Foundation, Mount Sinai Health System, and Healthcare Systems.[6] Agilent's Healthcare Solutions faces cost containment challenges in the healthcare industry, which might impose some concern in the future.

- **Chemical Analysis:** This business group provides analytical instrumentation, systems, and services for chromatography, spectroscopy, and bioinstrumentation. Major customers include Bayer AG, E. I. Du Pont de Nemours and Company, Exxon, Royal Dutch Shell, the Government of Korea, the States of Georgia, Texas, and California, Glaxo Wellcome PLC, Pfizer, Pharmicia and Upjohn, Roche Holdings, and SmithKline Beecham Clinical Laboratories, Inc.[7] There may be high costs associated with complying with the laws and regulations in the chemical industry, the FDA, and environmental issues that may adversely affect profitability.

Agilent Technologies reported separate financial statement data for each business unit since 1997. The balance sheet, income statement, and statement of cash flows for the business units that will become Agilent Technologies is provided in Tables 4–7.

Additional Issues for Ned Barnholt to Consider

The change in corporate status could cause morale and personnel difficulties among employees as Agilent Technologies strives to make an identity as an independent company. If Agilent and Hewlett-Packard are going to truly be two separate companies, both face huge costs to establish management and infrastructure without the economies of scale of the other. After the separation from Hewlett-Packard, Agilent may face higher costs resulting from the diseconomies of scale resulting from decreased purchasing power.

Table 4   Consolidated Balance Sheet for the Years Ending October 31 (in millions, except for par value and share amounts)

	October 31,		
	1999	1998	1997
Assets:	(In thousands, except for par value and share amounts)		
Current assets			
Cash and cash equivalents	$ —	$ —	$ —
Accounts receivable	1,635	1,215	1,234
Inventory	1,499	1,485	1,432
Other current assets	404	375	265
Total current assets	3,538	3,075	2,931
Property, plant, and equipment, net	1,387	1,481	1,623
Other assets	519	431	452
Total assets	$ 5,444	$ 4,987	$ 5,006
Liabilities and Stockholder's Equity:			
Current liabilities:			
Accounts payable	$ 510	$ 435	$ 495
Employee compensation and benefits	550	574	604
Deferred revenue	241	205	157
Other accrued liabilities	380	385	267
Total current liabilities	1,681	1,599	1,523
Other liabilities	381	366	373
Stockholder's equity:			
Preferred stock; $.01 par value; 125,000,000 shares authorized; none issued and outstanding	0	0	
Common stock; $.01 par value; 2,000,000,000 shares authorized; 380,000,000 shares issued and outstanding in 1999	4	0	
Additional paid-in capital	3,378	0	
Shareholder's net investment	0	3,022	3,110
Total stockholder's equity	3,382	3,022	3,110
Total liabilities and stockholder's equity	$ 5,444	$ 4,987	$ 5,006

Sources: Agilent 1999 10-K, p. F-3 and Prospectus, p. F-3.

The semiconductor technology licensing and supply arrangements with Hewlett-Packard limits Agilent's ability to sell to other companies, thus possibly capping its business. Agilent's ability to compete for Hewlett-Packard's business may suffer because of the separation and decreased access to Hewlett-Packard's research and development strategy, technology plans, future product features, and product supply needs.

Agilent faced multiple international risk factors to compliment the potential growth opportunities it enjoys.

Among the threats it faces are foreign exchange risk and exposure, as well as economic, political, and other risks associated with international sales and operations, particularly in Korea and Japan. International relations will require Agilent to continue to carefully consider its actions and the relationships of its actions in different cultural environments.

The labor market was very tight and Agilent, along with similar firms, faced the challenge of attracting and retaining a technologically strong employee base. Ned had a talented workforce and the opportunity to

Table 5	Selected Key Figures by Division for the Years Ending October 31 (in millions)

	Total Segments	Test and Measurement	Semiconductor Products	Healthcare Solutions	Chemical Analysis
1999:					
Assets ($5,444)*	$ 5,055	$ 2,555	$ 1,014	$ 958	$ 528
Capital expenditures	$ 305	$ 185	$ 96	$ 15	$ 9
Investment in equity-method investees	$ 40	$ 13	$ 15	$ 0	$ 12
External revenue	$ 8,331	$ 4,082	$ 1,722	$ 1,501	$ 1,026
Internal revenue	45	4	40	1	0
Total net revenue	$ 8,376	$ 4,086	$ 1,762	$ 1,502	$ 1,026
Depreciation and amortization expense	$ 359	$ 152	$ 156	$ 35	$ 16
Earnings from operations	$ 747	$ 377	$ 133	$ 125	$ 112
1998:					
Assets ($4,987)	$ 4,686	$ 2,188	$ 1,134	$ 847	$ 517
Capital expenditures	$ 347	$ 155	$ 162	$ 22	$ 8
Investment in equity-method investees	$ 30	$ 11	$ 19	$ 0	$ 0
External revenue	$ 7,952	$ 4,100	$ 1,574	$ 1,340	$ 938
Internal revenue	39	0	39	0	0
Total net revenue	$ 7,991	$ 4,100	$ 1,613	$ 1,340	$ 938
Depreciation and amortization expense	$ 381	$ 133	$ 205	$ 28	$ 15
Earnings from operations	$ 379	$ 348	($ 106)	$ 62	$ 75
1997:					
Assets ($5,006)	$ 4,840	$ 2,305	$ 1,273	$ 793	$ 469
Capital expenditures	$ 497	$ 147	$ 316	$ 13	$ 17
Investment in equity-method investees	$ 18	$ 14	$ 4	$ 0	$ 0
External revenue	$ 7,785	$ 4,203	$ 1,479	$ 1,208	$ 895
Internal revenue	28	0	27	0	1
Total net revenue	$ 7,813	$ 4,203	$ 1,506	$ 1,208	$ 896
Depreciation and amortization expense	$ 313	$ 107	$ 177	$ 16	$ 13
Earnings from operations	$ 838	$ 674	$ 57	$ 30	$ 77
1996:					
Assets ($4,720)	$ 4,605	$ 2,214	$ 1,173	$ 763	$ 455
Capital expenditures	$ 502	$ 146	$ 326	$ 17	$ 13
Investment in equity-method investees	$ 15	$ 15	$ 0	$ 0	$ 0
External revenue	$ 7,379	$ 3,823	$ 1,470	$ 1,244	$ 842
Internal revenue	30	0	30	0	0
Total net revenue	$ 7,409	$ 3,823	$ 1,500	$ 1,244	$ 842
Depreciation and amortization expense	$ 325	$ 110	$ 181	$ 21	$ 13
Earnings from operations	$ 875	$ 606	$ 125	$ 106	$ 38

*The difference between total assets ($5,444) and total segment assets ($5,055) reflects a fixed charge paid to corporate for overhead allowance. Similar charges are reflected in each year.

Sources: Agilent 1999 10-K, pp. F-25, F-27, and Prospectus pp. F-25, F-27.

Table 6   Consolidated Statement of Earnings for the Years Ending October 31 (in millions, except for par value and share amounts)

	October 31,			
	1999	1998	1997	1996
Net Revenue:	(In millions, except for par value and share amounts)			
Products	$ 6,193	$ 6,098	$ 6,114	$ 5,756
Products to Hewlett-Packard	832	696	640	684
Services	1,306	1,158	1,031	939
Total net revenue	$ 8,331	$ 7,952	$ 7,785	$ 7,379
Costs and expenses:				
Cost of products	3,582	3,807	$ 3,455	$ 3,327
Cost of services	806	705	671	574
Research and development	997	948	880	805
Selling, general, and administrative	2,205	2,050	1,909	1,798
Total costs and expenses	$ 7,590	$ 7,510	$ 6,915	$ 6,504
Earnings from operations	741	442	870	875
Other income (expense), net	46	(46)	(47)	(21)
Earnings before taxes	787	396	823	854
Provision for taxes	275	139	280	312
Net earnings	$ 512	$ 257	$ 543	$ 542
Basic and diluted net earnings per share (380 average shares)	$ 1.35	$ .68	$ 1.43	$ 1.43

Sources: Agilent 1999 10-K, p. F-4 and Prospectus, p. F-4.

succeed; now the key decisions will belong to his management team.

Considering the timeframe of late 1999, one significant concern was the Y2K issue when calendars around the world changed from 1999 to 2000. The issues of dealing with Y2K will be the responsibility of Agilent Technologies, not the larger Hewlett-Packard although there is no reason why the two companies would not work together on this issue. However, if the stock price suffers due to this or another near-term event, the distribution rate to HP will also suffer.

The Decision to Go Public

The initial public offering (IPO) is the first offering of stock to the public. Since Agilent Technologies was a spin-off of Hewlett-Packard, its independent operation qualifies the first stock issuance as an IPO. The offering price in the primary market was determined by the underwriting syndicate lead by Morgan Stanley Dean Witter with a final price to be named on November 17,

the day before the IPO. Many companies go public to raise capital to fund expansion or pay off debt, but Agilent Technologies agreed to pay the entire net proceeds of the IPO to Hewlett-Packard as a separating dividend. Wealth would accumulate to Agilent shareholders after the IPO. Figure 1 depicts Hewlett Packard's stock price movement from the time of the announcement of the spin-off to November 18, the day of Agilent's IPO. The stock was volatile, the price increased from $65.33 to $68.06 upon the March 2 announcement of the spin-off. The price skyrocketed to a high of $115.75 on July 19, shortly before the name "Agilent Technologies" was unveiled. The stock fell again to the mid $60's only to jump $13.28 on November 18, 1999. Clearly, investors took the spin-off as a positive signal for Hewlett-Packard; would the signal be as strong for Agilent Technologies?

Most IPO's trade on the NASDAQ, less than 25 percent trade on the NYSE.[8] For years, it was argued the NASDAQ was the market of choice for small firms and favored technology stocks. Because of the lower costs associated with the NASDAQ and the market

Table 7   Consolidated Statement of Cash Flow for the Years Ending October 31 (in millions)

	October 31,			
	1999	1998	1997	1996
	(In millions)			
Cash flows from operating activities:				
Net earnings	$ 512	$ 257	$ 543	$ 542
Adjustment to reconcile net earnings to net cash provided by operating activities:				
Depreciation and amortization	475	477	409	401
Deferred taxes on earnings	(12)	(140)	(26)	(1)
Non-cash restructuring and asset impairment charges	51	85		
Write-down of investments		37		
Changes in assets and liabilities:				
Accounts receivable	(431)	18	(20)	67
Inventory	(40)	(67)	(57)	(181)
Accounts payable	75	(60)	72	(11)
Other current assets and liabilities	(52)	130	57	84
Other, net	(117)	14	(13)	(20)
Net cash provided by operating activities	461	751	965	881
Cash flows from investing activities:				
Investment in property, plant and equipment	(434)	(410)	(582)	(559)
Disposition of property, plant and equipment	74	78	81	64
Acquisitions, net of cash acquired	(55)	(2)	(9)	(6)
Cash proceeds of divestitures	100	57		
Other, net	6	5	(5)	(7)
Net cash used in investing activities	(309)	(272)	(515)	(508)
Net cash transfers to Hewlett-Packard	(152)	(479)	(450)	(373)

Sources: Agilent 1999 10-K, p. F-5 and Prospectus, p. F-6.

environment, many companies chose the NASDAQ. Agilent Technologies was so highly sought that the New York Stock Exchange (NYSE) offered the company the coveted ticker symbol "A" if they listed on the NYSE. In recent years, many high growth companies went to the NASDAQ and the NYSE was eager to have the opportunity to persuade a company such as Agilent to list with them. The offer worked, Agilent agreed to list on the NYSE and open business on the day of its IPO, November 18, 1999.

> Our listing on the New York Stock Exchange represents an important milestone for Agilent as we continue our transition to an independent company. It is especially fitting that our stock will be symbolized by the single letter "A", reinforcing Agilent's leadership position in the marketplace,

our commitment to technological innovation, and our unique heritage and core values.

On July 30, 1999, Agilent issued ten million shares of common stock to Hewlett-Packard for $10 million. These shares were split 38 for 1 on October 21, 1999, which increased Hewlett-Packard's ownership in Agilent Technologies to 380 million shares. These shares were to be retained by Hewlett-Packard until mid-2000 at which time they could be sold. This posed a risk for Agilent shareholders if many of these shares hit the secondary markets at the same time, but a cost necessary to pursue the spin-off. Agilent's stock price could drop significantly after the Hewlett-Packard shares are distributed in mid-2000. Hewlett-Packard owned 84.1 percent of Agilent Technologies as of the date of the IPO, thus maintaining effective control of the company. If for whatever reason,

FIGURE 1

Hewlett-Packard Stock Prices March 1–November 18, 1999

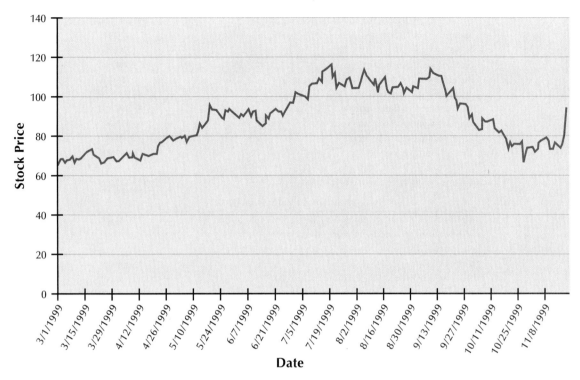

Hewlett-Packard does not complete its distribution, business could suffer. The relationship with Hewlett-Packard is critical to the short-term viability of Agilent.

Main underwriters Morgan Stanley Dean Witter and Goldman Sachs led the issuance of an additional 72 million shares on November 18, 1999. The price set for the issuance was $30 per share, which brought total gross receipts to $2.16 billion. Underwriter expenses are broken down in Table 8. Hewlett-Packard was granted the estimated net offering of $2.1 billion as a one-time dividend. Hewlett-Packard agreed to pay all underwriting expenses. Any gains to Agilent must come after the date of the initial public offering. The purchase of Agilent carried substantial risk because Hewlett-Packard paid a dividend and Agilent did not plan to. Stock held by index funds tied to the S&P 500 or the DJIA will have to be sold immediately after the Hewlett-Packard distribution, thus possibly causing a large sell-off of Agilent stock.

The Pricing Decision

On October 14, 1999, Salomon Smith Barney upgraded its report from "neutral" to "outperform" when it became clear the offering price would far exceed the initial price range of $11–14. Just a few days later on October 22, 1999, Agilent filed an amended registration with the SEC, amending its estimated offering price to $19–22 per share for an estimated total IPO of $1.1 billion for 57 million shares.[10] On November 17, the price was set at $30 and it was predicted the offering would be fully subscribed with substantial excess demand for this hot "new" stock.

From Here to Eternity …

Agilent went public on November 18, 1999 at a price of $30 per share. Options were granted and exercised for 7,560,432 shares at the offering price. It was fully subscribed with 60,000,000 shares offered in the United States and Canada and 11,400,000 shares sold abroad. The stock closed that day at $44, a first day gain of 46 percent. In sum, nearly 460,000,000 shares were outstanding on November 18, including the 380,000,000 in Hewlett-Packard shareholders hands. These shares could be traded in the secondary markets at a yet-to-be determined date in mid-2000. Pricing be what it may, the IPO was a sellout; now Barnholt was faced with even bigger issues.

Table 8   Underwriting Expenses for Agilent Technologies' Initial Public Offering

Type of Expense	Cost
Underwriting discounts and commissions	$91,800,000
Securities and Exchange Commission Registration Fee	$478,911
NASD filing fee	$30,500
NYSE original listing fee	$504,600
Blue Sky qualification fees and expenses	$5,000
Legal fees and expenses	$2,500,000
Accounting fees and expenses	$3,000,000
Transfer agent and registrar fees	$25,000
Printing and engraving fees	$500,000
Miscellaneous expenses	$455,989
Total underwriting and related expenses	$99,300,000

Additional Valuation Data

Risk-free rate of interest (proxied by the 90 day T-Bill rate)	5.4%
Market return (proxied by 10 year S&P average)	18%
Beta (proxied by Hewlett-Packard beta in October 1999)	1.2
Number of shares in IPO	72,000,000
Shares held by Hewlett-Packard until mid-2000	380,000,000
Total number of shares outstanding after the IPO	452,000,000

Ratio	Formula	Industry
Liquidity		
Current	Current Assets ÷ Current Liabilities	2.14
Quick	Current Assets − Inventory ÷ Current Liabilities	1.20
Asset Management		
Inventory Turnover	Sales ÷ Inventory	6.01
Days Sales Outstanding	Receivables ÷ (Annual Sales/360)	109
Fixed Asset Turnover	Sales ÷ Net Fixed Assets	12.80
Total Asset Turnover	Sales ÷ Total Assets	1.97
Debt Management		
Total Debt to Assets	Total Liabilities ÷ Total Assets	33.33%
Debt to Equity	Total Debt ÷ Total Equity	50.00%
Profitability		
Profit Margin on Sales	Net Income ÷ Sales	3.25%
Return on Assets	Net Income ÷ Total Assets	6.35
Return on Equity	Net Income ÷ Total Equity	13.91
Market Value		
Price to Earnings	Price per Share/Earnings per Share	38.55

Sources: Agilent 1999 10-K, p. 45, *Wall Street Journal*, 17 November 1999, http://www.yahoo.finance.

Our NYSE listing was an important step on our way to independence. Now that we are operating independently, Agilent's innovations in communications and life sciences, and the revenues that flow from them, will be visible in the marketplace. We now will be directly accountable for our results and to our shareholders.

—*Ned Barnholt, President and CEO of Agilent Technologies, November 18, 1999*[11]

Not all would be simple. Agilent would be under significant pressure to introduce products in an efficient, timely manner due to the high degree of obsolescence in its business lines. This increased pressure means that failure to meet these demands could significantly affect operating profits and cash flow and as a result, the company would have to deploy resources to address issues affecting the company. Operating profits, cash flows and subsequently, the stock price could be negatively impacted if its customers

FIGURE 2

Agilent Technologies' Closing Stock Prices After the IPO

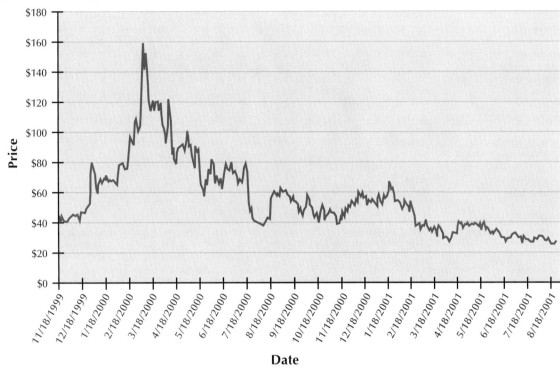

are in downward cycles. Agilent's customer base is wide and well diversified; thus, it should be able to buffer itself from some cyclical downturn. Figure 2 shows Agilent Technologies' closing stock price since the IPO.

Agilent has the opportunity to be a market leader in a rapidly growing industry with a significant head start from its long-term relationship with Hewlett-Packard. Agilent may now move to test other company's products, outside of Hewlett-Packard, which should provide significant growth potential. It is possible, and hoped by management, that Agilent would offer the stakeholders more apart from Hewlett-Packard than as an HP subsidiary. However, if Hewlett-Packard chooses a different semiconductor supplier or if business declines in this area, profits could decrease. The opportunity to continue to grow efficiently, move quickly and react to market needs and have better focus on the business units with strong competition at the door.

Clearly an exciting day, Barnholt had many things on his mind. Was the IPO properly priced? Where would

Agilent go from here? How would the company adequately identify and more importantly react to weaknesses and threats while capitalizing on strengths and opportunities? Barnholt and his employees faced many potential opportunities, but the road was not without its share of challenges. Clearly, Agilent was in his hands now and Wall Street would be watching closely.

Notes

1. Gouldson, Tim. "Realignment: The HP Way," *Canadian Electronics* 14, no. 3 (May 1999): 6.
2. Orshal, Judy. "HP Spins Off Instrumentation Unit," *Chemical Week* 161, no. 9 (10 March 1999): 41.
3. Agilent 1999 Annual Report, p. 7.
4. Agilent 1999 10-K, p. 15.
5. Ibid, p. 23.
6. Ibid, p. 30.
7. Ibid, p. 38.
8. http://ipo.com/member_services, accessed 28 April 2000.
9. Agilent Press Release.
10. Washington Post, p. E01, 23 October 1999.
11. Agilent Press Release.

Table 9   Key Financial Data, 1996–2005

Year	1996	1997	1998	1999	Avg (1)	2000	2001	2002	2003	2004	2005
Sales	$ 7,379	$7,785	$7,952	$ 8,331	$ 7,862	$9,827	$12,038	$14,446	$16,974	$19,520	$21,960
Net Income	$ 542	$ 543	$ 257	$ 512	$ 532	$ 665	$ 815	$ 978	$ 1,149	$ 1,322	$ 1,487
Depreciation	$ 401	$ 409	$ 477	$ 475	$ 246	$ 307	$ 376	$ 451	$ 530	$ 610	$ 686
Capital Spending	($ 502)	($ 497)	($ 347)	($ 305)	($ 413)	($ 516)	($ 632)	($ 758)	($ 891)	($ 1,025)	($ 1,153)
Changes in Working Capital			$ 68	$ 381	$ 225	$ 281	$ 344	$ 413	$ 485	$ 557	$ 627
Cash Flow	$ 441	$ 455	$ 455	$ 1,063	$ 604	$ 754	$ 924	$ 1,109	$ 1,303	$ 1,498	$ 1,686
PV of Years 2000–2005 (20.52%)	$ 3,653										
PV of Years 2006 Forth (at constant growth rate of 10%)	$16,024										
Total Value (000's)	$19,677										
Per share value	**$43.53**										

Assumptions

1. In calculating averages for 1996–1999, each year was used except for the net income in 1998, which was deflated due to extraordinary items. Therefore, in calculating a base net income, only 1996, 1997, and 1999 data were used. Clearly, this is a subjective decision that should be left up to the analyst.

2. For the base case scenario, growth rates for all accounts were assumed to be 25% in 2000, and decrease by 2.5 basis points each year until 2005, at which point the growth rate is 12.5%. After that time, a constant growth rate of 10% was used. The higher than average constant growth rate is justified by the growth potential for Agilent Technologies.

3. Non-constant growth is estimated for 6 years, after which the constant growth model is used. The time period for non-constant growth is subjective, generally from 4–10 years.

4. The discount rate for the cash flows is calculated using the CAPM and a constant growth rate of 10%.

5. The number of shares outstanding is assumed to be equal to the weighted average common shares outstanding as of the IPO, or 452 million shares.

Case 3

The AOL Time Warner Merger

Neil H. Snyder, Debbie Beisswanger, Lisa Jeffreys, and Jennifer Leemann,
University of Virginia

This is a historic moment in which new media has truly come of age. We've always said that America Online's mission is to make the Internet as central to people's lives as the telephone and television, and even more valuable, and this is a once-in-a-lifetime opportunity to turn this promise into reality. We're kicking off the new century with a unique new company that has unparalleled assets and the ability to have a profoundly positive impact on society. By joining forces with Time Warner, we will fundamentally change the way people get information, communicate with others, buy products and are entertained—providing far-reaching benefits to our customers and shareholders.
—*Steve Case, Chairman of the Board, AOL Time Warner*[1]

You've Got Mail

Steve Case and Time Warner's CEO, Gerald Levin, were long time acquaintances when they crossed paths in 1999 at the White House for a screening of Time Warner's "You've Got Mail." This film's title was inspired by AOL's email greeting,[2] and subtly foreshadowed the impending merger. A few months later, Levin invited Case to co-chair an international business forum in Paris.[3] The two men met again in China at *Fortune* magazine's global forum. After these meetings, Case and Levin realized that they shared similar views—"that corporations should stand for more than just profits."[4] Both men sat on the Board of the New York Stock Exchange and during a

mid-October 1999 coffee break, Case approached Levin with the idea of merging the two companies.[5] Levin felt the deal was a "natural fit," and readily agreed.[6] Less than three months later, they announced news of the merger in mid-town Manhattan.

The Announcement

News of a merger between American Online and Time Warner became public on January 10, 2000 in a press conference with Gerald Levin and Steve Case. Notable was the fact that Steve Case dressed formally in a tie and sports jacket while Gerald Levin was uncharacteristically dressed in an unbuttoned shirt and sports jacket.[7] Case announced, "This merger will launch the next Internet revolution."[8] A press release documenting this announcement can be found in Exhibit 1.

In the initial deal, America Online was to pay $183 billion in stock for Time Warner in exchange for 55 percent control of Time Warner, in addition to assuming $17 billion of Time Warner's debt.[9] Time Warner stockholders were to receive a premium of 1.5 shares in the new company while AOL stockholders' shares were to be converted one-for-one. AOL Time Warner was to trade under the ticker symbol AOL.[10] The merger aimed to "create the world's first fully integrated media and communications company for the Internet Century in an all-stock combination valued at $350 billion."[11] The merger shocked employees of both companies, as news of the deal had not been divulged. Even top mangers within AOL heard the news for the first time on January 10, according to Sean Kidder, Vice President of Strategic Infrastructure for AOL.[12]

Wall Street's Reaction to the News

Wall Street reacted to the news by initially driving Time Warner share prices, which were trading at 64 3/4 before the deal,[13] up to a high of $102. By the end of January 10, 2000, however, the price fell to $90.[14] America Online's shares, which sold at 73 ¾ before the deal,[15] closed at $71.25 after peaking at $80 earlier that day.[16] Two days after the announcement, the stock prices of both companies dropped $5 or more per share.[17] Jim

Exhibit 1   Press Release Announcing Merger

America Online and Time Warner Will Merge to Create World's First Internet-Age Media and Communications Company

- AOL Time Warner Will Be Premier Global Company Delivering Branded Information, Entertainment and Communications Across Rapidly Converging Media Platforms and Changing Technology
- Will Provide Far-Reaching Benefits to Consumers By Speeding Growth of Interactive Medium
- Will Accelerate Availability of Broadband Interactive Services Offering Vast Array of World-Class Content
- Will Drive Growth of Advertising and E-Commerce Across Unmatched Combination of Leading Brands
- Companies Also Announce New Marketing, Commerce, Content and Promotional Agreements

DULLES, VIRGINIA and NEW YORK, NEW YORK, January 10, 2000—America Online, Inc. [NYSE:AOL] and Time Warner Inc. [NYSE:TWX] today announced a strategic merger of equals to create the world's first fully integrated media and communications company for the Internet Century in an all-stock combination valued at $350 billion.

To be named AOL Time Warner Inc. with combined revenues of over $30 billion, this unique new enterprise will be the premier global company delivering branded information, entertainment and communications services across rapidly converging media platforms.

The merger will combine Time Warner's vast array of world-class media, entertainment and news brands and its technologically advanced broadband delivery systems with America Online's extensive Internet franchises, technology and infrastructure, including the world's premier consumer online brands, the largest community in cyberspace, and unmatched e-commerce capabilities. AOL Time Warner's unparalleled resources of creative and journalistic talent, technology assets and expertise, and management experience will enable the new company to dramatically enhance consumers' access to the broadest selection of high-quality content and interactive services.

By merging the world's leading Internet and media companies, AOL Time Warner will be uniquely positioned to speed the development of the interactive medium and the growth of all its businesses. The new company will provide an important new broadband distribution platform for America Online's interactive services and drive subscriber growth through cross-marketing with Time Warner's pre-eminent brands.

AOL Time Warner's brands will include AOL, *Time,* CNN, CompuServe, Warner Bros., Netscape, *Sports Illustrated, People,* HBO, ICQ, AOL Instant Messenger, AOL MovieFone, TBS, TNT, Cartoon Network, Digital City, Warner Music Group, Spinner, Winamp, *Fortune,* AOL.COM, *Entertainment Weekly,* and Looney Tunes. In addition to fully integrating its brands into a digital environment and bringing them closer to consumers, AOL Time Warner will have a wealth of creative resources to develop products specifically suited to interactive media.

Under the terms of a definitive merger agreement approved by unanimous votes at meetings of each company's board of directors, Time Warner and America Online stock will be converted to AOL Time Warner stock at fixed exchange ratios. The Time Warner shareholders will receive 1.5 shares of AOL Time Warner for each share of Time Warner stock they own. America Online shareholders will receive one share of AOL Time Warner stock for each share of America Online stock they own. The merger will be effected on a tax-free basis to shareholders. When complete, America Online's shareholders will own approximately 55% and Time Warner's shareholders will own approximately 45% of the new company. The stock will be traded under the symbol AOL on the New York Stock Exchange.

The merger will be accounted for as a purchase transaction and is expected to be accretive to America Online's cash earnings per share before the amortization of goodwill. This transaction is subject to certain closing conditions, including regulatory approvals and the approval of America Online and Time Warner shareholders, and is expected to close by the end of the year. Mr. Ted Turner, Vice Chairman of Time Warner, has agreed to vote his Time Warner shares, representing approximately 9% of the company's outstanding common stock, in favor of the merger.

Steve Case, Chairman and Chief Executive Officer of America Online, will become Chairman of the Board of the new company. Gerald M. Levin, Time Warner's Chairman and Chief Executive Officer, will become AOL Time Warner's Chief Executive Officer. As Chairman, Mr. Case will play an active role in helping to build and lead AOL Time Warner, focusing particularly on the technological developments and policy initiatives driving the global expansion of the interactive medium. As Chief Executive Officer, Mr. Levin will set the company's strategy, working closely with Mr. Case, and will oversee the management of the company. Mr. Levin will report to the board consisting of 16 members, with eight appointed by each of the current America Online and Time Warner boards.

Mr. Turner will become Vice Chairman of AOL Time Warner. Time Warner President Richard Parsons and America Online President and Chief Operating Officer Bob Pittman will be co-Chief Operating Officers of AOL Time Warner. J. Michael Kelly, Senior Vice President and Chief Financial Officer of America Online, will become the new company's Chief Financial Officer and Executive Vice President. A four-person integration committee, composed of Messrs. Pittman; Parsons; Kenneth J. Novack, America Online's Vice Chairman; and Richard Bressler, Chairman and Chief Executive Officer of Time Warner Digital Media, has been formed to ensure a smooth and rapid combination of the two companies. The Committee will make its recommendations to Messrs. Case and Levin. Messrs. Parsons, Pittman and Kelly will report to Mr. Levin.

Exhibit 1   Press Release Announcing Merger (continued)

Building a New Medium for the New Millennium

Mr. Case said: "This is an historic moment in which new media has truly come of age. We've always said that America Online's mission is to make the Internet as central to people's lives as the telephone and television, and even more valuable, and this is a once-in-a-lifetime opportunity to turn this promise into reality. We're kicking off the new century with a unique new company that has unparalleled assets and the ability to have a profoundly positive impact on society. By joining forces with Time Warner, we will fundamentally change the way people get information, communicate with others, buy products and are entertained—providing far-reaching benefits to our customers and shareholders.

Mr. Case added: "We have tremendous respect for Jerry Levin and Time Warner management, who have built the world's pre-eminent media company and have fostered an entrepreneurial culture that will mesh well with our own. Time Warner is the first major media company to not only recognize, but also fully embrace the interactive medium. I look forward to working with them to build the most valued and respected company in the world. By mobilizing the combined creative energies and extraordinary management talent of both companies, we will bring customers around the world an unmatched array of interactive services, with enriched multi-media content and e-commerce opportunities."

Mr. Levin said: "This strategic combination with AOL accelerates the digital transformation of Time Warner by giving our creative and content businesses the widest possible canvas. The digital revolution has already begun to create unprecedented and instantaneous access to every form of media and to unleash immense possibilities for economic growth, human understanding and creative expression. AOL Time Warner will lead this transformation, improving the lives of consumers worldwide."

Mr. Levin added: "I look forward to partnering with Steve Case—a visionary leader of the Internet—and his impressive management team. The opportunities are limitless for everyone connected to AOL Time Warner—shareholders, consumers, advertisers, the creative and talented people who drive our success, and the global audiences we serve."

Mr. Pittman said: "The value of this merger lies not only in what it is today but in what it will be in the future. We believe that AOL Time Warner will provide companies worldwide with a convenient, one-stop way to put advertising and commerce online as well as take advantage of the best in traditional marketing. We will accelerate the development of Time Warner's cable broadband assets by bringing AOL's hallmark ease-of-use to this platform. We expect America Online to help drive the growth of cable broadband audiences, and we will use our combined infrastructure and cross-promotional strengths to enhance the growth and development of both America Online and Time Warner brands around the world."

Mr. Parsons said: "This is a defining event for Time Warner and America Online as well as a pivotal moment in the unfolding of the Internet age. By joining the resources and talents of these two highly creative companies, we can accelerate the development and deployment of a whole new generation of interactive services and content. The heightened competition and expanded choices this will bring about will be of great benefit to consumers. For the creative and innovative people who are the lifeblood of our companies, it means a truly exciting range of new opportunities to explore and give shape to. For our shareholders, it means we'll be able to grow in ways we couldn't have as separate companies, producing superior returns in both the short and long term."

New Marketing, Commerce, Content and Promotional Agreements

Separate from the merger transaction, America Online and Time Warner also announced new marketing, commerce, content and promotional agreements that will immediately expand various relationships already in place between the two companies. These include:

- The AOL service will feature Time Warner's popular *InStyle* magazine, expanding on the popular content Time Warner already offers AOL members from *People, Teen People, Entertainment Weekly* and other content currently on the service.
- CNN.com and Entertaindom.com programming will be featured prominently on various America Online services.
- AOL members will have access to a wide range of Time Warner promotional music clips from Time Warner's unparalleled selection of popular artists.
- Time Warner and AOL MovieFone will participate in online-offline cross-promotion of Time Warner movies and related content, including live events.
- Broadband CNN news content will be distributed on AOL Plus, the rich media content offering designed for AOL members connecting via broadband, when it launches this spring.
- Time Warner will offer a number of special offers exclusively for AOL members, which will include everything from discounts on magazine subscriptions to premium cable subscriptions and movie passes.
- Building on the companies' current offline cross-promotional activities, including keywords on popular magazines like *People* and *Teen People*, Time Warner will dramatically expand cross-promotion of AOL in a number of their top offline media properties.
- The popular Warner Bros. retail stores will promote the AOL service, including through the in-store distribution of AOL disks.
- Time Warner will include AOL disks in promotional mailings and product shipments.
- America Online will make available on Road Runner popular America Online brands and products, including

Exhibit 1   Press Release Announcing Merger (continued)

AOL Instant Messenger, Digital City, AOL Search and AOL MovieFone.

The companies also said, with respect to broadband access, that AOL Time Warner will be committed to ensuring consumer choice of ISPs and content and that they hope this merger will persuade all companies operating broadband platforms to provide consumers with real choice.

Combination Creates Full Range of Growth Opportunities

In addition to today's announcements, America Online and Time Warner will have many other opportunities to combine their assets to create unique new expanded services to drive increased consumer usage, and marketing and promotion capabilities to fuel rapid growth for their shareholders and employees. These, among others, include:

- *Music:* The combination of Time Warner's prestigious music labels and roster of established stars and new artists with America Online's online marketing and e-commerce capacities will create powerful music destinations.

- *Entertainment:* America Online's AOL TV and MovieFone combined with Time Warner's cable networks and Warner Bros. movies and television will provide valuable programming, cross-promotional, and e-commerce opportunities.

- *Broadband:* AOL Time Warner's ability to offer the finest content will expand the already growing number of consumers seeking to access the Internet at high speeds via cable modem, DSL, wireless or satellite.

- *News:* AOL Time Warner will continue to enhance its online news offering with the world's most recognized and respected news media, including CNN, Time, and local all-news channels such as NY1 News.

- *Technology:* AOL Time Warner will be able to develop and leverage technology across all of the businesses, creating new opportunities to expand services and share infrastructure.

- *Telephony:* For businesses and consumers, AOL Time Warner will offer a major communications platform that combines America Online's popular instant messaging products with Time Warner's ability to offer local telephony over cable.

Kimsey, cofounder of AOL, commented on the stock price change, "We were surprised because we were expecting a reduction in the price of AOL and a rise in Time shares. What happened was the opposite and there was a greater drop than we expected."18 A comprehensive chart containing FAOL and Time Warner's five-year historical stock prices can be found in Exhibit 2.

The failed merger of USA Networks and Lycos in 1999 contributed to investors' concern regarding the AOL Time Warner merger.19 Merrill Lynch & Company analyst Henry Blodget commented, "The big question for shareholders is whether the market will accord the new entity a traditional valuation or an 'Internet valuation.'"20 Blodget also added that the value of the stock would be a "function of management's ability to instill confidence [in investors]." He predicted the stock price would fluctuate between $55 and $90 a share depending on management's ability to increase confidence in the deal. Steve Case and Gerald Levin underscored the similarities between AOL and Time Warner, as they are both subscription-based, distribution, and consumer brand-building operations.21

The volatile stock prices resulted also from a changing investor base. The Senior Managing Director of Wyser Pratte, a company that specializes in merger investments observed, "You're going to get a natural shift in investor base. Those people who own Time Warner would want to own a Time Warner-type of company and not to own

AOL."22 During the proposed Lycos/USA merger, Lycos' shareholders were displeased when an old economy company came together with a new economy tech firm. This indicated that Internet investors would look unfavorably upon consolidation with traditional companies.23 AOL stockholders did not want the company hindered by Time Warner's reputation as a "slow growth old media company." Likewise, Time Warner stockholders questioned the valuation of an Internet company like AOL.24 Michael Broder from AOL Investor Relations explained the inevitable withdrawal of short-term investors' money from AOL while the merger awaited approval. These shareholders are inclined to place their investments elsewhere while the market adjusts to the news and final approval of the deal.25

Wall Street began accepting the merger, seeing the strategic benefits of combining the two giants. However, the deal's closing date remained undetermined due to regulatory bodies' lengthy decision-making processes. The initial deal was expected to close in November, but as the year progressed, analysts pushed back their predictions for the deal's completion. Federal Trade Commission (FTC) negotiations intensified over cable access concerns, and Internet competitors sought assurance that they would be able to provide Internet service over Time Warner's cable systems.

In December 2000, the FTC unanimously voted to approve the merger. Share prices rose for both compa-

Exhibit 2   AOL and Time Warner Stock Five-Year Data

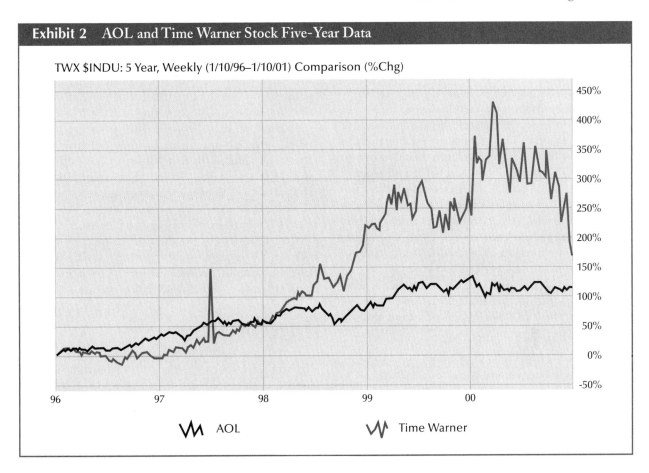

TWX $INDU: 5 Year, Weekly (1/10/96–1/10/01) Comparison (%Chg)

nies following this announcement—AOL by $1.55 and Time Warner by $1.90.[26] Nevertheless, almost a year after the deal's announcement, share prices were still declining. As of January 3, 2001 AOL shares hit a 52-week low of 32.39, down from its peak of $83.38; Time Warner also neared its 52-week low of 49.62. These significant declines may be attributed to the prolonged approval process. In addition, investors were concerned that Time Warner's declining advertising revenue would affect both companies' bottom lines.[27] On January 11, 2001 the Federal Communications Commission (FCC) approved the AOL Time Warner merger, and the company's stock began trading under the ticker symbol AOL.

AOL's History

In 1983, Steve Case worked for Control Video, a company that provided online services for Atari game players. The company faced major problems and needed reengineering so Case aided the CEO Jim Kimsey by raising funds to finance the company's reconstruction. In 1985, the recovered company changed its name to Quantum Computer and launched an online service known as Q-Link. Four years later, it expanded upon Q-Link with a new nationwide service known as America Online.

Headquartered in Dulles, Virginia, the company renamed itself America Online in 1991. A year later, the company went public on the NASDAQ trading under the ticker symbol AMER with shares selling for $11.50.[28] However, the company's stock value has grown 50,000 percent since the IPO.[29] In 1993, Case was appointed CEO of America Online, and he implemented a plan to focus on marketing as a competitive advantage over major competitors such as CompuServe, which AOL eventually purchased in 1998,[30] and Prodigy. With the unveiling of a Windows-based version of AOL, the company increased its number of users to 1 million by the end of 1994. The company went global in 1995 teaming with the German media giant Bertelsmann to create AOL Europe. AOL expanded its global reach further by entering Canadian and Japanese markets. AOL moved from trading on the NASDAQ to the NYSE in 1996 under the ticker symbol AOL. To combat intensifying competition, AOL began charging users a flat rate that increased proportionally to user's time spent online.

Bob Pittman, founder of MTV, joined AOL in 1997 as President.[31] With his guidance, the company scaled back marketing expenditures to focus on network traffic problems. As a result of these problems, AOL faced lawsuit threats from users unable to log online. AOL began offering refunds to unhappy subscribers in response.

AOL chose to sell its network service operations to WorldCom in return for CompuServe's online division and $147 million in cash. AOL then gained access to interactive TV with its purchase of NetChannel.[32] MovieFone and Netscape Communicator were also added to AOL's growing list of properties. AOL invested $1.5 billion in Hughes Electronics "to develop digital entertainment and Internet services, create a combination set-top box for DirecTV and AOL TV and collaborate on satellite Internet service DirectPC."

Today, AOL is the world's leader in interactive services, web brands, Internet technologies and electronic commerce services. AOL has four major lines of business

- The Interactive Services Group
- The Interactive Properties Group
- The AOL International Group
- The Netscape Enterprise Group

Exhibit 3 outlines the contents of each line of AOL's holdings in more detail.

Time Inc.'s History

In 1922, Henry Luce and Briton Hadden created a publishing giant known as Time Inc.[33] to bring world news and personal opinions to the poorly informed American public.[34] In 1923, the company published its first magazine, *Time*. It successfully encompassed the founder's goals and made a profit in four years.[35] The company was so successful that it launched *Fortune* and *Life* during the great depression—*Life* went on to become the most popular magazine ever. Despite Hadden's death in 1929, the company's portfolio continued to grow. The company continued adding properties: *Sports Illustrated* (1954), *Money* (1972), and *People* (1974).[36]

Time Life began to publish books in 1960.[37] Other additions to the product lines included the Book-of-the-Month Club and the publisher Brown & Company. The company briefly owned the textbook publisher Scott, Foresman & Company, but sold it in 1989.[38]

In 1970, Time Inc. decided to enter the cable television market. Thus, it acquired stakes in the American Television and Communications Corporation and founded Home Box Office (HBO).[39] By 1978, Time purchased complete control of American Television and Communications.[40]

Warner Brothers

Harry, Albert, Samuel, and Jack Warner founded Warner Brothers Pictures in 1923. Prior to founding the company, they operated movie theaters, but later moved into film distribution. The company initially hit financial problems but later recovered after patenting the vita phone process, introducing sound to films. Warner Brothers produced the first full-length film with sound in 1928 and in the next year introduced color as well. The success of these films made Warner Brothers a financial success and by the 1930s, it was producing 100 films a year.[41] Steven Ross' Kinney National Services acquired Warner Brothers in 1969 and later changed its name to Warner Communications. Since then, Warner Communications has become one of America's largest music producers and cable television operators.

Time Warner

Time Inc. and Warner Communications merged in 1989 to form Time Warner.[42] The $14 billion company was headed up by co-CEOs Steven Ross and Gerald Levin. Upon Ross' death in 1992, Levin became the sole CEO, and he became Chairman the following year. In 1996, Time Warner acquired Turner Broadcasting System for $7.6 billion,[43] making Ted Turner the new vice chairman. Turner Broadcasting brought WTBS, the Atlanta Braves, the Atlanta Hawks, CNN and TNT into Time Warner's portfolio. Today, Time Warner controls a variety of media content, as illustrated in Exhibit 4.

Customer Reach[44]

Neither AOL nor Time Warner has carved out a major global position as of 2001. In fact, AOL Time Warner conducts less than 20 percent of its business abroad. As a result of the marriage, the firm will go from a global "wannabe" to a true global competitor and capitalize on this growth potential.[45] By firmly controlling both content and distribution in the United States, the next hurdle becomes reaching customers in foreign countries.

Global adaptation of AOL's business model will take time and significant capital investment. The initial outlay to build fiber optics/cable lines does not present a cost problem for AOL Time Warner. However, the "last mile problem"—laying out cables to homes—will be expensive to solve. Solving this problem globally will be very expensive.

AOL Time Warner owns the number one Internet service provider and the number two cable company in the United States. On January 16, 2001, AOL passed the 27 million-subscriber mark on its flagship brand only 35

Exhibit 3   America Online Properties

Online Services
- America online—over 20 million subscribers
- CompuServe Interactive Services
- AOL Instant Messenger
- AOL.com portal
- Digital City
- AOL Europe
- ICQ
- The Knot, Inc.—wedding content (8% with QVC 36% and Hummer WinbladFunds 18%)
- MapQuest.com—pending regulatory approval
- Spinner.com
- DrKoop.com (10%)
  Other
  - Netscape Communications
  - Netscape Netcenter portal
  - AOL MovieFone
  - IAmaze
  - Quack.com

Joint Ventures with the following companies:
- Huhes Electronic Corp.
- 3Com
- Eastman Kodak Co.
- General Motors
- VarsityBooks.com
- Hewlett-Packard
- PurchasePro.com
- VeriSign Inc.
- Citigroup

days after reaching 26 million customers for an average of 28,500 net additions per day. AOL experienced its highest single subscriber day on Christmas Day 2000 when 70,000 new members signed on. As of March 20, 2001, AOL surpassed the 28 million mark with CompuServe contributing 3 million subscribers to the firm's overall reach. Interestingly, number two Earthlink and number 3 MSN have only 9 million customers combined. This disparity demonstrates AOL's dominance in the ISP market. To further illustrate AOL's dominance in this market, in January 2001 Americans spent one-third of all the time they were online with AOL Time Warner. By comparison, they spent seven percent of their time on Yahoo! and 6 percent on MSN.[46] Exhibit 5 contains AOL subscriber data over the past several years.

Time Warner owns various forms of subscription media, most of which dominate their respective categories. Turner Broadcasting is the leading revenue producer in basic cable, with three of the five top-rated basic cable networks. Also, CNN remains the most watched 24-hour news network. Time Warner's Home Box Office grew to 36.5 million US subscribers in 2000 between its HBO and Cinemax offerings. Regarding print media, Time Inc. has been in operation for over 75 years and has published more than 60 magazines with over 268 million readers. Warner Bros. television leads primetime programming with hits such as "Friends" and "ER." Additionally, Time Warner's New Line Cinema is one of the largest independent producers of theatrical motion pictures in the world, providing ample content for HBO and Cinemax. Musical endeavors include Warner Music, which operates in 68 countries and boasts well-known record companies such as Atlantic, Elektra, and Rhino. Finally, Time Warner Cable leads the cable television market with 12.7 million customers.

Time Warner's stake in the cable industry coupled with its joint venture with Road Runner broadband made it an attractive acquisition target for AOL.[47] The combination of Time Warner's content and cable with AOL's Internet distribution capabilities makes this merger a difficult one to duplicate. A comprehensive timeline documenting the history of AOL Time Warner merger can be found in Exhibit 6.

Financial Information

With 70 percent of mergers not producing the anticipated and desired results for shareholders it is imperative for AOL Time Warner to meet its financial expectations.[48] The combined AOL Time Warner was valued at $205 billion on the closing day of the deal, January 11, 2001.[49] Due to the devaluing of technology stocks in 2000, this figure pales in comparison to the initial value of the merger—$342 billion, quoted January 14, 2000.[50] Stock valuation for technology firms in general and for AOL Time Warner in particular has become a nightmare for Wall Street analysts due to the increasing uncertainty of the market and the structure of a company the likes of which has never existed in the history of the world. Clearly, AOL Time Warner is plowing new ground, and the investment community has not yet figured out how to value the new media enterprise.

Goldman, Sachs, & Company projects that AOL Time Warner will generate approximately $41.7 billion in total revenues in fiscal year 2001. Analysts expect Time Warner will contribute about 75 percent of the new company's revenues, while AOL will provide more than 50 percent of pre-tax income. This disparity results from Time Warner's high depreciation and interest charges whereas AOL's lower depreciation, large cash reserves, and minimal debt allow it to impact the joined firm's

Exhibit 4   Time Warner Properties

- Books
- Cable/DBS
- Movies and TV
- Magazines
- Music
- Online/other publishing
- Retail/theme parks/merchandise
- Turner Entertainment (includes cable, sports franchises, etc)

Time Warner—books
- Time Life Books
  - Time Life International
  - Time Life Education
  - Time Life Music
  - Time Life Audio Books
- Book of the month club
- Paperback book club
- Children's Book of the Month Club
- History Book Club
- Money Book Club
- HomeStyle Books
- Crafter's Choice
- One Spirit
- International
- Little, Brown & Company
- Bulfinch Press
- Back Bay Books
- Little, Brown & Company (U.K)
- Warner Books
- Warner Vision
- The Mysterious Press
- Warner Aspect
- Warner Treasures
- Oxmoor House (subsidiary of Southern Progress Corporation
- Leisure Arts
- Sunset Books
- TW Kids
- Leisure Arts

Time Warner—Cable/DBS
- HBO
- HBO Home Video
- HBO Pictures/HBO Showcase
- HBO Independent Productions
- HBO Downtown Productions
- HBO NYC Productions
- HBO Animation
- HBO Sports
- Cinemas
- Time Warner Sports International
- HBO Asia
- HBO en Espanol
- HBO Ole (with Sony)
- HBO Poland (with Sony)
- HBO Brazil (with Sony)
- HBO Hungary
- Cinemax Selecciones

Other Operations
- HBO Direct (DBS)
- Comedy Central (50% owned with Viacom)
- CNN
- CNN/SI
- CNN International
- CNN en Espanol
- CNN Headline News
- CNN Airport Network
- CNN fn
- CNN Radio
- CNN Interactive
- Court TV (with Liberty Media)
- Time Warner Cable
- Road Runner (high speed cable modem to the Internet, with MediaOne Group, Microsoft, and Compaq)
- Time Warner Communications (telephone service)
- New York City Cable Group (largest Cluster in world—over 1.1 million)
- New York 1 News (24 hour news channel devoted only to NYC)
- Time Warner Home Theater (Pay-per-view)
- Time Warner Security (residential and commercial security monitoring)
- Kablevision (53.75% cable television in Hungary)

Time Warner Inc. Film & TV Production/Distribution
- Warner Bros.
- Warner Bros. Studio
- Warner Bros. Television (Production)
- The WB Television Network
- Warner Bros. Television Animation
- Hanna-Barbera Cartoons
- Telepictures Productions
- Witt-Thomas Productions
- Castle Rock Entertainment
- Warner Home Video
- Warner Bros. Domestic Pay-TV
- Warner Bros. Domestic Television Distribution
- Warner Bros. International Television Distribution
- The Warner Channel (Latin America, Asia-Pacific, Australia, Germany)
- Warner Bros. International Theaters (owns/operates multiple theaters in over 12 countries)

Time Warner Inc.—Magazines
- Time
  - Time Asia
  - Time Atlantic
  - Time Canada
  - Time Latin America
  - Time South Pacific
  - Time Money
  - Time for Kids
- Fortune

- Life
- Sports Illustrated
  - Sports Illustrated Women/Sport
  - Sports Illustrated International
  - SI for Kids
- Inside Stuff
- Money
  - Your Company
  - Your Future
- People
  - Who Weekly (Australian edition)
  - People en Espanol
  - Teen People
- Entertainment Weekly
  - EW Metro
- The Ticket
- In Style
- Southern Living
- Progressive Farmer
- Southern Accents
- Cooking Light
- The Parent Group
  - Parenting
  - Baby Talk
  - Baby on the way
- This Old House
- Sunset
- Sunset Garden Guide
- The Health Publishing Guide
  - Health
  - Hippocrates
  - Costal Living
  - Weight Watchers
- Real Simple
- Asiaweek (Asian news weekly)
- President (Japanese business monthly)
- Dancyu (Japanese cooking)
- Wallpaper (UK)
- American Express Publishing Corporation (Partial ownership/management)
  - Travel & Leisure
  - Food & Wine
  - Your Company
  - Departures
  - SkyGuide
- Magazines listed under Warner Brothers label
  - DC Comics
  - Vertigo
  - Paradox
  - Milestone
- Mad Magazine

Time Warner Music
Warner Music Group—Recording Labels
- The Atlantic Group
- Atlantic Classics
- Atlantic Jazz
- Atlantic Nashville

Exhibit 4   Time Warner Properties (Cont'd)

- Atlantic Theater
- Big Beat
- Blackground
- Breaking
- Curb
- Igloo
- Lava
- Mesa/Bluemoon
- Modern
- 1 43
- Rhino Records
- Elektra Entertainment Group
- Elektra
- EastWest
- Asylum
- Elektra/Sire
- Warner Brothers Records
- Warner Brothers
- Warner Nashville
- Warner Alliance
- Warner Resound
- Warner Sunset
- Reprise
- Reprise Nashville
- American Recordings
- Giant
- Maverick
- Revolution
- Qwest
- Warner Music International
- WEA Telegram
- East West ZTT
- Coalition
- CGD East
- China
- Continental
- DRO East West

- Erato
- Faxer
- Finlandia
- Magneoton
- MCM
- Nonesuch
- Teldic

Other Recording Interests
- Waner/Chappell Music (publishing company)
- WEA Inc. (Sales, distribution, and manufacturing)
- Ivy Hill Corporation (printing and packaging)
- Warner Special Products

Joint Ventures
- Columbia House (with Sony-direct marketing)
- Music Sound Exchange (with Sony-direct marketing)
- Music Choice and Music Choice Europe (with Sony, EMI, General Instrument)
- Viva (with Sony, Pologram, EMI—German music video channel)
- Channel V (w/Sony, EMI, Bertelsmann, News Corp)
- Heartland Music (50%—direct order of country and gospel music)

Time Warner—Online/Other Publishing
- Road Runner
- Warner Publisher Services
- Time Distribution Services
- American Family Publishers (50%)
- Patherfinder
- Africana.com

Time Warner—Merchandise/Retail
- Warner Bros. Consumer Product

- Warner Bros. Studio Stores (as of December 1997, 170 stores worldwide in over 30 countries)

Theme Parks
- Warner Brothers Recreation Enterprises (owns/operates international theme parks)

Time Warner Inc.—Turner Entertainment
Entertainment Networks
- TBS Superstation
- Turner Network Television (TNT)
- Turner South
- Cartoon Network
- Turner Classic Movies
- Cartoon Network in Europe
- Cartoon Network in Latin America
- TNT & Cartoon Network in Asia/Pacific

Film Production
- New Line Cinema
- Fine Line Features
- Turner Original Productions

Sports
- Atlanta Braves
- Atlanta Hawks
- Atlanta Thrashers
- Turner Sports
- World Championship Wrestling
- Good Will Games
- Philips Arena

Other Operations
- Turner Learning
- CNN Newsroom (daily news program for classrooms)
- Turner Adventure Learning (electric field trips for schools)
- Turner Home Satellite
- Turner Network Sales

EBITDA (earnings before interest, taxes, depreciation, and amortization) more significantly.[51] A listing of AOL Time Warner's key ratios versus the industry can be found in Exhibit 7.

According to J.P. Morgan, AOL Time Warner will generate 33 percent of its revenue from content, 42 percent from subscription services, and 25 percent from advertising. Exhibit 8 contains a graphical depiction of AOL Time Warner's revenues. Analysts predict that advertising will be the fastest growing revenue builder for the new company. However, with the softening of the advertising market, many firms have reduced their advertising budgets.

Pre-acquisition, AOL's subscription services, advertising, and enterprise solutions constituted 63.9 percent, 28.8 percent, and 7.3 percent of total revenues, respectively. The subscription services revenue stems primarily from subscribers paying a standard monthly membership fee of $21.95. AOL's alliances with leading brands and retailers makes advertising the second largest source of revenue for the company. Enterprise solutions consist of product licensing fees, fees from technical support, and consulting and training services.

As a separate entity, Time Warner's essential revenue streams include cable systems, cable networks, and filmed entertainment. Analysts anticipate these components will contribute 30 percent, 28 percent, and 23 percent of 2001 forecast revenue growth, respectively. Time Warner cable investments in fiber optic and digital technology make it one of the most advanced cable television operations in the United States with 12.3 million customers. CNN, HBO, Cinemax, TBS, TNT, and the Cartoon Network are popular Time Warner cable network initiatives. Filmed

Exhibit 5   Growth of AOL Subscribers

Date Announced	AOL Members Announced (MM)	Avg Net Daily Adds
March 21, 2000	22.0	NA
March 31, 2000	22.208	20,800
June 16, 2000	23.0	10,421
June 30, 2000	23.201	14,357
September 5, 2000	24.0	11,925
September 30, 2000	24.643	25,720
October 24, 2000	25.0	14,875
December 12, 2000	26.0	20,408
January 16, 2001	27.0	29,412

Source: AOL Time Warner, Inc.

entertainment includes the creation, distribution licensing and marketing of movies, television programming and videos via Warner Brothers and New Line Cinema.

The benefits of the AOL Time Warner merger include a substantial decrease in divisional costs. These reductions will be obtained by fully exploiting Time Warner's content and AOL's delivery. The idea of an "evergreen" subscription renewal system will become a reality as AOL Time Warner reduces direct mailing costs in favor of renewal on the World Wide Web. Secondly, subscription based packages across various types of media will draw in more customers due to their convenience and all-inclusive nature. Online promotions of Time Warner entertainment will reduce money spent on newspaper and advertising media. Additionally, Warner Music can digitally distribute its' content rather than manufacture millions of compact discs. Finally, AOL Time Warner has the ability to raise prices accordingly as it delivers greater value and enhanced products to consumers.[52]

J.P. Morgan projects that AOL Time Warner's free cash flow over the next five years will reach $20 billion. This future cash flow will most likely be reinvested in one of the following ways:

- Investments in growth initiatives, such as interactive services via cable, online music services, etc.
- The buyback of AOL Time Warner stock
- Acquisitions (particularly global expansion)

This prediction is supported by the fact that on January 18, 2001, the company announced a two-year, $5 billion stock repurchase plan. This parallels Time Warner's historically active repurchasing behavior.

AOL Time Warner projects a 30 percent annual revenue growth rate. Some critics of the merger believe this projection is unrealistic. However, even if AOL Time

Warner produces a 15 percent annual growth rate for 15 years, it will generate a $2.4 trillion return for investors. If the company produces the desired 30 percent growth rate, the return for investors will be $4.8 trillion. Historically, companies of similar size meet short run expectations but fail to meet goals in the long run. Most merged companies within the first few years after the merger hit a brick wall, and begin to slow down financially.[53]

As a result of the merger, AOL Time Warner has the ability to take on more debt if necessary. The firm can take advantage of its financial strength to undertake an aggressive acquisition strategy. Also, this flexibility will allow AOL Time Warner to be on the cutting edge of new innovations and initiatives. ABN Ambro analyst David Londoner put it best when he said, "This merger creates a media powerhouse that may well be impossible to duplicate."[54]

The Federal Trade Commission

> The Federal Trade Commission worried that the AOL Time Warner deal would create a media octopus with such strong tentacles in so many areas that it could have undue influence over their provision of information and entertainment.
> —New York Times, *Dec. 15, 2000*[55]

Soon after the merger was announced, The FTC began reviewing potential antitrust issues regarding AOL Time Warner's industry leading consumer brands and leading Internet platform. The FTC believed Time Warner's 20 percent stake in the national cable market was significant enough to hamper competition. Both competitors and the FTC believed this percentage could lead to AOL gaining preferential treatment to high-speed Internet service.[56] Without restriction, the combined company would have the option to either block competitors' Internet

Exhibit 6   Timeline of AOL Time Warner

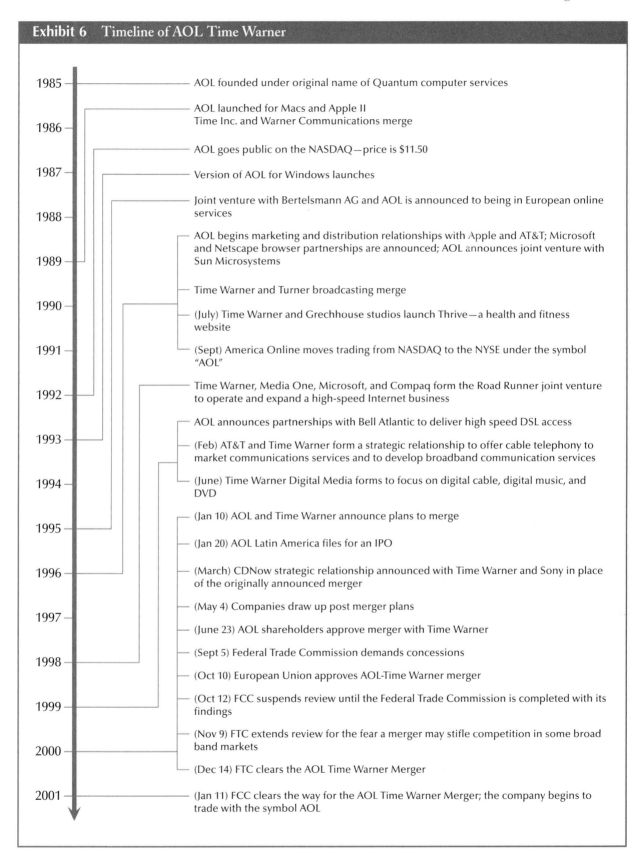

Year	Event
1985	AOL founded under original name of Quantum computer services
1986	AOL launched for Macs and Apple II Time Inc. and Warner Communications merge
1987	AOL goes public on the NASDAQ—price is $11.50 Version of AOL for Windows launches
1988	Joint venture with Bertelsmann AG and AOL is announced to being in European online services
1989	AOL begins marketing and distribution relationships with Apple and AT&T; Microsoft and Netscape browser partnerships are announced; AOL announces joint venture with Sun Microsystems
1990	Time Warner and Turner broadcasting merge (July) Time Warner and Grechhouse studios launch Thrive—a health and fitness website
1991	(Sept) America Online moves trading from NASDAQ to the NYSE under the symbol "AOL"
1992	Time Warner, Media One, Microsoft, and Compaq form the Road Runner joint venture to operate and expand a high-speed Internet business
1993	AOL announces partnerships with Bell Atlantic to deliver high speed DSL access (Feb) AT&T and Time Warner form a strategic relationship to offer cable telephony to market communications services and to develop broadband communication services
1994	(June) Time Warner Digital Media forms to focus on digital cable, digital music, and DVD
1995	(Jan 10) AOL and Time Warner announce plans to merge (Jan 20) AOL Latin America files for an IPO
1996	(March) CDNow strategic relationship announced with Time Warner and Sony in place of the originally announced merger
1997	(May 4) Companies draw up post merger plans (June 23) AOL shareholders approve merger with Time Warner
1998	(Sept 5) Federal Trade Commission demands concessions (Oct 10) European Union approves AOL-Time Warner merger
1999	(Oct 12) FCC suspends review until the Federal Trade Commission is completed with its findings
2000	(Nov 9) FTC extends review for the fear a merger may stifle competition in some broad band markets (Dec 14) FTC clears the AOL Time Warner Merger
2001	(Jan 11) FCC clears the way for the AOL Time Warner Merger; the company begins to trade with the symbol AOL

Exhibit 7   Ratio Comparisons for AOL Time Warner

AOL Time Warner, Inc.

NYSE: AOL

Sector: Technology

Industry: Computer Services

	Company	Industry	Sector
Valuation Ratios			
P/E Ratio (TTM)	96.99	69.5	35.12
Beta	2.61	1.92	1.74
Price to Sales (TTM)	15.59	9.65	7.51
Price to Book	15.23	10.6	6.97
Price to Tangible Book	17.09	13.44	8.43
Price to Cash Flow	64.66	46.65	31.14
Price to Free Cash Flow (TTM)	109.36	36.73	39.8
% Owned Institutions	55.11	31.89	41.83
Dividends			
Dividend Yield	0	0.56	1.16
Payout Ratio	0	2.9	3.75
Growth Rates (%)			
Sales	36.09	29.32	31.55
EPS	10.78	24.81	29.88
Capital Spending—5 yr. Growth Rate	58.97	24.71	-14.79
Financial Strength			
Quick Ratio	1.66	1.85	2.34
Current Ratio	1.88	2.08	2.9
LT Debt to Equity	0.25	0.37	0.22
Total Debt to Equity	0.25	0.42	0.29
Interest Coverage	N/A	15.61	12.3
Profitability Ratios			
Gross Margin	51.38	46.36	54.33
Effective Tax Rate	38.88	39.21	34.71
Management Effectiveness			
Return on Assets	10.69	5.1	11.86
Return on Investments	13.61	8.37	13.54
Return on Equity	17.97	11.6	17.49

Source: Forbes.com

service over its cable systems or increase their subscription fees for access. Additionally, Time Warner's roughly 20 percent share of the movies and music markets raised concerns about content exclusivity.[57]

AOL Time Warner's unwillingness to accede to regulator's demands for open access to cable systems and content distribution made negotiations with the FTC lengthy. If AOL and Time Warner did not agree to concessions preserving competition, the FTC was prepared to sue both companies. On December 15, 2000, both parties finally agreed to a five-year decree requiring them to:

- Open their cable systems to three rival ISPs— Earthlink, Microsoft MSN, and one other beneficiary to be named.

- Refrain from sabotaging content from rival Internet or interactive TV firms via a nondiscrimination provision.

- Continue to promote AOL's high-speed Internet service over DSL phone lines ("FTC approves AOL, Time Warner Deal" Tech Investor, *USA Today*).

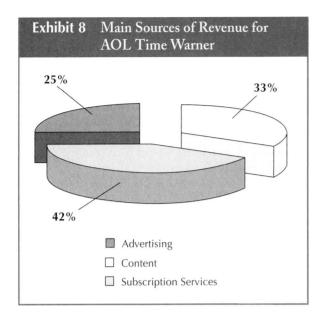

Exhibit 8 Main Sources of Revenue for AOL Time Warner

- 25%
- 33%
- 42%

☑ Advertising
☐ Content
☐ Subscription Services

The FTC's 5–0 unanimous vote ensured passage to the next hurdle for approval from the Federal Communications Commission.

The Federal Communications Commission

When the deal was announced, AOL and Time Warner executives believed the merger would be finalized by the end of calendar year 2000, especially since they received the FTC's stamp of approval. Speculation existed that the FCC would not impose any restrictions, making this final step of approval seemingly insignificant.[58] However, the FCC believed further regulation was necessary and began building upon the FTC's conditions.

One of the FCC's major concerns involved AOL's dominating instant messaging services that consist of AOL Instant Messaging (IM) and ICQ. Other competitors providing similar real-time message exchange programs pales by comparison to AOL's 80 percent market share including more than 140 million users worldwide.[59] With so many rivals offering comparable technology, the interoperability of all these systems became a major point of concern for competitors. Interoperability allows two users to exchange real-time messages between competing instant messaging services such as Yahoo! Chat and AOL IM.[60]

Instant messaging and other concerns were addressed in talks that lasted less than a month. On January 11, 2001, one year and a day after the announcement of the merger, the FCC declared, "You've got approval"[61] with a unanimous 5–0 vote. AOL, Time Warner, and the FCC agreed to conditions that were "designed to protect the open, competitive nature of the Internet," as stated by FCC Commissioner William Kennard:[62]

- *Instant messaging*—guarantees interoperability in its IM services before offering "advanced IM-based high-speed services," such as videoconferencing.
- *ISP choice*—prevents AOL Time Warner from interfering in customer choice over ISPs and requires the company to make available a list of competing, unaffiliated services on request.
- *First screen*—requires AOL Time Warner to allow competing ISPs to control the first screen that consumers call up when they access the Net.
- *Billing*—requires AOL Time Warner to grant ISPs direct billing relationships with their customers.
- *Performance quality*—requires AOL Time Warner to give unaffiliated ISPs the same quality of service guaranteed to affiliated ISPs.
- *Disclosure*—prevents AOL Time Warner from blocking any ISP from disclosing its terms of contract through confidentiality agreements.
- *Enforcement*—establishes rules for resolving disputes between ISPs and AOL Time Warner.
- *Investments*—requires AOL Time Warner to notify the FCC if it increases its stakes in the parent companies of DirecTV, General Motors, or Hughes Electronics.
- *Relationship with AT&T*—requires AT&T to divest a 25 percent stake in Time Warner Entertainment. AT&T cannot offer any AOL Time Warner ISP exclusive access to AT&T cable systems nor can it enter any agreement that limits AT&T's ability to offer such services to ISPs unaffiliated with AOL Time Warner.[63]

The regulatory battle ended with the FCC's decision and the newly combined AOL Time Warner began trading under the ticker symbol AOL that same day.

The European Union

Since AOL and Time Warner generated more than a combined 250 million euros in sales (US $213 million) each year within the European Union, the European Commission took great interest in ensuring that the proposed merger between the two companies would in no way hinder competition in the European market. The commission focused specifically on the merger's impact on music distribution and pay-for-content Internet access in the EU. After a four-month comprehensive investigation, the commission finally granted its conditional approval to the merger on October 11, 2000.

Following the conditions of the approval, AOL and Time Warner guaranteed not to block competitors from the emerging media and entertainment markets. Time

Warner initially proposed to merge with recording company EMI plc of Britain to create a major music company. However, faced with great opposition by European regulators, Time Warner dropped its joint venture plan with EMI to move ahead with its AOL merger.

Following the European Commission's request, AOL agreed to detach German media giant Bertelsmann AG from its joint ventures in AOL Europe and AOL CompuServe in France. Without the forced breaks, the Commission feared that AOL would team up with Warner Music, EMI, and Bertelsmann's music unit, BMG. With links to three of the world's five major music companies, AOL would be able to dominate the online music distribution market and the market for music players. In addition, by combining the market shares of Bertelsmann and Time Warner, AOL Time Warner would have been the European leader in music publishing with one third of the total market.

By separating AOL and Bertelsmann, Europe's largest media company, the Commission believes it can ensure that competition within the music industry in Europe remains strong. According to the European Commission, "The proposed undertakings will prevent AOL from having access to Europe's leading source of music publishing rights, thereby eliminating risk of dominance in the emerging market for online delivery of music over the Internet and software-based music players."

Risks

AOL Time Warner is the global media powerhouse of the future. Analysts predict good things for the company, however certain events may cause uncertainty for the future.

J.P. Morgan analysts identified the following three investment risks: execution risk, economic volatility, and a potential strike by screen actors and writers. Execution risk focuses solely on how the management team exploits all areas of the new firm and utilizes the full potential of all AOL Time Warner products. According to J.P. Morgan, the new management team will have to realize all synergies and successfully merge the new and old media products. Time Warner properties will have to move smoothly into AOL's existing capabilities. Additionally, the firm will have to keep innovating in the media industry to stay competitive. Finally, AOL Time Warner must utilize AOL's innovative ideas and plug the existing Time Warner products into its network to make the merger pay off for investors.[64]

The economy will affect AOL Time Warner. Economic factors are completely uncontrollable and unpredictable, yet AOL Time Warner needs to find ways to make its investors happy with large returns. As stated previously, the company projects an average growth rate of 30 percent per year. Realizing this projection will take the hard work and discipline for everyone at AOL Time Warner.[65]

Another potential risk is a strike by screen actors or writers. If they strike, the negative impact on broadcast networks will be significant. AOL Time Warner now owns the Warner Brothers, HBO, Cinemax, TNT, and TBS and all of these television networks could be severely affected financially by a strike.[66]

Analysts seem to have overlooked some of the risks that AOL Time Warner will face. One problem is protecting intellectual property on the Internet. The company simply must protect its copyrights on content. The shutdown of Napster in early 2001 set the precedent for valuing content. AOL Time Warner will also have to manage revenues and costs for intellectual property distributed on the Internet. It will have to produce returns for investors and not follow the business model of Amazon.com.[67]

Another problem media companies are dealing with is customer unwillingness to pay add-on subscription fees. Most media companies' business plans depend on consumers paying subscription fees. Digital services that require add-on fees include broadband, digital cable, personal video recorders, satellite radio, interactive video games, other Web content, Internet on TV, and wireless Internet. Macroeconomist Christian Weller of the Economic Policy Institute says, "We are pushing the limit in terms of what people can spend. It's hard to say where people are going to make the adjustment, but entertainment and recreation are easier to cut than financial services, medical services, and education." In 2000, the average suburban consumer spent $122 a month for cable, long-distance, Internet, cellular phones, pagers, etc. It is impossible to know how much more consumers would be willing to pay. For AOL Time Warner to reap profits, it must convince consumers that the growing media possibilities of the future will be worth their investment.[68]

Culture Differences

"Corporations are like small societies, complete with their own language, dress, philosophies, creation myths and worldviews."[69] Culture may be the most striking difference between AOL and Time Warner. The two companies clearly do not speak the same language. The New York based Time Warner's genteel, buttoned-down culture clashes with AOL's fast-paced and highly reactive management culture. To accentuate the growing relationship between the two firms, at the announcement of the merger Case and Levin swapped business attire for the event. Case showed up with a button-down shirt-and-tie look that emphasized Time Warner's corporate culture while Levin donned the more Web savvy, open collared look.[70] This was clearly a strategic move to show the merging of the two cultures. Analysts predict that America Online's culture will prevail, and this may cause internal disputes.[71]

Steve Case developed the concept for AOL while delivering pizzas for Pizza Hut, and he conceived the casual culture of the company at that time. Even so, AOL maintains a reputation for quick response by its management. Case believes in acquiring talented people and integrating them into the AOL infrastructure. Thus, he has focused AOL's acquisition strategy on getting the talent behind an idea, not necessarily the idea itself,[72] and he has demonstrated his ability to infuse talented people and their ideas into the casual but fast-paced AOL culture.

After the AOL Time Warner merger announcement in January 2000, Case said the new management team would be in place by the following May. Exhibit 9 shows the current management team at the company. Of the twenty-two senior corporate executives, fourteen represent former AOL employees. A small yet powerful group of former AOL employees report directly to Case, while Parsons and Pittman report to Levin. Some critics question whether Pittman's close relationship with Case will hinder the decision-making process and ultimately squeeze Levin out of the mix. However, others do not think this will be a problem. New York Stock Exchange Chairman Richard Grasso supports the duo of Levin and Pittman, saying, "I think at the surface comparative level, they will appear to be wildly different. But there are some very comparative similarities to the makeup of each. They are extraordinarily intelligent and very creative in how they approach problems."[73] Clearly, the new management team weighs heavily in AOL's favor, and this fact may create problems down the road.

Levin is now the CEO of AOL Time Warner, and he comes from an old-media culture. He will play a pivotal role in the new AOL Time Warner, and some analysts believe he represents the "connective tissue that can bridge the old and new media of these companies together."[74] Levin believes he can bring together the two companies as he brought together Time Inc. and Warner Communications Inc. in 1990.[75]

Steve Case, Gerald Levin, Richard Parsons, Robert Pittman, and Ted Turner are powerful players in the media business, and any combination of personalities like these may create problems. As one analyst said, "On top of dissimilarities between the two companies you have some of the feistiest characters in the business. In addition to Case and Levin, you have the 'Mouth of the South' Ted Turner

involved." Many critics believe that a number of the top executives at AOL Time Warner will have a hard time taking a back seat in decision making because of their former executive roles at AOL or Time Warner. Responding to this concern Case said, "Yes, there are a lot of cooks in the kitchen, but this is quite a feast that we want to serve."[76]

AOL Time Warner's management decided in May 2000, shortly after the merger announcement, that Ted Turner would not play an executive role in the combined company. Turner said he learned he was fired during a phone call with Gerald Levin. Levin told Turner that Turner Broadcasting would be reorganized and that Turner Broadcasting's employees would no longer to report to Turner. Instead, they would report to AOL Time Warner Co-Chief Operating Officer Robert Pittman.[77]

Competition

AOL Time Warner is the fourth largest company in the United States, behind Microsoft, General Electric, and Cisco Systems.[78] Most of its rivals have been growing larger as well due to rapid consolidation in the media, telecommunications, and ISP industries. In fact, the 15 largest merger deals ever took place within 21 months after the Travelers Group and Citicorp merger in April 1998.[79]

Despite overwhelmingly fierce competition, AOL Time Warner maintains a competitive advantage over the rest. While Earthlink, Microsoft, and hundreds of ISPs continue to offer competitive packages, there remains one intangible that proves more valuable than any discount or deal—AOL's brand recognition and marketing success. Other ISPs are merely pipes into consumer's homes. The AOL Time Warner merger sets a precedent in the industry by bringing media, telecommunications, and cable companies together, and it forces competitors to rethink their business models. Exhibit 10 shows a financial comparison of AOL Time Warner and several of its competitors.

Vivendi Universal

> Anyone who doesn't believe AOL Time Warner has changed the competitive landscape is kidding themselves.
> —*Edgar Bronfman Jr, Vice Chairman of Vivendi Universal.80*

Vivendi Universal came about as the product of France's Vivendi SA and its pay-TV unit Canal Plus acquiring the Canadian entertainment and liquor company Seagram in June 2000.[81] Vivendi owns media and communications properties in addition to water treatment businesses and is about three times the size of Seagram.[82] The extensive music and media content carried by Seagram—Universal

Exhibit 9   Senior Corporate Executives at AOL Time Warner

Executive	New Position in AOL Time Warner	Formerly With
Stephen Case—is actively involved in leading and building AOL Time Warner, with a particular focus on technological developments, policy initiatives, and strategic investments that are driving the global expansion of the interactive medium. He was formerly Chairman and CEO of America Online, Inc., since co-founding it in 1985.	Chairman of the Board	AOL
Gerald Levin—Formerly with Time Warner, and Chairman and CEO of Time Warner Inc., since 1993. He led the merger between Time Inc., and Warner Communications in 1990, and also helped with the merger of Turner Broadcasting System.	Chief Executive Officer	Time Warner
Richard Parsons—Served on the committee that worked to make a quick combination of AOL and Time Warner. He was elected President of Time Warner on October 1,1994 and was a member of the Time Warner Board of Directors since January 1991	Co-Chief Operating Officer	Time Warner
Robert Pittman—was a member of America Online's Board of Directors since 1995 and was appointed President and CEO of its AOL Networks in 1996. Two years later he was named President and COO of America Online	Co-Chief Operating Officer	AOL
R. E. "Ted" Turner—Previously with Time Warner, he served as Vice Chairman since 1996. Originally with Turner Broadcasting Systems, he served as President and CEO since 1963.	Vice Chairman and Senior Advisor	Time Warner
Kenneth Novack—For the past 11 years, he was the Vice Chairman of America Online and a member of its Board of Directors.	Vice Chairman	AOL

Studios, Universal Music Group, theme parks, and a minority stake in the USA Networks—made it an attractive fit for Vivendi CEO Jean-Marie Messier's Internet strategy. Since coming on board four years ago, he has been the driving force behind an aggressive strategy that "seeks control of the content and the conduit."

The all-stock transaction valued at $30 billion positions Vivendi Universal as the second major hybrid media/Internet firm. Vivendi Universal projects annual revenues of more than $55 billion in 2001, and the company has no debt due to the sale of Seagram's $7–$8 billion drink business.[83] Seagram's final price tag represented a 33 percent premium over the company's stock price before the merger announcement underscoring the trend of industry consolidation and merger overvaluations.

Vivendi recently launched a mobile Internet portal called Vizzavi in a joint venture with Vodafone Airtouch.[84] Also, minority stakes in the BskyB satellite television network and French telecom network Cegetel help to diversify Vivendi's operations.[85]

Despite Vivendi Universal's promised success and competitive resources, some analysts believe the only ground on which serious competition with AOL Time Warner will take place is in Europe.[86] As stated previously, neither AOL nor Time Warner is particularly "global." Thus, analysts believe AOL Time Warner and Vivendi Universal will compete aggressively in Europe to win a foothold and then seek to consolidate their positions as quickly as they can.

Concerning the Vivendi/Seagram merger, Ken Schachter of TechWeb Finance said, "Is it on par with the AOL Time Warner merger? Vivendi isn't AOL, and Seagram isn't Time Warner."[87] Analysts seem to think that while this company will see success, they will not rival AOL Time Warner. That may change, however, given the potential acquisition of NewsCorp. Talks between Vivendi Universal's Messier and NewsCorp's Rupert Murdoch regarding a merger have been made public, but to this date, nothing has materialized.

Viacom

Viacom Inc. owns properties including Paramount Pictures, MTV, VHI, TNN, Blockbuster, Oprah Winfrey,

Exhibit 9   Senior Corporate Executives at AOL Time Warner (Cont'd)

Executive	New Position in AOL Time Warner	Formerly With
Richard Bressler	Executive Vice President and Chief Executive Officer, AOL Time Warner Investments	Time Warner
Paul Cappuccio	Executive Vice President, General Counsel and Secretary	AOL
David Colburn	Executive Vice President and President of Business Development	AOL
J. Michael Kelly	Executive Vice President and Chief Financial Officer	AOL
Lennert Leader	President, Venture Group, AOL Time Warner Investments	AOL
Kenneth Lerer	Executive Vice President	AOL
William J. Raduchel	Executive Vice President and Chief Technology Officer	AOL
Mayo Stuntz, Jr.	Executive Vice President	AOL
George Vradenburg, III	Executive Vice President, Global and Strategic Policy	AOL
Edward Adler	Senior Vice President, Corporate Communications	Time Warner
Kathy Bushkin	Senior Vice President and President, AOL Time Warner Foundation	AOL
Marshall Cohen	Senior Vice President	AOL
Richard Hanlon	Senior Vice President, Investor Relations	AOL
Spencer B. Hays	Senior Vice President and Deputy General Counsel	Time Warner
Andrew Kaslow	Senior Vice President, People Development	Time Warner
John LaBarca	Senior Vice President, Financial Operations	Time Warner

and Howard Stern.[88] In fall 2000, it purchased CBS Corporation for $34.45 billion, making it the largest media deal to date.[89] CBS gained a TV and film studio to provide shows for its network, while Viacom gained major advertising outlets to promote the films and shows produced by Paramount and Spelling Entertainment TV studio.[90] Regarding Net strategies, Viacom brands its properties on the web with MTVi (MTV Interactive, combining MTV.com, VH1.com, SonicNet, and Imagine Radio), Nickelodeon.com, and the spun-off CBS MarketWatch. According to Chairman Sumner Redstone, "We don't think we have to own or be owned by an Internet company in order to get the value for our products."[91]

In February 1999, Viacom launched an online initiative called the "Buggles Project" to serve as a one-stop, all-genre destination.[92] The site boasts its customizability via Project Nozzle, a feature devoted to children with connections to Nickelodeon's content.[93] Personalized news, concert information, and targeted advertising are among the numerous offerings for adults. Viacom's recent acquisition of BET for $3 billion along with its

BET.com online portal gives it additional online presence to complement MTV and Nickelodeon.[94] Whether it's stand-alone Internet offerings will rival those of AOL Time Warner remains to be seen.

Yahoo! Inc.

The announcement of the AOL Time Warner merger in January 2000 sparked many rumors that Yahoo! would be the next web company to gobble up a media giant.[95] In particular, reports stated that Yahoo! was seriously considering buying Disney to keep itself on level playing field with AOL Time Warner despite Yahoo! President Jeff Mallett's insistence that the company was "in no rush to merge."[96] Additionally, he felt that AOL would not be able to take full advantage of Time Warner's properties such as CNN, Warner Bros, and People since they are already available on the web.[97]

Currently, Yahoo! is in no position to even consider the acquisition of a media company, especially one the size of Disney—its simply does not have the resources for such a purchase. Yahoo!'s stock plummeted from $250 at the

Exhibit 10 Financial Strength Comparisons with Competitors (as of March 13, 2001)

	Total Debt/Equity	Long-term Debt/Assets	Current Total Debt (in mill.)	Current Ratio	Quick Ratio	Current Inventory Turnover
AOL	0.26	0.15	$ 1,646.00	1.9	1.7	Not Calculable
VIAB	0.54	0.23	$ 12,876.90	1.1	0.6	6.8
DIS	0.39	0.15	$ 10,315.00	1.1	0.7	29.5
NWS	0.52	0.23	$ 9,201.00	1.5	1.2	7.8

AOL = America Online   **VIAB** = Viacom   **DIS** = Disney   **NWS** = News Corp.

Source: Quicken.com

beginning of 2000 to less than $35 by year-end.[98] Its market capitalization also fell from $130 billion to less than $20 billion, making the acquisition of Disney, with a market cap of $61 billion, a near impossibility.[99] Given these statistics, Yahoo! may become an acquisition target for entertainment content providers.

NewsCorp

NewsCorp is one of the world's largest media companies with total annual revenues of about $14 billion.[100] The company enjoys diversified global operations in five continents and total assets of $38 billion.[101] It boasts 83 percent ownership of Fox Entertainment Group and is the world's leading publisher of English-language newspapers (over 175 different newspapers worldwide).[102]

Regarding net strategies, NewsCorp produces its own entertainment and information through its Fox Studio and network, Fox Sports, and HarperCollins book company. Currently, it has satellite distribution capabilities in Asia, Europe, and Latin America. NewsCorp controls Sky Global Networks, Inc., a rollup of satellite TV assets and investments that the company hopes to take public.[103] If NewsCorp is able to accomplish this objective, it will be moving rapidly toward developing a global broadband pipeline via satellite, enabling TV and Internet beaming,[104] and it would establish NewsCorp as a powerful player in the content delivery game.

NewsCorp CEO Rupert Murdoch has been aggressive in his pursuit of Hughes Electronics Corporation DirecTV satellite operation since it was put on the market in late 2000.[105] Owned by General Motors, Hughes pulled in $7.3 billion in revenues in 2000, of which $6.3 billion came from the DirecTV division.[106] GM is looking for a deal consisting primarily of stock.[107] NewsCorp, on the other hand, has not traditionally run its business to please investors, making its stock less desirable than that of other media companies. Disney and Viacom both backed away

from the deal, fearing a bidding war and dilution of shareholder value. While Vivendi is considering a joint venture with Hughes and boasts "the strongest balance sheet in the media industry"[108] according to CEO Messier, NewsCorp will most likely acquire the satellite company, expanding its satellite holdings and increasing its ability to keep up with AOL Time Warner.

Walt Disney Company

> I don't see any pressure on us to make deals just to get bigger. The only deals we're going to make are those that make our earnings and share price bigger.
> —*Walt Disney CEO Michael Eisner.*[109]

Walt Disney Internet Group is the Internet media business of the Walt Disney Company and manages many popular web sites and services. Some of these sites include Disney.com, Family.com, ESPN.com, NFL.com, ABC.com (the leading broadcast network site), and many other entertainment and news properties.[110] Online commerce through DisneyStore.com and related Disney e-tailers gives the Walt Disney Internet Group a rather large web presence.[111] The combined websites run by this wing of the Walt Disney Company make up the seventh largest web property, attracting more than 21 million visitors (25 percent of the web universe) per month.[112]

Disney's main Internet project started with Go.com in November 1999. This online effort was the result of a merger between Infoseek Corporation and the Walt Disney Company's online unit, Buena Vista Internet Group.[113] By late 2000, however, Disney pulled the plug on Go.com after it did not meet expectations.

Despite the failure of Disney's Go.com online initiative, Disney quickly revamped its strategy and relaunched Go.com in early 2001. The results of this move have yet to be determined. Disney, however, remains the most profitable media company and is in no rush to buy an Internet firm. Michael Eisner, however, remains rather defensive when discussing merger issues and the implications surrounding the AOL Time Warner marriage. While admitting that Disney is still "in the acquisition business," he insists that Disney will not get into a merger frenzy.[114] In a February 2001 interview with BusinessWeek Online, Eisner spoke with dismay about the AOL Time Warner deal:

> "We're not going to make acquisitions to make journalists' headlines or to make bankers wealthy. I know I wouldn't have given away 65% of my company to make that deal. They may have been right, maybe AOL really is important for distribution, but not at that cost. Maybe we'll make a deal with AOL. Maybe we'll let them put ABCNews.com on their front page. They should be so lucky."[115]

Bertelsmann

> We have to find a second AOL.
> —*Thomas Middelhof, Bertelsmann CEO.*[116]

Bertelsmann is a German media powerhouse overseeing companies such as Random House, Doubleday, Arista Records, RCA, and over 100 worldwide magazines and newspapers.[117] This firm sees AOL Time Warner as a benchmark company that should be emulated and feels that its online access will truly be protected by the "preferred provider" clauses in the AOL Time Warner merger contracts.[118] Concerning online endeavors, Bertelsmann sells books, music, magazines, and TV shows over other people's networks or Internet portals such as AOL or Lycos. It also uses partners to sell books and music directly to consumers via bol.com in Europe and Asia and bn.com in the US.[119]

Bertelsmann, currently holding the number three spot in the media industry, hopes to become the number one firm in the global music business and media e-commerce.[120] A hefty investment in Napster as well as ongoing negotiations to merge Bertelsmann's Arista and RCA music labels with those of Britain's EMI are priming this company to become an even more significant player in the media field.[121] However, developing "pipe" to consumers via cable, wireless, or broadcast is not of utmost concern for Bertelsmann. Instead, it is focusing on content from all types of media. After all, Bertelsmann's Internet business contributed just 2.5 percent of sales in the fiscal year ended June 30, 2000.[122] This has not stopped Middelhoff from trying to embrace the net age by encouraging a more casual, "AOL style" work environment for his firm. Memos have been banned—emails are the only acceptable form of inter-office communication. Additionally, ties are not allowed at management board meetings.[123] These culture changes along with a focused corporate objective poise Bertelsmann for the coming shift in the media industry.

Earthlink

Earthlink is the world's second largest Internet service provider with 4.7 million subscribers.[124] It earned this position after a February 2000 merger with MindSpring hoping "to create the best Internet experience for our members by focusing on delivering the basics of Internet service."[125] So far, Earthlink has maintained a loyal customer base and has provided an attractive alternative to Microsoft's MSN service with 4 million subscribers.[126]

As part of the concessions made by AOL Time Warner to pass federal regulatory hurdles, Earthlink was included in an agreement to share access to Time Warner's cable lines. It expects to start selling fast Internet access over these lines in June or July of 2001.[127] While the majority of Earthlink's users are dial-up subscribers, the company has launched an aggressive initiative to offer fast connections. Along these lines, it expects to offer such high-speed services via satellites in April 2001 with Hughes Electronics.[128]

Further efforts to remain competitive with AOL Time Warner include a potential purchase of Earthlink by Microsoft.[129] A failed $400 rebate offer by MSN was terminated due to poor returns and has Microsoft re-thinking its online strategies.[130] An acquisition of Earthlink would double its customer base and put the combined company in a better position to compete with AOL Time Warner. Alan Mosher, an ISP analyst with Probe Research, believes this combination is necessary for both firms for increasing credibility with consumers, promotional power, and access to more partnerships. He says, "The only way you can start to compete effectively is to grow quickly. By combining the No. 2 and No. 3 together you start to become more attractive to advertisers and e-commerce companies."[131] While Microsoft denies any rumors of this merger, the deal faces another obstacle—Sprint. Sprint owns a 27 percent share of Earthlink and has the authority to refuse such acquisition offers.[132]

The Role of Cable Companies in Industry Consolidation

Starting in 1998, cable companies spent about $45 billion on capital expenditures to improve high-speed web access, digital video, and telephony as a delivery system.[133] These investments are part of an industry-wide trend toward vertical integration of entertainment and communication channels. To remain profitable, both cable companies and telecommunications firms have begun implementing "bundled packages" where services ranging from interactive

TV to phone service to Internet access are included in one bill. Cable companies, however, seem to be adapting to the industry change at a more rapid rate. With 84 percent of its industry upgrade to be completed by the end of 2001, the cable industry far surpasses that of the 40 percent upgrade figure seen from the Baby Bells.[134] With a majority of capital expenditures completed, these firms will turn their focus back to cost cutting and debt reduction.[135] In turn, these new revenues sources from bundled services as well as reduced debt should help to increase cable companies' attractiveness to investors. In the coming years, cable television systems will compete with the telephone network in providing two-way, high-speed digital communications to consumers. Exhibit 11 contains cable subscriber statistics since 1999.

While only seven percent of the country's 70 million wired houses take advantage of some of these new services being offered, wealthier customers contribute significantly to sales.[136] And should bad economic times develop, these cable companies can fall back on their programming delivery, which has been essentially immune to economic downturns, for sources of cash flow. In 2000, however, S&P's index of eight stocks in broadcasting, television, and cable was up 9.8 percent compared to a 6.6 percent drop in the S&P 500.[137] Cable industries are simply not as vulnerable to low consumer expectations as Internet stocks have proven to be.

As competition continues to grow fierce in this hybrid market, consumers are expected to respond accordingly. TCI's @Home and Time Warner's Road Runner introduced the first cable-based digital data services in the late 1990s.[138] Analysts predict that Comcast, America's third largest cable provider, will increase the number of subscribers for its new services from 1.75 million in 2000 to 8.3 million in 2005, creating quite a significant leap.[139] This number could grow much larger, however. Cox will continue to play a key role in the industry, but only behind the two leading behemoths, AT&T and AOL Time Warner.

The Role of Telecommunications Companies in Industry Consolidation

> The long-distance business as we know it won't exist in a few years.
> —*Jeffrey Kagan, Atlanta-based telecommunications analyst*[140]

Competitive pricing pressures characterize the telecommunications industry, giving consumers more freedom and choice than ever before. For many years, long-distance

carriers capitalized on price elasticity—they reduced prices and demand rose as anticipated, thus enhancing revenues. Since phones first came on the scene, the inflation-adjusted costs per minute for long distance have changed as follows: $100 in 1915, $10 in 1945, $1 in 1970, and $0.10 in 2001.[141] At some point, however, prices must reach an equilibrium point where demand will not meet supply regardless of price cuts. Basic economic theory coupled with new opportunities for cheap long-distance have put a squeeze on telecoms to find a new driving source of revenue.

Alternative forms of communication support the trend toward free long distance that can be seen right now. With new long-distance plans that cost next to nothing and Internet communication such as AOL Instant Messenger, people have come to rely less on traditional long distance telephone calling. Despite quality and reliability questions, people are also turning to web telephoning for the cheapest rates. Firms keep innovating in order to provide long-distance services at a lower cost with more efficient system structures.[142] To continue in business, long-distance firms must innovate and find new ways to make up for the 2/3 drop in revenues from long distance the industry has already experienced and the continuing decline analysts anticipate.[143]

Telecommunications companies have attacked this challenge via acquisitions and diversification. By expanding offerings to include Internet service providing and satellite television and incorporating them into "bundled services," these firms often times try to entice consumers to purchase a bundle with the bonus of free long distance. This indicates that long-distance will be considered as more of an accessory than a stand-alone product in the coming years.[144] For long-distance companies, about 80 percent of business is voice while 20 percent is data—this ratio will most likely flip-flop in the coming years with ongoing consolidation of content distributors and content providers.[145] A listing of recent telecommunications mergers can be found in Exhibit 12.

High Speed Internet Access: Broadband Technologies

> The most obvious benefits to AOL come from the potential of using Time Warner's 13 million cable subscribers as a gateway for AOL service, especially in their high-end cable modem business. Time Warner provides the homes and AOL provides the distribution.
> —*Jeff Logsdon, managing director & member of the board of directors, Seidler Companies (Investment Bank).*[146]

Almost 300 million people were online worldwide by the end of 2000.[147] This figure is expected to grow to over 500 million in the next few years as lower prices for personal computers and increased competition in the ISP industry have fueled demand for Internet access.[148] Teens total more than 27 percent of Internet users while 87 percent of college students are online.[149] These numbers show promise of a large, Internet savvy market maturing and embracing new technologies.

A majority of residential Internet users have "narrowband" access via a modem and telephone.[150] Unfortunately, dial-up systems are not conducive to having people online for long intervals. Broadband technologies offer high speed and high volume to accommodate today's more sophisticated content on the World Wide Web. Despite the growing availability of these services, the deployment of residential broadband is supply-side limited.[151] As consumers become more active online, demand will continue to increase for high-speed connections. Exhibit 13 shows projections for high-speed Internet access use in the coming years.

Digital Subscriber Line (DSL)

Digital subscriber lines are the telecommunications industry's response to dial-up limitations and increased demand for more bandwidth—or the amount of data that can flow through the lines.[152] For a monthly flat rate, DSL provides high-speed connectivity far superior to dial-up access. This "always on" connection links one's computer to the telephone line, allowing the customer to surf the web and talk on the phone at the same time.[153] This does not hold true for dial-up access, where a telephone line may be used for only one or the other. Installation requires a telecommunications company to split the voice phone line for sending Internet data at high frequencies and old-fashioned telephone calls at lower frequencies.[154]

DSL utilizes more bandwidth than the average copper telephone line.[155] Thus, increased speed ranks among DSL's greatest advantages aside from its "always-on" aspect. However, DSL has its drawbacks as well. Installation requires the cooperation of both a telecom company and an ISP—when these two elements are not in sync, problems may arise when setting up the system. Secondly, the customer must be closer than 18,000 feet from the telephone company's central office in order to be in an area that is available for DSL service.[156]

Despite inheriting cable lines from Time Warner, AOL realizes that to serve the entire market, multiple approaches to broadband services must be employed.[157]

Exhibit 11 MSO Subscribers by Quarter (sorted by Q3:00) (in thousands)

Basic Cable Subs	Q3:99	Q4:99	Q1:00	Q2:00	Q3:00
AT&T	16,383	16,383	16,036	16,100	16,304
Time Warner Cable	13,000	12,600	12,700	12,617	12,600
Comstat	7,447	7,068	7,128	7,113	7,529
Charter	6,179	6,138	6,152	6,214	6,318
Cox	6,019	6,077	6,147	6,138	6,163
Adelphia	5,483	4,990	5,004	5,146	5,543
Est. Total Basic Subs	61,072	60,255	59,735	59,921	61,055
Digital Cable Subs					
AT&T	1,560	1,856	2,025	2,239	2,512
Time Warner Cable	248	430	613	889	1,300
Comcast	401	598	770	943	1,134
Est. Total Digital Subs	2,811	3,720	4,492	5,487	6,984
Data Subs					
AT&T	297	427	565	689	888
Time Warner Cable	245	330	447	573	719
Cox	155	204	260	320	399
Est. Total Data Subs	1,078	1,488	1,936	2,417	3,060

Note: Sorted by Q3:00 totals
Source: JP Morgan Company Reports

Its DSL initiatives include partnerships with SBC Communications and the Baby Bells to offer these high-speed services to its customers.

Cable Modems

> Cable is in the lead now and this deal [AOL Time Warner] will do nothing but cement that lead.
> —*Michael Harris, Kinetics Strategies President*

Currently, cable modems are the most popular form of high bandwidth web access. Cable networks providing television services are already in place with lines capable of carrying large amounts of data.[158] An estimated 3.8 million households or almost 70 percent of the population in North America had cable television by the end of September 2000.[159]

Like DSL, cable modems providing Internet access run through the same lines from which the user receives television service. Therefore, large capital expenditures for infrastructure upgrades are necessary to enable cable lines to transmit information to and from the user. Cable television alone can only receive data.[160] Additional capital expenditures are required to maintain the existing pipes, as they are subject to extreme wear and tear.

Because cable networks are shared by all users, speed may decrease during peak usage hours of the day. This shared network concept has also heightened security concerns and fear of hackers on the web.[161]

Currently, AOL Time Warner serves less than 20 percent of the nation's cable market.[162] To broaden its scope in this area, it has entered into negotiations to obtain access to AT&T's cable lines, which reach almost 50 percent of the nation's homes.[163]

Satellite

In 2000, about 11.8 million subscribers received satellite delivered television.[164] With an 18-inch dish positioned on a subscriber's home, universality becomes satellite's biggest advantage. Like cable, it is a shared medium, resulting in decreased speeds during periods of high volume. Additionally, satellite data transmission can be affected by weather and atmospheric conditions. Currently, two-way satellite connections are rather poor. Large investments have been funneled toward improving transmission and allowing for two-way data exchange.

AOL Time Warner cut a deal in 1999 with Hughes Electronics and DirecTV to provide high-speed net services via satellite and to fully exploit its AOL Anywhere initiative.[165] The deals can be summed up as follows:[166]

- Hughes Network Systems will design and build the dual purpose AOL TV set-top receiver.

- DirecTV will collaborate with AOL on a new service that combines digital satellite television programming from DirecTV with AOL TV's enhanced interactive television Internet service.

Fiber Optics

> Even higher communication speeds will be made possible through fiber optic networks. Fiber optics, which use laser light to send digital data through thin strands of glass, have been used for many years to provide the highest speed links for the "trunk" lines that carry long distance voice and data traffic within telecommunications networks. Over the past decade, carriers have installed thousands of miles of fiber across the continent and under the oceans that are capable of carrying millions of telephone messages simultaneously at data rates in excess of one billion bits (one gigabit) per second.
> —*Richard Adler, Telecommunications specialist.*[167]

Fiber optics, or optical fiber cables, constitute yet another form of broadband web access. These lines have tremendous data capacity that will be useful as networks become overly saturated with transmissions.[168] Thus, it comes as no surprise that AOL Time Warner executives see fiber optics as the technology of the future. Inexpensive initial expenditures are offset by the costly layout of these cables to homes. This phenomenon is known as the "last mile problem," where the challenge lies in transmitting data over the last leg of its journey right into the consumer's home. As of 2001, this technology is still being tested, as many technical barriers exist.

The Future of the Telecommunications Industry[169]

The telecommunications industry of the future should be different from the current environment in five ways:[170]

- It will be digital.
- It will be broadband (high speed).
- It will be "always on."
- It will be ubiquitous.
  It will be intelligent.

In the future, computers and network-based services will be available virtually any place and any time. Exhibit 14 shows broadband service line data, further

Exhibit 12 Telecommunications Industry Statistics—Recent Telecom Mergers

Acquirer	Company Acquired	Announced Date	Value in Billions
Vodafone/Airtouch	Mannesmann	1/14/00	$180
America Online	Time Warner	1/10/00	$156
MCI WorldCom	Sprint	10/5/99	$113
SBC	Ameritech	5/11/98	$62
Vodafone	Air Touch	1/18/99	$60
AT&T	Media One	4/22/99	$56
AT&T	TCI	6/24/98	$53
Bell Atlantic	GTE	7/28/98	$53

Source: www.plunkettresearch.com

supporting the projections for increased high-speed Internet use in the coming years. A variety of smart information/communication devices will evolve from PCs and televisions. Examples of such innovative technologies include large, flat screens with brilliant 3D high-definition displays and small, portable, wearable devices that allow consumers to stay connected to all aspect of their daily lives, regardless of location. Today's desktop, laptop PCs, and Personal Digital Assistants (PDAs) will seem primitive compared to the interconnected devices of the future. These devices will be wired with local networks to which a variety of devices will be able to communicate with one another—from home appliances to high-technology computing devices.

Exhibits 15 and 16 present remarks made by Steve Case and Jerry Levin on Investor's Day 2001. Exhibit 17 is the transcript of a Question and Answer session after the company released first quarter 2001 financial data.

Exhibit 13 Residential High-Speed Households by Technology, 1999–2005 (in millions)

	1999	2000	2001	2002	2003	2004	2005
Cable	1.25	4.1	7.12	9.57	11.88	14.19	16.13
DSL	.58	1.93	4.22	6.88	9.38	11.87	14.22
Wireless	.01	.06	.19	.95	1.96	3.04	4.71
Other	0	.01	.10	.15	.30	.50	.80

Source: The Strategis Group

Exhibit 14 Number of Advanced Services (Broadband) Lines (over 200 Kbps in both directions)

Technology	December '99	June '00	%Change
ADSL	185,950	325,901	75
Other Wireline*	609,909	747,028	22
Coaxial Cable	879, 671	1,434,237	63
Fiber	307,315	301,551	n.m**
Satellite & Fixed Wireless	7,816	3,639	n.m**
Total Lines	1,990,662	2,812,366	41

*Includes symmetric DSL and traditional telephone company high speed lines such as T1 and T3 lines.
**Not meaningful due to previously unidentified inconsistencies in reported data.

Source: FCC

Exhibit 15 Remarks by Steve Case on Investor's Day 2001[171]

Introduction: AOL Time Warner CEO, Jerry Levin

We have all of our colleagues here tonight, but there's always someone who's first among equals. You're going to hear the phrase "iconic brands" a lot tomorrow. We have one person (we actually have several) who is himself an icon and a brand.

He's the only person in the company who has been Time's "Man of the Year," in 1991. He's the most extraordinary person I think any one of us has ever met. He continues to do marvelous things, not only as an inspiration to our company, but as you may know or read, he's started yet another foundation for the issue of nuclear proliferation, with Sam Nunn. He has been active in trying to get journalistic integrity into Russia. And when we talk about the social commitment of AOL Time Warner, there's no one who embodies that more than Ted Turner.

We're pleased to be hosting an Investor Day—the former Time Warner had not had one in a long time—and this is a major event. This is a wonderful Company and we couldn't wait to close the merger. For me, the epiphany occurred when our next speaker called me up on the telephone and made this outrageous proposal that we put the two companies together. To which I said, "No way in hell is that going to happen!"

As many of you may know, my preoccupation is really with people, about management, and how to make things work. Leadership requires you to have clear, simple objectives, stated with conviction, with persistence, and insistence. And that's really what defines Steve Case because, when you look at the growth, and the development, and now the absolute distinction of the AOL driving AOL Time Warner, it has come from those characteristics. So we thought it would be appropriate to hear from Steve and hear about the broader perspective. Steve Case.

AOL Time Warner Chairman, Steve Case:

Tomorrow, when you go to the Equitable Center for the Investor Day presentations, you may note that the event is historic in our short history, because that's where we announced this merger just over a year ago. So it will be nice to go back to that particular venue, to talk about what we're going to do in the years going forward.

What I want to do this evening is to give you an overall sense of what we're trying to do. You'll hear a lot tomorrow from what you'll agree is an exceptional management team, about our plans for the future, and particularly our plans for the next year. We've talked about our goal of having revenue in 2001 of at least $40 billion, EBITDA of at least $11 billion. Some have said, "In this slowing economy, that seems like those are hard numbers to hit. Don't you want to back-pedal a little bit?" The answer is, "No, we're not going to back-pedal. We do believe we can achieve those numbers."

The reason for our confidence is that we have real plans and an exceptional management team in place. But while we're making those numbers, we will also make the investments that we think are appropriate to drive our growth three to five years out.

It's important to remember that we didn't do this merger simply to achieve our 2001 objectives. We did this merger because we think we're at the right place, at the right time, with the right management, the right brands, and the right technology assets. We have the wind at our back, as the world moves—in what I think will be a startling way over the next five or ten years—to a more converged, interactive world. We think AOL Time Warner is the best-positioned Company in the world to benefit from that convergence—and to drive it.

Our goal is to become the most respected and the most valuable company in the world. We will achieve it both by making the numbers—and by making a difference. You'll hear a lot tomorrow about our near-term goals for each of our businesses, as well as a glimpse of the long-term strategy.

I hope you'll leave with a renewed confidence that we are going to be able to meet our short-term objectives. But I hope you will also leave with a tremendous confidence that we'll be able to achieve the greatness that we are aspiring to achieve because of the quality of this team, because of how well this new management is functioning as a team, and because of the rather unique dynamics that now exist in the market.

People are recognizing that something is happening, that the world is moving in a different direction, and that the next ten years are going to be quite a bit different than the last ten years.

The last ten years really were marked by clear segments between industries, with clear leadership within each of those industries. There was a clear demarcation in terms of products and services in the eyes of consumers. The telephone was one thing, music was another, the PC and the consumer's Internet experience was a third, and television was yet another. Consumers usually would go to different stores to feed their PC habit or their music habit. And there were no bridges between these worlds—they really were separate, almost isolated, worlds. Some companies emerged in each of those industries, and achieved great success.

But the challenge is to look forward and try to understand what's going to happen five or ten years from now, and what strategic changes are necessary to enable a company to be a leader a decade from now. That's what's driving AOL Time Warner. We recognize that we need to execute against our short-term plans, but, as I have said time and time again, our real focus is on the longer-term future.

The trends here are extraordinary, and, despite short-term economic cycles, are really unstoppable. We clearly are moving to a more converged world where people are integrating a whole variety of interactive products and services more and more in their lives.

I expect we will see a "flight to quality"—to the companies that have exceptional management teams. I expect a flight to companies that have a diversified mix of revenue streams, and that have a whole variety of different brands that appeal to different segments of the market. And, also, to companies with a business model that enables them to generate significant profit, significant cash flow, and healthy growth rates, which will allow

Exhibit 15 Remarks by Steve Case on Investor's Day 2001 (continued)

the company to invest in the future and achieve more and more scale, particularly more and more global scale.

So, as you think about this new world and about how things are coming together in a unique way, I think that you will conclude that AOL Time Warner really stands alone as the leader of the pack. It's really ours to lose, and we don't intend to lose it. We do think that we have an enormous opportunity here to capitalize on these significant consumer trends to run our businesses in a somewhat different fashion. And not just to achieve our results this year—which we will achieve—but also to achieve our goal of being the most valuable and respected company in the world.

When we have articulated this goal, some have said, "You've got to be kidding! Have you looked at GE's market cap? Have you looked at Microsoft?" And we have, but we think the next wave is going to be about convergence; and the real winners are not the people who, in the gold rush, sold the pots and pans, but rather the people who owned the gold.

The gold, we think, will be the content brands, and a unique relationship with audiences. We are going to be a company with different revenue streams: subscriber revenues, plus advertising and e-commerce revenue, plus content revenue.

When we held our first Board meeting of AOL Time Warner about ten days ago, we told the Board that in order to achieve the goal of being the most valuable and most respected company, we have to embrace a new approach. And that means thinking about the Company more broadly, not just thinking narrowly about divisions.

It means building a new culture and a new compensation system that rewards cross-business collaboration. It means thinking less like an American company and more like a global company. It means thinking boldly about major new initiatives that can create whole new industries, not simply how we can incrementally tweak our existing businesses. And it also means thinking about how we can make a difference in people's lives and make a difference in the communities that we serve.

To translate that from this somewhat aspirational, somewhat abstract goal—"We want to be the most valuable company in the world"—to something a bit more specific, and to give you a road map to track as these years play out, we've outlined seven goals that embody this new approach.

The first is a recognition that to become the most valuable and most respected company, we've got to demonstrate right out of the starting gate that we mean what we say and that we live up to our commitments. That includes living up to the commitments we made to you, in terms of the financial targets we've set. We know we need to be firing on all cylinders.

In retrospect—even though we may have wished the merger process was a little more streamlined—we've been able to use this year very constructively to think about how to operate this new company in a new way, and to build alignment among the executives.

We are committed to achieving our short-term goals, while also being committed to taking a longer-term view. And we recognize that in order to achieve greatness, we have to demonstrate that we have a plan, we have a team, and that we're executing against that plan.

Our second goal is to fundamentally transform the consumer experience. As I said before, among businesses and consumers, there is the beginning of recognition that things that used to be viewed as separate are beginning to converge. And that, I think, is the biggest opportunity: to fundamentally reinvent the way people get information, how they're entertained, how they communicate, how they buy products, and how they're educated.

The question is, how do you knit together the PC, the TV, the phone, and the stereo? And how do you build bridges between what had been separate industries? That, I think, is an enormous opportunity.

What underlies the trend towards convergence is consumers' fundamental desire for more simplicity and more integration. They're curious about some of the new products in the marketplace, but they're getting increasingly frustrated by the fact that each requires a whole new set of patterns, in which they have to set up another address book, or stock portfolio, and need to relearn how to perform basic functions.

People are saying, "Why can't I just do the stuff that I like to do, using all these different devices, connected to all these different networks? Why doesn't someone figure out a way to make it work together more seamlessly?"

One of the reasons people haven't figured that out is because it's hard. Another reason is because it's very difficult to get alignment, with a common vision in a converging world, if you spread these businesses across lots of disparate, separate companies with their own objectives. It's important to be flexible and open-minded about how value chains might migrate. And, if you're in all parts of the value chain, you have the flexibility to be more aggressive than if you're trying to protect a particular way of doing things.

I think that you probably see this trend in your own lives. You may be adopting more technologies, but wishing they worked together more conveniently, and more seamlessly.

If you are in the advertising business, you have an equally daunting challenge in a new world with more choices, more fragmentation, and more disintegration of the mass audience that was so easy to market to, particularly in the '60s and '70s—the glory days of packaged-goods marketing.

Advertisers are asking, how do you engage with consumers? And how do you not just build the brand, but also provide more information? And how do you provide, where possible, the ability to actually transact the sale?

So, when we talk about AOL Time Warner leveraging and driving this converging world and connecting the dots for consumers, we need to recognize that there's a similar opportunity to connect the dots for advertisers, and to create new kinds of integrated packages that allow people to do things in a new way.

I think it's important to understand the legacy of this company. Jerry talked about Ted Turner and the creation of cable

Exhibit 15   Remarks by Steve Case on Investor's Day 2001 (continued)

networks: Ted was the first person to recognize what satellite could do, and created TBS as a national superstation. CNN has had a transformative impact on the world, with the ability to change events.

But, similarly, AOL and Time Warner have been the leaders of the pack for more than a century. Henry Luce created the first news magazine, and the first photo journalism. Jack Warner at Warner Bros. was one of the instrumental players in making movies part of our everyday lives. Time Warner Cable System was the first to invest in interactive services over 20 years ago.

Jerry Levin was the founder of HBO, taking what was a not-very-successful local movie service and turning it into an extremely successful national service. You'll hear tomorrow about what AOL has done to popularize interactive services, to make the Internet more of a household word, and to build Instant Messaging into a new kind of communications phenomenon.

So AOL Time Warner is a company that has pioneered more businesses than any other company, anywhere in the world, with a legacy of innovation that is unmatched. So, as we've set our sights on this converging future, it's important to recognize that we bring to bear a tremendous perspective and a legacy of bold, pioneering innovation.

It's also important to understand that we need to be a global company. This is our third goal. We've made good progress expanding internationally with the AOL brand and many Time Warner businesses over the years. But the reality is that we're still predominantly an American company, with less than 20% of our revenue from outside the United States.

You can count on dramatic growth in our international business over the years ahead. In five years, my guess is that about one-third of our revenue will come from outside the United States; in ten years, about half our revenue will be international.

That creates an enormous opportunity, for extending our existing brands and businesses, for establishing joint ventures or developing local partnerships, and for being quite a bit more aggressive with investments, particularly larger strategic investments, especially in the next year or two. We'll be able to plant some flags in new markets and new regions. Over time, particularly as we've executed against our 2001 strategy—and as we would hope and expect to have a significantly higher stock price, therefore a stronger currency—you could also expect some acquisitions in the global space.

The bottom line is, if we're going to be the most valuable and the most respected company in the world, we have to be a global company, and we're aiming for half our revenues to come from outside the United States. We want to get there sooner rather than later. When you look at the revenue growth rates of this company, you need to factor in the enormous untapped potential in many very exciting markets around the world. We've got some initial projects that both AOL and Time Warner have launched in Europe and Asia, but we're pretty much missing in action in China. We won't be, in a few years.

The fourth goal is to reinvent our corporate culture and to move to a more integrated view, with more of a team approach—thinking of AOL Time Warner as one company. This move has gotten lots of attention. The big challenge here is integration and people. Are the people going to stay? Are they going to work together? Is it going to be an integrated approach, or the more historical divisional approach?

We understand that this is something that we need to focus on. We benefit from the fact that all these businesses have an intense consumer-centric point of view. And we also have taken steps over the past year to move quite dramatically to a more integrated approach, in terms of management as well as how we reward performance.

We moved towards a compensation system where every employee of AOL Time Warner is a stockholder, and everybody benefits if the stock goes up. We've moved away from a compensation that rewarded divisional performance to a compensation structure that is skewed towards company-wide performance.

Equally important is the change in perspective—the recognition that it requires a new team-building approach—not just to make the numbers in the short run by being more efficient in terms of costs, or by helping each other generate revenues, but, more significantly, to drive the longer-term vision of a converged world. We need to take down walls and build bridges, and that's been a very significant by-product of the past year as we were waiting for the merger to be approved.

A related goal is that we believe in talent. We believe that's true within each of our businesses, and it's also true in the management of all of our businesses. So, attracting and keeping the best people in the world will continue to be a major focus for us. We already have a world-class management team and a world-class Board of Directors, but we want to continue to build on this foundation. And we have built on it, even though a lot of the pundits said in January when we announced this merger, "When the merger closes, let's see how many people have left."

The fact is that the executive team is intact, and we've added new talent over the past year, and that will, I think, continue to be the point. We're not losing executives as is common in mergers—we're gaining executives, because there are a lot of people who are excited about what we're doing and who want to be part of this exciting future. They are recognizing that AOL Time Warner is uniquely positioned.

So it's not just about keeping people; it's also about attracting new people and then knitting them together into a team dynamic, so we can execute against this strategy of making the numbers in the short run and making a difference in the long run, by recognizing that we're living in a converging world.

The sixth goal is also important, and that's to focus on building what might be called "our public capital." We recognize that we are already among the most valuable companies in the world, already one of the most watched companies in the world because of the nature of what we do. Time Magazine, CNN, Madonna, AOL, Instant Messaging, "The Sopranos"—the list is endless. Our

Exhibit 15 Remarks by Steve Case on Investor's Day 2001 (continued)

products touch people's lives and, as a result, people are interested in what we're doing and pay attention to the company.

I also think—in fact, I know—that people expect more from us than they do from most other companies. We shoulder more responsibility than a typical company and we recognize that. We're focused quite intently on making sure that the decisions we make from a business standpoint, as well as the coalitions we forge from a policy standpoint, are supportive of the continued rapid growth of this medium.

We're focused, particularly, on knocking down some of the policy walls that currently exist, to make way for this wave of convergence. We recognize that we need to be a different kind of company. We need to shoulder this public-interest responsibility, and, as Jerry has said many times—including the day we announced the merger on January 10th—that was part of Henry Luce's will.

So this is part of the legacy of Time Warner, and will be part of the legacy for AOL Time Warner. We are not just operating the Company in the shareholders' interest, but operating it in the public interest as well, by being a leader and dealing with complicated issues, like privacy, taxation, and regulation.

We will do so not just to help our own business, although that's certainly a by-product. Indeed, to the extent that a company is viewed as a respected company, and one that can be trusted, the company gains more flexibility, for instance, for acquisitions.

But what's really driving us is the recognition that we do have an opportunity to be the most respected company, and that we shoulder an unusual set of responsibilities. We need to recognize that each and every day, as we make our business decisions and as we focus on trying to shape and frame the policy framework, not just in this country but around the world.

A related point, and the final goal, is that we don't want to just make the numbers—although we recognize it's important and we will make the numbers—we also want to make a difference. It's part of the unique nature of this company. We recognize that the more you make the numbers, the more flexibility you have to make a difference in a variety of ways.

We're going to use a variety of different approaches. We recognize that we can leverage the businesses we've got, as we did at AOL with Helping.org, which became the leading online site to stimulate volunteerism and philanthropy, or as Time has done with its reading program, which is the leading reading program in the nation today.

We will certainly leverage our businesses, which are unique and can be helpful in programs like improving education. We will also target particular initiatives that we think can benefit from our attention, such as trying to bridge the digital divide. So that, as we create a more integrated world, a more converged world, we're not leaving people behind. We recognize that we have an obligation and a responsibility to make a difference.

This conviction is deep down in our souls, but it is also, I think, tremendously motivational to the people of AOL Time Warner. People do want to make money, they do want the stock to go up, they do want their options to be more valuable, of course. But they also want to make a difference.

And that's not just a slogan we put on slides, but something that really is built into the DNA of AOL Time Warner. People are very excited about the unique role that AOL Time Warner can play, and recognize that it's not just something we should do because it's pragmatic, but something we must do because we want to be the world's most valuable and most respected company. We want to be measured by a different standard than other companies, we want people to expect more from us, and that's exactly the focus we'll be bringing over the years ahead.

I hope this gives you some kind of context, so, as you think about what you hear tomorrow, I do believe you will leave with much more confidence in the team and how well it's working together, and how we have built this cross-divisional teamwork with a collaborative focus, and how we do things every day.

You'll hear how we compensate people, and see that we really do have the ability to make these numbers, and we will make these numbers. At the same time, you'll recognize that our focus—and certainly my predominant focus—is not on this quarter, or even this year (thankfully, Jerry, Mike, Bob and Dick will have that focus, don't worry), but, rather, on what this company looks like five years from now.

And it's the possibilities of what this company can be five years from now that is so exciting to me and to Jerry and to the others on the management team. We recognize that this is an important year—it is a "show-me" year. And we intend to show you, while, at the same time, making the appropriate investments to drive our future growth, and to position the Company in a unique space as the most valuable and most respected company in the world.

We don't have all the answers. We've learned over time that consumers sometimes act in ways that aren't the way you expect. But we do have a pretty strong conviction. I'd say this conviction is stronger than we had ten years ago at AOL when we really bet on the growth of online services; or the conviction that Jerry had ten years ago, when everybody was saying cable systems were some kind of sinkhole, and he doubled down in the cable business. We believe that the world is changing, and that the next ten years are going to be quite different than the last ten years.

It's going to require a more integrated view of the market, a more converged view of the consumer experiences, a more omnibus view of how to serve advertisers, and a more integrated view of how to run companies. If we're successful in doing that—and we believe we will be—we will emerge as the most valuable and most respected company in the world.

We recognize that's a high mountain to aspire to climb, but that's the mountain we choose to climb, and, indeed, we feel comforted that we've got the wind at our back with an extraordinary future ahead of us.

I'd like to close by thanking you for being here tonight, and for showing an interest in AOL Time Warner. Together, we really can create an enormously exciting company, and the most valuable and the most respected company on earth.

Exhibit 16 Remarks by Gerald Levin on Investor's Day 2001[172]

You should have the earnings release that went out this morning, along with the trending schedules with consolidated and divisional metrics. We also put out a series of releases that cover the waterfront, in terms of advertising, cable, HBO, and other commercial arrangements. For the first time we have a fact book that pretty much details every part of the Company and has a good statement of the Company's mission and values.

When Mike Kelly speaks, he will get into guidance for Calendar Year 2001 and Q1, and we will put out a release, which will also be posted to our website. Then, throughout the day, you're going to hear from every part of the Company.

We originally thought that the birthing period for this new company would be the standard nine months; it turned out to be one year and a day. While it may have been frustrating to some, it was actually very helpful, because we really put in place the Company during that period. So, actually, I'm kind of pleased.

Frankly, the way I look at the Company is as a global large-cap growth company with growth metrics that are really quite astonishing, with a very healthy balance sheet. Actually, it's kind of a blue chip powerhouse because we have this tremendous commitment to make a difference. And when I say global, as you heard from Steve last night, our highest priority, over a sustained period of time, is to make this truly a global company, not only in terms of revenues that are generated outside of the Unites States, but also in terms of perspective. You're going to hear a lot during the day from the various companies and what that means.

This is not a media company anymore; it's not an Internet company. It truly is a one-of-a-kind company that's taking its place on the world's stage with a growth aspiration that really is unmatched and unassailable.

I honestly believe that the transformations that are taking place in the way people conduct their lives, are essentially going to be led by this Company. So not only has nothing dissuaded me from the opportunity I thought I saw a year ago, but now we've made it come together, by creating our new plan. This is a remarkable company, with remarkable flexibility.

When I'm done you'll hear from Mike Kelly, the Chief Financial Officer, who will deliver the meat of the financial presentation. We will hear from Bob Pittman, who will talk about the AOL December Quarter.

But Mike will not only take you through guidance; he'll also give you our balance-sheet strategy. You'll then hear from Pittman and Dick Parsons, because in May we put in place the organization based on the taxonomy in the Company, with subscriptions, advertising and content.

This afternoon, you'll hear the principal unit CEO presentations. Joe Collins will speak first on Cable; Barry Schuler for AOL; Don Logan for Time Inc; Terry McGuirk for the Turner Networks; Roger Ames for Music; Barry Meyer for Warner Bros.; and then Jeff Bewkes for HBO.

I think what you'll see is that I've had this opportunity to orchestrate things for some time now. There are a lot of announcements that came out this morning, but that doesn't mean that we've built up a backlog of announcements cutting across the Company. For example, the 400 commercial arrangements—and a lot of my colleagues who really fashioned this are here—we've been doing this for the last six or eight months. It's just that we had to call them a certain thing and keep it, to a certain extent, under wraps. And you'll see the soul of this new machine is a monetizing machine. I'm just orchestrating, on a continuing basis, how we do that.

Now I know that in some minds, there is the concept of the risk of execution. I am very comfortable that we have already created a new culture. I think you will see—and it's for you to question and observe—the kind of integration and the spirit that's here.

I believe there is a new culture. It's not just an Internet 24/7 culture, it's not just a media-centric culture; but it's very much—even though this is a large Company—an entrepreneurial style. Last night, Steve indicated the number of new companies that the people in our Company have started, and I can go down a tremendous list. This is a very flexible company; but, most significantly, it's committed to change. I love change. Change is good—fast-paced change.

You've got to be able to handle change, and you've got to be first to market. But that's not just what the predecessor companies were; that's what this new company is. It is very nimble, and you can see that by the stream of activity.

We're saying that we hit the ground running. That's not just a euphemism, because that's basically what's happened. We've changed the compensation of the company. You don't do that overnight. We looked at this very carefully, and I'm very pleased that we did two things that are really very significant for a company like ours.

First, everyone in the Company got a stock-option grant. Secondly, all of what we'll call the divisional cash plans were based on divisional performance, and we've now traded those for stock options. So, from a compensation point of view and perspective, there's essentially a view that it's all based on value creation. It's a profound change. And, yes, we changed the mix of compensation between equity-based and cash. You don't do that overnight.

We're going to run this Company through the strongest financial group that I've ever seen. You now have a set of metrics and detailed trending schedules, not only consolidated, but by each business. What this reflects is an internal document that we created almost six months ago.

We pay attention to the balance sheet. We're a triple B+ Company, so we will stay that way and have conservative ratios: a leverage ratio of 3:1 and coverage ratio of 4:1. We pay attention to every basis point; we get every single dollar we can get out of it. We want financial flexibility. We want to be very intelligent about fixed and variable, maturity schedules, what we do with our NOLs. As you know, we filed a shelf and we have a share repurchase program.

But with this Company, as before, we're going to measure capital allocation against the repurchase of our stock. We have

Exhibit 16 Remarks by Gerald Levin on Investor's Day 2001 (continued)

very high hurdle rates; we're going to watch capital expenditures, development costs, production spending, working capital. But our operating cash flow is growing, so the return on incremental capital is truly spectacular.

Most interesting to me is the fact that, when you put all this together, in 2001, cash and capacity is $14 billion; over our planned period it's $50 billion. Now this is after we have provided for—and I'm looking at all my colleagues—all of your requirements. On top of that, we have to be very aggressive; and you heard last night the objective we have for the overall company. So we expect to be—and through our investing activities, and, again, with this global perspective—a hyperactive Company.

I'm very comfortable with the fact that we've not only reaffirmed the guidance given a long time ago, but on a consolidated basis, we're paying real attention now to top line across the Company: revenue growth, EBITDA, free cash flow (that's what it's all about). And I'm pleased that we added cash earnings-per-share, because, from an accounting point of view, you deal with the goodwill. We have a metric that comes closest to paying attention to our capital structure. So that's the way we're going to run the Company, through the prism of these metrics.

If I had to use just one word for AOL Time Warner, it would be subscriptions. It's one reason why the cultures are so compatible. We have this 130-million subscription number, and we've made it an underlying metric. There's so much you can do in terms of acquisition, retention, upselling. But it's the format of the consumer relationship that enables you to rent your facilities and to do something that we euphemistically call advertising—which will be our fastest-growing part of the Company—but it's all built on this consumer relationship.

Let me just say a couple of things about the businesses. Let me declare affirmatively that AOL is the crown jewel of this company. I say that without qualification. When you look at the December quarter, when you look at the subscription acquisition that's taken place recently, when you look at the advertising, direct marketing, e-commerce line, it's enormous. Essentially, it is the fastest-growing subscription service on the fastest-growing medium in the world.

And I'm not just talking about the technological base of AOL, which will be extremely important to the Company, but I'm really talking about the habit structure of the AOL customer. This is a golden franchise that can be leveraged throughout Time Warner. In fact, I think as you hear people talk today, you will see that what we've done is plug all of our businesses into the AOL growth engine.

Having said that, I'm also a cable guy; that hasn't changed. And when you look at the relative metrics, you'll see that close to 60% of the company comes from AOL and Cable. Even the kind of growth activity that can take place—particularly now that we have digital set-top boxes and high-speed cable modems—the growth activity at Cable is very significant to the growth trajectory of the whole company.

But there's one other factor: everything the company is working on that's interesting in terms of transformation—whether that's interactive television, video-on-demand, subscription video-on-demand, interactive advertising, IP telephony, multiple ISPs, high-definition television—everything that I've described. Subscription services for music, downloading, all require bandwidth capability that uses digital television, IP screening capability, still serving the old analog boxes; the only place you can find that happens to be through cable.

So, from a laboratory perspective—which is what this Company is all about, an innovation Company—to be able to go to Cable and develop the P&L dynamic for an HBO subscription-on-demand, is very important.

Regarding Networks and the way we're reporting … we have Cable Networks, Pay Networks and Broadcast Networks. I am very pleased with where the Turner Networks are. You're going to hear a lot about the rebirth at CNN. We announced this morning CNN Money, something we've wanted to do for some time. Now we can put CNN in the family of the Time Inc. magazines and AOL Personal Finance, with distribution through Time Warner Cable.

We have some jewels there at Turner—one of them is called the Cartoon Network, and you'll hear more about this from Terry McGuirk. In terms of value creation on a global basis, it's one of the most interesting assets we have.

The WB, in all its iterations, has carved out an amazing niche in that broadcast arena.

HBO, as you'll hear from Jeff Bewkes, is at the top of its game, certainly in terms of programming, but also 37 million subscriptions grew by 1.2 million this year, and is still the largest of its kind.

Publishing—Don Logan is very boring; it's the 36th quarter in a row of up performance, another record year. The most curious thing is that Time Inc. and AOL are the most similar businesses in the house. It's just amazing—from a subscription dynamic, in terms of the demographics that are served—and it's not an accident that we're already up to almost 800,000 new magazine subscriptions generated by AOL. And there's now a substantial amount of activity at Time Inc. generating registrations for AOL.

But there's a remarkable synergy between AOL and Time Inc. It's why, again, I'm so comfortable, because I grew up in a Time Inc. subscription environment. Just look at subscriptions—now 130 million—and we're going to talk about how we're going to 140 million.

Advertising, but not traditional advertising; and e-commerce, but hitting the direct-marketing side of companies—that's an AOL invention, but it's not new to us, because Time Inc. has been the largest direct marketer in the country.

So we organized all those businesses under Bob Pittman, and his assignment is to monetize that footprint. You may ask, "what about the advertising environment?" but we're in a different zone. And some of the announcements this morning reflect that. You're going against a marketing budget. It's not the measured-media budget, it's not big network upfronts and scatter markets

Exhibit 16   Remarks by Gerald Levin on Investor s Day 2001 (continued)

and CPMs, and I would say to you that this is not traditional cross-selling; it's the leverage of the AOL tradition.

By the way, we're an advertiser, so Time Inc. has, in effect, used the AOL machine to generate subscriptions. It's that leverage, when you go to companies, that we can now make money flow into Turner and flow into the magazines. At the same time, there is a flight to quality, and it helps to be number one. It also helps to be a big advertiser because we can use a lot of our own medium. So that is Mr. Pittman's assignment.

We then took a look at content. It has different characteristics. There's a journalistic integrity that needs to be understood and preserved, there's the creative process of telling stories, whether it's through movies, television, music or literature. But here is the interesting thing—all of those businesses are profoundly affected within the new Company.

It is my aspiration that we can change the way this material is promoted and distributed, taking advantage of the digital technology. Because of the value of our catalogs and libraries. It's the only business I know where the inventory keeps going up in value because new technologies are discovered and new distribution formats arise.

I think the biggest technology and the biggest distribution format—putting to shame the CD or the VCR, and even now the DVD (although that is really driving our growth, and we're going to do a little DVD audio later on)—is precisely this ability to get material directly into the hands of people at home who might not have gone out to buy it through traditional distribution channels.

In that sense, you could look at market shares for current production across all of our businesses. The key fact is to look at the libraries. At the end of the day, the end of the week, the end of the year, we have added to our library. Of course, Warner Bros., New Line, HBO, CBS, TNT are producing new product, as are our Music catalog and our catalog in Publishing.

At AOL Time Warner, we realized that there's a lot of Internet construction going on and certain companies have high valuations while that infrastructure is played out.

But, eventually, what is it about? It's all about communications; we've got that. It's all about story-telling, entertainment; it's all about information to kind of conduct your life. That's what we do, and, eventually that's the gold, that's the nugget, that's the soul, and that's really what this Company has. So, instead of having isolated areas of digital activity—as we tried to do at Time Warner, and as you see what's happening, at company after company—we have now made this the central part of the Company...it's in our fiber. It makes a huge difference.

Let me get back to the basic point: this is all about execution. We clearly have in place the assets, we clearly have in place any transforming business you want to make. There are people in this audience who are working on interactive television. Now, some of us have been working on that for many, many years.

And, essentially, digital life's management is already being done, because we have the distribution system, the customer relationships, we have the material, we have the broadband outlet, we have the technology. So I'm very comfortable with the "risk of execution," because of the results that are coming out, the financial discipline that's in this Company, and finally and most importantly, the group of people assembled here today.

Exhibit 17   Question and Answer Session about 1st Quarter 2001 Results[173]

Q: What's driving your confidence in the strength in advertising spending in the second half of the year?
Kelly: Overall, we're starting to see some signs of take-off in the advertising market. Also, if you look at the performance both at AOL and Cable, you saw very strong performance in the first quarter because there's confidence going into the 2nd and 3rd quarters.

The other thing to think about is that we really didn't start delivering on the cross-platform opportunity until we got into the quarter, so we're still ramping that up. It has the ability for us to generate additional revenue as we get into the year. So we do feel, quite strongly, that we're well-positioned for the year.
Levin: Our company just rides above the normal market dynamics here, and you can see it in the results. And the results in the first quarter, since we hit our targets, gives us confidence, not only in AOL's profound partnership concept, which is really driving unique forms of relationships, hitting direct marketing expenditures. But it's driving revenues into the traditional parts of Time Warner. So, yes, you're going to get a different take on this approach and the marketplace from our company. And that gives us confidence, as Mike said, for the year.
Q: What role is pricing going to play in hitting your EBITDA targets?
Pittman: I assume you're talking about the AOL pricing. We have made no announcements about a price increase and no decision. But if the question is, "Do you need it to hit the quarter?" The answer is no.

But that misses the point of how we use our money. Not everything we do in a quarter goes to the bottom line—part of it goes to the bottom line, and part of it goes to invest in new projects we think are very important for the future.

When we come up with a new project that we think is very important to our future—it can be a great new earnings growth for us, or help increase our leadership position—we aren't going to take the money from earnings. We take the money by finding another project which isn't living up to its potential, getting rid of it, and repurposing the money. We find other efficiencies in the business, or we use price increases, not only for the AOL service,

Exhibit 17   Question and Answer Session about 1st Quarter 2001 Results (continued)

but other places within our stable of products; or we begin selling something we've not been selling, to fund that new project.

That's how we think about price increases. It's given us an enormous amount of flexibility over the years to not only do what we have to do to deliver the return people expect, but also the ability to build new products constantly.

Levin: Let me underscore what Bob said, not only as it relates to AOL, but to all our subscriptions. Certainly, there is pricing that's taking place, there's unit growth, and it all revolves around that's what we get paid to do, to make the judgments about when you've delivered sufficient features and you're invested in the habit structure, and to keep that annuity income flowing. And we do that all the time: we do that in Magazines, we do it in Cable, and we do it at AOL.

Q: Would you give us your current thinking on how the open-access issue is going to unfold over the coming 12–24 months?

Levin: In Columbus, Ohio we are actually putting in place all of the systems that are necessary to deliver multiple ISPs. We retain the same enthusiasm about the importance of this, because we think the broadband platform that's created is the platform over which we can deliver a lot of services. Obviously, this is helpful with the introduction of AOL's broadband service and the marketing expenditures that will take place in our Cable systems. So, later in the year we expect to begin to roll this out.

Q: How much upfront ad spending do you expect for the year? Where does AOL Time Warner have a competitive advantage?

Levin: Our competitive advantage is riding a concept of partnership deals through the distribution strength of the AOL sales and promotional platform that no one else has. You see it in the AOL numbers, and now in the AOL Time Warner numbers. That's the distinct competitive advantage.

Pittman: Last year was an extraordinary year in terms of the amount of dollars taken out on the upfront. I think you're going to see the pendulum swing the other way. Everyone—buyers and sellers—would agree it was probably not the best thing for a smooth-functioning marketplace.

I think this year you're going to see, both for reasons of the buyers and sellers, an upfront that swings in the other direction. I think you're going to see much more of an emphasis on the scatter-dollar spending, as opposed to spending it upfront. But I think that relates primarily to the TV media side of the business.

A lot of the cross-company deals are actually coming today probably more from the AOL relationship, and expanding out into the media, and I think that will operate somewhat independently from the normal media buying.

On the AOL service, we think that less than 10 percent—maybe only 5 percent—of the money is coming out of media budgets. In the TV business, I'd say all are coming out of the media budgets, and magazines are somewhere in between. Actually, part of the bundling is not only TV advertising and not only magazine advertising. But, if you buy into our view of what advertising is—which is that we're renting a customer relationship to an unaffiliated third party—it actually extends

into licensing, it extends into product placement, and it extends into a lot of non-traditional areas of advertising. Again, that's one of the great strengths of the company.

Q: Would you discuss the open-access question from the AOL side? Could you begin the mass audience rollout of AOL broadband with just the Time Warner systems? Or is it really fundamental that you have other cable companies open? And can you update us on your discussions with those other cable companies? What are the gating factors there?

Levin: Obviously, Time Warner Cable represents about 20 percent of the marketplace, but it's disproportionately important because of where the system configuration is, and the aggression and enthusiasm with which we approach new businesses.

So AOL Plus, and therefore the AOL broadband service, has the distinct advantage because Time Warner Cable is putting in place not only the systems, but the kind of marketing, billing, and customer service understanding needed. So we view this as a demonstration project. And yes, in all the conversations with the rest of the cable industry on the part of AOL, the key will be not only the deal structure itself—although we now have deal structures beyond AOL and Time Warner Cable—it will be the performance demonstration, about which we're quite confident.

We're quite confident about the marketplace demand for the AOL Plus service—we already know that. There already are probably close to two million broadband customers who are using AOL Plus. It's a tremendous opportunity because the AOL habit structure has expanded or extrapolated in that sense, so we're very optimistic and very confident about the money to be made not only by AOL, but by the Cable company. And this has been the history of the cable television history—the introduction of new services has followed the good performance. We've done this many, many times. We did it with HBO and Bob Pittman did it with MTV.

Pittman: If you take the broader view of broadband, we also think DSL and satellite play a role. AOL already has those agreements in place. With our discussions with cable operators, as Jerry mentioned, they're not doing it to do us any favors—they're interested because they can make more money. They will make more money offering multiple ISPs than they're going to make selling just one ISP, no matter what that ISP is.

I think they've also seen indications that the power of a brand like AOL is good for their business. I don't know if you saw the full-page ads that Cablevision was running, with no agreement with AOL, saying, "Your AOL will run better over … " and they were selling their service to merely support the AOL service. Again, we have millions of people now using the AOL Plus broadband service, using somebody else's carrier, but running AOL over it.

The surprising statistic for AOL is that, even in that environment, you would think most of the people would downgrade to $9.95 unlimited and bring their own access. Instead, the majority of people are paying $21.95 unlimited narrow-band access. The reason is that people not only are still using narrow brand—remember, they want the fastest speed they can get in whatever

Exhibit 17   Question and Answer Session about 1st Quarter 2001 Results (continued)

location—but they expect to use it, and know they're going to use it. So, again, I think AOL is in a pretty good position.

Q: On the balance sheet we saw your non-current inventories going up by almost $800 million and Music was up $460; what's going on there?

Kelly: This is the first quarter we've gone back and pushed down purchase accounting. Primarily, what you see in the Music line is the reevaluation of our copyrights, which is the assignment of the valuations we push back down. The increase all relates to purchasing accounting, accounting adjustments, and reevaluating those inventories as you look back out.

Regarding the increase on the inventory line, we have sped up some of our production spend, in light of what might be happening out on the West Coast later on this year, to prepare ourselves. So there is a stated effort to get some of that production spend on, which takes it to the inventories overall. We also have some other payments that we pushed through there. We have one in there for Major League Baseball; we have a large payment that we put out earlier.

Overall, it is really timing of spending, thinking about what may happen in the late spring and summer, as well as some other one-time payments that we've pushed through.

Q: Would you walk us through the experience with HBO as it relates to VOD?

Parsons: When you look at HBO, one of the exciting things we've hit upon is the idea of subscription-on-demand. HBO is really the flagship within our company to develop that, working very closely with Time Warner Cable, and with other cable companies as well. What we've seen is that consumers have a propensity to buy a finite cost item so that they don't have to watch the clock—we saw that with AOL, too.

And we think, obviously, where there's as much unique content that HBO has, plus all the movies, that it is a powerful engine and an understandable package for the consumer. They're going into test video on demand in a month or so, so we're very excited about it. And, by the way, the initial research says it can be very important to us.

Levin: This is quite significant because it indicates that we do think in terms of subscriptions, even with video-on-demand, which is normally thought of as a unit purchase. But we believe that you can convert a brand that has great consumer acceptance, and here you have 15 channels for HBO and Cinemax. If we can deliver on an impulse basis any program that's on HBO, and we're testing delivery that day, that week, that month—we have all the rights to that—and you charge an additional monthly fee, then we can test everything: six bucks, eight bucks, ten bucks.

Our assumption is that because of the power of the HBO brand and the power of programs like "The Sopranos," that that's an easy concept for consumers … maybe it's a little hard to figure out what Replay and TiVo are, but this is essentially the same thing, using a significant brand.

We believe it will work, and to give you some index of that, throughout the year we're testing in three or four other cable

operators' systems, because there's that almost immediate understanding or acceptance of subscription video-on-demand. It may be the template for future services.

Q: Within the AOL division, on the average monthly revenue per sub, it would appear that the subscription revenue came in a bit light. I'm wondering if that's because of bundling deals. And could you comment on what percentage of your new subscribers added in the quarter came from bundling? And how should we expect average monthly revenue per sub to trend, going forward?

Pittman: About a year ago, we began doing more marketing programs that are reflected as a reduction of revenue rather than as a marketing cost. And, over the year, you've seen an increase in the percentage of those programs, so that's primarily the impact.

Kelly: In light of what's been happening with PC manufacturers, PC sales and everything else that's sitting out there today, I think AOL had an extraordinary quarter, in terms of our subscriber growth. We added a little over 2 million subscribers for the quarter, worldwide, and we had very, very strong domestic adds coming through that.

So the impact of the marketing game of bundling, retention, and the timing of when you add those subs, it obviously has an impact, overall, in terms of revenue-per-member. We did see it come down a little bit this quarter; I think we're in that same general range as we look out in the second half of the year. We just talked about more aggressively rolling out broadband and other services, and we should see that number come back up in the second half of the year.

Q: Congratulations on a good quarter in a tough environment. My question on pricing is, what are you finding in terms of traction and experience in some of the new services you've rolled out, like AOLbyPHONE, in terms of incremental pricing opportunities? And how do you think that shapes up over the course of this year?

Pittman: I think you've hit upon it. When we talk about how we've got this subscriber relationship-not only can we rent it to other people, but we can use it ourselves-AOLbyPhone is an indication of using it ourselves. I think we're getting pretty good traction of all of the services. Clearly, we're in the early-adopter phase.

So I do think there are opportunities there, and I think, longer term, you can certainly expect to see that other layer of revenue sitting on top of that AOL subscription relationship, much the same as in Cable. Joe has built a basic cable subscription relationship, but the real growth of the company comes from taking those people and selling them a digital platform, and then building stuff on top of the digital platform. We're doing exactly the same thing on AOL.

Q: On the competitive side, Microsoft is going to be launching its operating system, XP, this year, and there's going to be a lot of integration with MSN. Could you talk a little bit about how AOL competes in that environment with 7.0, in terms of some of the feature sets?

Pittman: I think this is this year's version of what Microsoft is doing. So, how do we compete in the world? The way we've always

Exhibit 17   Question and Answer Session about 1st Quarter 2001 Results (continued)

competed, which is we look at the consumer, we build services the consumer wants, and that's our focus. And it's quite different for companies that look at technology or look at software as being their focus. And I think we will be very strong, as long as we continue to listen to the consumer and respond quickly.

That's not to say we don't appreciate Microsoft as a competitor because, boy, they are a strong competitor and a tough competitor. But, again, I have great confidence in Barry Schuler and the folks at AOL to continue to keep their eye on the ball, which, in our case, is the consumer.

Q: Following on an earlier question, can you talk a little bit more about what, specifically, you've seen in terms of advertising? Are you seeing some signs of a pickup? Then, if things don't recover on the advertising front going through the year, given the importance of that in most of the models, can you talk about some of the things you can do to manage the business to make the numbers, anyway, this year?

Kelly: Let me talk more broadly, as we look at the model, overall. We look at all the platforms we have out there, and how we drive even this quarter's results: we saw strong subscription growth across the board, we saw strong content growth across the board, as well as strong advertising growth. The advertising issue is more circled back in on two units overall, the other unit showing strong growth in terms of advertising. AOL and Cable are leading the charge.

But we continue to look for cost opportunities, we continue to look at projects that we're looking to launch maybe in the latter half of the year that we have some timing; we can gate when we actually start spending money on each of the individual projects. So, across all of our different platforms, across the different businesses, across literally the thousands of initiatives that we have going across the company, we've got a lot of dollars and leverage to go back and take a look at and manage, to go ahead and produce the results that we're going to deliver, overall.

Pittman: I would add that we've spent billions of dollars ourselves on marketing. So there is an upside and a downside to all of these issues and, obviously, we have benefited whenever we can get some extra opportunities from the cost side of our business, in terms of pushing out our products.

But I would say that if you look at the advertising business, you really have to break it into two components: The media side of the business is where all this stuff is going on, the media budgets. People still have to sell services—every company is worried about their growth for the next quarter—and marketing does work, so they're all going to spend the money.

Where we have the more strategic relationships and we're dealing with integrated company plans, we are not seeing much weakness and don't expect to. Where you're looking at media budgets, I always think it's a little like the *Mad Magazine's* "Spy Versus Spy." You get into a market like this and it's media buyer versus media seller, and it's a bit of a game. The question is, when does this sort of break and go, "Okay, here's the money"? and let's get on with it. I can't predict the moment at which that

happens, but I think we are certainly recognizing the fact that the money to market products is still there; it's still an imperative. And it's just a matter of how it's expressed.

The good news for us is that we have market leaders who, in times like this, are generally at the core of someone's media buy, not on the periphery. And, generally, in soft times, while people can do without the periphery, they can't do without the core. So I think we're in a pretty good position, no matter what happens.

Levin: Depending on what year you take, we may be the fifth-largest advertiser. So Bob has at his disposal the very efficient use of those advertising dollars.

Secondly, I challenge anyone who is drawing conclusions from this current economic environment, to take a look at new-product introduction across all the traditional businesses that will be taking place throughout the year, particularly in the second half of the year. And you'll see announcements like that; they're all going to have to advertise.

Kellner: You also can grow your rating-point inventory. If your CPM numbers are dropping off a bit, as long as your rating-point inventory grows, you can increase your total numbers. In the case of the WB, you have an 18 percent increase and its core demographics up part of the season, so that's driving that business. TBS is at almost an all-time high with enormous growth in the 4th quarter and 1st quarter. TNT is at an all-time high in the 1st quarter so far, Cartoon Network is at an all-time high. So you have a lot of additional inventory to sell as you go into what is not going to be the robust marketplace. But if we do our jobs properly, we have this inventory to sell and we can take share away from the competition, many of which have lost share. ABC has lost an enormous amount of share in the past year.

Q: On Publishing — circulation and advertising were both up strongly—how much of that growth was *Times Mirror*, how much of it was cost-cutting, and how much is driven by AOL marketing?

Kelly: We don't release numbers for subscription and advertising separately for *Times Mirror*, either separately for the unit or overall; but, suffice it to say that the advertising revenue for Publishing would be up, even normalizing for the *Times Mirror* acquisition. The subscription stuff goes back and forth from launches last year, publications that we closed like *Life*, so, going back and forth, that number becomes much more problematic to do the comparison. But a true comparison is really that the advertising market and publishing would be up on a year-over-year basis.

Q: The advertising growth on Cable was incredibly robust. Is that being driven by adding more channels with digital boxes, and how much of it was pricing gain?

On the basic cable subscriber area, will you get to 2 percent growth this year, given .07 percent in the 1st quarter? Then, finally, if you can, could you update us on the VOD rollout and the results you've seen so far? And, also, where you are in self-installations for data?

Levin: On basic cable advertising, these are real numbers. We've said in the past that this is a very strong opportunity for us because, as against all other local forms of advertising—including

Exhibit 17   Question and Answer Session about 1st Quarter 2001 Results (continued)

newspaper and radio and broadcast television—local cable has an advantage. And every time we start a new news service that's like starting a new television station.

The other thing that's happening is increasing the sophistication of our sales staff, so it's not just some mathematical mechanic that relates to more insertion of equipment, or more channels, or more digital. And I look, over time, at the increasing or enhanced sophistication of this capability, so it will be very strong.

And, even on an annualized basis, that revenue line for the basic cable business is now very strong and matches some of our other revenue lines.

With respect to the basic cable growth, I think we've made it very clear that our focus is entirely on digital boxes and cable modems; that's where the margins are; these are the platforms for all of our future services. So we will add basic cable subscribers, but our emphasis is on the new revenue-generating units. And take a look at our EBITDA margin in cable, not only the monthly per-subscriber number, but our EBITDA margin is now up to 47 percent. So a lot of that is because of this growth; that's where our emphasis will be.

With respect to video-on-demand, we're in three cable systems—in Hawaii, Tampa and Austin. And, even though we don't quite have all the films yet, it's proving to tell us what we knew—from way-back-when in Orlando—that the consumer really wants the movies or any material when the consumer wants it.

And when the phone rings, the consumer needs to be able to stop it and go answer the phone. That's why we're pushing not only video-on-demand, but subscription video-on-demand.

As for self-provisioning, presumably for cable modems, even if you look at some of the advertising here in New York for Road Runner, there is an increased emphasis on the ability to get it yourself and install it. That's significant, and I give the cable industry real credit for establishing standards to be able to do this. So, increasingly, that's going to make the margins even higher.

Q: Are you rethinking a pricing strategy, given the DSL umbrella?

Levin: I'll go back to my basic statement about all of our subscription services. Where you have heavy consumer demand and high unit growth, and your research tells you that the features are being absorbed—like they can't live without it—that's the kind of thing we're starting to see with high-speed Internet access.

You've already seen DSL pricing going up and that's something else that we're taking a look at. It's a very good position for us to be in and it kind of tells us that there's a lot of not only unit growth, but pricing flexibility, not only as it relates to AOL, but across our cable services.

Q: Could you comment on negotiations, if any, with AT&T and the status of Time Warner Entertainment?

Levin: I don't think there's anything else for us to say other than you're aware of our public statements that "discussions continue."

Notes

1. Press Release.
2. Roberts, Johnnie. "The Merger," *Newsweek International*, 24 January 2000.
3. Ibid.
4. Ibid.
5. Interview with Rich Cisek and other AOL Time Warner management.
6. Interview.
7. Sutel, Seth. "Lots of good cheer at AOL/Time Warner announcement" Associated Press Newswires, 10 January 2000 23:59.
8. David Streitfeld, "Internet-Media Merger Could Begin a Trend. Similar Deals Likely to Follow Analysts Predict," *Washington Post,* 11 January 2000, Business Section.
9. Thomas E. Weber, Martin Peers, and Nick Wingfield, "Two Titans in a Strategic Bind Bet on a Futuristic Mega Deal," *The Wall Street Journal,* 11 January 2000, B1.
10. Ibid.
11. Time Warner Inc. "America Online and Time Warner Will Merge to Create World's First Internet-Age Media and Communications Company" http://cgi.timewarner.com/cgibin/corp/news/index.cgi?template=article&article_id=100009.
12. Interview.
13. Stephanie Stoughton and Hiawatha Bray, "Investors See Reason to Flee Deal AOL-Time Warner Merger Spurs Many to Drop Shares of Both," *The Boston Globe,* 28 February 2000, Business pg.1.
14. Gretchen Morgenson, "AOL Time Warner May Inflate Internet Stock Values Even More. Yet Its Own Could Falter," *The New York Times,* 11 January 2000, sec. C16.
15. Stephanie Stoughton and Hiawatha Bray, "Investors See Reason to Flee Deal AOL-Time Warner Merger Spurs Many to Drop Shares of Both," *The Boston Globe,* 28 February 2000, Business pg.1.

16. Gretchen Morgenson, "AOL Time Warner May Inflate Internet Stock Values Even More. Yet Its Own Could Falter," *The New York Times*, 11 January 2000, sec. C16.
17. Floyd Norris, "Media Megadeal: Market Place; Two Stocks: One Swings, the Other Doesn't," *The New York Times*, 12 January 2000, sec. C7.
18. David Koop, "AOL Says Share Prices Should Stabilize Soon," *Dow Jones International News*, January 31, 2000. http://ptg.djnr.com/ccroot/asp/pub-lib/story.asp.
19. Alex Berenson, "Media Megadeal: The Deal," *The New York Times*, 13 January 2000, sec. C1.
20. Floyd Norris, "Media Megadeal: Market Place; Two Stocks: One Swings, the Other Doesn't," *The New York Times*, 12 January 2000, sec. C7.
21. Gretchen Morgenson, "AOL Time Warner May Inflate Internet Stock Values Even More. Yet Its Own Could Falter," *The New York Times*, 11 January 2000, sec. C16.
22. Alex Berenson, "Media Megadeal: The Deal," *The New York Times*, 13 January 2000, sec. C1.
23. Ibid.
24. Starobin, Paul. "A New Net Equation: One Lesson of the AOL Time Warner Deal: Profits Matter After All," *Business Week,* 31 January 2000, 38.
25. Broder, Michael. "AOL Investor Relations," *Interview,* 9 February 2001.
26. Watts, William. "FTC Approves AOL-Time Warner Deal" CBS.MarketWatch.com. 14 December 2000.
27. Alec Klien, "For AOL, Good News and Bad," *Washington Post*, 3 January 2001, E01.
28. Historical Dates for America Online, Inc. http://www.corp.aol.com.whoweare/who_timeline.html.
29. Ianthe Jeanne Dugan, "AOL's Stock Falls, Cutting Value of Deal," *Washington Post,* 12 January 2000.
30. CompuServe Interactive Services, Inc. Hoovers Online www.hoovers.comm /premium/profile/2/0,2147,43062,00.html 9 April 2000

31. Peter Goodman and John Schwartz, "Deal Stirs Concerns About Internet Access," *Washington Post,* 11 January 2000, E1.
32. Georgianis, Meria. "AOL To Spend $10B Over 5 Years to Add Network Access, Pres Says." *Dow Jones Newswires,* 1 October 1998. http://ptg.djnr.com/ccroot/asp/publib/story.asp.
33. Time Warner Inc. Encyclopedia Britannica. http://www.Britannica.com/seo/t/timewarner-inc/
34. Luce, Henry R. Encyclopedia Britannica wysiwyg://9/http://www .Britannica.com/bco...,50420+1+49235,000.html?querry=henry%20luce
35. Ibid.
36. Time Warner Inc. Encyclopedia Britannica. http://www.Britannica.com/seo/t/timewarner-inc/
37. Ibid.
38. Ibid.
39. Ibid.
40. Ibid.
41. Warner Brothers. Encyclopedia Britannica. Wysiwyg://26/http://www.Britannica.com/bc...123,00.html?query=warner%20communications
42. Thomas E. Weber, Martin Peers, and Nick Wingfield, "Two Titans in a Strategic Bind Bet on a Futuristic Mega Deal," *The Wall Street Journal,* 11 January 2000, B1.
43. Ibid.
44. AOL Time Warner corporate website.
45. Interview with Mario Vecchi.
46. Leslie Walker, "AOL Time Warner Sites Dominate Web Traffic Data," *The Washington Post,* 27 February 2001.
47. AOL Time Warner corporate website.
48. Gunther, Marc. "Understanding AOL's Grand Unified Theory of the Media Cosmos," *Fortune,* 8 January 2001.
49. Goldman Sachs Analyst Report 2000.
50. "AOL Buyout of Time Warner: Merger Frenzy Sweeping Corporate America" 14 January 2000. World Socialist Website.
51. Gunther, Marc. "Understanding AOL's Grand Unified Theory of the Media Cosmos," *Fortune,* 8 January 2001.
52. J.P. Morgan Analyst Reports.
53. (*Fortune* Feb 7 2000, p. 84 AOL + TWX by Carol J. Loomis.
54. Gunther, Marc. "Understanding AOL's Grand Unified Theory of the Media Cosmos," *Fortune,* 8 January 2001.
55. Saul Hansell, "Media Megadeal: The New Company; Two Become One or What?" *The New York Times,* 15 December 2000.
56. Ibid.
57. Paul Davidson, "Time Warner Resists FTC Demands," *USA Today,* 29 November 2000.
58. Ross, Patrick & Hansen, Evan: "FCC OK's AOL Time Warner Merger" 11 January 2001. ZDNet.com.
59. Edmund Sanders, "AOL, Time Warner Clear FCC Hurdle," *Los Angeles Times,* 12 January 2001.
60. Ross, Patrick & Hansen, Evan: "FCC OK's AOL Time Warner merger" January 11, 2001. ZDNet.com
61. Edmund Sanders, "AOL, Time Warner Clear FCC Hurdle," *Los Angeles Times,* 12 January 2001.
62. Ross, Patrick & Hansen, Evan: "FCC OK's AOL Time Warner merger" January 11, 2001. ZDNet.com.
63. Ross, Patrick & Hansen, Evan: "AOL, Time Warner complete merger with FCC blessing" January 11, 2001. CNET News.com
64. J.P. Morgan Analysts Reports.
65. Ibid.
66. Ibid.
67. Interview.
68. David Liebermann, "Tolls stack up on the tech highway," *USA Today,* 4 April 2001.
69. John Geriland and Eva Sonesh-Kedar, "The Odd Couple," *The Standard,* 24 January 2000.
70. Johnson, Tom; Case, Levin: An Odd Couple, 11 January 2001. Cnnfn.com.
71. Shock, David. "AOL-Time Warner: A Conquest, Not a Marriage." *Business Week,* 29 June 2000.
72. Interview.
73. Johnson, Tom; Case, Levin: An Odd Couple, January 11, 2001. Cnnfn.com.
74. Shock, David. "AOL-Time Warner: A Conquest, Not a Marriage." *Business Week,* 29 June 2000.
75. Ibid.
76. Gunther, Marc. "Understanding AOL's Grand Unified Theory of the Media Cosmos," *Fortune,* 8 January 2001.
77. http://www.drudgereport.com.
78. "AOL Buyout of Time Warner: Merger Frenzy Sweeping Corporate America" 14 January 2000. World Socialist Website.
79. Ibid.
80. Orwall, Bruce, "AOL-Time Warner competitors resist me-too deals—for now," *The Wall Street Journal,* 15 December 2000.
81. "Shareholders Approve Vivendi-Seagram Deal," *Bloomberg News,* 5 December 2000.
82. Gecker, Jocelyn: "A French Media Titan" 20 June 2000. The Associated Press—abcnews.com.
83. Gecker, Jocelyn: "A French Media Titan" 20 June 2000. The Associated Press—abcnews.com.
84. Schachter, Ken: "Merger Is Little Threat to AOL Time Warner" 20 June 2000. TechWeb Finance.
85. Ibid.
86. Ibid.
87. Ibid.
88. Viacom corporate website www.viacom.com.
89. "CBS and Viacom to Merge in Biggest Media Deal Ever" 7 September 1999. Fox Market Wire.
90. Ibid.
91. Orwall, Bruce, "AOL-Time Warner competitors resist me-too deals—for now," *The Wall Street Journal,* 15 December 2000.
92. Krigel, Beth Lipton: "Viacom Makes Major Online Push" 23 February 1999. CNET News.com.
93. Ibid.
94. Viacom Press Release from corporate website www.viacom.com
95. "Yahoo: No Rush to Merge" 12 January 2000. www.abcnews.com.
96. Ibid.
97. Ibid.
98. Orwall, Bruce, "AOL-Time Warner competitors resist me-too deals—for now," *The Wall Street Journal,* 15 December 2000.
99. Ibid.
100. NewsCorp corporate website www.newscorp.com.
101. Ibid.
102. Ibid.
103. Orwall, Bruce, "AOL-Time Warner competitors resist me-too deals—for now," *The Wall Street Journal,* 15 December 2000.
104. Ibid.
105. Grover, Ron: "Why DirecTV Will Wind Up in Murdoch's Orbit" 22 January 2001. *BusinessWeek* Online.
106. Ibid.
107. Ibid.
108. Ibid.
109. "Disney's Eisner: 'We Are the Most Profitable'" 8 February 2001. *BusinessWeek* Online
110. Yahoo! Finance Company Profile for Walt Disney Internet Group.
111. Ibid.
112. Walt Disney corporate website.
113. Yahoo! Finance Company Profile for Walt Disney Internet Group
114. "Disney's Eisner: 'We Are the Most Profitable'" 8 February 2001. *BusinessWeek* Online.
115. Ibid.
116. Ewing, Jack. "A New Net Powerhouse?" *BusinessWeek,* 13 November 2000, 47–52.
117. Ibid.
118. Ibid.
119. Ibid.
120. Ewing, Jack. "A New Net Powerhouse?" *BusinessWeek,* 13 November 2000, 47–52.
121. Ibid.
122. Ibid.
123. Ibid.

124. Grice, Corey: "ISP Industry Tryst for Earthlink and MSN?" 12 February 2001. CNET News.com.

125. Earthlink corporate website: www.earthlink.com/about/history/index.html

126. Grice, Corey: "ISP Industry Tryst for Earthlink and MSN?" 12 February 2001. CNET News.com.

127. "Earthlink May Sell AOL's Web Access by June," 13 February 2001. Bloomberg News.

128. Ibid.

129. Grice, Corey: "ISP Industry Tryst for Earthlink and MSN?" 12 February 2001. CNET News.com.

130. Ibid.

131. Ibid.

132. Ibid.

133. Anderson, James A, "Cable: Wired for Growth" Sector Scope, *BusinessWeek* Online.

134. Ibid.

135. Ibid.

136. Ibid.

137. Ibid.

138. Adler, Richard. "Telecommunications Technology in 2009," http://www.naruc.org/Pennindx.htm.

139. Ibid

140. "Talk is cheap via a computer" 3 April 2000. Newshouse News Service.

141. Harris, Wiltshire, & Grannis LLP. "Communications Update," December 2000/January 2001.

142. Ibid.

143. "Long Distance Carriers Should Connect Investors to Profits," 13 June 2000. Standard & Poor's.

144. Harris, Wiltshire, & Grannis LLP "Communications Update," December 2000/January 2001.

145. "Talk is cheap via a computer" April 3, 2000. Newshouse News Service.

146. Chetwynd, Haring, Seiler, Soriano. "Notable Quotables" Tech Report—www.usatoday.com.

147. Plunkett Research, Ltd. www.plunkettresearch.com Overview of the Telecommunications Industry.

148. Ingram, Mike, "World Internet usage grows to 300 million" 15 September 2000. World Socialist Web Site.

149. Plunkett Research, Ltd. www.plunkettresearch.com Overview of the Telecommunications Industry.

150. Kruger, Lennard G. & Gilroy, Angele A.: "Broadband Internet Access: Background and Issues" 28 November 2000. Congressional Research Service Issue Brief.

151. "High Speed Access to Pass Dial-Up in 2005" 22 January 2001. www.cyberatlas.com.

152. "Aware's Perspective on AOL/Time Warner Merger & The Effect It Will Have on the DSL Market" 12 January 2000. www.aware.com.

153. "What is DSL?" copyright 2001. www.00dsl.com.

154. Paonita, Anthony. "DSL or Cable: Which is Better?" *New York Law Journal*, 10 October 2000.

155. Ibid.

156. Ibid.

157. "Aware's Perspective on AOL/Time Warner Merger & The Effect It Will Have on the DSL Market" January 12, 2000. www.aware.com.

158. Paonita, Anthony. "DSL or Cable: Which is Better?" *New York Law Journal*, 10 October 2000.

159. Kruger, Lennard G. & Gilroy, Angele A.: "Broadband Internet Access: Background and Issues" 28 November 2000. Congressional Research Service Issue Brief.

160. Ibid.

161. Ibid.

162. Shook, David: "AOL's Narrow Broadband Vision" 17 January 2001. *BusinessWeek* Online.

163. "The Broadband Edge" www.abcnews.com.

164. Kruger, Lennard G. & Gilroy, Angele A.: "Broadband Internet Access: Background and Issues" 28 November 2000. Congressional Research Service Issue Brief.

165. "The Broadband Edge" www.abcnews.com.

166. AOL Time Warner corporate website.

167. Adler, Richard. "Telecommunications Technology in 2009" http://www.naruc.org/Pennindx.htm.

168. Kruger, Lennard G. & Gilroy, Angele A.: "Broadband Internet Access: Background and Issues" 28 November 2000. Congressional Research Service Issue Brief.

169. Adler, Richard. "Telecommunications Technology in 2009" http://www.naruc.org/Pennindx.htm.

170. Ibid.

171. aoltimewarner.com.

172. aoltimewarner.com.

173. aoltimewarner.com.

Case 4

AT&T: Twenty Years of Change

Dominik Woessner, *The American Graduate School of International Management*

In October 2000, AT&T Corporation (AT&T) announced a sweeping restructuring plan that would break the company up into separate wireless, broadband, business long distance, and consumer long distance companies. This announcement was the culmination of 20 years of change for the company that once dominated virtually all of U.S. telecommunications. AT&T hoped that the restructuring would attract new investors and provide cash to reduce the enormous debt load that had accumulated through various acquisitions. AT&T also announced that it would sell non-strategic assets. The result of the restructuring meant that AT&T businesses, for the third time in twenty years, would be split apart and forced to establish new corporate identities.

Early Years

The company that later became AT&T started in 1875, when Alexander Graham Bell received funding from two financial backers, Gardiner Hubbard and Thomas Sanders, to complete his work on the telephone (see Exhibit 1 for a history of AT&T). The following year, Bell succeeded in his invention of the telephone and earned a patent. In 1877 the three men founded the Bell Telephone Company, and one year later the first telephone exchange opened in New Haven under license from Bell Telephone. Within the following three years, telephone exchanges with licenses from the company were set up in most major cities and towns in the United States.

In 1882 the company, now called American Bell Telephone Company, acquired a majority interest in the Western Electric Company, which became the firm's manufacturing unit. In addition, American Bell acquired most of its licensees across the United States during those

years, which resulted in the company becoming known as the Bell system, or more colloquially as Ma Bell.

The American Telephone and Telegraph Company (AT&T) was incorporated in 1885 as a wholly owned subsidiary of American Bell, with the objective of building and operating a long distance network. Fourteen years later, in 1899, AT&T became the parent company of the Bell system when it acquired the assets of American Bell.

Bell's second patent expired in 1894, which resulted in the incorporation of over 6,000 new telephone companies during the following ten years. Bell Telephone and its licensees were no longer the only companies that could legally operate telephone systems in the United States. With new areas getting wired and other areas getting competition, the number of telephones increased from 285,000 to 3,317,000 during the ten years from 1894–1904. The problem, however, was that there was no interconnection, meaning that subscribers to different telephone companies could not call each other.[1]

The Bell System

In 1907 AT&T's president Theodore Vail formulated the principle that the telephone and its technology would operate most efficiently as a monopoly providing universal service. Initially, the United States government accepted this principle, which led to an agreement in 1913 known as the Kingsbury Commitment. AT&T agreed to connect competitors to its network and divest its controlling interest in Western Union Telegraph.

Several times over the next few decades, federal administrations investigated the U.S. telephone monopoly. The only notable result, however, was an anti-trust lawsuit filed in 1949, alleging company abuses. This led to a settlement in 1956, whereby AT&T agreed to restrict its activities to the regulated business of the national telephone system and government work. But the restriction did not influence the rapid development of the system and its steady progress towards its goal of universal service. The penetration of telephone service into American households increased from 50 percent in 1945 to 90 percent in 1969.

Exhibit 1   History of AT&T

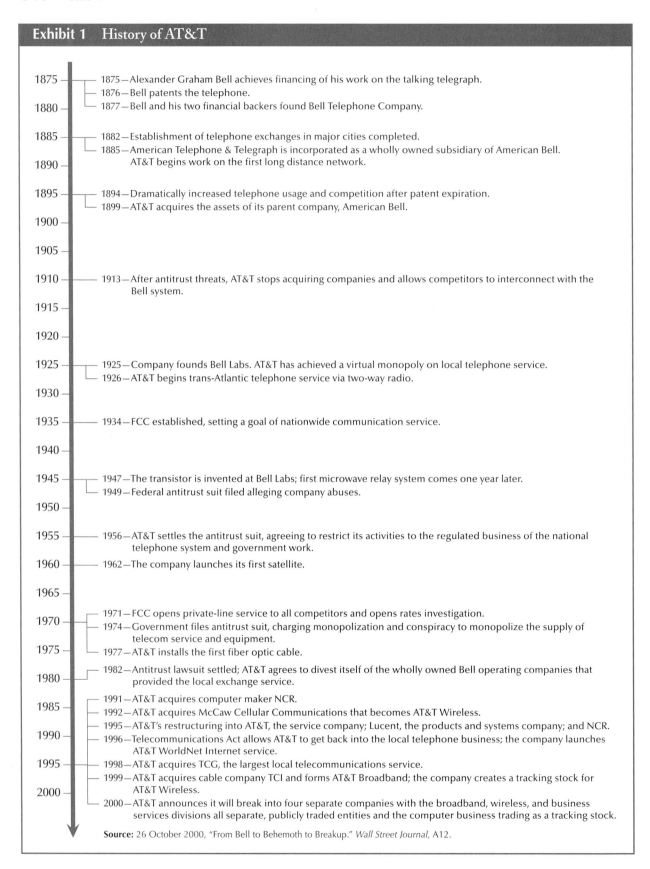

1875 — 1875—Alexander Graham Bell achieves financing of his work on the talking telegraph.
       1876—Bell patents the telephone.
1880 — 1877—Bell and his two financial backers found Bell Telephone Company.

1885 — 1882—Establishment of telephone exchanges in major cities completed.
       1885—American Telephone & Telegraph is incorporated as a wholly owned subsidiary of American Bell.
1890 —   AT&T begins work on the first long distance network.

1895 — 1894—Dramatically increased telephone usage and competition after patent expiration.
       1899—AT&T acquires the assets of its parent company, American Bell.
1900 —

1905 —

1910 — 1913—After antitrust threats, AT&T stops acquiring companies and allows competitors to interconnect with the
             Bell system.
1915 —

1920 —

1925 — 1925—Company founds Bell Labs. AT&T has achieved a virtual monopoly on local telephone service.
       1926—AT&T begins trans-Atlantic telephone service via two-way radio.
1930 —

1935 — 1934—FCC established, setting a goal of nationwide communication service.

1940 —

1945 — 1947—The transistor is invented at Bell Labs; first microwave relay system comes one year later.
       1949—Federal antitrust suit filed alleging company abuses.
1950 —

1955 — 1956—AT&T settles the antitrust suit, agreeing to restrict its activities to the regulated business of the national
             telephone system and government work.
1960 — 1962—The company launches its first satellite.

1965 —

1970 — 1971—FCC opens private-line service to all competitors and opens rates investigation.
       1974—Government files antitrust suit, charging monopolization and conspiracy to monopolize the supply of
             telecom service and equipment.
1975 — 1977—AT&T installs the first fiber optic cable.

1980 — 1982—Antitrust lawsuit settled; AT&T agrees to divest itself of the wholly owned Bell operating companies that
             provided the local exchange service.

1985 — 1991—AT&T acquires computer maker NCR.
       1992—AT&T acquires McCaw Cellular Communications that becomes AT&T Wireless.
       1995—AT&T's restructuring into AT&T, the service company; Lucent, the products and systems company; and NCR.
1990 — 1996—Telecommunications Act allows AT&T to get back into the local telephone business; the company launches
             AT&T WorldNet Internet service.
1995 — 1998—AT&T acquires TCG, the largest local telecommunications service.
       1999—AT&T acquires cable company TCI and forms AT&T Broadband; the company creates a tracking stock for
             AT&T Wireless.
2000 — 2000—AT&T announces it will break into four separate companies with the broadband, wireless, and business
             services divisions all separate, publicly traded entities and the computer business trading as a tracking stock.

Source: 26 October 2000, "From Bell to Behemoth to Breakup." *Wall Street Journal,* A12.

The rapid development of the telecommunications industry was mainly due to the technology developed at AT&T's Bell Telephone Laboratories subsidiary. One of the new technologies, microwave relay systems, provided an alternative to copper wires for long distance telephone transmission in the late 1940s. With the launch of its first communications satellite in 1962, AT&T provided an additional alternative for international communications. Furthermore, the transition to electronic components allowed more powerful and less-expensive customer and network equipment.

As AT&T grew, its culture became more and more rigid. According to one source,

> AT&T's safety from competition also fostered a management culture that ultimately would play a large part in the company's undoing. AT&T's managers saw profit as a way to support and extend the monopoly, not an end in itself. Cost control was an issue less for corporate efficiency than for ensuring that outlays didn't upset the company's regulatory overseers. With customers taken for granted, sales representatives received a straight salary, no commissions, and were warned not to oversell … This culture of control created managers who were averse to risk.[2]

Eventually, the Federal Communications Commission (FCC) signaled its interest in more competition and allowed competitors to use some of Bell Labs' technology and, therefore, competition became established in the general long distance service by the mid-1970s. In 1974 the U.S. government filed an antitrust lawsuit against AT&T, believing that a monopoly was still valid for the local exchanges, but no longer for long distance, manufacturing, and research and development. Competition was deemed appropriate for those segments.

The lawsuit was settled in 1982 when AT&T agreed to divest itself of the wholly owned Bell operating companies that provided local exchange service, creating the "Baby Bells" (see Exhibit 2 for AT&T's share price over the past twenty years). The government, in return, agreed to lift the constraints of the 1956 agreement.[3]

The Divestiture—AT&T and the Regional Bell Operating Companies

The AT&T divestiture took place on January 1, 1984. The Bell System was replaced by a new AT&T and seven operating companies, known as RBOCs (regional Bell operating companies), or Baby Bells. The new AT&T retained $34 billion of the $149.5 billion in assets and 373,000 of its previous 1,009,000 employees. The Bell logo was given to the regional telephone companies. Most significantly, AT&T lost its ability to reach almost every consumer in the United States by its wires and bills. With the divestiture, the "last mile" would be controlled by the RBOCs.

Although the new AT&T could build on great technological and personnel strength, the transition from a regulated monopoly (the Bell System) to a competitive environment required the reinvention of the company as a competitive player and a significant change in corporate culture. In addition, the company had to keep up with emerging technologies, such as fiber optic transmission. Therefore, with the long distance telephone service becoming more competitive, it was inevitable that AT&T's long distance market share would fall. From 1984 to 1996, market share fell from over 90 percent in 1984 to 50 percent in 1996.[4]

In addition to AT&T's long distance service, its manufacturing operations faced increasing challenges during its transition from monopoly to competition. Prior to the divestiture, AT&T purchased most of its equipment from its own manufacturing subsidiary, AT&T Network Systems. Now, AT&T's equipment arm had to compete for business with the now-independent RBOCs. Increasingly, the RBOCs saw AT&T more as a competitor than a partner.

Lastly, the Telecommunications Act of 1996 allowed the regional Bells and other competitors to compete in long distance service. This act increased the pressure on AT&T and the other long distance operators such as Sprint and MCI–WorldCom. The 1996 act also paved the way for the former regional Bells, Verizon Communications,[5] SBC Communications Inc.,[6] Qwest Communications International Inc.,[7] and BellSouth Corp., to become the strategically best-positioned telecommunications firms in the United States (Exhibit 3 shows AT&T's share price trend in comparison with the regional Bell operating companies; Exhibit 4 shows market capitalization for AT&T and the RBOCs immediately after the 1984 divestiture and in 2000). Because the regional Bells and their descendants controlled local networks, it had proved very difficult for new operators to succeed. In 2001 AT&T was lobbying state regulators to break the regional Bells into two companies: one that would sell services such as basic dial tone and DSL, and another that would lease the network to both competitors and to the incumbent local phone company. The regional Bells countered this position by arguing that they should not have to provide access to their network at a discounted price.

Exhibit 2   AT&T Share Prices

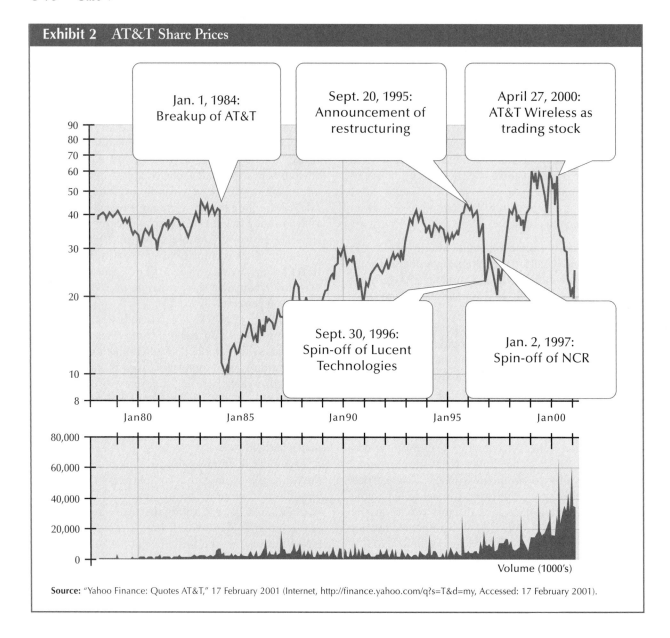

Source: "Yahoo Finance: Quotes AT&T," 17 February 2001 (Internet, http://finance.yahoo.com/q?s=T&d=my, Accessed: 17 February 2001).

AT&T's Strategy after the Divestiture

In 1984 AT&T was a firm without a local network into offices and homes. Instead of building its own network to match the regional Bells' facilities, AT&T had to negotiate agreements with the regional Bells to lease parts of their networks and resell the service to its own customers. But AT&T realized that, eventually, given the high fees for leased access, the company would have to find news ways of reaching the last mile. Options investigated included fixed wireless technology and cable television lines. Although AT&T would become the biggest cable provider, universal access to all American households, a privilege held before 1984,[8] was lost forever.

One result of the 1984 divestiture agreement was that AT&T's business activities were no longer restricted to the regulated business of the national telephone system and government work. Although AT&T was steadily losing market share after 1984, the company continued to generate enormous positive cash flows. A decision was made to diversify away from a reliance on telecom service and equipment manufacturing. AT&T acquired several companies in the early 1990s. In 1991 AT&T acquired computer maker NCR Corp. for $7.4 billion in a hostile takeover. The rationale for the acquisition was

Exhibit 3   Industry Stock Price Development, AT&T Corporation

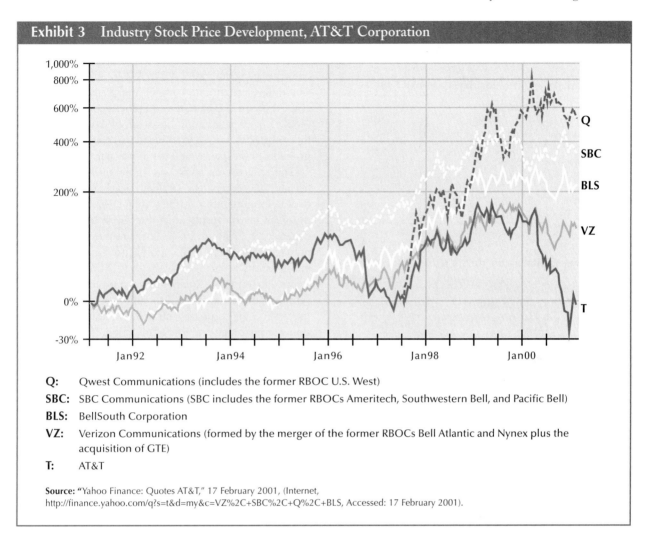

Q: Qwest Communications (includes the former RBOC U.S. West)

SBC: SBC Communications (SBC includes the former RBOCs Ameritech, Southwestern Bell, and Pacific Bell)

BLS: BellSouth Corporation

VZ: Verizon Communications (formed by the merger of the former RBOCs Bell Atlantic and Nynex plus the acquisition of GTE)

T: AT&T

Source: "Yahoo Finance: Quotes AT&T," 17 February 2001, (Internet, http://finance.yahoo.com/q?s=t&d=my&c=VZ%2C+SBC%2C+Q%2C+BLS, Accessed: 17 February 2001).

that with the convergence of communications and computing, AT&T could link these different businesses and capture unique synergies.[9] In a 1994 acquisition, AT&T acquired the then U.S. leader in the wireless business, McCaw Cellular Communications Inc., for $11.5 billion.[10] The McCaw deal established AT&T as a leading force in the fast-growing wireless telecommunications industry and gave the company direct access to consumers for the first time in a decade.[11]

The Restructuring—Lucent and NCR Spin-offs

AT&T's strategy became increasingly problematic as the 1990s progressed. There were few synergies between the telecom operator and manufacturing businesses. As well, the two businesses became obstacles to each other's growth. Both businesses were becoming more complex

and more global, leading to questions about the viability of AT&T as a single diversified corporation.

The result was a second divestiture involving AT&T, although this time it was voluntary and not mandated by the government. In addition to the changing telecom environment and increasing deregulation, problems at the company's NCR computer subsidiary were a catalyst for the restructuring of AT&T into three companies: a systems and equipment company (which became Lucent Technologies), a computer company (NCR), and a communications services company (which remained AT&T).[12, 13]

In January 1996 AT&T announced that a post-tax charge of approximately $4 billion was necessary to cover the costs of implementing the restructuring. The expenses included the elimination of nearly 40,000 jobs over three years, with about 70 percent completed by the end of 1996. The charge reduced fourth quarter net income by about

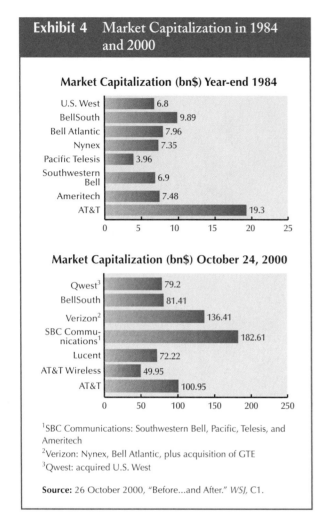

Exhibit 4   Market Capitalization in 1984 and 2000

Market Capitalization (bn$) Year-end 1984

U.S. West	6.8
BellSouth	9.89
Bell Atlantic	7.96
Nynex	7.35
Pacific Telesis	3.96
Southwestern Bell	6.9
Ameritech	7.48
AT&T	19.3

Market Capitalization (bn$) October 24, 2000

Qwest[3]	79.2
BellSouth	81.41
Verizon[2]	136.41
SBC Communications[1]	182.61
Lucent	72.22
AT&T Wireless	49.95
AT&T	100.95

[1]SBC Communications: Southwestern Bell, Pacific, Telesis, and Ameritech

[2]Verizon: Nynex, Bell Atlantic, plus acquisition of GTE

[3]Qwest: acquired U.S. West

Source: 26 October 2000, "Before…and After." *WSJ*, C1.

$2.50 a share, with earnings for the first nine months of 1995 at about $1.77 per share (see Exhibit 2).

AT&T completed its spin-off of Lucent Technologies on September 30, 1996, by providing its shareholders with 525 million shares of the new company. The spin-off included its telecom network, switching and transmission equipment business, as well as its famous Bell Labs. The new company had revenue totaling about $20 billion and 125,000 employees.[14]

As mentioned above, the spin-off was necessary because of the absence of synergies across AT&T's business and because of the emergence of new competitors. An analyst described AT&T's dilemma:

> Not too many years ago, AT&T had two global competitors: MCI Communications and Sprint. Today you'd be hard pressed to find any telecom service company not competing with AT&T.

The new telecom competitors, including cable firms, RBOCs, and mobile service companies, had many options from whom to buy their equipment. By a company's placing an order with AT&T, AT&T not only would have insight into competitors' plans, AT&T could also use the profits from the equipment contracts against them. However, after the spin-off of Lucent removed these obstacles, Lucent was able to win contracts it would probably never have won when it was part of AT&T.[15]

The spin-off of NCR was more difficult to digest because the company's strategy clearly failed. AT&T's decade-long ambition to be a major force in the computer industry resulted in the $7.4 billion hostile takeover of NCR in 1991. The computer subsidiary's management was left alone to operate semi-autonomously for two years, but AT&T eventually stepped in as the subsidiary's losses mounted. This intervention, however, decreased the unit's performance even more, since the corporate culture clash resulted in confusion, complacency, and loss of direction. In addition, the commitment to becoming one of the world's top three PC makers resulted in a product line and an expense structure that was out of line with market demand. From 1993 to 1996, the computer unit lost about $5.9 billion and forced AT&T to inject about $2.8 billion into the business. The NCR spin-off was done by distributing 101.4 million NCR shares on December 31, 1996. The spin-off valued NCR at $3.96 billion, which meant that AT&T had lost about $10 billion in its NCR debacle.[16]

Armstrong's Vision

Michael Armstrong was appointed Chairman and CEO of AT&T in November 1997. Prior to joining AT&T, Armstrong was CEO of Hughes Electronics Corp. Armstrong wrote in the 1998 Annual Report:

> We're transforming AT&T from a long distance company to an "any-distance" company. From a company that handles mostly voice calls to a company that connects you to information in any form that is useful to you—voice, data, and video. From a primarily domestic company to a truly global company.[17]

Following Armstrong's appointment, AT&T began to implement the vision of a global company by integrating the cable, wireless, and long distance businesses. In January 1998 the company announced a refocused strategy and cost-cutting measures to make AT&T the low-cost provider in the communications industry. The company planned to achieve a significant amount of the savings by cutting the workforce in its long distance business by 15,000 to 18,000 people over the following two years and by offering a voluntary retirement program for managers.[18]

In addition, AT&T initiated a series of joint ventures and acquisitions (see Exhibit 5 for major AT&T deals 1998–2000). One goal was to broaden the company's scope to areas such as data networking services, digital voice encryption, broadband cable telephony, and video telephony. The other goal was to increase AT&T's global reach.[19]

Transforming AT&T

In 1998 AT&T acquired Teleport Communications Group (TCG) for $11.5 billion. TCG was the leading local telecommunication service provider for business customers in the United States. TCG was an attractive target for AT&T, because it provided networks that were an alternative to those of the regional bells. The TCG acquisition was intended to provide AT&T with the ability to offer high-speed service to businesses in major U.S. urban areas. The acquisition of TCG allowed AT&T to save tens of millions of dollars in access charges previously paid to connect its customers to the Baby Bells' networks.

In support of the TCG acquisition, AT&T argued that the incentive was to acquire access to local business customers and provide these customers with a complete communications solution by integrating TCG's local services with AT&T's end-to-end telecommunications services packages for business customers. Within two years, however, almost all of TCG's former top executives had left the company, many because they missed the entrepreneurial spirit that existed at TCG prior to the acquisition.

The biggest steps made towards the vision of an integrated cable, wireless, and long distance company were undertaken in 1999 and 2000. In 1999 AT&T acquired Telecommunications, Inc. (TCI), the second largest cable company in the United States, for $55 billion. Armstrong said at the time:

> The closing of the merger is a major step forward in the transformation of AT&T from a long distance into an "any distance" company.[20]

After the TCI deal was announced, AT&T's stock fell about 12 percent from the day before the announcement. AT&T next completed an acquisition of MediaOne, a Denver-based cable operator, in a cash and stock transaction valued at approximately $56 billion. The two cable acquisitions resulted in AT&T becoming the leading cable television operator in the nation. The FCC approved the deal on June 15, 2000, but insisted that AT&T would have to undergo a serious revamping within one year. The FCC gave AT&T three choices: divest MediaOne's 25 percent stake in Time Warner

Exhibit 5   AT&T Deals

1998

July 24—Acquisition of Teleport Communications Group Inc. (TCG) for $11.5 billion.

July 26—AT&T and British Telecom announced the creation of a global venture equally owned by the two companies.

1999

February 1—AT&T announced the formation of a joint venture with Time Warner to offer AT&T's broadband cable telephony service to residential and small business customers over Time Warner's existing cable television systems in 33 states.

March—Merger with Tele-Communications Inc. (TCI) worth 37.3 billion. TCI becomes AT&T's newest business unit: AT&T Broadband & Internet Services.

May—AT&T completed its acquisition of the IBM Global Network business. AT&T agreed to acquire the IBM Global Network business for $5 billion in cash in December 1998. AT&T renamed the business AT&T Global Network Services.

June 1—AT&T Canada Corp. merged with MetroNet Communications Corp.

August—AT&T acquired Honolulu Cellular Telephone Company from BellSouth.

August—AT&T finalized transactions with British Telecommunications to jointly acquire a 33% equity stake in Rogers Cantel Mobile Communications, Inc. for an aggregate of approximately $934 million.

2000

February—AT&T and Dobson Communications Corporation completed the acquisition of American Cellular Corporation for approx. $2.4 billion, through a newly created joint venture.

March 28—AT&T acquired GRC International, Inc. for $15.00 per share.

April 10—AT&T, through its subsidiary Liberty Media Group, acquired 100% of Four Media's issued and outstanding common stock by converting it into the right to receive 0.16129 of a share of AT&T's Class A Liberty Media Group Stock and $6.25 in cash.

June—AT&T acquired Wireless One Network L.P.

June 9—AT&T's subsidiary Liberty Media Corp. acquired Ascent Entertainment Group, Inc. for $15.25 per share.

June 15—AT&T completed a merger with MediaOne in a cash and stock transaction valued at approximately $56 billion. AT&T shares had an aggregate market value of approximately $21 billion and cash payments totaled approximately $24 billion. In addition, the transaction included debt and other obligations of MediaOne totaling approximately $11 billion.

July—AT&T closed its purchase of the remaining partnership interests in the Bay Area Cellular Telephone Company, a joint partnership of AT&T Wireless and Vodaphone/Airtouch.

August—AT&T completed its investment of $1.4 billion in Net2Phone giving AT&T a 39% voting stake and a 32% economic stake in Net2Phone for a total cash investment of approximately $1.4 billion.

Source: "Company Data Report: AT&T Corp.," (Internet, http://www.fisonline.com/mds/find.csv, Accessed: 21 March 2001).

Entertainment; sell Liberty Media Group, a minority stake in Rainbow Media Holdings Inc. and MediaOne's programming networks; or sell 9.7 million cable subscribers, which was more than half of the company's current subscribers. These requirements didn't tarnish Armstrong's enthusiasm for the deal:

> The combination of AT&T and MediaOne means that far more American consumers will have a real choice and lower prices in local phone service, faster Internet access, and better cable TV. By year-end, most of our networks will be upgraded, making analog and digital video, high-speed Internet access, cable telephony and interactive television available to more of our customers.[21]

The acquisition of the cable Internet and TV services led to the creation of AT&T's newest division: AT&T Broadband and Internet Services. In addition, the deals would again give the company access to local phone services and (theoretically, since there were questions about technological viability) positioned AT&T as a one-stop shop for a wide range of communications services. AT&T was, in a sense, back in the position it was in 1984, when AT&T was broken up.[22]

Despite Armstrong's positive statements, two crucial issues had to be solved. One, AT&T had to accelerate cable system upgrades in order to introduce digital and telephony services to cable customers. Two, AT&T had to succeed in negotiations with other cable operators to achieve its goal of offering branded telephony coverage to at least 60 percent of U.S. homes.[23, 24] In anticipation of succeeding with these tasks, AT&T forecasted cable telephony revenues of $6 billion within five years. To achieve this goal, the company would require a compounded annual growth rate of 111 percent.[25]

Failed Strategy

In total, Armstrong's vision of transforming AT&T into a global company offering TV, local and long distance telephone services, and Internet services resulted in investments of $115 billion in cable systems. Unfortunately, the reality of creating the vision was much more difficult than Armstrong anticipated. The idea of providing an array of communications services, most of them delivered digitally by cable, proved to be harder than expected because of the expensive and time-consuming process of upgrading cable lines to make them suitable for voice phone calls. By 2001 AT&T was only able to upgrade about 65 percent of the cable lines within its cable network, which matched only about one-fourth of AT&T's 60 million total customer base. In doing the upgrade, AT&T spent as much as $5 billion and moved aggressively to secure new customers. Had the firm waited, newer Internet technologies would have substantially lowered the upgrade cost. According to analysts, AT&T was spending about $1,200 to add a phone subscriber to the cable network. By 2001 new technologies had lowered the cost of converting cable to allow phone service to about $700 per subscriber. The majority of cable companies (with the exception of AT&T and Cox Communications) decided to wait for cable phone technologies to mature before investing significant sums on upgrades. In addition, AT&T did not succeed in striking a deal with other cable operators to lease their lines, which was necessary in order to broaden AT&T's cable telephony customer base. Although AT&T announced a joint venture with Time Warner cable business in February 1999, the two companies failed to reach an agreement.[26]

The result was that AT&T's prediction of millions of cable telephony customers by the end of 2001 had to be downgraded to no more than 650,000, the number the company should have achieved by the end of 2000.[27] Coupled with the failure to build the cable telephony business, AT&T's core long distance business was shrinking and many analysts expected the price of long distance voice service to drop to nearly zero. The long distance business, which made up about 80 percent of AT&T's revenues in 1997, was projected to decrease to only 35 percent of revenues by the end of 2002. Moreover, the company had not succeeded in entering local phone service competition with the regional Bells. In addition, the acquisitions of TCI and MediaOne left the company with $64 billion in debt, making AT&T one of the industry's most indebted companies and leaving the company's stock price far behind its competitors (see Exhibit 3).[28] The industry consensus was that AT&T overpaid for MediaOne because of concerns that rivals might acquire the company. As well, AT&T's expectations that it could easily sell some of MediaOne's stakes in other companies proved to be unfounded.

Two areas of the business that were growing were AT&T Wireless, expected to grow by about 30 percent in 2000, and AT&T's high-speed services, sold under the brand Excite@Home, which was gaining customers rapidly.

Finally, AT&T failed in another area. In 1997 AT&T entered the Internet service provider business with WorldNet. In a few months, the company attracted about a million customers. At the time, WorldNet was growing faster than America Online. When sales began to slow,

AT&T chose not to make the marketing investments necessary to maintain growth rates. By late 2000 WorldNet had about two million customers and America Online had twenty-one million.

Disappointing Results

AT&T's third quarter results for 2000 confirmed an overall downward trend. Earnings in the Business Services division grew less than expected and revenue in the consumer long distance business fell 11 percent. AT&T Broadband reported revenue growth of 10.8 percent, less than the 13 percent forecasted by analysts. As mentioned earlier, the only bright spot was AT&T Wireless, which grew 37 percent, compared to the same period one year before. However, AT&T's revenues, totaling $16.97 billion, increased only slightly by 3.7 percent. In addition, the company's third quarter earnings of 38 cents per diluted share were down 24 percent compared to the same period a year ago (see Exhibits 6 and 7 for 2000 financial results).

Michael Armstrong blamed falling long distance prices for the company's disappointing performance and subsequently lowered the company's earnings projections for the fourth quarter of 2000 as well as the whole year. Moreover, the company said that it will review its dividend policy by the end of the year and might, for the first time ever, cut its dividend of currently $3.38 billion a year, or 88 cents a share. According to the company, AT&T needed to conserve cash to pay down debt that carried an interest expense of $2.1 billion for the first three quarters ($3.2 billion for the year

2000). On top of all the negative financial news, Moody's Investor Service, the debt rating company, put AT&T's ratings on review.[29]

Breakup Plans

> It's hard to escape the feeling that a corporate funeral took place today. It's really the end of an icon and no matter how they try to put a positive spin on it, it's the death of a corporate giant.
> Ken McGee, Analyst Gartner Group

On October 25, 2000, AT&T announced a plan to split the company into four parts: AT&T Broad-band, AT&T Wireless, AT&T Business Services, and AT&T Consumer Services (see Exhibit 8 for an overview of the planned restructuring). Under the breakup plan, the parent company would own the Business Services and Consumer Services (long distance) units. A tracking stock[30] would be introduced for the Consumer Services unit at the end of 2001. AT&T's 85 percent stake in AT&T Wireless, already traded as a tracking stock, would be converted into a common stock and spun off in mid-2001. Finally, the cable business was to be separated as a tracking stock, followed by an IPO in 2002.

The announced intent of the breakup was to give the individual companies more flexibility in raising money for repaying debt or for acquisitions. As well, the breakup was designed to boost the company's stock price by separating the various divisions into more easily understood stand-alone businesses (see Exhibit 9 for a comparison of AT&T's share price and three industry sector share price

Exhibit 6 AT&T Income Statement				
	12/31/2000	12/31/1999	Variance	%
Net sales	$65,981,000	$62,391,000	$3,590,000	5.75
Cost of revenue	31,105,000	29,071,000	2,034,000	7.00
Gross profit	34,876,000	33,320,000	1,556,000	4.67
Depreciation and amortization	10,267,000	7,439,000	2,828,000	38.02
Interest expense	3,183,000	1,651,000	1,532,000	92.79
Income tax expense	3,342,000	3,257,000	85,000	2.61
Income from con't operation	4,669,000	3,428,000	1,241,000	36.20
Net income	4,669,000	3,428,000	1,241,000	36.20
EPS—con't oprs	0.890	1.770	(0.880)	(49.72)
EPS—net income	0.890	1.770	(0.880)	(49.72)
EPS—from con't oprs—diluted	0.880	1.740	(0.860)	(49.43)
EPS—net income—diluted	0.880	1.740	(0.860)	(49.43)

Source: "Company Data Report: AT&T Corp.," 2001 (Internet, http://www.fisonline.com/mds/find.csv, Accessed: 21 March 2001).

Exhibit 7   AT&T Balance Sheet

	12/31/2000	12/31/1999	Variance	%
Cash and cash equivalents	$ 2,228,000	$ 1,024,000	$ 1,204,000	117.58
Net receivables—receivables, net	13,659,000	11,740,000	1,919,000	16.35
Inventories	4,074,000	3,633,000	441,000	12.14
Other current assets	0	0	0	0.00
Total current assets	17,087,000	13,884,000	3,203,000	23.07
Long-term investments	68,551,000	57,826,000	10,725,000	18.55
Fixed assets	51,161,000	39,618,000	11,543,000	29.14
Other assets	122,511,000	71,962,000	50,549,000	70.24
Total assets	242,223,000	169,406,000	72,817,000	42.98
Accounts payable	6,455,000	6,771,000	(316,000)	(4.67)
Current long-term debt	31,947,000	12,633,000	19,314,000	152.89
Other current liabilities	12,465,000	8,803,000	3,662,000	41.60
Total current liabilities	50,867,000	28,207,000	22,660,000	80.33
Total long-term debt	33,092,000	21,591,000	11,501,000	53.27
Total liabilities	139,025,000	90,479,000	48,546,000	53.65
Preferred stock	0	0	0	0.00
Total common equity	103,198,000	78,927,000	24,271,000	30.75
Total liabilities and equity	242,223,000	169,406,000	72,817,000	42.98

Source: "Company Data Report: AT&T Corp.," 2001 (Internet, http://www.fisonline.com/mds/find.csv, Accessed: 21 March 2001).

graphs). However, given AT&T's market capitalization of about $90 billion excluding debt and the company's stake in AT&T Wireless, which accounted for about half the value, the combined equity value of the remaining businesses was only $45 billion.[31] Given the disappointing performance of these divisions, few analysts expected that valuations would be higher just because they were managed as separate businesses.

Notes

1. "About AT&T: Origins," 28 February 2001 [Internet: http://www.att.com/history/history1.html, Accessed: 28 February 2001].
2. Cynthia Crossen, Deborah Solomon, 26 October 2000, "AT&T takes on a humbler role," *WSJ*, p. A12.
3. "About AT&T: The Bell System," 28 February 2001 [Internet, http://www.att.com/history/history3.html, Accessed: 28 February 2001].
4. "About AT&T: Post-Divesture AT&T," 28 February 2001 [Internet, http://www.att.com/history/history4.html, Accessed: 28 February 2001].
5. Verizon: Nynex, Bell Atlantic, plus acquisition of GTE.
6. SBC Communications: Southwestern Bell, Pacific, Telesis and Ameritech.
7. Qwest: Acquired U.S. West.
8. Crossen and Solomon, 2000.
9. Acquisition by converting 71.4 million shares of NCR common stock into approximately 203 million shares of AT&T's common stock as well as assuming and converting 2.9 million NCR stock options.
10. Acquisition of McCaw by converting 197.5 million shares of McCaw common stock into shares of AT&T common stock as well as assuming and converting 11.3 million McCaw stock options.
11. "About AT&T: Post-Divesture AT&T," 28 February 2001, [Internet, http://www.att.com/history/history4.html, Accessed: 28 February 2001].
12. "About AT&T: Post-Divesture AT&T," 28 February 2001 [Internet, http://www.att.com/history/history4.html, Accessed: 28 February 2001].
13. In addition to the restructuring into three publicly traded companies, AT&T sold its 86 percent interest in AT&T Capital, a diversified equipment leasing and finance company providing financing support for AT&T equipment sales.
14. "Company Data Report: AT&T Corp.," 2001 [Internet, http://www.fisonline.com/mds/find.csv, Accessed: 21 March 2001].
15. Brian Deagon, 26 September 1996, "Lucent, free from AT&T, finds room to be nimble," *Investor's Business Daily*, p. A8.
16. "Spinoff Sets NCR's Value at $3.96 Billion," 17 December 1996, *New York Times (National Edition)*, p. C18.
17. "Annual Reports & SEC Filings: Annual reports," 1999 [Internet, http://www.att.com/ar-1998/shareowners/, Accessed: 26 March 2001].
18. "Company Data Report: AT&T Corp.," 2001 [Internet, http://www.fisonline.com/mds/find.csv, Accessed: 21 March 2001].
19. In 1998 AT&T announced Concert, a Joint Venture with British Telecom, which combined the two company's trans-border assets and operations. The Joint Venture included their existing international networks, all of their international traffic, all of their trans-border products for business customers, and AT&T and BT's multinational accounts in selected industry sectors.
20. Sylvia Dennis, 9 March 1999, "AT&T Closes TCI Merger/Acquisition," *Newsbytes News Network*.
21. Brian Krebs, 15 June 2000, "AT&T Completes MediaOne Purchase," *Newsbytes News Network*.
22. Sylvia Dennis, 9 March 1999, "AT&T Closes TCI Merger/Acquisition," *Newsbytes News Network*.
23. Long-term agreements were sought with Time Warner Cable, Comcast Corp., Cox Communications, Cablevision Systems, and other cable operators.
24. Diane Mermigas, 15 March 1999, "The old TCI meets the new: Hindery ponders future as AT&T," *Electronic Media*, p. 1 ff.
25. Tom Kerver, Charles Paikert, 14 June 1999, "Now Comes the Really Hard Part: Execution," *CableVision* 23 (20), p. 27 f.
26. The joint venture was supposed to offer AT&T branded cable telephony service to residential and small-business customers over Time Warner's existing cable

Exhibit 8   Restructuring Plan

	AT&T Broadband	AT&T Wireless	AT&T Business Services	AT&T Consumer Services
Plans	Tracking stock for summer of 2001 and independent stock in 2002	Spin-off stake in current tracking stock, forming common stock by mid 2001	Will be the parent company and legally own the AT&T brand name	AT&T tracking stock by third quarter 2001
Offerings	Video, cable telephony, pay-TV, high-speed Internet access, and video-on-demand; will assume AT&T's interest in Excite@Home	Mobile phones, calling plans and data services to individuals, businesses and government agencies	Long distance calling, Internet hosting, and data networking to corporate customers	Residential long distance service and dial-up and DSL-based Internet access
Strengths	Nation's largest cable-TV company	Invented "one rate" calling plan; many business customers	Still the largest phone service provider to corporations	Reputation of reliability, loyal base of long-time customers
Weaknesses	Systems need upgrading, incompatible billing systems	Rising competition in national networks, one-rate plans	Facing growing competition; sales-force problems	Revenue gains drying up as long distance price plummets
Major Competitors	Time Warner, Charter Communications, Cox, Comcast	Verizon, Sprint PCS, Cingular (BellSouth-SBC joint venture)	Worldcom, Sprint, Qwest	Worldcom, Sprint, Verizon, SBC
Headquarters	Englewood, Colo.	Redmond, Wash.	Basking Ridge, N.J.	Basking Ridge, N.J.
Current Head	Daniel E. Somers, president	John D. Zeglis, CEO	Richard R. Roscitt, president	Robert Aquilina, Howard McNally, co-presidents
Employees	37,000	18,260	38,000	18,000
Subscribers	16.1 million	12.6 million	About six million	60 million

Source: "Four for the Future," 26 October 2000, *WSJ*, B1.

television systems in 33 states. "Company Data Report: AT&T Corp.," 2001 [Internet, http://www.fisonline.com/mds/find.csv, Accessed: 21 March 2001].

27. Leslie Cauley, 18 October 2000, "Armstrong's Vision of AT&T Cable Empire Unravels on the Ground," *WSJ*, p. A1.

28. Richard Waters, 28 February 2001, "Ma Bell starts to empty nest in effort to cut debts," *Financial Times*, p. 20.

29. Deborah Solomon, Nikhil Deogun, 26 October 2000, "AT&T: Disconnected," *WSJ*, p. B1.

30. Tracking stocks are designed to represent the results of a unit without actually owning the underlying assets of the operation.

31. Deborah Solomon, Nikhil Deogun, 26 October 2000, "AT&T splits amid ongoing business declines," *WSJ*, p. B4.

Exhibit 9   AT&T Share Price vs. Industry Sector Share Price Performance

AT&T

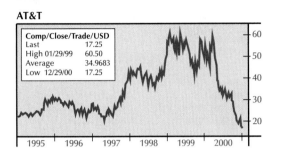

Comp/Close/Trade/USD	
Last	17.25
High 01/29/99	60.50
Average	34.9683
Low 12/29/00	17.25

DJUSFC (Dow Jones U.S. Fixed Line Communication)

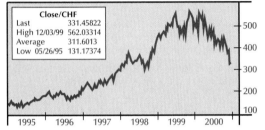

Close/CHF	
Last	331.45822
High 12/03/99	562.03314
Average	311.6013
Low 05/26/95	131.17374

DJUSWC (Dow Jones U.S. Wireless Communication)

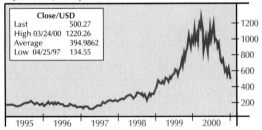

Close/USD	
Last	500.27
High 03/24/00	1220.26
Average	394.9862
Low 04/25/97	134.55

BBCI (Bloomberg Broadcasting and Cable Index)

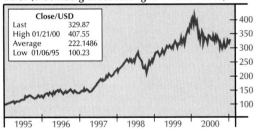

Close/USD	
Last	329.87
High 01/21/00	407.55
Average	222.1486
Low 01/06/95	100.23

Source: Bloomberg

Case 5

Beijing Jeep Co. and the WTO

Michael N. Young and Justin Tan, *The University of Western Ontario*

In May of 2000, the Beijing Jeep Corporation, Ltd. (BJC) faced one of the most challenging periods of its relatively short, tumultuous history. Founded in China in 1984, BJC was a pioneer in the Chinese automotive industry. It was one of the first joint ventures between an American company and a Chinese enterprise. At its initial founding, it was hailed with great fanfare by the American media as a potential saviour of the American automobile industry, which at that time was being battered by Japanese competition. This was to be a "beachhead" by which the Americans could access the Asian market and beat the Japanese on their own turf. Early in its operations, BJC was given preferential treatment on tariffs and foreign exchange. The company had also spent many years cultivating relationships with senior government officials—what the Chinese refer to as *guanxi*—to help it achieve its objectives. And since over 40 percent of its product's content was produced in China, BJC had operated as a local manufacturer under heavy protection from imports for all of its short life.[1]

All of this appeared to be on the brink of changing. Trade negotiators for the United States and the People's Republic of China had reached an agreement the previous November after 13 years of on-again-off-again negotiations, where they announced the agreement of terms for China's entry into the World Trade Organization (WTO). Although the Chinese authorities still needed the approval of the major European countries of the WTO, the blessing of the U.S. negotiating team was seen as the major hurdle. Now that the hurdle had been cleared, it meant that China's entry was probably just a matter of time. The terms of the agreement called for a steep reduction in tariffs for imported automobiles from nearly 100 percent to 25 percent by 2006.[2] This would lower the entry barriers to the Chinese automotive industry in which BJC already competed. However, the news was not all bad for BJC, for it meant BJC would pay lower tariffs on components of its Jeep Cherokees that were imported from the United States. Still, these lower tariffs were not enough to offset the potential flood of imported vehicles that could pose serious competition for BJC. As one analyst for the Chinese auto industry stated: "The entire auto industry is under attack from the WTO." This was in addition to the loss of market share and falling profits of the previous three years.

To make matters worse, the more formidable of BJC's two partners, DaimlerChrysler, was beset with its own problems and was in no position to assist BJC. DaimlerChrysler was the world's third largest car company. It had come into existence a little over a year earlier when Daimler Benz of Germany merged with the Chrysler Corporation of the United States. This international merger had created a whole host of unforeseen integration problems, and the company was preoccupied with sorting out its own affairs.[3] Thus, on the threshold of the 21st century, BJC was beset with unprecedented challenges that appeared to threaten its very survival.

Beijing Jeep's History

A British writer declared more than 150 years ago: "If only we could persuade every person in China to lengthen his shirt tails by a foot, we could keep the mills of Lancashire working 'round the clock."[4] In the early 1980s, American Motors Corporation (AMC), along with other foreign enterprises, wished to tap into the vast Chinese Market. Todd Clare, AMC's vice-president (VP) for international operations who directed the China operation, stated that the volume of cars sold in the United States was stable at about 15 million a year. The Western European market was also saturated. Thus, in the United States or Western Europe, one could sell more cars only by stealing another firm's market share—a "zero sum" game. Latin America's economies were showing little promise, and Africa's economies were worse. Yet China's market, with over a billion people, had been largely unexplored. The potential seemed enormous, for China covered about 6.5 percent of the world's land mass and was home to one-fifth of the world's population.[5]

Thus, AMC initiated the pioneering Sino-American joint venture with Beijing Automotive Works (BAW) shortly after China opened its doors in 1978 under the economic reforms of the late paramount leader Deng Xiaoping. At this time, the PRC was attracting worldwide attention because of its large potential market, low labor cost, newly introduced economic reforms, and its strategic location. AMC was not alone; Mercedes-Benz, Fiat, British Leyland, Volkswagen, and Ford, following the lead of Japanese companies such as Toyota, Nissan, Mitsubishi, and Daihatsu, soon sent emissaries to evaluate business prospects in China. In May 1983, after four years of negotiations, AMC and the Beijing Automotive Works agreed to form a joint venture, the Beijing Jeep Corporation Limited (BJC), to produce jeeps in the Chinese capital city of Beijing.

The deal was a landmark. It was the largest manufacturing agreement up to that time between a foreign corporation and a Chinese enterprise. AMC would own a 31.35 percent stake by contributing US$8 million in cash and another US$8 million in technology. The Chinese agreed to put up the equivalent of US$35 million in cash and assets for 68.65 percent of the new company. The board of directors of BJC would consist of seven Chinese members and four Americans. For the first three years, an American would hold the title of president and CEO, and then the job would alternate between the Chinese and Americans. The American media seemed pleased with the deal.[6] China was still seen as a land of limitless potential and serious obstacles to profitability were often overlooked. Although AMC had reported major losses for the three years before the deal, investors brushed that aside; AMC's stock increased 40 percent within two weeks of the announcement. At a press conference, Joseph E. Cappy, AMC's executive vice-president, said AMC would reinvest profits to increase AMC's equity share to 49 percent. "For American Motors, [Beijing Jeep] has meant not only an entry into the Chinese market, but the establishment of a strategic manufacturing base in the Pacific rim of Asia," Cappy said.[7]

The euphoria of both sides soon gave way to reality as the two sides attempted to get down to the business of producing automobiles. First of all, bringing the two sides together was not an easy task, because of cultural differences. In addition, the two sides did not share the same goals. The Chinese hoped to assimilate the sophisticated technology and eventually rank among the world's most advanced auto producers, while the Americans hoped to establish a base in Asia that would enable them to manufacture cars at low cost and compete in this growing region.[8] Also, the Americans learned that although the deal was signed, the "real" negotiations had just begun. Chinese business people were much more accustomed to doing business based on personal relationships and the charisma of business leaders, and they tended to view contracts nonchalantly. The Americans on the other hand viewed contracts as binding, and put much less emphasis on the aspects of personality in business.[9]

After the venture started in January 1984, the two sides disagreed over the product to be produced. According to the initial agreement, BJC was to continue manufacturing the old BJ series (based on a Soviet version of the American Second World War Jeep) while developing a new generation of Jeeps. The Americans wanted the new product to be similar to AMC's existing line of jeeps, but the Chinese wanted a military jeep for the army, historically BAW's most important customer. The army wanted a four-door vehicle with a removable top so that soldiers could open fire from inside the car and quickly hop in and out. Such a vehicle could not be designed based on AMC's existing jeeps, and developing the vehicle would cost at least US$700 million. Neither China nor AMC had that kind of money. So AMC officials tried to convince the Chinese to assemble AMC's newest product—the Jeep Cherokee—from parts kits imported from the United States. The Chinese partners reluctantly agreed. Thus, AMC switched its objective from "making money selling cars" to "making money selling kits." But a new problem emerged: Where would BJC obtain the foreign exchange for the kits? Whenever large-scale foreign exchange was conducted, a special license was required. BJC had not formally cleared this with the Chinese government.

Thus, later in 1985, AMC had hundreds of Cherokee kits in the United States ready to ship to China, but BJC had trouble getting a government import license and no hard currency to pay for the kits. Moreover, housing costs for AMC's staff rose 38 percent when luxury hotels increased their rates. BJC was virtually broke, and the plant was shut down for two months in early 1986.[10] Don St. Pierre, then BJC's American president, appealed to the top Chinese leaders. It took special intervention by then-Premier Zhao Ziyang. Large loans, new capital funds and foreign exchange were provided under a special, confidential agreement. BJC was also given preferential import tariffs and was given special permission to convert AMC's share of dividends into U.S. dollars and send them back to the United States. In return, the company was expected to spread good news worldwide about China. Chinese officials held BJC up as a "model joint venture." That is, the officials held up BJC to lure other companies to invest much-needed foreign exchange and transfer advanced technology. All along, the foreign firms were not aware of the special deals.[11]

Given the resolution of these problems, the company was back in business. In early 1986, the venture had about 4,300 employees, including 800 administrators, engineers, and technicians. Its main activities were producing chassis frames and body panels, welding, painting and final assembly. Labor costs were low: wages at the BJC plant were US$.60 cents an hour, compared to labor costs (including fringe benefits) of about US$22 an hour in the United States and US$12 an hour in Japan. In 1985, United States Vice-President George Bush visited the factory and gave his blessing.

From AMC to Chrysler

Although things were running smoothly for BJC, AMC continued to lose money and market share. It was becoming apparent that the situation could not continue, and in 1987, Chrysler acquired AMC. Chrysler's CEO, Lee Iacocca, made it clear that AMC's Jeep was one of the main reasons for the acquisition. "For Chrysler, the attractions are Jeep, the best-known automotive brand name in the world…," Iacocca said. The Jeep division gave Chrysler an instant entry into the booming 4WD truck market.[12] Chrysler bought the Jeep name and gained overseas operations in Egypt, Venezuela and China. Chrysler announced that it had no intention of altering operations at BJC. Nonetheless, the Chinese were concerned, since they had little knowledge of Chrysler, and they were also unaccustomed to the takeovers and other aspects of American-style capitalism.

To alleviate China's potential fears, Chrysler hinted that because it had more financial resources and more people at its disposal, it was maybe willing to invest more. In 1988, in accordance with the initial joint venture, Don St. Pierre handed the presidency of BJC over to Chen Xulin, his hand-picked successor, and Chrysler continued to hold out the prospect of big plans for China. In mid-1987, Chrysler's vice-president Bob Lutz signed a deal under which Chrysler sold new engine technology to China. Chinese officials were discussing the possibility of manufacturing passenger cars in Changchun, and Chrysler hoped to land that contract. In addition, Chrysler began discussing the possibility of a major expansion of BJC. There was even talk of manufacturing trucks. At one point the Chinese suggested that Chrysler invest as much as US$80 million to US$100 million for the expansion. Yet Chrysler officials moved cautiously, avoiding any commitment of new money. The First Automotive Corp. of Changchun gave the contract for passenger cars to Audi, a subsidiary of Volkswagen.

Still, Chrysler continued to be a good corporate citizen. After the Tiananmen Square incident on June 4, 1989, Chrysler was among the first Western companies to send executives and their families back to Beijing, after they had been relocated temporarily to Chrysler's Tokyo office.[13] Thereafter, Chrysler continued to show a commitment to the joint venture, and in the process, cultivated much-valued good relations with the Chinese authorities. In October 1988, then Chairman and CEO Lee Iacocca visited China. He inspected BJC and said, "I really have a feeling that they are creating history." In 1990, BJC began producing engines at a new engine facility. And from 1990 to 1992, annual Cherokee production went from 7,100 units to 20,808 units while production of the BJ-2000 series went from 41,400 to 57,878 units. Exhibit 1 shows production volumes of BJC since its inception. In 1993, an enhanced version of the BJ-2020 was launched. The Chinese president, Jiang Zemin, who had trained in China and the Soviet Union as an automotive and electrical engineer and had an in-depth knowledge of the automobile industry, inspected the company in 1995. In 1996 the venture acquired ISO-9000 certification. Exhibit 2 displays a time line of major events in BJC's history.

The Daimler Benz-Chrysler Merger

In November 1998, Daimler Benz merged with Chrysler Corporation to form the world's third largest car company, DaimlerChrysler. The company had since been beset with merger problems, such as the exodus of many top executives from Chrysler.[14] Professor E. Han Kim, an

Exhibit 1   Production History—Production Volume

Calendar Year	Cherokee	BJ-series	Total
1984	n/a	16,400	16,400
1985	300	20,600	20,900
1986	1,500	22,800	24,300
1987	3,500	23,700	27,200
1988	5,000	26,700	31,700
1989	6,600	32,500	39,100
1990	7,100	34,300	41,400
1991	15,797	35,000	50,797
1992	20,808	37,070	57,878
1993	10,400	33,300	43,700
1994	15,500	46,000	61,500
1995	26,127	55,024	80,151
1996	26,051	45,282	71,333
1997	19,700	31,883	51,583
1998 (thru Nov.)	8,236	19,552	27,788

Source: DaimlerChrysler fact sheet

expert on mergers and acquisitions, believed that the merger was a good decision, but that the culture clash first needed to be addressed. He stated:

> If they can somehow overcome this huge difference in corporate culture, which is the problem that they are really facing, they can achieve their full potential of synergistic gains. It's not only the savings, but greater revenue, increased perception in terms of quality, and growth in the product line. I think that could be perhaps as big, or bigger, than the savings in cost.

Kim believed that the company's United States operations had lost good executives wary of a German takeover.

> I think that was in part due to this culture clash between the German style of management and the American style of management, or the dominance of the Germans. When we look at these companies, really the biggest asset they have is people, and if you lose the people, that's it.[15]

Investors were not optimistic about the merger prospects. In January 1999, DaimlerChrysler's average closing share price was around US$108; by late May 2000, the share was trading at around US$55.[16] This represented a loss of nearly 50 percent of value in a year and four months. Thus, the Chinese feared that DaimlerChrysler, beset with merger problems, might not focus much attention on BJC, which played a relatively small role in its corporate structure. DaimlerChrysler owned 42.4 percent of BJC; the other 57.6 percent was owned by Beijing Automobile Works. In 1998, Beijing Jeep's total revenues were approximately equivalent to US$399 million, of which DaimlerChrylser's share was about US$169 million. This represented about one-tenth of one percent of DaimlerChrysler's US$131,782 billion total sales.

The Political and Economic Climate in China

In 2000, China's political economy was still undergoing a major transformation, begun in 1978 by Deng Xiaoping. China planned to achieve 'socialist modernization' through economic reform and opening up to the outside world. This included the use of financial markets and the establishment of joint ventures. Thus, China was the first communist nation in the world to have stock exchanges and the only socialist country to initiate building a "market style modern enterprise system" through a corporatization and shareholding framework.[17] As a result of economic reforms and the introduction of market mechanisms, provincial and local administrators and managers had more decision-making autonomy and new profit-sharing incentives had been put into place. Even though economic activities were still subject to a substantial amount of state intervention, the Chinese economy moved a step closer to a market system.

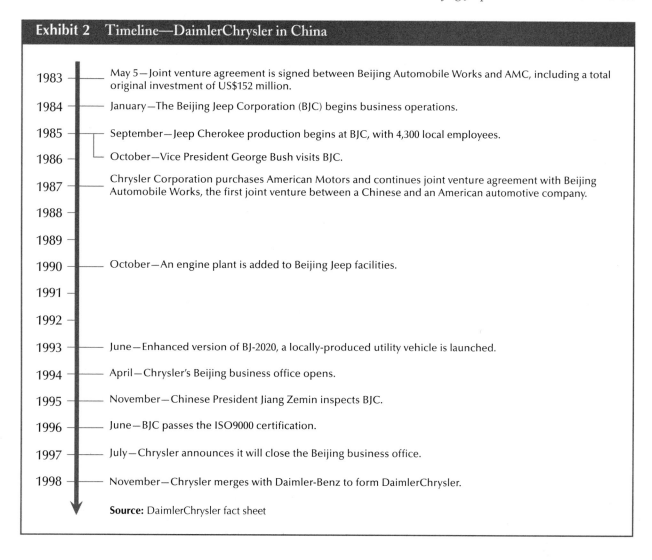

Exhibit 2   Timeline—DaimlerChrysler in China

1983 — May 5—Joint venture agreement is signed between Beijing Automobile Works and AMC, including a total original investment of US$152 million.

1984 — January—The Beijing Jeep Corporation (BJC) begins business operations.

1985 — September—Jeep Cherokee production begins at BJC, with 4,300 local employees.

1986 — October—Vice President George Bush visits BJC.

1987 — Chrysler Corporation purchases American Motors and continues joint venture agreement with Beijing Automobile Works, the first joint venture between a Chinese and an American automotive company.

1988

1989

1990 — October—An engine plant is added to Beijing Jeep facilities.

1991

1992

1993 — June—Enhanced version of BJ-2020, a locally-produced utility vehicle is launched.

1994 — April—Chrysler's Beijing business office opens.

1995 — November—Chinese President Jiang Zemin inspects BJC.

1996 — June—BJC passes the ISO9000 certification.

1997 — July—Chrysler announces it will close the Beijing business office.

1998 — November—Chrysler merges with Daimler-Benz to form DaimlerChrysler.

Source: DaimlerChrysler fact sheet

It was still not clear what the end result of the process of reforms would be. There was political conflict between the hard-liners and the reformers during the transition of the power structure, and there was likely to be political and social unrest during this process. While industrial enterprises had acquired more autonomy, the central government still had substantial power and influence over business activities, due to its control of the majority of raw materials and the distribution system. The government was also the largest customer and product distributor.[18]

From 1992 to 1996, China attracted more total foreign investment than any other developing country. During the latter part of the 1990's however, foreign investors began to doubt China's commitment to market reforms. In the first 10 months of 1999, contracted foreign investment in the mainland was about US$40 billion, down 35 percent on the corresponding period the previous year and the first such fall since Beijing started

its open-door policy in 1979. Although this was partly due to over-capacity in certain industries, it was also caused by slowing economic growth, inadequate laws and regulatory protection, and lack of access to markets. These factors were causing foreign firms to reconsider investing in China.[19]

One representative of a United States telecommunications was quoted as saying:

Foreign companies made major commitments to China over the past four years on assumptions of continuing liberalization of the investment climate and a market of 1.2 billion consumers. Now there is a perception that the process of liberalization, of reducing bureaucratic procedures, taxes and obstacles to doing business has come to a halt. There is a question about China's real commitment to a market economy.

Some believed that there was a policy battle within the Chinese leadership between those who wanted a market economy and those who wanted a South Korean-style system dominated by big state corporations.[20]

China's Entry into the World Trade Organization

On November 15, 1999, U.S. trade representative Charlene Barshefsky and China Trade Minister Shi Guangsheng reached an agreement on terms for China's entry into the WTO. The agreement had followed 13 years of stalemated negotiations that seemed to follow the general ebbs and flows of Sino-U.S. relations. For example, the negotiations were postponed by the bombing of the Chinese Embassy in Belgrade, Yugoslavia, by American military pilots in May of 1999.

In order to join the WTO, China had to agree to liberalize its financial markets. It also had to allow for more foreign investment in firms engaged in electronic commerce, entertainment, travel and tourism, and other industries. In addition, trade tariffs had to be reduced on a wide range of agricultural and manufactured products—including a reduction in the tariffs on imported automobiles from 100 percent to 25 percent by 2006.[21] Barshefsky stated: "This deal is crucial to China's economic reform because investment dollars will flow to other countries if China remains mired in rules and inefficiencies." Indeed, it was difficult to overestimate the importance of WTO entry to China's economic landscape. Political analyst Wang Shan called entry into the WTO the most important political event in China since Deng Xiaoping launched his ground-breaking reforms. The terms of the deal would reverberate deep inside Chinese society. If handled well, the WTO's terms would help China become more competitive, more modern, even more pluralistic. If managed poorly, the country could face an explosion of rural poverty and the disintegration of central control, warned an economist in Beijing.[22]

The Chinese Automotive Industry

In 2000, most cars in China were publicly owned or used as taxis, and were either imported or joint venture models. The proportion of old vehicles still in daily use was much higher than in Western countries, and the government wished to see these older vehicles replaced to improve safety and energy efficiency. There were about 1.7 million township enterprises and 150,000 urban collectively owned enterprises that were more autonomous than state-owned enterprises. As these enterprises developed, it was anticipated that more vehicles would be needed. Owners of private cars were mainly business people, especially private entrepreneurs.

A survey of the residents of Beijing, Shanghai, Guangzhou, Chengdu, Nanjing, and nine other major cities conducted in early 2000, indicated that private purchases of sedans would reach 910,000 that year. This represented an increase of around 390 percent over the same period in 1999, in which 2.6 percent of households surveyed indicated they had purchased vehicles. These optimistic projections were gaining the attention of carmakers from around the world. According to the same survey, 7.8 percent of households in those cities already owned vehicles, with 4.2 percent owning sedans and 0.4 percent owning Jeeps.[23] Thus, it appeared that the industry was poised for dramatic growth.

The situation was particularly attractive for Jeep, as China was perhaps the world's biggest potential market for four-wheel drive (4WD) vehicles because of its rugged, rural landscape and heavy emphasis on agriculture. Although there had been a road-building campaign and the government was committed to developing the highways system in its western, more rural areas, the need for Jeeps would likely continue to be great. Compared to the United States, China had less-rigid emission control and safety standards, but it was in the process of upgrading the standards. As in other parts of the world, the Chinese government had tried to regulate car sales by raising and lowering taxes and third-party motor vehicle insurance had been mandatory since February 15, 1989.

Major Domestic Competitors

In 2000, the Chinese automotive industry could be described as fragmented. There were around 136 domestic producers. Yet, some 40 percent of the capacity lay idle, and about half of all vehicle manufacturers were losing money.[24] But there was likely to be major consolidation in the next few years as import tariffs were reduced, and the remaining firms attempted to improve efficiency through increasing economies of scale.[25] In July of 1999, the State Council of the Central Government announced intentions to accelerate the restructuring of the auto sector. The State Machine-Building Industry Bureau would be in charge of the restructuring, with the goal of merging China's top 13 largest auto manufacturers into three conglomerates. The State Council hoped to transform the automobile sector into a "pillar industry." The three conglomerates would be based on Changchun's First Automobile Works (Group) Corp. (FAW), Shanghai Automotive Industry Corp., and Wuhan's Dongfeng Motor Co. Together, the top 13 domestic automakers produced roughly 1.4 million units, or 92 percent of national output in 1998.[26]

According to a source at the United States-China Business Council, the new restructuring policy was based on supporting strong companies and closing struggling ones. The policy aimed initially to close small township and village enterprises that received funding from local governments and produced substandard vehicles and parts. Provincial authorities would work to identify enterprises operating under poor manufacturing conditions and violating intellectual property rights. By late 1999, the list of enterprises slated for closure was announced. Small joint venture players that had already developed a niche in the China market by producing mini-buses and automobiles, such as Nanjing-based Yuejin Auto (Group) Co. and Jiangxi-based Jiangxi Jiangling Auto Co., were unlikely to be affected by the new policy.[27]

Now that China's entry into the WTO seemed likely, government planners realized that China's domestic industry was ill-prepared for global competition. They hoped that the new plan would reinvigorate ongoing efforts to eliminate duplicate investment and spur consolidation. The new plan coincided with the promulgation of China's 10th "Five-Year Plan" and the announcement of a new "Guiding Catalogue for Foreign Investment" which was to be released in year 2000. Both of these documents would reportedly be critical in setting the future course of the industry.[28] However, local governments viewed auto manufacturing as an important source of tax revenue and employment. This hindered central government efforts to consolidate the scattered and inefficient industry.

Foreign Joint Ventures

Chinese consumers were demanding better cars, and this was putting increasing pressure on domestic producers, while opening doors for high-quality foreign companies. "I see a watershed point in the auto industry here," said Michael Dunne, the managing director of Automotive Resources Asia Ltd., a Beijing- and Bangkok-based consulting firm.[29] Volkswagen, Audi, Honda, DaimlerChrysler, Citroen, Daihatsu, Suzuki, and Subaru all had joint venture manufacturing plants in China.[30] Japanese automakers had been selling in China since the early 1970s. Toyota decided that China was beginning to prosper and began to sell trucks, buses, luxury cars, taxis and motorcycles. Soon after, Nissan, Daihatsu, Suzuki, Mitsubishi, and others followed. Between 1983 and 1984, Japan's auto exports to China increased sevenfold, from 10,800 to 85,000, and China became Japan's second largest foreign car market after the United States. The massive imports of vehicles resulted in rapid depletion of foreign currency reserves and resulted in cancellations of further import licenses. The Chinese government had established some incentives, including taxes, bank loans, and foreign exchange, to encourage foreign companies operating in China to reinvest earnings or export their product. For example, a new tax law allowed a joint venture to avoid import tariffs when 40 percent of the value of a vehicle was produced in China.

General Motors

General Motors used the marketing and sales strategy from its Saturn division in the United States to produce and sell new Buicks in China that were manufactured by a 50/50 joint venture with Shanghai Automotive Industry Co. in Shanghai. The strategy seemed to be working; the new cars were selling well and there was a long waiting list despite a price that was the equivalent of about US$45,000 at the official exchange rate.[31] General Motors' Philip Murtaugh, executive vice-president for Shanghai GM, was fiercely proud of his operation and the respect it showed for the Chinese people. "The growth forecast for the Asian auto market was 15 to 20 percent a year. Some economists believe somewhere around 2025, China's auto industry will be the same size as North America's. [GM Chairman Jack Smith] is intent on the company participating in that growth," Murtaugh said. GM's investment in the project was around US$1.5 billion, and the joint venture was capable of producing about 100,000 units per year. Shanghai GM was planning to add a second vehicle, a minivan in 2000, and a small car later if approved by the government.[32]

This was not the first time that GM had sold cars to the Chinese; the last emperor owned a Buick and so did Communist leader Chou En-Lai. And Buick had sold 10,000 to 15,000 cars per year in China in the 1920s and 1930s, said Jay Hunt, Shanghai GM director of marketing and distribution.[33] GM demanded that Chinese suppliers match United States quality standards. Forty percent of the vehicle's value was produced by Chinese labor and parts, a requirement for reducing duties on imported parts. GM expected to hit 60 percent local content in the second year and 80 percent in the third or fourth year.[34]

At the Shanghai plant, 1,800 workers were needed to staff one eight-hour shift. The workers received training and wages well above the local norm, earning an average US$350 per month, plus benefits worth the same amount, including a housing subsidy, health care, company-provided breakfasts and lunches, shuttle service to and from work, and incentive bonuses. The plant employed a few more employees than it normally would in the United States.

The 200,000 square-metre integrated plant was built in 1997 and 1998 on a 500,000 square-metre site. It was laid out for efficiency and was similar to GM plants in

Argentina, Thailand, and Poland. The plant contained areas for stamping, storage, a body shop, engine, transmission, trim, chassis, general assembly lines, a paint booth, and a small sales showroom. The Shanghai operation built its own automatic transmissions and 2.98 litre V6 engines on site (the central government levied heavy taxes on cars with engines 3.0 litres or larger and did not allow for low-level bureaucrats to own them).

Supplier costs were higher than they probably should have been, partly because many state-run companies and joint ventures had not traditionally been concerned with costs or profits. "The biggest challenge the industry faces here in China is cost and quality competitiveness," said vice-president Murtaugh. "We are showing we can compete on quality. But our costs are still 25 percent to 30 percent above North America." General Motors had also teamed up with another partner, Jinbei Automotive GM, to make a version of its Chevrolet Blazer in the northeastern city of Shenyang. This would compete directly with BJC. Yet, at 300,000 yuan, the cars cost about 10 percent more than BJC's Cherokee.[35]

Volkswagen

Volkswagen (VW) dominated the China auto market with about 55 percent of sales. The company was bringing on production of five modern vehicles over the next three years, including the luxury Audi A6 and the VW Passat and Jetta. The number one German automaker was doubling its investment in China to six billion marks ($3.28 billion). Still, Volkswagen was not resting on its laurels. "China is becoming much more competitive, with demand more like it is in Western markets," said Stefan Jacoby, the VW vice-president in charge of the Asian-Pacific region.[36]

Much of Volkswagen's success had been in supplying China's demand for taxicabs, as anyone who visited the mainland in 2000 could determine; most of the taxis in use in the urban areas were Santanas or Jettas. Shanghai Volkswagen catered to this large market segment. For example, in June 1999, Shanghai Volkswagen began a new policy to expand its sales to the taxi service sector. Under the new policy, any local taxi company that bought 100 units of Santana cars or 50 units of Santana 2000GLS would get an extra unit of the same model. Also, the sales corporation offered a 15,000 kilometre (km), third-class, free maintenance warranty in addition to the 7,500 km, first-class, free maintenance for any Santana 2000GLS used as a taxi. Approximately 40 percent of Santanas made in 1998 went to the taxi sector. VW Santanas accounted for over 80 percent of the taxis in Shanghai. Volkswagen did not offer a sports utility

vehicle, and thus did not compete directly with the Cherokee or BJ models.

Honda

Honda was Japan's third-largest automaker. It manufactured its Accord in China at a joint venture with Denway Investment in Guangzhou. In December of 1999, the joint venture, named Guangzhou Honda, announced it would add models, raise output and sales of passenger cars, and increase the ratio of locally purchased parts to 80 percent within three years. A spokesman for the company said it wanted to boost local sales amid rising competition as rival automakers expanded vehicle production.

From March 2000, Guangzhou Honda began producing 2000 cubic centimeters (cc) Accords in addition to the 2300cc model it was already producing.[37] Honda said it hoped to increase government sales with the addition of the new model as Chinese officials can use only cars with low exhaust emission levels. Honda said it was also aiming to boost Accord sales to individual buyers as the model was favored by China's growing business community. The company said the ratio of locally sourced parts used at Honda Guangzhou reached 45 percent in November and that the next target was 60 percent, ahead of an eventual goal of 80 percent. "We adhere to the concept of producing cars where the demand is and meeting customer needs directly," a Honda official said.

Higher local-content ratios allowed the carmaker to avoid taxes on imported parts, the company said. Honda was producing 10,000 sedans at the joint-venture plant, which it acquired from Peugeot Citroen in 1997. The factory was scheduled to reach full capacity of 30,000 within two years, Guangzhou Honda president Koji Kadowaki said in June 1999. At that time Honda also announced a boost in annual output to 50,000, as low prices and a crackdown on smuggling sparked demand for its China-made Accords.[38]

Toyota

Although Toyota had been reluctant to enter the Chinese market, it hoped to control 10 percent of the Chinese market within five to 10 years of starting local production, according to Koji Hasegawa, managing director in charge of Asian operations. "The China market is still very young, but the potential is huge," said Hasegawa. "If we can offer an attractive vehicle to these customers, we can compete with Volkswagen."[39]

In 1998, Toyota shipped 27,000 cars and trucks to China, giving it a 1.7 percent market share. In November of 1999, Toyota was still awaiting approval from the Chinese government to start local production, most likely with local partner Tianjin Automotive Works. It was thought they would produce compact cars similar to the popular Vitz model in Japan. In preparation, Toyota had built up a network of more than 60 service stations, which it hoped to turn into dealerships. Hasegawa said Toyota planned eventually to offer three vehicles to the Chinese market: a compact car, a van, and a pick-up truck.[40] Exhibit 3 shows the market share of the major competitors in the Chinese Automotive Industry.

Beijing's Jeep Operations

Jeep was the second most recognizable foreign brand name in China, after Coca-Cola and before Head and Shoulders shampoo.[41] Still, the late 1990s was not a good period for BJC's performance. Profits fell from $216 million yuan in 1996 to $20 million yuan in 1997,[42] and for 1998, there was a loss.[43] Andy Okab, the vice-president of Chrysler Corporation's Beijing Jeep said that during 1999, the company cut its workforce from 7,100 to 4,800, through early retirement, lay-offs and by moving staff from permanent basis to contract basis, and reduced its bank loans by 25 percent and inventory from more than 800 million yuan to 350 million yuan. Okab added: "We were below break-even last year."

Beijing Jeep's current top management team consisted of one American, F.B. Krebs, as the general manager. The deputy general manager was Yunde Zhu, followed by the senior executives, Yuanzhu Li, Kaiying Zhou and Meidong Wang.[44]

Thus, BJC was continually losing market share. After its foundation in 1984, its total output was allocated to state companies and little sales or marketing was required. Sales to the army still accounted for 30 percent of the total, but industry growth was concentrated in taxi companies and the wealthy, mostly in the cities, who wanted comfortable passenger cars like the Santana, the Citroen ZX, and Jetta.[45] On top of that, a road-building campaign that had included 4,735 kilometres of highway had lessened the need for jeeps. Yet the company maintained that there was enormous potential demand for its vehicles in rural and mountainous areas. Unfortunately these were poor areas where people did not have the money to buy the company's vehicles.[46]

In the longer term, there was a question mark over the company's place in the mainland's overall car strategy. Following Chrysler's merger with Daimler-Benz, BJC was undergoing an evaluation by the new company. There had even been rumors that DaimlerChrysler may try to get out of its China operations to focus on the more immediate concerns of its merger integration problems. One analyst stated that the venture was looking like a lost cause. It was "saddled with an aged plant, bloated workforce and two outdated models," and that "even confirmed optimists are discouraged by the plethora of problems confronting the company."[47]

Still, DaimlerChrysler denied that it was thinking of pulling out. "No one in his right mind can recommend packing up and leaving," Okab said. "So much has changed in the past five years and so much could change in the next five years."[48] Jerry Hsu, vice-president for sales and marketing for Chrysler Asia-Pacific said that in the last quarter of 1999, Chrysler sent

Exhibit 3   Production Statistics by Model for China's Automotive Industry

Model Names	Sales Sept 1999	Sales Sept 1998	% Change in Sales	Market Share	Production in 1999	Production in 1998	% Change in Production
Santana (VW)	31,421	17,584	78.7	45.08	20,502	17,377	18.0
Jetta (VW)	7,622	5,358	42.3	10.93	7,840	5,235	49.8
Audi 2000	480	730	-34.2	0.69	102	654	-84.4
Buick (GM)	3,788	0	0.0	5.43	4,069	0	0.0
Small Hongqi	1,710	478	257.7	2.45	1,662	387	329.5
Fukang-Citroen	4,743	4,564	3.9	6.80	4,066	4,600	-11.6
Charade (Daihatsu)	12,542	7,585	65.4	17.99	11,262	10,069	11.8
Alto	5,254	3,274	60.5	7.54	6,464	3,417	89.2
Guangzhou Honda	1,251	0	0.0	1.8	1,199	0	0.0
Beijing Jeep	816	907	-10.0	1.17	520	723	-28.1
Subaru	86	0	0.0	0.12	0	0	0.0
Total	69,713	40,480	72.2	100.0	57,686	42,462	35.9

Source: *Asia Pulse*, November 22, 1999.

teams to redirect sales and marketing. To reduce costs, the firm had in the past six months reduced the workforce from 8,100 to 7,000. He denied rumors that Chrysler was considering leaving the mainland. Said Okab: "We remain firmly committed to China as a key part of our strategy. We believe in the economy and in the future."

Conor O'Clery, another Chinese automotive industry analyst, believed that BJC had been left behind by changes in the mainland's car market from being dominated by companies and state institutions to one in which the individual was becoming the most important customer. BJC's production scale was too small to allow price cuts to match those of its competitors and the high petrol consumption of its vehicles deterred many potential urban buyers. The previous year, private buyers had purchased about 40 percent of national output of 1.57 million vehicles, including 470,000 passenger cars, up from 1.45 million in 1996, and were expected to account for 50 percent in 1999.[49]

The lowest price for the Cherokee jeep was 128,000 yuan (approximately US$15,000).[50] Research had shown there was demand for this vehicle without some luxury features, so BJC planned a third-quarter launch of a model priced at less than $100,000 yuan.[51] The Cherokee assembled in China was powered by a 2.5 litre AMC petrol engine from the United States. There was a question, however, of whether the Cherokee was really suitable for China, or whether the more basic BJ200 series was better (see Exhibits 4 and 5). For example, Erming Xu, professor of strategic management and dean of the business school at the People's University in Beijing, stated the Cherokee was not an ideal model choice for China in that it did not fit a broad market niche. It was a bit too plush for the rural areas, and yet it was not as smooth riding as a sedan, which was popular in urban areas. He went further to state that the Cherokee seemed to be produced for United States residents living in suburbs who liked to go exploring on the weekends; among these residents, sport utility vehicles (SUVs), as the Cherokee is often classified, were typically second cars that supplemented the primary model of transportation, which was a sedan. The suburbs were still in the infant stages of development in China, and most people could not afford a first car, much less a second. In fact, the Cherokee had been modified to suit the Chinese market. BJC engineers made design changes on the chassis frame and suspension to make it more sturdy, and optional extras had been deleted. In short, the vehicle was not as luxurious as the United States version. BJC officials announced in February of 1999, that they were introducing a new "no-frills" version of the Cherokee.[52]

O'Clery, a Beijing-based analyst, stated that,

> Like many other foreigners in China, I drive a Beijing Jeep. Actually there isn't much choice. The huge duty on foreign imports makes other cars extremely expensive. The Cherokee is considered to be a high-class vehicle.

Beijing Jeeps were produced in different versions, but they were all based on a relatively heavy-gauge chassis frame, which gave the vehicle strength and a stiff base on which to mount the sturdy mechanicals: engine, a three-speed manual gearbox, 4WD transmission, long travel, semi-elliptic leaf spring suspension, and a high- and low-speed transfer box. Both the BJ212 and the civilian version BJ212A were not fuel-efficient. The BJ212 had been exported from China to the Netherlands, France and Australia in small numbers. Some had to be modified and upgraded to meet current safety regulations applying to those export markets. The original BJ212 design was later replaced by a modified version, BJ212L. The entire BJ series was originally based on a Soviet commander car. The BJ121K version had all the features of the BJ121A plus a canvas top with side windows, which covered the whole vehicle; it could also double as a 10-seat rural bus.

The local Beijing officials were trying to help the ailing carmaker since it was a major supplier of good paying jobs in the city—an indication that BJC still has some connections with powerful people. For example, in 1999, city authorities issued an edict that all sports utility vehicles—except those manufactured by BJC—would be barred from driving on the second and third ring roads between Monday and Friday. Any Beijing resident knew that trying to get anywhere without being able to drive on the city's two main circular arteries would amount to a considerable test of patience and ingenuity. Therein, historically, lies one of the main appeals of the Beijing Jeep. However, such anti-tariff tactics barriers appeared to be on the way out with the WTO on the horizon. Yet there was the question of how well the WTO changes could be enforced, at least in the short-run.[53]

Strategic Challenges

Thus, as the year 2000 got under way, the managers of Beijing Jeep were faced with challenges and opportunities. On one hand, as the Asian crisis faded, the Chinese economy promised growth rates that would put more consumers within reach of owning an automobile. Total private automobile sales were projected to nearly quadruple over that of 1999; thus, the dream of the vast Chinese market appeared to be becoming a reality.[54] Yet on the

Exhibit 4   Advertisement for Beijing Jeep Cherokee BJ7250 EL

Safety

We thought about Safety—with each and every passenger in mind. We've incorporated double sided galvanized steel for 24 percent increased stiffness and durability. The collision-absorbing steering column and the buffer zone work synergistically to reduce frontal impact injury. The three-point safety belts are available for on all seats and provide effective protection for passengers. Parents can relax while the "rear door child protection locks" are engaged, improving their children's safety.

New Safety Features

- Increased stiffness
- Collision absorbing steering column and buffer zone
- Three-point safety belts
- Rear door child protection locks

Utilization

We thought about Versatility—and developed a vehicle adaptable for various road terrains. Understanding the desires of our customers to carry everything from groceries to heavy equipment, we included the rear-folding seat to give a spacious luggage/cargo area. Cherokee's comfortable interior design is a result of our dedication to fully meet the ergonomic requirements and provide a luxurious ride.

Performance

We thought about overall performance—and succeeded in designing the Super Cherokee for quick response and all-round drive-ability. The available engines provide our customers with the power they want (standard 2.5L or more powerful 4.0L). Our off-road ability is ensured by the outstanding break-over angle approach angle and departure angle. Our state-of-the-art international suspension system adapts to the different Chinese road conditions as well as to different traveling speeds. The optional full-time 4WD shift-on-the-fly can be left in the four FULL–TIME mode over any road surfaces, including dry, paved road without damaging the drive train or reducing fuel economy all 4WD models have. Shift-on-the fly capability allows the customer to shift from 2WD to 4WD without slowing down or getting out of the vehicle to lock the hubs.

Value

We thought about value—and designed a vehicle with priceless capabilities. The comfort and convenience of the Super Cherokee go above and beyond customer expectations. Our guarantee is to passenger safety and superior performance. The exceptional value far exceeds the price of the Super Cherokee.

Environmental Protection

We thought about the environment—and equipped the Super Cherokee with an R134a air conditioner to ensure environmental protection. The addition of a catalytic converter to the electronic fuel injection engine insures compliance with the requirements of China's strict emission regulations.

Multiple Utilizations of the Super Cherokee

We thought of multiple utilizations of the Super Cherokee—and made it adaptable to an infinite range of roads, including: city, mountain, village high slopping fields, low-lying land, forest, wilderness, grasslands, deserts, snow covered, rain slick, mud covered, etc. We designed the Super Cherokee to accommodate a vast number of different professional and trade uses, including:

- Engineering
- Fire fighting
- Irrigating work
- Rescuing
- Banking
- Electric power works
- Military functions
- Medical and health works
- Security jobs, procurator
- Court functions
- Farming
- Forestry work
- Animal husbandry
- Fishery work

The Super Cherokee accommodates all personality styles, including: natural, unrestrained, tenacious, determined, fashion-minded, thrill-seeking, distinguished, family-minded, business-minded, pleasure seekers, etc.

- Adaptable to an infinite range of roads
- Accommodates a vast number of different professions
- Accommodates all personality styles

We thought about everything—and built a Jeep vehicle that is perfect for you. Take the keys to a legendary Jeep and you've taken ownership of something much bigger: rugged off-road trails, scenic mountaintops, freedom previously unknown and the company of like minds whose common bonds are adventure, discovery, comfort, convenience and prestige, all at an affordable price. The confidence a Jeep provides in all places at all times allows a peace of mind you've never known.

Source: BJC Web site—Company URL: http://www.Beijing-jeep.com/.

Exhibit 5   Advertisement for Beijing Jeep BJ2020SY

China is a country with a vast land mass area with every possible terrain and climate. The numerous complex road conditions (i.e., dry Gobi desert, sandy lands of Inner Mongolia and summertime seasonal rivers, the long winters that bring snow and ice in the Northeast, the rolling hills and narrow roads in the hot, humid climates of Yunnan, Guizhou and Sichuan Provinces) put any vehicle to the test of endurance. Despite the complex roads and inclement weather, Beijing Jeep Corporation, Ltd. provides a variety of models to take you where you want to go.

Highly skilled Beijing Jeep Corporation, Ltd. engineers have developed the hard-top Kuangchao Series, BJ2020SY, BJ2020SM and the BJ2020SMW, by using the most advanced technology. The option of an air conditioner is available to improve passenger comfort. There is always a model to meet your needs.

The BJ2020SY is equipped with a reinforced fibreglass removable hardtop. The robust hardtop is resistant to corrosion, resistant to aging, resistant to impact, durable and lightweight. Enjoy warm, sunny weather, with the wind in your hair when the hardtop is removed.

BJ2020SM has a metal roof, which seals out the environmental elements, such as rain, cold in the winter and heat in the

summer. In addition to the BJ2020SM's metal roof, the BJ2020SMW is designed with a lift gate for easy loading and unloading. Fold the rear seat forward for a spacious cargo area.

Source: BJC Web site—Company URL: http://www.Beijing-jeep.com/.

---

other hand, the competition for that market was steadily intensifying, and the WTO promised to lower the barriers on, what had been for BJC, a somewhat protected market.

As the first major foreign joint venture, BJC had learned to do things the hard way. The company had painstakingly cultivated guanxi with central and local government officials over the years. Guanxi is sometimes said to be a response to poorly developed market and regulatory institutions. Yet if the WTO improved the institutional and regulatory structure, it was possible that BJC's guanxi advantage would count for less in the future. As China was being pulled into the world economy, competition in its markets would more closely resemble that of the rest of the world. Until recently, BJC had been the darling of the government policy makers in Beijing, and it was once held up as a model joint venture. That honeymoon period was now over. American, German and Japanese automobile companies had all expressed their intentions to create or expand joint venture plans in the near future. BJC was no longer "the only game in town" when it came to joint ventures. It would be forced to compete with the best that the world had to offer.

It appeared that the venture could benefit from more technology, management expertise, and investment from its major foreign partner, DaimlerChrysler. BJC was losing money and market share, and it had two outdated models and 15-year old-technology. But how could it get more commitment from this organization, which was facing

disgruntled investors and merger problems of its own? Also, DaimlerChrysler was reluctant to transfer technology due to the historically weak record of property rights protection in China. There was even open speculation among some Chinese auto analysts that DaimlerChrysler was considering pulling out of the BJC venture totally.

Another point worth considering was the product line. Should BJC attempt to leverage the guanxi it had built up with Chinese authorities over the years and focus on government contracts, or should it concentrate on the growing middle class and market to individual consumers? Should the company focus more on the old BJ Jeeps that seemed to be more suitable for the masses, or should it attempt to go upscale and try to sell Grand Cherokees?

Thus, BJC was at a crossroads in the organization's history. Whichever path the company took was going to be full of challenges and opportunities, as the vast Chinese economy was in the midst of making a major historical transformation.

Notes

1. J. Mann, *Beijing Jeep: A Case Study of Western Business in China* (Boulder, Colorado: Westview Press, 1997).
2. D. Roberts, and P. Mangusson, "Welcome to the Club: China's Deal to Join the WTO Holds Both Promise and Peril," *Business Week*, 29 November 1999, 34.
3. K. Bradsher, "A Struggle Over Culture and Turf at Auto Giant," *New York Times*, 24 September 1999, C1.
4. C. O'Clery, "Making China Good for US Motors," *The Irish Times*, 20 July 1998, 10.

5. Mann, *Beijing Jeep*.
6. Mann, *Beijing Jeep*.
7. Ibid.
8. Ibid.
9. Ibid.
10. N. Fletcher, "Chrysler China Venture Finds Road to Success," *Journal of Commerce and Commercialization*, 12 May 1989, 1A.
11. Mann, *Beijing Jeep*, 223.
12. O'Clery, "Making China Good for U.S. Motors," 10.
13. Mann, *Beijing Jeep*.
14. B. Klayman, "Year Later, DaimlerChrysler Struggles With Identity," *Toronto Star*, 13 November 1999.
15. R. Kisiel, "DailmerChrysler Turns 1: Bigger…But Better?" *Automotive News*, 15 November 1999, 1.
16. Invest-O-Rama, http://home.sprintmail.com/, 2000.
17. C. Yao, *Stock Market and Futures in the People's Republic of China* (New York: Oxford University Press, 1998).
18. "China Against the Tide: The Succession Struggle and Prospects for Reform in China After the Peking Spring," *The Economist Intelligence Unit* (London), 1990 (Special Report 2025).
19. M. O'Neill, "Foreign Ventures Lose Allure: Outside Investors Begin to Doubt the Mainland's Free-Market Dream," *South China Morning Post*, 11 December 1999.
20. Ibid.
21. Roberts, "Welcome to the Club."
22. M. Liu et al, "A Tale of Two Cities: Beijing," *Newsweek*, 29 November 1999, 54.
23. "China Car Sales Forecast to Jump 390 Percent," *Jinrong Shibao* (Financial News—Beijing), 25 April 2000.
24. R. Jacob, and T. Burt, "China's Walls Will Crumble but Only One Brick at a Time," *Financial Times*, 30 May 2000, 12.
25. Roberts, "Welcome to the Club."
26. "Chinese Automobile Industry Will Be Restructured," *Modern Plastic,* no. 76 (November 1999): 24A.
27. Ibid.
28. Ibid.
29. R.L. Simison, "Nascent Demand in China for Better Cars Buoys Buick," *Asian Wall Street Journal*, 25 October 1999.
30. C.W. Craig, "As the Sun Sets on the 20th Century, it is Rising on the Chinese Automotive Market," *Detroit Free Press*, 27 October 1999.
31. Simison, "Nascent Demand."
32. Ibid.
33. T. Lassa, "Shanghai Century: When Better Buicks are Built, China will Build 'Em," *Auto Week* (25 November 1999): 4.
34. Simison, "Nascent Demand."
35. "GM to Sell Expensive Sport Vehicles in China," *Business Day* (4 June 1999).
36. Simison, "Nascent Demand."
37. "Honda Gears up for Competition," *Hong Kong Standard*, 8 December 1999.
38. Ibid.
39. A. Harney, "Toyota Targets Chinese Market," *Financial Times*, 24 November 1999. 31.
40. Ibid.
41. O'Clery, "Making China Good."
42. Mann, *Beijing Jeep*.
43. M. O'Neill, "Beijing Jeep on Rocky Roads as Profits Tumble," *South China Morning Post*, 21 January 1998, B4.
44. Graham & Whiteside Ltd. The Major Company Database 2000.
45. O'Clery, "Making China Good."
46. Ibid.
47. M. Chrysler, "Is DailmerChrysler Backing off from Beijing Jeep?" *Ward's Auto World* 35, no. 10 (1999): 63.
48. O'Clery, "Making China Good."
49. Ibid.
50. Mann, *Beijing Jeep*.
51. M. O'Neill, "Beijing Jeep Races After Sales with Few-Frills Cherokee," *South China Morning Post*, 18 February 1999, B3.
52. Ibid.
53. Jacob, "China's Wall Will Crumble."
54. "China Car Sales," *Jinrong Shibao* (Financial News), 2000.

Case 6

Blinds to Go: Evaluating the BlindsToGo.com Retail E-Commerce Venture

Ken Mark and Michael Pearce, *The University of Western Ontario*

Introduction

Senior management at Montreal-based Blinds To Go (BTG) had received sales, spending, and survey results from their retail e-commerce venture, BlindsToGo.com. In early July 2000, Nkere Udofia, vice-chairman of BTG, wanted to evaluate the results of this online venture.

Surpassing US$100 million in store revenues, Blinds To Go, a retailer and fabricator of window dressings, had achieved a blistering pace of retail growth in the past few years, sparked by an infusion of capital from Harvard Private Capital, the investment arm of Harvard University. Continuing this trend towards an eventual initial public offering (IPO) in the next few years, they were aiming to add 40 to 50 retail stores per year, funded entirely out of current cash flow, to their current complement of 120 stores across North America.

When Blindstogo.com, the online project of BTG, was first proposed in mid-1999, its board of directors was luke-warm to the idea. However, after six months of operation and seeing other retailers start to go online, and the tremendous valuation being given to dot.coms, the board was now encouraging BTG to devote more resources to this venture.

Montreal's Shiller Family, Originators of the Blinds To Go Concept

Consummate salesmen, David Shiller and his sons took this high-touch retail concept that Shiller had started in 1954 and turned it into a multimillion-dollar business. "In our original 'Au Bon Marche' store," explained Stephen Shiller, president of BTG, "we fed our customers, kept them busy while they waited for about an hour for their blinds to be ready. The factory was literally next to the store and we offered one hour delivery—we certainly kept the customer happy!" The aggressive commission-based approach to sales had resulted in a high-energy environment where above-average salespeople sold Cdn$10,000 worth of blinds per week with a six percent commission.

BTG was capitalizing on a niche in the US$2 billion market for window coverings dominated by large manufacturers and similarly large retailers. A retail fabricator, BTG manufactured and sold only their own brand of blinds, and was able to offer 48-hour delivery of their customer's customized orders. BTG took six separate steps and between one to three hours to manufacture a set of blinds, versus the industry average for a customized order turnaround (assuming they had the parts in stock) of four to six weeks.

BTG's retail fabricator competitors included 3 Day Blinds with US$100 million in sales, House of Blinds with US$20 million in sales, and the rest of the smaller retail fabricators accounting for another US$220 million in sales.[1]

Blinds To Go Retail Stores

With over 20,000 varieties of blinds in stock, BTG's sales associates could offer almost any choice of blinds to their walk-in customers. Each associate was trained to bond with the customers, shepherd them through the choices, offer advice, answer any questions—ultimately, the goal was to address all customer objections and finish the encounter with an average sale of Cdn$226.

Retail stores' sales average over $1.0 million per store with an advertising budget comprising between three to eight percent of revenues. Blinds To Go achieved average weekly store traffic of 300 to 900 people. The company leased real estate and built each store for an average of US$500,000. Refurbished stores (located in already established buildings) usually cost US$300,000 to build. Maintenance, including rent, utilities, and staff expenses, generally cost BTG in the range of US$300,000 to US$400,000 per year. The biggest issue BTG faced in its expansion campaign was attracting, hiring, and retaining qualified staff. Some new stores had delayed openings because of this staff shortage.

BTG staff had an average close rate of 30 to 40 percent, with low performance stores at 20 to 30 percent and high performance stores at 50 to 60 percent (see Exhibit 1).

BlindsToGo.com— The Internet Initiative

In January 2000, BlindsToGo.com was launched. BTG approached a small Web site builder in Chicago to develop and host the site (development of functionality), and another small company in Boston to design the layout of the site (see Exhibit 2). The process was managed by BTG and the site cost US$500,000 to build and US$40,000 per month to host and maintain. The BTG e-commerce site allowed people to browse the varieties of blinds, put in their specifications, and purchase blinds online (www.blindstogo.com).[2]

The site was created with the customer interface and ease of ordering as the main objectives. With this in mind, sections of the site were built in an attempt to replicate the in-store experience (see Exhibit 3). BTG's site was designed to be the leading blinds site that leapfrogged its fragmented online competition with focus and functionality. Jeff Rayner, vice-president of marketing at BTG, placed his online blinds Web site competition in two camps—order-taking sites that received customer orders and passed them on to manufacturers, and catalogue sites that posted their houseware catalogues online.[3] Neither group had sites with any substantial functionality, save for an online order form. Rayner felt that currently, the field was wide open for a nationally branded blinds solution.

When it was created, BTG set out that the measures of success for the site would rank in the following order: total sales, number of catalogue requests, closing rate and shopping cart rate.[4] Because this was their first online venture, BTG did not set specific targets for each metric at this early stage. BTG management felt that sales associates who answered the incoming phone calls originating from the site should always refer customers to stores in their region, gaining synergy between site and stores in established markets.

Some BTG store managers (all stores were corporately owned and store managers were compensated based on revenues) were concerned about the impact of Blindstogo.com cannibalizing their store sales. But senior management was able to ease the concerns of the stores by explaining that blindstogo.com was a new venture that would support the brand and was meant as a complement and support to store operations.

Six months after launch and selling over US$60,000 per month, BTG had received some site results. They had in their hands a slice of daily data from June (Exhibit 4), weekly Web site data from June (Exhibit 5), year-to-date results (Exhibit 6), Live Person Chat results (Exhibit 7), and the results of their online survey conducted in April 2000 (Exhibit 8).

BTG believed that the people who visited the site were the same people who visited their stores. With regard to fulfillment, it took equal time to fulfill an online order versus an offline order, with the exception that the online order would need to be shipped to the customer.

Exhibit 1   Setting Up the Sale (BTG Company Files)

Bonding

Greet the customer and welcome them to Blinds To Go. Determine their needs by asking open-ended questions.

Product Selection

Work with the customer to find the perfect product for their needs. Address any objections as they come up. Ensure that the worksheet is properly and completely filled out.

Present Price with Confidence

Reaffirm factory-direct pricing and lifetime guarantee.

Deduct Coupon

Verify and approve coupon if customer has one.

Introduce Customer to Manager

Walk through the order with the manager and have the manager greet customer.

Source: Blinds To Go Company Files.

Exhibit 2   Blinds to Go Homepage

Source: www.blindstogo.com, January, 2001

Conclusion

Udofia thought,

> We have now dipped our toes into the water. Is the board right—should we push forward aggressively? Is this going to be a break-even business? Or is this just a distraction to the organization? We are people constrained—do we continue to divert valuable management time to this opportunity?

Notes

1. 1997 figures. Sullivan Marketing Group. In 1997, Blinds To Go achieved US$32 million in store sales.
2. Site accessed August 20, 2000.
3. These sites included http://www.blindsgalore.com, www.americanblindsand-wallpaper.com, and www.smithandnoble.com. Rayner believed that there were about three other sites with similar functionality.
4. The Shopping Cart Rate referred to the percentage of sales that occurred online without human assistance.

Exhibit 3   Blinds To Go In-store Experience Pages

Whether in a Blinds To Go™ Superstore or on the website, our sales associates are the most knowledgeable sales associates in the industry. Each has completed intensive training in one of our Blinds To Go™ Universities. For help with choosing the right blind for you, contact one of our sales associates via email or at 877-842-0411 or try our new interactive wizard by answering the questions below.

I want a blind that is:

○ Room Darkening   ○ Adjustable   ○ Light Filtering

Which room are you decorating?

○ Living Room   ○ Dining Room   ○ Bedroom   ○ Den
○ Kitchen   ○ Bathroom   ○ Other

I am primarily concerned with:

○ Good Value   ○ Both - but mostly Value   ○ Both - but mostly Style   ○ Style

▶ find my blind! ◀

Existing Worksheet | Ask the Blinds Expert | Customer Reviews | Why Blinds To Go | Order the Idea Book

Source: www.blindstogo.com/blindstogo/products/expert, January 2001.

Exhibit 3　Blinds To Go In-store Experience Pages (continued)

Why Shop at Blinds To Go™?

Our History: Blinds and shades are in our roots. Since 1954 our mission has been to provide you, our customer with the best quality, value and customer service.

The largest selection: We search across the world and research the latest fashion trends to bring you the best and largest selection of blinds and shades. Visit us often, as we build our online product lines with the latest styles!

The lowest prices: We manufacture everything you see on our site, so you get the lowest price! No middleman, no retail markups!

We are The Experts: We understand blinds. Every Blinds To Go salesperson/service rep goes through Blinds To Go University, and is trained to be blinds and shade experts and to "treat the customer like family".

The Fastest Delivery: We use national carriers like UPS to get your order from our factory to your door, and everything is custom made to your needs!

100% Lifetime Guarantee!

A Lifetime Guarantee! : All our products are backed with a 100% lifetime guarantee. So, you can rest assured that you are buying the best window treatments that will last for years!

Source: www.blindstogo.com, January 2001.

Exhibit 4 June 11–17, 2000 Daily Web Site Results

June 11th to 17th 2000 - Week 3

	Totals	Sun	Mon	Tue	Wed	Thu	Fri	Sat
Total Net Sales (US$)	12,860.0	2,125.0	3,025.0	2,542.5	722.5	75.0	4,037.5	332.5
Number of Sales	42.5	5.0	7.5	7.5	7.5	2.5	7.5	5.0
Average Sale (US$)	308.0							
In Region Sale	30	3	8	5	8	3	3	3
Out of Region Sale	12.5	3	—	3	—	—	5	3
% out of Region	29%							
Advertising (US$)	1,648							
Online	1,648							
Offline	—							
Advertising as % of sales	13%							
Unique Visitors	6,028	648	1,103	1,003	913	910	850	603
Click Thru Rate	740	70	88	100	120	125	133	105
Sales as % of Unique Visits	0.70%							
Phone calls	135	5	30	13	25	30	10	23
Live Chats	80	13	15	10	8	18	18	—
E-mails	155	13	28	30	28	33	20	5
Phone Catalogues	58	—	10	18	13	10	5	3
Total Call Centre	428	30	83	70	73	90	53	30
Web Catalogue Requests	350	40	65	50	63	60	38	35
Phone Catalogues	—							

Source: Blinds To Go Company Files.

Exhibit 5 June Month-to-Date Web Site Results

	Totals	Week 1	Week 2	Week 3	Week 4
Total Net Sales (US$)	48,388	15,723	19,805	12,860	
Number of Sales	102	32	27	43	
Average Sale (US$)	258				
In Region Sale	127.5	52.5	45.0	30.0	
Out of Region Sale	60.0	27.5	20.0	12.5	
% out of Region	32%				
Advertising (US$)	5,050				
Online	5,050	1,955	1,448	1,648	
Offline	—				
Advertising as % of sales	10%				
Unique Visitors	17,726	5,890	5,808	6,028	
Click Thru Rate	2,105	818	548	740	
Sales as % of Unique Visits	1.07%				
Phone calls	315	68	113	135	
Live Chats	158	38	40	80	
E-mails	333	70	108	155	
Phone Catalogues	253	145	50	58	
Total Call Centre	1,058	320	310	428	
Web Catalogue Requests	1,078	400	328	350	
Phone Catalogues	195	145	50		

Source: Blinds To Go Company Files.

Exhibit 6   2000 Year-to-Date Web Site Results

	Totals	Jan	Feb	Mar	Apr	May	Jun
Total Net Sales (US$)	226,640.2	852.5	12,662.2	41,502.5	61,797.5	61,437.5	48,388.0
Number of Sales	917.0	10.0	40.0	212.5	295.0	257.5	102.0
Average Sale (US$)	228.0						
In Region Sale	675.0	10.0	32.5	130.0	202.5	172.5	127.5
Out of Region Sale	327.5	—	7.5	82.5	92.5	85.0	60.0
% out of Region	33%	0%	19%	39%	31%	33%	32%
Advertising (US$)	555,528	375	36,770	324,503	113,290	75,540	5,050
Online	75,643	375	25,270	18,888	19,293	6,768	5,050
Offline	479,883	—	11,500	305,613	93,998	68,773	—
Advertising as % of sales	245%						
Unique Visitors	149,249	3,125	16,988	35,043	32,325	44,043	17,726
Click Thru Rate	46,133	—	—	11,253	12,330	20,445	2,105
Sales as % of Unique Visits	0.87%						
Total Call Centre	4,650	—	—	1,688	1,308	598	1,058
Web Catalogue Requests	4,763	—	—	1,508	920	1,258	1,078
Phone Catalogues	213	—	—	—	103	235	195

Source: Blinds To Go Company Files.

Exhibit 7   Live Person Chats

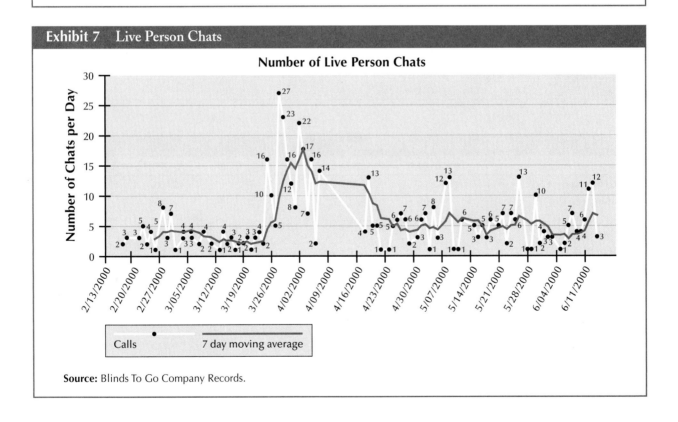

Source: Blinds To Go Company Records.

Exhibit 8 Online Survey—April 10, 2000

Q1—How did you hear about blindstogo.com?   **Q2—Rating of overall experience**

	%	Sample Size	Store	Friend	Banner	Newspapers/Mailer	TV	Catalogue	Others	Very Good	Good	Average	Bad
IN REGION (STORES)		35											
Toronto	20%	7	5	2		4				4	3		
DC/Balt	14%	5	2			3					3	2	
Boston	6%	2	1			1				1	1		
Richmond	9%	3	1		1	1	1				1	1	1
NY Metro	31%	11	5	2		4				6	4		
Philly	6%	2	1				1				2		
Detroit	14%	5			1	3	1			2	2		
subtotal			15	4	2	16	3	—	—	13	16	3	1
OUT OF REGION (NO STORES)		19											
Charlotte	5%	1							Magazine		1		
Austin	42%	8			2	3	3			3	5		
Orlando	26%	5				5					5		
Las Vegas	21%	4			1	1	3			2	2		
Others	5%	1			1					1			
subtotal			—	—	4	9	6	—	1	6	13	—	1
UN-IDENTIFIED subtotal		13	1	3	—	3	2	—	2	3	3	5	1
Category Total		67	16	7	6	28	11	—	3	22	32	8	2

Q3—Why did you choose not to buy from us? N=67; ANS=83

	Price	Selection	Site Troubles	Unclear Shipping Policy	Security Concerns	Just Looking for Info	Others	Total
All Regions	13	8	3	1	1	25	32	83
	16%	10%	4%	1%	1%	30%	39%	100%

Q4—Open-ended comments

	Site Visuals Needed	Color	Material	Overall Needed	Site Troubles	Site Visuals Subtotal	Not Enough Selection	Price	Need Cdn$	Skeptical About Quality	Positive Disposition	No Online Help	Security Problems	Site Navigation	Total
IN	15	4	—	3	2	24	6	5	3	—	1	2	1	3	45
OUT	7	3	1	—	1	12	6	5	—	—	1	—	2	1	27
Un-identified	7	—	—	—	—	7	2	2	2	1	—	—	1	3	18
Category Total	29	7	1	3	3	43	14	12	5	1	2	2	4	7	90
						48%	16%	13%	6%	1%	2%	2%	4%	8%	100%

Source: Blinds To Go Company Files.

Case 7

Cessna: Turbulence at 2000

Robert N. McGrath and Blaise P. Waguespack, *Embry-Riddle Aeronautical University*

Considering how low-risk the venture seemed at face value, it really had represented quite a gamble. In 1986 Cessna, a subsidiary of Textron, announced a complete moratorium on the production of single-engine, piston-driven general aviation aircraft because the costs of managing product liability problems had become prohibitive. The problem was industry-wide, of course. Cessna's competitors had made similar withdrawals, and Piper had even filed for Chapter 11 protection. Nevertheless, Cessna was giving up on the most successful aircraft design of all time, the Cessna 172 Skyhawk. Since it debuted in the 1950's, more aircraft of this type had been manufactured than any other in the history of aviation. Then in 1994, President Clinton signed into law legislation that would unburden the general aviation aircraft manufacturing industry of an enormous portion of its historical liability exposure. This single act triggered an industry-wide rejuvenation, and Cessna immediately announced that it would restart production of the venerable 172. It was a gamble not only because it would re-expose Cessna to a traditional liability headache after ten years of forgetting at the operational level, but because the market itself was unsure to accept a 1950's design well past the turn of the century. But it worked. The "new" Skyhawk was an immediate success, and success seemed only to accelerate through the end of the decade.

But indeed, the liability problem would not go away. In the background of marketing success, customer complaints continued to form a pattern. The new Cessna 172 had incorporated an accepted wing design, but one that was known to imperfectly address an age-old aviation problem—water in the fuel. When water gets into an aircraft's fuel tank, and it is not drained thoroughly and correctly, the engine can quit at altitude and cause fatalities. The problem seemed to be coming to a head. Cessna had not ignored the complaints, but had not been successful enough to ward off a pointed and threatening response from the Federal Aviation Administration. An attorney who at times represented Cessna, but also represented claimants, publicly accused Cessna management of burying its head, and the FAA became frustrated enough with Cessna's management of the situation to request a complete production shutdown.[1]

Product Liability in General Aviation

The term "product liability" addresses the issue of who bears risks associated with accidents.[2] In effect, this amounts to determining which party is at fault (and the extent of that responsibility) when a product fails to perform to a required standard or reasonable expectation. In principle, the objectives of liability statutes include the compensation of victims, the avoidance of injuries, the equitable spreading of risks, and the stimulation of safety-related innovation. In an important 1963 case, the Supreme Court of the United States ruled that even if a manufacturer of a product took reasonable care in the production of its goods, and had no prior knowledge that a product was defective in its manufacture or design, the manufacturer was nevertheless responsible, and wholly liable for associated damages. This "strict" interpretation of liability inaugurated a decades-long precedent where more and more types of liability burdens were consistently shifted from consumers to producers.

Because of the technological complexity of aircraft, their operating environments, and the egregious injuries that occurred during accidents, product liability expenses became enormous in the general aviation industry after the 1963 decision. Legal defenses became not only difficult, but easy to distort by a plaintiff. For example, full compliance with FAA standards became interpreted as merely the accomplishment of design and manufacture minimums; i.e., plaintiffs successfully argued that manufacturers that produced to FAA standards were trying to do as *little* as possible. The best efforts of the manufacturers' scientists and engineers, so difficult to understand by lawyers and judges, not to mention juries, were easily assailed.

It was sometimes argued that in this environment, innovation was stymied rather than stimulated, since the risks of newness became so much greater than the risks

---

Printed by permission of Robert N. McGrath and Blaise P. Waguespack, Embry-Riddle Aeronautical University.

of holding on to the tried-and-true. It was entirely possible, though difficult to show conclusively, that flight safety in general aviation was retarded, not improved, because of the "strict" liability standard. Nevertheless, immediate consumer sovereignty reigned supreme.

By the late 1980s the average amount per claimant per occurrence became about $10 million; the average total cost (losses plus defense expenses) became about $530,000. Even though manufacturers won over 80 percent of cases that went to trial, General Aviation's Big Three asserted that the annual cost incurred from all product liability expenditures was from $70–100,000 *per aircraft delivered.* Consequently, liability insurance expenses skyrocketed, from an industry-wide $24 million in 1978, to $210 million in 1985. The problem became so acute that insurers eventually became reticent to accept this business at all. Quipped one official of Lloyd's of London, "We are quite prepared to insure the risks of aviation, but not the risks of the American legal system."[3] In this environment, Cessna withdrew from the single engine aircraft market altogether, Beech substantially reduced levels of production, and Piper was forced to file for Chapter 11 status.

Many industry participants and followers felt that the demise of general aviation manufacturing was principally the result of these legal conditions, and responded. Lobbies such as the General Aviation Manufacturers Association (GAMA) and the Aircraft Owners and Pilots Association (AOPA) convinced legislators such as Representatives Dan Glickman and Nancy Kassebaum (both Republicans from Kansas) to introduce product liability reform bills. Consumer groups, organized labor, and the Association of Trial Lawyers of America (ATLA) successfully battled these movements for several years, but eventually the General Aviation Revitalization Act of 1994 was signed into law by President Bill Clinton on August 17 of that year.[4]

The most significant effect of this bill was to relinquish manufacturers from the liability for products more than eighteen years old. This relief to manufacturers might seem benign, but it was seen as a great breakthrough for several reasons. First, since the average age of a general aviation aircraft was more than 28 years, a very substantial window of litigation opportunity was erased. Second, since the most recent surge in production occurred in the late 1970s, more and more general aviation aircraft necessarily would become immune from liability in the near future. Therefore, advocates hailed this legislation as the beginning of a true revitalization for general aviation aircraft development and manufacturing. Detractors, of course, wailed at the deterioration of consumer sovereignty and, from one side of legal theory, innovation incentive.

The General Aviation Industry

The term "General Aviation," like terms used to describe other industries, was not entirely definitive, but could be generalized.[5] The General Aviation Industry included a light aircraft segment, a business aviation segment, and a regional/charter aircraft segment; it excluded the commercial airlines (with some ambiguities regarding regional/local carriers) and the military. In effect this mostly differentiated private from commercial aviation. More specifically, general aviation aircraft were considered to be single and multi-piston-engine powered fixed wing airplanes (as opposed to helicopters) weighing less than 12,500 pounds (i.e., "light" aircraft) and turboprop and jet powered aircraft (i.e., business or executive aircraft).

On the high end, the term General Aviation clearly distinguished firms like Boeing and Lockheed-Martin from the "Big Three" of general aviation: Beech, Cessna, and Piper (Exhibit 1). During the 1980's, Cessna manufactured about 100,000 general aviation aircraft; Piper manufactured about 50,000, and Beech manufactured about 24,000. Production by the mid 1990's fell to fractions of these figures.

Most of the revenues and the best profit margins were at the top end of the industry, in the turbofan (business jet) and turboprop product classes. There, the dominant players were Gulfstream, Bombardier (Learjet and other lines), and Cessna. Whereas piston-driven aircraft were usually priced in "six figures," business jets were usually priced in seven or eight figures. On the low end, General Aviation was distinct from "kitplanes" and "experimental aircraft" technologically, but more importantly, in the ways that players in those niches were regulated, which formed a fairly formidable barrier to entry.

Historically, the industry was earmarked by cyclical patterns, tied to the larger national economic picture. For example, aircraft sales plummeted after the economic recessions of 1960, 1970, and 1975, followed by industry recoveries that paralleled recoveries of the national economy as a whole. Oil embargoes also hurt, as did the chronically rising costs of maintenance and spare parts.

There have been two major slumps in production. Immediately following the at-large overexpansion of the 1960's (aircraft sales peaked at 15,768 in 1966), only 7,242 aircraft were sold in 1970. More recent developments were even more dramatic. After a recovery of 125 percent in a six-year period (1977 sales totaled 17,000), and an industry peak of 17,811 aircraft sold in 1979, production then crashed by 95.5 percent, to a point where only 811 aircraft were sold in 1993, and 444 in 1994. During the same period the number of U.S. manufacturers fell from 29 to 16; meanwhile, elsewhere in the world, the number of

Exhibit 1   General Aviation Airplane Shipments, CY 2000

Firm	Units	Billings
American Champion	96	n/a
Aviat Aircraft	91	$13,000,000
Bellanca	1	n/a
Boeing Business Jets	14	$518,500,000
Cessna Aircraft		
172 Skyhawk	150	
172S Skyhawk	340	
182 Skylane	267	
206A Stationair	53	
T206 Stationair	102	
208 Caravan I	16	
208B Caravan IB	76	
C25 CJ1	56	
525 CJ2	8	
500 Citation Bravo	54	
560 Citation Encore	6	
560XL Citation Excel	79	
650 Citation VII	12	
750 Citation X	37	
Total	1,256	$2,218,985,998
Cirrus Designs	95	n/a
Commander Aircraft	20	n/a
Gulfstream	71	$2,522,600,000
Lancair	5	$1,600,000
(Bombardier) Learjet	133	$1,197,683,525
Maule Air	57	$5,990,035
Micco Aircraft Company	6	$1,025,000
Mooney Aircraft	100	n/a
Raytheon (Beech)		
Bonanza A36	85	
Bonanza B36TC	18	
Baron 58	50	
King Air C90B	46	
King Air B200	59	
King Air 350	46	
1900D Airliner	54	
Beechjet 400A	51	
Hawker 800XP	67	
Total	476	$1,922,002,000
The New Piper Aircraft Company		
Warrior III	43	
Archer III	102	
Arrow	18	
Saratoga II	28	
Saratoga II TC	70	
Malibu Mirage	63	
Meridian	18	
Seminole	11	
Seneca V	42	
Total	395	$156,985,832
BY TYPE		
Single Engine Piston	1,810	
Multi-Engine Piston	103	
Turboprop	315	
Turbojet	588	
Grand Total	2,816	$8,558,372,390

Source: GAMA

manufacturers rose from 15 to 29. In 1980, U.S. manufacturers employed 40,000 people; in 1991, the figure was about 21,580. Whereas U.S. firms traditionally captured 20–30 percent of the world market in addition to their dominance at home, in 1981 the U.S. became a net importer of general aviation aircraft, and by 1988 net importation of foreign aircraft accounted for $700 Million of the larger national trade imbalance. Whereas 3,395 aircraft were exported in 1979, 440 were exported in 1986. Whereas U.S. manufacturers held 100 percent of home market share in 1980, by the mid-1990's this figure was less than 70 percent.

By that time the industry and many of its stakeholders had reacted in ways aimed at improving overall industry strength. In addition to the revitalization act, the federal government restored some of the subsidization of veterans' flight training programs. (Veterans had long been an important source of new pilots, as flight training was a GI benefit. However, this had become curtailed.) A Republican Congress restored the investment tax credit (which had also become curtailed) incentivizing the purchase of general aviation aircraft as well as many other durable goods. The FAA developed a comprehensive plan for industry improvement, consistent with its overall mission of advocating all aviation interests. The plan aimed at improving general aviation's image while reducing some of the regulatory burden that the agency itself imposed. The Airplane Owners and Pilots Association launched a project designed to attract 10,000 new student pilots, and largely achieved this goal. The National Business Aircraft Association actively promoted the value-addition that business flying had the potential to bring to individual firms, under the catchy slogan "No plane, No gain." Expansion of university programs in aviation-related degrees and actual flight training programs expanded significantly.

As the century concluded, the industry was well on its way to recovery (Exhibits 2 and 3). Between 1994 and 2000, 25,000 manufacturing jobs had been created, aircraft production was up 100 percent, exports more than doubled, many new products were being developed, and the number of student pilots was increasing. In 2000 general aviation was a $17 billion industry in 2000, and exporting about one-third of total production generated $51 billion in overall economic activity. General aviation aircraft carried 145 million passengers every year, flying over 27 million hours. Whereas the airlines served about 600 communities, general aviation airports served more than 5,400 (www.generalaviation.org).

Airworthiness of Aircraft

In the United States, matters regarding aviation were regulated by the Federal Aviation Administration (FAA) (www.faa.gov). This agency accomplished the safety-related aspect of its mission through an extensive system of Federal Aviation Regulations (FARs). One of the clearest and well known of these dictates was that the owner-operator of an aircraft was responsible for never leaving the ground unless the airplane was "airworthy" (FAR 23). This responsibility was true even if a safety-related activity such as maintenance was outsourced, or contracted out. In large-scale civilian operations, such as in the airline industry, there was always a very clear division of labor amongst specialists such as pilots/crews, the maintenance function, and so forth. This made the responsibility of the owner/operator for airworthiness only that much more important to maintain in its clarity.

In general aviation, on the other hand, there still remained a cultural vestige of bygone eras. In the beginnings of aviation, pilots often maintained their own aircraft; in fact this was something of a necessity given the poor support infrastructures of those eras. As the 20th century ended, many general aviation aircraft owners employed professionals to perform maintenance, especially periodic (100-hour) inspections and repairs that needed expertise and consumed large amounts of resources. But some still preferred to do much of the maintenance themselves, such as (50-hour) activities that were somewhat analogous to minor tune-ups and oil changes in the auto world. The FARs did not prohibit owners from performing maintenance; the issue was airworthiness by whatever means. But always, one act of maintenance that had always stayed with the operator—really the pilot—was the pre-flight check. A pre-flight check was a general visual inspection of critical features of an aircraft immediately before a flight. This was something of a "last chance" before flying to make sure the craft was airworthy, and must always be done before every flight.

FAA-regulated industries also had a fairly complex way of handling reported problems, including those that could affect airworthiness (FAR 39). The following description is a simplification. Problem reporting and correction had no clear starting or ending point, but this discussion will begin with the manufacturer. When a problem was identified involving the design or manufacture of an aircraft, manufacturers had very methodical and thorough internal review procedures to judge the seriousness of the suspected/known problem. After some engineering work and managerial oversight (as much as necessary), a decision was made that essentially balanced the nature of the problem, the likelihood of its occurrence, the consequences of its occurrence, and the risks in terms of both safety and cost. In aircraft manufacturing, safety, reliability, and maintainability engineering were advanced and mutually reinforcing professions.

When a problem was judged to be serious, the manufacturer commonly published a Service Bulletin (SB) and mailed a copy to each registered owner of the aircraft type, and to the FAA. Often the SB would recommend some corrective action, though technically it could not legally mandate compliance. Of course, the manufacturer could word an SB in stern language, making clear the gravity of a situation as well as its impact on general

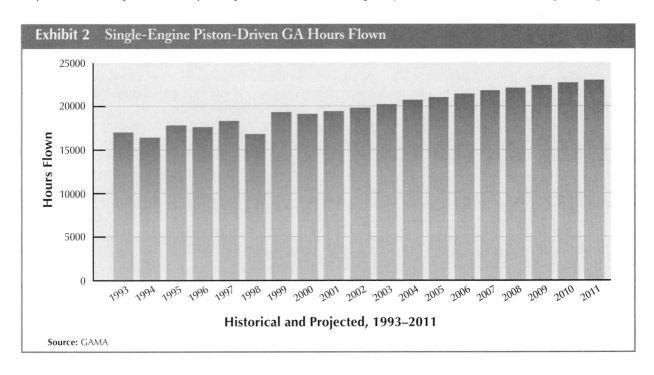

Exhibit 2   Single-Engine Piston-Driven GA Hours Flown

Historical and Projected, 1993–2011

Source: GAMA

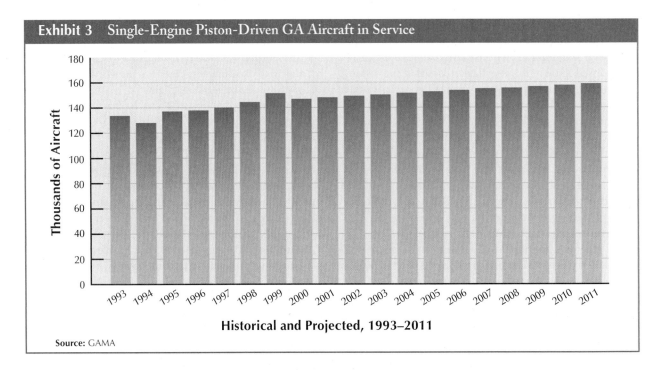

Exhibit 3   Single-Engine Piston-Driven GA Aircraft in Service

Historical and Projected, 1993–2011

Source: GAMA

warranty policies and specific contracts. However, sometimes the FAA judged an SB as being serious enough to be translated into law. It would do this by publishing an Airworthiness Directive (AD), which could legally force owners into complying with an SB. But it did not necessarily take an SB to trigger an AD. The FAA was empowered to issue ADs based on its own judgement alone, such as when it "grounded" airlines at times of accidents. Finally, and what was different than in other industries, it was the owner's responsibility to incur the cost of an AD, not the manufacturers'. Manufacturers could offer ways to relieve some or all of the cost, but complying with ADs and SBs could mount to be a significant portion of the overall cost of owning an aircraft, especially one with initial design or manufacturing problems. A typical Cessna policy, for example, was to warrant some, unspecified SBs during a two-year warranty period.

In the broader scheme of things, the FAA's role in ensuring airworthiness went far up the supply chain. In addition to governing actual aviation operations and organizations, the FAA was also responsible for making sure the manufacturing infrastructure produced airworthy aircraft. From the moment a manufacturer began designing an aircraft, the FAA was involved. Aircraft designs first needed to be "certified" as being airworthy, as did all production processes. Even some raw materials, component and spare parts suppliers needed to be certified by the FAA as having designs and production systems that would deliver airworthiness.

On the owners' side of things, this system was extended, and allowed them to call manufacturers' attention to problems occurring in the field. An owner could file a Service Difficulty Report (SDR,) for example, to officially record and detail a specific problem. When an SDR reached a manufacturer and entered its internal review system, the cycle would be basically renewed, in the sense that an SDR could trigger an internal investigation, the publication of Service Bulletins, consequent Airworthiness Directives, and so forth. But again, it did not necessarily take an SDR, or an AD, to trigger an internal investigation by a manufacturer. Many routine proposed engineering changes were always on a manufacturer's docket, most to make minor improvements.

No doubt this system made an important contribution to what was generally known to be safe. Exhibit 4 shows the figures specific to general aviation. The situation was stable and continuously improving.

Textron and Cessna

Dozens of acquisitions, divestitures, reorganizations and other moves peppered the history of Textron, which could trace its history to the establishment of the Franklin Rayon Corporation in 1928, which became known as Textron American, Inc., in 1955, after a merger with the American Woolen Company and Robbins Mills, Inc.[6] In subsequent decades, the corporate profile changed greatly. By the year 2000, Textron was known as a high-tech conglomerate, employing about 71,000 people in dozens of subsidiaries operating in two major business sectors: Manufacturing and Financial Services. Exhibit 5 portrays Textron's official view of itself and clearly states its strategic imperatives. The Manufacturing segments concentrated on the following product types: Aircraft, Automotive, Fastening Systems, and Industrial Products (Exhibit 5 shows selected financials). The Aircraft segment consisted of Bell Helicopter and Cessna. Overall, this business segment performed well in both civilian and military markets, adept at marketing its products through its own worldwide sales force as well as through a network of independent representatives. Key success factors were price, financing terms, product performance, reliability, and long-term product support.

A critical program in Bell Helicopter was the continuing development of the V-22 Osprey tilt rotor aircraft, many years in development and with much worldwide potential.[7] After taking many years to develop and achieve operational status as a U.S. Marine troop carrier, it's airworthiness came into serious question after a number of accidents. In the late 1990's 30 Marines were killed in four crashes, causing the Marine Corps to ground the fledgling fleet. Production of a total eventual delivery of 300 aircraft was postponed; each Osprey cost $70 million. The accidents also cast dark clouds on the development of a civilian version. Cessna was well known as the world's largest designer and manufacturer of general aviation aircraft; in particular, Cessna designed and manufactured light and mid-sized business jets, utility turboprop aircraft, and single and multi-engine piston-drive aircraft. Cessna was a fairly recent acquisition, having been purchased on February 28, 1992, from the General Dynamics Corporation for $605 million in cash. Two efforts were particularly exciting: new variants of the Citation X, a large business jet; and the ongoing production of the Cessna models 172, 182, and 206 piston-engine aircraft. In 2000 Cessna delivered 188 Citation business jets, and 912 of the 172/182/206 family. Similar to the profile of Bell Helicopter, Cessna marketed its products through both its own worldwide sales force and through independent representatives, principally relying on product reliability, product support, and superb brand name recognition.

The business jet segment was projected to grow by as much as 59 percent between 2000 and 2005; by 2010, 6,800 business jets might be purchased, worth nearly $89 billion.[8] Entry-level jets (such as the Cessna Citation family) were projected to garner 1,200 of this total. The Citation class aircraft, first introduced in 1969, had been one of the most successful in its product class ever. The 4000th Citation was projected for delivery in 2003; the 5000th in 2005. A production backlog through the year 2006 meant more than $6 billion to the company. The most advanced Citations cost around $12 million.

The Cessna 172

The original Cessna 172 was introduced to the general aviation market in 1955; not entirely original even then, since it shared many engineering features and componentry with other Cessna models.[9] Key to its success in the early years was aggressive advertising, which presented the plane as being comparable, in ease of operation, to the

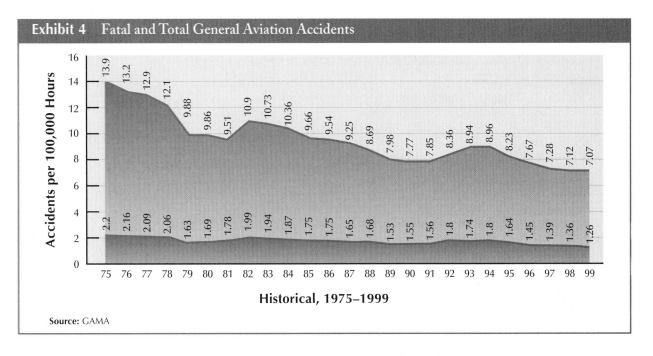

Exhibit 4   Fatal and Total General Aviation Accidents

Historical, 1975–1999

Source: GAMA

automobile. It even had features like doors on both sides and a steering wheel-like pilot control yoke, rather than the control sticks that were still ubiquitous at the time. More superficially, interior furnishings and exterior paint jobs emulated the automotive fashions of the day.

The first year the Cessna 172 was on the market, it outsold its cash-cow predecessor Cessna 170 by a margin of ten to one, prompting management to discontinue the old model in favor of the new, recognizing it as the company's future in general aviation. (Most significantly, the Cessna 170 was a "taildragger," while the Cessna 172 featured a "tricycle" landing gear configuration.) Virtually no design changes were deemed necessary until 1960, when the tail design was changed to a more swept-back look—a feature

---

Exhibit 5   Official Textron Statements

MISSION: Textron is a $13 Billion global, multi-industry company focused on delivering inspired solutions to our customers and compelling growth and value to our shareholders. In the Aircraft, Automotive, Fastening Systems, Industrial Products and Finance Industries, customers around the world know us for our powerful brands such as Bell Helicopters, Cessna Aircraft, Kauter, Lcyoming, E-Z-GO and Greenlee, among others. Our market-leading companies are redefining industries and generating compelling growth and profitability through a steadfast commitment to enterprise excellence.

Return on Invested Capital is our compass as we build a company whose powerful brands and enterprise excellence drive compelling growth.

Creating Powerful Brands

- *Build on our existing brand equity:* Use our established brand leadership to grow faster than our markets. Increase the value of our products and move into related new markets.
- *Simplify our portfolio:* Manage only market-leading, global brands and businesses that hold first or second positions in attractive markets.
- *Focus on "profit adding" versus "profit sustaining" investments:* Invest in higher growth, higher return businesses, with an emphasis on well-branded companies that are leaders in their respective market niches.
- *Invigorate our brand builders:* Give employees the freedom to find new revenue streams, develop out-of-the-box ideas and bring a passion to everything we do.

Achieving Enterprise Excellence

- *Emphasize Supply Chain Management:* Reduce material costs through strategic sourcing that leverages the "power of the whole" versus the "sum of the parts."
- *Create value through e-business strategies:* Build strategic internet alliances to increase productivity and reduce costs.
- *Create centers for shared services:* Actively look for and invest in those areas of expertise where consolidation across the enterprise makes sense.
- *Assimilate newly acquired companies with greater speed:* Move quickly to generate value from synergies across the enterprises.
- *Build on the foundation of Textron Quality Management:* Continue to drive the principles of Textron Quality Management (TQM). TQM is the institutionalization of professional controls and disciplines in every process and function we perform—from administration to engineering and manufacturing.

Delivering Compelling Growth

Delivering compelling growth means meeting the following financial goals:

- ROIC of 400 points above our weighted average cost of capital
- Organic growth of approximately 5% annually
- Segment profit margins in excess of 13% by 2005
- Earnings per share growth averaging 10% per year
- Debt to capital ratio of 30% to 35%

As these goals apply to Cessna Aircraft:

Creating Powerful Brands

- Produce business jets that represent the best value in the industry.
- Develop a broad range of business jets that support a "step-up" strategy—one that gives customers a logical "next step" in their Cessna purchases.
- Extend our brand into adjacent, high growth markets like fractional share ownership.

Achieving Enterprise Excellence

- Focus on operating improvements to add value at every step of the manufacturing process.
- Through Cessna 2020, employ Lean Manufacturing, Process Brand Management and Six Sigma performance tools.

incorporated for aerodynamic reasons, but one that was immediately popular for its looks as well. Minor changes occurred about every year thereafter, such as better streamlining (the distinguishing characteristic of the 172B Skyhawk, perhaps the version that most clearly embedded itself in general aviation history), shorter landing gear

struts, a wrap-around rear window, electric flaps, a baggage door, a larger fuel tank, and new contours that improved its range.

The airplane's original engine was the Continental O-300, very expensive to repair and overhaul and troublesome in terms of its tendency for valve failures and

Exhibit 6   Selected Textron Financial Data (000,000)

	2000	1999	1998	1997	1996
			(In millions)		
Revenues					
Aircraft	4,394	4,019	3,380	3,217	2,774
Automotive	2,924	2,868	2,356	2,072	1,577
Fastening Systems	2,137	2,082	1,758	1,498	1,355
Industrial Products	2,944	2,422	2,013	1,738	1,654
Finance	591	463	367	350	327
Total Revenues	13,090	11,854	9,874	8,875	7,687
Income					
Aircraft	451	362	338	313	261
Automotive	244	220	171	141	135
Fastening Systems	182	190	186	167	148
Industrial Products	343	301	232	188	163
Finance	190	128	113	108	96
Total Profit	1,410	1,201	1,040	917	803
Special Charges, Net	(483)	1	(87)	—	—
Gain on Sale of Division	—	—	97	—	—
Total Operating Income	927	1,202	1,050	917	803
Corporate Expenses	(184)	(143)	(141)	(152)	(125)
Interest Expense, Net	(152)	(29)	(146)	(117)	(138)
Income Taxes	(308)	(381)	(294)	(250)	(211)
Distribution Net Taxes	(26)	(26)	(26)	(26)	(23)
Income from Operations	277	623	443	372	306
Financial Position					
Total Assets	16,370	16,393	13,721	11,330	11,514
Debt					
Manufacturing	2,084	1,767	2,615	1,221	1,507
Finance	4,667	4,551	2,829	2,365	2,441
Preferred Securities of Subsidiary Trusts					
Manufacturing	484	483	483	483	483
Finance	28	29	—	—	—
Shareholder's Equity	3,994	4,377	2,997	3,228	3,183
Manufacturing Debt to Total Capital	32%	27%	43%	25%	29%
Investment Data					
Capital Expenditures	527	532	475	374	312
Depreciation	382	349	292	254	213
Research and Development	721	670	613	602	576

carburetor icing. This engine was replaced in 1968 by the Lycoming O-320-E2D, a proven design that was instantly popular when installed in the 172. In 1977 another engine change was made, but this time for the worse; the Lycoming O-320-H2AD caused camshaft and valve damage, and was plagued by abrupt engine failures related to the design and operation of oil pumps and accessory drive gears. A product recall in 1977–78 fixed some of these problems, and complete resolution was accomplished in 1981 with the installation of the Lycoming O-320-D2J engine.

Little could Cessna's management foresee in 1955 that the 172 would become the world's most popular airplane ever, in the sense that in the ensuing 31 years, some 36,010 individual aircraft would be sold, the largest number of aircraft of any single type of aircraft sold in aviation history. From its introduction to the mid-1980s, models A through P were introduced. By the mid-eighties, however, prospects in the general aviation industry were so dire that Cessna pulled out of the single-engine piston engine product line altogether.

As soon as production ceased, the marketplace missed the Cessna 172. Consumers loved this airplane so much that bodies of hobbyists emerged, focused on keeping the 172 alive in various ways. The 172 had become something of a legend in its own time and realm, and owners of the 172 discovered that as long as their airplanes were maintained well, they actually appreciated in value. Simple supply and demand evidenced itself in the very strong "used" market for 172s that developed rapidly. The airplane's continuing popularity stemmed from its excellent safety record, operating economy, and low maintenance costs. Of course, in terms of performance it was always somewhat ho-hum, being the "family car" of general aviation.

Inspired by the 1994 tort reform, Cessna announced in 1994 that Cessna would introduce a new version of the venerable 172. Start-up costs would be about $75 million. The new 172s would be produced by the company's Pawnee division, and manufactured in new facilities located in Independence, Kansas, with first deliveries planned for the summer of 1996. Though this new facility meant an important shift from Cessna's traditional Wichita production site, it meant lower overhead (first, the Wichita facility produced Cessna's jet aircraft; second, the Independence site would be new both physically and philosophically, being benchmarked against GMs Saturn methods of production as well as ISO 9001) and more manageable flight testing conditions. Plans called for the eventual manufacture of about 2000 planes per year, 600 in the first year, which should garner $300 million. The new business was expected to swell Cessna's payroll from 6,000 employees to over 7,500. Instant market leadership was expected, and full-scale production margins were expected to be double-digit.

The "new" 172 was to not be much different in appearance from the 172 legend, incorporating only a few aerodynamic improvements to reduce drag. The most significant improvements would be changes to the engine which would make it quieter, an electronic ignition with back-up magneto, an all-metal florescent-lit instrument panel, a standard backup instrument vacuum system, a gravity-feed 50-gallon wet wing, improved interior crashworthiness (improved seat tracking and seat adjustment system), a standard step-ladder, handle, toe-step and hand-grip provisions, redesigned cowling fasteners, corrosion-proofing, the addition of more modern avionics (the electronic componentry in airplanes), an improved autopilot, and a "derated" (200 hp to 160 hp) fuel-injected, four cylinder, Lycoming IO-360 engine; the derating would be accomplished by the installation of low-compression pistons and by limiting takeoff power to 2500 rpm.

Decisions regarding these changes were based on the thousands upon thousands of hours of operating experience accumulated on previous models and, of course, cost considerations. Cessna estimated that the nonrecurring costs of developing an airplane of this type "from scratch" would have been something like $25 million, through to FAA certification, and would optimistically have taken about three and a half years. Even these assumptions were based on traditional aluminum construction; state-of-the-art airframes partially fabricated of space-age composite materials were only that much more costly, difficult and time-consuming to produce and certify.

Also, it made good sense to re-invest in a design that many felt to be one of the safest of any aircraft.[10] The Skyhawk had a fatal accident rate of .56 per 100,000 hours, compared to 1.50 for all single-engine piston aircraft, and 2.13 for multi-engine piston aircraft. Upon a detailed examination of each accident, one interpretation offered the view that if accidents related to poor judgment and bad flying technique were removed from the data, Skyhawk's figure would be closer to .06. In total reported accidents, Skyhawk's record was 5.01 accidents per 100,000 hours, compared to 8.67 for other piston singles, and 6.56 for multi-engine pistons.

Ground was broken for the new manufacturing facility on May 19, 1995. On July 3, 1996—about fourteen months after the groundbreaking—production of single-piston aircraft officially began. The new facility was to manufacture not only the new 172, but also the Cessna 182 Skylane, and the Cessna 206 Stationaire, all in the same or proximate product classes, and all similar in design and appearance. The Independence plant had about 250,000 square feet of main assembly area, as well as paint and support facilities that totaled about another 150,000 square feet. Altogether, Cessna's Wichita and Independence sites could boast about 4.4 million square feet of production capacity, or about 1,900 acres. Production line flow began on July 10, and the first customer took delivery of a 172 in January of 1997. Its inaugural price was $124,500, and there were many imaginative financing and ownership schemes created by Cessna's sales and technical support function. The first new Skylane was delivered in April of 1997. In November of 1998, deliveries of the Stationair models began.

Success was immediate, steady, and continued.[11] Encouraged by the market's early response, Cessna developed and in March 1998, introduced the Skyhawk SP. "SP" stood for Special Performance. Taking the advice that had come directly from customer feedback as well as from the Cessna Sales Team Authorized Representatives, the SP package represented the incorporation of many incremental improvements in the 172's performance specifications.

The year 1999 was a true milestone year. On October 21, Cessna announced the delivery of the 1000th new Skyhawk[12] and the delivery of the 2000th aircraft overall, from the Independence site. Of the 1,210 aircraft that the company delivered by the end of that year, 899 had been single-piston models such as the 172. This represented an 11 percent increase over the prior year's delivery of 1,077 total aircraft, and a 14 percent increase over the prior year's delivery of 775 single-piston aircraft. More impressively, order placements grew 60 percent. Understandably encouraged, Cessna announced a "Millenium Edition" of Skyhawks, Skylanes, and Stationaires, which featured redesigned interiors, distinctive exterior striping, better Honeywell navigation avionics, and special accessory collections. The idea proved so successful that the planned production run sold out, and a second was produced which also sold out.[13] In January of 2000, Cessna celebrated the end of the century by announcing record company performance in terms of revenue and backlog. Sales revenues were $2.2 billion, and had never been higher in the company's 72 years of existence. The production backlog was 1,102 aircraft, worth more than $5.3 billion.

As the year 2000 ended things looked even rosier. Total revenues had reached $2.8 billion and backlog had reached 1,385 aircraft, worth about $6.6 billion.[14] In 2000 1,541 aircraft had been ordered, of which 912 were single-piston. Two new derivatives of the Skylane had been successfully introduced, Skyhawks were continuously improved at the performance margins, the company had opened up a new service center in Sacramento, California, and plans were made to open another in Orlando, Florida. A large parts distribution center was also planned. By mid-2001 the advertised price for basic 172 derivatives ranged from about $172,000 to $180,000 The company employed 13,000 people and was clearly doing well.

AvGas and Water Do Not Mix

The problem was nothing new, especially in aviation. Aviation Gasoline (AvGas) is not friendly to water when it comes to performance in piston-driven aircraft.[15] When water gets into a tank of AvGas (the main fuel tanks are usually in an aircraft's wings) and is not removed, there is a distinct possibility that the water will get to the engine and snuff out combustion. This can happen at any time, including at altitude. Obviously, this is a very hazardous condition and indeed, many aviators have suffered the consequences over the decades.

Keeping water out of a fuel system is not as easy as it might sound. For example, aircraft undergo temperature extremes, whereby condensation can be released from the fuel itself. Simpler and more obvious sources can be fueling an aircraft with contaminated fuel or seepage through imperfect seals and gaskets.

Depending on the aircraft design, manufacturers approached the problem differently. There were several basic wing/fuel system designs; two of the more common were a fuel bladder system and what's called a "wet wing." In the much older bladder design, fuel was contained in the wings in large flexible bladders. In the wet wing design, there were no bladders. Fuel was contained in hollows in the wings. Pilots liked wet wings because they held more fuel and thus allowed greater aircraft range, but the design did not inherently correct the water contamination problem.

Cessna began using the wet wing design in 1967, gradually replacing bladder designs in many aircraft. New Cessna 172s incorporated the wet wing design. As was typical in general aviation, Cessna 172 pilots were trained, and told in their operating manuals, to check for water in the fuel tanks during pre-flight inspections. To inspect for water, pilots were instructed to open each of 13 sumps, or drains, located where water was likely to pool.

Since Cessna's production of single-engine piston aircraft had been restarted in 1996, 2,149 accidents involving these aircraft had been reported. About 25 involved water in the fuel, and several deaths had occurred. In those two cases, however, it was found that the pilots had failed to perform proper pre-flight checks. But several dozen cases, where water was found in the fuel tanks, had been closed without final, conclusive determinations of cause. Still, Cessna reported that there were fewer problems reported with wet wings than with the old bladder design.

The FAA had been aware of the general problem for many years, of course, and had worked with manufacturers to constantly improve the situation. In 1982, Cessna added additional instructions to its flight manuals for single-engine aircraft. If water was originally found upon opening drains, pilots were to "gently rock" the wings and lower the tail in order to drain any remaining water. Cessna also issued a Service Bulletin to the same effect, and pilots came to refer to the procedure as "rock and roll."

In 1983, the daughter of a former FAA medical examiner was killed with her husband in a Cessna 182 equipped with fuel bladders. The husband had found water in the fuel tanks during pre-flight inspection and had "rock and rolled" the plane. Cessna was sued and the two parties settled out of court. Later that year, the FAA issued an Airworthiness Directive, instructing Cessna owners to inspect for bladder wrinkles in which water could be retained. Cessna followed with a Service Bulletin.

In 1992 Cessna sent owners a Service Bulletin warning them about continued problems and a proposed fix. At cost, Cessna would sell to owners kits for installing four more drains under each tank. Cessna reiterated this SB in 1996, feeling that compliance would add a definite margin of safety.

In 1998 the engine of a wet-wing Cessna 172 quit for the third time in a short period, and the pilot had to make an emergency landing. He called the local FAA office, which responded. Together they performed the standard pre-flight check and tried to take off, but the engine sputtered and died. Afterwards, they drained about a pint of water from the fuel tanks. The pilot then decided to install the extra drain kit that Cessna had recommended for years, but the problem continued at least one more time.

Determined, the pilot performed a simple test. He poured a pre-measured amount of water into the tanks, and drained it according to the standard procedure. Not all came out. The test was repeated by another FAA official and results were similar. The official then wrote his supervisors in Washington recommending a review of the fuel tank design. Washington officials sent two inspectors to the scene who, after performing a similar "experiment," did not differ substantially in their evaluation.

After an FAA review of accident and Service Difficulty Reports, Cessna was notified on March 13, 2000 of this specific problem aircraft in a letter. The FAA also noted "We believe this condition may exist on all Cessna high-wing integral-wing fuel-tank-equipped airplanes,"[16] a description which fit about 20,000 aircraft in the field. Cessna was simultaneously ordered to propose specific design changes to remedy the situation, for all airplanes within the FAA's concern, within two months.

Cessna responded on April 10 by rejecting any reason for concern, citing FAA documents which certified the design as meeting regulatory requirements. However, Cessna promised to conduct a "significant investigative program" and provide details "in the near future."[17] On May 30, 2000, the FAA asked Cessna for a voluntary halt to production. Cessna's management was stunned, and immediately dispatched six executives to the regional FAA office in Kansas City. After a one-day shutdown, production was restarted.

Through the middle of 2001, the FAA and Cessna were still testing 172s in a Cessna facility in Wichita. Relations between the two teams were tense.

Notes

1. Guidera, J. "Air and Water: FAA Tests Put Cloud Over Cessna's Revival of Single-Engine Line—Accidents Blamed on Flaws Fuel System Ignite Debate on Popular Plane—Losing Power at 3,000 Feet," *The Wall Street Journal*, 30 April 2001.

2. Huber, P.W. & Litan, eds., *The Liability Maze* (Washington, D.C: The Brookings Institute, 1991); Eichenberger, J. "The Day After," *The Aviation Consumer* (1 October 1994): 16–17; Stern, W.M. "A Wing and Prayer," *Forbes*, 25 April 1994, 42–43; Barnard, T. "Courts and Crashes: Why $70,000 of an Aircraft's Cost is for Product Liability Lawsuits," *Canadian Aviation* (July 1985): 33–35; Harrison, K.H. "Drastic Insurance Rate Hikes Sock it to General Aviation," *Aviation International News* (1 May 1995): 25–28; Truitt, L.J., & Tarry. "The Rise and Fall of General Aviation: Product Liability, Market Structure, and Technological Innovation," *Transportation Journal* (Summer 1995): 52–70.

3. Truitt, L.J., & Tarry. "The Rise and Fall of General Aviation: Product Liability, Market Structure, and Technological Innovation," *Transportation Journal* (Summer 1995): 56.

4. Banks, H. 1994. "Cleared for Takeoff," *Forbes*, 12 September 1994: 116–122; "Clearing a Runway for Planemakers," *Business Week* (20 March 1995): 84–95; "General Aviation Experiences a Rebirth," *Design News* (11 September 1995): 27–28.

5. FAA Aviation Forecasts: Fiscal Years 1996–2007. 1996 Washington, D.C: United States Department of Transportation; "Five Year Results: A Report to the President and Congress on The General Aviation Revitalization Act," General Aviation Manufacturer's Association, www.generalaviation.org.

6. *Moody's Industrial Manual, 2000.* New York: Moody's Investor's Services, Inc.

7. Fulgham, D.A. & R.W. Wall 2000. "MV-22 Crash Spurs Sweeping Reviews," *Aviation Week and Space Technology* (18–25 December 2000): 14–15.

8. "Outlook Bright for Business Aviation," *Flying* (January 2000): 31.

9. Charles, B. 1996. "Something's Coming," Air Progress (January): 14–15; "First 'New' C-172s to Fly in Late 1996," *Aviation Week and Space Technology* (5 June 1995): 64–65; Stewart, C. "Affordable Classic," *Air Progress* (October 1995): 30–43.

10. Collins, Richard L. 2000. "Cessna 172 Safety Report," *Flying* (April 2000): 85–87.

11. Goyer, R. 2000. "1,000th New Skyhawk," *Flying* (January 1999): 31.

12. "Cessna Celebrates Delivery of 1000th New Skyhawk," Cessna press release, Independence, Kansas, 21 October 1999; "Cessna Ends the Century With Record Performance," Cessna press release, Wichita, Kansas, 25 January 2000.

13. "Cessna Single Engine Millenium Edition Aircraft Sold out," Cessna press release, Lakeland Florida, 9 April 2000.

14. "Cessna Ends 2000 With Solid Increase in Sales," Cessna press release, Wichita, Kansas, 25 January 2001.

15. Guidera

16. Ibid.

17. Ibid.

Case 8

Citibank: The Confia Acquisition in Mexico (A)

Robert Grosse, *The American Graduate School of International Management*

Introduction

In August of 1998, Citibank-Mexico President Julio de Quesada was sitting in his office on the Paseo de la Reforma in Mexico City reminiscing about the wild ride that his organization had taken during the previous four years. From the depths of the "Tequila Crisis," when Mexico's peso devalued by more than 100 percent at the end of 1994 to the final payment of $US180 million to the Mexican government for the purchase of Banco Confia at the end of July 1998, Citibank's Mexican business had swung from peak to trough and back on several occasions. He was wondering if anyone would believe the incredible series of events that he had just experienced.

Citibank had operated in Mexico for almost seventy years, since opening its first office in Mexico City in August 1929. The bank had never had a large presence in the retail sector, being limited by Mexican law since the early 1970s to the operation of a single office and to dealing largely with the international sector. In spite of the legal limitations, Citibank built up a large loan portfolio and fee-based business by the beginning of the 1980s. Much of the bank's business was actually booked in New York, where the capital base was sufficient to extend more than $US3 billion of credits to a variety of Mexican government and corporate borrowers. The office in Mexico City was responsible for dealing with local clients and developing peso-based business, as well as providing the day-to-day links with borrowers in cross-border, dollar-denominated loans.

When Mexico's government declared its inability to service the foreign commercial bank debt in August 1982, and then governments in Argentina, Brazil, and elsewhere followed suit, Citibank was one of the hardest-hit lenders, with its loan portfolio in Latin America worth almost twice the value of shareholders' equity.

Table 1 depicts the degree of exposure of the main U.S. lenders in Latin America at the time.

Citibank in Mexico decided to ride out the storm, looking for ways to generate payments on its government loans, negotiating debt-to-equity swaps for other banks and companies, but fundamentally remaining committed to the Mexican market. Most other U.S. banks, in fact, closed their Mexican operations during the debt crisis of the 1980s.

By the early 1990s, Mexico's government had restructured its foreign debt with a Brady Plan agreement and had joined GATT (General Agreement on Tariffs and Trade), agreeing to open the economy to foreign trade and to permit foreign firms greater operating freedom in Mexico. Citibank was well positioned to build its local business, but still constrained by Mexican banking law from expanding into a branch network or taking over a local bank. When the North American Free Trade Agreement (NAFTA) began to function in January 1994, U.S. banks were finally permitted to compete on more similar terms to Mexican, domestically-owned banks. Citibank did not immediately jump to either build new branches or to buy a local bank. This turned out to be a very fortuitous decision when the Tequila Crisis hit on December 20, 1994. Mexico's government devalued the peso by 15 percent on that date, and stated a policy of allowing the peso to float freely in the foreign exchange market. An unexpectedly sharp speculative spike took the peso from about 3.4 pesos per dollar briefly to almost 8 pesos per dollar in early 1995, before settling back to about 7 pesos per dollar by the end of 1995. This dramatic devaluation caused huge burdens on many Mexican companies and banks, as their peso-denominated assets became worth less than half as much as before in dollar terms, while their dollar-denominated liabilities remained at their earlier values.

The economic situation in Mexico in 1995 thus turned out to be extremely difficult for Mexican and foreign firms alike. Citibank-Mexico's position was not as complicated as those of the large domestic banks because its loan portfolio was much smaller in local currency business. However, the lending from Citibank-New York

Table 1	U.S. Bank Exposure in Latin America as a Percentage of Capital						
Bank	Argentina	Brazil	Mexico	Venezuela	Chile	Total	Capital#
Citibank	18.2	73.5	54.6	18.2	10.0	174.5	5,989
Bank of America	10.2	47.9	52.1	41.7	6.3	158.2	4,799
Chase Manhattan	21.3	56.9	40.0	24.0	11.8	154.0	4,221
Morgan Guaranty	24.4	54.3	34.8	17.5	9.7	140.7	3,107
Manufacturers Hanover	47.5	77.7	66.7	42.4	28.4	262.8	2,592
Chemical	14.9	52.0	60.0	28.0	14.8	169.7	2,499
Bankers Trust	13.2	46.2	46.2	25.1	10.6	141.2	1,895
Crocker National	38.1	57.3	51.2	22.8	26.5	196.0	1,151

capital in millions of current U.S. dollars

Source: William Cline, *International Debt and the Stability of the World Economy*. Washington, D.C.: Institute for International Economics, September 1983, p. 34.

Table 2	Summary of Confia's Income Statements (in Millions of Pesos)		
	1994	**1995**	**1996**
		(In millions of pesos)	
Net Interest Income Before Provisions	1,250.5	1,607.9	981.7
Net Interest Margin	9.03%	7.27%	2.57%
Provisions for Loan Losses	(296.9)	(1,319.0)	(229.2)
Non-Interest Income	307.3	413.1	459.6
Total Net Income	1,260.9	701.9	1,212.1
Other Income and Expenses	(74.8)	42.5	112.5
Operating Expenses	(960.2)	(1,536.9)	(1,740.5)
Benefit from Deferred Tax & Profit Sharing	0	320.9	0
Earnings Before Tax and Profit Sharing	225.9	471.5	415.9
Tax and Profit Sharing	(84.8)	(0.025)	0
Net Income	141.1	(471.5)	(415.9)

Source: Abaco Grupo Financiero. 1997.

once again was hurt by client defaults and other impairments in their foreign debt servicing. The impact was far less than in the 1980s crisis, but the short term crash in Mexico was evidenced by 1995's real national income growth of *negative* 6 percent.

The Mexican economy stayed in a nosedive for most of 1995, only beginning to recover early the following year. The impact on companies was to create enormous stress on their abilities to deal with financial commitments, as their sales declined due to the recession and their foreign-currency debts grew dramatically with the devaluation. In a large number of cases, companies failed and, rather than sell off assets to try to meet bank financing

obligations, they simply handed over title to houses, factories, offices, etc., to the bank lenders. The banks consequently were hit by a wall of non-performing loans and repossessions of physical assets that they could not sell in the depressed market.

It was clear even by mid-1995 that the Mexican financial system was in trouble, and that significant resources would be needed to bail out the banks. In June the Mexican government discreetly probed Citibank to see if there was interest in taking over any one of the heaviest-hit Mexican commercial banks and injecting new liquidity into the system. The banks mentioned in this context included Bancrecer, Bancremi,

Table 3   Summary of Confia's Balance Sheets (in Thousands of Pesos)

	1994	1995	1996	1997
	(In thousands of pesos)			
Current	458,212	1,708,625	1,240,140	1,859,375
Investments In Securities	2,255,367	551,292	853,878	966,336
Investments In Loans	15,711,326	18,749,431	25,944,351	15,426,635
Forwards & Repurchase Agreements	1,663,915	2,079,379	1,502,365	510
Past-due	983,478	2,756,891	1,611,167	15,495,741
Sundry Debtors	43,895	96,050	494,142	394,593
Foreclosed Assets	85,924	459,235	684,385	921,933
Other Investments & Furniture And Equipment	325,713	587,810	657,506	251,223
Revaluation & Shares Real Estate	41,550	124,960	171,950	
Fixed Assets	264,068	372,229	426,379	1,037,364
Differred Charges	199,042	819,910	865,364	553,121
Total Assets	22,032,490	28,305,812	34,451,627	36,906,831
Demand Liabilities	2,535,496	3,612,408	5,570,289	5,284,595
Time Deposits	10,421,730	16,980,632	20,395,862	25,563,232
Banks Correspondents & Loans	5,374,852	1,691,984	3,510,826	7,102,731
Forwards & Repurchase Agreements	1,672,933	2,096,115	1,500,238	28
Other Deposits & Provisions & Reserves	206,980	271,538	236,748	732,509
Preventive Provisions For Loan Losses	526,699	1,704,853	907,231	22,742,721
Subordinated Non Conv. Debentures	400,000	400,000	750,000	740,195
Total Liabilities	21,138,690	26,757,530	32,871,194	62,166,011
Capital Stock	97,258	430,000	1,117,463	2,150,102
Capital Reserves	317,832	154,149	179,949	359,046
Subordinated Mandatory Conv. Debentures	115,000	1,091,839	750,500	750,500
Surplus/Deficit Shares & Other Assets	222,212	343,140	423,902	472,971
Net Sub. None Dist. Profit & Prior Year Earnings Sub.	439	663	(2,451)	0
Prior Year Loss	0	0	(472,981)	(1,445,749)
Net Income	141,059	(471,510)	(415,948)	(27,546,050)
Undone Income	0	0	1	0
Total Stockholders Equity	893,800	1,548,281	1,580,434	(25,259,180)
Total Liabilities Equity	22,032,490	28,305,812	34,451,627	36,906,831

Source: Abaco Grupo Financiero.

Banco Union, and Banpais, all of which had been intervened by the authorities due to their inadequate capitalization as a result of the crisis.

Citibank's strategy in Mexico in the early 1990s mirrored the bank's global two-part strategy, based on a global organization divided into corporate and retail divisions. The goal of the former division was to build the corporate business through lending and service-provision to large- and medium-sized Mexican companies and foreign companies operating in Mexico. The goal of the retail business was to build relationships with high net worth clients and to limit the number of small-scale clients and activities. The retail bank was allowed, after a change in Mexican banking legislation in 1987, to expand into additional branches, and six additional, highly computerized branches were set up in the early 1990s. Up to the time of the Confia negotiations, the branches were used mainly for credit card services and some check cashing, while not building up any substantial retail business. Most corporate clients continued to deal only with the main office on Paseo de la Reforma in Mexico City. In both retail and corporate divisions, the strategy was explicitly *not* to build a large branch network in Mexico.

Brief History of Citibank

City Bank of New York was founded in 1812 by Colonel Samuel Osgood, first commissioner of the U.S. Treasury. The bank opened offices in London and Shanghai in 1902 and in Buenos Aires in 1914. It was renamed National City Bank of New York during that period. By 1939 the bank had more than 100 foreign offices.

In 1955 the bank merged with First National Bank of New York to become First National City Bank. During the 1970s the bank became the United State's largest credit card issuer (which it remains today) and was a leader in offshore lending. The bank was renamed Citibank in 1974, during the leadership of Walter Wriston. It passed Bank of America to become the largest U.S. bank in 1981. In 1998 Citibank merged with Travelers, a huge insurance and investment banking firm, to form Citigroup.

The bank's organizational structure since 1994 (before the Travelers merger) divided business into a Global Consumer Division and a Global Finance Division. The Global Consumer Division was responsible for meeting the needs of retail clients, including deposit taking, consumer lending, asset management, and other services. The Global Finance Division was responsible for dealing with needs of corporate and government clients, and those of other financial institutions. Services offered by this division included corporate lending, funds transfer, foreign exchange, and a number of investment banking functions.

Citibank was the leading global bank in the United States in 1999. With more than 100 years of experience in international lending, and with affiliates in 98 countries outside of the United States, Citi was far ahead of the competition. U.S. banks had predominantly remained at home with their business, largely as a result of the huge size of the U.S. domestic market, the largest financial market in the world, which had been generally adequate for bank expansion through the years. Also, the banking industry historically had been one of the most highly regulated, so that domestic banks from any country were mostly limited to domestic business and very small and narrowly defined banking activity in other countries (such as trade financing and lending to local clients); for the most part, taking domestic deposits in other countries had been forbidden in the 20th century.[1]

Citibank built a network of international banking offices around the world, beginning in 1902, but expanding especially rapidly after World War II. In Latin America, Citibank and Bank of America competed in the post-War period to build networks of wholesale banking offices. By 1929 both had offices in Mexico City, Buenos Aires, Sao Paulo, and Santiago. By the 1970s, Citibank had a representative office in almost every Latin American country, and Bank of America was not far behind. The main competitors for these multinational banks were largely a handful of British (Barclays and Lloyds) and Canadian (Bank of Nova Scotia and Royal Bank of Canada) banks.

Citibank Strategy

Citibank in the mid- and late-1990s was pursuing a global strategy based on the division of activities into institutional (Global Finance) and consumer (Global Consumer) divisions. Each of these divisions was pursuing a relatively independent strategic plan, with emphasis on sharing resources and opportunities where possible. Figure 1 depicts the organizational structure into which the Mexican operations fit in 1995–98. The Global Consumer bank had had a goal set in the 1980s of gaining clients around the world so that Citibank would number one in every five people in the world as clients in one form or another. This goal was revised in the early 1990s, as the bank chose to focus on fewer customers in the middle and upper segments of the income scale.

Given the prohibition against foreign banks taking control of domestic banks in most countries of the world through the 1980s, Citibank was at a disadvantage in seeking local clients for retail services outside of the United States. The retail division was largely able to focus on international services and private banking services to higher income clients in its foreign offices. The bank thus developed a strategy of seeking out such clients and offering them a wide array of services, including cross-selling corporate banking services to their companies. Nevertheless, the goal of penetrating consumer markets around the world was clearly unrealistic at the mass-market level, so Citibank focused on the narrower target of what is known in banking as Segments A and B of the income scale, i.e., the top end.

The Global Finance division expanded very successfully during the 1980s and early 1990s into significant financial markets around the world through the establishment of typically small operations, in the form of representative offices, branches, and occasionally locally-incorporated banks. By investing quite small amounts of capital in the physical locations, Citibank was still able to provide world-leading service in corporate lending, cash management, trade finance, foreign exchange, and an additional broad array of financial services based on its global capitalization and willingness to innovate to meet customer needs.

In less-developed countries, the Global Finance affiliates reported through the Emerging Markets Group to the central Global Finance office, while the Global

FIGURE 1

Citibank Partial Organization Chart—1995, 1996

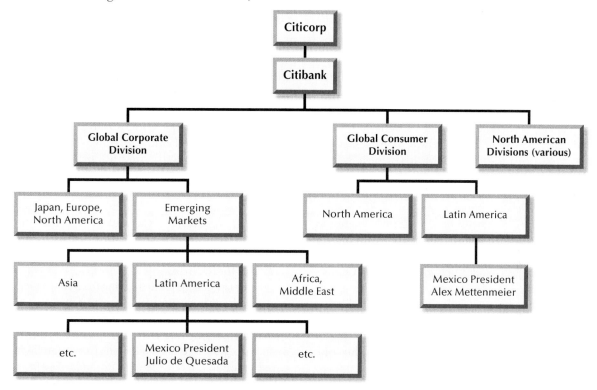

Consumer affiliates reported first through regional headquarters, then to the home office. This two-sided reporting structure applied to the bank's activities in Mexico and the other 74 emerging markets where the bank operated in the mid-1990s. The Emerging Markets Group was clearly set on minimizing the bank's exposure through physical facilities, aiming to build market share through electronic banking mechanisms and investment banking, non-credit activities. The Consumer Division was not pushing for extensive branch networks in emerging markets in the early 1990s, but with the announcement of the embedded bank strategy in 1994, Mexico was targeted for expansion of retail activity.

Brief History of Confia

Confia was originally formed as the Banco Azucarero (the sugar growers bank) in 1932. It changed its name in 1941 to Banco de Industria y Comercio, to represent a broader client base and focus. In 1977 it merged with Grupo Atlas to form Banca Confia. At that point Confia had 132 branches throughout Mexico.

In 1982 the Mexican government intervened in the bank due to the debt crisis and the bank's inadequate capitalization. All of the original shareholders' equity was lost. For the rest of that decade Confia was operated by the Mexican government.

Confia was purchased from the government by Jorge Lankenau in 1991, during the reprivatization of all of the Mexican banks that had been nationalized during the external debt crisis in 1982. Lankenau placed Confia into the holding company for his stock brokerage and insurance firms, Abaco Grupo Financiero. In 1992 the bank changed its name to Confia, S.A. The bank initially added 122 branches to the Abaco financial group, and subsequently this branch network was extended to almost 300 branches and 40 electronic modules.

Under Lankenau's leadership Confia gained a reputation for offering excellent retail service, efficient operation, and generally high quality. Just as with every other Mexican bank, Confia was devastated by the Tequila Crisis, and quickly became overwhelmed by devalued assets in pesos, revalued liabilities in dollars, and massive defaults by its corporate and individual borrowers in 1995. This situation led to the initial search for a short-term lender, and then to the forced need for a buyer of the bank.

Lankenau's efforts to prop up the bank led him to take funds from other affiliates of Abaco Grupo Financiero, which were lost as the bank sank into unmanageable debt. Shareholders in the group sued Lankenau in 1997 for taking almost $US200 million out of the brokerage firm and putting the money into the bank, thus losing it in the bank's failure. This legal maneuvering led to a highly publicized flight by Lankenau, and his ultimate imprisonment in November of 1997.

The Initial Strategic Alliance

The first link between Citibank and Confia was established in 1995 when the recently arrived General Manager of Citibank-Mexico, Julio de Quesada, negotiated an agreement with Confia President Jorge Lankenau, to utilize Confia branches for collection services to Citibank clients throughout Mexico.

This was a logical extension of Citibank's interest in offering service to major clients in locations around the country, but without requiring Citibank to establish an expensive branch network to offer that service. Confia's more than 300 branches across Mexico, with major strengths in the three big industrial centers of Mexico City, Monterrey, and Guadalajara, was an excellent distribution network from Citibank's point of view.

Likewise, the fit with Confia was good, since this bank was focused more on the middle market companies in Mexico, and was not such a direct competitor with Citibank as the three Tier-1 Mexican banks (Banamex, Bancomer, and Serfin). It turned out that both of the banks' leaders, De Quesada and Lankenau, had graduated from the University of Pennsylvania's Wharton School, and they hit it off very well. The relationship with Citibank was helpful to Confia in building its image of quality, and conversely it was helpful to Citibank to acquire the use of Confia branches to collect payments to Citi's clients throughout Mexico for deposit and transfer in their accounts. For example, Coca-Cola was able to receive payments from distributors around the country at their local Confia branches, and these payments were rapidly credited to Coca-Cola's account at Citibank in Mexico City through the collections agreement.

The Crisis at Confia

The initial strategic alliance with Confia progressed well in 1995, though it was not a major influence on Citibank success in Mexico. The Tequila Crisis had intervened to depress the business environment in Mexico, and demand for the products and services of Citibank's clients was hurt just as the rest of the economy. Nevertheless, the alliance was successful, and both banks profited from it. Overall, however, Confia and other Mexican financial institutions were very hard hit by the economic crisis.

In early 1996 Confia was becoming overwhelmed by the problems generated by the Tequila Crisis. Its capital had fallen far too low to support its outstanding assets, and the Mexican government was pressuring the bank to inject new capital from the owners. Citibank's first discussion of financial support with Jorge Lankenau was in March of 1996 at a bankers' meeting in Cancun, when he asked de Quesada for a bridge loan for $US50 million until he could get investors to put up that much money for recapitalizing the bank. This credit was debated within Citibank, and final approval was given in May of 1996. Interestingly, the issue of possible acquisition of an ownership stake in Confia was raised in these discussions, but Lankenau was not interested in giving up any control of the bank at that time. In fact, Lankenau rejected the loan offer because Citibank demanded to have shares of the bank put in escrow as collateral for the loan.

The situation deteriorated during the rest of 1996, such that Confia was still unable to come up with the funds necessary to recapitalize the bank. In early 1996, the Mexican government had begun to probe Citibank to see if the bank were interested in buying Confia, just as it had asked in relation to other weak Mexican banks a year earlier. Talks began in May of 1996 with the Mexican banking commission (Comision Nacional Bancaria y de Valores). The government gave Citibank a green light to buy Confia, if shareholders agreed—following similar treatment that had been given to BBV (which purchased Banco Mercantil Probursa in 1994) and Banco Santander (which purchased Grupo Financiero InverMexico in 1995).

Jorge Lankenau contracted with the investment bank, SBC Warburg, in mid-1996 to look for new capital contributions from investors in international capital markets. His intention was to maintain control over Confia and to attract minority investors or even lenders to raise the needed funding. Warburg was not able to deliver a strategic partner or a number of investors sufficient to recapitalize the bank adequately to meet Mexican government requirements. By early 1997 Lankenau changed his assignment to Warburg and asked the investment bank to look for a buyer for Confia. At that point he was aiming to rescue as much of his own capital as possible from the bank, and had resigned himself to losing control.

Citibank's Internal Perspective on Confia

Citibank's initial response was to consider the idea of an acquisition, despite the bank's own internal position against expansion in Mexico through building a branch network. The possibility of buying Confia constituted a window of opportunity, and it seemed to be one worth considering carefully. Interestingly, the bank itself was split on the issue, with the retail/consumer division in favor of acquiring Confia and building a major retail presence in the country, and the corporate/wholesale division of the Emerging Markets Group opposed to the risky investment that would expose the bank to having real physical assets throughout Mexico.

Citibank's local management team saw the situation as a real opportunity to be seized. Although they recognized the need to carefully examine Confia's books and market situation, the Citibank team saw Confia as a high-quality local retail provider whose personnel and offices could be quickly incorporated into Citibank's consumer banking business. In addition they saw the need for Citibank to respond to the Spanish challenge presented in the acquisitions by Banco Santander, Banco Bilbao-Vizcaya, and Banco Central Hispano (now merged with Santander—which bought Banco Internacional)—all during the previous two years. Citibank was in the position of being the long-time leading foreign bank in Mexico, but heading to become a second-rate player behind the Spanish banks, HongKong & Shanghai Bank (part owner of Banca Serfin), and Bank of Boston.

By acquiring Confia, Citibank would obtain not only the 300-branch network, but also client relationships with 30,000 mid-sized corporate clients and 280,000 retail clients throughout Mexico. Given the situation of the Tequila Crisis, both types of clients would initially be poor lending targets, since many of them were in default on their existing loans from Confia. However, the retail clients would offer an enormous deposit base throughout the country, and thus a major source of low-cost peso funding. The corporate clients would complement Citibank's 540 existing major corporate clients in Mexico, and could initially be served with fee-based services such as cash management and foreign exchange, as well as other non-credit services. Beyond this, Confia also would give Citibank access to the public sector market due to Confia's relationships with individual Mexican States, municipalities, and the social security system.

At the time Citibank was in the throes of a strategic shift in emerging markets. Given the economic opening that was occurring in many formerly restricted markets, opportunities were arising to capture significant market share in domestic banking activities that had previously been reserved for locally owned institutions only. In many Latin American countries, the way was open for foreign bank expansion, and several of Citibank's global competitors (such as HongKong Bank and Bank of Montreal) were already taking advantage by buying local banks. Citibank defined a new strategy of becoming an embedded bank in nine key emerging markets including Mexico. This meant gaining sufficient local size to compete successfully with the leading local banks in a wide range of lending and deposit activities and services. By pursuing such a strategy in Mexico, Citibank would have to build a much greater local presence.

An initial review of the situation led Citibank-Mexico's management to look at the three Tier 1 banks as possible acquisition targets. (See Table 4 for financial information about selected Mexican banks.) In addition to their very weak balance sheets due to the crisis, Banamex and Bancomer were eliminated from further consideration because of their very large size in the local market. Citibank did not want to be accused of dominating the Mexican banking system and taking unfair advantage of its large size and financial strength to do so. Banca Serfin was also examined, but the bank was viewed as being in extremely weak condition, both managerially and financially, and thus it was dropped from consideration as well. This last decision was made despite the Mexican government's request for Citibank to consider acquiring Serfin (which was later, in 1999, intervened in by the government and put up for resale—a process that was incomplete at year end 1999).

In late 1996 Citibank Mexico put together a team of President Julio De Quesada, Treasurer Eloy Molina, and Legal Counsel Jose Luis Rodriguez Macedo to investigate in more detail the possible acquisition of Confia. These three leaders of the bank proceeded to explore the feasibility of this strategy, the likely price needed to buy the bank, and the legal requirements that would have to be met. They took it as given that Confia would make an excellent platform for expanding Citibank's retail business in Mexico, and also the corporate business aimed at companies outside of Mexico City, where Citibank had no direct representation.[2]

Setting a Price on Confia

The Citibank team found that the financial analysis of Confia was quite complicated, because they were evaluating a bank in distressed condition rather than a typical going concern. While Confia's branches were mostly profitable, and the bank's deposit base was fairly secure, the loan portfolio was tremendously impaired, to the

Table 4	**Financial Condition of Mexican Banks at Year-end 1997 (in Millions of Pesos)**

Summary of Balance Sheet (1997)

	BANAMEX	BANCOMER	BANPAIS	BBV	CITIBANK	SERFIN	BANORTE	BITAL
Total Loans	152,198	174,479	20,089	41,963	10,755	106,646	20,871	54,812
Past-due Loans	28,057	22,116	0	1,323	167	11,364		
Total Assets	**250,949**	**219,319**	**22,316**	**62,880**	**15,608**	**147,620**	**26,315**	**73,956**
Loan-loss Reserves	15,556	12,729	32	1,191	127	6,476	1,571	4,050
Deposits	210,056	187,803	20,242	56,337	12,745	131,872	17,934	52,013
Stockholder Equity	22,144	19,462	762	3,700	1,729	N.d.	1,787	6,028
Net Income	2,103	2,371	21	302	50	-1,833	149	278
Fobaproa Bonds	29,773	33,877	20,060	23,289	0	52,347		
Total Liabilities Equity	**250,949**	**219,319**	**22,316**	**62,880**	**15,608**	**147,620**	**26,315**	**73,956**
Past-due/Total Loans	18.40%	12.70%	0.00%	3.20%	1.60%	10.70%		

Sources: Mexican Companies Books 4th Quarter 1998, Mexican Bank Reference Guide, December 1997

Summary of Income Statement (1997)

	BANAMEX	BANCOMER	BANPAIS	BBV	CITIBANK	SERFIN	BANORTE	BITAL
Net Interest Income	10,724	10,150	81,326	2,543	758	4,318	699	3,343
Noninterest Income	7,162	5,664	62,224	403	442	1,335	526	2,911
Noninterest Expense	9,985	11,357		2,475	831	5,940	805	6,469
Loan Loss Provision	5,324	3,805		111	70	1,029	173	1,222
Net Income	2,103	2,371	21	302	50	-1,833	149	278

Sources: Mexican Bank Reference Guide, December 1997, Latin Banking Guide & Directory 1998–1999.

point where it appeared that more than 50 percent of loans could be in arrears or default. This situation made it extremely difficult to place a value on Confia, except in the context of a negotiated deal in which some of the bad debt could be eliminated.

The method used by Molina and the Citibank financial team was to work through the Confia portfolio loan by loan and to assign values to the individual parts. This asset value was then compared with the value of liabilities such as peso deposits and loans to the bank (often in dollars). The full analysis was not undertaken until Citibank decided to pursue an agreement with the government. An initial look at Confia's books in July of 1997 led Citibank to anticipate a need for more than $US1 billion of new financial resources to cover bad debts. The bank's more than $US4 billion of loans ultimately were judged to be worth less than half of face value, leaving shareholders' equity with a negative value. Confia financial statements are presented at the end of the case. It took Citibank's finance team more than a year to work through the entire process, which was hampered severely by inadequate documentation of loans and an antiquated system for consolidating branch information at the home office.[3]

The Acquisition Process

Citibank pursued the analysis of Confia during the spring of 1997, and came to a general agreement with the Mexican government that it would make a formal offer to purchase Confia. At the same time the government was looking for other possible acquirers for Confia. Bids were sought from several foreign banks, among which Bank of Boston, Argentaria (Spain), General Electric Capital Corporation, and Bank of America seemed to be the most interested candidates.

This effort by the Mexican government to generate a bidding process was hampered by several factors. The first problem arose with the legal prosecution of Jorge Lankenau for his shifting of funds between affiliates of Abaco Grupo Financiero, and defrauding shareholders in the stockbroking firm. This created legal concerns with respect to the potential financial liabilities of Confia as a part of the Abaco group. These concerns were resolved, though Lankenau continued to claim that the bank was being illegally taken from him during his prosecution.

The situation was also complicated because the financial condition of Confia even without Lankenau's problems was quite weak due to the Mexican financial situation. The broad economy was growing again by 1997, but the banking system was still in jeopardy, with billions of dollars of non-performing loans burdening the balance sheets of the banks. Confia was in such weak condition that the Mexican government was at the point of forcing it to find an acquisition partner or close down. As pointed out above, the government sought out bidders for the bank—even though it was technically under intervention at that time.

Citibank agreed with the government in May of 1997 to pursue the acquisition, with a price to be set as soon as it was possible to conclude the evaluation process. In July the two sides began working on a Memorandum of Understanding (MOU) to define the terms of an acquisition and the timetable for legal steps and payments. On August 27, 1997, the Comision Nacional Bancaria y de Valores manage rially intervened in Confia, taking control from Lankenau's Abaco Grupo Financiero. This gave the government the right to dispose of Confia as it saw fit. Citibank and the Government of Mexico on the same day signed the Memorandum of Understanding, detailing a sequence of steps for setting a value for the purchase (KPMG Peat Marwick was contracted to do this), allowing Citibank to perform a due diligence evaluation of the bank, and defining an initial timetable for carrying out the process. This defined a full commitment on both sides for the acquisition to proceed once the financial and other details were settled.[4]

The two processes of placing a value on the bank and examining its activities in the due diligence analysis took months to carry out. Once the KPMG study was completed, Citibank negotiated in more detail with the government as to how much of the loan portfolio would be purchased and how much of it would be passed on to FOBAPROA (the Mexican equivalent of the U.S. Resolution Trust Company, established to dispose of the financial assets and institutions that went bankrupt in the 1980s during the savings and loan crisis). Table 5 shows an approximation of the balance sheet of Confia at year-end 1997, accounting for the bad loans in the portfolio that were identified in Citibank's due diligence process.

Initially, the government wanted Citibank to purchase 50 percent of the loan portfolio, whereas Citibank wanted as little as possible, judging most of it to be uncollectible. By May of 1998 Citibank agreed to buy the entire loan portfolio, to pay only about 25 percent of its face value, and to act as collection agent for FOBAPROA to try to collect on the rest of the portfolio over a five-year period.

Announcement of a Deal (May 8, 1998)

The official announcement of a deal was made public on May 8, 1998. Citibank agreed to pay $US135 million for the assets and liabilities of the bank, plus a premium of $US45 million for goodwill (prin cipally, the branch network).[5] This represented a market valuation of Confia's balance sheet. The government announced a legal intervention of Confia, giving it the right to sell Confia to Citibank. The agreement included an actual transfer of the funds to be made on May 20, 1998, after which Citibank would take control.

Table 5	Confia Approximate Balance Sheet, Adjusted for Bad Loans, December 31, 1997 (in Millions of U.S. Dollars)			
Assets			**Liabilities**	
Net Loans, Marked-to-Market	990		Deposits	2700
Other Assets	235		Other Liabilities	1200
Necessary Loan Loss Reserves	2800		Required Minimum Capital	125
Total Assets	4025		Total Liabilities + Equity	4025

Notes:

1. The net loans are adjusted for existing loan loss reserves. This means that FOBAPROA had to inject an additional $US 2.8 billion for the additional reserves needed.

2. Adjusted deposits were approximately the same as nominal deposits, since they were largely marked-to-market anyway.

3. The required minimum capital is the amount that the Mexican authorities would require for a financial institution with the deposit base of Confia. This also had to be injected by FOBAPROA.

On the basis of this information, and assuming that FOBAPROA would contribute the funds needed for reserves and capital, Citibank had to make an offer to buy Confia.

Operation Casablanca

On May 18, 1998, the U.S. Justice Department announced a series of indictments of Mexican banks and individuals, along with several banks and individuals from Venezuela and the Bahamas, for criminal money laundering. Confia was prominently present in the list, along with Serfin and Bancomer, among others. Several officers of the bank were accused of receiving drug money from undercover Federal agents and for soliciting money for laundering purposes. The undercover operation that led to these indictments was called Operation Casablanca.

This new shocking revelation caused Citibank to withhold payment for the acquisition and led to another frantic period of evaluating the liability of the bank, examining the alternatives for dealing with the problem, and ultimately proposing a solution so that Citibank could carry out the acquisition. In its due diligence process, Citibank had not uncovered the illegal activity. In the context of its valuation of the bank, KPMG had reported that Confia's anti-money laundering controls were inadequate, and at that time a program was instituted to put in place an acceptable system. The net result was that neither KPMG nor Citibank was guilty of any misdeeds, but their client Confia certainly was.

Citibank-Mexico's legal counsel, Jose Luis Rodriguez Macedo, examined the situation in great detail and came to the conclusion that Citibank could not run the risk of Confia being convicted of the charges, and that Citibank had to somehow deal with them without itself becoming liable subsequently. He was initially at a loss to see how to avoid the problem and still acquire Confia. The U.S. Justice Department was adamant about pursuing the prosecution, and would not negotiate a fine without admission of guilt.[6]

Rodriguez Macedo finally came up with what turned out to be a viable and innovative solution. He recommended splitting Confia into a shell company with the original name, which would keep the indictment and legal liability. All of the assets and liabilities of Confia would be spun off into a new company, and Citibank would buy that company. In this way, the Justice Department was satisfied that they prosecuted Confia and obtained an out of court settlement that allowed the U.S. Government to keep the seized funds ($US12 million). The Mexican Government and Citibank were satisfied because they did not end up with any legal liability for the episode after this settlement. And the Mexican government was especially pleased with this solution, since it meant that Citibank would take the problem bank off the government's hands and lend an appearance of greater soundness to the Mexican banking system.

It took until July for the money laundering crisis to be resolved, and then Citibank finally officially took ownership of Confia on July 31, 1998. The final payment for the acquisition was made on August 12, 1998. At that time Citibank became the proud owner of a branch network of almost 300 branches throughout Mexico, with a staff of more than 4000 employees.

The Relation of the Deal to the Travelers Merger

To add one more layer of complication to the entire process, Citicorp (the holding company for Citibank) announced in April 1998 its intent to merge with Travelers Company, a huge insurance and investment banking firm. The merged firm, Citigroup, would become the largest financial services firm in the United States. This merger was pursued over the same time period as the conclusion of the Confia acquisition, making the situation that much more difficult because of the organizational changes taking place at the top. These issues are discussed in case (B) in the Citibank series.

In fact, the Travelers merger did not have a great impact on the Confia acquisition, since Travelers had no insurance business in Mexico and only a very small presence of Salomon Smith Barney in Mexico City. The plans for future growth of these other activities to take advantage of Citibank's new expanded presence in Mexico began immediately, but there were no significant conflicts caused by the joining of Citibank and Travelers.

The Aftermath of the Acquisition

Once the legal arrangements were settled, Citibank moved into the process of assimilating the Confia personnel and organization. This process was largely completed by the end of 1999. The financial situation in Mexico remained quite fragile, with Banca Serfin under intervention by the government in July of 1999, and other banks remaining with severe bad debt burdens. The overall financial system was likewise under strain. FOBAPROA was reorganized and converted into a new agency called IPAB in late 1998. The cost of the financial restructuring and government bail-out of the financial institutions was estimated at almost $US100 billion by year-end 1999.

Citibank began to build up its domestic lending and deposit-taking business once the acquisition was completed, though again the financial system insecurity left a large question mark in Mexico for the entire sector.

Questions

1. What strategy should Citibank have followed in Mexico in 1995, after the Tequila Crisis and the opening of the Mexican banking system to greater foreign entry?
2. How much should Citibank have paid for Confia when they offered to buy the bank?
3. How does the recommended Mexico strategy fit within Citibank's (Citigroup's) global strategy?

Notes

1. U.S. banks were limited further to taking deposits in only one state until the legislation was changed in 1994. From the passage of the McFadden Act in 1927, U.S. banks and bank holding companies could only operate deposit taking locations in one state—though they were permitted to make loans, offer intern ational services, and provide other services nationwide. Banking deregulation in the 1990s eliminated the interstate banking prohibition and produced a tidal wave of nationwide banking consolidation.
2. Part of the embedded bank strategy included extending Citibank services to more middle-market companies, or ELCs (emerging local corporate clients). These were the bread and butter of Confia's corporate business

3. Confia had not implemented a computerized consolidation system for its accounting. Branch information, provided as computer printouts, was being manually re-entered into home-office computers, and only aggregate data were being presented—thus making detailed evaluation of the branch activities very difficult. The whole problem of inadequate computerized information, along with missing loan documentation in a number of instances, caused Citibank to take many months in the process of evaluating the books of Confia.
4. The MOU established clear lines of responsibility for dealing with Confia's existing liabilities and for recapitalizing the bank before Citibank would take over and pay for the acquisition. The terms of the agreement were set to depend on valuation of the loan portfolio and bad debts, plus other Confia assets and liabilities by an independent auditor approved by both Citibank and the Mexican government. The process identified in the MOU was followed through the subsequent months, and only unexpected events caused the final sale to be delayed until July of 1998.
5. Citibank was permitted to pay the premium with debt instruments of the Mexican government's foreign bank debt, which sold at a discount in the market, and allowed Citibank to eliminate some of its still-devalued Mexican loans from the 1980s. The Multiyear Restructuring Agreement (MYRA) loans were selling for slightly over half of face value, and Citibank was permitted to redeem them for face value in the transaction.
6. An admission of guilt and conviction of criminal money laundering was cause for any foreign bank to have its U.S. charter reviewed and revoked unless some other consideration(s) could justify a lesser penalty. This death penalty was extremely important to Banamex and Bancomer, both of which had important operations in the United States. But for Confia it was a less-severe sanction, since it did not have U.S. operations. Eventually, both Banamex and Bancomer paid large fines, but they did not receive the death penalty.

Case 9

CNET Networks, Inc.

William G. Shenkir, Neil H. Snyder, Allyn Dabkowski, Megan Edwards, Lane Green, Jeff Henderson, and Ashley Hogue, *University of Virginia*

As the Internet moves into its next phase, so does CNET Networks. We are incredibly well positioned as the leading player in the most important vertical, the global IT marketplace. We have only scratched the surface of the opportunity in the U.S. and it is multiplied as we see the demand for commerce-related information, services and marketplaces on a worldwide basis. This is an exciting time for our company and for me personally, as I step into the role of chairman.

—*Shelby Bonnie, November 29, 2000[1]*

With this statement, Shelby Bonnie assumed the role of Chairman of the Board of CNET Networks, Inc (CNET). His involvement with CNET began in 1993 when he joined Halsey Minor, founder of CNET, to become the company's third employee, and they moved aggressively to build one of the world's leading global media companies. Today, CNET is poised to grow rapidly as an e-commerce platform connecting buyers, sellers, and suppliers in the multi-trillion dollar global IT sales channel.

According to John "Bud" Colligan, a member of CNET's board, "Shelby has been here from the beginning and has helped build one of the strongest franchises on the Internet and in the IT supply chain. Shelby has been of critical importance to achieving the strategic growth that CNET has attained so far, and we believe he is the right man to take CNET Networks to the next level."[2]

History of the Company

CNET Networks (formerly CNET, Inc.) was the brainchild of Halsey Minor, a young analyst with Merrill Lynch Capital Markets in New York. One day while he was at home recuperating from the flu, Minor was channel surfing when it hit him.[3] He envisioned a television program designed to provide information and reviews about new technology and products. From this beginning, CNET has grown into a global media company providing original content Web sites and television programming that serves as a virtual Consumer Reports.[4] The company has become a trusted source of information about computers, the Internet, and technology as well as a primary data service provider for manufacturers, distributors, and sellers of computers and electronics.[5] CNET's content can be found on the Internet, television, and radio in over 100 countries worldwide.[6]

With the acquisition of mySimon.com in February 2000, CNET expanded its online buying guides to include over 200 categories of general consumer goods.[7] The mySimon.com acquisition is part of CNET's effort to rebrand itself as a general consumer shopping information service.[8] When CNET completed the mySimon.com acquisition, its name was changed to CNET Networks Inc. to reflect its growing diversity.[9] At the same time, CNET is growing quickly and adapting to the rapidly changing world of technology.[10]

In October 2000, CNET merged with Ziff Davis, Inc. owner of ZDNet, "a leading online content site focused on technology products and services."[11] ZD owns Computer Shopper and Smart Planet, and it has a stake in Red Herring Communications Inc. and a retained interest in ZDNet. Currently, Ziff-Davis is a wholly owned subsidiary of CNET. Prior to the merger, ZDNet was CNET's most formidable competitor.

In November 2000, ZDNet and MSN announced a strategic alliance making ZDNet the "premier provider of technology information and services … . The companies are teaming up to establish one place on the Internet where consumers can go to get computing information that helps them make smart buying decisions and be more productive using technology in their everyday lives."[12]

CNET is strengthening its position as the leading source of editorial, technical, and programming expertise in all aspects of modern media.[13] Currently, it is the leading provider of information about the world's biggest e-commerce market: technology.[14]

The IPO

In July 1996, CNET went public on the NASDAQ exchange. With Morgan Stanley acting as underwriter, CNET offered 2,000,000 shares of its common stock for $16 per share. In addition, the company sold 600,000 shares of common stock to Intel Corporation for 93 percent of the IPO price. Net of underwriting discounts, commissions, and estimated offering expenses, proceeds totaled $37.9 million.[15] After its debut, the stock price hovered between $15 and $21 for the following year.[16] Initial stockholders had to wait patiently for the stock to climb, as it barely moved during the two years after the IPO.[17] CNET's stock price reached a high of $79 per share in December 1999. On December 15, 2000, the stock price was $15.50 per share following the tech sell-off that started in April 2000.

CNET'S Business Model

Although CNET's operations have become increasingly complex with the addition of newly acquired companies, its core business model has stayed essentially the same. As Lawrence Marcus of Deutsche Banc Alex Brown put it, "We believe CNET has the best commerce model on the Web—sell nothing, but be the best impartial source of information and comparisons, connecting buyers to sellers."[18] Companies like Microsoft have copied CNET's business model, combining the power of the Internet medium with television.[19] Halsey Minor refers to CNET's business model as a "media model for linking buyers and sellers of technology products."[20]

Despite market volatility and the recent decline of CNET's stock price, analysts are generally optimistic about the company's long-term growth and profit potential. As of November 24, 2000, 13 out of 19 analysts recommended CNET as a Strong Buy, and the other 6 analysts recommended CNET as a Moderate Buy.[21]

The Board of Directors

- **Shelby Bonnie**—Chairman and CEO. Mr. Bonnie, a former managing director at Tiger Management, a New York investment firm, partnered with CNET founder Halsey Minor in 1993 as the company's third employee and third investor, and served as CNET's COO, CFO, and Vice Chairman before being elected CEO in March 2000.[22] He was elected Chairman in November 2000. Under Bonnie's guidance, CNET acquired ZDNet and "made CNET the ninth largest Web entity, with revenues of approximately $308 million in the first three quarters of 2000, and extended CNET's leadership model to more than 25 countries."[23] Mr. Bonnie received a B.S. in Commerce degree from the McIntire School of Commerce at the University of Virginia in 1986.

- **Dan Rosensweig**—President, CNET Networks. He oversees CNET Networks operations, corporate development including mergers and acquisitions, and corporate communications. Prior to joining CNET in October 2000, Mr. Rosensweig had been with Ziff-Davis for nearly 20 years, serving in many capacities, including CEO since March 1999, and ZDNet's president since June 1997.[24]

- **Randall T. Mays**—CFO, Clear Channel Communications, Inc.

- **John "Bud" Colligan**—Partner, Accel Partners.

- **Eric Hippeau**—President and Executive Managing Director, Softbank International Ventures.

- **Mitchell Kertzman**—President and CEO, Liberate Technologies.

- **Eric Robison**—Business analyst, Vulcan Northwest, Inc.

The Management Team

- **Shelby Bonnie**—Chairman and CEO.

- **Dan Rosensweig**—President.

- **Douglas Woodrum**—CFO. Before joining CNET in 1997, Mr. Woodrum was EVP and CFO, as well as co-founder, of Heritage Media Corporation for 10 years.

- **Richard Marino**—COO. Before joining CNET in 1999, Mr. Marino was CEO of PC World.

- **Ted Cahall**—CIO. Before joining CNET, Mr. Cahall held various management roles at Bank of America.

- **Barry Briggs**—President of Media. Before joining CNET, Mr. Briggs was president of ZDNet US.

- **Albert de Heer**—President of Channel Services. Before joining CNET, Mr. de Heer co-founded GDT SA. CNET acquired GDT SA in 1999.

- **Art Fatum**—President of International Media. Before joining CNET, Mr. Fatum was with ZDNet. Earlier, he was president and managing director, Europe, of AT&T Capital.

- **Josh Goldman**—President of mySimon. Before assuming his current position, Mr. Goldman was CEO of mySimon.

- **Alan Phillips**—President of Market Intelligence. Before joining CNET, Mr. Phillips was CIO of ZDNet.

CNET Properties[25]

Property	URL/Station	Launch Date
On the Web:		
CNET United States	CNET.com	June 1995
CNET Australia	Australia.CNET.com	January 1997
CNET Japan	Japan.CNET.com	May 1997
CNET Singapore	Singapore.CNET.com	March 1998
CNET Hong Kong	Hongkong.CNET.com	May 1998
CNET Taiwan	Taiwan.CNET.com	October 1998
CNET Malaysia	Malaysia.CNET.com	July 1999
CNET Korea	Korea.CNET.com	March 2000
CNET China	China.CNET.com	March 2000
CNET India	India.CNET.com	August 2000
mySimon	mySimon.com	April 1998
In Broadcast:		
CNET TV.com	CNBC	September 1996
CNET News.com	National Syndication	October 1999
CNET Radio	910 AM in San Francisco/San Jose or online at CNET Radio	January 2000
Other:		
CNET Data Services	—	July 1999
CNET Media Productions	—	January 2000
CNET Media Services	—	February 2000
Apollo Solutions	—	June 1998

- **Robin Wolaner**—EVP of Media Group. Before joining CNET, Ms. Wolaner was president and CEO of Sunset Publishing Corporation, a unit of Time Publishing Ventures.
- **Heather McGaughey**—SVP of Human Resources. Before joining CNET, Ms. McGaughey worked for Time Inc.

CNET Web Sites[26]

CNET.com

CNET's flagship site, CNET.com is the definitive online source for information on new Internet technologies, products, and trends, with a focus on Internet performance and productivity. The award-winning CNET.com has been singled out by leading Web services and national media sources as one of the Internet's best sites in both content and design.

CNET Builder.com

CNET Builder.com is the Internet's central source for product reviews and industry news for the Web builder community including designers, developers, and producers. The site features reviews of Web development tools; industry and technology news; and Builder Download—powered by CNET Download.com— which provides software for Web production. CNET Builder.com also offers interactive forums that enable Web builders to discuss issues and news pertaining to their community.

CNET News.com

CNET News.com is the premier online service devoted entirely to technology news, with 24-hour-a-day coverage created exclusively for the World Wide Web. With a staff of more than 30 reporters, producers, and designers, CNET News.com delivers breaking news from the world of computing and technology, as well as live event coverage, in-depth analysis of industry issues, and exclusive interviews with industry newsmakers. CNET News.com also offers CNET Radio, which provides audio coverage of the Internet and computing news and trends, as well as interviews with key industry newsmakers. Produced exclusively for the Web, CNET Radio is updated three times a day. CNET News.com is carried on CNBC, the world leader in live business news, available to more than 147 million homes worldwide, including 70 million in the United States.

CNET Computers.com

CNET Computers.com is the Internet's most useful guide to buying computer products. The site helps users of all levels find the computer products that are best for their business or home. CNET Computers.com's dynamic product directory offers comprehensive information on the top nationally distributed computer products and is updated daily to include the most current models, features, and prices. The directory is seamlessly integrated with original product reviews by CNET's staff of experts and offers links to nationally recognized resellers who stock each model. With CNET Computers.com, Web users have a quick and easy way to find all the information they need on which computer products to buy and where to buy them.

CNET Enterprise

Designed to help IT and business professionals make buying decisions, CNET Enterprise provides critical information on the software and services that can make or break your business strategies. From network management to application hosting, CNET Enterprise covers the spectrum. We focus on business functions instead of buzzwords, making it easy to explore and evaluate the technology you need.

CNET Gamecenter.com

Serious gamers trust CNET Gamecenter.com for the most timely and authoritative game news and reviews; exclusive game download premieres, powered by CNET Download.com; and complete coverage of game hardware. The site is the first stop for gamers awaiting demos of the industry's biggest titles, as CNET Gamecenter.com had the greatest number of exclusive download premieres—more than 50 in 1997 alone. These gamers also recognize CNET Gamecenter.com as the only site of its kind that enhances the community side of gaming.

CNET Search.com

CNET Search.com is an innovative departure from traditional search portals. Some highlights of this metasearch include comprehensive coverage, topical searching, and speed. A single query to Search.com checks every major search source. Search.com's metasearch channels organize more than 700 databases into special collections available for searching on demand. Search.com delivers an integrated view of 'ten searches for the wait of one' along with unsurpassed options for metasearch customization.

CNET Download.com

CNET Download.com compiles the Internet's top free-to-download software titles in the CNET Software Library, which comprises more than 250,000 shareware, freeware, and demo titles. CNET Download.com gives users an easy-to-use site that makes finding and downloading software quick and painless for the next generation of Web user. Visitors to CNET Download.com find today's most popular titles right at their fingertips, including must-have utilities, the hottest games, and the latest browsers and browser plug-ins that enable audio and video on the Internet. The site also features product highlights and descriptions to help users understand the use and benefit of each title. Users wishing to locate specific titles can choose from a "Quick," "Simple," or "Power" search.

CNET Shopper.com

CNET Shopper.com is an independent source of information for users that provides a comprehensive, organized resource for determining where to buy computer products on the Internet. CNET Shopper.com indexes and compares more than 1 million prices from 100 major resellers and contains data on more than 100,000 products. CNET Shopper.com offers instant information on product availability and direct links to product detail pages—and is one of the fastest, most up-to-date, and efficient shopping resources on the Web.

CNET TV.com

CNET.TV.COM is the companion Web site to CNET's five broadcast and cable television series—*CNET Central, The Web, The New Edge, Cool Tech, and TV.COM*—and its *Tech Reports* technology inserts. The Web site provides television viewers with a complementary source of information on the topics from each week's shows, an email connection to their favorite hosts, and relevant outside links for in-depth exploration of the Internet. CNET TV.com, in its fourth year, is the longest running technology program in syndication. The program is syndicated by TWI to 70 percent of the country, including 9 out of the 10 top broadcast markets. CNET Television has garnered over 20 national awards including Computer Press Awards for four consecutive years, winning "Best Overall Television Show" and "Best Television Segment," from 1996–1999.

CNET Web Services

CNET Web Services provides a niche directory that will help the computer user find all of the tools necessary to create a web site; from Web Hosting, to Web Design, to finding an ISP. The directory, comprised of the three sections mentioned above, is organized in such a way to make the information easily accessible for all levels of expertise. A customer can search for a Web Host, Web Designer, or ISP they already know of, or do a search from scratch. Either way, the customer is guaranteed to find information that is provided and maintained by the diligent Web Services team.

CNET Data Services

CNET Data Services (CDS), a division of CNET Europe S.A., provides technology industry players a range of services to build and maintain electronic product information that fuels electronic commerce platforms. We supply affordable, accurate, timely, structured and indexed electronic product information on PC hardware, peripherals and software from any manufacturer, and continue to expand our reach into new categories. The service's multi-lingual and multi-market functionality enables customers to deliver locally-focused information on a global scale.

CNET's Stake in NBCi

CNET owns 11 percent of NBCi as a result of its sale of Snap.com to NBC (a division of General Electric). It attracts more than 16 million users monthly who are searching for information, broadband and streaming content, and services like free e-mail. Advertising accounts for about 55 percent of NBCi sales, and the remainder comes from e-commerce and direct marketing services. In 1999, NBCi had sales of $35.6 million, which represented a 27.9 percent increase over 1998 sales, but the company showed a loss of $86.8 million in 1999.[27]

The Competition

CNET's initial content focused on a fairly narrow market of technologically savvy shoppers. This market, referred to as the technology content market, includes International Data Group (IDG), Internet.com, and smaller, more specialized sites.[28] Each of these competitors competes in a slightly different marketing niche. For example, much of IDG's focus is on technology publishing, with some 290 periodicals and a 75 percent interest in IDG Books Worldwide. Their titles include PCWorld, For Dummies, and CliffsNotes.[29]

Internet.com targets technology professionals and Web developers with industry news and product reviews located on more than 100 Web sites and 12 information channels. It also has a venture capital fund to invest in Internet media companies.

To compete more effectively with these strong content-based firms, CNET entered into a reciprocal partnership with the Associated Press in January 2000.[30] This partnership puts CNET in a strong position to compete in the technology content arena.

As CNET diversifies its operations, it faces an increased number and variety of competitors. The expansion into shopping services through the purchase of mySimon.com places CNET in competition with "comparison shopping" sites like BottomDollar.com, online shopping malls like Yahoo Shopping, and personal shopping services like Respond.com.

James Vogtle, director of electronic commerce research for the Boston Consulting Group, stated that CNET "get[s] instant credibility in other product categories."[31] In another venture, CNET launched an auction site for used, refurbished, and surplus computer products, which places it in competition with eBay.com. CNET, however, includes volumes of information and reviews that help buyers make informed purchase decisions.[32]

Competitors by Industry

Internet and Online Content Providers

America Online Inc. America Online Inc. is the worldwide leader in interactive services, Web brands, Internet technologies and electronic commerce services. AOL owns and operates CompuServe Internet services, Netscape Communicator client software, and other networks. Recently, AOL has been in the spotlight for its acquisition of Time Warner in a deal worth $183 billion in stock and debt (Time Warner is discussed separately below). Access to Time Warner's extensive entertainment and media archives, as well as its production capabilities makes AOL the leader in the Internet and Online content market, and it completely changes the future of entertainment and news.[33] Another important partnership with Sun Microsystems, will move AOL further into the realm of business-to-business e-commerce.[34] This joint venture will compete directly with Commerce One, one of CNET's strategic allies.[35]

EarthWeb Inc. EarthWeb Inc. focuses on the global IT Community, specifically IT professionals. It is the leading provider of Internet-based services for this market, offering online business-to-business services and IT content. The company operates more than 15 sites, offering access to extensive IT tutorials, manuals and similar resources. EarthWeb's sites also include job information for the IT professional, bulletin boards and a shopping site with over 33,000 products.[36]

Internet.com Corp. Internet.com's network of Web sites offers information geared towards industry professionals and Web developers. The sites offer email newsletters, discussion forums, and moderated e-mail discussions on topics of interest to this technologically savvy group of customers. Through 12 information channels, the company produces Internet industry news, product reviews, and information on how to use various Web sites. Realizing the importance of investing, the company has established two venture capital funds charged with the task of investing in Internet media companies.[37]

Lycos Inc. Best known as a search engine, Lycos Inc. aggregates content distributed through the Web as well as offering a network of globally branded media properties and guides to online content. The company provides a wide range of services, including free Internet access, chat rooms, e-mail, auction sites, and homepages. After a failed merger with USA Networks in 1999, Lycos began an aggressive acquisition strategy and formed LycosLabs, an incubator and financier for up to 12 Internet start-ups each year. Lycos also competes with

CNET through Lycos Radio Network, which delivers music and videos through streaming media technology, and through LYCOShop, its Internet shopping site.[38]

VerticalNet Inc. VerticalNet's Web sites serve as forums for business-to-business communities and their related business transactions. Referred to as "vertical trade communities," these sites allow businesses to exchange information directly and to perform e-commerce transactions without the use of additional middlemen. VerticalNet's efforts to expand beyond these vertical communities have prompted the company to enter the realm of online shopping and auction sites.[39]

Auctions

eBay Inc. Anyone interested in buying or selling just about anything can do it on eBay.com, the leading auction site on the Internet. The site offers items for sale in more than 3000 categories. In order to facilitate the sale and transport of larger items, eBay operates regional sites where buyers and sellers can deal in closer proximity. Also eager to join the business-to-business market, eBay established eBay Business Exchange, which auctions over 60,000 different goods, including computers and other IT products useful in smaller businesses. With its success, eBay is steadily acquiring companies and developing similar sites in Germany, Australia, and Japan. Recently, eBay announced its plans to develop person-to-person and merchant-to-person auction sites for Disney's Go Network.[40]

Entertainment

Time Warner Now under the control of AOL, Time Warner is the world's leading media and entertainment company, with its core operations in cable networks, publishing, music, film, and cable and digital media. The company has an amazing wealth of news and entertainment content, which it hopes to distribute through AOL's global networks. The leverage of these two previously separate companies will allow them to steer the direction of the information age. With strong print and television news divisions, as well as a position as the United States' number one multiple-system cable operator, the company is in a position to dominate the entertainment sector and the future of information communication through Internet and cable TV.[41]

Development Tools, Operating Systems and Utility Software

Microsoft Corp. As the frontrunner in the computer world, Microsoft's strengths reach into all areas of the world of technology. As a software developer, the company is best known for its Windows operating systems. In addition, Microsoft produces server and business/consumer applications, software development tools, and Internet/Intranet products and services. Microsoft has also established strong positions in interactive television, e-commerce services, and cable companies.[42] CNET's recent advertising agreement with Microsoft Corp. shows an effort to "join the competition" by accessing Microsoft's strong customer base. Through its MSN Hotmail e-mail service, Microsoft will provide CNET's newsletter free of charge to its over 30 million subscribers.[43]

Internet and Intranet Service Providers

Intraware Inc. Intraware Inc. provides Internet-based business software services specifically aimed toward technology professionals and vendors. It is a "meeting place" for software vendors and IT professionals who want to upgrade, market, buy, sell, and distribute products. Intraware's sites include IT Knowledge Center, which focuses on software, intraware.shop, a software buying service, and SubscripNet, a service that monitors software updates and licenses.[44]

Internet and Online Service Providers

Excite@Home Excite@Home offers broadband content and interactive services to consumers over digital cable TV and phone lines. It also offers free Web access to its narrowband dial-up Web access customers through its FreeWorld service. The content of the Internet portal focuses on business, careers, and travel. The company now owns the e-commerce company iMall, which competes with CNET's mySimon.com. Also, in a joint venture with Dow Jones, the company recently launched a joint venture, Work.com to develop a broadband business portal.[45]

Retail Specialty

Egghead.com Inc. Egghead.com Inc. sells technology products for the office and home. From computer hardware to electronics, the site offers access to retailers as well as an auction site for goods. As a somewhat unique feature, Egghead.com's auction site offers bargain prices on excess and closeout goods and services. Media Metrix, PC Data, and Nielson/Net Ratings continue to rate Egghead.com as one of the top e-commerce sites, especially commending its only slight drop-off in traffic after the holiday season in 2000.[46]

Computer and Software Retailing

Cyberian Outpost Inc. Cyberian Outpost Inc. sells computer products globally, targeting consumers and the small/home office marketplace with over 160,000 hardware, software, and peripheral products. The company offers more extensive gadget and home entertainment products through deals with Brookstone and Tweeter

Home Entertainment. Cyberian Outpost also operates a Web auction site dealing specifically with computers and other hardware.[47]

Music, Video, Book, and Entertainment Software Retailing and Distribution

Amazon.com Inc. Amazon.com Inc. is the world's leading online retailer. Although it is best known for selling books, the company has branched into all kinds of consumer products and services. Today, Amazon.com also operates Internet sites offering auction services, calendar/reminder services, Web shopping comparison services and a comprehensive movie database. Amazon.com defined the "spend-to-grow" style of business that set the stage for many of the Internet startups to follow it. The company invests very broadly in e-ventures trying, like other Internet companies, to pick those acquisitions that will give it competitive advantage. CNET competes with Amazon.com both in the shopping arena with mySimon.com, and in the consumer product reviews and information market.[48]

TV Broadcasting

Discovery Communications, Inc. Discovery Communications owns and operates the Discovery Channel, Discovery People, The Learning Channel, Animal Planet, and the Travel Channel. These outlets provide programming for the science-minded adventurer in over 145 countries worldwide. Through its retail stores, the company sells videos, CD-ROMs, computer software and other natural science products. Realizing the growing strength of the Internet, the company is broadening its focus to include computer and technology science material on its channels, which will compete with the TV program that started CNET.[49]

Publishing—Periodicals

Imagine Media, Inc. Imagine Media is a subsidiary of The Future Network, a UK publishing company featuring the titles: *Maximum PC*, *PSM* (PlayStation Magazine), and *Business2.0*. These publications are targeted at specific niches of CNET's core 'techie' consumer group. In addition to these publications, the company operates two Web networks, Maximum PC Network and MacDaily Network, which bring the company's content to the Web.[50]

International Data Group Commonly known as IDG, International Data Group is the top global publisher of technology information. With some 290 periodicals and a 75 percent interest in IDG Books Worldwide, the company owns titles including: *PCWorld*, *For Dummies*, *Cliffs Notes*, *The Industry Standard*, and *CIO*. These publications reach over 75 countries and support over 240 Web sites. IDG's content rivals that of CNET's and it is aimed at a very similar group of consumers.[51]

Commonalities

Several commonalities are apparent when looking at CNET and its competitors. All of them are adopting strong investment strategies, and they are constantly adding to and adapting their basic business models. Recognizing the growing popularity and reach of the Internet, they are trying to broaden their markets, reaching beyond the "techie" consumers into the mainstream. For example, many of them are offering basic Internet applications like e-mail, bulletin boards, and chat rooms to extend their reach. The success of eBay has prompted the development of a host of new auction sites, each with a different spin.

Strategy for the Future

Although CNET has established itself as an Internet 'high-flyer,' it must reach mainstream consumers and businesses on a global level in order to remain on top.[52] "Technology can support its growth only so long," says Peggy Lee O'Neill, an Internet analyst at Nielson/Net Ratings."[53] CS First Boston estimates that CNET can increase its revenue from non-tech operations from the current 2 percent of total revenue to 9 percent by 2001. To meet this challenge in the future, Bonnie's team has begun focusing on three main initiatives: business-to-business commerce, international expansion, and wireless opportunities.[54] In addition, CNET must continue to increase its Web site traffic through heightened brand awareness.[55]

In the business-to-business area, Bonnie intends to broaden CNET's customer base to include small to medium-size businesses.[56] CNET recently formed a strategic alliance with Commerce One, the leader in global e-commerce solutions, allowing CNET to deliver its information on technology services and products through Commerce One MarketSite, the premiere business-to-business marketplace portal.[57] The alliance will provide a business-to-business e-commerce solution capable of offering managers the most complete, detailed information available for consideration when making important purchasing decisions.[58] CNET estimates it can bring in $10 million in 2001 by selling information about technology products to other businesses.[59]

In addition to expanding its business-to-business capabilities, CNET is increasing its global reach. CNET is cultivating services and establishing sites in Asia and Europe to tap into the worldwide market for computers, which is currently growing faster than the U.S. market.[60] CNET is expanding into Asia through a joint venture, CNET Asia, with Singapore-based AsiaContent.com Ltd., an Internet

Exhibit 1   CNET Timeline of Critical Events

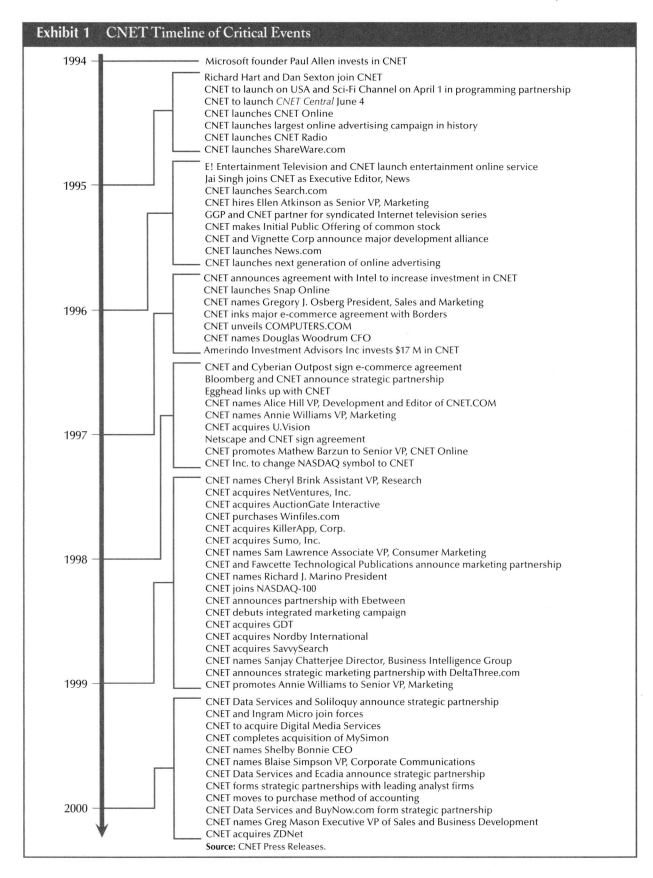

1994 — Microsoft founder Paul Allen invests in CNET

Richard Hart and Dan Sexton join CNET
CNET to launch on USA and Sci-Fi Channel on April 1 in programming partnership
CNET to launch *CNET Central* June 4
CNET launches CNET Online
CNET launches largest online advertising campaign in history
CNET launches CNET Radio
CNET launches ShareWare.com

1995 — E! Entertainment Television and CNET launch entertainment online service
Jai Singh joins CNET as Executive Editor, News
CNET launches Search.com
CNET hires Ellen Atkinson as Senior VP, Marketing
GGP and CNET partner for syndicated Internet television series
CNET makes Initial Public Offering of common stock
CNET and Vignette Corp announce major development alliance
CNET launches News.com
CNET launches next generation of online advertising

1996 — CNET announces agreement with Intel to increase investment in CNET
CNET launches Snap Online
CNET names Gregory J. Osberg President, Sales and Marketing
CNET inks major e-commerce agreement with Borders
CNET unveils COMPUTERS.COM
CNET names Douglas Woodrum CFO
Amerindo Investment Advisors Inc invests $17 M in CNET

1997 — CNET and Cyberian Outpost sign e-commerce agreement
Bloomberg and CNET announce strategic partnership
Egghead links up with CNET
CNET names Alice Hill VP, Development and Editor of CNET.COM
CNET names Annie Williams VP, Marketing
CNET acquires U.Vision
Netscape and CNET sign agreement
CNET promotes Mathew Barzun to Senior VP, CNET Online
CNET Inc. to change NASDAQ symbol to CNET

1998 — CNET names Cheryl Brink Assistant VP, Research
CNET acquires NetVentures, Inc.
CNET acquires AuctionGate Interactive
CNET purchases Winfiles.com
CNET acquires KillerApp, Corp.
CNET acquires Sumo, Inc.
CNET names Sam Lawrence Associate VP, Consumer Marketing
CNET and Fawcette Technological Publications announce marketing partnership
CNET names Richard J. Marino President
CNET joins NASDAQ-100
CNET announces partnership with Ebetween
CNET debuts integrated marketing campaign
CNET acquires GDT
CNET acquires Nordby International
CNET acquires SavvySearch
CNET names Sanjay Chatterjee Director, Business Intelligence Group
CNET announces strategic marketing partnership with DeltaThree.com

1999 — CNET promotes Annie Williams to Senior VP, Marketing

CNET Data Services and Soliloquy announce strategic partnership
CNET and Ingram Micro join forces
CNET to acquire Digital Media Services
CNET completes acquisition of MySimon
CNET names Shelby Bonnie CEO
CNET names Blaise Simpson VP, Corporate Communications
CNET Data Services and Ecadia announce strategic partnership
CNET forms strategic partnerships with leading analyst firms
CNET moves to purchase method of accounting
CNET Data Services and BuyNow.com form strategic partnership
CNET names Greg Mason Executive VP of Sales and Business Development
2000 — CNET acquires ZDNet

Source: CNET Press Releases.

media network of Web sites and advertising services.[61] CNET chose Asia as a starting point based on predicted exponential growth of the continent's Internet usage and a pre-existing relationship with AsiaContent.com.[62] CNET also maintains a European presence with its affiliate CNET Data Services, which offers a uniform database of technology product information in multi-lingual form.[63] Recent global initiatives also include investments in Israeli start-up, Hypernix, and global telephone provider, Deltathree.com.[64]

Bonnie believes wireless communication growth will help CNET by allowing shoppers access to CNET's reference reviews and price comparisons while in stores.[65] The acquisition of mySimon makes the move into wireless even more appealing to CNET. MySimon's shopping engine includes a variety of products beyond the technological realm, increasing CNET's benefit to consumers. In an effort to make this concept a reality, CNET recently established a relationship with Wysdom Inc., a leading wireless Internet Application Service Provider (ASP). CNET intends to offer Internet services, supported by Wysdom wireless solutions, to mobile devices.[66] This agreement will allow consumers to access the wealth of information that CNET has to offer anytime and anywhere.

Although these initiatives should help to fuel CNET's growth into the future, the firm must continue to focus on increasing its brand awareness among mainstream consumers to make such innovations worthwhile. CNET began to address its brand recognition issues in July of 1999 by launching a controversial $100 million advertising campaign.[67] Although share price fell 10 percent the day after the campaign was announced, management's decision resulted in increased traffic growth.[68] The campaign resulted in a 49 percent increase in the number of site visitors between July 1999 and August 2000.[69]

Exhibit 2   Risk Factors

WE HAVE A LIMITED OPERATING HISTORY, WHICH MAKES YOUR EVALUATION OF US DIFFICULT AND AFFECTS MANY ASPECTS OF OUR BUSINESS.

We have a limited operating history upon which you can evaluate us. Our prospects must be considered in light of the risks, expenses, and difficulties frequently encountered by companies in developing industries, particularly companies in the relatively new and rapidly evolving market for Internet products, content, and services. These risks for us include, but are not limited to:

- an evolving and unpredictable business model
- uncertain acceptance of new services
- competition
- management of growth

We cannot assure you that we will succeed in addressing such risks. If we fail to do so, our revenues and operating results could be materially reduced.

Additionally, our limited operating history and the emerging nature of the markets in which we compete makes the prediction of future operating results difficult or impossible. We cannot assure you that our revenues will increase or even continue at their current level or that we will maintain profitability or generate cash from operations in future periods. In addition, interest that we pay on our 5 percent convertible subordinated notes and costs of our acquisitions, including amortization of goodwill and other purchased intangibles and ongoing operating expenses, may further affect our operating results. We have incurred significant operating losses since inception. We may incur additional losses in the future. In view of the rapidly evolving nature of our business and our limited operating history, we believe that period-to-period comparisons of our operating results are not necessarily meaningful and should not be relied upon as indicating what our future performance will be.

WE MAY EXPERIENCE FLUCTUATIONS IN OUR QUARTERLY OPERATING RESULTS, AND MAY NOT BE ABLE TO ADJUST OUR SPENDING IN TIME TO COMPENSATE FOR ANY UNEXPECTED REVENUE SHORTFALL.

Our quarterly operating results may fluctuate significantly in the future as a result of a variety of factors, many of which are outside our control. We may be unable to adjust spending in a timely manner to compensate for any unexpected revenue shortfall. Accordingly, any significant shortfall in revenues in relation to our planned expenditures could materially reduce our operating results and adversely affect our financial condition.

Factors that may adversely affect our quarterly operating results attributable to our Internet operations include, among others:

- demand for Internet advertising
- the addition or loss of advertisers, and the advertising budgeting cycles of individual advertisers
- the level of traffic on our network of Internet channels
- the amount and timing of capital expenditures and other costs, including marketing costs, relating to our Internet, television and radio operations competition
- our ability to manage effectively our development of new business segments and markets
- our ability to successfully manage the integration of operations and technology of acquisitions and other business combinations
- our ability to upgrade and develop our systems and infrastructure
- technical difficulties, system downtime, Internet brownouts or denial of service or other similar attacks
- general economic conditions and economic conditions specific to the Internet and Internet media

Exhibit 2 Risk Factors (continued)

Due to all of the foregoing factors, it is likely that our operating results may fall below our expectations or the expectations of securities analysts or investors in some future quarter. If this happens, the trading price of our common stock would likely be materially and adversely affected.

OUR TELEVISION, RADIO, AND INTERNET CONTENT AND SERVICES MAY NOT BE ACCEPTED, WHICH COULD ADVERSELY AFFECT OUR PROFITABILITY.

Our future success depends upon our ability to deliver original and compelling Internet content and services that attract and retain users. We cannot assure you that our content and services will be attractive to a sufficient number of Internet users to generate revenues sufficient for us to sustain operations.

The successful development and production of content is subject to numerous uncertainties, including the ability to:

- anticipate and successfully respond to rapidly changing consumer tastes and preferences
- obtain favorable distribution rights
- fund new program development
- attract and retain qualified editors, producers, writers, technical personnel and television and radio hosts

If we are unable to develop content and services that allow us to attract, retain, and expand a loyal user base that is attractive to advertisers and sellers of technology products, we will be unable to generate revenue.

OUR FAILURE TO COMPETE SUCCESSFULLY COULD ADVERSELY AFFECT OUR PROSPECTS AND FINANCIAL RESULT.

The market for Internet content and services is new, intensely competitive, and rapidly evolving. It is not difficult to enter this market and current and new competitors can launch new Internet sites at relatively low cost. We cannot assure you that we will compete successfully with current or future competitors. If we do not compete successfully, our financial results may be adversely affected.

FAILURE TO EFFECTIVELY MANAGE OUR GROWTH COULD RESULT IN OUR INABILITY TO SUPPORT AND MAINTAIN OUR OPERATIONS

We have rapidly and significantly expanded our operations and anticipate that further expansion of our operations may be required in order to address potential market opportunities. This rapid growth has placed, and we expect it to continue to place a significant strain on our management, operational, and financial resources. We cannot assure you that:

- our current personnel, systems, procedures, and controls will be adequate to support our future operations
- management will be able to identify, hire, train, motivate, or manage required personnel
- management will be able to successfully identify and exploit existing and potential market opportunities

In addition, we could experience a negative impact on earnings as a result of expenses associated with growing our operations, whether through internal development or through acquisitions.

IF WE EXPERIENCE DIFFICULTIES WITH OUR SYSTEM DEVELOPMENT AND OPERATIONS, WE COULD EXPERIENCE A DECREASE IN REVENUES

Our Internet revenues consist primarily of revenues derived from the sale of advertisements and other fees from sellers of technology products on our Internet channels, in particular from arrangements with our advertising customers that provide for a guaranteed number of impressions. If our Internet channels are unavailable as a result of a system interruption, we may be unable to deliver the number of impressions guaranteed by these agreements. We cannot assure you that we will be able to accurately project the rate or timing of increases, if any, in the use of our Internet channels or will be able to, in a timely manner, effectively upgrade and expand our systems.

OUR FINANCIAL RESULTS WILL BE ADVERSELY AFFECTED IF WE FAIL TO SUSTAIN OUR ADVERTISING REVENUES OR LEAD FEES.

Our revenues through December 31, 1999 were derived primarily from the sale of advertising and other fees, such as lead fees, from sellers of technology products on our Internet channels and from advertising and license fees from producing our television programs. Most of our advertising contracts can be terminated by the customer at any time on very short notice. In addition, advertisers with longer term contracts sometimes breach their commitments and obtaining performance following breach can be costly and difficult. If we lose advertising customers, fail to attract new customers, or are forced to reduce advertising rates in order to retain or attract customers, our revenues and financial condition will be materially and adversely affected.

IF WE ARE UNABLE TO CONTINUE LICENSING THE CNET DATA SERVICES TRANSACTIVE PRODUCT DATABASE WE COULD FAIL TO ACHIEVE EXPECTATIONS FOR REVENUE GROWTH

CNET receives license fees for the license of the CNET Data Services transactive product database to manufacturers, distributors, and resellers of computer products. Our ability to meet expectations for revenue growth may depend in part upon our ability to continue to license this product to new customers. If we are unable to attract new customers for this product, we could fail to achieve revenue growth expectations.

IF OUR USER BASE DOES NOT CONTINUE TO GROW, WE COULD FAIL TO ACHIEVE EXPECTATIONS FOR REVENUE GROWTH

The rapid growth in the use of and interest in the Internet is a recent phenomenon. We cannot assure you that acceptance and use of the Internet will continue to develop or that we will be able to attract sufficient users to support growth expectations for our business.

We also cannot assure you that the Internet infrastructure will be able to support the demands placed upon it by:

Exhibit 2   Risk Factors (continued)

- an increase in number of users
- an increase in frequency of use
- an increase in bandwidth requirements of users

In addition, the Internet could lose its viability as a commercial medium due to delays in the development or adoption of new standards and protocols required to handle increased levels of Internet activity, or due to increased government regulation. If use of the Internet does not continue to grow or grows more slowly than expected, if we do not attract increasing users despite Internet growth, or if the Internet infrastructure does not effectively support growth that may occur, our revenues and financial condition would be materially and adversely affected.

IF THE INTERNET IS NOT ACCEPTED AS AN ADVERTISING MEDIUM WE COULD EXPERIENCE A DECREASE IN REVENUES

Many of our Internet advertising customers and potential customers have only limited experience with the Internet as an advertising medium and neither they nor their advertising agencies have devoted a significant portion of their advertising budgets to Internet-based advertising in the past. In order for us to generate advertising revenues, advertisers and advertising agencies must direct a significant portion of their budgets to the Internet and, specifically, to our Internet sites. Acceptance of the Internet among advertisers and advertising agencies also depends to a large extent on the growth of use of the Internet by consumers, which is very uncertain, and on the acceptance of new methods of conducting business and exchanging information. If Internet-based advertising is not widely accepted by advertisers and advertising agencies, our revenues and financial condition will be materially and adversely affected. In addition, users can purchase software that is designed to block banner advertisements from appearing on their computer screens as the user navigates on the Internet. This software is intended to increase the navigation speed for the user. Our revenues could be materially reduced if this software or other ad-blocking technology becomes widely-used.

IF OUR BRANDS ARE NOT ACCEPTED OR MAINTAINED, OUR FINANCIAL RESULTS COULD BE ADVERSELY AFFECTED.

Acceptance of our CNET and mySimon brand will depend largely on our success in providing high quality Internet and television content and services. If consumers do not perceive our existing services to be of high quality, or if we introduce new Internet channels or television or radio programs or enter into new business ventures that are not favorably received by consumers, we will not be successful in promoting and maintaining our brand. If we are unable to provide high quality content and services or fail to promote and maintain our brands, our revenues and financial condition will be materially and adversely affected.

INABILITY TO ATTRACT AND RETAIN KEY PERSONNEL COULD ADVERSELY AFFECT OUR ABILITY TO OPERATE

Our success depends to a large extent on the continued services of Halsey M. Minor, Shelby W. Bonnie and the other members of our senior management team. In particular, the loss of the services of Mr. Minor or Mr. Bonnie, our founders, could have an adverse effect on us due to their crucial role in our strategic development. Our success is also dependent on our ability to attract, retain, and motivate other officers, key employees, and personnel in a very competitive job environment. We do not have "key person" life insurance policies on any of our officers or other employees. The production of our Internet and television content and services requires highly skilled writers and editors and personnel with sophisticated technical expertise. We have encountered difficulties in attracting qualified software developers for our Internet channels and related technologies. If we do not attract, retain, and motivate the necessary technical, managerial, editorial, and sales personnel, there could be a material adverse effect on our business and operating results.

RISKS ASSOCIATED WITH TECHNOLOGICAL CHANGE COULD ADVERSELY AFFECT OUR ABILITY TO OPERATE

Characteristics of the market for Internet products and services include:

- rapid technological developments
- frequent new product introductions
- evolving industry standards

The emerging character of these products and services and their rapid evolution requires that we continually improve the performance, features, and reliability of our Internet content, particularly in response to competitive offerings. We cannot assure you that we will be successful in responding quickly, cost effectively, and sufficiently to these developments. In addition, the widespread adoption of new Internet technologies or standards could require us to make substantial expenditures to modify or adapt our Internet channels and services and could fundamentally affect the character, viability, and frequency of Internet-based advertising. Finally, technologies that we adopt could fail to perform according to expectations, resulting in system performance problems and increased costs. Any of these events could have a material adverse effect on our financial condition and operating results.

OUR FAILURE TO DEVELOP AND MAINTAIN RELATIONSHIPS WITH THIRD PARTIES COULD ADVERSELY AFFECT OUR FINANCIAL CONDITION

We rely on the cooperation of owners and operators of other Internet sites with whom we have syndication and other arrangements to generate traffic for our Internet sites. Our ability to advertise on other Internet sites and the willingness of the owners of these sites to direct users to our Internet channels through hypertext links are also critical to the success of our Internet operations. If we are unable to develop and maintain satisfactory relationships with such third parties on acceptable commercial terms, or if our competitors are better able to capitalize on these relationships, our financial condition and operating results will be materially and adversely affected.

Exhibit 2   Risk Factors (continued)

WE MAY HAVE DIFFICULTIES WITH OUR ACQUISITIONS AND INVESTMENTS, WHICH COULD ADVERSELY AFFECT OUR GROWTH AND FINANCIAL CONDITION

From time to time, we consider new business opportunities and ventures, including acquisitions, in a broad range of areas. Any decision by us to pursue a significant business expansion or new business opportunity could:

- require us to invest a substantial amount capital, which could have a material adverse effect on our financial condition and our ability to implement our existing business strategy
- require us to issue additional equity interests, which would be dilutive to our current stockholders, result in operating losses.
- place additional, substantial burdens on our management, personnel, and our financial and operational systems

We cannot assure you that we will have sufficient capital to pursue any investment or acquisition, that we will be able to develop any new Internet channel or service or other new business venture in a cost effective or timely manner or that these ventures would be profitable.

WE MAY HAVE DIFFICULTIES WITH OUR BUSINESS COMBINATIONS AND STRATEGIC ALLIANCES, WHICH COULD ADVERSELY AFFECT OUR GROWTH AND FINANCIAL CONDITION

We may choose to expand our operations or market presence by entering into:

- agreements
- business combinations
- investments
- joint ventures
- other strategic alliances with third parties

Any transaction will be accompanied by risks, which include, among others:

- the difficulty of assimilating the operations, technology and personnel of the combined companies
- the potential disruption of our ongoing business
- the possible inability to retain key technical and managerial personnel
- additional expenses associated with amortization of goodwill and other purchased intangible assets
- additional operating losses and expenses associated with the activities and expansion of acquired businesses
- the possible impairment of relationships with existing employees and advertising customers

We cannot assure you that we will be successful in overcoming these risks or any other problems encountered in connection with any transaction or that any transaction will be profitable.

WE DEPEND ON INTELLECTUAL PROPERTY RIGHTS, AND OTHERS MAY INFRINGE UPON THOSE RIGHTS, OR THESE RIGHTS MAY BECOME OBSOLETE, ADVERSELY AFFECTING OUR BUSINESS

We rely on trade secret, trademark and copyright laws to protect our proprietary technologies and content. We cannot assure you that:

- these laws will provide sufficient protection
- others will not develop technologies or content that are similar or superior to ours
- third parties will not copy or otherwise obtain and use our technologies or content without authorization

Any of these events could have a material adverse effect on our business.

WE MAY NOT BE ABLE TO ACQUIRE OR MAINTAIN OUR DOMAIN NAMES, WHICH COULD ADVERSELY AFFECT OUR ABILITY TO OPERATE OUR ONLINE DIVISION

We currently hold various Web domain names relating to our brand and sites. The acquisition and maintenance of domain names generally is regulated by government agencies and their designees. The regulation of domain names in the United States and in foreign countries is subject to change. We cannot assure you that we will be able to acquire or maintain relevant domain names in all countries in which we conduct business. Any inability to acquire or maintain domain names could have a material adverse effect on our business.

CHANGES IN REGULATIONS COULD ADVERSELY AFFECT THE WAY THAT WE OPERATE

It is possible that new laws and regulations will be adopted covering issues relating to the Internet, including:

- privacy
- copyrights
- obscene or indecent communications
- pricing, characteristics and quality of Internet products and services

The adoption of restrictive laws or regulations could:

- decrease the growth of the Internet
- reduce our revenues
- expose us to significant liabilities

We cannot be sure what effect any future material noncompliance by us with these laws and regulations or any material changes in these laws and regulations could have on our business.

WE HAVE CAPACITY CONSTRAINTS AND MAY BE SUBJECT TO SYSTEM DISRUPTIONS, WHICH COULD ADVERSELY AFFECT OUR REVENUES

Our ability to attract Internet users and maintain relationships with advertising and service customers depends on the satisfactory performance, reliability, and availability of our Internet channels and our network infrastructure. Our Internet advertising revenues directly relate to the number of advertisements delivered by us to users. System interruptions that result in the unavailability of our Internet channels or slower response times for users would reduce the number of advertisements and

Exhibit 2   Risk Factors (continued)

sales leads delivered and reduce the attractiveness of our Internet channels to users and advertisers. We have experienced periodic system interruptions in the past and believe that such interruptions will continue to occur from time to time in the future. Any increase in system interruptions or slower response times resulting from these factors could have a material adverse effect on our revenues and financial condition.

Our Internet, television, and radio operations are vulnerable to interruption by fire, earthquake, power loss, telecommunications failure, and other events beyond our control. Most of our servers and television production equipment are currently located in the Bay Area of California, an area that is susceptible to earthquakes. Since launching our first Internet site in June 1995, we have experienced system downtime for limited periods due to power loss and telecommunications failures, and we cannot assure you that interruptions in service will not materially and adversely affect our operations in the future. We do not carry sufficient business interruption insurance and do not carry earthquake insurance to compensate us for losses that may occur. Any losses or damages that we incur could have a material adverse effect on our financial condition.

OUR BUSINESS INVOLVES RISKS OF LIABILITY CLAIMS FOR OUR INTERNET, RADIO, AND TELEVISION CONTENT OR TECHNOLOGY, WHICH COULD RESULT IN SIGNIFICANT COSTS

As a publisher and a distributor of content over the Internet and television, we face potential liability for:

- defamation
- negligence
- copyright, patent, or trademark infringement
- other claims based on the nature and content of the materials that we publish or distribute

These types of claims have been brought, sometimes successfully, against online services. There is currently a trademark infringement claim pending against us based on the mySimon mark, as described in Item 3 Legal Proceedings. In addition, we could be exposed to liability in connection with material indexed or offered on our sites. There has been a recent increase in the granting and attempted enforcement of business process patents that cover practices that may be widely employed in the Internet industry. If we are found to violate any such patent and we are unable to enter into a license agreement on reasonable turns, our ability to offer our services could be materially and adversely affected. Although we carry general liability insurance, our insurance may not cover potential claims of defamation, negligence, and similar claims, it may or may not apply to a particular claim or be adequate to reimburse us for all liability that may be imposed. Any imposition of liability that is not covered by insurance or is in excess of insurance coverage could have a material adverse effect on our financial condition.

UNAUTHORIZED PERSONS ACCESSING OUR SYSTEMS COULD DISRUPT OUR OPERATIONS AND RESULT IN THE THEFT OF OUR PROPRIETARY INFORMATION

A party who is able to circumvent our security measures could misappropriate proprietary information or cause interruptions in our Internet operations. We may be required to expend significant capital and resources to protect against the threat of security breaches or to alleviate problems caused by breaches in security. For example, so-called "spiders" have and can be used in efforts to copy our databases, including our database of technology products and prices.

Concerns over the security of Internet transactions and the privacy of users may also inhibit the growth of the Internet, particularly as a means of conducting commercial transactions. To the extent that our activities or the activities of third party contractors involve the storage and transmission of proprietary information, such as computer software or credit card numbers, security breaches could expose us to a risk of loss or litigation and possible liability. We cannot assure you that contractual provisions attempting to limit our liability in these areas will be successful or enforceable, or that other parties will accept such contractual provisions as part of our agreements.

OUR INABILITY TO UTILIZE TECHNOLOGY THAT WE DO NOT OWN COULD DISRUPT OUR OPERATIONS

We rely on technology licensed from third parties. We cannot assure you that these third party technology licenses will be available or will continue to be available to us on acceptable commercial terms or at all.

WE MAY EXPERIENCE SEASONALITY IN OUR SALES, WHICH COULD HAVE A MATERIAL ADVERSE EFFECT ON OUR REVENUES AND OPERATING RESULTS

We believe that advertising sales in traditional media, such as television, are generally lower in the first and third calendar quarters of each year than in the respective preceding quarters and that advertising expenditures fluctuate significantly with economic cycles. Depending on the extent to which the Internet is accepted as an advertising medium, seasonality and cyclicality in the level of advertising expenditures generally could become more pronounced for Internet advertising. Seasonality and cyclicality in advertising expenditures generally, or with respect to Internet-based advertising specifically, could have a material adverse effect on our business, prospects, financial condition, and operating results.

We may also experience seasonality in our operating results, particularly in connection with our shopping services, which may reflect seasonal trends in the retail industry. The level of consumer retail spending generally decreases in the first and third calendar quarters. Adve rtising expenditures, which account for substantially all of our revenues, are also subject to seasonal fluctuations and are influenced by consumer spending patterns.

Exhibit 2   Risk Factors (continued)

OUR DEBT EXPOSES US TO RISKS THAT COULD ADVERSELY AFFECT OUR FINANCIAL CONDITION

As a result of the sale of our 5 percent convertible subordinatednotes in March 1999, we incurred $172.9 million of additional debt. We may incur substantial additional debt in the future. The level of our indebtedness, among other things, could:

- make it difficult for us to make payments on the notes
- make it difficult for us to obtain any necessary financing in the future for working capital, capital expenditures, debt service
- requirements or other purposes
- limit our flexibility in planning for, or reacting to changes in, our business
- make us more vulnerable in the event of a downturn in our business

We cannot assure you that we will be able to meet our debt service obligations, including our obligations under the notes.

WE MAY BE UNABLE TO PAY OUR DEBT SERVICE AND OTHER OBLIGATIONS, WHICH COULD ADVERSELY AFFECT OUR FINANCIAL CONDITION AND CAUSE US TO DEFAULT UNDER THE NOTES

The interest payable on our 5 percent convertible subordinated notes is $8,645,750 each year. If we experience a decline in revenues due to any of the factors described in this section, we could have difficulty paying interest and other amounts due on the notes or our other indebtedness. If we are unable to generate sufficient cash flow or otherwise obtain funds necessary to make required payments, or if we fail to comply with the various requirements of our indebtedness, we would be in default, which would permit the holders of our indebtedness to accelerate the maturity of the indebtedness and could cause defaults under our other indebtedness. Any default under our indebtedness could have a material adverse effect on our financial condition.

THE PRICE OF OUR COMMON STOCK IS SUBJECT TO WIDE FLUCTUATION

The trading price of our common stock is subject to wide fluctuations. Trading prices of our common stock may fluctuate in response to a number of events and factors, including:

- quarterly variations in operating results
- announcements of innovations
- new products, strategic developments, or business combinations by us or our competitors
- changes in our expected operating expense levels or losses
- changes in financial estimates and recommendations of securities analysis
- the operating and securities price performance of other companies that investors may deem comparable to us

- news reports relating to trends in the Internet
- other events or factors

In addition, the stock market in general, and the market prices for Internet-related companies in particular, have experienced extreme volatility that often has been unrelated to the operating performance of these companies. These broad market and industry fluctuations may adversely affect the trading price of our common stock.

WE HAVE A SUBSTANTIAL NUMBER OF SHARES OF COMMON STOCK THAT MAY BE SOLD, WHICH COULD AFFECT THE TRADING PRICE OF OUR COMMON STOCK

We have a substantial number of shares of common stock subject to stock option, and our notes may be converted into shares of common stock. We cannot predict the effect, if any, that future sales of shares of common stock or notes, or the availability of shares of common stock or notes for future sale, will have on the market price of our common stock. Sales of substantial amounts of common stock, including shares issued in connection with acquisitions, upon the exercise of stock options or warrants or the conversion of notes, or the perception that such sales could occur, may adversely affect prevailing market prices for our common stock and notes.

PROVISIONS OF OUR CERTIFICATE OF INCORPORATION, BYLAWS, AND DELAWARE LAW COULD DETER TAKEOVER ATTEMPTS

Some provisions in our certificate of incorporation and bylaws could delay, prevent, or make more difficult a merger, tender offer, proxy contest, or change of control. Our stockholders might view any transaction of this type as being in their best interest since the transaction could result in a higher stock price than the current market price for our common stock. Among other things, our certificate of incorporation and bylaws:

- authorize our board of directors to issue preferred stock with the terms of each series to be fixed by our board of directors
- divide our board of directors into three classes so that only approximately one-third of the total number of directors is elected each year
- permit directors to be removed only for cause
- specify advance notice requirements for stockholder proposals and director nominations

In addition, with some exceptions, the Delaware General Corporation Law restricts or delays mergers and other business combinations between us and any stockholder that acquires 15 percent or more of our voting stock.

Source: SEC 10-K, 12/31/99, pp.11–21.

Exhibit 3   CNET Networks, Inc., Acquisitions

Name	Date	Financing	Acctg.	$ Val.*	Acquired Company's Business	Benefit of Acquisition to CNET
U.Vision Inc.	5/98	Stock for Stock	Pooling	$17.8 M	Search engine indexing and comparing prices of computer products; convenient resource for determining where to buy computer products	U.Vision's pricing and sourcing capabilities complement CNET's range of services for computer buyers
NetVentures, Inc.	2/99	Stock for Stock	Pooling	$8.0 M	Owns and operates ShopBuilder.com, an online store-creation system. Develops innovative, low-cost e-commerce tools which allow small computer resellers to easily format catalogues for inclusion in comprehensive product directory	Enables sellers to take advantage of CNET's marketing power and further expands CNET's product and service segment
AuctionGate Interactive, Inc.	2/99	Stock for Stock	Pooling	$6.5 M	Owns and operates AuctionGate.com, an auction site specializing in computer products. Auction site for large and mid-sized vendors and consumers	Enables CNET to facilitate person-to-person and business-to-business auctions; further generates new revenue through listing fees from vendors
Winfiles.com	2/99	$5.75M cash; $5.75M note	Purchase	$11.5 M	A leading software downloading service; a location for Windows shareware, freeware, and demo software, all available for free download	Expands CNET's downloading services and enables CNET to take advantage of the market for software sales from these services
KillerApp Corp.	3/99	Stock for Stock	Pooling	$46 M	Network of shopping services allowing consumers to research and purchase products online; delivers real-time street pricing via Internet	Offers CNET users access to wider selection of computer products and prices; widens market through new shopping category, consumer electronics
Sumo, Inc.	4/99	Stock for Stock	Pooling		Develops internet directories as resource for information about quality Internet services and service providers	Allows CNET users to utilize both an extensive directory of Web services and providers and CNET's existing list of technology products and prices
GDT	7/99	$30M cash, $20M common stock	Purchase	$50 M	Multi-language, multi-market resource for technology product information	Gives CNET's shopping services an edge as the world's largest multi-language database of technology products
Nordby International, Inc.	7/99	$5M cash, $5M note, $10M common stock	Purchase	$20 M	Provider of research, opinion, and insight to clients interested in financial information	Enhances CNET's coverage of technology stocks
SavvySearch Limited	10/99	$4.4 M cash, $17.6 M common stock	Purchase	$22 M	Provides advanced Internet search capabilities through network of portal sites, users also benefit from high levels of customization	Brings CNET users more comprehensive information and resources from the Web, greater search speeds, customization levels, and scope of options
Manageable Software Services, Inc.	11/99	Stock for Stock	Purchase	$3 M	Provides automated PC management services to keep user's equipment up to date	**Caters to mainstream consumers who may not be as savvy in when and how to maintain their personal computer equipment*
MySimon	3/00	Stock for Stock	Pooling	$736 M	Comparison shopping destination assisting users in finding best values of any good or service sold on the Web	Creates the global leader in comparison shopping
Digital Media Services, Inc.	2/00	$18M cash and stock combination	Purchase	$18 M	Creation, production, and distribution of online point-of-sale merchandising tools which give shoppers product specific information and present promotions at point of sale	Enhance ability of CNET's vendors to reach their customers and to increase demand for their products with tools such as promotional offers, rebates, or product demos
Ziff-Davis Inc.	7/00	Stock for Stock	Pooling	$1.8 B	Print and Web based means of providing consumers with technology news and product information	Create more opportunities to bring together buyers and sellers; boost revenue and tighten up CNET's global expansion plans; providing a single stop for buyers and sellers worldwide
Apollo Solutions	7/00	Cash and stock combination	Purchase	$2M and 300,000 shares	Provides web-based application where Value Added Resellers, tech consultants and resellers can access current product information, pricing, and availability from many manufacturers and distributors, which increases the efficiency of the channel	CNET now can create a new Web-based service provider, which will provide companies in the IT channel the ability to make the process of buying and selling more efficient and accurate, from viewing products from multiple distributors to tracking final shipments to consumers.

*The dollar value of the acquisition has been reported at various amounts in some cases where stock was exchanged.

**Italicized information is inferred, as no press release was found giving CNET's acquisition strategy in acquiring Manageable Software Services, Inc.

Exhibit 4   CNET Networks Inc. Balance Sheets for Years Ending 12/31/95–12/31/99

	12/31/99	12/31/98	12/31/97	12/31/96	12/31/95
ASSETS					
Current assets:					
Cash and cash equivalents	$ 53,063	$ 51,534	$ 22,554	$ 20,156	$ 703
Investments in marketable debt securities	65,985	—	—	—	—
Investments in marketable equity securities	785,909	—	—	—	—
Accounts receivable, net of allowance	24,628	15,075	9,150	5,292	1,201
Accounts receivable, related party	—	1,711	—	—	—
Other current assets	18,743	1,705	1,135	941	206
Restricted cash	740	945	1,599	—	—
Total current assets	949,068	70,969	34,438	26,389	2,110
Investments in marketable debt securities	109,802	—	—	—	—
Property and equipment, net	30,044	15,326	19,554	11,743	2,393
Other assets	50,609	2,060	4,270	1,710	154
Goodwill	90,788	—	—	—	—
Total assets	$ 1,230,311	$ 88,354	$ 58,262	$ 39,842	$ 4,657
LIABILITIES AND STOCKHOLDERS' EQUITY					
Current liabilities:					
Accounts payable	$ 11,461	$ 3,477	$ 3,568	$ 2,912	$ 531
Accrued liabilities	16,398	6,593	10,081	2,973	707
Current portion of long-term debt	5,750	1,113	1,359	281	153
Income taxes payable	5,398	—	—	—	—
Deferred tax liability	306,352	—	—	—	—
Total current liabilities	345,359	11,182	15,007	6,166	1,391
Long-term debt	179,114	569	2,612	578	467
Total liabilities	524,473	11,751	17,619	6,744	1,858
Stockholders' equity:					
Convertible Preferred Stock	—	—	—	—	34
Common stock; $0.0001 par value	7	3	3	1	0
Additional paid in capital	218,670	127,770	94,696	62,425	15,144
Other comprehensive income, net of tax	121,409	—	—	—	—
Retained earnings (deficit)	365,752	(51,170)	(54,056)	(29,328)	(12,380)
Total stockholders' equity	705,838	76,603	40,643	33,098	2,799
Total liabilities and stockholders' equity	$ 1,230,311	$ 88,354	$ 58,262	$ 39,842	$ 4,657

Exhibit 5   CNET Networks Inc. Income Statements for 1995–1999

	1999	1998	1997	1996	1995
Revenues:					
Internet	104,887	50,419	26,717	10,134	393
Television	7,458	7,058	6,923	4,697	3,107
Total revenues	112,345	57,477	33,640	14,830	3,500
Cost of revenues:					
Internet	35,619	23,563	19,813	9,121	891
Television	8,341	6,741	6,904	6,213	4,742
Total cost of revenues	43,960	30,304	26,717	15,334	5,633
Gross profit (deficit)	68,385	27,173	6,923	(503)	(2,133)
Operating expenses:					
Sales and marketing	91,660	14,530	11,603	7,821	2,370
Development	7,561	3,454	13,609	3,438	2,264
General and administrative	15,266	7,154	6,849	3,772	1,703
Unusual items	—	(922)	9,000	—	—
Amortization of goodwill	15,036	—	—	—	—
Total operating expenses	129,523	24,216	41,061	15,032	6,337
Operating income (loss)	(61,138)	2,957	(34,138)	(15,535)	(8,470)
Other income (expense):					
Equity losses	—	(11,796)	(2,228)	—	—
Gain on sale of equity investments	734,138	10,450	11,027	—	—
Interest income, net	1,223	1,412	611	452	(137)
Loss on joint venture	—	—	—	(1,865)	—
Total other income	735,361	66	9,410	(1,413)	(137)
Income (loss) before income taxes	674,223	3,023	(24,728)	(16,949)	(8,607)
Income taxes	257,315	—	—	—	—
Net income (loss)	416,908	3,023	(24,728)	(16,949)	(8,607)
Other comprehensive income, net of tax:					
Unrealized holding gains arising during the period	121,409	—	—	—	—
Comprehensive income (loss)	538,317	3,023	(24,728)	—	—
Basic net income (loss) per share	5.80	0.05	(0.44)	(1.51)	(0.93)
Diluted net income (loss) per share	5.05	0.04	(0.44)		
Shares used in calculating basic per share data	71820	65783	55819	11240	9216
Shares used in calculating diluted per share data	83373	71623	55819		

Exhibit 6   CNET Networks Inc. Cash Flow Statements for 1995–1999 (continued)

	1999	1998	1997	1996	1995
Cash flows from operating activities:					
Net income(loss)	$416,908	$ 3,023	$ (24,728)	$ (16,949)	$ (8,607)
Adjustments to reconcile net loss to net cash provided (used) in operating activities:					
Depreciation and amortization	23,847	6,341	5,055	1,928	476
Amortization of program costs	8,131	5,802	6,549	4,673	3,155
Interest expense converted into preferred stock	—	—	—	222	118
Allowance for doubtful accounts	2,956	1,261	361	75	25
Investments for services provided	(6,021)	—	—	—	—
Gain on investment sales	(734,138)	—	—	—	—
Reserve for joint venture	—	—	(1,249)	1,865	—
Other	—	—	—	—	45
Warrant compensation expense	—	—	7,000	—	—
Changes in operating assets and liabilities:	—	—	—	—	—
Accounts receivable	(10,664)	(9,730)	(4,219)	(4,166)	(1,226)
Other current assets	(16,940)	455	(917)	30	(164)
Other assets	(3,805)	4,933	(1,515)	(1,237)	(122)
Accounts payable	7,978	329	229	2,380	454
Accrued liabilities	9,627	(3,253)	7,534	2,267	510
Income tax liabilities	5,399	—	—	—	—
Deferred tax liabilities	225,459	—	—	—	—
Net cash provided (used) in operating activities	(71,263)	9,161	(5,900)	(8,911)	(5,336)
Cash flows from investing activities:					
Purchase of marketable debt securities	(214,557)	—	—	—	—
Purchase of marketable equity securities	(15,950)	—	—	—	—
Proceeds from sale of marketable debt securities	37,539	—	—	—	—
Proceeds from sale of marketable equity securities	173,663	—	—	—	—
Privately held companies	(39,448)	—	—	—	—
Cash paid for acquisitions	(43,743)	(108)	—	—	—
Purchases of equipment, excluding capital leases	(22,373)	(4,879)	(12,213)	(10,739)	(1,862)
Purchases of programming assets	(8,312)	(6,084)	(5,826)	(5,438)	(3,133)
Deferred interest	(307)	—	—	—	—
Loan to joint venture	—	—	(1,638)	(1,777)	—
Investment in Vignette Corporation	—	—	—	(512)	—
Net cash used in investing activities	(133,488)	(11,071)	(19,677)	(18,466)	(4,994)

Exhibit 6   CNET Networks Inc. Cash Flow Statements for 1995–1999 (continued)

	1999	1998	1997	1996	1995
Cash flows from financing activities:					
Tax benefit from exercises of stock options	31,719	—	—	—	—
Net proceeds from issuance of convertible debt	167,220	—	—	4,544	6,909
Net proceeds from initial public offering	—	—	—	37,777	—
Allocated proceeds from issuance of warrants	—	—	—	164	187
Proceeds from stockholder receivable	—	—	—	595	—
Net proceeds from issuance of common stock	—	26,213	23,392	—	—
Net proceeds from employee stock purchase plan	934	723	705	170	—
Proceeds from debt	—	—	3,281	3,636	3,000
Net proceeds from exercise of options and warrants	8,086	6,246	1,176	141	—
Repayments of debt	—	—	—	—	—
Principal payments on capital leases	(42)	(416)	(239)	(105)	(231)
Principal payments on equipment note	(1,640)	(1,873)	(339)	(92)	(55)
Net cash provided by financing activities	206,277	30,893	27,976	46,829	9,810
Net increase in cash and cash equivalents	1,526	28,983	2,399	19,45	(521)
Cash and cash equivalents at beginning of period	51,537	22,554	20,155	703	1,224
Cash and cash equivalents at end of period	53,063	51,537	22,554	20,156	703
Supplemental disclosure of cash flow information:					
Interest paid	4,205	325	255	89	74
Taxes paid	2,625	—	—	—	—
Supplemental disclosure of noncash transactions:					
Non cash portion of investment	—	—	—	105	—
Issuance of debt for acquisitions	10,098	3,066	—	—	—
Capital lease obligations incurred	—	—	408	297	170
Note issued in exchange for equipment	—	—	—	138	549
Unrealized gain in marketable securities and investments, net of deferred tax liability	121,409	—	—	—	—
Issuance of common stock for acquisitions	50,553	—	—	—	—
Exercise of stock options through issuance of note receivable from stockholder	—	—	—	595	—
Conversion of preferred stock into common stock	—	—	—	43	—
Conversion of debt and interest into 208,548, 242,108, and 205,357 shares of convertible preferred stock, respectively	—	—	—	3,858	3,218

Exhibit 7   CNET Networks Inc. Common Size Balance Sheet (Percentage)

	Dec-99	Dec-98	Dec-97	Dec-96	Dec-95
Assets					
Cash & Equivalents	73.62	59.40	41.46	50.59	15.10
Net Receivables	2.00	19.00	15.70	13.28	25.79
Inventories	0.00	0.00	0.00	0.00	0.00
Prepaid Expenses	0.00	0.00	0.00	0.00	0.00
Other Current Assets	1.52	1.93	1.95	2.36	4.42
Total Current Assets	**77.14**	**80.32**	**59.11**	**66.23**	**45.31**
Gross Plant, Property & Equip	4.11	31.76	45.85	35.37	62.66
Accumulated Depreciation	1.67	14.42	12.29	5.90	11.27
Net Plant, Property & Equip	2.44	17.34	33.56	29.47	51.39
Investments at Equity	0.00	0.00	0.00	0.00	0.00
Other Investments	8.92	0.00	0.00	0.00	0.00
Intangibles	7.38	0.00	0.00	0.00	0.00
Deferred Charges	0.00	0.00	0.00	0.00	0.00
Other Assets	4.11	2.33	7.33	4.29	3.31
Total Assets	**100.00**	**100.00**	**100.00**	**100.00**	**100.00**
Liabilities and Stockholders' Equity					
Long Term Debt Due In One Year	0.47	1.26	2.33	0.71	3.29
Notes Payable	0.00	0.00	0.00	0.00	0.00
Accounts Payable	0.93	3.94	6.12	7.31	11.40
Taxes Payable	0.44	0.00	0.00	0.00	0.00
Accrued Expenses	1.33	6.79	11.75	7.46	15.18
Other Current Liabilities	24.90	0.67	5.55	0.00	0.00
Total Current Liabilities	**28.07**	**12.66**	**25.76**	**15.48**	**29.87**
Long Term Debt	14.56	0.64	4.48	1.45	10.03
Deferred Taxes	0.00	0.00	0.00	0.00	0.00
Investment Tax Credit	0.00	0.00	0.00	0.00	0.00
Minority Interest	0.00	0.00	0.00	0.00	0.00
Other Liabilities	0.00	0.00	0.00	0.00	0.00
Total Liabilities	**42.63**	**13.30**	**30.24**	**16.93**	**39.90**
Equity					
Preferred Stock—Redeemable	0.00	0.00	0.00	0.00	0.00
Preferred Stock—Nonredeemable	0.00	0.00	0.00	0.00	0.73
Total Preferred Stock	**0.00**	**0.00**	**0.00**	**0.00**	**0.73**
Common Stock	0.00	0.00	0.00	0.00	0.00
Capital Surplus	17.77	144.61	162.54	156.68	325.19
Retained Earnings	39.60	-57.92	-92.78	-73.61	-265.81
Less: Treasury Stock	0.00	0.00	0.00	0.00	0.00
Common Equity	57.37	86.70	69.76	83.07	59.37
Total Equity	57.37	86.70	69.76	83.07	60.10
Total Liabilities & Equity	100.00	100.00	100.00	100.00	100.00

Source: Research Insights

Exhibit 8   CNET Networks Inc. Common Size Income Statement (Percentage)

	Dec-99	Dec-98	Dec-97	Dec-96	Dec-95
Sales	100.00	100.00	100.00	100.00	100.00
Cost of Goods Sold	31.29	41.98	64.39	90.40	147.34
Gross Profit	68.71	58.02	35.61	9.60	-47.34
Selling, General, &					
Administrative Expense	101.91	43.93	95.30	101.36	181.06
Operating Income Before Deprec	-33.19	14.09	-59.70	-91.76	-228.40
Depreciation, Depletion, &					
Amortization	21.23	11.24	15.03	13.00	13.60
Operating Profit	-54.42	2.85	-74.72	-104.76	-242.00
Interest Expense	0.00	0.00	0.85	2.12	6.49
Non-Operating Income/Expense	654.56	0.12	28.82	-7.40	2.57
Special Items	0.00	1.63	-26.75	0.00	0.00
Pretax Income	600.14	4.61	-73.51	-114.29	-245.91
Total Income Taxes	229.04	0.00	0.00	0.00	0.00
Minority Interest	0.00	0.00	0.00	0.00	0.00
Income Before Extraordinary					
Items & Discontinued Operations	371.10	4.61	-73.51	-114.29	-245.91
Preferred Dividends	0.00	0.00	0.00	0.00	0.00
Available for Common	371.10	4.61	-73.51	-114.29	-245.91
Savings Due to Common					
Stock Equivalents	0.00	0.00	0.00	0.00	0.00
Adjusted Available for Common	371.10	4.61	-73.51	-114.29	-245.91
Extraordinary Items	0.00	0.00	0.00	0.00	0.00
Discontinued Operations	0.00	0.00	0.00	0.00	0.00
Adjusted Net Income	371.10	4.61	-73.51	-114.29	-245.91

Source: Research Insights

Exhibit 9   CNET Networks, Inc. Annual Ratio Report (Ratio, Except as Noted)

	Dec-99	Dec-98	Dec-97	Dec-96	Dec-95	Dec-94
Liquidity						
Current Ratio	2.75	6.35	2.29	4.28	1.52	@NA
Quick Ratio	2.69	6.19	2.22	4.13	1.37	@NA
Working Capital Per Share	8.17	0.88	0.33	0.38	0.07	@NA
Cash Flow Per Share	5.96	0.13	-0.34	-0.28	-0.75	@NA
Activity						
Inventory Turnover	@NC	@NC	@NC	@NC	@NC	@NA
Receivables Turnover	5.43	4.35	4.66	4.57	@NC	@NA
Total Asset Turnover	0.17	0.77	0.69	0.67	@NC	@NA
Average Collection Period (Days)	66.00	83.00	77.00	79.00	@NC	@NA
Days to Sell Inventory	0	0	0	0	@NC	@NA
Operating Cycle (Days)	66	83	77	79	@NC	@NA
Performance						
Sales/Net Property, Plant & Equip	3.74	3.68	1.72	1.26	1.46	@NA
Sales/Stockholder Equity	0.16	0.74	0.83	0.45	1.25	@NA
Profitability						
Operating Margin Before Depr (%)	-33.19	14.09	-59.70	-91.76	-228.40	@NA
Operating Margin After Depr (%)	-54.42	2.85	-74.72	-104.76	-242.00	@NA
Pretax Profit Margin (%)	600.14	4.61	-73.51	-114.29	-245.91	@NA
Net Profit Margin (%)	371.1	4.61	-73.51	-114.29	-245.91	@NA
Return on Assets (%)	33.89	2.94	-42.44	-42.54	-184.82	@NA
Return on Equity (%)	59.07	3.39	-60.84	-51.21	-311.28	@NA
Return on Investment (%)	47.11	3.37	-57.17	-50.33	-263.53	@NA
Return on Average Assets (%)	63.23	3.55	-50.41	-76.18	@NC	@NA
Return on Average Equity (%)	106.57	4.44	-67.07	-94.52	@NC	@NA
Return on Average Investment (%)	86.66	4.32	-64.29	-91.76	@NC	@NA
Leverage						
Interest Coverage Before Tax	@CF	@CF	-85.46	-52.81	-36.92	@NA
Interest Coverage After Tax	@CF	@CF	-85.46	-52.81	-36.92	@NA
Long-Term Debt/Common Equity (%)	25.38	0.74	6.43	1.75	16.89	@NA
Long-Term Debt/Shrhldr Equity(%)	25.38	0.74	6.43	1.75	16.68	@NA
Total Debt/Invested Capital (%)	20.89	2.18	9.18	2.55	18.98	@NA
Total Debt/Total Assets (%)	15.03	1.9	6.82	2.16	13.31	@NA
Total Assets/Common Equity	1.74	1.15	1.43	1.2	1.68	@NA
Dividends						
Dividend Payout (%)	0	0	0	0	0	@NA
Dividend Yield (%)	0	0	0	0	@NA	@NA

Source: Research Insights

Exhibit 10   A Financial Analysis of CNET Relative to Its Competition

	NI ($Mil)	D/E	P/E	EPS	Market Cap ($Mil)	Price 20-Apr	52 wk High	52 wk Low	% Change
CNET Networks	**416.9**	**0.25**	**5.5**	**$5.80**	**$2,349**	**$27.75**	**$79.88**	**$26.75**	**66.5**
Internet and Online Content Providers									
America Online Inc.	762.0	0.11	154.3	0.37	137,334	60.19	95.81	38.47	59.8
EarthWeb Inc.	NA	NA	NE	-3.78	102	10.50	61.00	8.13	86.7
Internet.com Corp.	-22.0	0.00	NE	-1.08	394	15.75	72.25	9.19	87.3
Lycos Inc.	-52.0	0.00	NE	-0.60	3,964	36.06	93.63	28.56	69.5
VerticalNet Inc.	-53.5	0.65	NE	-0.86	3,055	41.63	148.38	13.56	90.9
Ziff-Davis Inc.—ZDNet	1.9	0.00	628.1	0.03	189	42.88	42.88	11.63	72.9
Auctions									
eBay Inc.	10.8	0.02	0	0.10	19,560	150.25	255.00	70.28	72.4
Entertainment/Media									
Time Warner	1960.0	1.99	72.6	1.51	117,820	90.06	105.50	57.19	45.8
Software and System Development*									
Microsoft Corp.	7785.0	0.00	49.6	1.54	408,659	78.94	119.94	73.00	39.1
Internet and Intranet Service Providers									
Intraware Inc.	-28.0	NA	NE	-1.14	396	16.13	99.00	14.00	85.9
Internet and Online Service Providers									
Excite@Home	-1457.6	0.10	NE	-4.61	6,902	17.94	84.84	17.06	79.9
Retail Specialty									
Egghead.com Inc.	-154.9	0.00	NE	-4.29	157	4.13	26.50	4.00	84.9
Computer Software Retailing									
Cyberian Outpost Inc.	-35.6	NA	NE	-1.52	134	4.63	17.50	3.63	79.3
Music, Video, Book and Entertainment*									
Amazon.com Inc.	-720.0	5.51	NE	-2.20	18,306	52.38	113.00	40.81	63.9
TV Broadcasting									
Discovery Communications Inc.									
Publishing—Periodicals									
Imagine Media, Inc.									
International Data Group									

* title slightly modified from paper

Exhibit 11 Comparison of 1999 Revenues and Earnings

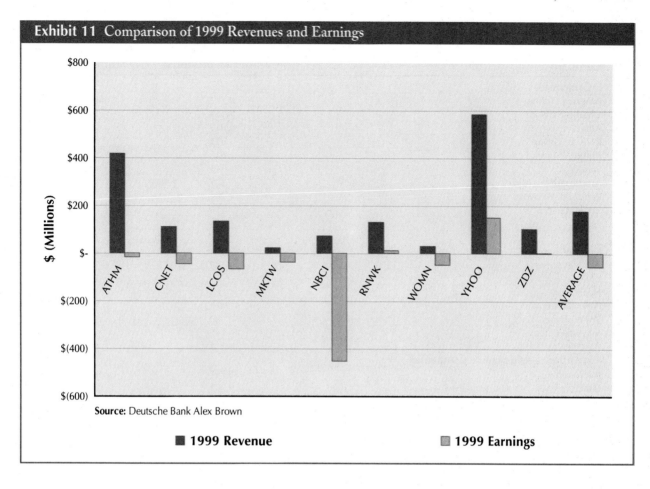

Source: Deutsche Bank Alex Brown

■ **1999 Revenue**   ▢ **1999 Earnings**

Exhibit 12 The Fortune e-50[70]

Company	Revenues ($ millions)	Year Founded
E-Companies		
America Online	4,777	1985
Charles Schwab	4,113	1986
Amazon.com	1,015	1994
E*Trade Group	621	1982
Knight/Trimark Group	618	1995
Yahoo	341	1995
Ameritrade Holding	301	1992
EarthLink Network	254	1994
Priceline.com	189	1998
CMGI	176	1986
eBay	125	1995
DoubleClick	103	1996
RealNetworks	89	1994
CNet	79	1995
Healtheon	68	1995
FreeMarkets	N/A	1995
Phone.com	68	1994
InfoSpace	37	1996
VerticalNet	8	1995
Net Software And Service Companies		
Microsoft	19,747	1975
Oracle	9,063	1977
Intuit	848	1983
Network Associates	785	1992
Cambridge Tech. Partners	628	1991
TMP Worldwide	585	1967
Citrix Systems	323	1989
Macromedia	167	1992
Exodus Communications	108	1992
Verisign	85	1995
BroadVision	71	1993
Inktomi	71	1996
Ariba	45	1996
Security First Technologies	44	1995
Razorfish	36	1995
Net Hardware Companies		
IBM	87,448	1911
Lucent Technologies	38,303	1995
Intel	28,194	1968
Dell Computer	21,670	1984
Cisco Systems	12,154	1984
Sun Microsystems	11,726	1982
EMC	4,459	1979
Qualcomm	3,937	1981
Network Appliance	335	1992
Broadcom	335	1991
JDS Uniphase Corp.	282	1999
Juniper Networks	31	1992
Net Communication Companies		
AT&T	56,968	1875
MCI WorldCom	30,720	1983
Qwest Communications	3,424	1997
Global Crossing	691	1997

Exhibit 13 CNET Press Release—3rd Quarter 2000 Performance

CNET Networks, Inc. Reports 99 Percent Annual Increase In Revenue And Increased Profitability In The Third Quarter

SAN FRANCISCO, CA—October 24, 2000—CNET Networks, Inc. (Nasdaq: CNET), today reported net revenues totaling $56.4 million for the third quarter ended September 30, 2000, compared to net revenues of $28.4 million for the third quarter of 1999, an increase of 99 percent. Income, excluding goodwill amortization, net gains on investment sales, and income taxes, was $6.2 million or $0.07 per diluted share for the third quarter. Including goodwill amortization, net gains on investment sales, and income taxes, CNET Networks' net loss for the third quarter of 2000 was $43.6 million, or $0.50 per share, versus net income of $29.3 million or $0.35 per diluted share in the same period last year.

Including the recently acquired ZDNet businesses, pro forma net revenues for the third quarter of 2000 were $110.5 million, up more than 53 percent, compared to pro forma net revenues of $72.1 million from the third quarter of 1999. CNET Networks and ZDNet online businesses showed revenue increases of 76.5 percent year over year. CNET Networks, including the results of the acquired ZDNet businesses, generated pro forma earnings before interest, income taxes, depreciation and amortization (EBITDA) of $16.7 million in the third quarter, representing a 15 percent margin. Pro forma earnings per share (EPS), including the results of the acquired ZDNet businesses, before goodwill amortization, net gains on investment sales and income taxes were $0.08.

"Both CNET Networks and ZDNet delivered very strong financial performances in the quarter, confirming that the merger was done from a position of strength for both companies," said Shelby Bonnie, CEO of CNET Networks, Inc. "The success of CNET and ZDNet demonstrate the tremendous importance of the Web as an information medium for technology products and services, and we've only begun to leverage the scale of CNET's multiple global media brands and channel services to empower buyers, sellers and suppliers. The merger of ZDNet is already making CNET Networks' business possibilities and global opportunities even more significant and attainable."

Q3 Operating Highlights, Pro Forma Including ZDNet:

- CNET Networks reaches approximately 24 million people online around the globe and reported 380 million international page views in the quarter.

- In the United States alone, CNET Networks ranks as a top 10 Web property, with an online audience of 17.6 million unique monthly visitors and a 22 percent reach, as measured by Media Metrix.

- CNET Networks reached 43 percent of professionals in the MIS/technical universe who are active online at work, and nearly 25 percent of all executives and managers who work online and have purchase decision-making power, according to Nielsen NetRatings.

- Aggregated average daily page views grew to 33.8 million, an increase of 57 percent over the third quarter of 1999.

- Internet revenue per 1000 page views increased 13 percent over the third quarter of 1999 to $31.18.

- Total aggregated unique customers were approximately 1,300 and 90 percent unduplicated when comparing the total customers of both CNET Networks and ZDNet.

- Daily leads to merchants reached 278,000, up 52 percent and revenue per lead reached an average of $0.78 in the quarter.

- CNET Networks estimates that its 25 million total leads out to merchants resulted in over $535 million in commerce during the third quarter.

- CNET Networks delivered 495 million user-requested email newsletters in the third quarter on over 90 different subjects to approximately 24.5 million email subscriptions to over 9.3 million unique email subscribers.

- CDS grew its multilingual product database to more than 500,000 products, up from 300,000 in the second quarter and 170,000 in the first quarter and increased site licenses to 120 in the third quarter from 90 in the second quarter of 2000.

- Headcount stood at 1,840 at the end of the quarter.

- MySimon achieved the number one position as the largest comparison-shopping aggregator and was cited by *Forbes*, the *Wall Street Journal*, and *Money* magazine as the best of breed in its space.

Focusing on Key Initiatives as Part of New Organizational Structure

CNET Networks has introduced a new organizational structure and business architecture to enable the organization to operate effectively, move quickly to address new opportunities, to innovate, and to continue to be a leader in the industry. Last week, the company announced five new business units—Media, International Media, Channel Services, Consumer Services and Market Intelligence—that will take advantage of the combined strengths and incredibly strong management teams from CNET Networks and ZDNet.

Media—CNET Media includes all aspects of the US-based ZDNet and CNET media brands, providing a trusted source of information and services to individuals and businesses of all sizes, empowering them to make informed buying decisions for technology products and services. Focused on CNET Network's domestic media, it includes the broadest portfolio of trusted, award-winning brands in the technology marketplace in multiple platforms, from online, television, radio and print to wireless. As the technology category becomes more and more important to people and businesses, CNET Networks' scale makes it the clear number one, with:

Exhibit 13 CNET Press Release—3rd Quarter 2000 Performance (continued)

- 33.8 million page views per day
- 24.5 million subscriptions to different email lists
- 1.5 million daily downloads
- 500,000 products with information, pricing and availability
- 20,000 expert reviews of technology products
- 80 fresh technology related news stories each day

"Technology products and services are considered purchases that require detailed research and access to objective, trusted information sources," Bonnie added. "Given that IT professionals are now using the Net as their preferred source of information on IT products and services, we are committed to evolving the ways that we can bring information to buyers by providing advertisers innovative new ways to deliver that information."

International Media—One of the most successful global companies in the Internet space, CNET Networks has 23 sites worldwide, including wholly owned operations in Europe, Asia and Australia, as well as joint ventures and licensees. Together, CNET Networks and ZDNet delivered approximately 380 million page views to their international sites in the third quarter, up 100 percent from the 190 million page views in the third quarter of 1999, representing 12 percent of the total, worldwide page views. During the third quarter, ZDNet continued aggressive expansion of its international footprint. ZDNet Australia became a wholly owned Web property. The company also executed a joint venture agreement with Jasubhai Interactive, India's preeminent online IT information and services resource, which turned ZDNet India from a licensed to a joint ventured site. In addition, ZDNet expanded into Latin America by signing syndication agreements with five leading Latin American Internet portals, including Globo, iG-Internet Grátis, Patagon, StarMedia, and Terra.

Channel Services—CNET Networks has made significant progress in creating an expansive range of product information and service offerings available to all channel participants, including manufacturers, distributors, resellers, value added resellers (VARs), resellers and IT consultants. CNET Channel Services is comprised of: CNET Data Services (CDS), a database of more than 500,000 technology and consumer electronics products; CNET Media Services (CMS), which produces marketing tools like product demos and online coupons that are distributed within the IT supply chain via CDS; and CNET Apollo, a browser-based application, targeted at 30,000 Value Added Resellers (VARS), that is coupled with CDS' data to streamline business transactions in a centralized product marketplace. In addition to adding 200,000 more product SKUs and 33 percent more site licenses to CDS, in Q3 CNET Media Services launched Netbate product coupons and CNET Apollo increased its customer base to 28 with 260 unique users. Apollo's service enabled approximately $700 million in annualized commerce transacted using Apollo's Web-based application.

Consumer Services—The vision for this unit is to provide users with as much information as possible on specific products and services, in the broadest range of consumer categories, using the Web as a powerful tool to search, compare, and ultimately guide users toward purchase decisions. We continue to leverage CNET Networks' technology, edit, data and audiences to help mySimon grow in leadership. Currently, mySimon—the leading independent comparison shopping service on the Internet, according to an October 2000 report by Nielsen NetRatings—searches millions of products at thousands of stores online, and offers robust product and price comparison capabilities. Its revenue stream is derived mainly from a combination of lead fees to participating merchants, advertising programs and licensing fees. CNET's Consumer Services business unit is poised to provide a key growth path for CNET Networks and a way to further extend the company's proven model into other categories.

Market Intelligence—a brand-new business initiative for CNET Networks, will focus on creating a new revenue stream by compiling and organizing a vast database of user traffic information as a basis for a range of research and consulting services. Its purpose is to compile and organize the enormous repository of data the company generates through its combined businesses, and create revenue streams by selling licenses and subscriptions to marketers who will use the data to help design, build and market their products or services. All Market Intelligence products and services will adhere to CNET Networks' strict online privacy policy. Created in the belief that, in the next five years, leading Web companies will have the ability to track and manage data as a core competency, this is a key area of investment for CNET Networks.

"Marrying CNET Media, Market Intelligence, and CNET Channel Services allows CNET to be a critical partner to the leading IT companies throughout the supply channel," said Bonnie. "We help our partners sell more efficiently and we help our users buy better. Our goal is to create informed customers and efficient marketplaces online and this quarter reflects our success."

CNET Networks Completed Acquisition of ZDNet on October 17, 2000

CNET Networks acquired the outstanding common stock of Ziff-Davis, Inc., with each share of ZD common stock (NYSE: ZD) was converted into 0.3397 shares of CNET Networks common stock and each share of ZDNet common stock (NYSE: ZDZ) was converted into 0.5932 shares of CNET Networks common stock. CNET issued approximately 47 million shares of common stock in the transaction. CNET Networks now has approximately 134 million shares outstanding, of which about 67 percent will be held by persons other than Softbank and CNET officers and directors.

Exhibit 13 CNET Press Release—3rd Quarter 2000 Performance (continued)

Investments

CNET Networks continues to have one of the strongest balance sheets in the industry with cash and marketable securities valued at approximately $460 million. The company currently has more than $340 million in cash and marketable debt securities as well as investments in 14 publicly traded companies valued at approximately $130 million and investments in more than a dozen privately held companies.

Outlook

For the combined businesses of CNET Networks, Inc., management estimates net revenues will be in the range of $120 million to $125 million for the fourth quarter of 2000. The company expects to grow revenues to approximately $580 million in 2001 and is targeting annual revenue growth of 25 to 30 percent in 2002. Based on these revenue goals, management believes reasonable EBITDA targets are between $18 million and $21 million (15.0 percent to 16.8 percent margins) in the fourth quarter of 2000, approximately $145 million (25 percent margin) in 2001, and an EBITDA margin of approximately 27 to 30 percent in 2002. For further guidance, please refer to the addendum that follows the financial statements.

Source: The information in this section was obtained directly from cnet.com.

Notes

1. Bonnie, Shelby. CNET Networks Press Release, 29 November 2000.
2. Colligan, John. CNET Networks Press Release, 29 November 2000.
3. Key, Angela. "CNET: Revenge of the Preppies," *Fortune Magazine*, 21 June 1999.
4. www.edger-online.com IPO Express: Company Profile: CNET Inc. 22 March 2000.
5. "CNET to Provide Internet Services to Mobile Devices Powered by Wysdom Wireless Solutions," *PR Newswire*, 20 March 2000.
6. http://ptg.djnr.com Dow Jones Interactive, Company and Industry Center, Company Reports, CNET Networks, Inc. 21 March 2000.
7. Tessler, Joelle. "CNET purchase of mySimon expands scope," *Mercury News*, 20 January 2000.
8. http://ptg.djnr.com Dow Jones Interactive, Company and Industry Center, Company Reports, CNET Networks, Inc. 21 March 2000.
9. Zito, Kelly. "CNET Expands, Purchases MySimon.com." *The San Francisco Chronicle*, 21 January 2000.
10. "CNET to Provide Internet Services to Mobile Devices Powered by Wysdom Wireless Solutions," *PR Newswire*, 20 March 2000.
11. http://yahoo.marketguide.com
12. http://yahoo.marketguide.com
13. www.edger-online.com IPO Express: Company Profile: CNET Inc. 22 March 2000.
14. Key, Angela. "CNET: Revenge of the Preppies," *Fortune Magazine*, 21 June 1999.
15. CNET Networks Inc., 10QSB, 15 August 1996.
16. Greenberg, Herb. "Is any Internet stock a safe bet?" *Fortune Magazine*, 9 December 1996.
17. Grady, Barbara. "CNET Yearns to Be Tech Voice for the Masses," *MSN Money Central*, 10 December 1999.
18. Grady, Barbara. "CNET Yearns to Be Tech Voice for the Masses," *MSN Money Central*, 10 December 1999.
19. *ADWEEK Eastern Edition*. "Halsey Minor: CEO CNET," 13 April 1998.
20. "CNET, Inc. Announces Fourth Quarter Financial Results," *PR Newswire*, 3 February 2000.
21. http://biz.yahoo.com/z/a/c/cnet.html.
22. CNET Press Release, November 2000.
23. CNET Press Release, November 2000.
24. www.cnet.com/aboutcnet.
25. This information was taken directly from the cnet.com website.
26. This information was taken directly from the cnet.com website.
27. www.hoovers.com/co/capsule/0/0,2163,60/00,00.html.
28. "CNET reaches 1 Out of Every 5 Internet Users at Work." *PR Newswire*, 22 February 2000.
29. www.idg.com, Hoovers Online.
30. "AP CNET Partnership," *AP Newswire*, 31 January 2000.
31. Tessler, Joelle. "CNET purchase of mySimon expands scope," *Mercury News*, 20 January 2000.
32. "CNET launches auction site for technology products," *AP Newswire*, 18 May 1999.
33. http://ptg.djnr.com Dow Jones Interactive, Company and Industry Center, Executive Reports, America Online, Inc. 20 April 2000.
34. www.aol.com, Hoovers Online.
35. http://ptg.djnr.com Dow Jones Interactive, Company and Industry Center, Executive Reports, America Online, Inc. 20 April 2000.
36. http://ptg.djnr.com Dow Jones Interactive, Company and Industry Center, Executive Reports, EarthWeb Inc.
37. http://ptg.djnr.com Dow Jones Interactive, Company and Industry Center, Executive Reports, internet.com Corp.
38. http://ptg.djnr.com Dow Jones Interactive, Company and Industry Center, Executive Reports, Lycos Inc.
39. http://ptg.djnr.com Dow Jones Interactive, Company and Industry Center, Executive Reports, VerticalNet Inc.
40. http://ptg.djnr.com Dow Jones Interactive, Company and Industry Center, Executive Reports, eBay Inc.
41. http://ptg.djnr.com Dow Jones Interactive, Company and Industry Center, Executive Reports, Time Warner Inc.
42. http://ptg.djnr.com Dow Jones Interactive, Company and Industry Center, Executive Reports, Microsoft Corp.
43. http://ptg.djnr.com Dow Jones Interactive, Company and Industry Center, Company Reports, CNET, "CNET Networks, Microsoft in Online Ads Pact," 17 April 2000.
44. http://ptg.djnr.com Dow Jones Interactive, Company and Industry Center, Executive Reports, Intraware Inc.
45. http://ptg.djnr.com Dow Jones Interactive, Company and Industry Center, Executive Reports, Excite@Home
46. *Business Wire*. "Egghead.com First Quarter Results Demonstrate Drive Toward Profitability," 19 April 2000.
47. http://ptg.djnr.com Dow Jones Interactive, Company and Industry Center, Executive Reports, Cyberian Outpost, Inc.
48. http://ptg.djnr.com Dow Jones Interactive, Company and Industry Center, Executive Reports, Amazon.com Inc.
49. www.discovery.com, Hoovers Online.
50. www.imaginemedia.com, Hoovers Online.
51. www.idg.com, Hoovers Online.
52. Grady, Barbara. "CNET Yearns to Be Tech Voice for the Masses," *MSN Money Central*, 10 December 1999.
53. *Business Week*, 30 October 2000, 116.
54. Fost, Dan. "CNET's Dynamic Duo Changing Roles as Minor Follows His Bliss/Bonnie to Run the Show as CEO While Partner Helps Other Firms Grow," *The San Francisco Chronicle*, 16 March 2000.
55. Morrison, Mary E. "CNET Ad Pro Thrives on Risks, Results; Williams Promoted to Senior VP-Marketing for Work on Campaign," *Business Marketing*, 1 December 1999.
56. Fost, Dan. "CNET's Dynamic Duo Changing Roles as Minor Follows His Bliss/Bonnie to Run the Show as CEO While Partner Helps Other Firms Grow," *The San Francisco Chronicle*, 16 March 2000.

57. *PR Newswire*. "CNET and Commerce One Sign Agreement to Provide IT Supplier Content for E-Commerce Portal," November 10, 1999.

58. *PR Newswire*. "CNET and Commerce One Sign Agreement to Provide IT Supplier Content for E-Commerce Portal," 10 November 1999.

59. *Business Week*, 30 October 2000, 118.

60. Fost, Dan. "CNET's Dynamic Duo Changing Roles as Minor Follows His Bliss/Bonnie to Run the Show as CEO While Partner Helps Other Firms Grow," *The San Francisco Chronicle,* 16 March 2000.

61. Lande, Laurie. "CNET to Increase Asia Operations in SK—India," *Dow Jones Business News*, 26 January 2000.

62. Lande, Laurie. "CNET to Increase Asia Operations in SK—India," *Dow Jones Business News*, 26 January 2000.

63. *PR Newswire*. "CNET Data Services Expands Customer Base," 1 February 2000.

64. *Israel Business Today.* "CNET Invests in Israeli Internet Company," 10 August 1999, 20.

65. Fost, Dan. "CNET's Dynamic Duo Changing Roles as Minor Follows His Bliss/Bonnie to Run the Show as CEO While Partner Helps Other Firms Grow," *The San Francisco Chronicle,* 16 March 2000.

66. *PR Newswire.* "CNET to Provide Internet Services to Mobile Devices Powered by Wysdom Wireless Solutions," 20 March 2000.

67. Morrison, Mary E. "CNET Ad Pro Thrives on Risks, Results," *Business Marketing,* 1 December 1999.

68. Grady, Barbara. "CNET Yearns to Be Tech Voice for the Masses," *MSN Money Central,* 10 December 1999.

69. *Business Week*, 30 October 2000, 118.

70. The information in this section was obtained directly from cnet.com.

Case 10

Cognex Corporation: "Work Hard, Play Hard"

Marilyn T. Lucas and Alan N. Hoffman, *Bentley College*

"To preserve and enhance vision," recited Bill Silver with his hand held vertically on the bridge of his nose, as he entered the office of Robert Shillman. With his usual smile, the CEO looked up from the Cognex Corporation's 1998 Annual Report, and returned the corporate salute, adopted from "The Three Stooges." Silver, the Vice-President of Research and Development, joined Shillman to discuss the future of Cognex Corporation, the company they started together 18 years ago. In spite of its leading position as a manufacturer of machine vision systems, Cognex has hurdled over changes in the industry in recent years. It has survived an industry shakeout of competitors in the early 1990s and managed to sustain stable growth during the slump of the semiconductor industry. However, competitors have recently begun to tap into the OEM market (Original Equipment Manufacturer), the cornerstone of Cognex's business, and have beaten Cognex to the punch in the international marketplace. Finally, the 1998 Annual Report shows that Cognex' revenues and profits have fallen from the peak levels they had reached in 1997 (Exhibits 1–3).

Robert Shillman, Bill Silver, and their fellow executives must decide which direction the company should take to realize growth and remain the number one manufacturer of machine vision systems.

Company Background

Two brand new bicycles and $100,000 constituted the initial investment made by Robert Shillman to start Cognex Corporation. A professor in human visual perception at Massachusetts Institute of Technology (MIT)

Reprinted by permission of Marilyn T. Lucas and Alan N. Hoffman, Bentley College.

Acknowledgements: The authors would like to thank Joseph Breen, Nan MacSwan, Lawrence Isaac, Kerry Armstrong, Nancy Manley, and Kendra Schoentag for their valuable comments and suggestions.

near Boston, Shillman had a vision for the future of machine imaging analysis. In the summer of 1981, with the help of the bicycles, he convinced two graduate students, Marilyn Matz and Bill Silver, to work for him. This small group of artificial intelligence experts went on to form the Cognex Corporation and develop machine vision devices.

The machine vision technology works by capturing an image of a part through a video camera, converts it to digital data and, via software, analyzes the data and derives answers about the image, such as where an object is located and whether or not it is defective. This information can then be sent to other equipment—such as a robotic arm to remove the defective part—and/or fed to an automated feedback loop.

In the early days of the company, machine vision technology was limited to black and white image analysis. Although reliable, this technology was slow to process, and the systems used were extremely expensive to develop and implement. In 1982, harnessing the use of algorithms written by Silver, Cognex pioneered the industry's first optical character recognition system and built the company's first machine vision system, called DataMan. This system was not only able to quickly process grayscale image data to locate patterns and shapes, but also to reliably read numbers. Priced at approximately $30,000, this revolutionary product was sold directly to end-users on the factory floor, and its success attracted many investors, allowing Cognex to grow rapidly in the early 1980s. This machine vision market, however, became quickly flooded with competitors, all looking to find a place in this new profitable segment.

In the mid-eighties, Cognex modified its strategy and decided to target Original Equipment Manufacturers (OEMs), which had the technical expertise for systems integration. The company designed the first machine vision system built on a single printed circuit board, called the Cognex 2000, specifically to support OEMs. Two years later, Cognex also introduced the world's first custom vision chip, the VC-1, which quadrupled the processing power of the company's machine vision systems without increasing their size.

Exhibit 1   Cognex Corporation: Financial Highlights

	1998	1997	1996	1995	1994
For The Year:					
Revenue	$ 121,844	$ 155,340	$ 122,843	$ 104,543	$ 62,484
Net Income	20,203	40,536	30,369	23,034	16,072
Diluted Net Income Per Share	.47	.91	.69	.55	.43
At Year-End:					
Working Capital	184,363	199,570	152,817	119,402	88,619
Total Assets	247,928	261,840	201,253	162,172	112,946
Long-Term Debts	–	–	–	–	–
Stockholders' Equity	222,875	236,142	182,689	143,916	103,608

In 1989, the company had its initial public offering. Within one year, the price of the company's stock jumped from $2.75 per share to $33.50 per share. In the following five years, Cognex successfully introduced many products, including the Cognex 5000, the first machine vision system designed to plug into a personal computer, and in 1994, after $5 million in research and development, a revolutionary user-friendly machine vision system—the Checkpoint vision system.

Dr. Bob

Dr. Robert Shillman enjoyed life in academia—his research on the study of human visual perception was innovative and his unique style gave him a reputable presence among the community at MIT. However, he had the idea that artificial intelligence could replicate the accurate process of human vision to make computers that can "see." With such an innovative technology, he could introduce new manufacturing applications and open the doors to the machine vision industry. With a life savings of $100,000 and two top students, he left MIT to start Cognex in the summer of 1981.

In his management style, Robert Shillman has instilled the philosophical attitude that "work is the meaning of life." He is theatrical and believes in the "work hard, play hard" attitude. Cognex' employees, from the newest to the vice-presidents, all recognize that those who work hard will be rewarded. But "Dr. Bob," as he is referred to around the office, has also designated Halloween to be the official company holiday, requiring that all employees wear a costume to work on that day. His unique style has contributed to international recognition. Now President, Chief Executive Officer, and Chairman of Cognex, Shillman was named *Inc. Magazine's* Entrepreneur of the Year in 1990, and received the Achievement Award in Leadership from the Automated Imaging Association in 1992.

The "Cognoid" Spirit

Cognex, derived from Cognition Experts, has a corporate culture that is as unique as its highest-ranking officer. The "work hard, play hard" attitude fosters an environment of people dedicated to the cause of the Cognex mission: to remain the number one manufacturer of machine vision systems. Only the best and the brightest are recruited to work for the company. A recent advertisement in the *Boston Globe* extended an invitation to those who liked candy to apply to Cognex Corporation (a ritual at Cognex is to give out free Goobers candy to all employees on the company's monthly movie night). Once initiated into the employee roll book, employees are fondly referred to as "Cognoids."

A 110 percent effort is expected, but the company acknowledges the importance of its human capital. It proposes many highly innovative reward programs designed to recognize and thank its employees for their hard work and dedication. Payback includes fringe benefits like no other company. In every other paycheck, all employees receive a coupon for a free car wash. Friday evening socials are regular events, offering an array of food and beverages for employees to gather and relax with each other. Every other month, Cognex rents a local movie theater and invites each employee and a guest to enjoy a free movie and open concession stand. Once a year, Dr. Shillman gives out the President's award to all employees who surpass the company's high expectations and who demonstrate superior job performance, a positive attitude, and a commitment to excellence. The award consists of a plaque and a bonus check ranging from $1,000 to $10,000. Finally, Cognex commemorates

Exhibit 2   Cognex Corporation—Consolidated Balance Sheets

	December 31,	
	1998	1997
Assets	(In thousands, except per share amount)	
Current Assets:		
Cash and Investments	$ 158,458	$ 178,014
Accounts Receivable, Less Reserves of $2,583 and $1,940 in 1998 and 1997, Respectively	20,987	25,095
Revenues in Excess of Billings	4,945	3,723
Inventories	10,812	7,784
Deferred Income Taxes	3,936	3,453
Prepaid Expenses and Other	8,141	5,937
Total Current Assets	207,279	224,006
Property, Plant, and Equipment, Net	34,225	32,995
Deferred Income Taxes	2,237	1,377
Other Assets	4,157	3,462
	$ 247,928	$ 261,840
Liabilities & Stockholders' Equity		
Current Liabilities:		
Accounts Payable	$ 2,488	$ 3,332
Accrued Expenses	11,653	13,712
Accrued Income Taxes	916	2,684
Customer Deposits	4,894	3,112
Deferred Revenue	2,965	1,596
Total Current Liabilities	24,436	22,916
Other Liabilities	2,137	1,262
Commitments		
Stockholders' Equity:		
Common Stock, $ .002 Par Value—		
Authorized: 120,000,000 Shares, Issued: 42,453,980 and 41,859,395 Shares in 1998 and in 1997, Respectively	87	84
Additional Paid-in Capital	97,531	91,082
Treasury Stock, at Cost, 2,307,140 and 103,139 Shares in 1998 and 1997, Respectively	(41,353)	(1,436)
Retained Earnings	166,571	146,368
Accumulated Other Comprehensive Income	41	44
Total Stockholders' Equity	$ 222,875	$ 236,142
	$ 247,928	$ 261,840

employees' three-, five-, 10-, and 15-year anniversaries with Perseverance Awards. After three years of service, each employee receives a Seiko watch engraved with his or her start date. After five years of service, employees receive a gold Cognex pin and an all-expense paid weekend getaway to a choice of locations. On their 10-year anniversaries, employees receive an extravagant one-week vacation in addition to a beautiful Atmos clock.

And on the milestone of a 15-year anniversary, "Cognoids" receive a 10-day vacation to their choice of one of the Wonders of the World.

Cognex' Products

Cognex designs products, referred to as machine vision systems, to improve the speed and quality of inspection in

Exhibit 3   Cognex Corporation—Consolidated Statements of Income

	Year Ended December 31,		
	1998	1997	1996
	(In thousands, except per share amount)		
Revenue	$ 121,844	$ 155,340	$ 122,843
Cost of revenue	37,296	42,273	38,855
Gross margin	84,548	113,067	83,988
Research, development, and engineering expenses	24,662	22,481	19,434
Selling, general, and administrative expenses	37,973	35,810	26,261
Charges for acquiring technology	2,100	3,115	
Income from operations	19,813	51,661	38,293
Investment income	6,756	5,947	4,726
Other income	733	718	678
Income before provision for income taxes	27,302	58,326	43,697
Provision for income taxes	7,099	17,790	13,328
Net income	$ 20,203	$ 40,536	$ 30,369
Net income per common and common equivalent share:			
Basic	$ .49	$ .98	$ .75
Diluted	$ .47	$ .91	$ .69
Weighted-average common and common equivalent shares outstanding:			
Basic	40,978	41,322	40,594
Diluted	43,203	44,702	43,814

manufacturing processes. The complexity, higher volume and lower cost of consumer items have made it virtually impossible to use human operators to perform the task of detecting errors and irregularities in those items. Machine vision is basically an electronic and computer-based method of inspecting materials during production. Its use enables companies to reduce manufacturing costs, with a decrease in the number of defective products, efficiency gains, and increased productivity. Industrial applications of machine vision include tasks such as inspecting, measuring, verifying, identifying, recognizing, grading, sorting, counting, locating and manipulating parts, monitoring/controlling production processes, and more. In short, machine vision is a substitute for the human eye in a number of inspecting processes that occur during manufacturing applications with tight limits on speed, cost, reliability, size, or safety.

Machine vision systems consist of software and hardware components that are customized for specific manufacturing needs. Cognex' family of produces offers a choice of hardware platforms, development modes and price/performance points. Customers typically choose systems that are programmable in C or programmable with a "point and click" interface and specify deployment options on either set or integrated board level machines or on a stand-alone, rack mountable system. For example, the revolutionary Checkpoint series of vision systems, introduced in 1994, offers a "point and click" development environment with a flexible graphical user interface (GUI) based on Microsoft Windows. This system drastically simplifies the implementation of automated visual inspection since it does not require in-depth knowledge of vision technology nor programming expertise from the automation engineers to customize for their specific needs. With Checkpoint, a computer can inspect parts on an assembly line in as few as ten milliseconds, measure each one precisely, and this results in inspection speeds 10 to 100 times faster than with conventional methods.

New Product Introduction

To maintain its leadership position in the machine vision industry, Cognex' team of expert engineers has traditionally developed and introduced new products. The new products of the last few years have helped the company, not only to expand on existing markets, but also to venture in new application areas for machine vision.

In 1997, Cognex introduced a new product known as PatMax. This software technology represented an entirely new method of pattern finding, which fundamentally changed the way machine vision systems locate objects. This ability to locate, with very high accuracy, just about any object, has enormous potential applications in a variety of new areas. In 1998, Cognex introduced the next generation of programmable machine vision systems, the MVS-8000™ product family, based on DSTTEL-MMX. Prior to this year, all Cognex' softwares only ran on proprietary hardware, based on the Motorola 68K line of microprocessors. With this ability to run directly on the customer's own PC, the MVS-8000™ series became the most successful product introduction ever for Cognex with more than 1,000 systems shipped in its first year. Finally, an addition to the product line in 1998 was a new surface inspection vision system. The SmartView™ Modular Camera Network (MCN) was the world's first modular surface inspection vision system for detecting, measuring, and classifying defects on products made in continuous processes. It allows for more complex applications for machine vision.

The Machine Vision Industry

There are two basic segments in the machine vision market: Original Equipment Manufacturers (OEMs) and the factory floor customers.

The OEMs are companies that manufacture standard products sold as capital equipment for the factory floor. These customers possess the technical expertise necessary to build Cognex's machine vision systems directly into their products, which are then sold to end-users.

The factory floor customers can be further subdivided between system integrators and end-users. System integrators are companies that create complete, automated inspection solutions for end-users on the factory floor. For example, in designing a custom inspection system for, say, examining sneakers or aspirin bottles, they combine proper lighting, robotics, machine-vision devices, and other necessary components. Because of the wide variety of automation problems they encounter, system integrators typically purchase a wide variety of Cognex products, ranging from programmable systems to application-specific solutions tailored to solving particular manufacturing tasks.

End-users are companies that "build" products—such as phones, metal, pens, and paper—on the factory floor. This market includes all high-volume product manufacturers who are interested in increasing the quality of their products and lowering their manufacturing costs. End-users include the automotive industry (e.g., gauging dimensions on automotive brake pads), medical devices (e.g., inspecting heart catheters), banking and financing (e.g., performing detailed inspection on financial cards), keyboard and display (e.g., inspecting the LCD on a cellular phone), consumer products (e.g., color inspection of eyeliner pencils), computer printing (e.g., ink jet and laser printer inspection), and the packaging industry (e.g., inspecting caps and lids on cans). While they may purchase capital equipment containing machine vision or contract a system integrator to build an inspection system, many end-users choose to purchase machine vision directly to solve specific applications on their product lines. Unlike OEMs and system integrators, these customers typically have little or no computer programming or machine vision experience and are interested in a more user-friendly product.

Cognex' Early Days

In 1981, the company's initial strategy was to sell and install customized vision systems directly to end-users. However, within four years, it became clear to Cognex' management that the strategy of providing turnkey vision systems to end-users was not profitable. In this arena, over 100 competitors were vying for business, and all were being hampered by the cost of custom engineering each system to individual customer needs. As a result, Cognex turned to OEMs. Its new strategy was to develop and sell high volumes of standard machine vision hardware and software products to OEMs, who would have the technical expertise to configure Cognex' machine vision systems directly into their products, which would then be sold to end-users. This strategy allowed the company to focus its strength in research, development and engineering.

In the 1980s, Cognex' focus was on OEMs in the semiconductor and electronics industries. These were two industries strongly affected by miniaturization, and this made the use of machine vision technology essential. The semiconductor industry originally adopted this technology to perform wafer identification, alignment and dicing, while the electronics industry used it to align printed circuit boards for screen printers/paste dispensers, guide surface-mount device robots and inspect surface mount devices, disk drives and keyboards. Cognex was first to enter the semiconductor market with a product that contained the VC-1 chip and quadrupled the processing power of the existing machines. In late 1986, Cognex struck a deal with General Signal's Electroglas division, which made test equipment for silicon wafers. Cognex had attempted to acquire General Signal as a customer before this new direction, but the product was rejected as too costly. This time, General Signal was so interested that it bought a piece of Cognex to get access to the technology.

In 1990, Cognex had two-thirds of the market for vision systems bought from outside vendors by makers of semiconductor and electronic equipment. Some of Cognex' customers included IBM, NEC, and Hewlett-Packard, which helped sales grow 50 percent in 1989 to $16 million; profits jumped 56 percent to $3.7 million. Cognex also found success by selling to its competitors (OEMs who build their own machine vision systems), which represented about half of the approximately $200 million machine vision market of the late 1980s.

The Early and Mid-1990s

The North American consumption of machine vision systems over 1990–96 showed annual increases of 15 percent or better. The industry performance in 1996 saw a revenue gain of 16.3 percent, from $894 million in 1995 to $1040 million in 1996. Similarly, the number of units shipped grew 21.3 percent, from 16,372 in 1995 to a total of 19,868 units in 1996.

In 1995, 75 percent of Cognex' customer base represented the OEM market and the corporation claimed the leading market share at 38 percent. In fact, the company grew its OEM market by 60 percent with 50 new customers. The factory floor customer base represented 25 percent, with a second place finish in market share of 14 percent behind Rockwell International. Cognex, however, grew its factory floor market by 96 percent with the addition of 140 new customers. In 1995, both of these markets were growing at a rapid pace.

In the OEM market segment Cognex' closest competitors were ICOS and AISI who had a combined market share of 32 percent. The remaining market (30 percent) was comprised of in-house developers. On the factory floor side of the business, the market was more fragmented with the clear leader being Rockwell International, grabbing only 16 percent of the share. It appeared as though this market was growing at a more rapid pace than that of the OEM market. However, the revenue potential and gross margins (77 percent) were lucrative enough to make both market segments extremely attractive.

The 1998 Market

In 1998, the majority of Cognex' customers are still OEMs. Although Cognex lists metals, papers, and plastics as other materials for machine vision inspection markets,

the overwhelming application base still lies in semiconductor and electronics inspection. However, easy-to-use produces, such as the Checkpoint vision system, have enabled Cognex to further penetrate the end-user market, which shows great promise for machine vision. In fact, while analysts estimate the current OEM market to be worth $170 million and the end-user (or factory floor) market to be worth $150 million, many believe that the factory floor market potential is in excess of $1 billion, a figure which creates many exciting prospects for Cognex. Opportunities for machine vision applications have been identified in industries such as:

- Aerial/satellite image analysis
- Agriculture
- Document processing
- Forensic science, including fingerprint recognition
- Health Screening
- Medicine
- Military applications
- Publishing
- Research, particularly in physics, biology, astronomy, materials engineering, etc.
- Security and surveillance
- Traffic control

Cognex wants to capitalize on this large growth area by reducing its exposure to the cyclical semiconductor and electronic industries. In 1998, Cognex grew its end-user business by six percent to $3,112,000 due to increased volume from customers in general manufacturing industries; meanwhile, business in Europe has increased 14 percent over the previous year. Due to devoting additional sales and marketing resources to grow its end-user customer base, the company saw end-user revenue grow to 43 percent of its total revenue in 1998 from 32 percent of total revenue in 1997.

Troubled Times …

The company's revenues for 1998, however, decreased by 22 percent to nearly 122 million dollars from 155 million dollars. This decrease of revenue from the previous year is due primarily to decreased volume from the company's OEM customers. Sales to OEM customers, most of whom make capital equipment used by manufacturers in the semiconductor and electronics industries, decreased by 34 percent from the previous year. Geographically, revenues decreased nearly $14 million, or 23 percent in North America, and $20.5 million, or 30 percent in Japan from the previous year, as most of the company's large OEM customers are based in these regions, while they increased $3 million, or 14 percent, in Europe.

This worldwide slowdown in the production and use of chips, resulting in a slowdown in the purchase of capital equipment for both semiconductor and electronics products, began in early 1996. Naturally, when customers slowed down their rate of purchasing, they delayed orders for vision systems until they had better "visibility," and consequently Cognex' domestic and global sales revenue decreased and its growth slowed. From 1995–1996, domestic OEM sales revenues decreased 24 percent from $21 million to $17 million. Similarly, global sales revenue to Japanese OEM customers also decreased from nearly $14 million to $9 million during this period. Cognex was forced to write off $4.2 million of obsolete inventory as a result of overproduction and reduced its production plans for 1996. Lower sales order fulfillment rates in these industries reduced Cognex' profitability, and in the fall of 1996, the value of Cognex' stock plummeted. This was no surprise as 35 percent of its annual sales stem from these troubled semiconductor and electronics markets.

Cognex has since made a deliberate attempt to begin to diversify into other industries, through both acquisition and product innovation. In 1995, Cognex acquired Acumen Inc., a developer of wafer identification products, which allowed the company to penetrate the factory floor market with 143 new end-user customers. Later in 1996, Cognex acquired Isys Controls Inc. known for their surface inspection technology. On July 31, 1997, Cognex acquired Mayan Automation, Inc. (Mayan), a developer of low-cost machine vision systems used for surface inspection. Finally, in 1998, Cognex formed a business relationship with Rockwell Automation, a leading supplier of factory automation products (e.g., components and systems), which also sells machine vision and has an extensive global distribution network to many Fortune 100 companies. This *preferred supplier* relationship with Rockwell Automation allowed Cognex to be introduced to all Rockwell's customers worldwide, in industries such as automotive, consumer products, and pharmaceutical manufacturing, where Cognex had previously little name recognition or market penetration.

A Changing Market

The focus of the machine vision industry is changing from technology to applications. Machine vision systems provide the most value-added benefits to operations through application engineering. In addition, machine vision tends to be demand inelastic. Since the product is less differentiated than the full solution, price reductions will have little impact on demand. From 1985–1995 there has been a 75 percent decline in the cost of hardware and software associated with machine vision systems. Falling prices have caused pressure in all segments of the real time image processing systems industry. This industry is expected to surpass $5 billion dollars by the year 2002.

Moreover, current trends in the personal computer and machine vision industries do not complement each other. For example, the speeds of central processor units on standard computers advance monthly. On the other hand, production lead times on high performance vision processor boards are eighteen to twenty-four months. Since machine vision systems need to operate on diverse hardware platforms, their application software could be customized and updated for different hardware platforms.

Competition

The increased use and availability of information technology has also resulted in increased competition. For example, Nikon Inc. introduced the Veritas CNC to assist OEM and end-users in computer chip inspection. Electro Scientific Industries acquired Applied Intelligent Systems Inc. to further their expertise in developing process control and visual inspection systems for the assembly of semi-conductor chips. As competition increases to provide the highest quality machine vision system at the lowest price, existing operating margins of approximately 75 percent could be affected as industry players compete for market share.

Opportunities for Growth

Machine vision is not widely known outside of the semiconductor and electronic industries. The business climate in the U.S. and throughout the world is reaching a highly or hypercompetitive stage in which companies need to continually cut costs by streamlining processes to remain viable. The use of machine vision in the production process accomplishes this. It is Cognex' challenge to communicate these advantages and benefits to other industries in pursuit of diversification.

Cognex sales are predominately generated from two economies: the U.S. at 41 percent and Japan at 46 percent. Its penetration into the European market is virtually untapped at 11 percent. Since its core business has always been in the OEM segment of the semiconductor industry, it is understandable as to why the geographic distribution would appear as such. However, there are limitless opportunities for machine vision technology throughout manufacturing processes across geographic and industry boundaries, as noted by the President: "Our goal is to exploit every available opportunity for our machine vision technology." The opportunities become limitless with global implications. Cognex has taken the first steps into the pharmaceutical (11 percent of total revenue) and automotive industries (nine percent of total revenue). They have also established satellite offices in Singapore and Korea to break into the manufacturing bases there as the Pacific Rim, because of its low labor rates and favorable incentives, offers many opportunities

A solid reputation, strong sales force, commitment to customer service, and research and development are the factors that contributed to the number one position Cognex captured and maintained in the OEM market. Cognex was the first to introduce efficient machine vision processing into the production of semiconductor components, and entered the market with a viable product, in which it continually tweaked to meet the ever-changing needs of its customer base. Its highly trained technical sales force, comprised of top quality and experienced engineers, focused, not only on understanding the needs and requirements of its customers in such a highly technical market (OEM), but also on developing and nurturing potential and existing relationships. The purchase of OEM equipment is an expensive undertaking in which the face of the manufacturing process is forever altered. As a result, the relationships that are established are longer in duration and require a solid foundation.

In being the first to introduce efficient machine vision processing into the production of semiconductor components, Cognex quickly established a solid name with a reliable reputation, which fostered its leading position. However, this has not been the case in the factory floor market segment, for it is a fragmented market. Cognex still intends to increase its sales to these customers 50 percent. Without a reputation, or leading position to drive this objective, Cognex needs to develop a solid strategy for clearly identifying itself as the optimum solution. The factory floor applications provide a challenge to create differentiated products that are specific enough to end-users' needs in diverse manufacturing processes, but yet still standardized enough to make it profitable to produce. This requires depth and flexibility in the design and application process.

Customer Service and Research & Development

Building a solid relationship with the potential customer prior to signing any agreement is quite extensive by the engineers at Cognex. This commitment to the relationship is maintained throughout the life of the contract, as set forth by the culture within the company. This emphasis on customer service contributes to the loyalty of Cognex' customer base. Cognex' company directives

state that all customer inquiries be responded to within a 24-hour time frame by a group of technicians who are on call at all times. Additionally, educational services are offered by Cognex to its customers to train their workforce. For its global customers, regional sales and distribution facilities exist to respond more quickly to these customers' needs, with all written or verbal support presented in the native language.

A direct output of the tight relationship between the Cognex engineers and their customers is the feedback provided by customers on product quality and enhancements. Since the sales force is mainly comprised of engineers, the discussions with customers can be quite technical in nature. This information is then tunneled to the research and development staff at Cognex. The company regards research and development as a top priority. This is one of the ways in which Cognex has developed and maintained its leadership position in the machine vision industry. For nearly two decades, it has invested tens of millions of dollars in R&D expense to invent and improve its products.

In order to focus all of its financial and labor resources on R&D, Cognex chose to outsource its manufacturing operation by January of 1997. The in-house manufacturing operations created a strain on its management and financial resources due to the large monetary outlays for capital equipment and the day-to-day operations. This forced the company to re-evaluate its business in terms of manufacturing, and it chose to outsource in order to lower costs, increase profitability, and focus on its core business—Cognex is unique among its competitors in terms of this decision. This was done in attempt to give strength to the R&D department in terms of developing produces to compete effectively in the factory floor marketplace that is more relevant to diversified industries like aerospace, automotive, and pharmaceuticals.

Cognex' commitment to new product development and to the creation and nurturing of potential or existing relationships is evident in the composition of its workforce. Thirty-nine percent of the total staff is dedicated to sales and marketing efforts, while 34 percent is focused on R&D. Cognex protects its investment in R&D with the use of patents, copyrights and trade agreements. Full disclosure agreements are signed by all Cognex employees, suppliers, consultants, and customers. In situations when computer codes need to be disclosed to the customer, legal confidentiality agreements are instituted.

Cognex' "Vision" of the Future …

Having survived the 1996–1997 crash of the semiconductor industry, Cognex needs to insulate itself against this kind of industry-wide volatility in the future. There are several corporate strategies to choose from. They range from expanding globally to diversifying its target markets.

One strategic alternative for Cognex would be to diversify away from OEMs and compete more aggressively in the factory floor marketplace. Although Cognex benefited greatly from its first-mover advantage, a dysfunctional consequence was that it never fully developed an effective marketing campaign. This will leave Cognex vulnerable as its first-mover advantage erodes.

Because the general manufacturing factory floor market is so competitive, Cognex will need to strengthen its marketing capabilities. More widely recognized names such as Allen-Bradley have already established themselves in this market. A significantly larger investment in training is required for factory floor workers than is needed for OEMs, as the OEM customers have a more technical background. However, Cognex' new graphical user interface reduces the need for training and offers a better match for the factory floor worker. With this product innovation Cognex has inadvertently positioned itself for a whole new market. Factory floor customers, who already have hardware platforms, and yet are in the market for an upgrade on software, represent a large target market.

Finally, Cognex never had to be concerned with decoupling its hardware and software solutions, and therefore only offers bundled packages to its customers. It should be noted that Cognex' competitors, however, are successful with selling hardware and software solutions separately. And that flexibility and compatibility are crucial to meet the diverse needs of the customer base.

Another strategic alternative would be to expand into Europe to minimize the company's dependence on Japan. Unlimited opportunities exist for Cognex' core products globally because of the rapid expansion of manufacturing outside the U.S. due to lower labor rates and lucrative incentives. Although Cognex has established itself as a leader in the industry through its strength in engineering, it lacks strong marketing to complement its expertise in technology. Outside the semiconductor industry, the use of machine vision to enhance production processes is still in its infancy. Yet, manufacturing inspection processes involving high speed and small parts are hardly unique to the semiconductor industry. There exist many industries with a variety of applications that Cognex can explore as potential opportunities to expand its business. But, if a strategy to expand geographically is pursued, reverse engineering becomes an even stronger threat, since intellectual property laws are weak abroad.

The Pacific Rim represents yet another untapped growth expansion opportunity. Cognex maintains a strong presence in Japan, and its name recognition should help it penetrate the Pacific Rim. In pursuing rapid geographical expansion, two viable strategic vehicles are acquisitions and strategic alliances. If Cognex could find a complementary business to align itself with, this alliance could enable a transfer of technology, which may lead to diversification. But, as in any alliance, the company would risk sharing its technical know-how with this transfer of technology.

Finally, the high profit margins in the machine vision industry continue to attract new competitors, and Cognex must prepare itself for this heightened level of competition. To stay on top Cognex needs to make some serious strategic decisions.

Works Consulted

"An Adventurers Guide to Machine Vision," Cognex Corporation, Annual Report 1998.

"Activity Book," Cognex Corporation, Annual Report 1997.

Barrow, Tom, "Eye on Machine Vision: New Technologies, Old Markets Fuel Vision Field's Growth," *Robotics World* (Summer 1998): 30.

"Machine-Vision Industry Eyes Future Growth," *Machine Design* (20 August 1999) 80.

"North American Machine Vision Market Tops $1.5 Billion; Worldwide Market Hits $4.6 Billion," *Robotics World* (May/June 1999): 12.

Stevens, Tim, "Shill the Showman: CEO Dr. Robert Shillman's Unique Management Style and Dogged Drive for Perfection Have Powered Cognex Corporation to Explosive Growth," *Industry Week* 243, no. 20 (7 November 1994): 26.

Teresko, John, "New Eyes in Manufacturing," *Industrial World* (19 April 1999): 47.

Case 11

The Comeback of Caterpillar, 1885–2001

Isaac Cohen, *San Jose State University*

For three consecutive years, 1982, 1983, and 1984, the Caterpillar Company lost one million dollars a day. Caterpillar's major competitor was a formidable Japanese company called Komatsu. Facing a tough global challenge, the collapse of its international markets, and an overvalued dollar, Caterpillar had no choice. It had to reinvent itself, or die.

Caterpillar managed to come back as a high-tech, globally competitive, growth company. Over a period of 15 years, and throughout the tenure of two CEOs— George Schaefer (1985–1990) and Donald Fites (1990–1999)—Caterpillar had transformed itself. George Schaefer introduced cost-cutting measures and employee involvement programs, outsourced machines, parts, and components, and began modernizing Caterpillar's plants. Donald Fites diversified Caterpillar's product line and reorganized the company structurally. He also completed Caterpillar's plant modernization program, revitalized Caterpillar's dealership network, and altered radically Caterpillar's approach to labor relations.

As Donald Fites retired in February 1999, Glen Barton was elected CEO. Barton was in an enviable position. The world's largest manufacturer of construction and mining equipment, and a *Fortune* 100 company, Caterpillar generated 21 billion dollars in revenues in 1998, the sixth consecutive record year. Leading its industry while competing globally, Caterpillar recorded a $1.5 billion profit in 1998, the second best ever.[1]

Notwithstanding Caterpillar's dramatic comeback, Barton could not count on the continual prosperity of the company because the U.S. construction industry was moving into a grinding economic downturn. At the time Barton completed his first year as CEO, on February 1, 2000, the company announced its 1999

result: sales declined by 6 percent and earnings by 37 percent. In March 2000, Caterpillar share price was trading close to its 52-week low ($36 against a high of $66) and one industry analyst declared: "The stock for the foreseeable future is dead money."[2]

What should Barton do? Should Barton follow the strategies implemented by Schaefer and Fites to enhance Caterpillar's competitive position relative to its principal rivals, Komatsu, John Deere, and CNH Global (CNH was the product of a 2000 merger between the Case Corp. and New Holland)? Should he, instead, reverse some of the policies introduced by his predecessors? Or should he, rather, undertake whole new strategies altogether?

To assess Barton's strategic choices in improving Caterpillar's results, the case looks back at the experience of his two predecessors. How precisely did both Schaefer and Fites manage to turn Caterpillar around?

The Heavy Construction Equipment Industry

The heavy construction equipment industry supplied engineering firms, construction companies, and mine operators. The industry's typical product line included earthmovers (bulldozers, loaders, and excavators), road building machines (pavers, motor graders, and mixers), mining related equipment (off-highway trucks, mining shovels), and large cranes. Most machines were offered in a broad range of sizes, and a few were available with a choice of wheels or crawler tracks. Most were used for the construction of buildings, power plants, manufacturing plants, and infrastructure projects such as roads, airports, bridges, tunnels, dams, sewage systems, and water lines. On a global basis, earthmoving equipment accounted for about half of the industry's total sales in the 1990s (Exhibit 1). Among earthmovers, hydraulic excavators accounted for 45 percent of the sales. Excavators were more productive, more versatile, and easier to use in tight spaces than either bulldozers or loaders. Off-highway trucks that hauled minerals, rocks, and dirt, were another category of fast selling equipment.[3]

Global demand for heavy construction machinery grew at a steady rate of 4.5 percent in the 1990s. The rate of growth, however, was faster among the developing nations of Asia, Africa, and Latin America than among the developed nations. In the early 2000s, North America and Europe were each expected to account for 25 percent of the industry's sales, Japan for 20 percent, and the developing nations for the remaining 30 percent.[4]

The distinction between original equipment and replacement parts was an essential feature of the industry. Replacement parts and "attachments" (work tools) made up together over a quarter of the total revenues of the heavy construction equipment industry (Exhibit 1), but accounted for a substantially larger share of the industry's earnings for two reasons: first, the sale of replacement parts was more profitable than that of whole machines; and second, the market for replacement parts was less cyclical than that for original equipment.[5] As a rule of thumb, the economic life of a heavy construction machine was 10 to 12 years, but in many cases, especially in developing countries, equipment users kept their machines in service much longer, perhaps 20 to 30 years, thus creating an ongoing stream of revenues for parts, components, and related services.[6]

Another characteristic of the industry was the need to achieve economies of scale. According to industry observers, the optimal scale of operation was about 90,000 units annually, in other words, up to a production level of 90,000 units a year, average equipment unit cost declined as output increased, and therefore capturing a large market share was critical for benefiting from economies of scale.[7] The relatively low volume of global sales—200,000 to 300,000 earthmoving equipment units per year (1996)[8]—further intensified competition over market share among the industry's leading firms.

Successful marketing also played an important role in gaining competitive advantage. A widespread distribution and service network had always been essential for competing in the heavy construction equipment industry because "downtime" resulting from the inability to operate the equipment at a construction site was very costly. Typically, manufacturers used a worldwide network of dealerships to sell machines, provide support, and offer after sales service. Dealerships were independent, company owned, or both, and were normally organized on an exclusive territorial basis. Since heavy construction machines operated in a tough and inhospitable environment, equipment wore out and broke down frequently, parts needed to be rebuilt or replaced often, and therefore manufacturers placed dealers in close proximity to equipment users, building a global service network that spread all over the world.

Manufacturers built alliances as well. Intense competition over market share drove the industry's top firms to form three types of cooperative agreements. The first were full-scale joint ventures to share production. Caterpillar's joint venture with Mitsubishi Heavy Industries was a notable case in point. The second were technology-sharing agreements between equipment manufacturers and engine makers to ensure access to the latest engine technology. The joint venture between Komatsu and Cummins Engine, on the one hand, and the Case Corporation and Cummins, on the other, provided two examples. The third type of agreements were technology sharing alliances between major global firms and local manufacturers whereby the former gained access to new markets, and in return, supplied the latter with advanced technology. Caterpillar utilized such an arrangement with Shanghai Diesel in China, and Komatsu did so with the BEML company in India.[9]

History of Caterpillar

At the turn of the century, farmers in California faced a serious problem. Using steam tractors to plow the fine delta

Exhibit 1	Global Demand of Heavy Construction Equipment by Major Categories, 1985–2005			
Item	1985	1994	2000	2005*
Earthmoving Equipment	50%	49%	49%	49%
Off Highway Trucks	8%	7%	7%	7%
Construction Cranes	9%	11%	10%	10%
Mixers, Pavers, and Related Equipment	6%	6%	7%	7%
Parts & Attachments	27%	27%	27%	26%
Total Demand (billions)	**$38**	**$56**	**$72**	**$90**

* Percentages do not add up to 100 because of rounding.

Source: Andrew Gross and David Weiss, "Industry Corner: The Global Demand for Heavy Construction Equipment," *Business Economics*, July 1996, p. 56.

land of the San Joaquin valley, California farmers fitted their tractors with large drive wheels to provide support on the moist soil; nevertheless, despite their efforts, the steamer's huge wheels—measuring up to 9 feet high—sank deeply into the soil. In 1904, Benjamin Holt, a combine maker from Stockton, California, solved the problem by replacing the wheels with a track, thereby distributing the tractor's weight on a broader surface. Holt, in addition, replaced the heavy steam engine with a gasoline engine, thus improving the tractor's mobility further by reducing its weight (a steam tractor weighed up to 20 tons). He nick-named the tractor "Caterpillar," acquired the "Caterpillar" trademark, and applied it to several crawler-type machines that his company manufactured and sold. By 1915 Holt tractors were sold in 20 countries.[10]

Outside agriculture, crawler tractors were first used by the military. In 1915, the British military invented the armor tank, modeling it after Holt's machine, and during World War I, the United States and its allies in Europe utilized Holt's track-type tractors to haul artillery and supply wagons. In 1925, the Holt Company merged with another California firm, the Best Tractor Company, to form Caterpillar (Cat). Shortly thereafter, Caterpillar moved its corporate headquarters and manufacturing plants to Peoria, Illinois. The first company to introduce a diesel engine on a moving vehicle (1931), Caterpillar discontinued its combine manufacturing during the 1930s and focused instead on the production of road-building, construction, logging, and pipe-laying equipment. During World War II, Caterpillar served as the primary supplier of bulldozers to the U.S. Army; its sales volume more than tripled between 1941 and 1944 to include motor graders, diesel engines, and electric generators, apart from tractors and wagons.[11]

Demand for Caterpillar products exploded in the early post-war years. Cat's equipment was used to reconstruct Europe, build the U.S. interstate highway system, erect the giant dams of the Third World, and lay out the major airports of the world. The company managed to differentiate itself from its competitors by producing reliable, durable and high quality equipment, offering a quick after-sales service, and providing a speedy delivery of replacement parts. As a result, during the 1950s and 1960s, Caterpillar had emerged as the uncontested leader of the heavy construction equipment industry, far ahead of any rival. By 1965, Caterpillar had established foreign manufacturing subsidiaries—either wholly owned or joint ventures—in Britain, Canada, Australia, Brazil, France, Mexico, Belgium, India, and Japan. Caterpillar's 50/50 joint venture with Mitsubishi in Japan, established in 1963, had become one of the most successful, stable, and enduring alliances among all American-Japanese joint ventures.[12]

Caterpillar's distribution and dealership network also contributed to the company's worldwide success. From the outset, the company's marketing organization rested on a dense network of independent dealers who sold and serviced Cat equipment. Strategically located throughout the world, these dealers were self-sustaining entrepreneurs who invested their own capital in their business, derived close to 100 percent of their revenues from selling and supporting Cat equipment, and cultivated close relationships with Caterpillar customers. On average, a Caterpillar dealership had remained in the hands of the same family—or company—for over 50 years. Indeed, some dealerships, including several located overseas, predated the 1925 merger that gave birth to Caterpillar.[13] In 1981, on the eve of the impending crisis, the combined net worth of Cat dealers equaled that of the company itself, the total number of employees working for Cat dealers was slightly lower than the company's own workforce.[14]

The Crisis of the Early 1980s

Facing weak competition both at home and abroad, Caterpillar charged premium prices for its high-quality products, paid its production workers union-scale wages, offered its shareholders high rates of return on their equity, and enjoyed superior profits. Then, in 1982, following a record year of sales and profits, Caterpillar suddenly plunged into three successive years of rising losses totaling nearly $1 billion. "Quite frankly, our long years of success made us complacent, even arrogant,"[15] Pierre Guerindon, an executive vice president at Cat conceded.

The crisis of 1982–84 stemmed from three sources: a global recession, a costly strike, and unfavorable currency exchange rates. First, the steady growth in demand for construction machinery, dating back to 1945, came to an end in 1980, as highway construction in the U.S. slowed down to a halt while declining oil prices depressed the worldwide market for mining, logging, and pipe-laying equipment. Second, Caterpillar's efforts to freeze wages and reduce overall labor cost triggered a seven-month strike (1982–83) among its U.S. employees. Led by the United Auto Workers (UAW) union, the strike accounted for a sizable portion of the company's three year loss. The third element in Caterpillar's crisis was a steep rise in the value of the dollar (relative to the Yen and other currencies) that made U.S. exports more expensive abroad, and U.S. imports (shipped by Caterpillar's competitors) cheaper at home. "The strong dollar is a prime factor in Caterpillar's reduced sales and earning … [and] is undermining manufacturing industries in the United States,"[16] said Cat's annual reports for 1982 and 1984.

Taking advantage of the expensive dollar, Komatsu Limited had emerged as Caterpillar's principal rival. Komatsu ("little pine tree" in Japanese) had initially produced construction machinery for the Japanese and Asian markets, then sought to challenge Caterpillar's dominance in the markets of Latin America and Europe, and eventually penetrated the United States to rival Caterpillar in its domestic market. Attacking Caterpillar head-on, Komatsu issued a battle cry, "Maru C," meaning "encircle Cat." Launching a massive drive to improve quality while reducing costs, Komatsu achieved a 50 percent labor productivity advantage over Caterpillar, and in turn, underpriced Caterpillar's products by as much as 30 percent. The outcome was a dramatic change in market share. Between 1979 and 1984 Komatsu global market share more than doubled to 25 percent while Caterpillar's fell by almost a quarter to 43 percent.[17]

Turnaround: George Schaefer's Caterpillar, 1985–1990

Competition with Komatsu and the crisis of 1982–84 forced Caterpillar to reexamine its past activities. Caterpillar's new CEO (1985), George Schaefer, was a congenial manager who encouraged Cat executives to openly admit the company's past mistakes. "We have experienced a fundamental change in our business—it will never again be what it was," Schaefer said as he became CEO. "We have no choice but to respond, and respond vigorously, to the new world in which we find ourselves."[18] Under Schaefer's direction, Caterpillar devised and implemented a series of strategies that touched upon every important function of the company, including purchasing, manufacturing, marketing, personnel, and labor relations.

Global Outsourcing

Traditionally, Caterpillar functioned as a vertically integrated company that relied heavily on in-house production. To ensure product quality as well as an uninterrupted supply of parts, Cat self-produced two-thirds of its parts and components, and assembled practically all of its finished machines. Under the new policy of "shopping around the world," Caterpillar sought to purchase parts and components from low-cost suppliers who maintained high quality standards. Working closely with its suppliers, Caterpillar moved towards the goal of outsourcing 80 percent of its parts and components.[19]

An additional goal of the policy was branding, that is, the purchase of final products for resale. Through its branding program, Caterpillar sold outsourced machines under its own brand name, taking advantage of its superior marketing organization, and keeping production costs down. Beginning in the mid-1980s, Cat contracted to buy lift trucks from a Norwegian company, hydraulic excavators from a West German manufacturer, paving machines from an Oklahoma corporation, off-highway trucks from a British firm, and logging equipment from a Canadian company, and resell them all under the Cat nameplate. Ordinarily, Caterpillar outsourced product manufacturing but not product design. By keeping control over the design of many of its outsourced products, Caterpillar managed to retain in-house design capability, and ensure quality control.[20]

Broader Product Line

For nearly a decade, the DC10 bulldozer had served as Caterpillar's signature item. It stood 15 feet tall, weighed 73 tons, and sold for more than $500,000 (1988). It had no competitors. But as demand for highway construction projects dwindled, Caterpillar needed to reevaluate its product mix because heavy equipment was no longer selling well. Sales of light construction equipment, on the other hand, were fast increasing. Between 1984 and 1987, accordingly, Caterpillar doubled its product line from 150 to 300 models of equipment, introducing many small machines that ranged from farm tractors to backhoe loaders (multi-purpose light bulldozers), and diversified its customer base. Rather than focusing solely on large clients, i.e. multinational engineering and construction firms like the Bechtel corporation—a typical user of heavy bulldozers—Cat began marketing its light-weight machines to a new category of customers: small-scale owner operators and emerging contractors. Still, the shift in Cat's product mix had a clear impact on the company's bottom line. Unlike the heavy equipment market where profit margins were wide, intense competition in the market for light products kept margins slim and pitted Caterpillar against John Deere and the Case corporation, the light equipment market leaders.[21]

Labor Relations

To compete successfully, Caterpillar also needed to repair its relationship with the union. In 1979, following the expiration of its collective bargaining agreement, Caterpillar experienced an 80-day strike, and three years later, in 1982, contract negotiations erupted in a 205-day strike, the longest company-wide work stoppage in UAW history.[22] Named CEO in 1985, George Schaefer led the next two rounds of contract negotiations.

Schaefer's leadership style was consensual. By contrast to the autocratic style of his predecessors, Schaefer advocated the free flow of ideas between officers, managers, and production workers, and promoted open communication at all levels of the company. A low-key CEO who often answered his own phone, Schaefer possessed exceptional people skills. Asked to evaluate Schaefer's performance, John Stark, editor of *Off Highway Ledger*, a trade journal, said: "Schaefer is probably the best manager the construction machinery industry has ever had."[23]

Schaefer's social skills led to a significant improvement in Cat's relations with the UAW. Not a single strike broke out over contract negotiations during Schaefer's tenure; on the contrary, each cycle of bargaining was settled peacefully. Under Schaefer's direction, furthermore, the union agreed to reduce the number of labor grades and job classifications, and to streamline seniority provisions; a move that enhanced management flexibility in job assignment, and facilitated the cross utilization of employees.[24] More important, improved labor relations contributed to the success of two programs that played a critical role in Caterpillar's turnaround strategy, namely, an employee involvement plan based on team work, and a reengineering effort of plant modernization and automation.

Employee Involvement

An industry-wide union famous for its cooperative labor-management efforts at the Saturn corporation, the NUMMI plant (a GM-Toyota joint-venture in Fremont California), and elsewhere, the UAW lent its support to Caterpillar's employee involvement program. Called the Employee Satisfaction Process (ESP), and launched by Schaefer in 1986, the program was voluntary. ESP members were organized in work teams, met weekly with management, and offered suggestions that pertained to many critical aspects of the manufacturing process, including production management, workplace layout, and quality enhancement. Implemented in a growing number of U.S. plants, the program resulted (1990) in productivity gains, quality improvements, and increased employee satisfaction. At the Cat plant in Aurora, Illinois, for example, the local ESP chairman recalled: the ESP program "changed everything: the worker had some say over his job. … [and t]op management was very receptive. We zeroed in on quality, anything to make the customer happy." Management credited the ESP teams at Aurora with a steep fall in the rate of absenteeism, a sharp decline in the number of union grievances filed, and cost savings totaling $10 million.[25] At another ESP plant, a Cat assembly-line worker told a *Fortune* reporter in 1988: "Five years ago the foreman wouldn't even listen to you, never mind the general foreman or plant supervisor. … Now everyone will listen." Caterpillar applied the ESP program to outside suppliers as well. Typically, ESP teams made up of Caterpillar machinists visited suppliers' plants to check and certify equipment quality. The certified vendors received preferential treatment, mostly in the form of reduced inspection, counting, and other controls. Only 0.6 percent of the parts delivered by certified suppliers were rejected by Caterpillar compared to a reject rate of 2.8 percent for non-certified suppliers.[26]

Plant with a Future

Caterpillar's employee involvement plan went hand in hand with a $1.8 billion plant modernization program launched by Schaefer in 1986.[27] Dubbed "Plant with a Future" (PWAF), the modernization program combined just-in-time inventory techniques, a factory automation scheme, a network of computerized machine tools, and a flexible manufacturing system. Several of these innovations were pioneered by Komatsu late in the 1970s. The industry's technological leader, Komatsu had been the first construction equipment manufacturer to introduce both the just-in-time inventory system, and the "quick changeover tooling," technique, a flexible tooling method designed to produce a large variety of equipment models in a single plant.[28]

To challenge Komatsu, top executives at Caterpillar did not seek to merely imitate the Japanese. This was not enough. They studied, instead, the modernization efforts of several manufacturing companies, and arrived at two important conclusions: it was necessary 1) to change the layout of an entire plant, not just selected departments within a plant; and 2) to implement the program company-wide, that is, on a global basis both at home and abroad. Implementing such a comprehensive program took longer than expected, however, lasting seven years: four under Schaefer's direction, and three more under the direction of his successor, Donald Fites.[29]

The traditional manufacturing process at Caterpillar, known as "batch" production, was common among U.S. assembly plants in a number of industries. Under batch production, subassembly lines produced components (radiators, hydraulic tanks, etc.) in small lots. Final assembly lines put together complete models, and the entire production system required large inventories of parts and components owing to the high level of "work in process" (models being built at any one time). Under batch production, furthermore, assembly tasks were highly specialized, work was monotonous and dull, and workers grew lax and made mistakes. Correcting assembly mistakes, it should be noted, took more time than the assembly process itself because workers needed to disassemble components in order to access problem areas. Parts delivery was also problematic. Occasionally, delays in delivery of parts to the assembly areas forced workers to leave the line in order to locate a missing part. Occasionally, the early arrival of parts before they were needed created its own inefficiencies.[30]

To solve these problems, Caterpillar reconfigured the layout of its manufacturing plants into flexible work "cells." Grouped in cells, workers used computerized machine tools to perform several manufacturing steps in sequence, processing components from start to finish and sending them "just-in-time" to an assembly area, as the following example suggests. To manufacture steel tractor-tread under the batch production layout, Cat workers were required to cut, drill, and heat-treat steel beams on three distinct assembly lines. Under cellular manufacturing, by contrast, all three operations were carried out automatically in single tractor-tread cells linked together by computers.[31]

Caterpillar, in addition, reduced material handling by means of an automated electrified monorail, which delivered parts to storage and assembly areas, traveling on a long aluminum track throughout the modernized plant. When parts arrived at the delivery point, a flashing light alerted the assembly line workers, semi-automatic gates (operated by infrared remote control) opened, and a lift lowered the components directly onto an assembly. Don Western, a manufacturing manager at Cat Aurora plant, observed: "Materials now [1990] arrive at the assembly point only when required—and in the order required. At most, we hold about a 4 hour supply of large parts and components on the line."[32]

Caterpillar, finally, improved product quality. Formerly, components moved down the assembly line continuously, not intermittently, and therefore workers were unable to respond quickly to quality problems. Managers alone controlled the speed of the line. Under the new assembly plan, on the other hand, components moved automatically between work areas and remained stationary during the actual assembly operation. More important, under the PWAF plan, managers empowered production workers to change the speed of the assembly line at will, granting them the flexibility necessary to resolve quality and safety problems.[33]

The PWAF program resulted in productivity and quality gains across the board in many of Caterpillar plants. At the Aurora plant in Illinois, for instance, factory workers managed to reduce the assembly process time fourfold, building and shipping a customer order in four rather than 16 days, and cutting product defects by one-half in four years (1986–1990).[34] At the Cat plant in Grenoble, France, to mention another case, workers slashed the time it took to assemble machinery parts from 20 to 8 days in three years (1986–1989). Company-wide changes were equally impressive: collectively, Caterpillar's 30 worldwide plants cut inventory levels by 50 percent and manufacturing space by 21 percent in three years.[35]

Looking back at Schaefer's five year long tenure, Caterpillar had reemerged as a globally competitive company, lean, flexible, and technologically advanced. Caterpillar's world market share rebounded from 43 percent to 50 percent (1984–1990),[36] revenues increased by 66 percent (1985–1989), and the company was profitable once again. As Caterpillar prospered, Komatsu was retrenching. In 1989, Caterpillar's sales totaled over $11 billion or nearly twice the sales reported by Komatsu, Caterpillar's profit margins exceeded Komatsu's, and the gap between the two companies—in terms of both market share and income on sales—was growing (Exhibit 2). Notwithstanding Schaefer's achievements, the transformation of Caterpillar was far from over. For one thing, the company stock lagged far behind its earnings; Cat shares underperformed the S&P 500 index by over 50 percent for five years (1987–1992).[37] For another, Caterpillar was facing an industry-wide downturn in both its domestic and international markets. Partly as a result of the cyclical nature of the construction equipment industry, and also as a result of an increase in the value of the dollar (a weak dollar in the late 1980s helped Caterpillar's foreign sales), Caterpillar revenues and profits fell. During the two years following Schaefer's retirement, the company actually lost money (Exhibit 6).

Replacing Schaefer in the winter of 1990, Donald Fites viewed Caterpillar's financial troubles as an opportunity to introduce change: "I certainly didn't count on … [a] recession … but [the recession] made it easier to accept the fact that we needed to change."[38] "It's hard to change an organization when you're making record profits."[39]

Leadership

Fites leadership style stood in a stark contrast to Schaefer's. "George was … a consensus builder" while "[Don] expects people to challenge him forcefully,"[40] one Cat executive said, and another (former Cat CEO Lee Morgan) described Fites as "one of the most determined men I've ever met."[41] Fites was a hard line executive, feared by his subordinates, respected by his peers, and cheered by Wall Street. An imposing man standing six-feet-five, Fites led by explicit command rather than persuasion, asserted the company's "right to manage" in face of mounting union opposition, and did not hesitate to cut thousands of management and production jobs at a stroke.

The son of a subsistence corn farmer, Fites had joined Caterpillar in 1956, rising through the ranks, and spending 16 years overseas. A career marketeer, he worked for Cat in South Africa, Germany, Switzerland, Brazil, Japan, and other countries. In 1971, Fites had earned an MBA from MIT, writing a thesis entitled "Japan Inc.: Can U.S. Industry Compete?" and soon thereafter, he received an assignment in Japan, serving nearly five years as the marketing director of Caterpillar-Mitsubishi joint venture. Fites' Japanese experience resonated throughout the remainder of his career. He was impressed, first of all, by the ways in which the Japanese trained their managers, rotating executives through functional departments in order to educate them in all aspects of the business. Returning from Japan to Peoria in the mid 1970s, Fites revamped Cat's product development process, utilizing an integrated approach based on Japanese-style functional teams. He also admired Japanese labor relations. Historically, American unions had been organized on an industry-wide basis and therefore labor relations in the United States were often adversarial. Trade unions in Japan, by contrast, were company-based organizations, loyal, cooperative, and in Fites' words, "deeply dedicated to the success of the [firm]."[42] Leading Caterpillar in the 1990s, Fites sought to bring Caterpillar's labor relations closer to the Japanese model.

Reorganization

A marketing manager, Fites was convinced that Caterpillar did not pay sufficient attention to customer needs because global pricing decisions were made at the company's headquarters in Peoria with little knowledge of the local market conditions around the world. In 1985, as he took charge of Cat's worldwide marketing organization, Fites delegated district offices the authority to set prices, thereby pushing responsibility down the chain of command to the lowest possible level. Promoted to President in 1989, Fites applied the same principle to Caterpillar's entire structure, developing a company-wide reorganization plan under Schaefer's direction.[43]

Caterpillar's old organizational structure was archaic. It was a functional structure suitable for a small company that operated just a few plants, all located within the United States. A centralized body with only four primary functions—engineering, manufacturing, marketing, and finance—the old structure served Caterpillar well until World War II, but as the company expanded globally in subsequent decades, the limitations of such a structure had become apparent. First, decisions were made at the top of each functional unit, and executives were reluctant to delegate authority to mid-level or low-level managers. Second, each functional unit tended to focus on its own goal rather than the enterprise's objectives (marketing was preoccupied with market share, engineering with product safety, manufacturing with assembly problems, etc.), making it difficult for top management to coordinate functional goals.[44] And third, the bureaucratization of the decision making process impaired effective communication. Under the old structure, Fites recalled, the flow of information upwards was "so filtered with various prejudices—particularly functional prejudice[s]—that you didn't know whether you were really looking at the facts or looking at someone's opinion."[45]

To equip Caterpillar with the flexibility, speed, and agility necessary to operate in the global economy, Fites broke the company into 17 semi-autonomous divisions or "profit centers," 13 responsible for products (tractors, engines, etc.), and four for services.[46] He then required each division to post a 15 percent rate of return on assets, and threatened to penalize any division that fell behind. He stood by his words. When Caterpillar's forklift division failed to improve its return on assets in 1992, Fites transferred it into an 80 percent–20 percent joint venture controlled by Mitsubishi.[47]

Caterpillar's new divisional structure facilitated downsizing. Under the new structure, Caterpillar cut 10,000 jobs in three years, 1990–1993 (Exhibit 3). Of the 7,500 employees who lost their jobs between January 1990 and August 1992, 2,000 were salaried managers and

---

Exhibit 2   George Schaefer's Caterpillar Highlights of Financial Data: Caterpillar vs. Komatsu

	Cat		Komatsu	
	Sales ($ bil.)	Income as % of sales	Sales ($ bil.)	Income as % of sales
1985	$6.7	2.9%	*	1.8%
1986	$7.3	1.0%	*	2.8%
1987	$8.2	3.9%	$5.1	1.3%
1988	$10.4	5.9%	$6.2	0.4%
1989	$11.1	4.5%	$6.0	2.6%

* Sales are available only in Yens: 1985, 796 billion Yen; 1986, 789 billion Yen.

Source: For Caterpillar, *Hoover's Handbook of American Business, 1995*, p. 329; For Komatsu, *Hoover's Handbook of World Business, 1995–96*, p. 291.

5,500 hourly workers.[48] As Caterpillar's sales grew from $10 billion to $15 billion in the first half of the 1990s, the number of managers employed by the company fell by 20 percent.[49] In addition, the move from a functional into a divisional structure, coupled with the drive for profit making, brought about a change in the methods of managerial compensation. Traditionally, Cat managers were paid in proportion to the size of the budget they controlled or the number of employees they supervised. Under the new plan, Caterpillar based all its incentive compensation schemes on return on assets.[50] Lastly, Caterpillar decentralized its research and development activities. With each division controlling its own product development programs and funding, R&D activities under the new plan were more customer driven than at any other period in the past.[51]

Marketing and Dealerships

Caterpillar's reorganization plan affected the company's distribution network as well. Under the new structure, dealers seeking assistance could contact any of the 17 product and service profit-centers directly, saving time and money; they no longer needed to call the General Office in their search for assistance within the company.[52] The new structure also facilitated a more frequent interaction between Caterpillar's managers and dealers, a development which resulted in "[v]irtually everyone from the youngest design engineer to the CEO" having "contact with somebody in [a] dealer organization [wrote Fites]." Ordinarily, low-level managers at Caterpillar communicated daily with their counterparts at Cat dealerships; senior corporate executives, several times a week.[53]

Exhibit 3	Donald Fites' Caterpillar: Employment and Sales	
	Number of Employees	Sales ($ bil.)
1990	60,000	11.4
1991	56,000	10.2
1992	52,000	10.2
1993	50,000	11.6
1994	54,000	14.3
1995	54,000	16.1
1996	57,000	16.5
1997	60,000	18.9
1998	64,000	21.0

Source: For 1990–1997: *Hoover's Handbook of American Business, 1999*, p. 329; for 1998: *Caterpillar Inc. 1999 Annual Report*, p. 1.

Caterpillar's network of dealerships was extensive. In 1999, 207 independent dealers served Caterpillar, 63 of whom were stationed in the U.S. and 144 abroad. The number of employees working for Cat dealers exceeded the company's own workforce (67,000) by nearly one third; the combined net worth of Cat dealers surpassed Caterpillar's stockholders' equity ($5.5 billion)[54] by nearly one quarter (Exhibit 4). Many of Caterpillar's dealerships were privately owned, a few were public companies. On average, the annual sales of a Caterpillar dealership amounted to $150 million (1996); several of the large dealerships, however, generated annual revenues of up to $1 billion.

To Caterpillar, the informal relationships between the company and its dealers were far more important than the formal contractual relations. Dealership agreements ran only a few pages, had no expiration date, and allowed each party to terminate the contract at will, following a 90-days notice. Notwithstanding the open-ended nature of the contract, turnover among Cat dealerships was extremely low. Caterpillar actively encouraged its dealers to keep the business in their families, running seminars on tax issues and succession plans for dealers, holding regular conferences in Peoria for the sons and daughters of "dealer Principals" (dealership owners), and taking concrete steps to encourage a proper succession from one generation to another.[55]

While Caterpillar had always protected its dealers against failure, under Fites' direction, Caterpillar did so more aggressively than before, assisting individual dealers who were subjected to intense price competition by rival manufacturers. To help a dealer, Caterpillar sometimes offered discounted prices, sometimes helped reduce the dealer's costs, and occasionally launched a promotion campaign in the dealer's service territory, emphasizing the lower lifetime cost of a Cat machine relative to a competitor's. Caterpillar also protected dealers during recessions. Despite the company's losses during the industry slump of 1991–92, Fites' Caterpillar helped vulnerable Cat dealers survive the downturn, stay in the business, and order equipment in advance of the 1993 upturn. Caterpillar's competitors, in contrast, saw several of their dealers go out of business during the recession.[56]

Fites' Caterpillar cooperated with dealers in other ways. During the 1990s, Caterpillar worked together with its dealers to conduct surveys among customers in order to improve customer service and parts delivery. Sending out 90,000 survey forms annually, Cat received a response rate of nearly 40 percent. Through its "Partners in Quality" program, Caterpillar involved dealers in quality control discussions, linking personnel at Cat plants and dealerships, and sponsoring quarterly meetings. Periodically, Caterpillar invited its entire body of independent dealers to a week-long conference in Peoria to review corporate strategy, manufacturing plants, and marketing policies. A firm believer in strong personal business ties, Fites explained:

> Dealers can call me or any senior corporate officer at any time, and they do. Virtually any dealer in the world is free to walk in my door. I'll know how much money he made last year and his market position. And I'll know what is happening in his family. I consider the majority of dealers personal friends. Of course, one reason I know the dealers so well is that I rose through our distribution organization.[57]

Caterpillar's worldwide distribution system, according to Fites, was the company's single greatest advantage over its competitors. It was a strategic asset whose importance was expected to grow in the future: "[u]ntil about 2010," Fites predicted, "distribution"—that is, after-sales support, product application, and service information—"will be what separates the winners from the losers in the global economy."[58] Contrasting American and Japanese manufacturing firms, Fites elaborated:

> Although many Japanese companies had the early advantage in manufacturing excellence, U.S. companies may have the edge this time around. … [T]hey know more about distribution than anyone else. … Quite frankly, distribution traditionally has not been a strength of Japanese companies. Marketing people and salespeople historically have been looked down upon in Japanese society[59]

Information Technology

Fites' Caterpillar invested generously in expanding and upgrading Caterpillar's worldwide computer network—a system linking together factories, distribution centers, dealers, and large customers. By 1996, the network connected 1,000 locations in 160 countries across 23 time zones, providing Caterpillar with the most comprehensive and fastest part delivery system in the industry. Although Caterpillar had long guaranteed a 48-hours delivery of parts anywhere in the world, by 1996, Cat dealers supplied 80 percent of the parts a customer needed at once; the remaining 20 percent—not stocked by the dealers—were shipped by the company on the same day the parts were ordered. With 22 distribution centers spread all around the world, Caterpillar serviced a total of 500,000 different parts, keeping over 300,000 in stock, and manufacturing the remainder on demand.[60]

A critical element in Caterpillar's drive for technological leadership was an electronic alert information system the company was developing under Fites. The new system was designed to monitor machines remotely, identify parts that needed to be replaced, and replace them before they failed. Once fully operational in the early 2000's, the new IT system was expected first, to help dealers repair machines before they broke down, thereby reducing machine downtime, on the one hand, and saving repair costs, on the other; and second, provide Caterpillar and its dealers with the opportunity to slash their inventory costs. In 1995, the value of the combined inventories held by Caterpillar and its dealers amounted to $2 billion worth of parts.[61]

Diversification

Fites' Caterpillar expanded its sales into farm equipment, forest products, and compact construction machines, introducing new lines of products, one at a time. Between 1991 and 1999, Caterpillar entered a total of 38 mergers and joint venture agreements, many of which contributed to the company's efforts to diversify.[62]

The growth in Caterpillar's engine sales was the company's largest. Caterpillar had traditionally produced engines for internal use only, installing them on

Exhibit 4 Caterpillar Dealerships, 1999			
	Inside U.S.	Outside U.S.	Worldwide
Dealers	63	144	207
Branch Stores	382	1,122	1,504
Employees	34,338	54,370	88,709
Service Bays	6,638	5,529	12,167
Estimated Net Worth	$3.22 bil.	$3.54 bil.	$6.77 bil.

Source: *Caterpillar Inc. 1999 Annual Report,* p. 43.

Cat machines, but beginning in the mid 1980s, as the company was recovering from its most severe crisis, Cat embarked on a strategy of producing engines for sale to other companies. In 1999, engine sales accounted for 35 percent of Cat's revenues, up from 21 percent in 1990, and Cat engines powered about one-third of the big trucks in the United States. Apart from trucking companies, Caterpillar produced engines for a variety of other customers including petroleum firms, electric utility companies, and shipbuilding concerns (Exhibit 6). Only 10 percent of the diesel engines manufactured by Caterpillar in 1999 were installed on the company's own equipment.[63]

Two important acquisitions by Caterpillar helped the company compete in the engine market. In 1996, Donald Fites purchased the MaK Company—a German maker of engines for power generation. Partly because governments of developing countries were reluctant to build large power plants, and partly because the utility industry in the United States deregulated and new electrical suppliers entered the market, worldwide demand for generators was fast increasing. The rise in demand helped Caterpillar increase its sales of power generators by 20 percent annually between 1995 and 1999.[64]

Similarly, in 1998, Fites bought Britain's Perkins Engines, a manufacturer of engines for compact construction machinery, for $1.3 billion. The new acquisition contributed to Caterpillar's efforts to increase its share in the small equipment market, which was growing at a rate of 10 percent a year. Perkins' best selling engine powered the skid steer loader. A compact wheel tractor operated by one person and capable of maneuvering in tight spaces, the skid dug ditches, moved dirt, broke up asphalt, and performed a wide variety of other tasks.[65]

Labor Relations

Perhaps no other areas of management had received more attention than Caterpillar's labor relations under Fites. For nearly seven years, 1991–1998, Fites fought the UAW in what had become the longest U.S. labor dispute in the 1990s. On the one side, a union official described the UAW relationship with Fites as "the single most contentious … in the history of the union;" on the other, a Wall Street analyst called Fites "the guy who broke the union, pure and simple."[66]

In part, Fites' opposition to the UAW was ideological: it "is not so much a battle about economics as it is a battle about who's going to run the company."[67] Yet economics did matter, and Fites was determined to ensure Caterpillar's global competitiveness by cutting the company's labor cost. His principal target was a UAW "pattern" agreement, a collective bargaining contract

modeled on agreements signed by the UAW and Caterpillar's domestic competitors, John Deere, the Case Corporation, and others (a pattern agreement tied separate labor contracts together so that changes in one led to similar changes in others within the same industry). Fites rejected pattern bargaining because Caterpillar was heavily dependent on the export of domestically manufactured products, selling over 50 percent of its American-made equipment in foreign markets, and thus competing head-to-head with foreign-based, global companies like Komatsu. Cat's U.S.-based competitors, by contract, exported a far smaller proportion of their domestically made goods. Because Cat's global competitors paid lower wages overseas than the wages paid by Cat's American-based competitors at home, Fites argued, Caterpillar could not afford paying the UAW pattern of wages.[68]

The first Caterpillar strike erupted in 1991, at a time Caterpillar's 17,000 unionized employees were working under a contract. The contract was set to expire on September 30, and Fites was prepared. He had built up enough inventory to supply customers for six months, giving Cat dealers special incentives to buy and stock parts and equipment in case a strike shut down the company's U.S. plants. Caterpillar's contract offer included three principal demands: no pattern on wages, flexible work schedules, and a two-tier wage system. The union rejected the offer outright and staged a strike. About 50 percent of the strikers were within six years of retirement, and as the strike prolonged, 30 percent of the strikers crossed the picket line. Five months into the strike, Fites threatened to replace the strikers permanently if they did not return to work within a week. Shortly thereafter, the union called off the strike, the strikers went back to work "unconditionally," and Cat's unionized employees continued working without a contract under the terms of the rejected offer.[69]

One casualty of the 1991–1992 strike was Caterpillar's Employee Satisfaction Process. The strike effectively put an end to Cat's ESP program, which George Schaefer had launched in 1986 and strove so painstakingly to preserve. As the climate of labor relations at Caterpillar deteriorated, the number of unresolved grievances increased. At the Aurora plant at Illinois, the number of grievances at the final stage before arbitration rose from less than 20 prior to the strike to over 300 in the year following the end of the strike. When Cat employees began wearing their own ESP buttons to read "Employee Stop Participating," Caterpillar terminated the program altogether.[70]

During 1992–94, Caterpillar's unionized employees continued to resist Fites' hard-line stand against the UAW. They organized shopfloor disruptions ("informational picketing"), slowdowns ("work to Rule"), wildcat strikes in selected plants, and picket lines at Cat's dealerships.[71] Fites, in the meantime, trained managers and office workers to operate factory machinery and reassigned many of them to the shopfloor of plants undergoing short-term work-stoppages. Once again, he was fully prepared for a long strike. The 1994–95 strike broke out in June 1994, lasted 17 months, was bitterly fought by the striking unionists, and came to an abrupt end when the UAW ordered its members to return to work "immediately and unconditionally" in order to save their jobs.[72] During the strike, Caterpillar supplemented its workforce with 5,000 reassigned white collar employees, 3,700 full-time and part-time new hires, 4,000 union members who crossed the picket line, and skilled workers borrowed from its dealerships. The company, furthermore, shifted work to non-union plants in the South. Additionally, Caterpillar supplied the U.S. market with equipment imported from its plants in Europe, Japan, and Brazil.[73] Operating effectively all through the strike, Caterpillar avoided massive customer defection, and managed to keep up production, expand sales, increase profits, and drive up the company stock price. In 1995, the company earned record profits for the second year in a row (Exhibit 5).

During the two years following the end of the strike, the shopfloor struggle between Cat management and the union resumed. Caterpillar issued strict rules of workplace conduct, limiting employees' behavior as well as speech. Union activists, in response, launched a work-to-rule campaign in Cat's unionized plants. The UAW, in addition, filed numerous charges with the National Labor Relations Board (NLRB), alleging that the company committed unfair labor practices. Accepting many of these charges, the NLRB issued formal complaints.[74] Meanwhile, in 1997, Caterpillar racked up record profits for the fourth year in a row (Exhibit 5).

In February 1998, at long last, Caterpillar and the union reached an agreement. The terms of the 1998 agreement clearly favored Caterpillar. First and most important, the contract allowed Caterpillar to break away from the long-standing practice of pattern bargaining. Second, the contract allowed Caterpillar to introduce a two-tier wage system and pay new employees 70 percent of the starting union scale. A third clause of the contract provided for a more flexible work schedule, allowing management to keep employees on the job longer than eight hours a day and during weekends (without paying overtime). The contract also granted management the right to hire temporary employees at certain plants without the union's approval, and reduce the number of union jobs below a certain level. Running for six years rather than the typical three years, the contract was expected to secure Caterpillar with a relatively long period of industrial peace.[75]

Several provisions of the contract were favorable to the union. The contract's key economic provisions included an immediate wage increase of 2–4 percent and future increases of 3 percent in 1999, 2001, and 2003; cost of living allowances; and substantial gains in pension benefits (the average tenure of the 1994–95 strikers was 24 years). Another provision favorable to the UAW was a moratorium on most plant closings. But perhaps the most significant union gain was simply achieving a contract, as AFL-CIO Secretary Treasurer Rich Trumka observed: "The message to corporate America is this: Here's one of the biggest companies, and they couldn't walk away from the union."[76]

Why, then, was Fites willing to sign a contract? Why did a company that operated profitably year after year without a contract, and operated effectively during strikes, suddenly seek to reach an agreement with the UAW?

Fites' decision was influenced by two developments. First, Caterpillar's record revenues and profits during

Exhibit 5	Caterpillar's Financial Results During the Labor Disputes of the 1990s			
	Sales ($Mil.)	Net Income ($Mil.)	Income as % of Sales	Stock Price FY Close
1991	10,182	(404)	—	10.97
1992	10,194	(2,435)	—	13.41
1993	11,615	652	5.6%	22.25
1994	14,328	955	6.7%	27.56
1995	16,072	1,136	7.1%	29.38
1996	16,522	1,361	8.2%	37.63
1997	18,925	1,665	8.8%	48.50

Source: *Hoover's Handbook for American Business*, 1999, p. 329.

1993–97 came to an end in 1998–99 as the industry was sliding into a recession. Revenues and profits were declining as a result of a strong dollar coupled with a weak demand for Cat products. Caterpillar, therefore needed a flexible wage agreement, stable employment relations, and a more cooperative workforce in order to smooth its ride during the impending downturn. Another reason why Fites sought accommodation with the union was the need to settle some 400 unfair labor practice charges filed by the NLRB against the company during the dispute. These charges were not only costly to adjudicate but could have resulted in huge penalties, which the company had to pay in cases where the NLRB ruled in favor of the UAW. One of Caterpillar's principal demands in the 1998 settlement—to which the UAW agreed—was dropping these unfair labor practice charges.[77]

The Future: Glen Barton's Caterpillar 1999–

As Fites retired in February 1999, Glen Barton, a 39-year Cat veteran, assumed the company's leadership. During his first year in office, Barton lost two potential allies on the Cat Board of Directors, Glen Schaefer and Donald Fites. In January 2000, Caterpillar's Board of Directors revised the company's corporate governance guidelines to prohibit retired Cat employees from sitting on the board. The move was intended to safeguard the interests of stockholders and prevent the company's inside directors from opposing swift actions proposed by the board's outside members.[78]

Barton faced other difficulties. In 1999, Caterpillar's profits fell 37 percent to $946 million, the worst results since 1993, and its North American market, which accounted for half of Cat's sales and nearly 2/3 of its profits, was in a slump.[79]

Barton believed that the downturn in the U.S. construction market could be offset by an upturn in the international market. He thought that Caterpillar could take advantage of its global positioning to cushion the U.S. decline by increasing sales in Asia and Latin America whose economies were rebounding. But being cautious, Barton also realized that he needed to ensure the future of Caterpillar in the long run. He therefore embarked on four growth strategies: the expansion into new markets; diversification; the development of a new distribution channel; and the build up of alliances with global competitors.

New Markets

In 1999, 80 percent of the world's population lived in developing countries, and Caterpillar's sales to developing nations accounted for only 23 percent of the total company's sales. Developing countries had limited access to water, electricity, and transportation, and therefore needed to invest in building highways, bridges, dams, and waterways. Under Barton's leadership, increased sales of Caterpillar's equipment to the developing nations of Asia, Latin America, Eastern Europe, and the Commonwealth of Independent States (the former Soviet Union) was a top strategic priority.[80]

Diversification

Just as globalization protected Caterpillar from the cyclical movements of boom and bust, so did diversification. Cat's expansion into the engine business is a case in point. In 1999, Caterpillar's overall sales fell by 6 percent, yet its engine sales rose by 5 percent. Cat's engine business itself was further diversified, with truck-engine sales making up just over one-third of all Cat's engine sales in 1999 (Exhibit 6).

Such a diversification, according to Barton, ensured the company that any future decline in truck engine sales could be offset, at least in part, by an

Exhibit 6	Cat Engine Sales to End Users, 1999, 2000	
	1999	2000
Trucks	34%	27%
Electric Power Generators	26%	33%
Oil Drilling Equipment	20%	19%
Industrial Equipment	11%	13%
Ships and Boats	9%	8%

Source: *Caterpillar Inc. 1999 Annual Report,* p. 24; and *2000 Annual Report.*

Exhibit 7	Caterpillar's Sales of Power Generators	
	Power Generator Sales ($Mil.)	Power Generator Sales As % of Total Revenues
1996	$1.2	7.3%
1997	$1.3	6.9%
1998	$1.6	7.6%
2000	$1.8	9.1%
2001	$2.3	11.4%

Source: David Barboza, "Cashing In On the World's Energy Hunger," *New York Times,* 22 May 2001.

increase in sales of non-truck engines. By 2010, Caterpillar's total engine sales were expected to double to nearly $14 billion.[81]

Of all Cat engine sales, the growth in sales of electric diesel generators—20 percent a year since 1996—had been the fastest (Exhibit 7). Caterpillar's energy business clearly benefited from the energy crisis. Large corporations, manufacturing facilities, internet server centers, and utility companies had installed back up diesel generators for standby or emergency use; in the nine months ending May 2001, Cat sales of mobile power modules (trailer equipped with a generator) quadrupled.[82]

The world's largest manufacturer of diesel generators, Caterpillar nevertheless faced a serious challenge in its efforts to transform itself into an ET (energy technology) company: diesel generators produced far more pollution than other sources of power. To address this problem,

Barton's Caterpillar accelerated its shift towards cleaner micro power. In 2001, only 10 percent of Caterpillar's generators were powered by natural gas; in 2011, the corresponding figure was expected to climb to 50 percent.[83]

To diversify the company in still another way, Barton planned to double its farm equipment sales in five years (1999–2004).[84] In the agricultural equipment market, caterpillar needed to compete head-to-head with the John Deere Co. and the CNH Corporation (former Case Corp. and New Holland), the leading U.S. manufacturers.

A New Distribution Channel

Under Barton's direction, Caterpillar expanded its rental equipment business, reaching a new category of customers both at home and abroad. Formerly, Caterpillar sold or rented equipment to rental centers, and these centers, in turn, re-rented the equipment to end-users.

Exhibit 8   Caterpillar: Five Year Financial Summary

(Dollars in million except per share data)	2000	1999	1998	1997	1996
Sales and Revenues	$ 20,175	$ 19,702	$ 20,977	$ 18,925	$ 16,522
Profits	$ 1,053	$ 946	$ 1,513	$ 1,665	$ 1,361
As % of Sales & Rev.	5.2%	4.8%	7.2%	8.8%	8.2%
Profits per Share	$ 3.04	$ 2.66	$ 4.17	$ 4.44	$ 3.54
Dividends per Share	$ 1.345	$ 1.275	$ 1.150	$ 0.950	$ 0.775
Return on Equity	19.0%	17.9%	30.9%	37.9%	36.3%
Capital Expenditures, Net	$ 723	$ 790	$ 925	$ 824	$ 506
R&D Expenses	$ 854	$ 814	$ 838	$ 700	$ 570
As % of Sales & Rev.	4.2%	4.1%	4.0%	3.7%	3.4%
Wage, Salaries, & Employee Benefits	$ 4,029	$ 4,044	$ 4,146	$ 3,773	$ 3,437
Number of Employees	67,200	66,225	64,441	58,366	54,968
December 31					
Total assets					
Consolidated	28,464	26,711	25,128	20,756	18,728
Machinery & Engines	16,554	16,158	15,619	14,188	13,066
Financial Products	14,618	12,951	11,648	7,806	6,681
Long term debt					
Consolidated	11,334	9,928	9,404	6,942	5,087
Machinery & Engines	2,854	3,099	2,993	2,367	2,018
Financial Products	8,480	6,829	6,411	4,575	3,069
Total debt					
Consolidated	15,067	13,802	12,452	8,568	7,459
Machinery & Engines	3,427	3,317	3,102	2,474	2,176
Financial Products	11,957	10,796	9,562	6,338	5,433

Source: *Caterpillar Inc. 2000 Annual Report*, p. 39

A special note: For additional financial data, as reported in the company's annual reports and other financial documents, check out the Caterpillar Web site at www.caterpillar.com

Rarely did Caterpillar rent directly to customers. Now Barton was making aggressive efforts to help Cat dealers diversify into rentals. Nearly half of all Cat's machines sold in North America in 2000 entered the market through the rental distribution channel, and the fastest growing segment of the business was short-term rentals. Implemented by Barton in 1999–2000, the Cat Rental Store Program was designed to assist dealers in operating a one-stop rental shop that offered a complete line of rental equipment from heavy bulldozers and tractors, to light towers, work platforms, and hydraulic tools.[85]

Joint Ventures

Increasingly, Caterpillar had used joint ventures to expand into new markets and diversify into new products. In November 2000, Barton's Caterpillar announced a plan to form two joint ventures with DaimlerChrysler, the world's leading manufacturer of commercial vehicles. One was for building medium-duty engines, the other was for manufacturing fuel systems. The combined share of the two companies in the medium-duty engine market was only 10 percent, yet the medium-duty engine market generated worldwide sales of $10 billion annually. The sales of fuel systems were even more promising. Fuel systems were designed to increase the efficiency of diesel engines and thereby reduce diesel emissions. Participating in the two joint ventures were Cat and DaimlerChrysler plants in four U.S. states (South Carolina, Georgia, Illinois, and Michigan) and at least five other countries.[86]

Future Prospects

Notwithstanding their initial prospects, Barton's strategic initiatives failed to address adequately two major concerns that could have affected the company's future. One had to do with the state of labor relations, particularly Cat's employee satisfaction program, which Schaefer had introduced and Fites terminated. Implemented effectively by Schaefer, the ESP program, we have seen, contributed to increased labor productivity, improved product quality, enhanced employee satisfaction, and reduced employee absenteeism. Should Barton, then, reintroduce Cat's employee satisfaction program and thereby improve the climate of labor relations at the company's U.S. plants? Would Barton be able to cooperate closely with the local union leadership to persuade shopfloor employees to join the program?

Another challenge Barton faced pertained to the impact of e-commerce. How could Caterpillar take advantage of the opportunities offered by e-commerce without undermining its distribution system? How, in other words, could Caterpillar benefit from utilizing the Internet for the marketing, distribution, and service of its products without weakening its strong dealers' networks?

Barton wondered, "What should I do next?"

A special note: For additional financial data, as reported in the company's annual reports and other financial documents, check out Caterpillar's web address at http://www.caterpillar.com

Notes

1. The Caterpillar Company 1999 Annual Report, p. 39
2. Michael Arndt, "This Cat Isn't so Nimble," *Business Week* (21 February 2000) 148. Online. Lexis-Nexis. Academic Universe; Mark Tatge, "Caterpillar's Truck-Engine Sales May Hit Some Breaking," *Wall Street Journal*, 13 March 2000.
3. Andrew Gross and David Weiss, "Industry Corner: The Global Demand for Heavy Construction Equipment," *Business Economics* 31, no. 3 (July 1996): 54–55.
4. Gross and Weiss, "Industry Corner," 54.
5. Gross and Weiss, "Industry Corner," 55.
6. Donald Fites, "Making Your Dealers Your Partners," *Harvard Business Review* (March-April 1996): 85.
7. U. Srinivasa Rangan, "Caterpillar Tractor Co.," in Christopher Bartlett and Sumantra Ghoshal, *Transatlantic Management: Text, Cases, and Readings in Cross Border Management* (Homewood IL.: Irwin, 1992), 296.
8. Fites, "Making Your Dealers Your Partners," 85.
9. Gross and Weiss, "Industry Corner," 58.
10. William L. Naumann, *The Story of Caterpillar Tractor Co.* (New York: The Newcomen Society, 1977), 7–9.
11. "Caterpillar Inc.," *Hoover's Handbook of American Business 1999* (Austin: Hoover Business Press, 1999), 328; "The Story of Caterpillar." Online. Caterpillar.Com. Retrieved, 9 March 2000.
12. Michael Yoshino and U. Srinivasa Rangan, *Strategic Alliances: An Entrepreneurial Approach to Globalization* (Boston: Harvard Business School Press, 1995), 93; Naumann, "Story of Caterpillar," 12–14; William Haycraft, *Yellow Power: The Story of the Earthmoving Equipment Industry* (Urbana Illinois: University of Illinois Press, 2000),118–122, 159–167, 196–203.
13. Fites, "Making your Dealers Your Partners," 94.
14. Rangan, "Caterpillar Tractor Co.," 304; James Risen, "Caterpillar: A Test of U.S. Trade Policy," *Los Angeles Times*, 8 June 1986. Online. Lexis-Nexis. Academic Universe.
15. Cited in Kathleen Deveny, "For Caterpillar, the Metamorphosis Isn't Over," *Business Week* (31 August 1987): 72.
16. Cited in Dexter Hutchins, "Caterpillar's Triple Whammy," *Fortune*, 27 October 1986, 91. See also Robert Eckley, "Caterpillar's Ordeal: Foreign Competition in Capital Goods," *Business Horizons* (March-April 1989): 81–83.
17. James Abegglen and George Stalk, Kaisha, the Japanese Corporation (New York: Basic Books, 1985), 62, 117–118; Yoshino and Rangan, *Strategic Alliances*, 94–95; "Komatsu Ltd.," *Hoover's Handbook of World Business* (1999): 320.
18. Quoted in Yoshino and Rangan, *Strategic Alliances*, 96.
19. Yoshino and Rangan, *Strategic Alliances*, 97; Eckley, "Caterpillar's Ordeal," 84.
20. Eckley, "Caterpillar's Ordeal," 84; *Business Week*, 31 August 1987, 73; Yoshino and Rangan, *Strategic Alliances*, 97.
21. Ronald Henkoff, "This Cat is Acting like a Tiger," *Fortune*, 19 December 1988, 67, 72, 76; *Business Week* (31 August 1987): 73.
22. Eckley, "Caterpillar Ordeal," 81, 83.
23. Quoted in *Fortune*, 19 December 1988, 76.
24. Eckley, "Caterpillar Ordeal," *Fortune*, 19 December 1988, 76; Alex Kotlowitz, "Caterpillar Faces Shutdown with UAW," *Wall Street Journal*, 5 March 1986. Online. ABI data base.
25. Barry Bearak, "The Inside Strategy: Less Work and More Play at Cat,", *Los Angeles Times*, 16 May 1995. Online. Lexis-Nexis. Academic Universe.
26. *Fortune*, 19 December 1988, 76.
27. Brian Bremner, "Can Caterpillar Inch its Way Back to Heftier Profits?" *Business Week* (25 September 1989): 75.

28. Abegglen and Stalk, Kaisha, 118.

29. *Fortune*, 19 December 1988, 72, 74; *Business Week* (25 September 1989): 75.

30. Karen Auguston, "Caterpillar Slashes Lead Times from Weeks to Days," *Modern Materials Handling* (February 1990): 49.

31. Barbara Dutton, "Cat Climbs High with FMS," *Manufacturing Systems* (November 1989): 16–22; *Business Week* (31 August 1987): 73; *Business Week* (25 September 1989): 75.

32. Quoted in Auguston, "Caterpillar Slashes Lead Times," 49.

33. Auguston, "Caterpillar Slashes Lead Times," 50–51.

34. Auguston, "Caterpillar Slashes Lead Times," 49, 51.

35. *Business Week* (September 25, 1989): 75.

36. Yoshino and Rangan, Strategic Alliances, 98.

37. Jennifer Reingold, "CEO of the Year," *Financial World* (28 March 1995): 68.

38. Quoted in "An Interview with Caterpillar Inc. Chairman and CEO Donald V. Fites," *Inter-Business Issues* (December 1992): 32.

39. Quoted in Tracy Benson, "Caterpillar Wakes Up," *Industry Week* (20 May 1991): 36.

40. Quoted in Reingold, "CEO of the Year," 74.

41. Quoted in Kevin Kelly, "Caterpillar's Don Fites: Why He Didn't Blink," *Business Week* (10 August 1992): 56.

42. Quoted in *Business Week* (10 August 1992): 56–57.

43. *Business Week* (10 August 1992): 57.

44. Quoted in Benson, "Caterpillar Wakes Up," 32.

45. "An Interview with Fites," *Inter Business Issues*, 32.

46. Benson, "Caterpillar Wakes Up," 33.

47. *Business Week* (10 August 1992): 56.

48. J. P. Donlon, "Heavy Metal," *Chief Executive* (September 1995): 50.

49. Andrew Zadoks, "Managing Technology at Caterpillar," *Research Technology Management* (January 1997): 49–51. Online. Lexis-Nexis. Academic Universe.

50. *Business Week* (10 August 1992): 56.

51. Donlon, "Heavy Metal," 50.

52. Benson, "Caterpillar Wakes Up," 36.

53. Fites, "Make Your Dealers Your Partners," 93.

54. Caterpillar Inc. 1999 Annual Report, 34.

55. Fites, "Make Your Dealers Your Partners," 89, 91–92, 94.

56. Fites, "Make Your Dealers Your Partners," 92–93.

57. Quoted in Fites, "Make Your Dealers Your Partners," 94, but see also 90, 93.

58. Quoted in Donlon. "Heavy Metals," 50.

59. Quoted in Fites, "Make Your Dealers You Partners," 86.

60. Myron Magnet, "The Productivity Payoff Arrives," *Fortune*, 27 June 1994, 82–83; Benson, "Caterpillar Wakes Up," 36; Fites, "Making Your Dealers Your Partners," 88–89.

61. Quoted in Steven Prokesch, "Making Global Connections in Caterpillar," *Harvard Business Review* (March-April 1996): 89, but see also 88, and Donlon, "Heavy Metals," 50.

62. "Caterpillar's Growth Strategies," Copyright 1999. Online. Caterpillar.Com

63. *Wall Street Journal*, 13 March 2000; David Barboza, "Aiming for Greener Pastures," *New York Times*, 4 August 1999.

64. De'Ann Weimer, "A New Cat on the Hot Seat," *Business Week* (9 March 1998): 61, *Wall Street Journal*, 13 March 2000.

65. *Business Week*, 9 March 1998; *Wall Street Journal*, 13 March 2000.

66. The quotations, in order, are from Reingold, "CEO of the Year," 72; Carl Quintanilla, "Caterpillar Chairman Fites to Retire," *Wall Street Journal*, 15 October 1998. Online. ABI data base.

67. Quoted in Reingold, "CEO of the Year," 72.

68. "An Interview with Fites," *Inter Business Issues*, 34–35; "What's Good for Caterpillar," *Forbes*, 7 December 1992. Online. ABI data base.

69. Michael Cimini, "Caterpillar's Prolonged Dispute Ends," *Compensation and Working Conditions* (Fall 1998): 5–6; Kevin Kelly, "Cat May be Trying to Bulldoze the Immovable," *Business Week* (2 December 1991): 116, "Cat VS. Labor: Hardhats, Anyone?" *Business Week* (26 August 1991): 48. Lexis-Nexis. Academic Universe.

70. Michael Verespej, "Bulldozing Labor Peace at Caterpillar," *Industry Week* (15 February 1993): 19. Online. ABI data base.

71. "Caterpillar: Union Bull," *Economist*, 9 January 1993, 61. Online. Lexis-Nexis. Academic Universe; Cimini "Caterpillar's Prolonged Dispute Ends," 7–9.

72. Cimini, "Caterpillar's Prolonged Dispute Ends," 9; Robert Rose, "Caterpillar Contract with UAW May be Tough to Sell to Workers," *Wall Street Journal*, 17 February 1998. Online. ABI data base; Reingold, "CEO of the Year," 72.

73. Cimini, "Caterpillar's Prolonged Dispute Ends," 8–9.

74. Cimini, "Caterpillar's Prolonged Dispute Ends," 9–10.

75. Carl Quintanilla, "Caterpillar Touts Its Gains as UAW Battle Ends," *Wall Street Journal*, 24 March 1998; Dirk Johnson, "Auto Union Backs Tentative Accord with Caterpillar," *New York Times*, 14 February 1998.

76. Quoted in Philip Dine, "Gulf Remains Wide in Caterpillar's Home," *St. Louis Post Dispatch*, 29 March 1998. Online. Lexis-Nexis. Academic Universe. See also Cimini, "Caterpillar's Prolonged Dispute Ends," 11.

77. "The Caterpillar Strike: Not Over Till Its Over," *Economist*, 28 February 1998.

78. *Business Week* (21 February 2000):148.

79. *Business Week* (21 February 2000):148.

80. "Growth Strategies." Caterpillar.Com, 2.

81. *Wall Street Journal*, 13 March 2000.

82. David Barboza, "Cashing In On the World's Energy Hunger," *New York Times*, 22 May 2001.

83. *New York Times*, 22 May 2001; "Energy Technology: Beyond the Bubble," *Economist*, 21 April 2001.

84. Heather Landy, "Putting More Cats Down on the Farm," *Chicago Sun Times*, 28 March 1999. Online. Lexis-Nexis. Academic Universe.

85. Michael Roth, "Seeing the Light," *Rental Equipment Register* (January 2000). Online. Lexis-Nexis. Academic Universe; Nikki Tait, "Cat Sharpens Claws to Pounce Again," *Financial Times* (8 November 2000). Online. Lexis-Nexis. Academic Universe.

86. Joseph Hallinan, "Caterpillar, DaimlerChrysler Team Up," *Wall Street Journal*, 23 November 2000.

Case 12

Competition in the Global Wine Industry: A U.S. Perspective

Murray Silverman, Richard Castaldi, Sally Baack, and Gregg Sorlien,
San Fransisco State University

The total volume of the global wine market in 1998 was measured at 6.8 billion gallons, with 25 percent of the total volume accounting for wine that was purchased outside the country from which the wine was produced.[1] This represents an increase over the 1991–95 period, during which the export segment of the market averaged approximately 17 percent by volume. The increasing trend for the export market since 1995 is due primarily to a change in the strategic priority that wine producing countries are placing on exporting as a method for growth. Historically, the market for wine was primarily one of local production and consumption. That paradigm has changed in the last few decades as a few of the more established wine drinking countries have seen their per capita consumption stagnate or decline (Table 1). At the same time, several wine producing countries around the world have begun to make an impact on the export market in an attempt to expand their industries beyond their limited local markets. The result of this shift in market focus for some of the older wine producing countries plus the rise of new wine producing countries around the world has caused an increase in the competitive nature of the global wine market.

Currently the U.S. is the fourth largest producer of wine in the world (Table 2) yet only accounts for approximately 4.2 percent of the total wine export market based on volume (Table 3). One reason for this disparity can be attributed to the low level of strategic importance placed on exporting by most U.S. wineries. In the past, a very common export strategy for U.S. companies was to export only the excess capacity that was on hand due to over production,[2] thus there was little focus on establishing a presence in the global market place. Foreign governments could also restrict U.S. wineries ability to operate by using anti-competitive actions such as implementing high tariffs for wine in retaliation for other trade issues, or implementing laws specifically designed to protect local wineries. The end result of these government interventions is that U.S. wines carry an increased cost burden over local wines and other imported wines, making it difficult to compete in the local markets.

In recognition of the opportunities presented by the global wine market and the threat that importers pose to the U.S. wine industry in 1998, the industry created a voluntary initiative called "WineVision." In direct acknowledgement of the shift in the global wine industry to a single worldwide marketplace, the vision of this organization is to make American wines the preeminent supplier to the global marketplace. Recognizing that much of this market development would be undertaken by individual brands, WineVision suggested that the ongoing threat, due to globalization, requires a well-funded, sustained, sophisticated response from a unified American wine industry. Therefore, WineVision has identified opportunities for an industry-wide initiative to provide brand promotion support, for example. The goal of WineVision was to help create strategies that would enable U.S. wineries to be more competitive and to increase the demand for U.S. wine both domestically and internationally. WineVision has focused on three main strategic priorities: 1) become the leader in sustainable practices—environmentally sound, socially responsible, and economically viable, 2) make wine an integral part of the American culture, 3) and position U.S. wine as the high-quality, high-value product (across price points) in global markets targeted for the greatest prosperity.[3]

Overview of Wine

The dynamics of the global wine industry are better understood through a brief history of wine as well as an overview of the wine making process. Some countries have longer historical and cultural ties with wine than others and that can affect the quality and perception of the product in the eyes of the consumer. Also, the conditions in which the wine grapes are raised and the processes used to make the wine can create a superior wine and therefore a competitive advantage.

This case was presented at the 2001 North American Case Research Association (NACRA) workshop. Copyright © 2001 by Murray Silverman, Richard Castaldi, Sally Baack, Gregg Sorlien, and NACRA. Reprinted with permission. All rights reserved.

Table 1   Per Capita Consumption of Wine in Selected Countries, 1995–1999 (in Liters)

Rank	Country	Population*	1996	1997	1998
1	Luxembourg	388,000	62.89	69.07	70.36
2	France	58,109,160	59.88	61.09	61.09
3	Italy	58,261,971	59.55	52.96	54.92
4	Slovenia	2,051,522	54.79	51.74	48.74
5	Croatia	4,547,000	37.61	47.26	47.66
6	Portugal	10,562,388	54.91	49.45	47.34
7	Switzerland	7,084,984	41.36	40.93	40.93
8	Argentina	34,292,742	38.97	39.05	39.52
9	Spain	39,404,348	36.69	37.02	38.07
10	Uruguay	3,222,716	29.88	33.57	35.13
33	United States	267,636,000	7.82	7.69	7.88

Source: Office International de la Vigne et du Vin (OIV) 1999.

Wine has been a part of Western history since the Neolithic Period (8,500–4,000 B.C.), when cultures first started to develop permanent communities, and stopped being nomadic hunter-gatherers.[4] One of the earliest written records of the consumption of wine is recorded in the Bible and the impact of wine on Mediterranean cultures became more pronounced over the years as the geopolitical situation stabilized in the region under the Roman Empire. Roman Imperialism helped to spread the production of wine across most of the countries in the Empire, which included most of North Africa and Southern Europe.[5] During that same era, wine became ingrained in the Christian faith and is still used in Christian mass today. The close tie between wine and the Christian faith aided to the spread of wine production and wine consumption across Europe in the ages after the fall of the Roman Empire and eventually throughout the world with the European Imperialism of the 15th–19th centuries. The wine producing and consuming countries listed in both Tables 2 and 3 are dominated by Western countries or ex-colonies, with most of them being historically Catholic.

There has never been a universally accepted system for naming styles of wine. Currently there are two prominent systems for naming wine, Varietal and Appellation. Appellation is a French term used to describe the region or specific area in which a wine is produced. In France when the Appellation naming convention was created, it was accepted that certain geographic locations, due to "terroir," the land where the grapes are grown, were better prepared to produce a specific type of grape, and therefore a specific style of wine. For example, that is why Champagne (wine with a degree of carbonation) comes from the Champagne region in France, east of Paris. Some Appellations that have been created around the world include, Bourdeaux (FR), Burgundy (FR), Chablis (FR), Champagne (FR), Tuscany (ITY), Maipo (CHL), Mendoza (ARG), New South Wales (AUS), Napa Valley (USA), and Sonoma County (USA).

Varietal is a descriptive naming convention based on the type of grape used to produce a wine. Varietal is predominately used as a U.S.-industry marketing tool to segment the market and is not specific to a geographic location. Some common Varietals today are; White Zinfandel,

Table 2   World Wine Production (in Millions of Gallons)

Country	1996	1997	1998
Italy	1,551	1,343	1,430
France	1,506	1,414	1,390
Spain	818	876	800
United States	498	580	539
Argentina	334	356	334
Germany	228	224	286
South Africa	230	232	215
Australia	177	162	195
Chile	100	120	144
Romania	202	176	132
Hungary	110	118	110
Yugoslavia	92	106	106
Rest of World	1,296	1,195	1,150
World Total	7,142	6,902	6,831

Source: IV International based on data from Office International de la Vigne et du Vin (OIV).

Table 3	Percent Share of the World Wine Production, Wine Consumption, Share of World Wine Market, and Share of Export Market 1998 (Based on Volume)				
Country*	% Share of Production	% Share of Consumption	% Share of World Market	% Share of Export Market	World Export Market Rank
Italy	21.0%	14.3%	20.8%	25.3%	1
France	20.4%	15.9%	20.3%	25.1%	2
Spain	11.7%	6.7%	10.6%	15.6%	3
United States	7.9%	9.3%	8.4%	4.2%	4
Argentina	4.9%	6.1%	6.4%	1.7%	10
Germany	4.2%	8.5%	4.1%	3.6%	5
Australia	2.9%	1.6%	2.3%	3.0%	8
Chile	2.1%	1.0%	2.0%	3.5%	6
Portugal	1.4%	2.2%	2.5%	3.4%	7
Others	23.5%	34.4%	22.6%	14.6%	
Total	100.0%	100.0%	100.0%	100.0%	

*sorted by % Share of Production

Source: Office International de la Vigne et du Vin (OIV) 1999.

Riesling, Chardonnay, Burgundy, Shiraz, Petite Shiraz, Merlot, Pinot Noir, Zinfandel, and Cabernet Sauvignon.

Terroir is a determining factor in the quality of the wine. It is not who makes it, or how they make it, but the quality of the grape that is used. It is the environmental factors that determine the flavors and sugar content in the grape. These factors are based on the temperature in the region, the amount of light that the grape vines are exposed to, the amount of rain that the area receives annually, and the characteristics of the soil. A vineyard that has all of these natural benefits still must have considerable agricultural work done to keep the vineyards healthy and free of insects and/or molds that damage the vines ability to produce quality grapes. The combinations of attributes that are needed to create a high quality grape are not very common throughout the world. The amount of good "terroir" is limited, and therefore the ability to produce fine wines is limited.

The wine making process is very complicated and as a result there are many opportunities to damage, as well as improve, the quality of the wine being produced. The wine making process starts in late fall, when the grapes are cut from the vine and laid on the ground in the sun to dry for a short period of time. This is done to increase the ratio of water to sugar content in the grape, thus creating the opportunity to make a sweeter wine. Then the grapes go into a vat and are crushed to remove the juice. The longer the skin of the grape remains with the juice, the darker the wine will be. If a white wine is desired, then the skins of the grapes are removed soon after the crush, but

if a red wine is desired then the skins of the grapes are left in with the juice for an extended period of time. The juice is then placed in a cask made of wood or vat made of stainless steel and aged for, on average, a year. The aging process allows the natural yeast from the sugar in the grape to ferment and produce alcohol. The aging process also allows the wine to absorb flavors from the container that it is aged in. After aging for the appropriate time, the wine is bottled, labeled, and shipped to the market.

Wine Producing Countries

In the global wine industry there are two broad categories for the classification of wine producing countries, the New World Producers and the Old World Producers. The larger New World Producers include the United States, Australia, Chile, and Argentina. The largest of the Old World producers are France and Italy. The New World (except the United States) and the Old World Producers industries are described in the following section.

Australia

Grape vines in Australia were first introduced in 1788 by English immigrants. The wine "industry" was born in the 1860s when European immigrants added the skilled workforce necessary to develop the commercial infrastructure. Despite the long history that they had at winemaking, the industry in Australia was stagnant until the 1960s when several key factors occurred to transform the industry and domestic market. Those key factors helped in the development of more innovative techniques to make higher quality wine while keeping costs down. The result was that the wineries were in a position to produce quality wine at many price points, and soon after, domestic and international demand began to rise. Since Australia has a very limited domestic market (population of only 17 million), the wineries realized that if the industry was to continue to grow it would have to do so in the international market.[6]

At the same time that the Australian wine industry was starting to show strong growth, the government was considering legislation that would severely tax wine in an attempt to gain revenue. To protect the industry, the local wineries joined together with government officials to develop a plan that would keep the government from doing this, and the result was the formulation of "Strategy 2025."[7] The consensus between the wineries and the government was that by growing the industry, the government and national economy would be better served than by instigating high taxes that could impede the growth of the wine industry. "Strategy 2025" is a business strategy that outlines how Australian wines will expand domestically and internationally. Their vision is that by the year 2025 the Australian wine industry will achieve $4.5 billion in annual sales by being the world's most influential and profitable supplier of branded wines and by pioneering wine as a universal first choice lifestyle beverage. They were even bold enough to name the specific markets that they would target. The top four markets targeted were the U.K., U.S., Germany, and Japan.[8] The top five markets that Australia shipped to in 1999 were the U.K., the U.S., New Zealand, Canada, and Germany. The U.K. accounted for over half of the revenue gained by Australia in the export market with $343 million, while the U.S. came in second place as a market for Australian wines with $160 million in revenue. The next three countries, New Zealand, Canada, and Germany only accounted for $97 million or 16.1 percent of the total revenue.[9] Japan was not in the list of top five countries that Australia exported to, despite being a strategic objective. Australia also plans on investing in the Asian Tigers as they develop due the large forecasted growth of their populations and economies. Australia was the eighth largest producer of wine in the world (Table 2) with output of 177 million gallons in 1996 and 195 million gallons in 1998. Australia had three percent of the total export market and was ranked eighth in the world for 1998 (Table 3).

Chile

The first vines were introduced to Chile in the 16th century by a Spanish priest. Over the years the cultivation slowly grew until the late 19th century when wine began to be produced on a large scale. Due to political and economic instability, the wine industry was not able to develop and take on a global perspective until 1979 when Chile began to focus on the exporting of natural resources to strengthen its economy.

The high Andean climate is very good for the production of high quality red wines. Chilean wines are higher in quality then their neighbor, Argentina, and in 1996, the government took an active role in maintaining the quality of wine for export by implementing the Denomination of Origin (DO). The DO is a set of laws that regulates the origin and variety of grape the wines use, as well as restricting the varietal labeling that is used to develop a consistent system. It has four wine producing regions that have appellations of origin and are monitored by the ministry of Agriculture. They are the Aconcagua, Maipo, Maule, and Rapel. In 1999 the top five markets that Chilean wines shipped to were the U.K., U.S., Canada, Denmark, and Japan. The U.K. accounted for the most revenue with $116 million, and the U.S accounted for $107 million. Canada, Denmark, and Japan accounted for $35, $25, and $24 million or 27 percent of the top five countries revenue.[10] Chile is the ninth largest producer of wine in the world (Table 2) with output of 100 million gallons in 1996 and 144 million gallons 1998. Despite being only the ninth largest producer, Chile had 3.5 percent of the total export market and was ranked sixth in the world for 1998 (Table 3).

Argentina

Like Chile, Argentina has a long history of making wine. However, the quality of the wine from Argentina was never as high, due to the small area of land that is capable of producing high quality grapes. The production of wine in Argentina has increased over the years (Table 2), but the wine produced tends to be for local consumption, not for export, due to low quality and government regulations. In recent years Argentina has developed several organizations to help boost the quality of the wines with the intent of increasing their presence in the export market. They include the Original Denomination (OD), Controlled Original Denomination (COD), and Guaranteed Controlled Original Denomination (GCOD). All of these organizations have the task of regulating the production and labeling of the wine to create a higher quality image in the global wine market. At present, there are many foreign companies that look to Chile to create joint ventures, but this is not the case in Argentina. The four main areas of wine production in Argentina are La Rioja, Mendoza, Rio Negro and San Juan. In 1999 the top markets for Argentine wine were Paraguay, the U.K., the U.S., Japan, Bolivia,

Uruguay, Chile, and Germany based on volume. The total volume of the top 8 countries was 58 millions of liters, with volume shipments for the countries being 12, 11, 10, 7, 5, 5, 4, and 4.[11] A significant portion of the volume, 45 percent of exports, went to other South American countries where the low cost/price of their product is a major factor. Argentina was the fifth largest producer of wine in the world (Table 2) with output of 334 million gallons in 1996 and 334 million gallons in 1998. Despite being the fifth largest producer in the world, Argentina held the tenth position in the total export market in the world for 1998 (Table 3).

France

France has been a long time world leader in the production of wine due to historical and cultural factors. In terms of volume, France was the number two producer of wine in the world (Table 2) with output of 1,506 million gallons in 1996 and 1,390 million gallons in 1998. The French developed the Vins d'appellation d'origine controlee (AOC) system centuries ago to help ensure that the quality of wine produced stays high. The AOC regulates the area of the production, the method used to produce and store the wine, as well as the minimum alcohol content of the wine. There are many regions in which quality grapes can be grown in France, and the dominant position that France has in the export market reflects this. Some of the appellations that are better known in France are Bordeaux, Burgundy, Champagne, and Rhone.

Italy

Italy, like France, also has a very old and established wine industry that relies on the appellation method to control the quality of their wines. Italy was the largest producer of wine in the world (Table 2) with output of 1,551 million gallons in 1996 and 1,430 million gallons in 1998. The two main organizations responsible for the control of the quality in Italian wine are the Denominazione di Origine Controllata and the Denominazione di Origine Controllata e Garantita. The second appellation control system was developed in recent years to help raise the quality of the wines produced.

New World Producers are using more modern methods of production thus creating more consistent high quality wine.[12] France was also in this situation since both countries tend to use older methods of production that have become a part of their "wine culture" instead of constantly innovating. All of the countries profiled, with the exception of Argentina, are capable of shipping brands that can compete at a wide range of price points. Argentine wines usually have a hard time competing in the premium market place, although there is one region capable of producing such wine. The French wines typically are capable of competing in the higher price classes, and it is not uncommon to find French wines that retail for over US$100. Italian wines tend to have more of an association of being good to have with meals and therefore do not tend to garner a price as high as French wines, but they do compete very well in the mid to lower price categories.

Major World Markets

Although several of the major wine-producing countries are also major markets, there are many countries and regions that do not have the capability to produce quality wines in large volumes, but have high demand for the product. This section will provide an overview of wine markets around the world and will reference the per capita consumption rates of select countries listed in Table 1.

In Australia, social behavior has driven the growth of the domestic market. These trends include a shift toward a Mediterranean style diet, the rise in the awareness of the health benefits of wine, recreational activities, and general entertainment.[13] As these trends have been increasing, so has Australia's per capita consumption. They were ranked 18th in the world for consumption (Table 1) in 1998 with 19.89 liters per person, up from 17.94 liters per person in 1996. The total market for imported wine in Australia for 1998 was 7.5 million gallons (Table 4), which translated into about a 5 percent market share for imported wines based on volume. According to *Strategy 2025*, this low market penetration by imported wine is attributed to the high quality and low price of the domestic brands, not because of government intervention to protect the market. In 1996, when *Strategy 2025* was written, six percent of the brands sold in Australia accounted for more then 75 percent of sales.

In 1998 Argentina was ranked eighth for per capita consumption in the world. Consumption in Argentina is showing a very slow growth trend, with 39.52 liters per person being consumed in 1998, up from 38.97 in 1996. The total market for imported wine in Argentina for 1998 was 1.3 million gallons (Table 4), which translated into about a .4 percent market share for imported wines based on volume. The high volumes of wine produced at low costs makes it very difficult for imported wines to come in and compete on price.

France and Italy were the number 2 and 3 countries in the world for per capita consumption in 1998 (Table 1). Both countries have a long history of wine production and consumption, yet despite this the consumption rate in France is relatively stagnant while Italy is showing a

Table 4	Wine Imports from 1996–1998 (in Thousands of Gallons)		
Country	1996	1997	1998
Germany	306.7	318.2	318.6
United Kingdom	197.0	211.8	233.9
France	140.0	153.8	148.0
United States	96.3	122.2	111.1
Japan	28.4	38.3	84.8
Russia	62.0	106.8	76.9
Netherlands	57.2	73.4	76.3
Canada	44.8	47.1	53.6
Switzerland	48.9	48.9	49.8
Denmark	40.3	44.3	46.1
Portugal	13.5	11.0	39.0
Sweden	30.2	28.0	29.6
Italy	4.5	30.4	28.3
Spain	30.2	3.9	23.6
Australia	3.7	5.5	7.5
Argentina	1.1	1.3	1.3
Chile	0.1	0.1	0.1
Rest of World	280.0	265.0	268.3
Total	1,384.9	1,510.0	1,596.8

Source: Office International de la Vigne et du Vin (OIV) 1999.

decrease. Italy, unlike France, has a very small market for imported wines. The import market sizes were roughly 13.4 percent and 2.8 percent in 1998 based on volume.

There are other countries and regions around the world that do not have the capability to produce large quantities of high quality wine, yet have markets that must be sustained through importing. These markets include the United Kingdom, Canada, Japan, and Asia. The United Kingdom's wine market is considered to be the "crucible" for the global wine market.[14] The U.K. has a very small domestic wine industry and also has good relationships with many of the wine producing countries in the world. That coupled with the long history of wine consumption the British have due to their historical association with the French and the Germans results in an open and competitive market. The British import market was second only to the German market in 1998, and the U.K. was ranked 23rd for per capita consumption in the same year with a trend of increasing consumption. The situation is very similar in Canada, except that there are more governmental constraints to competition in Canada. In 1998 Canada was ranked 30th in the world for per capita consumption with an increasing trend.

Although Japan has seen a steady increase in the size of its imported wine market (Table 4), they do not rank in the top 33 countries in the world for per capita consumption (Table 1). In fact, no Asia country has a high per capita consumption when compared to Western countries. This has to do with the lack of traditional and cultural trends that drive the consumption patterns in more established wine drinking countries. Asia does present a great opportunity for wine producers around the world because it is a very large market that has yet to be tapped. China alone has 1.4 billion potential consumers.

Overview of the U.S. Industry and Market

The total wine market in the United States for 1999 was $18.1 billion with an average growth rate of 8.5 percent since 1994. However, there has never been a cultural disposition for Americans to drink wine like has historically existed in Europe, despite being populated primarily by European immigrants. The two main reasons for this are, 1) the vineyard and production infrastructure was very small in the 19th century when the country was developing, and 2) the first alcoholic beverages to be mass produced and readily available nationwide in the U.S. were beer and whiskey. The low volume producers of wine were relegated to niche markets that were comprised of ethnic enclaves or individuals who wanted to enjoy a beverage with their food. The key differentiators between the drinks that were readily available, beer or whiskey, and wine became cuisine and the money necessary to attain the harder-to-reach imported wine. As a result of this, in the United States the consumption of wine became viewed as an elite drink, and was not embraced by the public.

Wine has been consumed on a national scale, but the attributes that categorized wine as an elite drink during the early days of the United States have carried forward into the present. The demographic breakdown of wine consumers does show that there are several distinct segments that comprise a majority of consumers. According to the *Adams Wine Handbook 1998*, women are slightly more likely to consume wine then men, with the majority of drinkers being in the "Baby Boomer" generation. They also tend to be college graduates who are professionals or managers and make over $60,000 annually. Furthermore, WR Hambrecht & Co. estimates that 15.7 million U.S. adults comprise the core of wine drinkers. The members of this segment have wine at least once a week and are credited with consuming approximately 88 percent of the wine by volume.[15]

The international image of the U.S. wine industry until the mid 1970's was that of a low quality jug wine producer. This image was prevalent due to the fact that the largest wineries of the time were high volume producers who targeted the mass market. The wineries that produced high quality wines were doing so in low volumes so their presence and reputation was understated by the Old World producers who had proven track records of producing world class wines. This changed in 1976 during a blind wine tasting contest in Paris, France where California wines from Napa Valley beat out several well-established European wines for the top honors. From that time forward, there has been a focus on developing high quality wines that can compete in the international market from the Northern California Appellations like Napa Valley and Sonoma County.

The U.S. has one of the most "open markets" in the world for imported wines. Despite this, California wines have traditionally dominated the domestic market for years due to the ideal growing conditions and favorable marketing and branding actions taken by some of California's larger wineries. The import segment has seen some fluctuations over the years and is currently on the rise, from 16 percent in 1992 to 17 percent in 1998, as more of the New and Old World producers start to implement targeted market strategies. California wines are also seeing increased competition from wines that are produced in Washington and New York states, as their market share has risen from 6.2 percent in 1992 to 14 percent in 1998.[16] Table 5 shows the balance of trade for the United States in wine for the years 1992–1998. The deficit has been shrinking in volume but has been growing in value over the time period. The total volume is up from the 1992 deficit number of 33,974 million gallons to 38,624 million gallons in 1998. But the 1998 number is down from the 1994 and 1996 numbers of over 40,000 million gallons. The trade deficit based on value has seen a surge in the past few time periods and currently stands at over $1.3 billion. With the value of the imports out pacing the value of exports while keeping a relatively flat volume, the value per gallon has risen for imports from $15.36 in 1992 to $17.14 in 1998. This trend clearly supports the theory that the import market is overwhelmingly targeting the premium wine segments.

Table 6 shows the top U.S. competitors for the years 1994, 1996 and 1998 based on volume. The top eight companies produced a total of 77.6 percent of the wine in the U.S. market based on volume, while an estimated 1600 plus other wineries produced the remaining 22.4 percent in 1998. A small number of companies dominating the majority of the production have been common for many years in the U.S. industry, however, the companies that have stayed in the top eight were not always the same. The reason for this can be attributed to a volatility that is inherent in the industry as companies initiate strategic divestitures and acquisitions to build better brand portfolios to compete in select market segments. This dominance of the

---

Table 5   United States Balance of Trade for Wine, 1990–1998

| By Volume | | | | |
Item	1992	1994	1996	1998
Imports	71,081	72,611	94,928	109,730
Exports	37,107	31,134	46,473	71,106
Trade Deficit	33,974	41,477	48,455	38,624
Ratio: Imports to Exports	1.9:1	2.3:1	2.0:1	1.5:1

| By Value | | | | |
Item	1992	1994	1996	1998
Total Value of Imports ($ millions)	$1,091.8	$1,050.0	$1,434.6	$1,880.8
Value per Gallon ($)	$15.36	$4.46	$15.11	$17.14
Total Value of Exports ($ millions)	$174.7	$192.1	$320.0	$531.9
Value per Gallon ($)	$4.71	$6.17	$6.89	$7.48
Trade Deficit ($ millions)	$917.1	$857.9	$1,114.6	$1,348.9
Ratio: Imports to Exports	6.2:1	5.5:1	4.5:1	3.5:1

Source: *Adams Wine Handbook,* 1999 / U.S. Department of Commerce.

market by such a few players results in their ability to leverage distributors to gain shelf space, put millions of dollars into marketing budgets, and to have leverage with suppliers for lower costs on inputs. The consolidation trend in the market has taken on a new twist in 2000. Instead of U.S. wineries consolidating with each other, foreign companies are looking to acquire U.S. wineries. This strategy enables the foreign producers to gain access to the U.S. market quickly and comprehensively. By purchasing a U.S. winery, the foreign producers can utilize the established distribution channel, existing suppliers, as well as the market knowledge of the acquired employees.

Table 7 shows how the customer preferences for the colors, or varietals, of wine in the years of 1990 to 1998 have shifted from white wines to red. White wines in 1990 accounted for 52.9 percent of the volume shipped, that number declined to 40.5 percent by 1998. This was due to the rise in demand for Red and Blush wines from 14.7 percent and 16.8 percent in 1990 to 31.9 percent and 21.4 percent in 1998 respectively. The category of Rose has dropped by over half of its market share from 15.6 percent to 6.2 percent.

Suppliers to the industry could be in the form of bottle manufactures, label printing services, or grape production. The capital investment that is required to start a winery depends on the scale of production. Very small wineries can start up with a minimal capital investment and can purchase grapes from select

Table 7 — Share of Bottled California Table Wine, Shipments by Color, 1990–1998 (Based on Volume)

Color	1990	1992	1994	1996	1998
Red	14.7%	19.6%	23.6%	27.2%	31.9%
Rose	15.6%	13.1%	9.2%	9.5%	6.2%
White	52.9%	48.7%	50.3%	46.8%	40.5%
Blush	16.8%	18.6%	16.9%	16.5%	21.4%
Total	100.0%	100.0%	100.0%	100.0%	100.0%

Source: *Adams Wine Handbook* 1999.

suppliers. However, it is not uncommon for competitors to out bid each other for grapes from suppliers that have a reputation for high quality grapes. Therefore, wineries choose to either purchase vineyards and assume the higher capital investment and agricultural maintenance costs or try to attain long-term contracts with grape suppliers.

In the United States, there is a law mandating the implementation of a 3-tier distribution system. The system is mandated by law because alcoholic beverages are a controlled substance and as such the government implemented a controlled system for getting those products to the markets. This law was enacted after the repeal of Prohibition in 1933. The wine producers must sell to a wholesaler, who then sells to an established customer base of grocery stores, liquor stores, hotels, and/or restaurants. Wineries are capable of using a 2-tier distribution system, which allows wineries to sell directly to the customers through gift shops located at the winery. Mailing lists and the internet can only be used in a limited number of states because most states have made direct shipments illegal. Direct sale volumes are very low when compared to the established 3-tier system. The distributors have a vested interest in keeping wineries from being able to use a 2-tier distribution system because every bottle that is sold directly to the customer does not generate revenue for them. As a result, there is an industry wide push by distributors to keep wine sales over the internet from being legal. One argument is that minors would be able to purchase wine by clicking a mouse. The role of the distribution channel is growing and taking on greater strategic importance as a trend of international and domestic consolidation grows. Recent examples of this would be the acquisition of grocery store chains like Kroger's by Albertson's and mega-store acquisitions like Wal-Mart purchasing a German chain called Wertkauf.[17] The result for wine producers is the ability to now gain access to more domestic and international markets without added

Table 6 — Domestic Table Wine Market, 1994–1998 (Based on Volume)

Company	% Market Share 1994	% Market Share 1996	% Market Share 1998
E & J Gallo Winery	34.3%	27.7%	27.5%
Canandaigua Wine	17.7%	15.5%	14.8%
The Wine Group	9.7%	11.4%	14.6%
Beringer Wine Estates*	3.2%	2.5%	4.0%
Robert Mondavi Winery	3.2%	3.6%	3.8%
Next 3 Competitors	13.7%	11.9%	12.9%
Others	19.2%	27.4%	22.4%
Total	100.0%	100.0%	100.0%

*Named "Wine World Estates" in 1994

Source: *Adams Wine Handbook,* 1999.

marketing and capital investments. At the same time, the number of distributors is declining due to the consolidation, so the ability of smaller wineries to find distributors to carry the low volume wines can be negatively impacted.

Like all branded products, image is a very important aspect to the sale of wine. With the target market for wine being educated professionals in the upper income brackets, the image of a high quality, low volume winery can have great appeal. An example of this are the so called "garage wines" being produced in France. The volume being produced by the wineries is very low and the quality and image of the wine is very high. Those attributes coupled with the fact that the wines are very hard to acquire, creates a showpiece-like aura. It is not uncommon for these wines to sell for over $500 a bottle.[18] Thus, the ability of small wineries to find niche markets and exploit them based on quality and image is very important. It is can also be very advantageous for small wineries to build strong associations with specific cuisine, lifestyle traits and local distribution channels to help set themselves apart. The competitive environment that small wineries are subject to is harsh. One analyst states that small wineries "stay small or perish,"[19] due to the tremendous obstacles that it takes to scale up from a low volume producer to a large volume producer. Table 8 gives a breakdown for the market segments based on the retail price per bottle with the corresponding volumes and value for each segment. Despite the fact that the Ultra-premium wine segment has only seven percent of the volume shipped, it accounts for 25 percent of the revenue. So small wineries can be profitable in this segment if they can correctly target and penetrate niche markets.

U.S. Wine Industry Exporting

For the past 14 years the United States has seen huge gains in the total volume and value of its wine exports as referenced in Table 9. Table 10 provides a country breakdown

Table 8	Estimated 1999 California Table Wine Shipments by Price Class		
Retail Price per Bottle	Price Segment	Percent of Total Volume	Percent of Total Revenue
Over $14	Ultra-Premium	7%	25%
$7 to $14	Super-Premium	16%	27%
$3 to $7	Popular Premium	33%	31%
Below $3	Jug Wine and Others	44%	17%
Total		100%	100%

Source: Estimated by Gomberg, Fredrikson, and Associates. Excludes exports.

Table 9	U.S. Wine Exports	
Year	Volume (Millions of Gallons)	Value (Millions of Dollars)
1999	75.4	$548.0
1998	71.9	$537.0
1997	60	$425.0
1996	47.5	$326.0
1995	38.8	$241.0
1994	35.2	$196.0
1993	34.9	$182.0
1992	38.9	$181.0
1991	33.1	$153.0
1990	29	$137.0
1989	21.9	$98.0
1988	16.9	$85.0
1987	11.9	$61.0
1986	7.3	$35.0

Source: U.S. Dept. of Commerce, National Trade Data Bank. Copyright: Wine Institute

for bottled table wine. The major markets for U.S wines include the U.K., Canada, Japan, the Netherlands, and Switzerland. Together they represent 76.7 percent of the total export market value for the U.S. Countries like the Netherlands and Switzerland have higher then average growth rates because they tend to be distribution hubs for the rest of Europe. Table 11 also gives a breakdown on the U.S. export market, but gives a breakdown based on regions, not countries. It is quite obvious that the European Union is the major market for U.S. wines, Canada alone is in second place and all of Asia comprises the third position.

A majority of U.S. wineries have not had a long history of exporting for several reasons. First, the U.S. industry is very fragmented and a majority of the wineries do not have the resources to pursue international expansion. Second, the image of U.S. wines was poor until the 1976 Paris wine tasting competition, so the demand was not there. Third, the domestic market was still developing over the years, so it was possible to grow without incurring the added costs of establishing an international presence. Now that more and more companies are looking to the international market for expansion, exporting issues are now making a more important impact on the wine industry. Access to foreign markets has also been a challenge for wineries due to trade barriers as well as the local business practices and customs that pose a barrier for entry.

There are many obstacles to doing business on a global scale because of diverse economic environments and

Table 10 U.S. Bottled Table Wine Exports to Selected Countries and World Totals, 1997–1999, by Value ($000)

Country	1997	1998	% Change (97–98)	1999	% Change (98–99)
United Kingdom	$ 98,373	$134,509	37%	$122,187	-9%
Canada	$ 58,877	$ 68,909	17%	$ 68,950	0%
Japan	$ 20,702	$ 55,226	167%	$ 46,235	-16%
Netherlands	$ 7,782	$ 43,273	456%	$ 68,249	58%
Switzerland	$ 14,331	$ 18,797	31%	$ 21,026	12%
Germany	$ 22,082	$ 15,663	-29%	$ 12,947	-17%
Denmark	$ 6,968	$ 9,156	31%	$ 11,052	21%
Ireland	$ 6,599	$ 10,191	54%	$ 10,678	5%
Belgium	$ 5,205	$ 7,107	37%	$ 5,937	-16%
Sweden	$ 10,011	$ 12,130	21%	$ 9,196	-24%
France	$ 4,632	$ 7,059	52%	$ 5,758	-18%
Mexico	$ 1,944	$ 1,384	-29%	$ 2,820	104%
Taiwan	$ 13,334	$ 5,247	-61%	$ 4,197	-20%
Hong Kong	$ 8,676	$ 5,005	-42%	$ 3,331	-33%
Singapore	$ 2,515	$ 1,799	-28%	$ 2,964	65%
Finland	$ 2,746	$ 2,131	-22%	$ 2,395	12%
Norway	$ 1,844	$ 2,452	33%	$ 2,458	0%
South Korea	$ 2,123	$ 790	-63%	$ 1,480	87%
Netherlands Antilles	$ 1,126	$ 1,304	16%	$ 989	-24%
China	$ 927	$ 391	-58%	$ 1,040	166%
Thailand	$ 2,261	$ 173	-92%	$ 501	190%
Country Total	$293,058	$402,696	37%	$404,390	0%
Other Countries	$ 14,910	$ 17,961	20%	$ 21,399	19%
World Total	$307,968	$420,657	37%	$425,789	1%

Source: U.S. Dept. of Commerce, "National Trade Data Bank". Copyright: Wine Institute.

multi-national political issues that are frequently played out in the form of trade issues. Some of the most common trade issues that need to be addressed in the international market place are subsidies, monopolies and tariffs. Currently, there are many countries around the world that subsidize their local industries by giving them money for research, brand building, and exporting. Government monopolies of liqueur stores and over wine production are also seen in several countries around the world. These countries instigate monopolies to help protect local producers or because they are socialist countries where the government tries to gain revenue by taxing and controlling the sale of alcoholic beverages. High tariffs are also very common around the world and can often be used as a political tool, because they are relatively easy to implement and can be country specific. The implementation of the World Trade Organization (WTO) was designed to help alleviate some of these trade issues and help to foster a more open market system on a global scale. To a degree the WTO has succeeded in loosening up trade barriers, but here are still many out there that can limit companies' competitive abilities.

Asia and the Pacific Rim accounted for 21 percent of U.S exports by value in 1997 (Table 11). Japan, Hong Kong, and Taiwan were the major markets in the region accounting for 81 percent of the revenue. In 1997, Japan and Hong Kong had a 21 percent and 30 percent tariff on U.S. wines while Taiwan's government monopoly instigated a flat US$3.62 tax per liter. The result was that the U.S. wineries were only able to compete in the premium categories, even if the quality of the wine would not warrant that price class.

The European Union (EU) accounted for 49 percent of U.S exports by value in 1997 (Table 11), making the

Table 11   U.S. Wine Exports by Region, 1993–1997, Value (US$000)

Region	1993	1994	1995	1996	1997
European Union	$ 72,485	$ 68,447	$ 96,841	$151,160	$205,629
Canada	$ 47,271	$ 52,424	$ 53,784	$ 72,440	$ 79,124
Asia	$ 31,535	$ 37,270	$ 49,114	$ 57,078	$ 89,503
Other Europe	$ 5,084	$ 8,545	$ 14,646	$ 16,566	$ 20,677
Mexico	$ 5,456	$ 7,151	$ 2,816	$ 3,961	$ 3,550
Latin America	$ 5,162	$ 5,972	$ 6,948	$ 7,791	$ 8,142
Caribbean	$ 10,440	$ 10,477	$ 11,620	$ 13,393	$ 13,314
Eastern Europe & Russian Federation	$ 1,989	$ 3,091	$ 1,739	$ 1,831	$ 1,768
Africa	$ 855	$ 687	$ 533	$ 709	$ 1,028
Middle East	$ 319	$ 151	$ 154	$ 307	$ 687
Other	$ 1,350	$ 1,640	$ 2,918	$ 914	$ 1,705
Total	$182,287	$196,271	$241,640	$326,589	$425,127

Source: The Wine Institute, *International Trade Barriers Report,* 1998.

EU the largest market for U.S. wines. In 1997 the EU subsidized local wineries with $US1 Billion (with $85 million for exports) and the countries of Spain, France, and Italy gave out further subsidies. Furthermore, the 1983 "Wine Accords" agreement with the European Union, an agreement in which the European Union formally recognized some of the U.S. systems for making wine, did not formally accept all methods of production. Instead they grant, on a regular basis, temporary recognition of U.S. practices for making and branding wine.

Canada has one of the most regulated markets for wine in the world and trade issues include state monopoly of liqueur stores, subsidies for the limited local production of wine, and a distribution system that curtails the ability of foreign companies to market their products. In Mexico, sales have dropped due to a trade dispute over brooms. As a result, tariffs on U.S. wines have gone up and Mexico now has a zero tariff trade agreement with Chile, whose wine sales are on the rise.[20]

As a result of the international business dynamic, there are several export methods that are primarily used by wineries to get their products to market. To be successful at exporting, the wineries must choose the proper channel or mix of channels to support the brand image of their wine and to achieve the necessary return on investment.

Agents and Brokers

An agent is a person or firm that will take ownership of the product and then sell into channels that the agent has already established. It can be very advantageous for a winery to partner with an agent that has a well-established network that can support their brand image. There can be several disadvantages to this system as well, such as no control over the channel used, marketing plans implemented by the agent could be different then the wine producer wants, and the producer has no access to data about the markets and consumers that purchase the product. The wineries are also very susceptible to competitive actions like brand proliferation that can cause an agent to drop competing brands in favor of a better selling brand or larger supplier. The agent is interested in profit, not necessarily the market penetration strategy of a wine brand that they currently carry. A broker is the same as an agent only they do not take ownership of the product. As a result all the same advantages and disadvantages apply with one addition, that revenue for the product can be delayed until it is sold to a retail establishment.

Distributors/Importers

The distributors/importers are locally based channels that sell to companies such as grocery stores, discount warehouse superstores, and hotel/resorts. As they take on a more global strategy for delivering their products/services, they give their suppliers the advantage of being able to access many more markets then was previously possible. An example of how a distributor/importer can supply an advantage is, in Europe, customers are starting to shift their preference for purchasing wine from specialty stores to larger "hyper" stores and grocery stores. In the past wine sales used to be sold through specialty stores, now 47.9 percent of consumers prefer to buy from "hyper" or super markets and 60–70 percent of the wine sold in Europe now goes through this channel.[21] Correctly positioning wines with distributors/importers can give a winery a competitive advantage in the market. This will continue to be very important as distributors/importers continue on their trend of global consolidations.

Direct

In the domestic market this method can be accomplished in several different ways: the Internet, sales through wine clubs, and sales through the winery gift shop. In the international market the dynamics are more complicated because of government regulations that can restrict sales of alcohol over the internet or through the mail. Also, it is not financially practical for small wineries to try to establish stores in every market, so in the international market this method may be very hard to implement.

Joint Ventures

A very common occurrence in the wine industry, they can be implemented for several different strategic reasons. To gain access to local markets so that foreign companies can work from within to gain an understanding of the market, branding advantages by being associated with national brands that are already established, technology exchange (usually the other countries benefit), and to blend the local wine and U.S. bulk wine to circumvent the local import regulations, and access to established distribution channels.

The mix of channels for reaching consumers can vary greatly depending on the market strategy that the winery adopts and the market segments that the wineries want to target. The most common retail channels are supermarkets, mega-stores, restaurants, hotel/resorts, airlines, airports (wine bars and restaurants), duty-free shops, and high-end liquor stores. Wineries decide which channels to use depending on the image and market segment they want their wine to portray and on their marketing budgets. Premium wine brands tend to be targeted to upscale restaurants, resorts, and high end liquor stores while large scale producers target larger market segments that are served through supermarkets and mega-stores.

Profiles of Selected U.S. Exporters

In the U.S. domestic wine market in 1999 there were over 1600 wineries in operation. Most of those wineries have very low volume production capabilities, so a small number of large volume producers dominate the market. Despite the strengths and weaknesses that are dictated by the size of the companies versus their competition, every

company has a need to get their product to the market and their customers. The following section provides a summary of a few select companies that have long histories in the industry, how they have adopted different strategies to go after specific market segments, and how they have leveraged their domestic strategies to help them in the international market.

E & J Gallo Winery

The largest winemaker in the world, their production capacity in 1998 was roughly equivalent to that of Argentina (Table 12). They also produce approximately a third of all the bottled wine consumed in the United States. Founded in 1933 in Modesto, California by two brothers, Ernest and Julio Gallo. They adopted early on the strategy of having their sales force "push" for very visible places in liquor stores and grocery stores to help drive sales. The visibility that the displays gave the products worked very well and sales grew at a fast rate. Their ability to build market share based on branding is one of their most successful strategies.

In order to get more control over their costs and to help position their products in the retail markets, the Gallo's also did a lot of forward integration into the distribution channel. This forward integration was considered one of their greatest competitive strengths and complemented their ability to get visible floor space in retail establishments. They also did backward integration into the suppliers for bottling plants, foil producers as well as owning a significant portion of their vineyards. The Gallo's were also pioneers in the development of new wine production techniques and growing high quality grapes. The innovations made in those two areas, helped them to be able to produce a consistently high quality wine for low costs. This enabled them to capture a very large portion of the low-end table wine market. After establishing a dominant position in the lower price/high volume wine segment, the Gallo's made the move into the higher price/low volume premium markets by pur-

Table 12	Winery Production Capabilities (in Thousands of Gallons)
Company	Capacity
E & J Gallo	330,000
Beringer Estates	17,800
Robert Mondavi	17,387
Wente	5,100

Source: *Wines & Vines*, July 2000.

Table 13	Number of Brands in the Top 75 in the U.S., 1996 and 1998 (Based on Volume)			
Company	# in Top 75 1996	Highest Rank 1996	# in Top 75 1998	Highest Rank 1998
E & J Gallo Winery	11	1	17	2
Robert Mondavi Corporation	1	8*	2	8
Beringer Wine Estates	3	10	2	9
Wente	0	N/A	0	N/A

*Includes volumes for ALL domestically produced Mondavi Wines

Source: *Adams Wine Handbook* 1997 and 1999.

chasing land in Napa and creating several new brands. Their ability to make those brands successful is demonstrated in Table 13. Gallo was able to increase the number of brands that they had in the top 75 based on volume, from 11 in 1996 to 17 by 1998.

The Gallo's have always been very aggressive competitors in an industry that likes to consider itself a "Gentleman's" industry. They were sued by Kendall-Jackson for creating a label very similar to one of their best selling products, the case was eventually settled out of court. E & J Gallo is not a publicly owned company, it is still family owned, so no financial data is available. The third generation of the Gallo family is currently taking over the operations of the winery, and they are continuing to use the techniques used by Ernest and Julio that made the company the largest wine producer in the world.

E & J Gallo exports to an estimated 86 country markets, but focuses for the most part on major markets such as Great Britain, Japan, Canada and Germany. Gallo sold about 13 percent of its production overseas in 1997, which is more then all other California wineries combined based on total volume (Table 14). The forward and backward integration strategy that enabled the Gallo's to be so successful domestically, have became an integral part of their export strategy according to the San Francisco wine consulting firm Gomberg, Fredrikson &

Associates.[22] An example of this is the company had a front isle display at Harrods' new wine shop in London. In the United Kingdom approximately 3 out of 5 bottles of California wine are Gallo brands. Gallo demonstrated their commitment to the U.K. when they launched a brand named Garnet Point in 1998 that was supposed to be tailored to appeal to British tastes. On September 29, 2000 Gallo announced a strategic alliance with Wal-Mart that would consist of a brand called Alcott Ridge Vineyards being sold through that channel worldwide.[23]

Robert Mondavi Corporation

A niche player in the wine market, Mondavi focuses exclusively on the premium market segment. Mondavi's production capacity is substantial considering the size of the market segment that they sell into, but is very small compared to Gallo (Table 12). The company was founded in 1966 by Robert Mondavi after he was asked to leave his previous position as sales manager at a winery owned by his family. Robert Mondavi was reportedly such an excellent salesman that the winery his family operated could not increase the production of the wine to keep up with his sales. While Robert Mondavi was part of the family wine business, he helped to create and bring to market several innovations. The use of cold fermentation in the production of wine, which created a lighter and fruitier

Table 14	Top California Wine Exporters (Based on Volume)			
1997 Rank	Company	Selected Brands	Exports*	% of Total Sales
1	E & J Gallo	Gallo, Turning Leaf	17,555	13%
4	Robert Mondavi	Woodbridge, Mondavi	1,302	8%
11	Wente	Wente, Concannon	485	61%
12	Beringer Estates	Beringer, Meridian	345	3%

*in millions of gallons

Source: *San Francisco Chronicle* research.

taste enabled him to differentiate the wine from European and other California wines. Another innovation that Mondavi implemented was the use of French oak barrels. The barrels were used to age the wine in, and gave the wine a distinctive flavor to rival the French wines that were dominating the international market at the time. He was also responsible for the changing of the accepted naming convention. He did that by combining the French appellation and California varietal naming conventions. This elevated the brand image of his wines as being higher quality due to the associations with French wines and the region where his wines were produced, Napa Valley. When Robert Mondavi left the family winery, he took with him all of the innovations that he had previously implemented, and set forth with the strategy to create a winery that would produce only the finest wines. An example of his dedication to making only premium wines is the joint venture that was formed with Baron Phillippe de Rothschild of France to produce the Opus One label. Opus One is considered one of the finest wines in the world and retails for over $100 per bottle. Robert Mondavi, being a dynamic sales man, never spent money on advertising. Instead he relied on trade shows, awards, salesmanship, and showmanship. Mondavi constantly states that love of wine comes from a way of life, and that way of life involves fine dining, travel, and love for the arts.

Mondavi sells to an estimated 77 countries and positions its products in restaurants, hotels, and other locations where a person would expect to find a premium and ultra-premium wine. This strategy is in line with the lifestyle image that Mondavi wants to promote along with his wine. Exporting and growing the global premium wine market is a priority for Mondavi who expects to export a minimum of 20 percent of their production to the global market in the future according to the 2000 annual report.

The Robert Mondavi Corporation went public in 1993, but the family still owns 92 percent of the stock. Financial information from their annual reports can be found in

Table 15. Their focus on the premium market has been very successful with double-digit growth rates in Net Revenue every year except one in the time period of 1995–1999.

Beringer Wine Estates, Inc.

Like Mondavi, Beringer has a market focus on the premium segment and has high production capacity for that segment (Table 12). The company was founded by Jacob and Frederick Beringer, two brothers who emigrated from the Rhine Valley in Germany. Beringer is the oldest continuously operating winery in Napa Valley, with their first crush occurring in 1877. The brothers came to America like most immigrants because of the new opportunities that the United States offered. They gained notoriety, both locally and internationally, by the turn of the century due to their high quality wines.

In 1971 the Beringer winery was sold by the family to Nestle USA, Inc. because the company was under performing. The family did not re-invest in the vineyards or in the production process, so the quality of the wines that were being produced was low compared to the wines that made them famous. The operating name for the company given to them by Nestle was Wine World Estates. They took a long-term approach and built up production and vineyards. Once the company was turned around it was sold in 1996 for $350 million and Beringer Wine Estates Inc. was formed. Soon after Beringer did several more acquisitions, focused on the high-end, then went public in 1997. The company's financial data can be found in Table 16. Beringer consistently had double-digit growth rates for their Net Income in the time period of 1995–1999.

In the fall of 2000, Beringer Wine Estates was purchased by Fosters Brewing Group Limited, the Australian parent company of Fosters Lager. Fosters Brewing Group acquired Beringer for US$1.2 billion and will combine Beringer's portfolio of wines with their wine subsidiary, Mildara Blass Limited. According to a Beringer press release[24] the merger has resulted in

Table 15	Robert Mondavi Winery Financial Summary (All Data in Millions)				
	1995	1996	1997	1998	1999
Net Revenue	$199.5	$240.8	$300.8	$325.2	$370.6
Gross Profit	$ 93.0	$117.9	$151.0	$151.3	$169.7
Operating Income	$ 28.9	$ 47.2	$ 71.2	$ 61.3	$ 6.6
Net Income	$ 12.3	$ 24.1	$ 38.1	$ 30.2	$ 34.5
Volume (9-liter case equivalent)	4.5	5.4	6.5	6.8	7.6

Source: *Robert Mondavi Corporation Income Statement.*

Table 16   Beringer Wine Estates Financial Summary (All Data in Millions)

	1995	1996	1997	1998	1999
Net Revenue	$202.0	$231.7	$269.5	$318.4	$376.2
Adjusted Gross Profit	$100.7	$116.1	$134.9	$163.7	$194.6
Adjusted Operating Income	$ 34.8	$ 43.9	$ 56.3	$ 70.5	$ 83.0
Adjusted Net Income	$ 16.8	$ 15.6	$ 15.1	$ 29.5	$ 39.3
Volume (9-liter case equivalent)	4.6	5	5.4	6.1	6.8
Total Assets	$289.9	$438.7	$467.2	$543.6	$644.3
Total Debt	N/A	$289.2	$319.1	$277.2	$328.0

Source: *Beringer Wine Estates 1999 Annual Report.*

making the largest premium wine company in the world with a combined revenue of $886 million in fiscal year 2000. Mildara Blass currently has 25 percent of the premium wine market in Australia and their main export markets are the United States, the U.K., and Europe. By purchasing a U.S. winery, Fosters Brewing Company Limited now has access to a broader distribution system with the purchase of Beringers, and can now leverage the U.S. system for the Australian produced wines and the Australian distribution system with the California wines. The result should be delivering a broader product line that appeals to more market segments with increased customer satisfaction and market share. For companies trying to break into a foreign market, establishing a distribution system can be very difficult to achieve due to the specialized knowledge of the market that is needed as well as the capital investment.

Wente

A family owned company that was founded in the Livermore Valley, California in 1885. Unlike the other companies previously discussed, Wente has long held to a strategy that focuses more on the export market then on the domestic market. Wente sells to an estimated 160 country markets and exported about 61 percent of their total production capacity in 1997 (Table 12). They implement specific marketing strategies on a country-by-country basis.[25] They do not focus on a few larger markets with limited service to smaller markets like their larger competitors. Instead, they have taken on more of a market development strategy that the company feels will lead to future opportunities, but in the mean time it also gives them many hurdles to leap.

A few examples of some of the distribution channels that Wente utilizes include opening wine bars in airports from Africa to the Pacific Rim. They are the number one

wine retailer in the world through duty-free shops in airports and they have created special gift boxes that contain French wines specifically for that channel to help drive sales. Wente also claims that they sell to more airlines then any other winery in the world with a focus in Asia and the Pacific Rim. The airlines include Thai Airways, All Nippon Airways, Singapore, Philippine, Cathay Pacific, Malaysian, Vietnam, Garuda, as well as Delta and United flights in the Pacific Rim. Wente invested heavily in the 1980's building up distributor relations in Japan. It paid off when a Japanese news program ran a segment that stated the health benefits of wine and they sold out their entire stock on hand. Wente also leverages traditional distribution channels and sells through restaurants, liquor stores, and hotels in the Chinese market.

Wente has formed many joint ventures throughout the world. Sometimes the joint ventures are in traditional markets with established wineries to help produce premium wines, other times the joint venture takes on more of a problem solving role to get access to local markets. A joint venture between Wente and Luigi Cecchi and Sons of Italy was made to produce an ultra-premium wine to be sold in the U.S. domestic market by 2003. Another joint venture was established with an Israeli winery named Segal Winery to produce a kosher wine. Examples of joint ventures formed to get access to foreign markets include a joint venture in India with The Indage Group to become the first company to import into the Indian market. The deal is not exclusive and the Indage group will also soon be entering into joint ventures with French and German wineries. The agreement stipulates that the foreign partners must export Indage wine to other markets and that all bottling of wine to be sold into India must be done locally. That was the only way the Indian government would allow the joint ventures to operate.[26] By arranging the joint venture that way, the government could offset the import and export credits between the participating countries. Another joint venture was formed with Bodegas de Santo Tomas, a Mexican winery, to sell a brand named Duetto in the United States and Mexico. The joint venture was formed to get around high import tariffs established by Mexico in retaliation for the American government penalizing Mexican companies for dumping cheap brooms in the U.S. market. Shipping bottled wine to Mexican markets became too expensive to compete in the local markets, so Wente started shipping bulk wine to Bodegas de Santo Tomas. The wine was then blended and bottled locally in Mexico to get around the import costs.[27]

Some other examples of problems that Wente has experienced in the foreign markets include having to pull out of Myanmar due to political pressure, pulling out of Russia when the currency collapsed, and marketing varietal wines in Africa to non-traditional foods such as zebra and antelope.[28]

Future Direction

With the competitive nature of the global wine market increasing, U.S. wineries will have a greater challenge competing in both the domestic and export markets. U.S. wineries have many strategic issues confronting them in the export market in particular. Given that the domestic market faces increasing pressure, the export markets take on an even greater strategic importance for U.S. wineries.

Notes

1. California Wine Export Program; "United States Wine Exports, Imports and Balance of U.S. Wine Trade 1999," Ivie International; 24 July 2000.
2. *Monterey County Herald*; "Monterey County, Calif., Wine Exports Increase," Monterey, Ca.; 14 November 1998.
3. Wine Vision, *American Wine in the 21st Century*, 6 July 2000.
4. University of Pennsylvania; Museum of Archaeology and Anthropology Web site; October 2000.
5. Britannica.com;search on wine; October 2000.
6. *Strategy 2025: The Australian Wine Industry*; Australian Wine Foundation; June 1996.
7. Franson, Paul. "U.S. Wineries Consider Long-Term Strategy to Maintain Competitiveness," Vineyard & Winery Management, May/June 1999.
8. *Strategy 2025: The Australian Wine Industry*; Australian Wine Foundation; June 1996.
9. Nicholson, Robert M. "New World Wine Exporters continued growth in '99," *Wines & Vines* July 2000.
10. Ibid.
11. Ibid.
12. Durkan, Andrew and Cousins, John. *Wine Appreciation* (NTC Publishing Group; Chicago, Il.), 1995.
13. *Strategy 2025: The Australian Wine Industry*; Australian Wine Foundation; June 1996.
14. Cartiere, Richard. "New World Global Wine Boom Shows No Sign of Faltering," *Wine Market Report*, 16 May 2000.
15. Koerber, Kristine. "Fueling Increased," *Wine Business Monthly* VII, no. 5 (May 2000).
16. *Adam Wine Handbook* (Adam Business Media, New York), 1999.
17. Cartiere, Richard. "New World Global Wine Boom Shows No Sign of Faltering," *Wine Market Report*, 16 May 2000.
18. Prial, Frank. "Controversy swirls around $1,000 garage wines," *New York Times*, 25 October 2000.
19. "On Your Mark-Get Set-Consolidate," *Wine Business Insider* 10, Issue 35 (2 September 2000).
20. Clawson, James B., Boone, Jeannie and Atkinson, Alan. *International Trade Barriers Report 1998* (JBC International; Washington D.C.), May 1998.
21. "Globalization, Who's leading the way?" *Wines & Vines* (April 2000).
22. Sinton, Peter. "California Wines Quenching in the World / Exports from the states have doubled in the past five years," *San Francisco Chronicle*, 23 January 1999.
23. Wal-Mart Press Release, 29 September 2000.
24. Beringer Wine Estates Press Release, 28 August 2000.
25. Sinton, Peter. "California Wines Quenching in the World / Exports from the states have doubled in the past five years," *San Francisco Chronicle*, 23 January 1999.
26. "Vintners uncork Indian market," *South China Morning Post* (Hong Kong), 21 March 1999.
27. "Multicultural Wine//Trade: A new red is being made with grapes from Northern California and Baja. The blend skirts Mexican tariffs," *Orange County Register*, 19 September 1998.
28. Sinton, Peter. "California Wines Quenching in the World / Exports from the states have doubled in the past five years," *San Francisco Chronicle*, 23 January 1999.

Reference Notes

Sawyer, Abby and Hammett, Jim. "American Appellations Earn Distinction as a Marketing Tool," *Wine Business Monthly* (June).

Johnson, Hugh. "All about Wine," www.reedbooks.co.uk.

Elliott-Fisk, Deborah. *The Geography of Soils* (University of California).

Marketing Intelligence Services Ltd.; "Gallo Garnet Point Wine," 21 September 1998.

Courtney, Kevin and Carson, L. Pierce. "Q & A, what he did right-and wrong- in the creation of his world wine empire," *Napa Valley Register*, 21 October 1998.

Beverage Industry; "Brown-Forman Taps Wines From Down Under," December 1999.

Duty-Free News International; "Wente and Bichot forge new partnership," 15 December 1999.

"California Vintners try to quench China's thirst for wine," *Contra Costa Times* (Walnut Creek, Ca.), 10 October 1997.

"California's Wente Vineyards halts shipments to Myanmar," *Contra Costa Times* (Walnut Creek, Ca.), 8 November 1996.

Impact; "Wente Bros," 15 December 1995.

Brown-Forman Corporation Annual Report 2000.

Case 13

The Department of Justice Versus Microsoft

Neil H. Snyder and Hilary Ritter, *University of Virginia*

A debate has developed in the United States over the application of antitrust laws, enacted to combat the monopolies of the 19th century, to powerful firms in high technology industries.[1] In the 19th century, firms employed a variety of tactics to insulate themselves from competition. Companies such as Standard Oil, which produced 90 percent of crude oil at the turn of the century, controlled enormous market share, vast financial resources, and the origin of raw materials. While the nature of high technology firms differs from that of the original trusts, their market power may be just as great and perhaps more durable.[2]

History of Antitrust Legislation

In 1890, Congress passed the Sherman Antitrust Act. This act makes it unlawful for companies to attempt to monopolize. A monopoly may be achieved through the specific intent to control prices or destroy competition, predatory conduct directed to accomplishing the unlawful purpose, and/or a dangerous probability of success.[3] If a firm engages in exclusionary activities to dominate a market, it is an unlawful monopoly. However, if a firm demonstrates superior skill and energy, an antitrust violation has not occurred, and the company is a lawful monopoly.[4]

The Sherman Act addresses actual, demonstrable harm to consumers. For example, the Act was aimed at protecting America's farmers from being charged high prices by large industrial combinations; it was also utilized to "bust" the Standard Oil trust in 1911.[5] Passed in 1914, the Clayton Act was designed to complement the Sherman Act and continue to promote competition. This Act dealt specifically with "mergers that tend to lessen competition or create a monopoly."[6] The mission of this act was to prevent possible or hypothetical harm to consumers, rather than to remedy actual damage.[7] This modification of antitrust law thrust the federal government into the occupation of market prognostication, and it becomes difficult to gauge whether consumer welfare is protected. By blocking a particular merger, for example, the government may claim that it averted disaster for consumers; however, the alternate result is unknown. It is an inherently uncertain process.[8]

Various federal court cases can be used as precedents in the application of antitrust law to high-tech firms such as Microsoft. In *United States v. E.I. duPont de Nemours and Company*, the Supreme Court identified monopoly power as "the power to control prices or exclude competition." Therefore, a monopolist is a company that can significantly heighten barriers to entry within a market. Another important precedent is *United States v. Griffith*, in which a monopolist is bound from using its dominance in one field as leverage to establish a monopoly in another.[9]

The Supreme Court did recognize the difference between lawful and unlawful monopolies. In *United States v. Grinnell Corporation*, the unlawful use of monopoly power involves "the possession of monopoly power in the relevant market and the willful acquisition or maintenance of that power as distinguished from growth or development as the consequent of a superior product, business acumen, or historic accident." The Supreme Court defined a "superior product" in *Berkey Photo, Inc. v. Eastman Kodak Co.* as one for which there is sufficient demand that warrants its production worthwhile to the consumer. "So long as the free choice of the consumers is preserved," the response to the product "can only be inferred from the reaction of the market." Monopolization, therefore, is not illegal; the use of monopoly power to prevent competition is.

How these precedents and antitrust law in general are applied to Microsoft, and other firms in high technology industries, will have a profound effect on the nature of competition, consumer welfare, and the structure of the national economy in the upcoming century.[10]

Microsoft was founded on April 4, 1975 by William H. Gates and Paul G. Allen as a Basic programming language shop.[11] Microsoft was incorporated on June 25,1981; in the same year, the company acquired the DOS operating system from Seattle Computer. They leased this technology to IBM for $50,000, and Microsoft's Disk Operating System (MS-DOS) debuted with IBM's personal computer.[12] Microsoft held its public offering in 1986. Throughout Microsoft's 22 year history, the computer industry evolved with the development of Microsoft products and services. Exhibit 1 highlights the major accomplishments achieved by Microsoft in the company's short history.

Microsoft Competitors

It has been claimed by competitors that the practices of Microsoft will prove a detriment to consumers, as its dominant position may allow for price increases and decreased innovation. In fact, the government's case deepened as a result of pressure from these competitors, rather than from the consumers that the laws are meant to protect.[13] Several companies and trade associations have formed a coalition, called the Project to Promote Competition and Innovation in the Digital Age ("ProComp"). The purpose of this organization is to mount an aggressive lobbying campaign against Microsoft to further pressure federal and state regulators to broaden their case against the software giant.[14]

Netscape Communications Corporation is a prominent member of the group. Their main contention involves the bundling of the Internet Explorer with Microsoft's Windows operating system, which is installed on more than 90 percent of the world's personal computers.[15] Executives from Netscape argue that computer makers will be reluctant to include other Internet browsers if Windows software is already equipped with a browser.[16] Robert Bork, former federal appellate court judge and retained counsel for Netscape, claims that Microsoft includes a programming code in their operating system "that makes it difficult to use competitors' [Internet] browsers, specifically Netscape's."[17]

The browser war between Netscape and Microsoft has been targeted as the major reason for Netscape's fourth-quarter earnings loss of $85 million. Daniel Rimer, an analyst with Hambrecht & Quist Inc., estimates that Netscape earned $110 million in 1997 from the sale of its web browser; by the fourth quarter, however, revenues from browser sales accounted for only $17 million, a reduction in $52 million from the same period a year prior. Rimer predicts that by June 1998, Netscape will have zero earnings from browser sales if the current trend continues.[18] Microsoft currently offers the Internet Explorer browser at no charge, which recently forced Netscape to do the same.

While Netscape currently retains an edge over Microsoft in the browser market, the software giant's share in the market increased 19 percent in the fourth quarter of 1996 (Exhibit 2).[19] This success convinced Netscape to also offer its browser at no charge. The dominance and lucrative nature (profit margins of 24 percent in 1997) of Microsoft software and business application products are such that it can afford to give away software in markets it does not control, such as browsers, to gain market share. Aggressive tactics like this threatens the existence of rival companies such as Netscape, which has felt losses as a result of the Microsoft challenge.[20] The combination of a technically sound, free product with wide availability has challenged Netscape's market position and caused the firm to question whether Microsoft is using its dominance in operating systems to leverage a monopoly in the Internet market.[21]

Sun Microsystems, another member of ProComp, is also challenging various business practices of Microsoft. Sun developed a product called Java, which is used to write software that can be used on a wide variety of computers, regardless of the operating system. This language is very useful in the development of feature rich Web publishing.[22] Microsoft recently released a version of Java that works exclusively with the Windows operating system or Apple Macintosh computers, contending that Java programs work best when configured for particular operating systems.[23] Microsoft has gone so far as to offer programmers new software "tools" that encourage the use of the Microsoft-friendly Java version. As with Netscape, Sun believes that Microsoft is attempting to use its dominance in PC operating systems to leverage control of computer programming technology. Rob Enderle, an analyst with Giga Information Systems, acknowledges that "Microsoft is attempting to take control of Java. The primary place that Java [applications] run today is on the PC desktop."[24] Exhibits 3 and 4 show company snapshots for both Sun Microsystems and Microsoft.

However, Sun's primary focus is not only the struggle over the integrity of the software market; it is also a struggle over profits. Analysts expect the battle between Sun and Microsoft for lucrative contracts from corporate customers to increase over the next two years. Each has a network operating system (NOS) that appeals to the corporate audience—Microsoft is poised to release its Windows NT 5.0 operating system with complementary software; Sun has its own software called Solaris (a version of Unix), a chip, called UltraSPARC, and a variety of sophisticated workstations and servers.[25] Sun fears that

Exhibit 1   Microsoft Milestones

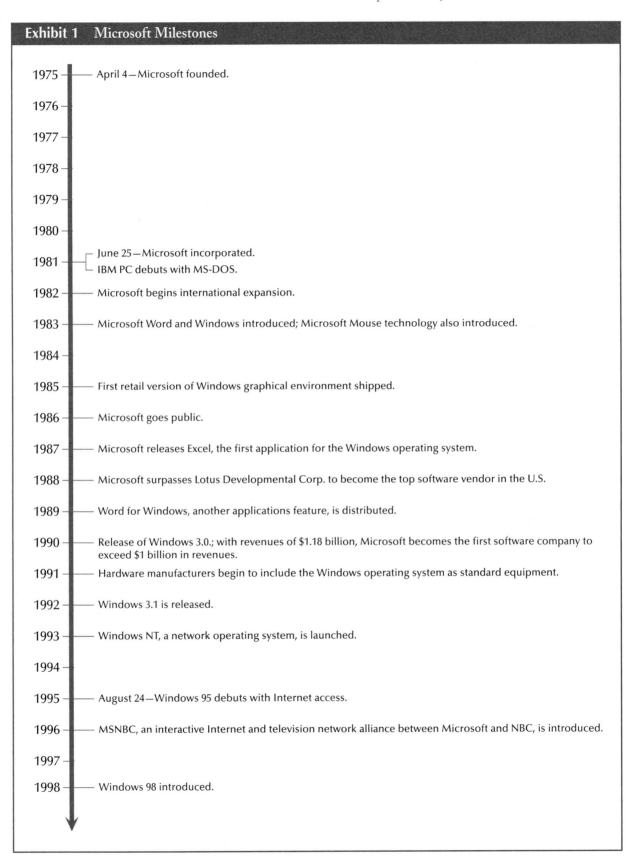

1975 — April 4—Microsoft founded.

1976

1977

1978

1979

1980

1981 — June 25—Microsoft incorporated.
       IBM PC debuts with MS-DOS.

1982 — Microsoft begins international expansion.

1983 — Microsoft Word and Windows introduced; Microsoft Mouse technology also introduced.

1984

1985 — First retail version of Windows graphical environment shipped.

1986 — Microsoft goes public.

1987 — Microsoft releases Excel, the first application for the Windows operating system.

1988 — Microsoft surpasses Lotus Developmental Corp. to become the top software vendor in the U.S.

1989 — Word for Windows, another applications feature, is distributed.

1990 — Release of Windows 3.0.; with revenues of $1.18 billion, Microsoft becomes the first software company to exceed $1 billion in revenues.

1991 — Hardware manufacturers begin to include the Windows operating system as standard equipment.

1992 — Windows 3.1 is released.

1993 — Windows NT, a network operating system, is launched.

1994

1995 — August 24—Windows 95 debuts with Internet access.

1996 — MSNBC, an interactive Internet and television network alliance between Microsoft and NBC, is introduced.

1997

1998 — Windows 98 introduced.

Exhibit 2 Market Share of Browsers	
Netscape	57%
Microsoft	31%
Other	12%

Source: *Web Week,* 3 March 1997.

Exhibit 3 Sun Microsystems: Company Snapshot		
Revenues	$ millions	8,598
	% change from 1996	21.2
Profits	$ millions	762
	% change from 1996	60.0
Assets	$ millions	4,697
Stockholder's Equity	$ millions	2,742
Market Value	$ millions 3/18/97	16,614.1
Profits as % of	Revenues	8.9
	Assets	16.2
	Stockholder's Equity	27.8
Earnings per Share	1997 $	1.96
	% change from 1996	62.0
	1987–97 annual growth rate (%)	30.3
Total Return to Investors	1997 (%)	55.2
	1987–97 annual rate (%)	25.3

Figures are for fiscal year ended June 30, 1997.

Microsoft's dominance in the PC market will cause programmers to use the software giant's version of Java, making Sun's technology undesirable or obsolete. Microsoft's Windows NT is gaining market share, while its competitors are losing share or just maintaining their current market position.

Sun has filed suit against Microsoft in federal court, alleging that Microsoft's inclusion of a version of Java in its Windows operating system is in direct violation of the contract that exists between the two firms. The suit is still pending. Currently, Sun is working towards a "100% pure" version of Java, the proliferation of which may reduce the need to buy Windows-equipped computers.[26]

James Barksdale, CEO of Netscape, and Scott McNealy, CEO of Sun, are calling for a vigorous application of antitrust law against their competitor, whom they accuse of using its market dominance to control commerce and content on the Internet and to govern software for emerging technologies.[27] Executives of both Netscape and Sun agree that existing laws are adequate to address their concerns over Microsoft; however, they are quick to discourage the federal government from regulating the freewheeling computer industry.[28] Jim Barksdale, CEO of Netscape Communications, agrees with Gates in that "[New legislation and regulations] are not needed. And I think it would have a harmful effect."[29] It seems that perhaps it is concerns over their business, rather than concern for the consumer, that is driving the campaigns of competitors. However, antitrust law was enacted to protect the consumer, not the competitor.

Consumer Advocacy Groups

Various industry groups, such as the aforementioned ProComp and a more secretive coalition called the Council for a Competitive Electronic Marketplace,[30] have been established to combat Microsoft and to pressure the federal government to broaden their antitrust investigation of the software giant. Consumer Advocacy groups and individuals have also joined the campaign against Microsoft, the most vocal of which is Ralph Nader. Nader claims that regulation against the software giant would benefit the consumer through increased competition and innovation. Nader claims that Microsoft has historically borrowed or bought technology (Exhibit 5), and is no example of innovation, yet the firm's operating system runs nearly 90 percent of personal computers. Microsoft's domination of desktop software applications has allowed a decreased number of new entrants or new products into this market, which has also served to decrease innovation. The creation of a Java version that is only compatible with the Windows operating system damages the idea that the same software may run on different computers, and further permits Microsoft to exercise the same type of control over MS Java Applications as it does over Windows applications. Nader also claims that the offering of the Internet Explorer for free is an attempt to leverage control of the browser market, which would give Microsoft control over standards for Internet publishing and electronic commerce. The navigation of the information superhighway will occur through strategically linked products, services, partners, and subsidiaries of Microsoft. Nader maintains that such actions are predatory and exclusionary to rivals, and are therefore monopolistic and detrimental to consumers.[31]

Exhibit 4   Microsoft: Company Snapshot

Revenues	$ millions	11,358
	% change from 1996	31.0
Profits	$ millions	3,454
	% change from 1996	57.4
Assets	$ millions	14,387
Stockholder's Equity	$ millions	10,777
Market Value	$ millions 3/18/97	199,046.4
Profits as % of	Revenues	30.4
	Assets	24.0
	Stockholders' Equity	32.0
Earnings per Share	1997 $	2.63
	% change from 1996	53.4
	1987–97 annual growth rate (%)	43.3
Total Return to Investors	1997 (%)	56.4
	1987–97 annual rate (%)	45.6

Figures are for fiscal year ended June 30, 1997.

Nader contends that such practices, and the subsequent dominance by Microsoft, will deter venture capitalists from funding any endeavor that may compete with Microsoft. Such an occurrence would stifle innovation. Nader further maintains that Microsoft is engaging in predatory pricing in an attempt to drive Netscape out of the browser business and discourage the entry of potential competitors. Predatory pricing refers to the practice of giving away a product below cost, or in the case of Microsoft's Internet Explorer, for free, to eliminate competitors. When the competitor(s) become obsolete, the firm engaged in this tactic then dramatically increases the price of the product to realize a return on their investment. This is the situation Nader claims Microsoft has created, at a detriment to the consumer.[32]

The Senate

On November 4, 1997, the Senate Judiciary Committee held a hearing on "competition, innovation, and public policy and the digital age," a hearing which provided an opportunity for Microsoft competitors to issue many allegations against the software giant. A statement issued by the committee said, "Given the committee's jurisdiction over antitrust and intellectual property law and policy, we would be remiss in carrying out our responsibilities were we not to examine the proper role for antitrust enforcement in high technology markets. Microsoft, as an industry leader, naturally will be one company whose market power and practices will receive some scrutiny."[33] The committee claims the hearings are part of an effort to examine the applicability of existing antitrust laws, originally written in the age of the railroad and steel monopolies, to the fast-changing and economically different field of software.[34] The focus of the Senate's inquiry is the soon-to-be released Windows 98, in which the Internet Explorer browser will be integrated.[35] Legal specialists say that the Senate inquiry may further pressure the Justice Department to broaden its case against Microsoft.[36]

Particular senators have found themselves embroiled in the battle between Microsoft and its competitors. Senator Orrin Hatch (R-Utah), Chairman of the Senate Judiciary Committee, is spearheading the campaign against Microsoft; he also represents the home state of a Microsoft competitor, Novell Inc.[37] Hatch has branded the software giant a monopoly, and recommends that the DOJ expand its case.[38] Disputing Sen. Hatch's claims is the congressman from Microsoft's home state, Senator Slade Gorton (R-Washington). Sen. Gorton questions whether the committee chairman can remain impartial and uphold his pledge to be fair to Microsoft in light of Sen. Hatch's vocal public skepticism of Microsoft.[39] As Chairman of the Senate Judiciary Committee, Hatch may pressure the DOJ to pursue a more vigorous antitrust investigation of Microsoft's businesses practices.[40]

The Department of Justice

Federal investigation into the business practices of Microsoft began in 1990, when the Federal Trade Commission questioned the firm for possible violations of the Sherman and Clayton Antitrust Acts. The Department of Justice (DOJ) formally undertook the case against Microsoft in 1993, alleging that the software giant has a monopoly in the operating systems market, which has been cemented through unlawful exercises of power. To avoid a lengthy and possibly losing battle, Microsoft agreed to sign a consent agreement with the DOJ in 1995 that addressed their illegal pricing policies and restrictive licensing and non-disclosure agreements.[41] The consent decree also disallowed Microsoft from using its dominance in the PC operating systems market to create additional monopolies.[42] However, the investigation into Microsoft's leverage into the markets of software development and on-line services continued. The DOJ also continued to investigate Microsoft's alleged use of vaporware, a term that refers to

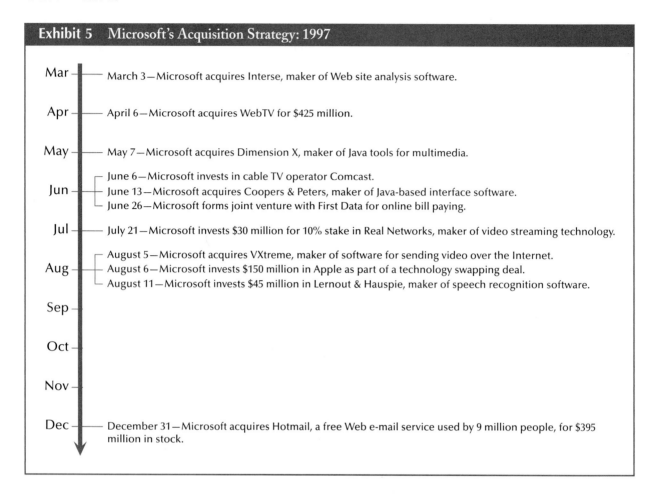

Exhibit 5   Microsoft's Acquisition Strategy: 1997

Mar — March 3—Microsoft acquires Interse, maker of Web site analysis software.

Apr — April 6—Microsoft acquires WebTV for $425 million.

May — May 7—Microsoft acquires Dimension X, maker of Java tools for multimedia.

Jun — June 6—Microsoft invests in cable TV operator Comcast.
June 13—Microsoft acquires Coopers & Peters, maker of Java-based interface software.
June 26—Microsoft forms joint venture with First Data for online bill paying.

Jul — July 21—Microsoft invests $30 million for 10% stake in Real Networks, maker of video streaming technology.

Aug — August 5—Microsoft acquires VXtreme, maker of software for sending video over the Internet.
August 6—Microsoft invests $150 million in Apple as part of a technology swapping deal.
August 11—Microsoft invests $45 million in Lernout & Hauspie, maker of speech recognition software.

Sep

Oct

Nov

Dec — December 31—Microsoft acquires Hotmail, a free Web e-mail service used by 9 million people, for $395 million in stock.

---

the announcement of products far prior to their release date to prevent consumers from purchasing competing products currently offered.[43]

In October 1997, the Justice Department filed suit against Microsoft, alleging that the company violated terms of the 1995 consent decree by forcing computer producers such as Compaq and Dell to install its Internet Explorer browser as a condition of licensing its Windows operating system. On December 11, 1997, U.S. District Judge Thomas Penfield Jackson issued a preliminary injunction against Microsoft, forcing the company to temporarily halt the practice of requiring computer manufacturers to install the Internet Explorer on its computers, until further investigation determines the legal implications of the practice. Throughout the investigation, it has been the contention of the DOJ that Microsoft is using its dominant position in the PC operating systems market to leverage control of the browser market, thereby stifling competing technologies and innovation.[44]

The pressure from Microsoft competitors and consumer advocates has caused the DOJ to broaden its investigation. This extended inquiry focuses on the accusation

that Microsoft is engaged in a variety of insidious practices to gain monopoly control over the Internet itself.[45] Such control may harm the consumers, in that Microsoft's dominant position would allow it to raise prices or prevent innovation. Further, the full integration of Internet Explorer into the Windows operating system, and the subsequent exclusive deals made with content providers, could allow Microsoft control over the information accessed over the Internet.[46] Exhibit 6 highlights the major steps involved in the investigation and subsequent suit filed.

Since 1994, American computer and software companies have accounted for the 30 percent increase in the country's gross domestic product. The industry's explosive growth has enabled the US to regain a supremacy in the global marketplace. The high-tech industry is the economic success story of the 1990's, and the driving force behind it is Microsoft, whose $3.4 billion in net income accounted for 41 percent of the profits of the ten largest publicly traded software companies.[47] It is this pervasiveness in the market that raises questions as to whether the Justice Department has a responsibility to limit the economic power a single company can exert over an

Exhibit 6   Major Legal Developments in Microsoft's Antitrust Disputes with the Department of Justice

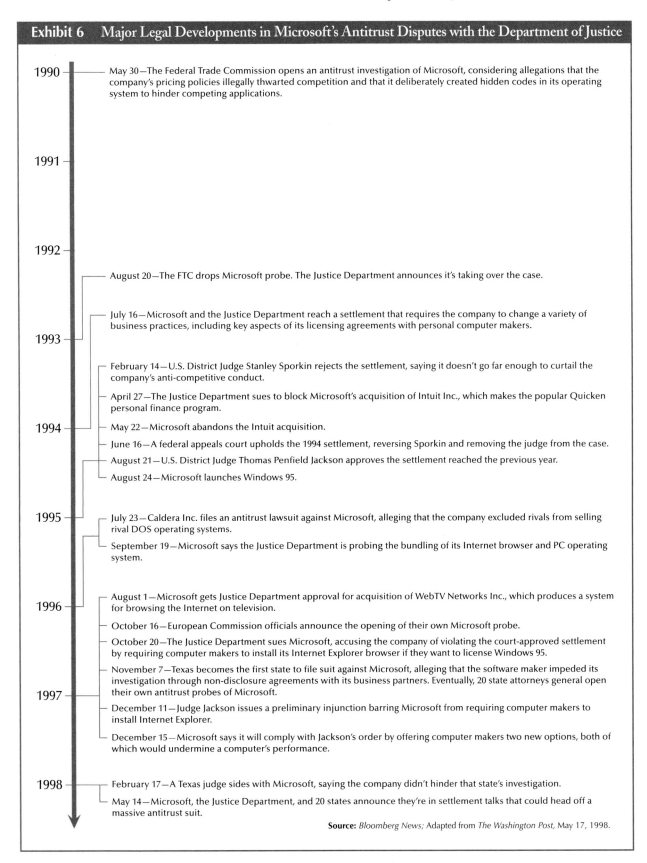

1990 — May 30—The Federal Trade Commission opens an antitrust investigation of Microsoft, considering allegations that the company's pricing policies illegally thwarted competition and that it deliberately created hidden codes in its operating system to hinder competing applications.

1991

1992

August 20—The FTC drops Microsoft probe. The Justice Department announces it's taking over the case.

July 16—Microsoft and the Justice Department reach a settlement that requires the company to change a variety of business practices, including key aspects of its licensing agreements with personal computer makers.

1993

February 14—U.S. District Judge Stanley Sporkin rejects the settlement, saying it doesn't go far enough to curtail the company's anti-competitive conduct.

April 27—The Justice Department sues to block Microsoft's acquisition of Intuit Inc., which makes the popular Quicken personal finance program.

1994 — May 22—Microsoft abandons the Intuit acquisition.

June 16—A federal appeals court upholds the 1994 settlement, reversing Sporkin and removing the judge from the case.

August 21—U.S. District Judge Thomas Penfield Jackson approves the settlement reached the previous year.

August 24—Microsoft launches Windows 95.

1995 — July 23—Caldera Inc. files an antitrust lawsuit against Microsoft, alleging that the company excluded rivals from selling rival DOS operating systems.

September 19—Microsoft says the Justice Department is probing the bundling of its Internet browser and PC operating system.

1996 — August 1—Microsoft gets Justice Department approval for acquisition of WebTV Networks Inc., which produces a system for browsing the Internet on television.

October 16—European Commission officials announce the opening of their own Microsoft probe.

October 20—The Justice Department sues Microsoft, accusing the company of violating the court-approved settlement by requiring computer makers to install its Internet Explorer browser if they want to license Windows 95.

November 7—Texas becomes the first state to file suit against Microsoft, alleging that the software maker impeded its investigation through non-disclosure agreements with its business partners. Eventually, 20 state attorneys general open their own antitrust probes of Microsoft.

1997 — December 11—Judge Jackson issues a preliminary injunction barring Microsoft from requiring computer makers to install Internet Explorer.

December 15—Microsoft says it will comply with Jackson's order by offering computer makers two new options, both of which would undermine a computer's performance.

1998 — February 17—A Texas judge sides with Microsoft, saying the company didn't hinder that state's investigation.

May 14—Microsoft, the Justice Department, and 20 states announce they're in settlement talks that could head off a massive antitrust suit.

Source: *Bloomberg News;* Adapted from *The Washington Post,* May 17, 1998.

industry. The challenge for the DOJ is to apply antitrust legislation written in the age of railroad and oil monopolies to fast-changing software technology industry.[48]

The DOJ may employ one of three strategies, each of which represents a main strand of anti-trust law. Antitrust policy has historically relied upon market forces, policing conduct, or major structural changes to protect competition. The first option is to leave Microsoft be. The second utilizes regulatory solutions which would restrict the firm's behavior and allow competitors a better chance for survival. The third alternative is the break up of Microsoft into two distinct companies.[49]

The DOJ must tread lightly, however, as any government action may handicap the nation's most dynamic economic sector.[50] The option to leave Microsoft alone protects the economy from this threat. In order to regulate Microsoft, the DOJ must establish that consumers have been harmed as a result of Microsoft's business practices, despite whether the firm has behaved illegally or is deemed so powerful that it stifles competition. Microsoft's current position is, in large part, a result of competing harder and smarter than its competitors. At present, the business practices of Microsoft are not hurting consumers, the economy, or causing a lack of innovation in the computer industry. Statistics support this contention. In 1997, 191 software companies were founded, twice as many as in 1990. Industry revenues rose from $39 billion in 1990 to $122 billion in 1997. The Windows operating system and the Windows NT programs have established economies of scale for PC makers, reducing the price of desktop computers from $2,192 in 1996 to $1,863 in 1998, a reduction of 15 percent.[51] These systems have also cultivated a prosperous software applications industry. As the industry's standard, Windows provides applications, companies, and programmers a mammoth market for their products.[52] Robert P. Taylor, law partner at Howrey & Simon in Menlo Park, California, argues against regulation, stating that, "The notion that we can make a system better that is functioning perfectly well should be viewed with skepticism."[53]

The computer industry is such that a seismic technological change occurs that alters the industry rules and shifts the balance of power. The most recent such event occurred in the 1980's, when IBM failed to anticipate the PC revolution and Microsoft rose to dominance.[54] History suggests that no one computing company will dominate for long; however, the industry has never dealt with ultra-competitiveness like that of Bill Gates. Critics argue that Microsoft has engaged in questionable business practices in order to gain increased market share, and that they have used their dominance in operating systems to leverage power in related markets. For example, by distributing the Internet

Explorer browser for free, Microsoft has garnered 37 percent of the Internet browser market in just three years. Microsoft is also including a Web server and other applications for free with the Windows NT system to corporate customers. Formidable competition is difficult, and in the absence of this there is no guarantee that Microsoft will not dramatically increase prices. Worries over such present and potential power make the "laissez faire" option unlikely.[55]

Therefore, the DOJ is considering employing a series of "surgical strikes"—lawsuits aimed at specific anticompetitive practices. This strategy is composed of four major remedies, each targeting a specific unfair act. The first is the "Fair Contract Remedy," consisting of guidelines that would limit Microsoft's ability to deter corporate partners from selling competitors' products through exclusionary deals. The "On Ramp Remedy" addresses Microsoft's practice of giving its own services and content priority spots on Windows. With Windows as the dominant operating system, it is the gateway to the Information Superhighway, and would give Microsoft the opportunity to dictate Internet content. The DOJ believes that such a remedy would promote competition among Internet-content companies.

The third guideline is called the "A La Carte Remedy," which would require Microsoft to sell its features separately, rather than including them free in a package. The goal of this rule is to force the firm to sell current technology for its actual cost of development. This remedy would theoretically help competitors such as Netscape; however, given the critical praise of the Internet Explorer, it is doubtful that such a ruling would alter the current landscape.[56] The fourth guideline considered is the "Public Access Remedy"; this would require Microsoft open its operating system to the public. This act would reduce the favoritism of Microsoft applications programs used with the operating system.[57] Joel Klein acknowledges the difficulties associated with these tactics, not wanting to "set in place a process where you become a de facto regulating commission monitoring all of their activities." The prospect of leaving Microsoft be, however, may be a greater threat.[58]

The final and most extreme option for the DOJ is the breakup of Microsoft into two entities. While such an action is rare, the hallmark of U.S. antitrust policy has been the breakup of excessively powerful companies. Microsoft competitors and various antitrust experts consider separation to be the best option. "There is an underlying chronic problem, which is that Microsoft has been endowed by history with control over the operating system," contends F.M. Scherer, a professor of corporate policy at Boston's John F. Kennedy School of Government. "That is essentially a structural characteristic ... [and]

you solve structural problems structurally, rather than by detailed regulation."[59]

In this scenario, the DOJ would break Microsoft into two entities: an operating systems company and an applications company. This may be the solution most promoting the free market system, as the two resulting Microsofts could compete in each market aggressively without government investigation or intervention. However, this action would force Gates to retain ownership in one company while divesting interest in the other—an attempt which Gates would battle ferociously. Such a split would disrupt the industry, and cause an "inefficient destruction of productive resources. They would have to cut some real important hoses and valves and connections," says Lloyd Constantine, an antitrust attorney.[60] The DOJ does not seem to be giving serious thought to this option; it is no surprise that the most vocal proponents of a breakup are Oracle's CEO Lawrence J. Ellison and Gary L. Reback, an attorney with the law firm Wilson, Sonsini, Goodrich, & Rosati, which represents a number of Microsoft competitors.[61]

Many of the options being considered by the DOJ would force Microsoft to alter many of its fundamental business practices. However, other remedies would appease antitrust lawyers and Microsoft competitors by forcing the company to alter the language of its licensing agreements; such a choice would have minimal impact on the software giant and market competition.[62]

The Justice Department must decide what anti-trust policy best promotes competition and innovation in the software industry. Each option carries with it a distinct set of risks and rewards, and no one appears to be a superior alternative. Currently, the case of the Department of Justice versus Microsoft will determine the utility of the department in this high tech age. Ultimately, the decision will determine the applicability of anti-trust law.[63]

Microsoft's Response

The Justice Department contends that the bundling of the Internet Explorer with the Windows operating system is in direct violation of the 1995 consent decree signed by Microsoft.[64] However, a clause in the agreement allows Microsoft to develop integrated products. Microsoft contends that the Internet browsing functionality is deeply imbedded in the Windows 95 operating system, and that they are a single, integrated product.[65] Microsoft maintains that the Internet Explorer and Windows 95 share important files, and the removal of such files would cripple the entire operating system.[66] To prove this point and comply with Judge Jackson's order, Microsoft offered PC makers two versions of Windows

95 that lack files shared with the Internet Explorer. One version contains no browser files and will not operate; the other lacks key functions offered with Windows 95.[67] "If you can't put Internet support in Windows, then Windows will fail," Gates remarked. "You know, our path is to make Windows better."[68] Gates concluded, "When Ford sells a car, a dealer isn't allowed to take out the engine and put a different one in. The basic right to define a product and test it on Windows and allow it to get to the consumer unadulterated is clearly the law of the country. There is no law of castrated products. Our license is for the whole product."[69]

This tactic found Microsoft facing the threat of contempt charges. Judge Jackson's order required Microsoft not to require PC makers to include the Internet Explorer browser as a condition of licensing the Windows 95 operating system. The DOJ believes that Microsoft ridiculed the judge's order by only offering computer manufacturers older or "commercially worthless" versions of Windows. To avoid contempt charges, Microsoft conceded to offer an up-to-date, fully functional version of Windows 95 without forcing manufacturers to install the browser as well.[70]

Microsoft has made other concessions in an attempt to appease the federal government and stave off the DOJ's antitrust suit. The company agreed to eliminate contracts Microsoft has with many business partners, called "content provider" companies, to exclusively promote Microsoft's Internet Explorer on their websites. Competitors, such as Netscape, claim that this practice was another attempt by Microsoft to leverage control of the browser market.[71] Microsoft also agreed to stop requiring PC manufacturers to display a channel bar, or list, of Microsoft selected Internet sites on the desktop of its Windows 98 software. Beginning in June 1998, Windows 98 will be installed in over 90 percent of all new PCs. Microsoft critics argue that the requirement unfairly harms those websites not selected by Microsoft, and would reduce the level of visitors to those sites.[72] However, despite this series of concessions, the heart of the Justice Department's antitrust suit remains intact, thus forcing Microsoft to continue defending its business practices.[73]

The confrontational nature of Microsoft's defense strategy has caused public relations damage to the company. Steve Ballmer, Microsoft's executive vice president, acknowledges that "we're a company that's viewed as having more power than we think we have. And the perception is that we're a harsh company that's using its power improperly."[74] Microsoft is currently considering ways to soften its image and reduce the perception of insensitivity to customers and competitors, including a possible internal code of conduct for the company.[75]

Despite the supposed damage, Microsoft was recently named the "Most Respected Company in the World" in a survey conducted of European CEOs by the *Financial Times* of London and Price Waterhouse.[76] Microsoft occupied the 137th rank of 1998's annual *Fortune* 500 List. Exhibits 7–11 highlight Microsoft's ranking in various lists compiled by *Fortune* magazine's 1998 Fortune 500 issue.

Many within the software industry agree that the threat to innovation is not a valid argument against Microsoft. Dale Beckles, a software executive from Toronto and Microsoft competitor, calls this field "probably the most competitive industry on Earth, and … the barrier for entry is so low." He fears not only the industry giants, such as Microsoft and IBM, but also "the individuals sitting in their garage that's a recent college student that is trying to come up with the next great idea to unseat Microsoft." All one has to do to see the level of innovation in the industry, Beckles argues, is "go to their local computer store and view the breadth and depth of products available."[77] Beckles also negates Ralph Nader's

argument that venture capitalists are reluctant to fund any endeavor that might compete with Microsoft. Beckles argues that venture capitalists are apt to question how one might "deal" not only with Microsoft, but with various other organizations, such as Sun and Netscape. The tremendous competition that exists, Beckles maintains, is the dynamic force behind differentiation within the industry, which adds value for the consumer.[78]

Microsoft's central agenda is to protect and extend the reach of its Windows operating system. The operating system is the "central nervous system" of a computer, and more than 90 percent of the world's PCs use some version the Windows system. This market share gives the company an advantage in new markets, such as Internet software, especially if this product is integrated into the system and offered at no additional charge. Other browser companies, such as Netscape, sell their technology as a stand-alone product.[79]

It is the practice of integration that presents a quandary for antitrust law. Antitrust laws exist to protect

Exhibit 7   Highest Returns on Assets

Rank	Company	500 Revenues Rank	1997 Profits as % of Assets
1	Coca-Cola	68	24.4
2	Intel	38	24.1
3	Microsoft	137	24.0
4	Schering-Plough	236	22.2
5	Dell Computer	125	22.1
6	Bristol-Myers Squibb	78	21.4
7	Western Digital	350	20.5
8	Cisco Systems	253	19.2
9	Lyondell Petrochemical	484	18.4
10	Merck	46	17.9
11	Oracle	280	17.8
12	Abbott Laboratories	129	17.4
13	Texas Instruments	148	16.6
14	3Com	455	16.5
15	Sun Microsystems	184	16.2
16	Minnesota Mining & Mfg.	89	16.0
17	Gap	249	16.0
18	EMC	477	15.4

Exhibit 8   Highest Returns on Revenues

Rank	Company	500 Revenues Rank	1997 Profits as % of Revenues
1	Microsoft	137	30.4
2	Intel	38	27.7
3	Coca-Cola	68	21.9
4	Schering-Plough	236	21.3
5	Merck	46	19.5
6	Bank of New York Co.	279	19.4
7	Bristol-Myers Squibb	78	19.2
8	CoreStates Financial Corp.	340	18.6
9	EMC	477	18.3
10	Berkshire Hathaway	150	18.2
11	Pfizer	124	17.7
12	Abbott Laboratories	129	17.6
13	Texas Instruments	148	17.1
14	Comerica	451	16.7
15	Cendant	295	16.4
16	Cisco Systems	253	16.3
17	Fleet Financial Group	193	16.1

Exhibit 9	Highest Return to Investors, 10 Year (Including Capital Gains or Losses plus Reinvested Dividends)		
Rank	Company	500 Revenues Rank	1987–97 Annual Rate %
1	Conseco	286	52.3
2	United Health Care	130	49.3
3	Microsoft	137	45.6
4	PacifiCare Health Systems	172	42.7
5	Home Depot	44	41.8
6	Cardinal Health	145	40.2
7	Cendant	295	39.7
8	BankAmerica Corp.	47	39.4
9	Fannie Mae	33	39.2
10	Applied Materials	364	37.8
11	Gap	249	37.3
12	Intel	38	35.9
13	Mattel	318	35.6
14	EMC	477	35.5
15	Oracle	280	35.4
16	Nike	168	33.6
17	Norwest Corp.	157	33.0
18	ServiceMaster	373	32.8

Exhibit 10	Highest Profits			
Rank	Company	500 Revenues Rank	1997 Profits $ Millions	Profits % Change from 1996
1	Exxon	3	8,460.0	12.7
2	General Electric	5	8,203.0	12.7
3	Intel	38	6,945.0	34.7
4	Ford Motor	2	6,920.0	55.6
5	General Motors	1	6,698.0	35.0
6	Philip Morris	9	6,310.0	0.1
7	Intl. Business Machines	6	6,093.0	12.2
8	AT&T	10	4,638.0	-21.5
9	Merck	46	4,614.1	18.9
10	Coca-Cola	68	4,129.0	18.2
11	State Farm Insurance Cos.	13	3,833.3	49.3
12	Chase Manhattan Corp.	27	3,708.0	50.7
13	Citicorp	21	3,591.0	-5.2
14	Wal-Mart Stores	4	3,526.0	15.4
15	Microsoft	137	3,454.0	57.4
16	Procter & Gamble	20	3,415.0	12.1

competitive markets in the interest of consumer welfare. By integrating traditionally stand-alone programs into its Windows operating system, Microsoft appears to be benefiting consumers by giving computer users more product for less money. Microsoft has consistently offered more features with its operating system, such as point and click icons. The results of a monopoly are typically decreased quality and increased prices. However, Microsoft products offer increased quality at lowered prices—computers have indeed become more powerful and easy to use thanks to Microsoft's increased additions to its operating system.[80]

However, as its market share has increased over the past two decades, Microsoft has eliminated competitors, and perhaps innovation. This presents a possible harm to consumers and to competitors. Other companies who experienced a profitable business through the sale of separate products may lose market share as Microsoft integrates the same technologies into the Windows operating system. However, unless it is proven that innovation is stifled as a result of decreased competition, Microsoft should be permitted to continue the practice of integration.[81]

Microsoft also maintains their commitment to continually innovate their products. The goal of Microsoft is to improve personal computing by regularly adding new features to its software.[82] Microsoft CEO Bill Gates debuted Microsoft's Windows 98 operating system on April 20, 1998, and plans to begin installation in May 1998. Windows 98 will include the Internet Explorer browser as a function of the operating system, an act that is sure to draw additional scrutiny.[83] Microsoft has also developed a program called Windows CE, a close cousin of Windows 95. This technology gives computer intelligence to electronic products, such as digital televisions and VCRs. Sony and Microsoft announced an agreement in April 1998 to cross license each other's technology and merge Windows CE with Sony's audio and visual technology. Microsoft's move into this emerging field is sure to draw further attention to issues of leverage.[84] Robert Herbold, COO of Microsoft, echoed the sentiment of Bill

Exhibit 11	Highest Market Value		
Rank	Company	500 Revenues Rank	$ Millions 3/14/98
1	General Electric	5	260,147
2	Microsoft	137	199,046
3	Coca-Cola	68	184,862
4	Exxon	3	158,784
5	Merck	46	156,965
6	Intel	38	125,741
7	Pfizer	124	114,196
8	Wal-Mart Stores	4	113,731
9	Procter & Gamble	20	113,635
10	Bristol-Myers Squibb	78	106,333
11	AT&T	10	105,879
12	Philip Morris	9	102,932
13	Johnson & Johnson	49	100,631
14	Intl. Business Machines	6	98,322
15	American International Group	26	87,964
16	Berkshire Hathaway	150	79,740
17	Lucent Technologies	37	78,367
18	Bell Atlantic	28	77,650
19	E.I. du Pont de Nemours	15	77,019

Gates, stating that "The principle at stake in this case is whether Microsoft—and every other software company—has the right to continually improve and add new innovations" for the benefit of consumers.[85]

The key issue in the case is to determine whether Microsoft is a monopoly, and if so, whether the software giant is using its dominant position to a competitive advantage which will prove harmful to consumers.[86] Microsoft spokesperson Mark Murray denies such a practice, citing the overwhelming evidence that "the software industry is healthy, competitive and producing greater benefits for consumers every year."[87] Gates has praised the growth in the computer industry, which claims over 7,500 software companies,[88] and stated in clear terms that, "Microsoft does not have monopoly power in the business of developing and licensing computer operating

systems. A monopolist, by definition, is a company that has the ability to restrict entry by new firms and unilaterally control prices. Microsoft can do neither."[89] Despite the fact that the Windows operating system is installed on 90 percent of personal computers, Gates acknowledges that such products become obsolete in as little as six months, which gives competitors ample opportunity to compete with the dominant firm. The constancy of Microsoft's supremacy can be attributed to, as Gates said, "the ingenuity of Microsoft engineers."[90] Charles Rule, former lawyer for the DOJ's antitrust division and current Microsoft consultant, contends that "if Microsoft [stopped innovating], and tried to act like the classic railroad monopoly, they'd get squashed" by competitors, including Netscape.[91] CNN's Jack Straw reminds that Microsoft has yet to be proven a monopoly. "If you are asserting that monopolies result in products that don't improve," Straw maintains, "I would point to the improvements in Windows over the last five years as proof that Microsoft is in fact not a monopoly."[92]

Microsoft denies any implication that it is using its dominance in the operating systems market to leverage control of the Internet browser market, as Netscape contends. The Internet boasts an excess of 50 million users, making it a huge and growing market for electronic commerce, information, and software. This vast size, Gates argues, makes it impossible for Microsoft to use its supremacy in operating systems to take control of the Internet. Gates asserts, "The Internet cannot be controlled or dominated because it is simply a constantly changing series of linkages."[93] In a letter to Microsoft shareholders, Gates contends:

> The Justice Department wants us to remove Internet functionality from the Windows 95 operating system. Despite what the Justice Department says, the issue here is not about choice. Computer manufacturers have always been free to install Netscape's browser, and many do. Customers are also free to use whichever browser they wish, and they are very sophisticated about making that choice. Even though early versions of Microsoft Internet Explorer were included with the first Windows 95, it didn't gain significant popularity until we came out with version 3, which won most of the reviews and was chosen by customers for its capabilities. Recent surveys show this as well. Only 20 percent of computer users are currently running the browser that came as part of their operating system. The rest have gotten theirs from the Web, Internet service providers or

elsewhere. So, clearly, customers have choice when it comes to browsers.[94]

Gates also denies any intention to turn the information superhighway into a sort of toll road, in which Microsoft could charge for use.[95] "We have no plan to use our platform software to charge any type of transaction fee," Gates remarked.

The current fear of Gates is partially the result of worried executives putting a face on their fear of the Internet. The Internet is radically changing existing relationships between companies and their customers; the threat of Microsoft, also known as the "J.D. Rockefeller of the Digital Age," is easier to envision than the threat of an amateur start-up. Jim Moore, President of the technology consulting firm GeoPartners Research based out of Cambridge, Massachusetts, argues, "What people really ought to feel threatened by is that their business is being transformed out from under them—not by Bill Gates, but by a worldwide knowledge revolution enabled by information technology."[96]

There is the assumption that Microsoft would soon dominate any market it entered, including the Internet. However, it has been observed that the Internet in particular, being a low cost software distribution channel, has allowed smaller competitors to compete with software giants. For example, in October 1996 *The Economist* predicted that the Internet Explorer would crush Netscape's browser. However, nearly a year later, *The Economist* retracted, acknowledging that Netscape retains 60 percent of the browser market.[97] In fact, two-thirds of all Internet surfers use other browsers, despite the free distribution and promised advantages of uniform interface of the Internet Explorer.[98] It was also predicted that the Microsoft Network (MSN) would overtake America Online's (AOL) market share. Currently, AOL has 10 million subscribers, compared to MSN's 2.3 million; analysts estimate that MSN is in fact losing millions of dollars a year.[99] Prognostication, therefore, may not be the best tool to determine the existence of a monopoly.

In response to the suit against Microsoft filed by Sun Microsystems, the software giant has filed a counter-suit, alleging that it was Sun who violated their contractual obligations. Tom Burt, Microsoft's Associate General Counsel, said "We have always used the Java language and Java Compatibility Logo in compliance with the terms of the contact freely signed by Microsoft and Sun. We believe that Sun has decided they do not like what they signed and are trying to use the courts to rewrite the agreement. We strongly believe that Microsoft has met all of its obligations under the agreement." The specifics regarding the case are sealed due to a Protective Order imposed by the court, as briefs related to the case contain confidential information about both firms. The case is not yet settled.[100]

Those critical of Microsoft's business practices liken the software industry to the oil, steel, and railroad monopolies of days past. The software industry, critics argue, exhibits a tendency toward monopoly, as the costs of developing the original product or network are so high that the firm that first acquires dominance gains a competitive advantage. This may allow that company to cut prices to obtain an even larger market share. As with the oil, steel, and railroad monopolies of the past, it benefits the consumer to have a standard software that is reliable and widely used.[101] The Justice Department contends that as the de facto industry standard, the bundling of the Internet Explorer and the Windows operating system allows Microsoft to further stifle competing technologies and software.[102]

However, Gates contends that old fears about the evils of the ancient monopolies do not apply to the intellectual and knowledge based nature of the computer industry, as "no company owns the factory for ideas."[103] Analysts in high-technology markets recognize that the issues in the Microsoft case are complex, as "operating systems are evolving creatures, adding more features and functions over time," according to Carl Shapiro, former chief economist in the DOJ's antitrust division.[104]

The nature of the software industry, which contributed over $100 billion to the national economy in 1997, may not be conducive to the existence of a monopoly. The computer industry is unlike any other, as constant innovations make it the fastest growing industry to date. The uniqueness of the industry hinders the ability of the federal government to write and enforce laws in this field. Perhaps the mistake of the Department of Justice was not to recognize Microsoft's pricing policies and licensing agreements as antitrust violations, and prosecute accordingly. Instead, the DOJ broadened their investigation at the behest of Microsoft competitors, thus allowing a five year period in which the software giant was able to monopolize the operating systems market.[105] The DOJ must set a precedent in which the limitations on a monopolist enjoying their innovation are defined, and exactly what constitutes leveraging in the software market. An entirely new set of rules may need to be set to regulate this unique industry. Until such actions are undertaken, the DOJ will only be able to control the computer industry through threat of litigation.[106]

Finances Statements

Exhibits 12 through 16 are financial statements for Microsoft.

Notes

1. Pitofsky, Robert. "Balancing Act on Big Business." *The Washington Post*, 9 February 1998.
2. Ibid.
3. Klayman, Elliott, Bagby, John, and Ellis Nan. "Restraints of Trade and Monopolies," *Irwin's Business Law* (1994): 1012.
4. Pitofsky, Robert. "Balancing Act on Big Business." *The Washington Post*, 9 February 1998.
5. Wyszomierski, Teresa. "Trust Busters Got Lost Long Before Microsoft." *The Washington Post*, 8 March 1998.
6. Klayman, Elliott, Bagby, John, and Ellis Nan. "Restraints of Trade and Monopolies," *Irwin's Business Law* (1994): 1012.
7. Wyszomierski, Teresa. "Trust Busters Got Lost Long Before Microsoft." *The Washington Post*, 8 March 1998.
8. Ibid.
9. Check, Dan. "The Case Against Microsoft." ourworld.compuserve.com, 1996.
10. Pitofsky, Robert. "Balancing Act on Big Business." *The Washington Post*, 9 February 1998.
11. Perkins, Anthony. "Why Microsoft Is Vulnerable." *The Red Herring Magazine*, www.redherring.com, 7 February 1998.
12. Microsoft Museum. www.microsoft.com
13. Wyszomierski, Teresa. "Trust Busters Got Lost Long Before Microsoft." *The Washington Post*, 8 March 1998.
14. Chandrasekaran, Rajiv. "Opponents Open Drive for Wider Antitrust Case," *The Washington Post*, 21 April 1998.
15. Saltzman, Marc. "The Browser Wars: From Computers to the Courtroom." *CNN Interactive*, 20 April 1998.
16. Corcoran, Elizabeth. "Gates to Unveil Windows 98, Awaits Legal Showdown," *The Washington Post*, 20 April 1998.
17. Chandrasekaran, Rajiv. "Opponents Open Drive for Wider Antitrust Case." *The Washington Post*, 21 April 1998.
18. Corcoran, Elizabeth. "Internet Pioneer Falters as It Tries to Shift Focus to Firms," *The Washington Post*, 11 January 1998.
19. Saltzman, Marc. "The Browser Wars: From Computers to the Courtroom." *CNN Interactive*, 20 April 1998.
20. Shiver, Jube. "Gates Scoffs at Assertion Microsoft Is a Monopoly," *The Los Angeles Times*, 4 March 1998.
21. Chandrasekaran, Rajiv. "Opponents Open Drive for Wider Antitrust Case." *The Washington Post*, 21 April 1998.
22. Nader, Ralph. "The Microsoft Menace." www.slate.com/Features/NaderMS/NaderMS.asp
23. Chandrasekaran, Rajiv. "In Java War, a New Microsoft Assault." *The Washington Post*, 12 March 1998.
24. Ibid.
25. Corcoran, Elizabeth. "Sun's Lonely Battle." *The Washington Post*, 8 February 1998.
26. Chandrasekaran, Rajiv. "In Java War, a New Microsoft Assault." *The Washington Post*, 12 March 1998.
27. Chandrasekaran, Rajiv. "Gates and Detractors Spar at Senate Hearing." *The Washington Post*, 4 March 1998.
28. Shiver, Jube. "Gates Scoffs at Assertion Microsoft Is a Monopoly," *The Los Angeles Times*, 4 March 1998.
29. CNN Interactive. "Microsoft 'Monopoly' Debated in Senate." 3 March 1998.
30. Birnbaum, Jeffrey. "D.C.'s Anti-Gates Lobby," *Fortune*, 12 January 1998.
31. Nader, Ralph. "The Microsoft Menace." www.slate.com/Features/NaderMS/NaderMS.asp
32. Newshour with Jim Lehrer Transcript. "Microsoft Explored," *Online Focus*, 13 January 1998. www.pbs.org/newshour
33. Paulson, Michael. "Senators Gorton, Hatch Remain at Odds Over Microsoft." *The Seattle Post-Intelligencer*, 1998.
34. Chandrasekaran, Rajiv. "Microsoft in Senate's Focus." *The Washington Post*, 3 March 1998.
35. Ibid.
36. Ibid.
37. Paulson, Michael. "Senators Gorton, Hatch Remain at Odds Over Microsoft." *The Seattle Post-Intelligencer*, 1998.
38. Chandrasekaran, Rajiv. "Gates and Detractors Spar at Senate Hearing," *The Seattle Post-Intelligencer*, 1998.
39. Paulson, Michael. "Senators Gorton, Hatch Remain at Odds Over Microsoft." *The Seattle Post-Intelligencer*, 1998.
40. Chandrasekaran, Rajiv. "Microsoft in Senate's Focus," *The Washington Post*, 3 March 1998.
41. Check, Dan. "The Case Against Microsoft." www.ourworldcompuserve.com
42. Black Edward. "Microsoft—Monopoly Hounds or Just Smart Business People?" *Online Newshour*, 21 January 1998.
43. Check, Dan. "The Case Against Microsoft." www.ourworldcompuserve.com
44. Wyszomierski, Teresa. "Trust Busters Got Lost Long Before Microsoft." *The Washington Post*, 8 March 1998.
45. Ibid.
46. Haines, Thomas, and Westneat, Danny. "Antitrust Probe Against Microsfot May Be Growing," *The Seattle Times*, 6 February 1998.
47. Cortese, Amy, & France, Mike et al. "What To Do About Microsoft." *Business Week*, 20 April 1998.
48. Chandrasekaran, Rajiv. "Justice Dept. Browsing a Range of Options in Microsoft Case," *The Washington Post*, 9 April 1998.
49. Cortese, Amy, & France, Mike, et al. "What To Do About Microsoft." *Business Week*, 20 April 1998.
50. Ibid.
51. Cortese, Amy & France, Mike, et al. "Scenario 1: Uncle Sam Leaves Bill Gates Alone." *Business Week*, 20 April 1998.
52. Ibid.
53. Ibid.
54. Ibid.
55. Cortese, Amy, & France, Mike, et al. "Scenario 2: Justice Slows the Giant With 'Surgical Strikes.'" *Business Week*, 20 April 1998.
56. Ibid.

Exhibit 12   Financial Highlights (in Millions, Except Earnings per Share)

| | Year Ended June 30, | | | | |
	1993	1994	1995	1996	1997
Revenue	$ 3,753	$ 4,649	$ 5,937	$ 8,671	$11,358
Net income	953	1,146	1,453	2,195	3,454
Earnings per share[1]	0.79	0.94	1.16	1.71	2.63
Return on revenue	25.4%	24.7%	24.5%	25.3%	30.4%
Cash and short-term investments	$ 2,290	$ 3,614	$ 4,750	$ 6,940	$ 8,966
Total assets	3,805	5,363	7,210	10,093	14,387
Stockholders' equity	3,242	4,450	5,333	6,908	10,777

[1]Earnings per share have been restated to reflect a two-for-one stock split in December 1996.

Exhibit 13　Income Statements (in Millions, Except Earnings per Share)

| | Year Ended June 30, | | |
	1995	1996	1997
Revenue	$5,937	$8,671	$11,358
Operating expenses:			
Cost of revenue	877	1,188	1,085
Research and development	860	1,432	1,925
Sales and marketing	1,895	2,657	2,856
General and administrative	267	316	362
Total operating expenses	3,899	5,593	6,228
Operating income	2,038	3,078	5,130
Interest income	191	320	443
Other expenses	(62)	(19)	(259)
Income before income taxes	2,167	3,379	5,314
Provision for income taxes	714	1,184	1,860
Net income	1,453	2,195	3,454
Preferred stock dividends	–	–	15
Net income available for common shareholders	$1,453	$2,195	$ 3,439
Earnings per share[1]	$ 1.16	$ 1.71	$ 2.63
Weighted average shares outstanding[1]	1,254	1,281	1,312

[1]Share and per share amounts have been restated to reflect a two-for-one stock split in December 1996.

57. Ibid.
58. Ibid.
59. Cortese, Amy, & France, Mike, et al. "Scenario 3: The Feds Split Microsoft in Two." *Business Week*, 20 April 1998.
60. Ibid.
61. Ibid.
62. Chandrasekaran, Rajiv. "Justice Dept. Browsing a Range of Options in Microsoft Case," *The Washington Post*, 9 April 1998.
63. Cortese, Amy, & France, Mike et al. "Epilogue: Weighing the Risks and Rewards." *Business Week*, 20 April 1998.
64. Lohr, Steve, & Markoff, John. "Why Microsoft Takes Hard Line With Government." *The New York Times*, 12 January 1998.
65. Newshour With Jim Lehrer Trancript. "Microsoft Explored." *Online Focus*, 13 January 1998, www.pbs.org/newshour/.
66. Chandrasekaran, Rajiv. "Microsoft Executive Questioned Sharply." *The Washington Post*, 15 January 1998.
67. Chandrasekaran, Rajiv. "Judge Criticizes Key Arguments Made By Microsoft Lawyer." *The Washington Post*, 14 January 1998.
68. Chandrasekaran, Rajiv. "Gates Fears Curb on Innovation." *The Washington Post*, 3 March 1998.
69. Corcoran, Elizabeth. "Gates to Unveil Windows 98, Awaits Legal Showdown." *The Washington Post*, 20 April 1998.
70. Associated Press. "U.S., Microsoft Settle Contempt Charges." *USA Today*, 22 January 1998.
71. Chandrasekaran, Rajiv. "Microsoft Again Makes Concessions on Browsers." *The Washington Post*, 10 April 1998.
72. Chandrasekaran, Rajiv. "Microsoft Abandons Another PC Mandate." *The Washington Post*, 8 January 1998.
73. Associated Press. "U.S., Microsoft Settle Contempt Charges." *USA Today*, 22 January 1998.
74. Corcoran, Elizabeth. "Microsoft Official Says Battle Is Taking a Toll." *The Washington Post*, 18 April 1998.
75. Bank, David, & Clark, Don. "Microsoft Looks at Ways to Soften Image Badly Damaged by Its Dispute With U.S." *The Wall Street Journal*.
76. Microsoft Press Pass. "Bill Gates Travels to Europe." 2 February 1998, www.microsoft.com/corpinfo/.
77. Newshour With Jim Lehrer Transcript. "Microsoft Explored." *Online Focus*, 13 January 1998, www.pbs.org/newshour
78. Ibid.
79. Lohr, Steve, & Markoff, John. "Why Microsoft Takes Hard Line With Government." *The New York Times*, 12 January 1998.
80. Ibid.
81. Ibid.
82. Corcoran, Elizabeth. "Gates to Unveil Windows 98, Awaits Legal Showdown." *The Washington Post*, 20 April 1998.
83. Ibid.
84. Corcoran, Elizabeth. "Windows' Little Brother Is Growing." *The Washington Post*, 8 April 1998.
85. Associated Press. "Microsoft Calls Justice's Antitrust Case 'Flawed.'" *The Washington Post*, 30 January 1998.
86. Haines, Thomas, & Westneat, Danny. "Antitrust Probe Against Microsoft May Be Growing." *The Seattle Times*, 6 February 1998.
87. Chandrasekaran, Rajiv. "Justice Dept. Browsing a Range of Options Against Microsoft." *The Washington Post*, 9 April 1998.
88. Herbold, Bob, & Kirkpatrick, David. "The View From Redmond." *Fortune*, 2 February 1998.

Exhibit 14 Cash Flow Statements (in Millions)

| | Year Ended June 30, | | |
	1995	1996	1997
Cash flows from operations			
Net income	$1,453	$2,195	$3,454
Depreciation and amortization	269	480	557
Unearned revenue	69	983	1,601
Recognition of unearned revenue from prior periods	(54)	(477)	(743)
Other current liabilities	404	584	321
Accounts receivable	(91)	(71)	(336)
Other current assets	(60)	25	(165)
Net cash from operations	1,990	3,719	4,689
Cash flows used for financing			
Common stock issued	332	504	744
Common stock repurchased	(698)	(1,385)	(3,101)
Put warrant proceeds	49	124	95
Preferred stock issued	–	–	980
Preferred stock dividends	–	–	(15)
Stock option income tax benefits	179	352	796
Net cash used for financing	(138)	(405)	(501)
Cash flows used for investments			
Additions to property, plant, and equipment	(495)	(494)	(499)
Equity investments and other	(230)	(625)	(1,669)
Short-term investments	(651)	(1,551)	(921)
Net cash used for investments	(1,376)	(2,670)	(3,089)
Net change in cash and equivalents	476	644	1,099
Effect of exchange rates on cash and equivalents	9	(5)	6
Cash and equivalents, beginning of year	1,477	1,962	2,601
Cash and equivalents, end of year	1,962	2,601	3,706
Short-term investments	2,788	4,339	5,260
Cash and short-term investments	$4,750	$6,940	$8,966

89. Grimaldi, James, & Westneat, Danny. "Gates: Microsoft 'Not a Monopoly.'" *The Seattle Times*, 3 March 1998.
90. Pearlstein, Steven, & Corcoran, Elizabeth. "Microsoft: Rewriting the Rules of Monopoly." *The Washington Post*, 4 March 1998.
91. Newshour With Jim Lehrer Transcript. "Microsoft Explored." *Online Newshour*, 13 January 1998, www.pbs.org/newshour
92. Straw, Jack. "Target: Microsoft." *CNN Interactive*, 20 April 1998.
93. Shiver, Jube. "Gates Scoffs at Assertion Microsoft is Monopoly." *The Los Angeles Times*, 4 March 1998.
94. Gates, Bill. "Letter to Microsoft Employees and Shareholders."
95. Grimaldi, James, & Westneat, Danny. "Gates: Microsoft 'Not a Monopoly.'" *The Seattle Times*, 3 March 1998.
96. Kirkpatrick, David. "Microsoft: Is Your Company Its Next Meal." *Fortune*, 1998 Fortune 500 List, www.pathfinder.com/fortune/fortune500.
97. Perkins, Anthony. "Why Microsoft Is Vulnerable." *The Red Herring Magazine*, 7 February 1998.
98. Rothstein, Edward. "Sympathy for the 'Evil Empire.'" *The New York Times*, 12 January 1998.
99. Perkins, Anthony. "Why Microsoft Is Vulnerable." *The Red Herring Magazine*, 7 February 1998.

Exhibit 15 Balance Sheets (in Millions)

	June 30,	
	1996	**1997**
Assets		
Current assets:		
Cash and short-term investments	$ 6,940	$ 8,966
Accounts receivable	639	980
Other	260	427
Total current assets	7,839	10,373
Property, plant, and equipment	1,326	1,465
Equity investments	675	2,346
Other assets	253	203
Total assets	$10,093	$14,387
Liabilities and stockholders' equity		
Current liabilities:		
Accounts payable	$ 808	$ 721
Accrued compensation	202	336
Income taxes payable	484	466
Unearned revenue	560	1,418
Other	371	669
Total current liabilities	2,425	3,610
Minority interest	125	–
Put warrants	635	–
Commitments and contingencies		
Stockholders' equity:		
Convertible preferred stock— shares authorized 0 and 100; shares issued and outstanding 0 and 13	–	980
Common stock and paid-in capital— shares authorized 4,000; shares issued and outstanding 1,194 and 1,204	2,924	4,509
Retained earnings	3,984	5,288
Total stockholders' equity	6,908	10,777
Total liabilities and stockholders' equity	$10,093	$14,387

100. "Microsoft Press Pass. "Microsoft Files Response Brief Against Preliminary Injunction in Sun Lawsuit." www.microsoft.com/corpinfo/, 6 February 1998.

101. Pearlstein, Steven, & Corcoran, Elizabeth. "Microsoft: Rewriting the Rules of Monopoly?" *The Washington Post*, 4 March 1998.

102. Wyszomierski, Teresa. "Trust Busters Got Lost Long Before Microsoft." *The Washington Post*, 8 March 1998.

103. Pearlstein, Steven, & Corcoran, Elizabeth. "Microsoft: Rewriting the Rules of Monopoly?" *The Washington Post*, 4 March 1998.

104. Lohr, Steve, & Markoff, John. "Why Microsoft Takes a Hard Line With Government." *The New York Times*, 12 January 1998.

105. Check, Dan. "The Case Against Microsoft." ourworld.compuserve.com, Spring 1996.

106. Ibid.

Exhibit 16 Stockholders' Equity Statements (in Millions)

	Year Ended June 30,		
	1995	1996	1997
Convertible preferred stock			
Convertible preferred stock issued	–	–	$ 980
Balance, end of year	–	–	980
Common stock and paid-in capital			
Balance, beginning of year	$1,500	$2,005	2,924
Common stock issued	332	504	744
Common stock repurchased	(30)	(41)	(91)
Proceeds from sale of put warrants	49	124	95
Reclassification of put warrant obligation	(25)	(20)	45
Stock option income tax benefits	179	352	792
Balance, end of year	2,005	2,924	4,509
Retained earnings			
Balance, beginning of year	2,950	3,328	3,984
Net income	1,453	2,195	3,454
Preferred stock dividends	–	–	(15)
Common stock repurchased	(668)	(1,344)	(3,010)
Reclassification of put warrant obligation	(380)	(210)	590
Net unrealized investment gains and other	(27)	15	285
Balance, end of year	3,328	3,984	5,288
Total stockholders' equity	$5,333	$6,908	$10,777

Case 14

Drkoop.com

Nicole Herskowitz, Michael Iverson, Fred Howard, Janet Mehlhop, and Pilar Speer,
University of Michigan

As Dennis Upah, cofounder of drkoop.com, sat in his small, dimly lit office sipping a glass of water, he thought back to an earlier conversation with his partner, C. Everett Koop, former surgeon general of the United States. He kept coming back to the comment that Dr. Koop had made: "I am excited about how the Web has greatly enhanced consumers' abilities to access health care information. I firmly believe that empowered consumers make better, more informed decisions with their physicians. Our new Web site gives Americans one premier location on the Net to find trusted, quality health care information."[1]

Since the drkoop.com launch in late 1998, the company had quickly grown to be the largest Web-based health information service, but revenues were far short of what was needed to make the new company profitable. Although the new company was focused on providing health care information, Dennis knew the site had to make a profit to keep shareholders happy and to ensure that the business would survive. He thought idly, "This tap water is terrible. I hope we soon turn a profit so we can afford a water cooler!" But he quickly jumped back to the issue that was troubling him: What strategy did drkoop.com need to pursue to sustain its early success? Sites offering medical advice were proliferating, and several competitors were mounting offensives to challenge drkoop.com.

The History of Medical Advice

People have sought knowledge about their ailments as far back as ancient times, when medicine men performed spells and advised people on their spiritual and mental health. In modern times, people have come to rely on their personal physicians for medical advice. For sicknesses like the flu or the common cold, there is a lot of information available from local pharmacists, the media, and friends, not to mention each individual's own personal experience with various remedies. For those who want detailed information or want to doctor themselves with assorted natural herbs, vitamin supplements, and other remedies available without a prescription, there are also numerous books, magazines, and health foods advisories. Numerous support organizations have sprung up in recent years to help people afflicted with cancer, diabetes, and other serious illnesses.

In addition to conducting its own R&D efforts to discover new prescription drugs to cure or prevent ailments of all types, the pharmaceutical industry contributes to health research organizations. Bristol-Myers Squibb, for example, donated $23 million through the Bristol-Myers Squibb foundation in 1997. A large portion of this money went to organizations such as the National Cancer Foundation and the National Diabetes Foundation. Pharmaceutical firms also help inform patients of new treatment options through media advertising. Web sites, other forms of publications, and extensive collaboration with patient support and prevention groups.

In late 1999, all pharmaceutical companies had extensive Web sites with numerous links and information options that addressed their primary treatment areas. Companies like Medtronic and Guidant had Web sites with specific areas dedicated to various types of cardiovascular problems. On Medtronic's site, for example, there were pages dedicated to ventricular fibrillation that not only featured medical advice but also contained many links to associated sites such as that of the American Heart Association.

Medical Advice on the Internet

The first Web sites pertaining to health care were created by pharmaceutical firms as part of their efforts to begin conducting business-to-business e-commerce with pharmaceutical distributors, drugstore chains, and physicians who wrote prescriptions. In the beginning, most pharmaceutical firms used their Web sites to advertise their products and services. However, they soon discovered that the aspect of the Internet that attracted the most users was information. Sites providing a wealth of free, informative, interesting, and valuable content began seeing thousands and then millions of unique hits each quarter. The appeal of good information quickly caught the attention of entrepreneurs who seized on the potential for providing medical information via the Internet.

Medical information Web sites were launched to provide the public with readily accessible and accurate information on a broad variety of health-related topics, curtailing the need for people to rely totally on a physician or medical specialist for answers to their questions or concerns. Site founders, recognizing "the value of the Internet as a viable tool for educating the public," saw themselves as performing a valuable public service by creating open access to tens of thousands of pages of reliable and trustworthy health care information.[2] The information on their sites was compiled from books and articles by well-known physicians, journals reporting medical research and the latest studies, information-providing partners, a medical advisory board, and various other medical experts.

Medical information Web sites began popping up left and right in the 1997–99 period. With competition on the rise, medical information providers were forced to add services to their sites in order to maintain growth in number of hits and unique viewers. Following the business models from other content provider Internet companies, the idea of "chat rooms" quickly found its way into the online health care scene. But to combat the potential for misleading or inaccurate information to be dispensed in chat rooms, most medical sites developed an "Ask the Expert" feature to help site users get accurate, timely answers to their questions. Several medical information providers had recruited experts, including physicians and specialists, to give advice to site users and respond to specific questions. Additionally, most medical sites, concerned with maintaining the integrity and objectivity of the information being provided, set up "stringent rules governing the ethics of the sites, including how advertising and editorial content should be addressed."[3]

Who Is Dr. Koop?

Dr. C. Everett Koop became a well-known public figure while serving as surgeon general in the Reagan administration. He played a prominent role in building public awareness of the acquired immune deficiency syndrome (AIDS) and was often in the public limelight crusading against the destructive effects of tobacco. As surgeon general, he was a strong proponent of tough antismoking regulations. Following his tenure as surgeon general. Dr. Koop continued his mission of encouraging good health.

His latest effort was to help found and launch drkoop.com as a provider of medical information.

Dr. Koop was born in Brooklyn, New York, in 1916. After earning his M.D. from Cornell University in 1941, he worked at Children's Hospital at the University of Pennsylvania for 35 years. During his tenure there, he built a reputation as one of the nation's best pediatric surgeons. From 1981 to 1989, Dr. Koop served as surgeon general of the U.S. Public Health Service and director of international health. In 1999, Dr. Koop continued to lead an active role in the health community and health education through writings, electronic media, public appearances, and personal contacts. He taught medical students at Dartmouth College, where the Koop Institute was based. He was chairman of the National Safe Kids Campaign, Washington, D.C., and produced 75 point-of-diagnosis videos during 1999–2001 for Time-Life Medical, of which he was chairman of the board.

The Web site was named after its 83-year-old cofounder to provide credibility and to give the site a competitive edge over rival medical information providers. Cofounder Dennis Upah believed Dr. Koop's name was an incredible asset. Upah said, "He's the most trusted man in health care. He's an icon. With that comes a tremendous responsibility and scrutiny."[4] In a recent survey by Bruskin-Goldring, almost 60 percent of consumers recognized Dr. Koop, and of that percentage, nearly half believed him to be a top authority on health care issues.[5] In return for use of his name. Dr. Koop agreed to receive a royalty equal to 2 percent of revenues from sales of the company's current products and up to 4 percent of revenues derived from sales of new products. However, this agreement was later modified; the royalty payments were eliminated and in their place Dr. Koop was granted rights to purchase 214,000 shares of drkoop.com's stock at an exercise price of $17.84. The rights vested at the rate of 8,900 shares per month.

Drkoop.com Is Born

After incorporating in July 1997, Empower Health Corporation launched the drkoop.com Web site on July 20, 1998, as a comprehensive consumer health care portal providing information on acute ailments, chronic illnesses, nutrition, and fitness and wellness, as well as access to medical databases, publications, and real-time medical news. The company said its mission was to "empower consumers with the information and resources they need to become active participants in the management of their own health." At the time, Dr. C. Everett Koop, the chairman of Empower, said, "I am excited about how the Web has greatly enhanced consumers' abilities to access health care information. I firmly believe that empowered consumers make better, more informed decisions with their physicians. Our new Web site gives Americans one premier location on the Net to find trusted, quality health care information."[6] The company went public in June 1999 at a price of $9; the stock price jumped to as high as $40 in July 1999 but then declined and traded in the $11–20 range during the last quarter of 1999 and in early 2000. The company's initial public offering raised about $85 million in new capital.

To build drkoop.com brand awareness, Empower Health partnered with USWeb Corporation, a specialist in Web audience development. Together, they devised a strategy built around innovative banner advertising and media placement of ads, search engine optimization, and online public relations and promotions.[7] In its first 90 days, the site attracted more than 1 million visitors. By June 1, 1999, the company had attracted 6 million unique users and signed up 280,000 registered members.

The initial success continued on into the second half of 1999, drawing over 15 million page views in October 1999.[8] In November 1999, Media Metrix ranked the site as the number one health Web site, and PC Data noted that it was the number one health Web site from March 1999 through November 1999. Media Metrix ranked drkoop.com as 25th in its News/Information/Entertainment category. During the fourth quarter of 1999, drkoop.com attracted 11.8 million unique visitors, who viewed 49.4 million pages. By January 2000, the company had 1 million registered users.

The Market Opportunity For Drkoop.com

Health care was the largest segment of the U.S. economy in the late 1990s, accounting for annual expenditures of roughly $1 trillion.[9] Health and medical information was one of the fastest-growing areas of interest on the Internet. According to Cyber Dialogue, an industry research firm, during the 12-month period ended July 1998, approximately 17 million adults in the United States searched online for health and medical information, and approximately 50 percent of these individuals made offline purchases after seeking information on the Internet. Cyber Dialogue estimated that approximately 70 percent of the persons searching for health and medical information online believed the Internet empowered them by providing them with information before and after they went to a doctor's office. Cyber Dialogue also estimated that the number of adults in the United States searching for online health and medical information would grow to approximately 30 million in the year 2000, and they would spend approximately $150 billion for all types of health-related products

and services offline.[10] Exhibit 1 shows the size of the various U.S. health care market segments. Medical information providers hoped to tap into a piece of this business.[11]

Drkoop.com's Business Model and Strategy

In the company's prospectus for its common stock offering in mid-1999, management described the objective and business model for drkoop.com:

> Our objective is to establish the drkoop.com network as the most trusted and comprehensive source of consumer health care information and services on the Internet. Our business model is to earn advertising and subscription revenues from advertisers, merchants, manufacturers, and health care organizations who desire to reach a highly targeted community of health care consumers on the Internet. We also earn revenues by facilitating e-commerce transactions, such as sales of prescription refills, vitamins and nutritional supplements, and insurance services offered by outside parties.

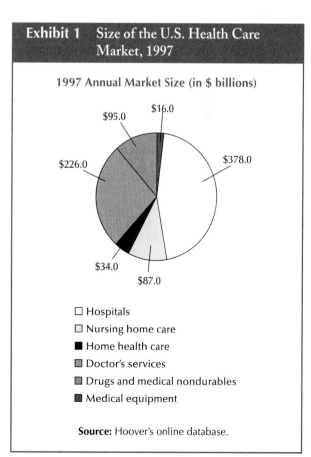

Exhibit 1   Size of the U.S. Health Care Market, 1997

1997 Annual Market Size (in $ billions)

$16.0
$95.0
$226.0
$378.0
$34.0
$87.0

☐ Hospitals
☐ Nursing home care
■ Home health care
▨ Doctor's services
▨ Drugs and medical nondurables
■ Medical equipment

Source: Hoover's online database.

Drkoop.com's strategy incorporated the following key elements:

- Establish the drkoop.com brand so that consumers associate the trustworthiness and credibility of Dr. C. Everett Koop with the company.

- Provide consumers with high-quality health care content to attract users to www.drkoop.com and promote their loyalty to the company's Web site.

- Distribute drkoop.com content to affiliated portals and other Web sites that (1) have established themselves as pathways for a broad variety of information and (2) have the potential to drive traffic to drkoop.com and provide broad exposure to the drkoop.com brand.

- Develop and expand online health care communities to allow users with similar health-related experiences to exchange information and gather news and knowledge in a secure, anonymous environment.

- Provide consumers with unique tools, such as one that educates consumers on the interaction among various drugs and other substances.

- Deploy a comprehensive personal medical record that will allow users to establish and maintain a life-long record of their health and medical information in a secure portion of the company's database.

- Provide an attractive Web site that can deliver advertising in a highly targeted manner, thereby commanding higher advertising rates.

- Facilitate e-commerce transactions offered by merchants, manufacturers, and service providers to a highly targeted community of health-conscious consumers.

Strategic Partnerships

A chief component of drkoop.com's strategy was to partner with organizations that would add to its content and service offerings, further expand its business model into traditional areas of the health care industry, and grow its viewing base. To develop content for its Web site, drkoop.com had partnered with the following eight organizations:

- *The American Council on Science and Health*—The ACSH was an independent, nonprofit, tax-exempt organization that conducted studies and did research in such areas as food, nutrition, chemicals, pharmaceuticals, lifestyles, the environment, and health. A board of 300 physicians, scientists, and policy advisers peer-reviewed all reports and published papers.

- *Cleveland Clinic Foundation*—The Cleveland Clinic integrated hospital patient care, research, and medical education in a private, nonprofit group practice with 1,000 salaried physicians. In 1999, *U.S. News and World Report* ranked the Cleveland Clinic best in the country for cardiac care and the fourth best hospital overall.

- *Dartmouth Medical School*—The Dartmouth Medical School provided consumer health and medical information on more than 60 medical topics along with analysis on leading medical research and trends written by staff and experts.

- *Lifescape.com*—Lifescape provided timely news articles, clinical information, and state-of-the-art assessment tools in areas relating to family, relationships, emotional health, and mental well-being.

- *Multum Information Services*—Multum provided drkoop.com with a comprehensive and up-to-date database of drug information that was the basis for drkoop.com's trademarked DrugChecker tool.

- *Screaming Media*—Screaming Media provided drkoop.com with late-breaking, real-time news and editorials on health and health care issues from over 50 wire services.

- *World Book*—World Book contributed use of its trusted and thorough World Book Rush-Presbyterian-St. Luke's Medical Center Medical Encyclopedia.

- *Shared Medical Systems*—SMS was a provider of software that enabled secure online data exchanges between patients, their physicians, and local health care organizations.

Going into 2000, drkoop.com had over one dozen agreements to be the exclusive or preferred provider of health care information for particular Web sites. The major ones were as follows:

- *Infoseek and Buena Vista Internet*—To enhance brand awareness and increase traffic on its Web site, drkoop.com entered into agreements with Infoseek Corporation and the Buena Vista Internet Group, a unit of the Walt Disney Company, to be the exclusive provider of health and related content on three Web sites of the Go Network: Go.com Health Center, ESPN.com Training Room, and the Family.com Health Channel. In addition, drkoop.com became the exclusive pharmacy and drugstore, health insurance, and clinical trials partner in the Go.com Health Center. Under the Infoseek agreement, drkoop.com was also the premier health content provider for ABCnews.com. The agreement was for the period April 1999 to April 2002 and called for drkoop.com to pay Infoseek and Buena Vista approximately $58 million in total consideration.

- *Adventist Health System*—In January 1999, drkoop.com exchanged 2,615,677 shares of preferred stock for $3.5 million in cash plus a 10 percent share of HealthMagic. HealthMagic was a subsidiary of Adventist Health Systems and a developer of a personal medical record application.[12] This partnership gave the company access to and use of a personal medical record application and secured Adventist as a customer in the Community Partner program.

- *FHC Internet*—FHC purchased 1.1 million shares of drkoop.com common stock at the offering price of $9 as part of an agreement for FHC to sponsor drkoop.com's mental health center.[13] FHC Internet was a subsidiary of Foundation Health Systems that specialized in the outsourcing of disease management programs for local health care organizations.

- *Quintiles International*—Quintiles entered into an agreement with drkoop.com to jointly develop a clinical trials information center. Quintiles was the world's largest provider of clinical research services to pharmaceutical companies and, as part of the agreement, purchased $5 million worth of shares of drkoop.com at the IPO price of $9. The clinical trials center provided visitors to the drkoop.com site with information about clinical trials that were currently going on across the country. Visitors could fill out an online prescreen form for various clinical trials, which was then forwarded to study sites. Drkoop.com received approximately $100 for each referral, Quintiles expected the agreement to help it speed recruit of candidates for clinical trials, lower prescreening costs, and create a larger pool of potential candidates for participation in clinical trials.[14]

- *America Online*—Drkoop.com's agreement called for it to provide medical info rmation services to America Online and CompuServe members as well as to AOL's Internet portals—AOL.com, Netscape.com, andd DigitalCity.com. To gain exposure to the 70-plus million users from the five entities combined and the benefits of AOL's sales force, drkoop.com agreed to pay AOL $589 million over the next four years and also to give AOL warrants to purchase 1.6 million shares of drkoop.com's stock at an exercise price of $15.94. Drkoop.com received an $8 million license fee for the use of a co-developed personal medical record.

- *Phar-Mor*—Drkoop.com's partnership with Phar-Mor, an online drugstore, involved Phar-Mor's sponsoring a monthly drkoop.com pharmacy newsletter. Users of Phar-Mor's Web site were directed to drkoop.com to gain necessary medical information while visitors to drkoop.com could click on links to Phar-Mor's Web site.

- *DrugEmporium*—DrugEmporium and drkoop.com signed an agreement in October 1999 whereby drkoop.com visitors could purchase over 20,000 discounted products sold by DrugEmporium, Shoppers at DrugEmporium could go directly to drkoop.com for further information on products they were considering. Further, drkoop.com's DrugChecker was integrated into the purchase of all prescription drugs at DrugEmporium, automatically checking for any potential problems.

- *Other Alliances and Comarketing Partnerships*—drkoop.com had partnered with such health care providers and HMOs as Highmark (one of the 10 largest insurers in the United States); MemorialCare (a large health care system serving more than 14 million residents in Los Angeles and Orange County); Scott and White Hospital and Clinic (one of the largest multispecialty hospitals in the United States); Promina Health Systems (a nonprofit health care organization serving 4.3 million residents in the Atlanta area); the Cleveland Clinic (with a staff of over 850 physicians); and the Baptist Health System (serving 3.5 million residents in the Miami, Florida, area). In addition to these agreements, drkoop.com had agreements to provide content, establish direct links to each other's Web sites, or otherwise gain market exposure with The Weather Channel, Physicians' Online, Salon.com Health & Body, SeniorNet, @Home, Roadrunner (the cable-based Internet service provider of Time Warner and Media One cable systems), Tallahassee Memorial HealthCare, and Yahoo Health.

Community Partners and Television Partners
Through the Community Partner Program, drkoop.com enrolled hospitals and health systems as local affiliates, allowing them to integrate the drkoop.com brand and content into their online initiatives. Participating health care organizations could draw on the content and resources at the drkoop.com Web site to supply their patients with online health care information and interactive capabilities, thus helping patients to educate themselves and make more informed decisions. In February 2000, there were more than 300 local health

care facilities participating in the Community Partner Program. In recent months, drkoop.com had also begun a Television Partner Program and was supplying content to 18 local television stations.

Using the Partnerships to Build a "Network"   The company saw all these content and affiliate partnerships as a central part of its strategy to create

> an Internet-based consumer health care network that … provides individuals with trusted health care content, services, and tools to empower them to better manage their health. Our network affiliates include other Internet portals. Web sites, health care organizations, and traditional sources of health and medical news. Establishing affiliations with traditional media outlets allows us to deliver quality health care content to a targeted audience. Affiliates provide local, relevant information directly to a local audience. Through this unique means of distribution, drkoop.com is building a leading network of health content and editorial-based, breaking health news on the Internet.[15]

Drkoop.com's Recent Marketing And Promotion Efforts

To build brand awareness and traffic, drkoop.com advertised on high-frequency Web sites such as Yahoo! Competitors were pursuing much the same approach. WebMD.com advertised on NetZero, a free Internet service provider for consumers, and Onhealth.com also advertised on Yahoo! Also, drkoop.com had entered into arrangements with local TV stations to give the stations content for health-related news stories in exchange for a drkoop.com "plug" at the end of a news story on a health issue.

In late 1999, drkoop.com launched a $10–$15 million advertising campaign to build brand recognition.[16] Management believed that growing competition among medical information providers on the Internet made higher levels of advertising necessary. The company had also employed Creative Artists Agency (CAA) to help build awareness and use of its Web site.[17]

Drkoop.com's Revenue Sources

The company generated revenue from selling advertising on its site, licensing its content to others, and partnerships with others. The big revenue generator was selling Web site ads. DrugEmporium was the only sponsor of the Web site. The site was covered with DrugEmporium advertisements and direct links to facilitate over-the-counter medication purchases. Advertising was also being sold to the company's Community Partners (local hospitals) and health insurance companies. Actual and projected financial statements for drkoop.com are shown in Exhibits 2, 3, and 4.

Information and Content at the Drkoop.com Web Site

The drkoop.com Web site contained over 70,000 pages of health information and tools for users. The tag line for the site mirrored Dr. Koop's belief that "the best prescription is knowledge." Going into 2000, the site served as a content and community portal with links to other information sources. Information at the site was organized around six categories:

- News
- Family
- Resources
- Wellness
- Community
- Conditions

Users could sign up to become drkoop.com members; membership enabled them to access interactive tools, community bulletin boards, and chat rooms. The site allowed members to customize their own drkoop.com homepage to cover whatever topics, health issues, and diseases that interested them.

News

The drkoop.com News section provided the latest and most critical information about health. Users could review recent and late-breaking information about product recalls, health-related editorials, health events, polls, special reports, and sports medicine. The site included reports and press releases from such sources as the American Council on Science and Health (ACSH) and the Occupational Safety and Health Administration (OSHA). Using drkoop.com's HealthSearch feature, members could readily locate archived articles relating to all types of health concerns. The search function not only scanned the drkoop.com site but also searched the MedLine database of medical journals and the National Cancer Institute's bibliographic database for relevant articles or abstracts.

Family

The Family section of the drkoop.com Web site was divided into subcategories, including Children, Men, Women, and Elderly. The Web site had received accolades as a superior health care destination for women and children. On November 8, 1999, eHealthCare World awarded

Exhibit 2   Actual and Projected Income Statements for drkoop.com, 1997–2001 (in Millions of $, Except for Per Share Data)

	Income Statement Data					Revenue-Cost-Margin Analysis				
	1997	1998	1999	2000*	2001*	1997	1998	1999	2000*	2001*
Revenues										
Advertising	–	–	$ 7.7	$23.3	$42.3	N/A	N/A	81.1%	72.7%	63.4%
Content licensing	–	–	1.7	6.7	17.1	N/A	N/A	17.9	20.8	25.6
Other	–	–	0.1	2.1	7.4	N/A	N/A	1.1	6.5	11.0
Total Revenues	–	$0.04	$ 9.5	$32.1	$66.7	N/A	N/A	100.0%	100.0%	100.0%
Cost of operations										
Production, content, and product development	$0.5	$ 4.4	$ 9.4	$20.8	$23.5	N/A	N/A	98.9%	64.9%	35.2%
Sales and marketing	–	2.0	45.6	34.6	35.8	N/A	N/A	480.0	107.7	53.6
Total cost of sales	$0.5	$ 6.4	$65.0	$55.4	$59.3	N/A	N/A	578.9%	172.6%	88.8%
Gross income	($0.5)	($ 6.4)	($47.9)	($23.3)	$ 7.4					
Gross margin %	NM	NM	NM	(72.6%)	11.1%					
General and administrative expense	$0.2	$ 2.6	$ 9.5	$10.6	$12.2	N/A	N/A	100.0%	33.0%	18.3%
Operating income	($0.6)	($ 9.0)	($57.4)	($33.9)	($ 4.8)					
Operating margin	NM	NM	NM	(105.6%)	(7.2%)					
Nonoperating income and expenses										
Interest (net)	–	–	$ 1.3	$ 1.7	$ 1.7	N/A	N/A	13.7%	5.3%	2.5%
Other	–	–	–	–	–	N/A	N/A	0.0	0.0	0.0
Pretax income	($0.6)	($ 9.0)	($56.1)	($32.2)	($ 3.1)	N/A	N/A	(590.5%)	(100.3%)	(4.6%)
Pretax margin	NM	NM	NM	(100.3%)	(4.6%)					
Provision for income taxes	–	–	–	–	$ 0.6					
Tax rate	0%	0%	0%	0%	(18%)					
Income before nonrecurring items	($0.6)	($ 9.0)	($56.1)	($32.2)	($ 3.6)	N/A	N/A	(590.5%)	(100.3%)	(5.4%)
Nonrecurring items	–	–	–	–	–					
Net income	($0.6)	($ 9.0)	($56.1)	($32.2)	($ 3.6)	N/A	N/A	(590.5%)	(100.3%)	(5.4%)

*Estimated

NM = Not meaningful. N/A = Not applicable.

Source: Company reports; Bear, Stearns & Co. Inc. estimates.

drkoop.com a gold medal in the category "Best Site for Women" based on meeting women's needs for its health and medical news, information, education, advice, support, and community events.[18]

Resources

Drkoop.com provided users with a variety of content and tools for users to personalize their experience at the Web site. Drkoop.com's Personal Drugstore was a central location where consumers could find information about prescription drugs and check drug interactions. DrugChecker, a proprietary drkoop.com technology, enabled consumers to ensure that their medications did not interact with each other or with food to cause adverse reactions. Such information was considered vital information, considering that the American Medical Association reported adverse drug interactions were the fourth leading cause of death in the United States. Over 100,000 deaths in 1997 were attributed to the adverse affects of prescription drugs.[19] Drkoop.com's DrugChecker technology received a gold medal as the "Best Interactive Assessment Tool" in the eHealthcare World awards.[20] Members could download the DrugChecker tool and add it to their personal Web site, free of charge. In late 1999, over 9,500 Web sites were making DrugChecker available.[21]

Drkoop.com's Personal Insurance Center helped consumers evaluate insurance plans through access to an insurance library, a glossary of terms, and expert advice.

Exhibit 3   Drkoop.com's Balance Sheet Data, 1998–1999, with Estimates for 2000–2001*
($ in Millions, Except for Share Data)

	December			
	1998	**1999**	**2000***	**2001***
Assets				
Current Assets:				
Cash and equivalents	–	$ 35.7	$ 19.9	$ 11.1
Accounts receivable	–	10.5	9.6	14.5
Other	–	22.6	5.9	5.9
Total current assets	$ 0.1	$ 68.9	$ 35.4	$ 31.5
Property, plant, and equipment	$ 0.3	$ 10.4	$ 1.0	$ 2.2
Investment	–	$ 5.0	$ 5.0	$ 5.0
Licenses	–	2.8	2.1	1.2
Other	–	12.4	–	–
Total assets	$ 0.4	$ 99.5	$ 43.6	$ 39.9
Liabilities and stockholders' equity				
Current liabilities				
Accounts payable	$ 0.8	$ 8.2	$ 5.0	$ 5.0
Accrued liabilities	0.5	9.6	2.7	2.7
Deferred revenue	–	3.4	0.7	0.7
Notes payable	0.5	–	0.3	0.3
Total current liabilities	$ 3.0	$ 23.2	$ 8.7	$ 8.7
Other	–	–	–	–
Redeemable preferred stock	$18.4	–	–	–
Preferred stock	–	–	–	–
Common stock	–	–	–	–
Capital in excess of par	–	$149.4	$133.5	$129.9
Retained earnings (deficit)	(19.6)	(75.7)	(94.9)	(94.9)
Other	(1.4)	(2.4)	(3.9)	(3.9)
Total stockholders' equity	($21.0)	$ 71.3	$ 34.8	$ 31.2
Total liabilities and stockholders' equity	$ 0.4	$ 99.5	$ 43.6	$ 39.9
Selected financial statistics				
Current ratio	0	7.7	4.1	3.6
Days sales outstanding	N/A	94	80.4	65.2
Book value/share	N/A	$ 2.23	$ 1.14	$ 0.99
Return on equity	N/A	N/A	N/A	N/A
Cash flow per share	($0.32)	($0.41)	($1.00)	($0.06)
Fee cash flow per share	($0.33)	($0.41)	($1.04)	($0.12)
Long-term debt/total capital	0%	0%	0%	0%

*Estimated

Source: Company reports; Bear, Stearns & Co. Inc. estimates.

Users could review frequently asked questions, search archived questions, and send their questions to insurance expert Jim Perry, the director of state affairs for the Council for Affordable Health Insurance. The Personal Insurance Center pages contained advertisements with direct links to several health insurance sites, including eHealthInsurance.com and Quotesmith.com, that provided online policy information and premium quotes.

Exhibit 4   Drkoop.com's Statement of Cash Flows, 1998–1999, with Projections for 2000–2001*
($ in Millions, Except for Share Data)

	1998	1999	2000*	2001*
Cash flows from operating activities				
Net income	($ 9.0)	($ 68.2)	($ 32.2)	($ 3.6)
Depreciation and amortization	0.1	1.4	1.8	1.8
Other	0.1	26.5	–	–
Change in current account				
Accounts receivable	–	(4.7)	(4.9)	(4.9)
Increase in other assets	–	–	–	–
Accounts payable	2.1	(0.1)	–	–
Accrued liabilities and other assets	–	(0.2)	–	–
Deferred revenue	–	(0.5)	–	–
Other	–	(6.0)	–	–
Cash provided by operating activities	($ 6.8)	($ 50.7)	($ 35.4)	($ 6.7)
Cash flows from investing activities				
Capital expenditures	($ 0.3)	($ 0.6)	($ 1.3)	($ 2.1)
Net cash used in investing activities	($ 0.3)	($ 0.6)	($ 1.3)	($ 2.1)
Cash flows from financing activities				
Net long-term financing	$ 0.5	–	–	–
Preferred stock issuances	6.6	$ 5.8	–	–
Common stock issuances	–	90.0	–	–
Other	–	12.0	–	–
Net cash provided in financing activities	$ 7.1	$ 107.8	–	–
Net increase (decrease) in cash	–	$ 56.6	($ 36.7)	($ 8.8)
Cash beginning of year	–	–	56.6	19.9
End of year	–	$ 56.6	$ 19.9	$ 11.1
Cash flow/share	($ 0.3)	($ 2.25)	($ 1.00)	($ 0.06)
Free cash flow (FCF) per share	($ 0.3)	($ 2.27)	($ 1.04)	($ 0.12)

	1998	1999	2000*	2001*
Cash flow from operations minus net loss (income)	$ 2.2	$ 17.5	($ 3.1)	($ 3.1)
EBITDA*	(9.0)	(41.6)	(32.1)	(3.0)
Free cash flow (FCF)	(6.5)	(50.1)	(34.1)	(4.6)

*Estimated.

* Earnings before interest, taxes, depreciation, and amortization.

Source: Company reports; Bear, Stearns & Co. Inc. estimates.

This section of the site was recognized for its extensive library of insurance articles, information on insurance programs by state, Medicare and Medicaid information, and tools for choosing an insurance policy.[22] Drkoop.com won a silver medal at the eHealthcare World Awards as the "Best Managed Care Site."

Prior to proliferating use of the Internet, information about clinical trial results and registration was limited for patients. Drkoop.com had recently begun disseminating information about clinical studies; this included such things as patient information, trial procedures, how research was conducted, and how consumers could participate in a

Quintiles clinical study. Drkoop.com had formed a partnership with Quintiles, the world's leading provider of health care services to the pharmaceutical industry and largest clinical trials management organization, whereby drkoop.com was compensated for successfully recruiting qualified participants into clinical trials.

Drkoop.com had a database and directory of health resources in local communities. A regional directory helped consumers locate hospitals; however, the directory listings were limited to hospitals that participated in the drkoop.com Community Partner Program.[23] A Physician Locator tool, provided by the American Board of Medical Specialties (ABMS), allowed members to search and verify the location and specialty of any physician certified by the member boards of the ABMS. When members clicked on the Physician Locator service, they were automatically transferred to the ABMS site. The Resources section also provided links to pharmacy sites where consumers could order and reorder their prescriptions with doctor approval. When asked if prescriptions will be given almost exclusively online, Donald Hackett, president and CEO of drkoop.com, did not expect the Internet to become the chief vehicle for providing prescriptions to patients. He said:

> Although I'm a technologist at heart, there's a tremendous amount of human interaction that needs to take place. But even when the consumer needs to schedule the appointment, you can eliminate waste from the system with new technology. This technology is about streamlining the screening process.[24]

Other resources included drkoop.com's rankings of other health sites (not including major competitors such as WebMD and onhealth.com) and a list of books recommended by drkoop.com experts and community leaders. Through an alliance with Amazon.com, users wishing to purchase any of the recommended books were automatically sent to the Amazon.com site.

Wellness

The primary topics in the Wellness section were fitness and prevention. There was advice on weight loss, along with diet-oriented chat rooms and recipes for diet foods. Consumers could use this section to plan a workout routine that matched diet and time constraints. The section's theme was that by staying healthy and fit, people could prevent many illnesses.

In further support of the wellness theme, there were pages devoted to one of Dr. C. Everett Koop's favorite subjects: the evils of smoking. In addition to extensive information on the effects of smoking on the body, there was information on quitting programs and support

groups. Much of the information concerning smoking reflected Dr. Koop's strong personal views.

Community

Drkoop.com's underlying philosophy of getting people together and giving them the tools and information to improve their health was much in evidence in the Community section of the Web site, which had more than 130 interactive chat rooms and message boards devoted to specific afflictions and health problems. Users could click on any of the 130-plus topics and join in on chat room discussions, read message board postings, and post messages sharing their own experiences and views. In addition, there were daily topics of discussion where participants could "listen in" on discussions not only with other patients, but also with doctors.

The Community section had a constant stream of banner ads and large sidebar ads from sites such as DrugEmporium.com; links to these sites made it convenient for site users to purchase health care products and services online. The ads often focused on the particular disease that the user was currently examining.

Conditions

The Conditions section was an online encyclopedia of medical advice. Visitors could research almost any disease or mental health issue they had questions about. It also offered shortcuts to advice pages for first aid and for common symptoms such as back pain or insomnia. The first-aid pages provided advice on a wide variety of topics, from animal bites to sunburn.

Site Disclaimer/Liability

The drkoop.com site had a disclaimer on every Web page that stated, "This information is not intended to be a substitute for professional medical advice. You should not use this information to diagnose or treat a health problem or disease without consulting with a qualified health care provider. Please consult your health care provider with any questions or concerns you may have regarding your condition."[25]

Site Awards

On November 4, 1999, drkoop.com won more awards than any other health care Web site at eHealthcare World Awards in New York. The site received two Gold and two Silver awards, in recognition of its trusted content and health care information for consumers. However, the drkoop.com Web site had been criticized by the American Medical Association for not providing sufficient information related to sponsorship and commerce relationships.

Drkoop.com's Medical Advisory Board

To help develop the content of the medical information and resources available at its website, drkoop.com had created a Medical Advisory Board consisting of Dr. C. Everett Koop and five others:

- Dr. Nancy Snyderman—a member of the company's board of directors, the medical correspondent for ABC (who made frequent appearances on *Good Morning America, 20/20,* and the *ABC Evening News),* a monthly columnist for *Good Housekeeping,* the author of a book on health care for women over 40, the author of several published papers and an associate clinical professor at the California Pacific Medical Center and the University of California–San Francisco.

- Dr. James F. Dickson III—a former deputy assistant secretary of health and assistant surgeon general, the author of over 50 published papers on surgery and biomedical research, the editor of six books, and a fellow of the American College of Surgeons.

- Dr. Bruce Hensel—an Emmy Award-winning medical, health, and science editor/reporter for NBC4's *Channel 4 News;* the host of *4 Your Health!;* a local Emmy Award-winning series of half-hour specials featuring the latest in medical breakthroughs, information, and technology; an associate professor of medicine at UCLA; and the winner of several other awards for medical education.

- Dr. Stanley Joel Reiser—a professor of humanities and technology in health care at the University of Texas–Houston Health Care Center, the author of over 120 articles and books, a noted speaker on medical topics, and recognized authority on medical ethics, the assessment of medical technologies, the role of values in governing health care organizations, and public health care policy.

- Dr. Michael Seth Shaw—president of Health Science Media (a health care education, communications, and media company in Atlanta, Georgia) since 1979; a graduate of Emory University School of Medicine; and a member of several medical organizations.

Competition and Profiles of Selected Rivals

Competition in the online medical information provider industry was strong and getting stronger. Hundreds of sites providing various kinds of medical information had emerged over the past two years. All of the most popular sites provided extensive consumer health information, chat rooms, expert advice, links to products and comprehensive and fully tailored health care publications for professionals of all specialties.

In addition to the companies that specialized primarily in online health and medical information, large medical and health care companies were establishing an Internet presence. Some provided medical information, but the primary focus of most such companies was on marketing health insurance and/or over-the-counter drug products. Most pharmaceutical companies had portions of their corporate Web sites dedicated to consumer health information. One big player in this area was Merck, which published an online "medical bible." The pharmaceutical companies were not direct competitors of medical information providers like drkoop.com because their main focus was to sell pharmaceutical products, but they were still players in the online medical information market.

Drkoop.com's management expected that competition among these sites to obtain content would likely increase the fees charged by high-quality content providers, perhaps driving up costs significantly. In addition, competition was forcing all medical information providers to try to set themselves apart on the basis of differentiating Web site features. The addition of new features required rivals to continue to improve the technology underlying their Web sites, also driving up costs significantly.

In October 1999, PC Data ranked drkoop.com as the number one dedicated health care site, based on Web site traffic, for the seventh consecutive month (see Exhibit 5).[26] According to PC Data, the site was the 43rd most popular site on the Internet overall.

Brief profiles of selected leading online medical information providers are presented below.

Healtheon/WebMD.com

Drkoop.com's strongest competitor was Healtheon/WebMD Corporation, which claimed to be the first comprehensive online health care portal.[27] The company was formed by a merger of Healtheon and WebMD in May 1999. Following the merger, the companies combined their consumer Web sites, MyHealtheon.com and MyWebMD.com, into one site (www.webmd.com). Healtheon/WebMD was building a system of software and services to automate such tasks as HMO enrollment, referrals, data retrieval, and claims processing for use by insurers, doctors, pharmacies, and consumers. The site also offered physician communications services, physician references, medical information and news, and personalized content to its users. Healtheon/WebMD had revenues of $28.7 million in the quarter ending September 1999.

Exhibit 5	Traffic Statistics on Medical Information Provider Web Sites, September, 1999

Company	Number of Unique Hits, September 1999
drkoop.com	5,539,000
onhealth.com	2,262,000
discoveryhealth.com	1,077,000
webmd.com	765,000
thriveonline.com	753,000
healthyideas.com	714,000
intelihealth.com	675,000
allhealth.com	596,000
AOLhealth.com	568,000
Healthcentral.com	532,000
medscape.com	415,000
ama-assn.org	404,000
mediconsult.com	225,000

In early December 1999, Rupert Murdoch's News Corp. formed a $1 billion partnership with Healtheon/WebMD in one of the largest media and Internet deals to date.[28]

News Corp. became a 10.8 percent owner of Healtheon/WebMD, providing $700 million in "branding services" over 10 years, purchasing $100 million of Healtheon/WebMD's stock, investing $100 million cash in the Internet company, and signing a $62.5 million five-year licensing deal to syndicate WebMD's daily broadcast content. In describing the partnership, News Corp. president and COO Peter Chemin said, "Companies traditionally re-purpose print or broadcast content for the Web. With this deal, we're using the Web as a source for original, unique programming which will be leveraged across all media owned by News Corp."[29] The goal of this partnership was to drive television viewers to medical Web sites and vice versa, creating single health care information brands across all media. Industry observers speculated that the News Corp. partnership could give Healtheon/WebMD an advantage in internationalizing online health care.

Mediconsult.com

Mediconsult's mission was to provide timely, comprehensive, and accessible information on chronic medical conditions, using the latest available technology to deliver information efficiently. Its Web site featured a fee-based service, *MediXpert,* which let visitors present a case to a medical specialist who responded with a confidential

report. Mediconsult had no affiliation with any HMO, hospital, or other health care organization in order to ensure unbiased, objective, credible information. Management insisted that all information on its site "pass a rigorous clinical review process before we deem it worthy" of the consumer.[30] The site also had a powerful search engine, Medisearch, which allowed quick keyword inquiries. Mediconsult reported revenues of $3.1 million for the quarter ending September 1999.

In September 1999, Mediconsult.com acquired Physicians Online in a stock deal valued at $180 million. The acquisition was expected to help Mediconsult.com take advantage of the recent introduction of online medical records and other services designed to connect doctors and patients and deliver health care.[31]

The Health Network.com

The Health Network was a 50/50 partnership between FOX Entertainment Group and AHN Partners, LP that combined the leading health cable television channel (The Health Network) with one of the most visited health information sites on the Internet (ahn.com, recently renamed TheHealthNetwork.com). The partnership promoted itself as a one-stop television and Internet site where consumers could find information, support, and the motivation needed to make decisions about leading a healthy life. The Health Network reached more than 17 million households in all 50 states through cable and satellite and could be seen via the Internet with live streaming video. Its Web site was the premier source of live medical events, such as the first live Internet birth and the first live Internet triplet birth.

Viewers, whether online or watching on television, were provided information by doctors and other experts in a clear, interesting, and easy-to-understand manner. In addition, the online site provided original programming, breaking news, exercise and nutrition guides, expert medical advice, and in-depth information. Online users could connect directly with both credible medical professionals and people who had similar interests in specific health categories such as women's health, parenting, and heart health.

Medscape

Medscape's home page was comprehensive, well organized, and user-friendly. It featured the Medscape Network (for students, nurses, physicians), Medscape Resources, My Medscape (records personalized info from previous visits), and an Editorial Board. In addition, Medscape published *Medscape General Medicine,* an online, peer-reviewed medical journal, and it offered a database of continuing medical education programs, an online bookstore, and physician Web sites for its members.

Medscape produced the consumer-oriented CBS *HealthWatch.* In July 1999, CBS acquired a 35 percent stake in Medscape in exchange for $157 million in advertising and branding services. The company had recently announced a content agreement with America Online. The three-year arrangement called for Medscape to develop co-branded health sites for AOL's 18 million subscribers. In exchange, Medscape will pay AOL $33 million for two years.

Medscape reported revenues of $3.1 million for the quarter ending September 1999.

The American Medical Association Web Site (www.ama-assn.org)

The American Medical Association (AMA) represented about 35 percent of U.S. doctors (down from 50 percent in 1975). A core objective of the AMA was to be the world leader in obtaining, synthesizing, integrating, and disseminating information on health and medical practice. The AMA published numerous journals, and its corporate Web site, a portion of which was accessible to members only, provided valuable online information. The general public could use the site to look for medical group and physician locators; to get medical advice about injuries, illnesses, and specific conditions; and to read about general health information. Consumers could also learn about the association's advocacy and legislative initiatives and read about topics on medical ethics and education.

Revenue erosion from declining membership was expected to cause the AMA to devote time and resources to enhancing and promoting the public part of its Web site as a way of rejuvenating its revenue stream.

OnHealth.com

OnHealth Network Company was a consumer health information company based in Seattle. Its Web site was not tied to a particular doctor group, health system, or insurance company. OnHealth.com offered both proprietary and syndicated content. Most information came from the *New England Journal of Medicine,* Cleveland Clinic, Beth Israel Deaconess Medical Center, and physicians who taught at Harvard, Columbia, and Stanford. A unique feature on the site's home page was the Herbal Index, which contained 140 descriptions of alternative health remedies. About 80 percent of OnHealth's audience was female.

The company had negotiated agreements to provide content to several Web sites, including America Online and WebTV. In December 1999, OnHealth.com signed an agreement with Ask Jeeves, Inc., a leading provider of natural-language question-answering services on the Web for consumers and businesses. This deal will provide OnHealth with prominent brand positioning.[32]

The site was supported by advertising. Advertisers included Johnson & Johnson and Pfizer. Site operators claimed that the information about a topic was not influenced by the advertisements displayed on that page, indicating, "If it ever appears otherwise to you, please let us know."[33]

Affiliates of Van Wagoner Capital Management owned about 39 percent of the company. OnHealth reported revenues of $1 million for the quarter ending September 1999.

iVillage's www.allHealth.com

iVillage's Web site targeted women aged 25 to 49 through more than 15 "channels" focusing on topics such as health, food, parenting, relationships, and shopping. The health sections of the site were at betterhealth.com or allhealth.com. The sites used the tag lines "Take Charge of Your Health!" and "Information you need from a Community you can trust."[34] Site features included extensive chat rooms, weekly polls, and shopping. iVillage members could "ask the experts" for medical advice. iVillage generated more than 80 percent of its revenue from advertising, but the company was looking to enlarge its online product offerings; its first step in this direction was a line of baby products offered at iBaby.com. In the quarter ending September 1999, iVillage reported revenues of $10.7 million.

Candice Carpenter, iVillage's CEO, commenting on the recent merger between Healtheon and WebMD, said, "I think it's pretty obvious there needs to be some (more) consolidation. We've got to clean this up a little. I don't know who's going to do it, but somebody should step up to the plate to do that job."[35]

Conflicts of Interest and Ethics Concerns

There was a growing concern among many medical information providers about the potential for conflicts of interests and potential liability in providing inaccurate information, diagnosis, and prescribing drugs online. In a proactive attempt to address such issues, Dr. C. Everett Koop initiated a meeting of interested parties. The meeting resulted in the formation of a coalition of 16 companies, including Healtheon/WebMD, Medscape Inc., America Online Inc., and drkoop.com, to develop an ethical code of conduct for Internet-based medical information providers. Alliance members accounted for 27 percent of total Internet audience traffic.[36] The group was working to create a set of recommended policies and practices for advertising, privacy, and content that would ensure the reliability of health information that consumers accessed through e-health providers. Donald Kemper, the chairperson of Hi-Ethics, stated that "our ultimate goal is to guide a future of consumer confidence in health care information."[37]

Future Outlook for Drkoop.com

Donald W. Hackett, president and CEO of drkoop.com, believed the company had a promising future:

> The successful execution of our business strategy has firmly positioned the company for growth. Our registered users are growing at a healthy pace, we are rapidly extending our reach, our advertising and sponsorship pipeline is strong, and the drkoop.com brand name continues to be recognized as an industry leader. Looking ahead, we intend to leverage the strength of our domestic business to accelerate expansion into international markets. We recently announced our first alliance with Australia's Medweb and anticipate continued international expansion in the first half of 2000.

Nonetheless, Hackett and company cofounder Dennis Upah knew the challenges ahead were formidable. Medical sites on the Internet were proliferating. Competition was becoming stronger. WebMD and Rupert Murdoch's News Corp. had announced plans to put more than $1 billion into developing their medical information site. Companies like Healtheon/WebMD were partnering with hospitals to provide services other than medical information. While there were many opportunities for medical information providers, it was far from clear which business model and strategy made the most sense for drkoop.com. And even more important, drkoop.com was "burning" through its cash reserves and looking at negative cash flows for some time to come. A number of investors were becoming increasingly concerned about the company's financial position and the viability of its business model.

Notes:

1. "Dr. Koop's Community," 1998 Business Wire, Inc., July 20, 1998.
2. ww.drkoop.com/aboutus/koop.
3. Ibid.
4. "i:2O drkoop.com's Dennis Upah," *Crain Communications,* November 1999.
5. PR Newswire Association, Inc., March 29, 1999.
6. "Dr. Koop's Community."
7. "USWeb Audience Development Practice Helps Establish Success of Leading Consumer Healthcare Site," 1998 Business Wire, Inc., November 19, 1998.
8. "drkoop.com Breaks 15 Million Page Views for October," PR Newswire, November 22,1999.
9. See Hoover's online database (www.hoovers. corn/industry /snap-shot/0,2204,23, OO.html). See also Thomas E. Miller and Scott Reents, "The Health Care Industry in Transition," *Cyber Dialogue,* 1998.
10. Miller and Reents, "The Health Care Industry in Transition."
11. Ibid.
12. Bear Stearns Equity Research, Health Care Industry, July 27, 1999.
13. Ibid.
14. Ibid.
15. Company documents.
16. "i:20 drkoop.com's Dennis Upah."
17. CAA provides strategic consulting services in marketing and technology areas and holds alliances with internet incubator, idealab! and communications consulting and advertising company, Shepardson, Stern and Kaminsky.
18. "drkoop.com Web Site Dominates Awards at eHealthcare World," PR Newswire, November 8, 1999.
19. "Dr. Koop's Community."
20. "drkoop.com Web Site Dominates Awards at eHealthcareWorld."
21. Ibid.
22. Ibid.
23. Hospitals that participate in the Community Partner Program pay $50,000 to $100,000 per year to license drkoop.com health care information to use on their Web sites. In addition, direct links are provided from the drkoop.com site to their individual Web sites.
24. "Posts," *The Standard,* June 28, 1999.
25. Disclaimer present on every page of the drkoop.com Web site.
26. PR Newswire Association, October 7, 1999, Financial News section.
27. www.ixl.com/success/webmd/index.html.
28. www.thestandard.coiWarticle/display/0,1151,6224,00.html.
29. thestandard.com.
30. www.mediconsult.com.
31. www.thestandard.com/article/display/0,1151,6224,00.html.
32. www.askjeeves.com. Investor Relations.
33. orihealth.com/chl/info/item.asp.
34. www. atlheatth.com.
35. www-thestandard-com/article/display/0,1151,4839,00.html.
36. "Leading E-Healthware Companies Form Alliance to Benefit Internet Consumers," Business Wire, November 4, 1999.
37. Ibid.

Case 15

Excellence at Motorola

E. Brian Peach and Kenneth L. Murrell, *The University of West Florida*

Introduction

1999. As the 20th century drew to a close, Motorola was one of the world's leading providers of wireless communications, semiconductors, and advanced electronic systems, components, and services. Major equipment businesses included cellular telephone, two-way radio, paging and data communications, personal communications, automotive, defense and space electronics and computers. Motorola semiconductors powered communication devices, computers and millions of other products. During the decade, Motorola's revenues tripled from approximately ten billion dollars in 1990 to almost thirty billion dollars in 1998.

Motorola History

1928–1949. The formative years for Motorola was the period of 1928–1949. Motorola had its beginnings in 1928 when Paul V. Galvin and his brother Joseph E. Galvin

---

Acknowledgements: This case could not have been completed without the active support and contributions of many Motorolans. Patrick (Pat) Canavan, Motorola's Senior Vice President and Director, Global Leadership and Organizational Development, sponsored our efforts within Motorola, helped us set up the interviews, and solved a number of problems that arose during our research.

RS Moorthy, Motorola's Director of Research and Strategic Capabilities, Global Leadership and Organizational Development, was a major adviser to our project, providing constant support and advice during the project. Known by many within Motorola for his cross-cultural knowledge management and ethical expertise, he participated in many of Motorola's ethics initiatives and is a key player in Motorola's Ethics Renewal Process. RS provided many invaluable insights into global ethics and cultural challenges facing global firms. He provided numerous documents that allowed us to see the ethical process from the inside. In addition, his staff coordinated our interviews and visits at Motorola and provided unfailing support for our requests.

A huge debt is owed to the many Motorola executives and employees who gave of their time to sit and talk with the case writers about Motorola and ethics. They were all passionate about their company and passionate about ethics. Clearly busy people, they often went past our scheduled appointment times to ensure they answered all of our questions. Robert W. (Bob) Galvin went well past his scheduled time, the entire discussion confirming his reputation as a true gentleman, and a man committed to ethics in business. Another executive followed us down the elevator and caught up with us in the lobby and talked for lengthy period to ensure we had a complete answer.

BJ Chakiris was a wise and thoughtful source of help. She provided critical helping to establish relations with Motorola and Pat Canavan, and made substantive suggestions in structuring the interviews and organizing the case. Our thanks to Peter Sorensen, Therese Yaeger, and Susan Stackley Stephens of Benedictine University. Peter and Therese worked with us in conceptualizing the case and assisted in a number of interviews. Susan helped with a number of interviews, taking notes and operating video equipment. Susan was also the go-to person when we needed something done in Chicago. She was a huge help in locating people, confirming appointments, and doing what needed to be done.

And finally, our thanks to Lynda Peach, who proofread the manuscripts, designed the website, and put up with Brian while we finished the case.

Financial support for this project was provided by a grant from the Shell Corporation, and a University of West Florida Research Grant.

Brian Peach
Ken Murrell
August 3rd, 1999

purchased the battery eliminator business of the bankrupt Stewart Storage Battery Company in Chicago and established the Galvin Manufacturing Corporation on September 25, 1928.[1] At that time, automobile manufacturers did not provide auto radios, and as the demand for battery eliminators declined, the Galvin Manufacturing Corporation produced auto radios that were sold and installed as an accessory by independent automotive distributors and dealers. Paul Galvin coined the name Motorola for the company's new products, linking the ideas of sound and motion. During the 1930s, the company developed police and home radio receivers, began a national advertising campaign, and developed innovative personnel programs. In the 1940s, Motorola developed the "handi-talkie" and "walkie-talkie" which were major contributions to communications in World War II. Serious research on FM communications and semiconductors began, leading to the establishment of a research laboratory in 1949. The name of the company was changed to Motorola, Inc. in 1947, and by the end of the decade, Motorola was supplying all three major auto manufacturers with radios, and had begun manufacturing televisions.

1950–1969. The decades of the 1950s and 1960s saw many advances in semiconductors, including smaller and more powerful transistors that were used in portable radios, auto radios, and a new product called pagers. With the increasing demand for semiconductor products, Motorola became a commercial producer and supplier of semiconductors for sale to other manufacturers, and established the Semiconductor Products Division in 1956. With the death of Paul Galvin in 1959, his son Robert W. Galvin oversaw the entry of Motorola into international markets, and by the end of the 1960s Motorola had established sales and manufacturing operations throughout the world. Motorola expanded its international presence by adding plants in many countries, including Australia, England, France, Germany, Israel, Japan, Korea, Malaysia, Mexico, and Puerto Rico.

1970s. The decade of the 1970s saw Robert W. Galvin continuing as Chief Executive Officer and Chairman of the Board, with William J. Weisz named President of Motorola in 1971 and Chief Operating Officer in 1972. During this period, Motorola produced components for consumer products such as quartz watches. In 1974, Motorola introduced its first microprocessor, the 6800, and later in 1979 introduced its first 16-bit microprocessor, the 68000. Motorola also expanded its presence in communications with a high capacity radio telephone system, computer controlled radio systems and products that use the trunking method. In 1979, Motorola accelerated its commitment to quality, with a

six-sigma company-wide quality program underway by the mid-1980s. In 1988 Motorola won the Malcolm Baldridge Quality Award, the first year it was given.

1980s. The 1980s saw a continuing emphasis by Motorola in the communications area including cellular and pager technologies, and Motorola provided a radio network for the Summer Olympic Games in Los Angeles. Contracts were received for cellular systems for New York, Philadelphia, Beijing, and Hong Kong, with system expansion contracts for the United Kingdom, Scandinavia, and Japan. In tandem with its quality initiative, Motorola increased its investment in employee education. The company-wide Motorola Training and Education Center (MTEC) was headquartered near Chicago in the new Galvin Center for Continuing Education, and in 1990, MTEC became Motorola University. Continuing a trend begun in the 1970s, Motorola moved away from consumer electronics and in 1987 Motorola produced its last auto radio. In 1988 George M. C. Fisher was named President of Motorola, and Gary L. Tooker was named Chief Operating Officer. Under George Fisher, Motorola concentrated its efforts on high technology including commercial, industrial and governmental markets, achieving record sales growth.

1990s. In 1990, 50 years after his father, Paul Galvin, invited him to perform his first assignment for the company, Robert W. Galvin moved to Chairman of the Executive Committee and Gary Tooker was elected CEO. Christopher B. Galvin, the third generation Galvin, was elected President and Chief Operating Officer, and later, on Jan 1, 1997 was named CEO. The 1990s witnessed the introduction of Motorola's third-generation 32-bit microprocessor, introduction of an array of digitally based products, and increased sophistication in embedded chips using DigitalDNA. Motorola developed and introduced a cellular communications system designed to reach every point on the globe based on an array of small satellites in low-Earth orbit called "Iridium." The decade also saw the opening of the Motorola Museum of Electronics where exhibits chronicle the closely intertwined evolution of Motorola and the electronics industry. "It is the voice of our past," said Robert W. Galvin, "But through the lessons and examples contained in this museum, we are better prepared to address our future."

Recent Performance

Corporate Growth

An impressive facet of Motorola's success is that it competes in industries noted for extraordinarily intense competition, constant exit of formerly significant competitors, and rapidly changing technology. Indeed, remaining on the cutting edge of technology is often insufficient—firms have to anticipate and lead the changes in technology. In addition, Motorola competes against some of the strongest and most competitive global firms in the world including an elite set of global competitors such as Intel and the very top Japanese firms in semiconductors. Two of the seven arenas the Japanese government has targeted with development support as critical industries of the future are semiconductors and communications—Motorola's major industries.

Motorola enjoyed some spectacular successes, especially in the early 1990s, when revenue and profit growth had investors and Wall Street cheering. However, the year 1998 was the culmination of a series of challenges and setbacks for Motorola, and its financial performance for 1998 resulted in its first loss in many years. Shareholder return averaged 54 percent from 1993 to 1995, but dropped to less than one percent annually from 1995 to 1998. Revenue growth had averaged 27 percent from 1993 to 1995 but sales in 1998 were $29.4 billion, down one percent from $29.8 billion in 1997. Motorola attributed the revenue decline to lost sales from various businesses that it had identified as non-strategic and poorly performing and from which it decided to exit. Profits dropped 33 percent from 1995 to 1997, and then turned negative in 1998. The 1998 loss, including special charges, was $962 million, or $1.61 per share, compared with earnings of $1.18 billion, or $1.94 per share, in 1997.[2] In addition to financial performance, other indicators were down. Motorola's domestic cellular phone market share dropped from 60 percent in 1994 to 45 percent in 1997, and 34 percent in 1998.[3] Worldwide, Nokia surpassed Motorola as the world's leading supplier of wireless phones in 1998. According to research firm Dataquest Inc., in 1998 Nokia sold more than 37 million wireless phones for a 23 percent market share, while Motorola sold 32 million phones for a 20 percent

market share. Ranking third and fourth were Ericsson with 15 percent and Panasonic with 8 percent.[4] The picture was bleaker in digital phones, where Motorola had only 9.3 percent of the US market for digital cellular handsets, and was ranked No. 5 in that sector behind rival brands such as Nokia and Sony.

Although Motorola's 1998 performance stands in stark contrast to its rapid growth and high profitability in the early 1990s, it had its genesis in a number of strategic and policy decisions Motorola made over the previous decade. These decisions, combined with external events such as the downturn in demand for major Motorola divisions (semiconductors and pagers), and the Asian economic meltdown, all led to a stunning reversal of fortune for Motorola. From a firm respected around the world for cutting edge technology and six-sigma quality, it found itself being criticized for its management style, behind in digital cellular phone technology, focusing on a wireless-equipment technology that only covered half the U.S. market potential, and losing customers due to quality and performance complaints.

Motorola's Challenges

Management Style and Practices

Motorola practices an informal, first-name-only culture that places high value on individual employees. Growing out of founder Paul Galvin's highly participative management style, Motorola in the late 1980s and early 1990s had a combination of a strong three man office of the chief executive and a highly decentralized organization structure that placed operating and strategic authority at the business unit level. Some functions, such as strategic planning, finance, human resources, legal, ethics and quality were retained at the corporate level, but autonomy to develop business unit strategies

Exhibit 1	Motorola Revenue Growth		
Year	Sales	Employees	Sales/Employee
1930	$287,256		
1940	$9,936,558	985	$10,088
1950	$177,104,669	9,325	$19,000
1960	$299,065,922	14,740	$20,300
1970	$796,418,521	36,000	$22,100
1980	$3,098,763,000	71,500	$43,340
1990	$10,885,000,000	105,000	$103,670
1998	$29,398,000,000	140,000	$210,000

Exhibit 2   Financial Highlights (Dollars in Millions, Except as Noted)[1,2]

	December 31,	
	1998	1997
Net sales	$29,398	$29,794
Earnings (loss) before income taxes	(1,374)	1,816
% to sales	(4.7)%	6.1 %
Net earnings (loss)	(962)	1,180
% to sales	(3.3)%	4.0 %
Diluted earnings (loss) per common share (in dollars)	(1.61)	1.94
Research and development expenditures	2,893	2,748
Capital expenditures	3,221	2,874
Working capital	2,091	4,181
Current ratio	1.18	1.46
Return on average invested capital	(6.2)%	(8.4)%
Return on average stockholders' equity	(7.6)%	(9.4)%
% of net debt to net debt plus equity	26.8 %	12.4 %
Book value per common share (in dollars)	$ 20.33	$ 22.21
Year-end employment (in thousands)	133	150

[1]http:\\www.motorola.com/investor

[2]A Five Year Financial Summary, Cash Flow, Balance Sheet, and Equity Report are provided as attachments.

Source: Motorola, Inc. and Subsidiaries

was given to the business units. This ultimately became at one and the same time both a source of strength and an Achilles heel for Motorola. Some divisions under strong managers became almost fiefdoms, referred to by some as "warring tribes."[5] At times the semiconductor group was unresponsive to needs of other divisions, refusing to make them chips. The head of the cellular phone operation was convinced that smaller analog phones were preferable to larger digital phones, and blocked attempts to accelerate digital development. The autonomy that had allowed Motorola's divisions to aggressively pursue opportunities without undue coordination in some cases led to stove pipe thinking in other cases that was unresponsive to the rapidly changing nature of the global marketplace. Divisions engaged in sub-optimized behavior as they endeavored to achieve goals at the expense of corporate competitiveness.

The management style of Motorola's leaders came under attack from outside critics as insular and tradition bound. Motorola's leadership culture was engineering based which had seemingly served it well as the company stayed on the forefront of technological advances. In the 1990s, this engineering-based culture was viewed by some as a liability in a world that increasingly was marketing dependent. Motorola tends towards longevity in employment because its core values are "Constant

Respect for People" and "Uncompromising Integrity," primary reasons it has been considered a great company to work for. Employee longevity was reflected by the fact that in 1997 it had 2000 employees celebrating their 25th anniversary at Motorola, a significant number given Motorola's total employment in 1952 was around 10,000. In addition, in 1998 67 percent of Motorola's top executives had been with Motorola for more than 20 years.[6] Viewed by many Motorola leaders as a source of strength and cohesion, it was viewed by critics as evidence that Motorola was inbred and out of touch at the top.

Digital Cellular Phones

Motorola invented the cellular phone and had excelled at improving analog technology, making its phones ever smaller and more feature rich. Motorola stumbled, however, when in an effort to maintain its high margins, it antagonized many of its major customers by attempting to leverage its dominant market share and limit wholesale sales to a few companies.[7] In another marketplace miscalculation, as digital cellular technology evolved, Motorola continued its emphasis on analog technology. The lack of a digital effort was complicated by the fact there are three competing digital technologies being developed: Time Division Multiple Access (TDMA) which is six times as fast as analog, Code Division Multiple Access (CDMA)

Exhibit 3   Consolidated Statements of Operations (in Millions, Except per Share Amounts)

| | December 31, | | |
	1998	1997	1996
Net sales	$29,398	$29,794	$27,973
Costs and expenses			
Manufacturing and other costs of sales	20,886	20,003	18,990
Selling, general, and administrative expenses	5,493	5,188	4,715
Restructuring and other charges	1,980	327	–
Depreciation expense	2,197	2,329	2,308
Interest expense, net	216	131	185
Total costs and expenses	30,772	27,978	26,198
Earnings (loss) before income taxes	(1,374)	1,816	1,775
Income tax provision (benefit)	(412)	636	621
Net earnings (loss)	$ (962)	$ 1,180	$ 1,154
Basic earnings (loss) per common share	$ (1.61)	$ 1.98	$ 1.95
Diluted earnings (loss) per common share	$ (1.61)	$ 1.94	$ 1.90
Diluted weighted average common shares outstanding	598.6	612.2	609.0

See accompanying condensed notes to consolidated financial statements.

Source: Motorola, Inc. and Subsidiaries

which is three times as fast as analog, and Global Standard for Mobile Communications (GSM) which is two to three times as fast and is the primary system in Europe.

Motorola had elected to abandon its early efforts on TDMA where it had a technological lead, to concentrate on CDMA, which it viewed as having greater market potential. This had two major impacts on Motorola. First, it eliminated Motorola from competing for customers that use TDMA. Second, Motorola lost the business of carriers that used CDMA such as AT&T that also wanted equipment that can work on all of the digital systems so that they could provide national coverage across CDMA and TDMA systems. National coverage equipment was provided by some of Motorola's competitors such as Nokia, which introduced a new cellular phone that worked on both analog and the two primary domestic digital networks.[8]

Lack of a digital product also hurt Motorola in Asian markets. Motorola had spent 20 years developing the Asian markets and dominated two-way radios and pagers. The Asian-Pacific region contributed 20 percent of Motorola's revenue in 1997. In Japan, after great difficulties in penetrating the market, Motorola had attained almost a 25 percent market share in 1995. But without a digital product, its share dwindled to 3 percent in 1998. In Thailand, one of Motorola's top three Asian markets,

sales also dropped, letting Nokia and Ericsson become the market leaders. As 1998 drew to a close, Nokia had 40 percent of the Thai market.[9] In China, Motorola lost its dominant position in the cellular phone market when China adopted GSM instead of CDMA, and this led to Ericsson and Nokia controlling approximately two thirds of the market in mid-1998.[10]

Wireless Technology   Motorola is a major supplier of wireless system infrastructure—the equipment that makes products such as cellular phones work, and Motorola has an excellent base station, the part that sends and receives signals from mobile phones. However, it had problems developing a reliable switching system, and this had become a critical part of the wireless infrastructure because digital switches make many of the new digital services possible. As a consequence, between 1990 and 1999 Motorola lost a number of customers and contracts because of poor switching capabilities. By 1998, Motorola had dropped to a 13 percent market share versus Lucent's 38 percent share.

Satellite Systems

Iridium   Motorola is a major backer and developer of Iridium. In 1999, Motorola owned 17.7 percent of Iridium, a satellite-based worldwide phone network that allows users to make and receive calls anywhere in the world. Iridium was intended to be an anywhere, anytime, communication device for anyone in the world that desired mobile communications on a global scale. As late as mid-1998, in the midst of Motorola's financial woes, Iridium was expected to be a significant part of the salvation for Motorola's difficulties. This based on the fact that Iridium had predicted it would garner a 40 percent share of an anticipated 12 million users by 2002 and projected it would generate revenues of over $2.5 billion by the year 2000.[11]

However, with the delayed introduction of Iridium to consumers, problems started occurring. The high user costs of $3000 to buy an Iridium handset and $2 to $7 per minute airtime charges, plus the increasing availability combined with dramatically falling costs of standard cellular phones made potential Iridium users reluctant to sign up. Iridium users also found the handsets to be bulky and hard to use. In addition, although the satellite system provides worldwide coverage, the handsets require a clear line of sight to the satellites, which precludes their use in buildings and other obstructed sites.

By mid-1999, Iridium had expended over $5 billion, shareholders were filing lawsuits, and analysts anticipated a possible bankruptcy for Iridium. The CEO, CFO, and top marketer all departed Iridium as its 10,000 subscribers were barely a fifth of the expected number, and revenues were $1.45 million, well short of covering operating expenses much less the $100 million quarterly debt service on its $3.4 billion in debt.[12] By mid-1999, Iridium's share price had dropped from $68 to $9, and its bonds were selling at 19 cents on the dollar. In July 1999, Motorola's share price dropped 13 percent when Motorola announced that Iridium had three options: out-of-court restructuring, Chapter 11 bankruptcy, or liquidation.[13] Although Motorola contended it had a contingency fund to cover possible Iridium losses, the size of Motorola's exposure made stockholders and the market uneasy.

Adding to Iridium's woes, during the 2000–2001 time period, it faced the prospect of additional direct competitors as three more hand-held mobile phone services were to be launched intensifying the competitive pressures. Ellipso, Globalstar, and ICO Global Communications were expected to be three new entrants to the rural areas of Latin America, Africa, and Southeast Asia. ICO was spending some $3 billion on its satellite system, and Ellipso was spending $1.5 billion. In addition to mainstream users, ICO expected rural villages to account for 10 percent of revenues, while for Ellipso, that percentage could be as high as 25 percent.[14]

Teledesic   Motorola was a 26 percent shareowner of Teledesic, which was planned as a $9 billion low earth orbit (LEO) satellite network and originally intended to begin operations in 2002. In addition to Motorola, billionaires Bill Gates of Microsoft, and Craig McCaw, who made his billions in the cellular phone industry, each had a 21 percent stake in Teledesic, Saudi investor Prince Alaweed Bin Talal had 11 percent, and Boeing had 4 percent. Teledesic planned to have 288 LEO satellites, and was designed to support millions of simultaneous users. Teledesic's business plan was aimed at providing business users access to the Internet at speeds up to 2,000 times faster than a dial-up modem.

In May 1999, Motorola shifted several hundred engineers from the Teledesic project, and rumors flew that Motorola was rethinking its support for Teledesic given its problems with Iridium. The satellite rocket launch industry had experienced a rash of satellite launch failures, and this raised concerns about possible increased costs for projects such as Teledesic in establishing their LEO network.[15]

Semiconductors   The semiconductor sector was a significant victim of the fiefdom mentality at Motorola. Decentralization had led to 23 product groups with 82,000 commodity products, yet the groups were reluctant to share designers or designs with each other. Each group had its own fabrication and systems design libraries and submicron laboratories. These problems were compounded by a worldwide drop in demand for semiconductors. The Semiconductor Division's share of Motorola's total revenues dropped from 31 percent in 1995 to 25 percent in 1998. The division generated losses of $1.2 billion in 1998, versus an operating profit of $1.2 billion in 1995, on sales of $7.3 billion in 1998 versus $8.5 billion in 1995.

External Economy

1998 saw continued weakness in Asian markets, an area that Motorola and most other firms had expected to be a rapidly growing economic force. Until the latter part of 1997, many Asian countries had been experiencing annual economic growth in the 6–9 percent range. The Asian miracle had come to a halt by January of 1998 as many Asian stock markets had dropped, some up to 70 percent, and some currencies had similarly depreciated against the dollar. Japan, once a major force in driving up technology demand in Asia continued in recession, and other areas of Asia were referred to as being in a meltdown economically. Japan's stock market Nikko index dropped from 40,000 in 1989 to 15,000 in 1997. Indonesia, Malaysia, and Thailand were especially hard hit. From 1990–1996, Malaysian exports had increased 18 percent per year, as its government had strongly supported investments in semiconductor production. Thailand's exports grew at 16 percent, Singapore 15 percent, and Hong Kong 14 percent. Businesses dealing in Asia had based their future plans on such high growth. With the abrupt end to the Asian miracle, businesses had to rethink. As an example, worldwide semiconductor sales dropped 8.4 percent from 1997 to 1998. Motorola's semiconductor division thus faced a market demand of $134.8 billion in 1998, well below an anticipated $160 billion market.[16]

Motorola's Actions

Management Practices

CEO Christopher Galvin took a number of actions in 1998 to reverse market share losses and return the firm to profitability. He reorganized Motorola into three major enterprises and replaced the heads of a number of divisions. The objective was to reduce inter-division competition and encourage sharing of ideas, reduce development costs and coordinate actions between Motorola's business units. He also instituted a company-wide rather than divisionally based bonus system for top executives to encourage cooperation.

Motorola's 1999 Organizational Structure

Communications Enterprise The Communications Enterprise (CE) combined Motorola's communications business sectors to establish a coordinated unit that provides integrated communications solutions to a variety of customers and consumers around the world. The CE comprised seven major business sectors (units) and represented approximately 70 percent of Motorola's global business in 1999.

Personal Communications Sector This business unit provided integrated communications solutions that enable consumers to carry voice, data, or video communications anywhere they go, anytime they want. Included within this sector is the Consumer Solutions Group, which seeks to identify and answer customer needs.

Commercial, Government, and Industrial Solutions Sector The three markets served by this business unit are distinct as well as global. This business unit provides integrated communications solutions that include systems, equipment, software, services, applications and content.

Network Solutions Sector This business unit is responsible for Motorola's cellular infrastructure. Functions include manufacturing, sales, and integration of cellular operations.

Global Telecom Solutions Group This business unit is responsible for identifying and serving the requirements of large global network operators, and coordinating with other Motorola businesses to deliver solutions that meet their needs.

Internet and Networking Group This business unit consists of Motorola's Internet, data networking, and software capabilities, and develops servers, applications, and Internet solutions.

Satellite Communications Group This business unit is a developer, system integrator, and prime contractor for satellite-based communications networks.

Network Management Group This business unit holds and manages Motorola's investments in land-based and satellite-based network operators.

Semiconductor Products Sector

This business unit provides digital solutions that enable customers to create new business opportunities in consumer networking and computing, transportation, and wireless communications markets. It also provides analog and digital semiconductors that are used in virtually every type of electronic equipment.

Integrated Electronic Systems Sector

This business unit designs and manufactures a broad range of electronic components, modules, and integrated electronic systems and products for automotive, computer, industrial, transportation, navigation, energy systems, consumer, and lighting markets.

Cellular Phones

Although analog phones had a large installed base, digital wireless phones in 1998 accounted for almost 85 percent of global sales of new phones. Total worldwide cellular phone sales increased 51 percent in 1998 with total sales value estimated at almost $28 billion.[17] Dataquest estimated that Motorola was still the leading supplier of analog wireless phones, but analog phones were only 15 percent of total sales. Motorola's total wireless sales rose by 27 percent in 1998, giving Motorola a 20 percent market share, while Nokia's mobile phones in 1998 were up by 81 percent for 23 percent of the world market.

Motorola realized that it had failed to anticipate the popularity of digital phones and was slow to bring its digital products to the market and would have to play catch up to Nokia and Ericsson. As part of its reorganization, Motorola put significant effort into developing digital products, and expected to recover some of its lost market share in 1999 and beyond with a number of new digital products.

By mid-1999, a number of new orders indicated that Motorola was making inroads in the digital cellular arena. A significant event occurred when Bell Atlantic ordered $250 million worth of CDMA phones. This effectively doubled Motorola's existing 10 percent CDMA share, allowing Motorola to gain market share on the CDMA leader, Qualcomm.[18] The central Chinese government decided in mid-1999 to adopt CDMA-based technology and Motorola increased its investment in two joint ventures. Analysts expected the CDMA adoption would help Motorola's profitability with these joint ventures. Internationally, Motorola announced in June 1999 that Brazil had placed a $400 million order for CDMA infrastructure and one million handsets. The agreement would expand Sao Paulo's current cellular system and add second-generation CDMA digital capabilities.

Motorola also continued to penetrate the GSM cellular market. In July 1999, it was awarded a $10.5 million to expand Oman's GSM digital cellular network. Motorola has supplied cellular infrastructure to nine Middle Eastern countries, and as of mid-1999 had been awarded over 90 GSM contracts in 40 countries.

Wireless Technology

Motorola remained as the only major cellular supplier in 1999 without a switching technology, which hurt its ability to provide complete solutions to customers. Motorola entered a joint venture with Cisco and Sun Microsystems to work on an advanced packet-switching technology to move voice, data and video from the Internet to wireless devices. The successful development of this technology would eliminate the need for circuit switching technology and move it ahead of Lucent and Nortel in this critical area as well as enable it to provide complete communications solutions.

Satellite Systems

Iridium

In 1998, Motorola had counted on Iridium to become a significant profit center in 1999. However, by mid-1999, Iridium was in serious trouble as it continued to have an insufficient subscriber base. To recover from the disappointing launch of its satellite-telephone service, Iridium cut prices and changed its marketing strategy from an anywhere, anytime phone to a narrower niche of industrial customers where cellular is not available. Motorola also introduced cheaper, more user-friendly phones. The new pricing effective July 1, 1999, cut per minute costs by as much as 65 percent, and phones became more affordable, dropping from about $3,000 to $1,000 or less. The service's pagers also were made more affordable. Motorola backed away from the mass consumer market, aiming marketing efforts at business travelers. Efforts to gain other Iridium users were put on hold until its phones became smaller and lighter.[19]

Teledesic

In July 1999, contracts were finalized for Motorola to build most of the satellites to be used in the Teledesic network. Cost estimates were revised to $9 billion, and the expected service date was moved to late 2003. Few details were available, but indications were that Motorola had limited its exposure on Teledesic. However, the positive move reassured industry observers about the likely success of Teledesic, and Motorola's stock rose $1.88 on the announcement.[20]

Semiconductors

The semiconductor division benefited from both organizational changes and improved demand. In mid-1999, Motorola was the third largest semiconductor manufacturer in the world after Intel and NEC. There was strong growth in the wireless, mobile, and connected devices markets, and Motorola had the number one share of embedded devices in autos, handheld organizers, and telecommunications switches. Motorola's 1998 market share in the embedded microprocessors sector was 36 percent, versus 30 percent for IBM, 12 percent for Hitachi, and seven percent for Intel.[21]

Motorola's semiconductor group changed its product emphasis. As part of a plan to get out of low-end chip manufacturing, Motorola laid off over 17, 000 employees. Believing the embedded chip future lies with whole systems on a chip, Motorola gave up $1.5 billion in annual revenues by selling the commodity component of its semiconductor division for $1.6 billion in cash.

Motorola introduced a new Digital DNA brand, with one of the first products being a set-top box that is involved in video, voice, data, DVD, and 3-D gaming. Hong Kong Telecom placed a $150 million order for the device. "Digital DNA" is a phrase coined by Motorola relating to its strategy in embedded systems. As the world becomes more dependent on technological devices, embedded systems become critical aspects of computing, communications, and consumer electronics. Digital DNA represents the "intelligent" properties of Motorola's embedded systems, allowing products to sense and adjust, or in effect, "think" for the user.[22] Development of a Digital DNA brand was expected to improve marketing and customer loyalty.

Conclusion

Motorola has taken a number of initiatives to address its changing environment and recent troubles. Chris Galvin restructured the firm and changed its incentive program. A new executive is in charge of the Communications Enterprise, which is 70 percent of Motorola's business. New leadership was brought in from competing firms, and a number of joint ventures and alliances were initiated. Three thousand engineers were redeployed to digital phones resulting in an array of digital products including StarTac that operates on digital and analog systems, two-way pagers, and an Internet phone for Nextel. Motorola's new vision is the creation of networks of devices that work smoothly together. Rather than an all-purpose device, Motorola intends to develop single-purpose devices that work together easily and well. In addition, Motorola plans on developing software to run on all these new devices.[23] With smart chips and Digital DNA working their way into a myriad of products, from shoes to doorknobs, Motorola plans to move beyond traditional digital products such as cellular phones, digital cameras, printers, and microwaves.

The stock market indicated it believed that Motorola had recovered its momentum. Motorola's stock price rose from $38 in October 1998 to near $100 in July 1999—a staggering $30 billion increase in market value. Second quarter 1999 earnings were $273 million, or 44 cents a share, beating projections by three cents a share and up from a bare $6 million in second quarter 1998.

However, a number of questions remain.

- Motorola's culture has been a key component of its success over the years. It has been known for seasoned leadership and high ethical standards. The restructuring and leadership changes instituted by Chris Galvin and his new leaders were taken to fix the problems generated by autonomous fiefdoms while retaining the essence of Motorola. Can Motorola reap the benefits of more coordinated actions without losing the entrepreneurial spark provided by autonomy? Are the changes sufficient to get the diverse parts of Motorola working together?

- Motorola was late to the digital market. Motorola is introducing new digital products and the vision

of separate but coordinated devices is enticing, but technologically difficult. Will the new digital products be sufficient to reverse the market share slide for Motorola's digital products? Do customers want specific solutions or a one-product-does-all approach? Will customers buy into DigitalDNA and respond to it as a brand name like Intel Inside?

- The Asian meltdown affected both Motorola's and the world economy's growth. Will the Asian economies recover, and will the recovery be soon enough to justify Motorola's continued investments?

- Motorola enjoyed rapid growth and the consequent influx of new employees, along with entry into many new markets and cultures. How will this affect its culture and values? Can it maintain its core values against the many competing value systems provided by other cultures? Should it maintain these values or accommodate local preferences?

All these questions and more greet Motorola and its leaders, employees, and stakeholders as it enters the next millennium.

Notes

1. For a more detailed history, see http://www.motorola.com/General/Timeline/
2. Motorola, *1998 Annual Report*; Additional financial performance data can be found at http:\\www.motorola.com/investor.
3. Williams, Elisa, "Motorola Measures Its Steps At Change," *Chicago Tribune*, 6 May 1998.
4. Van, Jon, "Nokia Leads In Wireless Phone Sales," *Chicago Tribune*, 9 February 1999.
5. Crockett, Roger. "How Motorola Lost Its Way," *Business Week*, 4 May 1998, 140–148.
6. Tetzeli, Rick. "And Now For Motorola's Next Trick," *Fortune*, 27 April 1997, 122.
7. Roth, Daniel. "Burying Motorola," *Fortune*, 6 July 1998, 28.
8. "Sales Surge For Wireless Makers," *Wall Street Journal*, 8 February 1999.
9. "Thailand: Motorola Undertakes A Marketing Drive," *Nation*, 27 October 1998.
10. "Motorola Expands Operations In China," *Wall Street Journal*, 12 June 1998.
11. Crockett, ibid.
12. Hawn, Carleen. "High Wireless Act," *Forbes*, 14 June 1999.
13. "Iridium Stock Off After Motorola Comments," *Reuters*. 14 July 1999.
14. "Satphone groups eye prospects in developing world's rural areas," *Financial Times*, 30 April 1999.
15. Joanna Glasner. 19 May 1999. Motorola Wavering On Teledesic? http://www.wirednews.com/news/news/business/story/19758.html
16. "Global Semiconductor Revenues Stagnate In '98," *Newsbytes News Network*, 1 April 1999.
17. "Sales Surge for Wireless Makers," *Wall Street Journal*, 8 February 1999.
18. Holstein, William J. "A Motorola Coaster," *U.S. News & World Report*, 21 June 1999, 42.
19. "Iridium to Cut Prices, Alter Marketing Strategy," *Wall Street Journal*, 22 June 1999.
20. Hawn, Carleen. "High Wireless Act," *Forbes*, 14 June 1999.
21. Joanna Glasner. Motorola On Board for Teledesic. http://www.wired.com/news/news/business/story/20655.html; Bruce Upbin, (31 May 1999). "Motorola Inside." *Forbes*.
22. Motorola, Guide 98.
23. Barboza, David. "Motorola Rolls Itself Over," *New York Times*, 14 July 1999.

Exhibit 4   Consolidated Statements of Cash Flows (in Millions)

	December 31,		
	1998	1997	1996
Operating			
Net earnings (loss)	$ (962)	$ 1,180	$1,154
Adjustments to reconcile net earnings (loss) to net cash provided by operating activities:			
Restructuring and other charges	1,980	327	–
Depreciation	2,197	2,329	2,308
Deferred income taxes	(933)	(98)	(162)
Amortization of debt discount and issue costs	11	10	8
Gain on disposition of investments in affiliates, net of acquisition charges	(146)	(116)	(78)
Change in assets and liabilities, net of effects of acquisitions and dispositions:			
Accounts receivable	(238)	(812)	101
Inventories	254	(880)	308
Other current assets	31	(114)	(69)
Accounts payable and accrued liabilities	(658)	830	398
Other assets and liabilities	(515)	(60)	220
Net cash provided by operating activities	1,021	2,596	4,188
Investing			
Acquisitions and advances to affiliates	(786)	(286)	(346)
Proceeds from dispositions of investments in affiliates	371	248	121
Capital expenditures	(3,221)	(2,874)	(2,973)
Proceeds from dispositions of property, plant, and equipment	507	443	282
Sales (purchases) of short-term investments	164	(37)	52
Net cash used for investing activities	(2,965)	(2,506)	(2,864)
Financing			
Proceeds from (repayment of) commercial paper and short-term borrowings	1,627	(100)	(260)
Proceeds from issuance of debt	773	312	55
Repayment of debt	(293)	(102)	(37)
Issuance of common stock	99	137	7
Payment of dividends	(288)	(286)	(261)
Net cash provided by (used for) financing activities	1,918	(39)	(496)
Effect of exchange rate changes on cash and cash equivalents	34	(119)	(40)
Net increase (decrease) in cash and cash equivalents	$ 8	$ (68)	$ 788
Cash and cash equivalents, beginning of year	$1,445	$1,513	$ 725
Cash and cash equivalents, end of year	$1,453	$1,445	$1,513
Supplemental Cash Flow Information			
Cash paid during the year for:			
Interest	$ 286	$ 211	$ 237
Income taxes	$ 388	$ 611	$ 506

See accompanying condensed notes to consolidated financial statements.
Source: Motorola, Inc. and Subsidiaries

Exhibit 5   Consolidated Balance Sheets (in Millions, Except per Share Amounts)

	December 31, 1998	December 31, 1997
Assets		
Current assets		
Cash and cash equivalents	$1,453	$1,445
Short-term investments	171	335
Accounts receivable, net	5,057	4,847
Inventories	3,745	4,096
Deferred income taxes	2,362	1,726
Other current assets	743	787
Total current assets	13,531	13,236
Property, plant, and equipment, net	10,049	9,856
Other assets	5,148	4,186
Total assets	$28,728	$27,278
Liabilities and Stockholders' Equity		
Current liabilities		
Notes payable and current portion of long-term debt	$2,909	$1,282
Accounts payable	2,305	2,297
Accrued liabilities	6,226	5,476
Total current liabilities	11,440	9,055
Long-term debt	2,633	2,144
Deferred income taxes	1,188	1,522
Other liabilities	1,245	1,285
Stockholders' equity		
Preferred stock, $100 par value issuable in series	–	–
Authorized shares: 0.5 (none issued)		
Common stock, $3 par value		
Authorized shares: 1998 and 1997, 1,400		
Issued and outstanding: 1998, 601.1; 1997, 597.4	1,804	1,793
Additional paid-in capital	1,894	1,720
Retained earnings	8,254	9,504
Non-owner changes to equity	270	255
Total stockholders' equity	12,222	13,272
Total liabilities and stockholders' equity	$28,728	$27,278

See accompanying condensed notes to consolidated financial statements.
Source: Motorola, Inc. and Subsidiaries

Exhibit 6   Consolidated Statements of Stockholders' Equity (in Millions, Except per Share MMAmounts)

	Non-owner Changes to Equity					
	Common Stock and Additional Paid-in Capital	Fair Value Adjustment to Certain Cost-based Investments	Foreign Currency Translation Adjustments	Minimum Pension Liability Adjustment	Retained Earnings	Compre-hensive Earnings (Loss)
Balances at January 1, 1996	$3,261	$ 77	$ (81)	$ –	$7,728	
Net earnings					1,154	1,154
Conversion of zero coupon notes	7					
Fair value adjustment to certain cost-based investments:						
Reversal of prior period adjustment		(77)				(77)
Recognition of current period unrecognized (loss)		(26)				(26)
Change in foreign currency translation adjustments			(40)			(40)
Stock options and other	64					
Dividends declared ($.46 per share)						(272)
Balances at December 31, 1996	$3,332	$ (26)	$(121)	$ –	$8,610	$1,011
Net earnings					1,180	1,180
Conversion of zero coupon notes	7					
Fair value adjustment to certain cost-based investments:						
Reversal of prior period adjustment		26				26
Recognition of current period unrecognized gain		533				533
Change in foreign currency translation adjustments			(119)			(119)
Minimum pension liability adjustment				(38)	(38)	
Stock options and other	174					
Dividends declared ($.48 per share)					(286)	
Balances at December 31, 1997	$3,513	$533	$(240)	$ (38)	$9,504	$1,582
Net loss					(962)	(962)
Conversion of zero coupon notes	3					
Fair value adjustment to certain cost-based investments:						
Reversal of prior period adjustment		(533)				(533)
Recognition of current period unrecognized gain		476				476
Change in foreign currency translation adjustments			34			34
Minimum pension liability adjustment					38	38
Stock options and other	182					
Dividends declared ($.48 per share)						(288)
Balances at December 31, 1998	$3,698	$476	$(206)	$ –	$8,254	$ (947)

Source: Motorola, Inc. and Subsidiaries

Exhibit 7   Five-Year Financial Summary (in Millions, Except as Noted)

	December 31,				
	1998	1997	1996	1995	1994
Operating Results					
Net sales	$29,398	$29,794	$27,973	$27,037	$22,245
Manufacturing and other costs of sales	20,886	20,003	18,990	17,545	13,760
Selling, general and administrative expenses	5,493	5,188	4,715	4,642	4,381
Restructuring and other charges	1,980	327	–	–	–
Depreciation Expense	2,197	2,329	2,308	1,919	1,525
Interest Expense, net	216	131	185	149	142
Total costs and expenses	30,722	27,978	26,198	24,255	19,808
Net gain on Nextel asset exchange	–	–	–	443	–
Earnings (loss) before income taxes	(1,374)	1,816	1,775	3,225	2,437
Income tax provision (benefit)	(412)	636	621	1,777	877
Net earnings (loss)	$ (962)	$ 1,180	$ 1,154	$ 2,048	$ 1,560
Net earnings (loss) as a percent of sales	(3.3)%	4.0%	4.1%	7.6%	7.0%
Per Share Data (in dollars)					
Diluted earnings (loss) per common share	$(1.61)	$1.94	$1.90	$3.37	$2.66
Diluted weighted average common shares outstanding	598.6	612.2	609.0	609.7	591.7
Dividends declared	$0.480	$0.480	$0.460	$0.400	$ 0.310
Balance Sheet					
Total assets	$28,728	$27,278	$24,076	$22,738	$17,495
Working Capital	2,091	4,181	3,324	2,717	3,008
Long-term debt	2,633	2,144	1,931	1,949	1,127
Total debt	5,542	3,426	3,313	3,554	2,043
Total stockholders' equity	$12,222	$13,272	$11,795	$10,985	$ 9,055
Other Data					
Current ratio	1.18	1.46	1.42	1.35	1.51
Return on average invested capital	(6.2)%	8.4%	8.4%	16.7%	17.5%
Return on average stockholders' equity	(7.6)%	9.4%	10.0%	20.2%	21.1%
Capital expenditures	$ 3,221	$ 2,874	$ 2,973	$ 4,225	$ 3,322
% to sales	11.0 %	9.6%	10.6%	15.6%	14.9%
Research and development expenditures	$ 2,893	$ 2,748	$ 2,394	$ 2,197	$ 1,860
% to sales	9.8 %	9.2%	8.6%	8.1%	8.4%
Year-end employment (in thousands)	133	150	139	142	132

See accompanying condensed notes to consolidated financial statements
Source: Motorola, Inc. and Subsidiaries

Exhibit 8   Financial Highlights (Dollars in Millions, Except as Noted)

	December 31,	
	1998[1]	1997[2]
Net sales	$29,398	$29,794
Earnings (loss) before income taxes	(1,374)	1,816
% to sales	(4.7)%	6.1%
Net earnings (loss)	(962)	1,180
% to sales	(3.3)%	4.0%
Diluted earnings (loss) per common share (in dollars)	(1.61)	1.94
Research and development expenditures	2,893	2,748
Capital expenditures	3,221	2,874
Working capital	2,091	4,181
Current ratio	1.18	1.46
Return on average invested capital	(6.2)%	8.4%
Return on average stockholders' equity	(7.6)%	9.4%
% of net debt to net debt plus equity	26.8 %	12.4%
Book value per common share (in dollars)	20.33	22.21
Year-end employment (in thousands)	133	150

[1]The loss before income taxes, net loss, and diluted loss per common share include special charges of $1.9 billion pre-tax, or $2.19 per share after-tax, resulting primarily from manufacturing consolidation, cost reduction, and restructuring programs.

[2]Earnings before income taxes, net earnings, and diluted earnings per common share include special charges of $306 million pre-tax, or 32 cents per share after-tax, resulting primarily from restructuring decisions to exit several unprofitable businesses.

Source: Motorola, Inc. and Subsidiaries

Exhibit 9   Consolidated Statements of Operations (in Millions, Except per Share Amounts)

	December 31,		
	1998	1997	1996
Net sales	$29,398	$29,794	$27,973
Costs and expenses			
Manufacturing and other costs of sales	20,886	20,003	18,990
Selling, general, and administrative expenses	5,493	5,188	4,715
Restructuring and other charges	1,980	327	–
Depreciation expense	2,197	2,329	2,308
Interest expense, net	216	131	185
Total costs and expenses	30,772	27,978	26,198
Earnings (loss) before income taxes	(1,374)	1,816	1,775
Income tax provision (benefit)	(412)	636	621
Net earnings (loss)	$(962)	$1,180	$1,154
Basic earnings (loss) per common share	$(1.61)	$1.98	$1.95
Diluted earnings (loss) per common share	$(1.61)	$1.94	$1.90
Diluted weighted average common shares outstanding	598.6	612.2	609.0

See accompanying condensed notes to consolidated financial statements.
Source: Motorola, Inc. and Subsidiaries

Case 16

Gannett Company, Inc.

Neil Snyder, Cary Chipley, and Rebekah Snyder, *University of Virginia*

Founded in 1906 by Frank Gannett and incorporated in 1923, Gannett Company is a leading information and communications company with $6.2 billion in annual revenue. Headquartered in Arlington, VA, Gannett runs and operates ninety-nine newspapers, including *USA Today*, and twenty-two broadcasting stations.[1]

The company also provides data services, a newswire service, and engages in marketing, commercial printing, and news programming. Although 95 percent of the company's revenues come from domestic operations in 43 states, Gannett also has operations in Guam, England, Belgium, Italy, Germany, and Hong Kong.[2] Gannett operates in the highly fragmented media industry, and the company's success is attributed to its size, which in turn is attributed in part to the company's ability to create economies of scale and market share, as well as diversify its products across regions.[3]

Gannett became a publicly traded company in 1967, and its financial strength is demonstrated by nine consecutive years of revenue growth between 1991 and 2000. Year on year revenue growth during this time was 22 percent with 2000 revenue of $6.2 billion, and operating cash flow increased 19 percent annually to $2.19 billion in 2000. Operating income grew at 16 percent per year during this time to $1.8 billion in 2000.[4] Exhibit 1 shows operating revenues by year between 1991 and 2000.

These impressive growth rates are attributed to a number of major accomplishments: technological advancement, strategic investments, strength in advertising demand, consistent profitability, high margins and returns, strong cash flow, visionary leadership, and commitment to increasing shareholder value.[5] Gannett's stock price over the last three-and-a-half decades reflects the company's success and improvement.

History

Much of Gannett's success can be attributed to its succession of visionary leaders over the last century. Since the company's inception in 1906 by Frank Gannett, Gannett has turned over its leadership only four times. Gannett began as a partial interest in the *Elmira Gazette* in Elmira, N.Y., from which the company gradually expanded through mergers with and acquisitions of other papers. By 1918, Gannett consisted of six papers, all located in New York. Recognizing the need for more formal management of his rapidly growing company, Frank Gannett hired his first general manager, Frank Tripp, in that year.[6]

Through 1947 Gannett experienced rapid expansion. The company bought 15 newspapers and also expanded into the radio broadcasting business with the purchase of seven radio stations. During this time, Gannett became known for its leadership in technology innovation. Since he was determined to move Gannett forward in the newspaper publishing industry, Frank Gannett invested early in several technologies that ultimately revolutionized newspaper publishing: the teletypsetter, shortwave radio sets, and color printing presses.[7] Frank Gannett believed that by pioneering the use of such new, yet uncertain, technologies he could increase the quality of Gannett's newspaper products and establish the company as a leader in the industry.

CEO #2

The first change in leadership at Gannett Company came with the election of Paul Miller as president and chief executive officer in 1957, which was shortly followed by the death of the company's founder Frank Gannett. Despite the company's tragic loss, Miller quickly transformed Gannett into a company with a national newspaper base, while also maintaining its commitment to quality. During Miller's reign Gannett went public in 1967 with a total of 33 daily and six weekly newspapers, six radio stations, and two television stations in operation.[8]

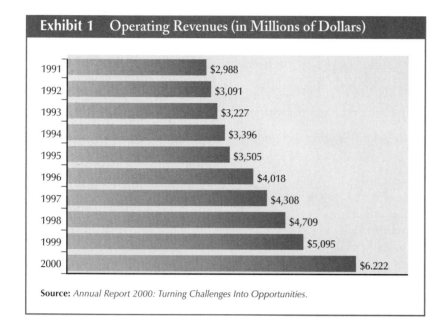

Exhibit 1   Operating Revenues (in Millions of Dollars)

Year	Revenue
1991	$2,988
1992	$3,091
1993	$3,227
1994	$3,396
1995	$3,505
1996	$4,018
1997	$4,308
1998	$4,709
1999	$5,095
2000	$6.222

Source: *Annual Report 2000: Turning Challenges Into Opportunities.*

CEO #3

The next shift in leadership began in 1966 when Allen H. Neuharth, who joined the company as president of the company's recent acquisition (Gannett Florida), was elected as president and chief operating officer of Gannett Company. Over the next several years Miller and Neuharth worked together closely, and in 1973 Miller relinquished his role as CEO to Neuharth, who boldly led the company through another period of steady growth and diversification. By 1979, Gannett had merged with Federated Publications, Speidel Newspaper Group, and Combined Communications. The company's portfolio totaled seventy-eight daily and twelve weekly newspapers, fourteen radio stations, seven television stations, outdoor advertising plants, a national news service, and a research firm by the end of the decade.[9]

CEO #4

In 1986, following two decades of successful growth and diversification of the company, Neuharth turned over his position as CEO to John J. Curley, who was president and chief operating officer of the company. Under Curley's leadership, Gannett created the first national newspaper—*USA Today*. After much research focusing on consumer needs and extensive technological development, *USA Today* was introduced on September 15, 1982 and was an instant success. By the end of 1983, the newspaper was circulating 1.3 million copies per day. In 1986, Gannett moved its headquarters from Rochester, NY to Arlington, VA to focus its attention on the increasingly popular cornerstone of its business— *USA Today.*[10]

Following the addition of *USA Today* to Gannett's long list of operations, the company made several more acquisitions under Curley's leadership, including Mulitmedia, Inc. in 1995, ten daily newspapers, five television stations, and two additional radio stations. The $2.3 billion Multimedia acquisition represented Gannett's largest acquisition up to that time and reduced the contribution of newspapers to Gannett's total revenue to 73 percent, down from 82 percent prior to the deal.[11]

In spite of Gannett's rapid growth and expansion, the company decided it was too diversified and decided to exit several lines of business to retain its focus on the company's core operations. This streamlining move included selling off its outdoor advertising division, research firm, and gradual sales of all its radio stations by the end of 1997. However, during this time Curley never lost sight of the company's need to stay at the forefront of technological development and implementation. In 1996, Gannett teamed up with Knight-Ridder and Landmark Communications to form InfiNet, a company providing Internet access and service to put newspapers online.[12]

CEO #5

Douglas McCorkindale, vice chairman and chief financial and administrative officer since 1985 and president since 1997, was the leader chosen to take Gannett into the new century.

John Curley officially handed over the title of CEO to McCorkindale on June 1, 2000. In the brief period that McCorkindale has been at the helm, he has successfully integrated Gannett's latest acquisitions: Newsquest plc (1999) and Newscom (2000), both large regional newspapers in England.[13] McCorkindale's fresh, aggressive approach to running the company resulted in $4.5 billion worth of acquisitions by the end of August 2000. They included nineteen daily newspapers across the Midwest, bringing Gannett's total collection to ninety-nine daily newspapers in the United States, fifteen dailies in the United Kingdom, and 500 non-daily publications worldwide, a weekly newspaper magazine, and twenty-two television stations.[14]

Today ...

Since its founding, Gannett has not lost sight of the importance of providing quality to its customers. The company stresses high quality in a document titled *Principles of Ethical Conduct for Newsrooms* and has been rewarded over the years for its success in producing quality products with forty-three Pulitzer Prizes and other awards.[15] In the 2000 *Fortune* 500 list, Gannett ranked 304 in overall revenues and second in revenues in the Publishing and Printing category.[16] Gannett has taken the Information Age by storm and has taken advantage of every opportunity to become the leader in the multimedia industry.

Revenue Composition

Gannett segments its business into two divisions: television broadcasting and newspaper publishing. Broadcasting revenues currently account for 14 percent of total revenues and are broken down into local advertising, national advertising, compensation from networks for carrying commercial network programs, and additional payments by advertisers for services such as advertising material production. Gannett has two ABC affiliates, six CBS affiliates, and thirteen NBC affiliates, all of which are contractual agreements that are subject to renewal approximately every five years.[17] In 1999, Gannett decided to divest its cable business, Multimedia Cablevision, Inc., for $2.7 billion.[18]

The revenue of Gannett's larger division, its newspaper division, accounts for 82 percent of total revenue and is broken down into three main components: advertising, circulation, and commercial printing. Exhibit 2 shows pertinent data relating to advertising, circulation, and printing.

Advertising accounts for the majority of newspaper revenue. In a 1996 survey, Gannett found that daily newspapers are the most preferred media source for advertisers.[19] Recognizing the importance of keeping its advertisers happy, Gannett implemented ADQ in 1995, a quality-improvement initiative for advertisement production, as a compliment to the existing Advance program, which focuses on increasing the number of advertisers. According to Newspaper Division vice president/customer programs, Joe Junod,

> ADQ's goal is simple: To improve quality and that will boost advertiser satisfaction and cut our costs. It's a way to improve the relationship between the advertising customer and the newspaper.[20]

In conjunction with Gannett's increased efforts to cover local news stories for its customers, in the early 1990's the company also began to seek out more medium and smaller advertisers. Gannett believes that its focus on local readership is attractive to smaller companies seeking more defined target markets. Although bigger names in advertising contributed the most to Gannett's profits, the company felt the need to reduce its reliance on big name advertisers.

Gannett operates the largest group of newspapers in the U.S. with daily circulation of 7.1 million copies. In 1999, the company acquired Newsquest, one of England's largest regional newspapers.[21] Gannett's biggest and subsequently most lucrative business venture was the decision to start *USA Today* in 1982. At the present time, *USA Today* circulates to more than 2.3 million people each day.[22] Exhibit 3 illustrates the circulation volume and revenues of all of Gannett's newspapers as of December 31, 2000, including *USA Today*, Newsquest, and all of its Internet operations.

Commitment to Customer Service

Gannett attributes its success in the newspaper publishing industry and its status as a leading news and information

---

Exhibit 2   Gannett Data on Advertising, Circulation, and Printing

Year	Advertising	%	Circulation	%	Commercial Printing & Other	%	Total
2000	$3,973	73	$1,121	21	$340	6	$5,434
1999	3,115	71	971	22	280	6	4,367
1998	2,773	70	958	24	257	6	3,988
1997	2,634	70	948	25	189	5	3,771
1996	2,418	69	918	26	166	5	3,502
1995	2,219	68	869	27	172	5	3,260

Source: *Annual Reports 1995–2000.*

Exhibit 3	Gannett Circulation Volume and Revenues on December 31, 2000		
Year	Circulation Revenues in Thousands	Daily Net Paid Circulation	Sunday Net Paid Circulation
2000	**$1,306,780**	**$8,368,000**	**$7,154,000**
1999	1,290,559	8,399,000	7,260,000
1998	1,290,236	8,486,000	7,375,000
1997	1,259,935	8,399,000	7,452,000
1996	1,198,944	8,369,000	7,536,000

Source: "Excerpts from the Form 10-K." *Annual Reports 1999: One Smart Cookie.*

source to its high brand recognition that it has built over the years through continual commitment to its customers. Through quality of management and flexibility, Gannett prides itself on superior customer service by focusing on local news—making sure the right stories reach the right people. Gannett believes communication with and feedback from its customers is necessary to make sure it continues to provide relevant products, stay on top of emerging trends, remain credible in the market, and build relationships.[23] Additionally, Gannett recognizes that the only way to gain trust in the eyes of the reader is to be accurate.[24]

In 1999, the newspaper division's editors and publishers met to form and write the company's "Principles of Ethical Conduct for Newsrooms" to focus attention on Gannett's high standards in order to maintain its reputation as a trustworthy publisher. These principles are:

- Seeking and reporting the truth in a truthful way
- Serving the public interest
- Exercising fair play
- Maintaining independence
- Acting with integrity[25]

Commitment to Employees

Gannett extends the same level of commitment to its employees that it does to its customers. In 1995, the company created the Enterprise Unit—a special department that gives reporters a break from their daily routines and enables them to experiment with different types of stories without the burden of time constraints. Reporters in the Enterprise Unit are on leave from normal daily responsibilities, and they research and write at their own rate. They can use their time in this unit to branch out

into different types of stories than they normally pursue and expand their horizons. This initiative has not only produced great satisfaction among reporters, but it has also resulted in unique coverage—a decided competitive advantage for the company.[26]

Internet Impact

Internet publishing requires additional resources above and beyond those of traditional newspaper publishers, such as national economies of scale and standardization of products and technology. Following the Internet trend of the 1990's, Gannett introduced online versions of many of its local newspapers to maintain its position as a leading information provider. From 1997 to 1999, Gannett doubled its number of online newspapers from thirty to sixty and increased its number of Internet products from 238 to over 480.[27]

In 1995, the company took *USA Today* online by introducing USATODAY.com. By the end of 1999, USATODAY.com was the only profitable online newspaper in the country. The Web site's most important attribute is its "breaking news" feature, which is largely responsible for the growth in user traffic seen each year, but it also provides interactive features that the print edition cannot offer.[28] During the fourth quarter of 1999, USATODAY.com's revenue was triple what it had been the same quarter a year earlier, and 15 million people were accessing the site each month.[29] Revenues from all of Gannett's Internet operations swelled during 1999, contributing $40 million to overall revenues; the company expects this growth trend to continue.[30]

Newspaper Publishing Industry

There is no better example of a fragmented industry than newspaper publishing, as it is composed of 30,000 publishers in the United States alone and includes larger multimedia companies in the industry. The newspaper industry serves five purposes in society. They are listed below:

- Education
- Entertainment
- Communication
- Persuasion
- Information[31]

The two largest components of a newspaper's cost structure are salaries and newsprint. Payroll accounts for 44 percent of Gannett's total expenses. Additionally, the company is the largest consumer of newsprint in North America. Newsprint accounts for 18.2 percent of Gannett's total expenses.

Exhibit 4   Advertising Media: Shares of the Market (in Percent)

MEDIA	1991	1992	1993	1994	1995	1996	1997	1998	1999
Newspapers	24.2	23.4	23.2	22.9	22.6	21.9	22.1	21.4	21.4
Magazines	5.2	5.3	5.3	5.3	5.3	5.1	5.2	4.9	4.7
Television	21.6	22.4	22.1	22.8	22	24.2	23.6	21.1	21
Radio	6.7	6.6	6.8	7	7	7	7.2	7.7	7.5
All other	42.3	42.3	42.5	42	43.1	41.7	41.9	44.9	45.4
Total	100	100	100	100	100	100	100	100	100
National	57.5	57.9	57.9	58.2	58.6	58.8	59	59.3	59.7
Local	42.5	42.5	42.1	41.8	41.4	41.2	41	40.7	40.3
Total	100	100	100	100	100	100	100	100	100

Source: "Consolidation within a fragmented industry," *Publishing: Industry Survey.* May 25, 2000.

Eighty percent of newspaper revenue comes from advertisements, and newspapers generate more revenue from advertisers than any other industry. Television is the newspaper industry's closest competitor in this regard. Exhibit 4 shows advertising market share by media type between 1991 and 1999.

From 1998 to 1999, newspapers increased their ad revenues by 5.4 percent from $43.9 to $46.3 billion.[32] An analysis of Gannett's actions and those of other major newspaper publishers over the years reveals that there is a substantial competitive advantage associated with size. The twenty largest newspapers capture 24 percent of the market in terms of average daily circulation. Further analysis reveals that the top ten newspaper companies—owning 270 newspapers—comprise a 45 percent market share.[33] In a time of rapidly changing technology, newspaper publishers have to adapt more quickly than ever to changes in their environments. The need to adapt is driven by "shifting target markets, competition from new media, advancing technologies, and changing circulation patterns."[34]

Circulation Patterns

Newspaper circulation is affected by, but not completely controlled by, newspaper readership. Newspaper circulation peaked in 1987 with a daily average circulation of 62.8 million copies, and since then it has been declining an average of 1 percent per year with only 55.8 million newspapers circulated daily in 1999. This decline is viewed as a gradual but significant one.

Newspaper readership, defined as the percentage of adults 18 and older who read newspapers, has been declining since 1970, reaching a low of 58.6 percent in 1998, down from an all-time high of 77.6 percent in 1970. In spite of declining circulation and readership over the last several decades and the increase in competition from other media, newspapers still represent the single most popular advertising medium for reaching consumers. The most difficult challenge newspapers face today is the ability to attract young readers, those between the ages of 18 and 24. Currently, only 48 percent of young adults read newspapers on a daily basis, compared to 59 percent for all adults.[35]

Other Industry Factors

The newspaper publishing industry relies heavily on labor. Newspapers must employ reporters, editors, photographers, art directors, copyreaders, graphic artists, proofreaders, illustrators, researchers, and copywriters, in addition to maintaining relationships with other news centers around the world.[36] Most newspapers utilize major wire services, such as Reuters and Associated Press (AP),[37] to retrieve their news, and most newspaper publishers do their printing in-house.[38]

Economic Implications

It is difficult to determine the effects of economic turmoil on newspaper publishers. On the one hand, most consumers tighten their spending during periods of economic stress when their disposable income decreases, and they tend to cut back on discretionary purchases such as newspapers. On the other hand, they may substitute newspapers for higher priced books and magazines when their incomes are under threat. Furthermore, it has been proven that the relationship between advertising expenditures and economic activity is relatively inelastic.

Although most advertisers cut spending during economic downturns, others see difficult economic times as an opportunity to increase market share, so they increase advertising spending.[39]

Impact of Technology

Among the trends impacting the newspaper publishing industry, technology is considered the most threatening. Changes in technology are expected to affect the industry in years to come with limitless possibilities that can emerge in the blink of an eye. Technology—including the Internet, CD-ROM products, and video games—has enabled most of the nation's newspapers to establish some sort of online version of their papers. These Web sites enable newspapers to offer extended features their print editions are physically unable to provide, such as electronic bulletin boards, e-mail capability, interaction with writers, sound and video clips, etc.

One of the most attractive characteristics of electronic information is the opportunity for the reader to manipulate it however he pleases. Although there is great fear about the impact online newspapers can have on print newspapers, the convenience of print newspapers has subdued worries about the extinction of print editions. Research has proven that online newspapers have the ability to "attract new readers who otherwise never would have read the print version."[40] The biggest roadblock encountered by newspaper publishers in the online business is their ability to make a profit. Costs involved in operating a news Web site, such as design, setup, maintenance, building readership, and obtaining ad revenues, are still extremely high.

Concerns

As recently as 1995, U.S. companies were unsure about how to effectively utilize the World Wide Web, and within the newspaper industry in particular there were many concerns. Large newspapers were not confident that the Internet would provide a new audience or that their papers could survive increased competition, both financially and creatively. As of 2001, results indicate the huge success of online newspapers, but in 1995 only a few newspapers were willing to risk the move online. Companies like *The Washington Post,* for example, introduced an electronic counterpart—washingtonpost.com. Companies that were successful in 1995 have had to completely restructure their sites to make them more interactive in order to thrive. They were challenged to exploit what people thought could be a fad, to find a way to produce profits, to market their product and shape it to meet the needs of their new audience, and to move forward in the face of failure and criticism.[41]

Competition

Newspapers compete with other print media, such as books and magazines, on three primary bases: content, service, and price. Price is largely determined by the amount of paper in inventory. Higher prices usually mean that a newspaper publisher currently has a large quantity of inventory. In an anticipation of rising costs, publishers usually stock up on inventory in order to avoid even higher prices in the near future.[42] For online newspapers, however, price is virtually irrelevant, as most Internet editions have been forced to provide their services to consumers for free. Those that have resisted offering their websites for free will likely feel the competitive pressure to do so in the near future.

Competition for advertising between newspapers and magazines is based on circulation levels, readership demographics, price, service, geographic market coverage, and effectiveness of advertising. In addition to local, regional, and national competition with each other, newspapers and magazines also compete against non-print media sources such as television, radio, outdoor advertising, and direct mail.[43]

M&A Activity

Due to the fragmented nature of competition in the newspaper publishing industry, mergers and acquisitions are expected to continue redefining and reshaping the industry. M&A activity is driven by the desire of companies to increase market share, the development of new markets and services, and possible synergies resulting from greater financial resources as well as brand recognition. Companies engaging in mergers and acquisitions are being forced to rethink their business strategies with regard to products offered, markets served, and methods of delivery. Following are two examples of recent transactions in the multimedia industry and the impacts on their respective companies:

1. Pearson plc, the world's largest educational publisher and owner of Penguin Books and *The Financial Times*, purchased Dorling Kindersley Holdings plc, an illustrated reference publisher, in March of 2000. This strategic move is an effort by Pearson to create new educational products through the use of Dorling's massive digital

library and specialized skills in the areas of image and content.[44]

2. The N.Y. Times Co. and Knight Ridder formed a purchasing consortium called KR/NYT Enterprises L.L.C. in April of 2000. The alliance is intended to leverage each company's expertise to reduce costs by identifying the best suppliers and create a more efficient purchasing process.[45] This combination is referred to as a B2B (business-to-business) venture.

The Internet Effect

In 1995, it was obvious to newspaper industry leaders that the Internet was the new frontier for information, but how were the newspapers to respond to this new medium? Four attributes that differentiate the Web from traditional media sources include:

1. Customization
2. Interactivity
3. Mobility
4. Timeliness[46]

Only two options for Internet transition were available to newspapers: "[1] set up its own Internet access site or [2] join an established access provider, such as America Online, Prodigy, Compuserve, or Genie."[47] If a newspaper creates its own Web site, it has more creative freedom and the possibility of more profits. However, this option is very expensive initially, and companies who thought the Internet was a passing fad could not justify the investment. Using an online service provider gives a novice newspaper publisher immediate expertise as well as subscribers.[48] Although this solution was the easiest, it did not turn out to be the best.

Just like the print editions of newspapers, the key to online success rests in advertising revenue. Newspapers must attract advertisers to their sites and keep them there, which is not easy or inexpensive. In 1995, many advertisers did not know how the Internet worked, nor were they convinced that there was an accurate way of counting how many "hits"[49] a Web site received. Another major concern for advertisers was the demographic composition of the people who would see their advertisements. Advertisers are careful to promote only where people are interested in their products in order to get the most for their money. In the beginning stages of the Internet, many of the "hits" on a Web site were speculated to be surfers, and therefore there was no certainty about who was viewing the site.[50]

Recognizing the necessity of introducing some form of a virtual newspaper, large numbers of newspaper publishers had to determine their competitive advantages as they sought to win reader loyalty. Gannett Vice President Frank Sutherland believes, "They key for newspapers is to tell readers things they don't already know—to break news no one else has and to give context to the news that no none else is giving."[51] Online newspapers all over the world including the BBC in England and Ha'Aretz and The Jerusalem Post in Israel are following his advice.

The Washington Post Paves the Way

In 1999, when washingtonpost.com did not seem to differentiate itself from the growing number of online newspapers, nor did it seem to be convincingly different from its print cousin, *The Washington Post* began doing its own advertising. *The Washington Post* spent six million dollars for six months of advertising to convince America that there was more on the Web than news.[52] This action led to the next stage of online newspaper publishing: the divorce of the online copy from the printed edition.

To create a product that was worth six million dollars in advertising, washingtonpost.com added features to make its Web site more interactive. It introduced "pm Extra" an afternoon newspaper of its own that included articles on events that had occurred since the printing of the hard copy that morning.[53] In so doing, washingtonpost.com placed an emphasis on original staff reporting, thus differentiating itself from the print edition through content and from their competitors through quality.[54]

Washingtonpost.com also began to make its ads interactive. In October 1999, the news site put a "Shopping Box" on every page except the first page. Inside the "Box" was an opportunity to buy something related to the page currently being viewed. "For example, a user visiting 'OnPolitics' will find a Shopping Box offering a politically oriented item for sale."[55] Along with interactive advertisements, washingtonpost.com schedules daily chat times where editors and reporters can answer the questions of readers, taking the interactive feature one step farther than just the question-and-answer format. A reader can have a real-time chat with any one of the *Post*'s reporters anywhere in the world. The goal is to "create value around that interaction." The result: "The '*Post*' has achieved this, simply and comprehensively."[56]

USA Today's Online Transition

Preparations for the transition of *USA Today* online began in 1995 only months before the Web site opened, when Gannett along with eight other newspaper companies founded the New Century Network (NCN). The purpose of the NCN is to provide national access to online services and products developed by local newspapers in an organized and coherent way. The goal of this collaboration is to guarantee the quality of news offered by local newspapers whether it be through print or electronic distribution. Through NCN, many of Gannett's newspapers developed electronic editions, including *USA Today*.[57]

1995   Two years after The Washington Post introduced its electronic version, USATODAY.com was launched in April of 1995 as a closed site-based service, meaning that customers had to pay a fee to access the site. However, in August 1995, USATODAY.com decided to open up its website for free use by its Internet customers.[58] USATODAY.com was able to foresee the benefits of opening up its website for free usage, and this prescience resulted in an explosion in usage on the Web site. The site received one million hits per day by October 1995, and the number of daily hits doubled to two million by January 1996.[59] Soon after USATODAY.com established its initial presence, Gatorade realized the opportunities available and became the Web site's first advertiser in October 1995.[60]

The two differentiating characteristics of USATODAY.com from the print edition are freedom and immediacy. Users can access information and news at their own leisure, as well as be selective about the news they wish to read. Secondly, the ability of the company to update its news and information almost instantly on the website, gives USATODAY.com an advantage over its printed counterpart. USATODAY.com runs continuous coverage around the clock and features "color photos, 3-D graphics, a front page update as often as a dozen times a day, and updated stock quotes and weather forecasts any time."[61]

1996   USATODAY.com increased the number of content pages from 20,000 to 70,000 over the course of the year and was already the most popular of all general-interest Web sites. The electronic version of the newspaper built up its advertiser base to more than eighty advertisers, including Microsoft, American Airlines, and Buick. Recognizing the importance of visibility, USATODAY.com began establishing partnerships with other Web sites in the form of links from partner's Web sites to its own. Some of these partnerships were with companies such as Intuit's Quicken, Berkley Systems', After Dark screen saver, Nifty (a Japanese online service), @HomeNetwork, and Sony electronics.[62]

1996 was also a good year due to the boost that *USA Today* and USATODAY.com received from the summer Olympics and the presidential election. These two events gave the newly established USATODAY.com a

chance to prove itself in the area of up-to-the-minute reporting of sports scores, as well as breaking news and voting results. With its global distribution, *USA Today* and its online counterpart are poised to reap the benefits of the trend towards global branding by advertisers, as they seek for the broadest form of distribution and reach for their advertisers.[63]

1997   For USATODAY.com, 1997 was characterized by escalating growth in terms of viewers, advertisers, and quality of talent. The number of content pages on the site doubled to 140, 000. In the area of advertising, big companies such as Honda and Oldsmobile introduced interactive advertisements on the Web site. During this period of rapid expansion, USATODAY.com never lost sight of its number one priority "to provide the most accurate and comprehensive news and information, in a convenient fashion."[64] In 1997, USA Today's emphasis on coverage did not go unnoticed by journalists, giving the newspaper a leg up in the industry in attracting top talent.[65]

1998   In only its fourth year of operation, USATODAY.com turned profitable in September 1998, reporting a small profit in the last quarter. A change in print edition format in the form of a new Friday travel section, a weekly health/behavior feature, and more coverage in the Money section was rolled over to USATODAY.com, contributing in part to the Web site's usage. USATODAY.com received 92 million hits, seven million page views, and 8.2 million different users each day. For the 58 Gannett newspapers with Web sites, online ad revenue doubled year on year.[66]

The increase in the number of users as well as the demographics of its readers attracted many advertisers to USATODAY.com. During the year, USATODAY.com formed relationships with many e-commerce vendors including Barnes & Noble, Preview Travel, Cyberian Outpost, CareerBuilder, and Music Boulevard. Shopping areas for these companies were integrated into various editorial sections throughout the Web site, including books, travel, technology, jobs, and music. For 1999, USATODAY.com's goals are to add more content and to find ways to leverage the electronic/print relationship.[67]

1999   For Gannett, 1999 was considered "the business of the Internet."[68] Not only did USATODAY.com confirm its position as the leader in electronic news and information, but Gannett also doubled the number of online products it offers to over 480 and now has over 60 domestic newspapers online. Since the introduction of its first newspapers online, Gannett has realized an increase in subscriptions for it print editions, which was at first surprising. However, further research showed that electronic editions leverage brand names and images, extending the reach of Gannett newspapers and attracting new readers who add to the company's top line.[69]

In 1999, Gannett generated $40 million in revenue from its Internet operations, with only a minimal loss. With revenues up 89 percent, USATODAY.com was profitable for all of 1999. By year-end, USATODAY.com readership was up 79 percent from the previous year, with fifteen million different users accessing the Web site each month. Advertisers and e-commerce vendors continued to flock to the most popular general news Web site in the nation. In an effort to further leverage its media relationships, thirteen of Gannett's TV stations launched Web sites in 1999, and the company plans for all of its TV markets to expand into Web business by 2001.[70]

2000   2000 was an exciting year for Gannett for many reasons. In terms of the Internet, the company grew revenues 58 percent reaching $63 million, and only lost a few million dollars. USATODAY.com underwent reconstruction, emerging with a newly redesigned website and once again produced record-breaking traffic with 2.4 billion page views, a 50 percent increase over 1999, and 25 million visitors per month.[71] Survey studies of some of Gannett's online and print newspapers, revealed that thousands of subscriptions to the print editions result from initial usage of electronic versions, reconfirming the positive impact online readership has on revenues.[72]

The summer Olympics proved to be a testing period for USATODAY.com, and the electronic newspaper emerged victorious. Internally, one of the biggest changes was that reporters wrote for the online edition before they wrote for its printed counterpart. USATODAY.com provided up-to-the-minute scores and results, as well as interactive features such as online chats with athletes. Although the company put significant financial and human resources into the event, the coverage resulted in a record 226 million page views in September, a 50 percent increase from the same time a year earlier.[73]

Gannett took this year to understand its online readers. A task force was formed to uncover the needs of Generation X readers (between the ages of 25–34), and the resulting recommendations were implemented to make sure the newspapers are appealing to its most important group of readers for the future. Gannett also implemented an initiative called Complete Community Coverage, to emphasize the importance of local news on its websites.[74]

Although USATODAY.com already has a presence in the wireless market, it is a small one as the company is investing most of its energy into the next wave of wireless technology. USATODAY.com believes the potential of the wireless market is enormous and that huge success will result when higher levels of data can be loaded at faster speeds. The company is already working with wireless producers to make sure USATODAY.com remains at the forefront of technology.[75]

The most monumental event for Gannett in 2000 was the introduction of its newest initiative: USA TODAY LIVE. This "new multimedia venture produces the USA TODAY content in electronic format and distributes it to Gannett TV stations and USATODAY.com."[76] This effort brings the product line full circle, with the content and credibility of the USA TODAY brand name available through yet another outlet. The program got off to a good start with successful coverage of the Concorde crash in Paris as its first story, and USA TODAY LIVE continued to gain integrity with its reports on the summer Olympics and the 2000 presidential election.[77] USATODAY.com benefited from this venture by implementing USA TODAY LIVE audio and video clips on its website.[78]

Success Factors

Core reader age of *USA Today* is one of the main factors contributing to the success of USATODAY.com's success on the Internet. *USA Today*'s core reader age is 42 years, whereas *The New York Times* and *The Los Angeles Times* core reader ages are 58 years. *USA Today*'s core readership age is lower than most of its competitors due to the form of delivery of the newspaper, through hotels rather than home delivery, and content, mainly sports and graphics. The simple fact that *USA Today*'s core reader age is lower than that of other national newspapers aided the development of the online edition since younger people are more familiar with the Web. USATODAY.com's core reader age is 34 years.[79]

More recently, Gannett's network approach and ability to push boundaries of newspaper publishing have driven the success of USATODAY.com. Currently the USA TODAY network (*USA Today*, USATODAY.com, and USA TODAY LIVE) reaches 25 percent of all households, and the goal is to raise this number to a level where the USA TODAY brand will be competing with its peer group, including MSNBC, ABC, NBC, CNN, and the WSJ. The company plans to achieve its objective by placing demands on its reporters and leveraging the crossover reporting capabilities achievable through a network approach, as well as promoting its wide distribution channels to advertisers who can purchase a color ad that will be seen worldwide.[80]

Today …

What does all of this mean for Gannett and *USA Today* and USATODAY.com? President and Publisher of USA TODAY Tom Curley sums it up this way:

> A reporter from USA TODAY can now say to a news source: I can get you in the largest newspaper, on one of the largest Web sites and on the largest local affiliate station group. Nobody else in media can make that claim.[81]

Going forward, USA TODAY is going to continue leveraging its assets to form a network that will be viewed as one brand through print publications, the Internet, and television. Curley gave an outlook on USA TODAY and the multimedia industry at a strategic leadership seminar in June 2000:

> In a word, today is about network. While there are many things to be determined in this era, one thing is already clear: A network will trump an individual product regardless of its form, quality, or perceived strength in the marketplace. The network must become our cause, no matter how much we might love what we do or how great our success. The newspaper that we fought so hard to keep alive and lately allowed ourselves some delight as it thrived is a part, not the whole. Vision cannot be acquired. Vision must come from within. The goal today is to help us as USA TODAY's leaders grasp the power and necessity of growing from newspaper into network.[82]

For advertisers, this network approach will instantly expand their reach to consumers. According to CEO Douglas McCorkindale, in 2001 the company is expecting, "that total Internet revenues may approach the $100 million mark and that these activities may be profitable for the year."[83]

Strategic Focus

Gannett's strategic outlook is one of commitment to continued growth. The company's focus is on "using [their] substantial cash flow to create and expand quality products and to make acquisitions in the news, information, and related fields."[84] This strategy has been with Gannett for decades, and the company defends its continued relevance by saying that it is the company's opportunities that change from year to year, not the strategy itself. From the viewpoint of *USA Today,* this mission has resulted in the vision of a network, combining its brand image, top-of-the-line media infrastructure, and new technology to develop one complete brand.

Gannett has already taken steps toward achieving this goal by joining its broadcasting division with USA TODAY. This effort will bring content from the national newspaper to local TV stations and bring the relationship full circle by using the stations to bring news and information to the newspaper and the online version.[85] USA TODAY CEO Tom Curley paints a picture of how USA TODAY has gotten where it is today and how it will move forward from here:

> … if there is any group in media that should be able to adjust to the new, different, startup or change it's this one. If you go back in our history, when did we ever know for sure what we were doing? Or can creating a network be harder than what we endured building the industry's best and only global distribution system? And who can forget all the smart people who asked what content could we possibly offer that the public doesn't already get in a dozen different ways and then ridiculed our look?

> And, yet, here we are, 18 years later, the top brand in print, with the biggest and strongest infrastructure in media, looking back on those who failed to adapt and hiring their brightest. The new technology gives us an incredible opportunity, if we can adapt. With print as our foundation, we can push beyond into other media, through more platforms, into a new era. We have the chance to become the top news brand. Period. No qualifiers about print. The top brand. This is the opportunity. This is the Ultimate Mile. This is what brings us together today."[86]

Next?

As Gannett continues to grow through improvement and development of new products, the company's overall goal to better serve its readers, viewers, listeners, advertisers and the industry while evolving into a communications giant remains the same. Concerning its Internet business, USATODAY.com's goal is to provide more depth in and breadth of information than its competitors in a visually appealing and user-friendly way.[87] The breadth and accuracy of coverage provided by USATODAY.com has helped establish the newspaper's credibility in the world of journalism, and USATODAY.com has leveraged this position to convince the world of advertising of its status.

Exhibit 5   Industry Characteristics

Internet Usage

	1999	1998
U.S. residents online (% of population)	37%	31%
Children (2–12 years old)	26%	20%
Teens (13–18 years)	47%	36%
College students	90%	86%
Adults (19–50 years)	48%	41%
Adults (51+ years)	18%	15%
Male share of net audience	51%	53%
Female share of net audience	49%	48%
Total U.S. Web users (mil.)	$100.1	$83.4
U.S. online ad revenues (bil. $)	$ 4.0	$ 1.9
U.S. offline ad revenues (bil. $, first 9 months)	$ 1.4	$ 0.3
Online holiday spending (bil. $)	$ 4.0	$ 1.5

Source: *Advertising Age.* Publishing Industry Survey, May 25, 2000, p. 1

Significant Publishing Industry Statistics

Newspapers	2000E	1999	1998
Advertising revenue (mil. $)			
National	7,675	6,734	5,721
Retail	22,700	20,900	20,331
Classified	19,340	18,642	17,873
Total	49,715	46,276	43,925
Circulation revenues (mil. $)			
Weekday	6,700	6,500	6,340
Sunday	4,175	4,050	3,925
Total	10,875	10,550	10,265
Magazines			
Number of magazines	230	220	205
Number of pages	248,245	255,146	230,237
Total advertising revenues	17,100	15,508	13,745
Advertising cost per page per thousand pages published:			
Black & white	$ 27.80	$ 26.10	$ 24.75
Four color	$ 35.95	$ 33.80	$ 31.75
Average single-copy price ($)	$ 3.75	$ 3.60	$ 3.45
Average yearly subscription price ($)	$ 36.50	$ 34.90	$ 33.00

Sources: Newspaper Association of America, McCann-Erickson, Publishers Information Bureau (PIB), Audit Bureau of Circulation, Standard Rate & Data Service. Publishing Industry Survey, May 25, 2000, p.5.

As stated in Gannett's business definition, the company "operate(s) with the belief that improving products and sound management will lead to higher profits for our shareholders." This attitude helps to explain the success Gannett has realized by pushing its limits and looking beyond newspapers for opportunity, enabling the company to become a diversified leader in news and information. Now that Gannett and USATODAY.com have established themselves as industry leaders on the Internet, and more broadly in the world of media, the company must maintain its position while building credibility.

Exhibits 5 through 14 present financial and other information on Gannett.

Notes

1. "Company Profile." Annual Report 2000: Turning Challenges Into Opportunities, p.1.
2. "Company Profile." Annual Report 2000: Turning Challenges Into Opportunities, p.1.
3. "Mergers and alliances make news; E-publishing gains respect." *Publishing Industry News* (25 May 2000): 11.
4. "Gannett Reports Record Fourth Quarter and 2000 Full-Year Earnings." Business Wire: Hoover's Online, 8 February 2001.
5. "Letter to Shareholders." Annual Report 1997: Listening … Leading, p.2.
6. "Company History," www.Gannett.com. p.1.
7. "Company History," www.Gannett.com. p.1.
8. "Company History," www.Gannett.com. p.2.
9. "Company History," www.Gannett.com. p.3.
10. "Company History," www.Gannett.com. p.3.
11. "Letter to Shareholders." Annual Report 1995, p.2.
12. "Company History," www.Gannett.com. p.4.
13. "Company History," www.Gannett.com. p.4.
14. "Company History," www.Gannett.com. p.5.
15. "The Company," www.Gannett.com. p.5.
16. "Company History," www.Gannett.com. p.1.
17. Excerpts from the Form 10-K, Annual Report 1999, www.Gannett.com, p.12.
18. Excerpts from the Form 10-K, Annual Report 1999, www.Gannett.com, p.15.
19. "Newspapers," Annual Report 1996, p.6.
20. "ADQ Reduces Errors and Credits." Annual Report 1995, p.6.
21. Excerpts from the Form 10-K, Annual Report 1999, www.Gannett.com, p.1.
22. Excerpts from the Form 10-K, Annual Report 1999, www.Gannett.com, p.2.
23. "Listening … Leading," Annual Report 1997: Listening … Leading, p.5.
24. "Listening … Leading," Annual Report 1997: Listening … Leading, p.7.
25. "Excerpts from the Form 10-K." Annual Report 1999: One Smart Cookie, p.7.
26. "USA TODAY." Annual Report 1995, p.10.
27. "Letter to Shareholders." Annual Report 1999: One Smart Cookie, p.3.
28. "USA TODAY." Annual Report 1999: One Smart Cookie, p.12.
29. "Newspapers." Annual Report 1999: One Smart Cookie, p.8.
30. "Letter to Shareholders." Annual Report 1999: One Smart Cookie, p.4.
31. "USA Today Online Case Discussion." http://dev.owen.vanderbilt. P.1
32. "Consolidation within a fragmented industry." Publishing: Industry Survey, May 25, 2000, p.11.
33. "Consolidation within a fragmented industry." Publishing: Industry Survey, May 25, 2000, p.12.
34. "Consolidation within a fragmented industry." Publishing: Industry Survey, May 25, 2000, p.12.
35. "Consolidation within a fragmented industry." Publishing: Industry Survey, May 25, 2000, p.17.

Exhibit 6   Competitor Statistics

Revenue Profile of Top Media Companies—1998

Company	Newspaper	Magazine	TV & Radio	Cable TV	Other Media
Time Warner	0	$3,309	$260	$10,719	0
AT&T Corp.	0	0	0	9872	0
CBS Corp.	0	0	6160	564	960.9
Walt Disney Corp.	0	398.6	4847	2295	0
NBC TV (General Electric Co.)	0	0	4900	369	0
News Corp.	121	0	3719.3	531.9	600
Gannett Co.	3953	0	725	232	0
America Online	0	0	0	0	4800
Cox Enterprises	1097.3	0	683.9	2102.5	0
Advance Publications	2493.3	1365.8	0	0	0
DirecTV (General Motors Co.)	0	0	0	0	3654.7
Hearst Co.	997.3	1563.2	731	0	0
Viacom	0	0	427	2607.9	0
Knight Ridder	2950.3	0	0	0	0
New York Times	2665	121	151.2	0	0
Cablevision Systems Corp.	0	0	0	2896.5	0
Comcast Corp.	0	0	0	2732.8	0
Times Mirror	2308.2	262.7	0	0	0
Tribune Co.	1498.6	0	1017	0	0
Clear Channel Communications	0	0	1376.9	0	702.1
Washington Post	846.8	399.5	357.6	298	0
AMFM Inc.	0	0	1581.4	0	0
Charter Communications	0	0	0	1539.1	0
Dow Jones & Co.	1479	0	0	0	0
Adelphia Communications	0	0	0	1419.8	

Source: *Advertising Age*. Publishing Industry Survey, May 25, 2000, p.6.

Top Media Companies, by Newspaper & Magazine Revenues

Company	Newspaper Revenue (mil. $) 1998	1997	Newspaper as % of all Media Revenue 1998	1997
Gannett Co.	3953	3582	80.5%	80.1%
Knight Ridder	2950	2770	100.0%	100.0%
New York Times	2665	2557	90.7%	89.2%
Advance Publications	2493	2386	64.6%	65.0%
Times Mirror	2308	2179	89.8%	89.8%
Tribune Co.	1499	1437	59.6%	60.8%
Dow Jones & Co.	1479	1444	100.0%	100.0%
Cox Enterprises	1097	1050	28.3%	30.3%
McClatchy Co.	1051	1012	100.0%	100.0%
Media News Group	1020	907	100.0%	100.0%
Hearst Corp.	997	950	30.3%	31.4%
Washington Post	847	813	44.5%	45.2%
E.W. Scripps	800	709	63.2%	64.6%
A.H. Bela Corp.	788	771	56.0%	56.6%
Central Newspapers	713	684	94.7%	95.6%

Source: *Advertising Age*. Publishing Industry Survey, May 25, 2000, p.11.

Exhibit 7   Divisional Operating Results (in Millions of Dollars)

Newspaper Operating Results

	2000	Change	1999	Change	1998	Change
Revenues	$5,434	24%	$4,367	10%	$3,988	11%
Expenses	$3,912	27%	$3,075	7%	$2,879	11%
Operating income	$1,522	18%	$1,292	16%	$1,109	11%
Operating cash flow	$1,825	22%	$1,499	16%	$1,294	11%

Source: *Annual Report 2000: Turning Challenges Into Opportunities,* p.25.

Newspaper Publishing Revenues

	2000	Change	1999	Change	1998	Change
Advertising	$3,973	28%	$3,115	12%	$2,773	12%
Circulation	$1,121	15%	$ 971	1%	$ 958	6%
Commercial printing and other	$ 340	21%	$ 281	9%	$ 257	16%
Total	$5,434	24%	$4,367	10%	$3,988	11%

Source: *Annual Report 2000: Turning Challenges Into Opportunities,* p.25.

Advertising Revenues

	2000	Change	1999	Change	1998	Change
Local	$1,312	1%	$1,301	1%	$1,287	2%
National	$ 792	10%	$ 717	13%	$ 632	9%
Classified	$1,860	4%	$1,782	7%	$1,662	9%
Total run-of-press	$3,964	4%	$3,800	6%	$3,581	7%
Preprint and other advertising	$ 693	10%	$ 630	8%	$ 585	3%
Total ad revenue	$4,657	5%	$4,430	6%	$4,166	6%

Source: *Annual Report 2000: Turning Challenges Into Opportunities,* p.26.

36. "Consolidation within a fragmented industry." Publishing: Industry Survey, May 25, 2000, p.17.
37. "Reuters supplies the global financial markets and the news media with the widest range of information and news products. These consist of real-time text, financial data, collective investment data from Lipper, numerical, textual, historical and graphical databases plus news, graphics, news video, and news pictures." "Company Description: Reuters Financial." http://about.reuters.com. p.1.
38. "Consolidation within a fragmented industry." Publishing: Industry Survey, May 25, 2000, p.18.
39. "Consolidation within a fragmented industry." Publishing: Industry Survey, May 25, 2000, p.28.
40. "Consolidation within a fragmented industry." Publishing: Industry Survey, May 25, 2000, p.15.
41. Computer Reseller News, Sept. 18, 1995, n649 p.47(2).
42. "Consolidation within a fragmented industry." Publishing: Industry Survey, May 25, 2000, p.24.
43. "Consolidation within a fragmented industry." Publishing: Industry Survey, May 25, 2000, p.18.
44. "Mergers and alliances make news; E-publishing gains respect." Publishing: Industry Survey, May 25, 2000, p.1.
45. "Mergers and alliances make news; E-publishing gains respect." Publishing: Industry Survey, May 25, 2000, p.4.
46. "USA Today Online Case Discussion." http://dev.owen.vanderbilty.edu. p.1.
47. *The Business Journal Serving Greater Sacramento*, Jan. 30, 1995, v.11 n45 pg.2.
48. *The Business Journal Serving Greater Sacramento*, Jan. 30, 1995, v.11 n45 pg.2.
49. A hit refers to accessing one information file, such as a page, text or graphic. Letter to Shareholders, Annual Report 1995, www.Gannett.com, p.3.
50. *San Diego Business Journal*, August 14, 1995 v.16 n.33 pg.3.
51. Sutherland, Frank. Annual Report 1997: Listening … Leading, p.7.
52. *Editor & Publisher*, Oct. 23, 1999, p.12.
53. *Editor & Publisher*, Sept. 4, 1999, p.45.
54. *Editor & Publisher*, Sept. 4, 1999, p.45.
55. *Editor & Publisher*, Feb. 14, 2000, p.42.
56. *Editor & Publisher*, Feb. 14, 2000, p.41.
57. "USA TODAY." Annual Report 1995, p.10.
58. "USA TODAY." Annual Report 1995, p.11.
59. "USA TODAY." Annual Report 1995, p.3.
60. "USA TODAY." Annual Report 1995, p.11.
61. "USA TODAY." Annual Report 1995, p.11.
62. "USA TODAY Online expands reach." Annual Report 1996: Dynamic by Definition, p.11.
63. "USA TODAY." Annual Report 1996: Dynamic by Definition, p.11.
64. "USA TODAY." Annual Report 1997: Listening … Leading, p.11.
65. "A Conversation with Hal Ritter, Managing Editor/News, USA TODAY." Annual Report 1997: Listening … Leading, p.11.
66. "A Quick Look." Annual Report 1998: More than Meets the Eye, p.11.
67. "Divisional Highlights." Annual Report 1998: More than Meets the Eye, p.10.
68. "Letter to Shareholders." Annual Report 1999: One Smart Cookie, p.3.
69. "Letter to Shareholders." Annual Report 1999: One Smart Cookie, p.3.
70. "Letter to Shareholders." Annual Report 1999: One Smart Cookie, p.4.
71. "USA TODAY Highlights." Annual Report 2000: Turning Challenges Into Opportunities, p.12.
72. "Letter to Shareholders." Annual Report 2000: Turning Challenges Into Opportunities, p.4.
73. "Collaboration was Key to Olympics Coverage." Annual Report 2000: Turning Challenges Into Opportunities, p.13.

Exhibit 8   Financial Performance Graphs

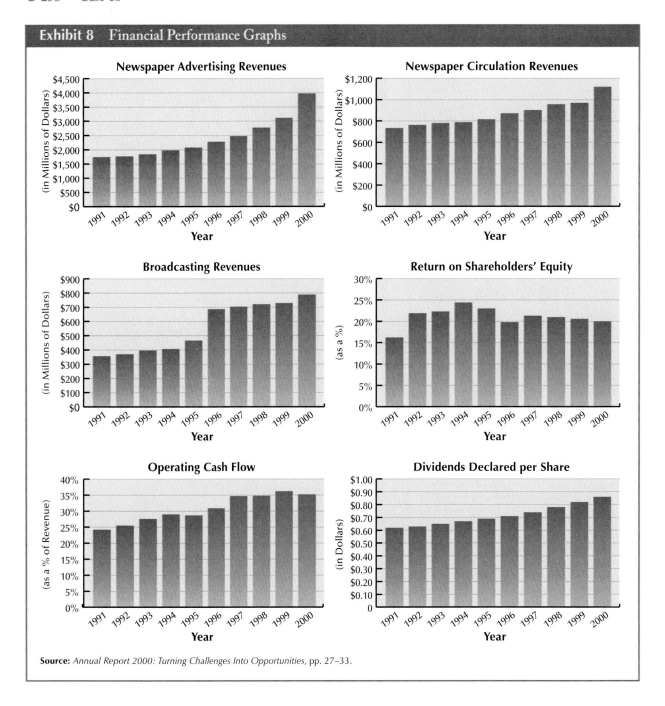

Source: *Annual Report 2000: Turning Challenges Into Opportunities*, pp. 27–33.

74. "Newspapers." Annual Report 2000: Turning Challenges Into Opportunities, p.7.

75. Curley, Tom. Arlington VA, November 16, 2000.

76. "USA TODAY Comes to Local TV News in Multimedia Venture." Annual Report 2000: Turning Challenges Into Opportunities, p.13.

77. "Letter to Shareholders." Annual Report 2000: Turning Challenges Into Opportunities, p.4.

78. "Collaboration was Key to Olympics Coverage." Annual Report 2000: Turning Challenges Into Opportunities, p.13.

79. Curley, Tom. Arlington VA, November 16, 2000.

80. Curley, Tom. Arlington VA, November 16, 2000.

81. Curley, Tom. Annual Report 2000: Turning Challenges Into Opportunities, p.13.

82. Curley, Tom. Strategic Leadership Seminar, Rosalyn, VA, June 15, 2000.

83. "Gannett Executives Speak at Credit Suisse First Boston Media Conference." www.Gannett.com, p.1.

84. "Gannett's Basic Game Plan." Annual Report 1999: One Smart Cookie, p.1.

85. "Letter to Shareholders." Annual Report 1999: One Smart Cookie, p.4.

86. Curley, Tom. Strategic Leadership Seminar, Rosalyn, VA, June 15, 2000.

87. "Letter to Shareholders." Annual Report 1996: Dynamic by Definition, p.5.

Exhibit 9   Other Financial Data

Two Largest Components of Operating Expenses

	2000	1999	1998
Payroll and employee expenses	0.44	0.45	0.451
Newsprint and other production expenses	0.182	0.192	0.21

Source: *Annual Report 2000: Turning Challenges Into Opportunities,* p. 30.

Working Capital Measurements

	2000	1999	1998
Current ratio	1.1-to-1	1.2-to-1	1.2-to-1
Accounts receivable turnover	7.4	7	7.2
Newsprint inventory turnover	7.3	7.3	7.5

Source: *Annual Report 2000: Turning Challenges Into Opportunities,* p. 32.

Broadcasting Expenses

	2000	Change	1999	Change	1998	Change
Revenues	$789	8%	$729	1%	$721	3%
Expenses	$429	10%	$391	4%	$377	1%
Operating income	$360	7%	$338	-2%	$344	5%
Operating cash flow	$425	6%	$400	-1%	$404	5%

Source: *Annual Report 2000: Turning Challenges Into Opportunities,* p.28.

Consolidated Operating Expenses (in Millions of Dollars)

	2000	Change	1999	Change	1998	Change
Cost of sales	$3,057	24%	$2,460	4%	$2,364	10%
Selling, general, & administrative expense	$ 972	23%	$ 792	12%	$ 705	5%
Depreciation	$ 195	15%	$ 169	3%	$ 164	7%
Amortization of intangible assets	$ 180	63%	$ 111	23%	$ 90	11%

Source: *Annual Report 2000: Turning Challenges Into Opportunities,* p.29.

Exhibit 10 Financial Summary (in Thousands, Except per Share Amounts)

	2000	Change	1999	Change	1998
Operating Revenues	$ 6,222,318	22.1%	$ 5,095,362	4.4%	$4,880,691
Operating Income	1,817,256	16.3%	1,563,101	12.8%	1,385,814
Income from continuing operations before non-recurring gains	971,940	9.6%	886,607	13.3%	782,818
Net non-operating gains			32,780		183,607
Income from continuing operations	971,940	5.7%	919,387	-4.9%	966,425
Earnings from discontinued operations, net	747,137		38,541		33,488
Net Income	1,719,077	79.5%	957,928	-4.2%	999,913
Income per share from continuing operations before non-recurring gains—diluted	3.63	15.2%	3.15	15.0%	2.74
Income per share from net non-operating gains—diluted			0.11	-82.8%	0.64
Income per share from continuing operations—diluted	3.63	11.3%	0.03	-99.2%	3.38
Income per share from discontinued operations—diluted	2.78		0.14		0.12
Net income per share—diluted	6.41	88.5%	3.40	-2.9%	3.50
Operating cash flow	2,193,171	19.0%	1,843,192	12.4%	1,639,277
Working capital	$ 128,335	-33.0%	$ 191,444	7.3%	$178,418
Long-term debt	5,747,856	133.3%	1,463,250	12.0%	1,306,859
Total assets	12,980,411	44.1%	9,006,446	29.0%	6,979,480
Capital expenditures	339,413	41.8%	239,438	8.6%	220,449
Shareholders' equity	5,103,410	10.2%	4,629,646	16.3%	3,979,824
Dividends per share	86	4.9%	1	5.1%	1
Average common shares outstanding—diluted	268,118	-4.8%	281,608	-1.4%	285,711

Source: *Annual Report 2000: Turning Challenges Into Opportunities,* p.25.

Exhibit 11 Gannett, Co. Balance Sheet (in Thousands of Dollars)

	2000	1999	1998	1997	1996
Assets					
Current assets:					
Cash	$ 69,954	$ 46,148	$ 60,103	$ 45,059	$ 27,179
Marketable securities	123,242	12	6,084	7,719	4,023
Trade receivables	875,363	800,682	664,540	638,311	569,095
Other receivables	56,469	80,753	52,619	45,316	47,850
Inventories	128,321	95,014	87,176	101,080	73,621
Prepaid expenses	48,987	52,613	35,863	47,149	44,837
Total current assets	1,302,336	1,075,222	906,385	884,634	766,605
Property, plant, and equipment					
Land	216,049	182,138	180,786	175,884	174,838
Buildings and improvement	1,101,696	886,655	839,210	840,157	770,456
Cable systems		424,907	413,059	548,219	481,053
Machinery, equipment and fixtures	2,525,182	2,259,362	2,123,468	2,140,148	1,926,058
Construction in progress	292,274	130,850	110,220	50,429	70,995
Total	4,135,201	3,883,912	3,666,743	3,754,837	3,423,400
Less accumulated depreciation	(1,673,802)	(1,660,060)	(1,602,960)	(1,562,795)	(1,429,340)
Net property, plant, and equipment	2,461,399	2,223,852	2,063,783	2,192,042	1,994,060
Intangible and other assets					
Excess of acquisition cost over the value of assets acquired	8,740,804	5,398,227	3,794,601	3,584,393	3,393,931
Investments and other assets	475,872	309,145	214,711	229,282	195,001
Total intangible and other assets	9,216,676	5,707,372	4,009,312	3,813,675	3,588,932
Total assets	$12,980,411	$9,006,466	$6,979,480	$6,890,351	$6,349,597
Liabilities & Shareholders' Equity					
Current liabilities:					
Current maturities of long-term debt			$7,812	$18,375	$23,302
Accounts Payable					
Trade	455,390	3,122,777	282,798	274,550	236,560
Other	37,853	36,312	29,485	25,710	25,278
Accrued liabilities					
Compensation	144,535	120,581	108,301	87,732	93,165
Interest	4,051	5,230	5,213	8,999	11,361
Other	177,318	145,684	114,708	137,944	126,832
Dividend payable	58,118	58,297	55,790	53,915	51,890
Income taxes	144,599	77,553	6,395	12,893	46,098
Deferred income	152,137	127,844	117,465	118,459	104,510
Total current liabilities	1,174,001	883,778	727,967	738,577	718,996
Deferred income taxes	274,829	479,547	442,359	402,254	396,170
Long-term debt	5,747,856	2,463,250	1,306,859	1,740,534	1,880,293
Postretirement medical/life insurance liabilities	403,528	304,400	308,145	312,082	301,729
Other long-term liabilities	276,787	245,825	214,326	217,168	121,591
Total liabilities	7,877,001	4,376,800	2,999,656	3,410,615	3,418,779
Shareholders' equity					
Common stock	324,421	324,421	324,421	324,421	162,210
Additional paid-in capital	170,715	153,267	126,045	104,366	86,126
Retained earnings	6,995,965	5,504,810	4,775,313	3,995,712	3,654,681
Accumulated other comprehensive income	(66,274)	25,377			
	7,424,827	6,007,875	5,225,779	4,424,499	3,903,017
Less treasury stock	(2,307,793)	(1,359,263)	(1,223,077)	(916,708)	(942,609)
Deferred compensation related to ESOP	(13,624)	(18,966)	(22,878)	(28,055)	(29,590)
Total shareholders' equity	5,103,410	4,629,646	3,979,824	3,479,736	2,930,818
Commitments and contingent liabilities					
Total liabilities and shareholders' equity	$12,980,411	$9,006,446	$ 679,480	$6,890,351	$6,349,597

Source: *Annual Report 2000: Turning Challenges Into Opportunities, Annual Report 1999: One Smart Cookie, Annual Report 1998: More Than Meets the Eye.*

Exhibit 12 Gannett, Co. Income Statement (in Thousands of Dollars)

	2000	1999	1998	1997	1996
Net operating revenue					
Newspaper advertising	$3,972,936	$3,115,250	$2,773,247	$2,634,334	$2,417,550
Newspaper circulation	1,120,991	971,114	958,456	948,141	917,677
Broadcasting	788,767	728,642	721,298	703,558	686,936
					232,500
All other	339,624	280,356	256,030	188,195	166,444
Total	6,222,318	5,095,362	4,709,031	4,474,228	4,421,107
Operating expenses	3,057,252	2,459,749	2,364,338	2,272,080	2,367,848
Cost of sales and operating expenses, exclusive of depreciation	971,895	792,421	705,416	706,201	699,484
Depreciation	195,428	169,460	163,776	152,964	193,011
Amortization of intangible assets	180,487	110,631	89,687	80,741	94,359
Total	4,405,062	3,532,261	3,323,217	3,211,986	3,354,702
Operating income	1,817,256	1,563,101	1,385,814	1,262,242	1,066,405
Non-operating income (expense)					
Interest expense	(219,228)	(94,619)	(79,412)	(98,242)	(135,563)
Interest income	27,209	5,739	19,318	6,517	6,727
Other	(16,297)	52,996	286,005	(15,564)	149,098
Total	(208,416)	(35,914)	225,911	(107,289)	20,262
Income before income taxes	1,608,840	1,527,187	1,611,725	1,154,953	1,086,667
Provision for income taxes	636,900	607,800	645,300	473,600	462,700
Income from continuing operations	971,940	919,387	966,425	681,353	623,967
Discontinued operations					
Income from the operation of discontinued operations	2,437	38,541	33,488	31,326	24,450
Gain on sale of cable business/discontinued operations	744,700				294,580
Net income	$1,719,077	$ 957,928	$ 999,913	$ 712,679	$ 943,087
Earnings per share—basic					
Earnings from continuing operations	$ 3.65	$ 3.29	$ 3.41	$ 2.41	$ 2.21
Earnings from discontinued operations:					
Discontinued operations, net of tax	0.01	0.14	0.12	0.11	0.09
Gain on sale of cable business, net of tax	2.79				1.05
Net income per share—basic	$ 6.45	$ 3.43	$ 3.53	$ 2.52	$ 3.35
Earnings per share—diluted					
Earnings from continuing operations	$ 3.63	$ 3.26	$ 3.38	$ 2.39	$ 2.20
Earnings from discontinued operations:					
Discontinued operations, net of tax	0.01	0.14	0.12	0.11	0.09
Gain on sale of cable business or discontinued operations, net of tax	2.77				1.04
Net income per share-diluted	$ 6.41	$ 3.40	$ 3.50	$ 2.50	$ 3.33

Source: *Annual Report 2000: Turning Challenges Into Opportunities, Annual Report 1999: One Smart Cookie, Annual Report 1998: More Than Meets the Eye.*

Exhibit 13 Gannett, Co. Statement of Cash Flows (in Thousands of Dollars)

	2000	1999	1998	1997	1996
Cash flows from operating activities					
Net income	$1,719,077	$ 957,928	$ 999,913	$ 721,679	$ 943,087
Adjustments to reconcile net income to operating cash flows					
Discontinued operations, net of tax	(747,137)	(38,541)	(33,488)	(31,326)	(319,120)
Income taxes on sale of cable business	(889,300)				
Depreciation	195,428	169,460	163,776	152,964	190,011
Amortization of intangibles	180,487	110,631	89,687	80,741	94,359
Deferred income taxes	(169,290)	21,983	40,105	(14,244)	68,254
Other, net, including gains on sales	(4,484)	(49,269)	(360,944)	(20,166)	(117,854)
Decrease (increase) in receivables	39,850	(70,014)	(29,732)	(41,684)	(50,046)
(Increase) decrease in inventories	(16,091)	(7,624)	11,054	(6,336)	16,489
Decrease (increase) in film broadcast rights				(644)	1,755
Increase (decrease) in accounts payable	8,833	(34,805)	(14,777)	(40,487)	(25,659)
Increase in interest and taxes payable	186,133	11,555	7,951	(26,336)	20,784
Change on other assets and liabilities, net	(1,179)	75,582	96,990	115,896	(218,191)
Net cash flow from operating activities	502,327	1,146,886	970,535	881,057	606,869
Cash flows from investing activities					
Purchase of property, plant, and equipment	(350,580)	(258,443)	(244,425)	(221,251)	(260,047)
Payments for acquisitions, net of cash acquired	(4,264,214)	(1,496,649)	(369,804)	(355,343)	
Change on other investments	(78,531)	(10,383)	(13,835)	(8,099)	(17,513)
Proceeds from sales of certain assets	2,714,362	38,450	665,001	40,859	778,716
Collection of long-term receivables				5,388	3,248
Net cash (used for) provided by investing activities	(1,978,963)	(1,727,025)	36,937	(538,466)	504,404
Cash flow from financing activities					
Proceeds from (payments of) long-term debt	2,799,161	915,865	(470,207)	(144,903)	(954,924)
Dividends paid	(228,391)	(226,274)	(218,853)	(206,557)	(197,417)
Cost of common shares repurchased	(967,242)	(163,228)	(328,956)		(1,443)
Proceeds from issuance of common stock	21,225	33,681	23,953	30,425	26,964
Net cash provided by (used for) financing activities	1,624,753	560,044	(994,063)	(321,035)	(1,126,820)
Effect of currency exchange rate	(1,081)	68			(236)
Increase (decrease) in cash/cash equivalents	147,036	(20,027)	13,409	21,576	(15,783)
Balance of cash/cash equivs. at begin. of year	46,160	66,187	52,778	31,202	46,985
Balance of cash/cash equivs. at end of year	$ 193,196	$ 46,160	$ 66,187	$ 52,778	$ 31,202

Source: *Annual Report 2000: Turning Challenges Into Opportunities, Annual Report 1999: One Smart Cookie, Annual Report 1998: More Than Meets the Eye.*

Exhibit 14 Gannett Pro Forma
             Operating Assumptions

USA Today

Advertising:

Advertising pages are expected to be up in the 4% to
5% range.

Rates will be up in the 3% range.

Circulation:

Volume is expected to be flat to slightly down.

There are no plans to increase circulation prices.

Television

Because of the absence of Olympic and political ad
spending, revenues will be in the range of a 1%
decrease to 1% increase.

Costs are expected to be up 1% to 2%.

Consolidated Gannett (including Acquisitions)

Capital Expenditures:

2001 Plan	$335,000,000
2000E	$345,000,000

Depreciation:

2001 Plan	$226,000,000
2000E	$199,000,000

Amortization of Intangibles (Goodwill and Other):

2001 Plan	$238,000,000
2000E	$181,000,000

Internet Expense:

We expect our debt at the beginning of the year to be
$5.7 billion. We have assumed that all of our free cash
flow will be used to pay down debt and that our
average interest rate will be 6.85%.

Tax Rate:

The tax rate for 2001 will be approximately the same as
this year at 39.6%.

Source: "Gannett's Operating Assumptions." www.gannett.com. pp.1–2.

Case 17

General Motors Corporation: Tooling Up and Scaling Back to Compete Globally

Neil Snyder, Ginny Sweet Simmons, Robin O'Neill, and Eleanor Tarkington,
University of Virginia

Although the French invented the first automobile in 1771, Americans created the modern automobile industry. It started in 1896 when the Duryea brothers from Springfield, Massachusetts produced thirteen automobiles. In that same year, the father of the modern automobile industry, Henry Ford, constructed his first car, the quadricycle, in Detroit, Michigan. In the early 1900s, Detroit became Motor City—the established city for the production and distribution of automobiles.[1]

Detroit in the early 1900's was like Silicon Valley in California today. According to John Rae, author of *The American Automobile Industry,* automobile manufacturers in Detroit invented "the concept of the automobile as an item of mass consumption," and they created "the technique of mass production." They also developed "a system of industrial organization for managing the large enterprises that the mass market for motor vehicles required."[2]

In the early-1920s, the United States automobile industry consolidated around three major competitors—General Motors, Ford, and Chrysler. Ford was the early frontrunner, but General Motors and Chrysler followed quickly. Eventually, they forged ahead of Ford. U.S. auto manufacturers produced high-quality, low-cost cars appealing to a rapidly expanding market, and competition between the Big Three (GM, Ford, and Chrysler) for leadership in the industry intensified. The Big Three retained their status as undisputed global leaders in automobile production until the early-1980s when imported cars, most notably from Germany and Japan, made their mark on the global scene. At that point, the automobile industry changed dramatically, and leading automobile producers to this day struggle to find ways to produce better, less expensive cars for an increasingly sophisticated car buyer in a very competitive market.

The Birth of an Auto Giant

In September 1908 in Flint, Michigan, William Durant created the company that would become General Motors (GM) in 1916. His goal was to design a vertically integrated company by "bringing together many small automobile producers and component and parts manufacturers into a single holding company." Buick, Oldsmobile, Cadillac, and Pontiac made up the original GM, and in 1918 Chevrolet was added to the list. "By 1920, more than thirty companies had been acquired by General Motors."[3]

The secret to success under Durant's structure was to market GM cars to different market segments without allowing divisions of the company to compete against one another. Unfortunately, he failed to achieve this goal because he did not adequately differentiate the car models in the GM line. Thus, divisions of the company fought with each other to attract car buyers, and when the business cycle turned down all car divisions suffered simultaneously. As one writer put it, "Durant created a performance nightmare: during good times performance was below potential, during bad times it was terrible."[4]

Durant's inability to make GM a top competitor and his failure to create an efficient management structure forced his resignation on November 30, 1920. That opened the door for Pierre duPont, whose family was the leading holder of GM stock, to take the helm of the company.[5] Soon after he took over, DuPont selected Alfred P. Sloan to be his successor, stating, "I greatly admire Mr. Sloan and his business methods and look upon him as one of the most able partners in the management of General Motors Corporation."[6] Immediately, Sloan initiated changes aimed at taking GM to the top of the United States automobile industry.

Sloan's first step was to create a decentralized management structure. Next, he appointed a special committee to develop a pricing structure that would help the company differentiate its cars. The committee made the following recommendations: (1) The company should produce a car in each price class, (2) there should be no price over-laps among divisions, and (3) there should be no wide price gaps between the offerings of the divisions.[7] The recommendations were adopted immediately.

With the new pricing strategy in place, Sloan turned his attention to marketing. His goal was to produce "a car for every purse and purpose."[8] To accomplish this objective he used a combination of makes, models, styles, colors, upholstery, and equipment to differentiate GM cars, satisfy consumers, and take the company to the coveted industry leader position.[9] In 1924, GM's share of the U.S. market was about 16 percent. By 1927, Sloan had worked his magic. GM held more than 43 percent of the market and was the recognized leader of the U.S. automobile industry.[10]

Leadership Changes at GM

Under Sloan's leadership from 1927 to 1956, GM was the market leader in automobiles with an average annual return on equity of 20 percent. Between the mid-1960s and early-1970s, GM's ROE declined to below 10 percent.[11] Despite the fact GM was still the largest and most powerful corporation in the world, by the 1970s GM lacked the ability to create, innovate, and change. As a result, competitors from the United States, Germany and Japan were chipping away at their lead. Tastes were changing. The global economy was changing. Smaller, more fuel-efficient cars were growing in popularity. At GM, however, things remained the same.

Leaders at GM had abandoned Alfred Sloan's wise counsel. The philosophies he put in place to take GM to the top of the industry were diluted and virtually unrec-ognizable at GM in the 1970s. Sloan had said,

> We should not be satisfied to go along ... when times are good, with no thought of the future. We should first devise scientific means of administration and control. ... We should proj-ect ourselves as much as possible into the future ... discount changing trends and influences and ... and be prepared at all times to alter the course of this ship of ours promptly and effec-tively should circumstances develop that required us to do so.[12]

In the 1980s, General Motors' president Roger Smith reorganized the company in an attempt to get the com-pany back on the right track. He is best remembered for plant closings and layoffs in Flint, Michigan that resulted in the loss of more than 30,000 jobs in the community and the production of an Oscar winning documentary

titled *Roger and Me*. Smith's efforts encountered tremen-dous resistance from the unions and GM's bureaucracy, and they ultimately failed to solve the company's prob-lems. Eventually, Smith was ousted by GM's board, and between 1979 and 1989, the company's market share in the U.S. fell from 47 percent to 35 percent.

However, leadership problems continued to plague the company. Robert Stempel succeeded Roger Smith at the helm of GM, but he was forced out in 1992 when out-side directors seized control of the company following a $4.5 billion loss. The board chose John F. Smith to replace Stempel. Smith joined GM in 1961, serving as comptroller, director of worldwide planning, President of GM-Canada, VP of GM-Europe Passenger Cars, President of GM-Europe, and vice chairman of GM. He became CEO and President in 1992, and chairman of the General Motors Board of Directors on January 1, 1996.[13]

Smith's goals were to cut costs, improve quality and service, and make GM a fierce global competitor. He went to work immediately to achieve his objectives. He closed inefficient plants, moved costly North American jobs to countries with lower labor costs, and cut an esti-mated $3 billion annually from GM's operating costs by revising and streamlining procedures. Finally GM was moving in the right direction. In the first quarter of 1998, GM posted the best quarterly performance in its history with a $1.6 billion net profit. The turnaround was a spec-tacular reversal from GM's 1991 $8.7 billion loss from North American operations.

Describing the change in attitude at GM, Smith said,

> We were often complacent, stubborn, and even arrogant in our so-called glory years. Worse, those traits made it easy to blind ourselves to the change that was sweeping through the industry in the 1970's and 80's...Ladies and gentlemen, we are not in denial anymore. We emerged from the crisis of 1992 with a firm determination to never allow past successes to blur current challenges and future requirements. We have shown that the organization has the fortitude required to change, and we are even more determined to keep the process of change moving. We will not be derailed on that journey called competitiveness[14]

Consolidation and Cost Pressure Characterize Today's Automobile Industry

The automobile industry is experiencing rapid transi-tion, cost pressure and consolidation. Top executives at

General Motors, Ford, and DaimlerChrysler told *USA Today* that "half the world's auto companies will fail or be absorbed within the next few years … Until then, worldwide overcapacity—80 factories worth—will keep prices low and force automakers into even more drastic cost cutting."[15]

DaimlerChrysler's Robert Eaton said, "Of the 30 top auto companies, less than 10 of them, as I count them, are making money—and these are relatively good times." Eaton added that "the auto industry worldwide has enough factories to manufacture about 21 million more cars and trucks than can be sold each year." That is equivalent to six Chryslers producing full time. According to Eaton, this is the most competitive market anyone in the car industry has ever seen in good times, and there is no end in sight. His forecast for the future sends shivers down the spines of auto executives—new car prices have come down for the last two years and "that's not likely to change."[16]

The automobile buyer is changing as well. According to Jacques Nasser, CEO of Ford, "Something on the order of 65% of customers don't like the car-buying process." DaimlerChrysler's Eaton adds that "our corporate future depends on serving the customer…If they don't like it, we better change." And change they must. Today's car buyer, equipped with computers and the Internet, are becoming quite sophisticated. They get their information together before they visit auto showrooms, and when they come in they know more than most car salesmen. That cannot last. According to GM's Smith, "We've got to bring our sales organization, our retail sales organization, to a higher level of technical competence to deal with this new generation of buyer." If they do not, they cannot survive the shakeout in the automobile industry. It is just that simple, and it is inescapable.[17]

Cost pressures are forcing automobile producers to scrutinize every facet of their operations, including parts purchases. At the same time, parts suppliers are seeking more autonomy from carmakers. Toyota and other Japanese car manufacturers are introducing new, upgraded models at prices that are dramatically lower than current versions and, in the process, putting tremendous pressure on U.S. auto manufacturers to maintain their existing prices or reduce them. With increasing pressure to cut costs, every automobile manufacturer in the world is anxious about the ability of parts suppliers to continue providing quality parts at prices low enough to enable them to remain competitive globally.

The quest to find less expensive inputs is creating opportunities for smaller parts suppliers around the world. Auto manufacturers are looking past Tier 1 suppliers to Tier 2 and Tier 3 suppliers who can meet their needs at a significantly lower cost. For example, GM Vice President-Worldwide Purchasing Harold Kutner says, "We are finding tremendous electronics companies in Israel at the Tier 2 and Tier 3 levels … In Brazil we're finding casters that are better, and in Russia we're finding aluminum components. And because we are global and because we have people in various parts of the world, we have the ability to help Tier 1s find Tier 2s and Tier 3s." Additionally, every car manufacturer is looking for and finding ways to drive costs out of the supply chain by purchasing raw materials such as steel and seating fabric in huge quantities, getting a volume discount, and then reselling to their suppliers at cost.

The stage is set for fierce competition and radical change. Nothing like this has happened in the automobile industry since its founding, and only a few players will survive. According to John Casesa, an analyst with Schroder & Co., "You're going to see a much more consolidated auto industry within the next five years. The faster the global economy turns down, the faster it will happen."[18] Ford Motor Company CEO Jacques Nasser says "for global competitors to be really competitive, their sales volume will have to be over five million cars a year," and Toyota's President Hiroshi Okuda says that "in the next century, there will be only five or six auto makers."[19] Today, there are only two automobile manufacturers selling more than five million cars a year—GM and Ford.

The Global 5 or 6 Takes Center Stage

When consolidation in the automobile industry is finished, Ford, DaimlerChrysler, Toyota, Honda, Volkswagen, and General Motors are the most likely companies to remain. However, if only five companies remain, one of these automobile giants will be merged with another company. Just what will happen to the other automobile manufacturers is unclear at this point. Some of them will cease to exist and others will play a minor role. For example, Renault of France announced in March 1999 that it was buying a $5.4 billion stake in Nissan of Japan after the world's major automobile producers declined to acquire the ailing Japanese firm. The deal is risky, because it combines two marginal automakers, one of which (Nissan) is $21 billion in debt.[20] But car manufacturers have very few options. They must either become competitive, or they will disappear. Exhibit 1 shows global industry statistics. Exhibit 2 shows 1998 financial comparisons between GM, Ford, Toyota, DaimlerChrysler, and Honda. Exhibit 3 shows the cash reserves of the global leaders.

Exhibit 1   Automobile Industry Statistics—1998: Top 6 Firms Globally

	GM	Ford	DaimlerChrysler	VW	Toyota	Honda
Global Market Share	13.30%	12.50%	7.80%	8.40%	7.60%	na
North Am. Market Share	30.20%	27.90%	19.0%—Chrysler	na	4.30%	5.90%
South Am. Market Share	20.00%	14.90%	1.80%	25.40%	1.50%	na
Asia-Pacific Market Share	0.70%	1.10%	na	na	20.00%	8.60%
W. Europe Market Share	10.90%	10.90%	6.4%—Daimler	19.40%	na	na
E. Europe Market Share	na	na	na	13.50%	na	na
Worldwide Vehicle Sales	7.5 M	6.8 M	4 M	4.58 M	4.45 M	2.34 M

Sources:
www.ai-online.com/articles/1098stats.htm
www.automotivedigest.com/member/news/global/000161.html
na means not available

Ford

With 18 subsidiaries, a work force of almost 364,000, and 1998 annual sales approaching $145 billion, Ford is smaller than General Motors, but more profitable. GM's 1998 annual sales were approximately $161 billion. In 1998, Ford sold 6.8 million vehicles worldwide compared to GM's 7.5 million, but it is making a big push to become the global leader in automobile sales—a position Ford has not held since 1931 when GM took that spot on the strength of Chevrolet's popularity. With the purchase of Volvo's car manufacturing business that sold 400,000 cars in 1998 and the soaring sales of Ford's Jaguar line, automobile industry experts believe Ford might indeed retake the lead.[21]

According to a report issued by Morgan Stanley, Dean Witter in October 1997, "Ford is the profit per unit leader in North America for the second year in a row."[22] It was not always so. In the early-1980s, Ford verged on bankruptcy, but they redesigned the company and implemented a program, called "Best in Class," that turned the company around. As a part of the "Best in Class" program, Ford literally took apart the top rated cars in the industry and used the best features of each car in designing their new offering, Taurus.[23] Additionally, "Quality is Job One" became the company's motto, and the focus on quality was just what the market wanted.

Ford has set its sights on achieving world market share leadership through quality, innovation, and acquisition. To accomplish this objective, in the early-1990s leaders at Ford announced their intention to become a "truly international corporation—a company without a country."[24] This goal recognizes the reality that country boundaries and allegiance to sovereign states tend to hinder firms in their ability to satisfy customer demands—

most notably their desire to purchase quality products at competitive prices. This philosophy will, in all likelihood, sweep the world's leading manufacturers and, in time, change the way we think about global business.

For the past decade, Ford's performance in foreign markets has been volatile. However, in 1997 Ford regained profitability in Europe, posting a $273 million profit. The company plans to expand in Europe cautiously in the future.[25] According to James Donaldson, president of Ford of Europe, "the goal has been to stay in the black this year as [the company] absorbs the costs of restructuring and of massive retooling" of its plants.[26] Ford is banking on the success of a new introduction in Europe called Focus that will replace Escort.[27]

Ford CEO Jacques Nasser believes Ford must continue to change or die. He said, "We're never done. That's what this business is about. You stop, or if you get to the point where you really start to be pleased with yourself, you're in trouble." At Ford, never stopping means many things, but it must include always looking for ways to cut costs. Nasser has developed a reputation for cost cutting and a nickname—Jac the Knife. He does not like the nickname, but he knows what he is doing is essential and inevitable. According to Nasser, "I never talk about cost-cutting. I always talk about the elimination of waste. But to me, you've got a choice. You can be inefficient and you can condone waste and lack of productivity and try to pass it on to the customers, and they won't accept it. Or you can let the shareholders pay for it and—guess what?—that won't last either. And you don't have a business."[28]

In December 1998, Ford announced that it would form a joint venture with AB Volvo, the world's smallest independent car company, to produce new cars for sale in Europe and the United States.[29] A few weeks later, the company agreed to acquire Volvo's car business, which has a

Exhibit 2   1998 Financial Comparisons: GM, Ford, Toyota, Honda

Income Statement

	GM	Ford	Toyota	Honda	DaimlerChrysler
Revenue	161,315	144,416	88,472	45,418	154,615
Cost of Goods Sold	130,174	117,989	69,493	31,362	121,692
Gross Profit	31,141	26,427	18,979	14,055	32,923
Gross Profit Margin	19.30%	18.30%	21.50%	30.90%	21.29%
SG&A Expense	17,330	9,414	13,345	10,556	19,041
Operating Income	13,811	17,013	5,634	3,499	13,882
Operating Margin	8.60%	11.80%	6.40%	7.70%	8.98%
Total Net Income	2,956	22,071	3,442	1,972	5,656
Net Profit Margin	1.80%	15.30%	3.90%	4.30%	3.66%

Balance Sheet

	GM	Ford	Toyota	Honda	DaimlerChrysler
Cash	10,869	4,836	9,292	2,553	7,731
Net Receivables	109,649	2,604	8,863	7,986	8,922
Inventories	12,207	5,656	5,571	4,548	13,840
Total Current Assets	148,559	39,860	48,281	17,391	88,456
Total Assets	257,389	237,545	104,957	36,451	159,738
Short-Term Debt	61,578	57,594	11,538	5,527	na
Total Current Liabilities	114,350	95,671	34,057	16,750	na
Long-Term Debt	52,574	74,564	21,093	5,130	na
Total Liabilities	242,405	214,136	59,336	24,279	73,361
Common Stock Equity	14,983	23,409	45,620	12,171	35,629

All dollar amounts in millions except per share amounts.
Source: Hoover's Online and DaimlerChrysler 1998 Annual Report

solid reputation for manufacturing safe and durable cars, for $6.5 billion.[30] On February 15, 1999, rumors circulated that Ford was making a bid to acquire BMW, the German maker of luxury cars.[31] Clearly, Ford understands the rules of the new automobile game and is taking steps to establish the company as a dominant global player.

DaimlerChrysler

"As DaimlerChrysler dawns, the 40 billion dollar merger of two legendary auto brands underlines the dramatic game of survival being played out among the world's carmakers."[32] The company must continue to increase quality and shave labor and benefit costs by more than $2,000 per car to be competitive with Nissan, America's most efficient producer. In addition, more than 25,000 production jobs must be eliminated.[33]

The merger between Daimler-Benz and Chrysler to form DaimlerChrysler was approved overwhelmingly by shareholders of both companies in September 1998, and it symbolized the dawning of a new global age.

Immediately, the phrase "The Big Three," applicable since the 1920s, became obsolete and the new catch phrase became "The Global Five." The consolidation of the automobile industry shifted into fifth gear as the leading automobile manufacturers in the world raced ahead to see who could create the most powerful new global company.

Although the DaimlerChrysler merger may have been shocking, it was not surprising. The new global reality is different—very different. "What once was a comfortable, predictable, nationalistic business is gone forever … The men who run Detroit's Big Three squinted at the horizon and offered descriptions of the future they see, one dominated by fewer car companies and smarter, more demanding consumers." Automobile manufacturers who do not understand the new reality will not survive.[34]

DaimlerChrysler faces some tough hurdles in merging the two cultures. As one reporter observed, "Anxiety fills the corridors, dining rooms, and office cubicles at Chrysler headquarters … Chrysler engineers and designers fear their pet projects might be jettisoned to serve the

Exhibit 3   Cash and Cash Equivalents in Billions of Dollars

	GM	Ford	Honda	DaimlerChrysler	VW	Toyota
Cash and Cash Equivalents in Billions of Dollars	16.6	23	3	25	12.4	23

Source: *Fortune*, 15 February 1999, 26.

priorities of the new DaimlerChrysler … ."[35] Chrysler insiders fear that Chrysler will become a subservient part of the Daimler whole. Their fear is founded in the belief that German businesses usually follow a bureaucratic pattern, whereas American businesses tend to allow more freedom for individual expression and innovation.

Ultimately, for the merger to succeed, each side will have to make concessions for an inter-culture common ground to be reached. As Robert J. Eaton, former Chrysler chairman and co-chairman of DaimlerChrysler, explains, "It's a bit like any marriage … after the honeymoon, a few issues come out. It's just inevitable."[36] Later he said, "I want to make sure all decisions are based on what is best for DaimlerChrysler, instead of what best pays homage to what had been Chrysler or Daimler-Benz as separate entities … This is not about nationalism. This is about business culture, and bringing all these people together as one team."[37]

The merger has some tremendous advantages. Both Eaton and Juergen E. Schrempp, former chairman of Daimler-Benz and co-chairman of DaimlerChrysler, point out that purchasing, production, marketing, and distribution efficiencies will boost profits by eliminating overlapping resources and cutting costs. Eaton said, "Business-integration teams already have outlined ways to cut operating costs by $1.4 billion in 1999, and by an overall $3 billion annually within two years."[38] Eaton and Schrempp know they must succeed because more global automotive deals are sure to follow. "It's inevitable; it's absolutely inevitable,"[39] says Eaton.

Toyota

Toyota Motor Corporation is the world's fifth largest automaker behind General Motors, Ford, DaimlerChrysler, and Volkswagen. Its product line includes the four-wheel drive vehicles 4Runner and Land Cruiser. Camry, Corolla, and Tercel are solid performers in the Toyota line with long histories of customer satisfaction, and its luxury line of Lexus cars are the standard by which luxury cars in the world are measured. Toyota is known for quality, reliability, and dependability, but it is best known for customer service. With its investment in the United States surpassing

$8 billion[40] and its constant commitment to excellence, Toyota is sure to be one of the Global 5 after the dust settles. Toyota Motor Sales, U.S.A. reported its best-ever October sales figure in 1998 with 121,216 vehicles sold for a stunning 26.8 percent gain over 1997.[41]

To achieve its global objectives, Toyota is pursuing growth opportunities throughout the world. Toyota CEO Hiroshi Okuda said, "globally, the company's performing like a charm … I am trying to push my colleagues to acquire more market share, and we have been successful so far."[42] Research and Development initiatives, including a joint venture with General Motors to develop a new inductive charging system for electric vehicles[43] and the search for ways to produce cleaner cars, have positioned Toyota as one of the most forward thinking firms in the industry.

Despite solid sales performance in the U.S. and Europe, the Asian financial crisis that started in the summer of 1997 hit Toyota hard. Its profits fell dramatically in the first half of 1998, because U.S. and European sales could not compensate for the slump in Japan and Southeast Asia. Due to the changing global conditions Okuda announced, "We're going to be particularly aggressive in Europe and the United States."[44] The global slump brought on by the rapid decline in Southeast Asian markets has intensified competition in the automobile industry and given added impetus to the consolidation of the industry.

Honda

Honda Motor Company is the third largest Japanese automaker behind Toyota and Nissan. Its most popular products in the United States include the Honda Accord, Civic, and Prelude, and its Acura line of luxury cars has earned a solid reputation for reliability. The Accord became America's best-selling car in 1989 and remained at the top until Toyota Camry took its place in the mid-1990s.

Despite the slump in Asian markets that stunned Toyota, Honda reported a sales increase of 12.1 percent in 1998, with a net profit of $1.29 billion. Although these figures were helped by the decline in the value of the yen relative to the dollar, Honda's tenacity in European and North American markets played an important part in the success of the company during 1998. Nevertheless, Honda must not become too dependent on robust U.S. and European markets and a weak yen to achieve financial success. Clearly, the biggest growth markets in the world are outside the United States and Europe. Together the U.S., Europe, and Japan represent only 17 percent of the world's population. Phenomenal growth opportunities exist in the remaining 83 percent of the world.

Volkswagen

Volkswagen is Europe's number one automaker. Its brand names include Volkswagen, Audi, Rolls-Royce, Lamborghini, SEAT, and SKODA. Volkswagen models include Golf, Passat, the New Beetle, and the Jetta, which is the best-selling European car in the United States. Manufacturing about 4.3 million cars annually, Volkswagen is a major global automotive competitor. The New Beetle model, which has experienced rave reviews and strong demand, boldly targeted both younger drivers seeking economy and older drivers nostalgic for the past. The company's aggressive pursuit of new markets and expansion of existing ones make Volkswagen a fierce global competitor with tremendous growth potential.

The Passat is making a big splash on the world scene. With a base price of $21,000 and a top price of just over $28,000, Passat is putting pressure on Lexus, Acura, DaimlerChrysler, and BMW. It is built like a luxury car, and it drives like the finest European road cars, but it costs thousands less than its competitors. In the United States, the Passat has been an especially big hit. Owners of BMWs, Range Rovers, and Mercedes are lining up in some cities to trade their cars in for the Volkswagen model. In 1999, Volkswagen expects to sell 500,000 cars in North America, and as Gerd Klaus, president of Volkswagen of America, says, "If you sell half a million cars in North America, you are not a niche player."[45]

Volkswagen's CEO, Ferdinand Piech, is a man of vision who has bold plans to take his company to global leadership in the automobile industry. In 1998, VW surpassed Toyota to become the third largest automobile producer in the world. Although many believe Toyota will reclaim its status once the Asian market stabilizes, Piech thinks otherwise. He dismisses the threat of a rebounding Toyota, focusing his attention instead on "knocking off Ford and GM."[46] VW's October 1998 sales reached $908 million for a 77 percent increase over 1997 sales figures.[47]

Under Piech's leadership, Volkswagen has established challenging objectives, and understandably so. VW's sales and profits are soaring despite the lackluster performance of the global economy. Perhaps the most amazing aspect of Volkswagen's stunning success is that just seven years ago the company was barely making ends meet. Piech attributes the remarkable turnaround to "platform consolidation,"[48] which has cut costs and improved manufacturing efficiency. As Piech ponders Volkswagen's future, he must be careful to avoid cannibalization of his existing markets. Using his words, "Make a VW as good-looking as the Audi, why buy the Audi."[49]

General Motors

"If it ain't broke, don't fix it!" That was the attitude at General Motors in the 1970s, 1980s and early-1990s. GM became satisfied with their successes and began to behave as though they were invincible. This philosophy simply cannot succeed in a global market that demands better and less expensive products. To remain competitive with the best firms in the world, General Motors and every other firm must run hard just to keep up. To pull away from the competition requires real genius. Excellent businesses must satisfy the demands of their customers for high quality products at reasonable prices, and they must continue to improve products and processes every day. For the better part of three decades, GM did not act like an excellent company, and their market share declined as a result.

Despite these problems, in 1997 General Motors had sales of about $178 billion and a workforce of 608,000.[50] GM, once a model of industrial achievement, came to represent mediocre quality and negligence toward industry trends that are changing the way automakers do business. GM's unwillingness to adapt to these global changes opened the door for Ford, Chrysler, Toyota and other auto manufacturers to attack their market and take their customers. Between the 1960s and the late-1990s, GM's market share declined from about 52 percent to roughly 30 percent.[51]

The root cause of GM's performance problems between the 1960s and 1992 was a lack of leaders who were willing to make the difficult decisions to get the company back on track.[52] Clearly, GM could not continue down this path and remain competitive. John Smith's ascension at GM in 1992 marked the dawning of a new day for the company and ended years of stagnation and arrogance. Now, leaders at GM are seeking dramatic improvements to regain their competitiveness. However, Ford, DaimlerChrysler, Toyota and other automakers are working just as hard to improve their competitive positions. As GM spokesperson notes, "When you look at what we've accomplished over the past few years, it's been very substantial. The problem is, the rest of the automotive world is moving, too. I guess we just have to crank it up a little faster."[53]

General Motors and Union Problems

In the summer of 1998, GM and the UAW ended a two-month strike that crippled the company's North American operations, led to layoffs of almost 200,000 workers, and cost the company more than $2.5 billion in lost profits.[54] More than 100 parts plants and 27 of GM's 29 assembly plants were forced to close during the strike, and dozens of suppliers serving GM were forced to lay off workers as well. Economists estimate the strike reduced 1998 Gross Domestic Product (GDP) in the United States by half a percent.[55]

Despite the negative effects of the strike on the company and the economy, GM needed to take a firm stand against union policies that had contributed greatly to the company's poor performance. For example, inflexible union work rules caused GM to lose $1,200 on every Chevrolet Cavalier sold in 1998, and GM's labor and benefit costs per vehicle sold were $4,439 higher than comparable costs for Nissan at its Smyrna, Tennessee plant (the most efficient auto manufacturing facility in the United States).[56]

The strike cost GM $75 million a day, a hefty price to pay, but the final settlement with the union provided very little help for the ailing company. Two issues in particular are problematic. First, "peg rates" have contributed greatly to GM's problems. Peg rates work like this. Workers are expected to produce a specific number of units per day, and if they produce more than the specified amount, they receive what amounts to bonus pay. On the face of it, peg rates sound like a good idea. They can be viewed as an incentive to increase production. However, technology has improved dramatically since peg rates were determined, and now workers can fulfill their obligation under the peg rate system with very little time and effort. Thus, they spend large portions of their workdays earning bonuses for exceeding work requirements that are far too low given productivity enhancements made since peg rates were determined.

For example, at GM's Flint, Michigan metal stamping plant, the average low-skill union worker earns $68,000 per year under the peg rate system.[57] Clearly, GM cannot compete with the best producers in the world when they pay their average low-skill workers such exorbitantly high wages. As Brent C. Smith, senior research associate at the University of Michigan Office for the Study of Automotive Transportation says, "The peg rate system is an archaic way of doing things. It is not a competitive way of doing things … It is just not acceptable."[58]

Second, many of GM's parts plants are not competitive. The quality of the parts they produce is no better than that of their competitors, and their costs are much too high. To solve this problem, GM has taken steps to outsource the production of several parts—including brakes. GM's Dayton, Ohio brake parts plant is a good example of a plant that is not competitive with the world's leading producers. In 1996, union workers in the Dayton plant called a strike when they learned GM was considering selling the plant. The strike lasted 17 days and cost GM almost $1 billion in lost earnings. They called another strike in 1998 for the same reason.

According to a GM spokesman, the plant is not competitive with outside producers who can make the brakes for much less money. GM has received offers for the plant, but as part of the strike settlement they agreed not to sell it until January 2000.[59] Outsourcing brake parts is a nobrainer, but GM is unable to make this move because of an inflexible union. It will not accept work rule changes demanded by competition in the global market, and it is willing to strike and bring the company to a virtual stand-still if its outdated work rules are not accepted by the company. In 1998, GM's profit per vehicle sold was $1,000 lower than Ford's.[60] Excessively high labor costs contribute greatly to this disparity, and it cannot continue if GM hopes to compete with the best automobile producers in the world.

Union leaders have failed to grasp one important truth—"manufacturing, once the cornerstone of the car business, is rapidly becoming a commodity operation that can be farmed out to whichever supplier offers the lowest price,"[61] and car manufacturers can assemble a vehicle by simply snapping together modular components.[62] Under these conditions, auto manufacturers have only one choice. To survive and remain competitive, they must purchase the least expensive inputs that satisfy their quality standards. It does not matter if those inputs are produced in China or Mexico or Singapore.

In September 1999, General Motors and the United Auto Worker's union agreed to a remarkable labor contract for the U.S. automobile industry. "GM has reportedly gone so far as to offer every UAW member with more than 10 years seniority a lifetime employment guarantee … .Under the current contract, GM is required to hire one person for every two workers who leave, a ratio that allows it to continue reducing its workforce. But GM may insist on eliminating or reducing that ratio … in exchange for job guarantees.[63] UAW president Stephen Yokich calls it the most generous contract he has seen in his career with the union.

As of the writing of this case, "the UAW workforce at GM has an average age of 48 with 23 years of service. UAW members can retire with full pension benefits after 30 years of service … .[Currently there are] 32,000 UAW workers [at GM] with 30 or more years of service, and the average retirement age is 57. Workforce attrition at GM was 6.8 percent in 1998."[64]

General Motors is Changing

As one industry observer noted, "Whoever says GM is not radically different than it was just five years ago simply isn't paying attention."[65] Between 1993 and 1997, GM increased its cash flow by $27 billion, fully-funded its pension fund that was under-funded by $12 billion in 1992, and generated $17.5 billion in cash that can be used to improve and expand operations. Most striking of all, however, GM posted a loss of $2.6 billion in 1992, but earned $6.7 billion in 1997. John Smith deserves credit for taking the steps necessary to turn the company around, but he has much more work to do to make GM competitive with the best automakers in the world.

Current changes taking place at GM point to a brighter future. For example, GM is taking steps to reduce confusion, save time, and eliminate duplication throughout the company. To achieve this objective, the company is focusing on using common processes, parts and vehicle platforms worldwide (GM plans to reduce the number of vehicle platforms used worldwide from 16 to eight). Savings from these and other changes are expected immediately at the five new plants GM is building around the world. Additionally, GM is cutting costs by streamlining development processes for cars and trucks. As a part of the largest global expansion in the company's history, GM is moving aggressively into the Asian market by building a new plant in China. Finally, by spinning off EDS in 1996 and Hughes Electronics in 1997, GM has repositioned itself as a growth company and freed up both EDS and Hughes Electronics to compete aggressively in their industries.

These changes are beginning to pay off. In 1997, GM's net income increased almost 37 percent (from $4.9 billion in 1996 to $6.7 billion in 1997), and its profit margin jumped from 3.4 percent in 1996 to 4.4 percent in 1997. Betting on the company's ability to compete successfully in the global market, in 1997 GM's board decided to repurchase $9 billion worth of the company's stock and invested $9.8 billion in capital improvements. Additionally, GM spent $4 billion in 1997 on studies designed to further improve the company's competitive position in the global market.

As the largest United States exporter of cars and trucks, GM currently has manufacturing, assembly, or component parts operations in 50 countries, and it has a presence in more than 190 countries. GM is large and diverse. Even if vehicle sales were not part of GM's operations, the company would still rank in the top 30 in the Fortune 500. Through more than 160 subsidiaries, joint ventures, and affiliates, General Motors has substantial interests in telecommunications and space, aerospace and defense, consumer and automotive electronics, financial and insurance services, locomotives, automotive systems, and heavy-duty automatic transmissions.

To improve its competitive position and grow the company, GM has made drastic cuts in its automobile production cycle time. According to John Smith, "Without question we're trying to grow the business and that's something I'm going to be focused on."[66] In 1995 GM's production cycle from design to manufacture was 36 months long. By 1998, the company had cut the production cycle to 24 months. In November 1998, GM announced a plan to reduce the production cycle to 18 months by investing $1.5 billion over five years to consolidate 40 engineering centers into four research and development sites.[67] According to Wesley Brown, an analyst with Nextrend, "Having all those research centers creates a communication problem. You have people working on identical projects without knowing it, because they are working in different buildings."[68]

While recognizing the importance of these changes, analysts are not entirely sanguine about the outlook for GM in the increasingly competitive global market. For example, they note that most of the changes made so far have been driven by the need to cut costs and take advantage of growth opportunities in potential new markets, like China and Eastern Europe. According Michael D. Prospero, an analyst for Pittsburgh-based PNC Institutional Investors Services, the plan to consolidate GM's North American and international automotive operations offered nothing more than the opportunity to catch up with Ford and Chrysler who had made similar changes years before. He said, "They're trying to play catch-up … but there's still so much waste in their operations. They're still behind the biggest competitors in areas such as production costs."[69]

Indeed, GM's successes have been eclipsed by aggressive cost-reductions and growth enhancements by Ford and Chrysler, as well as by rapidly changing global circumstances. For example, Toyota, BMW and Daimler-Benz have cut costs and changed the shape of global competition in the automobile industry by building manufacturing facilities in the United States to serve the North American market. Additionally, the merger of Daimler-Benz and Chrysler, and the promise of more stunning merger announcements to come, suggest that the global automobile industry is changing at warp speed. Candidly, GM's plan to consolidate globally is not innovative in light of these developments. As one industry expert said, "GM seems stuck in the quicksand of perpetual organization."[70]

Spinning-Off Delphi Automotive Systems

Delphi Automotive Systems is a diversified Tier 1 automobile parts supplier that sells to every manufacturer of light vehicles in the world.[71] With sales of $31.4 billion in 1997, Delphi would have ranked 25th on the list of all industrial companies in the U.S. if it were independent of GM.[72] Delphi has a long and proud history. Under GM, Delphi developed and introduced the electric self-starter, the in-dash radio, the turn signal, the catalytic converter, the airbag, the tilt steering wheel, independent front-wheel suspension, the energy-absorbing steering column, the electric power sliding door, and the integrated child safety seat. In 1997 alone, Delphi received more than 300 patents and introduced more than 50 new products and processes.[73]

On August 3, 1998, GM announced its intention to spin-off Delphi Automotive Systems in the first half of 1999. After separating from General Motors, Delphi Automotive will be the world's largest supplier of automobile parts, and it will be almost half the size the slimmed down GM. Lehman Brothers' analyst Joseph Phillippi believes the Delphi spin-off is "just what the doctor ordered."[74]

If the deal goes through as expected, both GM and Delphi will benefit greatly. Releasing Delphi will free GM from a portion of its stifling vertical integration, and it will help GM cut costs and improve margins.[75] According to GM Chairman John Smith:

> For General Motors, Delphi's independence will give us the power to reshape, re-energize, and refocus our company. It will further streamline General Motors, while simplifying our relationships among our sectors. And, like never before, it will allow us to focus on our core business—building the world's best cars and trucks.[76]

Independence from GM will enable Delphi to seek more business from Ford, DaimlerChrysler, and other automakers. As long as Delphi is a part of GM, they harbor fears that Delphi might reveal their secret car and truck plans to GM. According to Smith,

> Independence and public ownership mean Delphi will have the opportunity and resources to expand its consumer base and pursue global growth opportunities … It also means Delphi can better market its innovation—which has long been its hallmark—and complete its transformation into one of the world's leading high-technology companies.[77]

General Motors initiated the process of creating an independent Delphi Automotive Systems in 1991 when it organized the components business into the Automotive Components Group of GM. In 1994, Delphi became Delphi Automotive Components Group Worldwide as a separate division within GM, and it began a transformation from a North American based, captive component parts supplier to GM to a global supplier of components, integrated systems, and modules to a wide range of customers.[78] In 1995, it was renamed Delphi Automotive Systems, and in 1997 GM transferred Delco Electronics to Delphi. Thus, the announcement of the spin-off in August 1998 was no big surprise.

General Motors Board of Directors appointed a savvy group of business leaders to ensure Delphi's success as an independent company. Led by President and CEO J.T. Battenberg III, Delphi made bold moves in anticipation of the spin-off. Battenberg, lauded on Wall Street for his elimination of inefficiency, has been in charge of Delphi since 1992. At first Battenberg was reluctant to lead GM's parts empire. In the company, it was seen as a dead end for executives not chosen to lead an automotive sector, but eventually he realized that with 208 plants in 36 countries Delphi had the potential to become a powerful, independent global leader in automotive parts. With its global presence, Delphi will be able to follow its customers as they expand globally.[79]

Between 1992 and 1998, Battenberg aggressively streamlined Delphi, "targeting unprofitable plants, either consolidating, closing, or selling them. He dropped product lines where Delphi couldn't be a market leader. Since 1992, he has sold or closed 53 plants as Delphi's product line fell from 310 to 151 components."[80] Following the example of General Electric chairman Jack Welch, who's similarly aggressive tactics positioned GE as a global leader, Battenberg set challenging goals for Delphi, seeking to expand Delphi's customer base in an effort to secure half of its business from outside General Motors by 2002. In 1997, Delphi generated 35 percent of its sales from outside GM—up from 15 percent in 1992 when Battenberg took over.

Battenberg has surrounded himself with an aggressive team that is committed to making Delphi a world leader. Thomas H. Wyman, a GM Board member since 1985, serves as Delphi's lead independent director and chairman of the Board's Executive Committee. With vast experience at AT&T, CBS, Nestlè, Polaroid, Green Giant, and Pillsbury, Wyman's diverse background will be an asset to Delphi as it looks to the future as an independent company. Concerning Wyman, Battenberg said, "We are honored that Tom Wyman will be able to join the Delphi Board at its inception. His leadership and his strategic, global insights will be exceptionally valuable in helping us build our future growth."[81]

Alan S. Dawes is Chief Financial Officer of Delphi. Battenberg notes that "Alan brings extensive experience in finance and operations, having previously served as GM's assistant treasurer, assistant finance director, and executive-in-charge of operations for the former GM Automotive Components Group as well as general manager of Delphi Chassis."[82] John G. Blahnik is Delphi's Treasurer, leading a team to develop a new treasury system for Delphi. Guy C. Hachey is general manager of Delphi Chassis Systems. Donald L. Runkle is general manager of Energy and Engine Management, and leader of the Delphi Engineering Task Team. Delphi's Strategy Board is composed of Battenberg, Wyman, Dawes, Blahnik, Hachey, and Runkle.[83]

Believing that "achieving optimum performance requires systems expertise,"[84] Battenberg made clear at the outset his intention to build Delphi's strategy using a systems approach. This approach requires decision-makers to view an automobile as a group of interacting components. Delphi's strategy will showcase "fully integrated technology, quality components, systems, and modules, faster, lower-cost assembly, and better inventory control. When you put it all together, the Delphi Automotive Systems approach ensures a perfect match between components, systems, and the vehicles in which they are used."[85]

Delphi and the Union

Delphi has more than 200,000 employees, 167,000 of which belong to one of 53 unions.[86] The United Auto Workers union opposed the sale of Delphi Automotive Systems from the beginning. According to UAW Vice President Richard Shoemaker, "Should GM decide to proceed with the sale as announced, the UAW's record is clear: We can and will aggressively work to protect the rights and interests of UAW members impacted by the sale."[87] The timing of the spin-off announcement, which was made only five days after the settlement of the UAW strike against GM during the summer of 1998, contributed to the UAW's outrage. UAW President Stephen P. Yokich reiterated the union's position saying, "The UAW is on record as opposing the split-off or spin-off of GM's Delphi Operations and that remains our position."[88]

UAW opposition to the deal was no insignificant matter. The UAW strike during the summer of 1998 lasted only seven weeks, but it cost GM almost $2.5 billion in lost profits.[89] Surprisingly, 46 percent of the American public supported the union even though they knew very little about the reason for the strike.[90] Although the percentage of workers in the United States belonging to unions has been declining for several decades, unions started flexing their muscles in the 1996 elections. Their goals were to win public sympathy for their cause, to help re-elect President Bill Clinton, and to win democratic majorities in the Senate and House of Representatives. During 1997 and 1998, unions struck Northwest Airlines, General Motors, Bell Atlantic, and U.S. West, to name a few. Each of these strikes was costly. Since the UAW represents 25 percent of Delphi's workforce, the company cannot afford a battle with the union going into the public offering.[91]

Union opposition to the spin-off focused on several factors including the potential reduction of wage rates, possible losses in pensions and benefits, possible plant closings, and layoffs that could result once Delphi gains its independence. They also feared the implementation of a permanent two-tiered wage system. According to David Cole, director of the Office for the Study of Automotive Transportation at the University of Michigan, "Under the existing contract, new hires work under a temporary two-tiered system. They don't receive full union wages and benefits until they've worked at Delphi for a few years. New employees would be locked into the lower pay levels for good under a permanent two-tiered system, an arrangement the UAW has opposed in the past."[92]

Hoping to head off union problems, Battenberg said, "We intend to use this opportunity to engage in high-level dialogue with the leadership of the UAW and our other unions, and to enter a more constructive relationship with the employees of what will be a new *Fortune* 25 company."[93] Wyman suggested inviting a member of the UAW to sit on the board of Delphi in the hopes of opening communication lines with the UAW.[94]

The conflict between labor and management may continue for some time since Delphi wants to build more plants overseas and rid its U.S. plants of low-profit commodity parts. The union, on the other hand, wants the company to make more investments in U.S plants, and they fear that virtually all commodity parts will eventually be made in Mexico. Prices of commodity parts have dropped steadily for several years, and GM can no longer afford to make them in the United States where labor costs are high. However, Dan Thetford, president of the local union in a Flint, Michigan Delphi plant, said, "With the amount of cost cutting we'll get out of not being part of GM, I believe as a separate huge company we will be able to compete with anybody."[95] Time will tell if he is correct, but it is certain Delphi cannot compete effectively if it is a high cost producer.

Innovation—The Key to Delphi's Success

As an independent company, Delphi will have the ability to leverage its expertise in the integration of automotive systems and to take advantage of technological innovation.[96] Patenting more than one invention each day and, on the average, implementing one new product or process each week, Delphi is well known for its innovative activity. Between 1998 and 2000, Delphi introduced more than 139 major new products.[97]

Recognized by the most powerful firms in the automobile industry as a quality producer, in 1998 Delphi received GM's Worldwide Supplier of the Year Award, DaimlerChrysler's Gold Pentastar Award, Volkswagen's VW Formal Q Award, and Toyota's NUMMI Triple Crown Gold Award.[98] All these awards were bestowed on Delphi while it was a division of GM.

Evolution in automotive electronics has ushered in a world of opportunity for Delphi. For example, Volkswagen introduced Delphi's Electronic Power Steering, which replaces hydraulics-based systems. Additionally, "occupant protection" applications are being developed at Delphi employing "sensors and electronics, especially in 'smart airbags' that only deploy under specific conditions."[99] In 1998, "Delphi released a list of seven 'next-century winners'—high tech products, such as a system that automatically adjusts cruise control to avoid collisions—that it plans to introduce."[100] To be the global leader in automotive parts and achieve its goal of generating 50 percent of its sales from non-GM customers by the year 2002, Delphi must continue to innovate aggressively.

Delphi plans to be a leader in the production of products that are environmentally friendly, products that are "dedicated to protecting human health, natural resources, and the global environment."[101] By coupling technological innovation with environmentally friendly innovation, Delphi can position itself as the global automotive parts leader. In September 1998, the Mexican government recognized nine Delphi Automotive Systems plants for outstanding environmental achievements. Mexican Federal Environmental Protection Attorney Antonio Azuela de la Cueva emphasized that "in Mexico, Delphi is an environmental leader, a benchmark for the industry."[102] Environmentally friendly innovations by Delphi include Advanced Engine Management Systems, which achieves clean exhaust while maintaining fuel efficiency, Integrated Vehicle/Electronics Systems, requiring less packaging, 'X-by-Wire' Systems, reducing engine emissions, and ENERGEN (registered trademark), which addresses global warming concerns by improving fuel economy and reducing emissions.[103]

Delphi is expanding its strategic partnerships to a new global level while focusing on cutting edge technology. Nissan has begun importing auto batteries from Delphi for sale in the Japanese market as Nissan genuine service parts. Using batteries from Delphi's Korean facility will allow Nissan the shortest lead-time from shipment to delivery to Japan. Similarly, Delphi combined forces with Delco Electronics and Microsoft to unveil a Saab 9-5 sedan with a prototype Internet link. As automakers increasingly demand that suppliers develop whole systems instead of individual parts, Delphi has responded aggressively. According to Donald Runkle, "Delphi is a strong automotive supplier with capabilities to provide our customers with the entire engine management and converter value chain."[104]

On February 23, 1998, Delphi, Sun Microsystems, Microsoft, and Netscape unveiled the "Network Vehicle" at a trade show in Detroit. It featured an integration of wireless communications, global positioning via satellite, head-up displays, voice recognition, Java technology, Web access and other Internet components.[105] According to Battenberg, "Integrating electronics into 'smart' auto components is a key of Delphi's strategy to survive and grow after its independence from GM. Delphi's strength in technology will drive its success."[106]

Expanding Globally and Getting Ready for the IPO

Delphi is planning to cut costs aggressively and to expand its operations in the automobile aftermarket and non-automotive fields, such as aerospace and electronics systems. Together, 1997 sales in these markets was almost $11 billion, or roughly one third of Delphi's revenues. Delphi is attempting to reduce the cost of doing business in China through an agreement with Ford's Visteon Automotive Systems that enables the two companies to exchange and purchase parts from each other. Taking advantage of low labor costs, Delphi has invested $250 million in a wholly owned facility in China and in 10 joint ventures with Chinese parts makers. Additionally, the company opened a technical center in Beijing in 1998. Delphi currently has 17 operations in South America and predicts it will generate sales of $1.5 billion annually in South America early in the 21st century.

Delphi's experience with the design and assembly process at GM has prepared the company to add value to all its customers. According to Battenberg, Delphi will provide manufacturing flexibility and quicker cycle times by "taking modularity to the next level, by delivering customers value throughout the entire vehicle design, assembly, and manufacturing process."[107] Battenberg believes Delphi will become the "one-stop" component provider for the needs of all automobile manufacturers.[108]

In a letter to General Motors' employees dated August 3, 1998, GM chairman John Smith wrote,

Indeed, we are making Delphi independent because, quite simply, it is time. It is the right thing—and best thing—for all of us with a stake in General Motors … The independence of Delphi is possible because of [its] … dedicated focus on customer satisfaction and product and process improvements … Together, GM and Delphi share a rich and proud history. Separately though, Delphi can write its own history and control its own destiny.[109]

Delphi Becomes an Independent Company

On Friday February 5, 1999, GM sold 100 million shares of Delphi Automotive Systems stock, or 18 percent of the company, to the public and raised $1.7 billion in cash. It was the seventh largest domestic new issue in history. That day, Delphi was the most actively traded stock on the New York Stock Exchange, rising more than eight percent in value to 18 7/16 per share.[110] GM plans to distribute the remaining 82 percent of Delphi to GM shareholders during 1999, and by the beginning of the 21st century Delphi will be a completely independent company.[111]

Notes

1. Rae, John B. *The American Automobile Industry* (Boston: Twayne Publishers, 1984), 29.
2. Rae, John B. *The American Automobile Industry* (Boston: Twayne Publishers, 1984), 31.
3. Smith, Roger. *Building on 75 Years of Excellence: The General Motors Story* (New York: Newcomen Society of the United States, 1984), 13.
4. Kuhn, Arthur. *GM Passes Ford, 1918-1938: Designing the General Motors Performance-Control System* (University Park: Pennsylvania State University Press, 1986), 36.
5. Kuhn, Arthur. *GM Passes Ford, 1918-1938: Designing the General Motors Performance-Control System* (University Park: Pennsylvania State University Press, 1986), 43.
6. Kuhn, Arthur. *GM Passes Ford, 1918-1938: Designing the General Motors Performance-Control System* (University Park: Pennsylvania State University Press, 1986), 45.
7. Kuhn, Arthur. *GM Passes Ford, 1918-1938: Designing the General Motors Performance-Control System* (University Park: Pennsylvania State University Press, 1986), 84.
8. Smith, Roger. *Building on 75 Years of Excellence: The General Motors Story* (New York: Newcomen Society of the United States, 1984), 15.
9. Kuhn, Arthur. *GM Passes Ford, 1918-1938: Designing the General Motors Performance-Control System* (University Park: Pennsylvania State University Press, 1986), 88.
10. Kuhn, Arthur. *GM Passes Ford, 1918-1938: Designing the General Motors Performance-Control System* (University Park: Pennsylvania State University Press, 1986), 313.
11. Kawahara, Akira. *The Origin of Competitive Strength: Fifty Years of the Auto Industry in Japan and the U.S.* (Tokyo: New York: Springer, 1998), 106.
12. Kuhn, Arthur. *GM Passes Ford, 1918-1938: Designing the General Motors Performance-Control System* (University Park: Pennsylvania State University Press, 1986), 4.
13. www.generalmotors.com
14. www.generalmotors.com
15. Healey, James R. and Micheline Maynard. "Big Three: Auto Firms Will Dwindle," *USA Today*, 24 September 1998, 1.
16. Healey, James R. and Micheline Maynard. "Big Three: Auto Firms Will Dwindle," *USA Today*, 24 September 1998, 1.
17. Healey, James R. and Micheline Maynard. "Detroit Enters the Global Automaker Era," *USA Today*, 24 September 1998, 1.
18. Naughton, Keith. "The Global Six," *Business Week*, 25 January 1999, 16.
19. Naughton, Keith. "The Global Six," *Business Week*, 25 January 1999, 16.
20. Sugawara, Sandra. "Renault to Buy Large Stake in Nissan," *The Washington Post*, 28 March 1999, A-24.
21. "Henry Ford's Possible Revenge," *U.S. News & World Report*, 8 March 1999, 51.
22. Girsky, S.J., et.al. "Chrysler/Ford/General Motors—Company Report," Morgan Stanley, Dean Witter, 28 January 1998, The Investext Group: 1996.
23. Snyder, Neil and Angela Clontz. *The Will to Lead* (Chicago: Irwin Professional Publishing, 1997), 177.
24. Snyder, Neil and Angela Clontz. *The Will to Lead* (Chicago: Irwin Professional Publishing, 1997), 212.
25. Kurylko, Diana. "European Profits are a Priority: New Focus World Car is Crucial," *Automotive News*, 14 September 1998, 41.
26. Simison, Robert L. "Higher Profits Seen by Ford, GM in Europe," *The Wall Street Journal*, 30 September 1998, A-3.
27. Kurylko, Diana. "European Profits are a Priority: New Focus World Car is Crucial," *Automotive News*, 14 September 1998, 41.
28. Healey, James R. and Micheline Maynard. "Detroit Enters the Global Automaker Era," *USA Today*, 28 September 1998, 1.
29. Brown, Warren. "Volvo, Ford Discuss Joint Car Venture," *The Washington Post*, 24 December 1998, D-2.
30. Brown, Warren. "Ford to Pay $6.5 Billion For Volvo's Car Business," *The Washington Post*, 28 January 1999, E-1.
31. http://www.usatoday.com/money/world/mw1.htm
32. Seaman, Barrett and Ron Stodghill. "Here Comes the Road Test," Time.com, http://cgi.pathfinder.com/time/mag…518/business.here_comes_the_6html, 18 May 1998, 1.
33. Brown, Warren. "Two Stars, in Alignment: Merger Will Make Chrysler a Global Big Five Player," *The Washington Post*, 20 September 1998, H-1.
34. Healey, James R. and Micheline Maynard. "Detroit Enters the Global Market Era," *USA Today*, 28 September 1998, 1.
35. Brown, Warren. "Two Stars, in Alignment: Merger Will Make Chrysler a Global Big Five Player," *The Washington Post*, 20 September 1998, H-1.
36. Klayman, Ben. "Chrysler, Daimler's Biggest Challenges Ahead of Them," Yahoonews, 18 September 1998, http://biz.yahoo.co/rf/980918/baf.html.
37. Brown, Warren. "'Day One' for DaimlerChrysler," *The Washington Post*, 18 November 1998, C-13.
38. Brown, Warren. "'Day One' for DaimlerChrysler," *The Washington Post*, 18 November 1998, C-13.
39. Healey, James R. and Micheline Maynard. "Detroit Enters the Global Market Era," *USA Today*, 28 September 1998, 2.
40. www.toyota.com/times/local/docs
41. www.toyota.com/times/local/docs
42. www.infoseek.co/Content?ar…&sv=IS&1K=&col=NX&kt=A&ak=news1486
43. www.toyota.com/times/local/docs
44. www.infoseek.co/Content?ar…&sv=IS&1K=&col=NX&kt=A&ak=news1486
45. Holstein, William. "VW's Sixties Flashback," *U.S. News & World Report*, 8 March 1999, 50.
46. Healy, James R. "Some '99 Models Offer Big Price Cuts," *USA Today*, 16 September 1998, 1.
47. Healy, James R. "Some '99 Models Offer Big Price Cuts," *USA Today*, 16 September 1998, 1.
48. Healy, James R. "Some '99 Models Offer Big Price Cuts," *USA Today*, 16 September 1998, 1.
49. Healy, James R. "Some '99 Models Offer Big Price Cuts," *USA Today*, 16 September 1998, 1.
50. Chandler, Clay. "For the Economy, Strike is Small," *The Washington Post*, 29 July 1998, A-14.
51. Chandler, Clay. "For the Economy, Strike is Small," *The Washington Post*, 29 July 1998, A-14.
52. Snyder, Neil, James Dowd, and Dianne Houghton. *Vision, Values & Courage* (New York: The Free Press, 1994).

53. Brown, Warren and Frank Swoboda. "GM Faces New Global Realities," *The Washington Post*, 12 July 1998, H-1.
54. Hamilton, Martha and Betty Burkstrand. "Strikers Approve Accord with GM," *The Washington Post*, 29 July 1998, E-1.
55. Hamilton, Martha and Betty Burkstrand. "Strikers Approve Accord with GM," *The Washington Post*, 29 July 1998, E-1.
56. Brown, Warren and Frank Swoboda. "GM Faces New Global Realities," *The Washington Post*, 12 July 1998, H-1.
57. Burkstrand, Beth. "GM, UAW Reach Tentative Accord," *The Washington Post*, 29 July 1998, A-1.
58. Burkstrand, Beth. "GM, UAW Reach Tentative Accord," *The Washington Post*, 29 July 1998, A-1.
59. Burkstrand, Beth. "GM, UAW Reach Tentative Accord," *The Washington Post*, 29 July 1998, A-1.
60. Skrzycki, Cindy. "Getting Into Gear Will Take GM Weeks," *The Washington Post*, 29 July 1998, A-14.
61. Naughton, Keith. "The Global Six," *Business Week*, 25 January 1999, 16.
62. *Business Week*, 25 January 1999, http://web3.infotrac-custom.com.
63. Swoboda, Frank. "Lifetime Jobs a Key In Auto Union Talks," *The Washington Post*, 11 September 1999, E-1.
64. Swoboda, Frank. "Lifetime Jobs a Key In Auto Union Talks," *The Washington Post*, 11 September 1999, E-1.
65. Brown, Warren and Frank Swoboda. "GM Faces New Global Realities," *The Washington Post*, July 12, 1998, H-1.
66. Evanoff, Ted. "The Boss Says Pick Up the Pace," *The Detroit Free Press*, 7 October 1998, 1.
67. Brown, Warren. "GM's Consolidation Plan Fails to Impress Investors," *The Washington Post*, 7 October 1998, C-11.
68. Brown, Warren. "GM's Consolidation Plan Fails to Impress Investors," *The Washington Post*, 7 October 1998, C-11.
69. Brown, Warren. "GM's Consolidation Plan Fails to Impress Investors," *The Washington Post*, 7 October 1998, C-11.
70. Healy, James. "Some '99 Models Offer Big Price Cuts," *USA Today*, 16 September 1998, 1.
71. Delphi Automotive Systems Incorporated Prospectus, 2 February 1999, 4.
72. Delphi Automotive Systems Incorporated Prospectus, 2 February 1999, 4.
73. Delphi Automotive Systems Incorporated Prospectus, 2 February 1999, 76.
74. Maynard, Micheline. "Delphi Spin-off is 'Just What the Doctor Ordered' for GM," *USA Today*, 4 August 1998, B-3.
75. Tait, Nikki. "Spin-Off May Provide More Opportunities in Supplies," *The Financial Times*, 1 March 1999, 2.
76. Agence France-Presse, "GM to Spin Off its Delphi Unit Next Year," 3 August 1998.
77. Agence France-Presse, "GM to Spin Off its Delphi Unit Next Year," 3 August 1998.
78. Delphi Automotive Systems Incorporated Prospectus, 2 February 1999, 63.
79. Delphi Automotive Systems Incorporated Prospectus, 2 February 1999, 67.
80. Pittsburgh Post-Gazette, "GM's Delphi Automotive Spin-off a Newborn that Looks Like a Grownup," 6 August 1998, F-8.
81. M2 Presswire, "GM: Delphi Appoints Lead Director," 18 August 1998.
82. M2 Presswire, "GM: GM Announces Executive Appointments," 12 August 1998.
83. M2 Presswire, "GM: GM Announces Executive Appointments," 12 August 1998.
84. www.dephiauto.com
85. www.dephiauto.com
86. Delphi Automotive Systems Incorporated Prospectus, 2 February 1999, 17 and 90.
87. Burkstrand, Beth. "GM, UAW Deal to End Strike," *The Washington Post*, 29 July 1998, E-1.
88. Burkstrand, Beth. "GM, UAW Deal to End Strike," *The Washington Post*, 29 July 1998, E-1.
89. Burkstrand, Beth. "GM, UAW Reach Tentative Accord," *The Washington Post*, 29 July 1998, A-1.
90. Dionne, E.J. Jr. "The GM Fight," *The Washington Post*, 4 August 1998, A-15.
91. Greenhouse, Steven. "Unions, Growing Bolder, No Longer Shun Strikes," *The New York Times*, 7 September 1998, A-12.
92. Gallun, Alby. "Overtime and Job Anxiety for GM's Delphi Workers," *The Business Journal—Milwaukee*, 28 August 1998, 49.
93. GM IPO Announcement, August 1998.
94. Warner, Fara. "GM Names Wyman, a Director, to Lead New Board of Delphi Automotive Systems," *The Wall Street Journal*, 18 August 1998, B-14.
95. Blumenstein, Rebecca and Fara Warner, "GM to Make Delphi Unit Independent," *The Wall Street Journal*, 4 August 1998, A-3.
96. AFX News, "GM/Delphi—Separation to Enable Companies to Focus on Own Business," 3 August 1998.
97. www.delphiauto.com
98. Delphi Automotive Systems Incorporated Prospectus, 2 February 1999, 71.
99. Puchalsky, Andrea. "Delphi CEO Says 2002 Goal is Reachable; GM Committed to Spin-off," Dow Jones Online News, 29 September 1998.
100. Koenig, Bill. "Reinventing Delco: High-tech Products Expected to Fuel Growth," *The Indianapolis News/Indianapolis Star*, 15 October 1998, 1.
101. www.delphiauto.com
102. PR Newswire, "Delphi Goes Over the Forty Mark for Mexican Environmental Awards," 11 September 1998.
103. www.delphiauto.com
104. www.delphiauto.com
105. Newcomb, Kelly. "The 'Network Vehicle'—Good Idea, Bad Idea," TechMall:http//techmall.com/techdocs/nb-vehicle.html.
106. Williams, Fred. "Delphi's New Temperature Control System Expected to Boost Sales," *Buffalo News*, 2 March 1999, A-9.
107. "Delphi Positioned to be Automotive Industry's Best Single-Point Contact for Modular Solutions," PR Newswire, 1 March 1999.
108. Delphi Automotive Systems Incorporated Prospectus, 2 February 1999, 68.
109. PR Newswire, "Letter to Employees From GM Chairman John F. Smith, Jr.," 3 August 1998.
110. "IPO Market Rebounds," *USA Today*, 5 February 1999, http://www.usatoday.com/money/mds023.htm.
111. www.ipocentral.com/ml_ipo57829ml.html.

Case 18

Kerkhov Karpets, Inc.

Rick Mull, Roy A. Cook, and Janet Bear Wolverton, *Fort Lewis College*

The early morning drizzle in north Georgia seemed to underscore the importance of the decision now facing Jan and Mark. Together, they needed to formulate a strategy in reaction to the shocking news that the current owner of the firm where they worked, Kerkhov Karpets, Inc., Harm Van de Berg, wanted to sell the firm to another company.

For several years now, they had been the key managers in Kerkhov Karpets, Inc., the U.S. distributing arm of Nederlander Tapijt, a major flooring manufacturer and exporter based in Jan's homeland, the Netherlands. Although Jan carried the title of President, both he and Mark realized their dependence on each other in running the firm's operations. Since Jan and Mark had controlled virtually every strategic and operating decision of the firm over the past few years, they realized that they held a strong bargaining position.

Jan and Mark wanted to make Van de Berg an offer for the firm, but the amount they should offer as well as the terms of the offer and how it should be presented had yet to be determined.

Compatible Business Partners

Although Jan and Mark were quite different in their interests outside of business, they considered each other as good friends. In operating their business, they made a great team. While they saw eye-to-eye on most important issues, they could be frank with each other in their differences. Further, it seemed that in areas where one might be weak, the other had strengths to cover those shortcomings. For these reasons, going into business together seemed a viable option.

Jan Mulder was a Dutch national. Although accepted by one of the most prestigious colleges in the Netherlands, he had opted to attend Mesa State College in Grand Junction, Colorado. He had graduated with a business degree in 1988 after four years at Mesa State. He relished the good times he

had in college and particularly enjoyed life in the United States. After graduating, he worked for six months at a large Denver, Colorado bank, beginning as a teller.

Disappointed with the speed of his progression through the bank, he quit and returned to the Netherlands. He placed an ad in a large Dutch newspaper to find a Dutch company that might want someone with his education and experience to work in the United States. His efforts landed him a job with the Atlanta, Georgia-based U.S. corporate headquarters of Nederlander Tapijt. His initial responsibilities were primarily in sales, but he also carried the title of vice-president. Jan moved to Atlanta and began his new job in August 1989.

Jan and his wife Marcella were both avid hikers, enjoyed unwinding in the outdoors, and loved to travel. Jan made frequent business trips to Las Vegas, Chicago, Hong Kong, and the Netherlands, averaging about a dozen such trips per year. Marcella took advantage of the frequent flyer miles Jan earned and regularly traveled with him to Hong Kong, the Netherlands, and Colorado.

Mark Shaffer, on the other hand, was born and raised in the United States and attended the University of Georgia where he earned a degree in chemistry in 1987. He worked at various jobs until he began at Kerkhov Karpets, Inc. in 1992. Mark had little formal business training and little or no computer skills, accounting knowledge, or legal training. However, he excelled in dealing with people and that meant sales. In 1994, he became the Vice President of Sales for Kerkhov Karpets, Inc. Mark and his wife Robin did not travel much and enjoyed what some might consider domestic activities such as reading and maintaining their home in the suburbs of Atlanta.

The Company and Product History

Kerkhov Karpets, Inc. primarily imported carpet from the Netherlands for resale in the United States and had operated since 1984. Jan had been with the firm since 1989 and president since 1992. The firm was one of many businesses operating nationwide in the carpet industry and had established a solid reputation and a diversified client base over the years. Although the firm was periodically involved in other directly related activities such as the sale of carpet for car-mats, Kerkhov Karpets, Inc.'s primary business remained unchanged.

The firm offered three lines of products. The most recent addition was a line of carpets made from vegetable fiber twine imported from Mexico. It accounted for 25 percent of total sales. The other two lines accounted almost equally for the remaining sales volume and were imported from the Netherlands. They were polypropylene fiber indoor/outdoor carpets and wool Berber carpets. Although the three lines had distinct pricing, the firm wholesaled each line at an industry average markup of 40 percent.

The indoor/outdoor product used a 100 percent polypropylene fiber available only in Europe. It used a coarser fiber than similar U.S.-manufactured carpets and was more durable and resistant to ultra-violet decay. The U.S. market for this type of carpet was too small for major U.S. manufacturers to consider the significant capital equipment expenditures required to produce the product in the United States. A single machine could produce over seven million square yards annually. Additionally, the coarser fibers used in this process were available only in Europe.

Nederlander Tapijt, who manufactured a wide variety of quality carpets for European wholesalers, created Kerkhov Karpets, Inc. as the sole U.S. distributor of its carpets in 1984. They based the firm in northern Georgia, which is considered the "center" of the U.S. carpet industry. The parent firm was based in the Netherlands and was the manufacturer of the polypropylene and wool Berber carpets carried by Kerkhov Karpets, Inc. Nederlander Tapijt is the sole European wholesale distributor of these carpets as well.

After several years of operations, Van de Berg, who was working with the parent firm at the time, convinced Nederlander Tapijt to allow him to purchase the U.S. operations. In 1993, he borrowed $500,000 in cash from his father-in-law and purchased Kerkhov Karpets, Inc. from its parent company. At the time of this purchase, Van de Berg entered into a five-year agreement with Nederlander Tapijt to purchase the polypropylene and wool Berber carpet lines solely from Nederlander Tapijt and distribute them.

Other than as an investment, Van de Berg had little to do with the U.S. operations. Thus, Jan had moved into the president's position and had been in complete control of the operation of Kerkhov Karpets, Inc., United States since 1992. During this time, Van de Berg continued to work in the Netherlands for Nederlander Tapijt and focused on the manufacturing side of the business.

Opportunity Knocks

Four years after purchasing Kerkhov Karpets from Nederlander Tapijt, Van de Berg left Nederlander Tapijt and decided to build a competing manufacturing facility in the Netherlands. To obtain the required bank financing, Van de Berg and his father-in-law needed a large amount of cash to fund equity capital. To get these funds, Van de Berg decided to sell Kerkhov Karpets, Inc.

Van de Berg looked for someone to buy the firm, "forgetting" to tell Jan and Mark about his plans to sell. Jan and Mark first heard about the sale when Van de Berg called from the Netherlands to tell them that he had received an offer for Kerkhov Karpets, Inc. from a moderate-sized, U.S.-based carpet manufacturer. Van de Berg also told Jan that, because of his key position in the firm, the buyer was only interested in making the purchase if Jan remained with the firm.

Particularly important to Van de Berg was the cash offered by the purchasing firm. Although he asked a total of $1.25 million cash for Kerkhov Karpets, Inc., he had not received a final selling price offer or, more importantly, a cash offer amount from the interested firm. Van de Berg told Jan he hoped the firm would offer at least $500,000 cash, since he would be willing to finance the remaining balance. Jan and Mark talked at length about the possibility of buying the firm and gathered the following information about their own operations and the industry.

Management and Employees

Kerkhov Karpets operated with twelve full-time employees. The key employees are listed below.

Facilities

Kerkhov Karpets, Inc. maintained its only office just outside of Atlanta, Georgia. This building was a 30,000 square foot warehouse, which included roughly 3,000 square feet of offices. All inventories, equipment,

Table 1	Key Employees	
Name	Title	Years w/ Company
Van de Berg*	Owner of 100% shares	9
Jan Mulder	President	8
Mark Shaffer	Sales Manager	5

* Although receiving all financing from his father-in-law, Van de Berg was the owner of record of all outstanding shares.

computers, and support staff were located in the warehouse. The firm inventoried an average of one million square yards of carpet at any given time, or about one-fifth of its total annual volume. This level of inventory was required since the lead-time for receiving imported carpet was roughly eight weeks. The firm's other assets included a carpet cutting machine, two forklifts, a computer server, and ten computer terminals. Kerkhov Karpets, Inc. owned all of this equipment.

Future Prospects

Although the future ownership and direction of the firm was uncertain at this time, one thing was clear. Without Jan and Mark and the "goodwill" they had established, the firm would not continue generating its current level of business. The market for Kerkhov Karpets, Inc.'s carpet was primarily based on the efforts and reputation of Jan and Mark; all parties understood that only if they remained with the firm could it maintain its current level of growth.

Ironically, although Van de Berg wanted to sell the firm, he needed distributors for his new venture into the production end of the business. He told Jan that whoever purchased the company must agree to use his (Van de Berg's) new firm as the primary supplier of carpet for a least three and maybe as much as five years. This was a favorable condition for Jan and Mark since it would allow them to continue to have a ready supply of product for resale.

Industry Outlook

Kerkhov Karpets, Inc. derived a majority of its business from two different market segments, remodeling and new construction. Kerkhov Karpets, Inc. had experienced high historical growth rates relative to the industry. With its small but specialized market niche, it is likely that Kerkhov Karpets will be able to maintain high growth rates into the foreseeable future.

Jan and Mark realized that identifying similar firms and obtaining relevant information for those firms would be critical to establishing a meaningful comparison and valuation for their company. They identified two firms, FiberTech and Jorgenson Industries, which were relatively similar to Kerkhov Karpets, Inc. A synopsis of information and data for these two firms is presented in Exhibit 1.

In addition to the information presented in Exhibit 1, Jan and Mark talked at length about the future prospects for the firm. They arrived at several basic conclusions (assumptions). First, they agreed that sales should continue to grow at recent levels of about 12.5 percent annually for the next five years. They also believed that no other expense reductions, beyond Van de Berg's $150,000 annual salary, could

be realized, and that their tax rate would remain at 40 percent. In addition, they decided that current working capital levels should support any foreseeable growth. Finally, they agreed that annual capital expenditures would roughly equal annual depreciation, meaning that net income would approximate the firm's free cash flow.

The Decision

Both Jan and Mark were disturbed at the way the attempted sale was being handled. They had worked hard during the formative years of the firm, accepting lower-than-average industry wages in anticipation of future rewards. They did not want to start this process again with new owners. After discussing the issues for several days, they finally agreed that staying with the firm was unpalatable unless they were the new owners. Thus, the decision to purchase the firm from Van de Berg was made.

To proceed, they needed two things: (1) to arrive at a fair market value for the company, and (2) to determine a financial structure for the purchase. Fortunately, Jan's brother Rute was an international tax accountant with a strong financial analysis background. They asked Rute to help with the analysis. Rute said that, although valuation was "as much an art as a science," he would help point them in the right direction with some basic information and analysis techniques.

Learning about the Valuation Process

Jan and Mark began by discussing with Rute the process involved in determining a reasonable value for the firm. Rute pointed out that they should consider the firm's value from two standpoints. First, they should value the firm as an ongoing enterprise, and this should be the maximum that they would be willing to offer. Next, they should consider the firm's worth to Harm without either of them continuing to work for the firm, and this should be considered a minimum offer. Through negotiation, they could then arrive at an offer acceptable to Harm.

In terms of the valuation process, Rute first noted that if they were a publicly-traded firm, using the Capital Asset Pricing Model (CAPM) would be a reasonable approach. However, since they were a private firm, many of the assumptions underlying the CAPM were violated. Thus, there is no theoretically quantifiable formula for determining income capitalization rates in private firms. Historically, strong, well-positioned, small, publicly-traded firms with solid product lines and high degrees of collateralizable assets have had total equity discount rates of approximately 20 percent. Based on historical data, private firms have been found to have equity returns that

Exhibit 1   Current Relevant Data for FiberTech and Jorgenson Industries

FiberTech

Year	Sales (000's)	NI (000's)	EPS	Price	PE Ratio
1997	734,016	22,659	1.16	13.69	11.8
1996	352,512	8,827	0.58	12.35	21.3
1998	I/B/E/S*Projected P/E ratio				9.6
1999	I/B/E/S*Projected P/E ratio				8.2

Jorgenson Industries

Year	Sales (000's)	NI (000's)	EPS	Price	PE Ratio
1997	2,630,034	129,172	0.89	12.91	14.5
1996	2,320,810	100,623	0.72	19.88	27.6
1998	I/B/E/S*Projected P/E ratio				13.1
1999	I/B/E/S*Projected P/E ratio				11.0

Sales Multipliers For FiberTech and Jorgenson Industries

FiberTech Industries

Year	Sales (000's)	Market Value (000's)	Sales Multiplier
1997	$734,016	$640,560 – $247,275	0.873 – 0.337
1996	352,512	258,723 – 116,351	0.734 – 0.330

Jorgenson Industries

Year	Sales (000's)	Market Value (000's)	Sales Multiplier
1997	$2,630,034	$1,748,350 – $1,503,581	0.665 – 0.572
1996	2,320,810	1,779,109 – 1,010,248	0.767 – 0.435

*Institutional Brokers Estimate System (I/B/E/S)

are 30–40 percent higher than those of public companies. Thus, capitalization rates in the range of 26–28 percent or even more could be warranted.

The three methods suggested were:

- the income capitalization method,
- the P/E multiple method, and
- the Sales Multiplier method.

He told them that each method had its own advantages and disadvantages and that they would have to research which specific method or combination of methods might be appropriate for their company. Rute told Jan that it was common for valuation professionals to use a weighted-average of three different methods to estimate the value of a firm, with the weights based on a subjective confidence for each valuation method.

He told Jan that each of the three methods did have some common ground. Each method would require them to forecast a set of financial projections for the next five years, and he suggested using a percent of sales forecasting method. They would need to forecast sales, net income, and the firm's free cash flow. After that, they would need to develop appropriate "adjustment factors" to estimate the firm's value. They would need to examine current market data on interest rates, risk premiums, and the other relevant industry data they had already obtained to estimate the following three adjustment factors:

- A "discount rate" to capitalize income for the income capitalization method,
- A forecasted "P/E ratio" for the P/E multiple method, and
- A "sales multiplier" for the sales multiplier method.

Rute noted that, in general, small firms such as Kerkhov Karpets, Inc. were considered more risky than publicly-traded companies. Thus, they would need to make some reasonable, but subjective, adjustments to their findings. To help with these adjustments, Rute noted that conducting a ratio analysis using information contained in the balance sheet (see Exhibit 2) and the income statement (see Exhibit 3) might prove helpful in evaluating the strength of the firm, and thus more appropriate risk adjustment factors.

He specifically told Jan and Mark to use their comparable firm information as a starting point. They should then evaluate their firm, its risk, and make adjustments to those comparable firm values.

Rute also instructed them that it was common practice to use only five years of projections in the valuation process. Thus, they should project both sales and revenues for the next five years and use a simple average of these forecasts in the valuation process.

Exhibit 2   Kerkhov Karpets, Inc. Condensed Balance Sheets (in thousands)

	1996	1997
Assets		
Cash	$ 97	$ 6
Accounts Receivable	865	620
Inventory	1,361	1,300
Prepaid Expenses	5	20
Total Current Assets	$ 2,328	$ 1,946
Gross Fixed Assets	357	329
Accumulated Depreciation	38	52
Intangibles (Net)	–	–
Other Non-Current Assets	–	–
Total Assets	$ 2,723	$ 2,327
Liabilities & Net Worth		
Accounts and Notes Payable	$ 1,268	$ 846
Notes Payable—Short-Term	1,244	760
Accruals	12	20
Taxes Payable	3	31
Total Current Liabilities	$ 2,527	$ 1,657
Long-Term Debt	–	–
Common Stock	50*	440*
Paid-In Captial	62	62
Treasury Stock	–	–
Retained Earnings	84	168
Total Liability & Net Worth	$ 2,723	$ 2,327

*Domestic banks are often reluctant to lend to international firms with low equity ratios. As a preemptive move, Van de Burg contributed personal funds to the firm's equity in anticipation of future loan requests.

Exhibit 3   Kerkhov Karpets, Inc. Condensed Income Statements (in thousands)

	1996	1997
Sales	$ 4,569	$ 5,031
Cost of Sales	3,074	3,313
Gross Profit	$ 1,495	$ 1,718
Operating Expenses	1,316	1,485
Depreciation	14	14
Operating Profit	$ 165	$ 219
Interest Expense	95	102
All Other Expenses (Net)	–	–
Profit Before Tax	$ 70	$ 117
Taxes	6	34
Net Profit	$ 64	$ 83

Preparing an Offer

Jan and Mark also specifically asked Rute to help with structuring the financing of a possible offer. Knowing that they had essentially no funds of any significance to put up for the purchase, Rute pointed out that they had basically two options. They could either borrow the money from a lender or ask Van de Berg to finance the purchase.

Rute noted that it was unlikely that they would be able to borrow the funds for such a risky purchase. He suggested, since Harm had previously indicated a willingness to finance the purchase, that they proceed along this path. Jan and Mark concurred and agreed to develop and present Harm with a set of terms for financing the purchase.

The work that needed to be completed was substantial, but significant. If all went according to plan, Jan and Mark would soon own their own company. All they had left to do was "do their homework," devise a purchase plan, and make an offer Van de Berg "couldn't refuse."

Case 19

Kikkoman Corporation in the Mid-1990's: Market Maturity, Diversification and Globalization

Marilyn Taylor, Norihito Tanaka, and Joyce Claterbos, *University of Missouri at Kansas*

In early 1996 Mr. Yuzaburo Mogi, president of Kikkoman Corporation, faced a number of challenges. Analysts indicated concern with Kikkoman's slow sales growth and noted that the company's stock had underperformed on the Nikkei Exchange in relation to the market and to its peers for several years. Throughout the world, ongoing changes in taste preferences and dietary needs presented threats to the company's traditional food lines. The company marketed its branded products in ninety-four countries and had to consider which products and markets to emphasize as well as which new markets to enter. As Mr. Mogi described the company's focus, "...we are now concentrating on further enhancing our ability to serve consumers in Japan and overseas. The basic keynotes of this effort are expansion of soy sauce markets, diversification, and globalization."

In Japan, Kikkoman had long dominated the soy sauce market and its mid-1990's market share position of 27 percent was well beyond the 10 percent of its next closest competitor. However, its share of the soy sauce market had continued to decline from its high of 33 percent in 1983, falling from 28 percent in 1993 to 27.2 percent in 1994. Further, although the company's worldwide sales had increased slightly overall from 1994 to 1995, sales of soy sauce in Japan had decreased over 1 percent during that period.

The U.S. market had provided significant opportunity in the post-World War II period. However, the company's U.S. market share for soy and other company products was essentially flat. In addition, three competitors had built plants in the United States beginning in the late 1980's. Mr. Mogi was aware that Kikkoman's choices in the U.S. market would provide an important model for addressing higher income mature markets.

With a market capitalization of nearly 160 billion yen,[1] Kikkoman Corporation was the world's largest soy sauce producer, Japan's nineteenth largest food company, and also Japan's leading soy sauce manufacturer. The company was the oldest continuous enterprise among the two hundred largest industrials in Japan. The company began brewing shoyu, or naturally fermented soy sauce, in the seventeenth century and had dominated the Japanese soy industry for at least a century. The company held 50 percent of the U.S. soy sauce market and 30 percent of the world market. Kikkoman had thirteen manufacturing facilities in Japan and one each in the United States, Singapore, and Taiwan. The company was one of the few traditional manufacturers to successfully establish a presence worldwide. (See Exhibits 1 and 2 for locations of and information on the company's principal subsidiaries. See Exhibits 3 and 4 for consolidated financial statements.)

Kikkoman in Japan

The Beginnings in Noda

In 1615 the widow of a slain samurai warrior fled 300 miles from Osaka to the village of Noda near Edo (now called Tokyo). With her five children, the widow Mogi embarked upon rice farming and subsequently began brewing shoyu, or soy sauce. The quality of the Mogi family's shoyu was exceptional almost from its beginnings. At the time households produced shoyu for their own use or local farmers made and sold excess shoyu as a side enterprise to farming. As more people moved to the urban areas in the seventeenth and eighteenth centuries, there was increased demand for non-home production. Households developed preferences for the product of a particular brewer. (See Appendix A: The Making of Soy Sauce.)

Shoyu had come to Japan with the arrival of Buddhism in the sixth century. The teachings of Buddhism prohibited eating meat and fish. Residents of the Japanese islands turned from meat-based to vegetable-based flavorings. One of the favorites became a flavorful seasoning made from fermented soy beans. A

Exhibit 1   Locations of Principle Subsidiaries

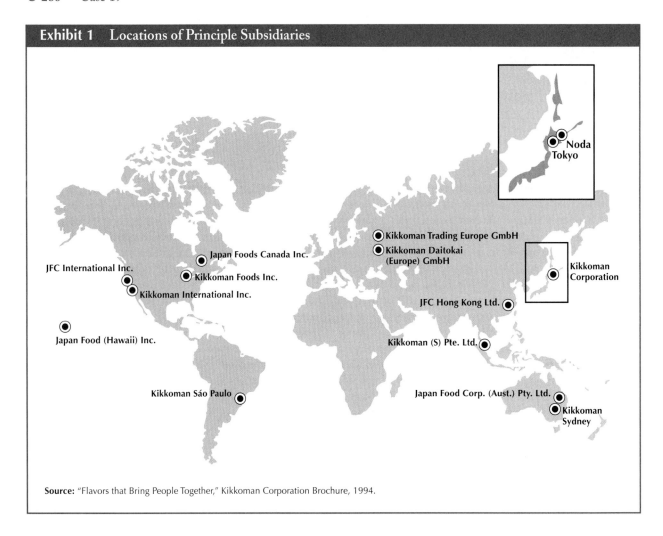

Source: "Flavors that Bring People Together," Kikkoman Corporation Brochure, 1994.

Japanese Zen Buddhist priest who had studied in China brought the recipe to Japan. The Japanese discovered that adding wheat gave the sauce a richer, more mellow flavor.

Over the eighteenth century Noda became a major center for shoyu manufacturing in Japan. Shoyu's major ingredients, soybeans and wheat, grew readily in the rich agricultural Kanto plain that surrounded Noda. The trip to the major market of Edo took only one day on the Edo River. The various shoyu producing families in the Noda area actively shared their knowledge of fermentation. The Mogi family and another Noda area family, the Takanashi family, were especially active in the industry. By the late eighteenth century the two families had become interrelated through marriage. Their various enterprises made considerable investment in breweries, and family members began ancillary enterprises such as grain brokering, keg manufacture, and transportation.

Japan's Shoyu Distribution System and Industry Structure

Japan's neophyte and fragmented shoyu industry had two distribution systems during this time. In the rural areas the shoyu breweries sold their products directly to households. In the cities urban wholesalers distributed shoyu, vinegar, and sake. The wholesalers purchased bulk shoyu and established their own brands. The wholesalers controlled pricing, inventory, distribution, and marketing knowledge. They would distribute branded shoyu only on consignment. During the 1800's the wholesalers formed alliances that gave them near-monopolistic power over the Tokyo market. As the shoyu manufacturers became more efficient, they found it impossible to lower prices or make other adjustments to increase their market share.

The Mogi and Takanashi families took several steps to counteract the wholesalers' dominance. The Takanashi family had diversified into wholesaling some years prior

Exhibit 2   Consolidated Subsidiaries as of FY 1995

Subsidiary	Country	Paid-in Capital (¥m/$m)	Kikkoman Equity (%)
Japan Del Monte	Japan	900	99.7
Mann's Wine	Japan	900	100
Pacific Trading	Japan	72	66.7
Morishin	Japan	30	66.7
Kikkoman Foods, Inc.	U.S.	U.S.$ 6	100
Kikkoman International	U.S.	U.S.$ 3.5	92.6
JFC International	U.S.	U.S.$ 1.2	98
Kikkoman Trading Europe	Germany	DM 1.5	75
Kikkoman Pte	Singapore	S$ 7.5	100
Kikkoman Trading Pte	Singapore	S$ 0.4	100
Tokyo Food Processing	U.S.	U.S.$0.02	100
Hapi Products	U.S.	U.S.$0.05	100
Rex Pacific	U.S.	U.S.$ 1.5	100

Source: Table 4: Consolidated Subsidiaries, UBS Securities Limited, May 28, 1996, as reported by *Investext*.

and were part of the wholesalers' alliance. One Mogi family intermarried with a wholesaler's family—a traditional strategy in Japan for cementing strategic alliances. In addition the Mogi and Takanashi families worked to increase brand recognition and dominance. In 1838 Mogi Saheiji applied for and received the shogunate's recognition of his family's premier brand named Kikkoman. He aggressively promoted the brand by sponsoring professional storytellers and sumo wrestlers, embossing paper lanterns and umbrellas with the Kikkoman trademark, and putting ornate gold labels from Paris on his Kikkoman shoyu kegs. In the latter part of the nineteenth century Kikkoman shoyu won recognition in several world's fairs.

In reaction to depressed market prices and fluctuating costs of inputs, a number of the Noda shoyu brewers formed the Noda Shoyu Brewers' Association in 1887. The association purchased raw materials, standardized wages, and regulated output quality. The members' combined efforts resulted in the largest market share at the time, 5–10 percent of the Tokyo market, and widespread recognition of the high quality of Noda shoyu.

Noda brewers, and especially the Mogi and Takanashi families, began research and development activities early. The Japanese government encouraged the Noda shoyu brewers to conduct research in the recovery and processing of the two by-products of shoyu manufacture, shoyu oil and shoyu cake. In the early 1900's the Association began to fund a joint research and development laboratory

The Shoyu Industry in the Twentieth Century

In 1910 there were still 14,000 known makers of shoyu in Japan. However, a number of changes led to consolidation. Manufacturing shifted from a small-batch, brewmaster-controlled production process to a large-batch, technology-controlled process. Mogi families in Noda invested in modernized plants and a fifth-grade Japanese geography reader featured a state-of-the-art Kikkoman facility. A national market also developed, thanks to the development of a railway system throughout most of the country. In addition, consumer tastes shifted to the Tokyo-style shoyu produced by eastern manufacturers such as the Noda Shoyu Brewers' Association.

Consumers also began to purchase shoyu in smaller glass bottles rather than in the traditional large wooden barrels that sometimes leaked and were expensive to build and difficult to store. Raw materials also became more expensive as the brewers increasingly sought higher quality imported soybeans (from Manchuria, China, and Korea) and salt (from England, Germany, and China). The Association members controlled costs by purchasing in bulk and demanding high quality materials from suppliers.

The Noda Shoyu Company: 1918–1945—A Family Zaibatsu[2]

In 1918, seven Mogi families and a related Takanashi family combined their various enterprises into a joint stock holding company called the Noda Shoyu Company. The merger was in reaction to the market upheaval caused by

Exhibit 3   Consolidated Profit and Loss Statement (¥ m)

	1989	1990	1991	1992	1993	1994	1995
Sales	195,851	196,925	206,861	211,671	203,491	200,976	203,286
COGS	117,062	118,808	122,872	124,882	118,504	117,809	119,656
Gross Profit	78,789	78,117	83,989	86,789	84,987	83,167	83,629
Gross Profit Margin (%)	40.2	39.7	40.6	41	41.8	41.4	41.1
SG&A Expenses	71,227	71,876	74,181	76,019	74,320	72,689	72,836
SG&A Exp. (%)	36.4	36.5	35.9	35.9	36.5	36.2	35.8
Operating Profit	7,562	6,240	9,807	10,769	10,666	10,477	10,792
Operating Margin (%)	3.9	3.2	4.7	5.1	5.2	5.2	5.3
Net Non-Op. Income	-572	-1,042	-1,564	-1,895	-2,282	-2,197	-2,305
Recurring Profit	6,990	5,197	8,243	8,873	8,384	8,280	8,487
Recurring Margin (%)	3.6	2.6	4	4.2	4.1	4.1	4.2
Net Extraordinary Income	181	1,165	1,317	59	108	1,434	-1,177
Pretax Profit	7,170	6,363	9,559	8,932	8,493	9,714	7,310
Tax	3,327	3,299	4,726	5,178	4,597	4,157	3,569
Tax Rate (%)	46.4	50.7	49.4	58	54.1	42.8	48.8
Minority Interest	56	78	37	34	1	-52	46
Amortization of Consol. Dif.	0	0	-35	1	5	0	-314
Equity in Earnings	1,097	1,464	1,188	1,245	887	1,002	996
Net Profit	4,697	4,694	6,166	4,928	4,688	6,614	4,447
Shares Outstanding (m)	169.08	169.71	169.97	178.61	187.62	187.77	197.2
EPS	27.8	27.7	31.3	25	23.8	33.5	22.6
EPS Change (%)	80	-0.4	13.3	-20.2	-4.9	41	-32.8
Cash Flow per Share	20.8	46.5	48	41.9	44.4	58.5	46.8
Average Exchange Rate (yen/USD)	137.96	144.79	134.71	126.65	111.20	102.21	94.06

Sources: Table 9: UBS Securities Limited, May 28, 1996, *The World Almanac*, 1998 (original source: IMF).

World War I. The new company was a small zaibatsu with nearly a dozen companies in manufacturing fermented grain-based products, transportation, and finance. Unlike early shoyu manufacturing where ownership, management, and operations were clearly separated, the Mogi and Takanashi families owned, managed, and operated their firm. Initially the family produced thirty-four different brands of shoyu at various price points. The Kikkoman brand had a history of heavy promotion for over forty years, greater Tokyo market share, and a higher margin than the company's other brands. The Kikkoman brand became the company's flagship brand. The new corporation continued its long-standing emphasis on research and development and aggressively pursued new manufacturing processes, increased integration, and acquisition of other shoyu companies.

After the Mogi Takanashi coalition, the company aggressively pursued a strong nationwide sole agent system and direct distribution. The combined company also continued Kikkoman's well-known advertising activities. Kikkoman had carried out the first newspaper advertising in 1878. In 1922 the company carried out the firm's first advertising on the movie screen.

During the 1920's the company aggressively modernized with machines such as hydraulic presses, boilers, conveyors, and elevators. The company's modernization efforts were emulated by competitors and the results were increased supply and heightened industry competition. The changes brought about by increased automation led to severe labor unrest. One particularly long strike against the Kikkoman company in the late 1920's almost destroyed the participating labor union. After the strike ended, Kikkoman rehired about a third of the striking employees. The company centralized and reorganized the work processes to accommodate improved technology, restructured work practices, and established

Exhibit 4   Consolidated Balance Sheet (¥ m)

	1990	1991	1992	1993	1994	1995
Current Assets	81,611	88,092	89,705	103,152	105,220	107,339
Cash and Deposits	13,254	17,570	18,261	28,826	36,381	37,366
Accounts Receivable	43,579	44,661	44,503	46,009	44,246	44,439
Securities	315	1,012	1,316	3,310	3,306	3,307
Inventories	21,769	21,300	22,484	21,469	18,579	19,258
Fixed Assets	94,631	97,999	105,231	113,940	112,183	119,411
Tangible Assets	52,087	53,254	59,276	67,649	65,795	72,684
Land	11,768	12,011	11,910	15,156	15,613	11,540
Investments	26,371	29,597	31,771	33,051	34,083	35,006
Total Assets	177,583	187,316	195,955	218,561	218,805	228,308
Liabilities and Owner's Equity						
Current Liabilities	48,040	52,626	54,014	50,272	46,663	63,400
Short-term Borrowings	18,846	18,908	19,046	17,462	14,838	15,741
Fixed Liabilities	58,374	58,850	62,351	85,532	85,143	71,710
Long-term Borrowings	4,457	4,549	4,723	3,274	3,091	2,312
Bonds and CBs[a]	26,565	26,346	26,231	46,170	44,776	29,921
Minority Interest	1,223	1,166	1,157	1,103	1,024	427
Total Liabilities	107,638	112,673	117,522	136,909	132,832	135,538
Shareholders' Equity	69,945	74,673	78,434	81,651	85,973	92,770
Total Liabilities and Equity	177,583	187,316	195,955	218,561	218,805	228,308

[a]There were two CBs issued Jan. 90 exercisable at ¥ 1,522. The other two were issued July 93 and were exercisable at ¥ 969. With the share price at approximately ¥ 100, the total dilution factor was about 18 percent, with 80 percent of that dependent on the two CBs exercisable at ¥ 969. Of 228 (¥ m) in 1995, about 170 belonged to the parent (i.e., Japan corporation) company.

Source: Nikkei Needs as reported in Table 12: Consolidated Balance Sheet, UBS Securities Limited, May 28, 1996.

methods to monitor and reward workers for their performance. However, the company also established efforts to improve the identity of the workers with the company. Internal communications carried the message that all employees were members of one family, or ikka, united in a common purpose, i.e., the production of shoyu. The Noda Shoyu Company was also heavily involved in the city of Noda and supported many of its cultural and charitable activities as well as the local railroad, bank, town hall, cultural center, library, fire station, elementary school, hospital, recreation facilities and association, and much of the city's water system.

Kikkoman's International Activities

Kikkoman's initial export activities began in the late seventeenth century with Dutch and Chinese traders. The Dutch began to export shoyu to Holland and the rest of Europe while the Chinese served the southeast Asian markets. The shoyu brewers relied on agents for these early export transactions. During the nineteenth century, one Mogi patriarch opened a factory in Inchon, Korea. Demand for the increasing export, marketing, and direct investment continued to come primarily from Japanese and other peoples living abroad whose traditional cuisines called for shoyu. In 1910 the Noda city brewers' international activities were recognized when the Japanese government selected Noda shoyu to appear in a public relations publication introducing Japan's industries overseas.

Noda Shoyu Company continued to expand internationally between World War I and World War II. Acquisition of raw materials from abroad continued. The company added a manufacturing facility for shoyu and miso in Manchuria and two shoyu factories in North America. Other facilities in Japan were expanded or updated to support increasing international sales.

The company established sales offices in China and Korea to market shoyu, miso, and sake. By the late 1930's the company exported 10 percent of its output, about half to Asian region—especially Korea, China, and Indonesia—and half to Hawaii and California. Almost all of the exports were the Kikkoman brand and were sold through food import/export firms to the company's traditional customers.

Post-World War II Kikkoman in Japan

At the end of World War II Kikkoman operated only in Japan. Activities elsewhere had been closed. To meet the need for capital, Kikkoman issued publicly-traded stock in 1946, reducing family ownership markedly. (See Exhibit 5 for changes in ownership from 1917 to 1993.) The post-World War II period brought a number of social changes to Japanese society. Japanese families began the change to nuclear rather than extended family formation. Food tastes changed leading, among other trends, to a decline in per capita consumption of shoyu. Compared with other industries, demand for soy sauce grew very slowly. In 1942 demand for soy sauce in Japan was 1.7 times greater than in 1918. Demand in the 1960's was expected to be 2.2 times greater than that in 1918. However, modernization led to increased output.

Kikkoman had received considerable recognition for its advertising efforts prior to World War II. After the war, the company began to market even more aggressively in Japan. These efforts included establishing the company's strong nationwide distribution system throughout Japan; mounting aggressive activities in marketing research, advertising, and consumer education; and changing to a new and more Western image. As a result of Kikkoman's marketing efforts, the company's market share rose sharply. (See Exhibit 6 for national output of shoyu and the company's market share from 1893 to 1994.) By 1964 the company officially changed its name to Kikkoman Shoyu and in 1980 became Kikkoman Corporation. The word *Kikkoman* is a combination of "kikko" (the shell of a tortoise) and "man" (ten thousand). It was taken from an old Japanese saying, "A crane lives a thousand years and a tortoise ten thousand years." (Implying, in other words, "May you live as long!") In essence, the Kikkoman brand connotes a long-lasting living thing. Kikkoman had become well known for its advertising skill in Japan and had found that the word *Kikkoman* was easy for Americans to pronounce.

The company also diversified its product line using its expertise in shoyu manufacture, fermentation, brewing, and foods marketing. This diversification included a 1963 venture to market Del Monte products in Japan. In 1990 the company bought the Del Monte assets and marketing rights for the Del Monte brand name in the Asia-Pacific region. (See Exhibit 7 for Kikkoman Corporation's Product lists as of 1949, 1981, and 1994.) Kikkoman's R&D expertise led to activities in biotechnology and products such as enzymes, diagnostic reagents, and other biologically-active substances used to test for micro-organisms in water samples in hospitals, food processing factories, and semiconductor plants. The company also developed a number of patents at home and overseas. The company became involved in both the import and export of wines. It also undertook activities in food processing machinery. In spite of the diversification, Kikkoman's domestic sales were still about 55 percent soy sauce-related.

In the 1990's soy sauce continued as a perennial favorite in Japan's cuisine, although demand was essentially flat. Among the remaining 3,000 shoyu companies in Japan, Kikkoman produced 360,000 kl in Japan, or about 27 percent of the country's output. (See Exhibit 6.) The company

---

Exhibit 5   Noda Shoyu Company and Kikkoman Corporation Ownership

Shareholder Name	Holdings (% of Total Shares or Assets)			
	1917	1925	1955	1993
Mogi-Takanashi-Horikiri Brewing Families	100%[a]	34.6%	15.0%[b]	2.3%
Senshusha Holding Company		62.0%	3.1%	3.4%
Insurance and Banking Companies			9.9%[c]	20.5%[c]
All Others		3.6%	71.1%	73.6%

[a]Eight holdings ranging from 1.4 percent to 29.3 percent.
[b]Five holdings ranging from 1.5 percent to 4.4 percent.
[c]In 1955 and 1993, including Meiji Mutual Insurance Co., Mitsubihi Trust Bank; in 1955, including Kofukan Foundation and Noda Institute of Industrial Science; in 1993, including, Nitsuit Trust Bank, Nippon Life Insurance, Sumitomo Trust, and Yasuda Trust.

Sources: W. Mark Fruin, *Kikkoman—Company, Clan, and Community* (Cambridge, MA, Harvard University Press, 1983), pp. 98, 121, 249, *Japan Company Handbook*, Toyo Keizai, Inc., 1993, p. 207.

Exhibit 6	National Output and Company Market Share of Shoyu (in Kiloliters)[a]	
Year	National Output (Japan)	Noda Shoyu Share
1893	230,360	3.5%
1903	317,500	4.5%
1913	430,435	6.1%
1923	624,764	5.1%
1933	576,026	10.1%
1943	680,955	12.0%
1953	822,179	14.1%
1963	1,051,730	21.4%
1973	1,277,887	31.4%
1983	n.a.	33.0%
1993	n.a.	28.0%[c]
1994	1,323,529[b]	27.2%[c]

[a]1 kiloliter = 264 gallons.
[b]Derived from Kikkoman's production of 360,000 kl and its 27.2 percent market share. Residents of Japan consumed about 2.6 gallons of soy sauce per capita yearly. In contrast, U.S. citizens consumed about 10 tablespoons.
[c]As reported by UBS Securities Limited, May 28, 1996 in *Investext*. This source also reported that demand for soy sauce was flat in Japan and production between 1984 and 1994 had declined about 5.1 percent.

Source: W. Mark Fruin, *Kikkoman—Company, Clan, and Community* (Cambridge, MA, Harvard University Press, 1983), pp. 40–41.

faced price pressures, especially on its base product of soy sauce, mainly due to the competitive pressures at the retail level in Japan and the aggressive introduction of private brands. Sales in the Del Monte line also decreased in the early 1990's. To improve performance, Kikkoman began to reduce its product line from a high of 5,000 items to an expected eventual 2,500. One bright spot was the growth in wines and spirits. In addition, Kikkoman also introduced successful new soy sauce-related products in 1993, 1994, and 1995 in the form of two soup stocks and steak soy sauce. Profit increases in the early 1990's came primarily from higher-priced luxury products. (See Exhibits 8 and 9 for parent company financial statements.) The company recognized that continuing success in its mature domestic market would depend on continuous development of new applications and variations of its older products as well as development of new products.

Kikkoman in the United States in the Post World War II Era

U.S. Market Potential The various Mogi family branches and Noda Shoyu Company had expanded company efforts beyond Japan since the early 1800's. By the end of World War II. the various family enterprises and the Noda Shoyu Company had ended all activities outside Japan. Japanese expatriates living in various countries and other peoples whose traditional cuisine used shoyu comprised the company's primary pre-World War II markets. In 1949 Kikkoman started to export soy sauce, mainly to the United States. In the 1950's, consumption of soy sauce began to decline in Japan. Noda Shoyu Company made the decision to invest heavily in expanding the international sales of Kikkoman brand shoyu to overseas markets. Prior to World War II, Noda Shoyu's major overseas markets were Asia and Hawaii. After the war the company decided to focus on the mainland United States because: 1) political and economic conditions in Asia were very unstable, 2) the Japanese community in Hawaii had relearned shoyu brewing during World War II and there were many small Hawaiian shoyu breweries that would have made competition intense in that market, and 3) the United States had a healthy and rapidly growing economy.

Several changes in the U.S. market made that market attractive to Noda Shoyu Company. First, Americans who had been in Asia during or just after World War II developed a taste for Japanese goods, including food. Second, the company expected that as Asians in the United States became more Americanized, their consumption of traditional foods—including soy sauce—would decline. Third, American eating habits were shifting to more natural foods and to food that could be prepared quickly. Noda Shoyu Company moved to target both Asians and non-Asians in its marketing efforts.

During the 1956 U.S. presidential elections, Noda Shoyu bought air time to advertise Kikkoman brand products. Yuzaburo Mogi, son of the head of the company's Planning Department, urged this move to U.S. television advertising.

U.S. Distribution Activities

During the years immediately after World War II Japanese companies in general relied on a small group of internationalized and entrepreneurial Japanese and Japanese-American individuals. Sale of food products in the United States involved a complex distribution system with heavy reliance on food brokers as promoters to local wholesalers and retailers. Food brokers required careful training by a knowledgeable sales team in how to use the product, especially where the product was unusual or unfamiliar to consumers. Food brokers marketed the product to wholesalers and large retailers, took orders for the product, and relayed the orders on to the manufacturer or, in the case of foreign manufacturers, the manufacturer's agent. The manufacturer or agent then made delivery of the product to the wholesaler or retailer and handled all billing and accounts,

Exhibit 7   Kikkoman Corporation Products and Product Lines

1949	1981	1994
Kikkoman Brand soy sauce, sauce, memmi, and tsuyu (soup bases)	**Kikkoman Brand** soy sauce, mild soy sauce (lower salt, 8%), light color soy sauce (usu-kuchi), teriyaki barbecue marinade and sauce, Worcestershire sauce, tonkatsu sauce, memmi and tsuyu (soup bases), sukiyaki sauce, instant soy soup mix, instant osumono (clear broth soup mix)	**Kikkoman Brand** soy sauce, mild soy sauce (lower salt, 8%), light color soy sauce (usu-kuchi), teriyaki sauce, Worcestershire sauce, tonkatsu sauce, memmi (soup base), sukiyaki sauce, sashimi soy sauce, lemon flavored soy sauce, mirin (sweet rice wine), Aji-Mirin, plum wine, instant miso (soybean pasta) soups, egg flower soup mixes, rice crackers, tofu, neo-genmai (puffed brown rice), genmai soups, oolong tea, tsuyudakono (soup base), ponzu soy sauce, soy sauce dressing, oyster sauce, bonito stock
Manjo Brand mirin (sweet rice wine), sake, shochu, whiskey	**Manjo Brand** mirin (sweet rice wine), shochu, plum wine	**Manjo Brand** triangle, komaki
	Yomonoharu Brand sake	**Yomonoharu Brand**
	Del Monte Brand* tomato ketchup, juice, puree, paste, chili sauce, Mandarin orange juice	**Del Monte Brand** tomato ketchup, juice, fruit drinks, Mandarin orange juice
	Disney Brand fruit juice (orange, pineapple, grape), nectar (peach, orange)	
	Mann's Brand[a] wine and sparkling wine, brandy	**Mann's Brand** koshu, koshu (vintage), zenkoji, blush, brandy
	Higeta Brand shoyu, tsuyu, Worcestershire sauce	
	Ragu Brand spaghetti sauces	
	Kikko's Brand tomato ketchup	**Beyoung** protein powder, wheat germ
	Monet Brand cognac	**Imported Wines** aujoux, chateau tatour, borie-manoux, franz reh and sohn, pol roger

*Marketed, not manufactured, by Kikkoman.
[a]The company established its Mann Wine subsidiary in 1964.

Sources: W. Mark Fruin, *Kikkoman—Company, Clan, and Community* (Cambridge, MA, Harvard University Press, 1983), pp. 275–276, "Flavors that Bring People Together," Kikkoman Corporation Brochure, 1994.

paying the broker a commission for his/her marketing representation. The food broker was an important link between the manufacturer and the wholesaler or retailer. Food brokers were evaluated based on their ability to persuade retailers and wholesalers to carry products and to feature them prominently.

In 1957 the company formed Kikkoman International, Inc. (KII), a joint venture between Noda Shoyu Company in Japan and Pacific Trading of California. KII was incorporated in San Francisco to serve as the marketing and distribution center for Kikkoman products in the United States. Most of the products were produced by Noda Shoyu Company, but some were purchased from other manufacturers and sold under the Kikkoman label.

Over the next ten years, sales grew 20–30 percent a year. In 1960 the Safeway grocery store chain agreed to have some of its stores carry Kikkoman Soy Sauce. Noda Shoyu opened regional sales offices for KII in Los Angeles

Exhibit 8	Parent Company Revenues by Product Line (¥ m)				
	1994	1995	Percent Change	1996E	Percent Change
Soy Sauce	74,666	73,843	-1.1	75,000	1.6
Food	15,091	16,310	8.1	18,500	13.4
Del Monte	24,692	19,857	-19.6	19,000	-4.3
Alcohol	24,993	25,925	3.7	27,000	4.1
Others	4,159	4,285	3	4,500	5
Total	143,601	140,220	-2.4	144,000	2.7

Source: Table 5: UBS Securities Limited, May 28, 1996, as available on *Investext*.

(1958), New York City (1960), Chicago (1965), and Atlanta (1977). Retail marketing activities included in-store demonstrations, advertising campaigns in women's magazines that emphasized soy sauce use in American cuisine, and limited television commercials. The company used brokers as their distribution channels to supermarkets and wholesalers for the small oriental retail stores. The company encouraged food brokers through contests and training. For the food service and industrial market segments, the company carried out industrial magazine ad campaigns and special educational programs. The company also formed partnerships with associations such as the American Veal Manufacturers' and the Avocado Association to feature Kikkoman Soy Sauce in their product advertisements.

Other major international companies had to modify their products for the United States. However, Kikkoman marketed the same soy sauce in the United States as in Japan. The company's experience in its campaign to "westernize" soy sauce for the Japanese market applied to the campaign in the United States. In the United States Kikkoman provided the traditional, low-sodium, preservative-free, and dehydrated soy sauce. The company also marketed tailor-made sauces, other food extracts, and agents.

Exploration of Potential U.S. Manufacturing Capacity

As early as 1965 Kikkoman Corporation began to explore the possibility of manufacturing in the United States. However, the company determined that sales in North America were insufficient to support the economies of scale required for a minimum efficient scale production facility. Instead, in 1968 Kikkoman Corporation contracted with a subsidiary of Leslie Salt Company of Oakland, California to bottle the Kikkoman Soy sauce shipped in bulk from Japan and to blend and bottle teriyaki sauce, a major ingredient of which was soy sauce. These bottling

efforts constituted Kikkoman's first post-World War II manufacturing efforts in the United States. Bottling in the United States reduced customs and tariff costs. However, moving goods back and forth from the United States and Japan added considerably to the company's costs. In the mid 1980's Japan imported 95 percent and 88 percent of its soy beans and wheat respectively. The United States was Japan's major source of supply. Transportation of raw materials (e.g., soybeans and wheat) to Japan was between 5 and 20 percent of preproduction costs while transportation costs of brewed soy sauce from Japan to the United States was 25 percent of production costs. Various import/export restrictions and tariffs increased the risk and expense of importing raw materials to Japan and exporting finished goods to the United States.

The North American market was potentially much larger than the Japanese market and Kikkoman had a greater share of the North American market than the company had in Japan. Yuzaburo Mogi hired a Columbia University classmate as a consultant and the company

Exhibit 9	Parent Company Balance Sheet (¥ m)		
	1993	1994	1995
Current Assets	78,463	81,805	80,749
Fixed Assets	88,007	86,029	89,599
Total	166,802	168,000	170,348
Short-term Liabilities	33,469	32,033	46,762
Long-term Liabilities	79,898	79,527	66,567
Equity	53,434	56,440	57,019
Total Liabilities and Equity	166,802	168,000	170,348

Source: UBS Securities Limited, May 28, 1996, Table 11 as reported by *Investext*.

formed a team to work with him to consider a U.S. plant. By 1970 the analyses, in spite of higher U.S. labor costs, favored construction of a U.S. manufacturing facility. As Yuzaburo Mogi put the company's motivation, "We made a decision to go after the American consumer."

Selection of Walworth, Wisconsin

The team considered over sixty potential sites in the East, West, and Midwest. The team chose the Midwest because of its central location and crop production. Ultimately the team selected a 200-acre dairy farm site in Walworth, Wisconsin. Walworth provided the best fit with the five criteria established by the company: a) access to markets (proximity to Milwaukee and Chicago as well as the geographic convenience of a mid-way point between the East and West coasts made shipping relatively efficient), b) ample supplies of wheat and soybeans (soybeans came from Wisconsin, wheat from North Dakota, and salt from Canada), c) a dedicated work force, d) a strong community spirit, and e) an impeccable supply of water. Kikkoman also appreciated Wisconsin's emphasis on a clean environment.

Walworth, Wisconsin was situated about two hours northwest of Chicago and about one hour west of Milwaukee. A community of about 1,100, Walworth was surrounded by some of the most productive farmland in the United States. The area included a number of other smaller communities whose economies depended primarily on farming and summer vacation home residences. The company hired a local consultant, lawyer Milton Neshek, who ultimately became General Counsel of Kikkoman Foods, Inc. Mr. Neshek described the original reaction to Kikkoman's purchase of prime farmland as mixed, "with a small faction on the town board opposed to the company coming in." Yuzaburo Mogi described the opposition as strong. Residents of the small, rural, close-knit farming community expressed concerns about the impact of a large, especially foreign, corporation in a small community, potential inflation of land values, and the possibility of industrial pollution.

One of Neshek's partners, Thomas Godfrey, visited Kikkoman facilities in Noda City, Japan. "When Kikkoman called me in 1971," said Godfrey, "and asked me to create a Wisconsin corporation for them so they could make soy sauce, I didn't even know what the hell soy sauce was. Nobody else around here did either." Walworth's Plant Manager, Bill Wenger, recalled his introduction to the company. In 1972 he was stationed with the U.S. Marines in Hawaii. His mother sent a newspaper clipping about the soy sauce plant suggesting that it might be a good place to begin his return to civilian

life. Wenger and his wife didn't know what soy sauce was either, but his wife went to the local grocery store and bought a bottle. As Wenger described it, the purchase was "..some horrible local Hawaiian brand. She brought it home and opened it. We looked at one another and said, '*@&…, this stuff is terrible.'" Another of the three American production managers employed at the plant had a similar tale. The production manager said, "The first year I worked here we never had any soy sauce in my home. My wife wouldn't buy it, wouldn't even allow it in the house. I finally brought home a bottle and put it on some meatloaf. Now we use it on just about everything. I put it on peaches. And we even have a local minister who puts it on his ice cream … I do too. It's good."

No other Japanese-owned manufacturing facility had been constructed in the United States at the time. Neshek's partner, Godfrey, visited Noda because, as he put it, "I had to see for myself what it was they were talking about. I had to make sure the factory wasn't going to pollute the air and water and stink up the place." Local Kikkoman representatives met with organizations such as the Local Grange, Farm Bureau groups, church groups, Rotary, and ladies clubs. Wisconsin's Governor Patrick Lucey came to one of the seven town meetings held to discuss the plant and explain the state's role and position. Yuzaburo Mogi described the process as "removing the fears of the local people and local council about the building of the new factory." The company was able to convince area residents that Kikkoman would not pollute the environment and would use local labor and other resources. The final vote of the County Zoning Board was 53 for, 13 against. The Town Board declined to oppose the Zoning Board's action. Among other issues, Kikkoman put a great deal of effort into reducing potential pollution. In talking about this process of "nemawashi," or root tending, Mr. Mogi emphasized the importance of a prosperous coexistence between the company and the local community. He said, "We've been doing business in Noda for 360 years. We learned a long time ago that to survive you need to coexist with the surrounding community."

Opening the New Plant

In January 1971 Kikkoman executives along with Japanese, Walworth, and Wisconsin officials held a ceremonial groundbreaking on the 200-acre site. A Cleveland, Ohio design and construction firm built the plant. Other American companies, many located in the region, built many of the critical components. The initial investment in the 10,000 kiloliter facility was $8 million and the plant was finished just in time to avoid the 1973 American embargo on the sale of soybeans to Japan.

Kikkoman's Walworth plant was the first Japanese investment in production capacity in the United States in the post-World War II period and the first plant Kikkoman built outside Japan after World War II. Opening ceremonies included dignitaries and officials from Wisconsin, Kikkoman, Japan, and the United States. The 700 invited guests heard the texts of telegrams from the Japanese Prime Minister and President Richard Nixon. The U.S. President referred to the plant as a " … visionary step (that) will mean meaningful trade relations and balance of trade and will enhance further friendships between our two countries."

From its opening in 1972 through the mid-1990's the company expanded the Walworth facility eight times to 500,000 square feet. Kikkoman invested in facilities or equipment every year with production increasing 8–10 percent per year. Originally the plant produced two products, soy sauce and teriyaki sauce. In the mid-1990's the plant produced eighteen products, including regular and light soy sauce, teriyaki steak sauce, sweet and sour sauce, and tempura dip. All but one used a soy base. The company had been very careful about pollution, treating its wastewater carefully so that there was no threat to nearby popular Geneva Lake. The Walworth town clerk said, "There's no noise, no pollution. I live about three-quarters of a mile from them, and once a day, I get a whiff of something that's like a sweet chocolate odor. It's no problem." The company marketed the plant's output in all fifty states plus Canada and Mexico. Soy sauce was shipped in many varieties including bottles ranging from 5 to 40 ounces, 1 to 5-gallon pails, and sometimes in stainless steel tank trucks for large customers. McDonald's, for example, used soy sauce in one of the Chicken McNuggets condiments.

Management of the Walworth Plant

The company maintained a state-of-the-art laboratory at the Walworth facilities. However, plant management pointed out that the most accurate test during production was the human nose. "Our people have worked with the product for so long, a whiff can tell them something is not quite right," said one Kikkoman director. The venture was described as "a prime example of the best combination of Japanese and American business and industrial savvy." As the plant's general manager, Michitaro Nagasawa, a Ph.D in Biochemistry from the University of Wisconsin, put it, "The productivity of this plant is the highest of all our plants … .It's an exceptional case in Kikkoman history … We took the sons and daughters of farmers, trained them and taught them about total quality management. They were raw recruits with no experience in making soy sauce. People with farm backgrounds are very diligent workers.

They will work seven days a week, twenty-four hours a day if necessary. They understand what hard work is."

The plant opened with fifty employees. Originally, fourteen Japanese Kikkoman employees and their families came to Walworth to train employees and get the plant functioning. The Japanese families scattered in groups of two or three to settle in Walworth and various nearby communities. Local women's community organizations "adopted" the Japanese wives, formed one-to-one friendships, and helped the Japanese wives become acclimated to the communities including learning to drive, using the local supermarkets, and hiring baby-sitters for their children. The Japanese husbands joined local service clubs. "That helped achieve an understanding between the Americans and Japanese and helped them to assimilate faster. It exposed Japanese people to a farming town which had had no Asian people before," noted Bill Nelson, Kikkoman Foods Vice President. Kikkoman established the practice of rotating its Japanese employees back to Japan after an average of five years in the United States. In the mid-1990's only seven Japanese families remained in the Walworth area, still spread throughout the local communities.

Community Contributions

Kikkoman Foods, Inc. was an active and contributing member of the community. The company donated time and funds on three levels. At the local level the company established Kikkoman Foods Foundation in 1993. The foundation, which was to be ultimately funded at the $3 million level, was formed to support area charitable activities. The company supported as many as thirty local projects a year including college scholarships for area students, local hospital activities, a vocational program that assisted people in developing employment related skills, and a nearby facility that preserved circus-related items. As Walworth's town clerk put it, "They sponsor just about everything—Community Chest (an organization similar to United Way), Boy Scouts, Girls Scouts, all the way down the line … They're very good neighbors." The clerk treasurer from a nearby town said, "You see their name in the paper almost every week helping out some organization."

At the state level, Kikkoman Foods, Inc. supported the University of Wisconsin educational system, established up to four Beloit College scholarships to honor Governor Lucey at his alma mater, and funded a Mogi Keizaburo scholarship at the Milwaukee School of Engineering. Members of the Board of Directors served on several public service boards and commissions. At the national level, Kikkoman Corporation, through its U.S. subsidiary Kikkoman Foods, Inc., supported Youth for Understanding exchange programs. At the fifth anniversary celebration Kikkoman's chairman reported that the plant had developed better than hoped for. At the tenth anniversary celebration of the Kikkoman plant the local Walworth paper reported, "In the ten years that Kikkoman Foods, Inc. has been located here, it has become an integrated part of the community. ... The company has truly become a part of the Walworth community, and not only in a business sense." In 1987, reflecting Kikkoman's contributions, Wisconsin's governor appointed Yuzaburo Mogi as Wisconsin's honorary ambassador to Japan.

Kikkoman's Japanese-American Management in the United States

In the mid-1990's Kikkoman operated its U.S. activities through two subsidiaries, Kikkoman Foods, Inc. (KFI) and Kikkoman International, Inc. (KII). KFI owned and operated the Walworth manufacturing plant. KII in San Francisco, California undertook marketing responsibilities, including wholesaler and distributor activities throughout the United States. The Boards of Directors for both subsidiaries had several members from the parent corporation but were primarily Americans from among local operations officers or local Walworth citizens (for KFI) or broader U.S. community (for KII). The KFI board met as a whole once a year and rotated the site of its annual stockholders' meeting between Japan and Wisconsin. An Executive Committee met monthly to consider operational decisions. The Executive Committee included Yuzaburo Mogi who attended two to three meetings in the United States every year and the head of Kikkoman Corporation's International Division. The remaining members of the Executive Committee included American and Japanese officers from the U.S. corporation. The KII Board operated in a similar manner but met only in the United States.

Yuzaburo Mogi believed that a long term commitment was essential for international success. A 1961 alumnus of Columbia University's Graduate School of Business, Mr. Mogi was the first Japanese to graduate from a U.S. university with an MBA degree. In the years following graduation he worked in various departments in Kikkoman including accounting, finance, computers, long-range planning, and new product development. In time he took on other roles including as a member of Kikkoman's board of directors (1979), managing director of the company (1982), executive management director (1989), and executive vice president (1994). The seventeenth generation of his family to brew soy sauce, Mr. Mogi had become Kikkoman's president in early 1995. He explained

his view regarding the necessity of a long term perspective, "We should do business from a longer range viewpoint. It will be very difficult to expect fruitful results in the short run under different and difficult circumstances. Failure will be inevitable in foreign countries if one proceeds with a short range view. In fact, it took Kikkoman sixteen years to become established in the United States."

Of the five senior managers at the Walworth facility, three were Japanese and two were American. The plant manager, the finance manager, and the laboratory manager were Japanese. It was expected that these three positions would continue to be Japanese appointments. One American manager described the situation, "We know we will only attain a certain level, but that's OK, though. I can accept that. Soy sauce has been made in Japan for centuries. It's their product, their technology. They have the history, the research."

The General Manager, i.e., plant manager, was the most senior person in authority at the plant and was responsible directly to headquarters in Japan. The appointment would be a person who had been with the company for many years. The finance manager's position required someone who was familiar with Japanese accounting systems and who was steeped in the Japanese emphasis on long-range profits. Japanese corporate headquarters controlled their foreign branches through their accounting and finance sections.

Mr. Mogi explained regarding the Japanese appointment to the position of laboratory manager, "The production of soy sauce is very sophisticated. Normally, we recruit graduates with a master's degree in Japan who have gone to universities that have specialized programs in soy sauce production. In America, there is no university that teaches soy sauce production techniques, so it is difficult to promote Americans into general manager positions." As Dr. Magasawa, General Manager at the Walworth plant put it in explaining the discriminating tastes the Japanese have developed since childhood, "The sensory system, passion, feeling, or sensitivity can't transfer. That is based on just experience. Our Vice President is a kind of god in this plant because he recognizes (even) a slight difference ... I don't have that. That's why I can't be Manufacturing Vice President ... I am a general manager—nothing special ... I am a biochemist (with) 39 years in Kikkoman, mostly in research."

Decisions at the Walworth plant, when possible, were made by consensus. KFI Vice President Bill Nelson described the plant management as American in content and Japanese in style with decisions arrived at from the bottom up and most matters of importance needing a consensus of employees. "It's hard, really, to get at because of the fact that nothing ... here should run in an

American style or a Japanese style or what have you. It was just simply—let's see what happens when you have both parties participate," he said. Nelson gave the example of an idea for changing summer working hours to start at 7 A.M. instead of 8 A.M. so that workers could leave earlier and enjoy more daylight. It was, Nelson, pointed out, unusual for a company to even entertain the idea. Nelson explained the process, " … instead of simply exploring it on a management level, here we started the process of asking individual employees what personal inconvenience would be experienced if the hours were changed."

Milton Nesheck observed that Japanese management and the middle management at the Walworth plant worked well together with long-range budgeting and strategic planning carried out by the Japanese executive team. He described the situation, " … our thirty employees feel like part of our family. … That makes management more responsive to employees. Decisions, whenever possible, are made by consensus." The fact that the plant has no labor union was no surprise to Nelson. As he put it, a union "has never been an issue here."

Yuzaburo Mogi summarized Kikkoman's approach to its U.S. operations and, in particular, its Walworth plant as a five-point approach:

> Kikkoman has been successful doing business in the U.S. by adapting to American laws, customers, and most importantly, its culture … (an) important matter to consider, especially when establishing a manufacturing plant in a foreign country, is the maintenance of what has come to be called "harmony" with society and the local community … a foreign concern should try to prosper *together* with society and the local community … . it is important to try to localize the operation … .(our) … . first commitment is the employment of as many local people as possible … Second we try to participate in local activities … trying to be a good corporate citizen (in Wisconsin) and contributing to society through our business activities. Third, we have been trying to avoid the so-called "Japanese-village." … by advising our people from Japan not to live together in one single community, but to spread out and live in several separate communities in order to become more familiar with the local people. Fourth, we try to do business with American companies … . The fifth commitment is our practice of delegating most authority to local management in order to better reflect local circumstances. Through this

process we are better able to make the most responsible decision. If we have an opinion, for example, we discuss it with other members at a local meeting in our American plant before reaching a decision. Kikkoman attempts to avoid a remote-control situation with letters or telephone calls from Japan … . If we have an opinion, we discuss it with other members at a local meeting in our American plant before reaching a decision.

The plant did encounter intercultural issues, however. For example, plant manager Bill Wenger pointed out "Communication can be a problem sometimes. The language barrier is one reason. And then there's the problem of saving face. If a mistake is made, the Japanese tend to cover up for one another so the person who made the mistakes doesn't lose face."

The company was a popular local employer in Walworth. Local unemployment was phenomenally low at 2 percent, but the Walworth plant had over 1,000 active applications on file for the plant's total 136 positions. However, turnover among plant employees was negligible. "No one quits unless it is a move by a spouse. Our absenteeism is minimal and as for tardiness—we just don't have it. We offer competitive wages and good benefits … employees feel like part of our family," said General Counsel Neshek. Company officials stated that they paid about 10 percent more than the state average of $9.71 per hour and employees did not have to contribute to the cost of their health insurance. As the company's vice president Shin Ichi Sugiyama put it, "In management our primary concern is always the employee." The employees reported, "We feel like they listen to us. Our opinion counts and we have the ability to make change, to better the company."

Mr. Sugiyama pointed out that the Walworth plant's productivity and quality had been about equal to that of Japanese plants. Productivity improved following the plant opening and by 1993 was actually the best of all the company's plants.

The U.S. Market in the 1990's[3]

U.S. Demand in the 1990's

After the opening of the Walworth plant, Kikkoman's U.S. sales growth slowed somewhat. However, Ken Saito, Kikkoman's brand manager for the Midwest, summarized the company's hopes, "Americans are more adventurous than Japanese when it comes to trying new foods. That's why we have developed some products only for the American market. But most Americans still are not familiar with how to use soy sauce." Thus, the company developed a number of non-Oriental recipes that call for soy sauce and other Kikkoman products, for example, teriyaki chicken wings and Pacific Rim pizza with sweet and sour sauce, beef and chicken fajitas, and grilled salmon with confetti salsa flavored with "lite" soy sauce. Kikkoman clearly expected Americans to increasingly use soy sauce for applications beyond Oriental foods and expected significant growth in the company's base product in the United States. As Saito put the company's optimism, "We figure the market in the United States will increase 100 times in the next decade." Kikkoman marketing coordinator, Trisha MacLeod articulated the goal as " ... to get consumers to realize soy sauce is the oldest man-made condiment, and that it can also be used in meatloaf, barbecue—across the spectrum."

MacLeod, pointed out, "Americans eat a lot more soy sauce than they realize." However, America's per capita consumption was barely ten tablespoons, translating into $300 million in North American sales. In contrast, Japanese per capita consumption was about 10.5 quarts per person which translated into about $1.4 billion in annual sales in Japan.

The population of Asian immigrants and families of Asian descent was projected to grow significantly in the United States. The California population increased 127 percent to 2.8 million during the 1980's. The total population of Asian Americans in the United States was estimated at 7.3 million in 1990, up 108 percent over the 1980's. Asian peoples represented the traditional main-stay market for Oriental foods. Asians had higher income and educational levels than any other ethnic group in the United States. However, each country represented a different cuisine and the different Asian ethnic groups required different marketing approaches. Asian populations had spread throughout many parts of the United States and retail outlets were learning how to highlight and display Oriental foods to spur sales. Restaurants greatly influenced American food-buying habits. One industry executive observed that almost all U.S. restaurant kitchens in the 1990's had soy sauce. A 1996 National Restaurant Association study indicated that ethnic foods were increasing in popularity. Thus, Oriental food manufacturers and distributors expected that Oriental food sales would increase sharply.

Some information in the mid-1990's suggested strong and increasing popularity for Oriental foods. U.S. sales of Oriental foods had slowed considerably. The most recent aggregate information regarding the demand for oriental food in the United States in the mid-1990s is shown in Exhibit 10.

By the late 1980's consumers began to indicate dissatisfaction with canned entrees, at $81 million in sales the second largest subcategory of Oriental foods. Sales of this subcategory had declined as much as 10 percent (1991 to 1992) and showed no signs of abating. Competition was intense with a third of all products sold on the basis of feature, price, and/or display promotion.

U.S. Major Competitors

Kikkoman's two major competitors in the United States were Chun King and LaChoy. Both companies made soy sauce by hydrolyzing vegetable protein. This European-derived method was faster and less expensive than the six-month fermentation process Kikkoman used. By 1971 Kikkoman surpassed Chun King in supermarket sales of soy sauce, becoming number two in the American marketplace. In 1976 Kikkoman outsold LaChoy brand soy sauce and became the number one retailer of soy sauce in the United States, a position it continued to hold in the mid-1990's. However, the company faced strong competitors in the Oriental foods category and in the sauces and condiments subcategory.

The new consumer focus was on Oriental food ingredients that individuals could add to home-cooked dishes. "People are cooking more Oriental foods at home," said Chun King's vice president of marketing, "Over 40 percent of U.S. households stir-fry at least once a month. Sauces are an opportunity to get away from the canned image." Indeed, sauces were the only growth area on the Oriental food category with 1992 sales rising 11 percent over the previous year. Rivals Chun King and LaChoy were flooding the Oriental foods aisle in American supermarkets with new products. LaChoy had about 40 percent of the shelf products in Oriental foods and Chun King about 20 percent.

However, there were more changes than just new products. In the early 1990's LaChoy and Chun King had revved up their marketing efforts under new ownership. La Choy was owned by ConAgra's Hunt-Wesson division.

Exhibit 10 U.S. Oriental Food Sales ($000,000)

Year	1992	1993	1994
Sales	$275	$305	$301

Source: Information Resources, Inc., Chicago, IL.

Among other initiatives ConAgra, a major U.S. food company, hired a new advertising firm for LaChoy.

A Singapore-based firm purchased Chun King in 1989 and brought in a new management team. As one observer put it, "The brand had really been neglected as part of Nabisco (its previous owner). It was just a small piece of a big pie." The new management team introduced a line of seasoned chow mein noodles and another of hot soy sauces. The firm's marketing plan included consumer promotions and a print ad campaign in women's magazines. Chun King's 1992 Oriental food sales were estimated at $30 million. In mid-1995 ConAgra purchased Chun King from the Singapore company and added the brand to its Hunt-Wesson division. ConAgra was no stranger to the Chun King brand. The large U.S. competitor had purchased Chun King's frozen food line in 1986 from Del Monte. It was expected that Hunt-Wesson would eventually consolidate manufacturing but continue to aggressively advertise the two brands separately. As a Hunt-Wesson executive put it, "They're both established leaders in their field and they both have brand strength."

LaChoy advertised itself as "the world's largest producer of Oriental Foods created for American tastes." The company led the Oriental foods category with sales (excluding frozen) of $87 million in 1992 and $104.4 million in 1994. Its products included chow mein noodles, bamboo shoots, sauces, and miscellaneous foods. About $28 million of the 1992 sales came from sauce and marinade sales. La Choy's manager of corporate communications indicated that the Chicago-based firm planned no increase in marketing spending in reaction to the new Chun King initiatives. However, the company did plan to advertise two new lines—Noodle Entrees and Stir-Fry Vegetables 'N Sauce. The company expected to expend most of its marketing support for the latter product line, a set of vegetables in four sauces formulated for consumers to stir-fry with their choice of meat.

Kikkoman and Other Competitors

Kikkoman remained the one bright spot in the Oriental food category of sauces and marinades. Kikkoman controlled $63 million of the $160 million sauces/marinades segment and supported its position with a moderate amount of advertising—$3.2 million in 1992, about the same as 1991. In its major product lines Kikkoman controlled about two-thirds of the California market and had about one third market share in other major U.S. sales regions. The company was test marketing a new line of sauces for addition to the consumer's own vegetables and meat.

Kikkoman also had to consider recent moves by several other competitors. Yamasa Shoyu Co., Ltd., Japan's second-largest soy sauce maker, had announced plans to build a factory in Oregon in mid-1994. This multi-generational company was founded in 1645 in Choshi city, Japan. Estimates on the cost of the Oregon factory ranged from $15 million to $20 million and the plant was expected to eventually employ fifty workers. Yamasa intended to produce soy sauce for the U.S. market using soybeans shipped from the Midwest. It took Yamasa four years to select the final site for its new plant. The company produced a number of products in addition to soy sauce, including other food and drugs made from biological raw materials such as soybean protein and wheat starch.

Hong Kong-based Lee Kum Kee, was a producer and importer of Chinese-oriented sauces and condiments. Lee Kum Kee had opened a sauce manufacturing plant in Los Angeles in 1991 to keep up with rising U.S. demand and to reduce dependence on imports, thus avoiding payment of import duties which could be as high as 20 percent. The company was a Hong Kong-subsidiary of one of Japan's leading soy sauce brewers. Lee Kum Kee retailed its sauces in big supermarket chains in all fifty states. Historically the company imported its soy sauce through an independent U.S.-based importer of the same name. The U.S. importer also imported about forty other food products, mostly marinades, curries, and sauces from the East. Lee Kum Kee found its sales propelled by the population doubling of Americans of Asian or Pacific Island descent.

Competitor San-J International of the San-Jirushi Corporation of Kuwana, Japan built a soy sauce plant in Richmond, Virginia in 1988. Hawaiian competitor Noh Foods of Hawaii innovated a line of Oriental dried seasonings and powdered mixes. In reaction, other manufacturers, including Kikkoman, produced copycat products. Noh Foods distributed its products in the United States, Europe, and Australia through distributors and trade show activities.

Kikkoman's International Position

The Kikkoman Vision

In the mid-1990's Kikkoman manufactured in four countries and marketed its brand products in over ninety countries. (See Exhibit 11 for comparison of domestic and non-Japan sales and operating profits.) Of the company's 3200 employees, over 1000 were in international subsidiaries and only 5 percent of those were Japanese. The company saw at least part of its

Exhibit 11 Consolidated Results FY 1995 (¥ m)

	Domestic	Non-Japan
Sales	162,426	40,860
Operating Profit	6,640	4,152
Operating Margin	4.0	10.1

Source: UBS Securities Limited, May 28, 1996. Table 7 as reported by *Investext*.

mission as contributing to international cultural exchange. Yuzaburo Mogi explained,

> Kikkoman believes that soy sauce marketing is the promotion of the international exchange of food culture. In order to create a friendlier world, I believe we need many types of cultural exchanges. Among these, there is one that is most closely related to our daily lives—the eating of food. Soy sauce is one of the most important food cultures in Japan. Hence the overseas marketing of soy sauce means the propagation of Japanese food culture throughout the world.

As one U.S. scholar who had studied the company extensively in the 1980's put it, "There is an evident willingness on the part of Kikkoman to experiment with new products, production techniques, management styles, and operational forms in the international arena." Yuzaburo Mogi put it similarly when he said, "It should be understood that adjustment to different laws, customs and regulations is imperative, instead of complaining about those differences."

Kikkoman in Europe

Kikkoman began its marketing activities in Europe in 1972. Kikkoman found Europeans more conservative and slower to try new tastes than Americans. The firm found Germany the least conservative and opened restaurants there in 1973. By the early 1990's the company had opened six Japanese steak houses in Germany. The restaurants gave their customers, over 90 percent of whom were non-Asian, the opportunity to try new cuisine. The Kikkoman trading subsidiary in Germany was the company's European marketing arm. Said the managing director for Kikkoman's European marketing subsidiary located in Germany, "Germany and Holland are big business for us, as both countries are very much into interesting sauces and marinades." Kikkoman's managing director of Europe made it clear that he had

aggressive plans to grow sales both by increasing the sales of soy sauce as well as extending the markets in which the company operated. The massive ready-made meal business in both the United States and Europe had huge potential for Kikkoman. The firm would need to market to end consumers at the retail level as well as to food manufacturers.

The company established its second overseas manufacturing facility in 1983. This facility supplied soy sauce to Australian and European markets. By the early 1990's Kikkoman had about 50 percent of the Australian soy sauce market. The United Kingdom brand debut occurred in 1986 and the 1992 UK market was estimated at 1 billion pounds. In 1993 the firm opened a 25,000 sq. ft. warehouse in London. With $1.66 billion (U.S.) in sales, Kikkoman had come a long way with "just" soy sauce. Overall analysts noted that the United States had experienced about 10 percent annual growth in soy sauce demand and expected Europe to expand similarly.

Kikkoman in Asia

In Asia the company opened a production facility in Singapore in 1983 and incorporated a trading company in 1990. Industry observers expected the company to enter the soy sauce market in China in the near future. In addition, other Asian countries offered various opportunities in sauces, condiments, and foods.

Kikkoman—The Challenges

The company the Mogi family had headed for nearly four centuries confronted a number of challenges on the global stage in the latter part of the 1990's. Kikkoman executives realized that the company's future could depend primarily on its mature domestic market. The multi-generation family firm would have to change its image as a maker of a mature product. As Mr. Mogi put it, "We … take pride in our ability to contribute to the exchange of cultures by using some of the world's most familiar flavors … we are now concentrating on further enhancing our ability to serve consumers in Japan and overseas … . Kikkoman continues as a company that is proud of its heritage, but nevertheless willing and able to adapt to the constantly evolving requirements of our customers and markets."

Notes

1. In early 1996 the exchange rate was about 95 yen per USD. Thus, in USD, Kikkoman's market value was about $1.7 billion. Sales at year end 1995 for the consolidated company were 203billion yen, or slightly less than $2 billion (See Exhibits 2 and 3 for consolidated financial data and Exhibits 8, 9, and 10 for parent company and domestic versus non-Japan revenues plus other selected financial information.)

2. *Zaibatsu*: Industrial and financial combines dissolved by occupation fiat after World War II, but which have reemerged as somewhat weaker entities. Some of these *zaibatsu* have developed into large conglomerates such as Mitsubishi. However, they should be distinguished from *keiretsu* (of which Mitsubishi is also one of largest). *Keiretsu* are informal enterprise group-based associations of banks, industrials, etc.

3. Information on the market and competitors was drawn primarily from InfoScan.

List of References for Kikkoman Corporation for CRJ*

Allen, Sara Clark . "Kikkoman, a Good Neighbor in Wisconsin," *Business,* Tuesday, June 11, 1996, np.

Bergsman, Steve. "Patience and Perseverence in Japan," *Global Trade,* Vol. 109, Issue 8 (August, 1989), p. 10, 12.

Campbell, Dee Ann. "Del Monte Foods to See European Foods Business," *Business Wire,* April 17, 1990, np.

Demestrakakes, Pan. "Quality for the Ages," *Food Processing,* Vol. 70, No. 6 (September, 1996).

"Fireflies Help Kill Germs," *Times Net Asia,* January 1, 1996.

Forrest, Tracy. "Kikkoman: a Way of Life," *Super Marketing,* January 28, 1994.

Forbish, Lynn. "Grand Oriental Celebration Held for Opening of Kikkoman Foods," *Janesville Gazette,* June 18, 1973, np.

Fruin, W. Mark. *op. cit.,* p. 280.

Hewitt, Lynda. "Liquid Spice," *Food Manufacture,* February, 1993, p. 23.

Hostveldt, John. "Japan's Kikkoman Corp. Brews Success Story in Walworth," *Business Dateline: The Business Journal—Milwaukee,* Vol. 3, No. 31, Sec. 3 (May 19, 1986), p. 17.

"In-store: Happy New Year's Feast," (Article on Kikkoman's In-store Promotion), *Brandsweek,* Vol. 37 (January 1, 1996), pp. 14–15.

Jansen, Leah. "Kikkoman Spices Up Walworth's Quality of Life," *Janesville Gazette,* January 21, 1984, np.

Jensen, Debra. "Kikkoman Executive Lauds Wisconsin, Lucey," *Gazette,* January 13, 1989, p. 1B.

Jensen, Don. "A Stainless Success Story," *Kenosha News,* Business Section, August 1, 1993.

La Choy's home page (http://www.hunt-wesson.com/lachoy/main/mission/).

LaGrange, Maria L. "RJR Sells Del Monte Operations for $1.4 Billion," *Los Angeles Times,* Vol. 108, Issue 297, September 26, 1989, p. 2.

Kikkoman Corporation: Flavors That Bring People Together (company brochure).

Kinugasa, Dean. "Kikkoman Corporation," 1979 (private translation by Norihito Tanaka and Marilyn Taylor 1994).

Mogi, Yuzaburo. "*Masatsunaki Kokusai Senryaku,*" (Tokyo, Japan: Selnate Publishing Co., Ltd., 1988) in English translation, p. 2.

Mogi, Yuzaburo. "The Conduct of International Business: One Company's Credo-Kikkoman, Soy Sauce and the US Market," *op. cit.,* p. 94.

Yuzaburo Mogi, "The Conduct of International Business: One Company's Credo—Kikkoman, Soy Sauce and the US Market," *op. cit.,* p. 93.

Ostrander, Kathleen. "Kikkoman's Success Tied to Proper Blend," *Business Datelines (Wisconsin State Journal),* March 1, 1992, p. 29.

Plett, Edith. "Kikkoman Foods Marks Fifth Year," *Janesville Gazette,* January 26, 1979, np.

Redman, Russell. "Hunt-Wesson Acquires Chun King," *Supermarket News,* Vol. 45, No. 19 (May 8, 1995), p. 101.

SBA Home Page, Wisconsin Gallery.

Schoenburg, Lorraine. "Governor Supports Kikkoman," *Janesville Gazette,* September 14, 1989, np.

Shima, Takeshi. "Kikkoman's Thousand-Year History," *Business JAPAN,* January, 1989, p. 65.

Kikkoman Corporation: Flavors That Bring People Together (company brochure).

"The Joy of Soy: How a Japanese Sauce Company Found a Happy Home in Walworth, Wisc.," *Chicago Tribune Magazine,* January 31, 1993, p. 13.

Wilkins, Mira. "Japanese Multinationals in the United States: Continuity and Change, 1879–1990, *Business History Review,* Vol. 64, Issue 4 (Winter, 1990), p. 585–629.

Yates, Ronald E. "Wisconsin's Other Brew," *Chicago Tribune Magazine,* January 31, 1993, p. 14.

* List of references from which information and quotations were drawn for this case. This list is part of a much broader set of sources that the authors consulted.

Appendix A: The Making of Soy Sauce

The Chinese began making jiang, a precursor of soy sauce, about 2,500 years ago. The most likely story of soy sauce's origins relates how Kakushin, a Japanese Zen priest who studied in China, returned to Japan in the middle of the thirteenth century and began preparing a type of miso, or soybean paste produced through fermentation, that became a specialty in that area. By the end of the thirteenth century, the liquid was called *tamari* and sold commercially along with the miso. Experimentation with the raw ingredients and methods for fermentation began. Vegetarianism also became popular in Japan during this time, and people were eager for condiments to flavor their rather bland diet. Soldiers also found the transportability of the seasonings useful.

Soy sauce evolved for tamari and miso by adding wheat to the soybean fermentations mash. The Japanese modified the shoyu to include wheat to gentle the taste so that it did not overwhelm the delicate flavors of Japanese cuisine. Most households made their shoyu during the slack time in agricultural cycles. Families harvested grains in the fall and processed them into mash. The mash fermented beginning in October–December to January–March when the shoyu was pressed from mash.

Regional differences among the soy sauces developed depending upon the mix of soybean, wheat, and fermentation techniques. Even in the last decade of the twentieth century, there were hundreds of local varieties of soy sauce available commercially in Japan.

Produced in the traditional way, soy sauce was a natural flavor enhancer. In the latter part of the twentieth century, ingredient-conscious consumers shied away from artificial flavor enhancers. Soy sauce responded to the challenge of finding ingredients to flavor foods. For vegetarian manufacturers, the "beefy" taste provided by the soy sauce without any meat extract was highly desirable.

There were two methods of manufacturing soy sauce—the traditional fermentations processed used to Kikkoman and the chemical method.

Soy Sauce Through Fermentation— Kikkoman's Traditional Method

Kikkoman's process was the traditional one and involved processing soy and wheat to a mash. Kikkoman had developed an innoculum of seed mold that the company added. The seed mold produced a growth, the development of which was controlled by temperature and humidity. The resulting mash (koji) was discharged into fermentation tanks where selected microorganism cultures and brine were added. The product (moromi mash) was aerated and mixed, then aged. During this process, enzymes formed into cells of the koji and provided the characteristics of the brewed sauce. The soybean protein changed to amino acid, and the enzymatic reaction that occurred between the sugar and amino acids produced the taste and color. Enzymes changed the wheat starch to sugars for sweetness, and special yeast developed changing some of the sugars to alcohol. Fermentation changed other parts of the sugar to alcohol that produced tartness. The brewing process determined flavor, color, taste, and aroma. The brine added to the koji mixture stimulated the enzymes and produced the reddish brown liquid mash. This process resulted in umami—or flavor-enhancing—abilities, as well as the brewed flavor components. The final mash was pressed between layers of cloth under constant pressure. After a pasteurization process to intensify color and aromas, the shoyu was filtered again and bottled. There were no flavorings, coloring, additives, or artificial ingredients in the product. According to produce developers, these complex flavors were not present in brewed soy sauce.

Chemically Produced Soy Sauce

Nonbrewed soy sauce could be made in hours. Soybeans were boiled with hydrochloric acid for fifteen to twenty hours. When the maximum amount of amino acid was removed from the soybeans, the mixture was cooled to end the hydrolysis action. The amino acid liquid was then neutralized, mixed with charcoal, and finally purified through filtration. Color and flavor were introduced via varying amount of corn syrup, salt, and caramel coloring. The resulting soy sauce was then refined and bottled.

Case 20

Kmart Corporation:
Seeking Customer Acceptance and Preference

James W. Camerius, *Northern Michigan University*

On June 1, 2000, the search for the new chairman and chief executive officer of Kmart Corporation was over. Charles C. Conaway, a 39-year-old drugstore chain executive, was selected to fill the position. His appointment meant that the strategic direction of the Kmart would come from a man who was previously unknown outside of the drugstore industry. He would have to provide an answer to a crucial question: How can Kmart respond to the challenges of industry leader Wal-Mart Stores, Inc. in the extremely competitive arena of discount retailing?

As president and chief operating officer of CVS Corporation, Mr. Conaway was the number two executive at the nation's largest drugstore chain, whose annual sales were about half those of Kmart's annual revenue of $36 billion. By all accounts, Mr. Conaway had made a sizable contribution in sales, earnings, and market value at CVS, Inc., headquartered in Woonsocket, Rhode Island. CVS had 1999 sales of $18 billion with 4,100 stores. Mr. Conaway, who became president and chief operating officer of CVS in 1998, was responsible for merchandising, advertising, store operations, and logistics. After joining the firm in 1992, he helped engineer the restructuring of the then-parent Melville Corporation, a diversified retailer, into a successful drugstore chain. Mr. Conaway said in an interview upon assuming his new position with Kmart that his primary task would be to improve customer service, productivity of resources and problems with out-of-stock merchandise. Setting the stage for a new direction, Mr. Conaway said, "Customer service is going to be at the top. We're going to measure it and we're going to tie incentives around it," he noted.

Floyd Hall, the previous Chairman, President, and Chief Executive Officer of Kmart since June of 1995, appeared pleased with the appointment. He had announced two years earlier that he had wanted to retire, and now he would be able to do so. Mr. Hall in the last five years had restored Kmart profitability and made improvements in store appearance and merchandise selection. Analysts had noted, however, that the firm was without a definable niche in discount retailing. Studies had shown that number one-ranked Wal-Mart, originally a rural retailer, had continued to be known for lower prices. Target Corporation, number three in sales, had staked out a niche as a merchandiser of discounted upscale products. Kmart was left without a feature that would give it competitive distinction in the marketplace.

Kmart's financial results reported in the fiscal first-quarter of 2000 noted that net income fell 61 percent to $22 million. The decline ended a string of fifteen consecutive quarters of profit increases that Floyd Hall felt had signaled a turnaround at the discount chain. Hall, however, was very optimistic about the company's future. The financial information over the previous periods had convinced him that a new corporate strategy that he introduced would revitalize Kmart's core business, its 2,171 discount stores, and put the company on the road to recovery. Industry analysts had noted that Kmart, once a industry leader, had posted eleven straight quarters of disappointing earnings prior to 1998 and had been dogged by persistent bankruptcy rumors. Analysts cautioned that much of Kmart's recent growth reflected the strength of the consumer economy and that uncertainty continued to exist about the company's future in a period of slower economic growth.

Kmart Corporation was one of the world's largest mass merchandise retailers. After several years of restructuring, it was composed largely of general merchandise businesses in the form of traditional Kmart discount department stores and Big Kmart (general merchandise and convenience items) stores as well as Super Kmart Centers (food and general merchandise). It operated in all fifty of the United States and in Puerto Rico, Guam, and the U.S. Virgin Islands. It also had equity interests in Meldisco subsidiaries of Footstar, Inc. that operated Kmart footwear departments. Measured in sales volume it was the third largest retailer and the second largest discount department store chain in the United States.

The discount department store industry was perceived by many to have reached maturity. Kmart, as part of that industry, had a retail management strategy that was developed in the late 1950s and revised in the early 1990s. The firm was in a dilemma in the terms of corporate strategy. The problem was how to lay a foundation to provide a new direction that would reposition the firm in a fiercely competitive environment.

The Early Years

Kmart was the outgrowth of an organization founded in 1899 in Detroit by Sebastian S. Kresge. The first S.S. Kresge store represented a new type of retailing that featured low-priced merchandise for cash in low-budget, relatively small (4,000 to 6,000 square foot) buildings with sparse furnishings. The adoption of the "5c and 10c" or "variety store" concept, pioneered by F.W. Woolworth Company in 1879, led to rapid and profitable development of what was then the S.S. Kresge Company.

Kresge believed it could substantially increase its retail business through centralized buying and control, developing standardized store operating procedures, and expanding with new stores in heavy traffic areas. In 1912, the firm was incorporated in Delaware. It had eighty-five stores with sales of $10,325,000, and, next to Woolworth's, was the largest variety chain in the world. In 1916 it was reincorporated in Michigan. Over the next forty years, the firm experimented with mail order catalogues, full-line department stores, self-service, a number of price lines, and the opening of stores in planned shopping centers. It continued its emphasis, however, on variety stores.

By 1957, corporate management became aware that the development of supermarkets and the expansion of drug store chains into general merchandise lines had made inroads into market categories previously dominated by variety stores. It also became clear that a new form of store with a discount merchandising strategy was emerging.

The Cunningham Connection

In 1957, in an effort to regain competitiveness and possibly save the company, Frank Williams, then President of Kresge, nominated Harry B. Cunningham as General Vice President. This maneuver was undertaken to free Mr. Cunningham, who had worked his way up the ranks in the organization, from operating responsibility. He was being groomed for the presidency and was given the assignment to study existing retailing businesses and recommend marketing changes.

In his visits to Kresge stores, and those of the competition, Cunningham became interested in discounting—particularly a new operation in Garden City, Long Island. Eugene Ferkauf had recently opened large discount department stores called E.J. Korvette. The stores had a discount mass-merchandising emphasis that featured low prices and margins, high turnover, large free-standing departmentalized units, ample parking space, and a location typically in the suburbs.

Cunningham was impressed with the discount concept, but he knew he had to first convince the Kresge Board of Directors, whose support would be necessary for any new strategy to succeed. He studied the company for two years and presented it with the following recommendation:

> We can't beat the discounters operating under the physical constraints and the self-imposed merchandise limitations of variety stores. We can join them—and not only join them, but with our people, procedures, and organization, we can become a leader in the discount industry.

In a speech delivered at the University of Michigan, Cunningham made his management approach clear by concluding with an admonition from the British author, Sir Hugh Walpole: "Don't play for safety, it's the most dangerous game in the world."

The Board of Directors had a difficult job. Change is never easy, especially when the company has established procedures in place and a proud heritage. Before the first presentation to the Board could be made, rumors were circulating that one shocked senior executive had said:

> We have been in the variety business for sixty years—we know everything there is to know about it, and we're not doing very well in that, and you want to get us into a business we don't know anything about.

The Board of Directors accepted H.B. Cunningham's recommendations. When President Frank Williams retired, Cunningham became the new President and Chief Executive Officer and was directed to proceed with his recommendations.

The Birth of Kmart

Management conceived the original Kmart as a conveniently located one-stop shopping unit where customers could buy a wide variety of quality merchandise at discount prices. The typical Kmart had 75,000 square feet, all on one floor. It generally stood by itself in a high-traffic, suburban area, with plenty of parking space. All stores had a similar floor plan.

The firm made an $80 million commitment in leases and merchandise for thirty-three stores before the first

Kmart opened in 1962 in Garden City, Michigan. As part of this strategy, management decided to rely on the strengths and abilities of its own people to make decisions rather than employing outside experts for advice.

The original Kresge 5 & 10 variety store operation was characterized by low gross margins, high turnover, and concentration on return on investment. The main difference in the Kmart strategy would be the offering of a much wider merchandise mix.

The company had the knowledge and ability to merchandise 50 percent of the departments in the planned Kmart merchandise mix, and contracted for operation of the remaining departments. In the following years, Kmart took over most of those departments originally contracted to licensees. Eventually all departments, except shoes, were operated by Kmart.

By 1987, the twenty-fifth anniversary year of the opening of the first Kmart store in America, sales and earnings of Kmart Corporation were at all-time highs. The company was the world's largest discount retailer with sales of $25,627 million and operated 3,934 general merchandise and specialty stores.

On April 6, 1987, Kmart Corporation announced that it agreed to sell most of its remaining Kresge variety stores in the United States to McCrory Corporation, a unit of the closely held Rapid American Corporation of New York.

The Nature of the Competitive Environment

A Changing Marketplace

The retail sector of the United States economy went through a number of dramatic and turbulent changes during the 1980s and early 1990s. Retail analysts concluded that many retail firms were negatively affected by increased competitive pressures, sluggish consumer spending, slower-than-anticipated economic growth in North America, and recessions abroad. As one retail consultant noted:

> The structure of distribution in advanced economies is currently undergoing a series of changes that are as profound in their impact and as pervasive in their influence as those that occurred in manufacturing during the nineteenth century.

This changing environment affected the discount department store industry. Nearly a dozen firms like E.J. Korvette, W.T. Grant, Arlans, Atlantic Mills, and Ames

passed into bankruptcy or reorganization. Some firms like Woolworth (Woolco Division) had withdrawn from the field entirely after years of disappointment. St. Louis-based May Department Stores sold its Caldor and Venture discount divisions, each with annual sales of more than $1 billion. Venture announced liquidation in early 1998.

Senior management at Kmart felt that most of the firms that had difficulty in the industry faced the same situation. First, they were very successful five or ten years ago but had not changed and, therefore, had become somewhat dated. Management that had a historically successful formula, particularly in retailing, was perceived as having difficulty adapting to change, especially at the peak of success. Management would wait too long when faced with a threat in the environment and then would have to scramble to regain competitiveness.

Wal-Mart Stores, Inc., based in Bentonville, Arkansas, was an exception. It was especially growth-orientated and had emerged in 1991 and continued in that position through 2000 as the nation's largest retailer as well as largest discount department store chain in sales volume. Operating under a variety of names and formats, nationally and internationally, it included Wal-Mart stores, Wal-Mart Supercenters, and Sam's Warehouse Clubs. The firm found early strength in cultivating rural markets, merchandise restocking programs, "everyday low-pricing," and the control of operations through company-wide computer programs that linked cash registers to corporate headquarters.

Sears, Roebuck, & Co., in a state of stagnated growth for several years, completed a return to its retailing roots by spinning off to shareholders its $9 billion controlling stake in its Allstate Corporation insurance unit and the divestment of financial services. After unsuccessfully experimenting with an "everyday low-price" strategy, management chose to refine its merchandising program to meet the needs of middle market customers, who were primarily women, by focusing on product lines in apparel, home, and automotive.

Many retailers such as Target Corporation (formerly Dayton Hudson), which adopted the discount concept, attempted to go generally after an upscale customer. The upscale customer tended to have a household income of $25,000 to $44,000 annually. Other segments of the population were served by firms like Ames Department Stores, Rocky Hill, Connecticut which appealed to outsize, older, and lower income workers, and by Shopko Stores, Inc., Green Bay, Wisconsin, which attempted to serve the upscale rural consumer.

Kmart executives found that discount department stores were being challenged by several other retail formats. Some retailers were assortment-oriented, with a much greater depth of assortment within a given product category. To illustrate, Toys-R-Us was an example of a firm that operated 20,000 square foot toy supermarkets. Toys-R-Us prices were very competitive within an industry that was very competitive. When the consumers entered a Toys-R-Us facility, there was usually no doubt in their minds if the product wasn't there, no one else had it. In the late 1990s, however, Toys-R-Us was challenged by Wal-Mart and other firms that offered higher service levels, more aggressive pricing practices, and more focused merchandise selections.

Some retailers were experimenting with the "off price" apparel concept where name brands and designer goods were sold at 20 to 70 percent discounts. Others, such as Home Depot and Menards, operated home improvement centers that were warehouse-style stores with a wide range of hard-line merchandise for both do-it-yourselfers and professionals. Still others opened drug supermarkets that offered a wide variety of high turnover merchandise in a convenient location. In these cases, competition was becoming more risk-oriented by putting $3 or $4 million in merchandise at retail value in an 80,000 square-foot facility and offering genuinely low prices. Jewel-Osco stores in the Midwest, Rite Aid, CVS, and a series of independents were examples of organizations employing the entirely new concept of the drug supermarket.

Competition was offering something that was new and different in terms of depth of assortment, competitive price image, and format. Kmart management perceived this as a threat because these were viable businesses and hindered the firm in its ability to improve and maintain share of market in specific merchandise categories. An industry competitive analysis is shown in Exhibit 1.

Expansion and Contraction

When Joseph E. Antonini was appointed chairman of Kmart Corporation in October 1987 he was charged with the responsibility of maintaining and eventually accelerating the chain's record of growth, despite a mature retail marketplace. He moved to string experimental formats into profitable chains. As he noted:

> Our vision calls for the constant and never-ceasing exploration of new modes of retailing, so that our core business of U.S. Kmart stores can be constantly renewed and reinvigorated by what we learn from our other businesses.

In the mid-1970's and throughout the 1980's, Kmart became involved in the acquisition or development of several smaller new operations. Kmart Insurance Services, Inc., acquired as Planned Marketing Associates in 1974, offered a full line of life, health, and accident insurance centers located in twenty-seven Kmart stores primarily in the South and Southwest.

In 1982, Kmart initiated its own off-price specialty apparel concept called Designer Depot. A total of twenty-eight Designer Depot stores were opened in 1982, to appeal to customers who wanted quality upscale clothing at a budget price. A variation of this concept, called Garment Rack, was opened to sell apparel that normally would not be sold in Designer Depot. A distribution center was added in 1983 to supplement them. Neither venture was successful.

Kmart also attempted an unsuccessful joint venture with the Hechinger Company of Washington, D.C., a warehouse home center retailer. However, after much deliberation, Kmart chose instead to acquire, in 1984, Home Centers of America of San Antonio, Texas, which operated 80,000 square foot warehouse home centers. The new division, renamed Builders Square, had grown to 167 units by 1996. It capitalized on Kmart's real estate, construction, and management expertise and Home Centers of America's merchandising expertise. Builders Square was sold in 1997 to the Hechinger Company. On June 11, 1999, Hechinger filed for Chapter 11 bankruptcy protection. As a result, Kmart recorded a non-cash charge of $354 million that reflected the impact of lease obligations for former Builders Square locations that were guaranteed by Kmart.

Waldenbooks, a chain of 877 bookstores, was acquired from Carter, Hawley, Hale, Inc. in 1984. It was part of a strategy to capture a greater share of the market with a product category that Kmart already had in its stores. Kmart management had been interested in the book business for some time and took advantage of an opportunity in the marketplace to build on its common knowledge base. Borders Books and Music, an operator of fifty large format superstores, became part of Kmart in 1992 to form the "Borders Group," a division that would include Waldenbooks. The Borders Group, Inc. was sold during 1995.

The Bruno's Inc., joint venture in 1987, formed a partnership to develop large combination grocery and general merchandise stores or "hypermarkets" called American Fare. The giant, one-stop-shopping facilities of 225,000 square feet, traded on the grocery expertise of Bruno's and the general merchandise of Kmart to offer a wide selection of products and services at discount

Exhibit 1   An Industry Competitive Analysis 1999

	Kmart	Wal-Mart	Sears	Target
Sales (millions)	$35,925	$165,013	$41,071	$33,702
Net Income (Mil.)	403	5,575	1,453	1,144
Sales growth	6.6%	20%	2.7%	10%
Profit margin	1.1%	3.4%	2.8%	3.4%
Sales/sq.ft	233	374	318	242
Return/equity	6.4%	22.9%	23%	19.5%

Number of Stores:

Kmart Corporation
  Kmart Traditional Discount Stores—202
  Big Kmart—1,860
  Super Kmart Centers—105
Wal-Mart Stores, Inc. (includes international)
  Wal-Mart Discount Stores—2,373
  Supercenters—1104
  SAM'S Clubs—512
Sears, Roebuck & Company
  Full-Line Stores—858
  Hardware Stores—267

Sears Dealer Stores—738
Sears Automotive Stores:
  Sears Auto Centers—798
  National Tire & Battery stores—310
Contract Sales
  The Great Indoors (Prototype decorating)—2
Target Corporation
  Target—912
  Mervyn's—267
  Department Store Division—64

Source: Company Annual Reports.

prices. A similar venture, called Super Kmart Center, represented later thinking on combination stores with a smaller size and format. In 2000, Kmart operated 105 Super Kmart Centers, all in the United States.

In 1988, the company acquired a controlling interest in Makro Inc., a Cincinnati-based operator of warehouse "club" stores. Makro, with annual sales of about $300 million, operated "member only" stores that were stocked with low priced fresh and frozen groceries, apparel, and durable goods in suburbs of Atlanta, Cincinnati, Washington, and Philadelphia. PACE Membership Warehouse, Inc., a similar operation, was acquired in 1989. The "club" stores were sold in 1994.

PayLess Drug Stores, a chain that operated super drug stores in a number of western states was sold in 1994 to Thrifty PayLess Holdings, Inc., an entity in which Kmart maintained a significant investment. Interests in The Sport Authority, an operator of large-format sporting goods stores, which Kmart acquired in 1990, were disposed of during 1995.

On the international level, an interest in Coles Myer, Ltd., Australia's largest retailer, was sold in November 1994. Interests in thirteen Kmart general merchandise stores in the Czech and Slovak Republics were sold to Tesco PLC at the beginning of 1996, one of the United Kingdom's largest retailers. In February 1998, Kmart stores in Canada were sold to Hudson's Bay Co., a Canadian chain of historic full-service department stores. The interest in Kmart Mexico, S.A.de C.V. was disposed of in FY 1997.

Founded in 1988, OfficeMax, with 328 stores, was one of the largest operators of high-volume, deep discount office products superstores in the United States. It became a greater than 90 percent-owned Kmart unit in 1991. Kmart's interest in OfficeMax was sold during 1995. In November 1995, Kmart also sold its auto service center business to a new corporation controlled by Penske Corporation. In connection with the sale, Kmart and Penske entered into a sublease arrangement concerning the operation of Penske Auto Service Centers.

During 1999, Kmart signed agreements with SUPERVALU, Inc. and Fleming Companies, Inc. under which they would assume responsibility for the distribution and replenishment of grocery-related products to all

Kmart stores. Kmart also maintained an equity interest in Meldisco subsidiaries of Footstar, Inc., operators of footwear departments in Kmart stores.

The Maturation of Kmart

Early corporate research revealed that on the basis of convenience, Kmart served 80 percent of the population. One study concluded that one out of every two adults in the United States shopped at a Kmart at least once a month. Despite this popular appeal, strategies that had allowed the firm to have something for everybody were no longer felt to be appropriate for the new millennium. Kmart found that it had a broad customer base because it operated on a national basis. Its early strategies had assumed the firm was serving everyone in the markets where it was established.

Kmart was often perceived as aiming at the low-income consumer. The financial community believed the Kmart original customer was blue collar, low income, and upper lower class. The market served, however, was more professional and middle class because Kmart stores were initially in suburban communities where that population lived.

Although Kmart had made a major commitment in more recent years to secondary or rural markets, these were areas that had previously not been cultivated. The firm, in its initial strategies, perceived the rural consumer as different from the urban or suburban customer. In re-addressing the situation, it discovered that its assortments in rural areas were too limited and there were too many preconceived notions regarding what the Nebraska farmer really wanted. The firm discovered that the rural consumer didn't always shop for bib overalls and shovels but shopped for microwave ovens and the same things everyone else did.

One goal was not to attract more customers but to get the customer coming in the door to spend more. Once in the store the customer was thought to demonstrate more divergent tastes. The upper income consumer would buy more health and beauty-aids, cameras, and sporting goods. The lower income consumer would buy toys and clothing.

In the process of trying to capture a larger share of the market and get people to spend more, the firm began to recognize a market that was more upscale. When consumer research was conducted and management examined the profile of the trade area and the profile of the person who shopped at Kmart in the past month, they were found to be identical. Kmart was predominately serving the suburban consumer in suburban locations.

In 1997 Kmart's primary target customers were women, between the ages of 25 and 45 years old, with children at home and with household incomes between $20,000 and $50,000 per year. The core Kmart shopper averaged 4.3 visits to a Kmart store per month. The purchase amount per visit was $40. The purchase rate was 95 percent during a store visit. The firm estimated that 180 million people shopped at Kmart in an average year.

In "lifestyle" research in markets served by the firm, Kmart determined there were more two-income families, families were having fewer children, there were more working wives, and customers tended to be homeowners. Customers were very careful how they spent their money and were perceived as wanting quality. This was a distinct contrast to the 1960's and early 1970's, which tended to have the orientation of a "throw away" society. The customer had said, "What we want is products that will last longer. We'll have to pay more for them but will still want them and at the lowest price possible." Customers wanted better quality products but still demanded competitive prices. According to a Kmart Annual Report, "Consumers today are well educated and informed. They want good value and they know it when they see it. Price remains a key consideration, but the consumers' new definition of value includes quality as well as price."

Corporate management at Kmart considered the discount department store to be a mature idea. Although maturity was sometimes looked on with disfavor, Kmart executives felt that this did not mean a lack of profitability or lack of opportunity to increase sales. The industry was perceived as being "reborn." It was in this context, in the 1990s, that a series of new retailing strategies, designed to upgrade the Kmart image, were developed.

The 1990 Renewal Program

The strategies that emerged to confront a changing environment were the result of an overall reexamination of existing corporate strategies. This program included: accelerated store expansion and refurbishing, capitalizing on dominant lifestyle departments, centralized merchandising, more capital investment in retail automation, an aggressive and focused advertising program, and continued growth through new specialty retail formats.

The initial 1990, five-year, $2.3 billion program involved virtually all Kmart discount stores. There would be approximately 250 new full-size Kmart stores, 620 enlargements, 280 relocations, and thirty closings. In addition 1,260 stores would be refurbished to bring their layout and fixtures up to new store standards. Another program, introduced in 1996, resulted in an additional

$1.1 billion being spent to upgrade Kmart stores. By year-end 1999, 1,860 new "Big Kmart" stores offered more pleasant shopping experiences thanks to the updated and easy-to-shop departmental adjacencies, better signing, lighting, wider aisles and more attractive in-store presentation.

One area receiving initial attention was improvement in the way products were displayed. The traditional Kmart layout was by product category. Often these locations for departments were holdovers from the variety store. Many departments would not give up prime locations. As part of the new marketing strategy, the shop concept was introduced. Management recognized that it had a sizable "do-it-yourself" store. As planning management discussed the issue, "nobody was aware of the opportunity. The hardware department was right smack in the center of the store because it was always there. The paint department was over here and the electrical department was over there." "All we had to do," management contended, "was put them all in one spot and everyone could see that we had a very respectable 'do-it-yourself' department." The concept resulted in a variety of new departments such as "Soft Goods for the Home," "Kitchen Korners," and "Home Electronic Centers." The goal behind each department was to sell an entire lifestyle-oriented concept to consumers, making goods complementary so shoppers would want to buy several interrelated products rather than just one item.

Name brands were added in soft and hard goods as management recognized that the customer transferred the product quality of branded goods to perceptions of private label merchandise. In the eyes of Kmart management, "if you sell Wrangler, there is good quality. Then the private label must be good quality."

The company increased its emphasis on trusted national brands such as Rubbermaid, Procter & Gamble, and Kodak, and put emphasis on major strategic vendor relationships. In addition it began to enhance its private label brands such as Kathy Ireland, Jaclyn Smith, Route 66, and Sesame Street in Apparel. Additional private label merchandise included K Gro in home gardening, American Fare in Grocery and Consumables, White-Westinghouse in appliances, and Penske Auto Centers in automotive services. Some private labels were discontinued following review.

Kmart hired Martha Stewart, an upscale Connecticut author of lavish best-selling books on cooking and home entertaining, as its "life-style spokesperson and consultant." Martha Stewart was featured as a corporate symbol for housewares and associated products in advertising and in-store displays. Management visualized her as the next Betty Crocker, a fictional character created some years ago by General Mills, Inc., and a representative of its interest in "life-style" trends. The "Martha Stewart Everyday" home fashion product line was introduced in 1995 and expanded in 1996 and 1997. A separate division was established to manage strategy for all Martha Stewart-label goods and programs. Merchandise was featured in the redesigned once-a-week Kmart newspaper circular that carried the advertising theme: "The quality you need, the price you want."

Several thousand prices were reduced to maintain "price leadership across America." As management noted, "it is absolutely essential that we provide our customers with good value—quality products at low prices." Although lowering of prices hurt margins and contributed importantly to an earnings decline, management felt that unit turnover of items with lowered prices increased significantly to "enable Kmart to maintain its pricing leadership that will have a most positive impact on our business in the years ahead."

A "centralized merchandising system" was introduced to improve communication. A computerized, highly automated replenishment system tracked how quickly merchandise sold and, just as quickly, put fast moving items back on the shelves. Satellite capability and a Point-of-Sale (POS) scanning system were introduced as part of the program. Regular, live satellite communication from Kmart headquarters to the stores would allow senior management to communicate with store managers and allow for questions and answers. The POS scanning system allowed a record of every sale and transmission of the data to headquarters. This enabled Kmart to respond quickly to what's new, what's in demand, and what would keep customers coming back.

The company opened its first Super Kmart Center in 1992. The format combined general merchandise and food with emphasis upon customer service and convenience and ranged in size from 135,000 to 190,000 square feet with more than 40,000 grocery items. The typical Super Kmart operated seven days a week, twenty-four hours a day and generated high traffic and sales volume. The centers also featured wider shopping aisles, appealing displays and pleasant lighting to enrich the shopping experience. Super Kmarts featured in-house bakeries, USDA fresh meats, fresh seafood, delicatessens, cookie kiosks, cappuccino bars, in-store eateries and food courts, and fresh carry-out salad bars. In many locations, the center provided customer services like video rental, dry cleaning, shoe repair, beauty salons, optical shops, express shipping services, as well as a full line of traditional Kmart merchandise. To enhance the appeal of the merchandise assortment, emphasis was placed on "cross merchandising." For example, toasters were featured above the fresh baked breads, kitchen gadgets were positioned across the aisle from produce, and baby centers featured everything from baby food to toys. At the end of 1999, the company operated 105 Super Kmart stores.

The Planning Function

Corporate planning at Kmart was the result of executives, primarily the senior executive, recognizing change. The role played by the senior executive was to get others to recognize that nothing is good forever. "Good planning," was perceived as the result of those who recognized that at some point they would have to get involved. "Poor Planning," was done by those who didn't recognize the need for it. When they did, it was too late to survive. Good planning, if done on a regular and timely basis, was assumed to result in improved performance. Kmart's Michael Wellman—then Director of Planning and Research—contended, "planning, as we like to stress, is making decisions now to improve performance tomorrow. Everyone looks at what may happen tomorrow, but the planners are the ones who make decisions today. That's where I think too many firms go wrong. They think they are planning because they are writing reports and are aware of changes. They don't say, 'because of this, we must decide today to spend this money to do this to accomplish this goal in the future.'"

Kmart management believed that the firm had been very successful in the area of strategic planning. "When it became necessary to make significant changes in the way we were doing business," Michael Wellman suggested, "that was accomplished on a fairly timely basis." When the organization made the change in the 1960's, it recognized there was a very powerful investment opportunity and capitalized on it—far beyond what anyone else would have done. "We just opened stores," he continued, "at a great, great pace. Management, when confronted with a crisis, would state, 'It's the economy, or it's this, or that, but it's not the essential way we are doing business.'" He noted, "Suddenly management would recognize that the economy may stay like this forever. We need to improve the situation and then do it." Strategic planning was thought to arise out of some difficult times for the organization.

Kmart had a reasonably formal planning organization that involved a constant evaluation of what was happening in the marketplace, what competition was doing, and what kinds of opportunities were available. Management felt a need to diversify because it would not be a viable company unless it was growing. Management felt it was not going to grow with the Kmart format forever. It

needed growth and opportunity, particularly for a company that was able to open 200 stores on a regular basis. Michael Wellman, Director of Planning and Research, felt that, "Given a 'corporate culture' that was accustomed to challenges, management would have to find ways to expend that energy. A corporation that is successful," he argued, "has to continue to be successful. It has to have a basic understanding of corporate needs and be augmented by a much more rigorous effort to be aware of what's going on in the external environment."

A planning group at Kmart represented a number of functional areas of the organization. Management described it as an "in-house consulting group" with some independence. It was made up of (1) financial planning, (2) economic and consumer analysis, and (3) operations research. The chief executive officer (CEO) was identified as the primary planner of the organization.

Reorganization and Restructuring

Kmart financial performance for 1993 was clearly disappointing. The company announced a loss of $974 million on sales of $34,156,000 for the fiscal year ended January 26, 1994. Chairman Antonini, noting the deficit, felt it occurred primarily because of lower margins in the U.S. Kmart stores division. "Margin erosion," he said, "stemmed in part from intense industry-wide pricing pressure throughout 1993." He was confident, however, that Kmart was on track with its renewal program to make the more than 2,350 U.S. Kmart stores more "competitive, on-trend, and cutting merchandisers." Tactical Retail Solutions, Inc., estimated that during Mr. Antonini's seven year tenure with the company, Kmart's market share in the discount arena fell to 23 percent from 35 percent. Other retail experts suggested that because the company had struggled for so long to have the right merchandise in the stores at the right time, it had lost customers to competitors. An aging customer base was also cited.

In early 1995, following the posting of its eighth consecutive quarter of disappointing earnings, Kmart's Board of Directors announced that Joseph Antonini would be replaced as chairman. It named Donald S. Perkins, former chairman of Jewel Companies, Inc. and a Kmart director, to the position. Mr. Antonini relinquished his position as President and Chief Executive Officer in March. After a nationwide search, Floyd Hall, 57, and former Chairman and CEO of the Target discount store division of the Dayton-Hudson Corporation, was appointed Chairman, President, and Chief Executive Officer of Kmart in June of 1995.

The company concluded the disposition of many non-core assets in 1996, including the sale of the Borders group, OfficeMax, the Sports Authority, and Coles Myer. During the 1990s, it also closed a large number of under-performing stores in the United States, and cleared out $700 million in aged and discontinued inventory in the remaining stores.

In 1996, Kmart converted 152 of its traditional stores to feature a new design that was referred to as the high-frequency format. These stores were named Big Kmart. The stores emphasized those departments that were deemed most important to core customers and offered an increased mix of high frequency, everyday basics, and consumables in the pantry area located at the front of each store. These items were typically priced at a one to three percentage differential from the leading com-petitors in each market and served to increase inventory turnover and gross margin dollars. In an addition to the pantry area, Big Kmart stores featured improved light-ing, new signage that was easier to see and read, and adjacencies that created a smoother traffic flow. In 1999, 588 stores were converted to the new Big Kmart format bringing the total to 1,860. Other smaller stores would be updated to a "best of Big Kmart" prototype.

Kmart launched its first e-commerce site in 1998. The initial Kmart.com offered a few products and was not considered a successful venture. In 1999, it partnered with SOFTBANK Venture Capital, who provided techni-cal expertise, experienced personnel, and initial capital to create an Internet site 60 percent owned by Kmart. BlueLight.com increased the number of Kmart products it offered online to about 65,000 from 1,250. It planned to boost the number to 100,000 by year-end 2000 and possibly to millions of items in the future.

Major changes were made to the management team. In total, twenty-three of the company's thirty-seven cor-porate officers were new to the company's team since 1995. The most dramatic restructuring had taken place in the merchandising organization where all four of the general merchandise managers responsible for buying organizations joined Kmart since 1995. In addition, fif-teen new divisional vice presidents joined Kmart during 1997. Significant changes also were made to the Board of Directors with nine of fifteen directors new to the com-pany since 1995.

At the end of his tenure, Floyd Hall announced that the company mandate in the year and century ahead was to create sustained growth that would profitably leverage all of the core strengths of the firm. The corporate mis-sion in 2000 was "to become the discount store of choice for low-and middle-income households by satisfying their routine and seasonal shopping needs as well as or better than the competition." Management believed that the actions taken by Charles Conaway, the new president,

would have a dramatic impact on how customers per-ceived Kmart, how frequently they shopped in the stores, and how much they would buy on each visit. Increasing customer's frequency and the amount they purchased each visit were seen as having a dramatic impact on the company's efforts to increase its profitability.

References

Berner, Robert, "Kmart's Earnings More Than Tripled in First Quarter," *Wall Street Journal*, 14 May 1998, A13.

Brauer, Molly, "Kmart in Black `in 6 Months,'" *Detroit Free Press*, 26 January 1996, E1.

Business Week, "Where Kmart Goes Next Now That It's No. 2," 2 June 1980, 109–110, 114.

Bussey, John, "Kmart Is Set To Sell Many Of Its Roots To Rapid-American Corp's McCrory," *Wall Street Journal*, 6 April 1987, 24.

Carruth, Eleanore, "Kmart Has To Open Some New Doors On The Future," *Fortune*, July 1977, 143–150, 153–154.

Coleman, Calmetta, "BlueLight.com Aims to Coax Kmart Shoppers Online," *Wall Street Journal*, 19 June 2000, B4.

Coleman, Calmetta, Kmart Lease Pledge May Slow Rebound, *Wall Street Journal*, 24 May 1999, A3.

Coleman, Calmetta, "Kmart's New CEO Outlines Plans for Fast Changes," *Wall Street Journal*, 27 July 2000, B4.

Coleman, Calmetta, "Kmart Sees $740 Million Pretax Charge From Closing 72 Stores, Other Changes," *Wall Street Journal*, 26, July 2000, B10.

Coleman, Calmetta, "Kmart Selects CVS President to be its CEO," *Wall Street Journal*, 1 June 2000.

Coleman, Calmetta, "Kmart's Wave of Insider Sales Continues Amid Questions About Retailer's Plans," *Wall Street Journal*, 23 June 1999, A4.

Dewar, Robert E., "The Kresge Company And The Retail Revolution," *University of Michigan Business Review*, 2 July 1975, 2.

Duff, Christina, and Joann S. Lubin, "Kmart Board Ousts Antonini As Chairman," *Wall Street Journal*, 18 January 1995, A3.

Elmer, Vickie, and Joann Muller, "Retailer Needs Leader, Vision," *Detroit Free Press*, 22 March 1995, 1A, 9A.

Frankel, Mark, (August 2, 1999), "Attention, Kmart Grocery Shoppers," *Business Week*, 2 August 1999, 49.

Guiles, Melinda G., "Attention, Shoppers: Stop That Browsing And Get Aggressive," *Wall Street Journal*, 16 June 1987, 1, 21.

Guiles, Melinda G., "Kmart, Bruno's Join To Develop 'Hypermarkets,'" *Wall Street Journal*, 8 September 1987, 17.

Ingrassia, Paul, "Attention Non-Kmart Shoppers: A Blue-Light Special Just For You," *Wall Street Journal*, 6 October 1987, 42.

Kmart Corporation, *Annual Report*, Troy, Michigan, 1990.

Kmart Corporation, *Annual Report*, Troy, Michigan, 1995.

Kmart Corporation, *Annual Report*, Troy, Michigan, 1996.

Kmart Corporation, *Annual Report*, Troy, Michigan, 1997.

Kmart Corporation, *Annual Report*, Troy, Michigan, 1999.

Kmart Corporation, *Kmart Fact Book*, Troy, Michigan, 1997.

Kranhold, Kathryn, "Kmart Hope to Steer Teens to Route 66," *Wall Street Journal*, 27 July 2000, B14.

Main, Jerry, "Kmart's Plan To Be Born Again," *Fortune*, 21 September 1981, 74–77, 84–85.

Rice, Faye, "Why Kmart Has Stalled," *Fortune*, 9 October 1989, 79.

Schwadel, Francine, "Kmart to Speed Store Openings, Renovations," *Wall Street Journal*, 27 February 1990, 3.

Saporito, Bill, "Is Wal-Mart Unstoppable?" *Fortune*, 6 May 1991, 50–59.

Sternad, Patrica, "Kmart's Antonini Moves Far Beyond Retail 'Junk' Image," *Advertising Age*, 25 July 1988, 1, 67.

Talaski, Karen, "Kmart to Invest $2 Billion," *The Detroit News*, 11 August 2000, 1C.

Talaski, Karen, "Kmart Profits Plunge Sharply," *The Detroit News*, 12 May 2000, 1B.

Wellman, Michael, Interview with Director of Planning and Research, 6 August 1984, Kmart Corporation.

Woodruff, David, "Will Kmart Ever Be a Silk Purse?" *Business Week*, 22 January 1990, 46.

Appendix A   Kmart Corporation Consolidated Balance Sheets and Operating Statements 1998–1999

Years Ended January 26, 2000, January 27, 1999 and January 28, 1998

	1999	1998	1997
Sales	$ 35,925	$ 33,674	$ 32,183
Cost of sales, buying, and occupancy	28,102	26,319	25,152
Gross margin	7,823	7,355	7,031
Selling, general, and administrative expenses	6,523	6,245	6,136
Voluntary early retirement programs	–	19	114
Continuing income before interest, income taxes and dividends on convertible preferred securities of subsidiary trust	1,300	1,091	781
Interest expense, net	280	293	363
Income tax provision	337	230	120
Dividends on convertible preferred securities of subsidiary trust, net of income taxes of $27, $27 and $26	50	50	49
Net income from continuing operations	633	518	249
Discontinued operations, net of income taxes of $(124)	(230)	–	–
Net income	$ 403	$ 518	$ 249
Basic earnings per common share			
Net income from continuing operations	$ 1.29	$ 1.05	$ .51
Discontinued operations	(.47)	–	–
Net income	$ .82	$ 1.05	$ .51
Diluted earnings per common share			
Net income from continuing operations	$ 1.22	$ 1.01	$ .51
Discontinued operations	(.41)	–	–
Net income	$ .81	$ 1.01	$ .51
Basic weighted average shares (millions)	491.7	492.1	487.1
Diluted weighted average shares (millions)	561.7	564.9	491.7

Appendix A Kmart Corporation Consolidated Balance Sheets and Operating Statements 1998–1999 (continued)

| | As of January 26, 2000 and January 27, 1999 | |
	1999	1998
Current Assets		
Cash and cash equivalents	$ 344	$ 710
Merchandise inventories	7,101	6,536
Other current assets	715	584
Total current assets	8,160	7,830
Property and equipment, net	6,410	5,914
Other assets and deferred charges	534	422
Total assets	$ 15,104	$ 14,166
Current Liabilities		
Long-term debt due within one year	$ 66	$ 77
Trade accounts payable	2,204	2,047
Accrued payroll and other liabilities	1,574	1,359
Taxes other than income taxes	232	208
Total current liabilities	4,076	3,691
Long-term debt and notes payable	1,759	1,538
Capital lease obligations	1,014	1,091
Other long-term liabilities	965	883
Company-obligated, mandatorily redeemable convertible preferred securities of a subsidiary trust holding solely 7–3/4% convertible junior subordinated debentures of Kmart (redemption value of $1,000)	986	984
Common stock, $1 par value, 1,500,000,000 shares authorized; 481,383,569 and 493,358,504 shares issued, respectively	481	493
Capital in excess of par value	1,555	1,667
Retained earnings	4,268	3,819
Total liabilities and Shareholders' Equity	$ 15,104	$ 14,166

Appendix B   Kmart Corporation Financial Performance 1990–1999

Year	Sales (000)	Assets (000)	Net Income (000)	Net Worth (000)
1990	$32,070,000	$13,899,000	$756,000	$5,384,000
1991	34,580,000	15,999,000	859,000	6,891,000
1992	37,724,000	18,931,000	941,000	7,536,000
1993	34,156,000	17,504,000	(974,000)	6,093,000
1994	34,025,000	17,029,000	296,000	6,032,000
1995	31,713,000	15,033,000	(571,000)	5,280,000
1996	31,437,000	14,286,000	(220,000)	6,146,000
1997	32,183,000	13,558,000	249,000	6,445,000
1998	33,674,000	14,166,000	518,000	6,963,000
1999	35,925,000	15,104,000	403,000	7,290,000

Source: *Fortune* financial analysis and Kmart Annual Reports.
After taxes and extraordinary credit or charges
Data from 1995, 1996, and 1997 reflects disposition of subsidiaries

Appendix C   Financial Performance Wal-Mart Stores, Inc. 1990–1999

Year	Sales (000)	Assets (000)	Net Income (000)	Net Worth (000)
1990	$ 32,601,594	$11,388,915	$1,291,024	$ 5,365,524
1991	43,886,900	15,443,400	1,608,500	6,989,700
1992	55,484,000	20,565,000	1,995,000	8,759,000
1993	67,344,000	26,441,000	2,333,000	10,753,000
1994	82,494,000	32,819,000	2,681,000	12,726,000
1995	93,627,000	37,541,000	2,740,000	14,756,000
1996	104,859,000	39,604,000	3,056,000	17,143,000
1997	117,958,000	45,384,000	3,526,000	18,503,000
1998	137,634,000	49,996,000	4,393,000	21,112,000
1999	165,013,000	70,349,000	5,575,000	25,834,000

Source: Wal-Mart annual reports/*Fortune* financial analysis.

Case 21

Lofty Ambitions at Cirrus Design and NASA

Robert N. McGrath and Blaise P. Waguespack, *Embry-Riddle Aeronautical University*

Momentum had been building steadily during the late 1990s and was still gaining strength through the early years of the 21st century. In 1994, the U.S. Congress passed the General Aviation Revitalization Act, legislation purposely created to reinvigorate the general aviation industry's collapse from the overwhelming cost of product liability lawsuits.[1] The act made airplanes over 18 years old exempt from liability prosecution, an enormous relief considering that the average age of a general aviation aircraft was then 27 years. By the year 2001, the industry was experiencing a vibrant rejuvenation, and prospects were good.

Also in 1994, the National Aeronautics and Space Administration (NASA) began a serious research effort towards making truly leapfrog improvements in general aviation. Programs, alliances, and consortia such as the Advanced General Aviation Transport Experiment (AGATE) Alliance and the General Aviation Propulsion (GAP) program were formed to advance technologies of many types.[2] These efforts blossomed into an extraordinary vision, one on a scale of the Apollo program. NASA became committed to making the small, private airplane the transportation mode of choice for private citizens, replacing much of the role of the automobile for intercity travel, and removing some of the burden from the airline/airport industries.[3] To do this, general aviation would need a virtual reinvention. By the year 2001, NASA's five-year research and demonstration budget for this effort had grown to $69 million, and the overall movement included more consortia of dozens of organizations from industry, government, and academia.[4] Was the image of the Jetson family ready to be turned into reality?

Also in 1994, the managers and engineers at Cirrus Design were early in the stage of developing prototypes for a truly innovative and economical general aviation aircraft.[5] Two brothers had boldly articulated that they could take general aviation aircraft to new levels of performance. By 2001 they were leading the way towards commercializing technologies that the traditional rivals had been slow to develop because of the risks. Full approvals from the Federal Aviation Administration (FAA) had been awarded, and Cirrus had a production backlog of over 600 aircraft. A transition from R&D to full-scale production was just getting organized, one that could change the nature of the company. But at the same time, continued R&D leadership from firms like Cirrus was badly needed so that NASA could realize its vision. Decades of product development work, continuously advancing the state of the art to unparalleled levels, was necessary. The brothers faced tough choices amongst golden, but different, opportunities.

General Aviation

The general aviation (GA) manufacturing industry was generally considered to consist of the makers of single and multi-engine (mostly twin engine) piston-driven (propeller) aircraft weighing less than 12,500 pounds, as well as small turboprop and turbofan (jet engine) aircraft mostly used for corporate/business aviation (Exhibit 1). Thus the industry could be divided along the lines of either technology or market segment in about the same way.[6]

As the new century began there were well over 200,000 general aviation aircraft registered in the United States, and over 250,000 citizens held private pilot licenses alone (Exhibit 2). Private pilots generally flew for leisure, sport, recreation, and because of the overall lure of flying. As a mode of transportation, though, small aircraft were very costly. In the corporate world, many firms owned very small fleets of business jets so that executives would not be slaves to the airline industry. Some corporate policies regarding their flight departments were prudent, while others were quite luxurious.

Printed by permission of Robert N. McGrath, Embry-Riddle Aeronautical University.

Exhibit 1   General Aviation Aircraft in Use, 1999

	Active GA Aircraft	Public Use	Corporate	Business	Personal	Instructional	Aerial Application	Aerial Observation	Sightseeing	External Load	Air Tours	Air Taxi	Medical	Other
Total	219,464	4,138	10,804	24,543	147,085	16,091	4,254	3,240	366	832	190	290	4,279	2,363
Piston Total	171,923	2,104	2,635	21,794	120,678	14,458	3,146	2,491	150	5	37	2,223	255	1,582
Single-engine	150,886	1,723	902	15,559	111,574	13,213	3,121	2,096	131	5	37	615	187	1,427
Twin-engine	20,930	364	1,733	6,216	9,087	1,245	25	395	8	0	0	1,607	68	137
Other	108	17	0	19	17	0	0	0	11	0	0	0	0	18
Turboprop Total	5,679	242	2,368	1,061	516	46	337	7	7	0	0	935	82	60
Single-engine	1,018	20	121	288	159	0	337	0	0	0	0	75	6	0
Twin-engine	4,641	201	2,246	773	357	46	0	7	0	0	0	860	76	60
Other	21	0	0	0	0	0	0	0	7	0	0	0	0	0
Turbojet Total	7,120	79	5,170	676	430	36	106	15	0	0	0	496	16	79
Twin-engine	6,387	79	4,633	621	412	36	0	15	0	0	0	496	9	69
Other	733	0	537	56	17	0	106	0	0	0	0	0	7	9

In a legal sense, aviation was circumscribed by statutory requirements. Federal Aviation Regulations (FARs) regulated private and executive aircraft under FAR Part 23, for example, while different sets of rules applied to other aspects of aviation.[7]

The fate of the industry was strongly tied to "macro" conditions such as the overall state of the economy, the ability to finance luxury items, energy costs, and demographics. Long boom-to-bust cycles were typical. Legislation that favored consumers' rights caused a long downslide from the 1960's through the mid-1990's, as the manufacturers accumulated stupendous product liability costs. By the mid-90s the industry was stagnant, and its infrastructure was falling apart. But the General Aviation Revitalization Act of 1994 changed all that, relieving GA of much of its liability exposure, and releasing pent-up demand (Exhibit 3–5). The industry was once again enjoying a boom cycle by the year 2001, without a foreseeable slowdown.

While general aviation manufacturing was dominated by the members of the General Aviation Manufacturer's Association (GAMA,) this organization was heavily represented by U.S.-based firms, and sometimes the international element was overlooked . The Big Three of general aviation were considered to be Cessna, a subsidiary of Textron, Inc., Beech, a subsidiary of Raytheon, and The New Piper Aircraft Company. These firms made the large majority of airplanes. In terms of revenue, however, there was a very great disparity between the low end and the high end. The low end was characterized by single-engine, piston/propeller, four seat aircraft, which typically cost from $150,000 to $300,000, while the high end was characterized by luxurious corporate jets, which could cost well over $10,000,000. The high end was dominated by Gulfstream, Bombardier, and Cessna.

Engine manufacturing was almost completely controlled by just two firms: Lycoming, a division of Textron, and Continental Motors, a division of Teledyne Technologies. Other supplier industries were more fragmented. GA manufacturers mostly outsourced engines, avionics (aviation electronics), and system components, and focused on the forward parts of the supply chain: the design and development of airframes, the final assembly of entire aircraft, marketing and sales, and product support.

NASA and SATS

The vision of aviation being a highway in the sky for millions of ordinary, private travelers had been around for decades, but had always been the province of futurists and science fiction writers. But as the century turned, social and economic pressures, alongside strides made in key technologies, made that vision seem more possible than ever before.

For one thing, the airline system was bursting at the seams, and the situation was only going to get worse if

Exhibit 2   U.S. Pilot Population

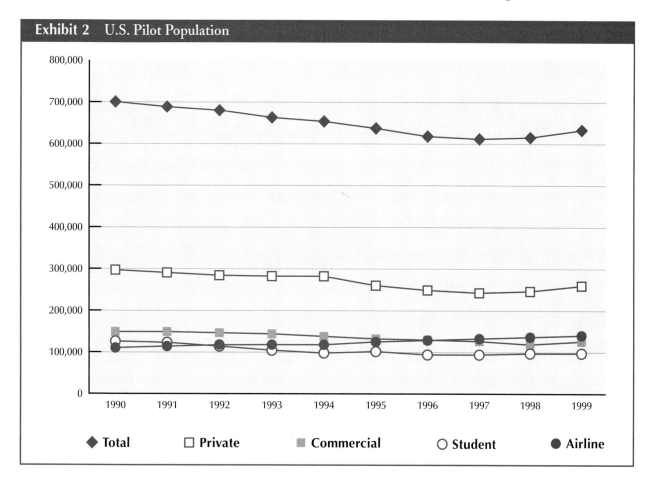

market predictions were accurate.[8] Four-fifths of all passengers passed through just 22 airport "hubs," creating enormous bottlenecks. The problem was so bad that bills were proposed in the U.S. legislature demanding the passage of a traveler's bill of rights into law. In a sense much of the problem was an infrastructure problem. Airlines had enough capacity and could always add more airplanes to their fleets, but airport expansion was a significant political, economic, social, and environmental challenge. And the Air Traffic Control system, while proven to be safe, was based on technologies that could not keep pace with the industry's needs.

Asking people to drive the long distances between many U.S. cities would not provide an answer on any large scale, only airplanes and sometimes railroads could efficiently transport many people over distances of hundreds of miles. The problem of expanding the U.S. railway system, however, faced higher hurdles than the airport expansion problem.

But the people at NASA observed something compelling, and hypothesized something else that was intriguing. While the airlines served about 600 cities in the United States, there were actually over 14,000 small airports, about 5,400 of which were underutilized but legitimate general aviation airports.[9] And while many people had long commutes just to get to a major airport, virtually everyone lived within a short commute of a general aviation airport.[10] Next to this observation, they hypothesized that as the information age really matured and came to define society, the value of a person's time would become a key, if not THE key, commodity. This changed the economics of transportation significantly.[11]

Altogether, then, the situation seemed to suggest the opportunity to develop a whole new transportation paradigm, one based on advanced general aviation airplanes. The concept was called the Small Aircraft Transportation System, or just SATS.[12] The official goal was to "reduce public travel time by half in 10 years and two-thirds in 25 years at equivalent highway system costs, increasing mobility for all of the nation's communities through advanced on-demand transportation … SATS increases the radius of action of daily life by tenfold, the first increase of such magnitude since the cars [sic] displaced horses for intercity travel."[13]

Exhibit 3   General Aviation Aircraft Shipments, 1990–1999

Year	Shipments		Units Shipped by Type				Exports					
	Total Units	Billings (Millions)	Single-Engine	Multi-Engine	Turbo Prop	Turbo Fan	Total Units	Billings (Millions)	Single-Engine	Multi-Engine	Turbo Prop	Turbo Jet
1990	1144	2008	608	87	281	168	458	872	224	57	86	91
1991	1021	1968	564	49	222	186	382	807	204	25	74	79
1992	941	1840	552	41	177	171	353	609	196	16	90	51
1993	964	2144	516	39	211	198	349	857	149	23	109	68
1994	928	2357	444	55	207	222	277	684	84	42	84	67
1995	1077	2842	515	61	255	246	315	816	130	30	85	70
1996	1115	3048	524	67	290	233	345	903	126	24	135	60
1997	1549	4593	898	86	223	342	449	1505	199	25	126	99
1998	2200	5761	1434	94	259	413	535	1640	268	30	131	106
1999	2504	7843	1634	114	239	517	562	2504	237	23	42	158

Source: GAMA.

To make it work, though, enormous levels of technological progress were necessary. As much or more progress had to be made in information technologies as at more obvious frontiers such as aerodynamics and propulsion. For one thing, the whole concept of air traffic control would have to be much different. SATS had to be based on the "free flight" concept to work, meaning that pilots would be given the discretion of how to get from point to point without much routing from a ground-based, human controller. This meant that the locus of control would be in the electronics in the airplanes themselves, to the point where traffic would be self-organizing.

Using satellite-based navigation information, each SATS aircraft will know its own position from takeoff till landing. It will broadcast that position and intent to all other SATS aircraft in the vicinity, and to local air traffic control facilities. In this manner, SATS flights can operate independently for the most part from the rigid routing and scheduling constraints of the commercial air traffic system.[14]

As such, the system would not depend on ground-based radar either. Airplanes would be equipped with all the necessary "situational awareness" electronics, and cockpit ergonomics, that it would take to ensure safe flight. The system would make great use of the wireless Internet, be intelligent enough to manage weather data very reliably, allow much greater traffic capacity in much more complex patterns, and in a word, make piloting an aircraft not just safe, but intuitively easy.

At least one generation of SATS aircraft and technologies was thought to be needed before the latent mass-market could be convinced of SATS' viability, with early market segments expected to be small groups of business travelers, personal leisure travelers, and small cargo distributors. More specifically, the early versions of SATS would probably be Private and corporate aircraft owned, rented, or leased by the operators or their clients. These aircraft will typically hold four to ten people, including the pilots. They will be equipped with digital avionics suites featuring satellite-based navigation systems, comprehensive integrated onboard computers allowing coordinated control and display of aircraft system operation and status, and synthetic vision to allow pilots to operate the aircraft in low visibility weather conditions. A 'highway' in the sky display will present a 3D perspective view of the path of flight, terrain, obstacles, traffic, and weather, with superimposed guides for the pilot to fly any flight plan.[15]

By the year 2001 significant progress had been made on many fronts. A revolutionary, small, lightweight, and economical jet engine was being prototyped, and strides had been made in diesel technology as well.[16] A fleet of aircraft had been equipped with first-generation avionics and was actively testing the control concept. Firms were completely revolutionizing cockpit instrumentation (the controls and displays used by pilots on an aircraft's dashboard.) Computer models had been developed by universities to examine air space limitations and overall economics, and results were encouraging. A dizzying

Exhibit 4   General Aviation Shipments

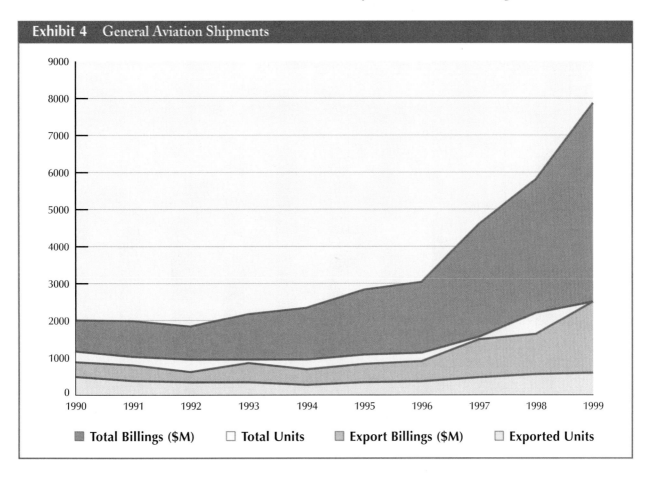

■ Total Billings ($M)   □ Total Units   ■ Export Billings ($M)   □ Exported Units

alphabet soup of acronyms and abbreviations for new technologies and studies had emerged. Plans were on progress to have an actual SATS infrastructure operating on a small scale in the state of Florida, to be used as a concept demonstrator and technology incubator, in the year 2005.

Cirrus Design

NASA depended on firms like Cirrus Design, and this firm had been important to NASA's vision for several years, leading or participating in important advancements in several fields. Partnered with the firm Terry Engineering of Wichita, Kansas, Cirrus had crash-tested four airplanes in the mid-90s.[17] The purpose was to help transfer the survivability characteristics of automobiles, racing cars, helicopters, etc., to SATS aircraft. Safety, after all, had to be advanced for SATS to really succeed. Cirrus also successfully developed an "Electroexpulsive Ice Protection System" for general aviation aircraft, a kind of de-icing technology necessary to bring flight safety up to the standards that SATS

would require.[18] The firm had also advanced the "Resin Transfer Molding" process: a relatively low-cost way of producing lightweight, consistent, complex three-dimensional shapes out of synthetic composite materials, the kind of space-age materials that were the subject of industry rumors and arguments for many years.[19]

By the late 1990s, Cirrus was widely recognized as one of two firms (with Lancair) that was commercializing anything close to a first-generation SATS aircraft: one with single-lever controls, a multi-function display of satellite navigation and airport information, graphical display of real-time weather, advanced lightweight composites, energy-absorbing structures, and more.[20] But this groundbreaking achievement did not happen overnight.[21]

Cirrus Design was founded by Alan and Dale Klapmeir in 1984 in Baraboo, Wisconsin, a time when the industry was not very dynamic. Existing industry rivals had become somewhat lethargic and generally focused on survival, making incremental improvements to proven designs and production processes, and avoiding serious technological risk. Yet the prices of

Exhibit 5   Shipments by Percentage

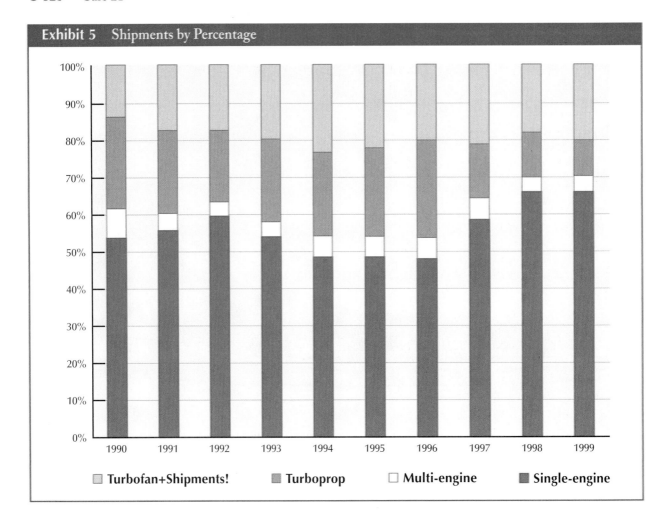

Legend: ■ Turbofan+Shipments!   ■ Turboprop   □ Multi-engine   ■ Single-engine

general aviation aircraft continued steadily upward, sometimes outpacing the Consumer Price Index by two-to-one. Conditions were such that many potential customers felt compelled to buy used instead of new aircraft (as long as aircraft were maintained well there were no real safety or performance problems).

Lovers of aviation, the Klapmeirs decided to try to change things. From the very beginning Cirrus was energized by their vision of almost single-handedly rejuvenating general aviation through creating high-quality and innovative aircraft that pilots would love. The early days of the firm were heavily influenced by the brightest engineers, mechanics, and technicians that the brothers could hire, all with a similar passion for aviation. Their first endeavor was to design and produce kit airplanes, and a design dubbed the VK-30 was unveiled at the 1987 Experimental Aircraft Association convention in Oshkosh, Wisconsin. As the name implies, kit aircraft were delivered in pieces, assembly being the responsibility of the purchaser. It

was a way of keeping prices reasonable, but it made it impossible to really compete in terms of airworthiness, especially official certificates granted by the FAA (under FAR Part 21). But producing such aircraft through the early years of the company helped it learn many fundamental lessons of how to do business in general aviation. The Klapmeirs did not plan on staying kit manufacturers for long, and ceased production of the VK-30 in 1992.

In 1993 Cirrus began construction of its headquarters and R&D facility in Duluth, Minnesota, a 30,000 square foot facility. The location was chosen because of its proximity to a large airport, availability of a talented labor pool, and quality of life. In 1994 construction had progressed enough to allow employees to begin moving in. Their main project was to begin development of four SR20 prototype aircraft. From the beginning, the customer was much involved. The Klapmeirs interviewed hundreds of pilots and learned that they wanted airplanes that were easier to operate than existing models, safer to fly, faster, more comfortable, and more affordable to buy, own, operate, and maintain. From the beginning, the SR20 was envisaged as a personal transportation vehicle, benchmarked against high-quality automobiles. The SR20 was to be a four-seat, fixed-landing gear, single-engine airplane. The interior was designed to be luxurious; the exterior was designed to be beautiful in its shape and style.

Perhaps the biggest gamble was composite construction, a materials technology that had been slow to become commercializeable in general aviation. "Composite" is a general term for several kinds of man-made, synthetic materials, and was surrounded in some controversy. While composite materials were used as viable substitutes for more traditional materials in aerospace and defense products for many years, incentives in general aviation were different. There, most manufacturers preferred and believed in traditional aluminum. Its overall performance was good, it was low-cost, and it had been around for many decades. With composites, however, manufacturers had more opportunities to make innovations in aerodynamic shapes and airframe construction.

A more sensational innovation was the development of what the firm named the Cirrus Airframe Parachute System, or CAPS. In short, CAPS was a parachute system not for passengers, but for the aircraft as a whole, to be used in truly dire emergencies when normal emergency procedures would not suffice. CAPS was positioned behind the baggage compartment, just forward of the tail. When the system was activated, parachute lines embedded in the fuselage would "unzip." The parachute would then suspend the airplane so that it would descend in a normal, level position.

Other features included a computerized, flat-panel, multi-function instrument display panel. The display was positioned lower than usual, and along with very large windows, facilitated much better vision and awareness of the pilot's surroundings. A single lever replaced the two traditionally-separate throttle and propeller controls. Designers simplified systems, incorporated state-of-the-art avionics, personal entertainment hook-ups, and more comfortable lighting. Fuel efficiency was also emphasized, and a Continental engine was chosen as the power plant.

One of the main objectives of the prototype program was to obtain "Type Certification." Type Certification was a term used by the Federal Aviation Administration (FAR Part 21) to acknowledge that the *design* of a new aircraft was "airworthy." This certification pertained only to design, though; obtaining the FAA certification that okayed production processes

would come later. Four prototypes would be produced (different kinds of prototypes were needed to test and demonstrate different aspects of the aircraft's design, construction, and performance). Under strict supervision from the FAA, two "conforming" prototypes (i.e., close to being the commercializable version) would be built, one optimized for testing aerodynamics, and the other optimized for testing systems and safety. Two "nonconforming" prototypes were built, one specifically designated to test CAPS.

Also in that year, of course, the U.S. Congress passed the General Aviation Revitalization Act. The timing could not have been better for Cirrus, as it invigorated a bullish climate throughout the industry that had not been experienced for many years.

In March of 1995, the first prototype was ready and made its maiden flight. The second prototype was completed in November, incorporating the planned improvements over the first prototype, as well as some of the ideas that became appreciated during the prototyping of the first aircraft.

Also in that year, the company was awarded a contract from the firm Isravation, for the design, development, and fabrication of a proof of concept prototype for a turboprop aircraft, the ST50. As well, Cirrus became a subcontractor for Alliant TechSystems, Inc., and manufactured the fuselage (main body), wings, and empennage (tail) for a system called the Tactical Unmanned Aerial Vehicle (TAUV) for the United States Department of Defense. The TAUV's design included composite materials in all three of the sections built by Cirrus. Contracts like these helped sustain cash flow while the SR20 was being developed, improved the firm's overall manufacturing competencies, and gave it invaluable experience with composites.

In March of 1996, Cirrus formally applied to the FAA for FAR Part 23 Type Certification of the SR20. Soon thereafter, management felt confident enough to proceed with Phase II of its expansion, from development and into small-scale production. Construction began of a second facility in the Grand Forks Industrial park in Grand Forks, North Dakota. This locale had the advantage of proximity to less-restricted air space, which would be needed during flight testing.

In March of 1997, testing of CAPS began, using weighted barrels to simulate the weight of an aircraft. Several dozen deployments of the parachute system were completed successfully. In April, production of the first production prototype began (a prototype built to demonstrate the quality of the production system). In October, the 67,5000 square foot facility in Grand Forks was opened.

In January of 1998, the first production prototype was completed and the plane made its maiden flight. With this aircraft, Cirrus began the process of verifying its design flight characteristics. Adjacent to the headquarters/R&D facility in Duluth, operations began in a new 111,000 square foot manufacturing facility, planned for an initial production rate of one airplane per week.

In June, the second production prototype was completed and flown. This aircraft was built especially to test the fuel, avionics and electrical systems, and for verifying fundamental ergonomic features such as the location of the flight controls, visibility, and ventilation. In the same month, formal flight tests began.

In October of that year, FAA Administrator Jane Garvey (the top official in the FAA) personally awarded to Cirrus Design the Type Certificate for the SR20 at the Airplane Owners and Pilots Association Convention in Palm Springs, California. This was, in effect, the official go-ahead to make and sell the product. Everyone at Cirrus rejoiced, and the whole industry became enthused—with some ambivalence among the manufacturing incumbents, of course.

In September, Cirrus announced a purchase and supply agreement with Ballistic Recovery Systems, Inc. (BRS) the producer of CAPS parachute units and the producer of 15,000 other systems like it, used in ultralight, microlight, and other general aviation aircraft.[22] In the partnership, Cirrus would receive warrants to acquire up to 19.3 percent of BRS stock. Cirrus agreed to take purchase of hundreds of parachutes over the five years of the agreement.

On March 23, 1999, one of two Cirrus test pilots to be killed, died in a crash of an SR20.[23] In the last seconds of flight, the pilot had reported a control problem and declared an emergency. The entire company grieved, but quickly resumed production as an internal review of the aircraft's design and production processes was begun. As it always does, the National Transportation and Safety Board (NTSB) also began an extensive investigation. It was common for an NTSB investigation to last several months, but everyone was optimistic that the problem would be resolved and that progress would regain its momentum. By that time, Cirrus had amassed nearly 3,000 flying hours in the SR20. The order backlog had grown to 281, worth more than $50,000,000. It was a crucial time for the company.

On April 29, the second production aircraft was completed and flown on an "experimental" basis, a level of airworthiness granted by the FAA for just such purposes.[24] This was the first flight since the test pilot fatalities. There were no problems. On June 9th, with 316 firm orders and renewed confidence, Cirrus announced that the price of an SR20 would be raised to $179,400.[25]

On June 19, Cirrus announced that it had completed an extensive re-evaluation of the control system. Cirrus pro-actively announced six design improvements to the wing and control system.[26] These improvements would have to be fully incorporated and tested, but this was accomplished in due course, and the FAA was satisfied.

On July 20 of 1999, the first SR20 delivery was made to a private family in Plymouth, Minnesota. Said Alan Klapmeier, "This is a great day for Cirrus design and general aviation. Dale and I are proud of our employees, shareholders and customers, all of whom helped make this day possible."[27] By that month, orders for the new aircraft reached 325; 100 were scheduled for delivery over the next 12 months.

On October 18 the first international sale was consummated with the delivery of an SR20 to Europe, specifically the Netherlands.[28] The plane was purchased by the firm General Enterprises, to be used as a demonstrator in the marketing of Cirrus Aircraft. The Cirrus European sales manager reported that there had been over 1,700 requests for a demonstration flight. Remarkably, 70 airplane orders had come from Europe without a demonstrator, and the SR20 design was receiving awards in Europe before one had even been delivered there.

In November the company announced a total of 420 confirmed orders, each backed by a non-refundable $15,000 deposit.[29] Sales had jumped 300 percent in the past year, or about 20 airplanes each month. But only eight had been delivered, and only nine more were on the production line. The firm Wings Aloft of Seattle, Washington was selected as its agent for customer training in the SR20, to be conducted in Duluth and under special license elsewhere. Cirrus also had 20 firm commitments from firms wishing to become authorized service centers, with ongoing discussions for about a dozen more.

During the first quarter of 2000, 15 SR20 aircraft were delivered.[30] The order backlog was more than 550 aircraft, one-fifth of which had come in since early November.[31] One SR20 was being made every five days, with plans to increase the rate to one every day by the end of the year, and production of two, and then three a day soon thereafter. The price rose to $188,300.[32] Employment was more than 450, and a second shift was added. The Civil Aviation Safety Authority of Australia (similar in its role to the FAA) granted its Type Acceptance Certificate in May, meaning that Cirrus could sell its product in that country.[33]

On May 19, Cirrus announced that fuselage assembly would be moved to Grand Forks, along with the existing manufacture there of interior fuselage parts, interior wing parts, interior cabin parts, cowlings, baggage doors and horizontal stabilizers.[34] Production of the wings and final assembly would remain in Duluth. By early April, 24 more aircraft had been delivered, and orders were than at 557.

On June 12, the FAA granted Cirrus its formal Production Certificate for the SR20.[35] The Production Certificate confirmed that Cirrus production processes conformed to very high standards of quality, but more to the point, allowed Cirrus to manufacture airplanes independently, without the constant oversight and presence of the FAA. This certificate also placed Cirrus proudly amongst the most legitimate of aircraft manufacturers. Four employees were also granted recognition by the FAA as Designated Manufacturing Inspection Representatives (DMIR), basically delegating much inspection responsibility to Cirrus. One of these employees granted the 39th SR20 its Airworthiness Certificate.

Later that month, the first SR20 was delivered to a private customer in Australia.[36] A total of 42 airplanes had been delivered, the workforce was at 539 people, and the backlog was over 600. In July the 50th SR20 was delivered, and production was two per week.[37]

In the background since the previous September, engineering was continuing on the SR22, a four-seat aircraft similar in overall design to the SR20, but bigger and heavier, including a much more powerful, 310 horsepower engine.[38] Other improvements included a better firewall, strengthened nose gear, repositioning of the landing light, and modifications to the wing structure that allowed a greater fuel capacity. In January of 2000 design of a conforming prototype began, and certification tests began in June. In October paperwork was submitted to the FAA for certification approval, and the new design was unveiled at the Airplane Owners and Pilots Association Convention in Long Beach, California. Because of the increased weight and power, demonstrating safety was a significant challenge. But in November, the FAA approved certification, and issued an amendment to the SR20 Production Certificate, authorizing the issuance of a Certificate of Airworthiness for the SR22.[39]

By October many existing customers had changed their minds, switching their orders from the SR20 to the SR22. The backlog for the SR20 was at 459, while the backlog for the SR22 was at 178. The base price for the SR22 was between $276,000 and $294,700, depending on how an aircraft was equipped. The base price for the SR20 ranged between $183,300 and $240,000

In November the FAA approved the Type Certificate for the SR22, only 14 months after engineering development had commenced, and nine months after the application had been submitted. Delivery of the first SR22 was planned to be made by the end of the year, with production blended in with the manufacture of the SR20s in Duluth.

In December, Cirrus delivered its 100th airplane.[40] Three hundred aircraft were being planned for delivery in the upcoming year. The backlog was at 640 aircraft, 450 SR20s and 192 SR22s.

In February of 2001, Alan Klapmeir announced that the company needed some restructuring, in order to accommodate anticipated growth, refine and streamline production processes, integrate production of the SR22, and reduce costs. The workforce needed to be reduced temporarily by 127 people, down to 512. Klapmeir said "Over the last 18 months, we have grown tremendously and have accomplished a great deal. It is now time for us to capture the gains we have made in production and focus on improving efficiency."[41]

On February 6th, the first SR22 was delivered.[42] In April, Cirrus announced that SR22s destined for Europe would be equipped with diesel engines manufactured by SMA, a French firm partnered with Aerospatiale (the French member of EADS/Airbus).[43] Diesel engines were much more fuel-efficient, and diesel fuel was less expensive. The SMA engine also performed better overall, in terms of power, acceleration, etc. These factors made diesel engines more attractive to customers located where fuel cost more than it did in the United States.

In the year 2001, Cirrus was still privately held, and had about 270 investors. The advertised base price for an SR20 was $197,600; for an SR22, $276,600.[44] The order backlog was at around 600, 20 percent destined for international customers. Cirrus had an innovative "one stop-shopping" program for finance and insurance, and more than 30 authorized service centers in the United States, Europe, and Australia.

Crossroads

Over its relatively brief but fast-paced existence, Cirrus' mission had not changed much. "Cirrus Design consists of an experienced team of highly trained and motivated people whose main purpose is the development and production of leading edge aviation technology. Cirrus is committed to the revitalization of general aviation through the design, manufacture and marketing of high quality, innovative designs that provide the greatest value to customers and pilots."[45] But within that broad dream, things were poised for a potential shift in strategy.

Although the firm had been in business for 17 years, in only about the past 10 years the company had rapidly gone from being a manufacturer of a sole kit model, to a subcontractor for large aerospace concerns, to being awarded full FAA certification for one of the most novel general aircraft designs in many years. Determined and talented people had been undaunted by the industry's collective "wisdom" about composites, and successfully managed extraordinary risks that the big players had learned to avoid. Demand had exploded to the point where the production rate would have to increase several times over just to keep pace with the rate of new orders coming in (Exhibit 6). Meanwhile, the company was committed to producing a bigger and better model than the original. The news was rapidly spreading around the world and modifications were needed to optimize the aircrafts' configurations for local operating environments, not the least of which were regulatory.

However, to move from research and development to low-rate production was one thing; to move to full-scale production was another. New efficient processes and technologies would have to replace the high-tech but hand-built atmosphere that was the earmark of early product development. That could easily mean an overall change in the culture of the firm, from one of fast-paced innovation and creativity to the controlled and productive use of assets. In short, they would feel the pressure to become more like the sleepy, "professionally managed" firms they originally vowed to challenge outright for rejuvenation of the industry. Worse, to become a major manufacturer could trigger a nasty response from the big incumbents. The cyclical nature of the industry suggested that sooner or later, incumbents would feel the pressure to compete more vigorously in all facets of the total products they provided.

But in NASA's view the industry was poised for much more than a rejuvenation; it seemed poised, in only a few more years, to begin an extended renaissance. Cirrus was already involved in producing SATS technologies, and was the kind of firm that gave much hope to NASA and the SATS consortia members. Its expertise in engineering and research, product design and development, product prototyping and technology transfer, risk-management, government relations, and strategic partnering all

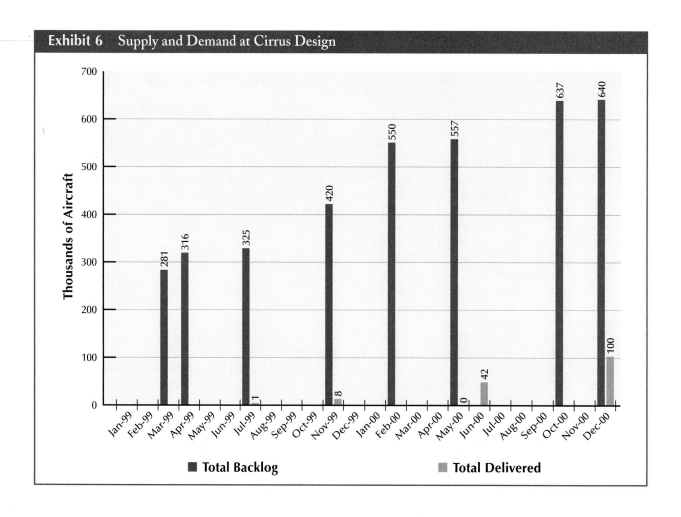

Exhibit 6   Supply and Demand at Cirrus Design

Thousands of Aircraft

- Mar-99: 281 (Total Backlog)
- Apr-99: 316 (Total Backlog)
- Jun-99: 325 (Total Backlog)
- Jul-99: 1 (Total Delivered)
- Oct-99: 420 (Total Backlog)
- Nov-99: 8 (Total Delivered)
- Jan-00: 550 (Total Backlog)
- Apr-00: 557 (Total Backlog)
- May-00: 0 (Total Delivered)
- Jun-00: 42 (Total Delivered)
- Oct-00: 637 (Total Backlog)
- Nov-00: 640 (Total Backlog)
- Dec-00: 100 (Total Delivered)

■ **Total Backlog**   ■ **Total Delivered**

seemed to be a perfect fit for the 21st-century transportation paradigm that was being nurtured.

It was a subtle choice, but one that had two diverging futures.

Notes

1. "Industry Statistics," General Aviation Manufacturer's Association, www.gama.com, June 2001.
2. "Light Plane Technologies Advance on Broad Front," NASA News Release no. 97-095, Langley Research Center, Hampton, Virginia; "Light Plane Technologies Coming to Market," Langley News Release no. 98-139, Langley Research Center, Hampton, Virginia.
3. Ross, R. "The New Commute: Embry-Riddle Researches a New Transportation System," *The Leader* (Spring 2000).
4. "NASA-led Technology Development Aimed at Increasing Mobility, Access for Smaller Communities," NASA Document FS-2001-03-59 LaRC, Langley Research Center, Hampton, Virginia.
5. "Cirrus Design Backgrounder," www.cirrus.design.com, June 2001; "Cirrus Design Mission Statement," www.cirrus.design.com, June 2001; "Cirrus Design Company Overview, Past," www.cirrus.design.com, June 2001; "Cirrus Design Company Overview, Present," www.cirrus.design.com, June 2001; "Cirrus Design Company Overview, Future," www.cirrus.design.com, June 2001; "Cirrus Design, Aircraft Introduction, Value," www.cirrus.design.com, June 2001; "Cirrus Design, Aircraft Introduction, Performance," www.cirrus.design.com, June 2001; "Cirrus Design, Aircraft Introduction, Innovation," www.cirrus.design.com, June 2001; "Cirrus Design, Aircraft Introduction, Comfort," www.cirrus.design.com, June 2001; "Cirrus Design, Aircraft Introduction, Safety," www.cirrus.design.com, June 2001; "Cirrus Design, Performance Specifications, SR20," www.cirrus.design.com, June 2001; "Cirrus Design, Performance Specifications, SR22," www.cirrus.design.com, June 2001; "Cirrus Design, FAQ: CAPS," www.cirrus.design.com, June 2001; "Cirrus Design, FAQ: Cirrus," www.cirrus.design.com, June 2001; "Cirrus Design, FAQ, Composites," www.cirrus.design.com, June 2001; "Cirrus Design, FAQ, Service," www.cirrus.design.com, June 2001; "The Cirrus SR20 Story," Cirrus Design News Release, Duluth, Minnesota, 28 July 1999.
6. "Industry Statistics," General Aviation Manufacturer's Association, www.gama.com, June 2001.
7. "Federal Code of Regulations, Federal Aviation Administration," www.faa.gov.
8. "NASA Small Aircraft Transportation System (SATS) Southeast SATSLab Consortium: An Introduction," Southeast SATSLab White Paper, sats.erau.edu, June 2001.
9. "NASA-led Technology Development Aimed at Increasing Mobility, Access for Smaller Communities," NASA Document FS-2001-03-59 LaRC, Langley Research Center, Hampton, Virginia; "National Aeronautics and Space Administration Small Aircraft Transportation System (SATS) Program Planning White Paper September 19, 2000," sats.erau.edu, 25 June 2001.
10. "Smart Airports to Extend Personal Aircraft Gains," NASA News Release 99-060, Langley Research Center, Hampton, Virginia, 31 July 1999.
11. "NASA Small Aircraft Transportation System (SATS) Southeast SATSLab Consortium: An Introduction," Southeast SATSLab White Paper, sats.erau.edu, June 2001.
12. Ross, R. "The New Commute: Embry-Riddle Researches a New Transportation System," *The Leader* (Spring 2000).
13. "NASA Small Aircraft Transportation System (SATS) Southeast SATSLab Consortium: An Introduction," Southeast SATSLab White Paper, sats.erau.edu, June 2001.
14. "Southeast SATSLab Consortium Overview of Master Plan: General Information and Program Plan," Southeast SATSLAb Consortium, sats.erau.edu, June 2001.
15. Ibid.
16. "'Smart' Airports to Extend Personal Aircraft Gains," Langley News Release no. 99-060, Langley Research Center, Hampton, Virginia.
17. "Light Plane Technologies Advance on Broad Front," NASA News Release no. 97-095, Langley Research Center, Hampton, Virginia.
18. "Low Cost Electromagnetic De-Icer for NAT Laminar Flow Airfoils," NASA SBIR Success Listings, sbir.gsfc.nasa.gov, July 2001.
19. "In Order to Bring Safe, Reliable, and Affordable General Aviation Aircraft," NASA SBIR Abstracts 1993, sbir.gsfc.nasa.gov, July 2001.
20. "Light Plane Technologies Coming to Market," Langley News Release no. 98-139, Langley Research Center, Hampton, Virginia; "High Tech Personal Airplanes Visit NASA Thursday," Langley News Release no. 99-009, Langley Research Center, Hampton, Virginia.
21. "Cirrus Design Backgrounder," www.cirrus.design.com, June 2001; "Cirrus Design Mission Statement," www.cirrus.design.com, June 2001; "Cirrus Design Company Overview, Past," www.cirrus.design.com, June 2001; "Cirrus Design Company Overview, Present," www.cirrus.design.com, June 2001; "Cirrus Design Company Overview, Future," www.cirrus.design.com, June 2001; "Cirrus Design, Aircraft Introduction, Value," www.cirrus.design.com, June 2001; "Cirrus Design, Aircraft Introduction, Performance," www.cirrus.design.com, June 2001; "Cirrus Design, Aircraft Introduction, Innovation," www.cirrus.design.com, June 2001; "Cirrus Design, Aircraft Introduction, Comfort," www.cirrus.design.com, June 2001; "Cirrus Design, Aircraft Introduction, Safety," www.cirrus.design.com, June 2001; "Cirrus Design, Performance Specifications, SR20," www.cirrus.design.com, June 2001; "Cirrus Design, Performance Specifications, SR22," www.cirrus.design.com, June 2001; "Cirrus Design, FAQ: CAPS," www.cirrus.design.com, June 2001; "Cirrus Design, FAQ: Cirrus," www.cirrus.design.com, June 2001; "Cirrus Design, FAQ, Composites," www.cirrus.design.com, June 2001; "Cirrus Design, FAQ, Service," www.cirrus.design.com, June 2001; "The Cirrus SR20 Story," Cirrus Design News Release, Duluth, Minnesota, 28 July 1999.
22. "Cirrus Design, Builder of the SR20 Aircraft, Opts for Stake in Parachute Maker, BRS," Ballisitic Recovery Systems, Inc. News Release, ST, Paul, Minnesota, 17 September 1999.
23. "Cirrus Proceeds With Delivery Plans," Cirrus Design News Release, Duluth, Minnesota, 2 April 1999.
24. "Cirrus Flies Second Production Prototype," Cirrus Design News Release, Duluth, Minnesota, 29 April 1999.
25. "SR20 Price Increases," Cirrus Design News Release, Duluth, Minnesota, 9 June 1999.
26. "NTSB Releases Cirrus SR20 Crash Information," Cirrus Design News Release, Duluth, Minnesota, 18 June 1999.
27. "Cirrus Delivers First SR20," Cirrus Design News Release, Duluth, Minnesota, 20 July 1999.
28. "Cirrus SR20 Arrives in Europe," Cirrus Design News Release, Duluth, Minnesota, 18 October 1999.
29. "Cirrus SR20 Orders Exceed 400," Cirrus Design News Release, Duluth, Minnesota, 19 November 1999.
30. "Cirrus Delivers 15 SR20 Aircraft in First Quarter," Cirrus Design News Release, Duluth, Minnesota, 9 April 2000.
31. "Cirrus SR20 Sales Top 500," Cirrus Design News Release, Duluth, Minnesota, 14 February 2000.
32. "Cirrus Announces Equipment & Price Change," Cirrus Design News Release, Duluth, Minnesota, 7 March 2000.
33. "Cirrus SR20 Certified in Australia," Cirrus Design News Release, Duluth, Minnesota, 11 May 2000.
34. "Fuselage Fabrication Moves to Grand Forks," Cirrus Design News Release, Duluth Minnesota, 19 May 2000.
35. "FAA Awards Production Certificate for SR20," Cirrus Design News Release, Duluth, Minnesota, 12 June 2000.
36. "Cirrus SR20 Arrives in Australia," Cirrus Design News Release, Duluth, Minnesota, 27 June 2000.
37. "Cirrus Design: General Aviation's Success Story," Cirrus Design News Release, Duluth, Minnesota, 26 July 2000.
38. "Cirrus Design Introduces the SR22," Long Beach, California, 20 October 2000.
39. "FAA Approves Type Certificate for Cirrus SR22," Cirrus Design News Release, Duluth, Minnesota, 30 November 2000.
40. "Cirrus Delivers its 100 SR20," Cirrus Design News Release, Duluth, Minnesota, 18 December 2000.
41. "Cirrus Design Restructuring for Growth," Cirrus Design News Release, Duluth, Minnesota, 2 February 2001.
42. "First Customer Delivery of SR22," Cirrus Design News Release, Duluth, Minnesota, 6 February 2001.

43. "SMA Diesel Engines in Cirrus Design Aircraft," Cirrus Design News Release, Friedrichshafen, Germany, 26 April 2001.

44. "Cirrus Announces Price Change for SR20," Cirrus Design News Release, Duluth, Minnesota, 1 February 2001.

45. "Cirrus Design Backgrounder," www.cirrus.design.com, June 2001; "Cirrus Design Mission Statement," www.cirrus.design.com, June 2001; "Cirrus Design Company Overview, Past," www.cirrus.design.com, June 2001; "Cirrus Design Company Overview, Present," www.cirrus.design.com, June 2001; "Cirrus Design Company Overview, Future," www.cirrus.design.com, June 2001; "Cirrus Design, Aircraft Introduction, Value," www.cirrus.design.com, June 2001; "Cirrus Design, Aircraft Introduction, Performance," www.cirrus.design.com, June 2001; "Cirrus Design, Aircraft Introduction, Innovation," www.cirrus.design.com, June 2001; "Cirrus Design, Aircraft Introduction, Comfort," www.cirrus.design.com, June 2001; "Cirrus Design, Aircraft Introduction, Safety," www.cirrus.design.com, June 2001; "Cirrus Design, Performance Specifications, SR20," www.cirrus.design.com, June 2001; "Cirrus Design, Performance Specifications, SR22," www.cirrus.design.com, June 2001; "Cirrus Design, FAQ: CAPS," www.cirrus.design.com, June 2001; "Cirrus Design, FAQ: Cirrus," www.cirrus.design.com, June 2001; "Cirrus Design, FAQ, Composites," www.cirrus.design.com, June 2001; "Cirrus Design, FAQ, Service," www.cirrus.design.com, June 2001.

Case 22

Moss Adams, LLP

Armand Gilinsky, Jr. and Sherri Anderson, *Sonoma State University*

In early January 2001, Jeff Gutsch, Senior Manager at Moss Adams, LLP, an accounting firm located in Santa Rosa, California, met with his team to discuss the progress of a new initiative for developing the firm's accounting practice to serve clients in the Northern California wine industry. At the meeting, Gutsch and his wine niche team reviewed the strategic plan for the coming year. (See Exhibit 1, "2001 Wine Niche Strategic Plan.")

The meeting took place just before the height of the busy tax and audit season. Gutsch, 39, had been concentrating on the firm's clients in its construction industry niche. He had not made as much headway developing new business with wine industry clients as he had hoped and opened the meeting by saying:

> I think the issue we are all struggling with is how to break into a well-established mature niche. Do we discount fees? If so, is that our desired position in servicing the wine industry? Do we advertise? Seems like a big commitment for something that we can't be sure will produce results. Do we just get on every panel we can and shake as many hands as we can? I'm still trying to find the right formula.

Chris Pritchard, an Accounting Manager who had worked with Gutsch for two years to develop the wine niche, said:

> Sorry, Jeff, but I've been too busy working in healthcare. Healthcare is taking off, so my time is limited on the wine side. There's something missing, sort of a spark in this niche. There's not as much of a hunger to close, to go out and actually close a deal, or at least go out and meet

with somebody. I think that's what's lacking for our success right now. I think we have all of the tools we need. But we don't have an aggressive nature to go out and start shaking hands and asking for business. We're doing everything else except asking for the business. We don't follow up.

Neysa Sloan, a Senior Accountant, nodded in assent:

> I personally do not see us making our objectives of gathering 20 percent of the market share in the regional wine industry over the next 3–5 years. Our marketing tactics are not up to the challenge. We need to seriously look at what we have done in the last year or two, what we are currently doing, and what we are proposing to do in regards to marketing. If we looked at this objectively, we would see that we have not gained much ground in the past using our current tactics—why would it work now? If you allowed more individuals to market and be involved, we might get somewhere.

Cheryl Mead, a Senior Manager whose specialty was conducting cost segregation* studies, commented:

> Growing wineries are looking for help. We need to focus on wineries that are expanding their facilities, and then grow with their growing businesses. Value-added services like cost segregation could represent as much as 40 percent of our wine industry practice. If we want to get in, we've got to do much more networking, marketing, and presentations. The challenge for us here in Santa Rosa is how to manage our resources. Career choices are changing; you can't be a generalist anymore. We need both people-related and technical skills, but those don't usually go hand-in-hand. We need someone who is famous in the field, a "who's who" in the wine accounting industry.

* Cost segregation is a process of breaking a large asset into its smaller components so that depreciation may be taken on an accelerated basis.

Exhibit 1   2001 Wine Niche Strategic Plan

Moss Adams LLP
Santa Rosa Office
Wine Industry Advisors
2001 Strategic Plan

Mission Statement

Our goal is to become the dominant accounting and business consulting firm serving the wine industry by providing superior, value-added services tailored to the needs of Northern California vineyards and wineries, as well as becoming experts in the industry.

- We expect to achieve this goal by December 31, 2004.

Five-Year Vision

We are recognized as the premier wine industry accounting and business consulting firm in Sonoma, Mendocino and Napa counties. We are leaders in the Moss Adams firm-wide wine industry group, helping to establish Moss Adams as the dominant firm in the Washington and Oregon wine regions. We have trained and developed recognized industry experts in tax, accounting and business consulting. Our staff is enthusiastic and devoted to the niche.

The Market

- A firm wide objective is to increase the average size of our business client. We expect to manage the wine niche with that objective in mind. However, during the first two to three years, we intend to pursue vineyards and wineries smaller than the firm's more mature niches would. When this niche is more mature we will increase our minimum prospect size. This strategy will help us gain experience, and build confidence in Moss Adams in the industry, as it is an industry that tends to seek firms that are well established in the Wine Industry.

- There are approximately 122 wineries in Sonoma County, 168 in Napa County and 25 in Mendocino County. Of these approximately 55 percent have sales over $1 million, and up to one-third have sales in excess of $10 million. In addition to these, there are over 450 vineyards within the same three counties.

- The wine industry appears to be extremely provincial. That combined with the fact that most of our stronger competitors (see "Competition" below) are in Napa County, we consider Sonoma County to be our primary geographic market. However Mendocino County has a growing wine industry, and we certainly will not pass up opportunities in Napa and other nearby counties in 2001.

Our Strengths

The Strengths Moss Adams has in competing in this industry are:

- We are large enough to provide the specific services demanded by this industry.

- Our firm's emphasis is on serving middle market businesses, while the "Big 5" firms are continually increasing their minimum client size. The majority of the wine industry is made up of middle market companies. This "Big 5" trend increases our market each year.

- We do not try to be all things to all people. We focus our efforts in specialized industries/niches, with the goal of ultimately becoming dominant in those industries.

- We emphasize value-added services, which create more client satisfaction, loyalty, and name recognition.

- We have offices located throughout the West Coast wine regions.

- We have individuals within the firm with significant wine industry experience, including tax, accounting and consulting. We also have experts in closely related industries such as orchards, beverage, and food manufacturing.

- Within California, we have some high profile wine industry clients.

- The majority of our niche members have roots in Sonoma County, which is important to Sonoma County wineries and grape growers.

- Our group is committed to being successful in and ultimately dominating the industry in Sonoma, Napa and Mendocino counties.

Challenges

- Our experience and credibility in the wine industry is low compared to other firms.

- There has been a perception in the Sonoma County area that we are not local to the area. As we continue to grow and become better known, this should be less of an issue.

If we can minimize our weaknesses by emphasizing our strengths, we will be successful in marketing to the wine industry, allowing us to achieve our ultimate goal of being dominant in the industry.

Competition

There are several CPA firms in northern California that service vineyards and wineries. The "Big 5" firms are generally considered our biggest competitors in many of the industries we serve, and some have several winery clients. But as noted earlier, their focus seems to be on larger clients, which has decreased their ability to compete in this industry. Of the firms with significant wine industry practices, the following firms appear to be our most significant competitors:

- Motto Kryla & Fisher—This firm is a well-established wine industry leader, with the majority of their client base located in Napa County, although they have many Sonoma County clients. They are moving away from the traditional accounting and tax compliance services, concentrating their efforts on consulting and research projects. We can

Exhibit 1   2001 Wine Niche Strategic Plan (continued)

take advantage of this, along with the perception of many in the industry that they are becoming too much of an insider, and gain additional market share.

- Dal Pagetto & Company—This firm was a split off from Deloitte & Touche several years ago. They are located in Santa Rosa, and have several vineyard and winery clients. At this time, they are probably our biggest Sonoma County competitor, however, they may be too small to compete once our momentum builds.

- Other firms that have significant wine industry practices that we will compete against include G & J Seiberlich & Co., Brotemarkle Davis & Co., Zainer Reinhart & Clarke, Pisenti & Brinker, Deloitte & Touche, and PriceWaterhouseCoopers. The first two are wine industry specialists headquartered in Napa County, and although very competitive there, they each do not appear to have a large Sonoma County client base. The next two are general practice firms with several wine industry clients. However, each of these firms has struggled to hold themselves together in recent years, and do not appear to have well coordinated wine industry practices. The last two firms listed above are "Big 5" firms that, as noted earlier, focus mostly on the largest wineries.

Annual Marketing Plan

Our marketing strategy will build on the foundation we laid during the prior two years. We have established the following as our marketing plan:

- Increase and develop industry knowledge and expertise:
  - ○ Work with other Moss Adams offices, particularly Stockton, to gain knowledge and experience from their experienced staff. Additionally, work with Stockton to have Santa Rosa Wine Niche staff assigned to two of their winery audits.
  - ○ Continue to attend industry CPE, including the Vineyard Symposium, the Wine Industry Symposium, the California State Society of CPAs sponsored wine industry conferences in Napa and San Louis Obispo, and selected Sonoma State University and UC Davis courses. We would like eight hours of wine industry specific CPE for each Senior Level and above committed member of the Wine Niche. Jeff will have final approval on who will attend which classes.
  - ○ Continue to build our relationship with Sonoma State University (SSU). Our wine niche has agreed to be the subject of a SSU case study on the development of a CPA firm wine industry practice. We feel this case study will help us gain additional insight into what it will take to be competitive, as well as give us increased exposure both at SSU and in the industry. We will also seek to become more involved in SSU's wine industry educational program by providing classroom guest speakers twice a year.

  - ○ Attract and hire staff with wine industry experience. We should strongly consider candidates who have attained a degree through the SSU Wine Business Program. We should also work to recruit staff within the office that have an interest in the industry.

- Continue to form alliances with industry experts both inside and outside the firm. We are building relationships with Ray Blatt of the Moss Adams Los Angeles office who has expertise in wine industry excise and property tax issues. Cheryl Mead of the Santa Rosa office has developed as a Cost Segregation specialist with significant winery experience.

- Develop and use relationships with industry referral sources:
  - ○ Bankers and attorneys that specialize in the wine industry. From these bankers and attorneys, we would like to see three new leads per year.
  - ○ Partner with other CPA firms in the industry. Smaller firms may need to enlist the services of a larger firm with a broader range of services, while the "Big 5" firms may want to use a smaller firm to assist with projects that are below their minimum billing size for the project type. We will obtain at least two projects per year using this approach.
  - ○ Leverage the relationships we have to obtain five referrals and introductions to other wine industry prospects per year.
  - ○ We will maintain a matrix of Sonoma, Mendocino, and Napa County wineries and vineyards, including addresses, controller or top financial officer, current CPA, and banking relationship. This matrix will be updated as new information becomes available. From this matrix, we will send at least one mailing per quarter.

- Increase our involvement in the following industry trade associations by attending regular meetings and getting to know association members. In one of the following associations, each committed niche member will seek to obtain an office or board position:
  - ○ Sonoma County Wineries Association
  - ○ Sonoma County Grape Growers Association
  - ○ Sonoma State University Wine Business Program
  - ○ Zinfandel Advocates and Producers
  - ○ Women for Winesense
  - ○ California Association of Winegrape Growers
  - ○ Wine Institute

- Establish an environment within the niche that promotes and practices the PILLAR concept. Encourage staff in the niche to be creative and strive to be the best. Provide interesting projects and events for the niche to make participation more interesting.

- Use the existing services that Moss Adams offers to market the firm which include:

Exhibit 1   2001 Wine Niche Strategic Plan (continued)

- ○ BOSS
- ○ Business Valuations
- ○ Cost Segregation
- ○ SCORE!
- ○ SALT
- ○ Business Assurance Services
- ○ Income Tax Compliance Services
- • Make use of Firm Resources
  - ○ Use Moss Adams' Info Edge (document management system) to share and refer to industry related proposals and marketing materials.
    - • All Wine Niche Proposals will be entered into and updated in InfoEdge as completed.
    - • All Wine Niche Marketing letters will be entered into InfoEdge as created.
- • Continue to have monthly wine industry niche meetings. We will review the progress on this plan at our March, April and September niche meetings. Within our niche, we should focus our marketing efforts on Sonoma County, concentrating on smaller prospects that we can grow with, which will enable us to increase our prospect

size over time. We would like to be in position to attract the largest wineries in the industry by 2004.

- • Establish a Quarterly CFO/Controller roundtable group, with the Moss Adams Wine Industry Group working as facilitator. We will have the Group established and have our first meeting in the summer.
- • Quarterly, at our niche meetings, monitor progress on the quantifiable goals in this strategic plan.

Summary

In 2001, one of our goals is to add a minimum of three winery clients to our client base. We feel this is a reasonable goal as long as we continue to implement our plan as written.

We believe we can make the wine industry niche a strong niche in the Santa Rosa office. The firm defines niche dominance as having a minimum of $500,000 in billings, a 20 percent market share, and having 40 percent of the services provided be in value-added service codes. We expect to become the dominant industry force in Sonoma, Mendocino and Napa Counties by 2004.

We are also willing to assist other offices within the firm establish wine industry niches, eventually leading to a mature niche within the firm. We believe with the proper effort, we can accomplish each of these goals.

Claire Calderon, also a Senior Tax Manager, said to the team:

> This is a hard niche to break into, Jeff. It takes a long time to develop relationships in specific industries. It could take a couple of years. First you find forums to meet people, get to know people, get people to trust you and then you get an opportunity to work on a project and you do a good job. It takes a while. Our goal is to become a trusted advisor and that doesn't happen overnight.

Gutsch replied:

> While consolidation is happening in the wine industry, many of the wineries we are targeting are still privately owned. When you're dealing with privately owned businesses it's much more personal than with public companies.

Calderon added:

> That might explain part of it, Jeff, but the reality is that there are two other fledgling niches that are doing well and going like gangbusters. This niche is off to a slow start!

Barbara Korte, a Senior Accountant, reassured him:

> Jeff, you have been very focused, very enthusiastic about this project. You've put a lot of time into it. As a leader, I think you are a real good manager.

At stake was the opportunity to generate significant incremental client fee revenues. More than 600 wine producers and vineyards (grape growers) were in business in the premium Northern California wine-growing region encompassing Napa, Sonoma, and Mendocino counties. According to the Summer 2000 issue of *Marketplace*, there were 168 wine producers and 228 vineyards in Napa; 122 wine producers and 196 vineyards in Sonoma; and 25 wine producers and 61 vineyards in Mendocino. Few of these operations were large, according to *Marketplace*. Napa and Sonoma each had 14 wine producers reporting over $10 million in sales, and Mendocino, only one.

Company Background

Moss Adams was a regional accounting firm. It had four regional hubs within the firm: southern California, northern California, Washington and Oregon. By late 2000, Moss Adams had become one of the 15 largest accounting firms in the United States, with 150 partners, 740 CPAs, and 1,200 employees. Founded in 1913 and headquartered in Seattle, the full-service firm specialized in middle-market companies, those with annual revenues of $10 million–$200 million.

Each office had a managing partner. Art King was the managing partner of the Santa Rosa office. [See Exhibit 2 for The Santa Rosa office organization chart.] The firm was considered mid-size and its client base tended to mirror that size. King reflected on Moss Adams' advantages of size and location:

> … it is an advantage to be a regional firm with a strong local presence. For one thing, there just aren't that many regional firms, especially out here on the West Coast. In fact, I think we're the only true West Coast regional firm. That gives us access to a tremendous number of resources that the larger firms have. We have the added advantage of being a big part of Sonoma County. Sonoma County companies want the same kind of services they can get from the Big Five operating out of places like San Francisco, but they also like to deal with local firms that are active in the community. Our staff is active in Rotary, 20–30, the local chambers of commerce, and so on, and that means a lot to the business-people in the area. Sonoma County companies will go to San Francisco for professional services, but only if they have to, so we offer the best of both worlds.

Each office within the firm was differentiated. An office like Santa Rosa had the ability to be strong in more niches because it was one of the dominant firms in the area. Moss Adams did not have to directly compete with the Big Five accounting firms as they are not interested in providing services to small to mid-size business. Since it was a regional firm, Moss Adams was able to offer a depth of services that most local firms were not able to match. This gave Moss Adams a competitive advantage when selling services to the middle market company segment.

Moss Adams provided services in four main areas of expertise: business assurance (auditing), tax, international, and consulting. Auditing comprised approximately 35-40 percent of Moss Adams's practice, the remainder being divided among tax work in corporate, partnerships, trusts and estates, and individual taxation. In its Santa Rosa office, Moss Adams serviced corporate business and high-wealth individuals.

On the international side, Moss Adams was a member of Moores Rowland International, a worldwide association of accounting firms. Moss Adams primarily worked with local companies that did business overseas or that wanted to set up a foreign location. It also did a lot of work with local companies that had parent firms located overseas.

On the consulting side, Moss Adams had about 80 full-time consultants, and this line of business represented probably 15–20 percent of the total practice. A large part of the consulting work performed by Moss Adams was in mergers and acquisitions. Its M&A division helped middle-market companies, which formed the bulk of its clientele, develop a coherent, consistent strategy, whether they were planning on selling the business and needed to find an appropriate buyer or were looking for a good acquisition target.

The Big Six (now Big Five) accounting firms had developed niche strategies in the eighties, and Moss Adams had been one of the first mid-level accounting firms in the nation to identify niches as a strategy. Adopting a niche strategy had allowed Moss Adams to target a basket of services to a particular industry of regional importance. As each practice developed a niche, it also identified the "famous people" in that niche. These people became the "go-to persons," the leaders of that niche.

The high technology sector represented one of the fastest-growing parts of Moss Adams's business. According to King:

> It's big in the Seattle area [where Moss Adams has its headquarters], and with the development of Telecom Valley, it's certainly becoming big in Sonoma County. We're finding that a great deal of our work is coming from companies that are offshoots of other large high-tech companies in the area. Financial institutions represent another client group that's growing rapidly, as is health care. With all of the changes in the health care and medical fields, there's been a good deal of turmoil. We have a lot of expertise in the health care and medical areas, so that's a big market for us. Have I seen a drop-off? No, not really. The interesting thing about the accounting industry is that even when the economy slows down, there's still a lot of work for a CPA firm. There might not be as many large, special projects as when the economy is really rolling, but the work doesn't slow down.

The Industry and the Market

Accounting was a large and relatively stable service industry, according to *The Journal of Accountancy*, the industry's most widely-read trade publication. The Big Five accounting firms (Andersen Worldwide, PriceWaterhouseCoopers,

Exhibit 2   Moss Adams' Santa Rosa, California Organizational Chart

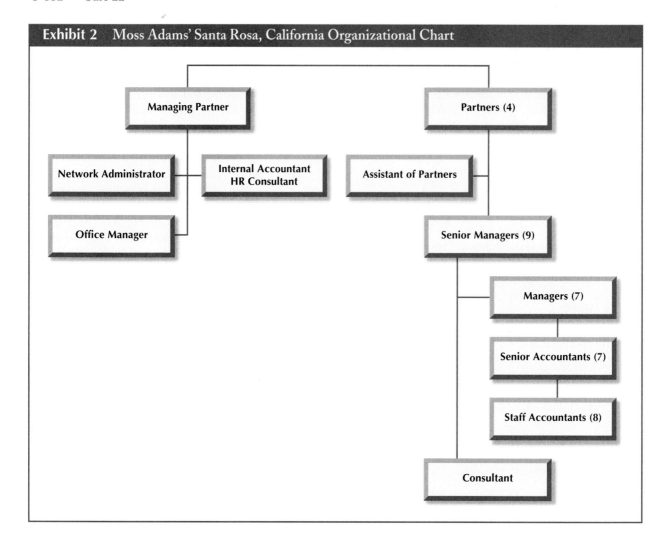

Ernst & Young, Deloitte & Touche, and KPMG) dominated the global market in 1998 with combined global revenue exceeding $58 billion, well over half the industry's total revenue. All of the Big Five firms reported double-digit growth rates in 1998. However, some of the most spectacular growth was achieved by firms outside the top 10, some of which registered increases of nearly 60 percent over 1997 revenues. Ninety of the top 100 firms had revenue increases, and 58 of them had achieved double-digit gains.

In 1999, accounting industry receipts in the U.S. exceeded $65 billion. The industry now employed greater than 632,000 people. However, the industry was expected to post more modest growth in revenues and employment into the 21st century. Finding niche markets, diversifying services, and catering to global markets were key growth strategies for companies in the industry. Large international firms, including the Big Five, had branched out into management consulting services in the late 1980s and early 1990s.

Accounting firms and certified public accountants (CPAs) nationwide began offering a wide array of services in addition to traditional accounting, auditing, and bookkeeping services. This trend was partially a response to clients' demand for "one-stop shopping" for all their professional services needs. Another cause was the relatively flat growth in demand for traditional accounting and auditing services over the past 10 years, as well as the desire of CPAs to develop more value-added services. The addition of management consulting, legal, and other professional services to the practice mix of large national accounting networks was transforming the industry.

Many firms began offering technology consulting because of growing client demand for Internet and electronic commerce services. *Accounting Today's* 1999 survey of CPA clients indicated that keeping up with technology was *the* strategic issue of greatest concern, followed by recruiting and retaining staff, competing with larger companies, planning for executive succession, and maximizing productivity.

However, according to *The CPA Journal*, the attractive consulting fees may have led many firms to ignore potential conflicts of interest in serving as an auditor and as a management consultant to the same client. The profession's standards could be jeopardized by the entrance of non-CPA partners and owners in influential accounting firms. Many companies facing these problems had split their accounting and management consulting operations. In January 2001, Arthur Andersen had spun off its consulting division and renamed it as "Accenture" to avoid accusations of impropriety.

Still, CPA firms could be expected to continue to develop their capabilities and/or strategic alliances to meet clients' demands. Some other areas of expansion among accounting firms included: administrative services, financial and investment planning services, general management services, government administration, human resources, international operations, information technology and computer systems consulting, litigation support, manufacturing administration, marketing, and research and development. Many small and medium-size independent firms were merging or forming alliances with large service companies such as American Express, H&R Block, and Century Business Services.

By the late 1990s, a trend toward consolidation got under way in the accounting industry. Several factors were fueling the drive toward consolidation. Large increases in revenue among the top 100 accounting firms between 1997 and 1998 may have been partially attributable to this trend toward consolidation. Consolidators wanted access to the large volume of business currently being done by independent CPAs. The trust that small businesses and individuals had in their CPAs was considered very valuable, and consolidators wanted to leverage the potential of an individual firm's integrity to expand their own businesses. Consolidation caused a decline in the number of independent accounting films that offered only tax and accounting services. The New York State Society of CPAs estimated that there was a strong possibility that up to 50 of the largest accounting firms in the United States would dissolve or merge with other entities by the end of the year 2000. In the San Francisco Bay Area, for example, the Big Five dominated the industry. [See Exhibit 3, "Top 20 Accounting Firms in the SF Bay Area."]

The Wine Industry Niche

The wine industry practice was a new niche for the Santa Rosa office, as well as Moss Adams in general. Moss Adams allowed any employee to propose a niche. All accounting firms bill at fairly standard rates so the more business that is generated the greater the profit. Moss Adams felt is was in their long-term best interest to allow employees to focus on areas in which they were interested. The firm would benefit from revenues generated, but more importantly employees would likely stay with a firm that allowed a degree of personal freedom and promoted professional growth.

Gutsch and Pritchard had begun this niche in mid-1998 for several reasons. First, both had an interest in the industry. Second, Sonoma and Napa counties had over two hundred wineries and numerous vineyard operations. Third, Moss Adams had expertise in related or similar business lines such as orchards, as well as significant related experience in providing services to the manufacturing sector. Finally, the wine industry had been historically serviced by either large firms that considered the typical winery a small client, or by smaller firms that were not able to offer the range of services that Moss Adams could provide.

Sara Rogers, a Senior Accountant and member of the wine niche team, recalled:

> It first started with Jeff Gutsch and Chris Pritchard and another Senior Manager, who was in our office until November, 1999. Anyway, I think it was their motivation that really started the group. The three of them were doing everything in building the niche. When the Senior Manager left, it sort of fell flat on its face for a little while. I think it got stagnant. Pretty much nobody said anything about it until last summer, when Jeff started the organization of it again and brought in more people, and then he approached people that he wanted to work with.

Gutsch felt that Moss Adams was in position to move forward to make the wine industry niche a strong niche both in the Santa Rosa office, and eventually the firm as a whole. He was committed to that goal and expected to achieve it within five years. Gutsch saw this niche as his door to future partnership. Moss Adams's marketing strategy included the following:

1. Develop industry marketing materials which communicate Moss Adams' strengths and commitment

2. Develop a distinctive logo for use in the industry

3. Create an industry brochure similar to that of the firm's construction industry group

4. Develop industry service information flyers such as the business lifecycle, R&E (Research & Exploration) credit, excise tax compliance and BOSS (Business Ownership Succession Services)

5. Develop relationships with industry referral sources (e.g. bankers and attorneys that specialized in the wine industry or current clients who served or had contacts in the industry)

6. Join and become active in industry trade associations

7. Use existing relationships with industry contacts to obtain leads into prospective wineries and vineyards

8. Use the existing services that Moss Adams offered to market the firm, particularly in Cost Segregation

9. Focus efforts on Sonoma County, as well as adjacent wine-growing regions, which would enable Moss Adams to increase its prospect size over time.

Pritchard reflected on those early days:

The first thing we did was to develop a database of regional wineries and send out an introduction letter. The other thing we did was to develop marketing materials. Jeff developed a logo. We used a top-down approach pyramid for an introduction letter, starting out general and then with an action step at the end to call us. So, we used that at first. Usually with that we'd get about two percent response which is good out of 300 letters or whatever we sent out.

However, according to King, the major issue in growing the wine industry practice was selling:

The thing about selling in public accounting is that you have to have a lot of confidence in what you do and what you can do for the client. You have to have confidence that you know something about the industry. If you go into a marketing meeting, or a proposal meeting and you're saying, "Well, we do a couple of wineries but we really want to do more and get better at

Exhibit 3   Top 20 Accounting Firms in SF Bay Area, Ranked by Number of Bay Area CPAs, June 2000

Rank	1999 Rank	Company	No. Bay Area CPAs	No. Company CPAs	No. Bay Area Employees	1999 Billings Bay Area	No. Partners in Bay Area	No. Company Partners	FYE	U.S. Net Revenue ($mil)	% Change Vs. Prev. Year
1	2	Deloitte & Touche LLP	439	8380	1437	NR	172	2066	May-99	$5,336.00	24.2
2	1	PricewaterhouseCoopers LLP	430	430	2000	NR	138	9000	Sep-99	6,956.00	18.7
3	3	KPMG Peat Marwick LLP	316	NR	1778	NR	157	6800	Jun-99	4,112.00	21.5
4	4	Arthur Andersen (ex. consulting)	312	6161	821	NR	63	3059	Aug-99	3,300.00	17.9
5	5	Ernst & Young LLP	300	NR	850	NR	77	2465	Sep-99	6,100.00	10.0
6	6	BDO Seidman LLP	72	1650	122	NR	15	360	Jun-00	408.00	36.9
7	14	Seiler & Co. LLP	44	44	110	NR	12	12	NR	NR	NR
8	7	Frank, Rimerman & Co. LLP	43	51	76	NR	12	13	May-99	17.23	9.2
9	9	Hood & Strong LLP	42	42	89	NR	12	12	NR	NR	NR
10*	10	Harb, Levy & Weiland LLP	38	38	80	NR	13	13	NR	NR	NR
10*	13	Ireland San Filippo LLP	38	38	81	12.7M	13	17	Apr-00	12.71	15.8
12	15	Burr, Pilger & Mayer	35	35	110	NR	10	10	NR	NR	NR
13	11	Armanino McKenna LLP	34	34	87	NR	13	13	NR	NR	NR
14	14	Novogradac & Co. LLP	31	36	80	NR	6	8	NR	NR	NR
15	12	RINA Accountancy Corp.	26	29	59	7.3M	13	14	NR	NR	NR
16*	16	Grant Thornton LLP	25	1300	90	NR	10	300	Jul-00	416.00	10.9
16*	18	Shea Labagh Dobberstein	25	25	35	NR	3	3	NR	NR	NR
18	18	Moss Adams LLP	24	800	39	NR	7	144	Dec-99	109.00	31.3
19	16	Lindquist, von Husen & Joyce	23	23	47	NR	5	5	NR	NR	NR
20	21	Lautze & Lautze	21	28	39	NR	9	11	NR	NR	NR

Sources: Viva Chan, *San Francisco Business Times,* June 16, 2000, v14 i46, p 28; Strafford Publications, *Public Accounting Reports,* Vol. XXIV, June, 2000.
NR = Not Reported
* indicates tie in ranking

it," you're not going to get the work. You gain confidence by knowing how to talk the language, knowing the buzzwords, knowing some of the players in the industry. You go into a meeting, all of a sudden you're on an equal footing with them. From a confidence standpoint, that's huge. You can't sell public accounting services unless you're confident about you and your firm and the people that are going to do the work. Over the last two years, Jeff has gone to the classes, gone to the meetings, and his confidence level is much higher than it was a year ago. When he goes into these meetings he's going to be at a level where he doesn't have to make excuses for not having a lot of winery clients, because we have a lot of activity in the wine and the beverage processing industries. So, I think that's going to help a lot. That's where he's going to have more success because we're getting the at bats, we just need to get some hits.

One of the roles of the Managing Partner was to mentor potential partners and help them attain the role of partner. The training process included marketing and helping them build a practice, according to King:

When we're talking with senior managers, I explain to them what they need to do to get to that next level. I had this conversation with Jeff because his primary focus when he came was, " I need to build a big practice, nothing else matters." He trusts the system now. He's transferred some clients to others and received some clients. You have to work well with people, you have to train people, you have to have some responsibilities, and you have to get along with your peers.

The firm's philosophy was to encourage people to really enjoy what they did. Anyone was allowed to propose a niche, even a Senior Manager. Pritchard explained:

Well, part of the way our firm works is, there is a "four-bucket" tier to make Partner. One of the buckets is to become a famous person and the fastest way of doing that is through the niche base; within a niche you get the experience and the reputation faster than you would as a generalist. Jeff is a Senior Manager, so now he's trying to figure a way to become partner. I work on Bonny Doon Winery. I have a grower client in Kenwood, so I do have some experience with that. I also like wine because I make wine. It's an untapped market in Sonoma County for our

firm. So we both got together—I had the entrepreneurial spirit to start and Jeff had the need.

King described in detail the "four bucket" evaluation system at Moss Adams:

We have four criteria that get evaluated by the partner and the compensation committee on a scale of one-to-ten. All of these are weighted equally, 25 percent, with a possibility of 40 points. The first is financial. We take a look at the potential partner's financial responsibilities, what their billings are, what their fee adjustments are, what their charge hours are. I've transferred many clients to people in the office. That's one way I help others grow their practices. I'm still responsible for some of those clients, because I'm the one who brought them in and I'm still the primary contact. My billing numbers may be this, but my overall financial responsibility may be bigger. That's an objective measure because we look at the numbers, we look at the trends.

The second is responsibility. Managing Partner of a big office gets more points than the Managing Partner of a smaller office does, who in turn gets more points than a person in charge of a niche, who in turn gets more points than a line partner. Somebody who is a Partner and is responsible for the tax department, let's say, might get an extra point or half a point, whereas someone in charge of a niche might get an extra point. If they're in charge of an office they get more points.

The third is personnel. Personnel is a very big initiative within Moss Adams. Upstream and downstream evaluations are conducted by our HR person for each office and measures staff retention and the quality of our mentoring program. Each partner is also evaluated up or down from an overall office rating score. For example, our office may get a "seven," but I may get an "eight" because I'm really good with people. Somebody who's really hard on people would get a lower rating.

The fourth and final "bucket" is peer evaluation. We have three other partners evaluate each partner. They evaluate the partner for training, mentoring, marketing, and involvement in their community. Then, evaluations are used by the Compensation Committee to review individual Partner compensation. They are also used for Partner counseling sessions.

King also assured a "soft landing" to the participants of the niche teams. This meant that if a niche didn't work out, he would assure the individual that another niche in the firm would be found for them. This, it was hoped, fostered entrepreneurial behaviors that had their potential upsides and downsides. According to King:

> A high level of practice responsibility for a partner would be $1 million in this office. The range is anywhere from $600,000 to $1 million in billings a year. The overall picture is, where we try to get people involved in at least two niches in the office, until a niche becomes large enough that you can spend full-time in it. The upside potentially of the wine niche would be a practice of from $500,000 to $1,000,000 based on Sonoma and maybe some Napa County wineries. So, the upside is a very mature, profitable niche that fits right into our model of our other niches of middle market companies that have the need, not only for client services, but also our value added services.

If for some reason the wine niche didn't take off, Jeff would become more involved in the manufacturing niche—well, wine is manufacturing anyway, but it's just a subset of manufacturing. It might slow his rate to partner. It could also turn out that—all of a sudden—Jeff gets four great referrals in the manufacturing niche this year, he builds this great big practice in manufacturing, and as a result he has less time for the wine niche. The downside is we've spent some money on marketing, and Jeff has spent some time on marketing when he could have been doing something else. Then, we abandon the project. If that happens, then Jeff's time becomes available and the money becomes available to go after some other initiative or something we're already doing or some new initiative. Nobody is going to lose his/her job over it. We haven't lost a lot of money over it.

The Aftermath

After the January 2001 meeting, Gutsch pondered how he should proceed to overcome some major roadblocks to building his team. King took Gutsch aside for counseling:

> … target the $10 million to under $20 million winery for which we can provide a full range of services. There's nobody else with our range of services that's really doing a good job in that area. There's an under-served market for those middle market companies. When you started, I knew it would take two or three years to really get the ball rolling. This is really going to be your year, Jeff. If it isn't, well, we'll re-evaluate at the end of the year. Our overall marketing budget is probably in the area of 1.5 percent to two percent of total client billings. In 1999, the first year for the wineries, we probably spent somewhere in the neighborhood of $5,000 to $8,000, which wasn't a lot but you joined some organizations and you did some training. Last year we probably spent $10,000 to $12,000. Now, Jeff, I know that some of our other offices spend a lot more on marketing than we do. We'll have to decide: is this the best use of your time? Is this the best use of our resources to try to go after an industry where we just tried for three years and haven't made any inroads?

The decision to develop a niche had been based upon a gut feeling. Moss Adams did not use any litmus test or hurdle rate of return to screen possible niches. This was because, with the exception of non-profits, most clients had similar fee realization rates. Moss Adams looked at the potential volume of business and determined whether it could handle that volume. Yet Moss Adams remained unknown in the wine industry. Time was running out.

Case 23

Peapod, Inc. and the Online Grocery Business

Alan B. Eisner and Nicole Belmont, *Pace University*

Acknowledgements: Many thanks to Arthur A. Thompson, Jr. for his helpful comments, edits, and improvements.

Peapod, Inc., co-founded by Andrew B. Parkinson and Thomas L. Parkinson in 1989, was a $68 million online grocery service that used both its own central warehouses and the retail stores of supermarket partners to fill customers' grocery orders. Peapod was the pioneer of the online grocery industry, getting its start on the Internet well before the Internet became a global phenomenon and well before such competitors as HomeGrocer.com, Webvan, and Netgrocer.com were even organized. However, the company had grown more slowly than first anticipated, revising its "trial and error" strategy several times to find a formula that would attract more customers and make the company profitable. In September 1999, co-founder Andrew Parkinson relinquished the position of CEO and turned the reins over to new president and CEO, Bill Malloy, who had been recruited from AT&T Wireless to fine tune and execute the Peapod's latest order fulfillment strategy and capitalize on what the co-founders believed was a blossoming opportunity in online grocery sales. Parkinson remained on as chairman of Peapod's board of directors.

Malloy faced three daunting challenges at Peapod. He had to prove that the company's newly revised business model was viable, that the company could be made profitable after six years of mounting losses, and that it could withstand competition from HomeGrocer.com, which had recently allied itself with Amazon.com, and from newly-formed Webvan, which raised over $350 million in its initial public offering of common stock in the second half of 1999.

Company Background

Founded in 1989 by brothers, Andrew and Thomas Parkinson, Peapod was an early pioneer in e-commerce,

inventing an online home-shopping service for grocery items years ahead of the commercial emergence of the Internet. With its tagline "Smart Shopping for Busy People," the company began providing consumers with a home shopping experience in the early 1990s, going so far as to install modems in their homes to provide an online connection. From its founding in 1989 until 1998, the company's business model involved filling customer orders by forming alliances with traditional grocery retailers. The company chose a retail partner in each geographic area where it operated and used the partner's local network of retail stores to pick and pack orders for delivery to customers. Peapod personnel would cruise the aisles of a partner's stores, selecting the items each customer ordered, pack and load them into Peapod vehicles, and then deliver them to customers at times chosen by customers. Peapod charged customers a fee for its service and it also collected fees from its retail supply partners for using their products in its online service. Over the next several years, Peapod built delivery capabilities in eight market areas:

Chicago, IL	San Francisco/San Jose, CA
Columbus, Ohio	Dallas, TX
Houston, TX	Austin, TX
Boston, MA	Long Island NY

The company steadily built a base of about 90,000 to 100,000 customers across all eight markets, filling over 700,000 orders annually in 1999. Peapod's revenues rose from $8.0 million in 1994 to $68.4 million in 1998—see Exhibit 1. Meanwhile, it made improvements in its Web site (www.peapod.com) and invested in proprietary software technologies to facilitate efficient order fulfillment and delivery routes, accumulate data on customer buying patterns, and better integrate pricing, merchandising, and product promotion. The company went public in June 1997, offering shares at $16. During 1999 and early 2000, Peapod's stock (listed on the Nasdaq National Market under the symbol "PPOD") traded mostly in the $8 to $12 range (for detailed financials see Exhibits 3 and 4).

Exhibit 1   Six-Year Summary of Peapod's Financial Performance, 1994–1999

6 Year Summary

Date	Sales (000$)	Net Income	EPS
1999	73,134	-28,450	-1.62
1998	69,265	-21,565	-1.27
1997	56,943	-12,979	-0.87
1996	27,642	-9,566	-0.82
1995	15,209	-6,592	-0.79
1994	8,005	-4,437	-0.75

In 1997, faced with mounting losses despite growing revenues, Peapod management determined that its original, partner-based business model entailed too high a cost structure for the company to achieve profitable growth. The co-founders opted to shift to a new order fulfillment business model utilizing a local company-owned and operated central distribution warehouse to store, pick, and pack customer orders for delivery. By mid-1999 the company had opened new distribution centers in 3 of the 8 markets it served—Chicago, Long Island, and Boston; a fourth distribution center was under construction in San Francisco. Peapod stocked its distribution centers with products purchased at wholesale from a variety of food and household products companies, including Kellogg's, Kraft, Colgate-Palmolive, Frito-Lay, Coca-Cola, Clorox, Kimberly-Clark, Procter & Gamble, Nabisco, Ralston Purina, Nestlè, Walgreens, and in some cases, traditional retailers. Peapod management had announced plans to use the centralized distribution model in all eight markets over time and in all new areas it entered. The company was reportedly losing money in five of the markets it served in mid-1999.

Peapod in Early 2000

Going into the new millennium, Peapod was the largest Internet supermarket with over 90,000 customers (based on a count of customers who had placed an order within the past twelve months). It had a 30 percent share of the estimated $235 million market for grocery products sold online.[1] The eight market areas where the company presently operated had an estimated 6.6 million households, representing approximately 7 percent of total U.S. households. Delivery operations in these areas were conducted out of twenty-two order fulfillment locations. Exhibit 2 shows the company's eight metropolitan markets, the number of households represented in each market, and the company's local retail supermarket partners. Peapod currently processed an average of 2,000 orders daily; average order size was $110–$115, but ran a bit lower in areas where the company utilized central distribution warehouses—Peapod stocked fewer items at its warehouses than were generally available from using the stores of supermarket partners to fill orders. Management believed that Peapod's average order size was about five times the in-store average of supermarkets and convenience stores.

Exhibit 2   Peapod's Metropolitan Markets, Household Exposure, and Retail Partners, February 2000

Metropolitan Market Area Served	Estimated Number of Area Households, 1998	Retail Partners	Peapod Distribution Center
Chicago, IL	1,732,000	Jewel Food Stores	Yes
Columbus, Ohio	398,00	Kroger	
Houston, TX	939,000	Randalls Food and Drug	
Boston, MA	1,242,000	Stop and Shop	Yes
San Francisco and San Jose, CA	840,000	Certified Grocers of California, Andronico's, and Walgreens	Yes
Dallas, TX	995,000	Tom Thumb	
Austin, TX	257,000	Randalls Food and Drug	
Long Island, NY	226,000	Giant/Edwards Super Foods Stores	Yes

Management's vision for the company was expressed in three statements:

- **Our Dream**—To fundamentally improve people's lives by bringing interactive shopping to a broad consumer market.
- **Our Mission**—To be the world's leading and preferred provider of interactive grocery shopping services.
- **Our Passion**—To amaze and delight each one of our customers.

Peapod's recent income statements and balance sheets are shown in Exhibits 3 and 4.

Peapod's Customers

Peapod's target market was a middle and upper-income household with PC savvy adults who were stressed for time and didn't particularly enjoy grocery shopping. This was the basis for its tag line "Smart Shopping for Busy People." The company's market research indicated that its typical customers were dual income households, households with children, and females between the ages

of 30 and 54. The incomes of customers covered a wide range, with a median annual income exceeding $60,000.

Peapod's Strategy

Peapod's strategy was to provide customers with a convenient, user-friendly, and personalized way of shopping for grocery items online 24 hours a day, seven days a week. Its online product offerings consisted of fresh meat, produce, deli, and bakery goods, plus name-brand canned and packaged goods, household items, and health and beauty products—essentially the same perishable and non-perishable name brand products typically found in local supermarkets or drug stores. Peapod's prices were competitive and it had weekly specials; manufacturer's coupons were accepted. Delivery was available seven days a week and could be scheduled for the same or next day at a time chosen by the customer. Peapod charged a fee for its online order and delivery service that varied by market area. In most markets customers had the option of paying a per order service charge (about $10 per delivery) or a flat rate for unlimited monthly deliveries.

Exhibit 3   Peapod's Statements of Income, 1996–1998 (in thousands, except per share data)

	1998	1997	1996
Revenues:			
Net product sales	57,305	43,487	22,015
Member and retailer	9,650	11,234	4,558
Interactive marketing	1,460	2,222	1,069
Licensing	850		
Total revenues	69,265	56,943	27,642
Costs and expenses:			
Cost of goods sold	53,903	40,823	20,485
Fulfillment operations	17,196	14,469	6,889
General and administrative	8,029	5,935	3,785
Marketing and selling	7,545	7,726	4,739
System development and maintenance	3,386	1,696	1,124
Depreciation and amortization	3,264	1,234	651
Total costs and expenses	93,323	71,883	37,673
Operating loss	-24,058	-14,940	-10,031
Other income (expense):			
Interest income	2,683	2,044	537
Interest expense	-190	-83	-72
Net loss	-21,565	-12,979	-9,566
Net loss per share:	-$1.27	-$0.87	-$0.82
Shares to compute loss per share:	16,964,439	14,915,734	11,664,956

Source: Company 10-K and 10-Q filings.

Exhibit 4   Peapod's Balance Sheets, 1997–1998 (in thousands, except per share data)

	1998	1997
Assets		
Current assets:		
Cash and cash equivalents	$4,341	$54,079
Marketable securities	15,836	8,798
Receivables	2,516	1,195
Prepaid expenses	186	444
Other current assets	974	228
Total current assets	23,853	64,744
Property and equipment:		
Computer equipment and software	4,010	4,499
Service equipment and other	2,147	1,053
Property and equipment, at cost	6,157	5,552
Accumulated depreciation	-2,252	-2,301
Net property and equipment	3,905	3,251
Non-current marketable securities	15,213	
Capitalized software development costs		998
Goodwill		117
Total assets	$42,971	$69,110
Liabilities and Stockholders' Equity		
Current liabilities:		
Accounts payable	$3,442	$7,514
Accrued compensation	802	1,258
Other accrued liabilities	2,688	926
Deferred revenue	1,000	1,969
Current obligations under capital lease	590	727
Total current liabilities	8,522	12,394
Deferred revenue	448	1,212
Obligations under capital lease, less current portion	395	701
Total liabilities	9,365	14,307
Stockholders' equity:		
Common stock, $.01 par value, 50,000,000 shares authorized; 17,245,828 and 16,852,557 shares issued in 1998 and 1997	172	169
Additional paid-in capital	64,319	63,148
Accumulated other comprehensive income		
Unrealized gain on available-for-sale securities	83	
Accumulated deficit	-30,060	-8,495
Treasury stock	-908	-19
Total stockholders' equity	33,606	54,803
Total liabilities and stockholders' equity	$42,971	$69,110

Source: Company 10-K and 10-Q filings.

The company's Web site was accessible to anyone using a Web browser, including personal computers, Web-enabled televisions, high-speed cable services, and wireless devices.

Peapod's Multi-Featured, Highly-Functional Website Technology

Peapod had built an easy-to-navigate Web site with a variety of highly functional features that management believed helped encourage repeat purchases and differentiated Peapod from other e-tailers and direct competitors. Customers could shop for items in several ways. One was to browse aisles, moving logically from general product category to individual items. Another was to conduct product searches based on brand or category name, which was particularly useful for coupon redemption or purchasing recipe ingredients. Shoppers could also sort items in any product category alphabetically or based on price, nutritional content (such as fat grams, calories, cholesterol, and sodium), sale items, and kosher status. Another feature stored a customer's last three grocery orders, eliminating the need to start a shopping list of frequently purchased items from scratch again. Other features included:

- An extensive library of product pictures, nutrition information, and product ingredients.
- An "Express Shop" feature that helped first-time shoppers build their order without having to browse through the aisles or search for items one at a time. For existing customers, Express Shop, in conjunction with the Previous Orders feature, allowed customers to easily add items to their order.
- A "SmartCart" feature that displayed a list of the items selected for purchase, as well as a running dollar total of the bill.
- The capability to generate Web pages based on a customer's shopping preferences, buying profile, and other variables so as to provide users with a customized shopping experience.
- A "Buddy E-Mail" feature that delivered order confirmations to two different e-mail addresses, something that was useful in households where shopping duties were shared among members.

Gomez Advisors, a leading provider of Internet research and analysis, in September 1999 rated Peapod's Web site first in terms of Ease of Use among all online grocers.

The company's Web site technology was designed to capture behavioral information from users—mouse clicks, time spent viewing each page, coupon redemptions, and other factors. The tracking data that was gathered allowed Peapod to generate dozens of metrics to evaluate the quality of its Web site and to identify opportunities to cross-sell additional goods and services.

Marketing and Advertising

The company's marketing objectives were attracting more users, retaining the business of current users, increasing the frequency with which users placed orders, growing average order size, and enhancing awareness of the Peapod brand. To achieve these objectives, the company used radio and newspaper advertising, direct mail, ads on local mass transit systems, Internet advertising, and branding on delivery trucks and employee uniforms. Company personnel drove attention-getting green Volkswagen "Pod Bugs" with the Peapod insignia to help promote local awareness about Peapod. In 1999, the company's marketing and advertising budget was about $6 million, the majority of which was focused on growing the customer base and helping the company achieve the operating scale needed for profitability.

One Internet marketing effort the company had come up with to attract new customers to Peapod's service was the Peapod Affiliate Program. Peapod started the program in April 1999 as a way of compensating other websites for promoting Peapod and providing links to Peapod from their site. Affiliates could earn a $15 commission for each referred visitor who placed an order with Peapod plus an additional $15 for a customer's third order.

To further promote consumer awareness of Peapod, the company had entered into an agreement with Hearst's HomeArts Network, a premier lifestyle site for women on the web, whereby Peapod would be the exclusive Internet grocery service promoted on The HomeArts Network. The network provided online programming, as well as features from Hearst's 11 women's magazines, including *Redbook, Good Housekeeping, Cosmopolitan*, and *Country Living*. The HomeArts Network had a user base that strongly matched the target Peapod customer. Peapod had also formed a marketing alliance with Excite, Inc. that made Peapod the exclusive online grocer on Excite's website. The agreement with Excite gave Peapod exposure to an estimated 35 percent of all Internet users.[2]

Peapod Packages

To help build a national presence and awareness of the Peapod brand, the company had begun promoting its "Peapod Packages" for shipment to any location. The company had put together preselected themed product assortments targeting such niche occasions as the Super Bowl, Christmas, Thanksgiving, the arrival of a new baby, or a birthday. There were also care packages for college students and recipe/meal solutions in a box. Shoppers could create their own Peapod Package. Peapod planned to expand the Peapod Package line to include specialty and gourmet foods and gifts.

Distribution Center Operations and Order Fulfillment Peapod's new $2 million distribution centers stocked over 12,000 dry grocery, frozen and dairy products, along with perishable products such as produce, meat, and prepared foods. Items were replenished on a just-in-time basis to optimize space utilization and ensure freshness.[3] While Peapod was opening distribution centers in each of its eight markets, it had stated its intention to continue its partnerships with its present retail supermarket allies, albeit on a reduced basis. Until its new central warehousing model was perfected, Peapod was temporarily relying on these partners to stock its central warehouse with perishables, health and beauty aids, and other items it did not currently stock and to fill orders for delivery to certain addresses not as convenient to its warehouse. Moreover, such alliances gave Peapod an advertising channel for promoting the website at its partners' brick-and-mortar locations.

A major component of Peapod's strategy was to optimize its order fulfillment process from a cost standpoint. As the company began shifting from supermarket partnerships to centralized warehousing, it had re-engineered its product distribution and order fulfillment practices to reduce costs, minimize out-of-stock frequencies, improve the accuracy of order picking at warehouses, make it economical to accommodate higher order volumes, and ensure that orders were delivered within the scheduled time frame. New warehousing, order picking, and delivery routing software and systems had been designed and put in place.

Order fulfillment was managed by a handheld scanning device that contained pick data for a given metropolitan market area and controlled the order selection process in a manner calculated to minimize the labor time for picking and packing orders. The list of items for a particular order was sorted according to the location of each item in the warehouse, thereby requiring only one pass through the warehouse and minimizing the pick time for each order. The handheld unit displayed each item to be picked and provided a variety of features for assuring accuracy and allowing flexibility for handling exceptions. As individual items appeared on the screen, the picker confirmed the proper item by scanning the item's uniform product code, and was alerted if the wrong item had been scanned. If an item was out of stock, the device noted the out-of-stock status and, if requested by the customer, automatically directed the picker to the customer-designated substitution. A list of out-of-stock items was automatically transmitted to the manager to generate replacement orders.

Delivery logistics were managed by a sophisticated computer program that provided time management information and point-to-point directions throughout the delivery route. The program accounted for traffic conditions, rush-hour volume, road construction, and other variables that could be predicted within the local area. Peapod drivers delivered the packages to the customers' doorstep or unloaded them in the kitchen (if requested) and obtained feedback from customers on the service. To build customer loyalty, Peapod tried to send the same delivery person to the homes of repeat customers. Peapod management was aggressively pursuing ways to fine-tune and improve all of the new systems it had implemented.

So far, order volume had not reached levels that allowed Peapod's warehouse and order fulfillment operation to realize scale economies. The costs of fulfillment operations were 30 percent of sales revenues during the first nine months of 1999, partly because the company was using both central warehouses and the local stores of its retail supermarket partners to fill orders. However, management expected this percentage to decline as the company moved through the period of getting its warehouses up and operating, as experience with the new systems accumulated, and as order volume increased. For the company to become profitable, order fulfillment costs had to drop to a much smaller percentage of revenues.

Nonetheless, Peapod believed that its business model would give it a significant competitive advantage over traditional grocery retailers. By utilizing the Internet to receive orders and central warehouse and distribution facilities to process them, Peapod eliminated the expenses associated with maintaining multiple retail locations in a metropolitan area. Moreover, its use of centralized inventory warehouses, utilizing just-in-time deliveries from suppliers, meant high inventory turns and reduced stockouts, while at the same time lowering waste and spoilage of perishable goods and reducing the shrinkage associated with store personnel and customer handling of in-store products. Peapod management expected the efficiencies of its business model would permit competitive pricing and, further, that its sophisticated Web technologies would result in being able to greater sales of higher margin products (private label goods). Thus, over time, it ought to have higher gross margins and better bottom-line profitability than traditional grocery retailers.

Research and Data Partnerships with Suppliers Peapod was leveraging the database it was accumulating from tracking user behavior and shopping patterns on its Web site. The company provided advertisers on its Web site with feedback on the effectiveness of marketing programs and it provided a forum for consumer goods companies to conduct targeted advertising, test electronic couponing, and gather data on online purchasing behavior. The company had created research panels of users at a cost which management believed was well below the costs of consumer panels used by Internet research firms. Peapod linked together users from its eight markets to form a national online network of panelists and users, enabling the company to collect information on user attitudes, purchasing behavior, and demographics. Peapod's database and membership profiles permitted it to deliver highly targeted ads and electronic coupons to users, as well as measuring the number of Web page exposures, click-throughs, coupon redemptions, and sales—all captured in a manner that permitted measuring the impact of a marketing program. Peapod had agreements to provide fee-based online marketing data and research services to a number of national consumer goods companies, resulting in revenues of $1.0 to $1.5 million annually. Management believed that as Peapod's customer base grew in size consumer goods companies would "increasingly view Peapod as a powerful advertising venue as well as a valuable research tool," thereby generating additional revenues for Peapod. Participating subscribers included Kellogg's, Kraft, Colgate-Palmolive, Frito-Lay, Coca-Cola, Clorox, Kimberly-Clark, Ralston Purina, and Nestle U.S.A.

Growth Strategies   Aside from its efforts to build order volume and add new customers in the eight markets where it already operated, Peapod's strategy to grow its business consisted of two major initiatives: one, expanding into additional market areas and, two, moving beyond groceries and adding altogether new products and services to its lineup of offerings to customers. Peapod management planned to use its central warehouse business model and new systems capabilities as the basis for expanding its service into a total of forty metropolitan areas with 400,00-plus households. The company planned to keep its investment costs down by building economical $2 million distribution centers. Moreover, by establishing a local order fulfillment network with recurring grocery purchases as a foundation, Peapod management believed it would have a pipeline into customer households through which it could provide an increasingly wide range of goods and services purchased online at little incremental cost. Peapod management believed that its "last mile" delivery network for groceries gave it an unparalleled opportunity to build the Peapod brand, establish personal relationships with individual customers through regular deliveries. Management planned to transform Peapod into a one-stop online shopping site offering home delivery of a host of different products and services, thereby dramatically improving profitability.

As one of the first steps to expand Peapod's product offerings, the company had recently formed a strategic product alliance with Walgreens. Under this agreement, Peapod would begin offering health and beauty products, household hardware and small appliances, electrical supplies, audio and videotapes, stationary and art supplies, and seasonal items supplied by Walgreens.[4]

The major impediment to Peapod's growth strategies was a potential shortage of capital. The company had nearly $13 million in cash and marketable securities going into fall 1999, but the size of the company's losses was creating negative cash flows from operations. The company was depleting its cash reserves to cover the negative cash flow deficits from current operations. Peapod management anticipated that its existing cash and marketable securities would be insufficient to fund the company's operations and capital requirements in 2000 and was currently evaluating financing opportunities. Analysts following the company forecast that Peapod's losses would amount to $17 to $20 million in 2000, equal to a negative $1.10 per share.

Management Changes

Peapod's top management team underwent significant change in 1999. Bill Malloy was brought in as President, Chief Executive Officer, and a member of the Board of Directors. Malloy had established an impressive record of successfully launching new operations and new services while managing rapid growth at AT&T Wireless, and he had been one of the key architects of AT&T's Digital One Rate strategy. Co-founder Andrew Parkinson, while turning over the role of President and CEO to Malloy, remained on as Chairman of the Board and began devoting his efforts full-time to Peapod's long-term strategy and business development. Malloy made several top management changes in the months following his appointment. Michael Brennan was promoted to Senior Vice President of Marketing and Product Management, George F. Douaire was made Senior Vice President of Peapod Interactive, and Robert P. Ziegler joined Peapod as Director of Chicago Operations. The top five officers under Malloy collectively had thirty-six years of experience in the online grocery business, and several officers had previous experience in packaged foods and consumer products as such companies as Kraft Foods and Procter & Gamble. Peapod employed approximately 475 full-time and 370 part-time employees in early 2000.

The Retail Grocery Industry

The U.S. retail grocery industry was a $430 billion business.[5] Sales of health and beauty aids amounted to an additional $200 to $225 billion. Forrester Research estimated the total sales of grocery and household items, health and beauty items, and beverages in all types of retail outlets amounted to a $720 billion U.S. market.

The top five supermarket chains in 1999 were Kroger, with $43.2 billion in sales; Albertson's, $35.9 billion; Wal-Mart, $27 billion from its grocery operations; Safeway, $26.5 billion; and Ahold, $20 billion.[6] Slow-growth and intense competition was driving supermarket industry consolidation. No supermarket chain had an industry market share much above 10 percent; the top five had a combined share under 30 percent. Supermarket sales had grown at an average of just 3.4 percent over the past ten years, partly because more consumers were shifting some of their purchases to drug chain, wholesale club, and discount chain "supercenter" formats. Traditional grocers' share of total U.S. food sales had dropped from 42 percent to 40 percent over the last ten years.[7]

Typical supermarkets carried an average of 30,000 items, were from 20,000 to 40,000 square feet in size, and averaged $12 million in sales annually. Consumers tended to be price-conscious and the industry was characterized by fierce price competition.

The supermarket business was a notoriously low-margin business with net profits of only 1 to 2 percent of revenues. Store profits depended heavily on creating a high volume of customer traffic and rapid inventory turnover, especially for perishables such as produce and fresh meat. Competitors had to operate efficiently to make money and tight control of labor costs and product spoilage was essential. Because capital investment costs were modest, involving mainly the construction of distribution centers and stores, it was not unusual for supermarket chains to realize 15 to 20 percent returns on invested capital.

Supermarket Chains as Potential Competitors in the Online Grocery Segment

Most supermarket chains were following developments in the online grocery industry carefully. While some observers believed that existing supermarket chains would be slow to enter into online sales for fear of cannibalizing their existing sales and undermining their brick-and-mortar investments, other industry observers expected supermarket chains to enter the online grocery segment, especially if online grocery sales took off. However, other supermarket industry analysts believed some existing supermarket chains would definitely not stand by idly and let online grocery companies steal market share without a fight. These analysts saw existing supermarket chains as potentially formidable competitors in the online segment because they had well-established supply chains, bought in volumes that gave them bargaining power with food and

household product suppliers, had well-known brand names, knew local markets, and could use their distribution centers and neighborhood stores as bases from which to make home deliveries. As many as one-third of U.S. grocery chains were said to have experimented with some type of delivery service.[8]

Albertson's had recently begun testing the market by offering online shopping to customers in the Dallas/Fort Worth, Texas, area. Albertson's was well established in the Dallas/Fort Worth area with numerous stores and a sizable market share of the supermarket business. If its online venture in the Dallas/Fort Worth area was deemed successful, management indicated that it would expand its online grocery service to other areas.

Clark's Supermarkets, a small family-owned Colorado chain, announced plans in early 2000 to experiment with online grocery sales at its stores. Clark's intended to put the items stocked in its stores online, allowing customers to log on to its website and select the items they wanted. The company had designed a special cart that allowed store personnel to cruise store aisles and pick five orders simultaneously. Clark's strategy was to run the items through its checkout counters, pack them, and have them ready for customer pickup at a time chosen by customers. For the time being, Clark's did not plan to deliver orders to customer's homes. Clark's store in Steamboat Springs was selected to be the pilot for the online experiment; if the service proved popular and successful, Clark's intended to make the service available in other Colorado locations where it had stores. Clark's saw online ordering capabilities as being a time saving service to customers; management did not expect the service to add substantially to the company's profitability.

The Online Grocery Segment

The online-grocery shopping business was in its infancy in 2000. Analysts believed that online grocery sales amounted to about $235 million in 1999, less than 0.25 percent of total supermarket industry sales. There were 45 companies in the online market and none were profitable yet.[9] So far, online grocery shopping had been slow to catch on, and industry newcomers had encountered high start-up and operating costs. Sales volumes were too small to permit profitability, as well as low profit margins for groceries and high costs. The problem, according to industry analysts, was that consumers had been largely disappointed in the service, selection, and prices that they had so far gotten from industry members.

However, some analysts expected online grocery sales to grow at a rapid pace as companies improved their service and selection, PC penetration of households rose, and consumers became more accustomed to making purchases online.[10] Forrester Research had forecast that online grocery sales could reach $3 billion by 2003 and as much as $85 billion by 2007. A two-year study by Consumer Direct Cooperative (CDC) concluded that online, consumer-direct grocery sales would account for between 8–12 percent of the total grocery market share by 2010.[11] CDC had also done a study of the types of online shoppers and which were most likely to shop for groceries online—see Exhibit 5. Most online grocery customers were believed to be either time starved or averse to grocery store visits.

A MARC Group study concluded "consumers who buy groceries online are likely to be more loyal to their electronic supermarkets, spend more per store 'visit,' and take greater advantage of coupons and premiums than traditional customers".[12] Another study found higher demand for produce online. Edward McLaughlin, head of the Food Industry Management Program at Cornell University, found that 12–16 percent of grocery expenditures through Peapod were for fresh produce compared to the supermarket average of about 10 percent.[13] He reasoned that this outcome was because "decisions made through a computer are more rational and choices are for healthier foods."

One of the problems with online grocery shopping was that consumers were extremely price sensitive when it came to buying groceries. The prices of many online grocers were above the prices at supermarkets and shoppers, in many cases, were unwilling to pay online grocers extra for the convenience of home delivery. Consumer price sensitivity meant that online grocers had to achieve a cost structure that would allow them to (1) price competitively, (2) cover the costs of picking and delivering individual grocery orders, and (3) have sufficient margins to earn attractive profits and returns on investment. Some analysts estimated that online grocers had to do ten times the volume of a traditional grocer in order to be successful.[14]

Gomez Advisor's Ratings of Online Grocers

Gomez Advisors provided user-oriented ratings of numerous types of online companies, ranging from banks to auction sites to travel agents to sellers of sporting goods. Many online shoppers were using the Gomez ratings to help them select which Internet providers to do business with. Gomez evaluated online grocers on five aspects:

- Ease of use—Whether the Web site had well-integrated features that minimized order time and that gave shoppers product comparison capabilities.
- Onsite resources—The breadth of product selection and the quality of information resources provided to users.

- Relationship services—Whether the grocer provided such "extras" as in-home visits with first-time customers, account representatives to answer questions, and willingness to fill unique orders.
- Overall cost—This criterion included product costs (based on non-promoted prices of a market basket of commonly purchased items), delivery charges, length and frequency of price promotions, and membership fees (including whether there were free trial periods for new members).
- Customer confidence—financially stability, reliability of customer service, and guarantees for what was sold.

Gomez also determined on the basis of its ratings which online grocers were most suitable for selective shoppers, bargain hunting shoppers, time-constrained shoppers, and meal solution shoppers. Exhibit 6 reports the Fall 1999 Gomez ratings of the top ten online grocers.

Profiles of Selected Peapod Competitors

Peapod management anticipated that the company would experience increasing competitive pressures in the online grocery segment. Competition was expected to come both from supermarket chains adopting "click-and-mortar" strategies and pursuing online sales as a new distribution channel to complement their traditional chain of retail outlets and from the aggressive market expansion efforts of the 45 companies already in the online segment. This section provides a brief look at three of Peapod's competitors in the online grocery business. Exhibit 7 provides a comparison of Peapod's prices for six selected items with those of Webvan, HomeGrocer.com, and Netgrocer.

Webvan Group, Inc.

Webvan's strategic intent was to become the market leader in the full-service online grocery and drugstore business. Louis Borders, a founder of booksellers Borders Group who left the company in 1992 to form his own investment firm, launched the Foster City (California) firm in June 1999 as one of the most ambitious e-commerce enterprises to date. Before going public, Webvan had attracted $122 million in investment capital from CBS, Yahoo, Softbank, Sequoia Capital, Benchmark Capital, and Knight-Ridder and had recruited the head of Andersen Consulting, George Shaheen, to be its president and CEO.[15] Webvan completed an initial public offering of its stock in November 1999, raising $375 million in capital by selling 9 percent of its shares. The shares, initially priced by Goldman Sachs at $13 to $15 a share, rose to as high as $34 per share before ending the first day's trading at $24.875.

> ### Exhibit 5   Types of Online Shoppers and Their Propensity to Be Attracted to Online Grocery Shopping
>
> | Types of Online Shoppers | Comments |
> |---|---|
> | Shopping avoiders | Dislike going to the grocery; prime candidate for online grocery shopping |
> | Necessity users | Have limited ability to go to the grocery store; strong candidate for using online grocery shopping as a substitute for in-store shopping |
> | New technologists | Young and comfortable with technology; certain to experiment with buying products online; amenable to online grocery shopping if it is a pleasant and satisfying experience |
> | Time-starved shoppers | Insensitive to price, don't mind paying extra to save time |
> | Responsibles | Have available time, get an enhanced sense of self-worth from grocery shopping |
> | Traditional shoppers | Older, may want to avoid technology and buying products online; very likely to prefer "touch and inspect" shopping in a grocery store |
>
> **Source:** A study by Consumer Direct Cooperative cited in Michael McGovern, "One Stop Shopping." *Transportation & Distribution,* Vol. 39, May 1998.

The company's prospectus forecasted that Webvan would post $11.9 million in revenues in 1999, $120 million in 2000, and $518.2 million in 2001. The prospectus also stated that company expectations were for a $73.8 million loss in 1999, a $154.3 million loss in 2000, and $302 million in losses in 2001.[16] The company shares traded in the $15 to $20 range in early 2000.

Webvan attracted about 10,000 customers in its first six weeks of operation in the San Francisco Bay area. The company had recruited several executives from Federal Express and was using FedEx's hub-and-spoke delivery system as a model for its own distribution system and delivery service. Webvan was using Wal-Mart as its example of breadth of product selection, Yahoo! as its model for speed, Amazon.com as its model for designing the kind of online shopping experience it wanted to provide, and eBay as its model for "warm-and-fuzzy" feel.[17] It had hired eighty software programmers to create proprietary systems that linked every aspect of its business processes and had recruited managers with expertise in logistics, grocery and drug retailing, and customer service.

Webvan's Strategy and Business Plan   To begin operations, Webvan had constructed a prototype 330,000 square-foot in Oakland to service an area of forty miles in any direction.[18] The $25 million facility included 4.5 miles of conveyor belts and temperature-controlled rooms to store wine, cigars, produce, meat, and frozen foods. It was designed to serve as many households as twenty to twenty-five supermarkets. The company planned to eventually stock 50,000 items, including an array of drugstore items, 300 varieties of fresh fruits and vegetables, 750 kinds of cheese, 500 types of cereal, 700 cuts of fresh meat and fish, 700 different wine labels, and chef-prepared meals that could be reheated in the microwave or oven. In the San Francisco market area, Webvan had formed alliances with leading local vendors to provide the freshest produce available; it planned to utilize such alliances in other markets as well. Webvan claimed that its prices were up to 5 percent less than in local grocery stores.

Webvan had entered into an agreement with Bechtel Group, one of the world's largest engineering and construction firms, to build Webvan's distribution centers and delivery systems in twenty-six markets over the next two years. Webvan's projected investment costs for its distribution centers and delivery systems amounted to $1 billion. The company's second distribution center had recently been built in Atlanta.

Webvan's tracking systems monitored customer orders starting with the time they were placed on the company's Web site. Orders were directed from the web site to the appropriate distribution center. Workers were located at order-picking stations scattered throughout each distribution center; their job was to pick items stocked in their area of the warehouse and put them in color-coded plastic tote bags that signaled whether the items were frozen, refrigerated, or dry. Pickers did not travel up and down aisles but instead moved no more than twenty feet in any direction to reach 8,000 bins of goods that were brought to the picker on rotating carousels. Once pickers completed their portion of a customer's order, the tote was transported on conveyors to other areas of the distribution center where pickers for the remaining items were located. After orders had made the necessary rounds through the warehouse, they were

Exhibit 6   Gomez Ratings of the Top Ten Online Grocers, Fall 1999

Company	Ease of Use	Overall Cost	Customer Confidence	Onsite Resources	Relationship Services	Overall Score	Comments
Peapod	9.07	7.96	5.41	7.90	3.75	6.97	Rated third (score of 6.17) for time-short shoppers looking for the best deal with the least hassle.
Homegrocer	7.33	7.41	4.82	7.74	5.00	6.67	Rated second best (score of 7.02) for selective shoppers wanting THE best quality products and delivery service; also rated second best (score of 6.80) for shoppers looking for specific meal solutions (recipes, seasonal foods, and prepared foods).
Webvan	8.22	7.16	2.63	7.32	5.00	6.36	Rated best (score of 7.23) for selective shoppers and best (score of 7.14) for shoppers looking for specific meal solutions.
Streamline	4.62	5.93	5.16	7.47	7.50	6.31	Rated best (score of 6.92) for time-short shoppers.
ShopLink	6.36	6.98	5.33	5.93	6.25	6.26	Rated second best for time-short shoppers (score of 6.70).
HomeRuns	5.56	8.75	4.97	3.41	2.50	5.18	Ranked best (score of 8.68) for bargain shoppers who love to browse and the thrill of shopping for the best deal.
NetGrocer	8.22	3.33	2.97	5.49	3.75	4.70	
Albertson's	4.67	8.16	3.99	0.90	2.50	4.13	Ranked second (score of 7.54) for bargain shoppers.
Grocer Online	5.42	3.46	6.64	0.36	2.50	3.73	
Your Grocer	4.53	3.84	5.91	2.70	5.00	3.68	

Source: www.gomez.com, February 6, 2000.

Exhibit 7   Comparative Prices of Selected Online Grocers, February 2000

Grocery Item	Peapod's Price	Webvan's Price	Homegrocer.com's Price	Netgrocer's Price
Lea & Perrin's Worcestershire Sauce (10 oz)	$2.19	$2.47	$2.25	$2.39
Campbell's Chunky Classic Chicken Noodle Soup (19 oz)	$2.45	$2.44	$2.19	$2.29
Bunch of green onions (scallions)	$0.50	$0.50	$0.49	Fresh produce not available
French's mustard squeeze (8 oz)	$0.97	$0.97	$0.95	$0.99
Maxwell House Instant Crystals (8 oz)	$4.89	$4.92	$5.49	$5.49
Kraft Macaroni and Cheese Deluxe (14 oz)	$2.39	$2.47	$2.29	$2.49

Source: Company Web sites.

loaded onto trucks refrigerated at thirty-five degrees Fahrenheit and taken to staging areas located throughout the metropolitan market area. From there totes were loaded onto one of the company's more than sixty vans for delivery to customers' homes. Staging areas were located so that Webvan's couriers did not have to travel more than ten miles in any direction from the staging area to reach a customer's home. The couriers were trained to be courteous, friendly, and act as customer service professionals and ambassadors for Webvan's service; they were not permitted to accept tips or gratuities. All of the logistics—how many items a tote bag should hold, how far pickers should travel to rotating carousels, how far trucks should travel from staging areas to make deliveries—had been carefully plotted to maximize efficiency.

Webvan management expected that each distribution center would be able to handle 8,000 orders a day (involving more than 225,000 items) and bring in $300 million in annual revenues.[19] Borders, Webvan's Chairman and founder, predicted that Webvan's business model would be so successful and efficient that the company would be able to charge lower prices than traditional supermarkets as well as rival online grocers.

Webvan offered free delivery on orders over $50 whereas most other online grocers waived delivery fees on orders over $75. And it did not charge a membership fee. Orders were delivered within a thirty minute window selected by the customer. Webvan's Web site offered customers recipes and use of a weekly menu planner.

HomeGrocer.com

Founded in 1997, HomeGrocer.com provided online grocery ordering and delivery service to customers in Seattle; Portland, Ore.; Orange County, Calif.; and portions of Los Angeles and San Bernardino County. HomeGrocer.com offered a broad selection of items, including fresh produce, meats, seafood, dairy products, local specialty foods, health and beauty aids, household items, fresh flowers, pet supplies, best-selling books, video games, and movies. HomeGrocer used a distribution center model also; in early 2000, it had four distribution centers and was adding others in the newly entered Los Angeles area. HomeGrocer.com's signature peach-logo delivery trucks had multiple compartments that permitted products to be stored at their appropriate temperatures without affecting the temperatures of the other products.

Customers could order groceries via the Internet until 11 p.m. and select a ninety minute window for next-day delivery. HomeGrocer.com offered free delivery for all first orders and those $75 or more, in addition to toll-free customer support for its members. To underscore its commitment to quality, the company offered an unconditional 100 percent satisfaction guarantee. HomeGrocer.com had been recognized by Feedback Direct, a leading online customer service authority, as one of the top fifty North American companies to consistently demonstrate superior customer service.

Although HomeGrocer.com was a fairly small business with fewer than 25,000 customers, it had ambitious plans to expand into twenty other markets in the near future, aided by a $42.5 million investment by Amazon.com.[20] Amazon's investment gave it a 35 percent stake in the company. Amazon had also recently invested in drugstore.com and Pets.com., and there had been speculation that Amazon might start to use HomeGrocer's vans to deliver CDs, books, prescription drugs to customer's homes. HomeGrocer.com had also received funding from the Barksdale Group, an investment firm run by James Barksdale, founder of Netscape, Martha Stewart Living Omnimedia Inc., Hummer Winblad Venture Partners, and Kleiner Perkins Caufield & Byers.[21] The company had filed plans with the Securities and Exchange Commission to issue shares of its common stock to the public in the first half of 2000.

Netgrocer

Netgrocer began operations in 1995 and offered nationwide distribution through a large central warehouse located in New Jersey. Netgrocer's product line included canned and packaged grocery items, paper products, cleaning products, organic and natural foods, international food items, dog and cat foods, laundry items, health and beauty products, dietary supplements, pain relief products, fragrances, baby products, a variety of electronics items (cameras, film, calculators, data organizers, audio accessories, batteries, and video games), CDs, and gifts. It generally offered prices of 10–20 percent less than supermarkets and free delivery for orders over $75. Netgrocer's orders were delivered by FedEx on the third business day after the order was received.

In 1999 Netgrocer relaunched its Web site following the removal of CEO Daniel Nissan and the firing of 80 percent of its staff. These changes, which occurred shortly after the company shelved its $38 million IPO, were attributed to market conditions and expense cuts. Since the launch of the new site, Netgrocer's average order size was up 40 percent and time spent on the site had increased dramatically.[22]

Notes

1. Peapod, Inc. Investor's Overview. www.peapod.com

2. "Peapod Signs Multi-Year Internet Marketing Deal with Excite." (http://www.peapod.com/v5/Html/Press/press045.html)

3. "Peapod Opens Centralized Operations Center in Chicago." Peapod Press Release, 25 January 1999.

4. "Peapod and Walgreen Co. Announce Product Alliance." Peapod Press Release, 10 March 1999.

5. King, Ronette. "Grocery Mergers Are Part of the Growing U.S. Trend." *Times-Picayune,* 13 October 1999, A4.

6. Bergmann, Joan. "Food for Thought: Going into the Grocery Industry." *Discount Merchandiser* (May 1999): 36.

7. Aufretier, Nora and Tim McGuire. "Walking Down the Aisles." *Ivey Business Journal* (March/April 1999): 49.

8. Belise, Laurent. "A Mouse in the Bakery Aisle." *Christian Science Monitor* Boston, Mass; (8 September 1998): 11.

9. Machlis, Sharon. "Filling Up Grocery Carts Online," *Computerworld* (27 July 1998): 4.

10. Machlis, Sharon. "Filling Up Grocery Carts Online," *Computerworld* (27 July 1998): 4.

11. Hennessy, Terry. "Sense of Sell," *Progressive Grocer* (August 1998): 107–110.

12. Woods, Bob. "America Online Goes Grocery Shopping for E-Commerce Bargains," *Computer News* (10 August 1998): 42.

13. "Net Profits: Making the Internet Work for You and Your Business," *Fortune,* Summer 1998, 240–243.

14. Fisher, Lawrence M. "On-Line Grocer is Setting up Delivery System for $1 Billion," *New York Times,* 10 July 1999, 1.

15. Himelstein, Linda. "Louis H. Borders," *BusinessWeek,* 27 September 1999, 28.

16. "Webvan Group files amended prospectus for Initial offering," *Wall Street Journal,* 13 October 1999, A8.

17. Linda Himelstein, "Can You Sell Groceries Like Books?" *Business Week,* 26 July 1999, EB 44.

18. Himelstein, "Can You Sell Groceries Like Books?" EB 45.

19. Himelstein, "Can You Sell Groceries Like Books?" EB 46.

20. Marlatt, Andrew. "Amazon Diversifies Further with $42M Stake in Grocer," *Internet World* (24 May 1999).

21. Beck, Rachel. "Online grocers work to build a market," *Houston Chronicle,* 30 May 1999 7.

22. Janoff, Barry. "Point, Click, Shop," *Progressive Grocer* (June 1999): 31.

Case 24

Perdue Farms, Inc.: Responding to Twenty-first Century Challenges

George C. Rubenson and Frank Shipper, *Salisbury University*

Background/Company History

> I have a theory that you can tell the difference between those who have inherited a fortune and those who have made a fortune. Those who have made their own fortune forget not where they came from and are less likely to lose touch with the common man. (Bill Sterling, 'Just Browsin' column in Eastern Shore News, March 2, 1988)

The history of Perdue Farms, Inc. is dominated by seven themes: quality, growth, geographic expansion, vertical integration, innovation, branding, and service. Arthur W. Perdue, a Railway Express Agent and descendent of a French Huguenot family named Perdeaux, founded the company in 1920 when he left his job with Railway Express and entered the egg business full-time near the small town of Salisbury, Maryland. Salisbury is located in a region immortalized in James Michener's *Chesapeake* that is alternately known as "the Eastern Shore" or "Delmarva Peninsula." It includes parts of Delaware, Maryland, and Virginia. Arthur Perdue's only child, Franklin Parsons Perdue was also born in 1920.

A quick look at Perdue Farms' mission statement reveals the emphasis the company has always put on quality (see Exhibit 1). In the 1920s, "Mr. Arthur," as he

Copyright © 2001 George C. Rubenson and Frank M. Shipper, Department of Management and Marketing, Franklin P. Perdue School of Business, Salisbury University.

Acknowledgements: The authors are indebted to Frank Perdue, Jim Perdue, and the numerous associates at Perdue Farms, Inc., who generously shared their time and information about the company. In addition, the authors would like to thank the anonymous librarians at Blackwell Library, Salisbury State University, who routinely review area newspapers and file articles about the poultry industry—the most important industry on the Delmarva Peninsula. Without their assistance, this case would not be possible.

was called, bought leghorn breeding stock from Texas to improve the quality of his flock. He soon expanded his egg market and began shipments to New York. Practicing small economies such as mixing his own chicken feed and using leather from his old shoes to make hinges for his chicken coops, he stayed out of debt and prospered. He tried to add a new chicken coop every year.

By 1940, Perdue Farms was already known for quality products and fair dealing in a tough, highly competitive market. The company began offering chickens for sale when "Mr. Arthur" realized that the future lay in selling chickens, not eggs. In 1944, Mr. Arthur made his son Frank a full partner in A. W. Perdue and Son, Inc.

In 1950, Frank took over leadership of the company that employed forty people. By 1952, revenues were $6,000,000 from the sale of 2,600,000 broilers. During this period, the company began to vertically integrate, operating its own hatchery, starting to mix its own feed formulations, and operating its own feed mill. Also, in the 1950s, Perdue Farms began to contract with others to grow chickens for them. By furnishing the growers with peeps (baby chickens) and the feed, the company was better able to control quality.

In the 1960s, Perdue Farms continued to vertically integrate by building its first grain receiving and storage facilities and Maryland's first soybean processing plant. By 1967, annual sales had increased to about $35,000,000. However, it became clear to Frank that profits lay in processing chickens. Frank recalled in an interview for *Business Week* (September 15, 1972) " . . . processors were paying us 10c a live pound for what cost us 14c to produce. Suddenly, processors were making as much as 7c a pound."

A cautious, conservative planner, Arthur Perdue had not been eager for expansion and Frank Perdue himself was reluctant to enter poultry processing. But, economics forced his hand, and in 1968, the company bought its first processing plant, a Swift and Company operation in Salisbury.

From the first batch of chickens that it processed, Perdue's standards were higher than those of the federal

Exhibit 1   Perdue Mission 2000

Stand on Tradition

Perdue was built upon a foundation of quality, a tradition described in our Quality Policy …

Our Quality Policy

We shall produce products and provide services at all times which meet or exceed the expectations of our customers.

We shall not be content to be of equal quality to our competitors.

Our commitment is to be increasingly superior.

Contribution to quality is a responsibility shared by everyone in the Perdue organization.

Focus on Today

Our mission reminds us of the purpose we serve…

Our Mission

Enhance the quality of life with great food and agricultural products.

While striving to fulfill our mission, we use our values to guide our decisions…

Our Values

- **Quality:** We value the needs of our customers. Our high standards require us to work safely, make safe food, and uphold the Perdue name.
- **Integrity:** We do the right thing and live up to our commitments. We do not cut corners or make false promises.
- **Trust:** We trust each other and treat each other with mutual respect. Each individual's skill and talent are appreciated.
- **Teamwork:** We value a strong work ethic and ability to make each other successful. We care what others think and encourage their involvement, creating a sense of pride, loyalty, ownership, and family.

Look to the Future

Our vision describes what we will become and the qualities that will enable us to succeed …

Our Vision

To be the leading quality food company with $20 billion in sales in 2020.

Perdue in the Year 2020

- **To our customers:** We will provide food solutions and indispensable services to meet anticipated customer needs.
- **To our consumers:** A portfolio of trusted food and agricultural products will be supported by multiple brands throughout the world.
- **To our associates:** Worldwide, our people and our workplace will reflect our quality reputation, placing Perdue among the best places to work.
- **To our communities:** We will be known in the community as a strong corporate citizen, trusted business partner, and favorite employer.
- **To our shareholders:** Driven by innovation, our market leadership and our creative spirit will yield industry-leading profits.

---

government were. The state grader on the first batch has often told the story of how he was worried that he had rejected too many chickens as not Grade A. As he finished his inspections for that first day, he saw Frank Perdue headed his way and he could tell that Frank was not happy. Frank started inspecting the birds and never argued over one that was rejected. Next, he saw Frank start to go through the ones that the state grader had passed and began to toss some of them over with the rejected birds. Finally, realizing that few met his standards, Frank put all of the birds in the reject pile. Soon, however, the facility was able to process 14,000 broilers per hour.

From the beginning, Frank Perdue refused to permit his broilers to be frozen for shipping, arguing that it resulted in unappetizing black bones and loss of flavor and moistness when cooked. Instead, Perdue chickens were (and some still are) shipped to market packed in ice, justifying the company's advertisements at that time that it sold only "fresh, young broilers." However, this policy also limited the company's market to those locations that could be serviced overnight from the Eastern Shore of Maryland. Thus, Perdue chose for its primary markets the densely populated towns and cities of the East Coast, particularly New York City, which consumes more Perdue chicken than all other brands combined.

Frank Perdue's drive for quality became legendary both inside and outside the poultry industry. In 1985, Frank and Perdue Farms, Inc. were featured in the book, *A Passion for Excellence,* by Tom Peters and Nancy Austin.

In 1970, Perdue established its primary breeding and genetic research programs. Through selective breeding, Perdue developed a chicken with more white breast meat than the typical chicken. Selective breeding has been so successful that Perdue Farms chickens are desired by other processors. Rumors have even suggested that Perdue chickens have been stolen on occasion in an attempt to improve competitor flocks.

In 1971, Perdue Farms began an extensive marketing campaign featuring Frank Perdue. In his early advertisements, he became famous for saying things like "If you want to eat as good as my chickens, you'll just have to eat my chickens." He is often credited with being the first to brand what had been a commodity product. During the 1970s, Perdue Farms also expanded geographically to areas north of New York City such as Massachusetts, Rhode Island, and Connecticut.

In 1977, "Mr. Arthur" died at the age of 91, leaving behind a company with annual sales of nearly $200,000,000, an average annual growth rate of 17 percent (compared to an industry average of 1 percent a year), the potential for processing 78,000 broilers per hour, and annual production of nearly 350,000,000 pounds of poultry per year. Frank Perdue said of his father simply "I learned everything from him."

In 1981, Frank Perdue was in Boston for his induction into the Babson College Academy of Distinguished Entrepreneurs, an award established in 1978 to recognize the spirit of free enterprise and business leadership. Babson College President Ralph Z. Sorenson inducted Perdue into the academy which, at that time, numbered eighteen men and women from four continents. Perdue had the following to say to the college students:

> There are none, nor will there ever be, easy steps for the entrepreneur. Nothing, absolutely nothing, replaces the willingness to work earnestly, intelligently towards a goal. You have to be willing to pay the price. You have to have an insatiable appetite for detail, have to be willing to accept constructive criticism, to ask questions, to be fiscally responsible, to surround yourself with good people and, most of all, to listen. (Frank Perdue, speech at Babson College, April 28, 1981)

The early 1980's saw Perdue Farms expand southward into Virginia, North Carolina, and Georgia. It also began to buy out other producers such as Carroll's Foods, Purvis Farms, Shenandoah Valley Poultry Company, and Shenandoah Farms. The latter two acquisitions diversified the company's markets to include turkey. New Products included value added items such as "Perdue Done It!," a line of fully cooked fresh chicken products.

James A. (Jim) Perdue, Frank's only son, joined the company as a management trainee in 1983 and became a plant manager. The latter 1980's tested the mettle of the firm. Following a period of considerable expansion and product diversification, a consulting firm recommended that the company form several strategic business units, responsible for their own operations. In other words, the firm should decentralize. Soon after, the chicken market leveled off and then declined for a period. In 1988, the firm experienced its first year in the red. Unfortunately, the decentralization had created duplication and enormous administrative costs. The firm's rapid plunge into turkeys and other food processing, where it had little experience, contributed to the losses. Characteristically, the company refocused, concentrating on efficiency of operations, improving communications throughout the company, and paying close attention to detail.

On June 2, 1989, Frank celebrated fifty years with Perdue Farms, Inc. At a morning reception in downtown Salisbury, the Governor of Maryland proclaimed it "Frank Perdue Day." The Governors of Delaware and Virginia did the same. In 1991, Frank was named Chairman of the Executive Committee and Jim Perdue became Chairman of the Board. Quieter, gentler, and more formally educated, Jim Perdue focuses on operations, infusing the company with an even stronger devotion to quality control and a bigger commitment to strategic planning. Frank Perdue continued to do advertising and public relations. As Jim Perdue matured as the company leader, he took over the role of company spokesperson and began to appear in advertisements.

Under Jim Perdue's leadership, the 1990s were dominated by market expansion into Florida and west to Michigan and Missouri. In 1992, the international business segment was formalized serving customers in Puerto Rico, South America, Europe, Japan, and China. By fiscal year 1998, international sales were $180 million per year. International markets are beneficial for the firm because U.S. customers prefer white meat while customers in most other countries prefer dark meat.

Food service sales to commercial consumers has also become a major market. New retail product lines focus on value added items, individually quick frozen items, home meal replacement items, and products for the delicatessen. The "Fit 'n Easy" label continues as part of a nutrition campaign using skinless, boneless chicken and turkey products.

The 1990s also saw the increased use of technology and the building of distribution centers to better serve the customer. For example, all over-the-road trucks were equipped with satellite two-way communications and geographic positioning, allowing real-time tracking, rerouting if needed, and accurately informing customers when to expect product arrival. Currently, nearly 20,000 associates have increased revenues to more than $2.5 billion.

Management and Organization

From 1950 until 1991, Frank Perdue was the primary force behind Perdue Farms' growth and success. During Frank's years as the company leader, the industry entered its high growth period. Industry executives had typically developed professionally during the industry's infancy. Many had little formal education and started their careers in the barnyard, building chicken coops and cleaning them out. They often spent their entire careers with one company, progressing from supervisor of grow-out facilities to management of processing plants to corporate executive positions. Perdue Farms was not unusual in that respect. An entrepreneur through and through, Frank lived up to his marketing image of "it takes a tough man to make a tender chicken." He mostly used a centralized management style that kept decision making authority in his own hands or those of a few trusted, senior executives whom he had known for a lifetime. Workers were expected to do their jobs.

In later years, Frank increasingly emphasized employee (or "associates" as they are currently referred to) involvement in quality issues and operational decisions. This later emphasis on employee participation undoubtedly eased the transfer of power in 1991 to his son, Jim, which appears to have been unusually smooth. Although Jim grew up in the family business, he spent almost fifteen years earning an undergraduate degree in biology from Wake Forest University, a master's degree in marine biology from the University of Massachusetts at Dartmouth, and a doctorate in fisheries from the University of Washington in Seattle. Returning to Perdue Farms in 1983, he earned an EMBA from Salisbury State University and was assigned positions as plant manager, divisional quality control manager, and vice president of Quality Improvement Process (QIP) prior to becoming Chairman.

Jim has a people-first management style. Company goals center on the three P's: People, Products and Profitability. He believes that business success rests on satisfying customer needs with quality products. It is important to put associates first because "If [associates] come first, they will strive to assure superior product quality—and satisfied customers." This view has had a profound impact on the company culture, which is based on Tom Peters view that "Nobody knows a person's 20 square feet better than the person who works there." The idea is to gather ideas and information from everyone in the organization and maximize productivity by transmitting these ideas throughout the organization.

Key to accomplishing this "employees first" policy is workforce stability, a difficult task in an industry that employs a growing number of associates working in physically demanding and sometimes stressful conditions. A significant number of associates are Hispanic immigrants who may have a poor command of the English language, are sometimes undereducated, and often lack basic health care. In order to increase these associates' opportunity for advancement, Perdue Farms focuses on helping them overcome these disadvantages.

For example, the firm provides English-language classes to help non-English speaking employees assimilate. Ultimately employees can earn the equivalent of a high-school diploma. To deal with physical stress, the company has an ergonomics committee in each plant that studies job requirements and seeks ways to redesign those jobs that put workers at the greatest risk. The company also has an impressive wellness program that currently includes clinics at ten plants. The clinics are staffed by professional medical people working for medical practice groups under contract to Perdue Farms. Employees can visit a doctor for anything from a muscle strain to prenatal care to screening tests for a variety of diseases and have universal access to all Perdue-operated clinics. Dependent care is available. While benefits to the employees are obvious, the company also benefits through a reduction in lost time for medical office visits, lower turnover, and a happier, healthier, more productive, and stable work force.

Marketing

In the early days, chicken was sold to butcher shops and neighborhood groceries as a commodity—that is, producers sold it in bulk and butchers cut and wrapped it. The customer had no idea what firm grew or processed the chicken. Frank Perdue was convinced that higher profits could be made if the firm's products could be sold at a premium price. But, the only reason a product can command a premium price is if customers ask for it by name—and that means the product must be differentiated

Exhibit 2   Perdue Farms Incorporated—Senior Management

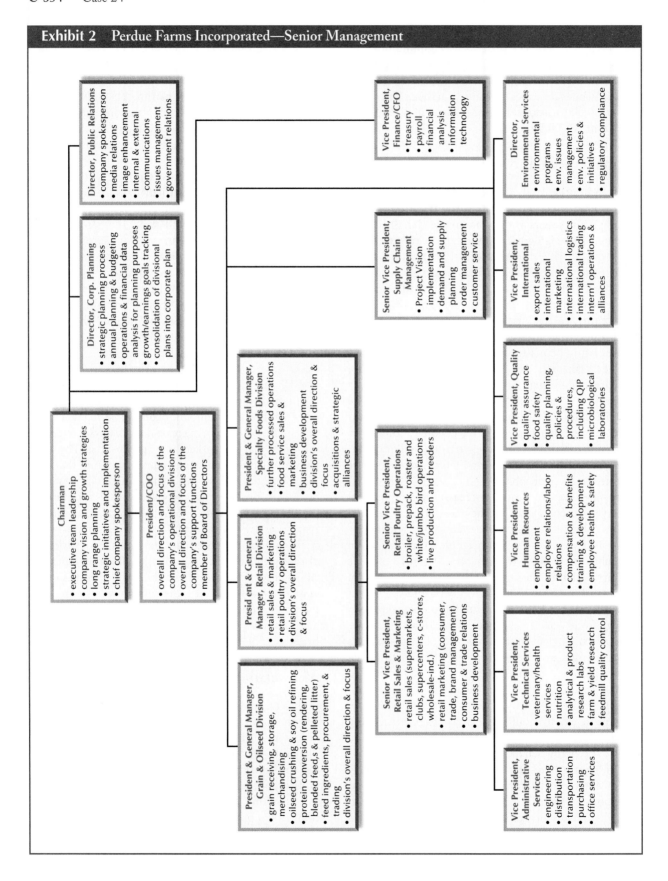

Chairman
- executive team leadership
- company vision and growth strategies
- long range planning
- strategic initiatives and implementation
- chief company spokesperson

President/COO
- overall direction and focus of the company's operational divisions
- overall direction and focus of the company's support functions
- member of Board of Directors

Director, Public Relations
- company spokesperson
- media relations
- image enhancement
- internal & external communications
- issues management
- government relations

Director, Corp. Planning
- strategic planning process
- annual planning & budgeting
- operations & financial data analysis for planning purposes
- growth/earnings goals tracking
- consolidation of divisional plans into corporate plan

Vice President, Finance/CFO
- treasury
- payroll
- financial analysis
- information technology

Director, Environmental Services
- environmental programs
- env. issues management
- env. policies & initiatives
- regulatory compliance

Senior Vice President, Supply Chain Management
- Project Vision implementation
- demand and supply planning
- order management
- customer service

Vice President, International
- export sales
- international marketing
- international logistics
- international trading
- intern'l operations & alliances

President & General Manager, Specialty Foods Division
- further processed operations
- food service sales & marketing
- business development
- division's overall direction & focus
- acquisitions & strategic alliances

President & General Manager, Retail Division
- retail sales & marketing
- retail poultry operations
- division's overall direction & focus

President & General Manager, Grain & Oilseed Division
- grain receiving, storage, merchandising
- oilseed crushing & soy oil refining
- protein conversion (rendering, blended feed,s & pelleted litter)
- feed ingredients, procurement, & trading
- division's overall direction & focus

Senior Vice President, Retail Poultry Operations
- broiler, prepack, roaster and white/jumbo bird operations
- live production and breeders

Vice President, Quality
- quality assurance
- food safety
- quality planning, policies & procedures, including QIP
- microbiological laboratories

Senior Vice President, Retail Sales & Marketing
- retail sales (supermarkets, clubs, supercenters, c-stores, wholesale-ind.)
- retail marketing (consumer, trade, brand management)
- consumer & trade relations
- business development

Vice President, Human Resources
- employment
- employee relations/labor relations
- compensation & benefits
- training & development
- employee health & safety

Vice President, Technical Services
- veterinary/health services
- nutrition
- analytical & product research labs
- farm & yield research
- feedmill quality control

Vice President, Administrative Services
- engineering
- distribution
- transportation
- purchasing
- office services

and "branded." Hence, the emphasis over the years on superior quality, broader breasted chickens, and a healthy golden color (actually the result of adding marigold petals in the feed to enhance the natural yellow color that corn provided).

In 1968, Frank Perdue spent $50,000 on radio advertising. In 1969, he added $80,000 in TV advertising to his radio budget—against the advice of his advertising agency. Although his early TV ads increased sales, he decided the agency he was dealing with didn't match one of the basic Perdue tenets: "The people you deal with should be as good at what they do as you are at what you do." That decision set off a storm of activity on Frank's part. In order to select an ad agency that met his standards, Frank learned more about advertising than any poultry man before him and, in the process, catapulted Perdue Farms into the ranks of the top poultry producers in the country.

He began a ten-week immersion on the theory and practice of advertising. He read books and papers on advertising. He talked to sales managers of every newspaper, radio, and television station in the New York area, consulted experts, and interviewed forty-eight ad agencies. During April 1971, he selected Scali, McCabe, Sloves as his new advertising agency. As the agency tried to figure out how to successfully "brand" a chicken—something that had never been done—they realized that Frank Perdue was their greatest ally. "He looked a little like a chicken himself, and he sounded a little like one, and he squawked a lot!"

McCabe decided that Perdue should be the firm's spokesman. Initially Frank resisted. But, in the end, he accepted the role and the campaign based on "It takes a tough man to make a tender chicken" was born. The firm's very first television commercial showed Frank on a picnic in the Salisbury City Park saying:

> A chicken is what it eats … And my chickens eat better than people do … I store my own grain and mix my own feed … And give my Perdue chickens nothing but pure well water to drink … That's why my chickens always have that healthy golden yellow color … If you want to eat as good as my chickens, you'll just have to eat my chickens.

Additional ads, touting high quality and the broader breasted chicken read as follows:

> Government standards would allow me to call this a grade A chicken … but my standards wouldn't. This chicken is skinny … It has scrapes and hairs … The fact is, my graders

reject 30 percent of the chickens government inspectors accept as grade A … That's why it pays to insist on a chicken with my name on it … If you're not completely satisfied, write me and I'll give you your money back … Who do you write in Washington? … What do they know about chickens?

> The Perdue Roaster is the master race of chickens.

> Never go into a store and just ask for a pound of chicken breasts … Because you could be cheating yourself out of some meat … Here's an ordinary one-pound chicken breast, and here's a one-pound breast of mine … They weigh the same. But as you can see, mine has more meat, and theirs has more bone. I breed the broadest breasted, meatiest chicken you can buy … So don't buy a chicken breast by the pound … Buy them by the name … and get an extra bite in every breast.

The ads paid off. In 1968, Perdue held about 3 percent of the New York market. By 1972, one out of every six chickens eaten in New York was a Perdue chicken. Fifty-one percent of New Yorkers recognized the label. Scali, McCabe, Sloves credited Perdue's "believability" for the success of the program. "This was advertising in which Perdue had a personality that lent credibility to the product. If Frank Perdue didn't look and sound like a chicken, he wouldn't be in the commercials."

Frank had his own view. As he told a Rotary audience in Charlotte, North Carolina, in March 1989, " … . the product met the promise of the advertising and was far superior to the competition. Two great sayings tell it all: 'nothing will destroy a poor product as quickly as good advertising,' and 'a gifted product is mightier than a gifted pen!'"

Today, branded chicken is ubiquitous. The new task for Perdue Farms is to create a unified theme to market a wide variety of products (e.g., fresh meat to fully prepared and frozen products) to a wide variety of customers (e.g., retail, food service, and international). Industry experts believe that the market for fresh poultry has peaked while sales of value added and frozen products continue to grow at a healthy rate. Although domestic retail sales accounts for about 60 percent of Perdue Farms revenues in FY2000, food service sales now account for 20 percent, international sales account for 5 percent, and grain and oilseed contribute the remaining 15 percent. The Company expects food service, international, and grain and oilseed sales to continue to grow as a percentage of total revenues.

Domestic Retail

Today's retail grocery customer is increasingly looking for ease and speed of preparation, i.e., value added products. The move toward value added products has significantly changed the meat department in the modern grocery. There are now five distinct meat outlets for poultry:

1. The fresh meat counter—traditional fresh meat includes whole chicken and parts
2. The delicatessen—processed turkey, rotisserie chicken
3. The frozen counter—individually quick frozen items such as frozen whole chickens, turkeys, and Cornish hens.
4. Home meal replacement—fully prepared entrees such as Perdue brand "Short Cuts" and Deluca brand entrees (the Deluca brand was acquired and is sold under its own name) that are sold along with salads and desserts so that you can assemble your own dinner
5. Shelf stable—canned products

Because Perdue Farms has always used the phrase "fresh young chicken" as the centerpiece of its marketing, value added products and the retail frozen counter create a possible conflict with past marketing themes. Are these products compatible with the company's marketing image and, if so, how does the company express the notion of quality in this broader product environment? To answer that question, Perdue Farms has been studying what the term "fresh young chicken" means to customers who consistently demand quicker and easier preparation and who admit that they freeze most of their fresh meat purchases once they get home. One view is that the importance of the term "fresh young chicken" comes from the customer's perception that "quality" and "freshness" are closely associated. Thus, the real issue may be "trust," i.e., the customer must believe that the product, whether fresh or frozen, is the freshest, highest quality possible and future marketing themes must develop that concept.

Food Service

The food service business consists of a wide variety of public and private customers including restaurant chains, governments, hospitals, schools, prisons, transportation facilities, and the institutional contractors who supply meals to them. Historically, these customers have not been brand conscious, requiring the supplier to meet strict specifications at the lowest price, thus making this category a less than ideal fit for Perdue Farms. However, as Americans continue to eat a larger percentage of their meals away from home, traditional grocery sales have flattened while the food service sector has shown strong growth. Across the domestic poultry industry, food service accounts for approximately 50 percent of total poultry sales while approximately 20 percent of Perdue Farms revenues come from this category. Clearly, Perdue Farms is playing catchup in this critical market.

Because Perdue Farms has neither strength nor expertise in the food service market, management believes that acquiring companies that already have food service expertise is the best strategy. An acquisition already completed is the purchase in September 1998 of Gol-Pak Corporation based in Monterey, Tennessee. A further processor of products for the food service industry, Gol-Pak had about 1600 employees and revenues of about $200 million per year.

International

International markets have generally been a happy surprise. In the early 1990s, Perdue Farms began exporting specialty products such as chicken feet (known as "paws") to customers in China. Although not approved for sale for human consumption in the United States, paws are considered a delicacy in China. By 1992, international sales, consisting principally of paws, had become a small, but profitable, business of about 30 million pounds per year. Building on this small "toehold," by 1998 Perdue Farms had quickly built an international business of more than 500 million pounds per year with annual revenues of more than $140 million, selling a wide variety of products to China, Japan, Russia, and the Ukraine (see Exhibit 3).

In some ways, Japan is an excellent fit for Perdue Farms products because customers demand high quality. However, all Asian markets prefer dark meat, a serendipitous fit with the U.S. preference for white breast meat because it means that excess (to America) dark meat can be sold in Asia at a premium price. On the downside, Perdue Farms gains much of its competitive advantage from branding (e.g., trademarks, processes, and technological and biological know-how) which has little value internationally because most of Asia has not yet embraced the concept of branded chicken.

To better serve export markets, Perdue Farms has developed a portside freezing facility in Newport News, Virginia. This permits poultry to be shipped directly to

Exhibit 3   International Volume

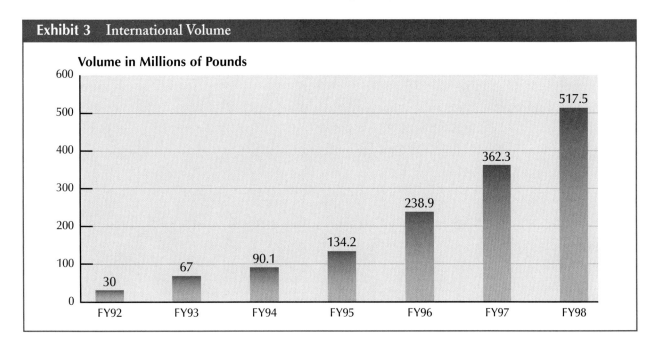

the port, reducing processing costs and helping to balance ocean shipping costs to Asia which are in the range of 2/3 cents per pound (contracting an entire ship equal to 300–500 truckloads).

Shipping poultry to Asia is not without problems. For example, in China, delivery trucks are seldom refrigerated. Thus, the poultry can begin to thaw as it is being delivered, limiting the distance it can be transported prior to sale. One shipload of Perdue Farms chicken bound for Russia actually vanished. It had been inappropriately impounded using forged documents. Although most of its dollar value was eventually recovered, it is important for firms to be aware of the possible difficulties of ocean shipping and the use of foreign ports.

Initial demand for product in Russia, Poland, and Eastern Europe was huge. By FY 1998, a significant portion of international volume was being purchased by Russia. Unfortunately, the crumbling of Russia's economy has had a devastating effect on imports and sales are currently off significantly. Such instability of demand, coupled with rampant corruption, makes risking significant capital unacceptable.

Import duties and taxes are also a barrier. In China, according to the USDA, import duty rates for poultry are a whopping 45 percent for favored countries and 70 percent for unfavored countries. And, there is a 17 percent value added tax for all countries. Import duties and taxes in Russia have been similarly high. Hence, profits can be expected to be slim.

Perdue Farms has created a joint partnership with Jiang Nan Feng (JNF) brand in order to develop a small processing plant in Shanghai. Brand recognition is being built through normal marketing tools. The products use the first "tray pack" wrapping available in Shanghai supermarkets. This new business shows promise because the sale in China of homegrown, fresh dark meat is a significant competitive advantage. Additionally, although government regulations do not presently permit importation to the United States of foreign-grown poultry, the future possibility of importing excess white meat from Shanghai to the United States is attractive since Asian markets, which prefer dark meat, will have difficulty absorbing all of the white breast meat from locally grown poultry. Perdue Farms' management believes that investments in processing facilities in Asia require the company to partner with a local company. Attempting to go it alone is simply too risky due to the significant cultural differences.

Operations

Two words sum up the Perdue approach to operations: quality and efficiency—with emphasis on the first over the latter. Perdue, more than most companies, represents the Total Quality Management (TQM) slogan, "Quality, a journey without end." Some of the key events are listed in Exhibit 4.

Both quality and efficiency are improved through the management of details. Exhibit 5 depicts the structure

Exhibit 4   Milestones in the Quality Improvement Process at Perdue Farms

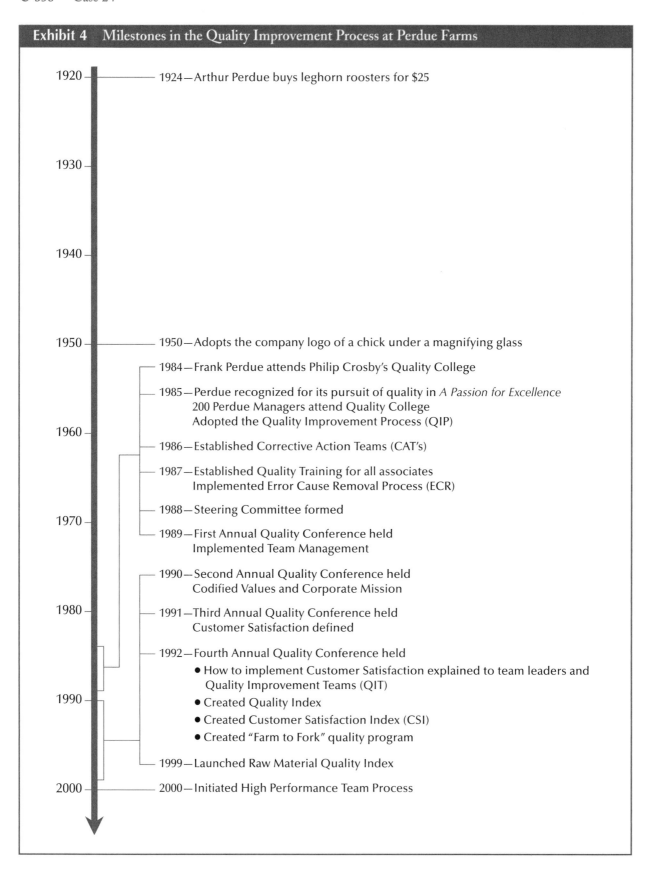

1920

1924—Arthur Perdue buys leghorn roosters for $25

1930

1940

1950

1950—Adopts the company logo of a chick under a magnifying glass

1984—Frank Perdue attends Philip Crosby's Quality College

1985—Perdue recognized for its pursuit of quality in *A Passion for Excellence*
200 Perdue Managers attend Quality College
Adopted the Quality Improvement Process (QIP)

1960

1986—Established Corrective Action Teams (CAT's)

1987—Established Quality Training for all associates
Implemented Error Cause Removal Process (ECR)

1988—Steering Committee formed

1970

1989—First Annual Quality Conference held
Implemented Team Management

1990—Second Annual Quality Conference held
Codified Values and Corporate Mission

1980

1991—Third Annual Quality Conference held
Customer Satisfaction defined

1992—Fourth Annual Quality Conference held
• How to implement Customer Satisfaction explained to team leaders and
Quality Improvement Teams (QIT)
• Created Quality Index

1990

• Created Customer Satisfaction Index (CSI)
• Created "Farm to Fork" quality program

1999—Launched Raw Material Quality Index

2000

2000—Initiated High Performance Team Process

Exhibit 5   Perdue Farms Integrated Operations

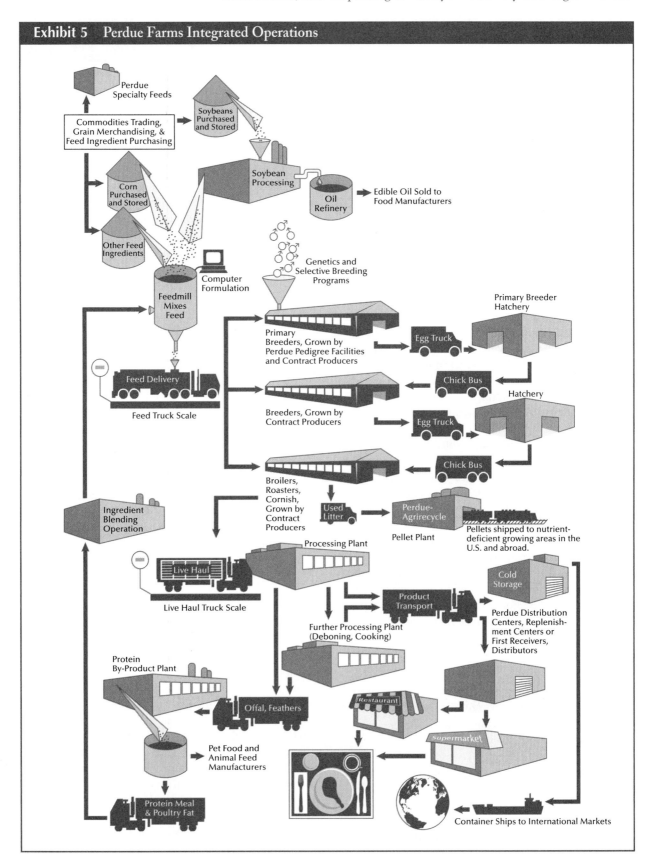

and product flow of a generic, vertically integrated broiler company. A broiler company can choose which steps in the process it wants to accomplish in-house and which it wants suppliers to provide. For example, the broiler company could purchase all grain, oilseed, meal, and other feed products. Or it could contract with hatcheries to supply primary breeders and hatchery supply flocks.

Perdue Farms chose maximum vertical integration in order to control every detail. It breeds and hatches its own eggs (nineteen hatcheries), selects its contract growers, builds Perdue-engineered chicken houses, formulates and manufactures its own feed (twelve poultry feedmills, one specialty feedmill, two ingredient blending operations), oversees the care and feeding of the chicks, operates its own processing plants (twenty-one processing/further processing plants), distributes via its own trucking fleet, and markets the products (see Exhibit 5). Total process control formed the basis for Frank Perdue's early claims that Perdue Farms poultry is, indeed, higher quality than other poultry. When he stated in his early ads that "A chicken is what it eats …. I store my own grain and mix my own feed … .and give my Perdue chickens nothing but well water to drink ….," he knew that his claim was honest and he could back it up.

Total process control also enables Perdue Farms to ensure that nothing goes to waste. Eight measurable items—hatchability, turnover, feed conversion, livability, yield, birds per man-hour, utilization, and grade—are tracked routinely.

Perdue Farms continues to ensure that nothing artificial is fed to or injected into the birds. No shortcuts are taken. A chemical-free and steroid-free diet is fed to the chickens. Young chickens are vaccinated against disease. Selective breeding is used to improve the quality of the chickens' stock. Chickens are bred to yield more white breast meat because that is what the consumer wants.

Exhibit 6   Quality Policy

- WE SHALL produce products and provide services at all times that meet or exceed the expectations of our customers.
- WE SHALL not be content to be of equal quality to our competitors.
- OUR COMMITMENT is to be increasingly superior.
- CONTRIBUTION TO QUALITY is a responsibility shared by everyone in the Perdue organization.

Exhibit 7   Perdue Farms Inc. Technological Accomplishments

- Conducts more research than all competitors combined
- Breeds chickens with consistently more breast meat than any other bird in the industry
- First to use digital scales to guarantee weights to customers
- First to package fully-cooked chicken products in microwaveable trays
- First to have a box lab to define quality of boxes from different suppliers
- First to test both its chickens and competitors' chickens on 52 quality factors every week
- Improved on time deliveries 20 percent between 1987 and 1993
- Built state of the art analytical and microbiological laboratories for feed and end product analysis
- First to develop best management practices for food safety across all areas of the company
- First to develop commercially viable pelletized poultry litter

---

To ensure that Perdue Farms' poultry continues to lead the industry in quality, the company buys and analyzes competitors' products regularly. Inspection associates grade these products and share the information with the highest levels of management. In addition, the company's Quality Policy is displayed at all locations and taught to all associates in quality training (see Exhibit 6).

Research and Development

Perdue is an acknowledged industry leader in the use of research and technology to provide quality products and service to its customers. The company spends more on research as a percent of revenues than any other poultry processor. This practice goes back to Frank Perdue's focus on finding ways to differentiate his products based on quality and value. It was research into selective breeding that resulted in the broader breast, an attribute of Perdue Farms' chicken that was the basis of his early advertising. Although other processors have also improved their stock, Perdue Farms believes that it still leads the industry. A list of some of Perdue Farms technological accomplishments is given in Exhibit 7.

As with every other aspect of the business, Perdue Farms tries to leave nothing to chance. The company employs specialists in avian science, microbiology, genetics, nutrition, and veterinary science. Because of its research and development capabilities, Perdue Farms is often involved in USDA field tests with pharmaceutical suppliers. Knowledge and experience gained from these tests can lead to a competitive advantage. For example, Perdue has the most extensive and expensive vaccination program in the industry. Currently, the company is working with and studying the practices of several European producers who use completely different methods. The company has used research to significantly increase productivity. For example, in the 1950s, it took fourteen weeks to grow a 3-pound chicken. Today, it takes only seven weeks to grow a 5-pound chicken. This gain in efficiency is due principally to improvements in the conversion rate of feed to chicken. The current rate of conversion is about two pounds of feed to produce one pound of chicken. Feed represents about 65 percent of the cost of growing a chicken. Thus, if additional research can further improve the conversion rate of feed to chicken by just 1 percent, it would represent estimated additional income of $2.5–3 million per week or $130–156 million per year.

Finance

Perdue Farms, Inc., is privately held and considers financial information to be proprietary. Hence, available data is limited. Stock is primarily held by the family with a limited amount held by Perdue Management. Common numbers used by the media and the poultry industry peg Perdue Farms' revenues for FY2000 at about $2.5 billion and the number of associates at nearly 20,000. Forbes magazine has estimated FY2000 operating profits at about 160 million and net profits at about 22 million.

The firm's compound sales growth rate has been slowly decreasing during the past twenty years, mirroring the industry, which has been experiencing market saturation and overproduction. However, Perdue has

compensated by using manpower more efficiently through improvements such as automation. For example, twenty years ago, a 1 percent increase in associates resulted in a 1.6 percent increase in revenue. Currently, a 1 percent increase in associates results in an 8.5 percent increase in revenues (see Exhibit 8).

Poultry operations can be divided into four segments: Retail Chicken (growth rate 5 percent), Food-service Chicken and Turkey (growth rate 12 percent), International Sales (growth rate 64 percent over past six years), and Grain and Oilseed (growth rate 10 percent). The bulk of Perdue Farms' sales continues to come from retail chicken—the sector with the slowest growth rate. The greatest opportunity appears to lie in food-service sales, where the company is admittedly behind, and international sales where political and economic instability in target countries make the risk to capital significant.

Perdue Farms has been profitable every year since its founding with the exception of 1988 and 1996. Company officials believe the loss in 1988 was caused by overproduction by the industry and higher administrative costs resulting from a decentralization effort begun during the mid-eighties. At that time, there was a concerted effort to push decisions down through the corporate ranks to provide more autonomy. When the new strategy resulted in significantly higher administrative costs due to duplication of effort, the company responded quickly by returning to the basics, reconsolidating and downsizing. The loss in 1996 was due to the impact of high corn prices. Currently, the goal is to constantly streamline in order to provide cost-effective business solutions.

Perdue Farms approaches financial management conservatively, using retained earnings and cash flow to finance most asset replacement projects and normal growth. When planning expansion projects or acquisitions, long-term debt is used. The target debt limit is 55 percent of equity. Such debt is normally provided by domestic and international bank and insurance companies. The debt strategy is to match asset lives with

Exhibit 8 Annual Compound Growth Rate Through FY2000			
	Revenue	Associates	Sales/Associate
past 20 years	10.60%	6.48%	3.87%
past 15 years	8.45%	4.48%	4.48%
past 10 years	7.39%	4.75%	2.52%
past 5 years	8.39%	0.99%	7.33%

liability maturities, and have a mix of fixed rate and variable rate debt. Growth plans require about two dollars in projected incremental sales growth for each dollar in invested capital.

Environment

Environmental issues present a constant challenge to all poultry processors. Growing, slaughtering, and processing poultry is a difficult and tedious process that demands absolute efficiency in order to keep operating costs at an acceptable level. Inevitably, detractors argue that the process is dangerous to workers, inhumane to the poultry, hard on the environment and results in food that may not be safe. Thus media headlines such as "Human Cost of Poultry Business Bared," "Animal Rights Advocates Protest Chicken Coop Conditions," "Processing Plants Leave a Toxic Trail," or "EPA mandates Poultry Regulations" are routine.

Perdue Farms tries to be pro-active in managing environmental issues. In April 1993, the company created an Environmental Steering Committee. Its mission is "….to provide all Perdue Farms work sites with vision, direction, and leadership so that they can be good corporate citizens from an environmental perspective today and in the future." The committee is responsible for overseeing how the company is doing in such environmentally sensitive areas as waste water, storm water, hazardous waste, solid waste, recycling, bio-solids, and human health and safety.

For example, disposing of dead birds has long been an industry problem. Perdue Farms developed small composters for use on each farm. Using this approach, carcasses are reduced to an end-product that resembles soil in a matter of a few days. The disposal of hatchery waste is another environmental challenge. Historically, manure and un-hatched eggs were shipped to a landfill. However, Perdue Farms developed a way to reduce the waste by 50 percent by selling the liquid fraction to a pet food processor that cooks it for protein. The other 50 percent is recycled through a rendering process. In 1990, Perdue Farms spent $4.2 million to upgrade its existing treatment facility with a state-of-the-art system at its Accomac, Virginia and Showell, Maryland plants. These facilities use forced hot air heated to 120 degrees to cause the microbes to digest all traces of ammonia, even during the cold winter months.

More than ten years ago, North Carolina's Occupational Safety and Health Administration cited Perdue Farms for an unacceptable level of repetitive stress injuries at its Lewiston and Robersonville, North Carolina processing plants. This sparked a major research program in which Perdue Farms worked with Health and Hygiene Inc. of Greensboro, North Carolina to learn more about ergonomics, the repetitive movements required to accomplish specific jobs. Results have been dramatic. Launched in 1991 after two years of development, the program videotapes employees at all of Perdue Farms' plants as they work in order to describe and place stress values on the various tasks. Although the cost to Perdue Farms has been significant, results have been dramatic with workers' compensation claims down 44 percent, lost-time recordables just 7.7 percent of the industry average, an 80 percent decrease in serious repetitive stress cases, and a 50 percent reduction in lost time or surgery back injuries (Shelley Reese, "Helping Employees get a Grip, *Business and Health*, Aug. 1998).

Despite these advances, serious problems continue to develop. In 1997, the organism Pfiesteria burst into media headlines when massive numbers of dead fish with lesions turned up along the Chesapeake Bay in Maryland. Initial findings pointed to manure runoff from the poultry industry. Political constituencies quickly called for increased regulation to ensure proper manure storage and fertilizer use. The company readily admits that " … .the poultry process is a closed system. There is lots of nitrogen and phosphorus in the grain, it passes through the chicken and is returned to the environment as manure. Obviously, if you bring additional grain into a closed area such as the Delmarva Peninsula, you increase the amount of nitrogen and phosphorus in the soil unless you find a way to get rid of it." Nitrogen and phosphorus from manure normally make excellent fertilizer that moves slowly in the soil. However, scientists speculate that erosion speeds up runoff threatening the health of nearby streams, rivers, and larger bodies of water such as the Chesapeake Bay. The problem for the industry is that proposals to control the runoff are sometimes driven more by politics and emotion than research, which is not yet complete.

Although it is not clear what role poultry-related nitrogen and phosphorus runoff played in the pfiesteria outbreak, regulators believe the microorganism feasts on the algae that grows when too much of these nutrients is present in the water. Thus, the EPA and various states are considering new regulations. Currently, contract growers are responsible for either using or disposing of the manure from their chicken houses. But some regulators and environmentalists believe that (1) it is too complicated to police the utilization and disposal practices of thousands of individual farmers and (2) only the big poultry companies have the financial resources to properly dispose of the waste. Thus, they want to make poultry companies responsible for all waste disposal, a move that the industry strongly opposes.

Some experts have called for conservation measures that might limit the density of chicken houses in a given area or even require a percentage of existing chicken houses to be taken out of production periodically. Obviously this would be very hard on the farm families who own existing chicken houses and could result in fewer acres devoted to agriculture. Working with AgriRecycle Inc. of Springfield, Missouri, Perdue Farms has developed a possible solution. The plan envisions the poultry companies processing excess manure into pellets for use as fertilizer. This would permit sale outside the poultry-growing region, better balancing the input of grain. Spokesmen estimate that as much as 120,000 tons, nearly one-third of the surplus nutrient from manure produced each year on the Delmarva peninsula, could be sold to corn growers in other parts of the country. Prices would be market driven but could be $25–30 per ton, suggesting a potential small profit. Still, almost any attempt to control the problem potentially raises the cost of growing chickens, forcing poultry processors to look elsewhere for locations where the chicken population is less dense.

In general, solving industry environmental problems presents at least five major challenges to the poultry processor:

- How to maintain the trust of the poultry consumer,
- How to ensure that the poultry remain healthy,
- How to protect the safety of the employees and the process,
- How to satisfy legislators who need to show their constituents that they are taking firm action when environmental problems occur, and
- How to keep costs at an acceptable level.

Jim Perdue sums up Perdue Farms' position as follows: " … .we must not only comply with environmental laws as they exist today, but look to the future to make sure we don't have any surprises. We must make sure our environmental policy statement is real, that

---

Exhibit 9   Perdue Farms Environmental Policy Statement

Perdue Farms is committed to environmental stewardship and shares that commitment with its farm family partners. We're proud of the leadership we're providing our industry in addressing the full range of environmental challenges related to animal agriculture and food processing. We've invested—and continue to invest—millions of dollars in research, new technology, equipment upgrades, and awareness and education as part of our ongoing commitment to protecting the environment.

- Perdue Farms was among the first poultry companies with a dedicated Environmental Services department. Our team of environmental managers is responsible for ensuring that every Perdue facility operates within *100 percent compliance of all applicable environmental regulations and permits.*

- Through our joint venture, Perdue AgriRecycle, Perdue Farms is investing $12 million to build in Delaware a first-of-its-kind pellet plant that will convert surplus poultry litter into a starter fertilizer that will be marketed internationally to nutrient-deficient regions. The facility, which will serve the entire Delmarva region, is scheduled to begin operation in April 2001.

- We continue to explore new technologies that will reduce water usage in our processing plants without compromising food safety or quality.

- We invested thousands of man-hours in producer education to assist our family farm partners in managing their independent poultry operations in the most environmentally responsible manner possible. In addition, all our poultry producers are required to have nutrient management plans and dead-bird composters.

- Perdue Farms was one of four poultry companies operating in Delaware to sign an agreement with Delaware officials outlining our companies' voluntary commitment to help independent poultry producers dispose of surplus chicken litter.

- Our Technical Services department is conducting ongoing research into feed technology as a means of reducing the nutrients in poultry manure. We've already achieved phosphorous reductions that far exceed the industry average.

- We recognize that the environmental impact of animal agriculture is more pronounced in areas where development is decreasing the amount of farmland available to produce grain for feed and to accept nutrients. That is why we view independent grain *and* poultry producers as vital business partners and strive to preserve the economic viability of the family farm.

At Perdue Farms, we believe that it is possible to preserve the family farm; provide a safe, abundant, and affordable food supply; and protect the environment. However, we believe that can best happen when there is cooperation and trust between the poultry industry, agriculture, environmental groups, and state officials. We hope Delaware's effort will become a model for other states to follow.

there's something behind it and that we do what we say we're going to do." (see Exhibit 9)

Logistics and Information Systems

The explosion of poultry products and increasing number of customers during recent years placed a severe strain on the existing logistic system, which was developed at a time when there were far fewer products, fewer delivery points, and lower volume. Hence, the company had limited ability to improve service levels, could not support further growth, and could not introduce innovative services that might provide a competitive advantage.

In the poultry industry, companies are faced with two significant problems—time and forecasting. Fresh poultry has a limited shelf life—measured in days. Thus forecasts must be extremely accurate and deliveries timely. On one hand, estimating requirements too conservatively results in product shortages. Mega-customers such as WalMart will not tolerate product shortages that lead to empty shelves and lost sales. On the other hand, if estimates are overstated, the result is outdated products that cannot be sold and losses for Perdue Farms. A common expression in the poultry industry is "you either sell it or smell it."

Forecasting has always been extremely difficult in the poultry industry because the processor needs to know approximately eighteen months in advance how many broilers will be needed in order to size hatchery supply flocks and contract with growers to provide live broilers. Most customers (e.g., grocers, food service buyers) have a much shorter planning window. Additionally, there is no way for Perdue Farms to know when rival poultry processors will put a particular product on special, reducing Perdue Farms sales, or when bad weather and other uncontrollable problems may reduce demand.

Historically, poultry companies have relied principally on extrapolation of past demand, industry networks, and other contacts to make their estimates. Although product complexity has exacerbated the problem, the steady movement away from fresh product to frozen product (which has a longer shelf life) offers some relief.

In the short run, Information Technology (IT) has helped by shortening the distance between the customer and Perdue Farms. As far back as 1987, PCs were placed directly on each customer service associate's desk, allowing them to enter customer orders directly. Next, a system was developed to put dispatchers in direct contact with every truck in the system so that they would have accurate

information about product inventory and truck location at all times. Now, IT is moving to further shorten the distance between the customer and the Perdue Farms service representative by putting a PC on the customer's desk. All of these steps improve communication and shorten the time from order to delivery.

In the longer run, these steps are not enough due to the rapidly expanding complexity of the industry. For example, today, poultry products fall into four unique channels of distribution:

- Bulk fresh—**Timeliness and frequency of delivery are critical to ensure freshness.** Distribution requirements are high volume and low cost delivery.
- Domestic frozen and further processed products—**Temperature integrity is critical**, distribution requirements are frequency and timeliness of delivery. This channel lends itself to dual temperature trailer systems and load consolidation.
- Export—**Temperature integrity, high volume, and low cost are critical.** This channel lends itself to inventory consolidation and custom loading of vessels.
- Consumer packaged goods (packaged fresh, prepared, and deli products)—**Differentiate via innovative products and services.** Distribution requirements are reduced lead time and low cost.

Thus, forecasting now requires the development of a sophisticated **supply chain management system** that can efficiently integrate all facets of operations including grain and oilseed activities, hatcheries and growing facilities, processing plants (which now produce more than 400 products at more than twenty locations), distribution facilities, and, finally, the distributors, supermarkets, food service customers, and export markets (see Exhibit 5). Perdue Farms underlined the importance of the successful implementation of supply chain management by creating a new executive position, Senior Vice President for Supply Chain Management.

A key step in overhauling the distribution infrastructure is the building of replenishment centers that will, in effect, be buffers between the processing plants and the customers. The portside facility in Norfolk, Virginia, which serves the international market, is being expanded and a new domestic freezer facility added.

Conceptually, products are directed from the processing plants to the replenishment and freezer centers based on customer forecasts that have been converted to an optimized production schedule. Perdue Farms trucks deliver these bulk products to the centers in finished or semi-finished form. At the centers, further finishing and

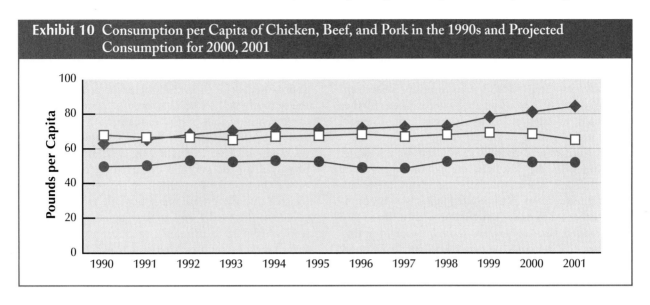

Exhibit 10 Consumption per Capita of Chicken, Beef, and Pork in the 1990s and Projected Consumption for 2000, 2001

packaging is accomplished. Finally, specific customer orders are custom palletized and loaded on trucks (either Perdue-owned or contracted) for delivery to individual customers. All shipments are made up from replenishment center inventory. Thus, the need for accurate demand forecasting by the distribution centers is key.

In order to control the entire supply chain management process, Perdue Farms purchased a multi-million dollar information technology system that represents the biggest non-tangible asset expense in the company's history. This integrated, state-of-the-art information system required total process re-engineering, a project that took eighteen months and required training 1200 associates. Major goals of the system were to (1) make it easier and more desirable for the customer to do business with Perdue Farms, (2) make it easier for Perdue Farms associates to get the job done, and (3) take as much cost out of the process as possible.

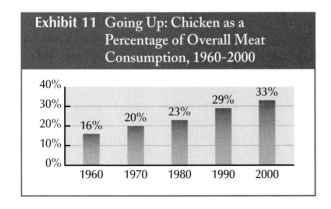

Exhibit 11 Going Up: Chicken as a Percentage of Overall Meat Consumption, 1960-2000

Industry Trends

The poultry industry is affected by consumer, industry, and governmental regulatory trends. Currently, chicken is the number one meat consumed in the United States with 40 percent market share (see Exhibits 10 and 11). Typical Americans consume about 81 pounds of chicken, 69 pounds of beef, and 52 pounds of pork annually (USDA data). Additionally, chicken is becoming the most popular meat in the world. In 1997, poultry set an export record of $2.5 billion. Although exports fell 6 percent in 1998, the decrease was attributed to Russia's and Asia's financial crisis and food industry experts expect this to be only a temporary setback. Hence, the world market is clearly a growth opportunity for the future.

The popularity and growth of poultry products is attributed to both nutritional and economic issues. Poultry products contain significantly less fat and cholesterol than other meat products. In the United States, the demand for boneless, skinless breast meat, the leanest meat on poultry, is so great that dark meat is often sold at a discount in the United States or shipped overseas where it is preferred over white meat.

Another trend is a decrease in demand for whole birds to be used as the base dish for home meals and an increase in demand for products that have been further processed for either home or restaurant consumption. For example, turkey or chicken hot dogs, fully-cooked sliced chicken or turkey and turkey pastrami—which neither looks nor tastes like turkey—can be found in most deli cases. Many supermarkets sell either whole or parts of hot rotisserie chicken. Almost all fast food restaurants have at least one sandwich based on poultry products. Many up-scale restaurants feature poultry products that are shipped to them frozen and partially prepared in order to simplify restaurant preparation. All these products have been further processed, adding value and increasing the potential profit margin.

The industry is consolidating, that is, the larger companies in the industry are continuing to buy smaller firms. Currently there are about thirty-five major poultry firms in the United States but this number is expected to drop to twenty or twenty-five within the next ten years. There are several reasons for this. Stagnant U.S. demand and general product oversupply create downward price pressure that makes it difficult for smaller firms to operate profitably. In addition, pressure for efficiency improvements requires huge capital outlays. Finally, mega-retailers such as Sam's Club and Royal Ahold (the Dutch owner of several U.S. supermarket chains) do not like to manage individual contracts with numerous smaller processors. Mega-retailers prefer to deal with mega-suppliers.

The industry is heavily regulated. The Food and Drug Administration (FDA) monitors product safety. The USDA inspects poultry as it arrives at the processing plant. After it is killed, each bird is again inspected by a USDA inspector for avian diseases, contamination of feces, or other foreign material. All poultry that does not meet regulations is destroyed under USDA supervision. USDA inspectors also examine the plant, equipment, operating procedures, and personnel for compliance with sanitary regulations. Congress has mandated that the USDA make this information available online. Additional intensive inspections of statistically selected samples of poultry products have been recommended by the National Academy of Sciences. Thus, additional FDA regulations for product quality are anticipated.

Although poultry produces less waste per pound of product than cattle or hogs, all meat industries are experiencing increased scrutiny by the Environmental Protection Agency (EPA) regarding the disposal of waste. In general, waste generated at processing plants is well controlled by regulation, monitoring, and fines. When an EPA violation occurs, the company that operates the plant can receive a substantial fine, potentially millions of dollars.

Still, the most difficult problems to deal with are those that occur as a cumulative result of numerous processors producing in a relatively limited area. For example, increasing poultry production in a given area intensifies the problem of disposal of manure. In man-made fertilizer, phosphorous and nitrogen exist in approximately a 1 to 8 ratio whereas in poultry manure the ratio can be 1 to 1. Thus, too much poultry manure can result in serious phosphorous run-off into streams and rivers, potentially resulting in aquatic disease and degradation of water quality. In 1997, an outbreak of pfiesteria, a toxic microbe, occurred in the tributaries of the Chesapeake Bay. Although the poultry industry insisted that there were many possible reasons for the problem, the media and most regulatory spokespersons attributed it primarily to phosphorous run-off from chicken manure. After much negative publicity and extensive investigation by both poultry processors and state regulatory agencies, the State of Maryland passed the Water Quality Act of 1998, which required nutrient management plans. However, many environmentalists continue to believe that the EPA must create additional, stricter federal environmental regulations. Recent regulatory activity has continued to focus on Eastern Shore agriculture, especially the poultry industry. However, new studies from the U.S. Geological Survey suggest that the vast majority of nutrients affecting the Chesapeake Bay come from rivers that do not flow through the poultry-producing regions of the Eastern Shore. The studies also found that improved agricultural management practices have reduced nutrient runoff from farmlands. Jim Perdue says "While the poultry industry must accept responsibility for its share of nutrients, public policy should view the watershed as a whole and address all the factors that influence water quality."

Other government agencies whose regulations impact the industry include The Occupational Safety and Health Administration (OSHA) for employee safety and the Immigration and Naturalization Service (INS) for undocumented workers. OSHA enforces its regulations via periodic inspections, and levies fines when non-compliance is found. For example, a Hudson Foods poultry plant was fined more than a million dollars for alleged willful violations causing ergonomic injury to workers. The INS also uses periodic inspections to find undocumented workers. It estimates that undocumented aliens working in the industry vary from 3 percent to 78 percent of the workforce at individual plants. Plants that are found to use undocumented workers, especially those that are repeat offenders, can be heavily fined.

The Future

The marketplace for poultry in the twenty-first century will be very different from the past. Understanding the wants and needs of generation Xers and echo-boomers will be key to responding successfully to these differences.

Quality will continue to be essential. In the 1970s, quality was the cornerstone of Frank Perdue's successful marketing program to "brand" his poultry. However, in the twenty-first century, quality will not be enough. Today's customers expect—even demand—all products to be high quality. Thus, Perdue Farms plans to use customer service to further differentiate the company. The focus will be on learning how to become indispensable to the customer by taking cost out of the product and delivering it exactly the way the customer wants it, where and when the customer wants it. In short, as Jim Perdue says, "Perdue Farms wants to become so easy to do business with that the customer will have no reason to do business with anyone else."

In the poultry business, customer purchase decisions, as well as company profitability, hinge on mere pennies. Thus, the location of processing facilities is key. Historically, Perdue Farms has been an Eastern Shore company and has maintained major processing facilities on the Eastern Shore. However, it currently costs about 1½ cents more per pound to grow poultry on the Eastern Shore versus what poultry can be grown for in Arkansas. This difference results from the cost of labor, compliance with federal and state environmental laws, resource costs (e.g., feed grain), and other variables. Clearly, selecting favorable sites for future growing and processing facilities is key. In the future, assuming regulations will permit the importation of foreign-grown poultry, producers could even use inexpensive international labor markets to further reduce costs. The opportunity for large growers to capture these savings puts increased pressure on small poultry companies. This suggests further consolidation of the industry.

Grocery companies are also consolidating in order to compete with huge food industry newcomers such as Walmart and Royal Ahold. These new competitors gain efficiency by minimizing the number of their suppliers and buying huge amounts from each at the lowest possible price. In effect, both mega-companies—the supplier and the buyer—become dependent on each other. Further, mega-companies expect their suppliers to do more for them. For example, Perdue Farms considers it possible that, using sophisticated distribution information programs, they will soon be able to manage the entire meat department requirements for several supermarket chains. Providing this service would support Perdue Farms' goal of becoming indispensable to their first line retail customer, the grocer.

The twenty-first century consumer will demand many options. Clearly, the demand for uncooked, whole chickens purchased at the meat counter has peaked. Demand is moving toward further processed poultry. To support this trend, Perdue Farms plans to open several additional cooking plants. In addition, a criterion for future acquisitions will be whether they support value added processing. Products from these plants will fill food service requirements and grocery sales of prepared foods such as delicatessen, frozen, home meal replacement, and shelf stable items. Additionally, the twenty-first century customer will be everywhere. Whether at work, at a sports event, in school, or traveling on the highway, customers expect to have convenient refreshment machines available with a wide selection of wholesome, ready-to-eat products. Designing a distribution system that can handle all of these options is extremely difficult. For example, the system must be able to efficiently organize hundreds of customer orders that are chosen from more than 400 different products that are processed and further prepared at more than twenty facilities throughout the southeast for delivery by one truck—a massive distribution task. As executives note, the company survived up until now using distribution techniques created as many as twenty years ago when there were a handful of products and processing facilities. However, the system approached gridlock during the late 1990s. Thus, Perdue Farms invested in a state of the art information processing system—a tough decision because "we could build two new processing plants for the price of this technology package."

International markets are a conundrum. On one hand, Perdue Farms' international revenue has grown from an insignificant side business in 1994 to about $140 million in 1999, approximately 5 percent of total revenues. Further, its contribution to profits is significant. Poultry is widely accepted around the world providing opportunities for further growth. But trying to be global doesn't work. Different cultures value different parts of the chicken and demand different meat color, preparation, and seasoning. Thus, products must be customized. Parts that are not in demand in a particular country must be sold at severely reduced prices, used as feed, or shipped frozen to a different market where demand exists. While this can be done, it is a distribution problem that significantly complicates an already diffi-cult forecasting model.

International markets can also be very unstable, exposing Perdue Farms to significant demand instabil-ity and potential losses. For example, in 1997, about 50 percent of Perdue Farms' international revenues came from Russia. However, political and economic prob-lems in Russia reduced 1999 revenues significantly.

This high level of instability, coupled with corruption that thrives in a country experiencing severe political and economic turmoil, introduces significant risk to future investment.

Clearly, the future holds many opportunities. But none of them comes without risk and Perdue Farms must carefully choose where it wants to direct its scarce resources.

Case 25

Philip Condit and the Boeing 777: From Design and Development to Production and Sales

Isaac Cohen, *San Jose State University*

Following his promotion to Boeing CEO in 1988, Frank Shrontz looked for ways to stretch and upgrade the Boeing 767—an eight-year-old wide-body twin jet—in order to meet Airbus competition. Airbus had just launched two new 300-seat wide-body models, the two-engine A330 and the four-engine A340. Boeing had no 300-seat jetliner in service, nor did the company plan to develop such a jet.

To find out whether Boeing's customers were interested in a double-decker 767, Philip Condit, Boeing Executive Vice President and future CEO (1996) met with United Airlines Vice President Jim Guyette. Guyette rejected the idea outright, claiming that an upgraded 767 was no match to Airbus' new model transports. Instead, Guyette urged Boeing to develop a brand new commercial jet, the most advanced airplane of its generation.[1] Shrontz had heard similar suggestions from other airline carriers. He reconsidered Boeing's options, and decided to abandon the 767 idea in favor of a new aircraft program. In December 1989, accordingly, he announced the 777 project and put Philip Condit in charge of its management. Boeing had launched the 777 in 1990, delivered the first jet in 1995, and by February 2001, 325 B-777s were flying in the services of the major international and U.S. airlines.[2]

Condit faced a significant challenge in managing the 777 project. He wanted to create an airplane that was preferred by the airlines at a price that was truly competitive. He sought to attract airline customers as well as cut production costs, and he did so by introducing several innovations—both technological and managerial—in aircraft design, manufacturing, and assembly. He looked for ways to revitalize Boeing's outmoded engineering production system, and update Boeing's manufacturing strategies. And to achieve these goals, Condit made continual efforts to spread the 777 program-innovations company wide.

Looking back at the 777 program, this case focuses on Condit's efforts. Was the 777 project successful and was it cost effective? Would the development of the 777 allow Boeing to diffuse the innovations in airplane design and production beyond the 777 program? Would the development of the 777's permit Boeing to revamp and modernize its aircraft manufacturing system? Would the making and selling of the 777 enhance Boeing competitive position relative to Airbus, its only remaining rival?

The Aircraft Industry

Commercial aircraft manufacturing was an industry of enormous risks where failure was the norm, not the exception. The number of large commercial jet makers had been reduced from four in the early 1980s—Boeing, McDonnell Douglas, Airbus, and Lockheed—to two in late 1990s, turning the industry into a duopoly, and pitting the two survivors—Boeing and Airbus—one against the other. One reason why aircraft manufacturers so often failed was the huge cost of product development.

Developing a new jetliner required an up front investment of up to $15 billion (2001 dollars), a lead time of five to six years from launch to first delivery, and the ability to sustain a negative cash flow throughout the development phase. Typically, to break even on an entirely new jetliner, aircraft manufacturers needed to sell a minimum of 300 to 400 planes and at least 50 planes per year.[3] Only a few commercial airplane programs had ever made money.

The price of an aircraft reflected its high development costs. New model prices were based on the average cost of producing 300 to 400 planes, not a single plane. Aircraft pricing embodied the principle of learning by doing, the so called "learning curve":[4] workers steadily improved their skills during the assembly process, and as a result, labor cost fell as the number of planes produced rose.

The high and increasing cost of product development prompted aircraft manufacturers to utilize subcontracting as a risk-sharing strategy. For the 747, the 767, and the 777, the Boeing Company required subcontractors to share a substantial part of the airplane's development costs. Airbus did the same with its own latest models. Risk sharing subcontractors performed detailed design work and assembled major subsections of the new plane while airframe integrators (i.e. aircraft manufacturers) designed the aircraft, integrated its systems and equipment, assembled the entire plane, marketed it, and provided customer support for twenty to thirty years. Both the airframe integrators and their subcontractors were supplied by thousands of domestic and foreign aircraft components manufacturers.[5]

Neither Boeing, nor Airbus, nor any other post-war commercial aircraft manufacturer produced jet engines. A risky and costly venture, engine building had become a highly specialized business. Aircraft manufacturers worked closely with engine makers—General Electric, Pratt and Whitney, and Rolls Royce—to set engine performance standards. In most cases, new airplanes were offered with a choice of engines. Over time, the technology of engine building had become so complex and demanding that it took longer to develop an engine than an aircraft. During the life of a jetliner, the price of the engines and their replacement parts was equal to the entire price of the airplane.[6]

A new model aircraft was normally designed around an engine, not the other way around. As engine performance improved, airframes were redesigned to exploit the engine's new capabilities. The most practical way to do so was to stretch the fuselage and add more seats in the cabin. Aircraft manufacturers deliberately designed flexibility into the airplane so that future engine improvements could facilitate later stretching. Hence the importance of the "family concept" in aircraft design, and hence the reason why aircraft manufacturers introduced families of planes made up of derivative jetliners built around a basic model, not single, standardized models.[7]

The commercial aircraft industry, finally, gained from technological innovations in two other industries. More than any other manufacturing industry, aircraft construction benefited from advances in material applications and electronics. The development of metallic and non-metallic composite materials played a key role in improving airframe and engine performance. On the one hand, composite materials that combined light weight and great strength were utilized by aircraft manufacturers; on the other, heat-resisting alloys that could tolerate temperatures of up to 3,000 degrees were used by engine makers. Similarly, advances in electronics revolutionized avionics. The increasing use of semiconductors by aircraft manufacturers facilitated the miniaturization of cockpit instruments, and more important, it enhanced the use of computers for aircraft communication, navigation, instrumentation, and testing.[8] The use of computers contributed, in addition, to the design, manufacture, and assembly of new model aircraft.

The Boeing Company

The history of the Boeing company may be divided into two distinct periods: the piston era and the jet age. Throughout the piston era, Boeing was essentially a military contractor producing fighter aircraft in the 1920s and 1930s, and bombers during World War II. During the jet age, beginning in the 1950s, Boeing had become the world's largest manufacturer of commercial aircraft, deriving most of its revenues from selling jetliners.

Boeing's first jet was the 707. The introduction of the 707 in 1958 represented a major breakthrough in the history of commercial aviation; it allowed Boeing to gain a critical technological lead over the Douglas Aircraft Company, its closer competitor. To benefit from government assistance in developing the 707, Boeing produced the first jet in two versions: a military tanker for the Air Force (k-135) and a commercial aircraft for the airlines (707-120). The company, however, did not recoup its own investment until 1964, six years after it delivered the first 707, and twelve years after it had launched the program. In the end, the 707 was quite profitable, selling 25 percent above its average cost.[9] Boeing retained the essential design of the 707 for all its subsequent narrow-body single-aisle models (the 727, 737, and 757), introducing incremental design improvements, one at a time.[10] One reason why Boeing used shared design for future models was the constant pressure experienced by the company to move down the learning curve and reduce overall development costs.

Boeing introduced the 747 in 1970. The development of the 747 represented another breakthrough; the 747 wide body design was one of a kind; it had no real competition anywhere in the industry. Boeing bet the entire company on the success of the 747, spending on the project almost as much as the company's total net worth in 1965, the year the project started.[11] In the short-run, the outcome was disastrous. As Boeing began delivering its 747s, the company was struggling to avoid bankruptcy. Cutbacks in orders as a result of a deep recession, coupled with production inefficiencies and escalating costs, created a severe cash shortage that pushed the company to the brink. As sales dropped, the 747's break-even point moved further and further into the future.

Yet, in the long run, the 747 program was a triumph. The Jumbo Jet had become Boeing's most profitable aircraft and the industry's most efficient jetliner. The new plane helped Boeing solidify its position as the industry leader for years to come, leaving McDonnell Douglas far behind, and forcing the Lockheed Corporation to exit the market. The new plane, furthermore, contributed to

Boeing's manufacturing strategy in two ways. First, as Boeing increased its reliance on outsourcing, six major subcontractors fabricated 70 percent of the value of the 747 airplane,[12] thereby helping Boeing reduce the project's risks. Second, for the first time, Boeing applied the family concept in aircraft design to a wide-body jet, building the 747 with wings large enough to support a stretched fuselage with bigger engines, and offering a variety of other modifications in the 747's basic design. The 747-400 (1989) is a case in point. In 1997, Boeing sold the stretched and upgraded 747-400 in three versions, a standard jet, a freighter, and a "combi" (a jetliner whose main cabin was divided between passenger and cargo compartments).[13]

Boeing developed other successful models. In 1969, Boeing introduced the 737, the company's narrow-body flagship, and in 1982 Boeing put into service two additional jetliners, the 757 (narrow-body) and 767 (wide-body). By the early 1990s, the 737, 757, and 767 were all selling profitably. Following the introduction of the 777 in 1995, Boeing's families of planes included the 737 for short-range travel, the 757 and 767 for medium-range travel, and the 747 and 777 for medium- to long-range travel (Exhibit 1).

In addition to building jetliners, Boeing also expanded its defense, space, and information businesses. In 1997, the Boeing Company took a strategic gamble, buying the McDonnell Douglas Company in a $14 billion stock deal. As a result of the merger, Boeing had become the world's largest manufacturer of military aircraft, NASA's largest supplier, and the Pentagon's second largest contractor (after Lockheed). Nevertheless, despite the growth in its defense and space businesses, Boeing still derived most of its revenues from selling jetliners. Commercial aircraft revenues accounted for 59 percent of Boeing's $49 billion sales in 1997 and 63 percent of Boeing's $56 billion sales in 1998.[14]

Exhibit 1   Total Number of Commercial Jetliners Delivered by the Boeing Company, 1958–2/2001*

Model	No. Delivered	First delivery
B-707	1,010 (retired)	1958
B-727	1,831 (retired)	1963
B-737	3,901	1967
B-747	1,264	1970
B-757	953	1982
B-767	825	1982
B-777	325	1995
B-717	49	2000
Total:	**10,158**	

* McDonnell Douglas commercial jetliners (the MD-11, MD-80, and MD-90) are excluded.

Sources: Boeing Commercial Airplane Group, *Announced Orders and Deliveries as of 12/31/97; The Boeing Company 1998 Annual Report,* p.35. "Commercial Airplanes: Order and Delivery Summary," http://www.Boeing.com/commercial/orders/index.html. Retrieved from Web 3/20/2001.

Following its merger with McDonnell, Boeing had one remaining rival: Airbus Industrie.[15] In 1997, Airbus booked 45 percent of the worldwide orders for commercial jetliners[16] and delivered close to 1/3 of the worldwide industry output. In 2000, Airbus shipped nearly 2/5 of the worldwide industry output (Exhibit 2).

Airbus' success was based on a strategy that combined cost leadership with technological leadership. First, Airbus distinguished itself from Boeing by incorporating the most advanced technologies into its planes. Second,

Exhibit 2   Market Share of Shipments of Commercial Aircraft, Boeing, McDonnell Douglas (MD), Airbus, 1992–2000

	1992	1993	1994	1995	1996	1997	1998	1999	2000
Boeing	61%	61%	63%	54%	55%	67%	71%	68%	61%
MD	17	14	9	13	13				
Airbus	22	25	28	33	32	33	29	32	39

Sources: *Aerospace Facts and Figures,* 1997–98, p. 34; *Wall Street Journal,* December 3, 1998, and January 12, 1999; *The Boeing Company 1997 Annual Report,* p. 19; Data supplied by Mark Luginbill, Airbus Communication Director, November 16, 1998, February 1, 2000, and March 20, 2001.

Airbus managed to cut costs by utilizing a flexible, lean production manufacturing system that stood in a stark contrast to Boeing's mass production system.[17]

As Airbus prospered, the Boeing company was struggling with rising costs, declining productivity, delays in deliveries, and production inefficiencies. Boeing Commercial Aircraft Group lost $1.8 billion in 1997 and barely generated any profits in 1998.[18] All through the 1990s, the Boeing Company looked for ways to revitalize its outdated production manufacturing system on the one hand, and to introduce leading edge technologies into its jetliners on the other. The development and production of the 777, first conceived of in 1989, was an early step undertaken by Boeing managers to address both problems.

The 777 Program

The 777 program was Boeing's single largest project since the completion of the 747. The total development cost of the 777 was estimated at $6.3 billion and the total number of employees assigned to the project peaked at nearly 10,000. The 777's twin-engines were the largest and most powerful ever built (the diameter of the 777's engine equaled the 737's fuselage), the 777's construction required 132,000 uniquely engineered parts (compared to 70,000 for the 767), the 777's seat capacity was identical to that of the first 747 that had gone into service in 1970, and its manufacturer empty weight was 57 percent greater than the 767's. Building the 777 alongside the 747 and 767 at its Everett plant near Seattle, Washington, Boeing enlarged the plant to cover an area of seventy-six football fields.[19]

Boeing's financial position in 1990 was unusually strong. With a 21 percent rate of return on stockholder equity, a long term debt of just 15 percent of capitalization, and a cash surplus of $3.6 billion, Boeing could gamble comfortably.[20] There was no need to bet the company on the new project as had been the case with the 747, or to borrow heavily, as had been the case with the 767. Still, the decision to develop the 777 was definitely risky; a failure of the new jet might have triggered an irreversible decline of the Boeing Company and threatened its future survival.

The decision to develop the 777 was based on market assessment—the estimated future needs of the airlines. During the fourteen year period, 1991–2005, Boeing market analysts forecasted an +100 percent increase in the number of passenger miles traveled worldwide, and a need for about 9,000 new commercial jets. Of the total value of the jetliners needed in 1991–2005, Boeing analysts forecasted a $260 billion market for wide body jets smaller than the 747. An increasing number of these wide body jets were expected to be larger than the 767.[21]

A Consumer Driven Product

To manage the risk of developing a new jetliner, aircraft manufacturers had first sought to obtain a minimum number of firm orders from interested carriers, and only then commit to the project. Boeing CEO Frank Shrontz had expected to obtain 100 initial orders of the 777 before asking the Boeing board to launch the project, but as a result of Boeing's financial strength on the one hand, and the increasing competitiveness of Airbus on the other, Schrontz decided to seek the board's approval earlier. He did so after securing only one customer: United Airlines. On October 12, 1990, United had placed an order for thirty-four 777s and an option for an additional thirty-four aircraft, and two weeks later, Boeing's board of directors approved the project.[22] Negotiating the sale, Boeing and United drafted a handwritten agreement (signed by Philip Condit and Richard Albrecht, Boeing's executive vice presidents, and Jim Guyette, United's Executive Vice President) that granted United a larger role in designing the 777 than the role played by any airline before. The two companies pledged to cooperate closely in developing an aircraft with the "best dispatch reliability in the industry" and the "greatest customer appeal in the industry." "We will endeavor to do it right the first time with the highest degree of professionalism" and with "candor, honesty, and respect" [the agreement read]. Asked to comment on the agreement, Philip Condit, said: "We are going to listen to our customers and understand what they want. Everybody on the program has that attitude."[23] Gordon McKinzie, United's 777 program director agreed: "In the past we'd get brochures on a new airplane and its options ... wait four years for delivery, and hope we'd get what we ordered. This time Boeing really listened to us."[24]

Condit invited other airline carriers to participate in the design and development phase of the 777. Altogether, eight carriers from around the world (United, Delta, American, British Airways, Qantas, Japan Airlines, All Nippon Airways, and Japan Air System) sent full-time representatives to Seattle; British Airways alone assigned 75 people at one time. To facilitate interaction between its design engineers and representatives of the eight carriers, Boeing introduced an initiative called "Working Together." "If we have a problem," a British Airways production manager explained, "we go to the source— design engineers on the IPT [Integrated Product Teams], not service engineer(s). One of the frustrations on the 747 was that we rarely got to talk to the engineers who were doing the work."[25]

"We have definitely influenced the design of the aircraft," a United 777 manager said, mentioning changes in the design of the wing panels that made it easier for airline mechanics to access the slats (slats, like flaps, increased lift on takeoffs and landings), and new features in the cabin that made the plane more attractive to passengers.[26] Of the 1,500 design features examined by representatives of the airlines, Boeing engineers modified 300. Among changes made by Boeing was a redesigned overhead bin that left more stand-up headroom for passengers (allowing a six-foot-three tall passenger to walk from aisle to aisle), "flattened" side walls which provided the occupant of the window seat with more room, overhead bin doors which opened down and made it possible for shorter passengers to lift baggage into the overhead compartment, a redesigned reading lamp that enabled flight attendants to replace light bulbs, a task formerly performed by mechanics, and a computerized flight deck management system that adjusted cabin temperature, controlled the volume of the public address system, and monitored food and drink inventories.[27]

More important were changes in the interior configuration (layout plan) of the aircraft. To be able to reconfigure the plane quickly for different markets of varying travel ranges and passenger loads, Boeing's customers sought a flexible plan of the interior. On a standard commercial jet, kitchen galleys, closets, lavatories, and bars were all removable in the past, but were limited to fixed positions where the interior floor structure was reinforced to accommodate the "wet" load. On the 777, by contrast, such components as galleys and lavatories could be positioned anywhere within several "flexible zones" designed into the cabin by the joint efforts of Boeing engineers and representatives of the eight airlines. Similarly, the flexible design of the 777's seat tracks made it possible for carriers to increase the number of seat combinations as well as reconfigure the seating arrangement quickly. Flexible configuration resulted, in turn, in significant cost savings; airlines no longer needed to take the aircraft out of service for an extended period of time in order to reconfigure the interior.[28]

The airline carriers also influenced the way in which Boeing designed the 777 cockpit. During the program definition phase, representatives of United Airlines, British Airways, and Qantas—three of Boeing's clients whose fleets included a large number of 747-400s—asked Boeing engineers to model the 777 cockpit on the 747-400's. In response to these requests, Boeing introduced a shared 747/777 cockpit design that enabled its airline customers to use a single pool of pilots for both aircraft types at a significant cost savings.[29]

Additionally, the airline carriers urged Boeing to increase its use of avionics for in-flight entertainment. The 777, as a consequence, was equipped with a fully computerized cabin. Facing each seat on the 777, and placed on the back of the seat in front, was a combined computer and video monitor that featured movies, video programs, and interactive computer games. Passengers were also provided with a digital sound system comparable to the most advanced home stereo available, and a telephone. About 40 percent of the 777's total computer capacity was reserved for passengers in the cabin.[30]

The 777 was Boeing's first fly by wire (FBW) aircraft, an aircraft controlled by a pilot transmitting commands to the moveable surfaces (rudder, flaps, etc.) electrically, not mechanically. Boeing installed a state of the art FBW system on the 777 partly to satisfy its airline customers, and partly to challenge Airbus' leadership in flight control technology, a position Airbus had held since it introduced the world's first FBW aircraft , the A-320, in 1988.

Lastly, Boeing customers were invited to contribute to the design of the 777's engine. Both United Airlines and All Nippon Airlines assigned service engineers to work with representatives of Pratt and Whitney (P&W) on problems associated with engine maintenance. P&W held three specially scheduled "airline conferences." At each conference, some forty airline representatives clustered around a full scale mock-up of the 777 engine and showed Pratt and Whitney engineers gaps in the design, hard-to-reach points, visible but inaccessible parts, and accessible but invisible components. At the initial conference, Pratt and Whitney picked up 150 airline suggestions, at the second, fifty, and at the third, ten more suggestions.[31]

A Globally Manufactured Product

Twelve international companies located in ten countries, and eighteen more U.S. companies located in twelve states, were contracted by Boeing to help manufacture the 777. Together, they supplied structural components as well as systems and equipment. Among the foreign suppliers were companies based in Japan, Britain, Australia, Italy, Korea, Brazil, Singapore, and Ireland; among the major U.S. subcontractors were the Grumman Corporation, Rockwell (later merged with Boeing), Honeywell, United Technologies, Bendix, and the Sunstrand Corporation (Exhibits 4 and 5). Of all foreign participants, the Japanese played the largest role. A consortium made up of Fuji Heavy Industries, Kawasaki Heavy Industries, and Mitsubishi Heavy Industries had worked with Boeing on its wide-body models since the early days of the 747. Together, the three Japanese subcontractors produced 20 percent of the value of the 777's airframe (up from 15 percent of the 767's). A group of 250 Japanese engineers had spent a year in Seattle working on the 777 alongside

Exhibit 3   The 777: Selected Design Features Proposed by Boeing Airline Customers and Adapted by the Boeing Company

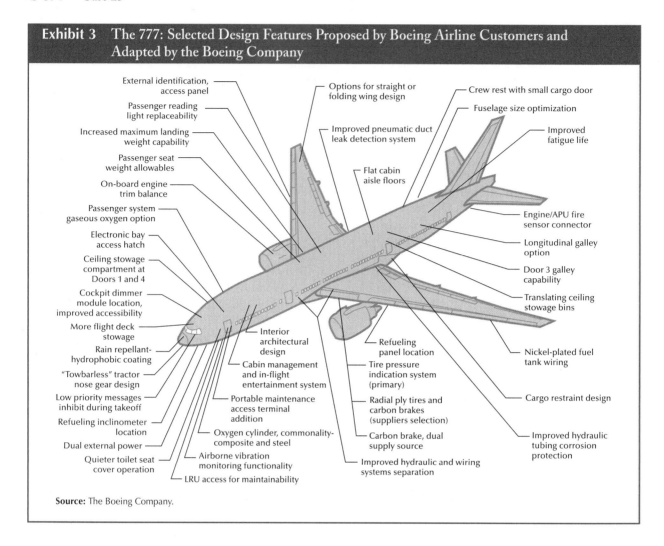

Source: The Boeing Company.

Boeing engineers before most of its members went back home to begin production. The fuselage was built in sections in Japan and then shipped to Boeing's huge plant at Everett, Washington for assembly.[32]

Boeing used global subcontracting as a marketing tool as well. Sharing design work and production with overseas firms, Boeing required overseas carriers to buy the new aircraft. Again, Japan is a case in point. In return for the contact signed with the Mitsubishi, Fuji, and Kawasaki consortium—which was heavily subsidized by the Japanese government—Boeing sold forty-six 777 jetliners to three Japanese air carriers: All Nippon Airways, Japan Airlines, and Japan Air System.[33]

A Family of Planes

From the outset, the design of the 777 was flexible enough to accommodate derivative jetliners. Because all derivatives of a given model shared maintenance, training, and operating procedures, as well as replacement parts and components, and because such derivatives enabled carriers to serve different markets at lower costs, Boeing's clients were seeking a family of planes built around a basic model, not a single 777. Condit and his management team, accordingly, urged Boeing's engineers to incorporate the maximum flexibility into the design of the 777.

The 777's design flexibility helped Boeing manage the project's risks. Offering a family of planes based on a single design to accommodate future changes in customers' preferences, Boeing spread the 777 project's risks among a number of models all belonging to the same family.

The key to the 777's design efficiency was the wing. The 777 wings, exceptionally long and thin, were strong enough to support vastly enlarged models. The first model to go into service, the 777-200, had a 209 foot-long fuselage, was designed to carry 305 passengers in three class configurations, and had a travel range of 5,900 miles in its original version (1995), and up to

Exhibit 4   777 Supplier Contracts

U.S. Suppliers of Structural Components

Astech/MCI	Santa Ana, CA	Primary exhaust cowl assembly (plug and nozzle)
Grumman Aerospace	Bethpage, NY	Spoilers, inboard flaps
Kaman	Bloomfield, CT	Fixed trailing edge
Rockwell	Tulsa, OK	Floor beams, wing leading edge slats

International Suppliers of Structural Components

Alenia	Italy	Wing outboard flaps, radome
AeroSpace Technologies of Australia	Australia	Rudder
Embraer-Empresa Brasiera de Aeronautica	Brazil	Dorsal fin, wingtip assembly
Hawker de Havilland	Australia	Elevators
*Mitsubishi Heavy Industries, Kawasaki Heavy Industries, and Fuji Heavy Industries	Japan	Fuselage panels and doors, wing center section, wing-to-body fairing, and wing in-spar ribs
Korean Air	Korea	Flap support fairings, wingtip assembly
Menasco Aerospace/Messier-Bugatti	Canada/France	Main and nose landing gears
Short Brothers	Ireland	Nose landing gear doors
Singapore Aerospace Manufacturing	Singapore	Nose landing gear doors

U.S. Suppliers of Systems and Equipment

AlliedSignal Aerospace Company, AiResearch Divisions	Torrance, CA	Cabin pressure control system, air supply control system, integrated system controller, ram air turbine
Bendix Wheels and Brakes Division	South Bend, IN	Wheel and brakes
Garrett Divisions	Phoenix/Tempe, AZ	Auxiliary power unit (APU), air-driven unit
BFGoodrich	Troy, OH	Wheel and brakes
Dowty Aerospace	Los Angeles, CA	Thrust reverser actuator system
Eldec	Lynnwood, WA	Power supply electronics
E-Systems, Montek Division	Salt Lake City, UT	Stabilizer trim control module, secondary hydraulic brake, optional folding wingtip system
Honeywell	Phoenix, AZ Coon Rapids, MN	Airplane information management system (AIMS), air data/inertial reference system (ADIRS)
Rockwell, Collins Division	Cedar Rapids, IA	Autopilot flight director system, electronic library system (ELS) displays
Sundstrand Corporation	Rockford, IL	Primary and backup electrical power systems
Teijin Seiki America	Redmond, WA	Power control units, actuator control electronics
United Technologies, Hamilton Standard Division	Windsor Locks, CT	Cabin air-conditioning and temperature control system, ice protection system

International Suppliers of Systems and Equipment

General Electric Company (GEC) Avionics	United Kingdom	Primary flight computers
Smiths Industries	United Kingdom	Integrated electrical load management system (ELMS), throttle control system actuator, fuel quantity indicating system (FQIS)

*Program partners

Source: James Woolsey, "777: Boeing's New Large Twinjet," *Air Transport World,* April 1994, p. 24.

8,900 miles in its extended version (1997). The second model to be introduced (1998), the 777-300, had a stretched fuselage of 242 ft (ten feet longer than the 747), was configured for 379 passengers (three-class), and flew to destinations of up to 6,800 miles away. In all-tourist class configuration, the stretched 777-300 could carry as many as 550 passengers.[34]

Digital Design

The 777 was the first Boeing jetliner designed entirely by computers. Historically, Boeing had designed new planes in two ways: paper drawings and full-size models called mock-ups. Paper drawings were two dimensional and therefore insufficient to account for the complex con-

Exhibit 5   The Builders of the Boeing 777

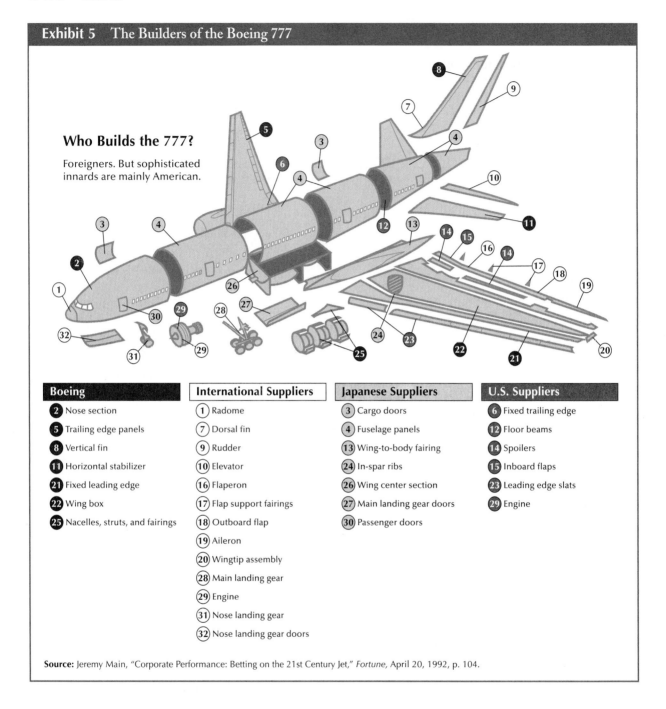

Who Builds the 777?

Foreigners. But sophisticated innards are mainly American.

Boeing

- ② Nose section
- ⑤ Trailing edge panels
- ⑧ Vertical fin
- ⑪ Horizontal stabilizer
- ㉑ Fixed leading edge
- ㉒ Wing box
- ㉕ Nacelles, struts, and fairings

International Suppliers

- ① Radome
- ⑦ Dorsal fin
- ⑨ Rudder
- ⑩ Elevator
- ⑯ Flaperon
- ⑰ Flap support fairings
- ⑱ Outboard flap
- ⑲ Aileron
- ⑳ Wingtip assembly
- ㉘ Main landing gear
- ㉙ Engine
- ㉛ Nose landing gear
- ㉜ Nose landing gear doors

Japanese Suppliers

- ③ Cargo doors
- ④ Fuselage panels
- ⑬ Wing-to-body fairing
- ㉔ In-spar ribs
- ㉖ Wing center section
- ㉗ Main landing gear doors
- ㉚ Passenger doors

U.S. Suppliers

- ⑥ Fixed trailing edge
- ⑫ Floor beams
- ⑭ Spoilers
- ⑮ Inboard flaps
- ㉓ Leading edge slats
- ㉙ Engine

Source: Jeremy Main, "Corporate Performance: Betting on the 21st Century Jet," *Fortune*, April 20, 1992, p. 104.

struction of the three dimensional airplane. Full-scale mock-ups served as a backup to drawings.

Boeing engineers used three classes of mock-ups. Made up of plywood or foam, class 1 mock-ups were used to construct the plane's large components in three dimensions, refine the design of these components by carving into the wood or foam, and feed the results back into the drawings. Made partly of metal, class 2 mock-ups addressed more complex problems such as the wiring and tubing of the airframe, and the design of the machine tools necessary to cut and shape the large components. Class 3 mock-ups gave the engineers one final opportunity to refine the model and thereby reduce the need to keep on changing the design during the actual assembly process or after delivery.[35]

Despite the engineers' efforts, many parts and components did not fit together on the final assembly line but rather "interfered" with each other, that is, overlapped in space. The problem was both pervasive and costly; Boeing engineers needed to rework and realign all overlapping parts in order to join them together.

A partial solution to the problem was provided by the computer. In the last quarter of the twentieth century, computer aided design was used successfully in car manufacture, building construction, machine production, and several other industries; its application to commercial aircraft manufacturing came later, both in the United States and in Europe. Speaking of the 777, Dick Johnson, Boeing chief engineer for digital design, noted the "tremendous advantage" of computer application:

> With mock-ups, the … engineer had three opportunities at three levels of detail to check his parts, and nothing in between. With Catia [Computer aided three dimensional, interactive application} he can do it day in and day out over the whole development of the airplane."[36]

Catia was a sophisticated computer program that Boeing bought from Dassault Aviation, a French fighter planes builder. IBM enhanced the program to improve image manipulation, supplied Boeing with eight of its largest mainframe computers, and connected the mainframes to 2,200 computer terminals that Boeing distributed among its 777 design teams. The software program showed on a screen exactly how parts and components fit together before the actual manufacturing process took place.[37]

A digital design system, Catia had five distinctive advantages. First, it provided the engineers with 100 percent visualization, allowing them to rotate, zoom, and "interrogate" parts geometrically in order to spotlight interferences. Second, Catia assigned a numerical value to each drawing on the screen and thereby helped engineers locate related drawings of parts and components, merge them together, and check for incompatibilities. Third, to help Boeing's customers service the 777, the digital design system created a computer simulated human—a Catia figure playing the role of the service mechanic—who climbed into the three dimensional images and showed the engineers whether parts were serviceable and entry accessible. Fourth, the use of Catia by all 777 design teams in the U.S., Japan, Europe, and elsewhere facilitated instantaneous communication between Boeing and its subcontractors and ensured the frequent updating of the design. And fifth, Catia provided the 777 assembly line workers with graphics that enhanced the narrative work instructions they received, showing explicitly on a screen how a given task should be performed.[38]

Design-Build Teams (DBT)

Teaming was another feature of the 777 program. About thirty integrated-level teams at the top and more than 230 design-build teams at the bottom worked together on the 777.[39] All team members were connected by Catia. The integrated-level teams were organized around large sections of the aircraft; the DBTs around small parts and components. In both cases, teams were cross-functional, as Philip Condit observed:

> If you go back…to earlier planes that Boeing built, the factory was on the bottom floor, and Engineering was on the upper floor. Both Manufacturing and Engineering went back and forth. When there was a problem in the factory, the engineer went down and looked at it….
>
> With 10,000 people [working on the 777], that turns out to be really hard. So you start devising other tools to allow you to achieve that—the design-build team. You break the airplane down and bring Manufacturing, Tooling, Planning, Engineering, Finance, and Materials all together [in small teams].[40]

Under the design-build approach, many of the design decisions were driven by manufacturing concerns. As manufacturing specialists worked alongside engineers, engineers were less likely to design parts that were difficult to produce and needed to be re-designed. Similarly, under the design-build approach, customers' expectations as well as safety and weight considerations were all incorporated into the design of the aircraft; engineers no longer needed to "chain saw"[41] structural components and systems in order to replace parts that did not meet customers expectations, were unsafe, or were too heavy.

The design of the 777's wing provides an example. The wing was divided into two integration-level teams, the "leading edge" (the foreword part of the wing) and the "trailing edge" (the back of the wing) team. Next, the trailing edge team was further divided into ten design-build teams, each named after a piece of the wing's trailing edge (Exhibit 6). Membership in these DBTs extended to two groups of outsiders: representatives of the customer airlines and engineers employed by the foreign subcontractors. Made up of up to twenty members, each DBT decided its own mix of insiders and outsiders, and each was led by a team leader. Each DBT included representatives from six functional disciplines: engineering, manufacturing, material, customer support, finance, and quality assurance. The DBTs met twice a week for two hours to hear reports from team members, discuss immediate goals and plans, divide responsibilities, set time lines, and take specific notes of all decisions taken.[42] Described by a Boeing official as "little companies," the DBTs enjoyed a high degree of autonomy from management supervision; team members designed their own tools, developed their own manufacturing plans, and wrote their own contracts with the program management, specifying deliverables, resources, and schedules. John Monroe, a Boeing 777 senior project manager remarked:

> The team is totally responsible. We give them a lump of money to go and do th[eir] job. They decide whether to hire a lot of inexpensive people or to trade numbers for resources. It's unprecedented. We have some $100 million plus activities led by non-managers.[43]

Employees' Empowerment and Culture

An additional aspect of the 777 program was the empowering of assembly line workers. Boeing managers encouraged factory workers at all levels to speak up, offer suggestions, and participate in decision making. Boeing managers also paid attention to a variety of "human relations" problems faced by workers, problems ranging from childcare and parking to occupational hazards and safety concerns.[44]

All employees entering the 777 program—managers, engineers, assembly line workers, and others—were expected to attend a special orientation session devoted to the themes of team work and quality control. Once a quarter, the entire "777 team" of up to 10,000 employees met offsite to hear briefings on the aircraft status. Dressed casually, the employees were urged to raise questions, voice complaints, and propose improvements. Under the 777 program, managers met frequently to discuss ways to promote communication with workers. Managers, for example, "fire fought" problems by bringing workers together and empowering them to offer solutions. In a typical "firefight" session, Boeing 777 project managers learned from assembly line workers how to improve the process of wiring and tubing the airframe's interior: "staffing" fuselage sections with wires, ducts, tubs, and insulation materials before joining the sections together was easier than installing the interior parts all at once in a preassembled fuselage.[45]

Under the 777 program, in addition, Boeing assembly line workers also were empowered to appeal management decisions. In a case involving middle managers, a group of Boeing machinists sought to replace a non-retractable jig (a large device used to hold parts) with a retractable one in order to ease and simplify their jobs. Otherwise they had to carry heavy equipment loads up and down stairs. Again and again, their supervisors refused to implement the change. When the machinists eventually approached a factory manager, he inspected the jig personally, and immediately ordered the change.[46]

Under the 777 program, work on the shop floor was ruled by the "Bar Chart." A large display panel placed at different work areas, the Bar Chart listed the name of each worker, his or her daily job description, and the time available to complete specific tasks. Boeing had utilized the Bar Chart system as a "management visibility system" in the past, but only under the 777 program was the system fully computerized. The chart showed whether assembly line workers were meeting or missing their production goals. Boeing industrial engineers estimated the time it took to complete a given task and fed the information back to the system's computer. Workers ran a scanner across their ID badges and supplied the computer with the data necessary to log their job progress. Each employee "sold" his/her completed job to an inspector, and no job was declared acceptable unless "bought" by an inspector.[47]

> ### Exhibit 6   The Ten DBTs ("little companies") Responsible for the Wing's Trailing Edge
>
> - **Flap Supports Team**
> - **Inboard Flap Team**
> - **Outboard Flap Team**
> - **Outboard Fixed Wing Team**
> - **Flaperon* Team**
> - **Aileron* Team**
> - **Inboard Fixed Wing and Gear Support Team**
> - **Main Landing Gear Doors Team**
> - **Spoilers** Team**
> - **Fairings*** Team**
>
> * The Flaperon and Aileron were moveable hinged sections of the trailing edge that helped the plane roll in flight. The Flaperon was used at high speed, the Aileron at low speed.
>
> ** The spoilers were the flat surfaces that lay on top of the trailing edge and extended during landing to slow down the plane.
>
> *** The fairings were the smooth parts attached to the outline of the wing's trailing edge. They helped reduce drag.
>
> **Source:** Karl Sabbagh, *21st Century Jet: The Making and Marketing of the Boeing 777* (New York: Scribner, 1996), p. 73.

Leadership and Management Style

The team in charge of the 777 program was led by a group of five vice presidents, headed by Philip Condit, a gifted engineer who was described by one Wall Street analyst as "a cross between a grizzly bear and a teddy bear. Good people skills, but furious in the market-place."[48] Each of the five vice presidents rose through the ranks, and each had a twenty-five to thirty years experience with Boeing. All were men.[49]

During the 777 design phase, the five VPs met regularly every Tuesday morning in a small conference room at Boeing's headquarters in Seattle in what was called the "Muffin Meeting." There were no agendas drafted, no minutes drawn, no overhead projectors used, and no votes taken. The homemade muffins served during the meeting symbolized the informal tone of the forum. Few people outside the circle of five had ever attended these weekly sessions. Acting as an informal chair, Condit led a freewheeling discussion of the 777 project, asking each VP to say anything he had on his mind.[50]

The weekly session reflected Boeing's sweeping new approach to management. Traditionally, Boeing had been a highly structured company governed by engineers. Its culture was secretive, formal, and stiff. Managers seldom interacted, sharing was rare, divisions kept to themselves, and engineers competed with each other. Under the 777 program, Boeing made serious efforts to abandon its secretive management style. Condit firmly believed that open communication among top executives, middle managers, and assembly line workers was indispensable for improving morale and raising productivity. He urged employees to talk to each other and share information, and he used a variety of management tools to do so: information sheets, orientation sessions, question and answer sessions, leadership meetings, regular workers as well as middle managers, Condit introduced a three-way performance review procedure whereby managers were evaluated by their supervisors, their peers, and their subordinates.[51] Most important, Condit made team-work the hallmark of the 777 project. In an address entitled "Working Together: The 777 Story" and delivered in December 1992 to members of the Royal Aeronautics Society in London,[52] Condit summed up his team approach:

> [T]eam building is … very difficult to do well but when it works the results are dramatic. Teaming fosters the excitement of a shared endeavor and creates an atmosphere that stimulates creativity and problem solving.

But building team[s] … is hard work. It doesn't come naturally. Most of us are taught from an early age to compete and excel as individuals. Performance in school and performance on the job are usually measured by individual achievement. Sharing your ideas with others, or helping others to enhance their performance, is often viewed as contrary to one's self interest.

This individualistic mentality has its place, but … it is no longer the most useful attitude for a workplace to possess in today's world. To create a high performance organization, you need employees who can work together in a way that promotes continual learning and the free flow of ideas and information.

The Results of the 777 Project

The 777 entered revenue service in June 1995. Since many of the features incorporated into the 777's design reflected suggestions made by the airline carriers, pilots, mechanics, and flight attendants were quite enthusiastic about the new jet. Three achievements of the program, in airplane interior, aircraft design, and aircraft manufacturing, stood out.

Configuration Flexibility

The 777 offered carriers enhanced configuration flexibility. A typical configuration change took only seventy-two hours on the 777 compared to three weeks in competing aircraft. In 1992, the Industrial Design Society of America granted Boeing its Excellence Award for building the 777 passenger cabin, honoring an airplane interior for the first time.[53]

Digital Design

The original goal of the program was to reduce "change, error, and rework" by 50 percent, but engineers building the first three 777's managed to reduce such modification by 60 percent to 90 percent. Catia helped engineers identify more than 10,000 interferences that would have otherwise remained undetected until assembly, or until after delivery. The first 777 was only 0.023 inch short of perfect alignment, compared to as much as 0.5 inch on previous programs.[54] Assembly line workers confirmed the beneficial effects of the digital design system. "The parts snap together like Lego blocks," said one mechanic.[55] Reducing the need for reengineering, replanning, retooling, and retrofitting, Boeing's innovative efforts were recognized yet again. In 1993, the Smithsonian Institution honored the Boeing 777 division with its Annual Computerworld Award for the manufacturing category.[56]

Empowerment

Boeing 777 assembly line workers expressed a high level of job satisfaction under the new program. "It's a whole new world," a fourteen-year Boeing veteran mechanic said, "I even like going to work. It's bubbly. It's clean. Everyone has confidence."[57] "We never used to speak up," said another employee, "didn't dare. Now factory workers are treated better and are encouraged to offer ideas."[58] Although the Bar Chart system required Boeing 777 mechanics to work harder and faster as they moved down the learning curve, their principal union organization, the International Association of Machinists, was pleased with Boeing's new approach to labor-management relations. A union spokesman reported that under the 777 program, managers were more likely to treat problems as opportunities from which to learn rather than mistakes for which to blame. Under the 777 program, the union representative added, managers were more respectful of workers' rights under the collective bargaining agreement.[59]

Unresolved Problems and Lessons Learned

Notwithstanding Boeing's success with the 777 project, the cost of the program was very high. Boeing did not publish figures pertaining to the total cost of Catia. But a company official reported that under the 777 program, the 3D digital design process required 60 percent more engineering resources than the older, 2D drawing-based design process. One reason for the high cost of using digital design was slow computing tools: Catia's response time often lasted minutes. Another was the need to update the design software repeatedly. Boeing revised Catia's design software four times between 1990 and 1996, making the system easier to learn and use. Still, Catia continued to experience frequent software problems. Moreover, several of Boeing's outside suppliers were unable to utilize Catia's digital data in their manufacturing process.[60]

Boeing faced training problems as well. One challenging problem, according to Ron Ostrowski, Director of 777 engineering, was "to convert people's thinking from 2D to 3D. It took more time than we thought it would. I came from a paper world and now I am managing a digital program."[61] Converting people's thinking required what another manager called an "unending communication" coupled with training and retraining. Under the 777 program, Ostrowski recalled, "engineers had to learn to interact. Some couldn't, and they left. The young ones caught on" and stayed.[62]

Learning to work together was a challenge to managers too. Some managers were reluctant to embrace Condit's open management style, fearing a decline in their authority. Others were reluctant to share their mistakes with their superiors, fearing reprisals. Some other managers, realizing that the new approach would end many managerial jobs, resisted change when they could, and did not pursue it whole-heartedly when they could not. Even top executives were sometimes uncomfortable with Boeing's open management style, believing that sharing information with employees was likely to help Boeing's competitors obtain confidential 777 data.[63]

Teamwork was another problem area. Working under pressure, some team members did not function well within teams and had to be moved. Others took advantage of their new-born freedom to offer suggestions, but were disillusioned and frustrated when management either ignored these suggestions, or did not act upon them. Managers experienced different team-related problems. In several cases, managers kept on meeting with their team members repeatedly until they arrived at a solution desired by their bosses. They were unwilling to challenge senior executives, nor did they trust Boeing's new approach to teaming. In other cases, managers distrusted the new digital technology. One engineering manager instructed his team members to draft paper drawings alongside Catia's digital designs. When Catia experienced a problem, he followed the drawing, ignoring the computerized design, and causing unnecessary and costly delays in his team's part of the project.[64]

Extending the 777 Revolution

Boeing's learning pains played a key role in the company's decision not to implement the 777 program companywide. Boeing officials recognized the importance of teamwork and Catia in reducing change, error, and rework, but they also realized that teaming required frequent training, continuous reinforcement, and ongoing monitoring, and that the use of Catia was still too expensive, though its cost was going down (in 1997, Catia's "penalty" was down to 10 percent). Three of Boeing's derivative programs, the 737 Next Generation, the 757-300, and the 767-400, had the option of implementing the 777's program innovations, and only one, the 737, did so, adopting a modified version of the 777's cross-functional teams.[65]

Yet the 777's culture was spreading in other ways. Senior executives took broader roles as the 777 entered service, and their impact was felt through the company. Larry Olson, director of information systems for the 747/767/777 division, was a former 777 manager who believed that Boeing 777 employees "won't tolerate going back to the old ways." He expected to fill new positions on Boeing's next program—the 747X—with former 777 employees in their 40s.[66] Philip Condit, Boeing CEO, implemented several of his own 777's innovations, intensifying the use of meeting among Boeing's managers, and promoting the free flow of ideas throughout the company. Under Condit's leadership, all mid-level managers assigned to Boeing Commercial Airplane Group, about sixty people, met once a week in to discuss costs, revenues, and production schedules, product by product. By the end of the meeting—which sometimes ran into the evening—each manager had to draft a detailed plan of action dealing with problems in his/her department.[67] Under Condit's leadership, more important, Boeing developed a new "vision" that grew out of the 777 project. Articulating the company's vision for the next two decades (1996-2016), Condit singled out "Customer satisfaction," "Team leadership," and "A participatory workplace," as Boeing's core corporate values.[68]

Conclusion: Boeing, Airbus and the 777

Looking back at the 777 program twelve years after the launch and seven years after first delivery, it is now (2002) clear that Boeing produced the most successful commercial jetliner of its kind. Airbus launched the A330 and A340 in 1987, and McDonnell Douglas launched a new 300-seat wide body jet in the mid 1980s, the three-engine MD11. Coming late to market, the Boeing 777 soon outsold both models. The 777 had entered service in 1995, and within a year Boeing delivered more than twice as many 777s as the number of MD11s delivered by McDonnell Douglas. In 1997, 1998,1999, and 2001, Boeing delivered a larger number of 777s than the combined number of A330s and A340s delivered by Airbus (Exhibit 7). A survey of nearly 6,000 European airline passengers who had flown both the 777 and the A330/A340 found that the 777 was preferred by more than three out of four passengers.[69] In the end, a key element in the 777's triumph was its popularity with the traveling public.

Notes

1. Rodgers, Eugene. *Flying High: The Story of Boeing* (New York: Atlantic Monthly Press, 1996), 415–416; Michael Dornheim, "777 Twinjet Will Grow to Replace 747-200," *Aviation Week and Space Technology* (3 June 1991): 43.
2. "Commercial Airplanes: Order and Delivery, Summary," http/www.boeing.com/commercial/orders/index.html. Retrieved from Web, 2 February 2000.
3. Donlon, J. P. "Boeing's Big Bet" (an interview with CEO Frank Shrontz), *Chief Executive* (November/December 1994): 42; Dertouzos, Michael, Richard Lester, and Robert Solow, *Made in America: Regaining the Productive Edge* (New York: Harper Perennial, 1990), 203.
4. John Newhouse, *The Sporty Game* (New York: Alfred Knopf, 1982), 21, but see also 10–20.
5. Mowery, David C. and Nathan Rosenberg. "The Commercial Aircraft Industry," in Richard R. Nelson, ed., *Government and Technological Progress: A Cross Industry Analysis* (New York: Pergamon Press, 1982), 116; Dertouzos et. al, *Made in America*, 200.
6. Dertouzos, et. al, *Made in America*, 203.
7. Newhouse, *Sporty Game*, 188. Mowery and Rosenberg, "The Commercial Aircraft Industry," 124–125.
8. Mowery and Rosenberg, "The Commercial Aircraft Industry," 102–103, 126–128.
9. Rae, John B. *Climb to Greatness: The American Aircraft Industry, 1920–1960* (Cambridge, Mass.: MIT Press, 1968), 206–207; Rodgers, *Flying High*, 197–198.
10. Spadaro, Frank. "A Transatlantic Perspective," *Design Quarterly* (Winter 1992): 23.
11. Rodgers, *Flying High*, 279; Newhouse, *Sporty Game*, Ch. 7.
12. Hochmuth, M. S. "Aerospace," in Raymond Vernon, ed., *Big Business and the State* (Cambridge: Harvard University Press, 1974), 149.
13. Boeing Commercial Airplane Group, *Announced Orders and Deliveries as of 12/31/97*, Section A 1.
14. *The Boeing Company 1998 Annual Report*, 76.
15. Formed in 1970 by several European aerospace firms, the Airbus Consortium had received generous assistance from the French, British, German, and Spanish governments for a period of over two decades. In 1992, Airbus had signed an agreement with Boeing that limited the amount of government funds each aircraft manufacturer could receive, and in 1995, at long last, Airbus had become profitable. "Airbus 25 Years Old," *Le Figaro*, October 1997 (reprinted in English by Airbus Industrie); Rodgers, *Flying High*, Ch. 12; *Business Week* (30 December 1996): 40.
16. Charles Goldsmith, "Re-Engineering, After Trailing Boeing for Years, Airbus Aims for 50% of the Market," *Wall Street Journal*, 16 March 1998.
17. "Hubris at Airbus, Boeing Rebuild," *Economist*, 28 November 1998.
18. *The Boeing Company 1997 Annual Report*, 19; *The Boeing Company 1998 Annual Report*, 51.

Exhibit 7	Total Number of MD11, A330, A340, and 777 Airplanes Delivered during 1995–2001						
	1995	**1996**	**1997**	**1998**	**1999**	**2000**	**2001**
McDonnell Douglas/ Boeing MD11	18	15	12	12	8	4	2
Airbus A330	30	10	14	23	44	43	35
Airbus A340	19	28	33	24	20	19	22
Boeing 777	13	32	59	74	83	55	61

Sources: For Airbus, Mark Luginbill Airbus Communication Director, February 1, 2000, and March 11, 2002. For Boeing, *The Boeing Company Annual Report*, 1997, p. 35, 1998, p. 35; "Commercial Airplanes: Order and Delivery, Summary," http//www.boeing.com/commercial/order/index.html. Retrieved from Web, February 2, 2000 and March 9, 2002.

19. Donlon, "Boeing's Big Bet," 40; John Mintz, "Betting It All on 777," *Washington Post*, 26 March 1995; James Woolsey, "777: A Program of New Concepts," *Air Transport World*, (April 1991): 62; Jeremy Main, "Corporate Performance: Betting on the 21st Century Jet," *Fortune*, 20 April 1992, 104; James Woolsey, "Crossing New Transport Frontiers," *Air Transport World* (March 1991): 21; James Woolsey, "777: Boeing's New Large Twinjet," *Air Transport World* (April 1994): 23; Michael Dornheim, "Computerized Design System Allows Boeing to Skip Building 777 Mockup," *Aviation Week and Space Technology* (3 June 1991): 51; Richard O'Lone, "Final Assembly of 777 Nears," *Aviation Week and Space Technology* (2 October 1992): 48.

20. Rodgers, *Flying High*, 42.

21. *Air Transport World* (March 1991): 20; *Fortune*, 20 April 1992, 102–103.

22. Rodgers, *Flying High*, 416, 420–24.

23. Richard O'Lone and James McKenna, "Quality Assurance Role was Factor in United's 777 Launch Order," *Aviation Week and Space Technology* (29 October 1990): 28–29; *Air Transport World* (March 1991): 20.

24. Quoted in the *Washington Post*, 25 March 1995.

25. Quoted in Bill Sweetman, "As Smooth as Silk: 777 Customers Applaud the Aircraft's First 12 Months in Service," *Air Transport World* (August 1996): 71, but see also *Air Transport World* (April 1994): 24, 27.

26. Quoted in *Fortune*, 20 April 1992, 112.

27. Rodgers, *Flying High*, 426; *Design Quarterly* (Winter 1992): 22; Polly Lane, "Boeing Used 777 to Make Production Changes," *Seattle Times*, 7 May 1995.

28. *Design Quarterly* (Winter 1992): 22; The Boeing Company, *Backgrounder: Pace Setting Design Value-Added Features Boost Boeing 777 Family*, 15 May 1998.

29. Boeing, *Backgrounder*, 15 May 1998; Sabbagh, *21st Century Jet*, p. 49.

30. Karl Sabbagh, *21st Century Jet: The Making and Marketing of the Boeing 777* (New York: Scribner, 1996), 264, 266.

31. Sabbagh, *21st Century Jet*, 131–132

32. *Air Transport World* (April 1994): 23,; *Fortune*, 20 April 1992, 116.

33. *Washington Post*, 26 March 1995; Boeing Commercial Airplane Group, 777 Announced Order and Delivery Summary...As of 9/30/99.

34. Rodgers, *Flying High*, 420–426; *Air Transport World* (April 1994): 27, 31; "Leading Families of Passenger Jet Airplanes," Boeing Commercial Airplane Group, 1998.

35. Sabbagh, *21st Century Jet*, 58.

36. Quoted in Sabbagh, *21st Century Jet*, 63.

37. *Aviation Week and Space Technology* (3 June 1991): 50, 12 October 1992, p. 49; Sabbagh *21st Century Jet*, p. 62.

38. George Taninecz, "Blue Sky Meets Blue Sky," *Industry Week* (18 December 1995): 49–52; Paul Proctor, "Boeing Rolls Out 777 to Tentative Market," *Aviation Week and Space Technology* (12 October 1992): 49.

39. *Aviation Week and Space Technology* (11 April 1994): 37; *Aviation Week and Space Technology* (3 June 1991): 35.

40. Quoted in Sabbagh, *21st Century Jet*, 68–69.

41. This was the phrase used by Boeing project managers working on the 777. See Sabbagh, *21st Century Jet*, Ch. 4.

42. *Fortune*, 20 April 1992, 116; Sabbagh, *21st Century Jet*, 69–73; Wolf L. Glende, "The Boeing 777: A look Back," The Boeing Company, 1997, 4.

43. Quoted in *Air Transport World* (August 1996): 78.

44. Richard O'Lone, "777 Revolutionizes Boeing Aircraft Development Process," *Aviation Week and Space Technology* (3 June 1992): 34.

45. O. Casey Corr. "Boeing"s Future on the Line: Company's Betting its Fortunes Not Just on a New Jet, But on a New Way of Making Jets," *Seattle Times*, 29 August 1993; Polly Lane, "Boeing Used 777 to Make Production Changes, Meet Desires of Its Customers," *Seattle Times*, 7 May 1995; *Aviation Week and Space Technology* (3 June 1991): 34.

46. *Seattle Times*, 29 August 1993.

47. *Seattle Times*, 7 May 1995, and 29 August 1993.

48. Quoted in Rodgers, *Flying High*, 419–420.

49. Sabbagh, *21st Century Jet*, 33.

50. Sabbagh, *21st Century Jet*, 99.

51. Dori Jones Young, "When the Going Gets Tough, Boeing Gets Touchy-Feely," *Business Week* (17 January 1994): 65–67; *Fortune*, 20 April 1992, 117.

52. Reprinted by The Boeing Company, Executive Communications, 1992.

53. Boeing, *Backgrounder*, 15 May 1998.

54. *Industry Week* (18 December 1995): 50–51; *Air Transport World* (April 1994): 24.

55. *Aviation Week and Space Technology* (11 April 1994): 37.

56. Boeing, *Backgrounder*, "Computing & Design/Build Process Help Develop the 777." Undated.

57. *Seattle Times*, 29 August 1993.

58. *Seattle Times*, 7 May 1995.

59. *Seattle Times*, 29 August 1993.

60. Glende, "The Boeing 777: A Look Back," 1997, 10; *Air Transport World* (August 1996): 78.

61. *Air Transport World* (April 1994): 23.

62. *Washington Post*, 26 March 1995.

63. *Seattle Times*, 7 May 1995; Rodgers, *Flying High*, 441.

64. *Seattle Times*, 7 May 1995; Rodgers, *Flying High*, 441–442.

65. Glende, "The Boeing 777: A Look Back," 1997, 10.

66. *Air Transport World*, August 1996, 78.

67. "A New Kind of Boeing," *Economist*, 22 January 2000, 63.

68. "Vision 2016," The Boeing Company 1997.

69. "Study: Passengers Voice Overwhelming Preference for Boeing 777," http/www.boeing.com/news/releases/1999. Retrieved from Web, 11/23/99.

Appendix A: Selected Features of the 777

Aerodynamic Efficiency

Aircraft operating efficiency depended, in part, on aerodynamics: the smoother the surface of the plane and the more aerodynamic the shape of the plane, the less power was needed to overcome drag during flight. To reduce aerodynamic drag, Boeing engineers sought to discover the optimal shape of the plane's major components, namely, the wings, fuselage, nose, tails, and nacelles (engine protective containers). Speaking of the 777's "airfoil," the shape of the wing, Alan Mulally, the 777's director of engineering (he later succeeded Condit as the project manager), explained:

> The 777 airfoil is a significant advance in airfoil design over ... past airplanes ... We arrived at this shape by extensive analysis in wind tunnel .... [W]e learned new things by testing the airfoil at ... near flight conditions as far as temperature ... pressures, and air distribution are concerned. And ... we've ended up with an airfoil that is a new standard at maximizing lift versus drag.[1]

The 777's advanced wing enhanced its ability to climb quickly and cruise at high altitudes. It also enabled the airplane to carry full passenger payloads out of many high elevation airfields served by Boeing customers. Boeing engineers estimated that the design of the 777 lowered its aerodynamic drag by 5–10 percent compared to other advanced jetliners.[2]

A Service Ready Aircraft

A two-engine plane needed special permission from the Federal Aviation Administration (FAA) to fly long over water routes. Ordinarily, the FAA first certified a twin-jet for one hour of flight away from an airport, then two hours, and only after two years in service, three hours across water anywhere in the world. For the 767, Boeing attained the three hours certification, known as ETOPS (extended range twin-engine operations) approval, after two years in service. For the 777, Boeing customers sought to obtain an ETOPS approval right away, from day one of revenue operations. Boeing 777 costumers also expected the new jet to deliver a high level of schedule reliability from the start (Boeing 767 customers experienced frequent mechanical and computer problems as the 767 entered service in 1982).[3]

To receive an early ETOPS approval, as well as minimize service disruptions, Boeing engineers made special efforts to produce a "service ready" plane. Using advanced computer technology, Boeing tested the 777 twice as much as the 767, improved and streamlined the testing procedure, and checked all systems under simulated flight conditions in a new $370 million high-tech lab called Integrated Aircraft System Laboratory. The Boeing Company, in addition, conducted flight tests for an extended period of time, using United pilots as test pilots. Following a long validation process that included taking off, flying, and landing on one engine, the FAA certified the 777 in May 1995.[4]

The 777 proved highly reliable. During the first three months of its revenue service, United Airlines experienced a schedule reliability of 98 percent, a level the 767 took eighteen months to reach. British Airways' first 777 was in service five days after delivery, a company record for a new aircraft. The next three 777s to join British Airways fleet went into service a day after they arrived at Heathrow.[5]

The Use of Composite Materials

Advanced composite materials accounted for 9 percent of the 777's total weight, the comparable figure for Boeing's other jetliners was 3 percent. Improved Alcoa aluminum alloys that saved weight and reduced corrosion and fatigue were used for the construction of the 777's upper wing skin; other non-metallic composites were used for the 777's rudder, fines, and the tails. To help reduce corrosion around the lavatories and galleys, Boeing pioneered the use of composite materials for the construction of the floor beam structure. Boeing made a larger use of titanium alloys on the 777 than on any previous aircraft. Substituting steel with titanium cut weight by half, and space by one quarter; titanium was also 40 percent less dense than steel, yet of equal strength. The use of heat resisting titanium in the 777's engine nacelle saved Boeing 180 pounds per engine, or 360 pounds per plane; the use of titanium rather than steel for building the 777's landing gear saved Boeing 600 pounds per plane. Although titanium was more expensive than steel or aluminum, the choice of its application was driven by economics: for each pound of empty weight Boeing engineers squeezed out of the 777, Boeing airline customers saved hundreds of dollars worth of fuel during the lifetime of the plane.[6]

Notes

1. Quoted in Sabbagh, *21st Century Jet*, 46–47.
2. Boeing *Backgrounder*, 25 May 1998; Michael Dornmeim, "777 Twinjet Will Grow to Replace 747-200," *Aviation Week and Space Technology* (3 June 1991): 43; Sabbagh, *21st Century Jet*, 286–87.
3. *Air Transport World* (April 1994): 27; *Fortune*, 20 April 1992, 117; Sabbagh, *21st Century Jet*, 139–140.
4. *Industry Week* (18 December 1995): 52; *Aviation Week and Space Technology* (11 April 1994): 39; *Seattle Times*, 7 May 1995; Boeing, *Backgounder*, 15 May 1998; Sabbagh, *21st Century Jet*, Ch. 24.
5. *Industry Week* (18 December 1995): 52; *Air Transport World* (August 1996): 71.
6. Steven Ashley, "Boeing 777 Gets a Boost from Titanium," *Mechanical Engineering* (July 1993): 61, 64–65; *Aviation Week and Space Technology* (3 June 1991): 49; Boeing, *Backgrounder*, 15 May 1998; *Air Transport World* (March 1991): 23–24.

Appendix B: The 777's Choice of Engines

Pratt and Whitney (P&W), General Electric (GE), and Rolls Royce (RR) had all developed the 777 jet engine, each offering its own make. Boeing required an engine that was more powerful, more efficient, and quieter than any jet engine in existence; the 777 engine was designed to generate close to 80,000 pounds of thrust (the forward force produced by the gases escaping backward from the engine) or 40 percent more power than the 767's.[1]

All three engine makers had been selected by Boeing airline customers (Exhibit 8). United Airlines chose the Pratt & Whitney engine. Partly because P&W supplied engines to United 747 and 767 fleets, and also because the design of the 777 engine was an extension of the 747's and 767's design, United management sought to retain P&W as its primary engine supplier.[2] British Airways, on the other hand, selected the GE engine. A major consideration in British Airways' choice was aircraft efficiency: fuel consumption of the GE engine was 5 percent lower than that of the two competing engines.[3] Other carriers selected the RR engine for their reasons pertaining to their own needs and interests.

A special note: For additional financial data, as reported in the company's annual reports and other financial documents, check out Boeing's Web address at: www.boeing.com

Notes

1. Boeing, *Backgrounder*, 15 May 1998.
2. Sabbagh, *21st Century Jet*, 12–122.
3. Arthur Reed, "GE90 Lives Up to Promises," *Air Transport World* (August 1996): 72.

Exhibit 8	The Choice of Engines: Boeing 777's Largest Customers
Air France	GE
All Nippon Airways	P&W
American Airlines	RR
British Airways	GE
Cathay Pacific Airways	RR
Continental Airlines	GE
Delta Airlines	RR
International Lease Finance Corp.	GE
Japan Air System	P&W
Japan Airlines	P&W
Korea Airlines	P&W
Malaysia Airlines	RR
Saudi Airlines	GE
Singapore Airlines	RR
Thai Airways International	RR
United Airlines	P&W

Source: Boeing Commercial Airplane Group, *777 Announced Order and Delivery Summary ... As of 9/30/99.*

Exhibit 9   Selected Financial Data (dollars in millions, except per share data)

	2000	1999	1998	1997	1996
Operation					
Sales and Revenues					
Commercial Airplanes	$ 31,171	$ 38,475	$ 36,998	$ 27,479	$ 19,916
Defense and Space*	20,236	19,051	19,879	18,125	14,934
Other	758	771	612	746	603
Accounting Differences	(844)	(304)	(1,335)	(550)	
Total	51,321	57,993	56,154	45,800	35,453
Net Earnings (Loss)	2,128	2,309	1,120	(178)	1,818
Earnings (Loss) per share	2.48	2.52	1.16	(0.18)	1.88
Cash dividends	504	537	564	557	480
Per Share	0.59	0.56	0.56	0.56	0.55
Other income (interest)	386	585	283	428	388
Research and Development	1,441	1,341	1,895	1,924	1,633
Capital expenditure	932	1,236	1,665	1,391	971
Depreciation	1,159	1,330	1,386	1,266	1,132
Employee salaries and wages	11,614	11,019	12,074	11,287	9,225
Year-end work force	198,000	197,000	231,000	238,000	211,000
Financial Position at 12/31					
Total assets	$ 42,028	$ 36,147	$ 37,024	$ 38,293	$ 37,880
Working capital	(2,425)	2,056	2,836	5,111	7,783
Plant and Equipment	8,814	8,245	8,589	8,391	8,266
Cash and Short-term Investments	1,010	3,454	2,462	5,149	6,352
Total debt	8,799	6,732	6,972	6,854	7,489
Customer and commercial financing assets	6,959	6,004	5,711	4,600	3,888
Shareholders' equity	11,020	11,462	12,316	12,953	13,502
Per share	13.18	13.16	13.13	13.31	13.96
Contractual Backlog					
Commercial airplanes	$ 89,780	$ 72,972	$ 86,057	$ 93,788	$ 86,151
Defense and Space*	30,820	26,276	26,839	27,852	28,022
Total	120,600	99,248	112,896	121,640	114,173

*Including Information

Source: *The Boeing Company 2000 Annual Report*, pp. 8, 98.

A special note: for additional financial data, as reported in the company's annual reports and other financial documents, check out the Boeing web address at www.boeing.com.

Case
26

The Rise and Fall of Iridium

THUNDERBIRD
THE AMERICAN GRADUATE SCHOOL
OF INTERNATIONAL MANAGEMENT

Andrew Inkpen, *The American Graduate School of International Management*

The Global Village just got a whole lot smaller. "After 11 years of hard work, we are proud to announce that we are open for business," said Edward F. Staiano, Iridium LLC Vice Chairman and CEO. "Iridium will open up the world of business, commerce, disaster relief and humanitarian assistance with our first-of-its-kind global communications service … .The potential uses of Iridium products is boundless," continued Staiano. "Business people who travel the globe and want to stay in touch with home and office, industries that operate in remote areas, disaster and relief organizations that require instant communications in troubled areas—all will find Iridium to be the answer to their communications needs." Using its constellation of sixty-six low-earth-orbit satellites, the Iridium system provides reliable communications from virtually any point on the globe. From ships at sea, to the highest mountains to remote locations, Iridium customers will be able to make and receive phone calls on their Iridium phone. For people traveling to urban areas in the developed world, Iridium offers a cellular roaming service featuring dual-mode phones that can be switched to operate with terrestrial wireless services.

—*Excerpts from Iridium press release, November 1, 1998*

On November 1, 1998, Iridium began commercial telephone service. Satellite paging service began two weeks later. To build the satellite network, Iridium spent $5 billion, which was raised from a combination of debt, an IPO, and equity investments by various corporate shareholders, including Motorola Inc. (Motorola), Kyocera Corporation

(Kyocera), and Sprint Corporation (Sprint). Motorola also served as the project's prime contractor.

The estimated number of subscribers needed for Iridium to break even was 400,000, and Iridium hoped to add 50,000 subscribers per month in 1999. However, a variety of problems plagued the company and by May 1999 Iridium had only 10,000 subscribers. In August 1999 Iridium defaulted on its debt and filed for Chapter 11 bankruptcy protection. In March 2000, with only 50,000 subscribers, Iridium terminated its services and announced that it would soon finalize a deorbiting plan for the sixty-six satellites. Motorola announced that it was "extremely disappointed" that Iridium did not emerge from bankruptcy protection. Motorola's estimated financial exposure to the bankruptcy of Iridium was $2.2 billion.

Satellite Communications

Various different systems could be utilized to provide mobile satellite services (MSS). The oldest technology utilized geostationary earth orbit designs. Geostationary satellites were positioned 22,300 miles above the earth's surface and rotated with the earth in a geosynchronous orbit. From the earth's surface, the satellite appears to be fixed above a particular point and a global system using geostationary satellites can be built using as few as three such satellites. However, these satellites were expensive, costing approximately $100 million apiece to build and another $10 million each to launch. In addition, the distance from the earth's surface to the satellite can cause a quarter of a second delay between sending and receiving, which can be annoying to callers.

Low-earth-orbit (the system utilized by Iridium) and medium-earth-orbit satellites did not have a time-delay problem and were much less expensive to produce and launch. However, instead of appearing stationary over a particular point on the earth's surface, these satellites flew overhead at speeds of more than 15,000 miles per hour. Tracking them from the ground and handing off calls from satellite to satellite was complicated and expensive. The expected failure rate of such satellites was around 10 percent and life expectancy ranged from five to seven years once the satellite was in orbit.

The Creation of Iridium

Iridium was designed to be a satellite-based, wireless personal communications network which would permit any type of telephone transmission, including voice, data, fax, and paging to reach its destination at any time, at any location in the world. The genesis for Iridium was in 1986 when the general manager of Motorola's Strategic Electronics Division (which was involved primarily in space-related business) formed a small R&D group within his division. Motorola's previous space-related experience had been as a subcontractor for defense contracts. Firms such as Lockheed Corporation were the prime contractors and outsourced the electronics work to Motorola and other companies. However, there was a belief in Motorola's space division that advances in electronics would allow Motorola to change the rules of space competition and become a prime contractor. The R&D group was asked to look for opportunities that could leverage Motorola's distinctive competence in high-density electronics. In addition, the group was asked to consider commercial and defense applications.

In 1987 the Strategic Electronics Division R&D group invented a satellite communication system (see Exhibit 1 for the timing of key events). The system, named Iridium, derived its name from the element Iridium, whose atomic number, seventy-seven, matched the number of low-earth-orbit satellites that the company had originally intended to launch. According to a senior Motorola manager:

> The space industry was almost entirely focused on defense business. The emphasis was on fail-safe systems, redundancy, and space-qualified parts. The result was always gigantic costs overruns. We took all the conventions of building a spacecraft and changed them. Iridium was designed as a statistically based system in which a single satellite failure would not be a catastrophic failure. We designed satellites with little redundancy and lowered the cost of building a satellite by a factor of ten. We did not need space-qualified parts, which were incredibly expensive and not very reliable because of their low volumes. We went to the Motorola automotive division to learn about components for high-volume manufacturing.

From late 1987 through 1988, Motorola analyzed the technological and commercial viability of Iridium. In the fall of 1989 Motorola's CEO, Robert Galvin, announced internally that the company would develop the Iridium project. In early 1990 an Iridium business unit was formed with about twenty people. Motorola announced the project in June 1990 with simultaneous press conferences in Beijing, London, Melbourne, and New York.

Radio spectrum was allocated to Iridium in 1992. Obtaining the spectrum required overcoming substantial resistance from INMARSAT, a global satellite communications company owned by about eighty governments. INMARSAT, whose principle service was emergency communications for ocean-going ships, waged an unsuccessful battle to keep Iridium from obtaining an operating license.

At the time Iridium was conceived, cellular or mobile phones were of limited use when users crossed international borders. Europe, for example, had many different mobile standards, which meant a German phone would usually not work in France or Italy. Motorola management saw an opportunity to build a communications network that had a common standard and allowed users to use their phones anywhere in the world. At the time, it was believed that the potential demand for such a service was enormous, especially for voice telephony from the business and military community. Prior to the system's launch, the company predicted a market of twelve million satellite phone users by 2002 and a 40 percent share for Iridium. The company also predicted 100 million cellular phone users by 2000.

Ownership Structure

Iridium, Inc. was incorporated in June 1991 and operated as a wholly owned subsidiary of Motorola. However, Motorola's intent was never to operate as a service provider. In July 1999 Iridium privately sold shares of common stock to various U.S. and foreign investors. By 1994 Iridium had $1.6 billion of equity financing in place. A further $315 million of equity was secured during the first quarter of 1996. In June 1997 Iridium shares went public at $20, raising $225 million. Investor demand for Iridium shares was strong.

As a result of three private placements of equity, five supplemental private placements with additional equity investors, and proceeds received from the initial public offering of Iridium common stock, Motorola's interest in Iridium was reduced to approximately 19 percent, for which it had paid $365 million. The Japanese components maker, Kyocera, and affiliates held an 11 percent stake in the company. Other investors included Sprint, Vebacom (Germany), Lockheed (U.S.), Raytheon (U.S.), Telecom Italia, a consortium built around the Japanese carrier, DDI, a consortia of Middle East, African, and South American companies, and companies from China, Canada, Thailand, South Korea, Russia, Taiwan, and India. Most of the companies involved in the consortia and equity placements were new telecom entrants or second carriers in the telecommunications field.

Exhibit 1   Significant Events

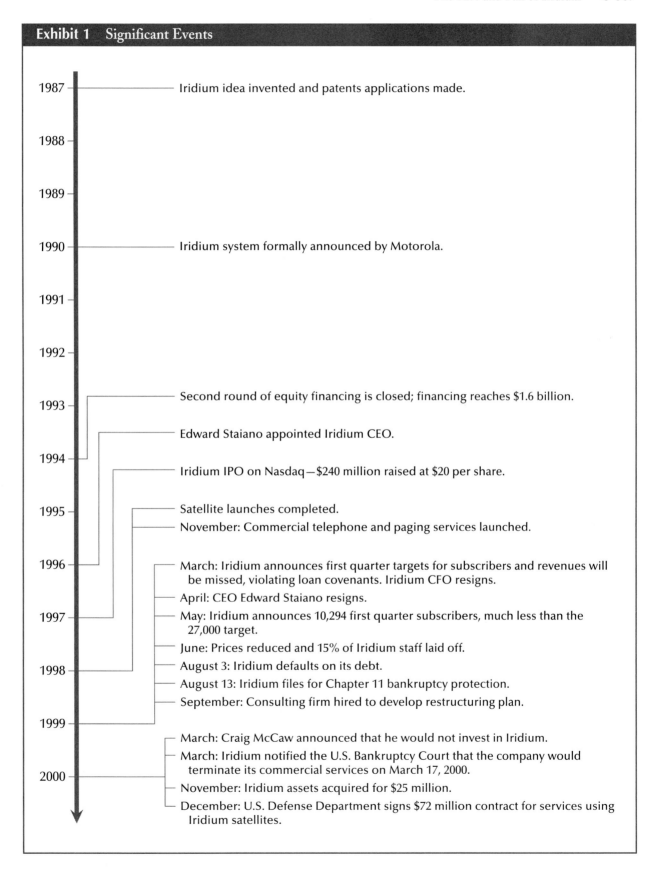

1987 — Iridium idea invented and patents applications made.

1988

1989

1990 — Iridium system formally announced by Motorola.

1991

1992

1993 — Second round of equity financing is closed; financing reaches $1.6 billion.

— Edward Staiano appointed Iridium CEO.

1994

— Iridium IPO on Nasdaq—$240 million raised at $20 per share.

1995 — Satellite launches completed.
— November: Commercial telephone and paging services launched.

1996 — March: Iridium announces first quarter targets for subscribers and revenues will be missed, violating loan covenants. Iridium CFO resigns.
— April: CEO Edward Staiano resigns.
1997 — May: Iridium announces 10,294 first quarter subscribers, much less than the 27,000 target.
— June: Prices reduced and 15% of Iridium staff laid off.
1998 — August 3: Iridium defaults on its debt.
— August 13: Iridium files for Chapter 11 bankruptcy protection.
— September: Consulting firm hired to develop restructuring plan.
1999
— March: Craig McCaw announced that he would not invest in Iridium.
— March: Iridium notified the U.S. Bankruptcy Court that the company would terminate its commercial services on March 17, 2000.
2000 — November: Iridium assets acquired for $25 million.
— December: U.S. Defense Department signs $72 million contract for services using Iridium satellites.

Background on Motorola and Kyocera

Motorola   In 1928 Paul Galvin and his brother, Joseph Galvin, purchased a bankrupt battery eliminator business in Chicago and formed the Galvin Manufacturing Corporation. The company's first product, a battery eliminator, enabled battery-operated home radios to operate on ordinary household current. In 1930 the company introduced the first practical and affordable car radio. Paul Galvin used the name Motorola for the company's new products, linking the ideas of motion and radio. The company's share of the car radio business increased rapidly and established the company as a leader in the U.S. market by 1936. In 1940 a communications division was established. Shortly after, this division developed the first hand-held two-way radio for the U.S. Army and the first commercial line of two-way FM radio communications products. By 1947 the Motorola trademark was so widely recognized that the Galvin Manufacturing Corporation changed its name to Motorola, Inc. Over the next five decades, Motorola developed a diverse mix of products that lead to the company becoming a global leader in providing integrated communications and electronic solutions. Over the years, in addition to car and two-way radios, Motorola developed televisions, pagers, transponders, cellular phones and systems, and semi-conductors. In 1999 Motorola's communications and electronic businesses focused on software-enhanced communications products and systems, networking and Internet-access products, digital and analog systems for broadband cable television, and semiconductors. Motorola was composed of three business units: Integrated Electronic Systems, Semiconductor Products, and the Communications Enterprise. Motorola was headquartered in Schaumburg, Illinois, and had a sales presence in almost every country. Sales for 1999 were $30.9 billion.

Kyocera   Founded in 1959 by Dr. Kazuo Inamori and seven colleagues as a manufacturer of a new advanced ceramic technology they had developed, Japan-based Kyocera diversified from electronic packages and components into optical and electronic systems. After more than four decades, Kyocera had grown into a global producer of high technology solutions in many areas, such as telecommunications, electronics, metal processing, automotive components, and solar energy. Kyocera operated with two fundamental objectives. The first was to continually improve its product offerings through the technological integration of its advanced materials into existing and emerging businesses. The second objective was to develop products responsive to marketplace needs through vertical integration. Kyocera management believed that production and marketing activities should be managed locally because of each country's unique culture. This belief made Kyocera one of the first Japanese companies with overseas facilities and marketing organizations. Kyocera was divided into three business segments: Ceramics and Related Products, Electronic Equipment, and Optical Instruments. In 1999 Kyocera was one of the world's leading producers of telecommunications equipment, including wireless phones. During 1999 Kyocera introduced the world's lightest CDMA cellular handset, the world's smallest satellite phone, and the world's first wireless, handheld videophone with color display. Kyocera's consolidated total net sales and operating revenue for fiscal year 1999 totaled ¥725 billion (yen) or $6.14 billion (at an exchange rate of ¥118/$).

Iridium Costs and Financing

The initial estimated cost of building the Iridium network was $3.5 billion. Based on the initial design, Motorola, as prime contractor, completed the project on time and on budget and above specifications. The capital cost consisted of two components: 1) the Space System contract for the design, development, production, and delivery of the satellites into orbit; and 2) the Terrestrial Network Development contract to design the gateway hardware and software. The $1.8 billion Operations and Maintenance (O&M) contract dealt with the day-to-day management of the satellites after deployment. The contract provided for monitoring, upgrading, and replacing hardware and software as necessary to maintain performance specifications. Motorola's Satellite Communications Division was general contractor for the space system and terrestrial network components and also had the contract to provide O&M.

Lockheed Corporation designed and constructed the satellite bus, and Raytheon Corporation designed the antenna for communication between the satellites and Iridium telephones. The Canadian firm, COMDEV, was responsible for the antennas for intersatellite and gateway links. Telesat, Siemens, Telespazio, and Bechtel were other key suppliers. Three suppliers from around the world were used to launch the satellites: Khrunichev Enterprise of the Russian Federation, China Great Wall Industry Corporation, and McDonnell Douglas (subsequently Boeing Corp).

Substantially all of the initial capital raised by Iridium was used to make payments to Motorola under the Space System contract, the Terrestrial Network Development contract, and the O&M contract. The Space System contract provided for a fixed price (subject to certain adjustments), scheduled to be paid by Iridium to Motorola over approximately a five-year period as milestones under the contract were completed. As of March 1, 1999,

Iridium had incurred all of the $3.435 billion estimated cost of the Space System contract and all but $5 million had been paid. As of March 1, 1999, Iridium had incurred $302 million of the $356 million estimated cost of the Terrestrial Network Development contract. According to the contract, Iridium was supposed to pay $120 million under the Terrestrial Network Development contract in 1999 and the remaining $10 million in 2000.

From July 1993 to December 1998, Iridium spent $4.8 billion. The expenditure was funded with 1) $500 million in secured bank debt; 2) $625 million in bank debt guaranteed by Motorola; 3) $1.62 billion from the issuance of debt securities; 4) $2.26 billion from the issuance of stock (private placement and IPO); and 5) $86 million of vendor financing. By March 1999 the amount of secured bank debt had increased to $800 million. The target leverage ratio was 60 percent, based on the theory that Iridium, once built, would resemble a utility with high margins, high fixed costs, and steady cash flows.

Motorola agreed to permit Iridium to defer its O&M obligations up to a total of $400 million until December 29, 2000. Total O&M payments were expected to be $2.89 billion over the initial five-year term of the contract between Motorola and Iridium. In addition to deferring O&M payments, Motorola guaranteed a significant amount of the bank financing and provided a guarantee in the event that additional bank financing up to $400 million was necessary.

Iridium Service

Motorola eventually launched sixty-six satellites into low-earth-orbit, approximately 485 miles above the earth's surface, and Iridium initiated service on November 1, 1998. Although a 10–15 percent failure rate for satellite deployment was normal, Motorola had a perfect record in satellite deployment. The satellites were mainly constructed and tested in Motorola's Satellite Communications Group facility in Chandler, Arizona. Because of the number of satellites, Motorola had to design a much more efficient production process than had been used previously by satellite manufacturers. Motorola developed an assembly line production process that allowed up to ten satellites to be under assembly at one time. Each satellite carried its own phone switching system and the network used complex satellite-to-satellite links that permitted phone calls to be switched in the sky. Although this feature substantially improved coverage and performance, the weight of the satellite increased very little because of advances in electronics. Based on statistical analysis, the satellites were expected to last about six years

before they would burn up in the earth's atmosphere, although sufficient fuel was provided for eight years.

Because of the nature of low- to medium-orbit satellites and the need to hand off calls from satellite to base station anywhere in the world, Iridium had to register user-link frequencies in every country around the world and obtain additional necessary operating permits. Nineteen strategic partners from around the world supported the Iridium system (Exhibit 2). Seventeen of the partners also participated in the operation and maintenance of twelve ground station "gateways" that linked the satellite system to terrestrial networks. The gateways, primarily telecom authorities and service providers in different countries, provided the terrestrial switching and call routing and served as regional distributors of Iridium services. The gateway partners shared in the revenue generated by Iridium calls. Although a few countries chose not to participate in the Iridium network, the countries that did participate made it possible to service most of the world's population.

The handsets were manufactured by Motorola and Kyocera and were seven inches long (plus antenna), weighed approximately one pound (Iridium promotional material described the handsets as "small, lightweight, hand-held telephones"), and retailed between $2,200 and $3,400. When Iridium service began, Iridium announced that Motorola and Kyocera, the manufacturers of Iridium satellite telephones and pagers, were expected to produce more than 100,000 satellite telephones in 1998. Service fees ranged from just under $2 per minute to as much as $7 per minute for some international calls.

Management

Edward Staiano, formerly the head of Motorola's cellular phone division, was appointed Iridium's CEO and vice chairman in 1996. Staiano became head of the cell phone division in 1984 and by 1996, division revenue was $11 billion. Staiano "personified the hardball, controlling leadership that got Motorola into trouble earlier in the year."[1] According to *Forbes*, one of Staiano's first major decisions was to ban all vacations at Iridium. The Iridium board was comprised of twenty-eight telecom executives and investor representatives from around the world. Except for two independent directors who received $20,000 per year and 1,000 options, none of the other directors received compensation from Iridium. Iridium operating companies were set up around the world (Exhibit 3).

Competition

In the mid-1990s, various experts and industry analysts were predicting that mobile satellite telephones would

Exhibit 2   Iridium Strategic Partners

- AIG Affiliated Companies
- Iridium Africa Corporation
- Iridium SudAmerica Corporation
- Iridium Middle East Corporation
- Khrunichev State Research and Production Space Center
- Lockheed Martin Corporation
- Iridium Canada, Inc.
- Iridium China (Hong Kong) Ltd.
- Iridium India Telecom Limited
- Iridium Italia S.p.A.
- Raytheon Company
- SK Telecom
- South Pacific Iridium Holdings Limited
- Sprint Iridium, Inc.
- Thai Satellite Telecommunications Co., Ltd.
- Motorola, Inc.
- Nippon Iridium (Bermuda) Limited
- Vebacom Holdings, Inc.
- Pacific Asia Communications Ltd.

experience huge growth rates over the subsequent decade. In a 1995 speech,[2] Steven Dorfman, president of Hughes Telecommunications and Space Company, one of the leading suppliers to the satellite industry, predicted that by the first years of the twenty-first century there would be twenty-five million satellite mobile telephones in use. Dorfman also predicted that the global satellite phone would be compatible for both terrestrial and satellite systems and would be used for voice, data, fax, and e-mail communications. Because satellites were not linked with borders, Dorfman argued that the traditional distinction between national and international telecom would soon disappear.

Largely in response to glowing predictions like that from Steven Dorfman, Iridium faced significant competition from MSS companies. The largest MSS competitors included Globalstar, Teledesic, and ICO Global Communications. Iridium had an eighteen-month lead over its MSS competition. As well, ground-based mobile networks were rapidly exploiting new technologies and building scale throughout the 1990s.

Globalstar

Globalstar had its roots in a 1989 plan at Ford Motor Company to use satellites to aid motorists. However, Ford's satellite unit was acquired by Loral Corporation in 1990 and Globalstar emerged in its present form through an alliance that Loral struck with several engineering firms

and large wireless providers. The investment in Globalstar totaled $3.8 billion and Loral owned 45 percent of the company. Other investors included Qualcomm, France Telecom, and AirTouch (now part of Vodaphone). The system began limited commercial service in late 1999.

The Globalstar network was built with fifty-two low-earth-orbit satellites. Unlike Iridium's satellites which had their own phone switching systems, Globalstar's satellites were like flying antennas, carrying calls to switching systems on the ground which were simple to operate and were linked into local networks. Globalstar's satellites, although simpler and cheaper than Iridium satellites, required ground switching systems and, therefore, coverage was restricted to land locations. Globalstar suffered a setback in September 1998 when twelve satellites were lost in a single failed launch on a Ukrainian/Russian rocket. Globalstar handsets weighed approximately 11 ounces and cost about $1,500. The price of calls was about $1.50 per minute and "get-acquainted" promotions offered Globalstar time for as little as $0.49 (U.S.) per minute. As of April 2000 Globalstar was available in twenty-seven countries with plans to increase to 80 nations by the middle of 2000.

Globalstar targeted wealthy business executives who required a service to cover areas where their cell phones did not work. It also focused on providing domestic service in developing countries and unwired regions, rather than on international traffic, as Iridium had. The company hoped that such customers would comprise approximately 15 percent of its total customers. In

Exhibit 3   Iridium Operating Companies

- Iridium Africa Services, (South Africa)
- Iridium Central America and Mexico
- Iridium China
- Iridium Communication Germany
- Iridium Eurasia (Moscow)
- Iridium India Telecom Limited
- Iridium Italia
- Iridium Korea Corporation
- Iridium Middle East Corporation (Dubai)
- Iridium North America
- Iridium Canada
- Nippon Iridium Corporation
- Pacific Iridium Telecom Corporation (Taiwan)
- Iridium Southeast Asia (Thailand)
- Iridium South Pacific (Australia)
- Iridium Brasil
- Iridium Cono Sur (Argentina, Bolivia, Chile, Paraguay, Uruguay)
- Iridium SudAmerica North (Venezuela)

addition, by June of 2000, the company would spend $40 million in advertising aimed at customers in narrow markets, such as fishing fleets and oil rigs. The system required one million subscribers to break even on an operating basis. According to Bernard Schwartz in 2000, "there is an addressable market of 40 million MSS users."[3]

Teledesic

Teledesic planned to launch 288 satellites in order to construct a web of two-way connections that could send data as quickly as sixty-four megabits-per-second through a global, broadband network. Teledesic was conceived by telecommunications pioneer, Craig McCaw, the company's chairman. The system was expected to cost in excess of $9 billion and besides McCaw, investors included Bill Gates, Saudi Prince Alwaleed Bin Talal, the Abu Dhabi Investment Company, Boeing, and Motorola. Motorola was selected as Teledesic's prime contractor, responsible for engineering and constructing the network. Prices were expected to be comparable to those of fixed line services and service was planned to begin in late 2003 or early 2004. Teledesic had cleared all major regulatory hurdles. Many analysts were skeptical and questioned whether there was a market for high-speed data communications to remote areas that fixed lines did not reach.

ICO Global Communications

London-based ICO Global Communications (ICO), with a system cost of $4.5 billion, was originally designed to use an array of twelve satellites to deliver global telecom service. ICO was a partnership of various companies, including British Telecom, Hughes Electronics, and TRW. ICO's initial public offering in the summer of 1998 fell well below expectations. In late July 1999, the company withdrew a $500 million rights offering and instead raised the money from large investors. Although the company attempted to save money by reducing the number of satellites in its system to ten and then to eight, it was expected that the company would fall short in its attempt to raise the necessary funds to launch its service in late 2000.

After ICO's shares plummeted from $16 in January to less than $5 in September 1999 as investors began to question the company's viability, ICO filed for bankruptcy protection. In November 1999, Craig McCaw, who also held a large stake in Teledesic, announced plans to invest in ICO, which was to be renamed New ICO. New ICO intended to focus on both voice and data communications and would be linked with Teledesic to provide *Internet-in-the-Sky* satellite communications services. Services were expected to begin in 2003.

Other Satellite Companies

Several other satellite projects were being developed, including ORBCOMM, a partnership between Orbital Sciences Corp. and Canada's Teleglobe. ORBCOMM launched 130 satellites for a messaging (not voice) network and had about $75 million in revenue in 1999. The system was primarily used by transportation companies. Several other systems were proposed but never developed. Hughes Electronics proposed a three satellite project called Spaceway. Another proposed system project called Ellipso involved a $1.5 billion dollar project for telephone service using seventeen satellites in elliptical orbits.

Ground-Based Wireless Services

Throughout the 1990's, while Iridium was being designed, ground-based wireless phone service grew rapidly around the world. A key factor in the growth of wireless phones was the adoption of a single standard, known as GSM, in Europe and parts of Asia. In the early 1980s, analog cellular telephone systems were growing rapidly in Europe. Each European country had developed its own cellular system, which was incompatible with equipment used in other countries. In 1982 the Conference of European Posts and Telegraphs (CEPT) formed a study group called the Groupe Spécial Mobile (GSM) to study and develop a pan-European public land mobile system. The proposed system had to meet certain criteria, including good subjective speech quality, low terminal and service cost, support for international roaming, and support for a range of new [unidentified] services and facilities that would presumably be developed.

In 1989, GSM responsibility was transferred to the European Telecommunication Standards Institute and GSM specifications were made public in 1990. Commercial GSM service began in 1991 and by 1993, there were thirty-six GSM networks in twenty-two countries, with twenty-five additional countries having already selected or considering GSM. This would eventually grow to more than 200 GSM networks in 110 countries. By the beginning of 1994 there were 1.3 million GSM subscribers worldwide; by February 1999 the number was 150 million. Including all cellular subscribers (analog and digital), there were more than 480 million subscribers worldwide by January 2000 and in a few years the number was expected to reach one billion. According to some observers, the rapid evolution to a single European standard took Motorola by surprise (although Iridium incorporated a GSM-based telephony architecture).

By 1999, Internet access via mobile phones had become commercially viable and the major telecom firms were moving rapidly to develop new technologies and standards. For example, in early 1999 Motorola introduced its Motorola's iDEN i1000plus phone with a built-in microbrowser to send and receive Internet e-mail and view web pages.

The Initial Market Response to Iridium

The Iridium company and board relied extensively on outside consultants for assistance in developing a marketing strategy. Iridium launched a $140 million global advertising campaign to create brand awareness two months before the phones were ready for sale. The campaign, using the slogan "Freedom to Communicate," emphasized that Iridium was the first truly global, personal telecommunications system. According to the ads, Iridium would allow voice, data, fax, and paging messages to be transmitted to anyone from virtually anywhere at any time. The target market was anyone who might require wireless telecommunications, which meant a target market of many millions. The ads, according to some observers, were "schmoozy and generic" and failed to distinguish Iridium from other wireless companies. Some time later, analysts speculated that too much emphasis on the technology was the root cause for the lack of focus in the marketing campaign.

In particular, the advertising message did not make it clear that Iridium's ability to communicate anytime, anywhere had some specific limitations. Without a special over-sized antenna to boost signal strength, Iridium phones were not designed to work in dense urban locations. In order to function, an Iridium phone had to be within a line of sight of one of the system's sixty-six satellites, which meant that the phones often would not function inside buildings. To design a satellite system with sufficient signal strength to penetrate buildings would have increased the Iridium cost by a factor of ten, according to a Motorola executive. Unfortunately, a common misconception in the business press was that Motorola changed the project specifications without complete communication to investors and potential users. In reality, the original specifications called for a design that allowed an Iridium phone to work in any location in the world but not necessarily inside a building. Testing was done from inside cars and using this as a baseline, the system actually built exceeded project specifications. From the beginning, the target market was:

International travelers who wanted to communicate with people in other countries from cars, airports, and other open areas. Anywhere meant any location on the globe, not anywhere on the globe from inside a building.

Nevertheless, as the *Wall Street Journal* reported, the advertising generated a large amount of potential interest in Iridium:

Over a matter of weeks, more than one million sales inquiries poured into Iridium's sales offices. They were forwarded to Iridium's partners—and many of them promptly disappeared, say several Iridium insiders. With no marketing channels and precious few sales people in place, most global partners were unable to follow up on the inquiries. A mountain of hot sales tips soon went cold.[4]

In addition, each Iridium satellite could handle only 1,100 simultaneous calls, limiting the company from achieving the economies of scale needed to offer its customers lower prices. In addition, sales personnel were not properly trained with Iridium and a shortage of telephones meant prospective customers were unable to try the product prior to purchase.

Iridium's subscriber base in the initial months of service fell far short of projections. In Iridium's 1998 annual report, management provided the following explanation for the slower than expected subscriber base and revenue:

Iridium believes that its slower than expected subscriber ramp-up and revenue generation have been primarily the result of problems with the initial distribution of subscriber equipment, a shortage of fully-trained service providers and sales personnel and a lack of effective marketing coordination among Iridium, its gateways and its service providers. During the initial roll-out of Iridium World Services, (i) Kyocera experienced significant difficulties in achieving Iridium's quality control standards and was unable to ship significant quantities of phones until early March of 1999, (ii) there were substantial difficulties in distributing phones and pagers to various markets around the world, (iii) although Motorola's satellite phones and pagers have been available since the commencement of commercial operations, the production of cellular cassettes for its dual mode satellite/cellular phones and some other accessories was delayed, and (iv) Iridium and its gateway operators had difficulty identifying and training service providers and their sales staffs. Iridium believes that Motorola and Kyocera have addressed most of these initial production and distribution problems. However, Iridium believes that it may take more time and effort to appropriately address the problems that have arisen in connection with the marketing and distribution of Iridium World Services.

Iridium left distribution up to its regional partners, but companies such as Sprint, which owned 3.5 percent of Iridium, were not selling the phones or service before the launch of the new system. Sprint's sales force did not push the service and its stores did not stock the handset. Therefore, Sprint, Motorola, and other partners, such as Telecom Italia, had to train their sales teams to sell the Iridium service. Moreover, business travelers, the primary target market, were reluctant to replace even a handful of small cellular phones with a large handset which weighed a pound, cost over $3,000 to purchase, was expensive to use, and could barely fit into a briefcase.

Service Problems

As prime contractor, Motorola's contract required delivery of the system by December 1998. Motorola met the deadline and in doing so, successfully created a new system for satellite design, manufacturing, and deployment. However, the completion of the contract should have been followed by a longer testing phase. The software had about twenty million lines of software code which inevitably, required debugging. Iridium starting selling the service before all testing and debugging was completed. When service problems resulted because of the lack of testing, the publicity was devastating, leading some observers to conclude that the system was prematurely turned on.

Financial Market Reaction

At year-end 1998 most financial analysts had buy recommendations for Iridium. Credit Suisse First Boston had a revenue projection for 2005 of $6.9 billion. Merrill Lynch, the firm that underwrote Iridium's initial public offering, was predicting about $6 billion. An investment analyst at Salomon Smith Barney wrote in February 1999: "Iridium presents a clear investment opportunity … Accordingly, we reiterate our Buy rating, maintain our $60 price target, and offer ten reasons to buy the stock immediately."5 Iridium's market capitalization was $5.6 billion at year-end 1998, down from almost $10 billion in May 1998.

New CEO

Iridium's secured bank loan contained various covenants. One group of covenants required Iridium to satisfy certain minimum revenue and subscriber levels, including conditions that at March 31, 1999, Iridium would have cumulative cash revenues of at least $4 million, cumulative accrued revenues of at least $30 million, at least 27,000 Iridium World Satellite Service subscribers and at least 52,000 total subscribers. In March 1999, Iridium announced that first-quarter revenue and customer targets dictated in its loan agreements would be missed and analysts predicted losses of more than $1.68 billion for 1999. The company's total revenue of $1.45 million had fallen far short of operating expenses and the company owed more than $100 million to creditors quarterly on its $3.4 billion debt. Iridium's shares sank from a high of $72 in 1998 to $9 in 1999 and its bonds traded at 19 cents on the dollar. Iridium also became the third most heavily shorted small-cap U.S. stock, with short-sellers holding 23 percent of its shares. Because of not meeting the revenue and subscriber targets, Iridium requested and received a waiver of compliance from lenders. Unfortunately, various events, including the financial crisis in Russia, continuing uncertainty in Asia, and the near collapse of Long Term Capital Management, meant that early 1999 was not a good time to seek concessions from lenders.

In April 1999, Staiano resigned as Iridium CEO and John Richardson, formerly head of Iridium's Africa unit, became interim CEO. Richardson immediately took action in an attempt to save the company. He revamped Iridium's marketing strategy and slashed prices. The company would no longer market itself as a rival to cellular services, but instead, position itself as a supplemental satellite service available where traditional cellular services were not. The focus would be on specialized markets, such as shipping and oil rigs. One new ad showed a North Atlantic fishing boat captain using an Iridium phone to find the port with the highest price for a catch of swordfish. According to Richardson:

> We have to do better than in past in terms of managing expectations of the consumer. Giving people the impression that you can use the phone in a nuclear bunker is clearly not the right way to … .6 The message about what this product was and where it was supposed to go changed from meeting to meeting. … One day we'd talk about cellular applications, the next day it was a satellite product. When we launched in November, I'm not sure we had a clear idea of what we wanted to be … . We did all the really

difficult stuff, like building the network and did all the no-brainer stuff at the end poorly."[7]

As to the possibility of liquidation publicly raised by Motorola, Richardson denied that liquidation was an option and offered this view:

What Motorola said about the alternatives [i.e., liquidation and bankruptcy] was, from an academic perspective, absolutely correct, but from our perspective, it's simply not on the radar screen.[8]

By May 1999, Iridium was still being used by only about 10,000 people—just one-fifth of what the company had promised. Many of these users, on offshore oil rigs or fishing boats or in remote locations such as northern Canada, were very satisfied with Iridium service. In a testimonial provided by Iridium, John Varty, producer of animal films in Africa, described the various ways that Iridium had become indispensable. For example, a lens broke while shooting a migration of over one million wildebeest—the largest migration in fourteen years. Using his Iridium phone, Varty was able to phone a Johannesburg company for guidance on how to repair the lens temporarily in the field.

Iridium announced on May 13 that it would be in technical default on $800 million of debt and the company's chief financial officer and top marketing executive resigned. On June 21, 1999, Iridium announced a new price-cutting strategy. In addition, the company attempted to sell its phones as a Y2K insurance policy, since the network orbited above the earth and would not be affected by any problems on the earth's surface. The company hoped to be able to create a new financial plan with investors and lenders by early July. In response to questions about a possible bankruptcy, Iridium's CFO said that a bankruptcy-court filing was not a realistic alternative because although such filings were relatively common in the United States, there was a significant stigma attached to them in other parts of the world. He went on to say:

We'd spend so much time explaining ourselves [to non-U.S. investors] that it could cost us a year's time in the market. … Our investors, partners and distributors do not feel that Iridium will quickly, if ever, recover from a bankruptcy.[9]

Bankruptcy

Business over the next few months did not improve. On August 5 1999, Iridium shares dropped below $6,

down from almost $50 earlier in the year. Prices for Iridium's bonds plummeted. On August 13, Iridium defaulted on its debt and filed for Chapter 11 bankruptcy protection after failing to meet bond payments and revenue targets promised to bankers. On September 1, Iridium announced that it had hired New York turnaround firm Alvarez & Marsal to help prepare a restructuring plan for the company. Iridium also announced that the firm was still in business and would emerge from the bankruptcy process as a stronger and more vibrant company.

Iridium continued to look for new investors to help rescue the company. Craig McCaw, one of Teledesic's major investors, had already saved ICO Global Communications from bankruptcy and appeared to be Iridium's greatest hope. By December, the talks between Iridium and McCaw appeared to be a failure, but negotiations were reopened in February of 2000. Iridium's bondholders were opposed to any deal because under McCaw's plan, the interests of unsecured debt holders and holders of existing Iridium common stock would likely be worthless.

McCaw's Eagle River Investments agreed to provide Iridium with $5 million, enough to finance the continued operation of the company through March 6, 2000. However, on March 20, McCaw announced that he would not rescue Iridium. By this time, the company had 55,000 subscribers and debts of $4.4 billion.

With the largest equity position in Iridium and its financial guarantees, Motorola stood to lose as much as $2.5 billion from its involvement as an investor and partner in Iridium. In 1999 Motorola wrote off its $365 million equity investment. Motorola's non-equity exposure included its guarantee of a $750 million bank loan, about $760 million in assets committed to Iridium, its holdings of $157 million of Iridium bonds, and vendor financing of $355 million.

Aftermath

In March of 2000, Iridium LLC notified the U.S. Bankruptcy Court that it had not been able to attract a qualified buyer for the service before the deadline set by the court and that the company would terminate its provisional commercial services after 11:59 pm on March 17, 2000. It was determined that the sixty-six satellites would be moved down, four at a time, into the earth's atmosphere where they would burn up. It was estimated that this process would take two years and cost between $30 million and $50 million.

Meanwhile, another satellite company, Orbitcall, offered a "911 rescue package" for Iridium's 50,000 subscribers, who otherwise would have been left without service after Motorola withdrew from the project. The trade-in offer included an Orbitcall M satellite phone and pre-paid airtime in exchange for the Motorola or Kyocera Iridium handsets.

In November 2000, a new company, headed by former Iridium CEO Ed Staiano and former Pan Am airlines CEO Dan Colussy, won bankruptcy court approval to buy Iridium assets for $25 million. In December 2000, the U.S. Department of Defense awarded Iridium LLC a two-year communications deal worth $72 million. The Defense Department said that it chose Iridium because its state-of-the-art technology could provide cryptographically secure communications to any open area on the planet.

Notes

1. Quentin Hardy, "Surviving Iridium," *Forbes*, September 6: 216–217.
2. Steven D. Dorfman, "Satellite Communications in the 21st Century," Speech to the Strategies Summit, Telecom '95 (ITU), Geneva, Switzerland, October 10, 1995.
3. Geoffrey Nairn, "Globalstar Optimistic Over Plan to Win Subscribers," *Financial Times*, March 15, 2000: XXVII.
4. Leslie Cauley, "Losses in Space—Iridium's Downfall: The Marketing Took a Back Seat to Science—Motorola and Partners Spent Billions on Satellite Links for a Phone Few Wanted," *Wall Street Journal*, August 18, 1999: A1.
5. John B. Coates, "Iridium World Communications," *Salomon Smith Barney Equity Research Report*, February 1, 1999: 2.
6. Ibid., 1999.
7. Carleen Hawn, "High Wireless Act," *Forbes*, June 14, 1999: 60–62.
8. Ibid., 1999.
9. Leslie Cauley, "Iridium Official Says Chapter 11 Isn't a Viable Option," *Wall Street Journal*, July 19, 1999: A4.

Other Sources

Art Brothers, "Long Distance: Phone Service Via Spacecraft Switches," *America's Network*, June 15, 1996: 118–.
Peter Brunt, "Iridium—Overview and Status," *Space Communications*, No. 2, 1996: 61–.
Roger Crockett, "Why Motorola Should Hang Up on Iridium," *Business Week*, August 30, 1999: 46.
Daniel Fisher, "Iridium for Truck Trailers," *Forbes*, October 4, 1999: 64–66.
Henry Goldblatt, "Just a Few Customers Shy of a Business Plan," *Fortune*, March 29, 1999: 40.
Quentin Hardy, "Surviving Iridium," *Forbes*, September 6: 216–217.
Paul Krugman, "When Did the Future Get So Boring," *Fortune*, September 27, 1999: 42–46.
Andy Reinhardt and Catherine Yang, "Risks Soar, The Rockets Don't," *Business Week*, May 31, 1999: 44.
Daniel Roth, "Motorola Lives!," *Fortune*, September 27, 1999: 305–306.
Gary Samuels, "Crowded Skies," *Forbes*, May 22, 1995: 98–.
Jonathon Sidener, "Iridium Ahead of, Then Behind Time," *The Arizona Republic*, March 26, 2000: D1, D5.
Debra Spark, "The Default Dilemma," *Business Week*, September 9, 1999: 76.
Catherine Yang and Roger Crockett, "Getting Iridium Of the Ground," *Business Week*, October 5, 1998: 76–80.
Joel Dreyfuss, "Calling Anywhere On Earth for Just $3,400," *Fortune*, March 1, 1999: 212.
www.gsmdata.com
www.iridium.com

The Scaffold Plank Incident

Stewart C. Malone and Brad Brown, *University of Virginia*

What had started as a typically slow February day in the lumber business had turned into a moral dilemma. With 12 inches of snow covering the ground, construction (and lumber shipments) had ground to a halt and on the 26th of the month, the company was still $5,000 below break-even point. In the three years since he had been in the business, Bob Hopkins knew that a losing February was nothing unusual, but the country seemed to be headed for a recession, and as usual, housing starts were leading the way into the abyss.

Bob had gone to work for a commercial bank immediately after college but soon found the bureaucracy to be overwhelming and his career progress appeared to be written in stone. At the same time he was considering changing jobs, one of his customers, John White, offered him a job at White Lumber Company. The job was as a "trader," a position that involved both buying and selling lumber. The compensation was incentive-based and there was no cap on how much a trader could earn. White Lumber, although small in size, was one of the bank's best accounts. John White was not only a director of the bank but one of the community's leading citizens.

It was a little after 8:00 a.m. when Bob received a call from Stan Parrish, the lumber buyer at Quality Lumber. Quality was one of White Lumber's best retail dealer accounts, and Bob and Stan had established a good relationship.

"Bob, I need a price and availability on 600 pieces of 3 x 12 Doug fir-rough-sawn—2 & better grade—16-feet long," said Stan, after exchanging the usual pleasantries.

"No problem, Stan. We could have those ready for pickup tomorrow and the price would be $470 per thousand board feet."

"The price sounds good, Bob. I'll probably be getting back to you this afternoon with a firm order," Stan replied.

Bob poured a third cup of coffee and mentally congratulated himself. Not bad, he thought—a two-truck

order and a price that guaranteed full margin. It was only a half-hour later that Mike Fayerweather, his partner, asked Bob if he had gotten any inquiries on a truck of 16-foot scaffold plank. As Bob said he hadn't, alarm bells began to go off in his brain. While Stan had not said anything about scaffold plank, the similarities between the inquiries seemed to be more than coincidence.

While almost all lumber undergoes some sort of grading, the grading rules on scaffold plank were unusually restrictive. Scaffold planks arc the wooden planks that are suspended between metal supports, often many stories above the ground. When you see painters and window-washers six stories in the air, they generally are standing on scaffold plank. The lumber had to be free of most of the natural defects found in ordinary construction lumber and had to have unusually high strength in flexing. Most people would not be able to tell certified scaffold plank from ordinary lumber, but it was covered by its own rules in the grading book, and if you were working ten stories above the ground, you definitely wanted to have certified scaffold plank underneath you. White Lumber did not carry scaffold plank, but its rough 3 x 12s certainly would fool all but the expertly trained eye.

At lunch, Bob discussed his concerns about the inquiry with Mike.

"Look, Bob, I just don't see where we have a problem. Stan didn't specify scaffold plank, and you didn't quote him on scaffold plank," observed Mike. "We aren't even certain that the order is for the same material."

"I know all that, Mike," said Bob, "but we both know that four inquiries with the same tally is just too big a coincidence, and three of those inquiries were for Paragraph 171 scaffold plank—It seems reasonable to assume that Stan's quotation is for the same stuff."

"Well, it's obvious that our construction lumber is a good deal cheaper than the certified plank. If Stan is quoting based on our 2 & better grade and the rest of his competition is quoting on scaffold plank, then he will certainly win the job," Mike said.

"Maybe I should call Stan back and get more information on the specifications of the job. It may turn out that this isn't a scaffold plank job, and all of these problems will just disappear."

The waitress slipped the check between the two lumbermen. "Well, that might not be such a great idea, Bob. First, Stan may be a little ticked off if you were suggesting he might be doing something unethical. It could blow the relations between our companies. Second, suppose he does say that the material is going to be used for scaffolding. We would no longer be able to say we didn't know what it was going to be used for, and our best legal defense is out the window. I'd advise against calling him."

Bob thought about discussing the situation with John White, but White was out of town. Also, White prided himself on giving his traders a great deal of autonomy. Going to White too often for answers to questions was perceived as showing a lack of initiative and responsibility.

Against Mike's earlier warnings, Bob called Stan after lunch and discovered to his dismay that the material was going to be used as scaffold plank.

"Listen, Bob, I've been trying to sell this account for three months and this is the first inquiry that I've had a chance on. This is really important to me personally and to my superiors here at Quality. With this sale, we could land this account."

"But, Stan, we both know that our material doesn't meet the specs for scaffold plank."

"I know, I know," said Stan, "but I'm not selling it to the customer as scaffold plank. It's just regular construction lumber as far as we are both concerned. That's how I've sold it, and that's what will show on the invoices. We're completely protected. Now just between you and me, the foreman on the job kinda winked at me and told me it was going to be scaffolding, but they're interested in keeping their costs down too. Also, they need this lumber by Friday, and there just isn't any scaffold plank in the local market."

"It just doesn't seem right to me," replied Bob.

"Look, I don't particularly like it, either. The actual specifications call for 2-inch thick material, but since it isn't actually scaffold plank, I'm going to order 3-inch planks. That is an extra inch of strength, and we both know that the load factors given in the engineering tables are too conservative to begin with. There's no chance that the material could fail in use. I happen to know that Haney Lumber is quoting a non-scaffold grade in a 2-inch material. If we don't grab this, someone else will and the material will be a lot worse than what we are going to supply."

When Bob continued to express hesitation, Stan said, "I won't hear about the status of the order until tomorrow, but we both know that your material will do this job ok—scaffold plank or not. The next year or two in this business are going to be lean for everyone, and our job—

yours and mine— is putting lumber on job sites, not debating how many angels can dance on the head of a pin. Now if Quality can't count on you doing your job as a supplier, there are plenty of other wholesalers calling here every day who want our business. You better decide if you are going to be one of the survivors or not. I'll talk to you in the morning, Bob."

The next morning, Bob found a note on his desk telling him to see John White ASAP. Bob entered John's oak-paneled office and described the conversation with Stan yesterday. John slid a company sales order across the desk, and Bob saw it was a sales order for the 3 x 12s to Quality Lumber. In the space for the salesman's name, Bob saw that John had filled in "Bob Hopkins." Barely able to control his anger, Bob said, "I don't want anything to do with this order. I thought White Lumber was an ethical company, and here we are doing the same thing that all the fly-by-nighters do," sputtered Bob in concluding his argument.

John White looked at Bob and calmly puffed on his pipe. "The first thing you better do, Bob, is to calm down and put away your righteous superiority for a moment. You can't make or understand a good decision when you are as lathered up as you are. You are beginning to sound like a religious nut. What makes you think that you have the monopoly on ethical behavior? You've been out of college for four or five years, while I've been making these decisions for forty years. If you go into the industry or the community and compare your reputation with mine, you'll find out that you aren't even in the same league."

Bob knew John White was right. He had, perhaps, overstated his case, and in doing so, sounded like a zealot. When he relaxed and felt as though he was once again capable of rational thought, he said, "We both know that this lumber is going to be used for a purpose for which it is probably not suitable. Granted, there is only a very small chance that it will fail, but I don't see how we can take that chance."

"Look, Bob, I've been in this business for a long time, and I've seen practices that would curl your hair. Undershipping (shipping 290 pieces when the order calls for 300), shipping material a grade below what was ordered, bribing building inspectors and receiving clerks, and so on. We don't do those things at my company."

"Don't we have a responsibility to our customers, though?" asked Bob.

"Of course we do, Bob, but we aren't policemen, either. Our job is to sell lumber that is up to specification. I can't and won't be responsible for how the lumber is used after it leaves our yard. Between the forest and the final user, lumber may pass through a dozen transactions before it reaches the ultimate user. If we are to assume responsibility for every one of those transactions, we would probably have time to sell about four boards a year. We have to assume, just like every other business, that our suppliers and our customers are knowledgeable and will also act ethically. But whether they do or don't, it is not possible for us to be their keepers."

Bob interjected, "But we have reason to believe that this material will be used as scaffolding. I think we have an obligation to follow up on that information."

"Hold on, just a second, Bob. I told you once we are not the police. We don't even know who the final user is, so how are we going to follow up on this? If Stan is jerking us around, he certainly won't tell us. And even if we did know, what would we do? If we are going to do this consistently, that means we would have to ask every customer who the final end user is. Most of our customers would interpret that as us trying to bypass them in the distribution channel. They won't tell us, and I can't blame them. If we carry your argument to its final conclusion, we'll have to start taking depositions on every invoice we sell.

"In the Quality Lumber instance, we are selling material to the customer as specified by the customer, Stan at Quality Lumber. The invoice will be marked, 'This material is not suitable for use as scaffold plank.' Although I'm not a lawyer, I believe that we have fulfilled our legal obligation. We have a signed purchase order and are supplying lumber that meets the specifications. I know we have followed the practices that are customary in the industry. Finally, I believe that our material will be better than anything else that could conceivably go on the job. Right now, there is no 2-inch dense 171 scaffold plank in this market, so it is not as though a better grade could be supplied in the time allotted. I would argue that we are ethically obligated to supply this lumber. If anyone is ethically at fault, it is probably the purchasing agent who specified a material that is not available."

When Bob still appeared to be unconvinced, John White asked him, "What about the other people here at the company? You're acting as though you are the only person who has a stake in this. It may be easy for you to turn this order down—you've got a college degree and a lot of career options. But I have to worry about all of the people at this company. Steve out there on the forklift never finished high school. He's worked here 30 years and if he loses this job, he'll probably never find another one. Janet over in bookkeeping has a disabled husband. While I can't afford to pay her very much, our health insurance plan keeps their family together. With the bills her husband accumulates in a year, she could never get him on another group insurance plan if she lost this job.

"Bob, I'm not saying that we should do anything and then try to justify it, but business ethics in the real world is not the same thing you studied in the classroom. There it is easy to say 'Oh, there is an ethical problem here. We better not do that.' In the classroom, you have nothing to lose by taking the morally superior ground. Out here, companies close, people lose their jobs, lives can be destroyed. To always say 'No, we won't do that' is no better than having no ethics at all. Ethics involves making tough choices, weighing costs and benefits. There are no hard-and-fast answers in these cases. We just have to approach each situation individually."

As Bob left John's office, he was more confused than ever. When he first entered his office, he had every intention of quitting in moral indignation, but John's argument had made a lot of sense to him, and he both trusted and respected John. After all, John White had a great deal more experience than he did and was highly respected in both the community and the lumber industry. Yet he was still uncomfortable with the decision. Was selling lumber to Quality merely a necessary adjustment of his ivory tower ethics to the real world of business? Or was it the first fork in the road to a destination he did not want to reach?

Case 28

7-Eleven Japan: Managing a Networked Organization

Ben M. Bensaou, H. Ochino, K. Mitani, and K. Noishiki, *INSEAD*

Toshifumi Suzuki had been a radical since his university days when he was a frequent student protester. Now, despite his unorthodox approach, the 64-year-old executive has become one of Japan's most esteemed company presidents. When, in the early 1970s, he proposed to bring from the United States the concept of the convenience store, he faced strong skepticism within Ito-Yokado, 7-Eleven Japan's parent company, and within the industry. Despite the opposition, he persevered and adapted the innovative concept to the Japanese context, starting a "revolution" in the Japanese distribution system. To explain the continual success of his company, Suzuki likes to explain that "we are not in the retail business but rather in the *information* business." To him, the bottle of shampoo sitting on the shelf at a Shizuoka store is a "bundle of information." This vision of the retail industry has led 7-Eleven Japan to be the first retailer to install, in 1991, an ISDN (Integrated Service Digital Network). Indeed, ever since the creation of the company in 1973, Suzuki has heavily invested in information technology (IT) applications to link his business processes to those of his business partners, the franchisees' stores, the wholesalers, and the manufacturers.

Critics in the industry, however, are now questioning whether the new and costly investments in networking technology are really necessary. 7-Eleven Japan indeed might have benefited from a first mover advantage, consistently improving its financial position, but it is now under the threat of competitors who have been implementing similar information systems. How can Suzuki sustain 7-Eleven's competitive advantage in a rapidly saturating domestic retail market? What does it take to stay number one in Japan? Is it time to expand internationally and export the CVS (convenience store) concept back to the United States and to new markets in Europe and Asia? How can Suzuki transfer to a Western context the unique capabilities he has created and nurtured in the domestic market over the last twenty years?

The Japanese Distribution System

Some Western experts view the Japanese distribution system as a major barrier to trade. They describe it as highly inefficient and hold it responsible for the high prices Japanese consumers pay. Traditional retailing in Japan consists of a conservative, multi-tiered, and outmoded system that brings together a large number of small wholesalers and retailers into a complex and exclusive network of tight relationships, based on not only economic efficiency but also human considerations (Exhibit 1). Japanese manufacturers generally control the distribution of their wares, and retailers have to select goods from wholesalers' limited offerings. In exchange, shops are able to return unsold goods to wholesalers. Stores then tend to be full of high-priced goods that consumers don't necessarily want. Today most Japanese small retailers are independent; yet belong to such informal but tight and cooperative vertical networks. These are held together by mutual interest and long-term personal as well as business relationships. These develop over time between well-known partners and are maintained and nurtured by personal contacts, frequent visits, gifts, mutual services, financing, and support in difficult times. Newcomers can only enter through introductions.

Already in feudal Japan, manufacturers were the ones controlling large, multi-tiered channels through which they marketed their products. At the time, the manufacturing class enjoyed much higher prestige than the merchant class. Their prestige and stature further increased later as they were credited with Japan's post-World War II economic success. In the Tokugawa era, Japan consisted of many small, largely self-contained provinces that developed their own local distribution system independently

This case was written by Ben M. Bensaou, Associate Professor of Information Technology and Management at INSEAD, with the participation of H. Uchino, K. Mitani, and M. Noishiki, INSEAD, MBA, on the basis of published documents. It is intended to be used as a basis for class discussion rather than to illustrate either effective or ineffective handling of an administrative situation. Copyright © 1997 INSEAD-EAC, Fontainebleau, France. All rights reserved.

Exhibit 1   International Comparisons of Distribution Systems

A. A Comparison of Distribution Structures

	Japan (1988)	US (1982)	UK (1984)	France (1987)	West Germany (1985)
Number of retail stores (000)	1,628	1,731	343	565	320
Population (millions)	121	231	56	55	61
Number of retail stores per 10,000 people	134	75	61	103	52
Number of wholesalers per 10,000 people	36	18	17	14	19
Number of retail stores per wholesaler	3.7	4.2	3.6	7.3	2.7
Number of employees per store	4.2	1.9	2.0	1.6	1.8
Number of retail stores per 10km	43.1	1.8	14.0	10.0	12.8

B. US and Japan's Retail Systems: Food and Non-Food Sectors

Number of Employees	US (1982) Food		US (1982) Non-Food		Japan (1985) Food		Japan (1985) Non-Food	
	Stores	Sales	Stores	Sales	Stores	Sales	Stores	Sales
0–2	23.7	2.5	50.6	7.9	60.1	17.0	56.0	10.6
3–9	46.1	13.7	31.0	25.0	35.0	50.5	38.1	39.8
10–19	12.6	9.2	10.2	17.0	3.1	4.0	4.0	13.5
20–49	11.2	29.0	6.0	20.9	1.5	18.6	1.5	10.7
50–99	5.0	29.7	1.6	13.1	0.3	8.2	0.3	5.1
100+	1.4	15.9	0.6	16.1	0.0	2.1	0.1	20.3
Total percentages	100.0	100.0	100.0	100.0	100.0	100.0	100.0	100.0
Percentage of total	9.5	22.6	90.5	77.4	41.2	31.3	58.8	68.7

Source: A. Goldman, 1992.

of each other. Mobility of goods and people across the four main islands was then extremely limited. To gain access to any area, producers had to rely on intermediaries who knew and could deal with customers in sometimes-remote villages. Over time, this practice led to the building of close relationships between the different players in this intricate distribution system.

Even today products typically pass through three or more levels of wholesalers—the national or primary wholesalers, the secondary wholesalers, and the local ones. The manufacturer designates the primary wholesaler who would coordinate the regional level and perform the handling, financing, physical distribution, warehousing, inventory promotion, and payment collection functions for him. In addition, since the 1950s, wholesalers are asked to accept on the manufacturers' behalf all the unsold products returned by the retailers. Before ending up in Mr. Nishida's store in Shibuya, Tokyo, an eyeglasses frame would travel from Horikawa Seisakusho's production site in Sabae, Fukui prefecture (500 kilometers from Tokyo), to the manufacturer's exclusive national wholesaler in Sabae. The large wholesaler then distributes its products through a close network of selected regional wholesalers all over Japan. The regional wholesaler in Fuchu (an eastern suburb of Tokyo) should carry the total inventory for the East Tokyo area. From his warehouse, the eyeglasses would be dispatched to one of the multiple local wholesalers and finally to retailers in the Shibuya-ku district.

Manufacturers still maintain a tight control over the relationships. They set the price at which the product needs to be sold and dictate the criteria on which are based the rebates they attribute to wholesalers and retailers. These rebates are based not only on quantity purchased, but also on loyalty and service, criteria that favor the small retailers and wholesalers. A large number and variety of rebates are offered in Japan. They include rebates for quantity, early payment, achieving sales targets, service performance, keeping inventory, sales promotion, loyalty to supplier, following manufacturers' pricing policies, cooperation with the manufacturer, and contributing to its success. The system was historically established by manufacturers to ensure total support for their products and their marketing strategies, and to exclude rival manufacturers from the channel. The negotiated and long-term nature of the rebates and the fact that they are secret increases manufacturers' power and strengthens their control over channel activities.

The Japanese retail sector in Japan is still dominated by small retailers (Exhibit 2). These local, small, "mom-and-pop" stores carry wide assortments in a narrow product line. They typically lack managerial and planning skills and thus have to rely on the wholesalers for inventory and distribution performance. In addition, given their limited size, they are often unable to bear the risks associated with carrying a wide range of products, and with financing and managing their own retail outlet. To support them, manufacturers and large wholesalers have implemented the product return system and various financing programs. Small shops, however, have been facing new threats, first coming from newly developed retail structures, such as department stores and supermarkets. In 1956, they lobbied the government for the introduction of the Department Stores Law, regulating the opening and business hours of larger outlets. Later, when the first superstores and supermarkets were met with wide customer acceptance, the government introduced more restrictive regulations, i.e., the Large Retail Stores (LRS) Law. Initially applied to stores with an area greater than 1,500 square meters, it was later extended in 1979 to stores 500 square meters and over. New guidelines were issued in 1982, giving more power to the local governments in these regulatory matters. Applications were now reviewed by special councils. The views of the local chamber of commerce and of the Council for Coordination of Commercial Activity (CCCA) regarding the impact of the proposed retail store on the local economy and on the small stores in the surrounding area weighed heavily in decisions. At present, no time limits existed on these negotiations and the process that originally took a year or so now took between seven and eight years, and in some instances even fifteen, to complete. Regulations have therefore effectively protected the small retailers and have helped the traditional sector to maintain its position. Under heavy pressure from abroad, changes to the LRS law have recently been proposed.

Despite these rigidities in the system, the intricacies of the multi-tiered channels and the high price of goods, consumer surveys indicate that Japanese consumers are generally content with their distribution system. Living in small houses or apartments with little storage space, Japanese housewives cherish shopping in specialty stores in their neighborhood and usually display a strong loyalty to the small, local stores. Relationships between customers and the storeowner tend to be long lasting. Some of these small stores are not necessarily run on a profit-making basis. Typically the store is part of the owner's residence, and in most instances, the wife and her retired husband work together. Overall the productivity of the distribution system has been low. Small retailers are unable to keep pace with rapidly changing consumer needs and invest in improving their operations. In a 1982 survey, annual sales per retailer in Japan amounted to $219,000 versus $600,000 in the United States (Exhibit 1).

The Forces for Change

In the 1950s, with rising income, rapid urbanization, and increased mobility, consumer preferences gradually changed. The concept of the *supermarket* was introduced to Japanese consumers around this time. These new stores, such as Daiei, Ito-Yokado, Seiyu, and Jusco, carried everyday items and sold them at low prices. They could offer competitive prices due to the large volume rebates they secured from large wholesalers. The 1970s and 1980s brought prosperity and affluence. Consumers did not just look for the cheapest product any more, but were now sensitive to the quality of the product and the service. At the same time, the social fabric of Japanese society was evolving. More women entered the labor force, the traditional, extended family structure started to disintegrate, and people wanted more leisure time. This period, in fact, represented a turning point in the evolution of the Japanese distribution system, as it moved from a manufacturer-centered system to a customer-oriented system. Listening to consumer needs became the critical success factor.

The Japanese retail industry flourished and grew to provide customers with a wide range of retail formats fiercely competing against each other. First, there was the large number of small traditional mom-and-pop stores that carried a narrow range of items but provided the convenience of neighborhood proximity. Large department stores, such as Mitsukoshi or Takashimaya (Exhibit 2), carried a wide range of items and catered to the high end of the market. Historically, these *hyakka-ten* were rich cloth merchants of the Edo or Tokugawa period (1600–1868) who later expanded their business to become large retailers. The supermarkets, on the other hand, carried a large range of items at discount prices that would appeal to the middle and low end of the market. Other players in the retail business included convenience stores, discount stores, and direct mail businesses, each of

Exhibit 2   The Key Players in the Japanese Retail Industry

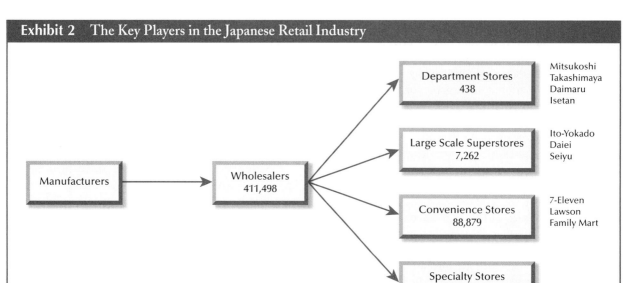

A. Supermarkets: 18% of the total retail market in 1991 (14,848,900 million ¥)

	Market Share	Operating Revenue (100 million ¥)	Income before Income Taxes (100 million ¥)	Employees
Daiei	10.1	20,259	275	46,045
Ito Yokado	8.9	14,596	972	32,076
Seiyu	6.9	10,950	160	23,657
Jusco	5.0	10,413	296	24,993
Nichii	4.9	7,671	291	20,025
Uny	3.6	5,558	174	12,461
Nagasakiya	2.8	4,374	41	11,009
Izumiya	2.6	4,002	151	n/a
Tsujitsuya	2.0	3,283	51	n/a
Maruetsu	2.2	3,213	82	10,722
Others	51.2	n/a	n/a	n/a

B. Department Stores: 8% of the Total Retail Market in 1991

	Market Share	Operating Revenue (100 million ¥)	Income before Income Taxes (100 million ¥)	Employees
Mitsukoshi	9.0	8,766	110	11,867
Takashimaya	8.6	8,430	134	9,782
Daimaru	6.2	6,083	61	7,312
Matsuzakaya	5.1	5,020	100	7,246
Isetan	4.8	4,682	141	5,683
Tokyo	4.2	4,106	92	4,945
Hankyu	3.6	3,552	114	5,440
Sogo	3.2	3,106	73	3,651
Hanshin	1.3	1,221	22	n/a
Matsuya	1.2	1,116	16	n/a
Others	52.8	n/a	n/a	n/a

them focusing on a different factor for success—convenience, discounts, and market targeting, respectively.

The Convenience Store Concept

Ito-Yokado was founded by Masatoshi Ito in 1946 as a 66-square-foot family clothing store in Tokyo. By 1960, Ito had expanded his business into a ¥384 million company. The same year, he visited the United States and saw multi-item superstores for the first time. Upon his return to Japan, he started a new chain of superstores offering a range of food and clothing products. He further expanded his business into other distribution areas, such as restaurants, department stores offering a full range of products, discount stores, and convenience stores. By 1988, the Ito-Yokado group had grown into the second largest retailer group in Japan and one of the most profitable ones, with thirty-two companies, 4,000 stores, and 60,000 employees (Exhibits 3, 4, and 5). It was at a business seminar in Tokyo in 1968 that Toshifumi Suzuki, Executive Manager of Ito-Yokado's New Business Development division, first heard of the concept of convenience stores, very popular in the United States at

the time. He came to realize that bringing small retailers into a new franchise of convenience stores would, on the one hand, provide the small shop owners with the management and merchandising skills they were lacking to survive, and on the other hand, provide customers with the benefits of the traditional, small neighborhood retailer. The restrictive LSR regulation did not encourage further development of the supermarket chain concept and provided the right context for an innovative solution that leveraged the pre-existence of a large number of protected small "neighborhood" stores.

Without his president's direct approval, Toshifumi Suzuki flew to the United States and directly negotiated with Southland, owner of 7-Eleven, to bring the U.S. convenience store concept to Japan. President Ito and others at Ito-Yokado were convinced that it was too early to introduce the concept into the Japanese distribution system, which was already saturated with a very large number of small retailers. Despite the commonly held skepticism and sometimes outright opposition within the mother company, Suzuki proceeded with his plans and in 1974 opened the first 7-Eleven convenience store in Japan

---

Exhibit 3   7-Eleven Japan and the Competition

A. Outlook of CVS Industry and Main Franchise Chains (1988)

CVS Chains	Sales (billion ¥)	No. of Stores	Parent Company
7-Eleven	780	3,940	Ito-Yokado
Lawsons	430	3,570	Daiei
Family Mart	264	1,725	Seibu Saisons
Sun-Every Yamazaki	223	2,061	Yamazaki Bread
Kmart	90	778	UNY

B. Outlook of CVS Industry and Main Franchise Chains (1988)

CVS Chains	Sales per Day (1$ = ¥125)	Store Space (m²)	Gross Margin (%)	Full-Time Clerks
7-Eleven	$4,048	98	27.4	4
Lawsons	3,156	100	28.8	8
Family Mart	3,200	90	26.5	6
Sun-Every Yamazaki	3,200	96	27.0	4
Kmart	2,794	132	22.0	4

C. Royalties

CVS Chains	Royalties (% of Gross Profit)	Contract Length (Years)
7-Eleven	45	15
Lawsons	32	10
Family Mart	35	10

Exhibit 4   7-Eleven Japan and Competition

A. Japan's Top Five Retailers by Total Store Sales (1996)

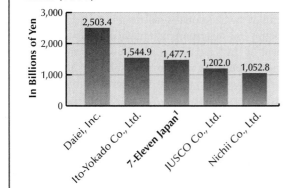

Note: [1]Sales of all 7-Eleven Japan stores.

B. Japan's Top Five Retailers by Ordinary Profit (1996)

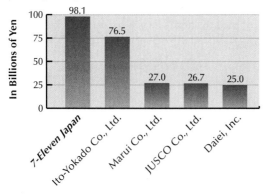

C. Sales by Japanese Convenience Stores

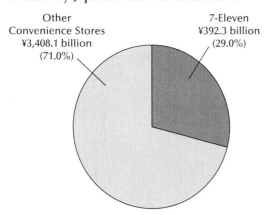

Other Convenience Stores ¥3,408.1 billion (71.0%)

7-Eleven ¥392.3 billion (29.0%)

☐ Convenience store sales are for fiscal 1994 and are taken from the *Nikkei Ryutsu Shinbun*.

■ The 7-Eleven sales figure is for the period ended February 28, 1995.

in Kohtoh-ku, an eastern suburb of Tokyo. He later explained: "At the time, I was young and very eager to find a way we could prosper together with small retailers. I was convinced that a convenience store franchise was the best solution." After the contract had been signed, Suzuki realized that the Southland concept of convenience store had to be adapted to the Japanese market and was convinced that the American operational know-how could not be directly transferred to the Japanese distribution system context. The challenge for 7-Eleven Japan was to develop new business systems all on its own. In particular, the differences in consumer behavior between the United States and Japan translated into large differences in the strategy and implementation Suzuki pursued for 7-Eleven Japan. Japanese consumers were generally more sensitive to product and service quality, more fickle, and less price sensitive. To meet such customer requirements within the constraints of limited shelf space and storage capacity, it was necessary to offer a wide range of well-targeted products and to provide additional services twenty-four hours a day, seven days a week.

Strategy

After graduating in economics from Chuo University, Suzuki worked for Tokyo Shuppan Hanbai, one of Japan's largest book wholesalers. At 31, he was noticed by one of his clients, Ito-Yokado, and was later asked to join the company. At the time, Ito-Yokado owned only four stores in the Tokyo area but was one of the fastest growing companies in Japan. At first Suzuki was in charge of personnel and advertisement. In 1970, years later, he became Executive Director for the New Business Development division. His most influential success was the creation of alliances with large regional retailers and with the Denny's chain of restaurants. His fundamental belief in the importance of customer satisfaction was repeatedly reinforced in all of his policies throughout his career. In particular, his obsession with customer satisfaction was at the origin of the 7-Eleven Japan practice of continuous item control, frequent delivery, and the heavy use of information technology (IT) applications. To get an objective assessment of customer needs, he preferred to rely on inexperienced people. In his view, "merchandising consists in identifying customer needs … and experience or expertise might contaminate a manager's judgment." Unlike many retail managers, he rarely visited stores. His approach was more analytical—hence his faith in a high-tech computer system to keep in touch with customer tastes. Suzuki's hunger for information gave birth to weekly meetings involving some 160 managers to discuss the tiniest matters affecting the

Exhibit 5   7-Eleven Japan Performance

A. Total Number of Retail Stores and of 7-Eleven Stores in Japan

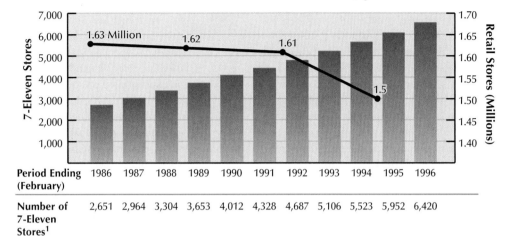

Period Ending (February)	1986	1987	1988	1989	1990	1991	1992	1993	1994	1995	1996
Number of 7-Eleven Stores[1]	2,651	2,964	3,304	3,653	4,012	4,328	4,687	5,106	5,523	5,952	6,420

Note: [1]Number of 7-Eleven stores includes stores in Hawaii.

B. Average Daily Sales at New Stores in Their First Fiscal Year of Operation

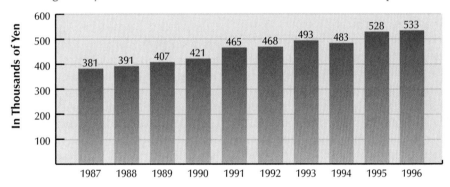

Source: 7-Eleven Japan, *An Introduction to Investors* (1996).

company, from curtain sales in northern Japan to the reasons peach sales flopped.

7-Eleven Japan had been changing its concept of "convenience store," constantly adjusting to changing consumer behavior. Suzuki described 7-Eleven stores as "stores where you can find a solution for any of your daily life problems. We always try to plan and design a store in such a way that young people, in particular, can get whatever they need at any time they want," Suzuki agreed that the productivity level of traditional small retailers was extremely low, mainly because most of these mom-and-pop stores had grown out of touch with consumer needs and thus were losing business to large retailers.

He subsequently built a strategy for his franchise business to address what he believed were the two main reasons for the failure of small, and even large, retailers: they ignored (1) the importance of convenience to the customer and (2) the quality of the products and the service. In surveys, customers typically complained about:

- The products they were looking for being sold out
- The long waiting lines at cashiers
- The stores being closed when they needed the service
- Product freshness
- The contact with store personnel

For 7-Eleven Japan, the first complaint was considered as the most critical problem to be dealt with. "If you cannot get me the fresh tofu I need for dinner tonight, I won't come back to your store," complained a housewife to her usual store. In essence, small retail stores were losing not only profit opportunity, but also customer loyalty. In response to this issue, 7-Eleven made it clear in its franchisee guidelines that "for them, thirty items sold out from a portfolio of 3,000 should represent a 'stock-out rate' of 100 percent and not 1 percent." The basic mission of a 7-Eleven Japan store was to provide solutions for all the problems of everyday life. A store offered a variety of high-quality products and services that were required on a daily or on a distress basis, or that just made life easier or more "convenient," Under Suzuki's leadership, 7-Eleven Japan had therefore developed three key principles to define a quality convenience store:

1. **Reduction of lost opportunity.** A missed opportunity to sell an item because it is sold out was believed to represent up to three times the value of the actually realized profit. Suzuki therefore encouraged the development of operational processes to reduce this opportunity cost: "We need to not simply identify what particular products customers like, but more importantly, we should accurately determine when, where, in which quantities, and at which price these products are needed."

2. **Supply of products just-in-time and in the quantity required.** The simplest way of reducing opportunity cost is to keep large inventories of a wide range of products. Unfortunately this solution could not be applied in convenience stores in Japan where shelf and storage space were limited and running large stocks was prohibitive. Moreover, planning customers' future needs presented major challenges. 7-Eleven Japan pursued a strategy of supplying products that were in demand on a just-in-time basis, thereby eliminating dead items and slow selling items and replacing them by the faster selling ones.

3. **Franchise strategy.** To support his fundamental concept of co-prosperity between large supermarkets and the traditional small retailers system, Suzuki adopted a franchise system. From the beginning, he did not invest in American-style "greenfield" stores, where it is the franchiser who buys the "walls," or builds the store from the ground up. On the contrary, 70 percent of 7-Eleven Japan stores were modified from old family-owned stores (e.g., rice, meat, or liquor stores). In other words, the storeowner provided part of the financing,

between U.S.$200,000 and 300,000, in addition to saving on the cost of land and the building. It was also the expression of the long-term commitment to store profitability by the owner. The relationship between franchiser and franchisee was also distinctly one of reciprocal obligations. The franchisee was an independent business that gave 7-Eleven Japan large royalties and a long-term commitment, and concentrated on the tasks of selling and effectively managing his inventory. In exchange, the franchiser provided the information back-up (i.e., data and analysis capabilities), implemented efficient operational systems to support planning and delivery of products, negotiated with the suppliers, advertised on a national scale, and developed new products that satisfied customers.

Outsourcing Policy

7-Eleven Japan was also known for its outsourcing policy and superior ability to manage supplier relationships. Suzuki explained that retailing is a "quick response business," and that his company should therefore concentrate only on what they do better and outsource the rest. Since its creation, the company had never directly owned any manufacturing and logistics operations. Although its competitors tried to develop their own capabilities to circumvent the inefficiency and complexity of the existing Japanese distribution system, 7-Eleven Japan identified an exclusive wholesaler for each region, assuring them of a long-term business relationship and large purchase volumes. In return for this exclusivity, these regional wholesalers were required to improve their operations and increase their performance standards. For instance, strict quality requirements in terms of freshness and taste were imposed. 7-Eleven Japan had even out-sourced its critical information technology. Although it had been spending about $80 million per year on IT, it had about twenty people running its electronic data system department. Their role was to develop a systems vision that fit with the business strategy, while the rest of the software and hardware design was subcontracted to the Nomura Research Institute (NRI), a subsidiary of Nomura Securities and the second largest systems integrator in Japan. In 1990, the company invested $200 million to replace its third-generation information systems. The multiple vendors involved, such as NTT and NRI, viewed the development of an IT infrastructure for 7-Eleven as a way of taking the lead over their own direct competitors.

"Selecting and negotiating with the various subcontractors, wholesalers, and small retailers was not easy," confides Suzuki. The long opening hours and the frequent deliveries did not attract many candidates at first. Also, the rationalized distribution system crafted by 7-Eleven—for instance, adopting a single exclusive regional wholesaler policy for each product category—created conflict within the traditional wholesale system. Over time, however, the 7-Eleven Japan system proved highly reliable and efficient, gradually drawing more and more proponents. In the early 1980s, while competitors were diversifying and opening more stores, 7-Eleven Japan concentrated on cost cutting and efficiency improvements. In its push for profitability, Ito-Yokado dropped inefficient wholesalers and forced the ones it retained to raise their standards. "It was tough for us because we had to make a huge investment to upgrade our information system for [them]" said a manager at a Tokyo-based wholesaler. "But if we'd refused, we'd have been cut off and gone out of business." Once those standards were met, wholesalers appreciated the feedback they were getting from the quick and precise sales data. Manufacturers also benefited, improving their sense of what customers wanted. "[Their] information system is so good that we can instantly find out which goods of ours are selling and how much," said a salesman at Tokyo Style, a large garment maker that makes an exclusive line for Ito-Yokado. By 1992, the company had built a network of 123 common distribution centers all over Japan, each of them created and operated by wholesalers and suppliers.

Implementation Processes

Item Selection

First of all, a store needs to display at least 3,000 distinct items in order to be perceived by the customer as a convenience store. However, the store space available for a 7-Eleven franchisee is on average about 100 square meters. It thus becomes critical to carry the proper range of products. For example, to recommend to franchisees items from the 3,000 different soft drink products available on the market (of which 1,200 are regularly replaced every year), 7-Eleven Japan used data analysis techniques to narrow down the list to 100 items. In one experiment, it was found that, under similar conditions, stores carrying a well-targeted range of only seventy items could sell 30 percent more than the regular stores with 100 items. 7-Eleven Japan also used point of sale (POS) systems to identify customer trends and enhance its product differentiation. It can test new products and new brands in days rather than weeks or months. Year to year, 70 percent of merchandise in a given store will be new.

This meant that 7-Eleven Japan was constantly monitoring and analyzing customer needs and tastes. It recently introduced a new innovation: weather forecasting and "human temperature studies." Weather terminals were used in stores to forecast orders for ice cream, bento boxes, sandwiches, oden (Japanese winter meal), and other items for which it had been observed that sales varied with weather conditions. Also, umbrellas kept in storage could be displayed if rain was forecast. Sandwiches do not sell well on rainy days, and on a sunny weekend, bentos sell extremely well. The weather also influenced the ingredients within a lunch box, and with three deliveries a day and orders for the next day accepted until 6:00 P.M., stores could precisely adjust their product mix to customer needs. The outlook of a store will typically be different in the morning or in the evening, whether the main customers are students on their way to school or "salarymen" on their way back.

7-Eleven Japan targeted all individuals living or working in the vicinity (i.e., within 300 meters walking distance) of the store. A new store opened only if there were enough population density within this area and no direct competition. The primary segmentation was therefore by geography. Then customers could be classified according to their shopping habits.

1. **Immediate consumption.** These are mainly younger people, often singles, who do not have much time to cook for themselves. They typically want to buy foods/drinks for instant consumption. The main competition for this segment is fast food chains, take-out food stores and restaurants, or easy home cooking.

2. **Distress and daily.** These are customers who make "distress" purchases or buy daily supplies, e.g., fresh bread, vegetables, or dairy products, while they may have done their weekly shopping at a discount store or supermarket. This is typically the local neighborhood population.

3. **One-stop shopping.** These are customers who typically like to do all their food shopping in their neighborhood stores. This can include older people attached to their local community, people without a car, or working men and women who have little time to go shopping (especially during working hours).

The distinction between these three categories of customers reflected their different requirements for products, time, and habits of purchase. The key value proposition to achieve for 7-Eleven Japan was therefore to deliver customer satisfaction for all three types of customers.

Item-by-Item Control

The items kept in stock and on the shelf were precisely selected for the targeted customers, and product quality was kept high. 7-Eleven discovered that customer loyalty was driven more by specific items than by item categories. The implication was that the franchiser needed to plan demand and delivery on an item-by-item basis and could not rely on aggregate estimates per category of item, due to the observed high variance within product categories. In other words, 7-Eleven Japan stores held just the right amount of stock for those selling items. Product turnover was high, and goods were always new and food extremely fresh. For instance, the shelf life of a "bento" lunchbox was three to four hours. Sales were registered on the POS system and slow or nonselling items were discontinued immediately. The product life cycle of branded drinks was short and tightly followed fashion. Stores could quickly switch from low-selling brands to the more fashionable ones according to sales data and the "top selling ranking" analysis. One could find all product types found at regular supermarkets, yet 7-Eleven Japan stores carried only a limited number of brands for each category. Sales by brands were also closely monitored and the portfolio of brands continually adjusted. Non-performing brands were ruthlessly deleted. To achieve such a tight item-by-item control, the Electronic Data Systems department proposed a POS (point of sale) system solution, whereby data could be gathered online about which product was selling and where. Using these statistics, store owners could adjust their product mixes and supply requests quickly enough to respond to movements in customer demand. The same data, aggregated over time, allowed franchiser and franchisees to forecast long-term demand and plan new product launches.

New Product Development

Early on, 7-Eleven Japan identified the fast-food business as a high growth niche where it could leverage its efficient planning and delivery systems (Exhibit 6). For instance, fast foods now represented 40 percent of the total items on shelves and 30.6 percent of total sales. The chain differentiated itself from the competition by focusing on quality control of ingredients, cooperation with producers at the development and preparation stages, and strict control of freshness during delivery. The commitment to fast-food products' quality reached all the way to top management. Board directors themselves met to taste the new "bento" lunch boxes as they were developed.

Freshness, Quality of Products

Price in Japanese convenience stores was typically at a 10 percent premium over the average price at a large supermarket. Customers were therefore ready to pay a premium for freshness, quality of products, and convenience. To meet customer requirements for quality, 7-Eleven Japan implemented a system of frequent and small lot deliveries (Exhibit 7). It had recently invested in temperature-controlled vans to preserve food quality and freshness.

Value-Added Services

To provide further convenience for its customers, 7-Eleven Japan decided to offer value-added services. It started a home delivery parcel service in cooperation with a large transportation company, first with Nittsu Corporation and afterwards with Yamato. Leveraging its extensive electronic network with manufacturers, suppliers, wholesalers, and retail stores, 7-Eleven Japan now provided online bill payment services for utilities (e.g., electricity and gas), insurance (e.g., life and car insurance), and telephone (e.g., NTT and KDD) (Exhibit 8). In 1992, it initiated a new mail order service business. In addition, beyond their direct retailing role, convenience stores had also become in urban areas a social center for younger crowds (Exhibit 8). They came and read magazines or bought concert tickets, music, or computer games.

Market Dominance Strategy

In its quietly aggressive way, Suzuki had been shaking up the conservative Japanese retail industry. His expansion strategy had been to penetrate new territory by building a critical mass of at least fifty to sixty franchisees (Exhibit 9). The resulting market presence contributed to:

- Distribution and logistics efficiency
- Operations and information systems effectiveness
- Franchisee support efficiency (i.e., field consultants)
- 7-Eleven corporate image
- Higher entry barriers for competitors

Service Quality

First, accessibility was important. Stores were located in dense neighborhoods and stayed open all day. The intuitive store layout made it easy to find items even for the first time. In a country where space is at a premium, stores must create a warm, friendly atmosphere that not only attracts customers but also gives them a much-valued sense of space and freedom. Shopping at 7-Eleven Japan did not only provide tangible/material

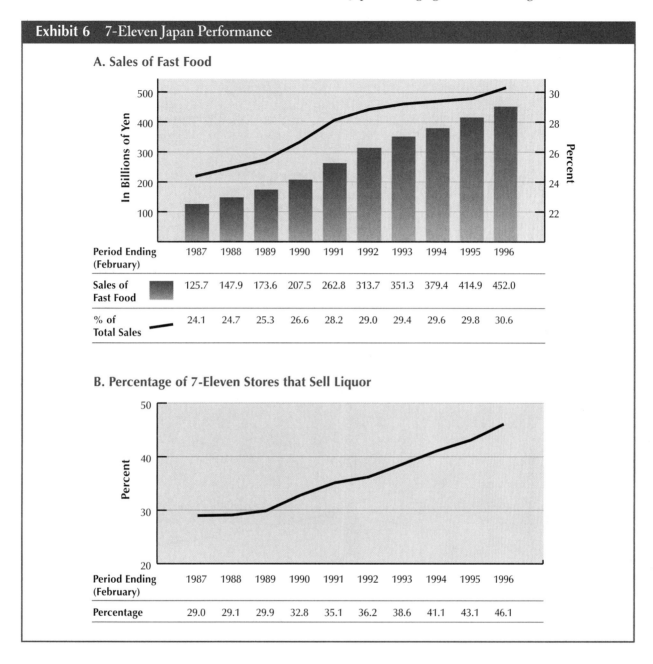

Exhibit 6   7-Eleven Japan Performance

A. Sales of Fast Food

Period Ending (February)	1987	1988	1989	1990	1991	1992	1993	1994	1995	1996
Sales of Fast Food	125.7	147.9	173.6	207.5	262.8	313.7	351.3	379.4	414.9	452.0
% of Total Sales	24.1	24.7	25.3	26.6	28.2	29.0	29.4	29.6	29.8	30.6

B. Percentage of 7-Eleven Stores that Sell Liquor

Period Ending (February)	1987	1988	1989	1990	1991	1992	1993	1994	1995	1996
Percentage	29.0	29.1	29.9	32.8	35.1	36.2	38.6	41.1	43.1	46.1

satisfaction (e.g., goods and foods to consume) but also intangible satisfaction, such as good service, safety, a sense of relaxation, and a feeling of belonging to a community. The design of the store was very important, and nothing at 7-Eleven Japan was left to chance. All parameters of store layout and design were analyzed and carefully chosen to deliver the value proposition to the customer. From the outside, the large 7-Eleven red and green logo flanked with red and green stripes around the store helped customers identify the store from the distance. The front side was a see-through window revealing the activity inside, in particular the crowd standing behind the window browsing through their favorite magazines and newspapers. Inside the store, the lighting was kept very bright (twice the brightness level at other stores). The store was always spotless, regularly cleaned, and safe, providing a comfortable, relaxing, and refreshing feeling to the visitor. Customers were reassured when they saw others in the store shopping or browsing and found that the store carried most of the branded products they knew. A visit to a 7-Eleven Japan store had

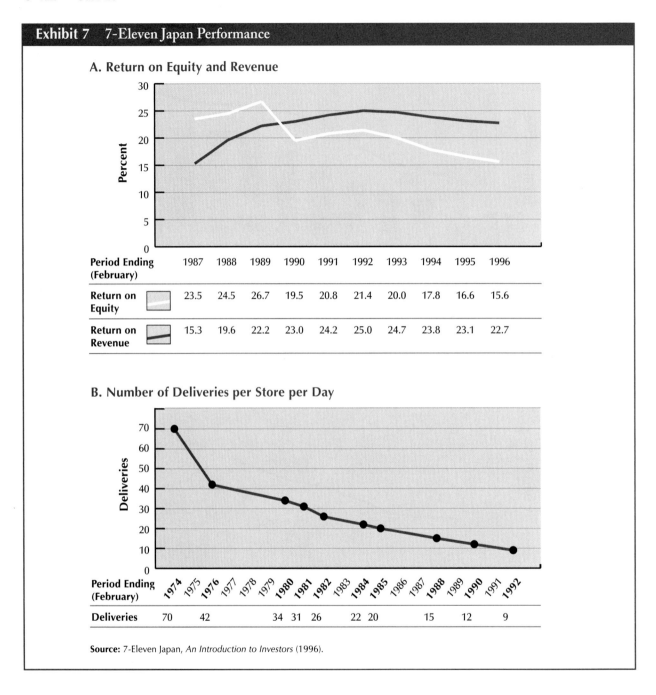

Exhibit 7   7-Eleven Japan Performance

A. Return on Equity and Revenue

Period Ending (February)	1987	1988	1989	1990	1991	1992	1993	1994	1995	1996
Return on Equity	23.5	24.5	26.7	19.5	20.8	21.4	20.0	17.8	16.6	15.6
Return on Revenue	15.3	19.6	22.2	23.0	24.2	25.0	24.7	23.8	23.1	22.7

B. Number of Deliveries per Store per Day

Period Ending (February)	1974	1975	1976	1977	1978	1979	1980	1981	1982	1983	1984	1985	1986	1987	1988	1989	1990	1991	1992
Deliveries	70	42					34	31	26		22	20			15		12		9

Source: 7-Eleven Japan, *An Introduction to Investors* (1996).

become for many a daily experience, "you get used to it, it becomes part of your daily routine."

The typical layout, the result of thorough research and experimentation, guides customers through various product categories, facilitating customer purchase decisions increasing their purchase desire, and therefore maximizing sales. Response time is dictated by customers. They may want to quickly choose a product/service and leave the store immediately, or alternatively, they may want to spend a long time in the store just browsing, relaxing, reading magazines, and enjoying the ambiance. After attracting the customer from outside, the store layout guides her from the magazine section, to the drinks section, the snacks, food, and finally dessert section before she faces the cashier surrounded by attractive items for impulse purchases and various added services. Also, the layout of the store, its product mix, and the items' allocation to shelf space may change during the day, during the week (weekdays different from weekends), and seasonally as customer

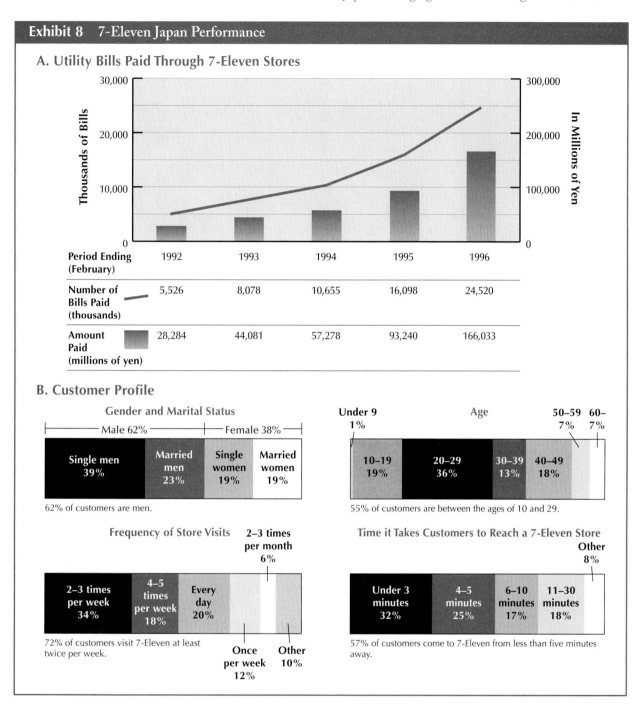

Exhibit 8   7-Eleven Japan Performance

A. Utility Bills Paid Through 7-Eleven Stores

Period Ending (February)	1992	1993	1994	1995	1996
Number of Bills Paid (thousands)	5,526	8,078	10,655	16,098	24,520
Amount Paid (millions of yen)	28,284	44,081	57,278	93,240	166,033

B. Customer Profile

Gender and Marital Status

Male 62% — Female 38%

Single men 39% | Married men 23% | Single women 19% | Married women 19%

62% of customers are men.

Age

Under 9 1% | 10–19 19% | 20–29 36% | 30–39 13% | 40–49 18% | 50–59 7% | 60– 7%

55% of customers are between the ages of 10 and 29.

Frequency of Store Visits

2–3 times per week 34% | 4–5 times per week 18% | Every day 20% | Once per week 12% | Other 10% | 2–3 times per month 6%

72% of customers visit 7-Eleven at least twice per week.

Time it Takes Customers to Reach a 7-Eleven Store

Under 3 minutes 32% | 4–5 minutes 25% | 6–10 minutes 17% | 11–30 minutes 18% | Other 8%

57% of customers come to 7-Eleven from less than five minutes away.

needs shift. If an item was doing well, it got its own section to make it more accessible to customers. Recently, when its regular partner, Sapporo Beer, failed to catch onto the "Ice" beer fever that came from the United States, 7-Eleven Japan successfully introduced a special section for Miller Ice beer, an American beer selling at ¥178 for 355 ml, when the domestic brand was priced at ¥225 for 350 ml.

Operations

Just-in-Time Delivery System

7-Eleven Japan developed the Combined Delivery System, whereby the same kind of products coming from different suppliers could be centralized in a CDC (Combined Delivery Center). This represented a revolution for the

Exhibit 9   7-Eleven Japan's Expansion Strategy

Global Expansion (15,490 stores in 22 countries)

Sweden	31	Malaysia	93
Norway	39	Singapore	77
Denmark	11	Philippines	83
UK	53	Guam	10
Spain	89	Canada	451
Turkey	9	USA	5,552
China	22	Mexico	221
Taiwan	1,158	Puerto Rico	12
Korea	110	Brazil	14
Hong Kong	328	Australia	153
Thailand	554	*Japan*	*6,420*

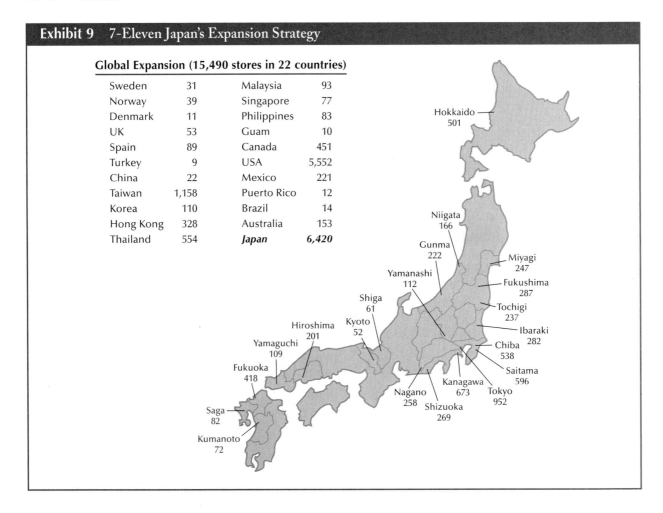

Hokkaido 501
Niigata 166
Gunma 222
Yamanashi 112
Miyagi 247
Fukushima 287
Shiga 61
Tochigi 237
Shiga 61
Kyoto 52
Ibaraki 282
Hiroshima 201
Chiba 538
Yamaguchi 109
Saitama 596
Fukuoka 418
Kanagawa 673
Tokyo 952
Nagano 258
Saga 82
Shizuoka 269
Kumanoto 72

suppliers whose products were traditionally delivered separately through exclusive channels. The benefit for 7-Eleven Japan was that it involved fewer deliveries from the producers to the wholesalers. Instead of ordering and then storing crates of a given product, a store operator may simply order the few items he judged were needed. Overall, in eighteen years, it managed to reduce the average number of vehicles visiting each store from seventy to nine a day (Exhibit 7). It also introduced the Temperature-Controlled Combined Delivery System, whereby items were grouped not by type, but on the basis of their required storage temperature: frozen foods were put together in a -20°C container, chilled products in a 5°C container, and rice balls and bentos in the 20°C compartment, while processed foods would stay in a room temperature area. By 10:00 a.m., all stores in the 7-Eleven Japan chain verified their data and placed orders needed that evening, as well as those needed the next morning and afternoon. Orders were transited by the host computer and were dispatched to the producers throughout the country by 10:30 a.m. Newly produced lunch boxes, for

instance, arrived at CDCs (Combined Delivery Centers) by 2:00 p.m. and would be delivered to the individual stores by 6:00 p.m. the same day.

Information Systems

Suzuki used to say: "Don't rely on the POS system. Information technology is merely a tool to achieve business strategy. We shouldn't use the technology unless we can understand what the information means on paper." However, after its first introduction of a high-capacity online network in 1989, 7-Eleven Japan began to explore new services that could take advantage of this new capability. In other words, while he was true to his original principle, Suzuki started to be influenced by technology when formulating his business strategy. When he opened his first store in 1974, order and sales data were orally exchanged back and forth between headquarters and the retail stores over regular telephone lines. However, as the number of stores increased, it became physically more difficult to do business this way. In 1975, for the first time, data was sent over phone lines directly to the mainframe computer at headquarters. Four years later, in collaboration with the computer vendor, NEC, 7-Eleven first developed and installed in each retail store a standalone order entry management system to support franchisees' activities. The next step, in 1979, was to put all these terminals online and to connect them to other business partners. This was the first example of a value-added network (VAN) in the industry (Exhibit 10).

The next challenge was to design and implement an electronic order booking system (EOB) and a point of sale system (POS). An EOB is a small, hand-held machine with a floppy disk drive that store managers use to key in the next orders as they walk around their store. The data on the diskette is then loaded onto the Terminal Controller (TC, i.e., the minicomputer within each store) and sent to the host system. On the other hand, a POS is a system with which a store operator can read bar codes on packages and automatically enter a sale into the system (Exhibit 11). Originally introduced in the United States, this type of system was used to increase the productivity and reliability of cashier operators because it reduced entry errors and triggered automatic replenishment. However, 7-Eleven Japan introduced its POS systems rather to collect sales data and to use the information for merchandising and item-by-item control processes. For instance, the cash register would not open until the operator entered the

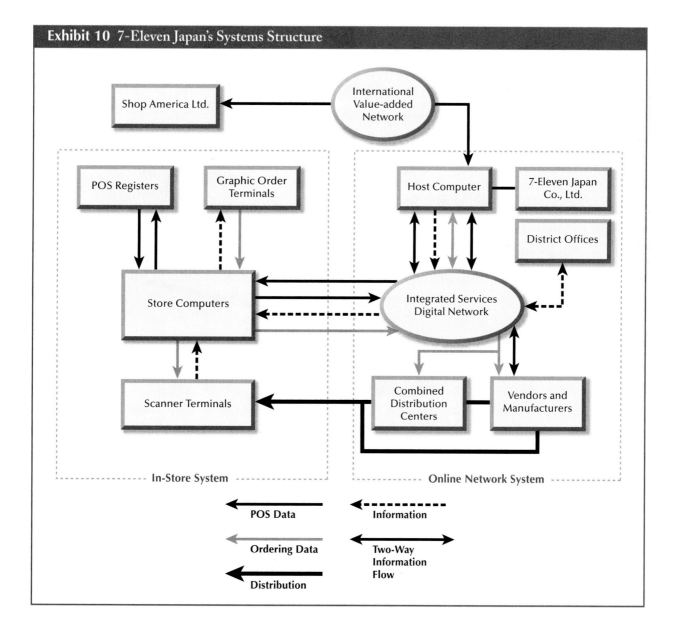

Exhibit 10 7-Eleven Japan's Systems Structure

data about the gender and estimated age of the customer. This data was also first loaded onto the TC in the back office and was later sent electronically to the host computer. In 1991, 7-Eleven installed, in collaboration with NTT and NRI, the first ISDN network in Japan, integrating all these separate information systems into a common network platform (Exhibit 11). This network linked all the franchise stores to corporate offices in Tokyo and all around Japan via optical fiber. ISDN allowed ten times more data to be exchanged thirty times faster and at one-fourth the cost of previous technologies. For example, headquarters had access to daily sales data on every single item for each of its 6,420 stores (in twenty-two of Japan's forty-seven prefectures, Exhibit 9) the afternoon of the next day. Before ISDN, it used to take more than a week. As a result, 7-Eleven Japan could capture and analyze consumer purchasing patterns virtually on a real-time basis (See Exhibit 9).

Operation Field Counselors (OFC)

In exchange for high royalties (Exhibit 3) and their long-term commitment, 7-Eleven Japan provided franchisees

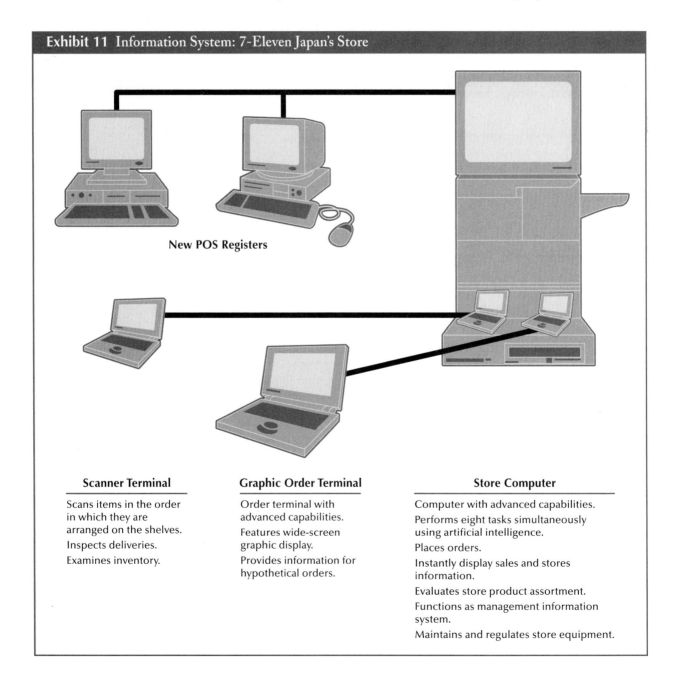

Exhibit 11 Information System: 7-Eleven Japan's Store

New POS Registers

Scanner Terminal	**Graphic Order Terminal**	**Store Computer**
Scans items in the order in which they are arranged on the shelves.	Order terminal with advanced capabilities.	Computer with advanced capabilities.
Inspects deliveries.	Features wide-screen graphic display.	Performs eight tasks simultaneously using artificial intelligence.
Examines inventory.	Provides information for hypothetical orders.	Places orders.
		Instantly display sales and stores information.
		Evaluates store product assortment.
		Functions as management information system.
		Maintains and regulates store equipment.

with constant service from field representatives. Japan was divided into sixty-six districts, serviced by a total of 1,000 Operation Field Counselors (OFCs). Reporting to a district manager, these OFCs provided the human backup to the 7-Eleven franchise system. Each of them supervised between six and seven stores, providing (i) advice on ordering and on the use of information systems and (ii) information on the portfolio of available items. The person-to-person contact with store managers was also a key element of the 7-Eleven franchise system. The counselors conveyed information, criticisms, and suggestions for improvements from and between store operators, all the way back to headquarters. Their frequent visits, two or three times a week, also had the effect of motivating the owners and staff of small remote stores. Once, a customer was put on a waiting list for a game CD and asked to come back on a specified date. The item was not in the store on the promised day. The OFC personally hand-delivered the CD to the customer that same evening.

Suzuki spends more than $1 million per year holding weekly meetings that bring together all the OFCs from all over Japan to headquarters in Tokyo. "It is not enough to exchange information. The information has no value unless it is understood and properly integrated by the franchisees and makes them work better," Suzuki repeats at each meeting. Before starting a new store, the new franchisees and their wives are first brought to the central training center for a month and then go through a two-month, on-the-job training in one of the regular stores. Training helps diffuse corporate policy and explain the need for high quality of data input and the importance of daily operation and service quality. Suzuki explains: "We became successful because we've concentrated on retailing, shared information with staff, and encouraged them constantly to respond to changes."

Business Performance

A look at average store sales at 7-Eleven Japan and its direct competitors shows average daily sales of $7,000, compared to $4,430 of the industry average (See Exhibit 12). In 1991, after seventeen years of sustained growth in sales and profits, 7-Eleven Japan showed no intention of slowing its expansion. Since its creation, the company had achieved one of the highest returns on equity in the industry, testifying to the performance of its outsourcing principle. Since 1993, sales for 7-Eleven Japan have been exceeding those of its parent company, the Ito-Yokado supermarket chain. The same year, 7-Eleven Japan's net income became the largest in the retail industry and remained number one.

However, the Japanese market was rapidly saturating as competition intensified. Since the 1970s, the number of CVS stores in Japan had multiplied twenty-fold to number some 50,000 stores, with one store for approximately 2,000 people. Total sales in Japanese convenience stores were in excess of the sales of all Japanese department stores. More Coca-Cola, batteries, and panty hose were sold in convenience stores than anywhere else in Japan. Lunch box (bento) sales in CVS stores were larger than the overall sales of McDonald's in Japan. Some competitors were preparing expansion strategies for countries outside Japan. At the same time, European retailers and distributors, for instance, were trying to develop convenience formats of their own. Ito-Yokado recently teamed up with the world's largest and second-largest retailers—Wal-Mart of the United States in 1993 and Germany's Metro in 1994. In 1990, Southland filed for bankruptcy after an attempt to win new customers with heavily discounted goods backfired. No other U.S. retailer was interested in trying to rescue the chain, so Southland turned to 7-Eleven Japan. Suzuki has been able to bail out the U.S. company—without yet introducing the information technology.

Mr. Nakauchi, CEO of Daiei, the number one supermarket chain in Japan and parent company of Lawson, a key competitor to 7-Eleven Japan, was recently quoted saying "In the twenty-first century, supermarkets will not be able to survive in Japanese retailing. Only discount stores and convenience stores will. Lifestyles will gradually change because of more women working, more single people, and the 24-hour society. Mothers will cook less at home and family members will not have as many meals at home. Therefore, supermarkets will be less necessary. Lunch boxes will become more popular, and this will increase demand at convenience stores for food and other items to be available at any time." This is a signal for even greater competition in the domestic convenience store industry, but also may be opening the doors to competition beyond the borders of Japan.

Exhibit 12 Information Systems and Distribution System Improvements and Performance (Average Stock Turnover Time, Daily Sales, and Gross Profit Margin per Store)

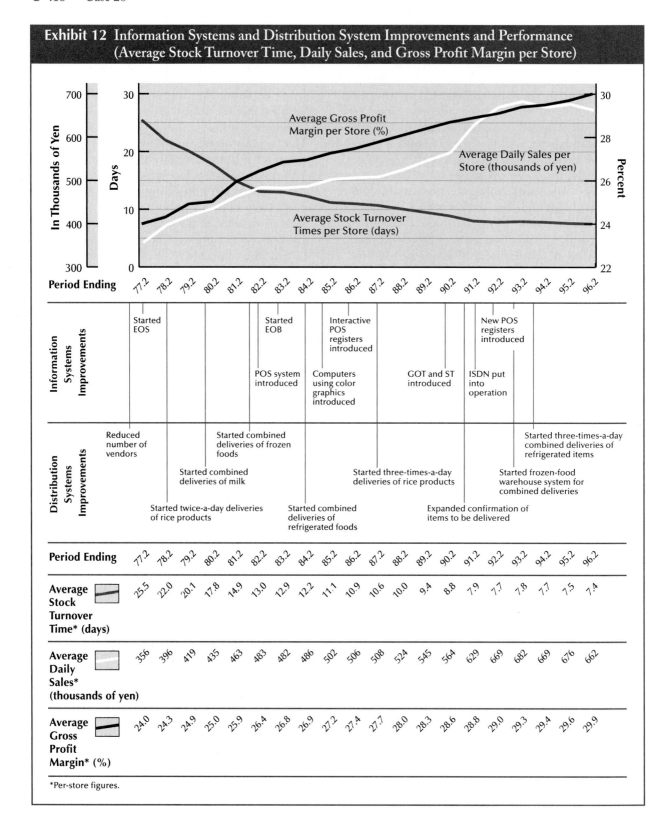

Period Ending	77.2	78.2	79.2	80.2	81.2	82.2	83.2	84.2	85.2	86.2	87.2	88.2	89.2	90.2	91.2	92.2	93.2	94.2	95.2	96.2
Average Stock Turnover Time* (days)	25.5	22.0	20.1	17.8	14.9	13.0	12.9	12.2	11.1	10.9	10.6	10.0	9.4	8.8	7.9	7.7	7.8	7.7	7.5	7.4
Average Daily Sales* (thousands of yen)	356	396	419	435	463	483	482	486	502	506	508	524	545	564	629	669	682	669	676	662
Average Gross Profit Margin* (%)	24.0	24.3	24.9	25.0	25.9	26.4	26.8	26.9	27.2	27.4	27.7	28.0	28.3	28.6	28.8	29.0	29.3	29.4	29.6	29.9

*Per-store figures.

Case 29

Rocky Mountain Chocolate Factory, Inc.

Walter Greene, *University of Texas Pan American* **and Dr. Jeff Totten,** *Bemidji State University*

Introduction

The first Rocky Mountain Chocolate Factory (RMCF) was opened in 1981 in Durango, Colorado, on the western slope of the Rocky Mountains. Franklin E. Crail, one of the co-founders of RMCF, was the company's chairman of the board, president, treasurer and director. The company began operations with the objective of becoming the premier chocolatier in the U.S. and in the world through product excellence and expansion of its franchise system. Frank Crail was now re-thinking the Company's future business expansion strategy.

Rocky Mountain Chocolate Factory had two store segments. The first focused on the traditional retail chocolate candy market through the 220 RMCF stores across the United States, Canada and Guam. The second segment focused on the hard candy retail market and was called Fuzziwig's Candy Factory. However, in late 1997, RMCF executives decided that the Fuzziwig's store segment did not meet its strategic long-term goals, and adopted a plan to divest itself of these operations by July 31, 1998.[1]

History

Frank Crail first operated a computer software company in the San Diego, California area in the 1970's. He and his wife decided to move to Durango, Colorado, for a change in lifestyle. After literally walking up and down the streets of Durango, asking people what was needed in the city, Crail went back to San Diego and researched the candy business. Then he opened the first RMCF store in 1981 in Durango.[2]

In 1982, the first franchise operation was opened in Colorado Springs, Colorado. The next major event for RMCF was the construction of a 12,000 square ft. factory in Durango, Colorado. In 1986, the company had grown enough to go public. RMCF is listed on the NASDAQ National Market Exchange. In 1993, RMCF opened its one-hundredth store and only a year later, in 1994, the 150th store was opened in Orlando, Florida. In that time, the Durango factory had been expanded twice, the first time to 28,000 square ft. and the second time to 53,000 square ft. As of April 30, 1998, the company had a total of 222 stores, 185 of them being franchises of RMCF and thirty-seven being company-owned stores operating in forty-three states, Canada and Guam. In addition, the company recently completed a master franchise agreement to establish a number of RMCF stores in Taiwan.[3]

Mission Statement

Rocky Mountain Chocolate Factory manufacturers high quality chocolate products, which are presented in unique, fun and inviting packaging and offered for sale to the general public in accessible, diverse environments.

Our goal: To become America's Chocolatier™.

Our image: American-made, old-fashioned quality presented with charm and excitement.

Our vision: For our Company and employees to build upon our reputation for honesty, integrity, creativity and customer service guided by common sense, fairness and caring.[4]

Company Objectives

RMCF had four main goals which it followed in order to fulfill its strategic goal of continuing to be a leading franchiser and operator of retail chocolate stores in the United States:

1. To manufacture a wide variety and assortment of world-class chocolates of the highest quality while at the lowest possible cost.

2. To have company-owned stores that serve as profit generators and as training and support leaders for the franchised operations.

3. To be the support system for the franchisees to insure their long-run success and profitability.

4. To provide merchandising and marketing support to company-owned operations as well as franchised stores.

Company Structure

The RMCF was composed of company-owned stores and franchises located in regional malls, tourist-oriented retail areas, ski resorts, specialty retail centers, airports, neighborhood centers, and factory outlet malls. Locations were selected on the basis of high tourism traffic. The company also had a factory located in Durango, Colorado. RMCF had two different types of stores, the RMCF and Fuzziwig's Candy Factory. The factory manufactured fine chocolates for both the company-owned stores and franchises; however, high quality chocolate candies were also hand-made at every RMCF store. The Durango factory made approximately 1.9 million pounds of chocolate confections annually. One hundred twenty-five people were employed at the plant; overall company employment was 350.[5]

The focus of RMCF was on franchise retailing, not on mail order. In 1995–96, *Success* Magazine placed Rocky Mountain in the seventh position of a list of the top 100 franchisers in the nation.

"We literally had to learn everything from scratch,'" Crail says. "How to be a retailer, how to be a manufacturer, how to be a franchiser, how to be a marketer. We develop all our own packaging … .We have a tremendous amount of vision as to where retail is going. We're more than just a chocolate company; our real expertise is in the franchise industry … .We're a full-service franchiser, … We find the location, negotiate the lease, design the store, coordinate the build-out, bring the franchisee here for training, send a district manager to the store opening, and have ongoing field support and regional and national conventions … . We do everything we can to give our franchisees the tools to be successful."[6]

Store Segments

Rocky Mountain Chocolate Factory stores were decorated in a distinctive early country Victorian design, which made an attractive setting for up to a variety of approximately 250 fine chocolates. Each store also had a selection of other items such as brittle, caramel apples, and fudge. Not all products were manufactured at the Rocky Mountain factory. Many chocolates were also prepared in the stores from company recipes. The franchise fee was

$19,500; the total investment required for a RMCF franchise license and to open a retail store was between $113,475 and $213,460, depending upon store size and location.[7] Candy making shows and demonstrations were a grand attraction for store customers. These stores tended to attract a "typically adult female market."[8] A line of sugar-free/no-sugar-added candies was introduced in fiscal year 1998, among 25 new products introduced.[9]

The first Fuzziwig's Candy Factory was opened in 1995, and it was a completely different atmosphere than that of Rocky Mountain Chocolate Factory stores. Fuzziwig's sold more than 250 varieties of non-chocolate candies. Selections consisted of hard-candies, fruit-flavored chewy candies, sugar-free candies, and some chocolate covered confections. Fuzziwig's store environment was geared toward families and children, because of its animated characters, props, lighting and sound. Fuzziwig's Candy Factories were decorated in the style of an Industrial Revolution Era factory, complete with the character of Professor Fuzziwig.[10] As the fastest-growing segment of the candy industry, hard candy was a lucrative business, with a customer base that spanned all age groups. Fuzziwig's was designed not only to appeal to the largest audience possible but also to stand out in the market.[11]

By the end of fiscal year 1997, the company had established fourteen Fuzziwig's stores, two of which were franchised. As Frank Crail admitted, store growth "has been slower than expected as a result of several factors, the most important one of which is the high cost of build-out and a larger 'footprint' of the store than can be economically justified in the most fruitful store environments. The Company is currently in the process of redesigning the Fuzziwig's store plan, including fixtures and animation, with the goal of reducing cost, allowing 'scalability' to lower space requirements with the goal of improving store economics."[12]

The company even licensed physical space in two Toys 'R' Us stores.[13] Yet, by late 1997, the company decided to discontinue the Fuzziwig's hard candy concept, due to lack of sufficient repeat business, according to Frank Crail. The concept and assets were to be sold in June 1998 to an unnamed buyer for $1.6 million.[14]

Competitive Factors

The retailing of confectionery products was extremely competitive. Many of RMCF's competitors had more name recognition, capital, marketing and other resources, e.g., Godiva (Belgian), Perugina (Italian), See's (American), and Teuscher (Swiss). In addition, there was strong competition among retailers for future outlets, store personnel and qualified franchisees. According to Susan Smith, Vice President, Chocolate Manufacturers Association of the U.S.A., the 170 member companies who wholesale chocolate produce approximately three billion pounds of chocolate each year for an estimated market of $12–13 billion retail. Smith noted that it's hard to estimate the industry's size given that it's so fragmented. Chocolate factories go up against independent companies who retail their own products.[15] A recent check of chocolate candy companies with Web pages on the Internet yielded a list of at least 125 companies, many of whom could be considered competitors for Rocky Mountain's stores. A search of "RMCF" on the Internet leads to about a dozen or so franchise store Web sites; however, the company itself did not appear to have a Web site.

While fine chocolates are primarily sold in specialty stores, RMCF also faces secondary competition from less expensive chocolates (e.g., Russell Stover and Whitman's), which are sold in drug, grocery, and discount stores. According to the National Confectioners Association and the Chocolate Manufacturers Association, 1997 confectionery sales increased 2.9 percent in food, drug, and mass merchant outlets. Sales of boxed chocolates increased 10.5 percent over 1996 sales. "Mass merchants led the way in 1997 with a 4.7 percent increase in dollar sales over 1996. Food stores produced a 3.5 percent increase while drug store sales were off 0.4 percent. Convenience store confectionery sales were even against 1996."[16]

In addition, fine chocolates compete with other product forms of snack foods, e.g., candy bars and nuts, for the consumer's snacking pleasure. Additional confectionery consumption statistics are shown in Table 1.

According to Crail, Rocky Mountain's strengths include:

1. A well known name;

2. Known for excellence, value, assortment and incomparable quality of its products;

3. Store ambiance;

4. Intelligence and background in implementing stringent standards for new store sites;

5. Specialization in retailing and distribution of chocolate and other candy products; and

6. Enforcement of important procedures and techniques at it's franchised and company-owned outlets. By managing the production of its own chocolate output, RMCF sought to improve its production quality standards for those products, extend proprietary products, control costs, manage production and delivery schedules, and identify potentially new distribution channels.

A survey conducted by *Money* magazine (February 1995) demonstrated that not all chocolate candies were created equal. The magazine's staff decided to test out the best premium-quality chocolates and ordered the "Forrest Gump" sampler ("You never know what you're gonna get."), a half-pound assortment box, from six of the most popular chocolatiers. A panel of thirty blindfolded judges (staff tasters) all agreed that the best chocolate was from the Rocky Mountain Chocolate Factory. Here are some of the remarks made by the judges about RMCF chocolates and its competitors:

(Note: second place was a tie, therefore two companies are listed in second place.)

5th Fanny May—Affordable, yes—but "too salty"

4th Godiva—overly "chemical taste" from the world-famous Belgian house, which has 116 U.S. stores.

3rd Teuscher—Swiss candymaker's package featured a mix of filled chocolates and truffles—the box's best

---

Table 1 Confectionary Consumption Statistics

- U.S. per capita consumption of confectionery grew from 17.9 pounds per person in 1983 to 25.5 pounds per person in 1997.
- Each American consumed an average of 11.7 pounds of chocolate in 1996.
- U.S. per capita chocolate consumption was 10.8 pounds in 1994, 11.5 pounds in 1995, and 12.1 pounds in 1997.
- In 1997, chocolate consumption totaled 3.23 billions pounds.
- Production of U.S. chocolate products grew from 1,126,400 metric tons in 1988 to 1,370,100 metric tons in 1995.

- Estimated seasonal sales (in millions) of confectionery for 1997 and 1998 were:

Halloween	$1,708	$1,767
Easter	1,495	1,670
Christmas	1,460	1,525
Valentine's	955	1,033

Source: Several reports under the category, "Stats" from the CandyUSA Web page, http://www.candyusa.org/, Chocolate Manufacturers Association & National Confectioners Association, downloaded on 10/27/1998.

stuff—but they lost points by sending the wrong order first time around.

2nd Perugina—Deemed "uneven," the Italian maker's sampler contained several marvelous dark pieces as well as some banana-flavor ditties described as, well, "yuckie."

2nd See's Candies—America's old-fashioned sweetheart, founded in 1921, turns out well-priced, "very good" chocolate.

1st place Rocky Mountain Chocolate Factory—Overall, Rocky Mountain won the coveted three-heart rating in our blind taste test because of "superior flavor" and "no chemical aftertaste," " richest chocolate," with intense, "natural" flavor.[17]

Economic Factors

The late 1980s and early 1990s were a period of high risks and uncertainty for all businesses in the U.S. Candy retailers and manufacturers were not immune to these risks. According to Rocky Mountain's management team, inflationary factors such as increases in the costs of ingredients and labor immediately affected company operations. Various facility leases had provisions for cost-of living adjustments and required the company to pay taxes, insurance and maintenance costs, all of which were exposed to inflation. Furthermore, projected lease costs for new store buildings included potential escalating cost of land and construction. The company would likely not be able to pass on its expansion costs to its customers.[18]

In addition, RMCF's sales and earnings were seasonal, with significantly higher sales and earnings occurring during the Christmas holidays and summer vacation seasons. This seasonality created irregularities in its quarterly production outputs. Furthermore, quarterly results had been, and would likely continue to be, affected by the timing of new outlet openings and the sale of franchises.[19]

Financial Results & Operations

Rocky Mountain Chocolate Factory's sales increased approximately $5 million between fiscal years 1995 and 1996 and between 1996 and 1997. At the same time, the company experienced increases in cost of sales, retail operating expenses, and store closure expenses. As a result, RMCF had a net loss of approximately $1.36 million in fiscal year 1997 after posting net incomes in preceding years, as shown in Exhibit 1. Nine company-owned stores were not making sufficient profits and had to be closed in 1997.[20] While store closure expenses remained a dragging factor in fiscal year 1998 along with the discontinuation of the Fuzziwig's retail concept,

RMCF managed to post a positive net income, as shown in Exhibit 2.

Balance sheets for fiscal years 1996 and 1997 are shown in Exhibit 3.[21] Statements of Operations are provided in Exhibit 1 for three years (1995–1997).[22] The 1998 fiscal year balance sheet and statement of operations are provided in Exhibit 2 and 4.[23] Note that sales and marketing expenses are shown separately from franchise costs for fiscal year 1998 (Exhibit 2). In the previous years, these expenses were listed as part of franchise costs (Exhibit 1). This change in reporting was made to reflect the increased focus on sales and marketing by the company, in terms of new products, customer service, additional promotional programs and alternative distribution sales personnel.[24]

Expansion Strategy

Sales of candy were primarily impulse driven. RMCF was building its name recognition so it could become a destination chocolatier. In other words, consumers would automatically recall the brand name when they wanted to give or get chocolate. If consumers began to seek out RMCF chocolates, the company would see an increase in the size of its gift business. Candy makers such as Fanny Farmer and Russell Stover had stronger gift business because of name recognition and longevity. Domestically, there was room for geographical expansion. RMCF stores were primarily located in the Rocky Mountain, Pacific, and Midwest regions of the United States. The Sunbelt and Eastern Seaboard regions offered possibilities, assuming premium high-traffic retail locations could be determined and acquired. The company was also considering foreign operations, including further expansion into the Canadian Market.[25] Several of its retail outlets had home pages on the Internet, and offered consumers the opportunity to purchase products online.[26]

With the decision to divest the Fuzziwig's Candy Factory store segment, which did not meet the strategic long-term goal of becoming a premier chocolatier, RMCF started pursuing distribution of products outside the franchised and company-owned stores. With limited viable real estate available and a desire to increase its market share, brand awareness, and customer base, RMCF began implementing an expansion strategy in fiscal 1998 and beyond. A major pilot program was launched with SAM's Club to offer selected company products in approximately eighty SAM's Club locations throughout the United States. The number of SAM's Club locations was to be expanded to 105 by October 1998, with more locations added in fiscal year 2000. A franchised store was

Exhibit 1   Statements of Operations

	February 28, 1997	February 29, 1996	February 28, 1995
Revenues			
Sales	$ 21,674,485	$ 16,094,995	$ 11,427,700
Franchise and royalty fees	2,597,985	2,648,303	2,188,434
	24,272,470	18,743,298	13,616,134
Costs and Expenses			
Cost of sales	11,508,384	8,598,798	5,985,970
Franchise costs	1,999,964	1,803,506	1,376,820
General and administrative	1,989,958	1,436,551	1,234,002
Retail operating expenses	8,087,052	4,746,026	2,749,511
Provision for store closure	1,358,398	–	–
Impairment loss—retail operations	597,062	–	–
Loss on write-down of assets	330,587	–	–
	25,871,405	16,584,881	11,346,303
Operating (loss) profit	(1,598,935)	2,158,417	2,269,831
Other Income (Expenses)			
Interest expense	(473,618)	(299,792)	(152,592)
Interest income	28,637	57,620	22,580
	(444,981)	(242,172)	(130,012)
Litigation settlements	(154,300)	–	–
Income (loss) before income tax expense	(2,198,216)	1,916,245	2,139,819
Income Tax Expense (Benefit)			
Current	149,414	583,488	749,516
Deferred	(981,928)	125,012	39,871
	(832,514)	708,500	789,387
Net Income (Loss)	$ (1,365,702)	$ 1,207,745	$ 1,350,432

opened on Guam and a master franchise agreement for Taiwan was also planned. Additionally, RMCF had received a commitment from AAFES (Army Air Force Exchange Services) to test candy-owned RMCF stores in two of AAFES largest domestic bases. The first military base store opened on August 1, 1998. Also, AAFES agreed to sell RMCF products in approximately 50 base exchanges by February 1999.[27]

Frank Crail provided this challenge in his letter to shareholders:

> Managing our brand will be the strategic focus for the future. Our continued growth and success

in the market place can only be achieved through creating a loyal and diverse customer base for our products. The progress we made in fiscal year 1998 was exciting, but merely sets the standard for future performance.[28]

Notes

1. Rocky Mountain Chocolate Factory, Inc. *FORM 10-K*, 28 February 1998, 3.
2. Bruce Goldberg, "Candy a Dandy Colorado Business," *Colorado Business Magazine* (September 1996): pp 56+; downloaded from the Internet on 27 October 1998.
3. Rocky Mountain Chocolate Factory, Inc. *FORM 10-K*, 28 February 1998, 1.

Exhibit 2   Statements of Operations

	February 28, 1998
Revenues	
Sales	$ 20,659,076
Franchise and royalty fees	3,104,906
	23,763,982
Costs and Expenses	
Cost of sales	10,960,966
Franchise costs	1,106,172
Sales and marketing	1,290,516
General and administrative	1,763,757
Retail operating expenses	6,043,810
Provision for store closure	–
Impairment loss—retail operations	–
Loss on write-down of assets	–
	21,165,221
Operating Income (Loss)	2,598,761
Other Income (Expenses)	
Interest expense	(664,852)
Litigation settlements	–
Interest income	114,732
Other, net	(550,120)
Income (Loss) before Income Tax Expense	2,048,641
Income Tax Expense (Benefit)	788,640
Income (Loss) from Continuing Operations	1,260,001
Discontinued Operations	
Income (loss) net of taxes	(90,849)
Provision for estimated loss on disposition	(929,234)
Total	(1,020,083)
Net Income (Loss)	$ 239,918

4. Mission Statement, Rocky Mountain Chocolate Factory, *1998 Annual Report*, 1.
5. Goldberg, pp. 56+.
6. Goldberg, pp. 56+.
7. Rocky Mountain Chocolate Factory, Inc., *Facts About Franchising With Rocky Mountain Chocolate Factory, Inc.*, Revised June 1998.
8. Fuzziweg's web site was at http://www.fuzziwigs.com/index.htm (as of 14 January 1998).
9. Franklin E. Crail, Letter to Our Shareholders, Rocky Mountain Chocolate Factory, *1998 Annual Report*, p.2.
10. Rocky Mountain Chocolate Factory, Inc., *Annual Report*, 1996, 11.
11. "Fuzziwig's Creates Candyland," *Chain Store Age Executive with Shopping Center Age* 72, no. 10 (October 1996): 74.
12. An Interview With CEO Frank Crail, "Rocky Mountain Chock Factory," *1997 Annual Report*, 6–7.
13. Bruce Horovitz, "Discovering Candyland. Toymakers Spy Sweet Success in Confections," *USA Today*, 4 March 1997, 1B.
14. Franklin E. Crail, Letter to Our Stockholders, Rocky Mountain Chocolate Factory, *1998 Annual Report*, 2.
15. Robert Schwab, "Sweet Deal," *The Denver Post*, 10 February 1997, C-01.
16. "A Review of Issues and Trends in the Confectionery Industry by the NCA," *Candy Industry* (June 1998): A2.
17. Elif Sinanoglu, "Smart Spending," *Money* (February 1995): 171.
18. *1998 Annual Report*, 8.
19. Ibid., 8.
20. Dina Bunn, "Nine Candy Stores Get Sour News," *Rocky Mountain News*, 15 April 1997: 3b.
21. RMCF *Annual Report*, 1997, 20–21.
22. Ibid., p. 22.
23. *1998 Annual Report*, 9–10.
24. *1998 Annual Report*, p. 6.
25. Susan Tiffany, "Rocky Mountain Candy Factory Celebrates 15 'Beary' Good Years," *Candy Industry* 161, no. 8 (August 1996): 24–29.
26. For example, see the outlets at Ocean City, MD (http://www.rmcfactory.com), Naperville, IL (http://www.napercafe.com/rmcf), Breckenridge, CO (http://www.mef-breck.com/factory.htm), and Burlington, WA (http://www.emcf-wa.com/main.htm). These web sites were all active as of 4 April 1998.
27. RMCF *FORM 10-K*, 28 February 1998, 5; "Rocky Mountain Chocolate Factory, Inc. Reports Record Revenue Income," *PR Newswire* (1 October 1998): pages 1–3 downloaded from http://investing.lycos.com on 28 October 1998.
28. Frank Crail, *1998 Annual Report*, 2.

Exhibit 3   Balance Sheet

	February 28, 1997	February 29, 1996	February 28, 1995
Assets			
Current Assets			
Cash and cash equivalents	$ 792,606	$ 528,787	$ 382,905
Accounts and notes receivable-trade, less allowance for doubtful accounts of $202,029 in 1997 and $28,196 in 1996	1, 729,971	1,463,901	1,179,019
Inventories	2,311,321	2,504,908	1,687,016
Deferred income taxes	722,595	59,219	68,586
Other	181,133	224,001	110,105
Total current assets	5,737,626	4,780,816	3,427,631
Property and Equipment—at Cost			
Land	122,558	122,558	122,558
Building	3,644,357	3,596,905	2,453,069
Leasehold improvements	2,213,116	1,753,165	803,160
Machinery and equipment	6,446,612	4,898,174	2,917,148
Furniture and fixtures	2,667,420	2,330,057	1,086,282
Transportation equipment	246,499	228,816	197,346
	15,340,562	12,929,675	7,579,563
Less accumulated depreciation and amortization	3,565,194	2,468,084	1,690,118
	11,775,368	10,461,591	5,889,445
Other Assets			
Accounts and notes receivable-trade, due after one year	82,774	111,588	136,132
Goodwill, net of accumulated amortization of $277,344 in 1997 and $253,740 in 1996	312,656	336,260	359,864
Deferred income taxes	43,044	—	—
Other	638,637	624,185	368,098
	1,077,111	1,072,033	1,072,033
Total Assets	$ 18,590,105	$ 16,314,440	$ 10,181,170
Liabilities and Stockholders' Equity			
Current Liabilities			
Short-term debt	—	1,000,000	—
Current maturities of long-term debt	847,881	134,538	182,852
Accounts payable-trade	799,671	998,520	839,117
Accrued compensation	465,338	335,926	222,713
Accrued liabilities	867,961	214,460	272,593
Income taxes payable	—	54,229	283,330
Deferred income	93,000	—	—
Total current liabilities	3,073,851	2,737,673	1,800,605
Long-Term Debt, Less Current Maturities	$ 5,737,312	$ 2,183,877	$ 2,313,895

(continued)

Exhibit 3 Balance Sheet (continued)

	February 28, 1997	February 29, 1996	February 28, 1995
Deferred Income Taxes	$ –	$ 275,508	$ 159,863
Commitments and Contingencies	–	–	–
Stockholders' Equity			
$1.00 cumulative convertible preferred stock-authorized 250,000 shares, $0.10 par value; issued and outstanding, 14,160 shares in 1995	–	–	1,462
Common stock-authorized 7,250,000 shares, $0.03 par value; issued 3,041,302 shares in 1997 and 3,034,302 in 1996	91,239	91,029	79,029
Additional paid-in capital	9,730,872	9,703,985	4,700,527
Retained earnings	972,565	2,338,267	1,130,522
	10,794,676	12,133,281	5,911,540
Less common stock held in treasury, at cost—129,003 shares in 1997, 129,153 shares in 1996, and 4,303 shares in 1995	1,015,734	1,015,899	4,733
	9,778,942	11,117,382	5,906,807
Total Liabilities	$ 18,590,105	$ 16,314,440	$ 10,181,170

Exhibit 4   Fiscal Year 1998 Balance Sheet

	1998
Assets	
Current Assets	
Cash and cash equivalents	$ 1,795,381
Accounts and notes receivable, less allowance for doubtful accounts ($214,152 & 202,029)	2,174,618
Refundable income taxes	483,448
Inventories	2,567,966
Deferred income taxes	257,176
Other	103,195
Net current assests of discontinued operations	44,351
Total Current Assets	7,426,135
Property and Equipment, Net	9,672,443
Other Assets	
Net non-current assets of discontinued operations	1,555,681
Accounts and notes receivable	279,122
Goodwill, less accumulated amoritization	596,152
Other	338,359
Total other assets	2,769,314
Total assets	$19,867,892
Liabilities & Stockholders' Equity	
Current Liabilities:	
Current maturities of long-term debt	1,132,900
Accounts payable	1,296,769
Accrued salaries and wages	707,737
Other accrued expenses	339,481
Deferred income	–
Total Current Liabilities	3,476,887
Long-Term Debt, Less Current Maturities	5,993,273
Deferred Income Taxes	378,272
Stockholders' Equity:	
Common stock, $ 0.03 par value; 7,250,000 shares authorized; 2,912,449 and 2,912,299 shares issued and outstanding	87,373
Additional paid-in capital	8,719,604
Retained earnings	1,212,483
Total stockholders' equity	10,019,460
Total Liabilities Stockholders' Equity	$19,867,892

Case 30

Robin Hood

Joseph Lampel, *New York University*

It was in the spring of the second year of his insurrection against the High Sheriff of Nottingham that Robin Hood took a walk in Sherwood Forest. As he walked he pondered the progress of the campaign, the disposition of his forces, the Sheriff's recent moves, and the options that confronted him.

The revolt against the Sheriff had begun as a personal crusade. It erupted out of Robin's conflict with the Sheriff and his administration. However, alone Robin Hood could do little. He therefore sought allies, men with grievances and a deep sense of justice. Later he welcomed all who came, asking few questions and demanding only a willingness to serve. Strength, he believed, lay in numbers.

He spent the first year forging the group into a disciplined band, united in enmity against the Sheriff and willing to live outside the law. The band's organization was simple. Robin ruled supreme, making all important decisions. He delegated specific tasks to his lieutenants. Will Scarlett was in charge of intelligence and scouting. His main job was to shadow the Sheriff and his men, always alert to their next move. He also collected information on the travel plans of rich merchants and tax collectors. Little John kept discipline among the men and saw to it that their archery was at the high peak that their profession demanded. Scarlock took care of the finances, converting loot to cash, paying shares of the take, and finding suitable hiding places for the surplus. Finally, Much the Miller's son had the difficult task of provisioning the ever-increasing band of Merrymen.

The increasing size of the band was a source of satisfaction for Robin, but also a source of concern. The fame of his Merrymen was spreading, and new recruits were pouring in from every comer of England. As the band grew larger, their small bivouac became a major encampment. Between raids the men milled about, talking and playing games. Vigilance was in decline, and discipline

was becoming harder to enforce. "Why," Robin reflected, "I don't know half the men I run into these days."

The growing band was also beginning to exceed the food capacity of the forest. Game was becoming scarce, and supplies had to be obtained from outlying villages. The cost of buying food was beginning to drain the band's financial reserves at the very moment when revenues were in decline. Travelers, especially those with the most to lose, were now giving the forest a wide berth. This was costly and inconvenient to them, but it was preferable to having all their goods confiscated.

Robin believed that the time had come for the Merrymen to change their policy of outright confiscation of goods to one of a fixed transit tax. His lieutenants strongly resisted this idea. They were proud of the Merrymen's famous motto: "Rob the rich and give to the poor." "The fanners and the townspeople," they argued, "are our most important allies. How can we tax them, and still hope for their help in our fight against the Sheriff?"

Robin wondered how long the Merrymen could keep to the ways and methods of their early days. The Sheriff was growing stronger and becoming better organized. He now had the money and the men and was beginning to harass the band, probing for its weaknesses. The tide of events was beginning to turn against the Merrymen. Robin felt that the campaign must be decisively concluded before the Sheriff had a chance to deliver a mortal blow. "But how," he wondered, "could this be done?"

Robin had often entertained the possibility of killing the Sheriff, but the chances for this seemed increasingly remote. Besides, killing the Sheriff might satisfy his personal thirst for revenge, but it would not improve the situation. Robin had hoped that the perpetual state of unrest, and the Sheriff's failure to collect taxes, would lead to his removal from office. Instead, the Sheriff used his political connections to obtain reinforcement. He had powerful friends at court and was well regarded by the regent, Prince John.

Prince John was vicious and volatile. He was consumed by his unpopularity among the people, who wanted the imprisoned King Richard back. He also lived

Prepared by Joseph Lampel, City University Business School, London. ©1985, revised 1991.

in constant fear of the barons, who had first given him the regency but were now beginning to dispute his claim to the throne. Several of these barons had set out to collect the ransom that would release King Richard the Lionheart from his jail in Austria. Robin was invited to join the conspiracy in return for future amnesty. It was a dangerous proposition. Provincial banditry was one thing, court intrigue another. Prince John had spies everywhere, and he was known for his vindictiveness. If the conspirators' plan failed, the pursuit would be relentless, and retributions swift.

The sound of the supper horn startled Robin from his thoughts. There was the smell of roasting venison in the air. Nothing was resolved or settled. Robin headed for camp promising himself that he would give these problems his utmost attention after tomorrow's raid.

Case 31

Wal-Mart Stores, Inc.: Strategies for Dominance in the New Millennium

James W. Camerius, *Northern Michigan University*

David Glass had recently announced that he was stepping down from his role as President and Chief Executive Officer (CEO) at Wal-Mart Stores, Inc. He stepped to the podium in early 2000 at a Kansas City convention of the company's store managers to introduce Wal-Mart's new CEO, Lee Scott, 51, to a crowd of cheering executives. "I'm not going anywhere; I'll be around to give everyone more help than they probably would like," Glass suggested. At 64-years-old, he would remain Chairman of the firm's Executive Committee.

Lee Scott was only the third CEO in the entire history of Wal-Mart. Sam Walton had built the company from the ground up. During the twelve years that David Glass held the position, sales grew from $16 billion to $165 billion. Lee Scott had been personally recruited by David Glass twenty-one years before from a Springdale, Arkansas, trucking company to come to Wal-Mart as a manager of the truck fleet. In his years at Wal-Mart he had established himself as a leader, innovator, and team player. Over the last four years he served as Chief Operating Officer (COO) and Vice Chairman of the company. He was aware that there were tremendous opportunities to serve new markets with the company's stores. His management mandate was drive the company to a new level of success in domestic and international markets.

A Maturing Organization

In 2000, Wal-Mart Stores, Inc., Bentonville, Arkansas, operated mass merchandising retail stores under a variety of names and retail formats including: Wal-Mart discount department stores; SAM's Wholesale Clubs, wholesale/retail membership warehouses; and Wal-Mart Supercenters, large combination grocery and general merchandise stores in all fifty states. In the International Division, it operated stores in Canada, Mexico, Argentina, Brazil, Germany, South Korea, United Kingdom, and Puerto Rico, and stores through joint ventures in China. It was not only the nation's largest discount department store chain, but had surpassed the retail division of Sears, Roebuck, & Co. in sales volume as the largest retail firm in the United States. It was also considered the largest retailer in the world, with sales of $165 billion in 1999. The McLane Company, Inc., a Wal-Mart subsidiary, sold a wide variety of grocery and non-grocery products to a variety of retailers including selected Wal-Marts, SAM's Clubs, and Supercenters. In 1999, *Discount Store News* honored Wal-Mart as "Retailer of the Century" with a commemorative issue of the periodical.

A financial summary of Wal-Mart Stores, Inc. for the fiscal years ended January 31, 1999 and January 31, 2000 is shown in Appendix A. An eleven-year financial summary for the fiscal years January 31, 1990 to January 31, 2000 is shown in Appendix B. Appendix C lists the Wal-Mart Board of Directors and Executive Officers on January 31, 2000.

The Sam Walton Spirit

Much of the success of Wal-Mart was attributed to the entrepreneurial spirit of its founder and Chairman of the Board, Samuel Moore Walton (1918–1992). Many considered him one of the most influential retailers of the century.

Sam Walton or "Mr. Sam" as some referred to him traced his down-to earth, old-fashioned, home-spun, evangelical ways to growing up in rural Oklahoma, Missouri, and Arkansas. Although he was remarkably blase about his roots, some suggested that it was the simple belief in hard work and ambition that had "unlocked countless doors and showered upon him, his customers, and his employees … , the fruits of…years of labor in building [this] highly successful company."

"Our goal has always been in our business to be the very best," Sam Walton said in an interview, "and, along with that, we believe that in order to do that, you've got to make a good situation and put the interests of your associates first. If we really do that consistently, they in turn will cause...our business to be successful, which is what we've talked about and espoused and practiced." "The reason for our success," he said, "is our people and the way that they're treated and the way they feel about their company." Many have suggested it was this "people first" philosophy, which guided the company through the challenges and setbacks of its early years, and allowed the company to maintain its consistent record of growth and expansion in later years.

There was little about Sam Walton's background that reflected his amazing success. He was born in Kingfisher, Oklahoma, on March 29, 1918, to Thomas and Nancy Walton. Thomas Walton was a banker at the time and later entered the farm mortgage business and moved to Missouri. Sam Walton, growing up in rural Missouri in the depths of the Great Depression, discovered early that he "had a fair amount of ambition and enjoyed working," he once noted. He completed high school at Columbia, Missouri, and received a bachelor of arts degree in economics from the University of Missouri in 1940. "I really had no idea what I would be," he once said, "At one point in time," adding as an afterthought, "I thought I wanted to become president of the United States."

A unique, enthusiastic, and positive individual, Sam Walton was "just your basic home-spun billionaire," a columnist once suggested. "Mr. Sam is a life-long small-town resident who didn't change much as he got richer than his neighbors," he noted. Walton had tremendous energy, enjoyed bird hunting with his dogs and flew a corporate plane. When the company was much smaller he could boast that he personally visited every Wal-Mart store at least once a year. A store visit usually included Walton leading Wal-Mart cheers that began, "Give me a W, give me an A..." To many employees he had the air of a fiery Baptist preacher. Paul R. Carter, a Wal-Mart executive vice-president, was quoted as saying, "Mr. Walton has a calling." He became the richest man in America, and by 1991 had created a personal fortune for his family in excess of $21 billion. In 1999, despite a division of wealth, five family members were still ranked among the richest individuals in the United States.

Sam Walton's success was widely chronicled. He was selected by the investment publication, *Financial World* in 1989 as the "CEO of the Decade." He had honorary degrees from the University of the Ozarks, the University of Arkansas, and the University of Missouri. He also received many of the most distinguished professional awards of the industry like "Man of the Year," "Discounter of the Year," "Chief Executive Officer of the Year," and was the second retailer to be inducted into the Discounting Hall of Fame. He was recipient of the Horatio Alger Award in 1984 and acknowledged by *Discount Stores News* as "Retailer of the Decade" in December of 1989. "Walton does a remarkable job of instilling near-religious fervor in his people," said analyst Robert Buchanan of A.G. Edwards. "I think that speaks to the heart of his success." In late 1989 Sam Walton was diagnosed to have multiple myeloma, or cancer of the bone marrow. He planned to remain active in the firm as Chairman of the Board of Directors until his death in 1992.

The Marketing Concept

Genesis of an Idea   Sam Walton started his retail career in 1940 as a management trainee with the J.C. Penney Co. in Des Moines, Iowa. He was impressed with the Penney method of doing business and later modeled the Wal-Mart chain on "The Penney Idea" as reviewed in Exhibit 1. The Penney Company found strength in calling employees "associates" rather than clerks. Penney's, founded in Kemerer, Wyoming in 1902, located stores on the main streets of small towns and cities throughout the United States. Early Walton 5 & 10s were on main streets and served rural areas.

Following service in the U.S. Army during World War II, Sam Walton acquired a Ben Franklin variety store franchise

---

Exhibit 1   The Penney Idea, 1913

1. To serve the public, as nearly as we can, to its complete satisfaction.

2. To expect for the service we render a fair remuneration and not all the profit the traffic will bear.

3. To do all in our power to pack the customer's dollar full of value, quality, and satisfaction.

4. To continue to train ourselves and our associates so that the service we give will be more and more intelligently performed.

5. To improve constantly the human factor in our business.

6. To reward men and women in our organization through participation in what the business produces.

7. To test our every policy, method, and act in this wise: "Does it square with what is right and just?"

Source: Trimble, Vance H., *Sam Walton: The Inside Story of America's Richest Man*, (New York: Dutton), 1990.

in Newport, Arkansas. He operated this store successfully with his brother, James L. "Bud" Walton (1921–1995), until losing the lease in 1950. When Wal-Mart was incorporated in 1962, the firm was operating a chain of fifteen stores. Bud Walton became a senior vice president of the firm and concentrated on finding suitable store locations, acquiring real estate, and directing store construction.

The early retail stores owned by Sam Walton in Newport and Bentonville, Arkansas, and later in other small towns in adjoining southern states, were variety store operations. They were relatively small operations of 6,000 square feet, were located on "main streets," and displayed merchandise on plain wooden tables and counters. Operated under the Ben Franklin name and supplied by Butler Brothers of Chicago and St. Louis, they were characterized by a limited price line, low gross margins, high merchandise turnover, and concentration on return on investment. The firm, operating under the Walton 5 & 10 name, was the largest Ben Franklin franchisee in the country in 1962. The variety stores were phased out by 1976 to allow the company to concentrate on the growth of Wal-Mart discount department stores.

Foundations of Growth   The original Wal-Mart discount concept was not a unique idea. Sam Walton became convinced in the late 1950's that discounting would transform retailing. He traveled extensively in New England, the cradle of "off-pricing." After he had visited just about every discounter in the United States, he tried to interest Butler Brothers executives in Chicago in the discount store concept. The first Kmart, as a "conveniently located one-stop shopping unit where customers could buy a wide variety of quality merchandise at discount prices" had just opened in Garden City, Michigan. Walton's theory was to operate a similar discount store in a small community and in that setting, he would offer name brand merchandise at low prices and would add friendly service. Butler Brothers executives rejected the idea. The first "Wal-Mart Discount City" opened in late 1962 in Rogers, Arkansas.

Wal-Mart stores would sell nationally advertised, well-known brand merchandise at low prices in austere surroundings. As corporate policy, they would cheerfully give refunds, credits, and rain checks. Management conceived the firm as a "discount department store chain offering a wide variety of general merchandise to the customer." Early emphasis was placed upon opportunistic purchases of merchandise from whatever sources were available. Heavy emphasis was placed upon health and beauty aids (H&BA) in the product line and "stacking it high" in a manner of merchandise presentation. By the end of 1979, there were 276 Wal-Mart stores located in eleven states.

The firm developed an aggressive expansion strategy. New stores were located primarily in communities of 5,000 to 25,000 in population. The stores' sizes ranged from 30,000 to 60,000 square feet with 45,000 being the average. The firm also expanded by locating stores in contiguous geographic areas. When its discount operations came to dominate a market area, it moved to an adjoining area. While other retailers built warehouses to serve existing outlets, Wal-Mart built the distribution center first and then spotted stores all around it, pooling advertising and distribution overhead. Most stores were less than a six-hour drive from one of the company's warehouses. The first major distribution center, a 390,000 square-foot facility, opened in Searcy, Arkansas, outside Bentonville in 1978.

National Perspectives   At the beginning of 1991, the firm had 1,573 Wal-Mart stores in thirty-five states with expansion planned for adjacent states. Wal-Mart became the largest retailer and the largest discount department store in the United States.

As a national discount department store chain, Wal-Mart Stores, Inc. offered a wide variety of general merchandise to the customer. The stores were designed to offer one-stop shopping in thirty-six departments that included family apparel, health and beauty aids, household needs, electronics, toys, fabric and crafts, automotive supplies, lawn and patio, jewelry, and shoes. In addition at certain store locations, a pharmacy, automotive supply and service center, garden center, or snack bar were also operated. The firm operated its stores with "everyday low prices" as opposed to putting heavy emphasis on special promotions, which called for multiple newspaper advertising circulars. Stores were expected to "provide the customer with a clean, pleasant, and friendly shopping experience."

Although Wal-Mart carried much the same merchandise, offered similar prices, and operated stores that looked much like the competition, there were many differences. In the typical Wal-Mart store, employees wore blue vests to identify themselves, aisles were wide, apparel departments were carpeted in warm colors, a store employee followed customers to their cars to pick up their shopping carts, and the customer was welcomed at the door by a "people greeter" who gave directions and struck up conversations. In some cases, merchandise was bagged in brown paper sacks rather plastic bags because customers seemed to prefer them. A simple Wal-Mart logo in white letters on a brown background on the front of the store served to identify the firm. Yellow smiley faces were used in in-store displays. In consumer studies it was determined that the chain was particularly adept at striking the delicate balance needed to convince customers its prices were low without making people feel that its stores were too cheap. In many ways, competitors like Kmart sought to emulate Wal-Mart by introducing people greeters, upgrading interiors, developing new logos and signage, and introducing new inventory response systems

A "Satisfaction Guaranteed" refund and exchange policy was introduced to allow customers to be confident of Wal-Mart's merchandise and quality. Technological advancements like scanner cash registers, hand held computers for ordering of merchandise and computer linkages of stores with the general office and distribution centers improved communications and merchandise replenishment. Each store was encouraged to initiate programs that would make it an integral part of the community in which it operated. Associates were encouraged to "maintain the highest standards of honesty, morality, and business ethics in dealing with the public.

The External Environment

Industry analysts labeled the 1980s and early 1990s as eras of economic uncertainty for retailers. Many retailers were negatively affected by increased competitive pressures, sluggish consumer spending, slower-than-anticipated economic growth in North America, and recessions abroad. In 1995, Wal-Mart management felt the high consumer debt level caused many shoppers to reduce or defer spending on anything other than essentials. Management also felt that the lack of exciting new products or apparel trends reduced discretionary spending. Fierce competition resulted in lower margins and the lack of inflation stalled productivity increases. By 1998 the country had returned to prosperity. Unemployment was low, total income was relatively high, and interest rates were stable. Combined with a low inflation rate, buying power was perceived to be high and consumers were generally willing to buy. At the beginning of the year 2000, the United States had experienced one of the longest periods of economic expansion in its history.

Many retail enterprises confronted heavy competitive pressure by restructuring. Sears, Roebuck & Company, based in Chicago, became a more focused retailer by divesting itself of Allstate Insurance Company and its real estate subsidiaries. In 1993, the company announced it would close 118 unprofitable stores and discontinue the unprofitable Sears general merchandise catalog. It eliminated 50,000 jobs and began a $4 billion, five-year remodeling plan for its remaining multi-line department stores. After unsuccessfully experimenting with an "everyday low-price" strategy, management chose to realign its merchandise strategy to meet the needs of middle market customers, who were primarily women, by focusing on

product lines in apparel, home, and automotive. The new focus on apparel was supported with the advertising campaign, "The Softer Side of Sears." A later company-wide campaign broadened the appeal: "The many sides of Sears fit the many sides of your life." Sears completed its return to its retailing roots by selling off its ownership in Dean Witter Financial Services, Discovery Card, Coldwell Banker Real Estate, and Sears mortgage banking operations. In 1999, Sears refocused its marketing strategy with a new program that was designed to communicate a stronger whole-house and event message. A new advertising campaign introduced with the slogan, "The good life at a great price. Guaranteed." In 2000, a new store format was introduced that concentrated on five focal areas: Appliances, Home Fashions, Tools, Kids, and Electronics. Other departments including men's and women's apparel assumed a support role in these stores.

The discount department store industry by the early-1990's had changed in a number of ways and was thought to have reached maturity by many analysts. Several formerly successful firms like E.J. Korvette, W.T. Grant, Atlantic Mills, Arlans, Federals, Zayre, Heck's, and Ames had declared bankruptcy and as a result either liquidated or reorganized. Venture announced liquidation in early 1998. Firms like Target Stores, and Shopko Stores began carrying more fashionable merchandise in more attractive facilities and shifted their emphasis to more national markets. Specialty retailers such as Toys "R" Us, Pier 1 Imports, and Oshmans had matured and were no longer making big inroads in toys, home furnishing, and sporting goods. The "superstores" of drug and food chains were rapidly discounting increasing amounts of general merchandise. Some firms like May Department Stores Company with Caldor and Venture and Woolworth Corporation with Woolco had withdrawn from the field by either selling their discount divisions or closing them down entirely. Woolworth's remaining 122 Woolco stores in Canada were sold to Wal-Mart in 1994. All remaining Woolworth variety stores in the United States were closed in 1997.

Several new retail formats had emerged in the marketplace to challenge the traditional discount department store format. The superstore, a 100,000–300,000 square foot operation, combined a large supermarket with a discount general merchandise store. Originally a European retailing concept, these outlets where known as "malls without walls." Kmart's Super Kmart, American Fare, and Wal-Mart's Supercenter Store were examples of this trend toward large operations. Warehouse retailing, which involved some combination of warehouse and showroom facilities, used warehouse principles to reduce operating expenses and thereby offer discount prices as a primary customer appeal. Home Depot combined the traditional hardware store and lumberyard with a self-service home improvement center to become the largest home center operator in the nation.

Some retailers responded to changes in the marketplace by selling goods at price levels (20 to 60 percent) below regular retail prices. These off-price operations appeared as two general types: (1) factory outlet stores like Burlington Coat Factory Warehouse, Bass Shoes, and Manhattan's Brand Name Fashion Outlet, and (2) independents like Loehmann's, T.J. Maxx, Marshall's, and Clothestime which bought seconds, overages, closeouts, or leftover goods from manufacturers and other retailers. Other retailers chose to dominate a product classification. Some super specialists like Sock Appeal, Little Piggie, Ltd., and Sock Market, offered a single narrowly defined classification of merchandise with an extensive assortment of brands, colors, and sizes. Others, as niche specialists, like Kids Mart, a division of Venator (Woolworth) Corporation targeted an identified market with carefully selected merchandise and appropriately designed stores. Some retailers like Silk Greenhouse (silk plants and flowers), Office Club (office supplies and equipment), and Toys "R" Us (toys) were called "category killers" because they had achieved merchandise dominance in their respective product categories. Stores like The Limited, Limited Express, Victoria's Secret, and The Banana Republic became mini-department specialists by showcasing new lines and accessories alongside traditional merchandise lines.

Kmart Corporation, headquartered in Troy, Michigan, became the industry's third largest retailer after Sears, Roebuck & Co. and second largest discount department store chain in the United States in the 1990's. Kmart had 2,171 stores and $35,925 million in sales at the beginning of 2000. The firm was perceived by many industry analysts and consumers in several independent studies as a laggard. It had been the industry sales leader for a number of years and had recently announced a turnaround in profitability. In the same studies, Wal-Mart was perceived as the industry leader even though according to the *Wall Street Journal*: "they carry much the same merchandise, offer prices that are pennies apart and operate stores that look almost exactly alike." "Even their names are similar," noted the newspaper. The original Kmart concept of a "conveniently located, one stop shopping unit where customers could buy a wide variety of quality merchandise at discount prices," had lost its competitive edge in a changing market. As one analyst noted in an industry newsletter: "They had done so well for the past twenty years without paying attention to market changes, now they have to." Kmart acquired a new, President and Chief Executive Officer in 2000. Wal-Mart and Kmart sales growth over the period 1990–1999 is reviewed in Exhibit 2. A competitive analysis is shown of four major retail firms in Exhibit 3.

Some retailers like Kmart had initially focused on appealing to professional, middle class consumers who lived in suburban areas and who were likely to be price sensitive. Other firms like Target, which had adopted the discount concept early, attempted to go generally after an upscale consumer. Some firms such as Fleet Farm and Pamida served the rural consumer, while firms like Value City and Ames Discount Department Stores chose to serve the urban consumer.

In rural communities Wal-Mart success often came at the expense of established local merchants and units of

Exhibit 2   Competitive Sales & Store Comparison, 1990–1999

	Kmart		Wal-Mart	
Year	Sales (000)	Stores[1]	Sales (000)	Stores[1]
1999	$ 35,925,000	2,171	$ 165,013,000	3,989
1998	33,674,000	2,161	137,634,000	3,999
1997	32,183,000	2,136	117,958,000	3,406
1996	31,437,000	2,261	104,859,000	3,054
1995	34,389,000	2,161	93,627,000	2,943
1994	34,025,000	2,481	82,494,000	2,684
1993	34,156,000	2,486	67,344,000	2,400
1992	37,724,000	2,435	55,484,000	2,136
1991	34,580,000	2,391	43,886,900	1,928
1990	32,070,000	2,350	32,601,594	1,721

[1] Number of general merchandise stores.

Exhibit 3   An Industry Comparative Analysis, 1999

	Wal-Mart	Sears[1]	Kmart	Target
Sales (Millions)	$ 165,013	$ 41,071	$ 35,925	$ 33,702
Net Income (Thousands)	$ 5,377	$ 1,453	$ 403	$ 1,144
Net Income Per Share	$ 1.21	$ 3.83	$ 1.29	$ 2.45
Dividends Per Share	$ 0.14	$ n/a	$ n/a	$ 0.40
% Sales Change	20.0%	2.7%	6.6%	9.9%

Number of Stores:

Wal-Mart United States
  Discount Stores - 1801
  SAM'S Clubs - 463
  Supercenters - 721
Wal-Mart International
  Discount Stores - 572
  SAM'S Clubs - 49
  Supercenters - 383
Sears Roebuck & Company (all divisions)[1]
  Sears Merchandise Group
    Full-line Department Stores - 858
    Hardware Stores - 267

Sears Dealer Stores - 738
Sears Auto Centers Stores - 798
NTB National Tire & Battery Stores - 310
K Mart Corporation
  Big Kmart - 1,860
  Traditional Kmart - 206
  Super Kmart - 105
Target Corporation
  Target - 912
  Mervyn's - 267
  Department Stores - 64

[1] Number of general merchandise stores
Source: *Corporate Annual Reports*

---

regional discount store chains. Hardware stores, family department stores, building supply outlets, and stores featuring fabrics, sporting goods, and shoes were among the first to either close or relocate elsewhere. Regional discount retailers in the Sunbelt states like Roses, Howard's, T.G.& Y., and Duckwall-ALCO, who once enjoyed solid sales and earnings, were forced to reposition themselves by renovating stores, opening bigger and more modern units, re-merchandising assortments, and offering lower prices. In many cases, stores like Coast-to-Coast and Ben Franklin closed upon a Wal-Mart announcement that it was planning to build in a specific community. "Just the word that Wal-Mart was coming made some stores close up," indicated one local newspaper editor.

Domestic Corporate Strategies

The corporate and marketing strategies that emerged at Wal-Mart were based upon a set of two main objectives that had guided the firm through its growth years. In the first objective the customer was featured, "customers would be provided what they want, when they want it, all at a value." In the second objective the team spirit was emphasized, "treating each other as we would hope to be treated, acknowledging our total dependency on our

Associate-partners to sustain our success." The approach included: aggressive plans for new store openings; expansion to additional states; upgrading, relocation, refurbishing and remodeling of existing stores; and opening new distribution centers. For Wal-Mart management, the 1990's were considered an era in which the firm grew to become a truly nationwide retailer that operated in all fifty states. At the beginning of 2000, Wal-Mart management predicted that over the next five years, 60 to 70 percent of sales and earnings growth would come from domestic markets with Wal-Mart stores and Supercenters, and another 10–15 percent from SAM'S Club and McLane. The remaining 20 percent of the growth would come from planned growth in international markets. As David Glass once noted, "We'll be fine as long as we never lose our responsiveness to the customer."

In the decade of the 1980's, Wal-Mart developed a number of new retail formats. The first SAM'S Club opened in Oklahoma City, Oklahoma in 1983. The wholesale club was an idea that had been developed by other firms earlier but which found its greatest success and growth in acceptability at Wal-Mart. SAM'S Clubs featured a vast array of product categories with limited selection of brand and model; cash-and carry business with limited hours; large (100,000 square foot), bare-bones facilities; rock bottom wholesale prices; and minimal promotion. The limited membership plan permitted wholesale members who bought membership and others who usually paid a percentage above the ticket price of the merchandise. A revision in merchandising strategy resulted in fewer items in the inventory mix with more emphasis on lower prices. A later acquisition of 100 Pace warehouse clubs, which were converted into SAM'S Clubs, increased that division's units by more than a third. At the beginning of 2000, there were 463 SAM'S Clubs in operation.

Wal-Mart Supercenters were large combination stores. They were first opened in 1988 as Hypermarket*USA, a 222,000 square foot superstore which combined a discount store with a large grocery store, a food court of restaurants, and other service businesses such as banks or video tape rental stores. A scaled down version of Hypermarket*USA was called the Wal-Mart Supercenter, similar in merchandise offerings, but with about 180,000 to 200,000 square feet of space. These expanded store concepts also included convenience stores, and gasoline distribution outlets to "enhance shopping convenience." The company proceeded slowly with these plans and later suspended its plans for building any more hypermarkets in favor of the Supercenter concept. At the beginning of 2000, Wal-Mart operated 721 Supercenters. The name, Hypermarket*USA, was no longer used to identify these large stores.

Wal-Mart also tested a new concept called the Neighborhood Market in a number of locations in Arkansas. Identified by the company as "small-marts," these green-and-white stores were stocked with fresh fruits and vegetables, a drive-up pharmacy, a 24-hour photo shop, and a selection of classic Wal-Mart hard goods. Management elected to move slowly on this concept, planning to open no more than ten a year. The goal was to ring the Superstores with these smaller stores to attract customers who were in hurry and wanted only a few items.

The McLane Company, Inc., a provider of retail and grocery distribution services for retail stores, was acquired in 1991. It was not considered a major segment of the total Wal-Mart operation.

Several programs were launched in Wal-Mart stores to "highlight" popular social causes. The "Buy American" program was a Wal-Mart retail program initiated in 1985. The theme was "Bring It Home to the USA" and its purpose was to communicate Wal-Mart's support for American manufacturing. In the program, the firm directed substantial influence to encourage manufacturers to produce goods in the United States rather than import them from others countries. Vendors were attracted into the program by encouraging manufacturers to initiate the process by contacting the company directly with proposals to sell goods that were made in the United States. Buyers also targeted specific import items in their assortments on a state-by-state basis to encourage domestic manufacturing. According to Haim Dabah, president of Gitano Group, Inc., a maker of fashion discount clothing which imported 95 percent of its clothing and now makes about 20 percent of its products here: "Wal-Mart let it be known loud and clear that if you're going to grow with them, you sure better have some products made in the U.S.A." Farris Fashion, Inc. (flannel shirts); Roadmaster Corporation (exercise bicycles); Flanders Industries, Inc. (lawn chairs); and Magic Chef (microwave ovens) were examples of vendors that chose to participate in the program.

From the Wal-Mart standpoint the "Buy American" program centered around value—producing and selling quality merchandise at a competitive price. The promotion included television advertisements featuring factory workers, a soaring American eagle, and the slogan: "We buy American whenever we can, so you can too." Prominent in-store signage, and store circulars were also included. One store poster read: "Success Stories—These items, formerly imported, are now being purchased by Wal-Mart in the U.S.A."

Wal-Mart was one of the first retailers to embrace the concept of "green" marketing. The program offered shoppers the option of purchasing products that were better for the environment in three respects: manufacturing, use, and disposal. It was introduced through full-page advertisements in the *Wall Street Journal* and *USA Today*. In-store signage identified those products that were environmentally safe. As Wal-Mart executives saw it, "customers are concerned about the quality of land, air, and water, and would like the opportunity to do something positive." To initiate the program, 7,000 vendors were notified that Wal-Mart had a corporate concern for the environment and to ask for their support in a variety of ways. Wal-Mart television advertising showed children on swings, fields of grain blowing in the wind, and roses. Green and white store signs, printed on recycled paper, marked products or packaging that had been developed or redesigned to be more environmentally sound.

The Wal-Mart private brand program began with the "Ol' Roy" brand, the private label dog food named for Sam Walton's favorite hunting companion. Introduced to Wal-Mart stores in 1982 as a low-price alternative to national brands, Ol' Roy became the biggest seller of all dog-food brands in the United States. "We are a (national) brand-oriented company first," noted Bob Connolly, Executive Vice President of merchandising of Wal-Mart. "But we also use private label to fill value or pricing void that, for whatever reason, the brands left behind. Wal-Mart's private label program included thousands of products that had brand names such as Sam's Choice, Great Value, Equate, and Spring Valley.

Wal-Mart had become the channel commander in the distribution of many brand name items. As the nation's largest retailer, and in many geographic areas the dominant distributor, it exerted considerable influence in negotiation for the best price, delivery terms, promotion allowances, and continuity of supply. Many of these benefits could be passed on to consumers in the form of quality name brand items available at lower than competitive prices. As a matter of corporate policy, management often insisted on doing business only with producer's top sales executives rather than going through a manufacturer's representative. Wal-Mart had been accused of threatening to buy from other producers if firms refuse to sell directly to it. In the ensuing power struggle, Wal-Mart executives refused to talk about the controversial policy or admit that it existed. As a representative of an industry association representing a group of sales agencies' representatives suggested, "In the Southwest, Wal-Mart's the only show in town." An industry analyst added, "They're extremely aggressive. Their approach has always been to give the customer the benefit of a corporate saving. That builds up customer loyalty and market share."

Another key factor in the mix was an inventory control system that was recognized as the most sophisticated in retailing.

A high-speed computer system linked virtually all the stores to headquarters and the company's distributions centers. It electronically logged every item sold at the checkout counter, automatically kept the warehouses informed of merchandise to be ordered and directed the flow of good to the stores and even to the proper shelves. Most important for management, it helped detect sales trends quickly and speeded up market reaction time substantially. According to Bob Connolly, Executive Vice President of Merchandising, "Wal-Mart has used the data gathered by technology to make more inventory available in the key items that customers want most, while reducing inventories overall."

At the beginning of 2000, Wal-Mart set up a separate company for its Web site with plans to go public. Wal-Mart.com Inc., based in Palo Alto, California, was jointly owned by Wal-Mart and Accel Partners, a Silicon Valley venture-capital firm. The site included a wide range of products and services that ranged from shampoo to clothing to lawn mowers as well as airline, hotel, and rental car bookings. After launching and then closing a SAM'S Club Web site, Wal-Mart had plans to reopen the site in mid-June 2000 with an emphasis on upscale items such as jewelry, housewares, and electronics, and full product lines for small business owners. SamsClub.com would be run by Wal-Mart from the company's Bentonville, Arkansas headquarters.

International Corporate Strategies

In 1994, Wal-Mart entered the Canadian market with the acquisition of 122 Woolco discount stores from Woolworth Corporation. When acquired, the Woolco stores were losing millions of dollars annually, but operations became profitable within three years. At the end of 1999, the company had 166 Wal-Mart discount stores in Canada and planned to open seventeen new stores in fiscal 2000. The company's operations in Canada were considered as a model for Wal-Mart's expansion into other international markets. With 35 percent of the Canadian discount and department store market, Wal-Mart was the largest retailer in that country.

With a tender offer for shares and mergers of joint ventures in Mexico, the company in 1997 acquired a controlling interest in Cifra, Mexico's largest retailer. Cifra, later identified as Wal-Mart de Mexico, operated stores with a variety of concepts in every region of Mexico, ranging from the nation's largest chain of sit-down restaurants to a softline department store. Retail analysts noted that the initial venture involved many costly mistakes. Time-after-time it sold the wrong products, including tennis balls that wouldn't bounce in high-altitude Mexico City. Large parking lots at some stores made access difficult as many people arrived by bus. In 2000, Wal-Mart operated 397 Cifra outlets in Mexico, in addition to twenty-seven Wal-Mart Supercenters and thirty-four SAM'S Club Stores.

When Wal-Mart entered Argentina in 1995, it also initially faced challenges adapting its U.S.-based retail mix and store layouts to the local culture. Although globalization and American cultural influences had swept through the country in the early 1990s, the Argentine market did not accept American cuts of meat, bright colored cosmetics and jewelry that gave prominent placement to emeralds, sapphires, and diamonds even though most Argentine women preferred wearing gold and silver. The first stores even had hardware departments full of tools wired for 110-volt electric power, the standard throughout Argentina was 220. Compounding the challenges was store layout that featured narrow aisles; stores appeared crowded and dirty.

Wal-Mart management concluded that Brazil offered great opportunities for Wal-Mart, with the fifth largest population in the world and a population that had a tendency to follow U.S. cultural cues. Although financial data was not broken out on South American operations, retail analysts cited the accounts of Wal-Mart's Brazilian partner, Lojas Americanas SA, to suggest that Wal-Mart lost $100 million in start-up costs of the initial sixteen stores. Customer acceptance of Wal-Mart stores was mixed. In Canada and Mexico, many customers were familiar with the company from cross-border shopping trips. Many Brazilian customers were not familiar with the Wal-Mart name. In addition, local Brazilian markets were already dominated by savvy local and foreign competitors such as Grupo Pao de Acucar SA of Brazil and Carrefour SA of France. And Wal-Mart's insistence on doing things "the Wal-Mart way" initially alienated many local suppliers and employees. The country's continuing economic problems also presented a challenge. In 2000, Wal-Mart planned to expand its presence by opening three more SAM'S Clubs in Brazil.

Because of stubborn local regulations, management felt it would be easier for Wal-Mart to buy existing stores in Europe than to build new ones. The acquisition of twenty-one "hypermarkets" in Germany at the end of 1997 marked the company's first entry into Europe, which management considered "one of the best consumer markets in the world." These large stores offered one-stop shopping facilities similar to Wal-Mart Supercenters. In early 1999 the firm also purchased seventy-four Interspar hypermarket stores. All of these German stores were identified with the Wal-Mart name and restocked with a new and revamped selection of merchandise. In a response to local laws that forced early store closings and forbid Sunday sales, the company simply opened stores earlier to allow shopping to begin at 7 A.M.

Wal-Mart acquired ASDA, Britain's third largest supermarket group, for $10.8 billion in July 1999. With its own price rollbacks, people greeter, "permanently low prices" and even "Smiley" faces, ASDA had emulated Wal-Mart's store culture for many years. Based in Leeds, England, the firm had 232 stores in England, Scotland, and Wales. While the culture and pricing strategies of the two companies were nearly identical, there were differences, primarily the size and product mix of the stores. The average Wal-Mart Supercenter in 1999 was 180,000 square feet in size and had about 30 percent of its sales in groceries. In contrast, the average ASDA store had only 65,000 square feet and did 60 percent of sales in grocery items.

The response in Europe to Wal-Mart was immediate and dramatic. Competitors scrambled to match Wal-Mart's low prices, long hours, and friendly service. Some firms combined to strengthen their operations. For example, France's Carrefour SA chain of hypermarkets combined forces with a competitor, Promodes, in a $16.5 billion deal. In 1999, Carrefour dominated the European market with 9,089 locations. It was also one of the world's largest retailers with market dominance not only in Europe, but in Latin America and Asia as well.

Wal-Mart's initial effort to enter China fell apart in 1996, when Wal-Mart and Thailand's Charoen Pokphand Group terminated an 18-month-old joint venture because of management differences. Wal-Mart decided to consolidate its operations with five stores in the Hong Kong border city of Shenzhen, one in Dalian, and another in Kumming. Although management had plans to open ten additional stores in China by the end of 2000, analysts concluded that the company was taking a low profile approach because of possible competitive response and government restrictions. Beijing restricted the operations of foreign retailers in China, requiring them, for instance, to have government-backed partners. In Shenzhen, it limited the number of stores Wal-Mart could open. Planned expansion in the China market came as China prepared to enter the World Trade Organization and its economy showed signs of accelerating. At the beginning of 2000, Wal-Mart also operated five Supercenters in South Korea.

The international expansion accelerated management's plans for the development of Wal-Mart as a global brand along the lines of Coca-Cola, Disney, and McDonald's. "We are a global brand name," said Bobby Martin, an early president of the International Division of Wal-Mart. "To customers everywhere it means low cost, best value, greatest selection of quality merchandise, and highest standards of customer service," he noted. Some changes were mandated in Wal-Mart's international operations to meet local tastes and intense competitive conditions. "We're building companies out there," said Martin. "That's like starting Wal-Mart all over again in South America or Indonesia or China." Although stores in different international markets would coordinate purchasing to gain leverage with suppliers, developing new technology and planning overall strategy would be done from Wal-Mart headquarters in Bentonville, Arkansas. At the beginning of 2000, the International Division of Wal-Mart operated 572 discount stores, 383 Supercenters, and forty-nine SAM'S Clubs. Wal-Mart's international unit accounted for $22.7 billion in sales in 1999. Exhibit 4 shows the countries in which stores were operated and the number of units in each country.

Decision Making in a Market-Oriented Firm

One principle that distinguished Wal-Mart was the unusual depth of employee involvement in company affairs. Corporate strategies put emphasis on human resource management. Employees of Wal-Mart became "associates," a name borrowed from Sam Walton's early association with the J.C. Penney, Co. Input was encouraged at meetings at the store and corporate level. The firm hired employees locally, provided training programs, and through a "Letter to the President" program, management encouraged employees to ask questions, and made words like "we," "us," and "our" a part of the corporate language. A number of special award programs recognized individual, department, and division achievement. Stock ownership and profit-sharing programs were introduced as part of a "partnership concept."

The corporate culture was recognized by the editors of the trade publication, *Mass Market Retailers*, when it recognized all 275,000 associates collectively as the "Mass Market Retailers of the Year." "The Wal-Mart associate," the editors noted, "in this decade that term has come to symbolize all that is right with the American worker, particularly in the retailing environment and most particularly at Wal-Mart." The "store within a store" concept, as a Wal-Mart corporate policy, trained individuals to be merchants by being responsible for the performance of their own departments as if they were running their own businesses. Seminars and training programs afforded them opportunities to grow within the company. "People development, not just a good 'program' for any growing company, but a must to secure our future," is how Suzanne Allford, Vice President of the Wal-Mart People

Division explained the firm's decentralized approach to retail management development.

"The Wal-Mart Way," was a phrase that was used by management to summarize the firm's unconventional approach to business and the development of the corporate culture. As noted in a report referring to a recent development program: "We stepped outside our retailing world to examine the best managed companies in the United States in an effort to determine the fundamentals of their success and to 'benchmark' our own performances." The name "Total Quality Management" (TQM) was used to identify this vehicle for proliferating the very best things we do while incorporating the new ideas our people have that will assure our future." In 1999, *Discount Store News* honored Wal-Mart Stores, Inc. as "Retailer of the Century" with a commemorative 200-page issue of the magazine.

The Growth Challenge

H. Lee Scott, Jr. indicated that he would never forget his first meeting with Sam Walton. "How old are you?" Walton asked the then 30-year-old Scott, who had just taken a job over-seeing Wal-Mart trucking fleet. "Do you think you can do this job?" asked Walton. When Scott said yes, Walton agreed and said "I reckon you can." More than twenty years later as Wal-Mart's new CEO, Scott was facing his toughest challenge yet: keeping the world's biggest retailer on its phenomenal roll and delivering the huge sales and earnings increases that investors had come to expect from Wal-Mart over the years. Analysts had correctly projected that Wal-Mart would surpass General Motors to be ranked No. 1 in revenue on the *Fortune* 500 list 2000. The combination of growth and acquisition had caused revenue to make huge leaps every year. In 1999 it went up 20 percent, from $139 billion in 1998 to $165 billion. Earnings also increased in 1999 by 21 percent, to nearly $5.4 billion. Industry analysts noted that this growth was on top of an 18 percent compound annual growth rate over the past decade.

Wal-Mart Stores, Inc. revolutionized American retailing with focus on low costs, high customer service, and everyday low pricing to drive sales. Although the company had suffered though some years of lagging performance, it had experienced big gains from its move into the grocery business with one-stop supercenters and in international markets with acquisition and new ventures. To keep it all going and growing was a major challenge. As the largest retailer in the world, the company and its leadership was challenged to find new areas to continue to grow sales and profits into the future. Lee Scott knew that an ambitious expansion program was called for to allow the company to meet these objectives.

Exhibit 4	Wal-Mart International Division, 1999
Country	**Stores**
Mexico	460
United Kingdom	236
Canada	166
Germany	95
Brazil	16
Puerto Rico	15
Argentina	10
China	8
South Korea	5

Source: Wal-Mart, Hoover's Online

References

Albright, Mark, "Changes in Store," *New York Times*, 17 May 1999, 10, 12.

Bergman, Joan, "Saga of Sam Walton," *Stores* (January 1988): 129–130.

Boudette, Neil E., "Wal-Mart Plans Major Expansion in Germany," *The Wall Street Journal*, 20 July 2000, A21.

Cummins, Chip, "Wal-Mart's Net Income Increases 28%, But Accounting Change Worries Investors," *The Wall Street Journal*, 10 August 2000, A6.

"David Glass's Biggest Job is Filling Sam's Shoes," *Business Month* (December 1988): 42.

Feldman, Amy, "How Big Can It Get?" *Money* (December 1999): 158.

Friedland, Johnathan and Louise Lee, "The Wal-Mart Way Sometimes Gets Lost in Translation Overseas," *The Wall Street Journal*, 8 October 1997, A1, A12.

Gustke, Constance, "Smooth Operator," *Worth* (March 2000): 41.

Helliker, Kevin, "Wal-Mart's Store of the Future Blends Discount Prices, Department-Store Feel," *The Wall Street Journal*, 17 May 1991, B1, B8.

Helliker, Kevin, and Ortega, Bob, "Falling Profit Marks End of Era at Wal-Mart," *The Wall Street Journal*, 18 January 1996, B1.

"How the Stores Did," *The Wall Street Journal*, 5 May 2000, B4.

Huey, John, "America's Most Successful Merchant," *Fortune*, 23 September 1991, 46–48.

Johnson, Jay L., "The Supercenter Challenge," *Discount Merchandiser* (August 1989): 70.

Komarow, Steven, "Wal-Mart Takes Slow Road in Germany," *USA Today*, 5 May 2000, 3B.

Krauss, Clifford, "Wal-Mart Learns A Hard Lesson," *International Herald Tribune* (6 December 1999): 15.

Larrabee, John, "Wal-Mart Ends Vermont's Holdout," *USA Today*, 19 September 1995, 4B.

Lee, Louise, "Discounter Wal-Mart is Catering to Affluent to Maintain Growth," *The Wall Street Journal*, 7 February 1996, A1.

Lee, Louise, and Joel Millman, "Wal-Mart to Buy Majority Stake in Cifra," *The Wall Street Journal*, 4 June 1997, A3.

Loomis, Carol J., "Sam Would Be Proud," *Fortune*, 17 April 2000, 131.

"Management Style: Sam Moore Walton," *Business Month* (May 1989): 38.

Marsch, Barbara, "The Challenge: Merchants Mobilize to Battle Wal-Mart in a Small Community," *The Wall Street Journal*, 5 June 1991, A1, A4.

Mason, Todd, "Sam Walton of Wal-Mart: Just Your Basic Homespun Billionaire," *Business Week* (14 October 1985): 142–143.

Mitchener, Brandon and David Woodruff, "French Merger of Hypermarkets Gets a Go-Ahead," *The Wall Street Journal*, 26 January 2000, A19.

Nelson, Emily, "Wal-Mart to Build a Test Supermarket in Bid to Boost Grocery-Industry Share," *The Wall Street Journal*, 19 June 1998, A4.

Nelson, Emily and Kara Swisher, "Wal-Mart Eyes Public Sale of Web Unit," *The Wall Street Journal*, 7 January 2000, A3.

"Our People Make the Difference: The History of Wal-Mart," Video Cassette, (Bentonville, Arkansas: Wal-Mart Video Productions, 1991).

Peters, Tom J., and Nancy Austin, *A Passion For Excellence*, (New York: Random House), 266–267.

Rawn, Cynthia Dunn, "Wal-Mart vs. Main Street," *American Demographics* (June 1990): 58–59.

"Retailer Completes Purchase of Wertkauf of Germany," *The Wall Street Journal*, 31 December 1997, B3.

Rudnitsky, Howard, "How Sam Walton Does It," *Forbes*, 16 August 1982, 42–44.

"Sam Moore Walton," *Business Month* (May 1989): 38.

Schwadel, Francine, "Little Touches Spur Wal-Mart's Rise," *The Wall Street Journal*, 22 September 1989, B1.

Sears, Roebuck and Co., *Annual Report*, Chicago, Illinois, 1999.

Sheets, Kenneth R., "How Wal-Mart Hits Main St.," *U.S. News & World Report*, 13 March 1989, 53–55.

Target Corporation, *Annual Report*, Minneapolis, Minnesota, 1999.

"The Early Days: Walton Kept Adding 'a Few More' Stores," *Discount Store News* (9 December 1985): 61.

Tomlinson, Richard, "Who's Afraid of Wal-Mart?" *Fortune*, 26 June 2000, 186.

Trimble, Vance H., *Sam Walton: The Inside Story of America's Richest Man*, (New York: Dutton), 1990.

Voyle, Susanna, "ASDA Criticised for Price Claims," *Financial Times* (8 December 1999): 3.

"Wal-Mart Spoken Here," *Business Week* (23 June 1997): 138.

Wal-Mart Stores, Inc., *Annual Report*, Bentonville, Arkansas, 2000.

Wal-Mart's ASDA Says CEO to Head Europe Expansion," *The Wall Street Journal Europe*, 3 December 1999, 6.

"Wal-Mart Takes A Stand," *The Economist* (22 May 1999): 31.

"Wal-Mart: The Model Discounter," *Dun's Business Month* (December 1982): 60–61.

"Wal-Mart Wins Again," *The Economist* (2 October 1999): 33.

Walton, Sam with John Huey, *Sam Walton Made in America*, (New York: Doubleday Publishing Company), 1992.

Wonacott, Peter, "Wal-Mart Finds Market Footing in China," *The Wall Street Journal*, 17 July 2000, A31.

"Work, Ambition—Sam Walton," Press Release, Corporate and Public Affairs, Wal-Mart Stores, Inc.

Zellner, Wendy, "Someday, Lee, This May All Be Yours," *Business Week* (15 November 1999): 84.

Zimmerman, Ann, "Wal-Mart Posts 19% Profit Rise, Exceeding Analysts' Expectations," *The Wall-Street Journal*, 10 May 2000, B8.

Zimmerman, Ann, "Wal-Mart to Open Reworked Web Site for SamsClub.com," *The Wall-Street Journal*, 6 June 2000, B8.

Appendix A Wal-Mart Stores, Inc. Consolidated Balance Sheets and Operating Statements, 1998–1999 (in millions except per share data)

	Fiscal Year Ended January 31,		
	2000	1999	1998
Revenues:			
Net Sales	$ 165,013	$ 137,634	$ 117,958
Other income net	1,796	1,574	1,341
	166,809	139,208	119,299
Costs and Expenses:			
Cost of sales	129,664	108,725	93,438
Operating, selling, and general and administrative expenses	27,040	22,363	19,358
Interest Costs:			
Debt	756	529	555
Capital leases	266	268	229
	157,726	131,885	113,580
Income Before Income Taxes, Minority Interest, Equity in Unconsolidated Subsidiaries, and Cumulative Effect of Accounting Change	9,083	7,323	5,719
Provision for Income Taxes			
Current	3,476	3,380	2,095
Deferred	(138)	(640)	20
	3,338	2,740	2,115
Income Before Minority Interest, Equity in Unconsolidated Subsidiaries, and Cumulative Effect of Accounting Change	5,745	4,583	3,604
Minority Interest and Equity in Unconsolidated Subsidiaries	(170)	(153)	(78)
Income Before Cumulative Effect of Accounting Change	5,575	4,430	3,526
Cumulative Effect of Accounting Change, net of tax benefit of $119	(198)	–	–
Net Income	$ 5,377	$ 4,430	$ 3,526
Net Income per Common Share:			
Basic Net Income per Common Share:			
Income before cumulative effect of accounting change	$ 1.25	$ 0.99	$ 0.78
Cumulative effect of accounting change, net of tax	(0.04)	–	–
Net Income per Common Share	$ 1.21	$ 0.99	$ 0.78
Average Number of Common Share	4,451	4,464	4,516
Diluted Net Income Per Common Share			
Income before cumulative effect of accounting change	$ 1.25	$ 0.99	$ 0.78
Cumulative effect of accounting change, net of tax	(0.04)	0.00	0.00
Net Income Per Common Share	$ 1.20	$ 0.99	$ 0.78
Average Number of Common Shares	4,474	4,485	4,533
Pro forma amounts assuming accounting change had been in effect in fiscal 2000, 1999, and 1998:			
Net income	$ 5,575	$ 4,393	$ 3,517
Net income per common share, basic and diluted	$ 1.25	$ 0.98	$ 0.78

Appendix A Wal-Mart Stores, Inc. Consolidated Balance Sheets and Operating Statements, 1998–1999 (in millions) (continued)

	January 31,	
	2000	**1999**
Assets		
Current Assets:		
Cash and cash equivalents	$ 1,856	$ 1,879
Receivables	1,341	1,118
Inventories		
At replacement cost	20,171	17,549
Less LIFO reserve	378	473
Inventories at LIFO cost	19,793	17,076
Prepaid Expenses and other	1,366	1,059
Total Current Assets	24,356	21,132
Property, Plant, and Equipment at cost:		
Land	8,785	5,219
Building and improvements	21,169	16,061
Fixtures and equipment	10,362	9,296
Transportation equipment	747	553
	41,063	31,129
Less accumulated depreciation	8,224	7,455
Net property, plant, and equipment	32,839	23,674
Property Under Capital Lease:		
Property under capital lease	4,285	3,335
Less accumulated amoritization	1,155	1,036
Net property under capital leases	3,130	2,299
Other Assets and Deferred Charges:		
Net goodwill and other acquired intangible assets	9,392	2,538
Other assets and deferred charges	632	353
Total Assets	$ 70,349	$ 49,996
Liabilities & Stockholders' Equity		
Current Liabilities:		
Commercial paper	$3,323	$ –
Accounts payable	13,105	10,257
Accrued liabilities	6,161	4,998
Accrued income taxes	1,129	501
Long-term debt due within one year	1,964	900
Obligations under capital leases due within one year	121	106
Total Current Liabilities	25,803	16,762
Long-term debt	13,672	6,908
Long-term obligations under capital leases	3,002	2,699
Deferred income taxes and other	759	716
Minority interest	1,279	1,799
Shareholders' Equity:		
Preferred stock ($.10 par value; 100 shares authorized, none issued)		
Common stock ($.10 par value; 5,500 shares authorized, 4,457 and 4,448 issued and outstanding in 2000 and 1999, respectively)	446	445
Capital in excess of par value	714	435
Retained earnings	25,129	20,741
Other accumulated comprehensive income	(455)	(509)
Total Shareholders' Equity	25,834	21,112
Total Liabilities and Shareholders' Equity	$ 70,349	$ 49,996

Appendix B   Wal-Mart Stores, Inc. 11-Year Financial Summary, 1990–2000
(in millions except per share data)

	2000	1999	1998	1997
Net Sales	$ 165,013	$ 137,634	$ 117,958	$ 104,859
Net sales increase	20%	17%	12%	12%
Comparative store sales increase	8%	9%	6%	5%
Other income—net	1,796	1,574	1,341	1,319
Cost of sales	129,664	108,725	93,438	83,510
Operating, selling, and general administrative expenses	27,040	22,363	19,358	16,946
Interest costs:				
Debt	756	529	555	629
Capital leases	266	268	229	216
Provision for income taxes	3,338	2,740	2,115	1,794
Minority interest and equity in unconsolidated subsidiaries	(170)	(153)	(78)	(27)
Cumulative effect of accounting change, net of tax	(198)	–	–	–
Net income	5,377	4,430	3,526	3,056
Per share of common stock:				
Basic net income	1.21	0.99	0.78	0.67
Diluted net income	1.20	0.99	0.78	0.67
Dividends	0.20	0.16	0.14	0.11
Financial Position				
Current assets	$ 24,356	$ 21,132	$ 19,352	$ 17,993
Inventories at replacement cost	20,171	17,549	16,845	16,193
Less LIFO reserve	378	473	348	296
Inventories at LIFO cost	19,793	17,076	16,497	15,897
Net property, plant, and equipment and capital leases	35,969	25,973	23,606	20,324
Total assets	70,349	49,996	45,384	39,604
Current liabilities	25,803	16,762	14,460	10,957
Long-term debt	13,672	6,908	7,191	7,709
Long-term obligations under capital leases	3,002	2,699	2,483	2,307
Shareholders' equity	25,834	21,112	18,503	17,143
Financial Ratios				
Current ratio	.9	1.3	1.3	1.6
Inventories/working capital	(13.7)	3.9	3.4	2.3
Return on assets*	9.8%***	9.6%	8.5%	7.9%
Return on shareholders' equity**	22.9%	22.4%	19.8%	19.2%
Other Year-End Data				
Number of domestic Wal-Mart stores	1,801	1,869	1,921	1,960
Number of domestic Supercenters	721	564	441	344
Number of domestic SAM's Club units	463	451	443	436
International units	1,004	715	601	314
Number of associates	1,140,000	910,000	825,000	728,000
Number of shareholders	341,000	261,000	246,000	257,000

*Net income before minority interest, equity in unconsolidated subsidiaries and cumulative effect of accounting change/average assets.

**Net income/average shareholders' equity.

***Calculated without giving effect to the amount by which a lawsuit settlement exceeded established reserves. See Managment's Discussion and Analysis.

Appendix B Wal-Mart Stores, Inc. 11-Year Financial Summary, 1990–2000 (in millions except per share data) (continued)

1996	1995	1994	1993	1992	1991	1990
$ 93,627	$ 82,494	$ 67,344	$ 55,484	$ 43,887	$ 32,602	$ 25,811
13%	22%	21%	26%	35%	26%	25%
4%	7%	6%	11%	10%	10%	11%
1,146	914	645	497	404	262	175
74,505	65,586	53,444	44,175	34,786	25,500	20,070
15,021	12,858	10,333	8,321	6,684	5,152	4,070
692	520	331	143	113	43	20
196	186	186	180	153	126	118
1,606	1,581	1,358	1,171	945	752	632
(13)	4	(4)	4	(1)	–	–
–	–	–	–	–	–	–
2,740	2,681	2,333	1,995	1,609	1,291	1,076
0.60	0.59	0.51	0.44	0.35	0.28	0.24
0.60	0.59	0.51	0.44	0.35	0.28	0.24
0.10	0.09	0.07	0.05	0.04	0.04	0.03
$ 17,331	$ 15,338	$ 12,114	$ 10,198	$ 8,575	$ 6,415	$ 4,713
16,300	14,415	11,483	9,780	7,857	6,207	4,751
311	351	469	512	473	399	323
15,989	14,064	11,014	9,268	7,384	5,808	4,428
18,894	15,874	13,176	9,793	6,434	4,712	3,430
37,541	32,819	26,441	20,565	15,443	11,389	8,198
11,454	9,973	7,406	6,754	5,004	3,990	2,845
8,508	7,871	6,156	3,073	1,722	740	185
2,092	1,838	1,804	1,772	1,556	1,159	1,087
14,756	12,726	10,753	8,759	6,990	5,366	3,966
1.5	1.5	1.6	1.5	1.7	1.6	1.7
2.7	2.6	2.3	2.7	2.1	2.4	2.4
7.8%	9.0%	9.9%	11.1%	12.0%	13.2%	14.8%
19.9%	22.8%	23.9%	25.3%	26.0%	27.7%	30.9%
1,995	1,985	1,950	1,848	1,714	1,568	1,399
239	147	72	34	10	9	6
433	426	417	256	208	148	123
276	226	24	10	–	–	–
675,000	622,000	528,000	434,000	371,000	328,000	271,000
244,000	259,000	258,000	181,000	150,000	122,000	80,000

The effects of the change in accounting method for SAM's club membership revenue recognition would not have a material impact on this summary prior to 1998. Therefore, pro forma information as if the accounting change had been in effect for all years presented has not been provided. See Management's Discussion and Analysis for discussion of the impact of the accounting change in fiscal 2000, 1999, and 1998.

The acquisition of the ASDA Group PLC and the Company's related debt issuance had a significant impact on the fiscal 2000 amounts in the summary. See Notes 3 and 6 to the Consolidated Financial Statements.

Appendix C Wal-Mart Stores, Inc. Board of Directors and Executive Officers, January 31, 2000

Directors

John A. Cooper, Jr.	Dr. Frederick S. Humphries	Donald G. Soderquist
Stephen Friedman	E. Stanley Kroenke	Dr. Paula Stern
Stanley C. Gault	Elizabeth A. Sanders	Jose Villarreal
David D. Glass	H. Lee Scott	John T. Walton
Roland Hernandez	Jack C. Shewmaker	S. Robson Walton

Officers

S. Robson Walton
Chairman of the Board

H. Lee Scott
President and CEO

David D. Glass
Chairman, Executive Committee of the Board

Donald G. Soderquist
Senior Vice Chairman

Paul R. Carter
Executive V.P. and Vice President, Wal-Mart Realty

Bob Connolly
Executive Vice President, Merchandise

Thomas M. Coughlin
Executive Vice President and President & CEO,
Wal-Mart Stores Division

David Dible
Executive Vice President, Specialty Division

Michael Duke
Executive Vice President, Logistics

Thomas Grimm
Executive Vice President and President & CEO,
SAM's Club

Don Harris
Executive Vice President, Operations

John B. Menzer
Executive Vice President and President & CEO
International Division

Coleman Peterson
Executive Vice President, People Division

Thomas M. Schoewe
Executive Vice President and CFO

Robert K. Rhoads
Senior Vice President, General Counsel, and
Secretary

J.J. Fitzsimmons
Senior Vice President, Finance and Treasurer

Source: Wal-Mart Stores, Inc., *2000 Annual Report.*

Case 32

Weaving an Effective Strategy: The Quaker Fabric Corp. Case

Anthony F. Chelte and Thomas J. Vogel, *Western New England College*

Quaker Fabric Corp. is a leading designer, manufacturer, and worldwide marketer of woven upholstery fabrics for residential furniture and one of the largest producers of Jacquard upholstery fabrics in the world. The company is also a leading developer and manufacturer of specialty yarns (including chenille yarns) that it both sells to external parties and uses in the production of its own fabrics. Quaker's product line is one of the most comprehensive in the industry, consisting of over 3,000 traditional, contemporary, transitional, and country fabric patterns intended to meet the styling and design, color, texture, quality, and pricing requirements of its customers.

The company manufactures its yarn and fabric products in its six manufacturing plants located in Fall River and Somerset, Massachusetts. Quaker also maintains domestic distribution centers in High Point, North Carolina, Tupelo, Michigan, and Los Angeles, California. To provide better service to its international customers, the company also has a distribution center in Mexico and is setting up a marketing and warehousing operation in Brazil to further expand its presence in Latin America. As of January 1, 2000, the company employed 2,363 persons. Quaker has the following for its mission statement:

> To be the premier supplier of upholstery fabrics and a major resource for specialty textile yarns, while holding the highest regard for our people, community, and environment.

Since going public in late 1993, Quaker has established a defined set of corporate strategies to help enhance its position as an industry leader. These strategies succeeded in increasing revenues from $181 million in 1994 to $251 million in 1999. Unfortunately, profits did not follow. In 1994, Quaker had a net income of $10 million (a return on sales of 5.5 percent). Despite the increased sales, the net income in 1999 was just $2 million (a return on sales of 0.8 percent). As one would expect, this financial performance had a negative impact on Quaker's stock price. After trading as high as $11 in early 1994, the price had dropped to a low of $3.69 in the fourth quarter of 1999. It seemed like an appropriate time to re-examine the corporate strategies currently in place.

Company History

On December 14, 1945, the company was incorporated in Pawtucket, Rhode Island under the name "General Textile Mill" by its co-founders Louis and Bernard Symonds. Since its incorporation, the company has experienced numerous corporate changes including the following:

- On October 6, 1947, the company's name was changed to Providence Pile Corporation.
- In 1966, the company moved to its current location in Fall River, Massachusetts.
- In 1979, the company changes its name to Quaker Fabric Corporation.
- In November 1993, the company begins trading on the NASDAQ stock exchange (symbol QFAB).

Through its history, Quaker established itself as a leading designer, producer, and marketer of woven upholstery fabrics for residential furniture markets in the United States and around the world. The company also designs and produces specialty yarns, primarily for use in the production of its own products. However, these specialty yarns are also sold to independent manufacturers of apparel and home furnishings.

Despite these impressive credentials, Quaker failed to impress Wall Street after its initial public offering in 1993. After peaking at $11.00 in early 1994, the company's stock price began a steady and severe descent to a low of $3.68 in early 1996. This decline was caused by

This case was presented at the 2001 North American Case Research Association (NACRA) workshop. Copyright © 2001 by Anthony Chelte, Thomas J. Vogel and NACRA. Reprinted with permission. All rights reserved.

Acknowledgements: The authors wish to acknowledge the assistance of Jennifer Doyle, Kim Rivers, and Lynn Byrd who provided an in-class case analysis of Quaker Fabric Corp. as part of the graduate course in Business Strategies.

many factors, but primarily poor industry and market conditions. In fact, 1995 was the first time in five years that company sales and income had decreased (sales decreased from $180.8 million in 1994 to $173.5 million in 1995). In response to the poor performance of 1995, management developed a comprehensive improvement plan incorporating three primary goals:

1. **Increase margins and earnings by growing sales.** To accomplish this, the company strengthened its marketing, merchandising, design, distribution, and new business development functions, expanded its network of international sales agents, introduced a branded line of better-end fabrics under its Whitaker label, developed products to meet the specific styling and design needs of its international and jobber customers, continued to broaden its product line, focused on opportunities to reduce delivery lead times and improve customer service, identified new markets and applications for its specialty yarn products, and prepared to enter the contract (office and institutional) market.

2. **Reduce raw material costs.** The company identified alternate suppliers for several of its key raw materials, employed more cost effective raw materials in certain of its products and implemented a company-wide program to reduce waste.

3. **Improve manufacturing efficiencies.** The company continued to pursue ISO 9001 certification, invested more than $10.8 million in new manufacturing equipment in 1996 to eliminate bottlenecks and meet its quality objectives, changed its new product development process to enhance coordination between the company's design and manufacturing areas, reduced set-up times, provided additional training to the company's managers and production area employees, and implemented a number of process improvements throughout the company's manufacturing areas.

The initiatives were a success. After their implementation, Quaker's sales and profitability increased substantially in 1996 to $198.9 million and $8.6 million respectively. It seemed as though 1995 was simply a bump in the road and the problems had been rectified. In fact, company performance improved even further in 1997. Sales jumped to $220.0 million (10 percent increase) and income to $11.1 million (24 percent increase). The year saw record order rates for fabrics and yarn. From a product line and distribution standpoint, it appeared that Quaker was in excellent shape. The unprecedented demand confirmed Quaker's status as an industry leader for product innovation. Finally, 1997 saw Quaker achieve ISO 9001 certification on a company-wide basis.

Unfortunately, the increased demand for its products created a new problem—i.e. production delivery time. At the end of 1997, Quaker had a backlog of orders totaling $53.4 million for its fabric and yarn, compared to just $29.1 million in the previous year. This resulted in increased delivery lead time. Although many customers were willing to make the "product/delivery tradeoff," management believed it was essential to take the necessary steps to increase the timeliness and efficiency of its production process. The result was a planned $67.0 million plant expansion that was begun in 1997 and scheduled to be completed in 1998. In addition to modernized machinery, the plan also included an investment in a new integrated, Y2K-compliant, Enterprise Resource Planning system to provide additional computerized support to the production operations. In the short-term, Quaker outsourced a small amount of the manufacturing and incurred other additional costs, such as overtime, in an attempt to maintain customer satisfaction. These additional costs had a negative impact on company margins.

The capital expansion program was completed in 1998 as scheduled. As a result, Quaker was able to provide its customers with improved service and shorter delivery lead times. The program helped the company increase sales to a record level of $252.6 million and reduce back orders at the end of the year to $31.9 million. To help finance the expansion program, Quaker issued 3 million shares of common stock for a net amount of $33.3 million. The remaining amount was financed through new debt issues.

However, to the surprise of company management, the increased efficiency did not lead to increased profits. Despite the large increase in sales, net income *decreased* in 1998 to $5.8 million. In particular, it was the second half of 1998 that was the major disappointment. During the third quarter, systems-related issues associated with the conversion to the new management information system depressed company production rates. During the fourth quarter, the order rate decreased significantly below expectations. This hindered the company's ability to absorb the fixed overheads associated with production. Net income for the last two quarters was below $1.0 million, compared to $5.7 million during these quarters in 1997. Selected quarterly information is presented in Exhibit 1.

In 1999, the depressed market continued and sales dropped below 1998 levels, finishing at $250.8 million. In addition, the company's net income and stock price continued to plummet. Quaker finished the year with net income of just $2.1 million. The stock price had dropped to a low of $3.50 in the fourth quarter, off nearly 83 percent from its record high of $20 obtained in early 1998.

Exhibit 1   Selected Quarterly Information for Quaker Fabric

	1999 Fiscal Year				1998 Fiscal Year				1997 Fiscal Year			
	First Quarter	Second Quarter	Third Quarter	Fourth Quarter	First Quarter	Second Quarter	Third Quarter	Fourth Quarter	First Quarter	Second Quarter	Third Quarter	Fourth Quarter
Net sales	56,140	64,463	61,305	68,916	62,730	64,075	60,331	65,422	53,198	52,475	55,130	58,371
Gross margin	10,337	13,127	12,332	13,792	13,591	14,594	12,137	12,350	13,099	13,006	12,656	13,012
Operating income	684	2,463	2,500	2,623	4,193	5,376	2,456	1,964	4,631	5,020	4,873	4,938
Net income (loss)	(382)	809	808	838	1,936	2,542	692	600	2,510	2,801	3,080	2,722
Earnings per share—basic	(0.02)	0.05	0.05	0.05	0.15	0.20	0.04	0.04	0.21	0.22	0.25	0.22
Earnings per share—diluted	(0.02)	0.05	0.05	0.05	0.15	0.19	0.04	0.04	0.20	0.21	0.23	0.21
Common stock price—high	6.69	6.00	6.25	5.00	17.67	20.17	17.00	7.63	12.33	11.33	15.92	16.17
Common stock price—low	3.50	4.00	4.13	3.00	11.42	13.00	4.38	3.91	8.67	8.67	10.00	11.00

It was certainly time for management to re-examine the company's strategy and goals. Exhibits 2 and 3 summarize Quaker's strategies and competitive strengths as summarized on their 1999 annual report. Exhibits 4, 5, and 6 present the financial statements for the company's fiscal years of 1997, 1998, and 1999.

The Industry

Total domestic upholstery fabric sales, exclusive of automotive applications, are estimated to be approximately $2.0 billion annually. The size of the international fabric market is estimated to be at least twice that of the domestic market. Due to the capital intensive nature of the fabric manufacturing process and the importance of economies of scale in the industry, the domestic industry is concentrated, with the top fifteen upholstery fabric manufacturers—including Quaker—accounting for over 80 percent of the total market. Most of the largest U.S. fabric producers have expanded their export sales, capitalizing on their size, distribution capabilities, technology advantages, and broad product lines. Within the Jacquard segment, price is a more important competitive factor in the promotional-end of the market than it is in the middle to better-end of the market, where fabric styling and design considerations typically play a more important role.

Demand for upholstery fabric is a function of demand for upholstered furniture. The upholstered furniture market has grown from $5.4 billion in 1991 to a projected $10.7 billion in 2000. Total upholstered furniture demand

is affected by population growth and demographics, consumer confidence, disposable income, geographic mobility, housing starts, and home sales. Although the domestic residential furniture industry is cyclical, periods of decline have been relatively brief.

The upholstery fabric covering a sofa, chair, or other piece of furniture is one of the most significant factors influencing a furniture buyer's selection. Purchase decisions are based primarily on the consumer's evaluation of aesthetics, comfort, durability, quality, and price. As a result, the fabric decisions a furniture manufacturer makes play a critical role in its ability to gain a product differentiation advantage at the retail level.

Quaker's principal competitors include: Burlington House Upholstery Division of Burlington Industries Inc., Culp, Inc., Joan Fabrics Corporation and its Mastercraft Division, and Valdese Weavers, Inc. Several of the companies with which the Company competes have greater financial resources than the Company. The Company's products compete with other upholstery fabrics and furniture coverings, including prints, flocks, tufts, velvets, and leather. For comparison purposes, Exhibit 7 reports certain financial information and ratios for Culp, Inc.

The long-term outlook for the fabric and upholstery industry will be influenced by certain trends:

- The furniture industry has been consolidating at both the retail and manufacturing levels for several years. As a result, fabric suppliers are required to deal with larger customers that require shorter

Exhibit 2   Quaker's Strategy (Abstracted from Quaker's 1999 Annual Report)

Quaker's strategy to further its growth and financial performance objectives includes:

- **Increasing Sales to the Middle to Better-End Segment.** To capitalize on the consolidation trend in the furniture industry, the company has positioned itself as a full-service supplier of Jacquard and plain woven fabrics to the promotional and middle to better-end of the market by offering a wide variety of fabric patterns at prices ranging from $2.50 to $35.00 per yard. Sales of the company's middle to better-end fabrics, which the company first began emphasizing in the early 1990s, have increased steadily and were $188.0 million, or 80.8 percent of total fabric sales in 1999.

- **Expanding International Sales.** The company has made worldwide distribution of its upholstery fabrics a key component of its growth strategy. Quaker has built an international sales and distribution network, dedicated significant corporate resources to the development of fabrics to meet the specific styling and design needs of its international customers, and put programs in place to simplify the purchase of products from Quaker. The company's international sales were $39.2 million in 1999.

- **Penetrating Related Fabric Markets.** Management believes the company's styling and design expertise, as well as its ISO 9001-certified operations, provide opportunities to penetrate the contract market and increase Quaker's share of the interior decorator and recreational vehicle

markets. Management believes Quaker's Ankyra 'TM' chenille yarns and fabric finishing abilities will provide the company with a product advantage in these markets.

- **Growing Specialty Yarn Sales.** Quaker is a leading producer of specialty yarns and management believes it is the world's largest producer of chenille yarns. Approximately 80 percent of the chenille yarn manufactured by the company is used in the production of the company's fabric. The balance is sold to apparel and home textile firms throughout the United States through Quaker's yarn sales division, Nortex Yarns. Sales of the company's specialty yarns were $22.4 million in 1999. The company's current line of specialty yarns includes over seventy-five different varieties of spun and chenille yarns, and Quaker's yarn design and development staff regularly creates innovative new specialty yarns for use in the company's fabrics and sale to the company's yarn customers.

- **Considering Acquisition Opportunities.** Although all of Quaker's growth to date has been the result of internal initiatives, the company has evaluated a number of acquisition candidates in the past and will continue to consider acquisition opportunities in the future. An ideal acquisition candidate would either support the company's new market development objectives or offer a unique and complementary product, manufacturing, or technical capability.

---

delivery lead times, customer-specific inventory management programs, and additional information technology-based support services. Large integrated fabric suppliers have an advantage over smaller competitors because of their ability to offer a broader range of product choices and meet the volume and delivery requirements of the large furniture manufacturers and retailers.

- There is a growing trend in the United States toward a more casual lifestyle, as evidenced by "casual Fridays" in the workplace and product shifts in the apparel and home furnishings industries. This trend has likely resulted in growing demand for less formal furniture upholstered with softer, more comfortable fabric.

- Pushed by consumers demanding immediate product delivery, the furniture industry has increased its focus on just-in-time manufacturing methods and shorter delivery lead times.

- Both consumers and furniture manufacturers have placed increased emphasis on product quality, enabling fabric manufacturers with effective quality control systems to gain a competitive advantage.

- Favorable demographic trends over the near term are expected to benefit from continued strength of the domestic economy as well as a move by the baby boom generation toward more upscale furniture as they approach retirement age and additional demand generated by that same group's purchases of vacation and retirement homes.

- Technological advances in the speed and flexibility of the Jacquard loom have reduced the cost of producing Jacquard fabrics, enabling them to compete more effectively with prints, velvets, flocks, tufts, and other plain woven products.

- Most of the largest U.S. fabric producers have expanded their export sales, leveraging their size and broad product lines. U.S. fabric producers with international distribution capabilities have also benefited from a growing demand for American styles and designs by foreign consumers.

- Fabrics entering the United States from China, India, and other countries with low domestic labor costs are resulting in increased price competition at the lower end of the upholstery fabric and upholstered furniture markets. In addition, competition in the

Exhibit 3   Quaker's Competitive Strengths (Abstracted from Quaker's 1999 Annual Report)

Management believes that the following competitive strengths distinguish Quaker from its competitors and that these strengths serve as a solid foundation for the company's growth strategy:

- **Product Design and Development Capabilities.** Management believes that Quaker's reputation for design excellence and product leadership is, and will continue to be, the company's most important competitive strength.

- **Focus on Jacquard Fabrics.** Management believes the detailed, copyrighted designs of the company's Jacquard fabrics have enabled it to compete primarily based on superior styling and design, rather than price.

- **Broad Product Offering.** The breadth and depth of Quaker's product line enables the company to be a full-service supplier of Jacquard and plain woven fabrics to

virtually every significant domestic manufacturer of upholstered furniture.

- **Vertical Integration.** Using Quaker's own specialty yarns in the production of its fabrics provides the company with significant design, cost, and delivery advantages.

- **Commitment to Customer Service.** The company is committed to offering its customers the best overall service levels in the industry and in 1998 launched a major internal supply chain management initiative intended to further that objective.

- **State-of-the-Art Manufacturing Equipment.** Management believes the company has one of the most modern, efficient, and technologically advanced manufacturing bases in the industry.

middle to better-end segment of the market is being affected by upper-end fabric imports from Europe.

Quaker's strategy to further its growth and financial performance objectives includes:

- **Increasing Sales to the Middle to Better-End Segment.** To capitalize on the consolidation trend in the furniture industry, the company has positioned itself as a full-service supplier of Jacquard and plain woven fabrics to the promotional and middle to better-end of the market by offering a wide variety of fabric patterns at prices ranging

from $2.50 to $35.00 per yard. Sales of the company's middle to better-end fabrics, which the company first began emphasizing in the early 1990s, have increased steadily and were $188.0 million, or 80.8 percent of total fabric sales in 1999.

- **Expanding International Sales.** The company has made worldwide distribution of its upholstery fabrics a key component of its growth strategy. Quaker has built an international sales and distribution network, dedicated significant corporate resources to the development of fabrics to meet the specific styling and design needs of its international

Exhibit 4   Quaker Fabric Corp. Consolidated Statements of Income (in Thousands Except per Share Data)

	FY Ended Jan. 1, 2000	FY Ended Jan. 2, 1999	FY Ended Jan. 3, 1998
Net sales	250,824	252,558	219,174
Cost of products sold	201,236	199,886	167,401
Gross margin	49,588	52,672	51,773
Selling, general and administrative expenses	41,318	38,683	32,311
Operating income	8,270	13,989	19,462
Other expense:			
Interest expense	5,127	5,405	3,700
Other, net	(46)	(28)	65
Income before provision for income taxes	3,189	8,612	15,697
Provision for income taxes	1,116	2,842	4,584
Net income	2,073	5,770	11,113
Earnings per common share—basic	0.13	0.42	0.90
Earnings per common share—diluted	0.13	0.40	0.85

Exhibit 5   Quaker Fabric Corp. Consolidated Balance Sheets (in Thousands Except per Share Data)

	Jan. 1, 2000	Jan. 2, 1999	Jan. 3, 1998	Jan. 4, 1997
ASSETS				
Current Assets:				
Cash	332	432	234	385
Accounts receivable	41,191	40,661	32,996	26,291
Inventories	40,890	46,594	32,176	26,957
Prepaid and refundable income taxes	1,563	1,311	25	694
Prepaid expenses and other current assets	7,440	6,791	4,688	3,617
Total current assets	91,416	95,789	70,119	57,944
Property, Plant, and Equipment, net	138,509	132,420	101,307	84,045
Other Assets:				
Goodwill, net of amortization	5,818	6,011	6,204	6,397
Deferred financing costs, net	293	252	251	322
Other assets	1,446	294	207	154
Total Assets	237,482	234,766	178,088	148,862
LIABILITIES AND STOCKHOLDERS' EQUITY				
Current Liabilities:				
Current portion of long-term debt	36	700	995	951
Current portion of capital lease obligations	1,026	1,861	1,167	1,532
Accounts payable	19,983	13,754	18,203	14,384
Accrued expenses	7,337	6,780	7,120	8,427
Total current liabilities	28,382	23,095	27,485	25,294
Long-term Debt	59,000	65,536	47,436	35,731
Capital Lease Obligations	2,672	3,475	5,336	6,504
Deferred Income Taxes	17,504	15,874	13,771	11,649
Other Long-term Liabilities	2,646	1,793	1,747	3,082
Stockholders' Equity:				
Common stock—$.01 par value per share	157	156	126	120
Additional paid-in capital	83,554	83,410	46,530	41,908
Retained earnings	44,915	42,842	37,072	25,959
Other accumulated comprehensive loss	(1,348)	(1,415)	(1,415)	(1,415)
Total stockholders' equity	127,278	124,993	82,313	66,572
Total Liabilities and Stockholders' Equity	237,482	234,766	178,088	148,832

customers, and put programs in place to simplify the purchase of product from Quaker. The company's international sales were $39.2 million in 1999.

- **Penetrating Related Fabric Markets.** Management believes the company's styling and design expertise, as well as its ISO 9001-certified operations, provide opportunities to penetrate the contract market and increase Quaker's share of the interior decorator and recreational vehicle markets. Management believes Quaker's Ankyra 'TM' chenille yarns and fabric finishing abilities will provide the company with a product advantage in these markets.

Exhibit 6   Quaker Fabric Corp. Consolidated Statements of Cash Flows (in Thousands)

	FY Ended Jan. 1, 2000	FY Ended Jan. 2, 1999	FY Ended Jan. 3, 1998
Cash Flows from Operating Activities:			
Net income	2,073	5,770	11,113
Adjustments to reconcile net income to net cash provided by operating activities:			
Depreciation and amortization	13,210	10,616	8,511
Stock option compensation expense	—	—	571
Deferred income taxes	1,630	2,103	2,122
Changes in operating assets and liabilities:			
Accounts receivable	(530)	(7,665)	(6,735)
Inventories	5,704	(14,418)	(5,219)
Prepaid expenses and other assets	(2,053)	(3,476)	(455)
Accounts payable and accrued expenses	6,786	(4,789)	2,512
Other long-term liabilities	853	46	(1,335)
Net cash provided by (used in) operating activities	27,673	(11,813)	11,085
Cash Flows from Investing Activities:			
Net purchases of property, plant and equipment	(18,630)	(41,487)	(25,484)
Net cash used for investing activities	(18,630)	(41,487)	(25,484)
Cash Flows from Financing Activities:			
Proceeds from the issuance of long-term debt	—	—	45,000
Net borrowings (repayments) of debt	(7,200)	17,805	(33,251)
Repayments of capital lease obligations	(2,038)	(1,167)	(1,533)
Capitalization of financing costs	(109)	(50)	(25)
Proceeds from issuance of common stock, net of offering expenses	—	36,484	3,267
Proceeds from exercise of common stock options	145	426	790
Net cash provided by (used in) financing activities	(9,202)	53,498	14,248
Effect of Exchange Rates on Cash	59	—	—
Net Increase (decrease) in Cash	(100)	198	(151)
Cash, Beginning of Period	432	234	385
Cash, End of Period	332	432	234

- **Growing Specialty Yarn Sales.** Quaker is a leading producer of specialty yarns and management believes it is the world's largest producer of chenille yarns. Approximately 80 percent of the chenille yarn manufactured by the company is used in the production of the company's fabric. The balance is sold to apparel and home textile firms throughout the United States through Quaker's yarn sales division, Nortex Yarns. Sales of the company's specialty yarns were $22.4 mil-

lion in 1999. The company's current line of specialty yarns includes over seventy-five different varieties of spun and chenille yarns, and Quaker's yarn design and development staff regularly creates innovative new specialty yarns for use in the company's fabrics and sale to the company's yarn customers.

- **Considering Acquisition Opportunities.** Although all of Quaker's growth to date has been the result of internal initiatives, the company has evaluated a

Exhibit 7   Selected Financial Information for Culp, Inc.

	FY Ended Apr. 30, 2000	FY Ended May 2, 1999	FY Ended May 3, 1998
Profitability			
Sales	488,079	483,084	476,715
Net income	9,380	3,102	15,513
Earnings per share	0.81	0.24	1.22
Gross margin	17.35%	15.75%	17.53%
Operating margin	5.07%	3.34%	6.41%
Net margin	1.92%	0.64%	3.25%
Return on assets	2.79%	0.91%	5.18%
Return on equity	7.33%	2.40%	12.80%
Liquidity			
Current ratio	2.64	3.05	2.72
Quick ratio	1.25	1.47	1.27
Statement of Cash Flows:			
Cash flows from operations	21,818	32,519	8,862
Cash flows from investing	(19,219)	(10,743)	(72,429)
Cash flows from financing	(2,101)	(23,579)	65,049
Efficiency			
Total Assets	342,878	330,612	354,815
Asset turnover	1.45	1.41	1.59
Collection period	54.49	54.50	49.95
Days to sell inventory	64.03	65.32	61.30
Operating cycle	118.52	119.82	111.25
Leverage			
Total debt / Total assets	0.63	0.61	0.63
Long-term debt / Equity	1.19	1.22	1.24
Interest coverage ratio	2.60	1.68	4.30
Stock Price			
Hi	11.06	19.13	22.19
Lo	5.00	5.13	16.50
Close	5.81	8.25	18.88

number of acquisition candidates in the past and will continue to consider acquisition opportunities in the future. An ideal acquisition candidate would either support the company's new market development objectives or offer a unique and complementary product, manufacturing, or technical capability.

Management believes that the following competitive strengths distinguish Quaker from its competitors and that these strengths serve as a solid foundation for the company's growth strategy:

- **Product Design and Development Capabilities.** Management believes that Quaker's reputation for design excellence and product leadership is, and will continue to be, the company's most important competitive strength.

- **Focus on Jacquard Fabrics.** Management believes the detailed, copyrighted designs of the company's Jacquard fabrics have enabled it to compete primarily based on superior styling and design, rather than price.

- **Broad Product Offering.** The breadth and depth of Quaker's product line enables the company to be a full-service supplier of Jacquard and plain woven fabrics to virtually every significant domestic manufacturer of upholstered furniture.

- **Vertical Integration.** Using Quaker's own specialty yarns in the production of its fabrics provides the company with significant design, cost, and delivery advantages.

- **Commitment to Customer Service.** The company is committed to offering its customers the best overall service levels in the industry and in 1998 launched a major internal supply chain management initiative intended to further that objective.

- **State-of-the-Art Manufacturing Equipment.** Management believes the company has one of the most modern, efficient, and technologically advanced manufacturing bases in the industry.

Case 33

Workbrain Corporation[1]

Trevor Hunter and Mary Crossan, *The University of Western Ontario*

It's almost as if I had another eye added to my head. This person would give me insight to see different perspectives, yet at the same time be part of the company. I don't like the term "outsider" but, really, it's like adding a new function to the business that allowed me to think in new directions.

—*David Ossip, President and CEO of Workbrain Corporation*

Introduction

Eric Green, the newly hired vice-president, Corporate Development at Workbrain Corporation, looked at his offer letter (which was one-half page long) and wondered how his role would evolve. There was no job description in the letter, and the president of the firm had given him some far-reaching and abstract goals. The position had been described to him as one that would mainly involve developing external partnerships with

some emphasis on the internal development of the firm. However, from Green's perspective, there were many issues that needed to be handled both on the internal and external sides of the business. At the time, the Workbrain sales team was in the process of securing a major client. There were some growth goals that needed to be achieved and there were no organizational protocols for making a sale in place. There was little time to organize his new office.

Eric Green

Eric Green had recently graduated from an MBA program in Fontainebleau, France. Having both practiced corporate law and been a management consultant, he had several years of corporate experience behind him, yet when he graduated he had entrepreneurial aspirations. It was through the process of trying to start his own business that he was made aware of Workbrain.

> A couple of my friends and I had worked together in a cyber-entrepreneurship class and we had put together a business plan that we were quite excited about. After school, we came back thinking we would shop it around to see what we would find.

> In the course of doing that I called a friend of mine who had been involved in the Internet for five years in Toronto who I figured would be a good person to run it by. He referred me to David Ossip saying that David was a strong technology guy and could probably shed some light on the industry. He also suggested that David was starting a company and that I might want to look at it.

> I went to the (old) Workbrain Web site and it didn't look that interesting. My friend called me later and said that David wanted me to call him and he felt I would be a good fit with his company. I thought he would want me to be an implementation consultant and that was not what I was looking to do. I was looking for

business development, with a more strategic focus. When I finally met with David we didn't talk about my business plan at all because what he told me about the company was a very powerful and compelling story. It was almost too good to be true; he was looking for somebody to do exactly what I wanted to do, and it was in a company at the exact stage of development that I wanted, in the industry I wanted.

Green's role was very loosely defined and there were high expectations of him. He was given a lot of responsibility but also a lot of autonomy to make the decisions he needed to make and David Ossip was completely on his side. Ossip described the role and the type of person he wanted to fill it:

> The individual I was looking for was someone who was very bright, who was a quick thinker, someone who could push the organization and really push me into growing it and who would be able to communicate the vision to the other people in the organization.
>
> I also wanted someone who could function as a recruiter to get other very bright people into the company. I needed a person who would be able to work out how we were going to get the right people we needed into the corporation, and how we were going to come up with an environment to keep them.
>
> Also, we had to define what these people would be doing. Because we were a new company, a lot of the time we would have to hire people before we had active projects and we had to make sure that they would be busy and productive even though they might be (in consultants' terms) on the beach.
>
> I wanted someone who could come in and think in almost textbook terms of how we could scale the business up and build an infrastructure while the rest of us were focused on more operational kinds of functions. It was right up front that I thought about this position.

Ossip did not have to sell Green on the job. Green knew Ossip's track record and was confident in his abilities. Although the job was not well defined, Green felt that the way it was presented to him, this job would offer him the challenges he wanted:

> He described the role as both external development and internal development. I knew coming in that I would be wearing many different hats.

On the external side I would be helping with the strategy, the marketing side and forming alliances. Since we knew that we wanted to partner with consulting firms, my background made me a good fit. On the internal side, I would be managing the strategic growth of the company, which was of interest to me since some of my experience was applicable to that as well.

> When I first joined the company we were in the middle of an RFP (request for proposal) development for a large client that we were pitching and it was a good opportunity to get involved right away. I was helping to draft documents about a system that I didn't really know. At the time I was the only person in the company who didn't have a technical background.

Workbrain

Workbrain was founded in 1999 by a group of former employees of a leading supplier of client-server labor management systems, headed by president and CEO, David Ossip. Years earlier, Ossip had founded this previously very successful company that had specialized in time and attendance management.

Ossip possessed a combination of technical, industry, and management experience that he turned into a successful business that was eventually purchased by a larger firm. When he sold the firm and began thinking about starting a new company, he was able to gather together a trusted group of former colleagues to form the management team out of which the concept for Workbrain was born.

The members of the Workbrain management team all had extensive contacts in various industries and were recognized for their firm's expertise. At the time of Green's arrival, Workbrain was not very large. Table 1 presents a list of all the employees and their roles. As can be seen, at the time, every employee was also a senior executive.

The firm had secured U.S.$5.5 million in start-up capital from investors. The main activities in the small offices they rented were either the preparation of the RFP or the development and testing of the system.

From his knowledge of the industry, Ossip recognized that an opportunity existed in the form of the millions of routine employee transactions that took place to track and manage hourly or "blue-collar" workforces (e.g., time-clock entries, employee scheduling, overtime allocation, etc.). Exhibit 1 presents the competitive position of Workbrain in relation to its indirect competitors. Several firms had developed automated systems to manage the activities of so-called

Table 1   Employee List

Name	Role
David Ossip	President and CEO
Martin Ossip	Executive Director
Ezra Kiser	VP and GM, US Operations
Scott Morrell	VP Technology
Raymond Nunn	VP Operations
David Stein	VP Sales
Eric Green	VP Corporate Development

"white-collared" or professional workers (e.g., expense reports, travel schedules, etc.); however, there were no firms that focused directly on the "blue-collar" workforce. Considering that in the United States alone it was estimated that there were 64 million "blue-collar" workers,[2] there was clearly an opportunity. The market was generally broken out on a "per seat" basis, which referred to a per employee calculation. Therefore, the market size calculation was found by taking the number of employees in target companies multiplied by the

dollar value per seat. The enterprise software industry generally priced its software between U.S.$100 to U.S.$300 per seat.

Workbrain's main product was an e-business application suite that combined workforce management, workplace administration, and workplace community process automation.

The market in which Workbrain operated was highly competitive, yet the other firms could all be described as indirect competitors. There were no other firms that had workforce management products specifically designed for the large "blue-collar" workforce. Those "blue-collar" workforce management systems that were available were either "shrink-wrapped systems" that were "optimized for smaller organizations with less complex hourly labor rules," or were "based on older client-server technologies" that were more difficult and costly to deploy.

A direct comparison with the workforce management industry leader, Kronos Inc. (which had an estimated 50 percent of the market), revealed that more than 75 percent of the company's installed base used UNIX and DOS-based applications that meant they had limited Internet functionality.[3] Internet functionality was the basis of

Exhibit 1   Competitive Positioning of Workbrain

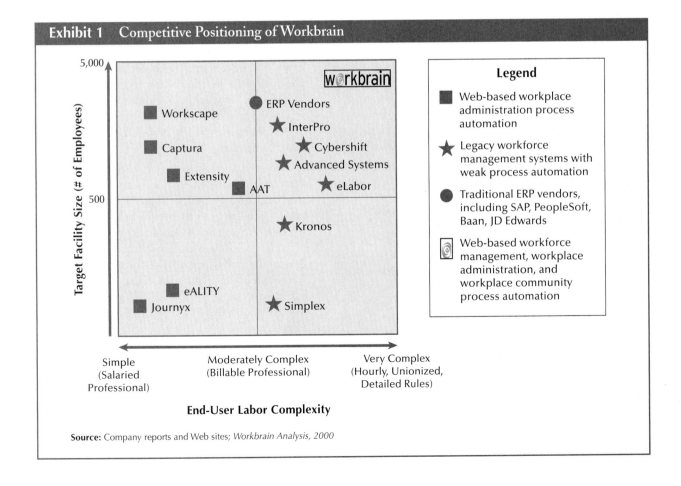

Source: Company reports and Web sites; *Workbrain Analysis, 2000*

Workbrain's product and was in line with industry analysts who predicted that much of the workforce management would soon be Web-based. The low implementation cost, flexible architecture and Web-based ease of operation gave Workbrain a strong competitive advantage.

Once the product was installed, managers of Workbrain's clients could more effectively automate hourly employee processes such as time and attendance tracking, activity-based costing, and employee scheduling. At the same time their clients' employees could, in turn, request shift changes, vacations, and overtime, administer their benefits claims, and carry out a host of other value-added, third-party transactions. In short, the product allowed Workbrain's clients to better manage their workforce through real time information transfer and analysis, while also providing the hourly employees more control over their activities and access to information that they needed to better perform their jobs and make their lives away from work easier, all through Web-based technology.

There were clear benefits to the clients in that the system would significantly reduce a number of administrative costs and payroll charges. It was estimated that form-processing costs ranged between $36 and $175 per submitted form[4] when one included the time spent filling in, submitting, approving, and auditing employee-related forms. For a facility employing 500 or more employees these costs would add up quickly. In addition, automated time and attendance systems reduced input errors and misrepresented working times that, on average, resulted in a loss equivalent to one percent to six percent of total payroll costs.[5] Improved labor analytics allowed managers to perform robust scenario analyses to determine impacts of potential labor policy changes and union contract terms on their firm's financials.

Ossip discussed one of the many examples of how a client could decrease costs by using Workbrain's product:

> Forms for any type of business process can be created and defined in real-time. This is just one of the many business objects embedded in our system. For example, if a company wanted to create something like a new safety glove requisition form project from scratch that required access passwords and security for every employee, the cost could easily reach $100,000 to get it started. When our system is installed, it would be a five-minute job. To send out a new type of process form, the new form is created first. Since everyone has a mailbox with complete messaging service built in, the new report is just a business object that is then messaged out to everyone. Our

system allows companies to create a data store that can be uploaded (things like procedure manuals, ISO checklists, etc. can be accessed). We make it more convenient for the employees to access the information they need to do their jobs.

Employees were presented with a number of services and functions designed to enhance their work and personal lives through a Web-based interface allowing them to contact their managers through any Internet access portal. Beyond directly work-related functions, a worker would be presented with email, and a business-to-employee "concierge" service through which they could take salary cash advances, make travel arrangements, and take advantage of e-procurement systems. These employee services would be provided through various alliances with partner firms who would gain direct access to many regular users with each additional contract. David Ossip described the product as follows (Exhibit 2 presents a screen shot of one of the Workbrain Web pages):

> The first level of contact is the employee self-service access, through kiosks onsite or from other Internet portals. Below that are the workforce management systems, which are our expertise—time and attendance plus labor analytics, shop floor data capture, attendance control, scheduling, etc. (Exhibit 3 presents a graphic of the concept) We believe that provides the client with an information layer that benefits them. In between the Workbrain transaction servers we can design different types of business objects that can either be provided by us or by other companies.

> If an employee wants to see her/his pay, there is a pay stub viewer. The employee can see the pay stub before it's printed. For benefit administration an employee can change the benefit plan to see different scenarios (this could be provided by a partner like Wattson Wyatt or Mercer Consulting in the form of additional modules). Another module might be incentive calculators, where an employee gets points based on things that are accomplished which can then be used to purchase things.

> The vision is the end-to-end total solution. We want to own the "blue-collar desktop." It is completely Web-based so it can be accessed from any Web portal. They can log-on, check their time, do their schedule, and at the same time they can use these other business objects that we have provided for them.

Exhibit 2   Workbrain Web page

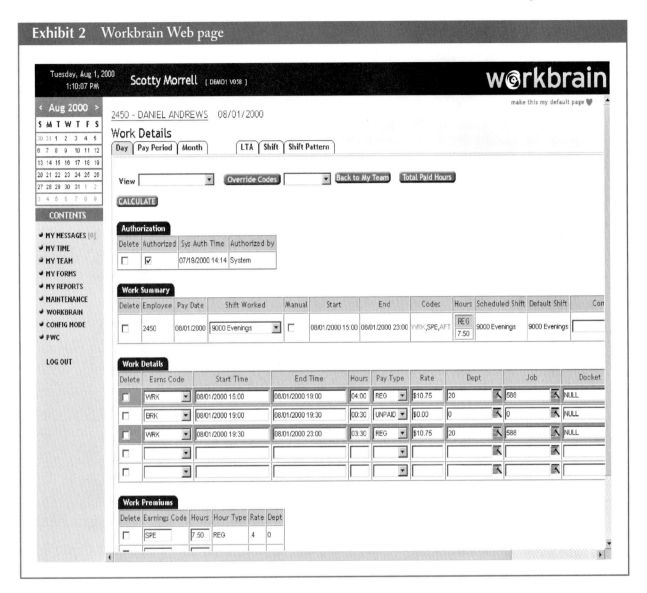

Our advantage is that our competitors only do one facet of the solution (i.e., the workflow automation or the workforce management) but they can't do the full end-to-end solution. We provide a very different viewpoint because all we are trying to do is make it friendlier. We believe that in the long run, in order for companies to retain people, they have to make the workplace more friendly or less frustrating to do things. That is what we are selling. That is the vision. It is not just our time and attendance management expertise that gives us our advantage. Our comprehensive approach (we view ourselves as consultants), the thoroughness of our proposals, and the quality of our work is what sets us apart.

It was clear that Ossip placed a high level of importance on the recruitment of alliance partners. Exhibit 4 presents Workbrain's strategy for alliances. The product was seen as a "win-win-win" situation for the client, their employees, and the partners since it brought everyone together in a virtual marketplace where job-shifts, benefits, processes, products, and services were exchanged in one arena.

Along with cutting-edge technology, there were two other keys to success that Ossip recognized: alliances and people, both of which fell under Green's responsibility. Exhibit 4 presents the firm's strategies for ensuring that these keys were in place. Distribution and content were the two important components to their strategy that alliances gave Workbrain.

Exhibit 3   Graphic of the Workbrain Concept

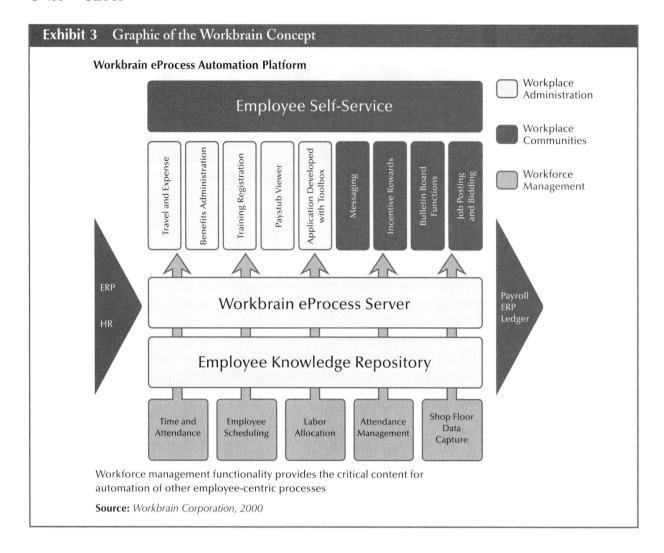

Workforce management functionality provides the critical content for automation of other employee-centric processes

Source: *Workbrain Corporation, 2000*

The Challenge

Workbrain was armed with what seemed like an industry-leading product, and highly skilled people to implement and service the systems and able salespeople to find clients. The key now was to develop an organization that would allow Ossip to bring his vision to reality and that job fell to Eric Green.

> One of the first things I did was to put together an organizational chart that described who did what. It only had about five boxes. I tried to get an idea of all the internal activities that went on in the company such as legal, accounting, operations, technology, and who owned what. There seemed to be no real definition of roles. It seemed as though everyone was just working on this RFP and everything was directed towards a client focus at that point.

> David didn't necessarily think in terms of organizational structure. I don't think that was really his interest. I think he was very much product-driven. He really loved the technology. He loved playing around with the coding. I guess I was the one who was supposed to be focusing on the internal growth and managing that growth.

> One of the major things I did was really push the recruiting forward. More than once I was referred to as the "fluffy" guy; it became a bit of a joke where people would say that if it was not selling or coding, then it was fluffy. For example, on my first day they were interviewing a candidate for the position of Director of Human Relations. I met with him and we really didn't click. At the end of the day we met to discuss whether we should make him an offer. Everyone was very nonchalant about

Exhibit 4   Workbrain's Alliance and Recruiting Strategy

Alliance Strategy

Workbrain recognizes that strategic alliances and partnerships are critical to the company's success, enabling the company to scale revenues quickly, leverage its resources and focus on software development. Accordingly, Workbrain will partner with best-in-class companies to establish and enhance its market position.

Partnership opportunities fall into four categories:

- *Sales and Marketing Partners.* Channel partners who will sell and co-market Workbrain solutions. The value to Workbrain would include expanded distribution and business scalability. As well, the value-added sales approach taken by some of these partners will position Workbrain as part of a broader business process redesign solution, potentially leading to higher prices and faster sales cycles. Value to partners would include a percentage of product sales and the ability to offer a broader set of solutions to clients. Such partners would include:

  ○ Systems consultants and management consultants with strong technology capabilities (e.g., PriceWaterhouseCoopers, Andersen Consulting, A.T. Kearney/EDS, Origin, Cambridge Technology Partners)

  ○ HR consultants with technology practices (e.g., Watson Wyatt, AON)

  ○ Enterprise software vendors (e.g., PeopleSoft, JD Edwards, SAP)

  ○ Application Service Providers (e.g., Corio, US Internetworking)

- *Implementation Partners.* Systems integrators and consultants who will lead and support the implementation of Workbrain solutions. As in the case of sales and marketing partnerships, implementation partners will help increase the scalability of Workbrain by not limiting the company's execution capacity. These partners will derive value by earning software configuration fees, systems integration fees, software development fees (e.g., designing additional modules to leverage the system's workflow infrastructure), and training fees. It is expected that in most cases, these partners will also have sold the Workbrain solution to the client. This group would, therefore, include the systems integration firms and the ASPs outlined above.

- *Solution Partners.* Hardware and software vendors whose products will be bundled with Workbrain to offer a more complete solution to clients. The benefits to Workbrain would include an enhanced value proposition and expanded solution portfolio, as well as a co-marketing channel. Solution Partners would derive value through hardware and software sales, as well as new and/or strengthened customer relationships. This group would include:

  ○ OEMs, including makers of PCs and servers (e.g., Dell, Compaq), Internet appliances (e.g., Netpliance), wireless devices (e.g., Palm, Research in Motion), and data capture devices (e.g., Synel Industries)

  ○ Enterprise software vendors (e.g., PeopleSoft, JD Edwards, SAP)

  ○ E-business software vendors and service providers (e.g., Ariba, Icarian, Healtheon/WebMD, RewardsPlus)

- *Commerce Partners.* Providers of goods and services who will enhance the value of the workplace community aspect of the Workbrain solution. These partnerships are fundamental to Workbrain to execute its vision to be the gateway for hourly employees to the outside world. By providing the 'sticky' content for hourly workers (e.g., payment and schedule information), Workbrain can build a large user base that would be attractive to other companies seeking to acquire customers. Transaction fees would be shared between the client, Workbrain, and the Commerce Partner. This group of partners would include:

  ○ Incentive management administrators (e.g., Maritz)

  ○ B2E aggregators (e.g., Perksatwork.com, employeesavings.com)

  ○ B2C vendors (e.g., Expedia.com, Citibank, E-trade, Paymybills.com, Amazon.com)

Workbrain is currently developing training and alliance programs to ensure that partners work effectively with Workbrain in executing all aspects of its strategy.

Rapid market penetration is key to Workbrain's long-term success. Although it is anticipated that in the longer term, the majority of software sales will be derived from channel partners, Workbrain is committed to building a strong direct sales force that will build market presence and complement our Sales and Marketing Partners.

Human Resources Strategy

Workbrain management recognizes that in today's competitive labor market, the ability to attract, develop, retain and inspire exceptional people is the single most important key success factor in building a great company. Workbrain's growth philosophy, therefore, focuses on excellence in recruiting, workplace environment and compensation policies.

- *Recruiting.* Workbrain is growing rapidly in Toronto and Atlanta by aggressively recruiting both experienced industry professionals and new graduates. Workbrain is looking primarily for results-oriented employees who understand the implementation needs of complex projects. Accordingly, the company's recruiting resources are focused on attracting experienced project managers from the industry segments that Workbrain serves. Workbrain management is leveraging their industry relationships to identify, recruit and train these sales and technology leaders with strong client contacts.

Exhibit 4   Workbrain's Alliance and Recruiting Strategy

Undergraduate, MBA, and IT recruiting is being conducted in conjunction with innovative human resources firms. Incentive compensation for *all* Workbrain employees recognizes their contribution to the firm's recruiting strategy.

- *Workplace Environment.* Workbrain management is intensely focused on creating an inspiring place to work, where risk-taking, results, creativity, and fun are all valued and rewarded. Responsibility is distributed to allow employees to make a real impact and to create uniquely stretching jobs. Cutting-edge productivity technologies and workplace amenities (including on-site health club memberships), flexible work hours, a relaxed workplace, and a genuine respect for work/life balance are all part of Workbrain's work environment.

- *Compensation.* All Workbrain employees receive highly competitive cash and equity-based compensation and best-in-class benefits, including health and dental insurance, continuing education, and a broad variety of employee perquisites.

Source: Workbrain Corporation, 2000

---

it and David liked him because he saw an immediate need to hire someone for the HR position—which is a credit to David because a lot of entrepreneurs just don't think HR is important. I didn't want to talk out of turn, but I really didn't feel he was right for the job for a few reasons. I left that day afraid that I had insulted some people, but we couldn't afford to make hiring mistakes, especially at that stage in the company's life. On the one hand there was a sense of urgency that we needed to fill roles and get people doing things, but if we made mistakes, it would have been a lot harder to correct them.

One of the things that seemed to be like a black hole was the whole selling process because David Stein, VP Sales, was used to doing almost everything. He is technical. He's a great salesman. He's very smart. He can do the documentation. He can do everything. He felt that all he needed to do was hire people like himself, but people like him were impossible to find. He had a very unique skill set. I put together charts and documents to visually communicate what it was that I wanted to get across. It helped David Stein separate some of the issues that he may have been co-mingling. I wanted him to create an organizational structure to allow him to understand the type of people he needed to hire and what skills they needed to possess. It put some clarity around what his organization needed to look like.

I was stressing recruiting, but it was really more strategic thinking. I was getting them (the senior managers) to realize that there were a lot of complementary skill sets out there. They didn't have to find every skill resident in one person. I think that since these guys worked in small companies where a few people did a lot of different things, especially in an industry where a person's experience is very industry-related, some people had to take a leap of faith that we could hire someone with general skills rather than industry-specific knowledge.

Another thing that was a bit concerning was that compensation seemed to be somewhat ad hoc. Salary levels and difficult compensation packages that included options were not really well thought out. I had to determine how much a VP or an analyst should be paid. I felt that we couldn't hire anyone until we really understood or knew what we were going to offer them in compensation.

Another important task was to develop job descriptions. We had to ask a lot of questions. What would this person be doing? What skills were we looking for and where could we find them? We needed to build processes to answer these questions. To do this we needed to start from the job descriptions and really think about what needed to get done and what each department was responsible for and who was going to do what.

There was one watershed moment where it seemed to me that it all became clear to everyone. I had been under the assumption that everyone had been working with the same vision and the same growth plan, that to me was represented by the business plan that was put together before I was hired. To me, the business plan was the company. What I later learned was that due to time constraints, some of the technical and implementation team had not been as involved in the planning process as they should have. There was some resentment that they had not been a part of it because some of them were founders of the firm. There was a disconnect about where they thought the company was going that had manifested itself in the way they were thinking about hiring.

At a meeting of the senior managers, which David Ossip could not attend, the department heads were discussing projects on the horizon, the expected value, and how many people they felt were needed for each project. I felt that we needed to hire about ten implementation people. They came out with numbers like 2.3 people for a project. I felt this was wrong and that it indicated that there was an assumption that we would grow using internally generated cash—I felt that we needed to get big fast. I suggested that the business would come but we needed to build up the infrastructure, which to me was the people.

There was definitely a lot of cynicism from the guys who came from a different environment who were not in this new economy, dot.com kind of thinking. To them it seemed ridiculous to hire people with nothing to do right now. I thought we had a lot to do. There was a lot of infrastructure to be developed for every group. All the materials and processes had to be developed because we were starting from scratch. We needed to get up to speed before we could take on another project and to me that seemed like a lot of work. People needed to be convinced that there was work to do that was not immediately realizing value or revenue.

At the conclusion of that meeting I think a lot of us were quite frustrated and I realized that a lot of those guys had never even seen the business plan. They weren't really quite sure what the vision was.

When David came back he saw that I was really frustrated. He called everyone into a meeting and walked everyone through the vision as he saw it and how the company should grow. This wasn't going to be a company that would grow using internally generated cash; we needed to build quickly. This is what we were promising investors. We were supposed to be 170 people by September 2001 and we had clear revenue targets. We couldn't do that by building incrementally. When David heard about the 2.3 people thing, he reiterated that we should not be thinking that way. We needed to get everyone on the same page and he said specifically that I was here to do that. Because I came from a big company, I thought like a big company and that's what we needed to be and, although I was pulling people in a different direction, that was the way we had to go.

That stands out in my mind as a real turning point in the company. It's not as if it changed overnight, but that started the sequence of events that started to get everyone on the same page. What was encouraging the whole time was that David had taken the step to hire someone like me in the first place because his last company didn't have anyone like me. To me that meant that as tough as this stuff might be to sell internally to get people thinking a certain way, I had his buy in.

It wasn't my vision. These guys had it before I got here. It disappeared for a little while under the bulk of the work that we had. I think that for the guys that came from the previous company it was a bit of a mind shift on a couple of fronts. On the product front, they had to stop thinking only in terms of time and attendance functionality and think more broadly, remembering that this was just one process within the system, and what we were building was a platform for all sorts of processes. Secondly, they had to stop thinking in terms of incremental growth and think more big bang. We were going to be up to sixty people after only eight months in business; that meant that we needed to think big. We needed big company processes. We needed to hire people dedicated to hiring and we needed to act like a big company. We needed to develop our infrastructure to support what we thought we were *going* to be. The people who came from the last company just had to get their heads around it.

In its first months of existence, Workbrain was on pace to exceed its revenue goals. However, the firm still needed to develop the crucial partnerships and client relationships that were required to secure investors in its next round of funding. With this success came more challenges in maintaining the vision, cementing and creating new processes and mental models within the firm. As divisions grew, the roles of the managers would have to be altered and new divisions would need to be created. As the firm grew, how could the culture Ossip espoused be maintained? The firm was staffed with and pursued highly talented, and thus much sought-after, people. How could they be retained? The task of answering these questions lay on the shoulders of Eric Green.

Notes

1. Some of the information in this case is taken from internal Workbrain documents authored by Daniel Debow, Matt Chapman, Eric Green and other members of the Workbrain management team.
2. U.S. Bureau of Statistics.
3. Hambrecht & Quist, 1999
4. American Express & AMR Research, 1997
5. American Payroll Association

Glossary

A

accounting controls Ensure that the financial information provided to internal and external stakeholders is accurate and follows generally accepted accounting practices (GAAP)

acquisition An organization buys a controlling interest in the stock of another organization or buys it outright from its owners

acquisition premium The percentage amount paid for shares of stock above their market value prior to the acquisition announcement

activist groups Organizations formed with the purpose of advancing a specific cause or causes; public interest groups represent the position of a broad cross-section of society, while special interest groups focus on the needs of smaller subgroups

administration Support activities of the value chain consisting of general management activities, such as planning and accounting

agency problem Exists when top managers attempt to maximize their own self interests at the expense of shareholders

aggressive strategy These firms use every available resource in an effort to overwhelm rivals, thus reducing the chance that any countermove will be effective

alliance An arrangement between two or more firms that establishes an exchange relationship but has no joint ownership involved

analyzer strategy Occupies a position in between a prospector strategy and a defender strategy; firms attempt to maintain positions in existing markets while locating growth opportunities on the fringes

antitrust laws Established by governments to keep organizations from getting large and powerful enough in one industry to engage in monopoly pricing and other forms of noncompetitive or illegal behavior

avoidance strategy Competitive strategy in which a firm avoids confrontation completely by focusing on a particular niche in the market in which other firms have little interest

B

bank-centered economies Banks and other financial institutions play the most significant role in the external capital markets

bargaining power Economic power that allows a firm or group of firms to influence the nature of business arrangements for factors such as pricing, availability of products or services, purchase terms, or length of contract

barriers to imitation Barriers intended to prevent existing competitors from imitating sources of cost savings or differentiation

basic research Activity associated with pushing back the boundaries of science as we know it

behavioral controls A special set of controls used to motivate employees to do things that the organization would like them to do, even in the absence of direct supervision; they include bureaucratic controls, clan control, and human resources systems

benchmarking A tool for assessing the best practices of direct competitors and firms in similar industries, then using the resulting "stretch" objectives as design criteria for attempting to change organizational performance

best value strategy A firm pursues elements associated with cost leadership and differentiation simultaneously

board of directors In publicly-owned companies, a group of individuals who are elected by the voting shareholders to monitor the behavior of top managers, therefore protecting their rights as shareholders

broad environment Forms the context in which the firm and its operating environment exist, including sociocultural influences, global economic influences, political/legal influences, and technological influences

buffering Techniques designed to stabilize and predict environmental influences and therefore soften the jolts that might otherwise be felt as the organization interacts with members of its external environment

builder-type culture Growth is the primary goal in the organization

bureaucratic control Rules, procedures, and policies that guide the behavior of organizational members

business angels Wealthy individuals who provide startup capital to entrepreneurs

business definition A description of the business activities of a firm, based on its products and services, markets, functions served, and resource conversion processes

business intelligence The collection and analysis of information on markets, new technologies, customers, competitors, and broad social trends, as well as information gained from internal sources

business-level strategy Defines an organization's approach to competing in its chosen markets

business-level strategy formulation Pertains to domain direction and navigation, or how businesses should compete in the business areas they have selected; sometimes these strategies are referred to as competitive strategies

business plan A plan that contains the details of how a new venture will be carried out

C

capital intensity The extent to which the assets of an organization are primarily associated with plants, equipment, and other fixed assets

capital requirements Costs associated with starting a business

CEO duality Occurs when the CEO also chairs the board of directors

change-style leadership The CEO formulates strategy and then plans the changes in structure, personnel, information systems, and administration required to implement it

Chapter XI A legal filing under the Federal Bankruptcy Code of the United States; allows an organization to work out a plan or arrangement for solving its financial problems under the supervision of a federal court

chief executive officer (CEO) Common title for the highest-ranking manager in a firm

chief information officer (CIO) A high-level manager who oversees the collection, analysis, and dissemination of information

clan control Socialization processes through which an individual comes to appreciate the values, abilities, and expected behaviors of an organization; closely linked to the concepts of culture and organizational ethics

code of ethics Communicates the values of the corporation to employees and other stakeholders

codified knowledge Knowledge that can be communicated completely via written means

collaboration strategy Firms combine resources in an effort to gain a stronger resource position; various forms of interorganizational relationships can lead to collaboration

collaborative-style leadership The CEO works with other managers to create a strategy; participants are then responsible for implementing the strategy in their own areas

collusion Formal price-setting cooperation among firms

commander-style leadership The CEO formulates strategy and then directs top managers to implement it

competitive dynamics The moves and countermoves of firms and their competitors

competitive tactics Techniques firms use—such as advertising, new product launches, cost reduction efforts, and quality improvements—to win market share, increase revenues, and increase profits at the expense of rivals

concentration A corporate-level strategy in which the firm has virtually all of its resource investments in one business area

conglomerate A large, highly diversified firm

consortia Specialized joint ventures encompassing many different arrangements; consortia are often a group of firms oriented towards problem solving and technology development, such as R&D consortia

control systems Systems used to measure and monitor firm activities and processes, as well as motivate or encourage behaviors that are conducive to desired organizational outcomes; the tools of strategy implementation

core knowledge Scientific or technological knowledge that is associated with actual creation of a product or service

core values The underlying philosophies that guide decisions and behavior in a firm; also called organizational values

corporate entrepreneurship Involves the creation of new business ventures within existing corporations

corporate-level distinctive competencies Derived from the ability to achieve shared competitive advantage across the business units of a multi-business firm

corporate-level strategy formulation Refers primarily to the selection of business areas in which the organization will compete and the emphasis each area is given; also includes strategies for carrying out the corporate-level strategy

corporate matrix structure The corporate-level counterpart to the project matrix structure described earlier; organizes operations along two dimensions, such as product and function

corporate raiders Organizations and individuals who engage in acquisitions, typically against the wishes of the managers of the target companies

craftsman-type culture Quality is the primary driver of the corporate culture

creative destruction The inevitable decline of leading firms because competitors will pursue creative opportunities to eliminate the competitive advantages they hold

crescive-style leadership The CEO encourages lower-level managers to formulate and implement their own strategic plans, while still filtering out inappropriate programs

crisis management Processes associated with preventing, detecting, or recovering from crises

cultural-style leadership The CEO formulates a vision and strategy for the company and then works with other managers to create a culture that will foster fulfillment of the vision

D

defender strategy A conservative strategy intended to preserve market share

deliberate strategy Implies that managers plan to pursue an intended strategic course

differentiation Requires the firm to distinguish its products or services on the basis of an attribute such as higher quality, more innovative features, greater selection, better service after sale, or more advertising

diversification Occurs when a firm expands its business operations into new products, functions served, markets, or technologies

divestiture A reverse acquisition; business assets are sold off or spun off as a whole business

domestic stage of international development Organizations focus their efforts on domestic operations, but begin to export their products and services, sometimes through an export department or a foreign joint venture

dominant logic Consists of the way managers deal with managerial tasks, the things they value, and their general approach to running their businesses; similar to a mental model

dot-coms Internet-based businesses; the name comes from the fact that many of these businesses have an Internet-based address that ends in .com, as in Amazon.com

downscoping Involves reducing diversification (refocusing) through selling off nonessential businesses that are not related to the organization's core competencies and capabilities

due diligence Involves a complete examination of a merger or acquisition, including such areas as management, equity, debt, sale of assets, transfer of shares, environmental issues, financial performance, tax issues, human resources, customers, and markets

E

e-commerce Describes business dealings that are electronically based, such as e-tailing (retailing through the Internet), exchanging data, business-to-business buying and selling, and e-mail communications

economic dependence Occurs when stakeholders rely on an organization to provide economic resources such as a salary, interest payments, tax revenues, or payment for goods and services supplied to the firm

economic environment Influences and trends associated with domestic or global economies, such as economic growth rates, interest rates, the availability of credit, inflation rates, foreign exchange rates, and foreign trade balances

economic perspective Defines the purpose of a business organization as profit maximization

economic power Derived from the ability to withhold services, products, capital, revenues, or business transactions that the organization values

economies of scale Cost savings that occur when it is more efficient to produce a product in a larger facility at higher volume

emergent strategy Implies that the existing strategy is not necessarily planned or intended, but rather a result of learning through a process of trial and error

emerging economies Economies that have historically been dominated by government influence, with poorly developed financial capital markets; some of these economies are now pursuing privatization programs that put economic assets in the hands of private citizens

employee stock ownership plan (ESOP) Reward system in which employees are provided with an attractive method for acquiring stock in the companies where they work

enactment The perspective that firms do not have to submit to existing environ-

mental forces because they can influence their environments

enterprise strategy Joins ethical and strategic thinking about the organization; it is the organization's best possible reason for the actions it takes

entrenchment Occurs when managers gain so much power that they are able to use the firm to further their own interests rather than the interests of shareholders

entrepreneurial discovery Entails channeling resources towards the fulfillment of a market need; the intersection of a need and a solution

entrepreneurial tasks Recognition or creation of an opportunity, creation of a business plan, securing startup capital, and actual management of the startup through its early stages

entrepreneurship The creation of new business

entry barriers Forces that keep new competitors out, providing a level of protection for existing competitors

environmental determinism The perspective that the most successful organization will be the one that best adapts to existing forces—in other words, the environment "determines" the best strategy

environmental discontinuities Major, unexpected changes in the social, economic, technological, political, or internal environments that necessitate change within organizations

environmental uncertainty A result of not being able to predict precisely what will happen with regard to the actions of external stakeholders and other external influences; results in organizational uncertainty

exit barriers Costs associated with leaving a business or industry

exporting Transferring goods to other countries for sale through wholesalers or a foreign company

external environment Stakeholders and forces outside the traditional boundaries of the firm; they can be divided into the broad and operating environments

F

family-centered economies Families hold a lot of the stock in large corporations, allowing them a lot of control

feedback control Provides managers with information concerning outcomes from organizational activities

feedforward control Helps managers anticipate changes in the external and

internal environments, based on analysis of inputs from stakeholders and the environment

financial controls Based purely on financial measures such as ROI

financial intermediaries A wide variety of institutions—including banks, stock exchanges, brokerage houses, investment advisors, mutual fund companies, pension fund companies, and other organizations or individuals—that may have an interest in investing in the firm

financial risk The risk that a firm will not be able to meet its financial obligations and may eventually declare bankruptcy

financial strategy Primary purpose is to provide the organization with the capital structure and funds that are appropriate for implementing growth and competitive strategies

first-movers Firms that stay at the forefront of technological advances in their industries

five forces of industry competition Forces that largely determine the type and level of competition in an industry and, ultimately, the industry's profit potential; they include customers, suppliers, entry barriers, substitute products or services, and rivalry among existing competitors

fixed costs Costs associated with plants, machinery, or other fixed assets

focus strategy A firm targets a narrow segment of the market through low-cost leadership, differentiation, or a combination of low cost and differentiation

Foreign Corrupt Practices Act (FCPA) A response to social concern about bribes paid by U.S. companies to foreign government officials; it defines the "rules-of-the-game" for U.S. companies when they operate in foreign countries

foreign exchange rates The rates at which currencies are exchanged across countries; this is a major source of uncertainty for firms operating in foreign countries

foreign trade balance A measure of the relative value of imports to exports from one country to another

formal power Occurs when stakeholders have a legal or contractual right to make decisions for some part of an organization

formal structure Specifies the number and types of departments or groups and provides the formal reporting relationships and lines of communication among internal stakeholders

franchising The services counterpart to a licensing strategy; a foreign firm buys the legal right to use the name and operating methods of a foreign firm in its home country

functional-level strategy The collective pattern of day-to-day decisions made and actions taken by managers and employees who are responsible for value-creating activities within a particular functional area

functional-level strategy formulation The details of how functional resource areas—such as marketing, operations, and finance—should be used to implement business-level strategies and achieve competitive advantage

functional strategy audit Through evaluation of functional-level strategies on the basis of internal consistency, consistency across functional areas, and the extent to which each functional strategy is supportive of the overall strategies of the firm

functional structure A business-level structure organized around the inputs or activities that are required to produce products and services, such as marketing, operations, finance, and R&D

G

generic business strategies A classification system for business-level strategies based on common strategic characteristics

global integration The process through which a multi-national organization integrates its worldwide activities into a single world strategy through its network of affiliates and alliances

global product/market approach Companies use one product design and market it in the same fashion throughout the world

global resource advantage A source of competitive advantage resulting from the ability of a global organization to draw from a much broader and more diversified pool of resources

global stage of international development The organization has become so global that it is no longer associated primarily with any one country

group-centered economies Groups of companies manage the use of Internal capital as a replacement for external capital markets

H

horizontal integration Involves acquisition of an organization in the same line of business

hostile acquisition An acquisition that is not desirable from the perspective of the managers of a target company; unexpected acquisition announcements typically are considered hostile

human resource management Support activities of the value chain associated with human-based activities such as recruiting, hiring, training, and compensation

human resources strategy The pattern of decisions about selection, training, rewards, and benefits

hypercompetition A condition of rapidly escalating competition

hypothesis development and testing Organizations should test their decisions to see if they are appropriate or likely to be successful; hypothesis development is a creative process, whereas hypothesis testing is an analytical process

I

inbound logistics Primary activities of the value chain that include activities associated with acquiring inputs that are used in the product

industry consolidation Occurs as competitors merge together

industry life cycle Portrays how sales volume for a product category changes over its lifetime, from the introduction stage through the commodity or decline stage

industry revolutionaries Firms that invent new business concepts

industry supply chain The sequence of activities in an industry from raw materials extraction through final consumption

information systems strategy Plan for using information systems to enhance organizational processes and strategy

inimitable resources Resources that are possessed by industry participants but are hard or impossible to completely duplicate

initial public offering (IPO) Entails sale of stock to the public and investors

intangible relatedness Occurs any time capabilities developed in one area can be applied to another area

intangible resources Organizational assets that are hard to quantify, such as

knowledge, skills, abilities, stakeholder relationships, and reputations

integrative knowledge Knowledge that helps integrate various activities, capabilities, and products

intelligent opportunism The ability of managers at various levels of the organization to take advantage of unanticipated opportunities to further intended strategy or even redirect a strategy

interlocking directorate Occurs when a director or executive of one firm sits on the board of a second firm or when two firms have directors who also serve on the board of a third firm

internal controls A set of controls that firms use to guide internal processes and behaviors; specifically, behavioral, process, and accounting controls

international expansion The process of building an expanding operational presence; this can lead to global resource advantages

international stage of international development Exports become an important part of organizational strategy; operations and marketing are tailored to the needs of each country

interorganizational relationships A term that includes many types of organizational cooperation or partnerships

intrapraneurship Corporate entrepreneurship, or the creation of new business ventures within existing corporations

J

joint venture An entity that is created when two or more firms pool a portion of their resources to create a separate jointly-owned entity

K

knowledge economy Refers to the importance of intangible people skills and intellectual assets to developed economies

L

learning curve Demonstrates that the time required to complete a task will decrease as a predictable function of the number of times the task is repeated

legal perspective Ethical behavior is defined as legal behavior

leverage A measure of a firm's long-term or total debt relative to its assets or equity; a common measure of financial risk

leveraged buyouts (LBOs) Private purchase of a business unit by managers, employees, unions, or private investors

licensing Selling the right to produce and/or sell a brand name product in a foreign market

limited partnership A business form in which the management responsibility and legal liability of partners are limited

liquidity A measure of a firm's ability to pay short-term obligations

low-cost leadership strategy A firm pursues competitive advantage through efficient cost production; also called cost leadership

M

market-centered economies Economies with well-developed infrastructures, business environments, and external capital markets

market development Involves repositioning a product or service to appeal to a new market

market penetration Competing with a single product or service in a single market

marketing and sales Primary activities of the value chain associated with processes through which customers can purchase the product and through which they are induced to do so

marketing strategy Plan for collecting information about customers or potential customers and using this information to project future demand, predict competitor actions, identify new business opportunities, create new products and services, and sell products and services

mental model A view of how the world works; mental models should include an understanding of both the internal and external organization and the interaction between the two

merger Occurs any time two organizations combine into one; acquisitions are the most common type of merger

mission statement Defines what the organization is and its reason for existing; often contains all of the elements of strategic direction—including vision, business definition, and organizational values

monopoly An industry in which one firm is the only significant provider of a good or service

multidivisional corporate-level structure A corporate-level structure in which each business exists as a separate unit reporting to top management

multidomestic product/market approach Entails handling product design, assembly, and marketing on a country-by-country basis by custom tailoring products and services around individual market needs

multi-market competition Firms compete in multiple markets simultaneously

multinational stage of international development The organization has marketing and production facilities throughout the world

N

network A hub and wheel configuration with a local firm at the hub organizing the interdependencies of a complex array of firms

network structure A business-level structure in which operating units or branches are organized around customer groups or geographical regions

newly industrialized economies (NIEs) Countries that have recently experienced high levels of growth in real gross domestic product

O

oligopoly An industry characterized by the existence of a few very large firms

operating environment Consists of stakeholders with whom organizations interact on a fairly regular basis—including customers, suppliers, competitors, government agencies and administrators, local communities, activist groups, unions, the media, and financial intermediaries

operating goals Established in an effort to bring the concepts found in the vision statement to a level that managers and employees can influence and control

operations Primary activities of the value chain that refer to transforming inputs into the final product

operations strategy Emerges from the pattern of decisions made within the firm about production or service operations

organizational crises Critical situations that threaten high priority organizational goals, impose a severe restriction on the amount of time in which key members of the organization can respond, and contain elements of surprise

organizational culture The system of shared values of an organization's members

organizational ethics A value system that has been widely adopted by members of an organization; often used interchangeably with the term "organizational values"

organizational fit Occurs when two organizations or business units have similar management processes, cultures, systems, and structures

organizational governance How the behavior of high-ranking managers is supervised and controlled; for example, the board of directors is responsible for ensuring that managerial behavior is consistent with shareholder interests

organizational scope The breadth of an organization's activities across businesses and industries

organizational structure Reporting relationships and the division of people into groups, teams, task forces, and departments within an organization

organizational values The underlying philosophies that guide decisions and behavior in a firm; also called core values or organizational ethics

outbound logistics Primary activities of the value chain related to storing and physically distributing a final product to customers

outsourcing Contracting with another firm to provide goods or services that were previously supplied from within the company; similar to subcontracting

owner/manager structure In this form, the owner is the top manager and the business is run as a sole proprietorship

P

Pacific Century Refers to a forecast that the world's growth center for the twenty-first century will shift across the Pacific Ocean to Asia

partnership A business form in which the partners each contribute resources and share in the rewards of the venture

patent Legal protection that prevents other companies from making use of a firm's innovation

performance-based compensation plan Reward system in which compensation varies depending on the success of the organization

pioneer-type culture The emphasis is on new product and new technology development

political environment Influences and trends associated with governments and other political or legal entities; political forces, both at home and abroad, are among the most significant determinants of organizational success

political power Comes from the ability to persuade lawmakers, society, or regulatory agencies to influence firm behavior

political strategies All organizational activities that have as one of their objectives the creation of a friendlier political climate for the organization

premise control Use of information collected by the organization to examine assumptions that underlie organizational vision, goals, and strategies

process controls Use immediate feedback to control organizational processes

product/market structure A business-level structure that organizes activities around the outputs of the organizational system, such as products, customers, or geographical regions

product/service development Introduction of new products or services related to an existing competence of the firm or development of truly new-to-the-world products not related to the core business of the firm

product/service differentiation Attributes associated with a product or service that cause customers to prefer it over competing products or services

pro-forma financial statements Forward-looking income statements, balance sheets, and cash flow statements that are based on predictions of what will happen in the future

project matrix structure A hybrid business-level structure that combines some elements of both functional and product/market structures

prospector strategy An offensive strategy in which firms aggressively seek new market opportunities and are willing to take risks

R

R&D/technology strategy Plan for developing new products and new technologies

radical innovations Major innovations that influence more than one business or industry

radical restructuring Major changes to a firm's direction, strategies, structures, and plans

reactor strategy Describes firms that don't have a distinct strategy; they simply react to environmental situations

reengineering A restructuring approach that involves the radical redesign of core business processes to achieve dramatic improvements in productivity cycle times and quality

related acquisitions Occur when the acquiring company shares common or complementary resources with its acquisition target

related diversification Diversification that stems from common markets, functions served, technologies, or products and services

religious perspective Religious teachings define appropriate behavior

reputation An economic asset that signals observers about the attractiveness of a company's offerings based on past performance

resource-based approach to strategic management Considers the firm as a bundle of resources; firms can gain competitive advantage through possessing superior resources

resource complementarity Occurs when two businesses have strengths in different areas

resource procurement Support activities of the value chain related to the purchase of inputs for all of the primary processes and support activities of the firm

restructuring Involves major changes to an organization's strategies, structure, and/or processes

retaliation strategy A firm threatens severe retaliation in an effort to discourage competitors from taking actions

retrenchment A turnaround strategy that involves tactics such as work force reductions, closing unprofitable plants, outsourcing unprofitable activities, implementation of tighter cost or quality controls, or new policies that emphasize quality or efficiency

S

S corporation Formerly called the Subchapter S corporation, this corporate form allows tax advantages in the United States that are similar to those associated with a partnership

salesman-type culture These firms are excellent marketers who create successful brand names and distribution channels, and pursue aggressive advertising and innovative packaging

service Primary activities of the value chain associated with providing service to enhance or maintain product value—such as repairing, supplying parts, or installation

situation analysis Analysis of stakeholders inside and outside the organization, as well as other external forces; this analysis should be conducted at both the domestic and international levels, if applicable

six sigma A philosophy based on minimizing the number of defects found in a manufacturing operation or service function

social responsibility The duty of an organization, defined in terms of its economic, legal, and moral obligations, as well as discretionary actions that might be considered attractive from a societal perspective

social stake Occurs when a stakeholder group is not directly linked to the organization, but is interested in assuring that the organization behaves in a manner that they believe is socially responsible

sociocultural environment Influences and trends that come from groups of individuals who make up a particular geographic region

spin-off A type of divestiture in which current shareholders are issued a proportional number of shares in the spun-off business

stakeholders Groups or individuals who can significantly affect or are significantly affected by an organization's activities

stakeholder approach to strategic management Envisions the firm at the center of a network of constituencies called stakeholders; firms can gain competitive advantage through superior stakeholder management

startup capital The financing required to begin a new venture

steward A leader who cares deeply about the firm, its stakeholders, and the society in which it operates

strategic business unit (SBU) structure A multidivisional structure in which divisions are combined into SBUs based on common elements they each possess

strategic control Refers to a combination of control systems that allows managers excellent control over their firms

strategic direction Pertains to the longer-term goals and objectives of the organization; this direction is often contained in mission and vision statements

strategic fit Refers to the effective matching of strategic organizational capabilities

strategic flexibility A firm can move its resources out of declining markets and into more prosperous ones in a minimum amount of time

strategic-group map Categorizes existing industry competitors into groups that follow similar strategies

strategic intent A vision of where an organization is or should be going; similar to the strategic concept of "vision" defined previously

strategic leadership Generally refers to leadership behaviors associated with creating organizational vision, establishing core values, developing strategies and a management structure, fostering organizational learning, and serving as a steward for the firm

strategic management A process through which organizations analyze and learn from their internal and external environments, establish strategic direction, create strategies that are intended to move the organization in that direction, and implement those strategies, all in an effort to satisfy key stakeholders

strategic planning process The formal planning elements of strategic management that result in a strategic plan; this process tends to be rather rigid and unimaginative

strategic reorientation A significant realignment of organization strategies, structure, and processes with the new environmental realities

strategic surveillance The process of collecting information from the broad, operating, and internal environments

strategic thinking A somewhat creative and intuitive process that leads to creative solutions and new ideas

strategy formulation The process of planning strategies, often divided into the corporate, business, and functional levels

strategy implementation Managing stakeholder relationships and organizational resources in a manner that moves the organization towards the successful execution of its strategies, consistent with its strategic direction

structural inertia Forces at work to maintain the status quo, which may include systems, structures, processes, culture, sunk costs, internal politics, and barriers to entry and exit

subcontracting Acquiring goods and services that used to be produced in-house from external companies

substitute products/services Products or services provided by another industry that can be readily substituted for an industry's own products/services

sustainable competitive advantage Exists when a firm enjoys a long-lasting business advantage compared to rival firms

synergy Occurs when the whole is greater than the sum of its parts

T

tacit knowledge Knowledge that is difficult to articulate in a way that is meaningful and complete

tangible relatedness Means that the organization has the opportunity to use the same physical resources for multiple purposes

tangible resources Organizational assets that can be seen, touched, and/or quantified, such as plants, money, or products

technological environment Influences and trends related to the development of technologies both domestically and internationally

technology Human knowledge about products and services and the way they are made and delivered

technology development Support activities of the value chain associated with learning processes that result in improvements in the way organizational functions are performed

thinking in time Recognition that the past, present, and future are all relevant to making good strategic decisions

top management team (TMT) Typically a heterogeneous group of three to ten top executives selected by the CEO; each member brings a unique set of skills and a unique perspective

trade association Organizations (typically nonprofit) that are formed by firms in the same industry to collect and disseminate trade information, offer legal and technical advice, furnish industry-related training, and provide a platform for collective lobbying

trade barriers Factors that discourage international trade, such as tariffs and import quotas

trademark Legal protection that prevents other companies from making use of a firm's symbol or brand name

traditional approach to strategic management Analysis of the internal and external environments of the organization to arrive at organizational strengths, weaknesses, opportunities, and threats (SWOT), which form the basis for developing effective missions, goals, and strategies

transaction cost economics the study of economic transactions and their costs

transaction costs The resources used to create and enforce a contract

transnational structure A corporate-level structure that organizes businesses along three dimensions: nation or region, product, and function

triad regions Three dominant economic regions in the world; namely, North America, Europe, and the Pacific Rim

U

United States Sentencing Guidelines (USSG) Compulsory guidelines courts must use to determine fines and penalties when corporate illegalities are proven

universalist perspective Appropriate behavior is defined by the question: "Would I be willing for everyone else in the world to make the same decision?"

unrelated acquisitions Occur between companies that don't share any common or complementary resources

unrelated diversification Diversification that is not based on commonality among the activities of a corporation

utilitarian perspective The most appropriate actions generate the greatest benefits for the largest number of people

V

value chain A representation of organizational processes, divided into primary and support activities that create value for the customer

venture capitalists Individuals or groups of investors that seek out and provide capital to entrepreneurs

vertical integration Exists when a firm is involved in more than one stage of the industry supply chain; a firm that vertically integrates moves forward to become its own customer or backward to become its own supplier

vision Expresses what the organization wants to be in the future

visionary leadership Pertains to envisioning what the organization should be like in the future, communicating the vision, and empowering followers to enact it

W

wholly-owned foreign subsidiary A business venture that is started from scratch; sometimes called a greenfield investment

Name Index

Subject Index